*For more resources, visit the Student Site
for the Value Edition of*

The American Promise

bedfordstmartins.com/roarkvalue

FREE Online Study Guide

Get instant feedback on your progress with

- Chapter self-tests
- Key terms review
- Map quizzes
- Timeline activities
- Note-taking outlines

FREE History research and writing help

Refine your research skills and find plenty of good sources with

- Suggested references for each chapter compiled by the textbook authors
- A database of useful images, maps, documents, and more at *Make History*
- A guide to online sources for history
- Help with writing history papers
- A tool for building a bibliography
- Tips on avoiding plagiarism

VALUE EDITION

The
American
Promise

A History of
the United States

FIFTH EDITION

VALUE EDITION

The
American
Promise

A History of
the United States

FIFTH EDITION

James L. Roark
Emory University

Michael P. Johnson
Johns Hopkins University

Patricia Cline Cohen
University of California, Santa Barbara

Sarah Stage
Arizona State University

Susan M. Hartmann
The Ohio State University

BEDFORD/ST. MARTIN'S

BOSTON ♦ NEW YORK

FOR BEDFORD/ST. MARTIN'S

Publisher for History: Mary V. Dougherty
Executive Editor for History: William J. Lombardo
Director of Development for History: Jane Knetzger
Developmental Editor: Jennifer Jovin
Senior Production Editor: Bridget Leahy
Assistant Production Manager: Joe Ford
Senior Marketing Manager for U.S. History: Amy Whitaker
Indexer: Leoni Z. McVey
Photo Researchers: Pembroke Herbert and Sandi Rygiel, Picture Research Consultants, Inc.
Permissions Manager: Kalina K. Ingham
Senior Art Director: Anna Palchik
Text Designer: Tom Carling, Carling Design, Inc.
Cover Designer: Billy Boardman
Cover Photo: Jeannette Rankin with American Flag. Congresswoman Jeannette Rankin is presented
   with the flag that flew at the House of Representatives during the passage of the suffrage
   amendment, January 21, 1918. © Bettman/CORBIS
Cartography: Mapping Specialists Limited
Composition: Cenveo Publisher Services
Printing and Binding: RR Donnelley and Sons

President: Joan E. Feinberg
Editorial Director: Denise B. Wydra
Director of Marketing: Karen R. Soeltz
Director of Production: Susan W. Brown
Associate Director, Editorial Production: Elise S. Kaiser
Managing Editor: Elizabeth M. Schaaf

Library of Congress Control Number: 2012932889

Manufactured in the United States of America.

7   6   5   4   3   2
f   e   d   c   b   a

For information, write: Bedford/St. Martin's, 75 Arlington Street, Boston, MA 02116
   (617-399-4000)

ISBN: 978–1–4576–1345-6 (Combined Edition)
ISBN: 978–1–4576–1346-3 (Vol. 1)
ISBN: 978–1–4576–1347-0 (Vol. 2)

Preface

As authors, we continue to be deeply gratified that *The American Promise* is one of the most widely adopted texts for the U.S. history survey, reaching students at all levels and helping instructors in all classroom environments. We know from years of firsthand experience that the survey course is the most difficult to teach and the most difficult to take, and we remain committed to making this book the most teachable and readable introductory American history text available. In creating this value edition, we set out to develop a resource that is both comprehensive and affordable.

Our experience as teachers continues to inform every aspect of our text, beginning with its framework. We have found that students need *both* the structure a political narrative provides *and* the insights gained from examining social and cultural experience. To write a comprehensive, balanced account of American history, we focus on the public arena — the place where politics intersects social and cultural developments — to show how Americans confronted the major issues of their day and created far-reaching historical change. To engage students in the American story and to portray fully the diversity of the American experience, we stitch into our narrative the voices of hundreds of contemporaries, provide a vivid and compelling art program, and situate American history in the global world in which students live. In this value edition, we provide the same high-quality material included in the parent text — the full narrative and select images, maps, and pedagogical tools — at a price that budget-conscious instructors and students will appreciate.

To extend the text, our array of multimedia and print supplements has never been more abundant or more impressive. A range of options — from video clips to lecture kits on CD-ROM and much more — offers instructors endless combinations to tailor *The American Promise* to fit the needs of their classroom. (See pages xii–xvi.) Students of all learning styles have more ways than ever to enhance their traditional textbook experience and make history memorable. The book companion site links to primary documents, including images, texts, and audiovisual files, and its Online Study Guide provides Web-based self tests, map exercises, and visual activities. By seamlessly connecting our text to its rich storehouse of digital resources, these supplements help students better understand the people whose ideas and actions shaped their times and whose efforts still affect our lives.

Our title, *The American Promise*, reflects our agreement with playwright Arthur Miller's conviction that the essence of America has been its promise. For millions, the nation has held out the promise of a better life, unfettered worship, equality before the law, representative government, democratic politics, and other freedoms seldom found elsewhere. But none of these promises has come with guarantees. As we see it, much of American history is a continuing struggle over the definition and realization of the nation's promise. Who are we, and what do we want to be? Abraham Lincoln, in the midst of what he termed the "fiery trial" of the Civil War, pronounced the nation "the last best hope of Earth." Kept alive by countless sacrifices, that hope has been marred by compromises, disappointments, and denials, but it still lives. We believe that our new edition of *The American Promise*, Value Edition, with its increased attention to human agency, will continue to show students that American history is an unfinished story and to make them aware of the legacy of hope bequeathed to them by generations of Americans stretching back more than four centuries, a legacy that is theirs to preserve and build on.

Features

In this value edition, we make sure to include carefully chosen illustrations and maps that extend and reinforce the narrative. The 155 contemporaneous **illustrations** — including paintings, photographs, and artifacts — make history tangible and emphasize the importance of material culture in the study of the past. **Comprehensive captions** for the illustrations in the book entice students to delve deeper into the text itself, and enrich the historical account. Our highly regarded **map program** rests on the old truth that "History is not intelligible without geography." For this new edition, we added blue to the formerly black-and-white color palette to make the maps more engaging and easier to decipher. Regional divisions, territorial expansion, and demographic changes are more apparent in this new design.

As part of our ongoing efforts to make *The American Promise* the most teachable and readable survey text available, we paid renewed attention to imaginative and effective pedagogy. Each chapter begins with a concise but colorful **opening vignette** that invites students into the narrative with lively accounts of individuals or groups who embody the central themes of the chapter. New vignettes in this edition include the Grimké sisters speaking out against slavery, Frederick Jackson Turner proclaiming his frontier hypothesis, migrant mother Florence Owens struggling to survive in the Great Depression, and the experience of Vietnam War veteran Frederick Downs Jr. Each vignette ends with a **narrative overview** of all of the chapter's main topics. Major sections within each chapter have **introductory paragraphs** that preview the subsections that follow and conclude with **review questions** to help students check their comprehension of main ideas. **Running heads** with dates and topical headings remind students of chronology. **Section headings,** now printed in color, draw students' attention as they work through the chapters to make studying easier. In addition, **key terms,** set in boldface type, highlight important people, events, and concepts. All chapters culminate in a **conclusion,** which reexamines central ideas and provides a bridge to the next chapter.

The two-page **Reviewing the Chapter** section at the end of each chapter provides a review guide to ensure student success. An illustrated chapter **Timeline** gives clear chronological overviews of key events. Three sets of questions elicit critical thinking and prompt students to make use of the facts they have mastered. **Review Questions,** repeated from within the narrative, focus on a specific topic or event, and **Making Connections** questions prompt students to think about broad developments within the chapter. An **all-new set of Linking to the Past** questions cross-reference developments in earlier chapters, encouraging students to make comparisons, see causality, and understand change over longer periods of time. **Online Study Guide cross-references** at the end of the review section point students to free self-assessment quizzes and other study aids.

Updated Scholarship

We updated the fifth edition in myriad ways to reflect our ongoing effort to offer a comprehensive text that braids all Americans into the national narrative and to frame that national narrative in a more global perspective. To do so, we have paid particular attention to the most recent scholarship and, as always, appreciated and applied many suggestions from our users that keep the book fresh, accurate, and organized in a way that works best for students.

In Volume One, we focused our attention on Native Americans, especially in the West, because of the publication of exciting new scholarship. In Chapter 6, we have incorporated into the narrative more coverage of Indians and their roles in various conflicts between the British and the colonists before the Revolution. Chapter 9 expands the coverage of American conflicts with Indians in the Southwest, adding new material on Creek chief Alexander McGillivray. Chapter 10 greatly increases the coverage of Indians in the West, with a new section devoted to the Osage territory and the impressive Comanche empire known as Comanchería.

Volume Two also includes expanded attention to Native Americans, but our main effort for the second half of the book has been to do more of what we already do best, and that is to give even more attention to women, African Americans, and the global context of U.S. history. In the narrative, we have added coverage of women as key movers in the rise of the Lost Cause after the Civil War, and we consider the ways in which the GI Bill disproportionately benefited white men after World War II. Chapter 16 includes new coverage of the Colfax massacre, arguably the single worst incidence of brutality against African Americans during the Reconstruction era. Chapter 27 provides new coverage of civil rights activism and resistance in northern states, and Chapter 28 increases coverage of black power and urban rebellions across the country.

Because students live in an increasingly global world and need help making connections with the world outside the United States, we have continued our efforts to incorporate the global context of American history throughout the fifth edition. This is particularly evident in Volume Two, where we have expanded coverage of transnational issues in recent decades, such as the 1953 CIA coup in Iran, the U.S. bombing campaign in Vietnam, and U.S. involvement in Afghanistan.

In addition to the many changes noted above, in both volumes we have updated, revised, and improved the text in response to both new scholarship and requests from instructors. New and expanded coverage areas include, among others, taxation in the pre-Revolutionary period and the early Republic, the Newburgh Conspiracy of the 1780s, the overbuilding of railroads in the West during the Gilded Age, the 1918–1919 global influenza epidemic, finance reform in the 1930s, post–World War II considerations of universal health care, the economic downturn of the late 2000s, the Obama presidency, and the most recent developments in the Middle East.

Acknowledgments

We gratefully acknowledge all of the helpful suggestions from those who have read and taught from previous editions of *The American Promise*, and we hope that our many classroom collaborators will be pleased to see their influence in the fifth edition. In particular, we wish to thank the talented scholars and teachers who gave generously of their time and knowledge to review this book: Patricia Adams, *Chandler-Gilbert Community College*; Susan Agee, *Truckee Meadows Community College*; Jennifer Bertolet, *George Washington University*; Michael Bryan, *Greenville Technical College*; Kim Burdick, *Delaware Technical and Community College*; Monica Butler, *Seminole State College, Sanford*; Andria Crosson, *University of Texas San Antonio*; Lawrence Devaro, *Rowan University and Camden County College*; Philip DiMare, *California State University, Sacramento*; Dorothy Drinkard-Hawkshawe, *East Tennessee State University*; Edward (Jim) Dudlo, *Brookhaven College*; John Duke, *Alvin Community College*; Aaron Edstrom, *University of Texas El Paso*; Brian Farmer, *Amarillo College*; Rafaele Fierro, *Tunxis Community College*; José Garcia, *University of Central Florida*; Cecilia Gowdy-Wygant, *Front Range Community College Westminster*; William Grose, *Wytheville Community College*; Stephanie Lee Holyfield, *University of Delaware*; Johanna Hume, *Alvin Community College*; W. Sherman Jackson, *Miami University*; Michael Jacobs, *University of Wisconsin Baraboo/Sauk County*; Kevin Kern, *University of Akron*; Barbara Martin, *University of Southern Indiana*; Alfonso John Mooney, *University of Oklahoma*; Christopher Paine, *Lake Michigan College*; George Sochan, *Bowie State University*; Joyce Thierer, *Emporia State University*; Kathryn Wells, *Central Piedmont Community College*; Steven White, *Bluegrass Community and Technical College*; and Tom Zeiler, *University of Colorado at Boulder*.

A project as complex as this requires the talents of many individuals. First, we would like to acknowledge our families for their support, forbearance, and toleration of our textbook responsibilities. Pembroke Herbert and Sandi Rygiel of Picture Research Consultants, Inc., contributed their unparalleled knowledge, soaring imagination, and diligent research to make possible the extraordinary illustration program.

We would also like to thank the many people at Bedford/St. Martin's who have been crucial to this project. No one contributed more than freelance developmental editor Michelle McSweeney, who managed the entire revision and oversaw the development of each chapter. The results of her dedication to excellence and commitment to creating the best textbook imaginable are evident on every page. We greatly appreciate the acute intelligence, attention to detail, and limitless tolerance for the authors' eccentricities that Michelle brought to this revision. We thank freelance editors Jan Fitter and Shannon Hunt for their help with the manuscript. Thanks also go to editorial assistant Laura Kintz for her assistance preparing the manuscript and to associate editor Jennifer Jovin, who developed the value edition and coordinated the supplements. We are also grateful to Jane Knetzger, director of development for history; William J. Lombardo, executive editor for history; and Mary V. Dougherty, publisher for history, for their support and guidance. For their imaginative and tireless efforts to promote the book, we want to thank Jenna Bookin Barry, Amy Whitaker, John Hunger, Sean Blest, and Stephen Watson. With great skill and professionalism, Bridget Leahy, senior production editor, and Kendra LeFleur and Kerri Cardone, production editors, pulled together the many pieces related to copyediting, design, and composition, with the able assistance of Elise Keller and the guidance of managing editor Elizabeth Schaaf and assistant managing editor John Amburg. Senior production supervisor Joe Ford oversaw the manufacturing of the book. Designer Tom Carling, and proofreader Janet Cocker attended to the myriad details that help make the book shine. Leoni McVey provided an outstanding index. The book's gorgeous covers were designed by Billy Boardman. New media editor Marissa Zanetti made sure that *The American Promise* remains at the forefront of technological support for students and instructors. Editorial director Denise Wydra provided helpful advice throughout the course of the project. Finally, Charles H. Christensen, former president, took a personal interest in *The American Promise* from the start, and Joan E. Feinberg, president, guided all editions through every stage of development.

Versions and Supplements

Adopters of *The American Promise,* Value Edition, and their students have access to abundant extra resources, including documents, presentation and testing materials, the acclaimed Bedford Series in History and Culture volumes, and much much more. See below for more information, visit the book's catalog site at **bedfordstmartins.com/roarkvalue/catalog**, or contact your local Bedford/St. Martin's sales representative.

Get the Right Version for Your Class

To accommodate different course lengths, *The American Promise,* Value Edition is available in several different formats:

- **Combined edition** (Chapters 1–31)
- **Volume 1: To 1877** (Chapters 1–16)
- **Volume 2: From 1865** (Chapters 16–31)

Your students can also purchase *The American Promise,* Value Edition in popular e-book formats for computers, tablets, and e-readers by visiting **bedfordstmartins.com/ebooks**. The e-book is available at a discount.

Online Extras for Students

The book's companion site at **bedfordstmartins.com/roarkvalue** gives students a way to read, write, and study, and to find and access quizzes and activities, study aids, and history research and writing help.

FREE Online Study Guide. Available at the companion site, this popular resource provides students with quizzes and activities for each chapter, including multiple-choice self-tests that focus on important concepts; flashcards that test students' knowledge of key terms; timeline activities that emphasize causal relationships; and map quizzes intended to strengthen students' geography skills. Instructors can monitor students' progress through an online Quiz Gradebook or receive email updates.

FREE Research, Writing, and Anti-plagiarism Advice. Available at the companion site, Bedford's **History Research and Writing Help** includes the textbook authors' **Suggested References** organized by chapter; **History Research and Reference Sources,** with links to history-related databases, indexes, and journals; **More Sources and How to Format a History Paper,** with clear advice on how to integrate primary and secondary sources into research papers and how to cite and format sources correctly; **Build a Bibliography,** a simple Web-based tool known as The Bedford Bibliographer that generates bibliographies in four commonly used documentation styles; and **Tips on Avoiding Plagiarism,** an online tutorial that reviews the consequences of plagiarism and features exercises to help students practice integrating sources and recognize acceptable summaries.

Resources for Instructors

Bedford/St. Martin's has developed a wide range of teaching resources for this book and for this course. They range from lecture and presentation materials and assessment tools to course management options. Most can be downloaded or ordered at **bedfordstmartins.com/roarkvalue/catalog**.

HistoryClass for The American Promise, **now with LearningCurve.** HistoryClass, a Bedford/St. Martin's Online Course Space, puts the online resources available with this textbook in one convenient and completely customizable course space. There you and your students can access an interactive e-book and primary sources reader; video clips, maps, images, documents, and links; chapter review quizzes including LearningCurve, a game-like adaptive quizzing system; interactive multimedia exercises; and research and writing help. In HistoryClass you can get all our premium content and tools and assign, rearrange, and mix them with your own resources. For more information, visit **yourhistoryclass.com**.

Bedford Coursepack for Blackboard, WebCT, Desire2Learn, Angel, Sakai, or Moodle. We have free content to help you integrate our rich content into your course management system. Registered instructors can download coursepacks with no hassle and no strings attached. Content includes our most popular free resources and book-specific content for *The American Promise,* Value Edition. Visit **bedfordstmartins.com/coursepacks** to see a demo, find your version, or download your coursepack.

Instructor's Resource Manual. The instructor's manual offers both experienced and first-time instructors tools for preparing lectures and running discussions. It includes chapter review material, teaching strategies, and a guide to chapter-specific supplements available for the text.

Guide to Changing Editions. Designed to facilitate an instructor's transition from the previous edition of *The American Promise* to the current edition, this guide presents an overview of major changes as well as of changes in each chapter.

Computerized Test Bank. The test bank includes a mix of fresh, carefully crafted multiple-choice, matching, short-answer, and essay questions for each chapter. It also contains the Historical Question, Documenting the American Promise, Seeking the American Promise, and Beyond America's Borders questions from the parent textbook and model answers for each. The questions appear in Microsoft Word format and in easy-to-use test bank software that allows instructors to easily add, edit, re-sequence, and print questions and answers. Instructors can also export questions into a variety of formats, including WebCT and Blackboard.

The Bedford Lecture Kit: **Maps, Images, Lecture Outlines, and i>clicker Content.** Look good and save time with *The Bedford Lecture Kit*. These presentation materials are downloadable individually from the Instructor Resources tab at **bedfordstmartins.com/roarkvalue/catalog** and are available on *The Bedford Lecture Kit* Instructor's Resource CD-ROM. They provide ready-made and fully customizable PowerPoint multimedia presentations that include lecture outlines with embedded maps, figures, and selected images from the parent textbook and extra background for instructors. Also available are maps and selected images in JPEG and PowerPoint formats; content for i>clicker, a classroom response system, in Microsoft Word and PowerPoint formats; the *Instructor's Resource Manual* in Microsoft Word format; and outline maps in PDF format for quizzing or handing out. All files are suitable for copying onto transparency acetates.

Make History — **Free Documents, Maps, Images, and Web Sites.** *Make History* combines the best Web resources with hundreds of maps and images, to make it simple to find the source material you need. Browse the collection of thousands of resources by course or by topic, date, and type. Each item has been carefully chosen and helpfully annotated to make it easy to find exactly what you need. Available at **bedfordstmartins.com/makehistory**.

Reel Teaching: Film Clips for the U.S. History Survey. This DVD provides a large collection of short video clips for classroom presentation. Designed as engaging "lecture launchers" varying in length from 1 to 15 or more minutes, the 59 documentary clips were carefully chosen for use in both semesters of the U.S. survey course. The clips feature compelling images, archival footage, personal narratives, and commentary by noted historians.

America in Motion: Video Clips for U.S. History. Set history in motion with *America in Motion*, an instructor DVD containing dozens of short digital movie files of events in twentieth-century American history. From the wreckage of the battleship *Maine*, to FDR's Fireside Chats, to Oliver North testifying before Congress, *America in Motion* engages students with dynamic scenes from key events and challenges them to think critically. All files are classroom-ready, edited for brevity, and easily integrated with PowerPoint or other presentation software for electronic lectures or assignments. An accompanying guide provides each clip's historical context, ideas for use, and suggested questions.

Videos and Multimedia. A wide assortment of videos and multimedia CD-ROMs on various topics in U.S. History is available to qualified adopters through your Bedford/St. Martin's sales representative.

Package and Save Your Students Money

For information on packages and discounts up to 50%, visit **bedfordstmartins.com/ roarkvalue/catalog**, or contact your local Bedford/St. Martin's sales representative.

***Reading the American Past,* Fifth Edition.** Edited by Michael P. Johnson, one of the authors of *The American Promise*, and designed to complement the textbook, *Reading the American Past* provides a broad selection of over 150 primary source documents, as well as editorial apparatus to help students understand the sources. Available at a 50% discount when packaged with the print text.

Reading the American Past e-Book. The reader is also available as an e-book. When packaged with the print or electronic version of the textbook, it is available at a 50% discount.

The Bedford Series in History and Culture. More than one hundred fifty titles in this highly praised series combine first-rate scholarship, historical narrative, and important primary documents for undergraduate courses. Each book is brief, inexpensive, and focused on a specific topic or period. For a complete list of titles, visit **bedfordstmartins.com/history/series**. Package discounts are available.

Rand McNally Atlas of American History. This collection of more than eighty full-color maps illustrates key events and eras from early exploration, settlement, expansion, and immigration to U.S. involvement in wars abroad and on U.S. soil. Introductory pages for each section include a brief overview, timelines, graphs, and photos to quickly establish a historical context. Available for $3.00 when packaged with the print text.

Maps in Context: A Workbook for American History. Written by historical cartography expert Gerald A. Danzer (University of Illinois at Chicago), this skill-building workbook helps students comprehend essential connections between geographic literacy and historical understanding. Organized to correspond to the typical U.S. history survey course, *Maps in Context* presents a wealth of map-centered projects and convenient pop quizzes that give students hands-on experience working with maps. Available for $2.00 when packaged with the print text.

The Bedford Glossary for U.S. History. This handy supplement for the survey course gives students historically contextualized definitions for hundreds of terms—from *abolitionism* to *zoot suit*—that they will encounter in lectures, reading, and exams. Available for $2.00 when packaged with the print text.

U.S. History Matters: A Student Guide to U.S. History Online. This resource, written by Alan Gevinson, Kelly Schrum, and the late Roy Rosenzweig (all of George Mason University), provides an illustrated and annotated guide to 250 of the most useful Web sites for student research in U.S. history as well as advice on evaluating and using Internet sources. This essential guide is based on the acclaimed "History Matters" Web site developed by the American Social History

Project and the Center for History and New Media. Available for $2.00 when packaged with the print text.

Trade Books. Titles published by sister companies Hill and Wang; Farrar, Straus and Giroux; Henry Holt and Company; St. Martin's Press; Picador; and Palgrave Macmillan are available at a 50% discount when packaged with Bedford/St. Martin's textbooks. For more information, visit **bedfordstmartins.com/tradeup**.

A Pocket Guide to Writing in History. This portable and affordable reference tool by Mary Lynn Rampolla provides reading, writing, and research advice useful to students in all history courses. Concise yet comprehensive advice on approaching typical history assignments, developing critical reading skills, writing effective history papers, conducting research, using and documenting sources, and avoiding plagiarism— enhanced with practical tips and examples throughout—have made this slim reference a best-seller. Package discounts are available.

A Student's Guide to History. This complete guide to success in any history course provides the practical help students need to be effective. In addition to introducing students to the nature of the discipline, author Jules Benjamin teaches a wide range of skills from preparing for exams to approaching common writing assignments, and explains the research and documentation process with plentiful examples. Package discounts are available.

Going to the Source: The Bedford Reader in American History. Developed by Victoria Bissell Brown and Timothy J. Shannon, this reader's strong pedagogical framework helps students learn how to ask fruitful questions in order to evaluate documents effectively and develop critical reading skills. The reader's wide variety of chapter topics that complement the survey course and its rich diversity of sources—from personal letters to political cartoons—provoke students' interest as it teaches them the skills they need to successfully interrogate historical sources. Package discounts are available.

America Firsthand. With its distinctive focus on ordinary people, this primary documents reader, by Anthony Marcus, John M. Giggie, and David Burner, offers a remarkable range of perspectives on America's history from those who lived it. Popular Points of View sections expose students to different perspectives on a specific event or topic, and Visual Portfolios invite analysis of the visual record. Package discounts are available.

Brief Contents

Preface   vii

Versions and Supplements   xii

Contents   xviii

Maps and Figures   xxxv

1   Ancient America, Before 1492... 1
2   Europeans Encounter the New World, 1492–1600 25
3   The Southern Colonies in the Seventeenth Century, 1601–1700 53
4   The Northern Colonies in the Seventeenth Century, 1601–1700 81
5   Colonial America in the Eighteenth Century, 1701–1770... 109
6   The British Empire and the Colonial Crisis, 1754–1775... 140
7   The War for America, 1775–1783... 173
8   Building a Republic, 1775–1789.. 207
9   The New Nation Takes Form, 1789–1800... 239
10   Republicans in Power, 1800–1824 267
11   The Expanding Republic, 1815–1840... 301
12   The New West and the Free North, 1840–1860 333
13   The Slave South, 1820–1860 365
14   The House Divided, 1846–1861.. 395
15   The Crucible of War, 1861–1865 425
16   Reconstruction, 1863–1877 459
17   The Contested West, 1865–1900.. 489
18   Business and Politics in the Gilded Age, 1865–1900 521
19   The City and Its Workers, 1870–1900 553
20   Dissent, Depression, and War, 1890–1900 586
21   Progressivism from the Grass Roots to the White House, 1890–1916 617
22   World War I: The Progressive Crusade at Home and Abroad, 1914–1920.................. 651
23   From New Era to Great Depression, 1920–1932... 683
24   The New Deal Experiment, 1932–1939... 716
25   The United States and the Second World War, 1939–1945 749
26   Cold War Politics in the Truman Years, 1945–1953.. 780
27   The Politics and Culture of Abundance, 1952–1960.. 809
28   Reform, Rebellion, and Reaction, 1960–1974 840
29   Vietnam and the End of the Cold War Consensus, 1961–1975.................................. 875
30   America Moves to the Right, 1969–1989 905
31   The Promises and Challenges of Globalization, Since 1989 939

Appendix   A-1

Glossary of Historical Vocabulary   G-1

Index   I-1

About the Authors   last book page

About the Cover Art   last book page

Contents

PREFACE   vii

VERSIONS AND SUPPLEMENTS   xii

BRIEF CONTENTS   xvii

MAPS AND FIGURES   XXXV

CHAPTER 1

Ancient America, Before 1492   1

OPENING VIGNETTE: An archaeological dig helps uncover ancient
North American traditions   1

Archaeology and History   3

The First Americans   4
  • African and Asian Origins 5   • Paleo-Indian Hunters 7

Archaic Hunters and Gatherers   8
  • Great Plains Bison Hunters 9   • Great Basin Cultures 9   • Pacific Coast
  Cultures 10   • Eastern Woodland Cultures 11

Agricultural Settlements and Chiefdoms   12
  • Southwestern Cultures 12   • Woodland Burial Mounds and Chiefdoms 14

Native Americans in the 1490s   15
  • Eastern and Great Plains Peoples 15   • Southwestern and Western Peoples 18
  • Cultural Similarities 18

The Mexica: A Mesoamerican Culture   19

Conclusion: The World of Ancient Americans   22

REVIEWING THE CHAPTER   23

CHAPTER 2

Europeans Encounter the New World,
1492–1600   25

OPENING VIGNETTE: Queen Isabella of Spain supports Christopher Columbus's
risky plan to sail west across the Atlantic   25

Europe in the Age of Exploration   27
  • Mediterranean Trade and European Expansion 28   • A Century of Portuguese
  Exploration 30

A Surprising New World in the Western Atlantic   31
  • The Explorations of Columbus 32   • The Geographic Revolution and the Columbian
  Exchange 34

xviii

Spanish Exploration and Conquest 36
  • The Conquest of Mexico 36 • The Search for Other Mexicos 39 • Spanish Outposts in Florida and New Mexico 40 • New Spain in the Sixteenth Century 41 • The Toll of Spanish Conquest and Colonization 45

The New World and Sixteenth-Century Europe 47
  • The Protestant Reformation and the Spanish Response 47 • Europe and the Spanish Example 48

Conclusion: The Promise of the New World for Europeans 49

REVIEWING THE CHAPTER 51

CHAPTER 3

The Southern Colonies in the Seventeenth Century, 1601–1700 53

OPENING VIGNETTE: Pocahontas "rescues" John Smith **53**

An English Colony on Chesapeake Bay 55
  • The Fragile Jamestown Settlement 56 • Cooperation and Conflict between Natives and Newcomers 57 • From Private Company to Royal Government 60

A Tobacco Society 60
  • Tobacco Agriculture 62 • A Servant Labor System 62 • The Rigors of Servitude 64 • Cultivating Land and Faith 66

Hierarchy and Inequality in the Chesapeake 67
  • Social and Economic Polarization 68 • Government Policies and Political Conflict 68 • Bacon's Rebellion 69

Toward a Slave Labor System 71
  • Religion and Revolt in the Spanish Borderland 72 • The West Indies: Sugar and Slavery 73 • Carolina: A West Indian Frontier 75 • Slave Labor Emerges in the Chesapeake 75

Conclusion: The Growth of English Colonies Based on Export Crops and Slave Labor 77

REVIEWING THE CHAPTER 79

CHAPTER 4

The Northern Colonies in the Seventeenth Century, 1601–1700 81

OPENING VIGNETTE: Roger Williams is banished from Puritan Massachusetts **81**

Puritans and the Settlement of New England 83
  • Puritan Origins: The English Reformation 84 • The Pilgrims and Plymouth Colony 85 • The Founding of Massachusetts Bay Colony 86

The Evolution of New England Society 89
  • Church, Covenant, and Conformity 89 • Government by Puritans for Puritanism 91 • The Splintering of Puritanism 92 • Religious Controversies and Economic Changes 94

The Founding of the Middle Colonies   97
- From New Netherland to New York 98   • New Jersey and Pennsylvania 99
- Toleration and Diversity in Pennsylvania 100

The Colonies and the English Empire   101
- Royal Regulation of Colonial Trade 101   • King Philip's War and the Consolidation of Royal Authority 103

Conclusion: An English Model of Colonization in North America   106

REVIEWING THE CHAPTER   107

CHAPTER 5

Colonial America in the Eighteenth Century,
1701–1770   109

OPENING VIGNETTE: The Robin Johns experience horrific turns of fortune in the Atlantic slave trade   **109**

A Growing Population and Expanding Economy in British North America   111

New England: From Puritan Settlers to Yankee Traders   112
- Natural Increase and Land Distribution 112   • Farms, Fish, and Atlantic Trade 113

The Middle Colonies: Immigrants, Wheat, and Work   116
- German and Scots-Irish Immigrants 116   • "God Gives All Things to Industry": Urban and Rural Labor 118

The Southern Colonies: Land of Slavery   121
- The Atlantic Slave Trade and the Growth of Slavery 122   • Slave Labor and African American Culture 125   • Tobacco, Rice, and Prosperity 127

Unifying Experiences   128
- Commerce and Consumption 129   • Religion, Enlightenment, and Revival 129
- Trade and Conflict in the North American Borderlands 131   • Colonial Politics in the British Empire 135

Conclusion: The Dual Identity of British North American Colonists   136

REVIEWING THE CHAPTER   138

CHAPTER 6

The British Empire and the Colonial Crisis,
1754–1775   140

OPENING VIGNETTE: Loyalist governor Thomas Hutchinson stands his ground in radical Massachusetts   **140**

The Seven Years' War, 1754–1763   142
- French-British Rivalry in the Ohio Country 142   • The Albany Congress 144
- The War and Its Consequences 146   • Pontiac's Rebellion and the Proclamation of 1763 147

The Sugar and Stamp Acts, 1763–1765   150
 • Grenville's Sugar Act 150 • The Stamp Act 151 • Resistance Strategies
and Crowd Politics 152 • Liberty and Property 154

The Townshend Acts and Economic Retaliation, 1767–1770   156
 • The Townshend Duties 156 • Nonconsumption and the Daughters of Liberty 157
 • Military Occupation and "Massacre" in Boston 159

The Destruction of the Tea and the Coercive Acts, 1770–1774   161
 • The Calm before the Storm 161 • Tea in Boston Harbor 162 • The Coercive Acts 163
 • Beyond Boston: Rural New England 164 • The First Continental Congress 165

Domestic Insurrections, 1774–1775   166
 • Lexington and Concord 166 • Rebelling against Slavery 168

Conclusion: The Long Road to Revolution   170

REVIEWING THE CHAPTER   171

CHAPTER 7
The War for America, 1775–1783   173

OPENING VIGNETTE: Deborah Sampson masquerades as a man to join
the Continental army   **173**

The Second Continental Congress   175
 • Assuming Political and Military Authority 175 • Pursuing Both War and Peace 177
 • Thomas Paine, Abigail Adams, and the Case for Independence 178 • The Declaration
of Independence 180

The First Year of War, 1775–1776   181
 • The American Military Forces 181 • The British Strategy 182 • Quebec, New York,
and New Jersey 183

The Home Front   186
 • Patriotism at the Local Level 186 • The Loyalists 187 • Who Is a Traitor? 189
 • Prisoners of War 189 • Financial Instability and Corruption 191

The Campaigns of 1777–1779: The North and West   192
 • Burgoyne's Army and the Battle of Saratoga 192 • The War in the West: Indian
Country 193 • The French Alliance 196

The Southern Strategy and the End of the War   197
 • Georgia and South Carolina 197 • Treason and Guerrilla Warfare 199
 • Surrender at Yorktown 200 • The Losers and the Winners 201

Conclusion: Why the British Lost   203

REVIEWING THE CHAPTER   205

CHAPTER 8
Building a Republic, 1775–1789   207

OPENING VIGNETTE: James Madison comes of age in the midst of revolution   **207**

The Articles of Confederation 209
- Congress and Confederation 209 • The Problem of Western Lands 211
- Running the New Government 211

The Sovereign States 213
- The State Constitutions 213 • Who Are "the People"? 214 • Equality and Slavery 216

The Confederation's Problems 218
- The War Debt and the Newburgh Conspiracy 219 • The Treaty of Fort Stanwix 220
- Land Ordinances and the Northwest Territory 222 • The Requisition of 1785 and Shays's Rebellion, 1786–1787 225

The United States Constitution 227
- From Annapolis to Philadelphia 227 • The Virginia and New Jersey Plans 228
- Democracy versus Republicanism 230

Ratification of the Constitution 231
- The Federalists 231 • The Antifederalists 232 • The Big Holdouts: Virginia and New York 234

Conclusion: The "Republican Remedy" 235

REVIEWING THE CHAPTER 237

CHAPTER 9
The New Nation Takes Form, 1789–1800   239

OPENING VIGNETTE: Brilliant and brash, Alexander Hamilton becomes a polarizing figure in the 1790s **239**

The Search for Stability 241
- Washington Inaugurates the Government 242 • The Bill of Rights 243
- The Republican Wife and Mother 244

Hamilton's Economic Policies 245
- Agriculture, Transportation, and Banking 245 • The Public Debt and Taxes 247
- The First Bank of the United States and the *Report on Manufactures* 248
- The Whiskey Rebellion 250

Conflict on America's Borders and Beyond 251
- Creeks in the Southwest 251 • Ohio Indians in the Northwest 253 • France and Britain 255 • The Haitian Revolution 258

Federalists and Republicans 259
- The Election of 1796 260 • The XYZ Affair 261 • The Alien and Sedition Acts 262

Conclusion: Parties Nonetheless 264

REVIEWING THE CHAPTER 265

CHAPTER 10
Republicans in Power, 1800–1824   267

OPENING VIGNETTE: The Shawnee chief Tecumseh attempts to forge a pan-Indian confederacy **267**

Jefferson's Presidency 269
- Turbulent Times: Election and Rebellion 270 • The Jeffersonian Vision of Republican Simplicity 271 • Dangers Overseas: The Barbary Wars 272

Opportunities and Challenges in the West 273
- The Louisiana Purchase 274 • The Lewis and Clark Expedition 275
- Osage and Comanche Indians 277

Jefferson, the Madisons, and the War of 1812 279
- Impressment and Embargo 279 • Dolley Madison and Social Politics 280
- Tecumseh and Tippecanoe 281 • The War of 1812 282 • Washington City Burns: The British Offensive 285

Women's Status in the Early Republic 286
- Women and the Law 287 • Women and Church Governance 288
- Female Education 288

Monroe and Adams 290
- From Property to Democracy 291 • The Missouri Compromise 292
- The Monroe Doctrine 294 • The Election of 1824 295 • The Adams Administration 296

Conclusion: Republican Simplicity Becomes Complex 297

REVIEWING THE CHAPTER 299

CHAPTER 11

The Expanding Republic, 1815–1840 301

OPENING VIGNETTE: The Grimké sisters speak out against slavery **301**

The Market Revolution 303
- Improvements in Transportation 304 • Factories, Workingwomen, and Wage Labor 305 • Bankers and Lawyers 307 • Booms and Busts 308

The Spread of Democracy 309
- Popular Politics and Partisan Identity 309 • The Election of 1828 and the Character Issue 310 • Jackson's Democratic Agenda 311

Jackson Defines the Democratic Party 312
- Indian Policy and the Trail of Tears 313 • The Tariff of Abominations and Nullification 316 • The Bank War and Economic Boom 317

Cultural Shifts, Religion, and Reform 319
- The Family and Separate Spheres 319 • The Education and Training of Youths 320 • The Second Great Awakening 321 • The Temperance Movement and the Campaign for Moral Reform 322 • Organizing against Slavery 324

Van Buren's One-Term Presidency 326
- The Politics of Slavery 326 • Elections and Panics 327

Conclusion: The Age of Jackson or the Era of Reform? 329

REVIEWING THE CHAPTER 331

CHAPTER 12
The New West and the Free North, 1840–1860   333

OPENING VIGNETTE: With the support of his wife, Abraham Lincoln struggles to survive in antebellum America   333

Economic and Industrial Evolution   335
- Agriculture and Land Policy 335
- Manufacturing and Mechanization 337   • Railroads: Breaking the Bonds of Nature 337

Free Labor: Promise and Reality   339
- The Free-Labor Ideal 340   • Economic Inequality 340   • Immigrants and the Free-Labor Ladder 341

The Westward Movement   342
- Manifest Destiny 343   • Oregon and the Overland Trail 343   • The Mormon Exodus 346   • The Mexican Borderlands 347

Expansion and the Mexican-American War   349
- The Politics of Expansion 349   • The Mexican-American War, 1846–1848 350
- Victory in Mexico 353   • Golden California 354

Reforming Self and Society   357
- The Pursuit of Perfection: Transcendentalists and Utopians 357   • Woman's Rights Activists 358   • Abolitionists and the American Ideal 360

Conclusion: Free Labor, Free Men   362

REVIEWING THE CHAPTER   363

CHAPTER 13
The Slave South, 1820–1860   365

OPENING VIGNETTE: Slave Nat Turner leads a revolt to end slavery   365

The Growing Distinctiveness of the South   367
- Cotton Kingdom, Slave Empire 367   • The South in Black and White 369
- The Plantation Economy 370

Masters and Mistresses in the Big House   374
- Paternalism and Male Honor 374   • The Southern Lady and Feminine Virtues 376

Slaves in the Quarter   378
- Work 378   • Family and Religion 380   • Resistance and Rebellion 381

The Plain Folk   382
- Plantation Belt Yeomen 383   • Upcountry Yeomen 383   • Poor Whites 384
- The Culture of the Plain Folk 385

Black and Free: On the Middle Ground   387
- Precarious Freedom 387   • Achievement despite Restrictions 388

The Politics of Slavery   389
- The Democratization of the Political Arena 389   • Planter Power 390

Conclusion: A Slave Society   392

REVIEWING THE CHAPTER   393

CHAPTER 14

The House Divided, 1846–1861　395

OPENING VIGNETTE: Abolitionist John Brown takes his war against slavery
to Harpers Ferry, Virginia　**395**

The Bitter Fruits of War　397
- The Wilmot Proviso and the Expansion of Slavery 397　• The Election of 1848 399
- Debate and Compromise 400

The Sectional Balance Undone　402
- The Fugitive Slave Act 402　• *Uncle Tom's Cabin* 403　• The Kansas-Nebraska Act 405

Realignment of the Party System　406
- The Old Parties: Whigs and Democrats 407　• The New Parties: Know-Nothings
and Republicans 408　• The Election of 1856 409

Freedom under Siege　411
- "Bleeding Kansas" 411　• The *Dred Scott* Decision 412　• Prairie Republican:
Abraham Lincoln 414　• The Lincoln-Douglas Debates 415

The Union Collapses　416
- The Aftermath of John Brown's Raid 417　• Republican Victory in 1860 417
- Secession Winter 419

Conclusion: Slavery, Free Labor, and the Failure of Political Compromise　421

REVIEWING THE CHAPTER　423

CHAPTER 15

The Crucible of War, 1861–1865　425

OPENING VIGNETTE: Runaway slave William Gould enlists in the U.S. navy　**425**

"And the War Came"　427
- Attack on Fort Sumter 428　• The Upper South Chooses Sides 428

The Combatants　430
- How They Expected to Win 431　• Lincoln and Davis Mobilize 432

Battling It Out, 1861–1862　434
- Stalemate in the Eastern Theater 434　• Union Victories in the Western Theater 437
- The Atlantic Theater 439　• International Diplomacy 439

Union *and* Freedom　440
- From Slaves to Contraband 440　• From Contraband to Free People 442　• The War
of Black Liberation 443

The South at War　444
- Revolution from Above 445　• Hardship Below 445　• The Disintegration
of Slavery 446

The North at War　447
- The Government and the Economy 447　• Women and Work at Home and at War 448
- Politics and Dissent 449

Grinding Out Victory, 1863–1865   450
- Vicksburg and Gettysburg 450 • Grant Takes Command 451 • The Election of 1864 454 • The Confederacy Collapses 454

Conclusion: The Second American Revolution   456

REVIEWING THE CHAPTER   457

CHAPTER 16

Reconstruction, 1863–1877   459

OPENING VIGNETTE: James T. Rapier emerges in the early 1870s as Alabama's most prominent black leader   **459**

Wartime Reconstruction   461
- "To Bind Up the Nation's Wounds" 461 • Land and Labor 463 • The African American Quest for Autonomy 464

Presidential Reconstruction   465
- Johnson's Program of Reconciliation 465 • White Southern Resistance and Black Codes 466 • Expansion of Federal Authority and Black Rights 467

Congressional Reconstruction   468
- The Fourteenth Amendment and Escalating Violence 468 • Radical Reconstruction and Military Rule 470 • Impeaching a President 471 • The Fifteenth Amendment and Women's Demands 472

The Struggle in the South   473
- Freedmen, Yankees, and Yeomen 473 • Republican Rule 475 • White Landlords, Black Sharecroppers 477

Reconstruction Collapses   479
- Grant's Troubled Presidency 479 • Northern Resolve Withers 480 • White Supremacy Triumphs 482 • An Election and a Compromise 484

Conclusion: "A Revolution But Half Accomplished"   486

REVIEWING THE CHAPTER   487

CHAPTER 17

The Contested West, 1865–1900   489

OPENING VIGNETTE: Frederick Jackson Turner delivers his "frontier thesis"   **489**

Conquest and Empire in the West   491
- Indian Removal and the Reservation System 493 • The Decimation of the Great Bison Herds 495 • Indian Wars and the Collapse of Comanchería 496 • The Fight for the Black Hills 497

Forced Assimilation and Resistance Strategies   498
- Indian Schools and the War against Indian Culture 499 • The Dawes Act and Indian Land Allotment 499 • Indian Resistance and Survival 500

Gold Fever and the Mining West   504
- Mining on the Comstock Lode 504 • The Diverse Peoples of the West 506 • Territorial Government 509

Land Fever   510
- Moving West: Homesteaders and Speculators 510   • Ranchers and Cowboys 513
- Tenants, Sharecroppers, and Migrants 514   • Commercial Farming and Industrial Cowboys 515

Conclusion: The West in the Gilded Age   517

REVIEWING THE CHAPTER   519

CHAPTER 18

Business and Politics in the Gilded Age, 1865–1900   521

OPENING VIGNETTE: Mark Twain and the Gilded Age   **521**

Old Industries Transformed, New Industries Born   523
- Railroads: America's First Big Business 525   • Andrew Carnegie, Steel, and Vertical Integration 527   • John D. Rockefeller, Standard Oil, and the Trust 528
- New Inventions: The Telephone and Electricity 530

From Competition to Consolidation   532
- J. P. Morgan and Finance Capitalism 532   • Social Darwinism, Laissez-Faire, and the Supreme Court 534

Politics and Culture   536
- Political Participation and Party Loyalty 536   • Sectionalism and the New South 536
- Gender, Race, and Politics 538   • Women's Activism 540

Presidential Politics   541
- Corruption and Party Strife 541   • Garfield's Assassination and Civil Service Reform 543   • Reform and Scandal: The Campaign of 1884 543

Economic Issues and Party Realignment   545
- The Tariff and the Politics of Protection 545   • Railroads, Trusts, and the Federal Government 546   • The Fight for Free Silver 547   • Panic and Depression 549

Conclusion: Business Dominates an Era   550

REVIEWING THE CHAPTER   551

CHAPTER 19

The City and Its Workers, 1870–1900   553

OPENING VIGNETTE: Workers build the Brooklyn Bridge   **553**

The Rise of the City   555
- The Urban Explosion: A Global Migration 557   • Racism and the Cry for Immigration Restriction 560   • The Social Geography of the City 563

At Work in Industrial America   564
- America's Diverse Workers 565   • The Family Economy: Women and Children 566
- White-Collar Workers: Managers, "Typewriters," and Salesclerks 568

Workers Organize   570
- The Great Railroad Strike of 1877 570   • The Knights of Labor and the American Federation of Labor 572   • Haymarket and the Specter of Labor Radicalism 574

At Home and at Play 575
- Domesticity and "Domestics" 576 • Cheap Amusements 577

City Growth and City Government 578
- Building Cities of Stone and Steel 578 • City Government and the "Bosses" 580
- White City or City of Sin? 582

Conclusion: Who Built the Cities? 583

REVIEWING THE CHAPTER   584

CHAPTER 20

Dissent, Depression, and War, 1890–1900   586

OPENING VIGNETTE: Frances Willard participates in the creation of the Populist Party in 1892 **586**

The Farmers' Revolt 588
- The Farmers' Alliance 589 • The Populist Movement 590

The Labor Wars 591
- The Homestead Lockout 591 • The Cripple Creek Miners' Strike of 1894 594
- Eugene V. Debs and the Pullman Strike 594

Women's Activism 597
- Frances Willard and the Woman's Christian Temperance Union 598 • Elizabeth Cady Stanton, Susan B. Anthony, and the Movement for Woman Suffrage 599

Depression Politics 600
- Coxey's Army 600 • The People's Party and the Election of 1896 602

The United States and the World 605
- Markets and Missionaries 606 • The Monroe Doctrine and the Open Door Policy 607 • "A Splendid Little War" 609 • The Debate over American Imperialism 611

Conclusion: Rallying around the Flag 614

REVIEWING THE CHAPTER   615

CHAPTER 21

Progressivism from the Grass Roots to the White House, 1890–1916   617

OPENING VIGNETTE: Jane Addams founds Hull House   **617**

Grassroots Progressivism 619
- Civilizing the City 620 • Progressives and the Working Class 621

Progressivism: Theory and Practice 624
- Reform Darwinism and Social Engineering 624 • Progressive Government: City and State 625

Progressivism Finds a President: Theodore Roosevelt 626
- The Square Deal 626 • Roosevelt the Reformer 630 • Roosevelt and Conservation 632
- The Big Stick 633 • The Troubled Presidency of William Howard Taft 635

Woodrow Wilson and Progressivism at High Tide   638
  • Progressive Insurgency and the Election of 1912 638   • Wilson's Reforms:
  Tariff, Banking, and the Trusts 639   • Wilson, Reluctant Progressive 641

The Limits of Progressive Reform   642
  • Radical Alternatives 642   • Progressivism for White Men Only 644

Conclusion: The Transformation of the Liberal State   647

REVIEWING THE CHAPTER   649

CHAPTER 22

World War I: The Progressive Crusade at Home and Abroad, 1914–1920   651

OPENING VIGNETTE: Doughboy George "Brownie" Browne sees combat on the front
lines in France   **651**

Woodrow Wilson and the World   653
  • Taming the Americas 654   • The European Crisis 655   • The Ordeal of American
  Neutrality 657   • The United States Enters the War 658

"Over There"   660
  • The Call to Arms 660   • The War in France 662

The Crusade for Democracy at Home   663
  • The Progressive Stake in the War 664   • Women, War, and the Battle
  for Suffrage 665   • Rally around the Flag — or Else 666

A Compromised Peace   668
  • Wilson's Fourteen Points 668   • The Paris Peace Conference 669   • The Fight
  for the Treaty 672

Democracy at Risk   673
  • Economic Hardship and Labor Upheaval 674   • The Red Scare 675   • The Great
  Migrations of African Americans and Mexicans 677   • Postwar Politics
  and the Election of 1920 679

Conclusion: Troubled Crusade   680

REVIEWING THE CHAPTER   681

CHAPTER 23

From New Era to Great Depression, 1920–1932   683

OPENING VIGNETTE: Henry Ford puts America on wheels   **683**

The New Era   685
  • A Business Government 686   • Promoting Prosperity and Peace Abroad 687
  • Automobiles, Mass Production, and Assembly-Line Progress 688   • Consumer
  Culture 689

The Roaring Twenties   690
  • Prohibition 691   • The New Woman 692   • The New Negro 694   • Entertainment
  for the Masses 696   • The Lost Generation 697

Resistance to Change   698
• Rejecting the Undesirables 699   • The Rebirth of the Ku Klux Klan 700   • The Scopes Trial 701   • Al Smith and the Election of 1928 702

The Great Crash   703
• Herbert Hoover: The Great Engineer 704   • The Distorted Economy 704   • The Crash of 1929 705   • Hoover and the Limits of Individualism 706

Life in the Depression   707
• The Human Toll 707   • Denial and Escape 710   • Working-Class Militancy 711

Conclusion: Dazzle and Despair   712

REVIEWING THE CHAPTER   714

CHAPTER 24

The New Deal Experiment, 1932–1939   716

OPENING VIGNETTE: "Migrant Mother" Florence Owens struggles to survive in the Great Depression   716

Franklin D. Roosevelt: A Patrician in Government   718
• The Making of a Politician 719   • The Election of 1932 720

Launching the New Deal   722
• The New Dealers 722   • Banking and Finance Reform 723   • Relief and Conservation Programs 725   • Agricultural Initiatives 727   • Industrial Recovery 728

Challenges to the New Deal   729
• Resistance to Business Reform 729   • Casualties in the Countryside 730   • Politics on the Fringes 732

Toward a Welfare State   733
• Relief for the Unemployed 734   • Empowering Labor 735   • Social Security and Tax Reform 737   • Neglected Americans and the New Deal 738

The New Deal from Victory to Deadlock   740
• The Election of 1936 741   • Court Packing 741   • Reaction and Recession 742   • The Last of the New Deal Reforms 743

Conclusion: Achievements and Limitations of the New Deal   745

REVIEWING THE CHAPTER   747

CHAPTER 25

The United States and the Second World War, 1939–1945   749

OPENING VIGNETTE: Colonel Paul Tibbets drops the atomic bomb on Hiroshima, Japan   749

Peacetime Dilemmas   751
• Roosevelt and Reluctant Isolation 751   • The Good Neighbor Policy 752   • The Price of Noninvolvement 753

The Onset of War   755
  • Nazi Aggression and War in Europe 755   • From Neutrality to the Arsenal of Democracy 757   • Japan Attacks America 758

Mobilizing for War   759
  • Home-Front Security 760   • Building a Citizen Army 760   • Conversion to a War Economy 761

Fighting Back   762
  • Turning the Tide in the Pacific 763   • The Campaign in Europe 764

The Wartime Home Front   765
  • Women and Families, Guns and Butter 766   • The Double V Campaign 767
  • Wartime Politics and the 1944 Election 768   • Reaction to the Holocaust 769

Toward Unconditional Surrender   770
  • From Bombing Raids to Berlin 770   • The Defeat of Japan 773
  • Atomic Warfare 775

Conclusion: Allied Victory and America's Emergence as a Superpower   776

REVIEWING THE CHAPTER   778

CHAPTER 26

Cold War Politics in the Truman Years, 1945–1953   780

OPENING VIGNETTE: Helen Gahagan Douglas, congresswoman and loyal Truman ally, supports the Marshall Plan, the creation of NATO, and the war in Korea   **780**

From the Grand Alliance to Containment   782
  • The Cold War Begins 783   • The Truman Doctrine and the Marshall Plan 786
  • Building a National Security State 788   • Superpower Rivalry around the Globe 790

Truman and the Fair Deal at Home   792
  • Reconverting to a Peacetime Economy 792   • Blacks and Mexican Americans Push for Their Civil Rights 794   • The Fair Deal Flounders 797   • The Domestic Chill: McCarthyism 798

The Cold War Becomes Hot: Korea   800
  • Korea and the Military Implementation of Containment 800   • From Containment to Rollback to Containment 802   • Korea, Communism, and the 1952 Election 802
  • An Armistice and the War's Costs 804

Conclusion: The Cold War's Costs and Consequences   805

REVIEWING THE CHAPTER   807

CHAPTER 27

The Politics and Culture of Abundance, 1952–1960   809

OPENING VIGNETTE: Vice President Richard Nixon debates Russian premier Nikita Khrushchev   **809**

Eisenhower and the Politics of the "Middle Way"   811
- Modern Republicanism 812   • Termination and Relocation of Native Americans 813
- The 1956 Election and the Second Term 815

Liberation Rhetoric and the Practice of Containment   815
- The "New Look" in Foreign Policy 816   • Applying Containment to Vietnam 817
- Interventions in Latin America and the Middle East 818   • The Nuclear Arms Race 820

New Work and Living Patterns in an Economy of Abundance   821
- Technology Transforms Agriculture and Industry 821   • Burgeoning Suburbs and Declining Cities 823   • The Rise of the Sun Belt 823   • The Democratization of Higher Education 826

The Culture of Abundance   827
- Consumption Rules the Day 827   • The Revival of Domesticity and Religion 828
- Television Transforms Culture and Politics 829   • Countercurrents 830

The Emergence of a Civil Rights Movement   832
- African Americans Challenge the Supreme Court and the President 832
- Montgomery and Mass Protest 834

Conclusion: Peace and Prosperity Mask Unmet Challenges   836

REVIEWING THE CHAPTER   838

CHAPTER 28

Reform, Rebellion, and Reaction,
1960–1974   840

OPENING VIGNETTE: Fannie Lou Hamer leads grassroots struggles of African Americans for voting rights and political empowerment   **840**

Liberalism at High Tide   842
- The Unrealized Promise of Kennedy's New Frontier 843   • Johnson Fulfills the Kennedy Promise 844   • Policymaking for a Great Society 845   • Assessing the Great Society 848   • The Judicial Revolution 849

The Second Reconstruction   850
- The Flowering of the Black Freedom Struggle 850   • The Response in Washington 853
- Black Power and Urban Rebellions 855

A Multitude of Movements   858
- Native American Protest 858   • Latino Struggles for Justice 859
- Student Rebellion, the New Left, and the Counterculture 861   • Gay Men and Lesbians Organize 863

The New Wave of Feminism   863
- A Multifaceted Movement Emerges 864   • Feminist Gains Spark a Countermovement 866

Liberal Reform in the Nixon Administration   868
- Extending the Welfare State and Regulating the Economy 868   • Responding to Environmental Concerns 869   • Expanding Social Justice 870

Conclusion: Achievements and Limitations of Liberalism   871

REVIEWING THE CHAPTER   873

CHAPTER 29

Vietnam and the End of the Cold War Consensus, 1961–1975   875

OPENING VIGNETTE: Lieutenant Frederick Downs, Jr., is wounded in Vietnam and returns home to a country divided over the war   875

New Frontiers in Foreign Policy   877
- Meeting the "Hour of Maximum Danger" 877 • New Approaches to the Third World 880
- The Arms Race and the Nuclear Brink 881 • A Growing War in Vietnam 882

Lyndon Johnson's War against Communism   884
- An All-Out Commitment in Vietnam 884 • Preventing Another Castro in Latin America 886 • The Americanized War 886 • Those Who Served 887

A Nation Polarized   888
- The Widening War at Home 889 • The Tet Offensive and Johnson's Move toward Peace 890 • The Tumultuous Election of 1968 892

Nixon, Détente, and the Search for Peace in Vietnam   893
- Moving toward Détente with the Soviet Union and China 893 • Shoring Up U.S. Interests around the World 895 • Vietnam Becomes Nixon's War 896 • The Peace Accords 898 • The Legacy of Defeat 900

Conclusion: An Unwinnable War   901

REVIEWING THE CHAPTER   903

CHAPTER 30

America Moves to the Right, 1969–1989   905

OPENING VIGNETTE: Phyllis Schlafly promotes conservatism   905

Nixon, Conservatism, and Constitutional Crisis   907
- Emergence of a Grassroots Movement 908 • Nixon Courts the Right 910 • The Election of 1972 911 • Watergate 912 • The Ford Presidency and the 1976 Election 913

The "Outsider" Presidency of Jimmy Carter   915
- Retreat from Liberalism 915 • Energy and Environmental Reform 917 • Promoting Human Rights Abroad 919 • The Cold War Intensifies 921

Ronald Reagan and the Conservative Ascendancy   922
- Appealing to the New Right and Beyond 923 • Unleashing Free Enterprise 924
- Winners and Losers in a Flourishing Economy 926

Continuing Struggles over Rights   928
- Battles in the Courts and Congress 928 • Feminism on the Defensive 929 • The Gay and Lesbian Rights Movement 930

Ronald Reagan Confronts an "Evil Empire"   932
- Militarization and Interventions Abroad 932 • The Iran-Contra Scandal 933
- A Thaw in Soviet-American Relations 934

Conclusion: Reversing the Course of Government   936

REVIEWING THE CHAPTER   937

CHAPTER 31
The Promises and Challenges of Globalization,
Since 1989   939

OPENING VIGNETTE: Colin Powell adjusts to a post-Cold War world   **939**

Domestic Stalemate and Global Upheaval: The Presidency of George H.W. Bush   942
- Gridlock in Government 942 • Going to War in Central America and the Persian Gulf 945 • The Cold War Ends 946 • The 1992 Election 949

The Clinton Administration's Search for the Middle Ground   950
- Clinton's Reforms 950 • Accommodating the Right 952 • Impeaching the President 953 • The Booming Economy of the 1990s 954

The United States in a Globalizing World   955
- Defining America's Place in a New World Order 956 • Debates over Globalization 957
- The Internationalization of the United States 959

President George W. Bush: Conservatism at Home and Radical Initiatives Abroad   961
- The Disputed Election of 2000 961 • The Domestic Policies of a "Compassionate Conservative" 962 • The Globalization of Terrorism 965 • Unilateralism, Preemption, and the Iraq War 967

The Obama Presidency: Reform and Backlash   970

Conclusion: Defining the Government's Role at Home and Abroad   972

REVIEWING THE CHAPTER   974

APPENDIX

The Declaration of Independence   A-1
The Articles of Confederation and Perpetual Union   A-4
The Constitution of the United States   A-9
Amendments to the Constitution (including the six unratified amendments)   A-17

GLOSSARY OF HISTORICAL VOCABULARY   G-1

INDEX   I-1

ABOUT THE AUTHORS   last book page

ABOUT THE COVER ART   last book page

Maps and Figures

CHAPTER 1

MAP 1.1 Continental Drift   5

MAP 1.2 Native North Americans about 1500   16

CHAPTER 2

MAP 2.1 European Trade Routes and Portuguese Exploration in the Fifteenth Century   28

MAP 2.2 Sixteenth-Century European Colonies in the New World   42

CHAPTER 3

MAP 3.1 Chesapeake Colonies in the Seventeenth Century   61

MAP 3.2 The West Indies and Carolina in the Seventeenth Century   74

CHAPTER 4

MAP 4.1 New England Colonies in the Seventeenth Century   88

MAP 4.2 American Colonies at the End of the Seventeenth Century   102

CHAPTER 5

MAP 5.1 Atlantic Trade in the Eighteenth Century   114

MAP 5.2 Zones of Empire in Eastern North America   132

CHAPTER 6

MAP 6.1 European Areas of Influence and the Seven Years' War, 1754–1763   143

MAP 6.2 Lexington and Concord, April 1775   167

CHAPTER 7

MAP 7.1 The War in the North, 1775–1778   184

MAP 7.2 The Indian War in the West, 1777–1782   195

MAP 7.3 The War in the South, 1780–1781   198

CHAPTER 8

MAP 8.1 Cession of Western Lands, 1782–1802   212

MAP 8.2 The Northwest Territory and Ordinance of 1785   223

CHAPTER 9

MAP 9.1 Travel Times from New York City in 1800   246

MAP 9.2 Western Expansion and Indian Land Cessions to 1810   254

CHAPTER 10

MAP 10.1 Jefferson's Expeditions in the West, 1804–1806   276

MAP 10.2 The War of 1812   284

MAP 10.3 The Missouri Compromise, 1820   294

CHAPTER 11
MAP 11.1 The Election of 1828   311
MAP 11.2 Indian Removal and the Trail of Tears   314

CHAPTER 12
MAP 12.1 Railroads in 1860   338
MAP 12.2 The Mexican-American War, 1846–1848   351
MAP 12.3 Territorial Expansion by 1860   354

CHAPTER 13
MAP 13.1 Cotton Kingdom, Slave Empire: 1820 and 1860   368
MAP 13.2 The Agricultural Economy of the South, 1860   371

CHAPTER 14
MAP 14.1 The Compromise of 1850   402
MAP 14.2 Political Realignment, 1848–1860   407

CHAPTER 15
MAP 15.1 Secession, 1860–1861   429
MAP 15.2 The Civil War, 1861–1862   435
MAP 15.3 The Civil War, 1863–1865   452

CHAPTER 16
MAP 16.1 A Southern Plantation in 1860 and 1881   478
MAP 16.2 The Reconstruction of the South   485

CHAPTER 17
MAP 17.1 The Loss of Indian Lands, 1850–1890   492
MAP 17.2 Federal Land Grants to Railroads and the Development of the West, 1850–1900   512

CHAPTER 18
MAP 18.1 Railroad Expansion, 1870–1890   524
MAP 18.2 The Election of 1884   544

CHAPTER 19
MAP 19.1 Economic Regions of the World, 1890s   556
MAP 19.2 The Impact of Immigration, to 1910   558

CHAPTER 20
MAP 20.1 The Spanish-American War, 1898   611
MAP 20.2 U.S. Overseas Expansion through 1900   612

CHAPTER 21
MAP 21.1 National Parks and Forests   634
MAP 21.2 The Election of 1912   640

CHAPTER 22

MAP 22.1 European Alliances after the Outbreak of World War I   656

MAP 22.2 Women's Voting Rights before the Nineteenth Amendment   666

MAP 22.3 Europe after World War I   671

CHAPTER 23

MAP 23.1 The Shift from Rural to Urban Population, 1920–1930   699

FIGURE 23.1 Manufacturing and Agricultural Income, 1920–1940   708

CHAPTER 24

MAP 24.1 Electoral Shift, 1928–1932   721

MAP 24.2 The Tennessee Valley Authority   726

CHAPTER 25

MAP 25.1 Western Relocation Authority Centers   761

MAP 25.2 The European Theater of World War II, 1942–1945   772

MAP 25.3 The Pacific Theater of World War II, 1941–1945   774

CHAPTER 26

MAP 26.1 The Division of Europe after World War II   784

MAP 26.2 The Korean War, 1950–1953   801

CHAPTER 27

MAP 27.1 The Interstate Highway System, 1930 and 1970   813

MAP 27.2 The Rise of the Sun Belt, 1940–1980   824

CHAPTER 28

MAP 28.1 The Rise of the African American Vote, 1940–1976   854

MAP 28.2 Urban Uprisings, 1965–1968   856

CHAPTER 29

MAP 29.1 U.S. Involvement in Latin America and the Caribbean, 1954–1994   878

MAP 29.2 The Vietnam War, 1964–1975   883

CHAPTER 30

MAP 30.1 Worldwide Oil Reserves, 1980   918

MAP 30.2 The Middle East, 1948–1989   920

CHAPTER 31

MAP 31.1 Events in the Middle East, 1989–2011   944

MAP 31.2 Events in Eastern Europe, 1989–2002   948

MAP 31.3 The Election of 2000   962

VALUE EDITION

The American Promise

A History of the United States

FIFTH EDITION

Ancient America

Before 1492

NOBODY TODAY KNOWS HIS NAME. BUT ALMOST A THOUSAND YEARS ago, more than four hundred years before Europeans arrived in the Western Hemisphere, many ancient Americans celebrated this man — let's call him Sun Falcon. They buried Sun Falcon during elaborate rituals at Cahokia, the largest residential and ceremonial site in ancient North America. (In this chapter, ancient North America refers to the giant landmass north of present-day Mexico.) Located near the eastern shore of the Mississippi River in what is now southwestern Illinois, Cahokia stood at the spiritual and political center of the world in the eyes of the 15,000 or 20,000 ancient Americans who lived there and thousands more in the hinterlands nearby. The way Cahokians buried Sun Falcon suggests that he was a very important person who represented spiritual and political authority.

What we know about Sun Falcon and the Cahokians who buried him has been discovered by archaeologists — scientists who study artifacts, or material objects, left behind by ancient peoples. Cahokia attracted the attention of archaeologists because of the hundreds of earthen mounds that ancient Americans built in the region. The largest surviving mound, Monks Mound, is a huge terraced pyramid rising one hundred feet from a base that covers sixteen acres (an acre is about the size of a football field), making it the biggest single structure ever built by ancient North Americans.

Atop the four terraces — or platforms — on Monks Mound, political and religious leaders performed ceremonies watched by thousands of Cahokia residents and visitors who stood on a fifty-acre plaza at the base of the mound. Exactly what the leaders did in these ceremonies is unknown.

1

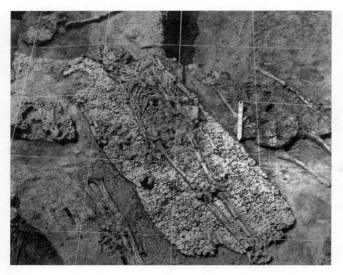

Cahokia Burial
The excavation of the ceremonial burial site at Cahokia revealed the remains of a man—presumably a revered leader—whom Cahokians buried atop a large cape or blanket in the shape of a bird, probably a raptor. Archaeologists superimposed the grid of white lines to record the precise location of each object. Covering the cape are more than 20,000 beads made of shells sewn onto an underlying fabric or animal skin (not visible). Nearby in the same mound, excavators found mass graves of scores of other Cahokians, many of them executed just before burial, evidently during ceremonies to honor their leader.
Courtesy Illinois State Museum: archival photograph.

Whatever they did was probably designed to demonstrate to onlookers the leaders' access to supernatural forces. Large garbage pits beside the plaza contain the bones of thousands of butchered deer, remnants of giant feasts that probably accompanied these ceremonies. At the far edge of the plaza, about a half mile from the base of Monk's Mound, Cahokians buried Sun Falcon in an oblong mound about 6 feet high and 250 feet long.

Before Cahokians lowered Sun Falcon into his grave sometime around AD 1050, they first placed the body of another man facedown in the dirt. On top of that man, Cahokians draped a large cape made of twenty thousand shell beads crafted into the likeness of a bird. They then put Sun Falcon faceup on the beaded cape with his head pointing southeast, aligned with the passage of the sun across the sky during the summer solstice at Cahokia. Experts speculate that Cahokians believed that Sun Falcon looked upward toward the life-giving light of the sun while the man beneath the beaded cape communicated with the dark interior of the earth. The people who buried Sun Falcon, it appears, sought to pay homage not only to him but also to the awe-inspiring forces of darkness and light, of earth and sun, that governed their lives.

To accompany Sun Falcon, Cahokians also buried hundreds of arrows with exquisitely crafted arrowheads, thousands of shell beads, and other rare and valuable artifacts that they believed Sun Falcon would find useful in the afterlife. Near the artifacts, Cahokians buried the bodies of seven other adults, including at least one person killed at the grave site, who probably were relatives or servants of Sun Falcon. Not far away, archaeologists discovered several astonishing mass graves. One contained 53 women, all but one between the ages of fifteen and twenty-five, who had been sacrificed by poison, strangulation, or having their throats slit. Other graves contained 43 more sacrificed women, 4 men whose arms had been tied together at the elbows and whose heads and hands had been chopped off, and 39 other men and women who had been executed at the burial site. In all, more than 270 people were buried in the mound with Sun Falcon.

To date, archaeologists have found no similar burial site in ancient North America. However, they have excavated only a tiny fraction of Cahokia. Who knows what remains to be discovered there and elsewhere?

Nobody knows exactly who Sun Falcon was or why Cahokians buried him as they did. Archaeologists believe that Sun Falcon's burial and the human sacrifices that accompanied it were major public rituals that communicated to the many onlookers the fearsome power he wielded, the respect he commanded, and the authority his survivors intended to honor and maintain. Much remains unknown and unknowable about him and his fellow Cahokians, just as it does with other ancient Americans. The history of ancient Americans is therefore necessarily incomplete and controversial. Still, archaeologists have learned enough to understand where ancient Americans came from and many basic features of the complex cultures they created and passed along to their descendants, who dominated the history of America until 1492.

▶ Archaeology and History

Archaeologists and historians share the desire to learn about people who lived in the past, but they usually employ different methods to obtain information. Both archaeologists and historians study **artifacts** as clues to the activities and ideas of the humans who created them. They concentrate, however, on different kinds of artifacts. **Archaeologists** tend to focus on physical objects such as bones, spear points, pots, baskets, jewelry, clothing, and buildings. Historians direct their attention mostly to writings, including personal and private jottings such as letters and diary entries, and an enormous variety of public documents, such as laws, speeches, newspapers, and court cases. Although historians are interested in other artifacts and archaeologists do not neglect written sources if they exist, the characteristic concentration of historians on writings and of archaeologists on other physical objects denotes a rough cultural and chronological boundary between the human beings studied by the two groups of scholars, a boundary marked by the use of writing.

Writing is defined as a system of symbols that record spoken language. Writing originated among ancient peoples in China, Egypt, and Central America about eight thousand years ago, within the most recent 2 percent of the four hundred millennia that modern human beings (*Homo sapiens*) have existed. Writing came into use even later in most other places in the world. The ancient Americans who buried Sun Falcon at Cahokia about AD 1050 and all those who inhabited North America in 1492 possessed many forms of symbolic representation, but not writing.

The people who lived during the millennia before writing were biologically nearly identical to us. But unlike us, they did not use writing to communicate across space and time. They invented hundreds of spoken languages; they moved across the face of the globe, learning to survive in almost every natural environment; they chose and honored leaders; they traded, warred, and worshipped; and, above all, they learned from and taught one another. Much of what we would like to know about their experiences remains unknown because it took place before writing existed.

Archaeologists specialize in learning about people who did not document their history in writing. They study the millions of artifacts these people created. They also scrutinize soil, geological strata, pollen, climate, and other environmental features to reconstruct as much as possible about the world ancient peoples inhabited. Although no documents chronicle ancient Americans' births and deaths or pleasures and pains, archaeologists have learned to make artifacts, along with their natural and human environment, reveal a great deal about the people who used them.

This chapter relies on studies by archaeologists to sketch a brief overview of ancient America, the long first phase of the history of the United States. Ancient Americans and their descendants resided in North America for thousands of years before Europeans arrived. For their own reasons and in their own ways, they created societies and cultures of remarkable diversity and complexity. Because they did not use written records, their history cannot be reconstructed with the detail and certainty made possible by writing. But it is better to abbreviate and oversimplify ancient Americans' history than to ignore it.

> **REVIEW** Why do historians rely on the work of archaeologists to write the history of ancient North America?

▶ The First Americans

The first human beings to arrive in the Western Hemisphere emigrated from Asia. They brought with them hunting skills, weapon- and tool-making techniques, and a full range of other forms of human knowledge developed millennia earlier in Africa, Europe, and Asia. These first Americans hunted large mammals, such as the mammoths they had learned in Europe and Asia to kill, butcher, and process for food, clothing, building materials, and many other purposes. Most likely, these first Americans wandered into the Western Hemisphere more or less accidentally, hungry and in pursuit of their prey.

African and Asian Origins

Human beings lived elsewhere in the world for hundreds of thousands of years before they reached the Western Hemisphere. They lacked a way to travel to the Western Hemisphere because millions of years before humans existed anywhere on the globe, North and South America became detached from the gigantic common landmass scientists now call **Pangaea**. About 240 million years ago, powerful forces deep within the earth fractured Pangaea and slowly pushed continents apart to approximately their present positions (Map 1.1). This process of **continental drift** encircled the land of the Western Hemisphere with large oceans that isolated it from the other continents long before early human beings (*Homo erectus*) first appeared in Africa about two million years ago. (Hereafter in this chapter, the abbreviation *BP* — archaeologists' notation for "years before the present" — is used to indicate dates earlier than two thousand years ago. Dates more recent than two thousand years ago are indicated with the common and familiar notation *AD* — for example, AD 1492.)

More than 1.5 million years after *Homo erectus* appeared, or about 400,000 BP, modern humans (*Homo sapiens*) evolved in Africa. All human beings throughout

MAP 1.1
Continental Drift
Massive geological forces separated North and South America from other continents eons before human beings evolved in Africa 1.5 million years ago.

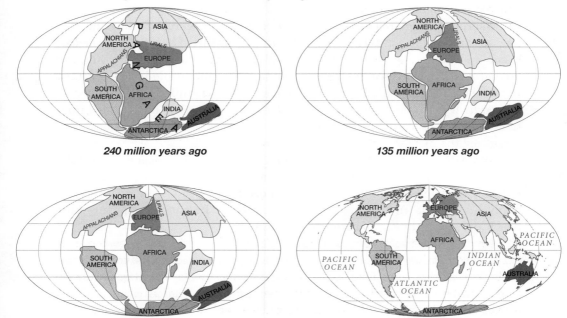

240 million years ago

135 million years ago

65 million years ago

Present day

the world today are descendants of these ancient Africans. Their DNA was the template for ours. Slowly, over many millennia, **Homo sapiens** migrated out of Africa and into Europe and Asia. Unlike North and South America, Europe and Asia retained land connections to Africa, allowing ancient humans to migrate on foot. Sometimes ancient people navigated rivers and lakes in small boats, but these vessels could not survive battering by the winds and waves of the enormous oceans isolating North and South America from the Eurasian landmass. For roughly 97 percent of the time *Homo sapiens* have been on earth, none migrated to the Western Hemisphere.

Two major developments made it possible for ancient humans to migrate to the Western Hemisphere. First, people successfully adapted to the frigid environment near the Arctic Circle. Second, changes in the earth's climate reconnected North America to Asia.

By about 25,000 BP, *Homo sapiens* had spread from Africa throughout Europe and Asia. People, probably women, had learned to use bone needles to sew animal skins into warm clothing that permitted them to become permanent residents of extremely cold regions such as northeastern Siberia. A few of these ancient Siberians clothed in animal hides walked to North America on land that now lies submerged beneath the sixty miles of water that currently separates easternmost Siberia from westernmost Alaska. A pathway across this watery chasm opened during the last global cold spell — the Wisconsin glaciation, which endured from about 25,000 BP to 14,000 BP — when snow piled up in glaciers, causing the sea level to drop as much as 350 feet below its current level. The falling sea level exposed a land bridge connecting Asian Siberia and American Alaska. This land bridge, which scientists call **Beringia**, opened a passageway hundreds of miles wide between the Eastern and Western Hemispheres.

Siberian hunters roamed Beringia for centuries in search of game animals. Grasses and small shrubs that covered Beringia supported herds of mammoths, bison, and numerous smaller animals. As the hunters ventured farther and farther east, they eventually became pioneers of human life in the Western Hemisphere. Their migrations probably had very little influence on their own lives, which continued more or less in the age-old ways they had learned from their Siberian ancestors. Although they did not know it, their migrations revolutionized the history of the world.

Archaeologists refer to these first migrants and their descendants for the next few millennia as **Paleo-Indians**. They speculate that these Siberian hunters traveled in small bands of no more than twenty-five people. How many such bands arrived in North America before Beringia disappeared beneath the sea will never be known.

When the first migrants came is hotly debated by experts. They probably arrived sometime after 15,000 BP. Scattered and inconclusive evidence suggests that they may have arrived several thousand years earlier. Certainly, humans who came from Asia — whose ancestors had left Africa hundreds of thousands of years earlier — inhabited the Western Hemisphere by 13,500 BP.

Paleo-Indian Hunters

When humans first arrived in the Western Hemisphere, massive glaciers covered most of present-day Canada. A narrow corridor not entirely obstructed by ice ran along the eastern side of Canada's Rocky Mountains, and most archaeologists believe that Paleo-Indians probably migrated through the ice-free passageway in pursuit of game. They may have also traveled along the Pacific coast in small boats, hunting marine life and hopscotching from one desirable landing spot to another. At the southern edge of the glaciers, Paleo-Indians entered a hunters' paradise. North, Central, and South America teemed with wildlife that had never before confronted wily two-legged predators armed with razor-sharp spears. The abundance of game presumably made hunting relatively easy. Ample food permitted the Paleo-Indian population to grow. Within a thousand years or so, Paleo-Indians had migrated to the tip of South America and virtually everywhere else in the Western Hemisphere, as proved by discoveries of their spear points in numerous excavations.

Early Paleo-Indians used a distinctively shaped spearhead known as a **Clovis point**, named for the place in New Mexico where it was first excavated. Archaeologists' discovery of Clovis points throughout North and Central America in sites occupied between 13,500 BP and 13,000 BP provides evidence that these nomadic hunters shared a common ancestry and way of life. Paleo-Indians hunted mammoths and bison — judging from the artifacts and bones that have survived from this era —

but they probably also hunted smaller animals. Concentration on large animals, when possible, made sense because just one mammoth kill supplied hunters with meat for weeks or, if dried, for months. Some Paleo-Indians even refrigerated killed mammoths by filling the intestines with stones and sinking the carcasses to the bottom of an icy lake to be retrieved and used later. In addition to food, mammoth kills provided hides and bones for clothing, shelter, tools, and much more.

About 11,000 BP, Paleo-Indians confronted a major crisis. The mammoths and other large mammals they hunted became extinct. The extinction was gradual, stretching over several hundred years. Scientists are not completely

Clovis Spear Straightener

Clovis hunters used this bone spear straightener about 11,000 BP at a campsite in Arizona, where archaeologists discovered it lying among the butchered remains of two mammoth carcasses and thirteen ancient bison. Similar objects often appear in ancient sites in Eurasia, but this is the only bone artifact yet discovered in a Clovis-era site in North America. Presumably Clovis hunters stuck their spear shafts through the opening and then grasped the handle of the straightener and moved it back and forth along the length of the shaft to remove imperfections and make the spear a more effective weapon.

Arizona State Museum, University of Arizona.

certain why it occurred, although environmental change probably contributed to it. About this time, the earth's climate warmed, glaciers melted, and sea levels rose. Mammoths and other large mammals probably had difficulty adapting to the warmer climate. Many archaeologists also believe, however, that Paleo-Indians probably contributed to the extinctions in the Western Hemisphere by killing large animals more rapidly than they could reproduce. Although some experts dispute this overkill hypothesis, similar environmental changes had occurred for millions of years without triggering the large-mammal extinctions that followed the arrival of Paleo-Indian hunters. Whatever the causes, Paleo-Indians faced a radical change in the natural environment within just a few thousand years of their arrival in the Western Hemisphere — namely, the extinction of large mammals. After the extinction, Paleo-Indians literally inhabited a new world.

Paleo-Indians adapted to the drastic environmental change of the big-game extinction by making at least two important changes in their way of life. First, hunters began to prey more intensively on smaller animals. Second, Paleo-Indians devoted more energy to foraging — that is, to collecting wild plant foods such as roots, seeds, nuts, berries, and fruits. When Paleo-Indians made these changes, they replaced the apparent uniformity of the big-game-oriented Clovis culture with great cultural diversity adapted to the many natural environments throughout the hemisphere, ranging from icy tundra to steamy jungles.

These post-Clovis adaptations to local environments resulted in the astounding variety of Native American cultures that existed when Europeans arrived in AD 1492. By then, more than three hundred major tribes and hundreds of lesser groups inhabited North America alone. Hundreds more lived in Central and South America. Hundreds of other ancient American cultures had disappeared or transformed themselves as their people constantly adapted to environmental change and other challenges.

> **REVIEW**   How and why did humans migrate into North America after 15,000 BP?

▶ Archaic Hunters and Gatherers

Archaeologists use the term *Archaic* to describe the many different hunting and gathering cultures that descended from Paleo-Indians and the long period of time when those cultures dominated the history of ancient America — roughly from 10,000 BP to somewhere between 4000 BP and 3000 BP. The term describes the era in the history of ancient America that followed the Paleo-Indian big-game hunters and preceded the development of agriculture. It denotes a **hunter-gatherer** way of life that persisted in North America long after European colonization.

Like their Paleo-Indian ancestors, **Archaic Indians** hunted with spears, but they also took smaller game with traps, nets, and hooks. Unlike their Paleo-Indian predecessors, most Archaic peoples used a variety of stone tools to prepare food from wild plants. A characteristic Archaic artifact is a grinding stone used to pulverize seeds into edible form. Most Archaic Indians migrated from place to place to harvest plants and hunt animals. They usually did not establish permanent villages, although they often returned to the same river valley or fertile meadow year after year. In regions with especially rich resources — such as present-day California and the Pacific Northwest — they developed permanent settlements. Many groups became excellent basket makers in order to collect and store food they gathered from wild plants. Archaic peoples followed these practices in distinctive ways in the different environmental regions of North America.

Great Plains Bison Hunters

After the extinction of large game animals, some hunters began to concentrate on bison in the huge herds that grazed the grassy, arid plains stretching hundreds of miles east of the Rocky Mountains. For almost a thousand years after the big-game extinctions, Archaic Indians hunted bison with Folsom points, named after a site near Folsom, New Mexico. In 1908, George McJunkin, an African American cowboy, discovered this site, which contained a deposit of large fossilized bones. In 1926, archaeologists excavated the site McJunkin had discovered and found evidence that proved conclusively for the first time that ancient Americans and giant bison — which were known to have been extinct for at least ten thousand years — were contemporaries. One Folsom point remained stuck between two ribs of a giant bison, where a Stone Age hunter had plunged it more than ten thousand years earlier.

Like their nomadic predecessors, Folsom hunters moved constantly to maintain contact with their prey. **Great Plains hunters** developed trapping techniques that made it easy to kill large numbers of animals. At the original Folsom site, careful study of the bones McJunkin found suggests that early one winter hunters drove bison into a narrow gulch and speared twenty-three of them. At other sites, Great Plains hunters stampeded bison herds over cliffs and then slaughtered the animals that plunged to their deaths.

Bows and arrows reached Great Plains hunters from the north about AD 500. They largely replaced spears, which had been the hunters' weapons of choice for millennia. Bows permitted hunters to wound animals from farther away, arrows made it possible to shoot repeatedly, and arrowheads were easier to make and therefore less costly to lose than the larger, heavier spear points. But these new weapons did not otherwise alter age-old techniques of bison hunting on the Great Plains. Although we often imagine ancient Great Plains bison hunters on horseback, in fact they hunted on foot, like their Paleo-Indian ancestors. Horses that had existed in North America millions of years earlier had long since become extinct. Horses did not return to the Great Plains until Europeans imported them in the decades after 1492, when Native American bison hunters acquired them and soon became expert riders.

Great Basin Cultures

Archaic peoples in the Great Basin between the Rocky Mountains and the Sierra Nevada inhabited a region of great environmental diversity. Some **Great Basin**

Indians lived along the shores of large marshes and lakes that formed during rainy periods, eating fish they caught with bone hooks and nets. Other cultures survived in the foothills of mountains between the blistering heat on the desert floor and the cold, treeless mountain heights. Hunters killed deer, antelope, and sometimes bison, as well as smaller game such as rabbits, rodents, and snakes. These broadly defined zones of habitation changed constantly, depending largely on the amount of rain.

Despite the variety and occasional abundance of animals, Great Basin peoples relied on plants as their most important food source. Unlike meat and fish, plant food could be collected and stored for long periods to protect against shortages caused by the fickle rainfall. Many Great Basin peoples gathered piñon nuts as a dietary staple. By diversifying their food sources and migrating to favorable locations to collect and store them, Great Basin peoples adapted to the severe environmental challenges of the region and maintained their Archaic hunter-gatherer way of life for centuries after Europeans arrived in AD 1492.

Pacific Coast Cultures

The richness of the natural environment made present-day California the most densely settled area in all of ancient North America. The land and ocean offered such ample food that **California peoples** remained hunters and gatherers for hundreds of years after AD 1492. The diversity of California's environment also encouraged corresponding variety among native peoples. The mosaic of Archaic settlements in California included about five hundred separate tribes speaking some ninety languages, each with local dialects. No other region of comparable size in ancient North America exhibited such cultural variety.

The Chumash, one of the many California cultures, emerged in the region surrounding what is now Santa Barbara about 5000 BP. Comparatively plentiful food resources — especially acorns — permitted Chumash people to establish relatively permanent villages. Conflict, evidently caused by competition for valuable acorn-gathering territory, frequently broke out among the villages, as documented by Chumash skeletons that display signs of violent deaths. Although few other California cultures achieved the population density and village settlements of the Chumash, all shared the hunter-gatherer way of life and reliance on acorns as a major food source.

Another rich natural environment lay along the Pacific Northwest coast. Like the Chumash, **Northwest peoples** built more or less permanent villages. After about 5500 BP, they concentrated on catching whales and large quantities of salmon, halibut, and other fish, which they dried to last throughout the year. They also traded with people who lived hundreds of miles from the coast. Fishing freed Northwest peoples to develop sophisticated woodworking skills. They fashioned elaborate wood carvings that denoted wealth and status, as well as huge canoes for fishing, hunting, and conducting warfare against neighboring tribes. Much of the warfare among Archaic northwesterners grew out of attempts to defend or gain access to prime fishing sites.

Chumash Necklace

Long before the arrival of Europeans, ancient Chumash people in southern California made this elegant necklace of abalone shell. The carefully formed, polished, and assembled pieces of shell illustrate the artistry of the Chumash and their access to the rich and diverse marine life of the Pacific coast. Since living abalone cling stubbornly to submerged rocks along the coast, Chumash divers presumably pried abalone from their rocky perches to obtain their delicious flesh; then one or more Chumash artisans recycled the inedible shell to make this necklace. Natural History Museum of Los Angeles County.

Eastern Woodland Cultures

East of the Mississippi River, Archaic peoples adapted to a forest environment that included many local variants, such as the major river valleys of the Mississippi, Ohio, Tennessee, and Cumberland; the Great Lakes region; and the Atlantic coast. Throughout these diverse locales, Archaic peoples pursued similar survival strategies.

Woodland hunters stalked deer as their most important prey. Deer supplied **Woodland peoples** with food as well as hides and bones that they crafted into clothing, weapons, and many other tools. Like Archaic peoples elsewhere, Woodland Indians gathered edible plants, seeds, and nuts, especially hickory nuts, pecans, walnuts, and acorns. About 6000 BP, some Woodland groups established more or less permanent settlements of 25 to 150 people, usually near a river or lake that offered a wide variety of plant and animal resources. The existence of such settlements has permitted archaeologists to locate numerous Archaic burial sites that suggest Woodland people had a life expectancy of about eighteen years, a relatively short time to learn all the skills necessary to survive, reproduce, and adapt to change.

Around 4000 BP, Woodland cultures added two important features to their basic hunter-gatherer lifestyles: agriculture and pottery. Gourds and pumpkins that were first cultivated thousands of years earlier in Mexico spread north to Woodland peoples through trade and migration. Woodland peoples also began to cultivate local species such as sunflowers, as well as small quantities of tobacco, another import from South America. Corn, which had been grown by Mesoamerican and South American peoples since about 7000 BP, slowly traveled north with migrants and traders and eventually became a significant food crop among Eastern Woodland peoples around 2500 BP. Most likely, women learned how to plant, grow, and harvest these crops as an outgrowth of their work gathering edible wild plants. Cultivated crops added to the quantity, variety, and predictability of Woodland food sources, but they did not alter Woodland peoples' dependence on gathering wild plants, seeds, and nuts.

Like agriculture, pottery probably originated in Mexico. Traders and migrants most likely brought pottery-making skills northward along with Mesoamerican and South American seeds. Pots were more durable than baskets for cooking and the storage of food and water, but they were also much heavier and therefore were shunned by nomadic peoples. The permanent settlements of Woodland peoples made the heavy weight of pots much less important than their advantages compared to leaky and fragile baskets. While pottery and agriculture introduced changes in Woodland cultures, ancient Woodland Americans retained the other basic features of their Archaic hunter-gatherer lifestyle, which persisted in most areas to 1492 and beyond.

> **REVIEW**   Why did Archaic Native Americans shift from big-game hunting to foraging and hunting smaller animals?

▶ Agricultural Settlements and Chiefdoms

Among Eastern Woodland peoples and most other Archaic cultures, agriculture supplemented hunter-gatherer subsistence strategies but did not replace them. Reliance on wild animals and plants required most Archaic groups to remain small and mobile. But beginning about 4000 BP, distinctive southwestern cultures slowly began to depend on agriculture and to build permanent settlements. Later, around 2500 BP, Woodland peoples in the vast Mississippi valley began to construct burial mounds and other earthworks that suggest the existence of social and political hierarchies that archaeologists term *chiefdoms*. Although the hunter-gatherer lifestyle never entirely disappeared, the development of agricultural settlements and chiefdoms represented important innovations to the Archaic way of life.

Southwestern Cultures

Ancient Americans in present-day Arizona, New Mexico, and southern portions of Utah and Colorado developed cultures characterized by **agricultural settlements** and multiunit dwellings called pueblos. All southwestern peoples confronted the challenge of a dry climate and unpredictable fluctuations in rainfall that made the supply of wild plant food very unreliable. These ancient Americans probably adopted agriculture in response to this basic environmental uncertainty.

About 3500 BP, southwestern hunters and gatherers began to cultivate corn, their signature food crop. The demands of corn cultivation encouraged hunter-gatherers to restrict their migratory habits in order to tend the crop. A vital consideration was access to water. Southwestern Indians became irrigation experts, conserving water from streams, springs, and rainfall and distributing it to thirsty crops.

About AD 200, small farming settlements began to appear throughout southern New Mexico, marking the emergence of the **Mogollon culture**. Typically, a Mogollon settlement included a dozen pit houses, each made by digging out a rounded pit about fifteen feet in diameter and a foot or two deep and then erecting poles to support a roof of branches or dirt. Larger villages usually had one or two bigger pit houses that may have been the predecessors of the circular kivas, the ceremonial rooms that became a characteristic of nearly all southwestern settlements. About AD 900, Mogollon culture began to decline, for reasons that remain obscure. Its descendants included the Mimbres people in southwestern New Mexico, who crafted spectacular pottery adorned with human and animal designs. By about AD 1250, the Mimbres culture disappeared, for reasons unknown.

Around AD 500, while the Mogollon culture prevailed in New Mexico, other ancient people migrated from Mexico to southern Arizona and established the distinctive **Hohokam culture**. Hohokam settlements used sophisticated grids of irrigation canals to plant and harvest crops twice a year. Hohokam settlements reflected the continuing influence of Mexican cultural practices that migrants brought with them as they traveled north. Hohokam people built sizable platform mounds and ball courts characteristic of many Mexican cultures. About AD 1400, Hohokam culture declined for reasons that remain a mystery, although the rising salinity of the soil brought about by centuries of irrigation probably caused declining crop yields and growing food shortages.

North of the Hohokam and Mogollon cultures, in a region that encompassed southern Utah and Colorado and northern Arizona and New Mexico, the **Anasazi culture** began to flourish about AD 100. The early Anasazi built pit houses on mesa tops and used irrigation much as their neighbors did to the south. Beginning around AD 1000 (again, it is not known why), some Anasazi began to move to large, multistory cliff dwellings whose spectacular ruins still exist at Mesa Verde, Colorado, and elsewhere. Other Anasazi communities — like the one whose impressive ruins can be visited at Chaco Canyon, New Mexico — erected huge stone-walled pueblos with enough rooms to house everyone in the settlement. Anasazi pueblos and cliff dwellings typically included one or more kivas used for secret ceremonies, restricted to men, that sought to communicate with the supernatural world. The alignment of Chaco buildings with solar and lunar events (such as the summer and winter solstices) suggests that Anasazi studied the sky carefully, probably because they believed supernatural celestial powers influenced their lives.

Drought began to plague the region about AD 1130, and it lasted for more than half a century, triggering the disappearance of the Anasazi culture. By AD 1200, the large Anasazi pueblos had been abandoned. The prolonged drought probably intensified conflict among pueblos and made it impossible to depend on the techniques of irrigated agriculture that had worked for centuries. Some Anasazi migrated toward regions with more reliable rainfall and settled in Hopi, Zuñi, and Acoma pueblos that their descendants in Arizona and New Mexico have occupied ever since.

Woodland Burial Mounds and Chiefdoms

No other ancient Americans created dwellings similar to pueblos, but around 2500 BP, Woodland cultures throughout the vast watershed drained by the Mississippi River began to build burial mounds. The size of the mounds, the labor and organization required to erect them, and differences in the artifacts buried with certain individuals suggest the existence of a social and political hierarchy that archaeologists term a **chiefdom**. Experts do not know the name of a single chief, nor do they know the organizational structure a chief headed. But the only way archaeologists can account for the complex and labor-intensive burial mounds and the artifacts found in them is to assume that one person — whom scholars term a *chief* — commanded the labor and obedience of very large numbers of other people, who made up the chief's chiefdom.

Between 2500 BP and 2100 BP, **Adena people** built hundreds of burial mounds radiating from central Ohio. In the mounds, the Adena usually accompanied burials with grave goods that included spear points and stone pipes as well as thin sheets of mica (a glasslike mineral) crafted into the shapes of birds, beasts, and human hands. Over the body and grave goods, Adena people piled dirt into a mound. Sometimes burial mounds were constructed all at once, but often they were built up slowly over many years.

About 2100 BP, Adena culture evolved into the more elaborate **Hopewell culture**, which lasted about five hundred years. Centered in Ohio, Hopewell culture extended throughout the enormous drainage of the Ohio and Mississippi rivers. Hopewell people built larger mounds than did their Adena predecessors and filled them with more magnificent grave goods. Burial was probably reserved for the most important members of Hopewell groups. Most people were cremated. Burial rituals appear to have brought many people together to honor the dead person and to help build the mound. Hopewell mounds were often one hundred feet in diameter and thirty feet high. Grave goods at Hopewell sites testify to the high quality of Hopewell crafts and to a thriving trade network that ranged from present-day Wyoming to Florida. Archaeologists believe that Hopewell chiefs probably played an important role in this sprawling interregional trade.

Hopewell culture declined about AD 400 for reasons that are obscure. Archaeologists speculate that bows and arrows, along with increasing reliance on agriculture, made small settlements more self-sufficient and therefore less dependent on the central authority of the Hopewell chiefs who were responsible for the burial mounds.

Four hundred years later, another mound-building culture flourished. The **Mississippian culture** emerged in the floodplains of the major southeastern river systems about AD 800 and lasted until about AD 1500. Major Mississippian sites, such as the one at Cahokia (see pages 1–3), included huge mounds with platforms on top for ceremonies and for the residences of great chiefs. Most likely, the ceremonial mounds and ritual practices derived from Mexican cultural expressions that were brought north by traders and migrants. At Cahokia, skilled farmers supported the large population with ample crops of corn. In addition to mounds, Cahokians erected what archaeologists call woodhenges (after the famous Stonehenge in England) — long wooden poles set upright in the ground and carefully arranged

Cahokia Tablet
This stone tablet excavated from the largest mound at Cahokia depicts a bird-man whose sweeping wings and facial features — especially the nose and mouth — resemble those of a bird. Crafted around AD 1100, the tablet probably played some role in rituals enacted on the mound by Cahokian people. Similar birdlike human forms have been found among other Mississippian cultures. Cahokia Mounds Historic Site.

in huge circles. Although the purpose of woodhenges is unknown, experts believe that Cahokians probably built them partly for celestial observations.

Cahokia and other Mississippian cultures dwindled by AD 1500. When Europeans arrived, most of the descendants of Mississippian cultures, like those of the Hopewell culture, lived in small dispersed villages supported by hunting and gathering, supplemented by agriculture. Clearly, the conditions that caused large chiefdoms to emerge — whatever they were — had changed, and chiefs no longer commanded the sweeping powers they had once enjoyed.

REVIEW How did food-gathering strategies influence ancient cultures across North America?

▶ Native Americans in the 1490s

On the eve of European colonization in the 1490s, Native Americans lived throughout North and South America, but their total population is a subject of spirited debate among scholars. Some experts claim that Native Americans inhabiting what is now the United States and Canada numbered 18 million to 20 million, while others place the population at no more than 1 million. A prudent estimate is about 4 million, or about the same as the number of people living on the small island nation of England at that time. The vastness of the territory meant that the overall population density of North America (excluding Mesoamerica) was low, just 60 people per 100 square miles, compared to more than 8,000 in England. Native Americans were spread thin across the land because of their survival strategies of hunting, gathering, and agriculture, although variations in climate and natural resources meant that some regions were more populous than others.

Eastern and Great Plains Peoples

About one-third of native North Americans inhabited the enormous Woodland region east of the Mississippi River; their population density approximated the

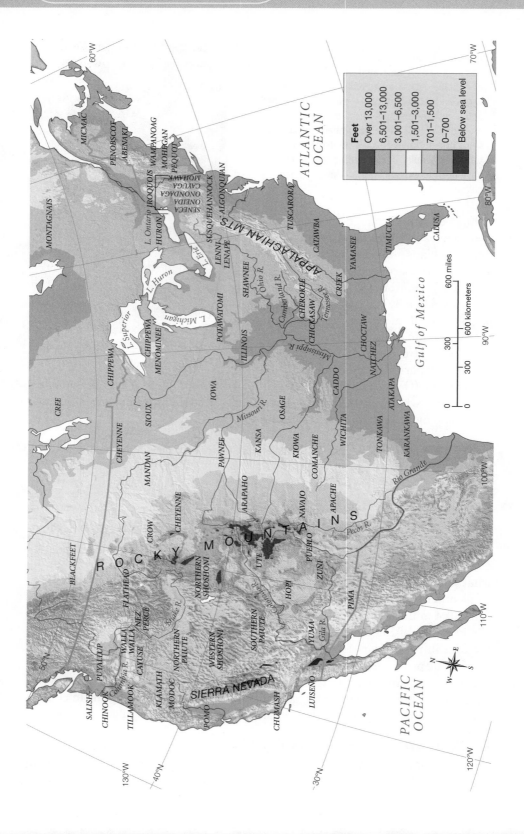

ATLANTIC OCEAN

PACIFIC OCEAN

Gulf of Mexico

Feet

Over 13,000
6,501–13,000
3,001–6,500
1,501–3,000
701–1,500
0–700
Below sea level

600 miles

600 kilometers

MICMAC
PENOBSCOT
ABENAKI
WAMPANOAG
MOHEGAN
PEQUOT
MONTAGNAIS
IROQUOIS
MOHAWK
CAYUGA
ONONDAGA
ONEIDA
SENECA
ALGONQUIAN
SUSQUEHANNOCK
LENNI LENAPE
TUSCARORA
CATAWBA
YAMASEE
TIMUCUA
CALUSA
HURON
SHAWNEE
Ohio R.
CHEROKEE
CHICKASAW
Tennessee R.
Cumberland R.
CREEK
CHOCTAW
NATCHEZ
CADDO
ATAKAPA
KARANKAWA
TONKAWA
WICHITA
Mississippi R.
ILLINOIS
POTAWATOMI
CHIPPEWA
MENOMINEE
L. Michigan
L. Huron
L. Superior
L. Erie
L. Ontario
CHIPPEWA
CREE
IOWA
SIOUX
MANDAN
CHEYENNE
CROW
CHEYENNE
Missouri R.
OSAGE
KANSA
PAWNEE
KIOWA
COMANCHE
ARAPAHO
NAVAJO
APACHE
Pecos R.
PUEBLO
UTE
Rio Grande
ZUNI
HOPI
PIMA
NORTHERN SHOSHONI
R O C K Y   M O U N T A I N S
BLACKFEET
FLATHEAD
WALLA WALLA
NEZ PERCE
CAYUSE
Columbia R.
Snake R.
NORTHERN PAIUTE
WESTERN SHOSHONI
SOUTHERN PAIUTE
Colorado R.
Gila R.
YUMA
LUISENO
POMO
CHUMASH
SIERRA NEVADA
MODOC
KLAMATH
TILLAMOOK
CHINOOK
SALISH
PUYALLUP
APPALACHIAN MTS.

N   E
W   S

60°W
70°W
80°W
90°W
100°W
110°W
120°W
130°W

50°N
40°N
30°N

average for North America as a whole (excluding Mesoamerica). Eastern Woodland peoples clustered into three broad linguistic and cultural groups: Algonquian, Iroquoian, and Muskogean.

Algonquian tribes inhabited the Atlantic seaboard, the Great Lakes region, and much of the upper Midwest (Map 1.2). The relatively mild climate along the Atlantic permitted the coastal Algonquians to grow corn and other crops as well as to hunt and fish. Around the Great Lakes and in northern New England, however, cool summers and severe winters made agriculture impractical. Instead, the Abenaki, Penobscot, Chippewa, and other tribes concentrated on hunting and fishing, using canoes both for transportation and for gathering wild rice.

Inland from the Algonquian region, **Iroquoian** tribes occupied territories centered in Pennsylvania and upstate New York, as well as the hilly upland regions of the Carolinas and Georgia. Three features distinguished Iroquoian tribes from their neighbors. First, their success in cultivating corn and other crops allowed them to build permanent settlements, usually consisting of several bark-covered longhouses up to one hundred feet long and housing five to ten families. Second, Iroquoian societies adhered to matrilineal rules of descent. Property of all sorts belonged to women. Women headed family clans and even selected the chiefs (normally men) who governed the tribes. Third, for purposes of war and diplomacy, an Iroquoian confederation — including the Seneca, Onondaga, Mohawk, Oneida, and Cayuga tribes — formed the **League of Five Nations**, which remained powerful well into the eighteenth century.

Muskogean peoples spread throughout the woodlands of the Southeast, south of the Ohio River and east of the Mississippi. Including the Creek, Choctaw, Chickasaw, and Natchez tribes, Muskogeans inhabited a bountiful natural environment that provided abundant food from hunting, gathering, and agriculture. Remnants of the earlier Mississippian culture still existed in Muskogean religion. The Natchez, for example, worshipped the sun and built temple mounds modeled after those of their Mississippian ancestors, including Cahokia.

Great Plains peoples accounted for about one out of seven native North Americans. Inhabiting the huge region west of the Eastern Woodland people and east of the Rocky Mountains, many tribes had migrated to the Great Plains within the century or two before the 1490s, forced westward by Iroquoian and Algonquian tribes. Some Great Plains tribes — especially the Mandan and Pawnee — farmed successfully, growing both corn and sunflowers. But the Teton Sioux, Blackfeet, Comanche, Cheyenne, and Crow on the northern plains and the Apache and other nomadic tribes on the southern plains depended on buffalo (American bison) for their subsistence.

◀ **MAP 1.2**
Native North Americans about 1500
Distinctive Native American peoples resided throughout the area that, centuries later, would become the United States. This map indicates the approximate location of some of the larger tribes about 1500. In the interest of legibility, many other peoples who inhabited North America at the time are omitted from the map.

Southwestern and Western Peoples

Southwestern cultures included about a quarter of all native North Americans. These descendants of the Mogollon, Hohokam, and Anasazi cultures lived in settled agricultural communities, many of them pueblos. They continued to grow corn, beans, and squash using methods they had refined for centuries.

However, their communities came under attack by a large number of warlike Athapascans who invaded the Southwest beginning around AD 1300. The Athapascans — principally Apache and Navajo — were skillful warriors who preyed on the sedentary pueblo Indians, reaping the fruits of agriculture without the work of farming.

About a fifth of all native North Americans resided along the Pacific coast. In California, abundant acorns and nutritious marine life continued to support high population densities, but this abundance retarded the development of agriculture. Similar dependence on hunting and gathering persisted along the Northwest coast, where fishing reigned supreme. Salmon were so plentiful that at **The Dalles**, a prime fishing site on the Columbia River on the border of present-day Oregon and Washington, Northwest peoples caught millions of pounds of salmon every summer and traded their catch as far away as California and the Great Plains. Although important trading centers existed throughout North America, particularly in the Southwest, it is likely that The Dalles was the largest Native American trading center in ancient North America.

Cultural Similarities

While trading was common, all native North Americans in the 1490s still depended on hunting and gathering for a major portion of their food. Most of them also practiced agriculture. Some used agriculture to supplement hunting and gathering; for others, the balance was reversed. People throughout North America used bows, arrows, and other weapons for hunting and warfare. None of them employed writing, expressing themselves instead in many other ways: drawings sketched on stones, wood, and animal skins; patterns woven in baskets and textiles; designs painted on pottery, crafted into beadwork, or carved into effigies; and songs, dances, religious ceremonies, and burial rites.

These rich and varied cultural resources of native North Americans did not include features of life common in Europe during the 1490s. Native North Americans did not use wheels; sailing ships were unknown to them; they had no large domesticated animals such as horses, cows, or oxen; their use of metals was restricted to copper. However, the absence of these European conveniences mattered less to native North Americans than their own cultural adaptations to the natural environment local to each tribe and to the social environment among neighboring peoples. That great similarity — adaptation to natural and social environments — underlay all the cultural diversity among native North Americans.

It would be a mistake, however, to conclude that native North Americans lived in blissful harmony with nature and one another. Archaeological sites provide ample evidence of violent conflict. Skeletons, like those at Cahokia, bear the marks of wounds as well as of ritualistic human sacrifice. Religious, ethnic, economic, and familial conflicts must have occurred, but they remain in obscurity because they left few archaeological traces. In general, fear and anxiety must have been at least as common among native North Americans as feelings of peace and security.

Native North Americans not only adapted to the natural environment but also changed it in many ways. They built thousands of structures, from small dwellings to massive pueblos and enormous mounds, permanently altering the landscape. Their gathering techniques selected productive and nutritious varieties of plants, thereby shifting the balance of local plants toward useful varieties. The first stages of North American agriculture, for example, probably involved Native Americans gathering wild seeds and then sowing them in a meadow for later harvest. It is almost certain that fertile and hardy varieties of corn were developed this way, first in Mesoamerica and later in North America. To clear land for planting corn, native North Americans set fires that burned off thousands of acres of forest.

Native North Americans also used fires for hunting. Great Plains hunters often started fires to force buffalo together and make them easy to slaughter. Eastern Woodland, Southwest, and Pacific coast Indians also set fires to hunt deer and other valuable prey. Hunters crouched downwind from a brushy area while their companions set a fire upwind; as animals raced out of the burning underbrush, hunters killed them.

Throughout North America, Indians started fires along the edges of woods to burn off shrubby undergrowth and encroaching tree seedlings. These burns encouraged the growth of tender young plants that attracted deer and other game animals, bringing them within convenient range of hunters' weapons. The burns also encouraged the growth of sun-loving food plants that Indians relished, such as blackberries, strawberries, and raspberries.

Because the fires set by native North Americans usually burned until they ran out of fuel or were extinguished by rain or wind, enormous regions of North America were burned over. In the long run, fires created and maintained light-dappled meadows for hunting and agriculture, cleared entangling underbrush from forests, and promoted a diverse and productive natural environment. Fires, like other activities of native North Americans, shaped the landscape of North America long before Europeans arrived in 1492.

REVIEW What cultural similarities were shared by the diverse peoples of the Western Hemisphere in the 1490s, and why?

▶ The Mexica: A Mesoamerican Culture

The vast majority of the 80 million people who lived in the Western Hemisphere in the 1490s inhabited Mesoamerica and South America, where the population approximately equaled that of Europe. Like their much less numerous counterparts

Mexican Human Sacrifice
This graphic portrayal of human sacrifice was drawn by a Mexican artist in the sixteenth century. It shows the typical routine of human sacrifice practiced by the Mexica for centuries before Europeans arrived. The victim climbed the temple steps and then was stretched over a stone pillar (notice the priest's helper holding the victim's legs) to make it easier for the priest to plunge a stone knife into the victim's chest, cut out the still-beating heart, and offer it to the bloodthirsty gods. The body of the previous victim has already been pushed down from the temple heights and is about to be dragged away. Scala/Art Resource, NY; Biblioteca Nazionale, Florence, Italy.

north of the Rio Grande, these people lived in a natural environment of tremendous diversity. They too developed hundreds of cultures, far too numerous to catalog here. But among all these cultures, the **Mexica** stood out. (Europeans often called these people Aztecs, a name the Mexica did not use.) Their empire stretched from coast to coast across central Mexico, encompassing between 8 million and 25 million people (experts disagree about the total population). We know more about the Mexica than about any other Native American society of the time, principally because of their massive monuments and their Spanish conquerors' well-documented interest in subduing them (as discussed in chapter 2). Their significance in the history of the New World after 1492 dictates a brief discussion of their culture and society.

The Mexica began their rise to prominence about 1325, when small bands settled on a marshy island in Lake Texcoco, the site of the future city of Tenochtitlán, the capital of the Mexican empire. Resourceful, courageous, and cold-blooded warriors, the Mexica were often hired out as mercenaries for richer, more settled tribes.

By 1430, the Mexica succeeded in asserting their dominance over their former allies and leading their own military campaigns in an ever-widening arc of empire building. Despite pockets of resistance, by the 1490s the Mexica ruled an empire that covered more land than Spain and Portugal combined and contained almost three times as many people.

The empire exemplified the central values of Mexican society. The Mexica worshipped the war god **Huitzilopochtli**. Warriors held the most exalted positions in the social hierarchy, even above the priests who performed the sacred ceremonies that won Huitzilopochtli's favor. In the almost constant battles necessary to defend and extend the empire, young Mexican men exhibited the courage and daring that would allow them to rise in the carefully graduated ranks of warriors. The Mexica considered capturing prisoners the ultimate act of bravery. Warriors usually turned over the captives to Mexican priests, who sacrificed them to Huitzilopochtli by cutting out their hearts. The Mexica believed that human sacrifice fed the sun's craving for blood, which kept the sun aflame and prevented the fatal descent of everlasting darkness and chaos.

The empire contributed far more to Mexican society than victims for sacrifice. At the most basic level, the empire functioned as a military and political system that collected **tribute** from subject peoples. The Mexica forced conquered tribes to pay tribute in goods, not money. Tribute redistributed to the Mexica as much as one-third of the goods produced by conquered tribes. It included everything from candidates for human sacrifice to textiles and basic food products such as corn and beans, as well as exotic luxury items such as gold, turquoise, and rare bird feathers.

Tribute reflected the fundamental relations of power and wealth that pervaded the Mexican empire. The relatively small nobility of Mexican warriors, supported by a still smaller priesthood, possessed the military and religious power to command the obedience of thousands of non-noble Mexicans and of millions of non-Mexicans in subjugated colonies. The Mexican elite exercised their power to obtain tribute and thereby to redistribute wealth from the conquered to the conquerors, from the commoners to the nobility, from the poor to the rich. This redistribution of wealth made possible the achievements of Mexican society that eventually amazed the Spaniards: the huge cities, fabulous temples, teeming markets, and luxuriant gardens, not to mention the storehouses stuffed with gold and other treasures.

On the whole, the Mexica did not interfere much with the internal government of conquered regions. Instead, they usually permitted the traditional ruling elite to stay in power — so long as they paid tribute. The conquered provinces received very little in return from the Mexica, except immunity from punitive raids. Subjugated communities felt exploited by the constant payment of tribute to the Mexica. By depending on military conquest and the constant collection of tribute, the Mexica failed to create among their subjects a belief that Mexican domination was, at some level, legitimate and equitable. The high level of discontent among subject peoples constituted the soft, vulnerable underbelly of the Mexican empire, a fact that Spanish intruders exploited after AD 1492 to conquer the Mexica.

REVIEW Why was tribute important in the Mexican empire?

▶ Conclusion: The World of Ancient Americans

Ancient Americans shaped the history of human beings in the New World for more than thirteen thousand years. They established continuous human habitation in the Western Hemisphere from the time the first big-game hunters crossed Beringia until 1492 and beyond. Much of their history remains irretrievably lost because they relied on oral rather than written communication. But much can be pieced together from artifacts they left behind at camps, kill sites, and ceremonial and residential centers such as Cahokia. Ancient Americans achieved their success through resourceful adaptation to the hemisphere's many and ever-changing natural environments. They also adapted to social and cultural changes caused by human beings — such as marriages, deaths, political struggles, and warfare — but the sparse evidence that has survived renders those adaptations almost entirely unknowable. Their creativity and artistry are unmistakably documented in their numerous artifacts. Those material objects sketch the only likenesses of ancient Americans we will ever have — blurred, shadowy images that are indisputably human but forever silent.

When European intruders began arriving in the Western Hemisphere in 1492, their attitudes about the promise of the New World were heavily influenced by the diverse peoples they encountered. Europeans coveted Native Americans' wealth, labor, and land, and Christian missionaries sought to save their souls. Likewise, Native Americans marveled at such European technological novelties as sailing ships, steel weapons, gunpowder, and horses, while often reserving judgment about Europeans' Christian religion.

In the four centuries following 1492, as the trickle of European strangers became a flood of newcomers from both Europe and Africa, Native Americans and settlers continued to encounter each other. Peaceful negotiations as well as violent conflicts over both land and trading rights resulted in chronic fear and mistrust. Yet even as the era of European colonization marked the beginning of the end of ancient America, the ideas, subsistence strategies, and cultural beliefs of native North Americans remained powerful among their descendants for generations and continue to persist to the present.

Reviewing Chapter 1

REVIEW QUESTIONS

1. Why do historians rely on the work of archaeologists to write the history of ancient America? (pp. 3–4)

2. How and why did humans migrate into North America after 15,000 BP? (pp. 4–8)

3. Why did Archaic Native Americans shift from big-game hunting to foraging and hunting smaller animals? (pp. 8–12)

4. How did food-gathering strategies influence ancient cultures across North America? (pp. 12–15)

5. What cultural similarities were shared by the diverse peoples of the Western Hemisphere in the 1490s, and why? (pp. 15–19)

6. Why was tribute important in the Mexican empire? (pp. 19–22)

MAKING CONNECTIONS

1. Explain the different approaches historians and archaeologists bring to studying people in the past. How do the different kinds of evidence they draw upon shape their accounts of the human past? In your answer, cite specific examples from the history of ancient America.

2. Discuss ancient peoples' strategies for surviving in the varied climates of North America. How did their different approaches to survival contribute to the diversity of Native American cultures? What else might have contributed to the diversity?

3. For more than twelve thousand years, Native Americans both adapted to environmental change in North America and produced significant changes in the environments around them. Discuss specific examples of Native Americans' adaptation to environmental change and the changes they caused in the North American landscape.

4. Rich archaeological and manuscript sources have enabled historians to develop a detailed portrait of the Mexica on the eve of European contact. How did the Mexica establish and maintain their expansive empire?

LINKING TO THE PAST

1. Did the history of ancient Americans make them unusually vulnerable to eventual conquest by European colonizers? Why or why not?

2. Do you think that ancient American history would have been significantly different if North and South America had never been disconnected from the Eurasian landmass? If so, how and why? If not, why not?

TIMELINE ca. 400,000 BP–AD 1492

NOTE: Major events are depicted below in chronological order, but the time scale between events varies from millennia to centuries.

(BP is an abbreviation used by archaeologists for "years before the present.")

ca. 400,000 BP • Modern humans (*Homo sapiens*) evolve in Africa.

ca. 25,000–14,000 BP • Wisconsin glaciation exposes Beringia, land bridge between Siberia and Alaska.

ca. 15,000 BP • First humans arrive in North America.

ca. 13,500–13,000 BP • Paleo-Indians in North and Central America use Clovis points to hunt big game.

ca. 11,000 BP • Mammoths and many other big-game prey of Paleo-Indians become extinct.

ca. 10,000–3000 BP • Archaic hunter-gatherer cultures dominate ancient America.

ca. 5000 BP • Chumash culture emerges in southern California.

ca. 4000 BP • Some Eastern Woodland peoples begin growing gourds and pumpkins and making pottery.

ca. 3500 BP • Southwestern cultures begin corn cultivation.

ca. 2500 BP • Eastern Woodland cultures start to build burial mounds, cultivate corn.

ca. 2500–2100 BP • Adena culture develops in Ohio.

ca. 2100 BP–AD 400 • Hopewell culture emerges in Ohio and Mississippi valleys.

ca. AD 200–900 • Mogollon culture develops in New Mexico.

ca. AD 500 • Bows and arrows appear in North America south of Arctic.

ca. AD 500–1400 • Hohokam culture develops in Arizona.

ca. AD 800–1500 • Mississippian culture flourishes in Southeast.

ca. AD 1000–1200 • Anasazi peoples build cliff dwellings at Mesa Verde and pueblos at Chaco Canyon.

ca. AD 1325–1500 • Mexica conquer neighboring peoples and establish Mexican empire.

AD 1492 • Christopher Columbus arrives in New World, beginning European colonization.

▶ FOR AN ONLINE BIBLIOGRAPHY, PRACTICE QUIZZES, WEB SITES, IMAGES, AND DOCUMENTS RELATED TO THIS CHAPTER, see the Book Companion Site at **bedfordstmartins.com/roarkvalue**.

▶ FOR DOCUMENTS RELATED TO THIS PERIOD, see Michael Johnson, ed., *Reading the American Past*, Fifth Edition.

Europeans Encounter the New World

1492–1600

TWO BABIES WERE BORN IN SOUTHERN EUROPE IN 1451, SEPARATED by about seven hundred miles and a chasm of social, economic, and political power. The baby girl, Isabella, was born in a king's castle in what is now Spain. The baby boy, Christopher, was born in the humble dwelling of a weaver near Genoa in what is now Italy. Forty-one years later, the lives and aspirations of these two people intersected in southern Spain and permanently changed the history of the world.

Isabella was named for her mother, the Portuguese second wife of King John II of Castile, whose monarchy encompassed the large central region of present-day Spain. She grew up amid the swirling countercurrents of dynastic rivalries and political conflict. Isabella's father died when she was three, and her half-brother, Henry, assumed the throne. Henry proved an ineffective ruler who made many enemies among the nobility and the clergy.

As a young girl, Isabella was educated by private tutors who were bishops in the Catholic Church, and her learning helped her become a strong, resolute woman. King Henry tried to control her and plotted to undermine her independence by arranging her marriage to one of several eligible sons of European monarchs. Isabella refused to accept Henry's choices and maneuvered to obtain Henry's consent that she would succeed him as monarch. She then selected Ferdinand, a man she had never met, to be her husband. A year younger than Isabella, Ferdinand was the king of Aragon, a region encompassing a triangular

Spanish Tapestry
This detail from a lavish sixteenth-century tapestry depicts Columbus (kneeling) receiving a box of jewels from Queen Isabella (whose husband, King Ferdinand, stands slightly behind her) in appreciation for his voyages to the New World. These gifts and others signified the monarchs' elation about the immense promise of the lands and peoples that Columbus encountered. The exact nature of that promise did not become clear until after the deaths of both Columbus and Isabella, when Cortés invaded and eventually conquered Mexico between 1519 and 1521. © Julio Conoso/Corbis Sygma.

slice of northeastern Spain bordering France and the Mediterranean Sea. The couple married in 1469, and Isabella became queen when Henry died in 1474.

Queen Isabella and King Ferdinand fought to defeat other claimants to Isabella's throne, to unite the monarchies of Spain under their rule, to complete the long campaign known as the Reconquest to eliminate Muslim strongholds on the Iberian Peninsula, and to purify Christianity. In their intense decades-long campaign to defend Christianity, persecute Jews, and defeat Muslims, Isabella and Ferdinand traveled throughout their realm, staying a month or two in one place after another, meeting local notables, hearing appeals and complaints, and impressing all with their regal splendor.

Tagging along in the royal cavalcade of advisers, servants, and assorted hangers-on that moved around Spain in 1485 was Christopher Columbus, a deeply religious man obsessed with obtaining support for his scheme to sail west across the Atlantic Ocean to reach China and Japan. An experienced sailor, Columbus had become convinced that it was possible to reach the riches of the East by sailing west. Columbus pitched his idea to the king of Portugal in 1484. The king's geography experts declared Columbus's proposal impossible: The globe was too big, the ocean between Europe and China was too wide, and no sailors or ships could possibly withstand such a long voyage.

Rejected in Portugal, Columbus made his way to the court of Isabella and Ferdinand in 1485 and joined their entourage until he finally won an audience with the monarchs in January 1486. They too rejected his plan. Doggedly, year after year Columbus kept trying to interest Isabella until finally she changed her mind. In mid-April 1492, hoping to expand the wealth and influence of her monarchy, she summoned Columbus and agreed to support his risky scheme.

Columbus hurriedly organized his expedition, and just before sunrise on August 3, 1492, three ships under his command caught the tide out of a harbor in southern Spain and sailed west. Barely two months later, in the predawn moonlight of October 12, 1492, he glimpsed an island on the western horizon. At daybreak, Columbus rowed ashore, and as the curious islanders crowded around, he claimed possession of the land for Isabella and Ferdinand.

Columbus's encounters with Isabella and those islanders in 1492 transformed the history of the world and unexpectedly made Spain the most important European power in the Western Hemisphere for more than a century. Long before 1492, other Europeans had restlessly expanded the limits of the world known to them, and their efforts helped make possible Columbus's voyage. But without Isabella's sponsorship, it is doubtful that Columbus could have made his voyage. With her support and his own unflagging determination, Columbus blazed a watery trail to a world that neither he nor anyone else in Europe knew existed. As Isabella, Ferdinand, and subsequent Spanish monarchs sought to reap the rewards of what they considered their emerging empire in the West, they created a distinctively Spanish colonial society that conquered and killed Native Americans, built new institutions, and extracted great wealth that enriched the Spanish monarchy and made Spain the envy of other Europeans.

▶ Europe in the Age of Exploration

Historically, the East — not the West — attracted Europeans. Around the year 1000, Norsemen ventured west across the North Atlantic and founded a small fishing village at L'Anse aux Meadows on the tip of Newfoundland that lasted only a decade or so. After the world's climate cooled, choking the North Atlantic with ice, the Norse left. Viking sagas memorialized the Norse "discovery," but it had virtually no other impact in the New World or in Europe. Instead, wealthy Europeans developed a taste for luxury goods from Asia and Africa, and merchants competed to satisfy that taste. As Europeans traded with the East and with one another, they acquired new information about the world they inhabited. A few people — sailors, merchants, and aristocrats — took the risks of exploring beyond

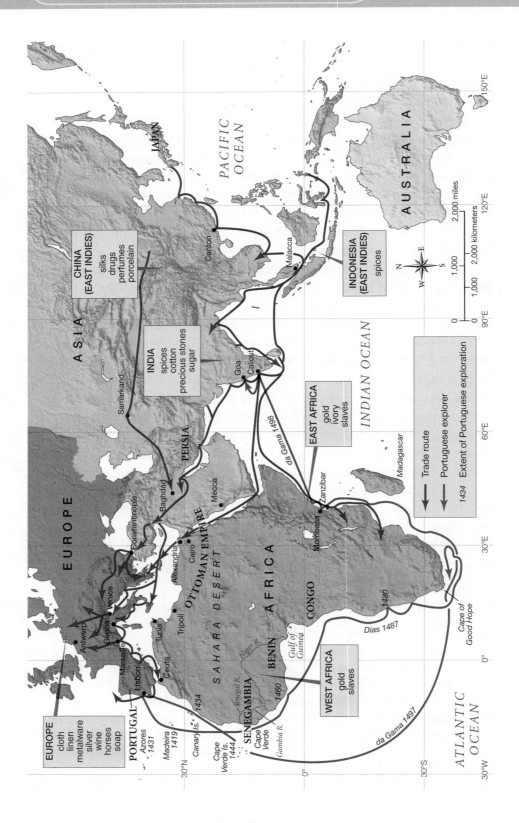

the limits of the world known to Europeans. Those risks were genuine and could be deadly. But sometimes they paid off in new information, new opportunities, and eventually the discovery of a world entirely new to Europeans.

Mediterranean Trade and European Expansion

From the twelfth through the fifteenth centuries, spices, silk, carpets, ivory, gold, and other exotic goods traveled overland from Persia, Asia Minor, India, and Africa and then were funneled into continental Europe through Mediterranean trade routes (Map 2.1). Dominated primarily by the Italian cities of Venice, Genoa, and Pisa, this lucrative trade enriched Italian merchants and bankers, who fiercely defended their near monopoly of access to Eastern goods. The vitality of the Mediterranean trade offered few incentives to look for alternatives. New routes to the East and the discovery of new lands were the stuff of fantasy.

Preconditions for turning fantasy into reality developed in fifteenth-century Europe. In the mid-fourteenth century, Europeans suffered a catastrophic epidemic of bubonic plague. The **Black Death**, as it was called, killed about a third of the European population. This devastating pestilence had major long-term consequences. By drastically reducing the population, it made Europe's limited supply of food more plentiful for survivors. Many survivors inherited property from plague victims, giving them new chances for advancement. The turmoil caused by the plague also prompted many peasants to move away from their homes and seek opportunities elsewhere.

Understandably, most Europeans perceived the world as a place of alarming risks where the delicate balance of health, harvests, and peace could quickly be tipped toward disaster by epidemics, famine, and violence. Most people protected themselves from the constant threat of calamity by worshipping the supernatural, by living amid kinfolk and friends, and by maintaining good relations with the rich and powerful. But the insecurity and uncertainty of fifteenth-century European life also encouraged a few people to take greater risks, such as embarking on dangerous sea voyages through uncharted waters to points unknown.

In European societies, exploration promised fame and fortune to those who succeeded, whether they were kings or commoners. Monarchs such as Isabella who hoped to enlarge their realms and enrich their dynasties also had reasons to sponsor journeys of exploration. More territory meant more subjects who could pay more taxes, provide more soldiers, and participate in more commerce, magnifying the monarch's power and prestige. Voyages of exploration also could

◀ **MAP 2.1**
European Trade Routes and Portuguese Exploration in the Fifteenth Century
The strategic geographic position of Italian cities as a conduit for overland trade from Asia was slowly undermined during the fifteenth century by Portuguese explorers who hopscotched along the coast of Africa and eventually found a sea route that opened the rich trade of the East to Portuguese merchants.

stabilize the monarch's regime by diverting unruly noblemen toward distant lands. Some explorers, such as Columbus, were commoners who hoped to be elevated to the aristocracy as a reward for their daring achievements.

Scientific and technological advances also helped set the stage for exploration. The invention of movable type by Johannes Gutenberg around 1450 in Germany made printing easier and cheaper, stimulating the diffusion of information, including news of discoveries, among literate Europeans; one such European was Isabella, who had an extensive personal library. By 1400, crucial navigational aids employed by maritime explorers such as Columbus were already available: compasses; hourglasses, which allowed for the calculation of elapsed time, useful in estimating speed; and the astrolabe and quadrant, which were devices for determining latitude. Many people throughout fifteenth-century Europe knew about these and other technological advances, but the Portuguese were the first to use them in a campaign to sail beyond the limits of the world known to Europeans.

A Century of Portuguese Exploration

With only 2 percent of the population of Christian Europe, Portugal devoted far more energy and wealth to the geographic exploration of the world between 1415 and 1460 than all other European countries combined. Facing the Atlantic on the Iberian Peninsula, the Portuguese lived on the fringes of the thriving Mediterranean trade. As a Christian kingdom, Portugal cooperated with Spain in the **Reconquest**, the centuries-long drive to expel the Muslims from the Iberian Peninsula. The religious zeal that propelled the Reconquest also justified expansion into what the Portuguese considered heathen lands. A key victory came in 1415 when Portuguese forces conquered Ceuta, the Muslim bastion at the mouth of the Strait of Gibraltar that had blocked Portugal's access to the Atlantic coast of Africa.

The most influential advocate of Portuguese exploration was **Prince Henry the Navigator**, son of the Portuguese king (and great-uncle of Queen Isabella of Spain). From 1415 until his death in 1460, Henry collected the latest information about sailing techniques and geography, supported new crusades against the Muslims, sought fresh sources of trade to fatten Portuguese pocketbooks, and pushed explorers to go farther still. Expeditions to Africa also promised to wrest wheat fields from their Moroccan owners and to obtain gold, the currency of European trade. Gold was scarce in Europe because the quickening pace of commerce increased the need for currency while purchases in the East drained gold away from Europeans.

Neither the Portuguese nor anybody else in Europe knew the immensity of Africa or the length or shape of its coastline, which, in reality, fronted the Atlantic for more than seven thousand miles — about five times the considerable distance from Genoa, Columbus's hometown, to Lisbon, the Portuguese capital. At first, Portuguese mariners cautiously hugged the west coast of Africa, seldom venturing beyond sight of land. By 1434, they had reached the northern edge of the Sahara Desert, where strong westerly currents swept them out to sea. They soon learned to ride those currents far away from the coast before catching favorable winds that turned them back toward land, a technique that allowed them to reach Cape Verde by 1444 (see Map 2.1).

To stow the supplies necessary for long periods at sea and to withstand the battering of waves in the open ocean, the Portuguese developed the caravel, a fast, sturdy ship that became explorers' vessel of choice. In caravels, Portuguese mariners sailed into and around the Gulf of Guinea and as far south as the Congo by 1480.

Fierce African resistance confined Portuguese expeditions to coastal trading posts, where they bartered successfully for gold, slaves, and ivory. Powerful African kingdoms welcomed Portuguese trading ships loaded with iron goods, weapons, textiles, and ornamental shells. Portuguese merchants learned that establishing relatively peaceful trading posts on the coast was far more profitable than attempting the violent conquest and colonization of inland regions. In the 1460s, the Portuguese used African slaves to develop sugar plantations on the Cape Verde Islands, inaugurating an association between enslaved Africans and plantation labor that would be transplanted to the New World in the centuries to come.

About 1480, Portuguese explorers, eager to bypass the Mediterranean merchants, began a conscious search for a sea route to Asia. In 1488, Bartolomeu Dias sailed around the Cape of Good Hope at the southern tip of Africa and hurried back to Lisbon with the exciting news that it appeared to be possible to sail on to India and China. In 1498, after ten years of careful preparation, Vasco da Gama commanded the first Portuguese fleet to sail to India. Portugal quickly capitalized on the commercial potential of da Gama's new sea route. By the early sixteenth century, the Portuguese controlled a far-flung commercial empire in India, Indonesia, and China (collectively referred to as the East Indies). Their new sea route to the East eliminated overland travel and allowed Portuguese merchants to charge much lower prices for the Eastern goods they imported and still make handsome profits.

Portugal's African explorations during the fifteenth century broke the monopoly of the old Mediterranean trade with the East, dramatically expanded the world known to Europeans, established a network of Portuguese outposts in Africa and Asia, and developed methods of sailing the high seas that Columbus employed on his revolutionary voyage west.

(REVIEW) Why did European exploration expand dramatically in the fifteenth century?

▶ A Surprising New World in the Western Atlantic

In retrospect, the Portuguese seemed ideally qualified to venture across the Atlantic. They had pioneered the frontiers of seafaring, exploration, and geography for almost a century. However, Portuguese and most other experts believed that sailing west across the Atlantic to Asia was literally impossible. The European discovery of America required someone bold enough to believe that the experts were wrong and that the risks were surmountable. That person was **Christopher Columbus**. His explorations inaugurated a geographic revolution that forever altered Europeans' understanding of the world and its peoples, including themselves. Columbus's landfall in the Caribbean initiated a thriving exchange between the people, ideas, cultures, and institutions of the Old and New Worlds that continues to this day.

The Explorations of Columbus

Columbus went to sea when he was about fourteen, and he eventually made his way to Lisbon, where he married Felipa Moniz, whose father had been raised in the household of Prince Henry the Navigator. Through Felipa, Columbus gained access to explorers' maps and information about the tricky currents and winds encountered in sailing the Atlantic. Columbus himself ventured into the Atlantic frequently and at least twice sailed to the central coast of Africa.

Like other educated Europeans, Columbus believed that the earth was a sphere and that theoretically it was possible to reach the East Indies by sailing west. With flawed calculations, he estimated that Asia was only about 2,500 miles away, a shorter distance than Portuguese ships routinely sailed between Lisbon and the Congo. In fact, the shortest distance to Japan from Europe's jumping-off point was nearly 11,000 miles. Convinced by his erroneous calculations, Columbus became obsessed with a scheme to prove he was right.

In 1492, after years of unsuccessful lobbying in Portugal and Spain, plus overtures to England and France, Columbus finally won financing for his journey from the Spanish monarchs, **Queen Isabella and King Ferdinand**. They saw Columbus's venture as an inexpensive gamble: The potential loss was small, but the potential gain was huge. They gave Columbus a letter of introduction to China's Grand Khan, the ruler they hoped he would meet upon reaching the other side of the Atlantic.

After scarcely three months of frantic preparation, Columbus and his small fleet — the *Niña* and *Pinta*, both caravels, and the *Santa María*, a larger merchant vessel — headed west. Six weeks after leaving the Canary Islands, where he stopped for supplies, Columbus landed on a tiny Caribbean island about three hundred miles north of the eastern tip of Cuba.

Columbus claimed possession of the island for Isabella and Ferdinand and named it San Salvador, in honor of the Savior, Jesus Christ. He called the islanders "Indians," assuming that they inhabited the East Indies somewhere near Japan or China. The islanders called themselves **Tainos**, which in their language meant "good" or "noble." The Tainos inhabited most of the Caribbean islands Columbus visited on his first voyage, as had their ancestors for more than two centuries. An agricultural people, the Tainos grew cassava, corn, cotton, tobacco, and other crops. Instead of dressing in the finery Columbus had expected to find in the East Indies, the Tainos "all . . . go around as naked as their mothers bore them," Columbus wrote. Although Columbus concluded that the Tainos "had no religion," in reality they worshipped gods they called *zemis*, ancestral spirits who inhabited natural objects such as trees and stones. The Tainos mined a little gold, but they had no riches. "It seemed to me that they were a people very poor in everything," Columbus wrote.

What the Tainos thought about Columbus and his sailors we can only surmise, since they left no written documents. At first, Columbus got the impression that the Tainos believed the Spaniards came from heaven. But after six weeks of encounters, Columbus decided that "the people of these lands do not understand me nor do I, nor anyone else that I have with me, [understand] them. And many times I understand one thing said by these Indians . . . for another, its contrary." The confused communication between the Spaniards and the Tainos suggests how strange each group seemed to the other. Columbus's perceptions of the Tainos were shaped by European attitudes, ideas, and expectations, just as the Tainos' perceptions of the Europeans were no doubt colored by their own culture.

Columbus and his men understood that they had made a momentous discovery, but they found it frustrating. Although the Tainos proved friendly, they did not have the riches Columbus expected to find in the East. In mid-January 1493, he started back to Spain, where Queen Isabella and King Ferdinand were overjoyed by his news. With a voyage that had lasted barely eight months, Columbus appeared to have catapulted Spain from the position of an also-ran in the race for a sea route to Asia into that of a serious challenger to Portugal, whose explorers had not yet sailed to India or China. The Spanish monarchs elevated Columbus to the nobility and awarded him the title "Admiral of the Ocean Sea." The seven Tainos Columbus had brought to Spain were baptized as Christians, and King Ferdinand became their godfather.

Soon after Columbus returned to Spain, the Spanish monarchs rushed to obtain the pope's support for their claim to the new lands in the West. When the pope, a Spaniard, complied, the Portuguese feared that their own claims to recently discovered territories were in jeopardy. To protect their claims, the Portuguese and Spanish monarchs negotiated the **Treaty of Tordesillas** in 1494. The treaty drew an imaginary line eleven hundred miles west of the Canary Islands. Land discovered west of the line (namely, the islands that Columbus discovered and any additional land that might be found) belonged to Spain; Portugal claimed land to the east (namely, its African and East Indian trading empire).

Isabella and Ferdinand moved quickly to realize the promise of their new claims. In the fall of 1493, they dispatched Columbus once again, this time with a fleet of seventeen ships and more than a thousand men who planned to locate the Asian mainland, find gold, and get rich. When Columbus returned to the island where he had left behind thirty-nine of his sailors (because of a shipwreck near the end of his first voyage), he received disturbing news. In his absence, his sailors had terrorized the Tainos by kidnapping and sexually abusing their women. In retaliation, the Tainos had killed all the sailors. This small episode prefigured much of what was to happen in encounters between Native Americans and Europeans in the years ahead.

Before Columbus died in 1506, he returned to the New World two more times (in 1498 and 1502) without relinquishing his belief that the East Indies were there, someplace. Other explorers continued to search for a passage to the East or some other source of profit. Before long, however, prospects of beating the Portuguese to Asia began to dim along with the hope of finding vast hoards of gold. Nonetheless, Columbus's discoveries forced sixteenth-century Europeans to think about the world in new ways. It was possible to sail from Europe to the western rim of the Atlantic and return to Europe. Most important, Columbus's voyages proved that lands and peoples entirely unknown to Europeans lay across the Atlantic.

The Geographic Revolution and the Columbian Exchange

Within thirty years of Columbus's initial discovery, Europeans' understanding of world geography underwent a revolution. An elite of perhaps twenty thousand people with access to Europe's royal courts and trading centers learned the exciting news about global geography. But it took a generation of additional exploration before they could comprehend the larger contours of Columbus's discoveries.

European monarchs hurried to stake their claims to the newly discovered lands. In 1497, King Henry VII of England, who had spurned Columbus a decade earlier, sent John Cabot to look for a **Northwest Passage** to the Indies across the North Atlantic. Cabot reached the tip of Newfoundland, which he believed was part of Asia, and hurried back to England, where he assembled a small fleet and sailed west in 1498. But he was never heard from again.

Three thousand miles to the south, a Spanish expedition landed on the northern coast of South America in 1499 accompanied by Amerigo Vespucci, an Italian businessman. In 1500, Pedro Álvars Cabral commanded a Portuguese fleet bound for the Indian Ocean that accidentally made landfall on the east coast of Brazil as it looped westward into the Atlantic.

By 1500, European experts knew that several large chunks of land cluttered the western Atlantic. A few cartographers speculated that these chunks were connected to one another in a landmass that was not Asia. In 1507, Martin Waldseemüller, a German cartographer, published the first map that showed the New World separate from Asia; he named the land America, in honor of Amerigo Vespucci.

Two additional discoveries confirmed Waldseemüller's speculation. In 1513, Vasco Núñez de Balboa crossed the Isthmus of Panama and reached the Pacific Ocean. Clearly, more water lay between the New World and Asia. **Ferdinand Magellan** discovered just how much water when he led an expedition to circumnavigate the globe in 1519. Sponsored by King Charles I of Spain, Magellan's voyage took him first to the New World, around the southern tip of South America, and into the Pacific late in November 1520. Crossing the Pacific took almost four months, decimating his crew with hunger and thirst. Magellan himself was killed by Philippine tribesmen. A remnant of his expedition continued on to the Indian Ocean and managed to transport a cargo of spices back to Spain in 1522.

In most ways, Magellan's voyage was a disaster. One ship and 18 men crawled back from an expedition that had begun with five ships and more than 250 men. But the geographic information it provided left no doubt that America was a continent separated from Asia by the enormous Pacific Ocean. Magellan's voyage made clear that it was possible to sail west to reach the East Indies, but that was a terrible way to go. After Magellan, most Europeans who sailed west set their sights on the New World, not on Asia.

Columbus's arrival in the Caribbean anchored the western end of what might be imagined as a sea bridge that spanned the Atlantic, connecting the Western Hemisphere to Europe. Somewhat like the Beringian land bridge traversed by the first Americans millennia earlier (see chapter 1), the new sea bridge reestablished a connection between the Eastern and Western Hemispheres. The Atlantic Ocean, which had previously isolated America from Europe, became an aquatic highway, thanks to sailing technology, intrepid seamen, and their European sponsors. This new sea bridge launched the **Columbian exchange**, a transatlantic trade of goods, people, and ideas that has continued ever since.

Spaniards brought novelties to the New World that were commonplace in Europe, including Christianity, iron technology, sailing ships, firearms, wheeled vehicles, horses and other domesticated animals, and much else. Unknowingly, they also carried many Old World microorganisms that caused devastating epidemics of smallpox, measles, and other diseases that would kill the vast majority of Indians during the sixteenth century and continue to decimate survivors in later centuries. European diseases made the Columbian exchange catastrophic for

Smallpox Victim in Hut
This sixteenth-century Mexican drawing shows a victim of smallpox lying in a hut made of branches. Spaniards brought smallpox to Mexico where it sickened and killed millions. A highly contagious and often fatal viral infection, smallpox spread like wildfire among Native Americans in the New World who, unlike most Europeans, had no previous exposure to the virus and therefore had developed no immunity to it. Smallpox and other European microbes decimated native Americans, greatly disfiguring and demoralizing many of those who survived. At the time, nearly everybody recognized the horrors of smallpox, but nobody knew how to prevent or cure it. Arxiu Mas.

Native Americans. In the long term, these diseases were decisive in transforming the dominant peoples of the New World from descendants of Asians, who had inhabited the hemisphere for millennia, to descendants of Europeans and Africans, the recent arrivals from the Old World.

Ancient American goods, people, and ideas made the return trip across the Atlantic. Europeans were introduced to New World foods such as corn and potatoes that became important staples in European diets, especially for poor people. Columbus's sailors became infected with syphilis in sexual encounters with New World women and unwittingly carried the deadly bacteria back to Europe. New World tobacco created a European fashion for smoking that ignited quickly and has yet to be extinguished. But for almost a generation after 1492, this Columbian exchange did not reward the Spaniards with the riches they yearned to find.

> **REVIEW** How did Columbus's discoveries help revolutionize Europeans' understanding of global geography?

▶ Spanish Exploration and Conquest

During the sixteenth century, the New World helped Spain become the most powerful monarchy in both Europe and the Americas. Initially, Spanish expeditions reconnoitered the Caribbean, scouted stretches of the Atlantic coast, and established settlements on the large islands of Hispaniola, Puerto Rico, Jamaica, and Cuba. Spaniards enslaved Caribbean tribes and put them to work growing crops and mining gold. But the profits from these early ventures barely covered the costs of maintaining the settlers. After almost thirty years of exploration, the promise of Columbus's discovery seemed illusory.

In 1519, however, that promise was spectacularly fulfilled by Hernán Cortés's march into Mexico. By about 1545, Spanish conquests extended from northern Mexico to southern Chile, and New World riches filled Spanish treasure chests. Cortés's expedition served as the model for Spaniards' and other Europeans' expectations that the New World could yield bonanza profits for its conquerors. Meanwhile, forced labor and deadly epidemics meant that native populations plummeted.

The Conquest of Mexico

Hernán Cortés, an obscure nineteen-year-old Spaniard seeking adventure and the chance to make a name for himself, arrived in the New World in 1504. Throughout his twenties, he fought in the conquest of Cuba and elsewhere in the Caribbean. In 1519, the governor of Cuba authorized Cortés to organize an expedition of about six hundred men and eleven ships to investigate rumors of a fabulously wealthy kingdom somewhere in the interior of the mainland.

A charismatic and confident man, Cortés could not speak any Native American language. Landing first on the Yucatán peninsula with his ragtag army, he had the good fortune to receive from a local chief of the Tobasco people the gift of a young girl named **Malinali**. She spoke several native languages, including Mayan and Nahuatl, the language of the **Mexica**, the most powerful people in what is now Mexico and Central America (see chapter 1). Malinali had acquired her linguistic skills painfully. Born into a family of Mexican nobility, she learned Nahuatl as a child. After her father died and her mother remarried, her stepfather sold her as a slave to Mayan-speaking Indians, who subsequently gave her to the Tobascans. Malinali, whom the Spaniards called Marina, soon learned Spanish and became Cortés's interpreter. She also became one of Cortés's several mistresses and bore him a son. (Several years later, after Cortés's wife arrived in New Spain, Cortés cast Marina aside, and she married one of his soldiers.) Malinali was the Spaniards' essential conduit of communication with the Indians. "Without her help," wrote one of the Spaniards who accompanied Cortés, "we would not have understood the language of New Spain and Mexico." Malinali allowed Cortés to talk and fight with Indians along the Gulf coast of Mexico as he tried to discover the location of the fabled kingdom. By the time Marina died, the people among whom she had grown up — who had taught her languages, enslaved her, and given her to Cortés — had been conquered by the Spaniards with her help.

In **Tenochtitlán**, the capital of the Mexican empire, the emperor **Montezuma** heard about some strange creatures sighted along the coast. (Montezuma and his people are often called Aztecs, but they called themselves Mexica.) He feared that the strangers were led by the god Quetzalcoatl, who was returning to Tenochtitlán to fulfill a prophecy of the Mexican religion. Marina had told Cortés about Quetzalcoatl, and when Montezuma's messengers arrived, Cortés donned the regalia they had brought, almost certain proof to the Mexica that he was indeed the god they feared. The Spaniards astounded the messengers by blasting their cannons and displaying their swords.

The messengers hurried back to Montezuma with their amazing news. The emperor sent representatives to bring the strangers large quantities of food and perhaps postpone their dreaded arrival in the capital. Before the Mexican messengers served food to the Spaniards, they sacrificed several human hostages and soaked the food in their blood. This fare disgusted the Spaniards and might have been enough to turn them back to Cuba. But along with the food, the Mexica also brought the Spaniards another gift, a "disk in the shape of a sun, as big as a cartwheel and made of very fine gold," as one of the Mexica recalled. Here was conclusive evidence that the rumors of fabulous riches heard by Cortés had some basis in fact.

In August 1519, Cortés marched inland to find Montezuma. Leading about 350 men armed with swords, lances, and muskets and supported by ten cannons, four smaller guns, and sixteen horses, Cortés had to live off the land, establishing peaceful relations with indigenous tribes when he could and killing them when he thought it necessary. On November 8, 1519, Cortés reached Tenochtitlán, where Montezuma welcomed him. After presenting Cortés with gifts, Montezuma ushered the Spaniards to the royal palace and showered them with lavish hospitality. The Spaniards were stunned by the magnificence that surrounded them.

One of Cortés's soldiers recalled that "it all seemed like an enchanted vision . . . [or] a dream." Quickly, Cortés took Montezuma hostage and held him under house arrest, hoping to make him a puppet through whom the Spaniards could rule the Mexican empire. This uneasy peace existed for several months until one of Cortés's men led a brutal massacre of many Mexican nobles, causing the people of Tenochtitlán to revolt. Montezuma was killed (whether by his own people or Spaniards is not certain), and the Mexica mounted a ferocious assault on the Spaniards. On June 30, 1520, Cortés and about a hundred other Spaniards fought their way out of Tenochtitlán and retreated about one hundred miles to Tlaxcala, a stronghold of bitter enemies of the Mexica. The friendly Tlaxcalans — who had long resented Mexican power — allowed Cortés to regroup, obtain reinforcements, and plan a strategy to conquer Tenochtitlán.

In the spring of 1521, Cortés and tens of thousands of Indian allies laid siege to the Mexican capital. With a relentless, scorched-earth strategy, Cortés finally defeated the last Mexican defenders on August 13, 1521. The great capital of the Mexican empire "looked as if it had been ploughed up," one of Cortés's soldiers remembered.

How did a few hundred Spaniards so far away from home defeat millions of Indians fighting on their home turf? For one thing, the Spaniards had superior military technology that partially offset the Mexicans' numerical advantages. They fought with weapons of iron and steel against the Mexicans' stone, wood, and copper. The muscles of Mexican warriors could not match the endurance of cannons and muskets fueled by gunpowder.

European viruses proved to be even more powerful weapons. Smallpox arrived in Mexico with Cortés, and in the ensuing epidemic thousands of Mexicans died and many others became too sick to fight. After Cortés evacuated Tenochtitlán, a plague — probably another smallpox outbreak — decimated the Mexican capital, "striking everywhere in the city and killing a vast number of our people," as one Mexican recalled. The sickness spread back along the network of trade and tribute feeding Tenochtitlán, weakening the entire Mexican empire and causing many to fear that their gods had abandoned them. "Cut us loose," one Mexican pleaded, "because the gods have died."

The Spaniards' concept of war also favored them. Mexicans tended to consider war a way to impose their tribute system on conquered people and to take captives for sacrifice. They believed that the high cost of continuing to fight would cause their adversaries to surrender and pay tribute. While Mexicans sought surrender, Spaniards sought total victory. As one Mexican described a Spanish attack, soldiers "stabbed everyone with iron lances and . . . iron swords. They stuck some in the belly, and then their entrails came spilling out. They split open the heads of some, . . . their skulls were cut up into little bits. Some they hit on the shoulders; their bodies broke open and ripped." To Spaniards, war meant destroying their enemy's ability to fight.

Politics proved decisive in Cortés's victory over the Mexicans. Cortés shrewdly exploited the tensions between the Mexica and the people they ruled in their empire (see chapter 1). Cortés reinforced his small army with thousands of Indian allies who were eager to seek revenge against the Mexica. Cortés's Indian allies fought alongside the Spaniards and provided a fairly secure base from which to maneuver against the Mexican stronghold of Tenochtitlán. Hundreds of thousands of other Indians aided Cortés by failing to come to the Mexicans' defense. In the end, the political tensions created by the Mexican empire proved to be its crippling weakness.

The Search for Other Mexicos

Lured by their insatiable appetite for gold, Spanish **conquistadors** (soldiers who fought in conquests) quickly fanned out from Tenochtitlán in search of other sources of treasure. The most spectacular prize fell to **Francisco Pizarro**, who conquered the **Incan empire** in Peru. The Incas controlled a vast, complex region that contained more than nine million people and stretched along the western coast of South America for more than two thousand miles. In 1532, Pizarro and his army of fewer than two hundred men captured the Incan emperor Atahualpa and held him hostage. As ransom, the Incas gave Pizarro the largest treasure yet produced by the conquests: gold and silver equivalent to half a century's worth of precious-metal production in Europe. With the ransom safely in their hands, the Spaniards murdered Atahualpa. The Incan treasure proved that at least one other Mexico did indeed exist, and it spurred the search for others.

Juan Ponce de León had sailed along the Florida coast in 1513. Encouraged by Cortés's success, he went back to Florida in 1521 to find riches, only to be killed in battle with Calusa Indians. A few years later, Lucas Vázquez de Ayllón explored the Atlantic coast north of Florida to present-day South Carolina. In 1526, he established a small settlement on the Georgia coast that he named San Miguel de Gualdape, the first Spanish attempt to establish a foothold in what is now the United States. This settlement was soon swept away by sickness and hostile Indians. Pánfilo de Narváez surveyed the Gulf coast from Florida to Texas in 1528, but his expedition ended disastrously with a shipwreck near present-day Galveston, Texas.

In 1539, Hernando de Soto, a seasoned conquistador who had taken part in the conquest of Peru, set out with nine ships and more than six hundred men to find another Peru in North America. Landing in Florida, de Soto literally slashed his way through much of southeastern North America for three years, searching for the rich, majestic civilizations he believed were there. After the brutal slaughter of many Native Americans and much hardship, de Soto died of a fever in 1542. His men buried him in the Mississippi River and turned back to Mexico, disappointed.

Tales of the fabulous wealth of the mythical Seven Cities of Cíbola also lured Francisco Vásquez de Coronado to search the Southwest and Great Plains of North America. In 1540, Coronado left northern Mexico with more than three hundred Spaniards, a thousand Indians, and a priest who claimed to know the way to what he called "the greatest and best of the discoveries." Cíbola turned out to be a small Zuñi pueblo of about a hundred families. When the Zuñi shot arrows at the Spaniards, Coronado attacked the pueblo and routed the defenders

Zuñi Defend Pueblo against Coronado
This sixteenth-century drawing by a Mexican artist shows Zuñi bowmen fighting back against the arrows of Coronado's men and the entreaties of Christian missionaries. Intended to document the support some Mexican Indians gave to Spanish efforts to extend the conquest into North America, the drawing depicts the Zuñi defender at the bottom of the pueblo aiming his arrow at a Mexican missionary armed only with religious weaponry: a crucifix, a rosary, and a book (presumably the Bible). Hunterian Museum Library, University of Glasgow. Glasgow University Library, Department of Special Collections.

after a hard battle. Convinced that the rich cities must lie somewhere over the horizon, Coronado kept moving all the way to central Kansas before deciding in 1542 that the rumors he had pursued were just that.

The same year Coronado abandoned his search for Cíbola, Juan Rodríguez Cabrillo's maritime expedition sought to find wealth along the coast of California. Cabrillo died on Santa Catalina Island, offshore from present-day Los Angeles, but his men sailed on to Oregon, where a ferocious storm forced them to turn back toward Mexico.

These probes into North America by de Soto, Coronado, and Cabrillo persuaded other Spaniards that although enormous territories stretched northward, their inhabitants had little to loot or exploit. After a generation of vigorous exploration, the Spaniards concluded that there was only one Mexico and one Peru.

Spanish Outposts in Florida and New Mexico

Disappointed by the explorers' failure to discover riches in North America, the Spanish monarchy insisted that a few settlements be established in Florida and New Mexico to give a token of reality to its territorial claims. Settlements in Florida would have the additional benefit of protecting Spanish ships from pirates and privateers who lurked along the southeastern coast, waiting for the Spanish treasure fleet sailing toward Spain.

In 1565, the Spanish king sent Pedro Menéndez de Avilés to create settlements along the Atlantic coast of North America. In early September, Menéndez founded **St. Augustine** in Florida, the first permanent European settlement within what became the United States. By 1600, St. Augustine had a population of about five hundred, the only remaining Spanish beachhead on North America's vast Atlantic shoreline.

More than sixteen hundred miles west of St. Augustine, the Spaniards founded another outpost in 1598. Juan de Oñate led an expedition of about five hundred people to settle northern Mexico, now called New Mexico, and claim the booty rumored to exist there. Oñate had impeccable credentials for both conquest and mining. His father helped to discover the bonanza silver mines of Zacatecas in central Mexico, and his wife was Isabel Tolosa Cortés Montezuma — the granddaughter of Cortés and the great-granddaughter of Montezuma.

After a two-month journey from Mexico, Oñate and his companions reached pueblos near present-day Albuquerque and Santa Fe. He solemnly convened the pueblos' leaders and received their oath of loyalty to the Spanish king and the Christian God. Oñate sent out scouting parties to find the legendary treasures of the region and to locate the ocean, which he believed must be nearby. Meanwhile, many of his soldiers planned to mutiny, and relations with the Indians deteriorated. When Indians in the Acoma pueblo revolted against the Spaniards, Oñate ruthlessly suppressed the uprising, killing eight hundred men, women, and children. Although Oñate's response to the **Acoma pueblo revolt** reconfirmed the Spaniards' military superiority, he did not bring peace or stability to the region. After another pueblo revolt occurred in 1599, many of Oñate's settlers returned to Mexico, leaving New Mexico as a small, dusty assertion of Spanish claims to the North American Southwest.

New Spain in the Sixteenth Century

For all practical purposes, Spain was the dominant European power in the Western Hemisphere during the sixteenth century (Map 2.2). Portugal claimed the giant territory of Brazil under the Tordesillas treaty but was far more concerned with exploiting its hard-won trade with the East Indies than with colonizing the New World. England and France were absorbed by domestic and diplomatic concerns in Europe and largely lost interest in America until late in the century. In the decades after 1519, the Spaniards created the distinctive colonial society of **New Spain**, which showed other Europeans how the New World could be made to serve the purposes of the Old.

The Spanish monarchy gave the conquistadors permission to explore and plunder what they found. The crown took one-fifth, called the "royal fifth," of any loot confiscated and allowed the conquerors to divide the rest. In the end, most conquistadors received very little after the plunder was divided among leaders such as Cortés and his favorite officers. To compensate his disappointed battle-hardened soldiers, Cortés gave them towns the Spaniards had subdued.

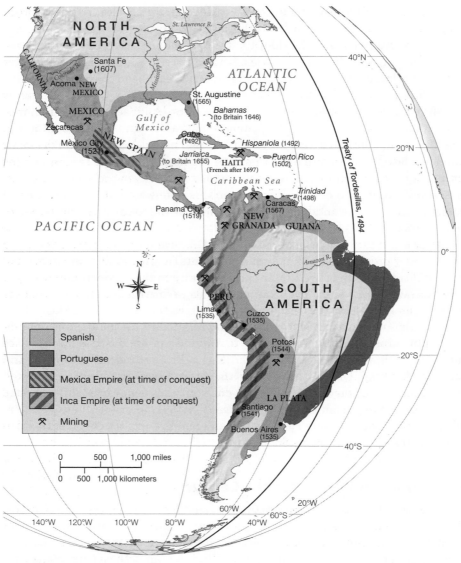

MAP 2.2
Sixteenth-Century European Colonies in the New World
Spanish control spread throughout Central and South America during the sixteenth century, with the important exception of Portuguese Brazil. North America, though claimed by Spain under the Treaty of Tordesillas, remained peripheral to Spain's New World empire.

The distribution of conquered towns institutionalized the system of *encomienda*, which empowered the conquistadors to rule the Indians and the lands in and around their towns. The concept of encomienda was familiar to Spaniards, who had used it to govern regions recaptured from Muslims during the Reconquest. Encomienda transferred to the Spanish *encomendero* (the man who "owned" the town) the tribute that the town had previously paid to the

Mexican empire. In theory, encomienda involved a reciprocal relationship between the encomendero and "his" Indians. In return for the tribute and labor of the Indians, the encomendero was supposed to be responsible for their material well-being, to guarantee order and justice in the town, and to encourage the Indians to convert to Christianity.

Catholic missionaries labored earnestly to convert the Indians. They fervently believed that God expected them to save the Indians' souls by convincing them to abandon their old sinful beliefs and to embrace the one true Christian faith. But after baptizing tens of thousands of Indians, the missionaries learned that many Indians continued to worship their own gods. Most priests came to believe that the Indians were lesser beings inherently incapable of fully understanding Christianity.

In practice, encomenderos were far more interested in what the Indians could do for them than in what they or the missionaries could do for the Indians. Encomenderos subjected the Indians to chronic overwork, mistreatment, and abuse. According to one Spaniard, the Indians' behavior justified the encomenderos' cruelty: "Everything [the Indians] do is slowly done and by compulsion. They are malicious, lying, [and] thievish." Economically, however, encomienda recognized a fundamental reality of New Spain: The most important treasure the Spaniards could plunder from the New World was not gold but uncompensated Indian labor.

The practice of coerced labor in New Spain grew directly out of the Spaniards' assumption that they were superior to the Indians. As one missionary put it, the Indians "are incapable of learning. . . . [They] are more stupid than asses and refuse to improve in anything." Therefore, most Spaniards assumed, Indians' labor should be organized by and for their conquerors. Spaniards seldom hesitated to use violence to punish and intimidate recalcitrant Indians.

Encomienda engendered two groups of influential critics. A few of the missionaries were horrified at the brutal mistreatment of the Indians. The cruelty of the encomenderos made it difficult for priests to persuade the Indians of the tender mercies of the Spaniards' God. "What will [the Indians] think about the God of the Christians," Friar Bartolomé de Las Casas asked, when they see their friends "with their heads split, their hands amputated, their intestines torn open? . . . Would they want to come to Christ's sheepfold after their homes had been destroyed, their children imprisoned, their wives raped, their cities devastated, their maidens deflowered, and their provinces laid waste?" Las Casas and other outspoken missionaries softened few hearts among the encomenderos, but they did win some sympathy for the Indians from the Spanish monarchy and royal bureaucracy. The Spanish monarchy moved to abolish encomienda in an effort to replace swashbuckling old conquistadors with royal bureaucrats as the rulers of New Spain.

In 1549, a reform called the *repartimiento* began to replace encomienda. It limited the labor an encomendero could command from his Indians to forty-five days per year from each adult male. The repartimiento, however, did not challenge the principle of forced labor, nor did it prevent encomenderos from continuing to cheat, mistreat, and overwork their Indians. Many Indians were put to work in silver mines, which required large capital investments and large groups of laborers. Silver mining was grueling and dangerous for the workers, but very profitable for the Spaniards who supervised them: During the entire sixteenth

Español con India,
Mestizo.

Mestizo con Española
Castizo.

Castizo con Española
Español.

Español con Mora.
Mulato.

Mulato con Española.
Morisco.

Morisco con Española
Chino.

Chino con India.
Salta atras.

Salta atras con Mulata.
Lobo.

Mixed Races

The residents of New Spain maintained a lively interest in each person's racial lineage. These eighteenth-century paintings illustrate forms of racial mixture common in the sixteenth century. In the first painting, a Spanish man and an Indian woman have a mestizo son; in the fourth, a Spanish man and a woman of African descent have a mulatto son; in the fifth, a Spanish woman and a mulatto man have a *morisco* daughter. The many racial permutations led the residents of New Spain to develop an elaborate vocabulary of ancestry. The child of a morisco and a Spaniard was a *chino*; the child of a chino and an Indian was a *salta abas*; the child of a salta abas and a mulatto was a *lobo*; and so on. Can you detect hints of some of the meanings of racial categories in the clothing depicted in these paintings? Bob Schalkwijk/INAH.

century, precious-metal exports from New Spain to Spain were worth twenty-five times more than the next most important export, leather hides.

For the Spaniards, life in New Spain after the conquests was relatively easy. Although the riches they won fell far short of their expectations, encomienda gave them a comfortable, leisurely life that was the envy of many Spaniards back in Europe. As one colonist wrote to his brother in Spain, "Don't hesitate [to come]. . . . This land [New Spain] is as good as ours [in Spain], for God has given us more here than there, and we shall be better off." During the century after 1492, about 225,000 Spaniards settled in the colonies. Virtually all of them were poor young men of common (non-noble) lineage who came directly from Spain. Laborers and artisans made up the largest proportion, but soldiers and sailors were also numerous. Throughout the sixteenth century, men vastly outnumbered women, although the proportion of women grew from about one in twenty before 1519 to nearly one in three by the 1580s.

The gender and number of Spanish settlers shaped two fundamental features of the society of New Spain. First, Europeans never made up more than 1 or 2 percent of the total population. Although Spaniards ruled New Spain, the population was almost wholly Indian. Second, the shortage of Spanish women meant that Spanish men frequently married Indian women or used them as concubines. For the most part, the relatively few women from Spain married Spanish men, contributing to a tiny elite defined by European origins.

The small number of Spaniards, the masses of Indians, and the frequency of intermarriage created a steep social hierarchy defined by perceptions of national origin and race. Natives of Spain — ***peninsulares*** (people born on the Iberian Peninsula) — enjoyed the highest social status in New Spain. Below them but still within the white elite were ***creoles***, the children born in the New World to Spanish men and women. Together, peninsulares and creoles made up barely 1 or 2 percent of the population. Below them on the social pyramid was a larger group of ***mestizos***, the offspring of Spanish men and Indian women, who accounted for 4 or 5 percent of the population. So many of the mestizos were born out of wedlock that the term *mestizo* (after the Spanish word for "mixed") became almost synonymous with *bastard* during the sixteenth century. Some mestizos worked as artisans and labor overseers and lived well, and a few rose into the ranks of the elite, especially if their Indian ancestry was not obvious from their skin color. Most mestizos, however, were lumped with the Indians, the enormous bottom slab of the social pyramid.

The society of New Spain established the precedent for what would become a pronounced pattern in the European colonies of the New World: a society stratified sharply by social origin and race. All Europeans of whatever social origin considered themselves superior to Native Americans; in New Spain, they were a dominant minority in both power and status.

The Toll of Spanish Conquest and Colonization

By 1560, the major centers of Indian civilization had been conquered, their leaders overthrown, their religion held in contempt, and their people forced to work for the Spaniards. Profound demoralization pervaded Indian society. As a Mexican poet wrote:

> Nothing but flowers and songs of sorrow are left in Mexico . . .
>
> where once we saw warriors and wise men. . . .
>
> We are crushed to the ground; we lie in ruins.
> There is nothing but grief and suffering in Mexico.

A Sign of Conquest
This skull of an Indian man in his fifties was excavated from the site of a Native American village in southwestern Georgia visited by de Soto's expedition in 1540. The skull shows that the man suffered a fatal sword wound above his right eye. Combined with slashed and severed arm and leg bones from the same site, the skull demonstrates the brutality de Soto employed against indigenous peoples on his journey through the Southeast. No native weapons could have inflicted the wounds left on this skull and the other bones. Robert L. Blakely.

Adding to the culture shock of conquest and colonization was the deadly toll of European diseases. As conquest spread, the Indians succumbed to virulent epidemics of measles, smallpox, and respiratory illnesses. They had no immunity to these diseases because they had not been exposed to them before the arrival of Europeans. The isolation of the Western Hemisphere before 1492 had protected ancient Americans from the contagious diseases that had raged throughout Eurasia for millennia. The new post-1492 sea bridge eliminated that isolation, and by 1570 the Indian population of New Spain had fallen about 90 percent from what it was when Columbus arrived. The destruction of the Indians was a catastrophe unequaled in human history. A Mayan Indian recalled that when sickness struck his village, "great was the stench of the dead. . . . The dogs and vultures devoured the bodies. The mortality was terrible." For most Indians, New Spain was a graveyard.

For the Spaniards, Indian deaths meant that the most valuable resource of New Spain — Indian labor — dwindled rapidly. By the last quarter of the sixteenth century, Spanish colonists felt the pinch of a labor shortage. To help supply laborers, the colonists began to import African slaves. Some Africans had come to Mexico with the conquistadors. One Mexican recalled that among Cortés's men were "some black-skinned one[s] with kink[y] hair." In the years before 1550, while Indian labor was still adequate, only 15,000 slaves were imported from Africa. Even after Indian labor began to decline, the relatively high cost of African slaves kept imports low, totaling approximately 36,000 from 1550 to the end of the century. During the sixteenth century, New Spain continued to rely primarily on a shrinking number of Indians.

REVIEW How did New Spain's distinctive colonial population shape its economy and society?

▶ The New World and Sixteenth-Century Europe

The riches of New Spain helped make the sixteenth century the Golden Age of Spain. After the deaths of Queen Isabella and King Ferdinand, their sixteen-year-old grandson became King Charles I of Spain in 1516. Three years later, just as Cortés ventured into Mexico, King Charles used judicious bribes to secure his selection as Holy Roman Emperor Charles V. His empire encompassed more territory than that of any other European monarch. He used the wealth of New Spain to protect the sprawling empire and promote his interests in the fierce dynastic battles of sixteenth-century Europe. He also sought to defend orthodox Christianity from the insurgent heresy of the Protestant Reformation. The power of the Spanish monarchy spread the clear message throughout sixteenth-century Europe that a New World empire could bankroll Old World ambitions.

The Protestant Reformation and the Spanish Response

In 1517, **Martin Luther**, an obscure Catholic priest in central Germany, initiated the **Protestant Reformation** by publicizing his criticisms of the Catholic Church. Luther's ideas won the sympathy of many Catholics, but they were considered extremely dangerous by church officials and monarchs such as Charles V who believed that just as the church spoke for God, they ruled for God.

Luther preached a doctrine known as "justification by faith": Individual Christians could obtain salvation and life everlasting only by having faith that God would save them. Giving monetary offerings to the church, following the orders of priests, or participating in church rituals would not bring believers closer to heaven. Also, the only true source of information about God's will was the Bible, not the church. By reading the Bible, any Christian could learn as much about God's commandments as any priest. Indeed, Luther called for a "priesthood of all believers."

In effect, Luther charged that the Catholic Church was in many respects fraudulent. He insisted that priests were unnecessary for salvation and that they encouraged Christians to violate God's will by promoting religious practices not specifically commanded by the Bible. The church, Luther declared, had neglected its true purpose of helping individual Christians understand the spiritual realm revealed in the Bible and had wasted its resources in worldly conflicts of politics and wars. Luther hoped his ideas would reform the Catholic Church, but instead they ruptured forever the unity of Christianity in western Europe.

Charles V pledged to exterminate Luther's Protestant heresies. The wealth pouring into Spain from the New World fueled his efforts to defend orthodox Catholic faith against Protestants, as well as against Muslims and Jews in eastern Europe and against any nation bold or foolhardy enough to contest Spain's supremacy. As the wealthiest and most powerful monarch in Europe, Charles V, followed by his son and successor Philip II, assumed responsibility for upholding the existing order of sixteenth-century Europe.

American wealth, particularly Mexican silver, fueled Spanish ambitions and made the Spanish monarchy rich and powerful among the states of Europe. But Charles V's and Philip II's expenses for constant warfare far outstripped the revenues arriving from New Spain. To help meet military expenditures, both kings raised taxes in Spain more than fivefold during the sixteenth century. Since the nobility, the wealthiest Spaniards by far, were exempt from taxation, the burdensome new taxes fell mostly on poor peasants. The monarchy's ambitions impoverished the vast majority of Spain's population and brought the nation to the brink of bankruptcy. When taxes failed to produce enough revenue to fight its wars, the monarchy borrowed heavily from European bankers. By the end of the sixteenth century, interest payments on royal debts swallowed two-thirds of the crown's annual revenues. In retrospect, the riches from New Spain proved a short-term blessing but a long-term curse.

Most Spaniards, however, looked upon New Spain as a glorious national achievement that displayed Spain's superiority over Native Americans and over other Europeans. As they surveyed their many accomplishments in the New World, they saw clear signs of progress. They had added enormously to their knowledge and wealth. They had built mines, cities, Catholic churches, and even universities on the other side of the Atlantic. These military, religious, and economic achievements gave them great pride and confidence that their European rivals often considered swaggering arrogance.

Europe and the Spanish Example

The lessons of sixteenth-century Spain were not lost on Spain's European rivals. Spain proudly displayed the fruits of its New World conquests. In 1520, for example, the German artist Albrecht Dürer wrote in his diary that he "marveled over the subtle ingenuity of the men in these distant lands" who created "things which were brought to the King . . . [such as] a sun entirely of gold, a whole fathom [six feet] broad." But the most exciting news about "the men in these distant lands" was that they could serve the interests of Europeans, as Spain had shown. With a few notable exceptions, Europeans saw the New World as a place for the expansion of European influence, a place where, as one Spaniard wrote, Europeans could "give to those strange lands the form of our own."

France and England tried to follow Spain's example. Both nations warred with Spain in Europe, preyed on Spanish treasure fleets, and ventured to the New World, where they too hoped to find an undiscovered passageway to the East Indies or another Mexico or Peru.

In 1524, France sent Giovanni da Verrazano to scout the Atlantic coast of North America from North Carolina to Canada, looking for a Northwest Passage. Eleven years later, France probed farther north with Jacques Cartier's voyage up the St. Lawrence River. Encouraged, Cartier returned to the region with a group of settlers in 1541, but the colony they established — like the search for a Northwest Passage — came to nothing.

English attempts to follow Spain's lead were slower but equally ill-fated. Not until 1576, almost eighty years after John Cabot's voyages, did the English again try to find a Northwest Passage. This time Martin Frobisher sailed into the frigid waters of northern Canada. His sponsor was the Cathay Company, which hoped to open trade with China. Like many other explorers, Frobisher was mesmerized by the Spanish example and was sure he had found gold. But the tons of "ore" he hauled back to England proved worthless, the Cathay Company collapsed, and English interests shifted southward to the giant region on the northern margins of New Spain.

English explorers' attempts to establish North American settlements were no more fruitful than their search for a northern route to China. Sir Humphrey Gilbert led expeditions in 1578 and 1583 that made feeble efforts to found colonies in Newfoundland until Gilbert vanished at sea. Sir Walter Raleigh organized an expedition in 1585 to settle Roanoke Island off the coast of present-day North Carolina. The first group of explorers left no colonists on the island, but two years later Raleigh sent a contingent of more than one hundred settlers to **Roanoke** under John White's leadership. White went back to England for supplies, and when he returned to Roanoke in 1590, the colonists had disappeared, leaving only the word *Croatoan* (whose meaning is unknown) carved in a tree. The Roanoke colonists most likely died from a combination of natural causes and unfriendly Indians. By the end of the century, England had failed to secure a New World beachhead.

REVIEW   How did Spain's conquests in the New World shape Spanish influence in Europe?

▶ Conclusion: The Promise of the New World for Europeans

The sixteenth century in the New World belonged to the Spaniards who employed Columbus and to the Indians who greeted him as he stepped ashore. The Portuguese, whose voyages to Africa and Asia set the stage for Columbus's voyages, won the important consolation prize of Brazil, but Spain hit the jackpot. Isabella of Spain helped initiate the Columbian exchange between the New World and the Old, which massively benefited first Spain and later other Europeans and which continues to this day. The exchange also subjected Native Americans to the ravages of European diseases and Spanish conquest. Spanish explorers, conquistadors, and colonists forced the Indians to serve the interests of Spanish settlers and the Spanish monarchy. The exchange illustrated one of the most important lessons of the sixteenth century: After millions of years, the Atlantic no longer was an impermeable barrier separating the Eastern and Western Hemispheres. After the voyages of Columbus, European sailing ships regularly bridged the Atlantic and carried people, products, diseases, and ideas from one shore to the other.

No European monarch could forget the seductive lesson taught by Spain's example: The New World could vastly enrich the Old. Spain remained a New World power for almost four centuries, and its language, religion, culture, and institutions left a permanent imprint. By the end of the sixteenth century, however, other European monarchies had begun to contest Spain's dominion in Europe and to make forays into the northern fringes of Spain's New World preserve. To reap the benefits the Spaniards enjoyed from their New World domain, the others had to learn a difficult lesson: how to deviate from Spain's example. That discovery lay ahead.

While England's rulers eyed the huge North American hinterland of New Spain for possible exploitation, they realized that it lacked the two main attractions of Mexico and Peru: incredible material wealth and large populations of Indians to use as workers. In the absence of gold and silver booty and plentiful native labor in North America, England would need to find some way to attract colonizers to a region that — compared to New Spain — did not appear very promising. During the next century, England's leaders overcame these dilemmas by developing a distinctive colonial model, one that encouraged land-hungry settlers from England and Europe to engage in agriculture and that depended on other sources of unfree labor: indentured servants from Europe and slaves from Africa.

Reviewing Chapter 2

REVIEW QUESTIONS

1. Why did European exploration expand dramatically in the fifteenth century? (pp. 27–31)

2. How did Columbus's discoveries help revolutionize Europeans' understanding of world geography? (pp. 31–36)

3. How did New Spain's distinctive colonial population shape its economy and society? (pp. 36–46)

4. How did Spain's conquests in the New World shape Spanish influence in Europe? (pp. 47–49)

MAKING CONNECTIONS

1. The Columbian exchange exposed people on both sides of the Atlantic to surprising new people and goods. It also produced dramatic demographic and political transformations in the Old World and the New. How did the Columbian exchange lead to redistributions of power and population? Discuss these changes, being sure to cite examples from both contexts.

2. Despite inferior numbers, the Spaniards were able to conquer the Mexica and maintain control of the colonial hierarchy that followed. Why did the Spanish conquest of the Mexica succeed, and how did the Spaniards govern the conquered territory to maintain their dominance?

3. Spanish conquest in North America brought new peoples into constant contact. How did the Spaniards' and Indians' perceptions of each other shape their interactions? In your answer, cite specific examples and consider how perceptions changed over time.

4. How did the astonishing wealth generated for the Spanish crown by its conquest of the New World influence European colonial exploration throughout the sixteenth century? In your answer, discuss ways it both encouraged and limited interest in exploration.

LINKING TO THE PAST

1. How did the legacy of ancient Americans influence their descendants' initial encounters and subsequent economic, social, and military relations with Europeans in the sixteenth century? (See chapter 1.)

2. Before the arrival of Europeans, Native Americans in the New World had no knowledge of Christianity, just as Europeans had no knowledge of Native American religions. To what extent did contrasting religious beliefs and assumptions influence relations among Europeans and Native Americans in the New World in the sixteenth century? (See chapter 1.)

TIMELINE 1480–1599

1480 • Portuguese ships reach Congo.

1488 • Bartolomeu Dias rounds Cape of Good Hope.

1492 • Christopher Columbus lands on Caribbean island that he names San Salvador.

1493 • Columbus makes second voyage to New World.

1494 • Portugal and Spain negotiate Treaty of Tordesillas.

1497 • John Cabot searches for Northwest Passage.

1498 • Vasco da Gama sails to India.

1513 • Vasco Núñez de Balboa crosses Isthmus of Panama.

1517 • Protestant Reformation begins in Germany.

1519 • Hernán Cortés leads expedition to find wealth in Mexico.
      • Ferdinand Magellan sets out to sail around the world.

1520 • Mexica in Tenochtitlán revolt against Spaniards.

1521 • Cortés conquers Mexica at Tenochtitlán.

1532 • Francisco Pizarro begins conquest of Peru.

1535 • Jacques Cartier explores St. Lawrence River.

1539 • Hernando de Soto explores southeastern North America.

1540 • Francisco Vásquez de Coronado starts to explore Southwest and Great Plains.

1542 • Juan Rodríguez Cabrillo explores California coast.

1549 • Repartimiento reforms begin to replace encomienda.

1565 • St. Augustine, Florida, settled.

1576 • Martin Frobisher explores northern Canadian waters.

1587 • English settle Roanoke Island.

1598 • Juan de Oñate explores New Mexico.

1599 • Acoma pueblos revolt against Oñate.

▶ FOR AN ONLINE BIBLIOGRAPHY, PRACTICE QUIZZES, WEB SITES, IMAGES, AND DOCUMENTS RELATED TO THIS CHAPTER, see the Book Companion Site at **bedfordstmartins.com/roarkvalue**.

▶ FOR DOCUMENTS RELATED TO THIS PERIOD, see Michael Johnson, ed., *Reading the American Past*, Fifth Edition.

3

The Southern Colonies in the Seventeenth Century

1601–1700

IN DECEMBER 1607, BARELY SIX MONTHS AFTER ARRIVING AT Jamestown with the first English colonists, Captain John Smith was captured by warriors of Powhatan, the supreme chief of about fourteen thousand Algonquian Indians who inhabited the coastal plain of present-day Virginia, near Chesapeake Bay. According to Smith, Powhatan "feasted him after their best barbarous manner." Then, Smith recalled, "two great stones were brought before Powhatan: then as many [Indians] as could layd hands on [Smith], dragged him to [the stones], and thereon laid his head, and being ready with their clubs, to beate out his braines." At that moment, Pocahontas, Powhatan's eleven-year-old daughter, rushed forward and "got [Smith's] head in her armes, and laid her owne upon his to save him from death." Pocahontas, Smith wrote, "hazarded the beating out of her owne braines to save mine, and . . . so prevailed with her father, that I was safely conducted [back] to James towne."

This romantic story of an Indian maiden rescuing a white soldier and saving Jamestown — and ultimately English colonization of North America — has been enshrined in the writing of American history since 1624, when Smith published his *Generall Historie of Virginia*. Historians believe that this episode

Ætatis suæ 21. A°. 1616.

Matoaks als Rebecka daughter to the mighty Prince Powhatan Emperour of Attanoughkomouck als Virginia converted and baptized in the Christian faith, and Wife to the wor.ll M.r Tho: Rolff.

Pocahontas in England
Shortly after Pocahontas and her husband, John Rolfe, arrived in England in 1616, she posed for this portrait dressed in English clothing suitable for a princess. The portrait captures the dual novelty of England for Pocahontas and of Pocahontas for the English. Ornate, courtly clothing probably signified to English observers that Pocahontas was royalty and to Pocahontas that the English were accepting her as befitted the "Emperour" Powhatan's daughter. The mutability of Pocahontas's identity is displayed in the identification of her as "Matoaks" or "Rebecka." National Portrait Gallery, Smithsonian Institution/Art Resource, NY.

happened more or less as Smith described it. But Smith did not understand why Pocahontas acted as she did.

Most likely, when Pocahontas intervened to save Smith, she was a knowing participant in an Algonquian ceremony that expressed Powhatan's supremacy and his ritualistic adoption of Smith as a subordinate chief, or *werowance*. What Smith interpreted as Pocahontas's saving him from certain death was instead a ceremonial enactment of Powhatan's willingness to incorporate Smith and the white strangers at Jamestown into Powhatan's empire. Powhatan routinely attached his sons and daughters to subordinate tribes as an expression of his protection and his dominance. By appearing to save Smith, Pocahontas was probably acting out Smith's new status as an adopted member of Powhatan's extended family.

Smith returned to England about two years after the adoption ritual. In Virginia, relations between Powhatan and the English colonists deteriorated into bloody raids by both parties. In 1613, the colonists captured Pocahontas and held her hostage at Jamestown. Within a year, she converted to Christianity and married one of the colonists, a widower named John Rolfe. After giving birth to a son named Thomas, Pocahontas, her husband, and the new baby sailed for England in the spring of 1616. There, promoters of the Virginia colony dressed her as a proper Englishwoman and arranged for her to go to a ball attended by the king and queen.

When John Smith heard that Pocahontas was in London, he went to see her. According to Smith, Pocahontas said, "You did promise Powhatan what was yours should bee his, and he the like to you; you called him father, being in his land a stranger, and by the same reason so must I doe you." It seems likely that Pocahontas believed that her incorporation into English society was a counterpart of the adoption ritual Powhatan had staged for John Smith in Virginia back in 1607.

Pocahontas died in England in 1617. Her son, Thomas, ultimately returned to Virginia, and by the time of the American Revolution his descendants numbered in the hundreds. But the world Thomas Rolfe and his descendants inhabited was shaped by a reversal of the power ritualized when his mother "saved" John Smith. By the end of the seventeenth century, Native Americans no longer dominated the newcomers who had arrived in the Chesapeake with John Smith.

During the seventeenth century, English colonists learned how to deviate from the example of New Spain (see chapter 2) by growing tobacco, a crop Native Americans had cultivated in small quantities for centuries. The new settlers grew enormous quantities of tobacco and exported most of it to England. Instead of incorporating Powhatan's people into their new society, the settlers encroached on Indian land and built new societies on the foundation of tobacco agriculture and transatlantic trade.

Producing large crop surpluses for export required hard labor and people who were willing — or could be forced — to do it. While New Spain took advantage of Native American labor, for the most part the Native Americans in British North America refused to be conscripted into the English colonists' fields. Instead, the settlers depended on the labor of family members, indentured servants, and, by the last third of the seventeenth century, African slaves.

By the end of the century, the southern colonies had become sharply different both from the world dominated by Powhatan when the Jamestown settlers first arrived and from contemporary English society. In ways unimaginable to Powhatan, Pocahontas, and John Smith, the colonists paid homage to the international market and the English monarch by working mightily to make a good living growing crops for sale to the Old World.

▶ An English Colony on Chesapeake Bay

When James I became king of England in 1603, he looked toward North America as a possible location for English colonies that could be as profitable as New Spain. In 1606, he granted the Virginia Company more than six million acres in North America in hopes of establishing the English equivalent of Spain's New World empire. Enthusiastic reports from the Roanoke voyages twenty years earlier (see chapter 2) claimed that in Virginia "the earth bringeth foorth all things in aboundance . . . without toile or labour."

Even if these reports were exaggerated, investors reasoned, perhaps some valuable exotic crop could be grown profitably. Maybe rich lodes of gold and silver awaited discovery, as they had in New Spain. Or maybe quick and easy profits could be grabbed in an occasional raid on the gold and silver stashed in the holds of Spanish ships that cruised up the Atlantic coast on their way to Spain. Such hopes failed to address the difficulties of adapting English desires and expectations to the New World already inhabited by Native Americans. The Jamestown settlement struggled to survive for nearly two decades, until the royal government replaced the private Virginia Company, which never earned a penny for its investors.

The Fragile Jamestown Settlement

Although Spain claimed all of North America under the 1494 Treaty of Tordesillas (see chapter 2), King James believed that England could encroach on the outskirts of Spain's New World empire. In 1588, England had successfully defended itself from the Spanish Armada, a large fleet of warships sent to invade England and bring it under Spanish rule. Now, the king hoped to flex England's muscles overseas and build new colonies in areas of North America that Spain could not defend. In effect, his land grant to the **Virginia Company**, a joint-stock company, was a royal license to poach on both Spanish claims and Powhatan's chiefdom.

English merchants had pooled their capital and shared risks for many years by using joint-stock companies for trading voyages to Europe, Asia, and Africa. The London investors of the Virginia Company, however, had larger ambitions: They hoped to found an empire that would strengthen England both overseas and at home. Richard Hakluyt, a strong proponent of colonization, claimed that a colony would provide work for swarms of poor "valiant youths rusting and hurtfull by lack of employment" in England. Colonists could buy English goods and supply products that England now had to import from other nations. More trade and more jobs would benefit many people in England, but the Virginia Company investors risked their capital because they fervently hoped to reap quick profits from the new colony.

In December 1606, the ships *Susan Constant*, *Discovery*, and *Godspeed* carried 144 Englishmen toward Virginia. They arrived at the mouth of Chesapeake Bay on April 26, 1607. That night while the colonists rested onshore, one of them later recalled, a band of Indians "creeping upon all foure, from the Hills like Beares, with their Bowes in their mouthes," attacked and dangerously wounded two men. The attack by **Algonquian Indians** gave the colonists an early warning that the North American wilderness was not quite the paradise described by the Virginia Company's publications in England. A few weeks later, they went ashore on a small peninsula in the midst of the territory ruled by **Powhatan**. With the memory of their first night in America fresh in their minds, they quickly built a fort, the first building in the settlement they named **Jamestown**.

The Jamestown fort showed the colonists' awareness that they needed to protect themselves from Indians and Spaniards. Spain planned to wipe out Jamestown when the time was ripe, but that time never came. Powhatan's people defended Virginia as their own. For weeks, the settlers and Powhatan's warriors skirmished repeatedly. English muskets and cannons repelled Indian attacks on Jamestown, but the Indians' superior numbers and knowledge of the Virginia wilderness made it risky for the settlers to venture far beyond the peninsula.

The settlers soon confronted dangerous, invisible threats: disease and starvation. Salt water and freshwater mixed in the swampy marshlands surrounding Jamestown, creating an ecological zone that allowed waterborne diseases to thrive, especially since the colonists' sanitation precautions were haphazard. During the summer, many of the Englishmen lay "night and day groaning in every corner of the Fort most pittiful to heare," wrote George Percy, one of the settlers. By September, fifty colonists had died. The colonists increased their misery by bickering among themselves, leaving crops unplanted and food supplies shrinking. "For the most part [the settlers] died of meere famine," Percy wrote; "there were never Englishmen left in a forreigne Countrey in such miserie as wee were in this new discovered Virginia."

Powhatan's people came to the rescue of the weakened and demoralized Englishmen. Early in September 1607, they began to bring corn to the colony for barter. Accustomed to eating food derived from wheat, English people considered corn the food "of the barbarous Indians which know no better . . . a more convenient food for swine than for man." The famished colonists soon overcame their prejudice against corn. Jamestown leader **Captain John Smith** recalled that the settlers were so hungry that "they would have sould their soules" for half a basket of Powhatan's corn. Indians' corn acquired by both trade and plunder managed to keep 38 of the original settlers alive until a fresh supply of food and 120 more colonists arrived from England in January 1608.

It is difficult to exaggerate the fragility of the early Jamestown settlement. One colonist lamented that "this place [is] a meere plantacion of sorrowes and Cropp of trobles, having been plentifull in nothing but want and wanting nothing but plenty." During the "starving time" winter of 1609–10, food became so short that one or two famished settlers resorted to eating their recently deceased neighbors. When a new group of colonists arrived in 1610, they found only 60 of the 500 previous settlers still alive. The Virginia Company sent hundreds of new settlers to Jamestown each year, each of them eager to find the paradise promised by the company. But most settlers went instead to early graves.

Cooperation and Conflict between Natives and Newcomers

Powhatan's people stayed in contact with the English settlers but maintained their distance. The Virginia Company boasted that the settlers bought from the Indians "the pearles of earth [corn] and [sold] to them the pearles of heaven [Christianity]." In fact, few Indians converted to Christianity, and the English devoted scant effort to proselytizing. Marriage between Indian women and English men also was rare, despite the acute shortage of English women in Virginia in the early years. Few settlers other than John Smith bothered to learn the Indians' language.

Powhatan's people regarded the English with suspicion, for good reason. Although the settlers often made friendly overtures to the Indians, they did not hesitate to use their guns and swords to enforce English notions of proper Indian behavior. More than once, the Indians refused to trade their corn to the settlers, evidently hoping to starve them out. Each time, the English broke the boycott by attacking the uncooperative Indians, pillaging their villages, and confiscating their corn.

The Indians retaliated against English violence, but for fifteen years they did not organize an all-out assault on the European intruders, probably for several reasons. Although Christianity held few attractions for the Indians, the power of the settlers' God impressed them. One chief told John Smith that "he did believe that our [English] God as much exceeded theirs as our guns did their bows and arrows." Powhatan probably concluded that these powerful strangers would make better allies than enemies. As allies, the English strengthened Powhatan's dominance over the tribes in the region.

They also traded with his people, usually exchanging European goods for corn. Native Virginians had some copper weapons and tools before the English arrived, but they quickly recognized the superiority of the intruders' iron and steel knives, axes, and pots, and they traded eagerly to obtain them. The trade that supplied the Indians with European conveniences provided the English settlers with a necessity: food.

But why were the settlers unable to feed themselves for more than a decade? First, as the staggering death rate suggests, many settlers were too sick to be productive members of the colony. Second, very few farmers came to Virginia in the early years. Instead, most of the newcomers were gentlemen and their servants. In John Smith's words, these men "never did know what a day's work was." The proportion of gentlemen in Virginia in the early years was six times greater than in England, a reflection of the Virginia Company's urgent need for investors and settlers. John Smith declared repeatedly that in Virginia "there is no country to pillage [as in New Spain]. . . . All you can expect from [Virginia] must be by labor." For years, however, colonists clung to English notions that gentlemen should not work with their hands and that tradesmen should work only in trades for which they had been trained. These ideas made more sense in labor-rich England than in labor-poor Virginia. In the meantime, the colonists depended on the Indians' corn for food.

The persistence of the Virginia colony created difficulties for Powhatan's chiefdom. Steady contact between natives and newcomers spread European diseases among the Indians, who suffered deadly epidemics in 1608 and between 1617 and 1619. The settlers' insatiable appetite for corn introduced other tensions within Powhatan's villages.

To produce enough corn for their own survival and for trade with the English required the Indians to spend more time and effort growing crops. Since Native American women did most of the agricultural work, their burden increased along with the cultural significance of their chief crop. The corn surplus grown by Indian women was bartered for desirable English goods such as iron pots, which replaced

Advertisement for Jamestown Settlers

Virginia imported thousands of indentured servants to labor in the tobacco fields, but the colony also advertised in 1631 for settlers like those pictured here. The notice features men and women equally, although men heavily outnumbered women in the Chesapeake region. How would the English experiences of the individuals portrayed in the advertisement have been useful in Virginia? Why would such individuals have wanted to leave England and go to Virginia? If indentured servants had been pictured, how might they have differed in appearance from these people? Harvard Map Collection, Pusey Library, Harvard University.

the baskets and ceramic jugs Native Americans had used for millennia. Growing enough corn to feed the English altered age-old patterns of village life. But from the Indians' viewpoint, the most important fact about the always-hungry English colonists was that they were not going away.

Powhatan died in 1618, and his brother **Opechancanough** replaced him as supreme chief. In 1622, Opechancanough organized an all-out assault on the English settlers. As an English colonist observed, "When the day appointed for the massacre arrived [March 22], a number of savages visited many of our people in their dwellings, and while partaking with them of their meal[,] the savages, at a given signal, drew their weapons and fell upon us murdering and killing everybody they could reach[,] sparing neither women nor children, as well inside as outside the dwellings." In all, the Indians killed 347 colonists, nearly a third of the English population. But the attack failed to dislodge the colonists. Instead, in the years to come the settlers unleashed a murderous campaign of Indian extermination that pushed the Indians beyond the small circumference of white settlement. Before 1622, the settlers knew that the Indians, though dangerous, were necessary to keep the colony alive. In the years after 1622, most colonists considered the Indians their perpetual enemies.

From Private Company to Royal Government

In the immediate aftermath of the 1622 uprising, the survivors became discouraged and demoralized because, as one explained, the "massacre killed all our Countrie . . . [and] burst the heart of all the rest." The disaster prompted a royal investigation of affairs in Virginia. The investigators discovered that the appalling mortality among the colonists was caused more by disease and mismanagement than by Indian raids. In 1624, King James revoked the charter of the Virginia Company and made Virginia a **royal colony**, subject to the direction of the royal government rather than to the company's private investors, an arrangement that lasted until 1776.

The king now appointed the governor of Virginia and his council, but most other features of local government established under the Virginia Company remained intact. In 1619, for example, the company had inaugurated the **House of Burgesses**, an assembly of representatives (called burgesses) elected by the colony's inhabitants. (Historians do not know exactly which settlers were considered inhabitants and were thus qualified to vote.) Under the new royal government, laws passed by the burgesses had to be approved by the king's bureaucrats in England rather than by the company. Otherwise, the House of Burgesses continued as before, acquiring distinction as the oldest representative legislative assembly in the English colonies. Under the new royal government, all free adult men in Virginia could vote for the House of Burgesses, giving it a far broader and more representative constituency than the English House of Commons had.

The demise of the Virginia Company marked the end of the first phase of colonization of the Chesapeake region. From the first 105 adventurers in 1607, the population had grown to about 1,200 by 1624. Despite mortality rates higher than during the worst epidemics in London, new settlers still came. Their arrival and King James's willingness to take over the struggling colony reflected a fundamental change in Virginia. After years of fruitless experimentation, it was becoming clear that English settlers could make a fortune in Virginia by growing tobacco.

REVIEW Why did Powhatan behave as he did toward the English colonists?

▶ A Tobacco Society

Tobacco grew wild in the New World, and Native Americans used it for thousands of years before Europeans arrived. Columbus observed Indians smoking tobacco on his first voyage to the New World. Many other sixteenth-century European explorers noticed the Indians' habit of "drinking smoke." During the sixteenth century, Spanish colonists in the New World sent tobacco to Europe, where it was an expensive luxury used sparingly by a few. During the next century, English colonists in North America sent so much tobacco to European markets that it became an affordable indulgence used often by many people.

By 1700, nearly 100,000 colonists lived in the Chesapeake region, encompassing Virginia, Maryland, and northern North Carolina (Map 3.1). They

MAP 3.1

Chesapeake Colonies in the Seventeenth Century

This map illustrates the intimate association between land and water in the settlement of the Chesapeake in the seventeenth century. The fall line indicates the limit of navigable water, where rapids and falls prevented travel farther upstream. Although Delaware had excellent access to navigable water, it was claimed and defended by the Dutch colony at New Amsterdam (discussed in chapter 4) rather than by the English settlements in Virginia and Maryland shown on this map.

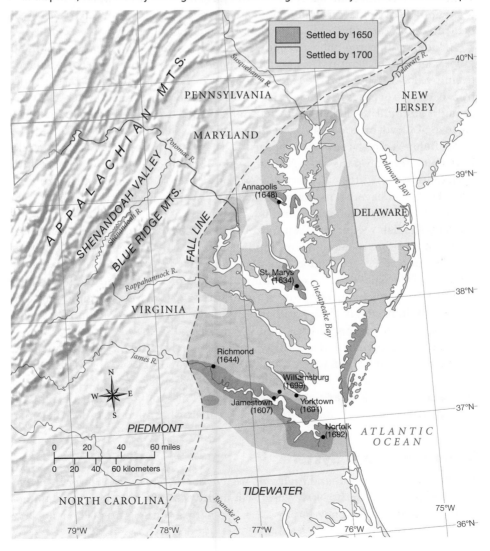

exported more than 35 million pounds of tobacco, a fivefold increase in per capita production since 1620. Clearly, Chesapeake colonists mastered the demands of tobacco agriculture, and the "Stinkinge Weede" (a seventeenth-century Marylander's term for tobacco) also mastered the colonists. Settlers lived by the rhythms of tobacco agriculture, and their endless need for labor attracted droves of English indentured servants to work in tobacco fields.

Tobacco Agriculture

Initially, the Virginia Company had no plans to grow and sell tobacco. "As for tobacco," John Smith wrote, "we never then dreamt of it." **John Rolfe** — future husband of **Pocahontas** — planted West Indian tobacco seeds in 1612 and learned that they flourished in Virginia. By 1617, the colonists had grown enough tobacco to send the first commercial shipment to England, where it sold for a high price. After that, Virginia transformed itself from a colony of rather aimless adventurers who had difficulty growing enough corn to feed themselves to a society of dedicated planters who grew as much tobacco as possible.

A demanding crop, tobacco required close attention and a great deal of hand labor year-round. Primitive tools and methods made this intensive cycle of labor taxing. Like the Indians, the colonists "cleared" fields by cutting a ring of bark from each tree (a procedure known as "girdling"), thereby killing the tree. Girdling brought sunlight to clearings but left fields studded with tree stumps, making the use of plows impractical. Instead, colonists used heavy hoes to till their tobacco fields. To plant, a visitor observed, they "just make holes [with a stick] into which they drop the seeds," much as the Indians did. Growing tobacco with such methods left little time for idleness, but the colonists enjoyed the fruits of their labor. "Everyone smokes while working or idling," one traveler reported, including "men, women, girls, and boys, from the age of seven years."

The English settlers worked hard because their labor promised greater rewards in the Chesapeake region than in England. One colonist proclaimed that "the dirt of this Province affords as great a profit to the general Inhabitant, as the Gold of Peru doth to . . . the Spaniard." Although he exaggerated, it was true that a hired man could expect to earn two or three times more in Virginia's tobacco fields than in England. Better still, in Virginia land was so abundant that it was extremely cheap compared with land in England.

By the mid-seventeenth century, common laborers could buy a hundred acres for less than their annual wages — an impossibility in England. New settlers who paid their own transportation to the Chesapeake received a grant of fifty acres of free land (termed a **headright**). The Virginia Company granted headrights to encourage settlement, and the royal government continued them for the same reason.

A Servant Labor System

Headrights, cheap land, and high wages gave poor English folk powerful incentives to immigrate to the New World. Yet many potential immigrants could not scrape together the money to pay for a trip across the Atlantic. Their poverty and the colonists' crying need for labor formed the basic context for the creation of a servant labor system.

About 80 percent of the immigrants to the Chesapeake during the seventeenth century came as **indentured servants**. Instead of a slave society, the seventeenth-century Chesapeake region was fundamentally a society of white servants and ex-servants.

Relatively few African slaves were brought to the Chesapeake in the first half century after settlement. The first known Africans arrived in Virginia in 1619 aboard the *White Lion*, an English privateer that had seized them from a Portuguese slave ship bound for South America. The "20. And odd Negroes," as John Rolfe called them, were slaves captured in Angola in west-central Africa. Virginia officials acquired them by giving the privateer captain supplies in exchange. A few more slaves trickled into the Chesapeake region during the next several decades. Until the 1670s, however, only a small number of slaves labored in Chesapeake tobacco fields. (Large numbers of slaves came in the eighteenth century, as chapter 5 explains.) Men and women of African descent occasionally became indentured servants, served out their terms of servitude, and became free. A few slaves purchased their way out of bondage and lived as free people, even owning land and using the local courts to resolve disputes, much as freed white servants did. These people were exceptions, however. Almost all people of African descent were slaves and remained enslaved for life.

A small number of Native Americans also became servants. But the overwhelming majority of indentured servants were white immigrants from England. To buy passage aboard a ship bound for the Chesapeake, an English immigrant had to come up with about £5, roughly a year's wages for an English servant or laborer. Earning wages at all was difficult in England since job opportunities were shrinking. Many country landowners needed fewer farmhands because they shifted from growing crops to raising sheep in newly enclosed fields.

Unemployed people drifted into seaports such as Bristol, Liverpool, and London, where they learned about the plentiful jobs in North America. Unable to pay for their trip across the Atlantic, poor immigrants agreed to a contract called an indenture, which functioned as a form of credit. By signing an indenture, an immigrant borrowed the cost of transportation to the Chesapeake from a merchant or ship captain in England. To repay this loan, the indentured person agreed to work as a servant for four to seven years in North America.

Once the indentured person arrived in the colonies, the merchant or ship captain sold his right to the immigrant's labor to a local tobacco planter. To obtain the servant's labor, the planter paid about twice the cost of transportation and agreed to provide the servant with food and shelter during the term of the indenture. When the indenture expired, the planter owed the former servant "freedom dues," usually a few barrels of corn and a suit of clothes.

Ideally, indentures allowed poor immigrants to trade their most valuable assets — their freedom and their ability to work — for a trip to the New World and a period of servitude followed by freedom in a land of opportunity. Planters reaped more immediate benefits. Servants meant more hands to grow more tobacco. A planter expected a servant to grow enough tobacco in one year to cover the price the planter paid for the indenture. Servants' labor during the remaining three to six years of the indenture promised a handsome profit for the planter. No wonder one Virginian declared, "Our principall wealth . . . consisteth in servants." But roughly half of all servants became sick and died before serving out their indentures, reducing planters' gains. Planters still profited, however, since they received a headright of fifty acres of land from the colonial government for every newly purchased servant.

About three out of four servants were young men between the ages of fifteen and twenty-five when they arrived in the Chesapeake. Typically, they shared the desperation of sixteen-year-old Francis Haires, who indentured himself for seven years because, according to his contract, "his father and mother and All friends [are] dead and he [is] a miserable wandering boy." Like Francis, most servants had no special training or skills, although the majority had some experience with agricultural work. "Hunger and fear of prisons bring to us onely such servants as have been brought up to no Art or Trade," one Virginia planter complained. A skilled craftsman could obtain a shorter indenture, but few risked coming to the colonies since their prospects were better in England.

Women were almost as rare as skilled craftsmen in the Chesapeake and more ardently desired. In the early days of the tobacco boom, the Virginia Company shipped young single women servants to the colony as prospective wives for male settlers willing to pay "120 weight [pounds] of the best leaf tobacco for each of them," in effect getting both a wife and a servant. The company reasoned that, as one official wrote in 1622, "the plantation can never flourish till families be planted, and the respect of wives and children fix the people on the soil." The company's efforts as a marriage broker proved no more successful than its other ventures. Women remained a small minority of the Chesapeake population until late in the seventeenth century.

The servant labor system perpetuated the gender imbalance. Although female servants cost about the same as males and generally served for the same length of time, only about one servant in four was a woman. Planters preferred male servants, as one explained, because they were "the mor[e] excellent and yousefull Cretuers," especially for field work. Although many servant women hoed and harvested tobacco fields, most also did household chores such as cooking, washing, cleaning, gardening, and milking.

The Rigors of Servitude

Servants — whether men or women, whites or blacks, English or African — tended to work together and socialize together. During the first half century of settlement, racial intermingling occurred, although the small number of blacks made it infrequent. Courts punished sexual relations between blacks and whites, but the court cases show that sexual desire readily crossed the color line. In general, the commonalities of servitude caused servants — regardless of their race and gender — to consider themselves apart from free people, whose ranks they longed to join eventually.

Servant life was harsh by the standards of seventeenth-century England and even by the frontier standards of the Chesapeake. Unlike servants in England, Chesapeake servants had no control over who purchased their labor — and thus them — for the period of their indenture. They were "sold here upp and downe like horses," one observer reported. Before their indentures expired, many servants were bought and sold several times. A Virginia servant protested in 1623 that his master "hath sold me for £150 sterling like a damnd slave." But tobacco planters' need for labor muffled complaints about treating servants as property.

For servants, the promise of indentured servitude that loomed large in their decision to leave England and immigrate to the Chesapeake often withered when they confronted the rigors of labor in the tobacco fields. James Revel, an eighteen-year-old thief punished by being indentured to a Virginia tobacco planter, declared he was a "slave" sent to hoe "tobacco plants all day" from dawn to dark. Severe laws aimed to keep servants in their place. Punishments for petty crimes stretched servitude far beyond the original terms of indenture. Richard Higby, for example, received six extra years of servitude for killing three hogs. After midcentury, the Virginia legislature added three or more years to the indentures of most servants by requiring them to serve until they were twenty-four years old.

Women servants were subject to special restrictions and risks. They were prohibited from marrying until their servitude had expired. A servant woman, the law assumed, could not serve two masters at the same time: one who owned her indentured labor and another who was her husband. However, the pre-dominance of men in the Chesapeake population inevitably pressured women to engage in sexual relations. About a third of immigrant women were pregnant when they married. Pregnancy and childbirth sapped a woman's strength, and a new child diverted her attention, reducing her usefulness as a servant. As a rule, if a woman servant gave birth to a child, she had to serve two extra years and pay a fine. However, for some servant women, premarital pregnancy was a path out of servitude: The father of an unborn child sometimes purchased the indenture of the servant mother-to-be and then freed and married her.

Harsh punishments reflected four fundamental realities of the servant labor system. First, planters' hunger for labor caused them to demand as much labor as they could get from their servants, including devising legal ways to extend the period of servitude. Second, servants hoped to survive their servitude and use their freedom to obtain land and start a family. Third, servants' hopes frequently conflicted with planters' demands. Since servants saw themselves as free people in a temporary status of servitude, they often made grudging, halfhearted workers. Finally, planters put up with this contentious arrangement because the alternatives were less desirable.

Planters could not easily hire free men and women because land was readily available and free people preferred to work for themselves on their own land. Nor could planters depend on much labor from family members. The preponderance of men in the population meant that families were few, were started late, and thus had few children. And, until the 1680s and 1690s, slaves were expensive and hard to come by. Before then, masters who wanted to expand their labor force and grow more tobacco had few alternatives to buying indentured servants.

Cultivating Land and Faith

Villages and small towns dotted the rural landscape of seventeenth-century England, but in the Chesapeake towns were few and far between. Instead, tobacco farms occupied small clearings surrounded by hundreds of acres of wilderness. Tobacco was such a labor-intensive crop that one field worker could tend only about two acres of the plants in a year (an acre is slightly smaller than a football field), plus a few more acres for food crops. A successful farmer needed a great deal more land, however, because tobacco quickly exhausted the fertility of the soil. Since each farmer cultivated only 5 or 10 percent of his land at any one time, a "settled" area comprised swatches of cultivated land surrounded by forest. Arrangements for marketing tobacco also contributed to the dispersion of settlements. Tobacco planters sought land that fronted a navigable river in order to minimize the work of transporting the heavy barrels of tobacco onto ships. A settled region thus resembled a lacework of farms stitched around waterways.

Most Chesapeake colonists were nominally Protestants. Attendance at Sunday services and conformity to the doctrines of the Church of England were

Jamestown Church Tower
This modern-day photograph shows the remains of the tower of the Anglican church that colonists constructed in Jamestown beginning in 1639. Nearby is the foundation of an older church, built in 1617, that also served as the site of the first meeting of the Virginia general assembly or House of Burgesses, the first representative legislative body in British North America. The churches illustrate the importance Virginia's leaders attached to maintaining the central British institution of worship and spiritual order in the fledgling colony. Courtesy of Preservation Virginia.

required of all English men and women. Few clergymen migrated to the Chesapeake, however, and too few of those who did were models of righteousness and piety. Certainly, some colonists took their religion seriously. Church courts punished fornicators, censured blasphemers, and served notice on parishioners who spent Sundays "goeing a fishing." But on the whole, religion did not awaken the zeal of Chesapeake settlers, certainly not as it did the zeal of New England settlers in these same years (as discussed in chapter 4). What quickened the pulse of most Chesapeake folk was a close horse race, a bloody cockfight, or — most of all — an exceptionally fine tobacco crop. The religion of the Chesapeake colonists was Anglican, but their faith lay in the turbulent, competitive, high-stakes gamble of survival as tobacco planters.

The situation was similar in the Catholic colony of Maryland. In 1632, England's King Charles I granted his Catholic friend **Lord Baltimore** about six and a half million acres in the northern Chesapeake region. In return, the king specified that Lord Baltimore pay him the token rent of "two Indian arrowheads" a year. Lord Baltimore intended to create a refuge for Catholics, who suffered severe discrimination in England. He fitted out two ships, the *Ark* and the *Dove*; gathered about 150 settlers; and sent them to the new colony, where they arrived on March 25, 1634. However, Maryland failed to live up to Baltimore's hopes. The colony's population grew very slowly for twenty years, and most settlers were Protestants rather than Catholics. The religious turmoil of the Puritan Revolution in England (discussed in chapter 4) spilled across the Atlantic, creating conflict between Maryland's few Catholics — most of them wealthy and prominent — and the Protestant majority, most of them neither wealthy nor prominent. During the 1660s, Maryland began to attract settlers, mostly Protestants, as readily as Virginia. Although Catholics and the Catholic faith continued to exert influence in Maryland, the colony's society, economy, politics, and culture became nearly indistinguishable from Virginia's. Both colonies shared a devotion to tobacco, the true faith of the Chesapeake.

> **REVIEW** Why did the vast majority of European immigrants to the Chesapeake come as indentured servants?

▶ Hierarchy and Inequality in the Chesapeake

The system of indentured servitude sharpened inequality in Chesapeake society by the mid-seventeenth century, propelling social and political polarization that culminated in 1676 with Bacon's Rebellion. The rebellion prompted reforms that stabilized relations between elite planters and their lesser neighbors and paved the way for a social hierarchy that muted differences of landholding and wealth and amplified racial differences. Amid this social and political evolution, one thing did not change: Chesapeake colonists' dedication to growing tobacco.

Social and Economic Polarization

The first half of the seventeenth century in the Chesapeake was the era of the **yeoman** — a farmer who owned a small plot of land sufficient to support a family and tilled largely by servants and a few family members. A small number of elite planters had larger estates and commanded ten or more servants. But for the first several decades, few men lived long enough to accumulate fortunes sufficient to set them much apart from their neighbors. On the whole, a rough frontier equality characterized free families in the Chesapeake until about 1650.

Until midcentury, the principal division in Chesapeake society was less between rich and poor planters than between free farmers and unfree servants. Although these two groups contrasted sharply in their legal and economic status, their daily lives had many similarities. Servants looked forward to the time when their indentures would expire and they would become free and eventually own land.

Three major developments splintered the equality during the third quarter of the century. First, as planters grew more and more tobacco, the ample supply depressed tobacco prices in European markets. Cheap tobacco reduced planters' profits and made saving enough to become landowners more difficult for freed servants. Second, because the mortality rate in the Chesapeake colonies declined, more and more servants survived their indentures, and landless freemen became more numerous and grew more discontented. Third, declining mortality also encouraged the formation of a planter elite. By living longer, the most successful planters compounded their success. The wealthiest planters also began to buy slaves as well as to serve as merchants, marketing crops for their less successful neighbors, importing English goods for sale, and extending credit to hard-pressed customers.

By the 1670s, the society of the Chesapeake had become polarized. Landowners — the planter elite and the more numerous yeoman planters — clustered around one pole. Landless colonists, mainly freed servants, gathered at the other. Each group eyed the other with suspicion and mistrust. For the most part, planters saw landless freemen as a dangerous rabble rather than as fellow colonists with legitimate grievances. **Governor William Berkeley** feared the political threat to the governing elite posed by "six parts in seven [of Virginia colonists who] . . . are poor, indebted, discontented, and armed."

Government Policies and Political Conflict

In general, government and politics strengthened the distinctions in Chesapeake society. The most vital distinction separated servants and masters, and the colonial government enforced it with an iron fist. Poor men such as William Tyler complained that "nether the Governor nor Counsell could or would doe any poore men right, but that they would shew favor to great men and wronge the poore." Most Chesapeake colonists, like most Europeans, assumed that "great men" should bear the responsibilities of government. Until 1670, all freemen could vote, and they routinely elected prosperous planters to the legislature. No former servant served in either the governor's council or the House of Burgesses after 1640. Yet Tyler and other poor Virginians believed that the "great men" used their government offices to promote their selfish personal interests rather than governing impartially.

As discontent mounted among the poor during the 1660s and 1670s, colonial officials tried to keep political power in safe hands. Beginning in 1661, for example, Governor William Berkeley did not call an election for the House of Burgesses for fifteen years. In 1670, the House of Burgesses outlawed voting by poor men, permitting only men who headed households and were landowners to vote.

The king also began to tighten the royal government's control of trade and to collect substantial revenue from the Chesapeake. A series of English laws funneled the colonial trade exclusively into the hands of English merchants and shippers. The **Navigation Acts** of 1650 and 1651 specified that colonial goods had to be transported in English ships with predominantly English crews. A 1660 act required colonial products to be sent only to English ports, and a 1663 law stipulated further that all goods sent to the colonies must pass through English ports and be carried on English ships manned by English sailors. Taken together, these navigation acts reflected the English government's mercantilist assumptions about the colonies: What was good for England should determine colonial policy.

Assumptions about **mercantilism** also underlay the import duty on tobacco inaugurated by the Navigation Act of 1660. The law assessed an import tax of two pence on every pound of colonial tobacco brought into England, about the price a Chesapeake tobacco farmer received. The tax gave the king a major financial interest in the size of the tobacco crop. During the 1660s, these tobacco import taxes yielded about a quarter of all English customs revenues, an impressive sign of the growing importance of the Chesapeake colonies in England's Atlantic empire.

Bacon's Rebellion

Colonists, like residents of European monarchies, accepted class divisions and inequality as long as they believed that government officials ruled for the general good. When rulers violated that precept, ordinary people felt justified in rebelling. In 1676, **Bacon's Rebellion** erupted as a dispute over Virginia's Indian policy. Before it was over, the rebellion convulsed Chesapeake politics and society, leaving in its wake death, destruction, and a legacy of hostility between the great planters and their poorer neighbors.

Opechancanough, the Algonquian chief who had led the Indian uprising of 1622 in Virginia, mounted another surprise attack in 1644 and killed about five hundred Virginia colonists in two days. During the next two years of bitter fighting, the colonists eventually gained the upper hand, capturing and murdering the old chief. The treaty that concluded the war established policies toward the Indians that the government tried to maintain for the next thirty years. The Indians relinquished all claims to land already settled by the English. Wilderness land beyond the fringe of English settlement was supposed to be reserved exclusively for Indian use. The colonial government hoped to minimize contact between settlers and Indians and thereby maintain the peace.

If the Chesapeake population had not grown, the policy might have worked. But the number of land-hungry colonists, especially poor, recently freed servants, continued to multiply. In their quest for land, they pushed beyond the treaty limits of English settlement and encroached steadily on Indian land. During the 1660s and 1670s, violence between colonists and Indians repeatedly flared along the advancing frontier. The government, headquartered in the tidewater region near the coast, far from the danger of Indian raids, took steps to calm the disputes and reestablish the peace. Frontier settlers thirsted for revenge against what their leader, Nathaniel Bacon, termed "the protected and Darling Indians." Bacon proclaimed his "Design not only to ruine and extirpate all Indians in Generall but all Manner of Trade and Commerce with them." Indians were not the only enemies Bacon and his men singled out. Bacon also urged the colonists to "see what spounges have suckt up the Publique Treasure." He charged that **grandees**, or elite planters, operated the government for their private gain, a charge that made sense to many colonists. In fact, officeholders had profited enough to buy slaves to replace their servants; by the 1660s, they owned about 70 percent of all the colony's slaves. Bacon crystallized the grievances of the small planters and poor farmers against both the Indians and the colonial rulers in Jamestown.

Hoping to maintain the fragile peace on the frontier in 1676, Governor Berkeley pronounced Bacon a rebel, threatened to punish him for treason, and called for new elections of burgesses who, Berkeley believed, would endorse his get-tough policy. To Berkeley's surprise, the elections backfired. Almost all the old burgesses were voted out of office, and they were replaced by local leaders, including Bacon. The legislature was now in the hands of minor grandees who, like Bacon, chafed at the rule of the elite planters.

In June 1676, the new legislature passed a series of reform measures known as Bacon's Laws. Among other changes, the laws gave local settlers a voice in setting tax levies, forbade officeholders from demanding bribes or other extra fees for carrying out their duties, placed limits on holding multiple offices, and restored the vote to all freemen. Under pressure, Berkeley pardoned Bacon and authorized his campaign of Indian warfare. But elite planters soon convinced Berkeley that Bacon and his men were a greater threat than Indians.

When Bacon learned that Berkeley had once again branded him a traitor, he declared war against Berkeley and the other grandees. For three months, Bacon's forces fought the Indians, sacked the grandees' plantations, and attacked Jamestown. Berkeley's loyalists retaliated by plundering the homes of Bacon's supporters. The fighting continued until late October, when Bacon unexpectedly died, most likely from dysentery, and several English ships arrived to bolster Berkeley's strength. With the rebellion crushed, Berkeley hanged several of Bacon's allies and destroyed farms that belonged to Bacon's supporters.

The rebellion did nothing to dislodge the grandees from their positions of power. If anything, it strengthened them. When the king learned of the turmoil in the Chesapeake and its devastating effect on tobacco exports and customs duties, he ordered an investigation. Royal officials replaced Berkeley with a governor more attentive to the king's interests, nullified Bacon's Laws, and instituted an export tax on every hogshead (large barrel) of tobacco as a way of paying the expenses of government without having to obtain the consent of the tightfisted House of Burgesses.

In the aftermath of Bacon's Rebellion, tensions between great planters and small farmers gradually lessened. Bacon's Rebellion showed, a governor of Virginia said, that it was necessary "to steer between . . . either an Indian or a civil war." The ruling elite concluded that it was safer for the colonists to fight the Indians than to fight each other, and the government made little effort to restrict settlers' encroachment on Indian land. Tax cuts also were welcomed by all freemen. The export duty on tobacco imposed by the king allowed the colonial government to reduce taxes by 75 percent between 1660 and 1700. In the long run, however, the most important contribution to political stability was the declining importance of the servant labor system. During the 1680s and 1690s, fewer servants arrived in the Chesapeake, partly because of improving economic conditions in England. Accordingly, the number of poor, newly freed servants also declined, reducing the size of the lowest stratum of free society. In 1700, as many as one-third of the free colonists still worked as tenants on land owned by others, but the social and political distance between them and the great planters did not seem as important as it had been in 1660. The main reason was that by 1700 the Chesapeake was in the midst of transitioning to a slave labor system that minimized the differences between poor farmers and rich planters and magnified the differences between whites and blacks.

REVIEW Why did Chesapeake colonial society become increasingly polarized between 1650 and 1670?

▶ Toward a Slave Labor System

Although forced native labor was already a common practice under New Spain's system of *repartimiento* (see chapter 2), repeated Indian uprisings in the Spanish colonies of New Mexico and Florida kept them marginal and unprofitable. English colonists, who had been unsuccessful in conscripting Indian labor, looked to another source of workers used by the Spaniards and Portuguese: enslaved Africans. On this foundation, European colonizers built African **slavery** into the most important form of coerced labor in the New World.

During the seventeenth century, English colonies in the West Indies followed the Spanish and Portuguese examples and developed sugar plantations with slave labor. In the English North American colonies, however, a slave labor system did not emerge until the last quarter of the seventeenth century. During the 1670s, settlers from Barbados brought slavery to the new English mainland colony of Carolina, where the imprint of the West Indies remained strong for decades. In Chesapeake tobacco fields at about the same time, slave labor began to replace servant labor, marking the transition toward a society of freedom for whites and slavery for Africans.

Religion and Revolt in the Spanish Borderland

While English colonies in the Chesapeake grew and prospered with the tobacco trade, the northern outposts of the Spanish empire in New Mexico and Florida stagnated. Spanish officials seriously considered eliminating both settlements because their costs greatly exceeded their benefits. Only about fifteen hundred Spaniards lived in Florida, and roughly twice as many inhabited New Mexico, yet both colonies required regular deliveries of goods and large subsidies because their populations proved unable to sustain themselves. One royal governor complained that "no [Spaniard] comes . . . to plow and sow [crops], but only to eat and loaf."

Instead of attracting settlers and growing crops for export, New Mexico and Florida appealed to Spanish missionaries seeking to convert Indians to Christianity. In both colonies, Indians outnumbered Spaniards ten or twenty to one. Royal officials hoped that the missionaries' efforts would pacify the Indians and be a relatively cheap way to preserve Spanish footholds in North America. The missionaries baptized thousands of Indians in Spanish North America during the seventeenth century, but they also planted the seeds of Indian uprisings against Spanish rule.

Dozens of missionaries came to Florida and New Mexico, as one announced, to free the Indians "from the miserable slavery of the demon and from the obscure darkness of their idolatry." The missionaries followed royal instructions that Indians should be taught "to live in a civilized manner, clothed and wearing shoes . . . [and] given the use of . . . bread, linen, horses, cattle, tools, and weapons, and all the rest that Spain has had." Stirrups adorned with Christian crosses on soldiers' saddles proclaimed the faith behind the Spaniards' swords, and vice versa. In effect, the missionaries sought to convert the Indians not just into Christians but also into surrogate Spaniards.

The missionaries supervised the building of scores of Catholic churches across Florida and New Mexico. Adopting practices common elsewhere in New Spain, they forced the Indians both to construct these churches

Spanish Stirrup
This seventeenth-century stirrup used by Spaniards on the northern frontier of New Spain illustrates the use of elaborate ornamentation and display to convey a sense of Spanish power. It is no accident that the stirrup is in the shape of a Christian cross, a vivid symbol of the Spaniards' belief in the divine source of their authority. © George H. H. Huey.

and to pay tribute in the form of food, blankets, and other goods. Although the missionaries congratulated themselves on the many Indians they converted, their coercive methods subverted their goals. A missionary reported that an Indian in New Mexico asked him, "If we [missionaries] who are Christians caused so much harm and violence [to Indians], why should they become Christians?"

The Indians retaliated repeatedly against Spanish exploitation, but the Spaniards suppressed the violent uprisings by taking advantage of the disunity among the Indians, much as Cortés did in the conquest of Mexico (see chapter 2). In 1680, however, the native leader **Pope** organized the **Pueblo Revolt**, ordering his followers, as one recounted, to "break up and burn the images of the holy Christ, the Virgin Mary, and the other saints, the crosses, and everything pertaining to Christianity." During the revolt, Indians desecrated churches, killed two-thirds of the Spanish missionaries, and drove the Spaniards out of New Mexico to present-day El Paso, Texas. The Spaniards managed to return to New Mexico by the end of the seventeenth century, but only by curtailing the missionaries and reducing labor exploitation. Florida Indians never mounted a unified attack on Spanish rule, but they too organized sporadic uprisings and resisted conversion, causing a Spanish official to report by the end of the seventeenth century that "the law of God and the preaching of the Holy Gospel have now ceased."

The West Indies: Sugar and Slavery

The most profitable part of the English New World empire in the seventeenth century lay in the Caribbean (Map 3.2). The tiny island of **Barbados**, colonized in the 1630s, was the jewel of the English West Indies. During the 1640s, Barbadian planters began to grow sugarcane with such success that a colonial official proclaimed Barbados "the most flourishing Island in all those American parts, and I verily believe in all the world for the production of sugar." Sugar commanded high prices in England, and planters rushed to grow as much as they could. By midcentury, annual sugar exports from the English Caribbean totaled about 150,000 pounds; by 1700, exports reached nearly 50 million pounds.

Sugar transformed Barbados and other West Indian islands. Poor farmers could not afford the expensive machinery that extracted and refined sugarcane juice, but planters with enough capital to grow sugar got rich. By 1680, the wealthiest Barbadian sugar planters were, on average, four times richer than tobacco grandees in the Chesapeake. The sugar grandees differed from their Chesapeake counterparts in another crucial way: The average sugar baron in Barbados owned 115 slaves in 1680.

African slaves planted, cultivated, and harvested the sugarcane that made West Indian planters wealthy. Beginning in the 1640s, Barbadian planters purchased thousands of slaves to work their plantations, and the African population on the island mushroomed. During the 1650s, when blacks made up only 3 percent of the Chesapeake population, they had already become the majority in Barbados. By 1700, slaves constituted more than three-fourths of the island's population.

For slaves, work on a sugar plantation was a life sentence to brutal, unremit-ting labor. Slaves suffered high death rates. Since slave men outnumbered slave women two to one, few slaves could form families and have children. These grim realities meant that in Barbados and elsewhere in the West Indies, the slave population did not grow by natural reproduction. Instead, planters continually purchased enslaved Africans. Although sugar plantations did not gain a foothold

MAP 3.2

The West Indies and Carolina in the Seventeenth Century

Although Carolina was geographically close to the Chesapeake colonies, it was culturally closer to the West Indies in the seventeenth century because its early settlers — both blacks and whites — came from Barbados. South Carolina maintained strong ties to the West Indies for more than a century, long after the arrival of many later settlers from England, Ireland, France, and elsewhere.

in North America in the seventeenth century, the West Indies nonetheless exerted a powerful influence on the development of slavery in the mainland colonies.

Carolina: A West Indian Frontier

The early settlers of what became South Carolina were immigrants from Barbados. In 1663, a Barbadian planter named John Colleton and a group of seven other men obtained a charter from England's King Charles II to establish a colony south of the Chesapeake and north of the Spanish territories in Florida. The men, known as "proprietors," hoped to siphon settlers from Barbados and other colonies and encourage them to develop a profitable export crop comparable to West Indian sugar and Chesapeake tobacco. The proprietors enlisted the English philosopher John Locke to help draft the *Fundamental Constitutions of Carolina*, which provided for religious liberty and political rights for small property holders while envisioning a landed aristocracy supported by bound laborers and slaves. Following the Chesapeake example, the proprietors also offered headrights of up to 150 acres of land for each settler, a provision that eventually undermined the *Constitutions'* goal of a titled aristocracy. In 1670, the proprietors established the colony's first permanent English settlement, Charles Towne, later spelled Charleston (see Map 3.2).

As the proprietors had planned, most of the early settlers were from Barbados. In fact, Carolina was the only seventeenth-century English colony to be settled principally by colonists from other colonies rather than from England. The Barbadian immigrants brought their slaves with them. More than a fourth of the early settlers were slaves, and as the colony continued to attract settlers from Barbados, the black population multiplied. By 1700, slaves made up about half the population of Carolina. The new colony's close association with Barbados caused English officials to refer routinely to "Carolina in ye West Indies."

The Carolinians experimented unsuccessfully to match their semitropical climate with profitable export crops of tobacco, cotton, indigo, and olives. In the mid-1690s, colonists identified a hardy strain of rice and took advantage of the knowledge of rice cultivation among their many African slaves to build rice plantations. Settlers also sold livestock and timber to the West Indies, as well as another "natural resource": They captured and enslaved several thousand local Indians and sold them to Caribbean planters. Both economically and socially, seventeenth-century Carolina was a frontier outpost of the West Indian sugar economy.

Slave Labor Emerges in the Chesapeake

By 1700, more than eight out of ten people in the southern colonies of English North America lived in the Chesapeake. Until the 1670s, almost all Chesapeake colonists were white people from England. By 1700, however, one out of eight people in the region was a black person from Africa. A few black people had lived in the Chesapeake since the 1620s, but the black population grew fivefold between 1670 and 1700 as hundreds of tobacco planters made the transition from servant to slave labor. Only relatively prosperous planters could afford to buy slaves, concentrating slave ownership among the elite.

E English of Reighly
In Esex N.º 2

Tobacco Wrapper
This wrapper labeled a container of tobacco from the English colonies sold at Reighly's shop in Essex. The wrapper was much like a brand, promising consumers consistency in quality and taste. The wrapper features two black slaves enjoying a pipe of the leaves they presumably helped grow. It also illustrates tobacco growing in a field and harvested leaves ready to be packed into a barrel, ferried to the ships waiting off-shore, and transported to Reighly's and other tobacconists in England. Reighly's owners didn't worry that depicting slaves would alienate their customers. The Granger Collection, New York.

Planters saw several advantages to purchasing slaves rather than servants. Although slaves cost three to five times more than servants, slaves never became free. Because the mortality rate had declined by the 1680s, planters could reasonably expect a slave to live longer than a servant's period of indenture. Slaves also promised to be a perpetual labor force, since children of slave mothers inherited the status of slavery. And unlike servants, they could be controlled politically. Bacon's Rebellion had demonstrated how disruptive former servants could be when their expectations were not met. A slave labor system promised to avoid the political problems caused by the servant labor system. Slavery kept discontented laborers in permanent servitude, and their color was a badge of their bondage.

The slave labor system polarized Chesapeake society along lines of race and status: All slaves were black, and nearly all blacks were slaves; almost all free people were white, and all whites were free or only temporarily bound in indentured servitude. Unlike Barbados, however, the Chesapeake retained a vast white majority. Among whites, huge differences of wealth and status still existed. By 1700, more than three-quarters of white families had neither servants nor slaves. Nonetheless, poor white farmers enjoyed the privileges of free status. They could own property, get married, have families, and bequeath their property and their freedom to their descendants; they could move when and where they wanted; they could associate freely with other people; they could serve on juries, vote, and hold political office; and they could work, loaf, and sleep as they chose. These privileges of freedom — none of them possessed by slaves — made lesser white folk feel they had a genuine stake in the existence of slavery, even if they did not own a single slave. By emphasizing the privileges of freedom shared by all white people, the slave labor system reduced the tensions between poor folk and grandees that had plagued the Chesapeake region in the 1670s.

In contrast to slaves in Barbados, most slaves in the seventeenth-century Chesapeake colonies had frequent and close contact with white people. Slaves and white servants performed the same tasks on tobacco plantations, often working side by side in the fields. Slaves took advantage of every opportunity to slip away from white supervision and seek out the company of other slaves. Planters often feared that slaves would turn such seemingly innocent social pleasures to political ends, either to run away or to conspire to strike against their masters. Slaves often did run away, but they were usually captured or returned after a brief absence. Despite planters' nightmares, slave insurrections did not occur.

Although slavery resolved the political unrest caused by the servant labor system, it created new political problems. By 1700, the bedrock political issue in the southern colonies was keeping slaves in their place, at the end of a hoe. The slave labor system in the southern colonies stood roughly midway between the sugar plantations and black majority of Barbados to the south and the small farms and homogeneous villages that developed in seventeenth-century New England to the north (as discussed in chapter 4).

REVIEW   Why had slave labor largely displaced indentured servant labor by 1700 in Chesapeake tobacco production?

▶ Conclusion: The Growth of English Colonies Based on Export Crops and Slave Labor

By 1700, the colonies of Virginia, Maryland, and Carolina were firmly established. The staple crops they grew for export provided a livelihood for many, a fortune for a few, and valuable revenues for shippers, merchants, and the English monarchy. Their societies differed markedly from English society in most respects, yet the colonists considered themselves English people who happened to live in North America. They claimed the same rights and privileges as English men and women, while they denied those rights and privileges to Native Americans and African slaves.

The English colonies also differed from the example of New Spain. Settlers and servants flocked to English colonies, in contrast to Spaniards who trickled into New Spain. Few English missionaries sought to convert Indians to Protestant Christianity, unlike the numerous Catholic missionaries in the Spanish settlements in New Mexico and Florida. Large quantities of gold and silver never materialized in English North America. English colonists never adopted the system of encomienda (see chapter 2) because the Indians in these areas were too few and too hostile and their communities too small and too decentralized compared with those of the Mexica. Yet some forms of coerced labor and racial distinction that developed in New Spain had North American counterparts, as English colonists employed servants and slaves and defined themselves as superior to Indians and Africans.

By 1700, the remnants of Powhatan's people still survived. As English settlement pushed north, west, and south of Chesapeake Bay, the Indians faced the new colonial world that Powhatan and Pocahontas had encountered when John Smith and the first colonists had arrived at Jamestown. By 1700, the many descendants of Pocahontas's son, Thomas, as well as other colonists and Native Americans, understood that the English had come to stay.

Economically, the southern colonies developed during the seventeenth century from the struggling Jamestown settlement that could not feed itself into a major source of profits for English merchants, shippers, and the king. The European fashion for tobacco provided livelihoods for numerous white families and riches for elite planters. But after 1700, enslaved Africans were conscripted in growing numbers to grow tobacco in the Chesapeake and rice in Carolina. The slave society that dominated the eighteenth-century southern colonies was firmly rooted in the developments of the seventeenth century.

A desire for land, a hope for profit, and a dream for security motivated southern white colonists. Realizing these aspirations involved great risks, considerable suffering, and frequent disappointment, as well as seizing Indian lands and coercing labor from servants and slaves. By 1700, despite huge disparities in individual colonists' success in achieving their goals, tens of thousands of white colonists who were immigrants or descendants of immigrants now considered the southern colonies their home, shaping the history of the region and of the nation as a whole for centuries to come.

Reviewing Chapter 3

REVIEW QUESTIONS

1. Why did Powhatan behave as he did toward the English colonists? (pp. 55–60)

2. Why did the vast majority of European immigrants to the Chesapeake come as indentured servants? (pp. 60–67)

3. Why did Chesapeake colonial society become increasingly polarized between 1650 and 1670? (pp. 67–71)

4. Why had slave labor largely displaced indentured servant labor by 1700 in Chesapeake tobacco production? (pp. 71–77)

MAKING CONNECTIONS

1. Given the vulnerability of the Jamestown settlement in its first two decades, why did its sponsors and settlers not abandon it? In your answer, discuss the challenges the settlement faced and the benefits different participants in England and the New World hoped to derive from their efforts.

2. Tobacco dominated European settlement in the Chesapeake during the seventeenth century. How did tobacco agriculture shape the region's development? In your answer, be sure to address the demographic and geographic features of the colony.

3. Bacon's Rebellion highlighted significant tensions within Chesapeake society. What provoked the rebellion, and what did it accomplish? In your answer, be sure to consider causes and results in the colonies and in England.

4. In addition to making crucial contributions to the economic success of seventeenth-century English colonies, Native Americans and enslaved Africans influenced colonial politics. Describe how European colonists' relations with these populations contributed to political friction and harmony within the colony.

LINKING TO THE PAST

1. How did England's colonization efforts in the Chesapeake and Carolina during the seventeenth century compare with Spain's conquest and colonization of Mexico? (See chapter 2.)

2. How did the development of the transatlantic tobacco trade exemplify the Columbian exchange? (See chapter 2.)

TIMELINE 1606–1680

1606   • Virginia Company receives royal charter.

1607   • English colonists found James-town settlement; Pocahontas "rescues" John Smith.

1607–1610 • Starvation plagues Jamestown.

1612   • John Rolfe begins to plant tobacco in Virginia.

1617   • First commercial tobacco shipment leaves Virginia for England.
            • Pocahontas dies in England.

1618   • Powhatan dies; Opechancanough becomes chief of the Algonquians.

1619   • First Africans arrive in Virginia.
            • House of Burgesses begins to meet in Virginia.

1622   • Opechancanough leads first Indian uprising against Virginia colonists.

1624   • Virginia becomes royal colony.

1630s   • Barbados colonized by English.

1632   • King Charles I grants Lord Baltimore land for colony of Maryland.

1634   • Colonists begin to arrive in Maryland.

1640s   • Barbados colonists begin to grow sugarcane with labor of African slaves.

1644   • Opechancanough leads second Indian uprising against Virginia colonists.

1660   • Navigation Act imposes mercantilist requirement that colonial products to be shipped only to English ports.
            • Virginia law defines slavery as inherited, lifelong servitude.

1663   • Royal charter granted for Carolina colony.

1670   • Charles Towne, South Carolina, founded.

1670–1700 • Slave labor system emerges in Carolina and Chesapeake colonies.

1676   • Bacon's Rebellion.

1680   • Pueblo Revolt.

▶ FOR AN ONLINE BIBLIOGRAPHY, PRACTICE QUIZZES, WEB SITES, IMAGES, AND DOCUMENTS RELATED TO THIS CHAPTER, see the Book Companion Site at bedfordstmartins.com/roarkvalue.

▶ FOR DOCUMENTS RELATED TO THIS PERIOD, see Michael Johnson, ed., *Reading the American Past*, Fifth Edition.

The Northern Colonies in the Seventeenth Century

1601–1700

ROGER WILLIAMS AND HIS WIFE, MARY, ARRIVED IN MASSACHUSETTS in February 1631. Educated at Cambridge University, the twenty-eight-year-old Williams was "a godly [Puritan] minister," noted Governor John Winthrop. But when Winthrop's Boston church asked Williams to become its minister, he refused because the church had not openly rejected the corrupt Church of England. New England's premier Puritan church was not pure enough for Roger Williams.

Williams and his wife moved to Plymouth colony for two years. While there, he spent a great deal of time among the Narragansett Indians. "My soul's desire was to do the natives good," he said. Williams believed that "Nature knows no difference between Europeans and [Native] Americans in blood, birth, [or] bodies . . . God having made of one blood all mankind." He sought to learn about the Indians' language, religion, and culture without trying to convert them to Christianity, insisting that all human beings — Christians and non-Christians alike — should live according to their consciences as revealed to them by God.

Believing that English claims were legally, morally, and spiritually invalid, Williams condemned English colonists for their "sin of unjust usurpation" of Indian land. In contrast, Massachusetts officials defended colonists' settlement on Indian land. If land "lies common, and hath never been replenished or subdued, [it] is free to any that possess or improve it," Governor Winthrop explained. Besides, he said, "if we leave [the Indians] sufficient [land] for their use, we may lawfully take the rest, there being more than enough for them and us."

In 1633, Williams became minister of the church in Salem, Massachusetts, where church members believed, like other New England Puritans, that churches and governments should enforce both godly belief and behavior according to biblical rules. They claimed that "the Word of God is . . . clear." In contrast, Williams believed that the Bible shrouded the Word of God in "mist and fog." Williams contended that devout and pious Christians could and did differ about what the Bible said and what God expected. That observation led him to denounce the emerging New England order as impure, ungodly, and tyrannical.

Williams disagreed with the New England government's requirement that everyone attend church services. He argued that forcing non-Christians to attend church was akin to requiring "a dead child to suck the breast, or a dead

New England
This 1677 map highlights the importance of water in the New England settlements. Why do you think roads and trails linking settlements are not shown? Rhode Island, haven for Roger Williams and other religious dissenters, is located on the left side, just below the center. The small numbers on the map indicate Indian attacks during King Philip's War.
© Massachusetts Historical Society, Boston, MA, USA/The Bridgeman Art Library.

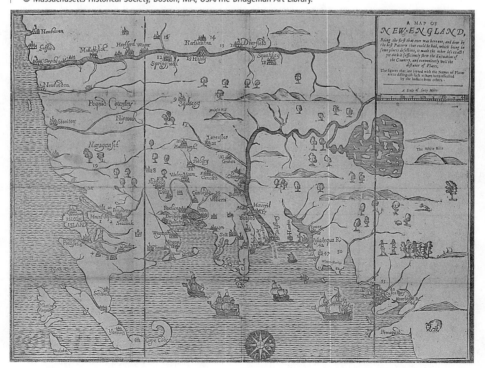

man [to] feast." This "False Worshipping" only promoted "spiritual drunkenness and whoredom." He believed that to regulate religious behavior would be "spiritual rape"; that governments should tolerate all religious beliefs because only God knows the Truth; that no person and no religion can understand God with absolute certainty. "I commend that man," Williams wrote, "whether Jew, or Turk, or Papist, or whoever, that steers no otherwise than his conscience dares." In Williams's view, toleration of religious belief and liberty of conscience were the only paths to religious purity and political harmony.

New England's leaders denounced Williams's arguments and banished him for his "extreme and dangerous" opinions. In January 1636, he escaped from an attempt to ship him back to England and fled south to Narragansett Bay, wandering for "fourteen weeks in a bitter winter season," Williams later wrote, "not knowing what bed or bread did mean." In the spring, he and his followers purchased land from the Narragansetts and established the colony of Rhode Island, which enshrined "Liberty of Conscience" as a fundamental ideal and became a refuge for other dissenters. Although New England's leaders expelled Williams from their holy commonwealth, his dissenting ideas arose from orthodox Puritan doctrines, which inspired him to draw his own conclusions and stick to them.

During the seventeenth century, New England's Puritan zeal cooled, and the promise of a holy New England faded. Late in the century, the new "middle" colonies of New York, New Jersey, and Pennsylvania were founded, featuring greater religious and ethnic diversity than New England. Religion remained important throughout all the colonies, but it competed with the growing faith that a better life required less focus on salvation and more attention to worldly concerns of family, work, and trade.

Throughout the English mainland colonies, settlements encroached on Indian land, causing violent conflict to flare up repeatedly. Political conflict also arose among colonists, particularly in response to major political upheavals in England. By the end of the seventeenth century, the English monarchy exerted greater control over North America and the rest of its Atlantic empire, but the products, people, and ideas that pulsed between England and the colonies energized both.

▶ Puritans and the Settlement of New England

Puritans who emigrated to North America aspired to escape the turmoil and persecution they suffered in England, a long-term consequence of the English Reformation. They also sought to build a new, orderly, Puritan version of England. Puritans established the first small settlement in New England in 1620, followed a few years later by additional settlements by the Massachusetts Bay Company. Allowed self-government through royal charter, these Puritans were in a unique position to direct the new colonies according to their faith. Their faith shaped the colonies they established in almost every way. Although many New England colonists were not Puritans, Puritanism remained a paramount influence in New England's religion, politics, and community life during the seventeenth century.

Puritan Origins: The English Reformation

The religious roots of the Puritans who founded New England reached back to the Protestant Reformation, which arose in Germany in 1517 (see chapter 2). The Reformation spread quickly to other countries, but the English church initially remained within the Catholic fold and continued its allegiance to the pope in Rome. Henry VIII, who reigned from 1509 to 1547, saw that the Reformation offered him an opportunity to break with Rome and take control of the church in England. In 1534, Henry formally initiated the **English Reformation**. At his insistence, Parliament passed the Act of Supremacy, which outlawed the Catholic Church and proclaimed the king "the only supreme head on earth of the Church of England." Henry seized the vast properties of the Catholic Church in England as well as the privilege of appointing bishops and others in the church hierarchy.

In the short run, the English Reformation allowed Henry VIII to achieve his political goal of controlling the church. In the long run, however, the Reformation brought to England the political and religious turmoil that Henry had hoped to avoid. Henry himself sought no more than a halfway Reformation. Protestant doctrines held no attraction for him; in almost all matters of religious belief and practice, he remained an orthodox Catholic. Many English Catholics wanted to revoke the English Reformation; they hoped to return the Church of England to the pope and to restore Catholic doctrines and ceremonies. But many other English people insisted on a genuine, thoroughgoing Reformation; these people came to be called **Puritans**.

During the sixteenth century, Puritanism was less an organized movement than a set of ideas and religious principles that appealed strongly to many dissenting members of the Church of England. They sought to eliminate what they considered the offensive features of Catholicism that remained in the religious doctrines and practices of the Church of England. For example, they demanded that the church hierarchy be abolished and that ordinary Christians be given greater control over religious life. They wanted to do away with the rituals of Catholic worship and instead emphasize an individual's relationship with God developed through Bible study, prayer, and introspection. Although there were many varieties and degrees of Puritanism, all Puritans shared a desire to make the English church thoroughly Protestant.

The fate of Protestantism waxed and waned under the monarchs who succeeded Henry VIII. When Henry died in 1547, the advisers of the new king, Edward VI — the nine-year-old son of Henry and his third wife, Jane Seymour — initiated religious reforms that moved in a Protestant direction. The tide of reform reversed in 1553 when Edward died and was succeeded by Mary I, the daughter of Henry and Catherine of Aragon, his first wife. Mary was a steadfast Catholic, and shortly after becoming queen, she married Philip II of Spain, Europe's most powerful guardian of Catholicism. Mary attempted to restore the pre-Reformation Catholic Church. She outlawed Protestantism in England and persecuted those who refused to conform, sentencing almost three hundred to burn at the stake.

The tide turned again in 1558 when Mary died and was succeeded by Elizabeth I, the daughter of Henry and his second wife, Anne Boleyn. During her long reign, Elizabeth reaffirmed the English Reformation and tried to position the English church between the extremes of Catholicism and Puritanism. Like her father, she was less concerned with theology than with politics. Above all, she desired a church that would strengthen the monarchy and the nation. By the time Elizabeth died in 1603, many people in England looked on Protestantism as a defining feature of national identity.

When Elizabeth's successor, James I, became king, English Puritans petitioned for further reform of the Church of England. James authorized a new translation of the Bible, known ever since as the King James version. However, neither James I nor his son Charles I, who became king in 1625, was receptive to the ideas of Puritan reformers. James and Charles moved the Church of England away from Puritanism. They enforced conformity to the Church of England and punished dissenters, both ordinary Christians and ministers. In 1629, Charles I dissolved Parliament — where Puritans were well represented — and initiated aggressive anti-Puritan policies. Many Puritans despaired about continuing to defend their faith in England and began to make plans to emigrate. Some left for Europe, others for the West Indies. The largest number set out for America.

The Pilgrims and Plymouth Colony

One of the first Protestant groups to emigrate, later known as **Pilgrims**, espoused an unorthodox view known as separatism. These **Separatists** sought to withdraw — or separate — from the Church of England, which they considered hopelessly corrupt. In 1608, they moved to Holland; by 1620, they realized that they could not live and worship there as they had hoped. **William Bradford**, a leader of the group, recalled that "many of their children, by . . . the great licentiousness of youth in [Holland], and the manifold temptations of the place, were drawn away by evil examples." Bradford and other Separatists believed that America promised to better protect their children's piety and preserve their community. Separatists obtained permission to settle in the extensive territory granted to the Virginia Company (see chapter 3). To finance their journey, they formed a joint-stock company with English investors. The investors provided the capital; the Separatists provided their labor and lives and received a share of the profits for seven years. In August 1620, the Pilgrim families boarded the *Mayflower*, and after eleven weeks at sea all but one of the 102 immigrants arrived at the outermost tip of Cape Cod, in present-day Massachusetts.

The Pilgrims realized immediately that they had landed far north of the Virginia grants and had no legal authority to settle in the area. To provide order and security as well as a claim to legitimacy, they drew up the **Mayflower Compact** on the day they arrived. They pledged to "covenant and combine ourselves together into a civil Body Politick, for our better Ordering and Preservation." The signers (all men) agreed to enact and obey necessary and just laws.

The Pilgrims settled at Plymouth and elected William Bradford their governor. That first winter, which they spent aboard their ship, "was most sad and lamentable," Bradford wrote later. "In two or three months' time half of [our] company died . . . being the depth of winter, and wanting houses and other comforts [and] being infected with scurvy and other diseases."

In the spring, Indians rescued the floundering Plymouth settlement. First Samoset and then Squanto befriended the settlers. Samoset had learned English from previous contacts with sailors and fishermen who had visited the coast to dry fish and make repairs years before the Plymouth settlers arrived. Squanto had been kidnapped by an English trader in 1614 and taken as a slave to Spain, where he escaped to London. There he learned English and finally made his way back home. Samoset arranged for the Pilgrims to meet and establish good relations with Massasoit, the chief of the **Wampanoag Indians**, whose territory included Plymouth. Squanto, Bradford recalled, "was a special instrument sent of God for their [the Pilgrims'] good. . . . He directed them how to set their corn, where to take fish, and to procure other commodities, and was also their pilot to bring them to unknown places." With the Indians' guidance, the Pilgrims managed to harvest enough food to guarantee their survival through the coming winter, an occasion they celebrated in the fall of 1621 with a feast of thanksgiving attended by Massasoit and other Wampanoags.

Still, the Plymouth colony remained precarious. Only seven dwellings were erected that first year, and a new group of threadbare, sickly settlers arrived in November 1621, requiring the colony to adopt stringent food rationing. The colonists quarreled with their London investors, who became frustrated when Plymouth failed to produce the expected profits.

Yet the Pilgrims persisted, living simply and coexisting in relative peace with the Indians. They paid the Wampanoags when settlers gradually encroached on Indian land. By 1630, Plymouth had become a small permanent settlement, but it failed to attract many other English Puritans.

The Founding of Massachusetts Bay Colony

In 1629, shortly before Charles I dissolved Parliament, a group of Puritan merchants and country gentlemen obtained a royal charter for the **Massachusetts Bay Company**. The charter provided the usual privileges granted to joint-stock companies, including land for colonization that spanned present-day Massachusetts, New Hampshire, Vermont, Maine, and upstate New York. In addition, a unique provision of the charter permitted the government of the Massachusetts Bay Company to be located in the colony rather than in England. This provision allowed Puritans to exchange their status as a harassed minority in England for self-government in Massachusetts.

To lead the emigrants, the stockholders of the Massachusetts Bay Company elected **John Winthrop**, a prosperous lawyer and landowner, to serve as governor. In March 1630, eleven ships crammed with seven hundred passengers sailed for Massachusetts; six more ships and another five hundred emigrants followed a few months later. Winthrop's fleet arrived in Massachusetts Bay in early June. Unlike

Seal of Massachusetts Bay Colony
In 1629, the Massachusetts Bay Company designed this seal depicting an Indian man inviting English settlers to "come over and help us." Of course, such an invitation was never issued. The seal was an attempt to lend an aura of altruism to the Massachusetts Bay Company's colonization efforts. In reality, colonists in Massachusetts and elsewhere were far less interested in helping Indians than in helping themselves. For the most part, that suited the Indians, who wanted no "help" from the colonists. What does the seal suggest about English views of Indians?
Courtesy of Massachusetts Archives.

the Separatists, Winthrop's Puritans aspired to reform the corrupt Church of England (rather than separate from it) by setting an example of godliness in the New World. Winthrop and a small group chose to settle on the peninsula that became Boston, and other settlers clustered at promising locations nearby (Map 4.1).

In a sermon to his companions aboard the *Arbella* while they were still at sea — probably the most famous sermon in American history — Winthrop proclaimed the cosmic significance of their journey. The Puritans had "entered into a covenant" with God to "work out our salvation under the power and purity of his holy ordinances," Winthrop declared. This sanctified agreement with God meant that the Puritans had to make "extraordinary" efforts to "bring into familiar and constant practice" religious principles that most people in England merely preached. To achieve their pious goals, the Puritans had to subordinate their individual interests to the common good. "We must be knit together in this work as one man," Winthrop preached. "We must delight in each other, make others' conditions our own, rejoice together, mourn together, labor and suffer together." The stakes could not be higher, Winthrop told his listeners: "We must consider that we shall be as a city upon a hill. The eyes of all people are upon us."

That belief shaped seventeenth-century New England as profoundly as tobacco shaped the Chesapeake. Winthrop's vision of a city on a hill fired the Puritans' fierce determination to keep their covenant and live according to God's laws, unlike the backsliders and compromisers who accommodated to the Church of England. Their resolve to adhere strictly to God's plan charged nearly every feature of life in seventeenth-century New England with a distinctive, high-voltage piety.

The new colonists, as Winthrop's son John wrote later, had "all things to do, as in the beginning of the world." Unlike the early Chesapeake settlers, the first Massachusetts Bay colonists encountered few Indians because the local population had been almost entirely exterminated by an epidemic probably caused by contact with Europeans more than a decade earlier. Still, as in the Chesapeake, the colonists fell victim to deadly ailments. More than two hundred settlers died

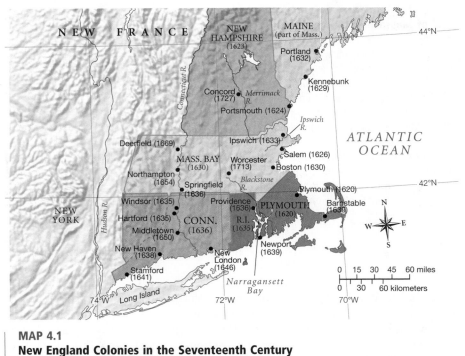

MAP 4.1

New England Colonies in the Seventeenth Century

New Englanders spread across the landscape town by town during the seventeenth century. (For the sake of legibility, only a few of the more important towns are shown on the map.)

during the first year, including one of Winthrop's sons and eleven of his servants. But Winthrop maintained a confidence that proved infectious. He wrote to his wife, "I like so well to be heer as I do not repent my comminge. . . . I would not have altered my course, though I had forseene all these Afflictions." And each year from 1630 to 1640, ship after ship followed in the wake of Winthrop's fleet. In all, more than twenty thousand new settlers came, their eyes focused on the Puritans' city on a hill.

Often, when the Church of England cracked down on a Puritan minister in England, he and many of his followers moved together to New England. Smaller groups of English Puritans moved to the Chesapeake, Barbados, and elsewhere in the New World, including New Amsterdam (present-day New York). By 1640, New England had one of the highest ratios of preachers to population in all of Christendom. Several ministers sought to carry the message of Christianity to the Indians in order to replace what missionary John Eliot termed the Indians' "unfixed, confused, and ungoverned . . . life, uncivilized and unsubdued to labor and order." They established "praying towns" to encourage Indians to leave their communities and adopt English ways. A few Indians moved to these towns and converted to Christianity, but for the most part the colonists focused less on saving Indians' souls than on saving their own.

The occupations of New England immigrants reflected the social origins of English Puritans. On the whole, the immigrants came from the middle ranks of

English society. The vast majority were either farmers or tradesmen, including carpenters, tailors, and textile workers. Indentured servants, whose numbers dominated the Chesapeake settlers, accounted for only about a fifth of those headed for New England. Most New England immigrants paid their way to Massachusetts, even though the journey often took their life savings. They were encouraged by the promise of bounty in New England reported in Winthrop's letter to his son: "Here is as good land as I have seen there [in England]. . . . Here can be no want of anything to those who bring means to raise [it] out of the earth and sea."

In contrast to Chesapeake newcomers, New England immigrants usually arrived as families. In fact, more Puritans came with family members than did any other group of immigrants in all of American history. A ship that left Weymouth, England, in 1635, for example, carried 106 passengers, all but eight of them part of a family unit. Unlike immigrants to the Chesapeake, women and children made up a solid majority in New England.

As Winthrop reminded the first settlers in his *Arbella* sermon, each family was a "little commonwealth" that mirrored the hierarchy among all God's creatures. Just as humankind was subordinate to God, so young people were subordinate to their elders, children to their parents, and wives to their husbands. The immigrants' family ties reinforced their religious beliefs with universally understood notions of hierarchy and mutual dependence. Whereas immigrants to the Chesapeake were disciplined mostly by the coercions of servitude and the caprices of the tobacco market, immigrants to New England entered a social order defined by the interlocking institutions of family, church, and community.

REVIEW Why did the Puritans immigrate to North America?

▶ The Evolution of New England Society

The New England colonists, unlike their counterparts in the Chesapeake, settled in small towns, usually located on the coast or by a river (see Map 4.1). Massachusetts Bay colonists founded 133 towns during the seventeenth century, each with one or more churches. Church members' fervent piety, buttressed by the institutions of local government, enforced remarkable religious and social conformity in the small New England settlements. During the century, tensions within the Puritan faith and changes in New England communities splintered religious orthodoxy and weakened Puritan zeal. By 1700, however, Puritanism still maintained a distinctive influence in New England.

Church, Covenant, and Conformity

Puritans believed that the church consisted of men and women who had entered a solemn covenant with one another and with God. Winthrop and three other men signed the original covenant of the first Boston church in 1630, agreeing to "Promisse, and bind our selves, to walke in all our wayes according to the Rule of the Gospell, and in all sincere Conformity to His holy Ordinaunces." Each new member of the covenant had to persuade existing members that she or he had fully experienced conversion. By 1635, the Boston church had added more than 250 names to the four original subscribers to the covenant.

Puritans embraced a distinctive version of Protestantism derived from **Calvinism**, the doctrines of John Calvin, a sixteenth-century Swiss Protestant theologian. Calvin insisted that Christians strictly discipline their behavior to conform to God's commandments announced in the Bible. Like Calvin, Puritans believed in **predestination** — the idea that the all-powerful God, before the creation of the world, decided which few human souls would receive eternal life. Only God knows the identity of these fortunate predestined individuals — the "elect" or "saints." Nothing a person did in his or her lifetime could alter God's inscrutable choice or provide assurance that the person was predestined for salvation with the elect or damned to hell with the doomed multitude. The gloomy inevitability and exclusivity of predestination contrasted sharply with Catholic doctrines that all human beings could potentially be granted eternal life by God, acting through the Catholic Church.

Despite the looming uncertainty about God's choice of the elect, Puritans believed that if a person lived a rigorously godly life — constantly winning the daily battle against sinful temptations — his or her behavior was likely to be a hint, a visible sign, that he or she was one of God's chosen few. Puritans thought that "sainthood" would become visible in individuals' behavior, especially if they were privileged to know God's Word as revealed in the Bible.

The connection between sainthood and saintly behavior, however, was far from certain. Some members of the elect, Puritans believed, had not heard God's Word as revealed in the Bible, and therefore their behavior did not necessarily signal their sainthood. One reason Puritans required all town residents to attend church services was to enlighten anyone who was ignorant of God's Truth. The slippery relationship between saintly behavior, observable by anybody, and God's predestined election, invisible and unknowable to anyone, caused Puritans to worry constantly that individuals who acted like saints were fooling themselves and others. Nevertheless, Puritans thought that **visible saints** — persons who passed their demanding tests of conversion and church membership — probably, though not certainly, were among God's elect.

Members of Puritan churches ardently hoped that God had chosen them to receive eternal life and tried to demonstrate saintly behavior. Their covenant bound them to help one another attain salvation and to discipline the entire community by saintly standards. Church members kept an eye on the behavior of everybody in town. Infractions of morality, order, or propriety were reported to Puritan elders, who summoned the wayward to a church inquiry. By overseeing every aspect of life, the visible saints enforced a remarkable degree of righteous conformity in Puritan communities. Total conformity, however, was never achieved. Ardent Puritans differed among themselves; non-Puritans shirked orthodox rules. Every community contained dissenters and recalcitrants, such as the Roxbury servant who declared that "if hell were ten times hotter, [I] would rather be there than [I] would serve [my] master."

Despite the central importance of religion, churches played no direct role in the civil government of New England communities. Puritans did not want to mimic the Church of England, which they considered a puppet of the king rather than an independent body that served the Lord. They were determined to insulate New England churches from the contaminating influence of the civil state and its merely human laws. Although ministers were the most highly respected figures in New England towns, they were prohibited from holding government office.

Puritans had no qualms, however, about their religious beliefs influencing New England governments. As much as possible, the Puritans tried to bring public life into conformity with their view of God's law. For example, fines were issued for Sabbath-breaking activities such as working, traveling, playing a flute, smoking a pipe, and visiting neighbors.

Puritans mandated other purifications of what they considered corrupt English practices. They refused to celebrate Christmas or Easter because the Bible did not mention either one. They outlawed religious wedding ceremonies; couples were married by a magistrate in a civil ceremony (the first wedding in Massachusetts performed by a minister occurred in 1686). They prohibited elaborate clothing and finery such as lace trim and short sleeves — "whereby the nakedness of the arm may be discovered." They banned cards, dice, shuffleboard, and other games of chance, as well as music and dancing. The distinguished minister Increase Mather insisted that "Mixt or Promiscuous Dancing . . . of Men and Women" could not be tolerated since "the unchaste Touches and Gesticulations used by Dancers have a palpable tendency to that which is evil." On special occasions, Puritans proclaimed days of fasting and humiliation, which, as one preacher boasted, amounted to "so many Sabbaths more."

Government by Puritans for Puritanism

It is only a slight exaggeration to say that seventeenth-century New England was governed by Puritans for Puritanism. The charter of the Massachusetts Bay Company empowered the company's stockholders, known as freemen, to meet as a body known as the General Court and make the laws needed to govern the company's affairs. The colonists transformed this arrangement for running a joint-stock company into a structure for governing the colony. Hoping to ensure that godly men would decide government policies, the General Court expanded the number of freemen in 1631 to include all male church members. Only freemen had the right to vote for governor, deputy governor, and other colonial officials. As new settlers were recognized as freemen, the size of the General Court grew too large to meet conveniently. So in 1634, the freemen in each town agreed to send two deputies to the General Court to act as the colony's legislative assembly. All other men were classified as "inhabitants," and they had the right to vote, hold office, and participate fully in town government.

A "town meeting," composed of a town's inhabitants and freemen, chose the selectmen and other officials who administered local affairs. New England town meetings routinely practiced a level of popular participation in political life that was unprecedented elsewhere in the world during the seventeenth century. Almost every adult man could speak out in town meetings and fortify his voice with a vote. However, all women — even church members — were prohibited from voting, and towns did not permit "contrary-minded" men to become or remain inhabitants. Although town meeting participants wrangled from time to time, widespread political participation tended to reinforce conformity to Puritan ideals.

One of the most important functions of New England government was land distribution. Settlers who wanted to establish a new town entered a covenant and petitioned the General Court for a grant of land. The court granted town sites to suitably pious petitioners but did not allow settlement until the Indians who inhabited a grant agreed to relinquish their claim to the land, usually in exchange for manufactured goods. For instance, William Pynchon purchased the site of Springfield, Massachusetts, from the Agawam Indians for "eighteen fathams [arm's lengths] of Wampum [strings of shell-beads used in trade], eighteen coates, 18 hatchets, 18 hoes, [and] 18 knives."

Having obtained their grant, town founders apportioned land among themselves and any newcomers they permitted to join them. Normally, each family received a house lot large enough for an adjacent garden as well as one or more strips of agricultural land on the perimeter of the town. Although there was a considerable difference between the largest and smallest family plots, most clustered in the middle range — roughly fifty to one hundred acres — resulting in a more nearly equal distribution of land in New England than in the Chesapeake.

The physical layout of New England towns encouraged settlers to look inward toward their neighbors, multiplying the opportunities for godly vigilance. Most people considered the forest that lay just beyond every settler's house an alien environment that was interrupted here and there by those oases of civilization, the towns. Footpaths connecting one town to another were so rudimentary that even John Winthrop once got lost within half a mile of his house and spent a sleepless night in the forest, circling the light of his small campfire and singing psalms.

The Splintering of Puritanism

Almost from the beginning, John Winthrop and other leaders had difficulty enforcing their views of Puritan orthodoxy. In England, persecution as a dissenting minority had unified Puritan voices in opposition to the Church of England. In New England, the promise of a godly society and the Puritans' emphasis on individual Bible study led New Englanders toward different visions of godliness. Puritan leaders, however, interpreted dissent as an error caused either by a misguided believer or by the malevolent power of Satan. Whatever the cause, errors could not be tolerated. As one Puritan minister proclaimed, "The Scripture saith . . . there is no Truth but one."

Shortly after banishing **Roger Williams** (see pages 81–83), Winthrop confronted another dissenter, this time a devout Puritan woman steeped in Scripture and absorbed by religious questions: **Anne Hutchinson**. The mother of fourteen children, Hutchinson served her neighbors as a midwife. After she settled into her new home in Boston in 1634, women gathered there to hear her weekly lectures on recent sermons. As one listener observed, she was a "Woman that Preaches better Gospell then any of your blackcoates . . . [from] the Ninneversity."

As the months passed, Hutchinson began to lecture twice a week, and crowds of sixty to eighty women and men assembled to listen to her.

Hutchinson expounded on the sermons of John Cotton, her favorite minister. Cotton stressed what he termed the "covenant of grace" — the idea that individuals could be saved only by God's grace in choosing them to be members of the elect. Cotton contrasted this familiar Puritan doctrine with the covenant of works, the erroneous belief that a person's behavior — one's works — could win God's favor and ultimately earn a person salvation. Belief in the covenant of works and in the possibility of salvation for all was known as **Arminianism**. Cotton's sermons strongly hinted that many Puritans, including ministers, embraced Arminianism, which claimed — falsely, Cotton declared — that human beings could influence God's will. Anne Hutchinson agreed with Cotton. Her lectures emphasized her opinion that many of the colony's leaders affirmed the Arminian covenant of works. Like Cotton, she preached that only God's covenant of grace led to salvation.

The meetings at Hutchinson's house alarmed her nearest neighbor, Governor John Winthrop, who believed that she was subverting the good order of the colony. In 1637, Winthrop had formal charges brought against Hutchinson and denounced her lectures as "not tolerable nor comely in the sight of God nor fitting for your sex." He told her, "You have stept out of your place, you have rather bine a Husband than a Wife and a preacher than a Hearer; and a Magistrate than a Subject."

In court, Winthrop interrogated Hutchinson, fishing for a heresy he could pin on her. Winthrop and other Puritan elders referred to Hutchinson and her followers as **antinomians**, people who believed that Christians could be saved by faith alone and did not need to act in accordance with God's law as set forth in the Bible and as interpreted by the colony's leaders. Hutchinson nimbly defended herself against the accusation of antinomianism. Yes, she acknowledged, she believed that men and women were saved by faith alone; but no, she did not deny the need to obey God's law. "The Lord hath let me see which was the clear ministry and which the wrong," she said. Finally, Winthrop had cornered her. How could she tell which ministry was which? "By an immediate revelation," she replied, "by the voice of [God's] own spirit to my soul." Winthrop spotted in this statement the heresy of prophecy, the view that God revealed his will directly to a believer instead of exclusively through the Bible, as every right-minded Puritan knew.

In 1638, the Boston church formally excommunicated Hutchinson. The minister decreed, "I doe cast you out and . . . deliver you up to Satan that you may learne no more to blaspheme[,] to seduce and to lye. . . . I command you . . . as a Leper to withdraw your selfe out of the Congregation." Banished, Hutchinson and her family moved first to Roger Williams's Rhode Island and then to present-day New York, where she and most of her family were killed by Indians.

The strains within Puritanism exemplified by Anne Hutchinson and Roger Williams caused communities to splinter repeatedly during the seventeenth century. **Thomas Hooker**, a prominent minister, clashed with Winthrop and other leaders over the composition of the church. Hooker argued that men and women who lived godly lives should be admitted to church membership even if they had not experienced conversion. This issue, like most others in New England, had both religious and political dimensions, for only church members could vote in Massachusetts. In 1636, Hooker led an exodus of more than eight hundred colonists from Massachusetts to the Connecticut River valley, where they founded Hartford and neighboring towns. In 1639, the towns adopted the Fundamental Orders of Connecticut, a quasi-constitution that could be altered by the vote of freemen, who did not have to be church members, though nearly all of them were.

Other Puritan churches divided and subdivided throughout the seventeenth century as acrimony developed over doctrine and church government. Sometimes churches split over the appointment of a controversial minister. Sometimes families who had a long walk to the meetinghouse simply decided to form their own church nearer their homes. These schisms arose from ambiguities and tensions within Puritan belief. As the colonies matured, other tensions developed as well.

Religious Controversies and Economic Changes

A revolutionary transformation in the fortunes of Puritans in England had profound consequences in New England. Disputes between King Charles I and Parliament, which was dominated by Puritans, escalated in 1642 to civil war in England, a conflict known as the **Puritan Revolution**. Parliamentary forces led by the staunch Puritan Oliver Cromwell were victorious, executing Charles I in 1649 and proclaiming England a Puritan republic. From 1649 to 1660, England's rulers were not monarchs who suppressed Puritanism but believers who championed it. In a half century, English Puritans had risen from a harassed group of religious dissenters to a dominant power in English government.

When the Puritan Revolution began, the stream of immigrants to New England dwindled to a trickle, creating hard times for the colonists. They could no longer consider themselves a city on a hill setting a godly example for humankind. Puritans in England, not New England, were reforming English society. Furthermore, when immigrant ships became rare, the colonists faced sky-high prices for scarce English goods and few customers for their own colonial products. As they searched to find new products and markets, they established the enduring patterns of New England's economy.

New England's rocky soil and short growing season ruled out cultivating the southern colonies' crops of tobacco and rice that found ready markets in Atlantic ports. Exports that New Englanders could not get from the soil they took instead from the forest and the sea. During the first decade of settlement, colonists traded with the Indians for animal pelts, which were in demand in Europe. By the 1640s, furbearing animals had become scarce unless traders ventured far beyond the frontiers of English settlement. Trees from the seemingly limitless forests of New England proved a longer-lasting resource. Masts for ships and staves for barrels of Spanish wine and West Indian sugar were crafted from New England timber.

The most important New England export was fish. During the turmoil of the Puritan Revolution, English ships withdrew from the rich North Atlantic fishing grounds, and New England fishermen quickly took their place. Dried, salted codfish found markets in southern Europe and the West Indies. The fish trade also stimulated colonial shipbuilding and trained generations of fishermen, sailors, and merchants, creating a commercial network that endured for more than a century. But this export economy remained peripheral to most New England colonists. Their lives revolved around their farms, their churches, and their families.

Although immigration came to a standstill in the 1640s, the population continued to boom, doubling every twenty years. In New England, almost everyone married, and women often had eight or nine children. Long, cold winters minimized the presence of warm-weather ailments such as malaria and yellow fever in the northern colonies, so the mortality rate was lower than in the South. The descendants of the immigrants of the 1630s multiplied, boosting the New England population to roughly equal that of the southern colonies.

During the second half of the seventeenth century, under the pressures of steady population growth and integration into the Atlantic economy, the red-hot piety of the founders cooled. After 1640, the population grew faster than church membership. All residents attended sermons on pain of fines and punishment, but many could not find seats in the meetinghouses. Boston's churches in 1650 could house only about a third of the city's residents. By the 1680s, women were the majority of church members throughout New England. In some towns, only 15 percent of the adult men were members. A growing fraction of New Englanders, especially men, embraced what one historian has termed "horse-shed Christianity": They attended sermons but loitered outside near the horse shed, gossiping about the weather, fishing, their crops, or the scandalous behavior of neighbors. This slackening of piety led the Puritan minister Michael Wigglesworth to ask, in verse:

> How is it that
> I find In stead of holiness Carnality;
> In stead of heavenly frames an Earthly mind,
> For burning zeal luke-warm Indifferency,
> For flaming love, key-cold Dead-heartedness. . . .
> Whence cometh it, that Pride, and Luxurie
> Debate, Deceit, Contention and Strife,
> False-dealing, Covetousness, Hypocrisie
> (With such Crimes) amongst them are so rife,
> That one of them doth over-reach another?
> And that an honest man can hardly
> Trust his Brother?

Most alarming to Puritan leaders, many of the children of the visible saints of Winthrop's generation failed to experience conversion and attain full church membership. Puritans tended to assume that sainthood was inherited — that the children of visible saints were probably also among the elect. Acting on this premise, churches permitted saints to baptize their infant sons and daughters, symbolically cleansing them of their contamination with original sin. As these children grew up during the 1640s and 1650s, however, they seldom experienced the inward transformation that signaled conversion and qualification for church membership. The problem of declining church membership and the watering-down of Puritan orthodoxy became urgent during the 1650s when the children of saints, who had grown to adulthood in New England but had not experienced conversion, began to have children themselves. Their sons and daughters — the grandchildren of the founders of the colony — could not receive the protection that baptism afforded against the terrors of death because their parents had not experienced conversion.

Puritan churches debated what to do. To allow anyone, even the child of a saint, to become a church member without conversion was an unthinkable retreat from fundamental Puritan doctrine. In 1662, a synod of Massachusetts ministers reached a compromise known as the **Halfway Covenant**. Unconverted children of saints would be permitted to become "halfway" church members. Like regular church members, they could baptize their infants. But unlike full church members, they could not participate in communion or have the voting privileges of church membership. The Halfway Covenant generated a controversy that sputtered through Puritan churches for the remainder of the century. With the Halfway Covenant, Puritan churches came to terms with the lukewarm piety that had replaced the founders' burning zeal.

Nonetheless, New England communities continued to enforce piety with holy rigor. Beginning in 1656, small bands of **Quakers** — members of the Society of Friends, as they called themselves — began to arrive in Massachusetts. Many of their beliefs were at odds with orthodox Puritanism. Quakers believed that God spoke directly to each individual through an "inner light" and that individuals needed neither a preacher nor the Bible to discover God's Word. Maintaining that all human beings were equal in God's eyes, Quakers refused to conform to mere temporal powers such as laws and governments unless God requested otherwise. For example, Quakers refused to observe the Sabbath because, they insisted, God had not set aside any special day for worship, expecting believers to worship faithfully every day. Women often took a leading role in Quaker meetings, in contrast to Puritan congregations, where women usually outnumbered men but remained subordinate.

New England communities treated Quakers with ruthless severity. Some Quakers were branded on the face "with a red-hot iron with [an] H. for heresie." When Quakers refused to leave Massachusetts, Boston officials hanged four of them between 1659 and 1661.

New Englanders' partial success in realizing the promise of a godly society ultimately undermined the intense appeal of Puritanism. In the pious Puritan communities of New England, leaders tried to eliminate sin. In the process, they diminished the sense of utter human depravity that was the wellspring of Puritanism. By 1700, New Englanders did not doubt that human beings sinned, but they were more concerned with the sins of others than with their own.

Witch trials held in Salem, Massachusetts, signaled the erosion of religious confidence and assurance. From the beginning of English settlement in the New World, more than 95 percent of all legal accusations of witchcraft occurred in New England, a hint of the Puritans' preoccupation with sin and evil. The most

Witches Show Their Love for Satan

Mocking pious Christians' humble obeisance to God, witches willingly debased themselves by standing in line to kneel and kiss Satan's buttocks — or so it was popularly believed. This seventeenth-century print portrays Satan with clawlike hands and feet, the tail of a rodent, the wings of a bat, and the head of a lustful ram attached to the torso of a man. Notice that women predominate among the witches eager to express their devotion to Satan and to do his bidding. UCSF Library/Center for Knowledge Management.

notorious witchcraft trials took place in Salem in 1692, when witnesses accused more than one hundred people of witchcraft, a capital crime. Bewitched young girls shrieked in pain, their limbs twisted into strange contortions, as they pointed out the witches who tortured them. According to the trial court record, the bewitched girls declared that "the shape of [one accused witch] did oftentimes very grievously pinch them, choke them, bite them, and afflict them; urging them to write their names in a book" — the devil's book. Most of the accused witches were older women, and virtually all of them were well known to their accusers. The Salem court hanged nineteen accused witches and pressed one to death, signaling enduring belief in the supernatural origins of evil and gnawing doubt about the strength of Puritan New Englanders' faith. Why else, after all, had so many New Englanders succumbed to what their accusers and the judges believed were the temptations of Satan?

REVIEW Why did Massachusetts Puritans adopt the Halfway Covenant?

▶ The Founding of the Middle Colonies

South of New England and north of the Chesapeake, a group of middle colonies were founded in the last third of the seventeenth century. Before the 1670s, few Europeans settled in the region. For the first two-thirds of the seventeenth century, the most important European outpost in the area was the relatively small Dutch colony of New Netherland. By 1700, however, the English monarchy had seized New Netherland, renamed it New York, and encouraged the creation of a Quaker colony in Pennsylvania led by William Penn. Unlike the New England colonies, the middle colonies of New York, New Jersey, and Pennsylvania originated as land grants by the English monarch to one or more proprietors, who then possessed both the land and the extensive, almost monarchical, powers of government. These middle colonies attracted settlers of more diverse European origins and religious faiths than were found in New England.

From New Netherland to New York

In 1609, the Dutch East India Company dispatched Henry Hudson to search for a Northwest Passage to the Orient. Hudson sailed along the Atlantic coast and ventured up the large river that now bears his name until it dwindled to a stream that obviously did not lead to China. A decade later, the Dutch government granted the West India Company — a group of Dutch merchants and shippers — exclusive rights to trade with the Western Hemisphere. In 1626, Peter Minuit, the resident director of the company, purchased Manhattan Island from the Manhate Indians for trade goods worth the equivalent of a dozen beaver pelts. New Amsterdam, the small settlement established at the southern tip of Manhattan Island, became the principal trading center in **New Netherland** and the colony's headquarters.

New Amsterdam

The settlement on Manhattan Island — complete with a windmill — appears in the background of this 1673 Dutch portrait of New Amsterdam. In the foreground, the Dutch artist placed native inhabitants of the mainland, drawing them to resemble Africans rather than Lenni Lenape (Delaware) Indians. The artist probably had never seen Indians and depended on well-known artistic conventions about the appearance of Africans to create his Native Americans. The portrait contrasts orderly, efficient, businesslike New Amsterdam with the exotic natural environment of America, to which the native woman on the left clings. © Collection of the New-York Historical Society.

N: AMSTERDAM, ou N: IORK
in Ameriq:

Unlike the English colonies, New Netherland did not attract many European immigrants. Like New England and the Chesapeake colonies, New Netherland never realized its sponsors' dreams of great profits. The company tried to stimulate immigration by granting patroonships — allotments of eighteen miles of land along the Hudson River — to wealthy stockholders who would bring fifty families to the colony and settle them as serflike tenants on their huge domains. Only one patroonship succeeded; the others failed to attract settlers, and the company eventually recovered much of the land.

Though few in number, New Netherlanders were remarkably diverse, especially compared with the homogeneous English settlers to the north and south. Religious dissenters and immigrants from Holland, Sweden, France, Germany, and elsewhere made their way to the colony. A minister of the Dutch Reformed Church complained to his superiors in Holland that several groups of Jews had recently arrived, adding to the religious mixture of "Papists, Mennonites and Lutherans among the Dutch [and] many Puritans . . . and many other atheists . . . who conceal themselves under the name of Christians."

The West India Company struggled to govern the motley colonists. Peter Stuyvesant, governor from 1647 to 1664, tried to enforce conformity to the Dutch Reformed Church, but the company declared that "the consciences of men should be free and unshackled," making a virtue of New Netherland necessity. The company never permitted the colony's settlers to form a representative government. Instead, the company appointed government officials who established policies, including taxes, that many colonists deeply resented.

In 1664, New Netherland became New York. Charles II, who became king of England in 1660 when Parliament restored the monarchy, gave his brother James, the Duke of York, an enormous grant of land that included New Netherland. Of course, the Dutch colony did not belong to the king of England, but that legal technicality did not deter the king or his brother. The duke quickly organized a small fleet of warships, which appeared off Manhattan Island in late summer 1664, and demanded that Stuyvesant surrender. With little choice, he did.

As the new proprietor of the colony, the Duke of York exercised almost the same unlimited authority over the colony as had the West India Company. The duke never set foot in New York, but his governors struggled to impose order on the unruly colonists. Like the Dutch, the duke permitted "all persons of what Religion soever, quietly to inhabit . . . provided they give no disturbance to the publique peace, nor doe molest or disquiet others in the free exercise of their religion." This policy of religious toleration was less an affirmation of liberty of conscience than a recognition of the reality of the most heterogeneous colony in seventeenth-century North America.

New Jersey and Pennsylvania

The creation of New York led indirectly to the founding of two other middle colonies, New Jersey and Pennsylvania. In 1664, the Duke of York subdivided his grant and gave the portion between the Hudson and Delaware rivers to two of his friends. The proprietors of this new colony, New Jersey, quarreled and called in a prominent English Quaker, **William Penn**, to arbitrate their dispute.

Penn eventually worked out a settlement that continued New Jersey's proprietary government. In the process, Penn became intensely interested in what he termed a "holy experiment" of establishing a genuinely Quaker colony in America.

Unlike most Quakers, William Penn came from an eminent family. His father had served both Cromwell and Charles II and had been knighted. Born in 1644, the younger Penn trained for a military career, but the ideas of dissenters from the reestablished Church of England appealed to him, and he became a devout Quaker. By 1680, he had published fifty books and pamphlets and spoken at countless public meetings, although he had not won official toleration for Quakers in England.

The Quakers' concept of an open, generous God who made his love equally available to all people manifested itself in behavior that continually brought them into conflict with the English government. Quaker leaders were ordinary men and women, not specially trained preachers. Quakers allowed women to assume positions of religious leadership. "In souls there is no sex," they said. Since all people were equal in the spiritual realm, Quakers considered social hierarchy false and evil. They called everyone "friend" and shook hands instead of curtsying or removing their hats — even when meeting the king. These customs enraged many non-Quakers and provoked innumerable beatings and worse. Penn was jailed four times for such offenses, once for nine months.

Despite his many run-ins with the government, Penn remained on good terms with Charles II. Partly to rid England of the troublesome Quakers, in 1681 Charles made Penn the proprietor of a new colony of some 45,000 square miles called Pennsylvania.

Toleration and Diversity in Pennsylvania

Quakers flocked to Pennsylvania in numbers exceeded only by the great Puritan migration to New England fifty years earlier. Between 1682 and 1685, nearly eight thousand immigrants arrived, most of them from England, Ireland, and Wales. They represented a cross section of the artisans, farmers, and laborers who predominated among English Quakers. Quaker missionaries also encouraged immigrants from the European continent, and many came, giving Pennsylvania greater ethnic diversity than any other English colony except New York. The Quaker colony prospered, and the capital city, Philadelphia, soon rivaled New York as a center of commerce. By 1700, the city's five thousand inhabitants participated in a thriving trade exporting flour and other food products to the West Indies and importing English textiles and manufactured goods.

Penn was determined to live in peace with the Indians who inhabited the region. His Indian policy expressed his Quaker ideals and contrasted sharply with the hostile policies of the other English colonies. As he explained to the chief of the Lenni Lenape (Delaware) Indians, "God has written his law in our hearts, by which we are taught and commanded to love and help and do good to one another . . . [and] I desire to enjoy [Pennsylvania lands] with your love and consent." Penn instructed his agents to obtain the Indians' consent by purchasing their land, respecting their claims, and dealing with them fairly.

Penn declared that the first principle of government was that every settler would "enjoy the free possession of his or her faith and exercise of worship towards

God." Accordingly, Pennsylvania tolerated Protestant sects of all kinds as well as Roman Catholicism. All voters and officeholders had to be Christians, but the government did not compel settlers to attend religious services, as in Massachusetts, or to pay taxes to maintain a state-supported church, as in Virginia.

Despite its toleration and diversity, Pennsylvania was as much a Quaker colony as New England was a stronghold of Puritanism. Penn had no hesitation about using civil government to enforce religious morality. One of the colony's first laws provided severe punishment for "all such offenses against God, as swearing, cursing, lying, profane talking, drunkenness, drinking of healths, [and] obscene words . . . which excite the people to rudeness, cruelty, looseness, and irreligion."

As proprietor, Penn had extensive powers subject only to review by the king. He appointed a governor, who maintained the proprietor's power to veto any laws passed by the colonial council, which was elected by property owners who possessed at least one hundred acres of land or who paid taxes. The council had the power to originate laws and administer all the affairs of government. A popularly elected assembly served as a check on the council; its members had the authority to reject or approve laws framed by the council.

Penn stressed that the exact form of government mattered less than the men who served in it. In Penn's eyes, "good men" staffed Pennsylvania's government because Quakers dominated elective and appointive offices. Quakers, of course, differed among themselves. Members of the assembly struggled to win the right to debate and amend laws, especially tax laws. They finally won the battle in 1701 when a new Charter of Privileges gave the proprietor the power to appoint the council and in turn stripped the council of all its former powers and gave them to the assembly, which became the only single-house legislature in all the English colonies.

REVIEW How did Quaker ideals shape the colony of Pennsylvania?

► The Colonies and the English Empire

Proprietary grants to faraway lands were a cheap way for the king to reward friends. As the colonies grew, however, the grants became more valuable. After 1660, the king took initiatives to channel colonial trade through English hands and to consolidate royal authority over colonial governments. Occasioned by such economic and political considerations and triggered by King Philip's War between colonists and Native Americans, these initiatives defined the basic relationship between the colonies and England that endured until the American Revolution (Map 4.2).

Royal Regulation of Colonial Trade

English economic policies toward the colonies were designed to yield customs revenues for the monarchy and profitable business for English merchants and shippers. Also, the policies were intended to divert the colonies' trade from England's enemies, especially the Dutch and the French.

MAP 4.2

American Colonies at the End of the Seventeenth Century
By the end of the seventeenth century, settlers inhabited a narrow band of land that stretched more or less continuously from Boston to Norfolk, with pockets of settlement farther south. The colonies' claims to enormous tracts of land to the west were contested by Native Americans as well as by France and Spain.

The Navigation Acts of 1650, 1651, 1660, and 1663 (see chapter 3) set forth two fundamental rules governing colonial trade. First, goods shipped to and from the colonies had to be transported in English ships using primarily English crews. Second, the Navigation Acts listed ("enumerated," in the language of the time) colonial products that could be shipped only to England or to other English colonies. While these regulations prevented Chesapeake planters from shipping their tobacco directly to the European continent, they interfered less with the commerce of New England and the middle colonies, whose principal exports — fish, lumber, and flour — were not enumerated and could legally be sent directly to their most important markets in the West Indies.

By the end of the seventeenth century, colonial commerce was defined by regulations that subjected merchants and shippers to royal supervision and gave them access to markets throughout the English empire. In addition, colonial commerce received protection from the English navy. By 1700, colonial goods (including those from the West Indies) accounted for one-fifth of all English imports and for two-thirds of all goods re-exported from England to the European continent. In turn, the colonies absorbed more than one-tenth of English exports. The commercial regulations gave economic value to England's proprietorship of the American colonies.

King Philip's War and the Consolidation of Royal Authority

The monarchy also took steps to exercise greater control over colonial governments. Virginia had been a royal colony since 1624; Maryland, South Carolina, and the middle colonies were proprietary colonies with close ties to the crown. The New England colonies possessed royal charters, but they had developed their own distinctively Puritan governments. Charles II, whose father, Charles I, had been executed by Puritans in England, took a particular interest in harnessing the New England colonies more firmly to the English empire. The occasion was a royal investigation following **King Philip's War**.

A series of skirmishes in the Connecticut River valley between 1636 and 1637 culminated in the Pequot War when colonists massacred hundreds of Pequot Indians. In the decades that followed, New Englanders established relatively peaceful relations with the more potent Wampanoags, but they steadily encroached on Indian land. In 1642, a native leader urged warring tribes to band together against the English. "We [must] be one as they [the English] are," he said; "otherwise we shall be gone shortly, for our fathers had plenty of deer and skins . . . but these English having gotten our land, they with scythes cut down the grass, and with axes fell the trees, and their cows and horses eat the grass, and their hogs spoil our clam banks, and we shall all be starved."

Such grievances accumulated until 1675, when the Wampanoags attacked English settlements in western Massachusetts. Metacomet — the chief of the Wampanoags (and son of Massasoit), whom the colonists called King Philip — probably neither planned the attacks nor masterminded a conspiracy with the Nipmucs and the Narragansetts, as the colonists feared. But when militias from Massachusetts and other New England colonies counterattacked all three tribes, a deadly sequence of battles killed more than a thousand colonists and thousands more Indians. The Indians destroyed thirteen English settlements and partially burned another half dozen. Mary Rowlandson, a minister's wife in Lancaster, Massachusetts, who was captured by Indians after her relatives were killed and wounded, recalled later that it was a "solemn sight to see so many Christians lying in their blood . . . like a company of sheep torn by wolves. All of them stripped naked by a company of hell-hounds, roaring, singing, ranting and insulting, as if they would have torn our very hearts out."

By the spring of 1676, Indian warriors ranged freely within seventeen miles of Boston. The colonists finally defeated the Indians, principally with a scorched-earth policy of burning their food supplies. But King Philip's War left the New England colonists with a large war debt, a devastated frontier, and an enduring hatred of Indians. "A Swarm of Flies, they may arise, a Nation to Annoy," a colonial officer wrote in justification of destroying the Indians, "Yea Rats and Mice, or Swarms of Lice a Nation may destroy." And in 1676, an agent of the king arrived to investigate whether New England was abiding by English laws.

Not surprisingly, the king's agent found all sorts of deviations from English rules, and the monarchy decided to govern New England more directly. In 1684, an English court revoked the Massachusetts charter, the foundation of the distinctive Puritan government. Two years later, royal officials incorporated Massachusetts and the other colonies north of Maryland into the **Dominion of New England**. To govern the dominion, the English sent Sir **Edmund Andros** to Boston. Some New England merchants cooperated with Andros, but most colonists were offended by his flagrant disregard of such Puritan traditions as keeping the Sabbath. Worst of all, the Dominion of New England invalidated all land titles, confronting every landowner in New England with the horrifying prospect of losing his or her land.

Events in England, however, permitted Massachusetts colonists to overthrow Andros and retain title to their property. When Charles II died in 1685, he was succeeded by his brother James II, a zealous Catholic. James's aggressive campaign to appoint Catholics to government posts engendered such unrest that in 1688 a group of Protestant noblemen in Parliament invited the Dutch ruler William III of Orange, James's son-in-law, to claim the English throne.

When William III landed in England at the head of a large army, James fled to France, and William III and his wife, Mary II (James's daughter), became co-rulers in the relatively bloodless "Glorious Revolution," reasserting Protestant influence in England and its empire. Rumors of the revolution raced across the Atlantic and emboldened colonial uprisings against royal authority in Massachusetts, New York, and Maryland.

In Boston in 1689, rebels tossed Andros and other English officials in jail, destroyed the Dominion of New England, and reestablished the former charter government. New Yorkers followed the Massachusetts example. Under the leadership of Jacob Leisler, rebels seized the royal governor in 1689 and ruled the colony for more than a year. That same year in Maryland, the Protestant Association, led by John Coode, overthrew the colony's pro-Catholic government, fearing it would not recognize the new Protestant king.

But these rebel governments did not last. When King William III's governor of New York arrived in 1691, he executed Leisler for treason. Coode's men ruled Maryland until the new royal governor arrived in 1692 and ended

Indians in New France

Native Americans used canoes as the most efficient form of transportation on waterways throughout North America. Heavy bundles of animal pelts, for example, were carried long distances from a remote trapping region to a fur trading post in canoes. This seventeenth-century drawing from New France illustrates Native Americans' "very amazing" skills in handling a canoe, in this case by standing up while netting and spearing fish. The figure on the right appears to be playing a flute, perhaps to attract fish. Why do you think the artist was so fascinated with the fishermen's tattoos and body paint? Gilcrease Museum, Tulsa, Oklahoma.

both Coode's rebellion and Lord Baltimore's proprietary government. In Massachusetts, John Winthrop's city on a hill became another royal colony in 1691. The new charter said that the governor of the colony would be appointed by the king rather than elected by the colonists' representatives. But perhaps the most unsettling change was the new qualification for voting. Possession of property replaced church membership as a prerequisite for voting in colony-wide elections. Wealth replaced God's grace as the defining characteristic of Massachusetts citizenship.

Much as colonists chafed under increasing royal control, they still valued English protection from hostile neighbors. Colonists worried that the Catholic colony of New France menaced frontier regions by encouraging Indian raids and by competing for the lucrative fur trade. Although French leaders tried to buttress the military strength of New France during the last third of the seventeenth century to block the expansion of the English colonies, most of the military efforts mustered by New France focused on defending against attacks by the powerful Iroquois. However, when the English colonies were distracted by the Glorious Revolution, French forces from the fur-trading regions along the Great Lakes and in Canada attacked villages in New England and New York. Known as King William's War, the conflict with the French was a colonial outgrowth of William's war against France in Europe. The war dragged on until 1697 and ended inconclusively in both Europe and the colonies. But it made clear to many colonists that along with English royal government came a welcome measure of military security.

REVIEW Why did the Glorious Revolution in England lead to uprisings in the American colonies?

► Conclusion: An English Model of Colonization in North America

By 1700, the northern English colonies of North America had developed along lines quite different from the example set by their southern counterparts. Emigrants came with their families and created settlements unlike the scattered plantations and largely male environment of early Virginia. Puritans in New England built towns and governments around their churches and placed worship of God, not tobacco, at the center of their society. They depended chiefly on the labor of family members rather than on that of servants and slaves.

The convictions of Puritanism that motivated John Winthrop and others to reinvent England in the colonies became muted, however, as New England matured and dissenters such as Roger Williams multiplied. Catholics, Quakers, Anglicans (members of the Church of England), Jews, and others settled in the middle and southern colonies, creating considerable religious toleration, especially in Pennsylvania and New York. At the same time, northern colonists, like their southern counterparts, developed an ever-increasing need for land that inevitably led to bloody conflict with the Indians who were displaced.

During the next century, the English colonial world would undergo surprising new developments built on the achievements of the seventeenth century. Immigrants from Scotland, Ireland, and Germany streamed into North America, and unprecedented numbers of African slaves poured into the southern colonies. On average, white colonists attained a relatively comfortable standard of living, especially compared with most people in England and continental Europe. While religion remained important, the intensity of religious concern that characterized the seventeenth century waned during the eighteenth century. Colonists worried more about prosperity than about providence, and their societies grew increasingly secular, worldly, and diverse.

Reviewing Chapter 4

REVIEW QUESTIONS

1. Why did the Puritans immigrate to North America? (pp. 83–89)

2. Why did Massachusetts Puritans adopt the Halfway Covenant? (pp. 89–97)

3. How did Quaker ideals shape the colony of Pennsylvania? (pp. 97–101)

4. Why did the Glorious Revolution in England lead to uprisings in the American colonies? (pp. 101–105)

MAKING CONNECTIONS

1. How did the religious dissenters who flooded into the northern colonies address the question of religious dissent in their new homes? Comparing two colonies, discuss their different approaches and the implications of those approaches for colonial development.

2. In his sermon aboard the *Arbella*, John Winthrop spoke of the Massachusetts Bay Colony as "a city upon a hill." What did he mean? How did this expectation influence life in New England during the seventeenth century? In your answer, be sure to consider the relationship between religious and political life in the colony.

3. Religious conflict and political turmoil battered England in the seventeenth century. How did political developments in England affect life in the colonies? In your answer, consider the establishment of the colonies and the crown's attempts to exercise authority over them.

4. To what extent did the New England and middle colonies become more alike during the seventeenth century? To what extent did they remain distinctive? In your answer, consider religions, economies, systems of governance, and patterns of settlement in the colonies.

LINKING TO THE PAST

1. How did the communal goals of New England settlers compare with the aspirations of the tobacco and rice planters of the southern colonies? (See chapter 3.)

2. To what degree did religious intolerance shape events in the New World colonies of Spain, France, and England? (See chapters 2 and 3.)

TIMELINE 1534–1692

1534	• King Henry VIII breaks with Roman Catholic Church; English Reformation begins.	**1656**	• Quakers arrive in Massachusetts and are persecuted there.
1609	• Henry Hudson searches for Northwest Passage.	**1660**	• Monarchy restored in England; Charles II becomes king.
1620	• Plymouth colony founded.	**1662**	• Many Puritan congregations adopt Halfway Covenant.
1626	• Manhattan Island purchased; New Amsterdam founded.	**1664**	• English seize Dutch colony, rename it New York.
1629	• Massachusetts Bay Company receives royal charter.		• Colony of New Jersey created.
1630	• John Winthrop leads Puritan settlers to Massachusetts Bay.	**1675–1676**	• King Philip's War.
1636	• Rhode Island colony established.	**1681**	• William Penn receives charter for colony of Pennsylvania.
	• Connecticut colony founded.	**1686**	• Dominion of New England created.
1636–1637	• Pequot War.	**1688**	• England's Glorious Revolution; William III and Mary II become new rulers.
1638	• Anne Hutchinson excommunicated.		
1642	• Puritan Revolution inflames England.	**1689–1697**	• King William's War.
		1692	• Salem witch trials.
1649	• English Puritans win civil war and execute Charles I.		

▶ FOR AN ONLINE BIBLIOGRAPHY, PRACTICE QUIZZES, WEB SITES, IMAGES, AND DOCUMENTS RELATED TO THIS CHAPTER, see the Book Companion Site at **bedfordstmartins.com/roarkvalue**.

▶ FOR DOCUMENTS RELATED TO THIS PERIOD, see Michael Johnson, ed., *Reading the American Past*, Fifth Edition.

5

Colonial America in the Eighteenth Century

1701–1770

THE BROTHERS AMBOE ROBIN JOHN AND LITTLE EPHRAIM ROBIN JOHN and their cousin Ancona Robin John lived during the 1750s and 1760s in Old Calabar on the Bight of Biafra in West Africa. The Robin Johns were part of a slave-trading dynasty headed by their kinsman Grandy King George, one of the most powerful leaders of the Efik people. Grandy King George owned hundreds of slaves whom he employed to capture and trade for still more slaves in the African interior. He sold these captives to captains of European slave ships seeking to fill their holds with human cargo for the transatlantic voyage to the sugar, tobacco, and rice fields in the New World. Old Calabar was a major contributor to the massive flow of more than 1.2 million slaves from the Bight of Biafra to the New World during the eighteenth century.

Grandy King George nearly monopolized the Old Calabar slave trade during the 1760s, allowing him to live in luxury, surrounded by fine British trade goods. British slave ship captains and Grandy King George's African rivals resented his choke hold on the supply of slaves and in 1767 conspired to trap the king and the Robin Johns, seize hundreds of their slaves, and destroy the king's monopoly. In the bloody melee, Grandy King George managed to escape, but other members of his family were less fortunate. Amboe Robin John was beheaded by the leader of the African attackers. Little Ephraim and Ancona Robin John were enslaved, packed aboard the ship Duke of York with more than 330 other slaves, and transported across the Atlantic to the West Indies.

Model of a Slave Ship
Jammed into the holds of slave ships, enslaved Africans made the dreaded Middle Passage to the New World. The model of a slave ship shown here was used in parliamentary debates by antislavery leaders in Britain to demonstrate the inhumanity of shipping people as if they were cargo. The model does not show another typical feature of slave ships: weapons. Slaves vastly outnumbered the crews aboard the ships, and crew members justifiably feared slave uprisings.
Wilberforce House, Hull City Museums and Art Galleries, UK/Bridgeman Art Library.

Unlike most slaves, the Robin Johns understood, spoke, and even wrote English, an essential skill they had learned as slave traders in Old Calabar. A French physician bought the Robin Johns and, according to Ancona, "treated [them] . . . upon ye whole not badly." After seven months, the Robin Johns escaped from their owner and boarded a ship "determined to get home," Little Ephraim wrote. But the ship captain took them to Virginia instead and sold them as slaves to a merchant who traded between the Chesapeake and Bristol, England. Their new master "would tie me up & whip me many times for nothing at all," Ancona testified, adding that he "was exceedingly badly man ever I saw." After their master died in 1772, the Robin Johns heard that a slave ship from Old Calabar had recently arrived in Virginia, and the captain promised to take them back to Africa if they would run away and come aboard his ship. Instead, he took the Robin Johns to Bristol and sought to sell them as slaves yet again.

While imprisoned "in this Deplorable condition" on a ship in Bristol harbor, the Robin Johns managed to smuggle letters to a Bristol slave trader they had known and dealt with in Old Calabar. With help from him and other English sympathizers, the Robin Johns appeared before Lord Mansfield, the chief justice of England, and appealed for their freedom on the grounds that they were unjustly enslaved because they "were free people . . . [who] had not done anything to forfeit our liberty." After complex negotiations, they won legal recognition of their freedom.

As free Africans in Bristol, the Robin Johns converted to Christianity under the ministry of the famous Methodists John and Charles Wesley, but they longed to return to Africa. In 1774, they left Bristol as free men on a slave ship bound for Old Calabar, where they resumed their careers as slave traders.

The Robin Johns' unrelenting quest to escape enslavement and redeem their freedom was shared but not realized by millions of Africans who were victims of slave traders such as Grandy King George and numberless merchants, ship captains, and colonists. In contrast, tens of thousands of Europeans voluntarily crossed the Atlantic to seek opportunities in North America — often by agreeing to several years of contractual servitude. Both groups illustrate the undertow of violence and deceit beneath the surface of the eighteenth-century Atlantic commerce linking Britain, Africa, the West Indies, and British North America. In the flux and uncertainty of the eighteenth-century world, many, like the Robin Johns, turned to the consolations of religious faith as a source of meaning and hope in an often cruel and unforgiving society.

The flood of free and unfree migrants crossing the Atlantic contributed to unprecedented population growth in eighteenth-century British North America. In contrast, Spanish and French colonies in North America remained thinly populated outposts of European empires interested principally in maintaining a toehold in the vast continent. While the New England, middle, and southern colonies retained regional distinctions, commercial, cultural, and political trends built unifying experiences and assumptions among British North American colonists.

▶ A Growing Population and Expanding Economy in British North America

The most important fact about eighteenth-century British America is its phenomenal population growth: In 1700, colonists numbered about 250,000; by 1770, they tallied well over 2 million. An index of the emerging significance of colonial North America is that in 1700, there were nineteen people in England for every American colonist; by 1770, there were only three. The eightfold growth of the colonial population signaled the maturation of a distinctive colonial society. That society was by no means homogeneous. Colonists of different ethnic groups, races, and religions lived in varied environments under thirteen different colonial governments, all of them part of the British empire.

In general, the growth and diversity of the eighteenth-century colonial population derived from two sources: immigration and **natural increase** (growth through reproduction). Natural increase contributed about three-fourths of the population growth, immigration about one-fourth. Immigration shifted the ethnic and racial balance among the colonists, making them by 1770 less English and less white than ever before. Fewer than 10 percent of eighteenth-century immigrants came from England; about 36 percent were Scots-Irish, mostly from northern Ireland; 33 percent arrived from Africa, almost all of them slaves; nearly 15 percent had left the many German-language principalities (the nation of Germany did not exist until 1871); and almost 10 percent came from Scotland. In 1670, more than 9 out of 10 colonists were of English ancestry, and only 1 out of 25 was of African ancestry. By 1770, only about half of the colonists were of English descent, while more than 20 percent descended from Africans. Thus, by 1770, the people of the colonies had a distinctive colonial — rather than English — profile.

The booming population of the colonies hints at a second major feature of eighteenth-century colonial society: an expanding economy. In 1700, after almost a century of settlement, nearly all the colonists lived within fifty miles of the Atlantic coast. The nearly limitless wilderness stretching westward made land relatively cheap compared with its price in the Old World. The abundance of land in the colonies made labor precious, and the colonists always needed more. The insatiable demand for labor was the fundamental economic environment that sustained the mushrooming population. Economic historians estimate that free colonists (those who were not indentured servants or slaves) had a higher standard of living than the majority of people elsewhere in the Atlantic world. The unique achievement of the eighteenth-century colonial economy was this modest economic welfare of the vast bulk of the free population.

REVIEW How did the North American colonies achieve the remarkable population growth of the eighteenth century?

▶ New England: From Puritan Settlers to Yankee Traders

The New England population grew sixfold during the eighteenth century but lagged behind the growth in the other colonies. Most immigrants chose other destinations because of New England's relatively densely settled land and because Puritan orthodoxy made these colonies comparatively inhospitable to those of other faiths and those indifferent to religion. As the population grew, many settlers in search of farmland dispersed from towns, and Puritan communities lost much of their cohesion. Nonetheless, networks of economic exchange laced New Englanders to their neighbors, to Boston merchants, and to the broad currents of Atlantic commerce. In many ways, trade became a faith that competed strongly with the traditions of Puritanism.

Natural Increase and Land Distribution

The New England population grew mostly by natural increase, much as it had during the seventeenth century. Nearly every adult woman married. Most married women had children — often many children, thanks to the relatively low mortality rate in New England. The perils of childbirth gave wives a shorter life expectancy than husbands, but wives often lived to have six, seven, or eight babies. Anne Franklin and her husband, Josiah, a soap and candle maker in Boston, had seven children. Four months after Anne died, Josiah married his second wife, Abiah, and the couple had ten more children, including their son Benjamin, who became one of the most prominent colonial leaders of the eighteenth century. Like many other New Englanders, Benjamin Franklin felt hemmed in by family pressures and lack of opportunity and left the region when he was seventeen years old "to assert my freedom," as he put it, first in New York and then in Philadelphia.

The growing New England population pressed against a limited amount of land. Compared to colonies farther south, New England had less land for the expansion of settlement. Moreover, as the northernmost group of British colonies, New England had contested northern and western frontiers. Powerful Native Americans, especially the Iroquois and Mahican tribes, jealously guarded their territory. The French (and Catholic) colony of New France also menaced the British (and mostly Protestant) New England colonies when provoked by colonial or European disputes.

During the seventeenth century, New England towns parceled out land to individual families. In most cases, the original settlers practiced **partible inheritance** — that is, they subdivided land more or less equally among sons. By the eighteenth century, the original land allotments had to be further subdivided to accommodate grandsons and great-grandsons, and many plots of land became too small to support a family. Sons who could not hope to inherit sufficient land to farm had to move away from the town where they were born.

During the eighteenth century, colonial governments in New England abandoned the seventeenth-century policy of granting land to towns. Needing revenue, the governments of both Connecticut and Massachusetts sold land directly to individuals, including speculators. Now money, rather than membership in a community bound by a church covenant, determined whether a person could obtain land. The new land policy eroded the seventeenth-century pattern of settlement. As colonists spread north and west, they tended to settle on individual farms rather than in the towns and villages that characterized the seventeenth century. New Englanders still depended on their relatives and neighbors, but far more than in the seventeenth century, they regulated their behavior in newly settled areas by their own individual choices.

Farms, Fish, and Atlantic Trade

A New England farm was a place to get by, not to get rich. New England farmers grew food for their families, but their fields did not produce huge marketable surpluses. Instead of one big crop, a farmer grew many small ones. If farmers had extra, they sold to or traded with neighbors. Poor roads made travel difficult, time-consuming, and expensive, especially with bulky and heavy agricultural goods. The one major agricultural product the New England colonies exported — livestock — walked to market on its own legs. By 1770, New Englanders had

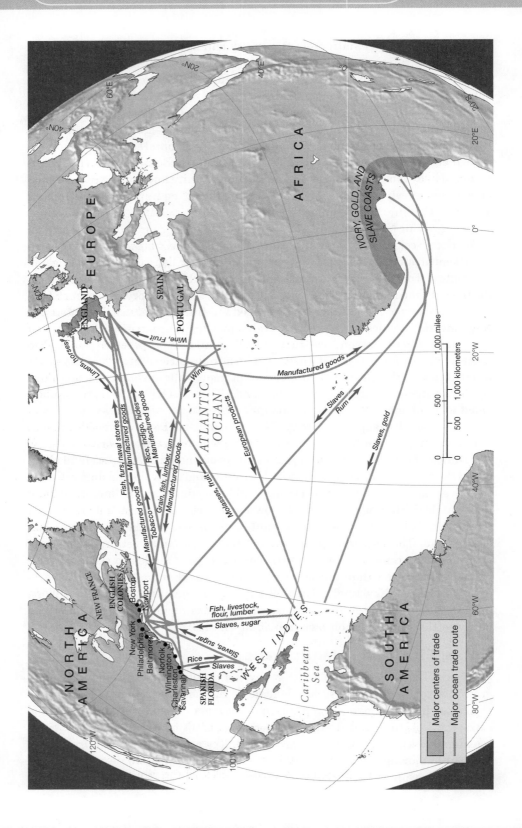

only one-fourth as much wealth per capita as free colonists in the southern colonies.

As consumers, New England farmers participated in a diversified commercial economy that linked remote farms to markets throughout the Atlantic world. Merchants large and small stocked imported goods — British textiles, ceramics, and metal goods; Chinese tea; West Indian sugar; and Chesapeake tobacco. Farmers' needs supported local shoemakers, tailors, wheelwrights, and carpenters. Larger towns, especially Boston, housed skilled tradesmen such as cabinet-makers, silversmiths, and printers. Shipbuilders tended to do better than other artisans because they served the most dynamic sector of the New England economy. Many New Englanders made their fortunes at sea, as they had since the seventeenth century.

Fish accounted for more than a third of New England's eighteenth-century exports; livestock and timber made up another third. The West Indies absorbed two-thirds of all New England's exports. Slaves on Caribbean sugar plantations ate dried, salted codfish caught by New England fishermen, filled barrels crafted from New England timber with molasses and refined sugar, and loaded those barrels aboard ships bound ultimately for Europeans with a sweet tooth. Almost all of the rest of New England's exports went to Britain and continental Europe (Map 5.1). This **Atlantic commerce** benefited the entire New England economy, providing jobs for laborers and tradesmen as well as for ship captains, clerks, merchants, and sailors.

Merchants dominated Atlantic commerce. The largest and most successful New England merchants lived in Boston at the hub of trade between local folk and the international market. Merchants not only bought and sold goods but also owned and insured the ships that carried the merchandise throughout the Atlantic world. Shrewd, diligent, and lucky merchants could make fortunes. The magnificence of a wealthy Boston merchant's home stunned John Adams, a thrifty Massachusetts lawyer who became a leader during the American Revolution and ultimately the second president of the United States. To Adams, the merchant's house seemed fit "for a noble Man, a Prince." Such luxurious Boston homes contrasted with the modest dwellings of Adams and other New Englanders, an indication of the polarization of wealth that developed in Boston and other seaports during the eighteenth century.

By 1770, the richest 5 percent of Bostonians owned about half the city's wealth; the poorest two-thirds of the population owned less than one-tenth. While the rich got richer and everybody else had a smaller share of the total wealth, the incidence of genuine poverty did not change much. About 5 percent of New Englanders qualified for poor relief throughout the eighteenth century. Overall,

◀ **MAP 5.1**
Atlantic Trade in the Eighteenth Century
This map illustrates the economic outlook of the colonies in the eighteenth century — east toward the Atlantic world rather than west toward the interior of North America. The long distances involved in the Atlantic trade and the uncertainties of ocean travel suggest the difficulties Britain experienced governing the colonies and regulating colonial commerce.

colonists were better off than most people in England. A Connecticut traveler wrote from England in 1764, "We in New England know nothing of poverty and want, we have no idea of the thing, how much better do our poor people live than 7/8 of the people on this much famed island."

The contrast with English poverty had meaning because the overwhelming majority of New Englanders traced their ancestry to England. New England was more homogeneously English than any other colonial region. People of African ancestry (almost all of them slaves) numbered more than fifteen thousand by 1770, but they barely diversified the region's 97 percent white majority. In the Narragansett region of Rhode Island, large landowners imported numerous slaves to raise livestock. But most New Englanders had little use for slaves on their family farms. Instead, slaves were concentrated in towns, especially Boston, where most of them worked as domestic servants and laborers.

By 1770, the population, wealth, and commercial activity of New England differed from what they had been in 1700. Ministers still enjoyed high status, but Yankee traders had replaced Puritan saints as the symbolic New Englanders. Atlantic commerce competed with religious convictions in ordering New Englanders' daily lives.

REVIEW Why did settlement patterns in New England change from the seventeenth to the eighteenth century?

▶ The Middle Colonies: Immigrants, Wheat, and Work

In 1700, almost twice as many people lived in New England as in the middle colonies of Pennsylvania, New York, New Jersey, and Delaware. But by 1770, the population of the middle colonies had multiplied tenfold — mainly from an influx of German, Irish, Scottish, and other immigrants — and nearly equaled the population of New England. Immigrants made the middle colonies a uniquely diverse society. By 1800, barely one-third of Pennsylvanians and less than half the total population of the middle colonies traced their ancestry to England. New settlers, whether free or in servitude, poured into the middle colonies because they perceived unparalleled opportunities. However, the increasing number of slaves arriving in bondage had little hope of sharing in such rewards.

German and Scots-Irish Immigrants

Germans made up the largest contingent of migrants from the European continent to the middle colonies. By 1770, about 85,000 Germans had arrived in the colonies. Their fellow colonists often referred to them as **Pennsylvania Dutch**, an English corruption of *Deutsch*, the word the immigrants used to describe themselves.

Most German immigrants came from what is now southwestern Germany, where, one observer noted, peasants were "not as well off as cattle elsewhere." Devastating French invasions of Germany during Queen Anne's War (1702–1713) made bad conditions worse and triggered the first large-scale migration. German immigrants included numerous artisans and a few merchants, but the great majority were farmers and laborers. Economically, they represented "middling folk," neither the poorest (who could not afford the trip) nor the better-off (who did not want to leave).

By the 1720s, Germans who had established themselves in the colonies wrote back to their friends and relatives, as one reported, "of the civil and religious liberties [and] privileges, and of all the goodness I have heard and seen." Such letters prompted still more Germans to pull up stakes and embark for America, to exchange the miserable certainties of their lives in Europe for the uncertain attractions of life in the middle colonies.

Similar motives propelled the **Scots-Irish**, who considerably outnumbered German immigrants. The "Scots-Irish" actually hailed from northern Ireland, Scotland, and northern England. Like the Germans, the Scots-Irish were Protestants, but with a difference. Most German immigrants worshiped in Lutheran or German Reformed churches; many others belonged to dissenting sects such as the Mennonites, Moravians, and Amish, whose adherents sought relief from persecution they had suffered in Europe for their refusal to bear arms and to swear oaths, practices they shared with the Quakers. In contrast, the Scots-Irish tended to be militant Presbyterians who seldom hesitated to bear arms or swear oaths. Like German settlers, however, Scots-Irish immigrants were clannish, residing when they could among relatives or neighbors from the old country.

In the eighteenth century, wave after wave of Scots-Irish immigrants arrived, culminating in a flood of immigration in the years just before the American Revolution. Deteriorating economic conditions in northern Ireland, Scotland, and England pushed many toward America. Most of the immigrants were farm laborers or tenant farmers fleeing droughts, crop failures, high food prices, or rising rents. They came, they told inquisitive British officials, because of "poverty," the "tyranny of landlords," and their desire to "do better in America."

Both Scots-Irish and Germans probably heard the common saying "Pennsylvania is heaven for farmers [and] paradise for artisans," but they almost certainly did not fully understand the risks of their decision to leave their native lands. Ship captains, aware of the hunger for labor in the colonies, eagerly signed up the penniless German emigrants as **redemptioners**, a variant of indentured servants. A captain would agree to provide transportation to Philadelphia, where redemptioners would obtain the money to pay for their passage by borrowing it from a friend or relative who was already in the colonies or, as most did, by selling themselves as servants. Many redemptioners traveled in family groups, unlike impoverished Scots-Irish emigrants, who usually traveled alone and paid for their passage by contracting as indentured servants before they sailed to the colonies.

Redemptioners and indentured servants were packed aboard ships "as closely as herring," one migrant observed. Seasickness compounded by exhaustion, poverty, poor food, bad water, inadequate sanitation, and tight quarters encouraged the spread of disease. On the sixteen immigrant ships arriving in Philadelphia in 1738, more than half the passengers died en route. When one ship finally approached land, a traveler wrote, "everyone crawls from below to the deck . . . and people cry for joy, pray, and sing praises and thanks to God." Unfortunately, their troubles were far from over. Redemptioners and indentured servants had to stay on board until somebody came to purchase their labor. Unlike indentured servants, redemptioners negotiated independently with their purchasers about their period of servitude. Typically, a healthy adult redemptioner agreed to four years of labor. Indentured servants commonly served five, six, or seven years.

"God Gives All Things to Industry": Urban and Rural Labor

An indentured servant in 1743 wrote that Pennsylvania was "the best poor Man's Country in the World." Although the servant reported that "the Condition of bought Servants is very hard" and masters often failed to live up to their promise to provide decent food and clothing, opportunity abounded in the middle colonies because there was more work to be done than workers to do it.

Most servants toiled in Philadelphia, New York City, or one of the smaller towns or villages. Artisans, small manufacturers, and shopkeepers prized the labor of male servants. Female servants made valuable additions to households, where nearly all of them cleaned, washed, cooked, or minded children. From the masters' viewpoint, servants were a bargain. A master could purchase five or six years of a servant's labor for approximately the wages a common laborer would earn in four months. Wageworkers could walk away from their jobs when they pleased, and they did so often enough to be troublesome for employers. Servants, however, could not walk away; they were legally bound to work for their masters until their terms expired.

Since a slave cost at least three times as much as a servant, only affluent colonists could afford the long-term investment in slave labor. Like many other prosperous urban residents, Benjamin Franklin purchased a few slaves after he became wealthy. But most farmers in the middle colonies used family labor, not slaves. Wheat, the most widely grown crop, did not require more labor than farmers could typically muster from relatives, neighbors, and a hired hand or two. Consequently, although people of African ancestry (almost all slaves) increased to more than thirty thousand in the middle colonies by 1770, they accounted for only about 7 percent of the total population and much less outside the cities.

Most slaves came to the middle colonies and New England after a stopover in the West Indies, as the Robin Johns did. Very few came directly from Africa. Enough slaves arrived to prompt colonial assemblies to pass laws that punished slaves much more severely than servants for the same transgressions. "For the least trespass," an indentured servant reported, slaves "undergo the severest Punishment." And slaves — unlike servants — could not charge masters with violating the terms of their contracts. A master's commands, not a written contract, set the terms of a slave's bondage. Small numbers of slaves managed to obtain their freedom, though few of them as dramatically as the Robin Johns.

But free African Americans did not escape whites' firm convictions about black inferiority and white supremacy.

Whites' racism and blacks' lowly social status made African Americans scapegoats for European Americans' suspicions and anxieties. In 1741, when arson and several unexplained thefts plagued New York City, officials suspected a murderous slave conspiracy and executed thirty-one slaves. On the basis of little evidence other than the slaves' "insolence" (refusal to conform fully to whites' expectations of servile behavior), city authorities burned thirteen slaves at the stake and hanged eighteen others. Although slaves were certifiably impoverished, they were not among the poor for whom the middle colonies were reputed to be the best country in the world.

Immigrants swarmed to the middle colonies because of the availability of land. The Penn family (see chapter 4) encouraged immigration to bring in potential buyers for their enormous tracts of land in Pennsylvania. From the beginning, Pennsylvania followed a policy of negotiating with Indian tribes to purchase additional land. This policy reduced the violent frontier clashes more common elsewhere in the colonies. Yet even the Penn family did not shrink from occasionally testing its agreement with Indians. In a dispute with tribes on the northern Delaware River in 1737, the Penns pulled out a document showing that local Indians had granted the colonists land that stretched as far as a man could walk in a day and a half. Under the terms of this infamous "Walking Purchase," the Penns sent out three runners, one of whom raced more than sixty miles in the time limit and doubled the size of the Penns' claim.

Few colonists drifted beyond the northern boundaries of Pennsylvania. Owners of the huge estates in New York's Hudson valley preferred to rent rather than sell their land, and therefore they attracted fewer immigrants. The **Iroquois Indians** dominated the lucrative fur trade of the St. Lawrence valley and eastern Great Lakes, and they vigorously defended their territory from colonial encroachment. Few settlers chose to risk having their scalps lifted by Iroquois warriors in northern New York when they could settle instead in the comparatively safe environs of Pennsylvania.

The price of farmland depended on soil quality, access to water, distance from a market town, and extent of improvements. One hundred acres of improved land that had been cleared, plowed, fenced, and ditched, and perhaps had a house and barn built on it, cost three or four times more than the same acreage of uncleared, unimproved land. Since the cheapest land always lay at the margin of settlement, would-be farmers tended to migrate to promising areas just beyond already improved farms. By midcentury, settlement had reached the eastern slopes of the Appalachian Mountains, and newcomers spilled south down the fertile valley of the Shenandoah River into western Virginia and the Carolinas. Thousands of settlers migrated from the middle colonies through this back door to the South. Abraham Lincoln's great-grandfather, John Lincoln — whose own grandfather, Mordecai, had migrated from England to Puritan Massachusetts in the 1630s — moved his family in the 1760s from Pennsylvania down the Shenandoah Valley into Virginia, where the future president's grandfather, also

Bethlehem, Pennsylvania

This view of the small community of Bethlehem, Pennsylvania, in 1757 dramatizes the profound transformation of the natural landscape wrought in the eighteenth century by highly motivated human labor. Founded by Moravian immigrants in 1740, Bethlehem must have appeared at first like the dense woods on the upper left horizon. In less than twenty years, precisely laid-out orchards and fields replaced forests and glades. By carefully penning their livestock (lower center right) and fencing their fields (lower left), farmers safeguarded their livelihoods from the risks and disorders of untamed nature. Individual farmsteads (lower center) and impressive multistory brick town buildings (upper center) integrated the bounty of the land with the delights of community life. Few eighteenth-century communities were as orderly as Bethlehem, but many effected a comparable transformation of the environment. Print Collection, Miriam and Ira D. Wallack Division of Art, Prints and Photographs, The New York Public Library. Astor, Lenox, and Tilden Foundations.

named Abraham, raised his family, including the future president's father, Thomas Lincoln.

Farmers like the Lincolns made the middle colonies the breadbasket of North America. They planted a wide variety of crops to feed their families, but they grew wheat in abundance. Flour milling was the number one industry and flour the number one export, constituting nearly three-fourths of all exports from the middle colonies. Pennsylvania flour fed residents in other colonies, in southern Europe, and, above all, in the West Indies (see Map 5.1). For farmers, the grain market in the Atlantic world proved risky but profitable. Grain prices rose steadily after 1720. By 1770, a bushel of wheat was worth twice as much (adjusted for inflation) as it had been fifty years earlier.

The standard of living in rural Pennsylvania was probably higher than in any other agricultural region of the eighteenth-century world. The comparatively widespread prosperity of all the middle colonies permitted residents to indulge in a half-century shopping spree for British imports. The middle colonies' per capita consumption of imported goods from Britain more than doubled between 1720 and 1770, far outstripping the per capita consumption of British goods in New England and the southern colonies.

Philadelphia stood at the crossroads of trade in wheat exports and British imports. By 1776, Philadelphia had a larger population than any other city in the entire British empire except London. Merchants occupied the top stratum of Philadelphia society. In a city where only 2 percent of the residents owned enough property to qualify to vote, merchants built grand homes and dominated local government. Many of Philadelphia's wealthiest merchants were Quakers. Quaker traits of industry, thrift, honesty, and sobriety encouraged the accumulation of wealth. A colonist complained that a Quaker "prays for his neighbors on First Days [the Sabbath] and then preys on him the other six."

The lower ranks of merchants included aspiring tradesmen such as **Benjamin Franklin**. In 1728, Franklin opened a small shop, run mostly by his wife, Deborah, that sold a little of everything: cheese, codfish, coffee, goose feathers, soap, and occasionally a slave. In 1733, Benjamin Franklin began to publish *Poor Richard's Almanack*, which preached the likelihood of long-term rewards for tireless labor and quickly became Franklin's most profitable product.

The popularity of *Poor Richard's Almanack* suggests that many Pennsylvanians thought less about the pearly gates than about their pocketbooks. Poor Richard's advice that "God gives all Things to Industry" might be considered the motto for the middle colonies. The promise of a worldly payoff made work a secular faith. Poor Richard advised, "Work as if you were to live 100 years, Pray as if you were to die Tomorrow."

William Penn's Quaker utopia became a center of worldly affluence whose most famous citizen, Franklin, was neither a Quaker nor a utopian. Quakers remained influential, but Franklin spoke for most colonists with his aphorisms of work, discipline, and thrift that echoed Quaker rules for outward behavior. Franklin's maxims did not look to the Quaker's divine inner light for guidance. Instead, they celebrated the spark of ambition and the promise of gain.

REVIEW Why did immigrants flood into Pennsylvania during the eighteenth century?

▶ The Southern Colonies: Land of Slavery

Between 1700 and 1770, the population of the southern colonies of Virginia, Maryland, North Carolina, South Carolina, and Georgia grew almost ninefold. By 1770, about twice as many people lived in the South as in either the middle colonies or New England. As elsewhere, natural increase and immigration accounted for the rapid population growth. Many Scots-Irish and German immigrants funneled from the middle colonies into the southern backcountry. Other immigrants were indentured servants (mostly English and Scots-Irish) who followed their seventeenth-century predecessors. But slaves made the most striking contribution to the booming southern colonies, transforming the racial composition of the population. Slavery became the defining characteristic of the southern colonies during the eighteenth century, shaping the region's economy, society, and politics.

The Atlantic Slave Trade and the Growth of Slavery

The number of southerners of African ancestry (nearly all of them slaves) rocketed from just over 20,000 in 1700 to well over 400,000 in 1770. The black population increased nearly three times faster than the South's briskly growing white population. Consequently, the proportion of southerners of African ancestry grew from 20 percent in 1700 to 40 percent in 1770.

Southern colonists clustered into two distinct geographic and agricultural zones. The colonies in the upper South, surrounding the Chesapeake Bay, specialized in growing tobacco, as they had since the early seventeenth century. Throughout the eighteenth century, nine out of ten southern whites and eight out of ten southern blacks lived in the Chesapeake region. The upper South retained a white majority during the eighteenth century.

In the lower South, a much smaller cluster of colonists inhabited the coastal region and specialized in the production of rice and indigo (a plant used to make blue dye). Lower South colonists made up only 5 percent of the total population of the southern colonies in 1700 but inched upward to 15 percent by 1770. South Carolina was the sole British colony along the southern Atlantic coast until 1732. (North Carolina, founded in 1711, was largely an extension of the Chesapeake region.) Georgia was founded in 1732 as a refuge for poor people from England. Georgia's leaders banned slaves from 1735 to 1750, but few settlers arrived until after 1750, when the prohibition on slavery was lifted and slaves flooded in. In South Carolina, in contrast to Georgia and every other British mainland colony, slaves outnumbered whites almost two to one; in some low-country districts, the ratio of blacks to whites exceeded ten to one.

The enormous growth in the South's slave population occurred through natural increase and the flourishing Atlantic slave trade. Slave ships brought almost 300,000 Africans to British North America between 1619 and 1780. Of these Africans, 95 percent arrived in the South and 96 percent arrived during the eighteenth century. Unlike indentured servants and redemptioners, these Africans did not choose to come to the colonies. Like the Robin Johns, most of them had been born into free families in villages located within a few hundred miles of the West African coast.

Although they shared African origins, they came from many different African cultures, including Akan, Angolan, Asante, Bambara, Gambian, Igbo, and Mandinga, among others. They spoke different languages, worshipped different deities, observed different rules of kinship, grew different crops, and recognized

Olaudah Equiano

Painted more than a decade after he had bought his freedom, this portrait evokes Equiano's successful acculturation to eighteenth-century English customs. His clothing and hairstyle reflect the fashions of a respectable young Englishman. In his *Interesting Narrative*, Equiano wrote that he "looked upon [the English] . . . as men superior to us [Africans], and therefore I had the stronger desire to resemble them, to imbibe their spirit and imitate their manners." Yet Equiano did not forsake his African roots. He honored his dual identity by campaigning against slavery. His *Narrative* was one of the most important and powerful antislavery documents of the time. Library of Congress.

different rulers. The most important experience they had in common was enslavement.

Captured in war, kidnapped, or sold into slavery by other Africans, they were brought to the coast, sold to African traders like the Robin Johns who assembled slaves for resale, and sold again to European or colonial slave traders or ship captains, who packed two hundred to three hundred or more aboard ships that carried them on the **Middle Passage** across the Atlantic and then sold them yet again to colonial slave merchants or southern planters.

Olaudah Equiano published an account of his enslavement that hints at the stories that might have been told by the millions of other Africans swept up in the slave trade. Equiano wrote that he was born in 1745 in the interior of what is now Nigeria. "I had never heard of white men or Europeans, nor of the sea," he recalled. One day when he was eleven years old, he was kidnapped by Africans, who sold him to other Africans, who in turn eventually sold him to a slave ship on the coast. Equiano feared that he was "going to be killed" and "eaten by those white men with horrible looks, red faces, and loose hair." Once the ship set sail, many of the slaves, crowded together in suffocating heat fouled by filth of all descriptions, died from sickness. "The shrieks of the women and the groans of the dying rendered the whole a scene of horror almost inconceivable," Equiano recalled. Most of the slaves on the ship were sold in Barbados, but Equiano and other leftovers were shipped off to Virginia, where he "saw few or none of our native Africans and not one soul who could talk to me." Equiano felt isolated and "exceedingly miserable" because he "had no person to speak to that I could understand." Finally, the captain of a tobacco ship bound for England purchased Equiano, and he traveled as a slave between North America, England, and the West Indies for ten years until he succeeded in buying his freedom in 1766.

Only about 15 percent of the slaves brought into the southern colonies came aboard ships from the West Indies, as Equiano and the Robin Johns did. All the other slaves brought into the southern colonies came directly from Africa, and almost all the ships that brought them (roughly 90 percent) belonged to British merchants. Most of the slaves on board were young adults, with men usually outnumbering women two to one. Children under the age of fourteen, like Equiano, typically accounted for no more than 10 to 15 percent of a cargo.

Mortality during the Middle Passage varied considerably from ship to ship. On average, about 15 percent of the slaves died, but sometimes half or more perished. The average mortality among the white crew of slave ships was often nearly as bad. In general, the longer the voyage lasted, the more people died. Recent studies suggest that many slaves succumbed not only to virulent epidemic diseases such as smallpox and dysentery but also to acute dehydration caused by fluid loss from perspiration, vomiting, and diarrhea combined with a severe shortage of drinking water.

Normally, an individual planter purchased at any one time a relatively small number of newly arrived Africans, or **new Negroes**, as they were called. New Negroes were often profoundly depressed, demoralized, and disoriented. Planters expected their other slaves — either those born into slavery in the colonies (often called **country-born** or **creole slaves**) or Africans who had arrived earlier — to help new Negroes become accustomed to their strange new surroundings. Planters' preferences for slaves from specific regions of Africa aided slaves' acculturation (or seasoning, as it was called) to the routines of bondage in the southern colonies. Chesapeake planters preferred slaves from Senegambia, the Gold Coast, or — like Equiano and the Robin Johns — the Bight of Biafra, which combined accounted for 40 percent of all Africans imported to the Chesapeake. South Carolina planters favored slaves from the central African Congo and Angola regions, the origin of about 40 percent of the African slaves they imported. Although slaves within each of these regions spoke many different languages, enough linguistic and cultural similarities existed that they could usually communicate with other Africans from the same region.

Seasoning acclimated new Africans to the physical as well as the cultural environment of the southern colonies. Slaves who had just endured the Middle Passage were poorly nourished, weak, and sick. In this vulnerable state, they encountered the alien diseases of North America without having developed a biological arsenal of acquired immunities. As many as 10 to 15 percent of newly arrived Africans, sometimes more, died during their first year in the southern colonies. Nonetheless, the large number of newly enslaved Africans made the influence of African culture in the South stronger in the eighteenth century than ever before — or since.

While newly enslaved Africans poured into the southern colonies, slave mothers bore children, which caused the slave population in the South to grow rapidly. Slave owners encouraged these births. Thomas Jefferson explained, "I consider the labor of a breeding [slave] woman as no object, that a [slave] child raised every 2 years is of more profit than the crop of the best laboring [slave] man."

Negro's houses

a fire

Boys playing under that Roof

a door

a Woman with her Child on her back

The African Slave Trade
The African slave trade existed to satisfy the New World's demand for labor and Europe's voracious appetite for New World products such as sugar, tobacco, and rice. African men, women, and children, like those pictured in this early-eighteenth-century engraving of a family residence in Sierra Leone, were kidnapped or captured in wars — typically by other Africans — and enslaved. Uprooted from their homes and kin, they were usually taken to coastal enclaves where African traders and European ship captains negotiated prices, made deals, and often branded the newly enslaved people. Courtesy, Earl Gregg Swen Library, College of William and Mary, Williamsburg, Virginia.

Although slave mothers loved and nurtured their children, the mortality rate among slave children was high, and the ever-present risk of being separated by sale brought grief to many slave families. Nonetheless, the growing number of slave babies set the southern colonies apart from other New World slave societies, where mortality rates were so high that deaths exceeded births. The high rate of natural increase in the southern colonies meant that by the 1740s the majority of southern slaves were country-born.

Slave Labor and African American Culture

Southern planters expected slaves to work from sunup to sundown and beyond. George Washington wrote that his slaves should "be at their work as soon as it is light, work til it is dark, and be diligent while they are at it." The conflict between the masters' desire for maximum labor and the slaves' reluctance to do more than necessary made the threat of physical punishment a constant for eighteenth-century slaves. Masters preferred black slaves to white indentured servants, not just because slaves served for life but also because colonial laws did not limit the force masters could use against slaves. As a traveler observed in 1740, "A new negro . . . [will] let a hundred men show him how to hoe, or drive a wheelbarrow; he'll still take the one by the bottom and the other by the wheel and . . . often die before [he] can be conquered." Slaves resisted their masters' demands, the traveler noted, because of their "greatness of soul" — their stubborn unwillingness to conform to their masters' definition of them as merely slaves.

Some slaves escalated their acts of resistance to direct physical confrontation with the master, the mistress, or an overseer. But a hoe raised in anger, a punch in the face, or a desperate swipe with a knife led to swift and predictable retaliation by whites. Throughout the southern colonies, the balance of physical power rested securely in the hands of whites.

Rebellion occurred, however, at Stono, South Carolina, in 1739. Before dawn on a September Sunday, a group of about twenty slaves attacked a country store, killed the two storekeepers, and confiscated the store's guns, ammunition, and powder. Enticing other slaves to join, the group plundered and burned more than half a dozen plantations and killed more than twenty white men, women, and children. A mounted force of whites quickly suppressed the rebellion. They placed the rebels' heads atop mileposts along the road, grim reminders of the consequences of rebellion. The **Stono rebellion** illustrated that eighteenth-century slaves had no chance of overturning slavery and very little chance of defending themselves in any bold strike for freedom. After the rebellion, South Carolina legislators enacted repressive laws designed to guarantee that whites would always have the upper hand. No other similar uprisings occurred during the colonial period.

Slaves maneuvered constantly to protect themselves and to gain a measure of autonomy within the boundaries of slavery. In Chesapeake tobacco fields, most slaves were subject to close supervision by whites. In the lower South, the **task system** gave slaves some control over the pace of their work and some discretion in the use of the rest of their time. A "task" was typically defined as a certain area of ground to be cultivated or a specific job to be completed. A slave who completed the assigned task might use the remainder of the day, if any, to work in a garden, fish, hunt, spin, weave, sew, or cook. When masters sought to boost productivity by increasing tasks, slaves did what they could to defend their customary work assignments.

Eighteenth-century slaves also planted the roots of African American lineages that branch out to the present. Slaves valued family ties, and, as in West African societies, kinship structured slaves' relations with one another. Slave parents often gave a child the name of a grandparent, aunt, or uncle. In West Africa, kinship identified a person's place among living relatives and linked the person to ancestors in the past and to descendants in the future. Newly imported African slaves usually arrived alone, like Equiano, without kin. Often slaves who had traversed the Middle Passage on the same ship adopted one another as "brothers" and "sisters." Likewise, as new Negroes were seasoned and incorporated into existing slave communities, established families often adopted them as fictive kin.

When possible, slaves expressed many other features of their West African origins in their lives on New World plantations. They gave their children traditional dolls and African names such as Cudjo or Quash, Minda or Fuladi. They grew food crops they had known in Africa, such as yams and okra. They constructed huts with mud walls and thatched roofs similar to African residences. They fashioned banjos, drums, and other musical instruments, held dances, and observed funeral rites that echoed African practices. In these and many other ways, slaves drew upon their African heritages as much as the oppressive circumstances of slavery permitted.

Tobacco, Rice, and Prosperity

Slaves' labor bestowed prosperity on their masters, British merchants, and the monarchy. Slavery was so important and valuable that one minister claimed in 1757 that "to live in Virginia without slaves is morally impossible." The southern colonies supplied 90 percent of all North American exports to Britain. Rice exports from the lower South exploded from less than half a million pounds in 1700 to eighty million pounds in 1770, nearly all of it grown by slaves. Exports of indigo also boomed. Together, rice and indigo made up three-fourths of lower South exports, nearly two-thirds of them going to Britain and most of the rest to the West Indies, where sugar-growing slaves ate slave-grown rice.

Tobacco was by far the most important export from British North America; by 1770, it represented almost one-third of all colonial exports and three-fourths of all Chesapeake exports. Under the provisions of the Navigation Acts (see chapter 4), nearly all of it went to Britain, where the monarchy collected a lucrative tax on each pound. British merchants then reexported more than 80 percent of the tobacco to the European continent, pocketing a nice markup for their troubles.

These products of slave labor made the southern colonies by far the richest in North America. The per capita wealth of free whites in the South was four times greater than that in New England and three times that in the middle colonies. At the top of the wealth pyramid stood the rice grandees of the lower South and the tobacco gentry of the Chesapeake. These elite families commonly resided on large estates in handsome mansions adorned by luxurious gardens, all maintained and supported by slaves. The extravagant lifestyle of one gentry family astonished a young tutor from New Jersey, who noted that during the winter months the family kept twenty-eight large fires roaring, requiring six oxen to haul four heavy cartloads of slave-cut firewood to the house every day. In contrast, yeoman families — who supported themselves on small plots of land with family labor — cut their own firewood and usually warmed themselves around just one fire.

The vast differences in wealth among white southerners engendered envy and occasional tension between rich and poor, but remarkably little open hostility. In private, the planter elite spoke disparagingly of humble whites, but in public the planters acknowledged their lesser neighbors as equals, at least in belonging to the superior — in their minds — white race. Looking upward, white yeomen and tenants (who owned neither land nor slaves) sensed the gentry's condescension and veiled contempt. But they also appreciated the gentry for granting favors, upholding white supremacy, and keeping slaves in their place. Although racial slavery made a few whites much richer than others, it also gave those who did not get rich a powerful reason to feel similar (in race) to those who were so different (in wealth).

The slaveholding gentry dominated the politics and economy of the southern colonies. In Virginia, only adult white men who owned at least one hundred acres of unimproved land or twenty-five acres of land with a house could vote. This property-holding requirement prevented about 40 percent of white men in Virginia from voting for representatives to the House of Burgesses. In South Carolina, the property requirement was only fifty acres of land, and therefore most adult white men qualified to vote. In both colonies, voters elected members of the gentry to serve in the colonial legislature. The gentry passed elected political offices from generation to generation, almost as if they were hereditary. Politically, the gentry built a self-perpetuating oligarchy — rule by the elite few — with the votes of their many humble neighbors.

The gentry also set the cultural standard in the southern colonies. They entertained lavishly, gambled regularly, and attended Anglican (Church of England) services more for social than for religious reasons. Above all, they cultivated the leisurely pursuit of happiness. They did not condone idleness, however. Their many pleasures and responsibilities as plantation owners kept them busy. Thomas Jefferson, a phenomenally productive member of the gentry, recalled that his earliest childhood memory was of being carried on a pillow by a family slave — a powerful image of the slave hands supporting the gentry's leisure and achievement.

REVIEW   How did slavery influence the society and economy of the southern colonies?

▶ Unifying Experiences

The societies of New England, the middle colonies, and the southern colonies became more sharply differentiated during the eighteenth century, but colonists throughout British North America also shared unifying experiences that eluded settlers in the Spanish and French colonies. The first was economic. All three British colonial regions had their economic roots in agriculture. Colonists sold their distinctive products in markets that, in turn, offered a more or less uniform array of goods to consumers throughout British North America. Another unifying experience was a decline in the importance of religion. Some settlers called for a revival of religious intensity, but most people focused less on religion and more on the affairs of the world than they had in the seventeenth century. Also, white inhabitants throughout British North America became aware that they shared a distinctive identity as *British* colonists. Thirteen different governments presided over these North American colonies, but all of them answered to the British monarchy. British policies governed not only trade but also military and diplomatic relations with the Indians, French, and Spanish arrayed along colonial borderlands. Royal officials who expected loyalty from the colonists often had difficulty obtaining obedience. The British colonists asserted their prerogatives as British subjects to defend their special colonial interests.

Commerce and Consumption

Eighteenth-century commerce whetted colonists' appetites to consume. Colonial products spurred the development of mass markets throughout the Atlantic world. Huge increases in the supply of colonial tobacco and sugar brought the price of these small luxuries within the reach of most free whites. Colonial goods brought into focus an important lesson of eighteenth-century commerce: Ordinary people, not just the wealthy elite, would buy the things that they desired in addition to what they absolutely needed. Even news, formerly restricted mostly to a few people through face-to-face conversations or private letters, became an object of public consumption through the innovation of newspapers and the rise in literacy among whites. With the appropriate stimulus, market demand seemed unlimited.

The Atlantic commerce that took colonial goods to markets in Britain brought objects of consumer desire back to the colonies. British merchants and manufacturers recognized that colonists made excellent customers, and the Navigation Acts gave British exporters privileged access to the colonial market. By midcentury, export-oriented industries in Britain were growing ten times faster than firms attuned to the home market. Most British exports went to the vast European market, where potential customers outnumbered those in the colonies by more than one hundred to one.

But as European competition stiffened, colonial markets became increasingly important. British exports to North America multiplied eightfold between 1700 and 1770, outpacing the rate of population growth after midcentury. When the colonists' eagerness to consume exceeded their ability to pay, British exporters willingly extended credit, and colonial debts soared. Imported mirrors, silver plates, spices, bed and table linens, clocks, tea services, wigs, books, and more infiltrated parlors, kitchens, and bedrooms throughout the colonies. Despite the many differences among the colonists, the consumption of British exports built a certain material uniformity across region, religion, class, and status. Buying and using British exports made the colonists look and feel more British even though they lived at the edge of a wilderness an ocean away from Britain.

The dazzling variety of imported consumer goods also presented women and men with a novel array of choices. In many respects, the choices might appear trivial: whether to buy knives and forks, teacups, a mirror, or a clock. But such small choices confronted eighteenth-century consumers with a big question: What do you want? As colonial consumers defined and expressed their desires with greater frequency during the eighteenth century, they became accustomed to thinking of themselves as individuals who had the power to make decisions that influenced the quality of their lives — attitudes of significance in the hierarchical world of eighteenth-century British North America.

Religion, Enlightenment, and Revival

Eighteenth-century colonists could choose from almost as many religions as consumer goods. Virtually all of the bewildering variety of religious denominations represented some form of Christianity, almost all of them Protestant. Slaves made up the largest group of non-Christians. A few slaves converted to Christianity in Africa or after they arrived in North America, but most continued to embrace elements of indigenous African religions. Roman Catholics concentrated in Maryland as they had since the seventeenth century, but even there they were far outnumbered by Protestants.

The varieties of Protestant faith and practice ranged across a broad spectrum. The middle colonies and the southern backcountry included militant Baptists and Presbyterians. Huguenots who had fled persecution in Catholic France peopled congregations in several cities. In New England, old-style Puritanism splintered into strands of Congregationalism that differed over fine points of theological doctrine. The Congregational Church was the official established church in New England, and all residents paid taxes for its support. Throughout the plantation South and in urban centers such as Charleston, New York, and Philadelphia, prominent colonists belonged to the Anglican Church, which received tax support in the South. But dissenting faiths grew everywhere, and in most colonies their adherents won the right to worship publicly, although the established churches retained official support.

Many educated colonists became deists, looking for God's plan in nature more than in the Bible. **Deism** shared the ideas of eighteenth-century European Enlightenment thinkers, who tended to agree that science and reason could disclose God's laws in the natural order. In the colonies as well as in Europe, **Enlightenment** ideas encouraged people to study the world around them, to think for themselves, and to ask whether the disorderly appearance of things masked the principles of a deeper, more profound natural order. From New England towns to southern drawing rooms, individuals met to discuss such matters. Philadelphia was the center of these conversations, especially after the formation in 1769 of the American Philosophical Society, an outgrowth of an earlier group organized by Benjamin Franklin, who was a deist. Leading colonial thinkers such as Franklin and Thomas Jefferson, among many other members, communicated with each other seeking both to understand nature and to find ways to improve society. Franklin's interest in electricity, stoves, and eyeglasses exemplified the shift of focus among many eighteenth-century colonists from heaven to the here and now.

Most eighteenth-century colonists went to church seldom or not at all, although they probably considered themselves Christians. A minister in Charleston observed that on the Sabbath "the Taverns have more Visitants than the Churches." In the leading colonial cities, church members were a small minority of eligible adults, no more than 10 to 15 percent. Anglican parishes in the South rarely claimed more than one-fifth of eligible adults as members. In some regions of rural New England and the middle colonies, church membership embraced two-thirds of eligible adults, while in other areas only one-quarter of the residents belonged to a church. The dominant faith overall was religious indifference. As a late-eighteenth-century traveler observed, "Religious indifference is imperceptibly disseminated from one end of the continent to the other."

The spread of religious indifference, of deism, of denominational rivalry, and of comfortable backsliding profoundly concerned many Christians. A few despaired that, as one wrote, "religion . . . lay a-dying and ready to expire its last breath of life." To combat what one preacher called the "dead formality" of church services, some ministers set out to convert nonbelievers and to revive the piety of the faithful with a new style of preaching that appealed more to the heart than to the head. Historians have termed this wave of revivals the **Great Awakening**. In Massachusetts during the mid-1730s, the fiery Puritan minister **Jonathan Edwards** reaped a harvest of souls by reemphasizing traditional Puritan doctrines of humanity's utter depravity and God's vengeful omnipotence. The title of Edwards's most famous sermon, "Sinners in the Hands of an Angry God," conveys the flavor of his message. In Pennsylvania and New Jersey, William Tennent led revivals that dramatized spiritual rebirth with accounts of God's miraculous powers, such as raising Tennent's son from the dead.

The most famous revivalist in the eighteenth-century Atlantic world was **George Whitefield**. An Anglican, Whitefield preached well-worn messages of sin and salvation to large audiences in England using his spellbinding, unforgettable voice. Whitefield visited the North American colonies seven times, staying for more than three years during the mid-1740s and attracting tens of thousands to his sermons, including Benjamin Franklin and Olaudah Equiano. Whitefield's preaching transported many in his audience to emotion-choked states of religious ecstasy. About one revival he wrote, "The bitter cries and groans were enough to pierce the hardest heart. Some of the people were as pale as death; others were wringing their hands; others lying on the ground; others sinking into the arms of their friends; and most lifting their eyes to heaven, and crying to God for mercy."

Whitefield's successful revivals spawned many lesser imitations. Itinerant preachers, many of them poorly educated, toured the colonial backcountry after midcentury, echoing Whitefield's medium and message as best they could. Bathsheba Kingsley, a member of Jonathan Edwards's flock, preached the revival message informally — as did an unprecedented number of other women throughout the colonies — causing her congregation to brand her a "brawling woman" who had "gone quite out of her place."

The revivals awakened and refreshed the spiritual energies of thousands of colonists struggling with the uncertainties and anxieties of eighteenth-century America. The conversions at revivals did not substantially boost the total number of church members, however. After the revivalists moved on, the routines and pressures of everyday existence reasserted their primacy in the lives of many converts. But the revivals communicated the important message that every soul mattered, that men and women could choose to be saved, that individuals had the power to make a decision for everlasting life or death. Colonial revivals expressed in religious terms many of the same democratic and egalitarian values expressed in economic terms by colonists' patterns of consumption. One colonist noted the analogy by referring to itinerant revivalists as "Pedlars in divinity." Like consumption, revivals contributed to a set of common experiences that bridged colonial divides of faith, region, class, and status.

Trade and Conflict in the North American Borderlands

British power defended the diverse inhabitants of its colonies from Indian, French, and Spanish enemies on their borders — as well as from foreign powers abroad. Each colony organized a militia, and privateers sailed from every port to prey on

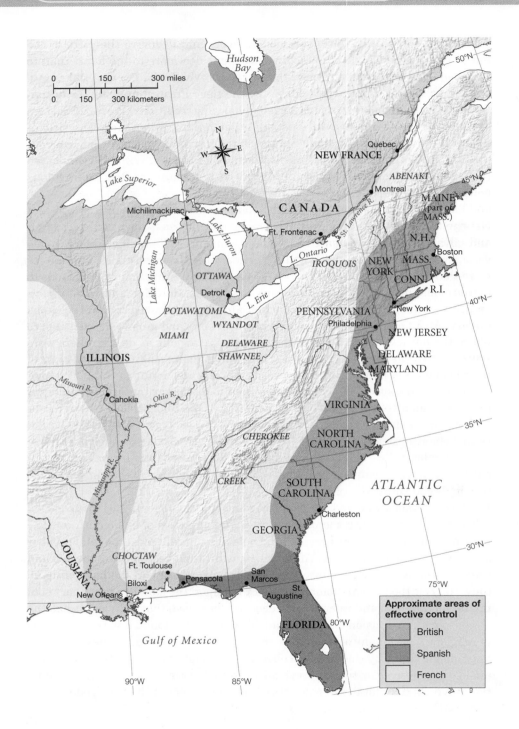

Hudson Bay

50°N

0   150   300 miles

0   150   300 kilometers

NEW FRANCE

Quebec

ABENAKI

Montreal

45°N

Lake Superior

MAINE
(part of
MASS.)

Michilimackinac

CANADA

N.H.

Lake Huron

Ft. Frontenac

L. Ontario

Boston

St. Lawrence R.

IROQUOIS

NEW
YORK

MASS.

Lake Michigan

CONN.

OTTAWA

R.I.

Detroit

L. Erie

New York

40°N

POTAWATOMI

PENNSYLVANIA

WYANDOT

Philadelphia

NEW JERSEY

MIAMI

DELAWARE

DELAWARE

SHAWNEE

MARYLAND

ILLINOIS

Missouri R.

Ohio R.

Cahokia

VIRGINIA

35°N

CHEROKEE

NORTH
CAROLINA

Mississippi R.

CREEK

SOUTH
CAROLINA

*ATLANTIC
OCEAN*

Charleston

GEORGIA

30°N

LOUISIANA

CHOCTAW

Ft. Toulouse

San
Marcos

75°W

Biloxi

Pensacola

St.
Augustine

New Orleans

FLORIDA

80°W

Gulf of Mexico

**Approximate areas of
effective control**

British

Spanish

French

90°W

85°W

foreign ships. But the British navy and army bore ultimate responsibility for colonial defense. Royal officials warily eyed the small North American settlements of New France and New Spain for signs of threats to the colonies.

Alone, neither New France nor New Spain jeopardized British North America, but with Indian allies they could become a potent force that kept colonists on their guard (Map 5.2). Native Americans' impulse to defend their territory from colonial incursions competed with their desire for trade, which tugged them toward the settlers. As a colonial official observed in 1761, "A modern Indian cannot subsist without Europeans. . . . [The European goods that were] only conveniency at first [have] now become necessity." To obtain such necessities as guns, ammunition, clothing, sewing utensils, and much more that was manufactured largely by the British, Indians trapped beavers, deer, and other furbearing animals throughout the interior.

British, French, Spanish, and Dutch officials monitored the fur trade to prevent their competitors from deflecting the flow of furs toward their own markets. Indians took advantage of this competition to improve their own prospects, playing one trader and empire off another. The Iroquois, for example, promised the French exclusive access to the furs and territory of the Great Lakes region and at the same time made the same pledge of exclusive rights to the British. Indian tribes and confederacies also competed among themselves for favored trading rights with one colony or another, a competition colonists encouraged.

The shifting alliances and complex dynamics of the fur trade struck a fragile balance along the frontier. The threat of violence from all sides was ever present, and the threat became reality often enough for all parties to be prepared for the worst. In the **Yamasee War of 1715**, Yamasee and Creek Indians — with French encouragement — mounted a coordinated attack against colonial settlements in South Carolina and inflicted heavy casualties. The Cherokee Indians, traditional enemies of the Creeks, refused to join the attack. Instead, they protected their access to British trade goods by allying with the colonists and turning the tide of battle, thus triggering a murderous rampage of revenge by the colonists against the Creek and Yamasee tribes.

Relations between Indians and colonists differed from colony to colony and from year to year. But the British colonists' nagging perceptions of menace on the frontier kept them continually hoping for help from the British to keep the Indians at bay and to maintain the essential flow of trade. In 1754, the British

◀ **MAP 5.2**
Zones of Empire in Eastern North America
The British zone, extending west from the Atlantic coast, was much more densely settled than the zones under French, Spanish, and Indian control. The comparatively large number of British colonists made them more secure than the relatively few colonists in the vast regions claimed by France and Spain or the settlers living among the many Indian peoples in the huge area between the Mississippi River and the Appalachian Mountains. Yet the British colonists were not powerful enough to dominate the French, Spaniards, or Indians. Instead, they had to guard against attacks by powerful Indian groups allied with the French or Spaniards.

colonists' endemic competition with the French flared into the Seven Years' War (also known as the French and Indian War), which would inflame the frontier for years (as discussed in chapter 6). Before the 1760s, neither the British colonists nor the British themselves developed a coherent policy toward the Indians. But both agreed that Indians made deadly enemies, profitable trading partners, and powerful allies. As a result, the British and their colonists kept an eye on both the French and Spanish empires and relations with the Indians.

The Spanish, in turn, were keeping an eye on the Pacific coast, where Russian hunters in search of seals and sea otters threatened to become a permanent presence on New Spain's northern frontier. To block Russian access to present-day California, officials in New Spain mounted a campaign to build forts (called **presidios**) and missions there. In 1769, an expedition headed by a military man,

Mission Carmel

This eighteenth-century drawing portrays a reception for a Spanish visitor at Mission Carmel in what is now Carmel, California. Lines of mission Indians dressed in robes flank the entrance to the chapel where a priest and his assistants await the visitor. During worship, priests wore lavishly decorated chasubles, which were intricately and colorfully embroidered to signify the magnificence of divine authority embodied in the priests and their Spanish sponsors. The reception ritual dramatized the strict hierarchy that governed relations among Spanish missionaries, ruling officials, and the subordinate Indians. University of California at Berkeley, Bancroft Library.

Gaspar de Portolá, and a Catholic priest, **Junípero Serra**, traveled north from Mexico to present-day San Diego, where they founded the first California mission, San Diego de Alcalá. They soon journeyed all the way to Monterey, which became the capital of Spanish California. There Portolá established a presidio in 1770 "to defend us from attacks by the Russians," he wrote. The same year, Serra founded Mission San Carlos Borroméo de Carmelo in Monterey to convert the Indians and recruit them to work to support the soldiers and other Spaniards in the presidio. By 1772, Serra had founded other missions along the path from San Diego to Monterey.

One Spanish soldier praised the work of the missionaries, writing that "with flattery and presents [the missionaries] attract the savage Indians and persuade them to adhere to life in society and to receive instruction for a knowledge of the Catholic faith, the cultivation of the land, and the arts necessary for making the instruments most needed for farming." Yet for the Indians, the Spaniards' California missions had horrendous consequences, as they had elsewhere in the Spanish borderlands. European diseases decimated Indian populations, Spanish soldiers raped Indian women, and missionaries beat Indians and subjected them to near slavery. Indian uprisings against the Spaniards occurred repeatedly, but the presidios and missions endured as feeble projections of the Spanish empire along the Pacific coast.

Colonial Politics in the British Empire

The plurality of peoples, faiths, and communities that characterized the North American colonies arose from the somewhat haphazard policies of the eighteenth-century British empire. Since the Puritan Revolution of the mid-seventeenth century, British monarchs had valued the colonies' contributions to trade and encouraged their growth and development. Unlike Spain and France — whose policies of excluding Protestants and foreigners kept the population of their North American colonial territories tiny — Britain kept the door to its colonies open to anyone, and tens of thousands of non-British immigrants settled in the North American colonies and raised families.

The open door did not extend to trade, however, as the seventeenth-century Navigation Acts restricted colonial trade to British ships and traders. These policies evolved because they served the interests of the monarchy and of influential groups in Britain and the colonies. The policies also gave the colonists a common framework of political expectations and experiences.

British attempts to exercise political power in their colonial governments met with success so long as British officials were on or very near the sea. Colonists acknowledged — although they did not always readily comply with — British authority to collect customs duties, inspect cargoes, and enforce trade regulations. But when royal officials tried to wield their authority in the internal affairs of the colonies on land, they invariably encountered colonial resistance. A governor appointed by the king in each of the nine royal colonies (Rhode Island and Connecticut selected their own governors) or by the proprietors in Maryland and Pennsylvania headed the government of each colony. The British envisioned colonial governors as mini-monarchs able to exert influence in the colonies much as the king did in Britain. But colonial governors were not kings, and the colonies were not Britain.

Eighty percent of colonial governors had been born in England, not in the colonies. Some governors stayed in England, close to the source of royal patronage, and delegated the grubby details of colonial affairs to subordinates. Even the best-intentioned colonial governors had difficulty developing relations of trust and respect with influential colonists because their terms of office averaged just five years and could be terminated at any time. Colonial governors controlled few patronage positions to secure political friendships in the colonies. Officials who administered the colonial customs service, for example, received their appointments through patronage networks centered in England rather than from colonial governors. Obedient and loyal to their superiors in Britain, colonial governors fought incessantly with the colonists' assemblies. They battled over governors' vetoes of colonial legislation, removal of colonial judges, creation of new courts, dismissal of the representative assemblies, and other local issues. Some governors developed a working relationship with the colonists' assemblies. But during the eighteenth century, the assemblies gained the upper hand.

Since British policies did not clearly define the colonists' legal powers, colonial assemblies seized the opportunity to make their own rules. Gradually, the assemblies established a strong tradition of representative government analogous, in their eyes, to the British Parliament. Voters often returned the same representatives to the assemblies year after year, building continuity in power and leadership that far exceeded that of the governor.

By 1720, colonial assemblies had won the power to initiate legislation, including tax laws and authorizations to spend public funds. Although all laws passed by the assemblies (except in Maryland, Rhode Island, and Connecticut) had to be approved by the governor and then by the Board of Trade in Britain, the difficulties in communication about complex subjects over long distances effectively ratified the assemblies' decisions. Years often passed before colonial laws were repealed by British authorities, and in the meantime the assemblies' laws prevailed.

The heated political struggles between royal governors and colonial assemblies that occurred throughout the eighteenth century taught colonists a common set of political lessons. They learned to employ traditionally British ideas of representative government to defend their own colonial interests. More important, they learned that power in the British colonies rarely belonged to the British government.

> **REVIEW** What experiences tended to unify the colonists in British North America during the eighteenth century?

▶ Conclusion: The Dual Identity of British North American Colonists

During the eighteenth century, a society that was both distinctively colonial and distinctively British emerged in British North America. Tens of thousands of immigrants and slaves gave the colonies an unmistakably colonial complexion and contributed to the colonies' growing population and expanding economy.

People of different ethnicities and faiths sought their fortunes in the colonies, where land was cheap, labor was dear, and — as Benjamin Franklin preached — work promised to be rewarding. Indentured servants and redemptioners risked temporary periods of bondage for the potential reward of better opportunities in the colonies than on the Atlantic's eastern shore. Slaves arrived in unprecedented numbers and endured lifelong servitude, which they neither chose nor desired but from which their masters greatly benefited.

None of the European colonies could claim complete dominance of North America. The desire to expand and defend their current claims meant that the English, French, and Spanish colonies were drawn into regular conflict with one another, as well as with the Indians upon whose land they encroached. In varying degrees, all sought control of the Native Americans and their land, their military power, their trade, and even their souls. Spanish missionaries and soldiers sought to convert Indians on the West Coast and exploit their labor; French alliances with Indian tribes posed a formidable barrier to westward expansion of the British empire.

Yet despite their attempts to tame their New World holdings, Spanish and French colonists did not develop societies that began to rival the European empires that sponsored and supported them. They did not participate in the cultural, economic, social, and religious changes experienced by their counterparts in British North America, nor did they share in the emerging political identity of the British colonists.

Identifiably colonial products from New England, the middle colonies, and the southern colonies flowed to the West Indies and across the Atlantic. Back came unquestionably British consumer goods along with fashions in ideas, faith, and politics. The bonds of the British empire required colonists to think of themselves as British subjects and, at the same time, encouraged them to consider their status as colonists. By 1750, British colonists in North America could not imagine that their distinctively dual identity — as British and as colonists — would soon become a source of intense conflict. But by 1776, colonists in British North America had to choose whether they were British or American.

Reviewing Chapter 5

REVIEW QUESTIONS

1. How did the North American colonies achieve the remarkable population growth of the eighteenth century? (pp. 111–112)

2. Why did settlement patterns in New England change from the seventeenth to the eighteenth century? (pp. 112–116)

3. Why did immigrants flood into Pennsylvania during the eighteenth century? (pp. 116–121)

4. How did slavery influence the society and economy of the southern colonies? (pp. 121–128)

5. What experiences tended to unify the colonists in British North America during the eighteenth century? (pp. 128–136)

MAKING CONNECTIONS

1. Colonial products such as tobacco and sugar transformed consumption patterns on both sides of the Atlantic in the eighteenth century. How did consumption influence the relationship between the American colonies and Britain? In your answer, consider how it might have strengthened and weakened connections.

2. Why did the importance of religion decline throughout the colonies from the seventeenth to the eighteenth century? How did American colonists respond to these changes?

3. How did different colonies attempt to manage relations with the Indians? How did the Indians attempt to manage relationships with the Europeans? In your answer, consider disputes over territory and trade.

4. Varied immigration patterns contributed to important differences among the British colonies. Compare and contrast patterns of immigration to the middle and southern colonies. Who came, and how did they get there? How did they shape the economic, cultural, and political character of each colony?

LINKING TO THE PAST

1. How did the British North American colonies in 1750 differ politically and economically from those in 1650? Were there important continuities? (See chapters 3 and 4.)

2. Is there persuasive evidence that colonists' outlook on the world shifted from the seventeenth to the eighteenth century? Why or why not? (See chapters 3 and 4.)

TIMELINE 1702–1775

1711– 1713 • Queen Anne's War triggers German migration to North America.

1711 • North Carolina founded.

1715 • Yamasee War.

1730s • Jonathan Edwards promotes Great Awakening.

1732 • Georgia founded.

1733 • Benjamin Franklin begins to publish *Poor Richard's Almanack*.

1739 • Stono rebellion.

1740s • George Whitefield preaches religious revival in North America.
• Majority of southern slaves are country-born.

1745 • Olaudah Equiano born.

1750s • Colonists begin to move down Shenandoah Valley.

1754 • Seven Years' War begins.

1769 • American Philosophical Society founded.
• First California mission, San Diego de Alcalá, established.

1770 • Mission and presidio established at Monterey, California.
• British North American colonists number more than two million.

1775 • Indians destroy San Diego mission.

▶ FOR AN ONLINE BIBLIOGRAPHY, PRACTICE QUIZZES, WEB SITES, IMAGES, AND DOCUMENTS RELATED TO THIS CHAPTER, see the Book Companion Site at **bedfordstmartins.com/roarkvalue**.

▶ FOR DOCUMENTS RELATED TO THIS PERIOD, see Michael Johnson, ed., *Reading the American Past*, Fifth Edition.

6

The British Empire and the Colonial Crisis

1754–1775

IN 1771, THOMAS HUTCHINSON BECAME THE ROYAL GOVERNOR OF THE colony of Massachusetts. Unlike most royal governors, who were British aristocrats sent over by the king for short tours of duty, Hutchinson was a fifth-generation American. A Harvard-educated member of the Massachusetts elite, from a family of successful merchants, he had served two decades in the Massachusetts general assembly. In 1758, Thomas Hutchinson was appointed lieutenant governor, and in 1760 he also became chief justice of the colony's highest court. He lived in the finest mansion in Boston. Wealth, power, and influence were his in abundance. He was proud of his connection to the British empire and loyal to his king.

Hutchinson had the misfortune to be a loyal colonial leader during the two very tumultuous decades leading up to the American Revolution. He worked hard to keep the British and colonists aligned in interests, even promoting a plan to unify the colonies with a limited government (the Albany Plan of Union) to deal with Indian policy. His plan of union ultimately failed, however, and a major war — the Seven Years' War — ensued, pitting the British and colonists against the French and their Indian allies in the backcountry of the American colonies. When the war ended and the British government began to think about taxing colonists to pay for it, Hutchinson had no doubt that the new British taxation policies were legitimate — unwise, perhaps, but legitimate.

Thomas Hutchinson

The only formal portrait of Thomas Hutchinson still in existence shows an assured young man in ruffles. Decades of turmoil in Boston failed to puncture his self-confidence. Doubtless he sat for other portraits, as did all the Boston leaders in the 1760s to 1780s, but no other likeness has survived. One portrait of him hung in his summer house outside Boston; a revolutionary crowd mutilated it and stabbed out the eyes. In 1775, Hutchinson fled to Britain, the country he regarded as his cultural home, only to realize how very American he was. Courtesy of the Massachusetts Historical Society.

Not everyone in Boston shared his opinion. Fervent, enthusiastic crowds protested against a succession of British taxation policies enacted after 1763 — the Sugar Act, the Stamp Act, the Townshend duties, the Tea Act, all landmark events on the road to the American Revolution. But Hutchinson maintained his steadfast loyalty to Britain. His love of order and tradition inclined him to unconditional support of the British empire, and by nature he was a measured and cautious man. "My temper does not incline to enthusiasm," he once wrote.

Privately, he lamented the stupidity of the British acts that provoked trouble, but his sense of duty required him to defend the king's policies, however misguided. Quickly, he became an inspiring villain to the emerging revolutionary movement. Governor Hutchinson came to personify all that was wrong with British and colonial relations. The man not inclined to enthusiasm unleashed popular enthusiasm all around him. He never appreciated that irony.

In another irony, Thomas Hutchinson was actually one of the first Americans to recognize the difficulties of maintaining full rights and privileges for colonists so far from their supreme government, the king and Parliament in Britain. In 1769, when British troops occupied Boston in an effort to provide civil order, he wrote privately to a friend in England, "There must be an abridgement of what are called English liberties. . . . I doubt whether it is possible to project a system of government in which a colony three thousand miles distant from the parent state shall enjoy all the liberty of the parent state." What he could not imagine was the possibility of giving up the parent state and creating an independent government closer to home.

Thomas Hutchinson was a loyalist; in the 1750s, most English-speaking colonists were affectionately loyal to Britain. But the Seven Years' War, which Britain and its colonies fought together as allies, shook that affection, and imperial policies in the decade following the war shattered it completely. Over the course of 1763 to 1773, Americans insistently raised serious questions about Britain's governance of its colonies. Many came to believe what Thomas Hutchinson could never accept — that a tyrannical Britain had embarked on a course to enslave the colonists by depriving them of their traditional English liberties.

The opposite of liberty was slavery, a condition of nonfreedom and coercion. Political rhetoric about liberty, tyranny, and slavery heated up the emotions of white colonists during the many crises of the 1760s and 1770s. But this rhetoric turned out to be a two-edged sword. The call for an end to tyrannical slavery meant one thing when sounded by Boston merchants whose commercial shipping rights had been revoked, but the same call meant something quite different in 1775 when sounded by black Americans locked in the bondage of slavery.

▶ The Seven Years' War, 1754–1763

For the first half of the eighteenth century, Britain was at war intermittently with France or Spain. Often the colonists in America experienced reverberations from these conflicts, most acutely along the frontier of New France in northern New England.

In the 1750s, international tensions returned, this time sparked by conflicts over contested land in America's Ohio Valley. The land, variously claimed by Virginians, Pennsylvanians, and the French, was actually inhabited by more than a dozen Indian tribes. The result was the costly **Seven Years' War** (its British name), known in the colonies as the French and Indian War, in which Americans and the British shared the hardships of battle and finally the glory of victory. Before it ended in 1763, fighting had extended through Europe, into the Caribbean, and even to India. The immense costs of the war — in money, death, and desire for revenge by losers and even winners — laid the groundwork for the imperial crisis of the 1760s between the British and Americans.

French-British Rivalry in the Ohio Country

For several decades, French traders had cultivated alliances with the Indian tribes in the Ohio Country, a frontier region they regarded as part of New France (Map 6.1). Cementing their relationships with gifts, the French established a profitable exchange of manufactured goods for beaver furs. But in the 1740s, Pennsylvania traders began to infringe on the territory. Adding to the tensions, a group of enterprising Virginians, including the brothers Lawrence and Augustine

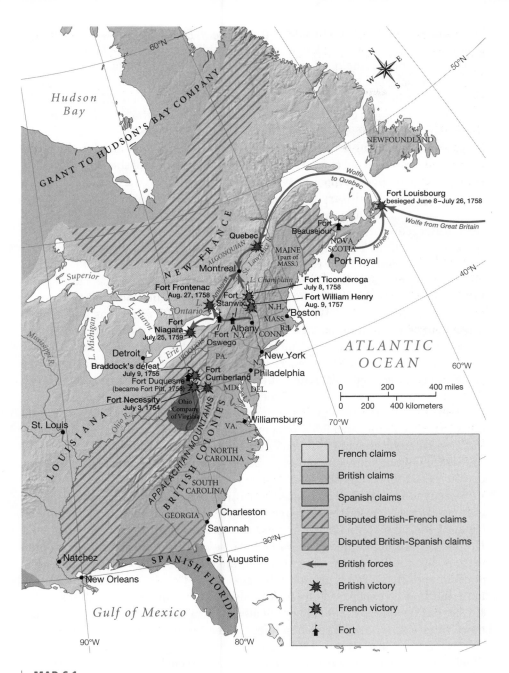

MAP 6.1

European Areas of Influence and the Seven Years' War, 1754–1763

In the mid-eighteenth century, France, Britain, and Spain claimed vast areas of North America, many of them already inhabited by various Indian peoples. The early flash points of the Seven Years' War were in regions of disputed claims where the French had allied with powerful native groups — the Iroquois and the Algonquian tribes — to put pressure on the westward-moving British and Americans.

Washington, formed the **Ohio Company** in 1747 and advanced into French-claimed territory. Their goal was to secure wilderness tracts to be resold later on to the exploding Anglo-American population seeking fresh land.

French soldiers began building a series of military forts to secure their trade routes and to create a western barrier to American population expansion. In response, the royal governor of Virginia, Robert Dinwiddie, also a shareholder in the Ohio Company, dispatched a messenger in 1753 to warn the French that they were trespassing on Virginia land. For this dangerous mission, he chose the twenty-one-year-old George Washington, half-brother of the Ohio Company leaders, who did not disappoint. Washington returned with crucial intelligence confirming French military intentions.

Impressed, Dinwiddie appointed the youth to lead a small military expedition west to assert and, if need be, defend Virginia's claim. Imperial officials in London, concerned about the French fortifications, had authorized the governor "to repell force by force," only if the French attacked first. By early 1754, the French had built Fort Duquesne at the forks of the Ohio River; Washington's delicate assignment was to chase the French away without actually being the aggressor.

In the spring of 1754, Washington set out with 160 Virginians and a small contingent of Mingo Indians, who were also concerned about the French military presence in the Ohio Country. The first battle of what would become known as the French and Indian War occurred early one May morning when the Mingo chief Tanaghrisson led a detachment of Washington's soldiers to a small French encampment in the woods. Who fired first was later a matter of dispute, but fourteen Frenchmen (and no Virginians) were wounded. While Washington, lacking a translator, struggled to communicate with the injured French commander, Tanaghrisson and his men intervened to kill and then scalp the wounded soldiers, including the commander, probably with the aim of inflaming hostilities between the French and the colonists.

This sudden massacre violated Washington's instructions to avoid being the aggressor and raised the stakes considerably. Fearing retaliation, Washington ordered his men to fortify their position, resulting in the makeshift "Fort Necessity." Reinforcements amounting to several hundred more Virginians arrived, but the Mingos, sensing disaster and displeased by Washington's style of command, fled. (Tanaghrisson later said, "The Colonel was a good-natured man, but had no experience; he took upon him to command the Indians as his slaves, [and] would by no means take advice from the Indians.") In early July, more than six hundred French soldiers aided by one hundred Shawnee and Delaware warriors attacked Fort Necessity, killing or wounding a third of Washington's men. The message was clear: The French would not depart from the disputed territory.

The Albany Congress

Even as Virginians, Frenchmen, and Indians fought and died in the Ohio Country, British imperial leaders hoped to prevent a larger war. One obvious strategy was to strengthen frayed British alliances with once friendly Indian tribes. Since 1692, Mohawks and New York merchants in the fur trade had participated in an alliance called the Covenant Chain, but lately the Mohawks felt neglected by British officials and left open to victimization by unsavory land speculators and Albany fur traders. British authorities in London directed the governor to convene a colonial conference to repair trade relations and secure the Indians' help — or at least their neutrality — against the looming French threat.

More than just New Yorkers and Mohawks were called to the Albany meeting, held in June and July 1754. Seven colonies sent a total of twenty-four delegates, making this an unprecedented pan-colony gathering. All six constituent tribes of the Iroquois Confederacy, of which the Mohawks were the easternmost tribe, also attended. The Mohawk chief Hendrick, a gray-haired man with long-term friendships with English and Dutch colonists, gave a powerful and widely cited speech at the congress, asserting that the recent neglect would inevitably reorient Indian trade relations to the French. "Look at the French, they are men; they are fortifying every where; but we are ashamed to say it; you are like women, bare and open, without any fortifications." Hendrick urged the assembled colonists to prepare for defense against the French.

Two delegates at the congress seized the occasion to push for yet more ambitious plans. Benjamin Franklin of Pennsylvania and Thomas Hutchinson of Massachusetts, both rising political stars, coauthored the **Albany Plan of Union**, a proposal for a unified but limited government to formulate Indian policy and coordinate colonial military forces. Key features included a president-general, appointed by the crown, and a grand council representing the colonies, meeting annually to consider questions of war, peace, and trade with the Indians. The writers of the Albany Plan humbly reaffirmed Parliament's authority; this was no bid for enlarged autonomy of the colonies. Hutchinson and Franklin easily persuaded the conference delegates to take the plan back to their respective assemblies.

To Franklin's surprise, not a single colony approved the Albany Plan. The Massachusetts assembly feared it was "a Design of gaining power over the Colonies," especially the power of taxation. Others objected that it would be impossible to agree on unified policies toward scores of quite different Indian tribes. The British government never backed the Albany Plan either; instead, it appointed two superintendents of Indian affairs, one for the northern and another for the southern colonies, each with exclusive powers to negotiate treaties, trade, and land sales with all tribes.

The Indians at the Albany Congress were not impressed with the Albany Plan either. The Covenant Chain alliance with the Mohawk tribe was reaffirmed, but the other nations left without pledging to help the British battle the French. At this very early point in the Seven Years' War, the Iroquois figured that the French military presence around the Great Lakes would discourage the westward push of American colonists and therefore better serve their interests.

The War and Its Consequences

By 1755, George Washington's frontier skirmish had turned into a major mobilization of British and American troops against the French. At first, the British expected a quick victory on three fronts. General Edward Braddock, recently arrived from England, marched his army toward Fort Duquesne in western Pennsylvania. Farther north, British troops moved toward Fort Niagara, critically located between Lakes Erie and Ontario. And William Johnson, a New Yorker recently appointed superintendent of northern Indian affairs, led forces north toward Lake Champlain, intending to defend the border against the French in Canada (see Map 6.1). Unfortunately for the British, the French were prepared to fight and had cemented respectful alliances with many Indian tribes throughout the region.

Braddock's march west was the first of a series of disasters for the British. Accompanied by George Washington and his Virginia soldiers, Braddock led 2,000 troops into the backcountry in July 1755. Although Indian guidance and support amounted to a mere 8 Oneida warriors, Braddock expected an easy victory with his big artillery and overwhelming numbers. One day short of reaching Fort Duquesne, in heavy woods where their cannons were useless, the British were ambushed by 250 French soldiers joined by 640 Indian warriors, including Ottawas, Ojibwas, Potawatomis, Shawnees, and Delawares. Surviving soldiers reported that they never saw more than a half dozen Indians at a time, so hidden were they in the woods. But the soldiers could hear them. One soldier wrote weeks later that "the yell of the Indians is fresh on my ear, and the terrific sound will haunt me until the hour of my dissolution." The disciplined British troops stood their ground, making them easy targets. In the bloody Battle of the Monongahela, named for a nearby river, nearly a thousand on the British side were killed or wounded. Washington was unhurt, though two horses in succession were shot out from under him. General Braddock was killed.

Braddock's defeat stunned British leaders. For the next two years, they stumbled badly, deploying inadequate numbers of troops. Colonial assemblies, unwilling to be forced to shoulder the costs of war, held back from contributing provincial troops. What finally turned the war around was the rise to power in 1757 of **William Pitt**, Britain's prime minister, a man ready to commit massive resources to fight France and its ally Spain worldwide. Pitt treated the assemblies as allies, not subordinates, and paid them to raise and equip provincial soldiers, an intensification of manpower that led at last to the capture of Forts Duquesne, Niagara, and Ticonderoga, followed by victories over the French cities of Quebec and finally Montreal, all from 1758 to 1760.

By 1761, the war subsided in America but expanded globally, with battles in the Caribbean, Austria, Prussia, and India. The British captured the French sugar islands Martinique and Guadeloupe and then invaded Spanish Cuba with an army of some four thousand provincial soldiers from New York and New England. By the end of 1762, France and Spain capitulated, and the **Treaty of Paris** was signed in 1763.

The triumph was sweet but short-lived. In the complex peace negotiations, Britain gained control of Canada, eliminating the French threat from the north. British and American title to the eastern half of North America, precisely what Britain had claimed before the war, was confirmed. France transferred all its territory west of the Mississippi River, including New Orleans, to Spain as compensation for Spain's assistance during the war. France retained Martinique and Guadeloupe, while Cuba, where two thousand Americans had died of injury or disease in the invasion, was restored to Spain.

In the aftermath of the war, Britain and the colonies, having worked as allies to defeat the French, began to eye each other warily. The British credited their mighty army for their victory and criticized the colonists for inadequate support. William Pitt was convinced that colonial smuggling — beaver pelts from French fur traders and illegal molasses in the French Caribbean — "principally, if not alone, enabled France to sustain and protract this long and expensive war." American traders, grumbled British leaders, were really traitors.

Colonists read the lessons of the war differently. American soldiers had turned out in force, they claimed, but had been relegated to grunt work by arrogant British commanders and subjected to unexpectedly harsh military discipline, ranging from frequent floggings (stealing a shirt brought a thousand lashes) to executions, the punishment for desertion. One Massachusetts army doctor avoided attending the punishments: "I saw not the men whiped, for altho' there is almost every Day more or less whiped or Piqueted [forced to stand on a sharpened stake], I've never had the curiosity to see 'm, the Shrieks and Crys" being more than he could bear.

Further, the British army did not always wage frontier warfare so brilliantly. Benjamin Franklin heard General Braddock brag that "these savages may, indeed, be a formidable enemy to your raw American militia, but upon the king's regular and disciplined troops, sir, it is impossible they should make any impression." Braddock's crushing defeat "gave us Americans," Franklin wrote, "the first suspicion that our exalted ideas of the prowess of British regulars had not been well founded."

Perhaps most important, the enormous expense of the Seven Years' War caused by Pitt's no-holds-barred military strategy cast a huge shadow over the victory. And the costs continued to mount, because British leaders decided in 1762 to maintain a force of ten thousand soldiers in North America to guard against potential hostilities with Indians or French Canadians. By 1763, Britain's national debt, double what it had been when Pitt took office, posed a formidable challenge to the next decade of leadership in Britain.

Pontiac's Rebellion and the Proclamation of 1763

One glaring omission marred the Treaty of Paris: The major powers at the treaty table failed to include the Indians. Minavavana, an Ojibwa chief of the Great Lakes region, put it succinctly to an English trader: "Englishman, although you have conquered the French, you have not yet conquered us! We are not your slaves.

These lakes, these woods and mountains were left to us by our ancestors. They are our inheritance; and we will part with them to none." Furthermore, Minavavana pointedly noted, "your king has never sent us any presents, nor entered into any treaty with us, wherefore he and we are still at war."

Minavavana's complaint about the absence of British presents was significant. To Indians, gifts cemented social relationships, symbolizing honor and establishing obligation. Over many decades, the French had mastered the subtleties of gift exchange, distributing textiles and hats and receiving calumets (ceremonial pipes) in return. British military leaders, new to the practice, often discarded the calumets as trivial trinkets, thereby insulting the givers. From the British view, a generous gift might signify tribute (thus demeaning the giver), or it might be positioned as a bribe. "It is not my intention ever to attempt to gain the friendship of Indians by presents," Major General Jeffery Amherst declared. The Indian view was the opposite: Generous givers expressed dominance and protection, not subordination, in the ceremonial practices of giving.

Despite Minavavana's confident words, Indians north of the Ohio River had plenty of cause for concern. Old French trading posts all over the Northwest were beefed up by the British into military bases. Fort Duquesne, renamed Fort Pitt to honor the victorious British prime minister, was fortified with new walls sixty feet thick at their base, ten at the top, announcing that this was no fur trading post. Americans settlers were beginning to cluster around Fort Pitt's protective sphere, further alarming the local Indians.

A religious revival among the Indians magnified feelings of antagonism toward the British. A Delaware prophet named Neolin reported a vision in which the Master of Life chastised Indians: "Whence comes it that ye permit the Whites upon your lands? Can ye not live without them?" Neolin urged a return to traditional ways, and his preaching spread quickly, gaining credence as the British bungled diplomacy and American settlers continued to penetrate western lands.

In 1763, a renewal of commitment to Indian ways and the formation of tribal alliances led to open warfare, which the British called **Pontiac's Rebellion**, after the chief of the Ottawas. (The coordinated uprising was actually the work of many men.) In mid-May, Ottawa, Potawatomi, and Huron warriors attacked Fort Detroit. Six more attacks on forts followed within weeks, and frontier settlements were also raided by nearly a dozen tribes from western New York, the Ohio Valley, and the Great Lakes region. By the fall, Indians had captured every fort west of Detroit. More than four hundred British soldiers were dead and another two thousand colonists killed or taken captive.

Not all of the attacks were instigated by Indians. The worst of a number of violent aggressions by Americans occurred in late 1763, when some fifty Pennsylvania vigilantes known as the Paxton Boys descended on a peaceful village of Conestoga Indians — friendly Indians, living not far from Philadelphia — and murdered and scalped twenty of them. The vigilantes, now numbering five hundred and out to make war on all Indians, marched on Philadelphia to try to capture and murder some Christian Indians held in protective custody there. British troops prevented that, but the Paxton Boys escaped punishment for their murderous attack on the Conestoga village.

In early 1764, the uprising faded. The Indians were short on ammunition, and the British were tired and broke. The British government recalled the imperious general Amherst, blaming him for mishandling the conflict, and his own soldiers toasted his departure. A new military leader, Thomas Gage, took command and began distributing gifts profusely among the Indians.

To minimize the violence, the British government issued the **Proclamation of 1763**, forbidding colonists to settle west of the Appalachian Mountains. More than just naming a boundary, the Proclamation offered assurances that Indian territory would be respected. It limited trade with Indians to traders licensed by colonial governors, and it forbade private sales of Indian land. But the Proclamation's language also took care not to identify western lands as belonging to the Indians. Instead, it spoke of lands that "are reserved to [Indians], as their Hunting Grounds."

Other parts of the Proclamation of 1763 referred to American and even French colonists in Canada as "our loving subjects," entitled to English rights and privileges. In contrast, the Indians were clearly rejected as British subjects and instead were described more vaguely as those "who live under our protection" and as "Tribes of Indians with whom We are connected." Of course, the British were not really well connected with any Indians, nor did they wish connections to form among the tribes. As William Johnson, the superintendent of northern Indian affairs, advised in 1764, "It will be expedient to treat with each nation separately . . . for could they arrive at a perfect union, they must prove very dangerous Neighbours."

The 1763 boundary was yet a further provocation to many Americans, and most especially to land speculators (like Virginia's Patrick Henry or the men of the Ohio Company) who had already staked claims to huge tracts of land west of the Appalachians and who had no desire to lose profitable resale opportunities. The boundary also proved impossible to enforce, despite the large British military presence. Surging population growth had already sent many hundreds of settlers, many of them squatters, west of the Appalachians.

By 1774, continuous hostilities and periodic bloodshed escalated into a conflict named Lord Dunmore's War, after Virginia's royal governor. In this short but deadly war, Virginia soldiers traversed the Appalachian Mountains to attack Mingo and Shawnee peoples south of the Ohio River, thereby establishing speculators' land claims in western Virginia and Kentucky. But they left the frontier aflame with such ethnic antagonism that would-be settlers were left fearful, uncertain about their future, and increasingly wary of British claims to be a protective mother country.

REVIEW How did the Seven Years' War erode relations between colonists and British authorities?

▶ The Sugar and Stamp Acts, 1763–1765

In 1760, **George III**, twenty-two years old, became king of England. Timid and insecure, George struggled to gain his footing in his new job. He rotated through a succession of leaders, searching for a prime minister he could trust. A half dozen ministers in seven years took turns dealing with one basic, underlying British reality: A huge war debt needed to be serviced, and the colonists, as British subjects, should help pay it off. To many Americans, however, that proposition seemed in deep violation of what they perceived to be their rights and liberties as British subjects, and it created resentment that eventually erupted in large-scale street protests. The first provocative revenue acts were the work of Sir George Grenville, prime minister from 1763 to 1765.

Grenville's Sugar Act

To find revenue, George Grenville scrutinized the customs service, which monitored the shipping trade and collected all import and export duties. Grenville found that the salaries of customs officers cost the government four times what was collected in revenue. The shortfall was due in part to bribery and smuggling, so Grenville began to insist on rigorous attention to paperwork and a strict accounting of collected duties.

The hardest duty to enforce was the one imposed by the Molasses Act of 1733 — a stiff tax of six pence per gallon on any molasses imported to British colonies from non-British sources. The purpose of the tax was to discourage trade with French Caribbean islands and to redirect the molasses trade to British sugar islands, but it did not work. French molasses remained cheap and abundant because French planters on Martinique and Guadeloupe had no use for it. A by-product of sugar production, molasses was a key ingredient in rum, a drink the French scorned. Rum-loving Americans were eager to buy French molasses, and for decades American importers lined the pockets of customs officials in order to avoid paying the tariffs.

Grenville's inspired solution was the **Revenue Act** of 1764, popularly dubbed the **Sugar Act**. It lowered the duty on French molasses to three pence, making it more attractive for shippers to obey the law, and at the same time raised penalties for smuggling. The act appeared to be in the tradition of navigation acts meant to regulate trade (see chapter 4), but Grenville's actual intent was to raise revenue. He was using an established form of law for new ends and accomplishing his goal by the novel means of lowering a duty.

The Sugar Act toughened enforcement policies. From now on, all British naval crews could act as impromptu customs officers, boarding suspicious ships and seizing cargoes found to be in violation. Smugglers caught without proper paperwork would be prosecuted, not in a local court with a friendly jury but in a vice-admiralty court located in Nova Scotia, where a single judge presided. The implication was that justice would be sure and severe.

Grenville's hopes for the Sugar Act did not materialize. The small decrease in duty did not offset the attractions of smuggling, while the increased vigilance

A Philadelphia Tavern Scene
This trade card advertises the pleasures that await customers at Isaac Jones's tavern on Front Street — smoking and drinking. These men are likely drinking rum, a favorite colonial beverage frequently imbibed in taverns in sociable groups. The Sugar Act of 1763 put into question the supply of West Indies molasses, politicizing an essential ingredient in rum. Library Company of Philadelphia.

in enforcement led to several ugly confrontations in port cities. Reaction to the Sugar Act foreshadowed questions about Britain's right to tax Americans, but in 1764 objections to the act came principally from the small numbers of Americans engaged in the shipping trades.

From the British point of view, the Sugar Act seemed to be a reasonable effort to administer the colonies. To American shippers, however, the Sugar Act was not just about regulating trade. The British supervision appeared to be a disturbing intrusion into the long-held colonial practice of self-taxation by elected colonial assemblies. Benjamin Franklin, Pennsylvania's lobbyist in London, warned that "two distinct Jurisdictions or Powers of Taxing cannot well subsist together in the same country."

The Stamp Act

By his second year in office, Grenville had made almost no dent in the national debt. So in February 1765, he escalated his revenue program with the **Stamp Act**, precipitating a major conflict between Britain and the colonies over Parliament's right to tax. The Stamp Act imposed a tax on all paper used for official documents — newspapers, pamphlets, court documents, licenses, wills, ships' cargo lists — and required an affixed stamp as proof that the tax had been paid. Unlike the Sugar Act, which regulated trade, the Stamp Act was designed plainly and simply to raise money. It affected nearly everyone who used any taxed paper but, most of all, users of official documents in the business and legal communities.

Grenville was no fool. Anticipating that the stamp tax would be unpopular — Thomas Hutchinson had forewarned him — he delegated the administration of the act to Americans, to avoid taxpayer hostility toward British enforcers. In each colony, local stamp distributors would be hired at a handsome salary of 8 percent of the revenue collected.

English tradition held that taxes were a gift of the people to their monarch, granted by the people's representatives. This view of taxes as a freely given gift preserved an essential concept of English political theory: the idea that citizens have the liberty to enjoy and use their property without fear of confiscation. The king could not demand money; only the House of Commons could grant it. Grenville agreed with the notion of taxation by consent, but he argued that the colonists were already "virtually" represented in Parliament. The House of Commons, he insisted, represented all British subjects, wherever they were.

Colonial leaders emphatically rejected this view, arguing that **virtual representation** could not withstand the stretch across the Atlantic. Colonists willingly paid local and provincial taxes, levied by their town, county, or colonial assemblies. Typically, such annual taxes were based on property valuation, with an emphasis on income-generating property, such as numbers of cultivated acres and of livestock. The taxes paid for government administrative expenses and for shared necessities like local roads, schools, and poor relief. In contrast, the stamp tax was a clear departure as a fee-per-document tax, levied by a distant Parliament on unwilling colonies.

Resistance Strategies and Crowd Politics

News of the Stamp Act arrived in the colonies in April 1765, seven months before it was to take effect. There was time, therefore, to object. Governors were unlikely to challenge the law, for most of them owed their office to the king. Instead, the colonial assemblies took the lead; eight of them held discussions on the Stamp Act.

Virginia's assembly, the House of Burgesses, was the first. At the end of its May session, after two-thirds of the members had left, **Patrick Henry**, a young political newcomer, presented a series of resolutions on the Stamp Act that were debated and passed, one by one. They became known as the **Virginia Resolves**. Henry's resolutions inched the assembly toward radical opposition to the Stamp Act. The first three stated the obvious: that Virginians were British citizens, that they enjoyed the same rights and privileges as Britons, and that self-taxation was one of those rights. The fourth resolution noted that Virginians had always taxed themselves, through their representatives in the House of Burgesses. The fifth took a radical leap by pushing the other four unexceptional statements to one logical conclusion — that the Virginia assembly alone had the right to tax Virginians.

Two more fiery resolutions were debated as Henry pressed the logic of his case to the extreme. The sixth resolution denied legitimacy to any tax law originating outside Virginia, and the seventh boldly called anyone who disagreed with these propositions an enemy of Virginia. This was too much for the other representatives. They voted down resolutions six and seven and later rescinded their vote on number five as well.

Their caution hardly mattered, however, because newspapers in other colonies printed all seven Virginia Resolves, creating the impression that a daring first challenge to the Stamp Act had occurred. Consequently, other assemblies were willing to consider even more radical questions, such as this: By what authority could Parliament legislate for the colonies without also taxing them? No one disagreed, in 1765, that Parliament had legislative power over the colonists, who were, after all, British subjects. Several assemblies advanced the argument that there was a distinction between *external* taxes, imposed to regulate trade, and *internal* taxes, such as a stamp tax or a property tax, which could only be self-imposed.

Reaction to the Stamp Act ran far deeper than political debate in assemblies. Every person whose livelihood required official paper had to decide whether to comply with the act. There were only three options: boycotting, which was within the law but impractical because of the reliance on paper; defying the law and using unstamped paper; or preventing distribution of the stamps at the source before the law took effect, thus ensuring universal noncompliance.

The first organized resistance to the Stamp Act began in Boston in August 1765 under the direction of town leaders, chief among them **Samuel Adams**, John Hancock, and Ebenezer Mackintosh. The first two, both Harvard graduates, were town officers. Adams, in his forties, had shrewd political instincts and a gift for organizing. Hancock, though not yet thirty, had recently inherited his uncle's shipping business and was one of the wealthiest men in Massachusetts. Mackintosh, the same age as Hancock, was a shoemaker and highly experienced street activist. Many other artisans, tradesmen, printers, tavern keepers, dockworkers, and sailors — the middling and lower orders — mobilized in resistance to the Stamp Act, taking the name "**Sons of Liberty**."

The plan hatched in Boston called for a large street demonstration highlighting a mock execution designed to convince Andrew Oliver, the designated stamp distributor, to resign. On August 14, 1765, a crowd of two thousand to three thousand demonstrators, led by Mackintosh, hung an effigy of Oliver in a tree and then paraded it around town before finally beheading and burning it. In hopes of calming tensions, the royal governor Francis Bernard took no action. The flesh-and-blood Oliver stayed in hiding; the next day he resigned his office in a well-publicized announcement. The Sons of Liberty were elated.

The demonstration provided lessons for everyone. Oliver learned that stamp distributors would be very unpopular people. Governor Bernard, with no police force to call on, learned the limitations of his power to govern. The demonstration's leaders learned that street action was effective. And hundreds of ordinary men not only learned what the Stamp Act was all about but also gained pride in their ability to have a decisive impact on politics.

Twelve days later, a second crowd action showed how well these lessons had been learned. On August 26, a crowd visited the houses of three detested customs and court officials, breaking windows and raiding wine cellars. A fourth target was the finest dwelling in Massachusetts, owned by the stiff-necked lieutenant governor and chief justice **Thomas Hutchinson**. Rumors abounded that Hutchinson had urged Grenville to adopt the Stamp Act. Although he had actually done the opposite, Hutchinson refused to set the record straight, saying curtly, "I am not obliged to give an answer to all the questions that may be put me by every lawless person." The crowd attacked his house, and by daybreak only the exterior walls were standing. Governor Bernard gave orders to call out the militia, but he was told that many militiamen were among the crowd.

The destruction of Hutchinson's house brought a temporary halt to protest activities in Boston. The town meeting issued a statement of sympathy for Hutchinson, but a large reward for the arrest and conviction of rioters failed to produce a single lead. Hutchinson assumed that Mackintosh had led the attack, under orders issued by Samuel Adams, but Adams denied involvement and professed shock at the "truly mobbish Nature" of the violence.

Essentially, the opponents of the Stamp Act in Boston had triumphed; no one replaced Oliver as distributor. When the act took effect on November 1, ships without stamped permits continued to clear the harbor. Since he could not bring the lawbreakers to court, Hutchinson, ever principled, felt obliged to resign his office as chief justice. He remained lieutenant governor, however, and within five years he became the royal governor.

Liberty and Property

Boston's crowd actions of August sparked similar eruptions by groups calling themselves Sons of Liberty in nearly fifty towns throughout the colonies, and stamp distributors everywhere hastened to resign. A crowd forced one Connecticut distributor to throw his hat and powdered wig in the air while shouting a cheer for "Liberty and property!" This man fared better than another Connecticut stamp agent who was nearly buried alive by Sons of Liberty. Only when the thuds of dirt sounded on his coffin did he have a sudden change of heart, shouting out his resignation to the crowd above. Luckily, he was heard. In Charleston, South Carolina, the stamp distributor resigned after crowds burned effigies and chanted "Liberty! Liberty!" The royal governor of Virginia glumly assessed the situation in a letter to British authorities: "The flame is spread through all the continent, and one colony supports another in their disobedience to superior powers."

Some colonial leaders, disturbed by the riots, sought a more moderate challenge to parliamentary authority. In October 1765, twenty-seven delegates representing nine colonial assemblies met in New York City as the **Stamp Act Congress**. For two weeks, the men hammered out a petition about taxation addressed to the king and Parliament. Their statement closely resembled the first five Virginia Resolves, claiming that taxes were "free gifts of the people," which only the people's representatives could give. They dismissed virtual representation: "The people of these colonies are not, and from their local circumstances, cannot be represented in the House of Commons." At the same time, the delegates carefully affirmed their subordination to Parliament and monarch in deferential language. Nevertheless, the Stamp Act Congress, by the mere fact of its meeting, advanced a radical potential — the notion of intercolonial political action.

The rallying cry of "Liberty and property" made perfect sense to many white Americans of all social ranks, who feared that the Stamp Act threatened their traditional right to liberty as British subjects. The liberty in question was the right to be taxed only by representative government. "Liberty and property" came from a trinity of concepts — "life, liberty, property" — that had come to be regarded as the birthright of freeborn British subjects since at least the seventeenth century. A powerful tradition of British political thought invested representative government with the duty to protect individual lives, liberties, and property against potential abuse by royal authority. Up to 1765, Americans had consented to accept Parliament as a body that represented them. But now, in this matter of taxation via stamps, Parliament seemed a distant body that had failed to protect Americans' liberty and property against royal authority.

Alarmed, some Americans began to speak and write about a plot by British leaders to enslave them. A Maryland writer warned that if the colonies lost "the right of exemption from all taxes without their consent," that loss would "deprive them of every privilege distinguishing freemen from slaves." In Virginia, a group of planters headed by Richard Henry Lee issued a document called the Westmoreland Resolves, claiming that the Stamp Act was an attempt "to reduce the people of this country to a state of abject and detestable slavery." The opposite meanings of *liberty* and *slavery* were utterly clear to white Americans, but they stopped short of applying similar logic to the half million black Americans they held in bondage. Many blacks, however, could see the contradiction. When a crowd of Charleston blacks paraded with shouts of "Liberty!" just a few months after white Sons of Liberty had done the same, the town militia turned out to break up the demonstration.

Politicians and merchants in Britain reacted with distress to the American demonstrations and petitions. Merchants particularly feared trade disruptions and pressured Parliament to repeal the Stamp Act. By late 1765, yet another new minister, the Marquess of Rockingham, headed the king's cabinet and sought a way to repeal the act without losing face. The solution came in March 1766: The Stamp Act was repealed, but with the repeal came the **Declaratory Act**, which asserted Parliament's right to legislate for the colonies "in all cases whatsoever." Perhaps the stamp tax had been inexpedient, but the power to tax — one prime case of a legislative power — was stoutly upheld. As yet, the Sugar Act lowered the molasses tax, and the Stamp Act was a complete bust; very little tax revenue had been extracted from the colonies.

REVIEW   Why did the Sugar Act and the Stamp Act draw fierce opposition from colonists?

▶ The Townshend Acts and Economic Retaliation, 1767–1770

Rockingham did not last long as prime minister. By the summer of 1766, George III had persuaded William Pitt to resume that position. Pitt appointed Charles Townshend to be chancellor of the exchequer, the chief financial minister. Facing both the old war debt and the cost of the British troops in America, not successfully shifted to the Americans, Townshend turned again to taxation. But his knowledge of the changing political climate in the colonies was limited, and his plan to raise revenue touched off coordinated boycotts of British goods in 1768 and 1769. Even women were politicized as self-styled "Daughters of Liberty." Boston led the uproar, causing the British to send peacekeeping soldiers to assist the royal governor. The stage was thus set for the first fatalities in the brewing revolution.

The Townshend Duties

Townshend proposed new taxes in the old form of a navigation act. Officially called the Revenue Act of 1767, it established new duties on tea, glass, lead, paper, and painters' colors imported into the colonies, to be paid by the importer but passed on to consumers in the retail price. A year before, the duty on French molasses had been reduced from three pence to one pence per gallon, and finally the Sugar Act was pulling in a tidy revenue of about £45,000 annually. Townshend naively assumed that external taxes on transatlantic trade would be acceptable to Americans.

The **Townshend duties** were not especially burdensome, but the principle they embodied — taxation through trade duties — looked different to the colonists in the wake of the Stamp Act crisis. Although Americans once distinguished between external and internal taxes, accepting external duties as a means to direct the flow of trade, that distinction was wiped out by an external tax meant only to raise money. John Dickinson, a Philadelphia lawyer, articulated this view in a series of articles titled *Letters from a Farmer in Pennsylvania*, widely circulated in late 1767. "We are taxed without our consent. . . . We are therefore — SLAVES," Dickinson wrote, calling for "a total denial of the power of Parliament to lay upon these colonies any 'tax' whatever."

A controversial provision of the Townshend duties directed that some of the revenue generated would pay the salaries of royal governors. Before 1767, local assemblies set the salaries of their own officials, giving them significant influence over crown-appointed officeholders. Through his new provision, Townshend aimed to strengthen the governors' position as well as to curb what he perceived to be the growing independence of the assemblies.

The New York assembly, for example, seemed particularly defiant. It refused to enforce Parliament's Quartering Act of 1765, which directed the colonies to shelter and supply British regiments still based in America. This was effectively a tax levied without consent, the assembly argued, because it required New Yorkers to pay money by order of Parliament. In response, Townshend pushed through the New York Suspending Act, which declared all the assembly's acts null and void until it met its obligations to the army. Both measures — the new compensation model for royal governors and the suspension of the governance functions of the New York assembly — struck a chill throughout the colonies. Many wondered whether legislative government was at all secure.

Massachusetts again took the lead in protesting the Townshend duties. Samuel Adams, now an elected member of the provincial assembly, argued that any form of parliamentary taxation was unjust because Americans were not represented in Parliament. Further, he argued that the new way to pay governors' salaries subverted the proper relationship between the people and their rulers. The assembly circulated a letter with Adams's arguments to other colonial assemblies for their endorsement. As with the Stamp Act Congress of 1765, colonial assemblies were starting to coordinate their protests.

In response to Adams's letter, Lord Hillsborough, the new man in charge of colonial affairs in Britain, instructed Massachusetts governor Bernard to dissolve the assembly if it refused to repudiate the letter. The assembly refused, by a vote of 92 to 17, and Bernard carried out his instruction. In the summer of 1768, Boston was in an uproar.

Nonconsumption and the Daughters of Liberty

The Boston town meeting led the way with **nonconsumption agreements** calling for a boycott of all British-made goods. Dozens of other towns passed similar resolutions in 1767 and 1768. For example, prohibited purchases in the town of New Haven, Connecticut, included carriages, furniture, hats, clothing, lace, clocks, and textiles. The idea was to encourage home manufacture and to hurt trade, causing London merchants to pressure Parliament for repeal of the duties.

Nonconsumption agreements were very hard to enforce. With the Stamp Act, there was one hated item, a stamp, and a limited number of official distributors. In contrast, an agreement to boycott all British goods required serious personal sacrifice. Some merchants were wary because it hurt their pocketbooks, and a few continued to import in readiness for the end of nonconsumption (or to sell on the side to people choosing to ignore the boycotts). In Boston, such merchants found themselves blacklisted in newspapers and broadsides.

A more direct blow to trade came from nonimportation agreements, but getting merchants to agree to these proved more difficult, because of fears that merchants in other colonies might continue to import goods and make handsome profits. Not until late 1768 could Boston merchants agree to suspend trade through a nonimportation agreement lasting one year starting January 1, 1769. Sixty signed the agreement. New York merchants soon followed suit, as did Philadelphia and Charleston merchants in 1769.

Doing without British products, whether luxury goods, tea, or textiles, no doubt was a hardship. But it also presented an opportunity, for many of the British products specified in nonconsumption agreements were household goods traditionally under the control of the "ladies." By 1769, male leaders in the patriot cause clearly understood that women's cooperation in nonconsumption and home manufacture was beneficial to their cause. The Townshend duties thus provided an unparalleled opportunity for encouraging female patriotism. During the Stamp

Edenton Tea Ladies
American women in many communities renounced British apparel and tea during the early 1770s. Women in Edenton, North Carolina, publicized their pledge and drew hostile fire in the form of a British cartoon. The cartoon's message is that brazen women who meddled in politics would undermine their femininity. Neglected babies, urinating dogs, wanton sexuality, and mean-looking women would be some of the dire consequences, according to the artist. The cartoon works as humor for the British because of the gender reversals it predicts and because of the insult it directs at American men. Library of Congress.

Act crisis, Sons of Liberty took to the streets in protest. During the difficulties of 1768 and 1769, the concept of **Daughters of Liberty** emerged to give shape to a new idea — that women might play a role in public affairs. Any woman could express affiliation with the colonial protest through conspicuous boycotts of British-made goods. In Boston, more than three hundred women signed a petition to abstain from tea, "sickness excepted," in order to "save this abused Country from Ruin and Slavery." A nine-year-old girl visiting the royal governor's house in New Jersey took the tea she was offered, curtsied, and tossed the beverage out a nearby window.

Homespun cloth became a prominent symbol of patriotism. A young Boston girl learning to spin called herself "a daughter of liberty," noting that "I chuse to wear as much of our own manufactory as pocible." In the boycott period of 1768 to 1770, newspapers reported on spinning matches, or bees, in some sixty New England towns, in which women came together in public to make yarn. Nearly always, the bee was held at the local minister's house, and the yarn produced was charitably handed over to him for distribution to the poor. Newspaper accounts variously called the spinners "Daughters of Liberty" or "Daughters of Industry."

This surge of public spinning was related to the politics of the boycott, which infused traditional women's work with new political purpose. But the women spinners were not equivalents of the Sons of Liberty. The Sons marched in streets, burned effigies, threatened hated officials, and celebrated anniversaries of their successes with raucous drinking in taverns. The Daughters manifested their patriotism quietly, in ways marked by piety, industry, and charity. The difference was due in part to cultural ideals of gender, which prized masculine self-assertion and feminine selflessness. It also was due to class. The Sons were a cross-class alliance, with leaders from the middling orders reliant on men and boys of the lower ranks to fuel their crowds. The Daughters dusting off spinning wheels and shelving their teapots were genteel ladies accustomed to buying British goods. The difference between the Sons and the Daughters also speaks to two views of how best to challenge authority: violent threats and street actions, or the self-disciplined, self-sacrificing boycott of goods?

On the whole, the anti-British boycotts were a success. Imports fell by more than 40 percent; British merchants felt the pinch and let Parliament know it. In Boston, the Hutchinson family — whose fortune rested on British trade — also endured losses, but even more alarming to the lieutenant governor, Boston seemed overrun with anti-British sentiment. The Sons of Liberty staged rollicking annual celebrations of the Stamp Act riot, and both Hutchinson and Governor Bernard concluded that British troops were necessary to restore order.

Military Occupation and "Massacre" in Boston

In the fall of 1768, Britain sent three thousand uniformed troops to occupy Boston. The soldiers drilled conspicuously on the town Common, played loud music on the Sabbath, and in general grated on the nerves of Bostonians. Although the situation was frequently tense, no major troubles occurred that winter and through most of 1769. But as January 1, 1770, approached, marking the end of the nonimportation agreement, it was clear that some merchants — such as Thomas Hutchinson's two sons, both importers — were ready to break the boycott.

Trouble began in January, when a crowd defaced the door of the Hutchinson brothers' shop with "Hillsborough paint," a potent mixture of human excrement and urine. In February, a crowd surrounded the house of customs official Ebenezer Richardson, who panicked and fired a musket, accidentally killing a young boy passing on the street. The Sons of Liberty mounted a massive funeral procession to mark this first instance of violent death in the struggle with Britain.

For the next week, tension gripped Boston. The climax came on Monday evening, March 5, 1770, when a crowd taunted eight British soldiers guarding the customs house. Onlookers threw snowballs and rocks and dared the soldiers to fire; finally one did. After a short pause, someone yelled "Fire!" and the other soldiers shot into the crowd, hitting eleven men, killing five of them.

The **Boston Massacre**, as the event quickly became called, was over in minutes. In the immediate aftermath, Hutchinson (now acting governor after Bernard's recall to Britain) showed courage in addressing the crowd from the balcony of the statehouse. He quickly removed the regiments to an island in the harbor to prevent further bloodshed, and he jailed Captain Thomas Preston and his eight soldiers for their own protection, promising they would be held for trial.

The Sons of Liberty staged elaborate martyrs' funerals for the five victims. Significantly, the one nonwhite victim shared equally in the public's veneration.

The Bloody Massacre Perpetrated in King Street, Boston, on March 5, 1770
This mass-produced engraving by Paul Revere sold for sixpence per copy. In this patriot version of events, the soldiers are posed as a firing squad, shooting under orders at an unarmed and bewigged crowd. Actually, the shots were chaotic, and the five fatalities were all from the lower orders of youth and laborers, not the sort to wear wigs. Among them was Crispus Attucks, a dockworker of African and Indian ethnicity, but Revere shows only whites among the wounded and dead. Anne S. K. Brown Military Collection, Providence, RI.

Crispus Attucks, a sailor and rope maker in his forties, was the son of an African man and a Natick Indian woman. A slave in his youth, he was at the time of his death a free laborer at the Boston docks. Attucks was one of the first American partisans to die in the revolutionary struggle with Britain, and certainly the first African American.

The trial of the eight soldiers came in the fall of 1770. They were defended by two young Boston attorneys, Samuel Adams's cousin John Adams and Josiah Quincy. Because Adams and Quincy had direct ties to the leadership of the Sons of Liberty, their decision to defend the British soldiers at first seems odd. But Adams was deeply committed to the idea that even unpopular defendants deserved a fair trial. Samuel Adams respected his cousin's decision to take the case, for there was a tactical benefit as well. It showed that the Boston leadership was not lawless but could be seen as defenders of British liberty and law.

The five-day trial resulted in acquittal for Preston and for all but two of the soldiers, who were convicted of manslaughter, branded on the thumbs, and released. Nothing materialized in the trial to indicate a conspiracy or concerted plan to provoke trouble by either the British or the Sons of Liberty. To this day, the question of responsibility for the Boston Massacre remains obscure.

REVIEW   Why did British authorities send troops to occupy Boston in the fall of 1768?

▶ The Destruction of the Tea and the Coercive Acts, 1770–1774

In the same week as the Boston Massacre, yet another new British prime minister, Frederick North, acknowledged the harmful impact of the boycott on trade and recommended repeal of the Townshend duties. A skillful politician, Lord North took office in 1770 and kept it for twelve years; at last King George had stability at the helm. Seeking peace with the colonies and prosperity for British merchants, North persuaded Parliament to remove all the duties except the tax on tea, kept as a symbol of Parliament's power.

The renewal of trade and the return of cooperation between Britain and the colonies gave men like Thomas Hutchinson hope that the worst of the crisis was behind them. For nearly two years, peace seemed possible, but tense incidents in 1772, followed by a renewed struggle over the tea tax in 1773, precipitated a full-scale crisis in the summer and fall of 1774.

The Calm before the Storm

Repeal of the Townshend duties brought an end to nonimportation. Trade boomed in 1770 and 1771, driven by pent-up demand. Moreover, the leaders of the popular movement seemed to be losing their power. Samuel Adams, for example, ran for a minor local office and lost to a conservative merchant. Then in 1772, several incidents again brought the conflict with Britain into sharp focus. One was the burning of the *Gaspée*, a Royal Navy ship pursuing suspected smugglers near Rhode Island. A British investigating commission failed to arrest anyone but announced that it would send suspects, if any were found, to Britain for trial on charges of high treason. This ruling seemed to fly in the face of the traditional English right to trial by a jury of one's peers.

When news of the *Gaspée* investigation spread, it was greeted with disbelief in other colonies. Patrick Henry, Thomas Jefferson, and Richard Henry Lee in the Virginia House of Burgesses proposed that a network of standing committees be established to link the colonies and pass along alarming news. By mid-1773, every colonial assembly except Pennsylvania's had a "committee of correspondence."

Another British action in 1772 further spread the communications network. Lord North proposed to pay the salaries of superior court justices out of the tea revenue, similar to Townshend's plan for paying royal governors. The Boston town meeting, fearful that judges would now be improperly influenced by their new paymasters, established a committee of correspondence and urged all

Massachusetts towns to do likewise. The first message, circulated in December 1772, attacked the salary policy for judges as the latest proof of a sinister British conspiracy to undermine traditional liberties: first taxation without consent, followed by military occupation, a massacre, and now a plot to subvert the justice system. By spring 1773, more than half the towns in Massachusetts had set up **committees of correspondence**, providing local forums for debate. These committees politicized ordinary townspeople, sparking a revolutionary language of rights and constitutional duties. They also bypassed the official flow of power and information through the colony's royal government.

The final incident shattering the relative calm of the early 1770s was the **Tea Act of 1773**. Americans had resumed buying the taxed British tea, but they were also smuggling large quantities of Dutch tea, cutting into the sales of Britain's East India Company. So Lord North proposed legislation giving favored status to the East India Company, allowing it to sell tea directly to a few selected merchants in four colonial cities, cutting out British middlemen. The appointed agents would resell the tea, collecting the three pence tax that had its origins in the Townshend duty on tea of 1767. The reduced shipping costs would lower the final price of the East India tea below that of smuggled Dutch tea, thus motivating Americans to obey the law.

Tea in Boston Harbor

In the fall of 1773, news of the Tea Act reached the colonies. Parliamentary legislation to make tea inexpensive struck many colonists as an insidious plot to trick Americans into buying the duted tea. The real goal, some argued, was the increased revenue that would pay the salaries of royal governors and judges. The Tea Act was thus a painful reminder of Parliament's claim to the power to tax and legislate for the colonies.

But how to resist the Tea Act? Nonimportation was not viable, because the tea trade was too lucrative to expect merchants to give it up willingly. Consumer boycotts seemed ineffective, because it was impossible to distinguish between duted tea (the object of the boycott) and smuggled tea (illegal but politically clean) once it was in the teapot. The appointment of official tea agents, parallel to the Stamp Act distributors, suggested one solution. In Charleston, Philadelphia, and New York, revived Sons of Liberty pressured tea agents to resign. Without agents, governors yielded, and tea cargoes either landed duty-free or were sent home.

Governor Hutchinson, however, would not bend any rules. Three ships bearing tea arrived in Boston in November 1773. The ships cleared customs, and the crews, sensing the town's extreme tension, unloaded all cargo except the tea. The captains wished to leave Boston with their tea on board, but because the ships had already cleared customs, Hutchinson would not grant them passage without paying the tea duty. To add to the difficulties, another long-standing law imposed a time limit on ships in the harbor. After twenty days, the required duty had to be paid, or local authorities would confiscate the cargo.

For the full twenty days, pressure built in Boston. Daily mass meetings energized citizens from Boston and surrounding towns, alerted by the committees of correspondence. On the final day, December 16, when for a final time Hutchinson refused clearance for the ships, a large crowd gathered at Old South Church to debate a course of action. No official plan was agreed on at that meeting, but immediately following it, 100 to 150 men, disguised as Indians, boarded the ships and dumped thousands of pounds of tea into the harbor while a crowd of 2,000 watched. In admiration, John Adams wrote: "This Destruction of the Tea is so bold, so daring, so firm, intrepid and inflexible, and it must have so important Consequences."

The Coercive Acts

Lord North's response was swift and stern: He persuaded Parliament to issue the **Coercive Acts**, four laws meant to punish Massachusetts for destroying the tea. In America, those laws, along with a fifth one, the Quebec Act, were soon known as the **Intolerable Acts**.

The first act, the Boston Port Act, closed Boston harbor to all shipping as of June 1, 1774, until the destroyed tea was paid for. Britain's objective was to halt the commercial life of the city.

The second act, called the Massachusetts Government Act, greatly altered the colony's charter, underscoring Parliament's claim to supremacy over Massachusetts. The royal governor's powers were augmented, and the governor's council became an appointive, rather than elective, body. Further, the governor could now appoint all judges, sheriffs, and officers of the court. No town meeting beyond the annual spring election of town selectmen could be held without the governor's approval, and every agenda item required prior approval. Every Massachusetts town was affected.

The third Coercive Act, the Impartial Administration of Justice Act, stipulated that any royal official accused of a capital crime — for example, Captain Preston and his soldiers at the Boston Massacre — would be tried in a court in Britain. It did not matter that Preston had received a fair trial in Boston. What this act ominously suggested was that down the road, more Captain Prestons and soldiers might be firing into unruly crowds.

The fourth act amended the 1765 Quartering Act and permitted military commanders to lodge soldiers wherever necessary, even in private households. In a related move, Lord North appointed General **Thomas Gage**, commander of the Royal Army in New York, as governor of Massachusetts. Thomas Hutchinson was out, relieved at long last of his duties. Military rule, including soldiers, returned once more to Boston.

The fifth act, the Quebec Act, had nothing to do with the four Coercive Acts, but it fed American fears. It confirmed the continuation of French civil law and government form, as well as Catholicism, for Quebec — an affront to Protestant New Englanders who had recently been denied their own representative government. The act also gave Quebec control of disputed land (and the lucrative fur trade) throughout the Ohio Valley, land also claimed by Virginia, Pennsylvania, and a number of Indian tribes.

The five Intolerable Acts spread alarm in all the colonies. If Britain could squelch Massachusetts — change its charter, suspend local government, inaugurate military rule, and on top of that give Ohio to Catholic Quebec — what liberties were secure? Fearful royal governors in a half dozen colonies dismissed the sitting assemblies, adding to the sense of urgency. A few of the assemblies defiantly continued to meet in new locations. Through the committees of correspondence, colonial leaders arranged to convene in Philadelphia in September 1774 to respond to the crisis.

Beyond Boston: Rural New England

Well before the delegates assembled in Philadelphia, all of New England had arrived at the brink of open insurrection. With a British general occupying the Massachusetts governorship and some three thousand troops controlling Boston, the revolutionary momentum shifted from urban radicals to rural farmers who protested the Massachusetts Government Act in dozens of spontaneous, dramatic showdowns. To get around the prohibition on new meetings, some towns refused to adjourn their last authorized town meeting. More defiant towns just ignored the law. Gage's call for elections for a new provincial assembly under his control sparked elections for a competing unauthorized assembly.

In all Massachusetts counties except one, crowds of thousands of armed men converged to prevent the opening of county courts run by crown-appointed jurists. No judges were physically harmed, but they were forced to resign and made to doff their judicial wigs or run a humiliating gantlet. In Suffolk County, the courts met in troop-filled Boston, making mass intimidation of judges impossible. One by one, however, the citizen jurors called to serve in court refused. By August 1774, farmers and artisans all over Massachusetts had effectively taken full control of their local institutions.

Unfettered by the crown, ordinary citizens throughout New England began serious planning for the showdown everyone assumed would come. Town militias stockpiled gunpowder "in case of invasion." Militia officers repudiated their official chain of command to the governor and stepped up drills of their units. Town after town withheld its tax money from the royal governor and diverted it to military supplies. Governor Gage felt under heavy threat, but he could do little. He beefed up fortifications around Boston and in general rattled his sword loudly, praying for reinforcements from Britain.

At this point in the struggle, confrontations did not lead to bloodshed. But one incident, the Powder Alarm, nearly provoked violence and showed how close New England farmers were to armed insurrection. On September 1, 1774, Gage sent troops to capture a supply of gunpowder just outside Boston. In the surprise and scramble of the attack, false news spread that the troops had fired on men defending the powder, killing six. Within twenty-four hours, several thousand armed men from Massachusetts, New Hampshire, and Connecticut streamed on foot to Boston to avenge the first blood spilled. At this moment, ordinary men became insurgents, willing to kill or be killed in the face of the British clampdown. Once the error was corrected and the crisis defused, the men returned home peaceably. But Gage could no longer doubt the speed, numbers, and deadly determination of the rebellious subjects.

All this had occurred without orchestration by Boston radicals, Gage reported. But British leaders found it hard to believe, as one put it, that "a tumultuous

Rabble, without any Appearance of general Concert, or without any Head to advise, or Leader to conduct" could pull off such effective resistance. Repeatedly in the years to come, the British would seriously underestimate their opponents.

The First Continental Congress

Every colony except Georgia sent delegates to Philadelphia in September 1774 to discuss the looming crisis in what was later called the **First Continental Congress**. The gathering included notables such as Samuel Adams and John Adams from Massachusetts and George Washington and Patrick Henry from Virginia. A few colonies purposely sent men who opposed provoking Britain, such as Pennsylvania's Joseph Galloway, to keep the congress from becoming too radical.

Delegates sought to articulate their liberties as British subjects and the powers Parliament held over them, and they debated possible responses to the Coercive Acts. Some wanted a total ban on trade with Britain to force repeal, while others, especially southerners dependent on tobacco and rice exports, opposed halting trade. Samuel Adams and Patrick Henry were eager for a ringing denunciation of all parliamentary control. The conservative Joseph Galloway proposed a plan (quickly defeated) to create a secondary parliament in America to assist the British Parliament in ruling the colonies.

The congress met for seven weeks and produced a declaration of rights couched in traditional language: "We ask only for peace, liberty and security. We wish no diminution of royal prerogatives, we demand no new rights." But from Britain's point of view, the rights assumed already to exist were radical. Chief among them was the claim that Americans were not represented in Parliament and so each colonial government had the sole right to govern and tax its own people. The one slight concession to Britain was a carefully worded agreement that the colonists would "cheerfully consent" to trade regulations for the larger good of the empire, so long as trade regulation was not a covert means of raising revenue.

To put pressure on Britain, the delegates agreed to a staggered and limited boycott of trade: imports prohibited this year, exports the following, and rice totally exempted (to keep South Carolinians happy). To enforce the boycott, they called for a Continental Association, with chapters in each town variously called committees of public safety or of inspection, to monitor all commerce and punish suspected violators of the boycott (sometimes with a bucket of tar and a bag of feathers). Its work done in under two months, the congress disbanded in late October, with agreement to reconvene the following May.

The committees of public safety, the committees of correspondence, the regrouped colonial assemblies, and the Continental Congress were all political bodies functioning defiantly without any constitutional authority. British officials did not recognize them as legitimate, but many Americans who supported the patriot cause instantly accepted them. A key reason for the stability of such unauthorized governing bodies was that they were composed of many of the same men who had held elective office before.

Britain's severe reaction to Boston's destruction of the tea finally succeeded in making many colonists from New Hampshire to Georgia realize that the problems of British rule went far beyond questions of nonconsensual taxation. The Coercive Acts infringed on liberty and denied self-government; they could not be ignored. With one colony already subordinated to military rule and a British army at the ready in Boston, the threat of a general war was on the doorstep.

> **REVIEW** Why did Parliament pass the Coercive Acts in 1774?

▶ Domestic Insurrections, 1774–1775

Before the Second Continental Congress could meet, violence and bloodshed came to Massachusetts. Fearing the threat of domestic insurrection, General (and Governor) Thomas Gage requested more troops from Britain and prepared to subdue rebellion. On the other side, New England farmers prepared to defend their homes against an intrusive power they feared was bent on enslaving them. To the south, a different and inverted version of the same story began to unfold, as thousands of enslaved black men and women seized an unprecedented opportunity to mount a different kind of insurrection — against planter-patriots who looked over their shoulders uneasily whenever they called out for liberty from the British.

Lexington and Concord

During the winter of 1774–75, Americans pressed on with boycotts. Optimists hoped to effect a repeal of the Coercive Acts; pessimists stockpiled arms and ammunition. In Massachusetts, militia units known as minutemen prepared to respond at a minute's notice to any threat from the British troops in Boston.

Thomas Gage soon realized how desperate the British position was. The people, Gage wrote to Lord North, were "numerous, worked up to a fury, and not a Boston rabble but the freeholders and farmers of the country." Gage requested twenty thousand reinforcements. He also strongly advised repeal of the Coercive Acts, but leaders in Britain could not admit failure. Instead, in mid-April 1775, they ordered Gage to arrest the troublemakers immediately, before the Americans got better organized.

Gage quickly planned a surprise attack on a suspected ammunition storage site at Concord, a village eighteen miles west of Boston (Map 6.2). Near midnight on April 18, 1775, more than fifteen hundred British soldiers moved west across the Charles River. Boston silversmith Paul Revere and William Dawes, a tanner, learned of the attack by a prearranged signal, two lanterns hung in a church belfry, and they raced ahead to alert the minutemen. When the British arrived at **Lexington**, a village five miles east of **Concord**, they were met by some seventy armed men assembled on the village green. The British commander barked out, "Lay down your arms, you damned rebels, and disperse." The militiamen hesitated

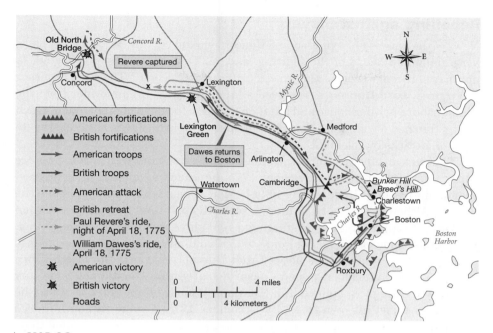

MAP 6.2
Lexington and Concord, April 1775
When British soldiers left Boston to raid a suspected arms supply in Concord, Paul Revere and
William Dawes set out to warn the patriots. Revere went by boat from Boston to Charlestown
and then by horse through Medford to Lexington. Dawes casually passed British sentries
guarding the narrow land route out of Boston and then rode his horse at full speed to Lexington.
Once there, Revere and Dawes urged Samuel Adams and John Hancock, guests in a Lexington
home, to flee to avoid capture. The two couriers then went on to Concord to warn residents of
the impending attack.

and began to comply, turning to leave the green, but then someone — nobody
knows who — fired. In the next two minutes, more firing left eight Americans
dead and ten wounded.

The British units continued their march to Concord, any pretense of surprise
gone. Three companies of minutemen nervously occupied the town center but
offered no challenge to the British, who searched in vain for the ammunition.
Finally, at Old North Bridge in Concord, British troops and three hundred to
four hundred local minutemen exchanged shots, killing two Americans and three
British soldiers.

By now, both sides were very apprehensive. The British failed to find the
expected arms, and the Americans failed to stop their raid. As the British returned
to Boston, militia units from the countryside converged on the Concord road and
ambushed them, bringing the bloodiest fighting of the day. In the end, 273 British
soldiers were wounded or dead; the toll for the Americans stood at about 95. It
was April 19, 1775, and the war had begun.

Rebelling against Slavery

News of the battles of Lexington and Concord spread rapidly. Within eight days, Virginians had heard of the fighting, and, as Thomas Jefferson reflected, "a phrenzy of revenge seems to have seized all ranks of people." The royal governor of Virginia, **Lord Dunmore**, removed a large quantity of gunpowder from the Williamsburg powder house and put it on a ship in the dead of night, out of reach of any frenzied Virginians. Next, he threatened to arm slaves, if necessary, to ward off attacks by colonists.

This was an effective threat; Dunmore understood full well how to produce panic among planters. In November 1775, he issued an official proclamation promising freedom to defecting able-bodied slaves who would fight for the British. Although Dunmore wanted to scare the planters, he had no intention of liberating all the slaves or starting a real slave rebellion. Female, young, and elderly slaves were not welcome to flee, and many were sent back to face irate masters. Astute blacks noticed that Dunmore neglected to free his own slaves. A Virginia barber named Caesar declared that "he did not know any one foolish enough to believe him [Dunmore], for if he intended to do so, he ought first to set his own free." By December 1775, around fifteen hundred slaves in Virginia had fled to Lord Dunmore, who armed them and called them his "Ethiopian Regiment." Camp diseases quickly set in: dysentery, typhoid fever, and smallpox. When Dunmore sailed for England in mid-1776, he took just three hundred black survivors with him. But the association of freedom with the British authorities had been established, and throughout the war thousands more southern slaves made bold to run away as soon as they heard the British army was approaching.

In the northern colonies as well, slaves clearly recognized the evolving political struggle with Britain as an ideal moment to bid for freedom. A twenty-one-year-old Boston domestic slave employed biting sarcasm in a 1774 newspaper essay to call attention to the hypocrisy of local slave owners: "How well the Cry for Liberty, and the reverse Disposition for exercise of oppressive Power over others agree, — I humbly think it does not require the Penetration of a Philosopher to Determine." This extraordinary young woman, **Phillis Wheatley**, had already gained international recognition through a book of poems endorsed by Governor Thomas Hutchinson and Boston merchant John Hancock and published in London in 1773. Possibly neither man fully appreciated the irony of his endorsement, however, for Wheatley's poems spoke of "Fair Freedom" as the "Goddess long desir'd" by Africans enslaved in America. At the urging of his wife, Wheatley's master freed the young poet in 1775.

Wheatley's poetic ideas about freedom found concrete expression among other discontented groups. Some slaves in Boston petitioned Thomas Gage, promising to fight for the British if he would liberate them. Gage turned them down. In Ulster County, New York, along the Hudson River, two blacks were overheard discussing gunpowder, and thus a plot unraveled that involved at least twenty slaves in four villages discovered to have ammunition stashed away.

Phillis Wheatley's Title Page
Phillis, born in Africa, became the slave of John Wheatley at age seven. Remarkably gifted in English, she wrote poetry and could read the Bible with ease by age sixteen. Her master took her to London in 1773, where this book of poems was published, gaining her great literary notice. The Wheatleys freed Phillis, who then married a free black man; two of their three children died in infancy, and her husband deserted her. Poetry alone could not support her, and she found work in a boardinghouse. By the end of 1784, Phillis and her remaining child had died. Library of Congress.

In Maryland, soon after the news of the Lexington battle arrived, blacks exhibited impatience with their status as slaves, causing one Maryland planter to report that "the insolence of the Negroes in this county is come to such a height, that we are under a necessity of disarming them. . . . We took about eighty guns, some bayonets, swords, etc." In North Carolina, a planned uprising was uncovered, and scores of slaves were arrested. Ironically, it was the revolutionary committee of public safety that ordered the whippings to punish this quest for liberty.

By 1783, when the Revolutionary War ended, as many as twenty thousand blacks had voted against slavery with their feet by seeking refuge with the British army. Most failed to achieve the liberation they were seeking. The British generally used them for menial labor, and disease, especially smallpox, devastated encampments of runaways. But some eight thousand to ten thousand persisted through the war and later, under the protection of the British army, left America to start new lives of freedom in Canada's Nova Scotia or Africa's Sierra Leone.

REVIEW How did enslaved people in the colonies react to the stirrings of revolution?

▶ Conclusion: The Long Road to Revolution

In the aftermath of the Seven Years' War, Britain and its American colonies were victorious, but almost none of the warring parties came away satisfied. France lost vast amounts of North American land claims, and Indian land rights were increasingly violated or ignored. As for the victors, Britain's huge war debt and subsequent revenue-generating policies distressed Americans and set the stage for the imperial crisis of the 1760s and 1770s. The years 1763 to 1775 brought repeated attempts by the British government to subordinate the colonies into contributing partners in the larger scheme of empire.

American resistance to British policies grew slowly but steadily. In 1765, loyalist Thomas Hutchinson shared with patriot Samuel Adams the belief that it was exceedingly unwise for Britain to assert a right to taxation because Parliament did not adequately represent Americans. By temperament and office, Hutchinson was obliged to uphold British policy. Adams, in contrast, protested the policy and made political activists out of thousands in the process.

By 1775, events propelled many Americans to the conclusion that a concerted effort was afoot to deprive them of all their liberties, the most important of which were the right to self-rule and the right to live free of an occupying army. Prepared to die for those liberties, hundreds of minutemen converged on Concord. April 19 marked the start of their rebellion.

Another rebellion under way in 1775 was doomed to be short-circuited. Black Americans who had experienced actual slavery listened to shouts of "Liberty!" from white crowds and appropriated the language of revolution swirling around them that spoke to their deepest needs and hopes. Defiance of authority was indeed contagious, but freedom for black slaves would not be fully granted in America for nearly a century.

In 1765, patriot leaders had wanted a correction, a restoration of the ancient liberty of self-taxation, but events over the next decade convinced many that a return to the old ways was impossible. Challenging Parliament's right to tax had led, step-by-step, to challenging Parliament's right to legislate over the colonies in any matter. By 1774, many in New England were willing to shoulder guns and risk death to free the colonies from Parliament's rule. Yet even after the battles of Lexington and Concord, a war with Britain seemed far from inevitable to colonists outside New England. In the months ahead, American colonial leaders pursued peaceful as well as military solutions to the question of who actually had authority over them. By the end of 1775, however, reconciliation with the crown would be unattainable.

Reviewing Chapter 6

REVIEW QUESTIONS

1. How did the Seven Years' War erode relations between colonists and British authorities? (pp. 142–149)

2. Why did the Sugar Act and the Stamp Act draw fierce opposition from colonists? (pp. 150–155)

3. Why did British authorities send troops to occupy Boston in the fall of 1768? (pp. 156–161)

4. Why did Parliament pass the Coercive Acts in 1774? (pp. 161–166)

5. How did enslaved people in the colonies react to the stirrings of revolution? (pp. 166–169)

MAKING CONNECTIONS

1. In the mid-eighteenth century, how did Native Americans influence relations between European nations? Between Britain and the colonies?

2. What other grievances, besides taxation, led colonists by 1775 to openly rebel against Britain?

3. How did the colonists organize to oppose British power so effectively? In your answer, discuss the role of communication in facilitating the colonial resistance, being sure to cite specific examples.

LINKING TO THE PAST

1. In Bacon's Rebellion in Virginia in 1676, backcountry farmers protested the rule of a royal governor who did not seem to have the economic interests of many Virginians at heart. Compare the administration of Sir William Berkeley of Virginia with that of Thomas Hutchinson of Massachusetts in the 1760s. Are there more differences than similarities? (See chapter 3.)

2. How does the growing ethnic and religious diversity of the mid-eighteenth-century colonies help explain the evolution of anti-British feeling that would culminate in insurrection in 1775? (See chapter 5.)

TIMELINE 1754–1775

1754
- Seven Years' War begins in North America.
- Albany Congress proposes Plan of Union (never implemented).

1755
- Braddock defeated in western Pennsylvania.

1757
- William Pitt fully commits Britain to war effort.

1760
- Montreal falls to British.
- George III becomes British king.

1763
- Treaty of Paris ends Seven Years' War.
- Pontiac's Rebellion.
- Proclamation of 1763.
- Paxton Boys massacre friendly Indians in Pennsylvania.

1764
- Parliament enacts Sugar (Revenue) Act.

1765
- Parliament enacts Stamp Act.
- Virginia Resolves challenge Stamp Act.
- Sons of Liberty stage dozens of crowd actions.
- Stamp Act Congress meets.

1766
- Parliament repeals Stamp Act and passes Declaratory Act.

1767
- Parliament enacts Townshend duties.

1768
- British station troops in Boston.

1768–1769
- Merchants sign nonimportation agreements.

1770
- Boston Massacre.
- Parliament repeals Townshend duties.

1772
- British navy ship *Gaspée* burned.

1773
- Parliament passes Tea Act.
- Dumping of tea in Boston harbor.

1774
- Parliament passes Coercive (Intolerable) Acts.
- Powder Alarm shows colonists' readiness to engage in battle with British.
- First Continental Congress meets; Continental Association formed.

1775
- Battles of Lexington and Concord.
- Lord Dunmore promises freedom to defecting slaves.

▶ FOR AN ONLINE BIBLIOGRAPHY, PRACTICE QUIZZES, WEB SITES, IMAGES, AND DOCUMENTS RELATED TO THIS CHAPTER, see the Book Companion Site at **bedfordstmartins.com/roarkvalue**.

▶ FOR DOCUMENTS RELATED TO THIS PERIOD, see Michael Johnson, ed., *Reading the American Past*, Fifth Edition.

The War for America

1775–1783

ROBERT SHURTLIFF OF MASSACHUSETTS WAS A LATECOMER TO THE American Revolution, enlisting in the Continental army months after the last decisive battle at Yorktown had been fought. The army needed fresh recruits as a holding action against the large British force still occupying New York City. Both sides were waiting for the peace treaty to be finalized in Paris — a process that would take nearly two years.

To secure those new recruits in a country exhausted by eight years of war, some towns offered cash bounties of $50 in silver. Beardless boys who had been children when the first shots were fired at Lexington now stepped forward, Shurtliff among them. Reportedly eighteen, the youth was single, poor, and at loose ends. With a muscular physique and a ready proficiency with a musket, Shurtliff won assignment to the army's elite light infantry unit, part of Washington's army of 10,000 men stationed along the Hudson River, north of New York City.

That is, 10,000 men and 1 woman. "Robert Shurtliff" was actually Deborah Sampson, age twenty-three, from Middleborough, Massachusetts. For seventeen months, Sampson masqueraded as a man, marching through woods, skirmishing with the enemy, and enduring the boredom of camp. Understating her age enabled her to blend in with the beardless boys, as did her competence as a soldier. With privacy at a minimum, she faced constant risk of discovery. Soldiers slept six to a tent, "spooning" their bodies together for warmth. Somehow, Sampson managed to escape detection. Although many thousands of women served the army as cooks, laundresses, and caregivers, they were never placed in combat. Not only was Sampson defrauding the

Deborah Sampson
In the mid-1790s, Deborah Sampson sat for this small portrait painted by Massachusetts folk artist Joseph Stone. An engraved copy of it illustrated *The Female Review*, a short book about Sampson's unusual military career and life published in 1797. Sampson, by then a wife and mother, displays femininity in this picture. Note her long curly hair, the necklace, and the stylish gown with a low, lace-trimmed neckline filled in (for modesty's sake) with a white neckerchief. Sampson the soldier had used a cloth band to compress her breasts; Sampson the matron wore a satin band to define her bustline. Rhode Island Historical Society.

military, but she was also violating a legal prohibition on cross-dressing. Why did she run this risk?

A hard-luck childhood had left Sampson both impoverished and unusually plucky. When she was five, her father deserted the family, forcing her mother to place the children in foster care. Deborah trained to be a servant in a succession of families. Along the way, she learned to plow a field and to read and write, uncommon skills for a female servant. Freed from servitude at age eighteen, she earned a living as a weaver and then as a teacher, low-wage jobs but also ones without supervising bosses. Marriage would have been her normal next step, but either lack of inclination or a wartime shortage of men kept her single and "masterless," rare for an eighteenth-century woman. But like most single females, she was also poor; the $50 bounty enticed her to enlist.

Sampson's true sex was finally discovered by a physician when she was hospitalized for a fever. She was discharged immediately, but her fine service record kept her superiors from prosecuting her for cross-dressing. What eventually made Sampson famous was not her war service alone — there were several other instances of women who wielded weapons in various battles — but her success in selling her story to the public. In 1797, now a middle-aged mother of three, she told her life story (a blend of fact and fiction) in a short book. During 1802–1803, she reenacted her wartime masquerade on a speaking tour of New England and New York. Once again, she was crossing gender boundaries, since women who were not actresses normally did not speak from public stages.

Except for her disguised sex, Sampson's Revolutionary War experience was similar to that of most Americans. Disruptions affected everyone's life, whether in military service or on the home front. Wartime shortages caused women and children to take up traditionally male labor. Soldiers fought for ideas, but they also fought to earn money. Hardship was widely endured. And Sampson's quest for personal independence — a freedom from the constraints of being female — was echoed in the general quest for political independence that many Americans identified as a major goal of the war.

Political independence was not everyone's primary goal at first. For more than a year after fighting began, the Continental Congress in Philadelphia resisted declaring America's independence. Some delegates cautiously hoped for reconciliation with Britain. The congress raised an army, financed it, and sought alliances with foreign countries — all while exploring diplomatic channels for peace.

Once King George III rejected all peace overtures, Americans loudly declared their independence, and the war moved into high gear. In part a classic war with professional armies and textbook battles, the Revolutionary War was also a civil war and at times a brutal guerrilla war between committed rebels and loyalists. It also had complex ethnic dimensions, pitting Indian tribes allied with the British against others allied with the Americans. And it provided an unprecedented opportunity for enslaved African Americans to win their freedom, either by joining the British, who openly encouraged slaves to desert their masters, or by joining the Continental army and state militias, fighting alongside white Americans.

▶ The Second Continental Congress

On May 10, 1775, nearly one month after the fighting at Lexington and Concord, the **Second Continental Congress** assembled in Philadelphia. The congress immediately set to work on two crucial but contradictory tasks: to raise and supply an army and to explore reconciliation with Britain. To do the former, they needed soldiers and a commander, they needed money, and they needed to work out a declaration of war. To do the latter, they needed diplomacy to approach the king. But the king was not receptive, and by 1776, as the war progressed and hopes of reconciliation faded, delegates at the congress began to ponder the treasonous act of declaring independence — said by some to be plain common sense.

Assuming Political and Military Authority

Like members of the First Continental Congress (see chapter 6), the delegates to the second were well-established figures in their home colonies, but they still had to learn to know and trust one another. They did not always agree. The Adams cousins John and Samuel defined the radical end of the spectrum, favoring independence. **John Dickinson** of Pennsylvania, no longer the eager revolutionary who had dashed off *Letters from a Farmer* in 1767, was now a moderate, seeking reconciliation with Britain. Benjamin Franklin, fresh off a ship from an eleven-year residence in London, was feared by some to be a British spy. Mutual suspicions flourished easily when the undertaking was so dangerous, opinions were so varied, and a misstep could spell disaster.

Most of the delegates were not yet prepared to break with Britain. Some felt that government without a king was unworkable, while others feared it might be suicidal to lose Britain's protection against its traditional enemies, France and Spain. Colonies that traded actively with Britain feared undermining their economies. Probably the vast majority of ordinary Americans were unable to envision independence. From the Stamp Act of 1765 to the Coercive Acts of 1774 (see chapter 6), the constitutional struggle with Britain had focused on the issue of parliamentary power, but almost no one had questioned the legitimacy of the monarchy.

The few men at the Continental Congress who did think that independence was desirable were, not surprisingly, from Massachusetts. Their colony had been stripped of civil government under the Coercive Acts, their capital was occupied by the British, and their blood had been shed at Lexington and Concord. Even so, those men knew that it was premature to push for a break with Britain. John Adams wrote his wife, Abigail, in June 1775: "America is a great, unwieldy body. Its progress must be slow. It is like a large fleet sailing under convoy. The fleetest sailors must wait for the dullest and slowest."

Yet swift action was needed, for the Massachusetts countryside was under threat of further attack. Even the hesitant moderates in the congress agreed that a military buildup was necessary. Around the country, militia units from New York to Georgia collected arms and trained on village greens in anticipation. On June 14, the congress voted to create the **Continental army**, choosing a Virginian, not a New Englander, as commander in chief. The appointment of **George Washington** sent the clear message that there was widespread commitment to war beyond New England.

Next the congress drew up a document titled "A Declaration on the Causes and Necessity of Taking Up Arms," which rehearsed familiar arguments about the tyranny of Parliament and the need to defend English liberties. This declaration was first drafted by a young Virginia planter, **Thomas Jefferson**, a radical on the question of independence. The moderate John Dickinson, fearing that the declaration would offend Britain, was allowed to rewrite it. However, he left intact much of Jefferson's highly charged language about choosing "to die freemen rather than to live slaves." Even a man as reluctant about independence as Dickinson acknowledged the necessity of military defense against an invading army.

To pay for the military buildup, the congress authorized a currency issue of $2 million. The Continental dollars were merely paper; they were not backed by gold or silver. The delegates somewhat naively expected that the currency would be accepted as valuable on trust as it spread in the population through the hands of soldiers, farmers, munitions suppliers, and beyond.

In just two months, the Second Continental Congress had created an army, declared war, and issued its own currency. It had taken on the major functions of a legitimate government, both military and financial, without any legal basis for its authority, for it had not yet declared independence from the authority of the king.

Pursuing Both War and Peace

Three days after the congress established the army, one of the bloodiest battles of the Revolution occurred. The British commander in Boston, Thomas Gage, had recently received troop reinforcements, including three talented generals (William Howe, John Burgoyne, and Henry Clinton), and new instructions to attack the Massachusetts rebels. But before Gage could take the offensive, the Americans fortified the hilly terrain of Charlestown, a peninsula just north of Boston, on the night of June 16, 1775.

The British generals could have closed off the peninsula to box in the Americans. But General **William Howe** insisted on a bold frontal assault, sending 2,500 soldiers across the water and up the hill in an intimidating but potentially costly attack. The American troops, 1,400 strong, turned them back twice with deadly short-range fire.

On the third assault, the British took the hill, mainly because the American ammunition supply gave out, and the defenders quickly retreated. The **battle of Bunker Hill** was thus a British victory, but an expensive one. The dead numbered 226 on the British side, with more than 800 wounded; the Americans suffered 140 dead, 271 wounded, and 30 captured. As General Clinton later remarked, "It was a dear bought victory; another such would have ruined us."

Unwilling to risk more raids into the countryside, Howe retreated to Boston instead of pursuing the fleeing Americans. If the British had had any grasp of the basic instability of the American units around Boston, they might have decisively defeated the Continental army in its infancy. Instead, they lingered in Boston, abandoning it without a fight nine months later.

Howe used the time in Boston to inoculate his army against smallpox because a new epidemic of the deadly disease was spreading in port cities along the Atlantic. Inoculation worked by producing a mild but real (and therefore risky) case of smallpox, followed by lifelong immunity. Howe's instinct was right: During the American Revolution, some 130,000 people on the American continent, most of them Indians, died of smallpox. When hundreds of Bostonians began to contract the disease, Howe ordered them to leave town, causing American leaders to fear that the British intended to spread smallpox into the countryside as a "weapon of defense."

A week after Bunker Hill, when General Washington arrived to take charge of the new Continental army, he found enthusiastic but undisciplined troops. Sanitation was an unknown concept, with inadequate latrines fouling the campground. The amazed general attributed the disarray to the New England custom of letting militia units elect their own officers, which he felt undermined deference. Washington spotted a militia captain, a barber in civilian life, shaving an ordinary soldier, and he moved quickly to impose more hierarchy and authority. "Be easy," he advised his newly appointed officers, "but not too familiar, lest you subject yourself to a want of that respect, which is necessary to support a proper command."

While military plans moved forward, the Second Continental Congress pursued its contradictory objective: reconciliation with Britain. Delegates from the middle colonies (Pennsylvania, Delaware, and New York), whose merchants depended on trade with Britain, urged that channels for negotiation remain open. In July 1775, congressional moderates led by John Dickinson engineered an appeal to the king called the **Olive Branch Petition**. The petition affirmed loyalty to the monarchy and strategically blamed all the troubles on the king's ministers and on Parliament. It proposed that the American colonial assemblies be recognized as individual parliaments under the umbrella of the monarchy. But **King George III** rejected the Olive Branch Petition and heatedly condemned the Americans as traitors. Reconciliation was now out of the question.

Thomas Paine, Abigail Adams, and the Case for Independence

Pressure for independence started to mount in January 1776, when a pamphlet titled *Common Sense* appeared in Philadelphia. **Thomas Paine**, its author, was an English artisan and coffeehouse intellectual who had befriended Benjamin Franklin in London. He came to America in the fall of 1774 with letters of introduction from Franklin to several Philadelphia printers, one of whom hired him. He soon met delegates from the Second Continental Congress, and, with their encouragement, he wrote *Common Sense* to lay out a lively and compelling case for complete independence.

In simple yet forceful language, Paine elaborated on the absurdities of the British monarchy. Why should one man, by accident of birth, claim extensive power over others? he asked. A king might be foolish or wicked. "One of the strongest natural proofs of the folly of hereditary right in kings," Paine wrote, "is that nature disapproves it; otherwise she would not so frequently turn it into ridicule by giving mankind *an ass for a lion*." Calling the British king an ass broke through the automatic deference most Americans still had for the monarchy. To replace monarchy, Paine advocated republican government based on the consent of the people. Rulers, according to Paine, were only representatives of the people, and the best form of government relied on frequent elections to achieve the most direct democracy possible.

Paine's pamphlet sold more than 150,000 copies in a matter of weeks. Newspapers reprinted it; men read it aloud in taverns and coffeehouses; John Adams sent a copy to his wife, Abigail, who passed it around to neighbors in Braintree, Massachusetts. New Englanders desired independence, but other colonies, under no immediate threat of violence, remained cautious.

Washington's Inscribed Copy of *Common Sense*

Thomas Paine, a recent immigrant to America, wrote *Common Sense* to advance the debate on independence. The pamphlet sold hundreds of thousands of copies, and Paine donated the proceeds to the Revolutionary cause. Shown here is George Washington's personal copy, with his name inscribed at the top. Paine returned to Europe in 1787 and quickly became involved in the French Revolution, defending it in a major pamphlet called *The Rights of Man*. He later wrote *The Age of Reason*, a book that among other things seemed to avow atheism. Boston Athenaeum.

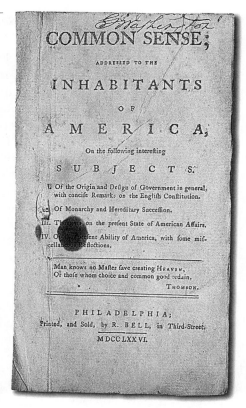

COMMON SENSE;

ADDRESSED TO THE

INHABITANTS

OF

AMERICA,

On the following interesting

SUBJECTS.

I. Of the Origin and Defign of Government in general, with concife Remarks on the Englifh Conftitution.

II. Of Monarchy and Hereditary Succeffion.

III. Thoughts on the prefent State of American Affairs.

IV. Of the prefent Ability of America, with fome mifcellaneous Reflections.

Man knows no Mafter fave creating HEAVEN,
Or thofe whom choice and common good ordain.
THOMSON.

PHILADELPHIA;
Printed, and Sold, by R. BELL, in Third-Street.
MDCCLXXVI.

Abigail Adams was impatient not only for independence but also for other legal changes that would revolutionize the new country. In a series of astute letters to her husband, she outlined obstacles and gave advice. She worried that southern slave owners might shrink from a war in the name of liberty: "I have sometimes been ready to think that the passion for Liberty cannot be Equally strong in the Breasts of those who have been accustomed to deprive their fellow Creatures of theirs." And in March 1776, she expressed her hope that women's legal status would improve under the new government: "In the new Code of Laws which I suppose it will be necessary for you to make I desire you would Remember the Ladies, and be more generous and favourable to them than your ancestors." Her chief concern was husbands' legal dominion over wives: "Do not put such unlimited power into the hands of the Husbands," she advised. "Remember all Men would be tyrants if they could." Abigail Adams anticipated a more radical end to tyranny than did Thomas Paine.

The Continental Congress was, in fact, not rewriting family law; that task was left to individual states in the 1780s. John Adams dismissed his wife's concerns. But to a male politician, Adams privately rehearsed the reasons why women (and men who were free blacks, or young, or propertyless) should remain excluded from political participation. Even though he concluded that nothing should change, at least Abigail's letter had forced him to ponder the exclusion, something few men — or women — did in 1776. Urgent talk of political independence was as radical as most could imagine.

The Declaration of Independence

In addition to Paine's *Common Sense*, another factor hastening independence was the prospect of an alliance with France, Britain's archrival. France was willing to provide military supplies and naval power only if assured that the Americans would separate from Britain. News that the British were negotiating to hire German mercenary soldiers further solidified support for independence. By May 1776, all but four colonies were agitating for a declaration. The holdouts were Pennsylvania, Maryland, New York, and South Carolina, the latter two containing large loyalist populations. An exasperated Virginian wrote to his friend in the congress, "For God's sake, why do you dawdle in the Congress so strangely? Why do you not at once declare yourself a separate independent state?" In early June, the Virginia delegation introduced a resolution calling for independence. The moderates still commanded enough support to postpone a vote on the measure until July. In the meantime, the congress appointed a committee, with Thomas Jefferson and others, to draft a longer document setting out the case for independence.

On July 2, after intense politicking, all but one state voted for independence; New York abstained. The congress then turned to the document drafted by Jefferson and his committee. Jefferson began with a preamble that articulated philosophical principles about natural rights, equality, the right of revolution, and the consent of the governed as the only true basis for government. He then listed more than two dozen specific grievances against King George. The congress merely glanced at the philosophical principles, as though ideas about natural rights and the consent of the governed were accepted as "self-evident truths," just as the document claimed. The truly radical phrase declaring the natural equality of "all men" was likewise passed over without comment.

For two days, the congress wrangled over the list of grievances, especially the issue of slavery. Jefferson had included an impassioned statement blaming the king for slavery, which delegates from Georgia and South Carolina struck out. They had no intention of denouncing their labor system as an evil practice. But the congress let stand another of Jefferson's fervent grievances, blaming the king for mobilizing "the merciless Indian Savages" into bloody frontier warfare, a reference to Pontiac's Rebellion (see chapter 6).

On July 4, the amendments to Jefferson's text were complete, and the congress formally adopted the **Declaration of Independence**. (See appendix, page A-1.) The New York delegation switched from abstention to endorsement on July 15, making the vote on independence unanimous. In early August, the delegates gathered to sign the official parchment copy. Four men, including John Dickinson, declined to sign; several others "signed with regret . . . and with many doubts," according to John Adams. The document was then printed, widely distributed, and read aloud in celebrations everywhere.

Printed copies did not include the signers' names, for they had committed treason, a crime punishable by death. On the day of signing, they indulged in gallows humor. When Benjamin Franklin paused before signing to look over the document, John Hancock of Massachusetts teased him, "Come, come, sir. We must be unanimous. No pulling different ways. We must all hang together." Franklin replied, "Indeed we must all hang together. Otherwise we shall most assuredly hang separately."

REVIEW   Why were many Americans initially reluctant to pursue independence from Britain?

▶ The First Year of War, 1775–1776

Both sides approached the war for America with uneasiness. The Americans, with inexperienced militias, were opposing the mightiest military power in the world. Also, their country was not unified; many people remained loyal to Britain. The British faced serious obstacles as well. Their disdain for the fighting abilities of the Americans required reassessment in light of the Bunker Hill battle. The logistics of supplying an army with food across three thousand miles of water were daunting. And since the British goal was to regain allegiance, not to destroy and conquer, the army was often constrained in its actions. These patterns — undertrained American troops and British troops strangely unwilling to press their advantage — played out repeatedly in the first year of war.

The American Military Forces

Americans claimed that the initial months of war were purely defensive, triggered by the British invasion. But the war also quickly became a rebellion, an over-throwing of long-established authority. As both defenders and rebels, many Americans were highly motivated to fight, and the potential manpower that could be mobilized was, in theory, very great.

Local defense in the colonies had long rested with a militia composed of all able-bodied men over age sixteen. Militias, however, were best suited for local and limited engagements, responding to conflict with Indians or slave rebellions. Such events were relatively infrequent, and the traditional militia training day in most communities had evolved into a holiday of drinking, marching, and shooting practice.

In forming the Continental army, the congress first set enlistment at one year, which proved to be too optimistic. Incentives produced longer commitments: a $20 bonus for three years of service, a hundred acres of land for enlistment for the duration of the war. For this inducement to be effective, of course, recruits had to believe that the Americans would win. Over the course of the war, some 230,000 men enlisted, about one-quarter of the white male adult population.

Women also served in the Continental army, cooking, washing, and nursing the wounded. The British army established a ratio of one woman to every ten men; in the Continental army, the ratio was set at one woman to fifteen men. Close to 20,000 "camp followers," as they were called, served during the war, many of them wives of men in service. Some 12,000 children also tagged along, and babies were born in the camps. Some women helped during battles, supplying drinking water or ammunition to soldiers. One soldier recalled a woman at the battle of Monmouth whose petticoats were shot off by a cannonball that whizzed between her outstretched legs. "Looking at it with apparent unconcern," he wrote of the gutsy woman, "she observed that it was lucky it did not pass a little higher, for in that case it might have carried away something else."

Black Americans at first were excluded from the Continental army by slave owner George Washington's orders. But as manpower needs abruptly increased, the Continental Congress permitted free blacks and even slaves to enlist, compensating their masters up to $400 for each man released. In Rhode Island and Connecticut, black Continental soldiers served in segregated units with white officers. While some of these men were involuntary substitutes sent by their owners, others were clearly inspired by ideals of freedom in a war against tyranny. For example, twenty-three Rhode Island blacks gave "Liberty," "Freedom," and "Freeman" as their surnames at the time of enlistment, expressing the hope that successful wartime service would bring them actual freedom and liberty. About 5,000 black men served in the Revolutionary War on the rebel side, nearly all from the northern states.

Military service helped politicize Americans during the early stages of the war. In early 1776, independence was a risky, potentially treasonous idea. But as the war heated up and recruiters demanded commitment, some Americans discovered that apathy had its dangers as well. Anyone who refused to serve ran the risk of being called a traitor to the cause. Military service became a prime way of demonstrating political allegiance.

The American army was at times raw and inexperienced, and often woefully undermanned. It never had the precision and discipline of European professional armies. But it was never as bad as the British continually assumed. The British would learn that it was a serious mistake to underrate the enemy.

The British Strategy

The American strategy was straightforward — to repulse and defeat an invading army. The British strategy was not as clear. Britain wanted to put down a rebellion and restore monarchical power in the colonies, but the question was how to accomplish this. A decisive defeat of the Continental army was essential but not sufficient to end the rebellion, for the British would still have to contend with an armed and motivated insurgent population. Furthermore, there was no single political nerve center whose capture would spell certain victory. The Continental Congress moved from place to place, staying just out of reach of the British. During the course of the war, the British captured and occupied every major port city, but that brought no serious loss to the Americans, 95 percent of whom lived in the countryside.

King George had told Parliament at the outset that once his army subdued the rebels, "I shall be ready to receive the misled with tenderness and mercy" as soon as "the unhappy and deluded multitude . . . shall become sensible of their error." While this was calmingly deceptive talk appropriate to the start of war, it did underscore the real tension in the British position. Britain's delicate task was to restore the old governments, not to destroy an enemy country. Hence, the British generals were at first reluctant to ravage the countryside, confiscate food, or burn villages. There were thirteen distinct political entities to capture, pacify, and then restore to the crown, and they stretched in a long line from New Hampshire to Georgia. Clearly, a large land army was required for the job. Without the willingness to seize food from the locals, the British needed hundreds of supply ships — hence their desire to capture the ports. The British strategy also assumed that many Americans remained loyal to the king and would come to their aid.

The overall British plan was a divide-and-conquer approach, focusing first on New York, the state judged to have the greatest number of loyal subjects. New York offered a geographic advantage as well: Control of the Hudson River would allow the British to isolate the rebellious New Englanders. British armies could descend from Canada and move up from New York City along the Hudson River into western Massachusetts. Squeezed between a naval blockade on the eastern coast and army raids in the west, Massachusetts could be driven to surrender. New Jersey and Pennsylvania would fall in line, the British thought, because of loyalist strength. Virginia was a problem, like Massachusetts, but the British were confident that the Carolinas would help them isolate and subdue Virginia.

Quebec, New York, and New Jersey

In late 1775, an American expedition was launched to capture the cities of Montreal and Quebec before British reinforcements could arrive (Map 7.1). This offensive was a clear sign that the war was not purely a reaction to the invasion of Massachusetts. A force of New York Continentals commanded by General Richard Montgomery took Montreal easily in September 1775 and then advanced on Quebec. Meanwhile, a second contingent of Continentals led by Colonel Benedict Arnold moved north through Maine to Quebec, a punishing trek through freezing rain with woefully inadequate supplies. Arnold showed heroic determination, but close to half of his men either died or turned back during the march. Arnold and Montgomery jointly attacked Quebec in December but failed to take the city. Worse yet, they encountered smallpox, which killed more men than had the battle for Quebec.

The main action of the first year of the war came not in Canada, however, but in New York, crucial to British strategy. In August 1776, some 45,000 British troops (including 8,000 German mercenaries, called **Hessians**) under the command of General Howe landed south of New York City. General Washington had anticipated this move and had relocated his army of 20,000 south from Massachusetts. The **battle of Long Island**, in late August 1776, pitted the well-trained British "redcoats" (slang referring to their red uniforms) against a very green Continental army. Howe attacked, inflicting many casualties (1,500 dead and wounded, with another 1,000 taken prisoner). A British general crowed, "If a good bleeding can bring those Bible-faced Yankees to their senses, the fever of independency should soon abate." Howe failed to press forward, however, perhaps remembering the costly victory of Bunker Hill, and Washington evacuated his troops to Manhattan Island in the dead of a foggy night. Knowing it would be hard to hold Manhattan, he withdrew farther north to two forts on either side of the Hudson River, allowing the British command to set up headquarters in the wealthy island city. For two months, the armies

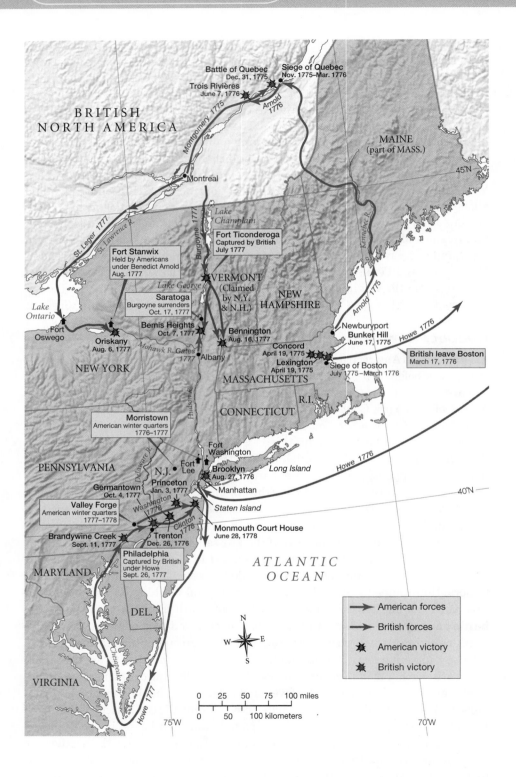

BRITISH
NORTH AMERICA

MAINE
(part of MASS.)

45°N

Montreal

Battle of Quebec
Dec. 31, 1775

Siege of Quebec
Nov. 1775–Mar. 1776

Trois Rivières
June 7, 1776

Arnold 1776

Montgomery 1775

Burgoyne 1777

Lake
Champlain

Fort Ticonderoga
Captured by British
July 1777

St. Leger 1777

St. Lawrence R.

Kennebec R.

Lake George

VERMONT
(Claimed
by N.Y.
& N.H.)

NEW
HAMPSHIRE

Fort Stanwix
Held by Americans
under Benedict Arnold
Aug. 1777

Saratoga
Burgoyne surrenders
Oct. 17, 1777

Bemis Heights
Oct. 7, 1777

Bennington
Aug. 16, 1777

Newburyport

Arnold 1775

Howe 1776

Lake
Ontario

Fort
Oswego

Oriskany
Aug. 6, 1777

Mohawk R. Gates
1777

Albany

Bunker Hill
June 17, 1775

Concord
April 19, 1775

Lexington
April 19, 1775

Siege of Boston
July 1775–March 1776

British leave Boston
March 17, 1776

NEW YORK

MASSACHUSETTS

R.I.

CONNECTICUT

Hudson R.

Morristown
American winter quarters
1776–1777

Fort
Washington

PENNSYLVANIA

Delaware R.

N.J.

Fort
Lee

Brooklyn
Aug. 27, 1776

Long Island

Howe 1776

40°N

Germantown
Oct. 4, 1777

Princeton
Jan. 3, 1777

Manhattan

Staten Island

Valley Forge
American winter quarters
1777–1778

Washington 1776

Clinton 1778

Monmouth Court House
June 28, 1778

Brandywine Creek
Sept. 11, 1777

Trenton
Dec. 26, 1776

Philadelphia
Captured by British
under Howe
Sept. 26, 1777

ATLANTIC
OCEAN

MARYLAND

DEL.

VIRGINIA

Chesapeake Bay

Howe 1777

N
W   E
S

75°W

70°W

	American forces
	British forces
	American victory
	British victory

0   25   50   75   100 miles
0   50   100 kilometers

Triumphal Entry of Royal Troops in New York, 1776
An artist in Germany portrayed British troops marching into New York City in September 1776, in rank and file as far as the eye can see. It looks like a peaceful take-over, with Americans watching quietly from windows and street corners. The picture shows a European-looking city, with blocks of far more substantial buildings than New York actually had. Clearly this artist was not familiar with the real New York. Just days before the British marched in, several hundred wooden buildings went up in smoke from a fire set by a disgruntled American woman. Museum of the City of New York, The J. Clarence Davies Collection.

engaged in limited skirmishing, but in November Howe finally captured Fort Washington and Fort Lee, taking another 3,000 prisoners.

Washington retreated quickly across New Jersey into Pennsylvania. Again Howe unaccountably failed to press his advantage. Had he attacked Washington's army at Philadelphia, he could have taken the city. Instead, he parked his German troops in winter quarters along the Delaware River. Perhaps he knew that many of the Continental soldiers' enlistment periods ended on December 31, making him confident that the Americans would not attack him. He was wrong.

◀ **MAP 7.1**
The War in the North, 1775–1778
After the early battles in Massachusetts in 1775, rebel forces invaded Canada but failed to capture Quebec. A large British army landed in New York in August 1776, turning New Jersey into a continual battle site in 1777 and 1778. Burgoyne arrived from England to secure Canada and attempted to pinch off New England along the Hudson River, but he was stopped at Saratoga in 1777 in the key battle of the early war.

On December 25, in an icy rain, Washington stealthily moved his army across the Delaware River and at dawn made a quick capture of the unsuspecting German soldiers. This impressive victory lifted the sagging morale of the patriot side. For the next two weeks, Washington remained on the offensive, capturing supplies in a clever attack on British units at Princeton. Soon he was safe in Morristown, in northern New Jersey, where he settled his army for the winter. Washington finally had time to administer mass smallpox inoculations and see his men through the abbreviated course of the disease.

All in all, in the first year of declared war, the rebellious Americans had a few proud moments but also many worries. The inexperienced Continental army had barely hung on in the New York campaign. Washington had shown exceptional daring and admirable restraint, but what really saved the Americans was the repeated reluctance of the British to follow through militarily when they had the advantage.

REVIEW Why did the British initially exercise restraint in their efforts to defeat the rebellious colonies?

▶ The Home Front

Battlefields alone did not determine the outcome of the war. Struggles on the home front were equally important. In 1776, each community contained small numbers of highly committed people on both sides and far larger numbers who were uncertain about whether independence was worth a war. Both persuasion and force were used to gain the allegiance of the many neutrals. Revolutionaries who took control of local government often used it to punish loyalists and intimidate neutrals, while loyalists worked to reestablish British authority. A major factor pushing neutrals to side with the revolution was the British treatment of prisoners of war. Adding to the turbulence of the times was a very shaky wartime economy. The creative financing of the fledgling government brought hardships as well as opportunities, forcing Americans to confront new manifestations of virtue and corruption.

Patriotism at the Local Level

Committees of correspondence, of public safety, and of inspection dominated the political landscape in patriot communities. These committees took on more than customary local governance; they enforced boycotts, picked army draftees, and policed suspected traitors. They sometimes invaded homes to search for contraband goods such as British tea or textiles.

Loyalists were dismayed by the increasing show of power by patriots. A man in Westchester, New York, described his response to intrusions by committees: "Choose your committee or suffer it to be chosen by a half dozen fools in your neighborhood — open your doors to them — let them examine your tea-cannisters and molasses-jugs, and your wives' and daughters' petty coats — bow and cringe and tremble and quake — fall down and worship our sovereign lord the mob. . . .

Should any pragmatical committee-gentleman come to my house and give himself airs, I shall show him the door." Oppressive or not, the local committees were rarely challenged. Their persuasive powers convinced many middle-of-the-road citizens that neutrality was not a comfortable option.

Another group new to political life — white women — increasingly demonstrated a capacity for patriotism as wartime hardships dramatically altered their work routines. Many wives whose husbands were away on military or political service took on masculine duties. Their competence to tend farms and make business decisions encouraged some to assert competence in politics as well. Abigail Adams managed the family farm in Massachusetts while John Adams was away for several years engaged in politics, in which Abigail took a keen interest. Eliza Wilkinson managed a South Carolina plantation and talked revolutionary politics with women friends. "None were greater politicians than the several knots of ladies who met together," she remarked, alert to the unusual turn female conversations had taken. "We commenced perfect statesmen."

Women from prominent Philadelphia families took more direct action, forming the **Ladies Association** in 1780 to collect money for Continental soldiers. A published broadside, "The Sentiments of an American Woman," defended their female patriotism: "The time is arrived to display the same sentiments which animated us at the beginning of the Revolution, when we renounced the use of teas [and] when our republican and laborious hands spun the flax."

The Loyalists

Around one-fifth of the American population remained loyal to the crown in 1776, and probably another two-fifths tried to stay neutral. With proper cultivation, this large base might have sustained the British empire in America. In general, **loyalists** of the elite classes often had strong cultural and economic ties to England; they thought that social stability depended on a government anchored by monarchy and aristocracy, and they feared democratic tyranny. Patriots seemed to them to be unscrupulous, violent, self-interested men who simply wanted power for themselves. There were many non-elite loyalists as well, with diverse and often highly local reasons for opposing the revolutionary leaders of their region.

The most visible loyalists (called **Tories** by their enemies) were royal officials, not only governors such as Thomas Hutchinson of Massachusetts but also local judges and customs officers. Wealthy merchants gravitated toward loyalism to maintain the trade protections of navigation acts and the British navy. Conservative urban lawyers admired the stability of British law and order. Among the ordinary colonists, some chose loyalism simply to oppose traditional adversaries. Backcountry Carolina farmers leaned loyalist out of resentment of the power of the lowlands gentry, generally of patriot persuasion. Tenant farmers of the Hudson River valley in New York, who harbored decades of grievances against rich landlords now active in the Continental Congress, also tended to side with the British. And, of course, southern slaves had their own resentments against the white slave-owning class and looked to Britain in hope of freedom.

Many Indian tribes hoped to remain neutral at the war's start, seeing the conflict as a civil war between the English and Americans. Eventually, however, most were drawn in, many taking the British side. The powerful Iroquois Confederacy divided: The Mohawk, Cayuga, Seneca, and Onondaga peoples lined up with the British; the Oneida and Tuscarora tribes aided Americans. One young Mohawk leader, **Thayendanegea** (known also by his English name, **Joseph Brant**), traveled to England in 1775 to complain to King George about land-hungry American settlers. "It is very hard when we have let the King's subjects have so much of our lands for so little value," he wrote; "they should want to cheat us in this manner of the small spots we have left for our women and children to live on." Brant pledged Indian support for the king in exchange for protection from encroaching settlers. In the Ohio Country, parts of the Shawnee and Delaware tribes started out pro-American but shifted to the British side by 1779 in the face of repeated betrayals by American settlers and soldiers.

Pockets of loyalism thus existed everywhere — in the middle colonies, in the backcountry of the southern colonies, and out beyond the Appalachian Mountains in Indian country. Even New England towns at the heart of the turmoil, such as Concord, Massachusetts, had a small and increasingly silenced core of loyalists who refused to countenance armed revolution. On occasion, husbands and wives, fathers and sons disagreed completely on the war.

Loyalists were most vocal between 1774 and 1776, when the possibility of a full-scale rebellion against Britain was still uncertain. They challenged the emerging patriot side in pamphlets and newspapers. In 1776 in New York City,

Rivington's New-York Loyal Gazette

Not all newspaper editors supported the Revolution. James Rivington of New York City heaped abuse on Washington and others, and earned a reputation for mean-spirited polemics. In return, rioters hanged him in effigy, broke up his press, and burned down his house. When New York became British headquarters, Rivington curried favor with the British command. Yet it appears now that long-standing rumors about his duplicity are likely true: by 1781, evidence suggests he was indeed passing codes to George Washington about British military plans. Courtesy, American Antiquarian Society.

547 loyalists signed and circulated a broadside titled "A Declaration of Dependence" in rebuttal to the congress's July 4 declaration, denouncing the "most unnatural, unprovoked Rebellion that ever disgraced the annals of Time."

Who Is a Traitor?

In June 1775, the Second Continental Congress declared all loyalists to be traitors. Over the next year, state laws defined as treason acts such as provisioning the British army, saying anything that undermined patriot morale, and discouraging men from enlisting in the Continental army. Punishments ranged from house arrest and suspension of voting privileges to confiscation of property and deportation. Sometimes self-appointed committees of Tory-hunters bypassed the judicial niceties and terrorized loyalists, raiding their houses or tarring and feathering them.

Were wives of loyalists also traitors? When loyalist families fled the country, their property was typically confiscated. But if the wife stayed, courts usually allowed her to keep one-third of the property, the amount due her if widowed, and confiscated the rest, so long as she was known to be "a steady and true and faithful friend to the American states," in the case of one Connecticut woman. This legal position supported a wife's autonomy to choose political sides, if she stayed in the United States. Yet what about a wife who favored the patriot side but was obligated by her fleeing loyalist husband to join him? After the Revolution, descendants of refugee loyalists filed several lawsuits to regain property that had entered the family through the mother's inheritance. In one well-publicized Massachusetts case in 1805, the outcome confirmed the traditional view of women as political blank slates. The American son of loyalist refugee Anna Martin recovered her dowry property on the grounds that she had no independent will to be a loyalist.

Tarring and feathering, property confiscation, deportation, terrorism — to the loyalists, such denials of liberty of conscience and of freedom to own private property proved that democratic tyranny was more to be feared than the monarchical variety. A Boston loyalist named Mather Byles aptly expressed this point: "They call me a brainless Tory, but tell me . . . which is better — to be ruled by one tyrant three thousand miles away, or by three thousand tyrants not a mile away?" Byles was soon sentenced to deportation.

Throughout the war, probably 7,000 to 8,000 loyalists fled to England, and 28,000 found haven in Canada. British strategy depended on using loyalists to hold occupied territory, but for many loyalists, that was impossible without British protection. In New Jersey, for example, 3,000 Jerseyites felt protected (or scared) enough by the occupying British army in 1776 to swear an oath of allegiance to the king. But then General Howe drew back to New York City, leaving them to the mercy of local patriot committees that pressured for new loyalty oaths to the Continental Congress. Despite the staunch backing of loyalists in 1776, the British could not build a winning strategy on their support.

Prisoners of War

The poor treatment of loyalists as traitors by the revolutionaries was more than matched by the horrendous treatment of American prisoners of war by the British.

Such captives were a predictable by-product of war, and George Washington fully expected the British to provide humane treatment, as was customary among European military powers. Among these civilities were provision of food, clothing, blankets, and laundry, all paid for by the captives' own government, and the possibility of release via prisoner exchanges. These customs recognized that captured soldiers were not common criminals subject to punishing incarceration. But British leaders refused to see the captives as foot soldiers employed by a sovereign nation. In their eyes, the captured Americans were traitors — and therefore worse than common criminals.

The British crowded their initial 4,000 prisoners on two dozen vessels anchored in the river between Manhattan and Brooklyn. The largest of these was the half-century-old HMS *Jersey*, stripped of its masts and guns. Built to house a crew of 400, the *Jersey*'s hull was packed with more than 1,100 prisoners of war. Survivors described the dark, stinking space below decks where more than half a dozen men died daily, wasted and parched from extreme thirst. Food and sanitation facilities were inadequate. A twenty-year-old captive seaman described his first view of the hold: "Here was a motley crew, covered with rags and filth; visages pallid with disease, emaciated with hunger and anxiety, and retaining hardly a trace of their original appearance. Here were men . . . now shriveled by a scanty and unwholesome diet, ghastly with inhaling an impure atmosphere, exposed to contagion and disease, and surrounded with the horrors of sickness and death."

The Continental Congress sent food and funds to supply rations to the prisoners, but only a fraction of the provisions reached the men; most of the supplies were diverted to British use. Washington fumed at General Howe and threatened severe treatment of British prisoners, but Howe remained uncooperative.

Treating the captives as criminals potentially triggered the Anglo-American right of habeas corpus, a central feature of English law since the thirteenth century, which guaranteed every prisoner the right to challenge his detention before a judge and to learn the charges against him. To remove that possibility, Parliament voted in early 1777 to suspend habeas corpus specifically for "persons taken in the act of high treason" in any of the colonies.

Despite the treatment of his own men, Washington insisted that captured British soldiers be treated humanely. From the initial group of Hessians taken on Christmas of 1776 to the several thousands more captured in American victories by 1778, America's prisoners of war were gathered in rural encampments that shifted location from Massachusetts to Virginia and points in between. Guarded by local townsmen, the captives typically could cultivate small gardens, move about freely during the day, and even hire themselves out to farmers suffering wartime labor shortages. Officers with money could purchase comfortable lodging with private families and mixed socially with Americans. Officers enjoyed the freedom to travel locally; many were even allowed to keep their guns as they waited for prisoner exchanges to release them.

As the war dragged on, such exchanges were negotiated out of necessity, when the British were desperate to regain valued officers. American officers benefited from these limited exchanges, but for ordinary soldiers and seamen, death — or the rare escape — was their fate. More than 15,000 men endured captivity in the prison ships during the war, and two-thirds of them died, a larger number than those who died in battle (estimated to be around 5,000). News of the horrors of the British death ships increased the revolutionaries' resolve and convinced some neutrals of the necessity of the war.

Financial Instability and Corruption

Wars cost money — for arms and ammunition, for food and uniforms, for soldiers' pay, for provisions for prisoners. The Continental Congress printed money, but its value quickly deteriorated because the congress held no reserves of gold or silver to back the currency. In practice, it was worth only what buyers and sellers agreed it was worth. When the dollar eventually bottomed out at one-fortieth of its face value, a loaf of bread that once sold for two and a half cents then sold for a dollar. States, too, were printing paper money to pay for wartime expenses, further complicating the economy.

As the currency depreciated, the congress turned to other means to procure supplies and labor. One method was to borrow hard money (gold or silver coins) from wealthy men in exchange for certificates of debt (public securities) promising repayment with interest. The certificates of debt were similar to present-day government bonds. To pay soldiers, the congress issued land grant certificates, written promises of acreage usually located in frontier areas such as central Maine or eastern Ohio. Both the public securities and the land grant certificates quickly became forms of negotiable currency. A soldier with no cash, for example, could sell his land grant certificate to get food for his family. These certificates soon depreciated, too.

Depreciating currency inevitably led to rising prices, as sellers compensated for the falling value of the money. The wartime economy of the late 1770s, with its unreliable currency and price inflation, was extremely demoralizing to Americans everywhere. In 1778, in an effort to impose stability, local committees of public safety began to fix prices on essential goods such as flour. Inevitably, some turned this unstable situation to their advantage. Money that fell fast in value needed to be spent quickly; being in debt was suddenly advantageous because the debt could be repaid in devalued currency. A brisk black market sprang up in prohibited luxury imports, such as tea, sugar, textiles, and wines, even though these items came from Britain. A New Hampshire delegate to the Continental Congress denounced the violation of the homespun association agreements of just a few years before: "We are a crooked and perverse generation, longing for the fineries and follies of those Egyptian task masters from whom we have so lately freed ourselves."

REVIEW   How did the patriots promote support for their cause in the colonies?

▶ The Campaigns of 1777–1779: The North and West

In early 1777, the Continental army faced bleak choices. General Washington had skillfully avoided defeat, but the minor victories in New Jersey lent only faint optimism to the American side. Meanwhile, British troops moved south from Quebec, aiming to isolate New England from the rest of the colonies by taking control of the Hudson River. Their presence drew the Continental army up into central New York, polarizing Indian tribes of the Iroquois nation and turning the Mohawk Valley into a bloody war zone. By 1779, tribes in western New York and in Indian country in the Ohio Valley were fully involved in the Revolutionary War. Most sided with the British and against the Americans. The Americans had some success in this period, such as the victory at Saratoga, but the involvement of Indians and the continuing strength of the British forced the American government to look to France for help.

Burgoyne's Army and the Battle of Saratoga

In 1777, British general **John Burgoyne** assumed command of an army of 7,800 soldiers in Canada and began the northern squeeze on the Hudson River valley. His goal was to capture Albany, near the intersection of the Hudson and Mohawk rivers (see Map 7.1). Accompanied by 1,000 "camp followers" (cooks, laundresses, and musicians) and some 400 Indian warriors, Burgoyne's army did not travel light. In addition to food and supplies for 9,200 people, the army carried food for the 400 horses hauling heavy artillery. Burgoyne also carted thirty trunks of personal belongings and fine wines.

In July, Burgoyne captured Fort Ticonderoga with ease. American troops stationed there spotted the approaching British and abandoned the fort without a fight. The British continued to move south, but the large army moved slowly on primitive roads through dense forests. Burgoyne lost a month hacking his way south; meanwhile, his supply lines back to Canada were severely stretched. Soldiers sent out to forage for food were beaten back by local militia units.

The logical second step in isolating New England should have been to advance troops up the Hudson from New York City to meet Burgoyne. American surveillance indicated that General Howe in Manhattan was readying his men for a major move in August 1777. But Howe surprised everyone by sailing south to attack Philadelphia.

To reinforce Burgoyne, British and Hessian troops stationed at Montreal traveled south and then east along the Mohawk River, joined there by Mohawks and Senecas of the Iroquois Confederacy. The British were counting on loyalism among the numerous Palatine Germans living in the Mohawk Valley to allow them an easy path to Albany (see Map 7.1). A hundred miles west of Albany, they encountered American Continental soldiers at Fort Stanwix, supported by Palatine German militiamen and Oneida Indians. Mohawk chief Joseph Brant led the Senecas and Mohawks in an ambush on the Germans and the Oneidas in a narrow ravine called Oriskany, killing nearly 500 out of

840 of them. On Brant's side, some 90 warriors were killed. Meanwhile, Continental defenders of Fort Stanwix forced their British and Indian attackers to retreat (see Map 7.1). The **Oriskany** and **Fort Stanwix** battles were very deadly; they were also complexly multiethnic, pitting Indians against Indians, German Americans (the Palatines) against German mercenaries, New York patriots against New York loyalists, and English Americans against British soldiers.

The British retreat at Fort Stanwix deprived General Burgoyne of the additional troops he expected. Camped at a small village called Saratoga, he was isolated, with food supplies dwindling and men deserting. His adversary at Albany, General Horatio Gates, began moving his army toward Saratoga. Burgoyne decided to attack first because every day his soldiers weakened. The British prevailed, but at the great cost of 600 dead or wounded redcoats. Three weeks later, an American attack on Burgoyne's forces at Saratoga cost the British another 600 men and most of their cannons. General Burgoyne finally surrendered to the American forces on October 17, 1777.

Americans on the side of the rebellion were jubilant. After the **battle of Saratoga**, the first decisive victory for the Continental army, a popular dance called "General Burgoyne's Surrender" swept through the country, and bookies in the major cities set odds at five to one that the war would be won in six months.

General Howe, meanwhile, had succeeded in occupying Philadelphia in September 1777. Figuring that the Saratoga loss was balanced by the capture of Philadelphia, the British government proposed a negotiated settlement — not including independence — to end the war. The American side refused.

Patriot optimism was not well founded. Spirits ran high, but supplies of arms and food ran precariously low. Washington moved his troops into winter quarters at Valley Forge, just west of Philadelphia. Quartered in drafty huts, the men lacked blankets, boots, stockings, and food. Some 2,000 men at Valley Forge died of disease; another 2,000 deserted over the bitter six-month encampment.

Washington blamed the citizenry for lack of support; indeed, evidence of corruption and profiteering was abundant. Army suppliers too often provided defective food, clothing, and gunpowder. One shipment of bedding arrived with blankets one-quarter their customary size. Food supplies arrived rotten. As one Continental officer said, "The people at home are destroying the Army by their conduct much faster than Howe and all his army can possibly do by fighting us."

The War in the West: Indian Country

Burgoyne's defeat in the fall of 1777 and Washington's long stay at Valley Forge up to June 1778 might suggest that the war paused for a time, and it did on the Atlantic coast. But in the interior western areas — the Mohawk Valley, the Ohio Valley, and Kentucky — the war of Indians against the American pro-independence side heated up. For native tribes, the struggle was not about taxation, representation, or monarchical rule; it was about independence, freedom, and land.

The ambush and slaughter at Oriskany in August 1777 marked the beginning of three years of terror for the inhabitants of the Mohawk Valley. Loyalists and Indians engaged in many raids on farms throughout 1778, capturing or killing the residents. In retaliation, American militiamen destroyed Joseph Brant's home village, Onanquaga. Although they failed to capture any warriors, they killed several children in hiding. A month later, Brant's warriors attacked the town of Cherry Valley, killing 16 soldiers and 32 civilians and taking 71 people captive.

The following summer, General Washington authorized a campaign to wreak "total destruction and devastation" on all the Iroquoian villages of central New York. Some 4,500 troops commanded by General John Sullivan implemented a deliberate campaign of terror in the fall of 1779. Forty Indian towns met with total obliteration; the soldiers looted and torched the dwellings and then burned cornfields and orchards. In a few towns, women and children were slaughtered, but in most, the inhabitants managed to escape, fleeing to the British at Fort Niagara. Thousands of Indian refugees, sick and starving, camped around the fort in one of the most miserable winters on record.

Much farther to the west, beyond Fort Pitt in the Ohio Valley, another complex story of alliances and betrayals between American militiamen and Indians unfolded. Some 150,000 native people lived between the Appalachian Mountains and the Mississippi River, and by 1779 neutrality was no longer an option. Most sided with the British, who maintained a garrison at Fort Detroit, but a portion of the Shawnee and Delaware tribes at first sought peace with the Americans. In mid-1778, the Delaware chief White Eyes negotiated a treaty at Fort Pitt, pledging Indian support for the Americans in exchange for supplies and trade goods. But escalating violence undermined the agreement. That fall, when American soldiers killed two friendly Shawnee chiefs, Cornstalk and Red Hawk, the Continental Congress hastened to apologize, as did the governors of Pennsylvania and Virginia, but the soldiers who stood trial for the murders were acquitted. Two months later, White Eyes, nominally an ally of and an informant for the Americans, died under mysterious circumstances. He was almost certainly murdered by militiamen, who repeatedly had trouble honoring distinctions between allied and enemy Indians.

West of North Carolina (today's Tennessee), the frontier war zone of the South, militias attacked Cherokee settlements in 1779, destroying thirty-six villages and burning fields and livestock. Indian raiders from north of the Ohio River, in alliance with the British, repeatedly attacked white settlements such as Boonesborough (in present-day Kentucky) (Map 7.2). In retaliation, a young

▶ **MAP 7.2**

The Indian War in the West, 1777–1782

The American Revolution involved many Indian tribes, most of them supporting the British. Iroquois Indians, with British aid, attacked American towns in New York's Mohawk Valley throughout 1778. In 1779, the Continental army destroyed forty Iroquois villages in central New York. Shawnee and Delaware Indians to the west of Fort Pitt tangled with American militia units in 1779, while tribes supported by the British at Fort Detroit conducted raids on Kentucky settlers, who hit back with raids of their own. Sporadic fighting continued in the West through 1782, ending with Indian attacks on Hannastown, Pennsylvania, and Fort Henry on the Ohio River.

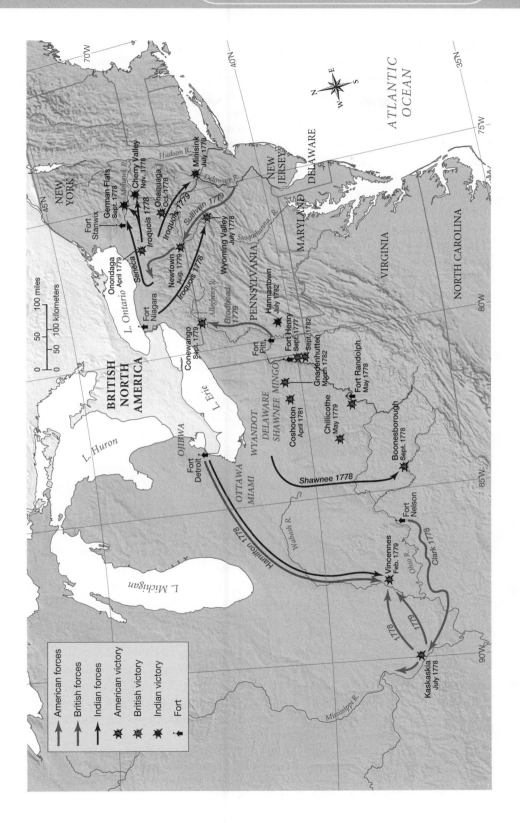

ATLANTIC OCEAN

BRITISH NORTH AMERICA

NEW YORK

NEW JERSEY

DELAWARE

MARYLAND

VIRGINIA

NORTH CAROLINA

PENNSYLVANIA

WYANDOT
DELAWARE
SHAWNEE MINGO

OJIBWA

OTTAWA
MIAMI

L. Huron

L. Michigan

L. Erie

L. Ontario

German Flats
Sept. 1778

Cherry Valley
Nov. 1778

Ohaquaga
Oct. 1778

Minisink
July 1779

Fort
Stanwix

Iroquois 1778

Iroquois 1779

Sullivan 1779

Seneca

Onondaga
April 1779

Newtown
Aug. 1779

Iroquois 1778

Wyoming Valley
July 1778

Fort
Niagara

Conewango
Sept. 1779

Brodhead
1779

Fort
Pitt

Fort Henry
Sept. 1777
Sept. 1782

Hannastown
July 1782

Gnadenhutten
March 1782

Coshocton
April 1781

Chillicothe
May 1779

Fort Randolph
May 1778

Boonesborough
Sept. 1778

Fort Detroit

Shawnee 1778

Hamilton 1778

Wabash R.

Ohio R.

Fort Nelson

Vincennes
Feb. 1779

Clark 1778

1778

1779

Kaskaskia
July 1778

Mississippi R.

Hudson R.

Mohawk R.

Delaware R.

Susquehanna R.

Allegheny R.

70W
75W
80W
85W.
90W.

35N
40N
45N

100 miles
100 kilometers
50
50
0
0

N
E
S
W

Legend:
- American forces
- British forces
- Indian forces
- American victory
- British victory
- Indian victory
- Fort

Virginian, George Rogers Clark, led Kentucky militiamen into what is now Illinois, attacking and taking the British fort at Kaskaskia. Clark's men wore native clothing — hunting shirts and breechcloths — but their dress was not a sign of solidarity with the Indians. When they attacked British-held Fort Vincennes in 1779, Clark's troops tomahawked Indian captives and threw their still-live bodies into the river in a gory spectacle witnessed by the redcoats. "To excel them in barbarity is the only way to make war upon Indians," Clark announced. And, he might have added, it was an effective way to terrorize British soldiers as well.

By 1780, very few Indians remained neutral. Violent raids by Americans drove Indians into the arms of the British at Detroit and Niagara, or into the arms of the Spaniards, who still held much of the land west of the Mississippi River. Said one officer on the Sullivan campaign, "Their nests are destroyed but the birds are still on the wing." For those who stayed near their native lands, chaos and confusion prevailed. Rare as it was, Indian support for the American side occasionally emerged out of a strategic sense that the Americans were unstoppable in their westward pressure and that it was better to work out an alliance than to lose in a war. But American treatment of even friendly Indians showed that there was no winning strategy for them.

The French Alliance

On their own, the Americans could not have defeated Britain, especially as pressure from hostile Indians increased. Essential help arrived as a result of the victory at Saratoga, which convinced the French to enter the war; a formal alliance was signed in February 1778. France recognized the United States as an independent nation and promised full military and commercial support. Most crucial was the French navy, which could challenge British supplies and troops at sea and aid the Americans in taking and holding prisoners of war.

Well before 1778, however, the French had been covertly providing cannons, muskets, gunpowder, and highly trained military advisers to the Americans. Monarchical France was understandably cautious about endorsing a democratic revolution attacking kingship. Instead, the main attraction of an alliance was the opportunity it provided to defeat archrival Britain. A victory would also open pathways to trade and perhaps result in France's acquiring the coveted British West Indies. Even an American defeat would not be a disaster for France if the war lasted many years and drained Britain of men and money.

French support materialized slowly. The navy arrived off the Virginia coast in July 1778 but then sailed south to the West Indies to defend the French sugar-producing islands. French help would prove indispensable to the American victory, but the alliance's first months brought no dramatic victories, and some Americans grumbled that the partnership would prove worthless.

REVIEW Why did the Americans need assistance from the French to ensure victory?

▶ The Southern Strategy and the End of the War

When France joined the war, some British officials wondered whether the fight was worth continuing. A troop commander, arguing for an immediate negotiated settlement, shrewdly observed that "we are far from an anticipated peace, because the bitterness of the rebels is too widespread, and in regions where we are masters the rebellious spirit is still in them. The land is too large, and there are too many people. The more land we win, the weaker our army gets in the field." The commander of the British navy argued for abandoning the war, and even Lord North, the prime minister, agreed. But the king was determined to crush the rebellion, and he encouraged a new strategy for victory focusing on the southern colonies, thought to be more persuadably loyalist. He had little idea of the depth of anger that would produce deadly guerrilla warfare between loyalists and patriots. The king's plan was brilliant but desperate, and ultimately unsuccessful.

Georgia and South Carolina

The new strategy called for British forces to abandon New England and focus on the South, with its large slave population thought to be ready to run to the king's forces. Such desertions, the British assumed, would disrupt the economy and unnerve rebellious white slave owners. Banking on loyalism among the nonslaveholding whites of Georgia and the Carolinas, the British hoped to build a safe foothold that would allow them to recapture the southern colonies one by one, moving north to the more problematic middle colonies and saving prickly New England for last.

Georgia, the first target, fell at the end of December 1778 (Map 7.3). A small army of British soldiers occupied Savannah and Augusta, and a new royal governor and loyalist assembly were quickly installed. Taking Georgia was easy because the bulk of the Continental army was in New York and New Jersey, keeping an eye on General **Henry Clinton**, Howe's replacement as commander in chief, and the French were still in the West Indies. The British in Georgia quickly organized twenty loyal militia units, and 1,400 Georgians swore an oath of allegiance to the king. So far, the southern strategy looked as if it might work.

Next came South Carolina. The Continental army put ten regiments into the port city of Charleston to defend it from attack by British troops shipped south from New York under the command of General Clinton. For five weeks in early 1780, the British laid siege to the city and took it in May 1780, in the process capturing 3,300 American soldiers, a tremendous loss for the patriots. Again, the king's new strategy seemed to be on target.

From Charleston, Clinton announced that slaves owned by rebel masters were welcome to seek refuge with his army. Several thousand responded by escaping to the coastal city. Untrained in formal warfare, they were of more immediate use to the British as knowledgeable guides to the surrounding countryside and as laborers in service to the army, building defensive earthworks and

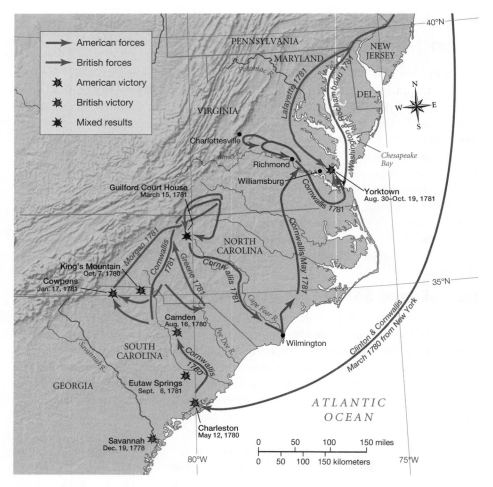

MAP 7.3
The War in the South, 1780–1781
After taking Charleston in May 1780, the British advanced into South Carolina and the foothills of North Carolina, leaving a bloody civil war in their wake. When the American general Horatio Gates and his men fled from the humiliating battle of Camden, Gates was replaced by General Nathanael Greene and General Daniel Morgan, who pulled off major victories at King's Mountain and Cowpens. The British general Cornwallis then moved north and invaded Virginia, but he was bottled up and finally overpowered at Yorktown in the fall of 1781.

fortifications. Escaped slaves with boat piloting skills were particularly valuable to the British as they navigated the inland river systems of the southern colonies.

Clinton returned to New York, leaving the task of pacifying the rest of South Carolina to General **Charles Cornwallis** and 4,000 troops. A bold commander, Lord Cornwallis quickly chased out the remaining Continentals and established military rule of South Carolina by midsummer. He purged rebels from government office and disarmed rebel militias. One officer under Cornwallis, Colonel

Banastre Tarleton, plundered food and supplies from large plantations, using insurgent blacks to terrify wealthy whites. As in Georgia, pardons were offered to Carolinians willing to prove their loyalty by taking up arms for the British.

By August 1780, American troops arrived from the North to strike back at Cornwallis. General Gates, the hero of Saratoga, led 3,000 troops, half of them experienced Continental soldiers and others newly recruited militiamen, into battle against Cornwallis at Camden, South Carolina, on August 16 (see Map 7.3). Right from the battle's start, militia units panicked; one unit managed to return fire, but others threw down unfired muskets and fled. The remaining Continentals, seriously outnumbered, faced heavy fire and soon gave up. When regiment leaders tried to regroup the next day, only 700 soldiers showed up; the rest were dead, wounded, captured, or still in flight. The **battle of Camden** was a devastating defeat, the worst of the entire war, and prospects seemed very grim for the Americans.

Treason and Guerrilla Warfare

Britain's southern strategy succeeded in 1780 in part because of information about American troop movements secretly conveyed by an American traitor: **Benedict Arnold**. The hero of several American battles, Arnold was a brilliant military talent but also a deeply insecure man who never felt he got his due in either honor or financial reward. Sometime in 1779, he opened secret negotiations with General Clinton in New York, trading information for money and hinting that he could deliver far more of value. When General Washington made him commander of West Point, a new fort on the Hudson River sixty miles north of

A Shaming Ritual Targeting the Great Traitor
In late September 1780, Philadelphians staged a ritual humiliation of Benedict Arnold, represented by an effigy with two faces and a mask, to manifest his duplicity. Behind him stands the devil, prodding him with a pitchfork and shaking a bag of coins near his ear, reminding all that Arnold sold out for money. While two fife players and a drummer keep the beat, soldiers and onlookers proceed to a bonfire, where the effigy was burned to ashes. Library of Congress.

New York City, Arnold's plan crystallized. West Point controlled the Hudson; its easy capture by the British might well have meant victory in the war.

Arnold's plot to sell a West Point victory to the British was foiled in the fall of 1780 when Americans captured the man carrying plans of the fort's defense from Arnold to Clinton. News of Arnold's treason created shock waves. Arnold represented all of the patriots' worst fears about themselves: greedy self-interest, like that of the war profiteers; the unprincipled abandonment of war aims, like that of turncoat southern Tories; panic, like that of the terrified soldiers at Camden. But instead of symbolizing all that was troubling about the American side of the war, Arnold's treachery was publicly denounced in a kind of displacement of the anxieties of the moment. Vilifying Arnold allowed Americans to stake out a wide distance between themselves and dastardly conduct. It inspired a renewal of patriotism at a particularly low moment.

Bitterness over Gates's defeat at Camden and Arnold's treason revitalized rebel support in western South Carolina, an area that Cornwallis thought was pacified and loyal. The backcountry of the South soon became the site of guerrilla warfare. In hit-and-run attacks, both sides burned and ravaged not only opponents' property but also the property of anyone claiming to be neutral. Loyalist militia units organized by the British were met by fierce rebel militia units whose members figured they had little to lose. In South Carolina, some 6,000 men became active partisan fighters, and they entered into at least twenty-six engagements with loyalist units. Some were classic battles, but on other occasions the fighters were more like bandits than soldiers. Guerrilla warfare soon spread to Georgia and North Carolina. Both sides committed atrocities and plundered property, clear deviations from standard military practice.

The British southern strategy depended on sufficient loyalist strength to hold reconquered territory as Cornwallis's army moved north. The backcountry civil war proved this assumption false. The Americans won few major battles in the South, but they ultimately succeeded by harassing the British forces and preventing them from foraging for food. In the fall of 1780, Cornwallis moved the war into North Carolina not because he thought South Carolina was secure — it was not — but because the North Carolinians were supplying the South Carolina rebels with arms and men (see Map 7.3). Then came word that 1,400 frontier riflemen had massacred loyalist troops at King's Mountain in western South Carolina, and the news sent Cornwallis hurrying back. The British were stretched too thin to hold even two of their onetime colonies.

Surrender at Yorktown

By early 1781, the war was going very badly for the British. Their defeat at King's Mountain was quickly followed by a second major defeat at the battle of Cowpens in South Carolina in January 1781. Cornwallis retreated to North Carolina and thence to Virginia, where he captured Williamsburg in June. A raiding party under Colonel Tarleton proceeded to Charlottesville, the seat of government, capturing members of the Virginia assembly but not Governor Thomas Jefferson, who escaped the soldiers by a mere ten minutes. (The slaves at Monticello, Jefferson's home, stood their ground and saved his house from plundering, but more than a dozen at two other plantations he owned sought refuge with the British.) These minor victories allowed Cornwallis to imagine he was succeeding in Virginia. His army, now swelled by some 4,000 escaped slaves, moved toward Yorktown, near Chesapeake Bay. As the general waited for backup troops by ship from British headquarters in New York City, smallpox and typhus began to set in among the black recruits.

At this juncture, the French-American alliance came into play. French regiments commanded by the Comte de Rochambeau had joined General Washington in Newport, Rhode Island, in mid-1780, and in early 1781 warships under the Comte de Grasse had sailed from France to the West Indies. Washington, Rochambeau, and de Grasse now fixed their attention on Chesapeake Bay. The French fleet got there ahead of the British troop ships from New York; a five-day naval battle left the French navy in clear control of the Virginia coast. This proved to be the decisive factor in ending the war, because the French ships prevented any rescue of Cornwallis's army.

On land, General Cornwallis and his 7,500 troops faced a combined French and American army of 16,000. For twelve days, the Americans and French bombarded the British fortifications at Yorktown; Cornwallis ran low on food and ammunition. He also began to expel the black recruits, some of them sick and dying. A Hessian officer serving under Cornwallis later criticized this British action as disgraceful: "We had used them to good advantage, and set them free, and now, with fear and trembling, they had to face the reward of their cruel masters." Many never made it back to their masters but died in the no-man's-land between the two armies, causing an American observer to record that "an immense number of Negroes have died in the most miserable manner in York." The twelve-day siege brought Cornwallis to the realization that neither victory nor escape was possible. He surrendered on October 19, 1781.

What began as a promising southern strategy in 1778 had turned into a discouraging defeat by 1781. British attacks in the South had energized American resistance, as did the timely exposure of Benedict Arnold's treason. The arrival of the French fleet sealed the fate of Cornwallis at the **battle of Yorktown**, and major military operations came to a halt.

The Losers and the Winners

The surrender at Yorktown spelled the end for the British, but two more years of skirmishes ensued. Frontier areas in Kentucky, Ohio, and Illinois still blazed with battles pitting Americans against various Indian tribes. The British army remained in control of three coastal cities — Savannah, Charleston, and New York — and in response, an augmented Continental army stayed at the ready, north of New York City. Occasional clashes occurred, like the ones in which light infantryman Deborah Sampson saw action, while cross-dressing as a male soldier. Skirmishes continued around Savannah and Charleston as well, involving white loyalists teamed up with runaway black insurgents.

The **Treaty of Paris**, also called the Peace of Paris, was two years in the making. Commissioners from America and Britain worked out the ten articles of peace, while a side treaty including Britain, France, Spain, and the Netherlands sealed related deals. The first article went to the heart of the matter: "His Britannic Majesty acknowledges the said United States to be free Sovereign and independent States." Other articles set the western boundary of the new country at the Mississippi River and guaranteed that creditors on both sides could collect debts owed them in sterling money, a provision especially important to British merchants. Britain agreed to withdraw its troops quickly, but more than a decade later this promise still had not been fully kept. A last-minute addition to the article about the British withdrawal prohibited the British from "carrying away any Negroes or other property of the American inhabitants." The treaty was signed on September 3, 1783.

News of the treaty signing was cause for celebration among most Americans, but not among the thousands of self-liberated blacks who had joined the British under promise of freedom. Boston King, a refugee from a South Carolina plantation, now huddled with his family at New York under protection of the British. He later wrote how the treaty's article prohibiting the British from evacuating any slaves "filled us with inexpressible anguish and terror." King and others pressed the British commander in New York, Sir Guy Carleton, to honor pretreaty British promises. Luckily, Carleton responded favorably. For all refugees able to state that they had been with the British for more than a year, he issued certificates of freedom — and hence they were no longer "property" to be returned. More than 4,000 blacks sailed out of New York for Nova Scotia, Boston King among them. As Carleton coolly explained to a protesting George Washington, "the Negroes in question . . . I found free when I arrived at New York, I had therefore no right, as I thought, to prevent their going to any part of the world they thought proper." British commanders in Savannah and Charleston followed Carleton's lead and aided the exit of perhaps 10,000 blacks from the United States.

The emancipation of slaves had never been a war goal of the British; destabilizing patriot planters and gaining manpower were their initial reasons for promises of freedom. Had the British won the war, they might well have reenslaved insurgent blacks to restore the profitable plantation economy of the South. For their part, blacks viewed British army camps as sites of refuge (not figuring on the devastations of epidemic diseases and food shortages) and had no reason to revere the British monarchy. In fact, some runaways had headed for Indian country instead.

The Treaty of Paris had nothing to say about the Indian participants in the Revolutionary War. Like the treaty ending the Seven Years' War, the 1783 treaty failed to recognize the Indians as players in the conflict. As one American told the Shawnee people, "Your Fathers the English have made Peace with us for themselves, but forgot you their Children, who Fought with them, and neglected you like Bastards." Indian lands were assigned to the victors as though they were uninhabited. Some Indian refugees fled west into present-day Missouri and Arkansas, and others, such as Joseph Brant's Mohawks, relocated to Canada. But significant numbers remained within the new United States, occupying their traditional homelands in areas west and north of the Ohio River. For them, the Treaty of Paris brought no peace at all; their longer war against the Americans would extend at least until 1795 and for some until 1813. Their ally, Britain, conceded defeat, but the Indians did not.

With the treaty finally signed, the British began their evacuation of New York, Charleston, and Savannah, a process complicated by the sheer numbers involved — soldiers, fearful loyalists, and runaway slaves by the thousands. In New York City, more than 27,000 soldiers and 30,000 loyalists sailed on hundreds of ships for England in the late fall of 1783. In a final act of mischief, on the November day when the last ships left, the losing side raised the British flag at the southern tip of Manhattan, cut away the ropes used to hoist it, and greased the flagpole.

REVIEW   Why did the British southern strategy ultimately fail?

▶ Conclusion: Why the British Lost

The British began the war for America convinced that they could not lose. They had the best-trained army and navy in the world; they were familiar with the landscape from the Seven Years' War; they had the willing warrior-power of most of the native tribes of the backcountry; and they easily captured every port city of consequence in America. A majority of colonists were either neutral or loyal to the crown. Why, then, did the British lose?

Beginning in 1775 and 1776, British royal officials fled the colonies, thereby abdicating civil power, which they never really regained. The Americans created their own government structures, from the Continental Congress to local committees and militias. Staffed by many who before 1775 had been the political elites, these new government agencies had remarkably little trouble establishing their authority to rule. The basic British goal — to turn back the clock to imperial rule — receded into impossibility as the war dragged on.

Another ongoing problem facing the British was the uncertainty of supplies. Unwilling to ravage the countryside until late in the war, the army depended on a steady stream of supply ships from home. Insecurity about food helps explain their reluctance to pursue the Continental army aggressively. And although any plan to repacify the colonies required the cooperation of the loyalists and neutrals, the British repeatedly failed to support them, leaving them to the mercy of vengeful rebels.

Finally, French aid looms large in any explanation of the British defeat. Even before the formal alliance, French artillery and ammunition proved vital to the Continental army. After 1780, the French army brought a new infusion of troops to a war-weary America, and the French navy made the Yorktown victory possible.

The war for America had lasted just over six years, from Lexington to Yorktown; negotiations and the evacuation took two more. It profoundly disrupted the lives of Americans everywhere. More than a war for independence from Britain, it required people to think about politics and the legitimacy of authority. The precise disagreement with Britain about representation and political participation had profound implications for the kinds of governance the Americans would adopt, both in the moment of emergency and later when states began to write their constitutions. The rhetoric employed to justify the revolution against Britain put the words *liberty*, *tyranny*, *slavery*, *independence*, and *equality* into common usage. These words carried far deeper meanings than a mere complaint over taxation without representation, meanings not lost on unfree groups — slaves, servants, wives — excluded from politics by their dependent status. In the decades to come, the Revolution unleashed a dynamic of equality and liberty that was largely unintended and unwanted by many of the political leaders of 1776. A half century later, the language of the Declaration of Independence would emerge as a potent force offering legitimacy to antislavery and woman's rights groups.

Reviewing Chapter 7

REVIEW QUESTIONS

1. Why were many Americans reluctant to pursue independence from Britain? (pp. 175–181)

2. Why did the British initially exercise restraint in their efforts to defeat the rebellious colonies? (pp. 181–186)

3. How did the patriots promote support for their cause in the colonies? (pp. 186–191)

4. Why did the Americans need assistance from the French to ensure victory? (pp. 192–196)

5. Why did the British southern strategy ultimately fail? (pp. 197–203)

MAKING CONNECTIONS

1. Even before the colonies had committed to independence, they faced the likelihood of serious military conflict. How did they mobilize for war? In your answer, discuss specific challenges they faced, noting the unintended consequences of their solutions.

2. Congress's adoption of the Declaration of Independence confirmed a decisive shift in the conflict between the colonies and Britain. Why did the colonies make this decisive break in 1776? In your answer, discuss some of the arguments for and against independence.

3. The question of whether the colonists would be loyal to the new government or to the old king was pivotal during the Revolutionary War. Discuss the importance of loyalty in the outcome of the conflict. In your answer, consider both military and political strategy.

4. American colonists and British soldiers were not the only participants in the Revolutionary War. How did Native Americans shape the conflict? What role did African Americans play? What benefits did these two groups hope to gain? Did they succeed?

LINKING TO THE PAST

1. Most Indian tribes joined with the French and opposed the British in the Seven Years' War; yet in the American Revolution, most tribes sided with the British and opposed the Americans. What accounts for this apparent shift in alliances? (See chapter 6.)

2. Consider the leading roles of Massachusetts and Virginia in the coming of the American Revolution. With such very different origins and such very different economic, demographic, and religious histories, how could these two so readily join in partnership in the break from British rule? (See chapters 3, 4, and 5.)

TIMELINE 1775–1783

1775
- Second Continental Congress convenes; creates Continental army.
- British win battle of Bunker Hill.
- King George III rejects Olive Branch Petition.
- Americans lose battle of Quebec.

1776
- *Common Sense* published.
- British evacuate Boston.
- July 4. Congress adopts Declaration of Independence.
- British take Manhattan.

1777
- British Parliament suspends habeas corpus for rebels.
- British take Fort Ticonderoga.
- Ambush at Oriskany; Americans hold Fort Stanwix.
- British occupy Philadelphia.
- British surrender at Saratoga.

1777–78
- Continental army endures winter at Valley Forge.

1778
- France enters war on American side.
- American militiamen destroy Mohawk chief Joseph Brant's village.
- White Eyes negotiates treaty with Americans; later mysteriously dies.
- British take Savannah, Georgia.

1779
- Militias attack Cherokee settlements in far western North Carolina.
- Americans destroy forty Iroquois villages in New York.
- Americans take Forts Kaskaskia and Vincennes.

1780
- Philadelphia Ladies Association raises money for soldiers.
- British take Charleston, South Carolina.
- French army arrives in Newport, Rhode Island.
- British win battle of Camden.
- Benedict Arnold exposed as traitor.
- Americans win battle of King's Mountain.

1781
- British forces invade Virginia.
- French fleet blockades Chesapeake Bay.
- Cornwallis surrenders at Yorktown; concedes British defeat.

1783
- Treaty of Paris ends war; United States gains all land east of Mississippi River.

▶ FOR AN ONLINE BIBLIOGRAPHY, PRACTICE QUIZZES, WEB SITES, IMAGES, AND DOCUMENTS RELATED TO THIS CHAPTER, see the Book Companion Site at **bedfordstmartins.com/roarkvalue**.

▶ FOR DOCUMENTS RELATED TO THIS PERIOD, see Michael Johnson, ed., *Reading the American Past*, Fifth Edition.

Building a Republic

1775–1789

JAMES MADISON GRADUATED FROM PRINCETON COLLEGE IN NEW
Jersey in 1771, not knowing what to do next with his life. Certainly, the
twenty-year-old had an easy fallback position. As the firstborn son of a
wealthy plantation owner, he could return to the foothills of Virginia and wait
to inherit substantial land and many slaves. But Madison was an intensely stu-
dious young man, uninterested in farming. Five years at boarding school had
given him fluency in Greek, Latin, French, and mathematics; and three years at
Princeton had acquainted him with the great thinkers, both ancient and
modern. Driven by a thirst for learning, young Madison hung around
Princeton for six months after graduation.

In 1772, he returned home, still adrift. He tried studying law, but his unim-
pressive oratorical talents discouraged him. Instead, he swapped reading lists
and ideas about political theory by letter with a Princeton classmate, prolong-
ing his student life. While Madison struggled for direction, the powerful winds
before the storm of the American Revolution swirled through the colonies. In
May 1774, Madison traveled north to deliver his brother to boarding school
and was in Philadelphia when the startling news broke that Britain had closed
the port of Boston in retaliation for the destruction of the tea. Turbulent
protests over the Coercive Acts turned him into a committed revolutionary.

Back in Virginia, Madison joined his father on the newly formed committee of public safety. For a few days in early 1775, the twenty-four-year-old
took up musket practice in a burst of enthusiasm for war, but it was quickly
plain that his greater contribution lay in the science of politics. In the spring of
1776, he gained election to the Virginia Convention, a Revolutionary assembly

James Madison, by Charles Willson Peale
Philadelphia artist Charles Willson Peale painted this miniature portrait of Madison in 1783, along with a matching miniature of Madison's fiancée, Kitty Floyd, the sixteen-year-old daughter of a New York delegate to the Continental Congress. Madison's portrait was mounted in a brooch (note the pin sticking out on the right) so that his lady love might wear it on her person, but Floyd returned the miniature to Madison when she broke off the engagement. Eleven years later, Madison tried romance again when New York congressman Aaron Burr introduced him to a young Virginia widow named Dolley Payne Todd. Madison was forty-three, and Todd was twenty-six; they married four months after meeting. Library of Congress.

replacing the defunct royal government. The convention's main task was to hammer out a state constitution with innovations such as frequent elections and limited executive power. Shy, self-effacing, and still learning the ropes, Madison mostly stayed on the sidelines, but Virginia's elder statesmen noted the young man's logical, thoughtful contributions. When his county failed to return him to the assembly in the next election, he was appointed to the governor's council, where he spent two years gaining experience in a wartime government.

In early 1780, Madison represented Virginia in the Continental Congress. Not quite twenty-nine, unmarried, and supported by his father's money, he was free of the burdens that made distant political service difficult for so many others. He stayed in the North for three years, working with men such as Alexander Hamilton of New York and Robert Morris of Pennsylvania as the congress wrestled with the chaotic economy and the ever-precarious war effort. In one crisis, Madison's negotiating skills proved crucial: He broke the deadlock over the ratification of the Articles of Confederation by arranging for the cession of Virginia's vast western lands. Those lands would soon appear on maps as the Northwest Territory, calling forth a series of western land ordinances, planned out by Madison's friend Thomas Jefferson, that exemplified the promise of and high hopes for the future of the new confederation government. But more often, service in the congress proved frustrating to Madison because the confederation government seemed to lack essential powers, chief among them the power to tax.

Madison resumed a seat in the Virginia assembly in 1784. But he did not retreat to a local point of view as so many other state politicians of the decade did. The economic hardships created by heavy state taxation programs — which in Massachusetts led to a full-fledged rebellion against state government — spurred Madison to pursue means to strengthen the government shared by the thirteen new states. In this, he was in the minority: To many Americans, it was not clear that the Articles of Confederation needed major revamping.

Madison thought the Articles did need overhauling. He worked hard to organize an all-state convention in Philadelphia in May 1787, where he took the lead in steering the delegates to a complete rewrite of the structure of the national government, investing it with considerably greater powers. True to form, Madison spent the months before the convention in feverish study of the great thinkers he had read in college, seeking the best way to constitute a government on republican principles. His lifelong passion for scholarly study, seasoned by a dozen years of energetic political experience, paid off handsomely. The United States Constitution was the result.

By the end of the 1780s, James Madison had had his finger in every kind of political pie on the local, state, confederation, and finally national level. He had transformed himself from a directionless and solitary youth into one of the leading political thinkers of the Revolutionary period. His personal history over the 1780s was deeply entwined with the path of the emerging United States.

▶ The Articles of Confederation

From 1775 to 1781, the Continental Congress met in Philadelphia and other cities without any formal constitutional basis. It took time to work out a plan of government that embodied Revolutionary principles. With monarchy gone, where would sovereignty lie? What would be the nature of representation? Who would hold the power of taxation? The resulting plan, called the **Articles of Confederation**, proved to be surprisingly difficult to implement, mainly because the thirteen states disagreed over boundaries in the land to the west of the states. Once the Articles were ratified and the active phase of the war had drawn to a close, the congress faded in importance compared with politics in the individual states.

Congress and Confederation

After the Declaration of Independence had been signed and circulated, the Continental Congress set a committee in motion to draft a document that would specify what powers the congress had and by what authority it existed. There was widespread agreement on key central governmental powers: pursuing war and peace, conducting foreign relations, regulating trade, and running a postal service. Yet the congress's attention was still mainly on the war, and so it took a year of tinkering before its members reached agreement on the Articles of Confederation in November 1777. The Articles defined the union as a loose confederation of states, characterized as "a firm league of friendship" existing mainly to foster a common defense. The structure of the government paralleled that of the existing Continental Congress. There was no national executive (that is, no president) and no national judiciary. Term limits of three years ensured rotation in congressional offices. State delegations could vary in size from two to seven, and each delegation cast a single vote. Routine decisions in the congress required a simple majority of seven states; for momentous decisions, such as declaring war, nine states needed to agree. To approve or amend the Articles required the unanimous consent both of the thirteen state delegations and of the thirteen state legislatures — giving any state an unrealistic and eventually crippling veto power. Most crucially, the Articles gave the national government no power of direct taxation.

Taxation was a necessity, since all governments require money and governments pursuing wars need even more. The congress issued bonds to finance most of the war's hefty and immediate costs (for supplies and manpower); the bonds were held in part by French and Dutch bankers but also by large numbers of middling to wealthy Americans. (Bondholders considered bonds with 6 percent interest an attractive investment, especially when they could be purchased with depreciating Continental dollars that were accepted at face value.) The congress also anticipated new peacetime expenses in addition to the large war debt and the expanding interest owed to bondholders. Trade regulation required a paid force of customs officers; a postal system required postmen, horses and wagons, and well-maintained postal roads; the western lands required surveyors; and Indian diplomacy (or war) added further large costs. Article 8 of the confederation document declared that taxes were needed to support "the common defence or general welfare" of the country, yet the congress also had to be sensitive to the rhetoric of the Revolution, which denounced heavy taxation by a distant and nonrepresentative power.

The congress hoped to solve this delicate problem with a two-step procedure. The congress would **requisition** (that is, request) money to be paid into the common treasury, and each state legislature would then levy taxes within its borders to pay the requisition. The Articles specified that state contributions were to be assessed in proportion to the property value of the state's land; thus, large and populous states paid more than did small or sparsely populated states. Requiring that the actual tax bill be passed by the state legislatures preserved the Revolution's principle of taxation only by direct representation. However, no mechanism compelled states to pay.

The lack of centralized authority in the confederation government was exactly what many state leaders wanted in the late 1770s. A league of states with rotating personnel, no executive branch, no power of direct taxation, and a requirement of unanimity for any major change seemed to be a good way to keep government in check. Yet there were problems, and the first was the requirement that every state ratify the Articles of Confederation. This mandatory unanimity stalled the acceptance of the Articles for four additional years, until 1781.

The Problem of Western Lands

The most serious disagreement over the Articles of Confederation involved the absence of any plan for the lands to the west of the thirteen original states. This absence was deliberate; an earlier draft of the Articles gave the congress the power to set state boundaries and to administer the sales of the western lands. But states with large land claims objected. A few states — Virginia and Connecticut, for example — had old colonial charters that located their western boundaries at the Mississippi River, and they insisted that their claims be recognized. Six more states also had plausible legal claims to extensive territories (Map 8.1). Five states lacked such land claims entirely, and they preferred that the congress preserve all the western lands as a national domain that would eventually be sold off to settlers and constitute new states, administered by the congress. Financial motives loomed large, for, as one Rhode Island delegate put it, "the western world opens an amazing prospect as a national fund; it is equal to our debt."

The eight land-claiming states were ready to sign the Articles of Confederation in 1777, since it protected their interests. Three states without claims — Rhode Island, Pennsylvania, and New Jersey — eventually capitulated and signed, "not from a Conviction of the Equality and Justness of it," said a New Jersey delegate, "but merely from an absolute Necessity there was of complying to save the Continent." But Delaware and Maryland continued to hold out, insisting on a national domain policy. In 1779, the disputants finally compromised: Any land a state volunteered to relinquish would become the national domain. When James Madison and Thomas Jefferson ceded Virginia's huge land claim in 1781, the Articles of Confederation were at last unanimously approved. (See appendix, page A-4.)

The western lands issue demonstrated that powerful interests divided the thirteen new states. The apparent unity of purpose inspired by fighting the war against Britain papered over sizable cracks in the new confederation.

Running the New Government

No fanfare greeted the long-awaited inauguration of the new government in 1781. The congress continued to sputter along, its problems far from solved by the signing of the Articles. Lack of a quorum often hampered day-to-day activities. The Articles required representation from seven states to conduct business and a minimum of two men from each state's delegation. But some days, fewer than fourteen men in total showed up. State legislatures were slow to select delegates, and many politicians preferred to devote their energies to state governments,

MAP 8.1

Cession of Western Lands, 1782–1802

The thirteen new states found it hard to ratify the Articles of Confederation without settling their conflicting land claims in the West, an area larger than the original states and occupied by Indian tribes. The five states objecting to the Articles' silence over western lands policy were Maryland, Delaware, New Jersey, Rhode Island, and Pennsylvania.

especially when the congress seemed deadlocked or, worse, irrelevant. Some had difficulty learning the art of formal debate. A Pennsylvanian reflected that "I find there is a great deal of difference between sporting a sentiment in a letter, or over a glass of wine upon politics, and discharging properly the duties of a senator."

It also did not help that the congress had no permanent home. During the war, when the British army threatened Philadelphia, the congress relocated to small Pennsylvania towns such as Lancaster and York and then to Baltimore. After hostilities ceased, the congress moved from Trenton to Princeton to Annapolis to New York City. Many delegates were reluctant to travel far from home, especially if they had wives and children. Consequently, some of the most committed delegates were young bachelors, such as James Madison, and men in their fifties and sixties whose families were grown, such as Samuel Adams.

To address the difficulties of an inefficient congress, executive departments of war, finance, and foreign affairs were created in 1781 to handle purely administrative functions. When the department heads were ambitious — as was Robert Morris, a wealthy Philadelphia merchant who served as superintendent of finance — they could exercise considerable executive power. The Articles of Confederation had deliberately refrained from setting up an executive branch, but a modest one was being invented by necessity.

REVIEW Why was the confederation government's authority so limited?

▶ The Sovereign States

In the first decade of independence, the states were sovereign and all-powerful. Only a few functions, such as declaring war and peace, had been transferred to the confederation government. As Americans discarded their British identity, they thought of themselves instead as Virginians or New Yorkers or Rhode Islanders. Familiar and close to home, state governments claimed the allegiance of citizens and became the arena in which the Revolution's innovations would first be tried. States defined who was a voter, and they also defined who would be free. Squaring slavery with Revolutionary ideals became a front-burner issue everywhere; northern states had more success ending this inconsistency than did southern states, where slavery was deeply entrenched in the economy.

The State Constitutions

In May 1776, the congress recommended that all states draw up constitutions based on "the authority of the people." By 1778, all had done so. Having been denied the unwritten rights of Englishmen, Americans wanted written contracts that guaranteed basic principles. A shared feature of all the state constitutions was the conviction that government ultimately rests on the consent of the governed. Political writers in the late 1770s embraced the concept of **republicanism** as the underpinning of the new governments. Republicanism meant more than popular elections and representative institutions. For some, republicanism invoked a way of thinking about who leaders should be: autonomous, virtuous citizens who placed civic values above private interests. For others, it suggested direct democracy, with nothing standing in the way of the will of the people. For all, it meant government that promoted the people's welfare.

Widespread agreement about the virtues of republicanism went hand in hand with the idea that republics could succeed only in relatively small units, so that the people could make sure their interests were being served. Nearly every state continued the colonial practice of a two-chamber assembly but greatly augmented the powers of the lower house. Two states, Pennsylvania and Georgia, abolished the more elite upper house altogether, and most states severely limited the term and powers of the governor. Instead, real power resided with the lower houses, constituted to be responsive to popular majorities, with annual elections and guaranteed rotation in office. If a representative displeased his constituents, he could be out of office in a matter of months. James Madison learned about such political turnover when he lost reelection to the Virginia assembly in 1777. Ever shy, he attributed the loss to his reluctance to socialize at taverns and glad-hand his constituents in the traditional Virginia style. His series of increasingly significant political posts from 1778 to 1787 all came as a result of appointment, not popular election.

Six of the state constitutions included **bills of rights** — lists of basic individual liberties that government could not abridge. Virginia passed the first bill of rights in June 1776, and many of the other states borrowed from it. Its language resembles the Declaration of Independence, which Thomas Jefferson was drafting that month in Philadelphia. The Virginia bill of rights states: "That all men are by nature equally free and independent, and have certain inherent rights, of which, when they enter into a state of society, they cannot by any compact deprive or divest their posterity; namely, the enjoyment of life and liberty, with the means of acquiring and possessing property, and pursuing and obtaining happiness and safety." Along with these inherent rights went more specific rights to freedom of speech, freedom of the press, and trial by jury.

Who Are "the People"?

When the Continental Congress called for state constitutions based on "the authority of the people," and when the Virginia bill of rights granted "all men" certain rights, who was meant by "the people"? Who exactly were the citizens of this new country, and how far would the principle of democratic government extend? Different people answered these questions differently, but in the 1770s certain limits to political participation were widely agreed upon.

One limit was defined by property. In nearly every state, candidates for the highest offices had to meet substantial property qualifications. In Maryland, candidates for governor had to be worth the large sum of £5,000, while voters had to own fifty acres of land or £30. In the most democratic state, Pennsylvania, voters and candidates simply needed to be property tax payers, large or small. Only property owners were presumed to possess the necessary independence of mind to make wise political choices. Are not propertyless men, asked John Adams, "too little acquainted with public affairs to form a right judgment, and too dependent upon other men to have a will of their own?" Property qualifications probably disfranchised from one-quarter to one-half of adult white males in all the states. Not all of them took their nonvoter status quietly. One Maryland man challenged the £30 rule: "Every poor man has a life, a personal liberty, and a right to his earnings; and is in danger of being injured by government in a variety of ways." Why restrict such a man from voting? Others noted that property-less men were fighting and dying in the Revolutionary War; surely they had legitimate political concerns. Finally, a few radical voices challenged the notion that wealth was correlated with good citizenship; maybe the opposite was true. But ideas like this were outside the mainstream. The writers of the new constitutions, themselves men of property, viewed the right to own and preserve property as a central principle of the Revolution.

Another exclusion from voting — women — was so ingrained that few stopped to question it. Yet the logic of allowing propertied females to vote did occur to a handful of well-placed women. Abigail Adams wrote to her husband, John, in 1782, "Even in the freest countrys our property is subject to the controul and disposal of our partners, to whom the Laws have given a sovereign Authority. Deprived of a voice in Legislation, obliged to submit to those Laws which are imposed upon us, is it not sufficient to make us indifferent to the publick Welfare?" A wealthy Virginia widow named Hannah Corbin wrote to her brother, congressional delegate Richard Henry Lee, to complain of her taxation without the corresponding representation. Her letter no longer exists, but Lee wrote in his reply that women would be "out of character . . . to press into those tumultuous assemblies of men where the business of choosing representatives is conducted."

Only three states specified that voters had to be male, so powerful was the unspoken assumption that only men could vote. Still, in one state, small numbers of women began to turn out at the polls in the 1780s. New Jersey's constitution of 1776 enfranchised all free inhabitants worth more than £50, language that in theory opened the door to free blacks as well as unmarried women who met the property requirement. (Married women owned no property, for by law their husbands held title to everything.) Little fanfare accompanied this radical shift, and some historians have inferred that the inclusion of unmarried women and blacks was an oversight. Yet other parts of the suffrage clause pertaining to residency and property were extensively debated when the clause was put in the state constitution, and no objections were raised at that time to its gender- and race-free language. Thus other historians have concluded that the law was intentionally inclusive. In 1790, a revised election law used the words *he or she* in reference to voters, making woman suffrage explicit. As one New Jersey legislator declared, "Our Constitution gives this right to maids or widows *black* or *white*." However, that legislator was complaining, not bragging, so his words do not mean that egalitarian suffrage was an accepted fact.

In 1790, only about 1,000 free black adults of both sexes lived in New Jersey, a state with a population of 184,000. The number of unmarried adult white women was probably also small and comprised mainly widows. In view of the property requirement, the voter blocs enfranchised under this law were minuscule. Still, this highly unusual situation lasted until 1807, when a new state law specifically disfranchised both blacks and women. Henceforth, independence of mind, that essential precondition of voting, was redefined to be sex- and race-specific.

In the 1780s, voting everywhere was class-specific because of property restrictions. John Adams urged the framers of the Massachusetts constitution not even to discuss the scope of suffrage but simply to adopt the traditional colonial property qualifications. If suffrage is brought up for debate, he warned, "there will be no end of it. New claims will arise; women will demand a vote; lads from twelve to twenty-one will think their rights not enough attended to; and every man who has not a farthing, will demand an equal voice with any other."

Equality and Slavery

Restrictions on political participation did not mean that propertyless people enjoyed no civil rights and liberties. The various state bills of rights applied to all individuals who were free; unfree people were another matter.

The author of the Virginia bill of rights was George Mason, a planter who owned 118 slaves. When he wrote that "all men are by nature equally free and independent," he meant that white Americans were the equals of the British and could not be denied the liberties of British citizens. Other Virginia legislators, worried about misinterpretations, added the phrase specifying that rights belonged only to people who had entered civil society. As one wrote, with relief, "Slaves, not being constituent members of our society, could never pretend to any benefit from such a maxim." One month later, the Declaration of Independence used essentially the same phrase about equality, this time without the modifying clause about entering society. Two state constitutions, for Pennsylvania and Massachusetts, also picked it up. In Massachusetts, one town suggested rewording the draft constitution to read "All men, whites and blacks, are born free and equal." The suggestion was not implemented.

Slowly, the Revolutionary ideals about natural equality and liberty began to erode the institution of slavery. Often, enslaved blacks led the challenge. In 1777, several Massachusetts slaves petitioned for their "natural & unalienable right to that freedom which the great Parent of the Universe hath bestowed equally on all mankind." They modestly asked for freedom for their children at age twenty-one and were turned down. In 1779, similar petitions in Connecticut and New Hampshire met with no success. Seven Massachusetts free men, including the mariner brothers Paul and John Cuffe, refused to pay taxes for three years on the grounds that they could not vote and so were not represented. The Cuffe brothers landed in jail in 1780 for tax evasion, but their petition to the Massachusetts legislature spurred the extension of suffrage to taxpaying free blacks in 1783.

Another way to bring the issue before lawmakers was to sue in court. In 1781, a woman called **Elizabeth Freeman** (Mum Bett) was the first to win freedom in a Massachusetts court, basing her case on the just-passed state constitution that declared "all men are born free and equal." Another Massachusetts slave, Quok Walker, charged his master with assault and battery, arguing that he was a freeman under that same constitutional phrase. Walker won and was set free, a decision confirmed in an appeal to the state's superior court in 1783. Several similar cases followed, and by 1789 slavery had been effectively abolished by a series of judicial decisions in Massachusetts.

Black Loyalists in Canada: Passport to Freedom
This rare sketch from 1788 portrays a black woodcutter who resided in Nova Scotia along with three thousand other black loyalists who had escaped to northeastern Canada between 1783 and 1785. Very few of the Nova Scotia refuges were able to acquire land, and after 1786 the British authorities stopped provisioning them. Most, like the man pictured here, were forced to become servants or day laborers for whites. Low wages created dissatisfaction, and racial tensions mounted. In 1791–1792, nearly a third of the black refugees in Nova Scotia left for Sierra Leone in West Africa, where British officials promised them land and opportunities for self-rule. William Booth, National Archives of Canada C-401621.

Pennsylvania's legislature enacted a **gradual emancipation** law in 1780, providing that infants born to a slave mother on or after March 1, 1780, would be freed at age twenty-eight. Not until 1847 did Pennsylvania fully abolish slavery, but slaves did not wait for such slow implementation. Untold numbers in Pennsylvania simply ran away and asserted their freedom. One estimate holds that more than half of young slave men in Philadelphia joined the ranks of free blacks, and by 1790, free blacks outnumbered slaves in Pennsylvania two to one.

Rhode Island and Connecticut adopted gradual emancipation laws in 1784. In 1785, New York expanded the terms under which individual owners could free slaves, but only in 1799 did the state adopt a gradual emancipation law; New Jersey followed suit in 1804. These were the two northern states with the largest number of slaves: New York in 1800 with 20,000, New Jersey with more than 12,000. In contrast, slaves in Pennsylvania numbered just 1,700. Gradual emancipation illustrates the tension between radical and conservative implications of republican ideology. Republican government protected people's liberties and property, yet slaves were both people and property. Gradual emancipation attempted to balance the civil rights of blacks and the property rights of their owners by delaying the promise of freedom.

South of Pennsylvania, in Delaware, Maryland, and Virginia, where slavery was critical to the economy, emancipation bills were rejected. All three states, however, eased legal restrictions and allowed individual acts of emancipation for adult slaves below the age of forty-five under new manumission laws passed in 1782 (Virginia), 1787 (Delaware), and 1790 (Maryland). By 1790, close to 10,000 newly freed Virginia slaves had formed local free black communities complete with schools and churches.

In the deep South — the Carolinas and Georgia — freedom for slaves was unthinkable among whites. Yet several thousand slaves had defected to the British during the war, and between 3,000 and 4,000 shipped out of Savannah and Charleston, destined for freedom. Adding northern blacks evacuated from New York City in 1783, the probable total of emancipated blacks who left the United States was between 8,000 and 10,000. Some went to Canada, some to England, and some to Sierra Leone on the west coast of Africa. Many hundreds took refuge with the Seminole and Creek Indians, becoming permanent members of their communities in Spanish Florida and western Georgia.

Although all these instances of emancipation were gradual, small, and certainly incomplete, their symbolic importance was enormous. Every state from Pennsylvania north acknowledged that slavery was fundamentally inconsistent with Revolutionary ideology. On some level, white southerners also understood this, but their inability to imagine a free biracial society prevented them from taking action. George Washington owned 390 slaves and freed not one of them in the 1780s, even when his friend the French general Lafayette urged him to do so as a model for others. In his will, written in 1799, Washington provided for the eventual freedom of his slaves — but only after his wife, Martha, died. She freed them one year later, preferring loss of income to the uneasy situation of her life being the only barrier to her slaves' freedom.

Emancipation in the 1780s, limited as it was, shows that the phrase of the Declaration of Independence — "all men are created equal" — was beginning to acquire real force as a basic principle. Yet a geographic pattern was taking shape: From the 1780s on, the North was associated with freedom and the South with slavery, with profound consequences for the next two centuries of American history.

REVIEW How did states determine who would be allowed to vote?

▶ The Confederation's Problems

In 1783, the confederation government faced three interrelated concerns: paying down the large war debt, making formal peace with the Indians, and dealing with western settlement. The federal debt remained a vexing problem, since the Articles of Confederation lacked the power to enforce its tax requisitions. Making matters worse, the debt suddenly escalated in 1783 when army officers threatened to stage a coup to secure pensions. Western lands suggested a promising source of income to reduce the federal debt, but competing land claims made it difficult for states to use the proceeds of land sales to retire state debts. The Indian inhabitants of those same lands had different ideas, of course.

From 1784 to 1786, the congress struggled mightily with these three issues. Some leaders were gripped by a sense of crisis, fearing that the Articles of Confederation were too weak. Others defended the Articles as the best guarantee of liberty because real governance occurred at the state level, closer to the people. A major outbreak of civil disorder in western Massachusetts quickly crystallized the debate and propelled the critics of the Articles into decisive and far-reaching action.

The War Debt and the Newburgh Conspiracy

For nearly two years, the Continental army camped at Newburgh, a town just north of the British-occupied city of New York, awaiting news of a finalized peace treaty that would send the British army home. The soldiers at Newburgh were bored, restless, and upset about the confederation government's wobbly financial standing. Military payrolls were far in arrears, and an earlier promise of generous pensions (half pay for life), made to all officers in 1780 in a desperate effort to retain them, seemed increasingly unlikely to be honored. In December 1782, officers petitioned the congress for immediate back pay for their men so that when peace arrived, no one would go home penniless. The petition carried an unspecified threat: "The uneasiness of the soldiers, for want of pay, is great and dangerous; any further experiments on their patience may have fatal effects."

Instead of rejecting the petition outright for lack of money, several members of the congress saw an opportunity to make an especially forceful case to the states for the necessity of taxation. One of these was **Robert Morris**, a Philadelphia merchant with a gift for financial dealings, who was the government's superintendent of finance. Morris single-handedly kept the books and wheedled loans from European bankers, using his own substantial fortune as collateral. He knew better than anyone how insolvent the United States was. In 1781 and later in 1786, Morris led an effort to amend the Articles to allow the government to collect a 5 percent **impost** (an import tax), yet each time it failed by one vote. The dissenters, Rhode Island and New York, collected state import duties at their bustling ports, so it was in their interest to block a national impost. Both states acknowledged the seriousness of the confederation's taxation problem — just not at the same time. The failure of the impost vote showed how unworkable the amendment provision of the Articles was. In this context, the petition from the army officers offered a new opening to pressure the states for the power to tax.

The result was a plot called the **Newburgh Conspiracy**, the country's first and only instance of a threatened military coup. Morris and several other congressmen offered encouragement to officers to act as if the army would march on the congress to demand its pay. No actual coup was envisioned; both sides simply wanted a more powerful central government to arise from the threat. Yet the risks were great, for not everyone would understand that this was a ruse. What if the soldiers, incited by their grievances, could not be held in check? One congressman was confident that the risk was worth taking. He wrote privately (and guardedly) about the officers' petition: "I am glad to see things in their present train. It must terminate in giving to Government that power without which Government is just a name."

General George Washington, sympathetic to the plight of unpaid soldiers and officers, had approved the initial petition. But the plotters, knowing of his reputation for integrity, did not inform him of their collusion with congressional leaders. In March 1783, when the general learned of these developments, he delivered an emotional speech to a meeting of five hundred officers, reminding them in stirring language of honor, heroism, and sacrifice. He urged them to put their faith in the congress, and he denounced the plotters as "subversive of all order and discipline." In essence, Washington asserted the key principle that civilian government takes precedence over the military. His audience was left speechless and tearful, and the plot was immediately defused.

In the midst of the crisis, congressman Robert Morris put forward his own threat, to resign. He complained that a government that could incur debts with no assured way to pay them, including the debts owed the soldiers, was unworkable: "I will never be the Minister of Injustice." Morris was not universally admired, for just a few years earlier he had left the congress amid accusations that he had unfairly profited from public service. But his threat to quit now, at this crucial juncture, sent shock waves around the country. Morris continued to work to find money to pay the soldiers, as did Washington. In the end, a trickle of money from a few states was too little and too late, coming after the army began to disband. For its part, the congress voted to endorse a plan to *commute*, or transform, the lifetime pension promised the officers into a lump-sum payment of full pay for five years. But no lump sum of money was available. Instead, the officers were issued "commutation certificates," promising future payment with interest, which quickly depreciated like other forms of public debt in the 1780s.

In 1783, the soldiers' pay issue added some $5 million to the rising public debt, forcing the congress to press for larger requisitions from the states. The confederation, however, had one new source of enormous untapped wealth: the extensive western territories, attractive to the fast-growing white population but currently inhabited by Indians.

The Treaty of Fort Stanwix

Although the Indians were excluded from the 1783 Treaty of Paris, the confederation government now recognized the need to formalize treaties that would end ongoing hostilities between Indians and settlers and secure land cessions. The congress was particularly concerned with the land inhabited by the **Iroquois Confederacy**, a league of six tribes, but now claimed by the states of New York and Massachusetts based on their colonial charters (see Map 8.1). The Massachusetts charter was older by four decades, but New York felt entitled because the disputed land bordered its territory. The tension between the two states was such that it struck a southern delegate as "the seeds of dissension which I think will not end without a civil war."

At issue was the revenue stream that land sales would generate. The congress summoned the Iroquois to a meeting in October 1784 at Fort Stanwix, on the upper reaches of the Mohawk River. The Articles of Confederation gave the congress (as opposed to individual states) the right to manage diplomacy, war, and "all affairs with the Indians, not members of any of the States." Although Massachusetts accepted the confederation's authority, New York's governor seized on the ambiguous language in the Articles, claiming that the Iroquois were in fact "members" of his state and that New York had sole rights to negotiate. He called his own meeting with the Iroquois at Fort Stanwix in September. Suspecting that New York might be superseded by the congress, the most important chiefs declined to come and instead sent deputies without authority to negotiate. The Mohawk leader Joseph Brant shrewdly identified the problem of divided authority that afflicted the confederation government: "Here lies some Difficulty in our Minds, that there should be two separate bodies to manage these Affairs." No deal was struck with New York.

Three weeks later, U.S. commissioners opened proceedings at Fort Stanwix with the Seneca chief Cornplanter and Captain Aaron Hill, a Mohawk leader, accompanied by six hundred Indians from the six tribes. The U.S. commissioners arrived with a security detail of one hundred New Jersey militiamen.

The Americans demanded a return of prisoners of war; recognition of the confederation's authority to negotiate, rather than that of individual states; and an all-important cession of a strip of land from Fort Niagara due south, which established U.S.-held territory adjacent to the border with Canada. This crucial change enclosed the Iroquois land within the United States and made it impossible for the Indians to claim to be *between* the United States and Canada. When the tribal leaders balked, one of the commissioners sternly replied, "You are mistaken in supposing that, having been excluded from the treaty between the United States and the King of England, you are become a free and independent nation and may make what terms you please. It is not so. You are a subdued people."

In the end, the treaty was signed, gifts were given, and six high-level Indian hostages were kept at the fort awaiting the release of the American prisoners taken during the Revolutionary War, mostly women and children. In addition, a significant side deal sealed the release of much of the Seneca tribe's claim to the Ohio Valley to the United States. This move was a major surprise and aggravation to the Delaware, Mingo, and Shawnee Indians who lived there. In the months to come, tribes not at the meeting tried to disavow the **Treaty of Fort Stanwix** as a document signed under coercion by virtual hostages. But the confederation government ignored those complaints and made plans to survey and develop the Ohio Territory.

New York's governor astutely figured that the congress's power to implement the treaty terms was limited. The confederation's financial coffers were nearly empty, and its leadership was stretched. So New York quietly began surveying and then selling the very land it had failed to secure by individual treaty with the Iroquois. As that fact became generally known, it pointed up the weakness of the confederation government. One Connecticut leader wondered, "What is to defend us from the ambition and rapacity of New York, when she has spread over that vast territory, which she claims and holds? Do we not already see in her the seeds of an over-bearing ambition?"

Land Ordinances and the Northwest Territory

The congress ignored western New York and turned instead to the Ohio Valley to make good on the promise of western expansion. Delegate Thomas Jefferson, charged with drafting a policy, proposed dividing the territory north of the Ohio River and east of the Mississippi — called the **Northwest Territory** — into nine new states with evenly spaced east-west boundaries and townships ten miles square. He at first advocated giving the land to settlers, rather than selling it, arguing that future property taxes on the improved land would be payment enough. Jefferson's aim was to encourage rapid and democratic settlement, to build a nation of freeholders (as opposed to renters), and to discourage land speculation. Jefferson also insisted on representative governments in the new states; they would not become colonies of the older states. Finally, Jefferson's draft prohibited slavery in the nine new states.

The congress adopted parts of Jefferson's plan in the Ordinance of 1784: the rectangular grid, the nine states, and the guarantee of self-government and eventual statehood. What the congress found too radical was the proposal to give away the land; the national domain was the confederation's only source of independent wealth. The slavery prohibition also failed, by a vote of seven to six states.

A year later, the congress revised the legislation with procedures for mapping and selling the land. The Ordinance of 1785 called for three to five states, divided into townships six miles square, further divided into thirty-six sections of 640 acres, each section enough for four family farms (Map 8.2). Property was thus reduced to easily mappable squares. Land would be sold by public auction at a minimum price of one dollar an acre, with highly desirable land bid up for more. Two further restrictions applied: The minimum purchase was 640 acres, and payment had to be in hard money or in certificates of debt from Revolutionary days. This effectively meant that the land's first owners would be prosperous speculators. The grid of invariant squares further enhanced speculation, allowing buyers and sellers to operate without ever setting foot on the acreage. The commodification of land had been taken to a new level.

Speculators usually held the land for resale rather than inhabiting it. Thus they avoided direct contact with the most serious obstacle to settlement: the dozens of Indian tribes that claimed the land as their own. The treaty signed at Fort Stanwix in 1784 was followed in 1785 by the Treaty of Fort McIntosh, which similarly coerced partial cessions of land from the Delaware, Wyandot, Chippewa, and Ottawa tribes. Finally, in 1786, a united Indian meeting near Detroit issued an ultimatum: No cession would be valid without the unanimous consent of the tribes. The Indians advised the United States to "prevent your surveyors and other people from coming upon our side of the Ohio river." For two more decades, violent Indian wars in Ohio and Indiana would continue to impede white settlement (see chapter 9).

In 1787, a third land act, called the **Northwest Ordinance**, set forth a three-stage process by which settled territories would advance to statehood. First, the congress would appoint officials for a sparsely populated territory who would adopt

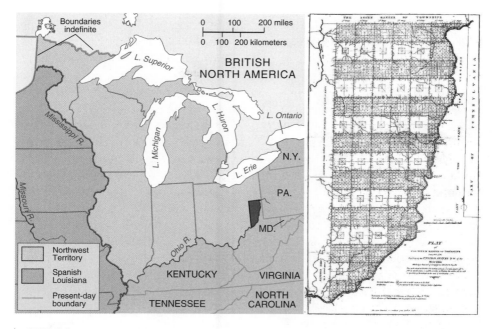

MAP 8.2

The Northwest Territory and Ordinance of 1785

Surveyors ventured into the eastern edge of the Northwest Territory in the 1780s and produced this first plat map (at right), showing the 6-mile square townships neatly laid out. Each township was subdivided into one-mile squares each containing sixteen 40-acre farms. Jefferson got his straight lines and right angles after all; compare this map to his on page 224. Cleveland Public Library, Map Collection.

a legal code and appoint local magistrates to administer justice. When the free male population of voting age and landowning status (fifty acres) reached 5,000, the territory could elect its own legislature and send a nonvoting delegate to the congress. When the population of voting citizens reached 60,000, the territory could write a state constitution and apply for full admission to the Union. At all three territorial stages, the inhabitants were subject to taxation to support the Union, in the same manner as were the original states.

The Northwest Ordinance of 1787 was perhaps the most important legislation passed by the confederation government. It ensured that the new United States, so recently released from colonial dependency, would not itself become a colonial power — at least not with respect to white citizens. The mechanism it established allowed for the successful and orderly expansion of the United States across the continent in the next century.

Nonwhites were not forgotten or neglected in the 1787 ordinance. The brief document acknowledged the Indian presence in the Northwest Territory and promised that "the utmost good faith shall always be observed towards the

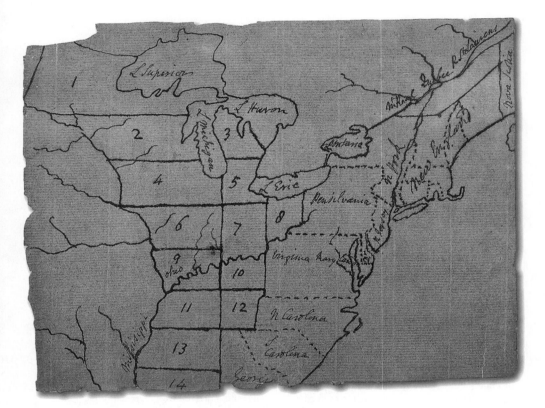

Jefferson's Map of the Northwest Territory
Thomas Jefferson sketched out borders for nine new states in his initial plan for the Northwest Territory in 1784 and additional anticipated states below the Ohio River. Straight lines and right angles held a strong appeal for him. But such regularity ignored inconvenient geographic features such as rivers and even more inconvenient political facts such as Indian territorial claims, most unlikely to be ceded by treaty in orderly blocks. Jefferson also submitted a list of distinctive names for the states. Number 9, for example, was Polypotamia, "land of many rivers" in Greek. Other proposed names were Sylvania, Michigania, Assenisipia, and Metropotamia. William L. Clements Library.

Indians; their lands and property shall never be taken from them without their consent; and, in their property, rights, and liberty, they shall never be invaded or disturbed, unless in just and lawful wars authorized by Congress." The 1787 ordinance further pledged that "laws founded in justice and humanity, shall from time to time be made for preventing wrongs being done to them, and for preserving peace and friendship with them." Such promises were full of noble intentions, but they were not generally honored in the decades to come.

Jefferson's original and remarkable suggestion to prohibit slavery in the Northwest Territory resurfaced in the 1787 ordinance, passing this time without any debate. Probably the addition of a fugitive slave provision in the act set southern congressmen at ease: Escaped slaves caught north of the Ohio River would be returned south. Also, abundant territory south of the Ohio remained available for the spread of slavery. The ordinance thus acknowledged and supported slavery even as it barred it from one region. Still, the prohibition of slavery in the Northwest Territory perpetuated the dynamic of gradual emancipation in the North. North-South sectionalism based on slavery was slowly taking shape.

The Requisition of 1785 and Shays's Rebellion, 1786–1787

Without an impost amendment and with public land sales projected but not yet realized, the confederation turned again to the states in the 1780s to contribute revenue to the central government. The amount requested was $3 million, four times larger than the previous year's requisition. Of this sum, 30 percent was needed for the operating costs of the government. Another 30 percent was earmarked to pay debts owed to foreign lenders, who insisted on payment in gold or silver. The remaining 40 percent was to go to Americans who owned government bonds, the IOUs of the Revolutionary years. A significant slice of that 40 percent represented the interest (but not the principal) owed to army officers for their recently issued "commutation certificates." This was a tax that, if collected, was going to hurt.

At this time, states were struggling under state tax levies. Several states without major ports (and the import duties that ports generated) were already asking a great deal of their farmer citizens in order to retire state debts from the Revolution. New Jersey and Connecticut fit this profile, and both state legislatures voted to ignore the requisition. In other states, like New Hampshire, town meetings voted to refuse to pay, on the grounds that the towns didn't have the money. In late 1786, a group of two hundred armed insurgents surrounded the New Hampshire capitol to protest the taxes but were driven off by a hastily called and armed militia. The shocked assemblymen pulled back from an earlier order to haul delinquent taxpayers into courts. Some states (Rhode Island, North Carolina, and Georgia) responded to their constituents' protests by issuing abundant amounts of paper money and allowing taxes to be paid in greatly depreciated currency.

Nowhere were the tensions so extreme as in Massachusetts. For four years in a row, a fiscally conservative legislature, dominated by the coastal commercial centers, had passed tough tax laws to pay state creditors who required payment in hard money, not cheap paper. Then in March 1786, the legislature in Boston loaded the federal requisition onto the bill. In June, farmers in southeastern Massachusetts marched on a courthouse in an effort to close it down, and petitions of complaint about oppressive taxation poured in from the western two-thirds of the state. In July 1786, when the legislature adjourned, having yet again ignored their complaints, dissidents held a series of conventions and called for revisions to the state constitution to promote democracy, eliminate the elite upper house, and move the capital farther west in the state.

Still unheard in Boston, the dissidents in six counties targeted the county courts, the local symbol of state authority. In the fall of 1786, several thousand armed men in each protest event forced bewildered judges to close their courts until the state constitution was revised. Sympathetic local militias did not intervene. The insurgents were not predominantly poor or debt-ridden farmers; they included veteran soldiers and officers in the Continental army as well as town leaders. One was a farmer and onetime army captain, Daniel Shays.

The governor of Massachusetts, James Bowdoin, once a protester against British taxes, now characterized the western dissidents as illegal rebels. He vilified Shays as the chief leader (he was not), and a Boston newspaper claimed that Shays planned to burn Boston to the ground and overthrow the government, a report that created panic. Another former radical, Samuel Adams, took the extreme position that "the man who dares rebel against the laws of a republic ought to suffer death." Those aging revolutionaries had little considered that representatives in a state legislature could seem to be as oppressive as monarchs. The dissidents challenged the assumption that popularly elected governments would always be fair and just.

Members of the Continental Congress had much to worry about. In nearly every state, the requisition of 1785 spawned some combination of crowd protests, threats to state authorities, demands for inflationary paper money, and emotional diatribes about greedy money speculators. The Massachusetts insurgency was the worst episode, and it seemed to be spinning out of control. In October 1786, the congress began to anticipate the need for armed intervention. But when it called for enlistments to triple the size of the federal army, fewer than 100 men responded. So Governor Bowdoin raised a private army, gaining the services of some 3,000 men with pay provided by wealthy and fearful Boston merchants.

In January 1787, the insurgents learned of the private army marching west from Boston, and 1,500 of them moved swiftly to capture a federal armory in Springfield to obtain weapons. But a militia band loyal to the state government beat them to the weapons facility and met their attack with gunfire; 4 rebels were killed and another 20 wounded. The final and bloodless encounter came at Petersham, where Bowdoin's army surprised the rebels on a freezing February morning and took 150 prisoners; the others fled into the woods, but most were soon rounded up and jailed. Daniel Shays escaped capture by fleeing to the self-declared independent republic of Vermont.

In the end, 2 men were executed for rebellion; 16 more sentenced to hang were reprieved at the last moment on the gallows. Some 4,000 men gained leniency by confessing their misconduct and swearing an oath of allegiance to the state. A special Disqualification Act prohibited the penitent rebels from voting, holding public office, serving on juries, working as schoolmasters, or operating taverns for up to three years.

Shays's Rebellion caused leaders throughout the country to worry about the confederation's ability to handle civil disorder. Inflammatory Massachusetts newspapers wrote about bloody mob rule; perhaps, some feared, similar "combustibles" in other states were awaiting the spark that would set off a dreadful political conflagration. New York lawyer John Jay wrote to George Washington, "Our affairs seem to lead to some crisis, some revolution — something I cannot foresee or conjecture. I am uneasy and apprehensive; more so than during the war." Benjamin Franklin, in his eighties, shrewdly observed that in 1776 Americans had feared "an excess of power in the rulers" but now the problem was perhaps "a defect of obedience" in the subjects. Among such leaders, the sense of crisis in the confederation had greatly deepened.

REVIEW Why did farmers in western Massachusetts revolt against the state legislature?

▶ The United States Constitution

Shays's Rebellion provoked an odd mixture of fear and hope that the government under the Articles of Confederation was losing its grip on power. A small circle of Virginians decided to try one last time to augment the powers granted to the government by the Articles. Their call for a meeting to discuss trade regulation led, more quickly than they could have imagined in 1786, to a total reworking of the national government.

From Annapolis to Philadelphia

Led by **James Madison**, the Virginians convinced the confederation congress to allow a September 1786 meeting of delegates at Annapolis, Maryland, to try again to revise the trade regulation powers of the Articles. Only five states participated, and the delegates rescheduled the meeting for Philadelphia in May 1787. The congress reluctantly endorsed the Philadelphia meeting and limited its scope to "the sole and express purpose of re-vising the Articles of Confederation." But at least one representative at the Annapolis meeting had more ambitious plans. **Alexander Hamilton** of New York hoped the Philadelphia meeting would do whatever was necessary to strengthen the federal government. Young Hamilton was suited for such bold steps. Born in impoverished circumstances in the West Indies, he had made his way into the elite circles of New York society (via talent, hard work, and a well-connected marriage) and now fully identified with the elite and their fear of democratic disorder.

The fifty-five men who assembled at Philadelphia in May 1787 for the **constitutional convention** were generally those who had already concluded that there were weaknesses in the Articles of Confederation. Few attended who were opposed to revising the Articles. Patrick Henry, author of the Virginia Resolves in 1765 and more recently state governor, refused to go to the convention, saying he "smelled a rat." Rhode Island declined to send delegates. Two men sent by New York's legislature to check the influence of fellow-delegate Alexander Hamilton left in dismay in the middle of the convention, leaving Hamilton as the sole representative of the state.

This gathering of white men included no artisans, day laborers, or ordinary farmers. Two-thirds of the delegates were lawyers. Half had been officers in the Continental army. The majority had served in the confederation congress and knew its strengths and weaknesses. Seven men had been governors of their states and

The Pennsylvania Statehouse
The constitutional convention assembled at the Pennsylvania statehouse to sweat out the summer of 1787. Despite the heat, the delegates nailed the windows shut to eliminate the chance of being heard by eavesdroppers, so intent were they on secrecy. The statehouse, built in the 1740s to house the colony's assembly, accommodated the Continental Congress at various times in the 1770s and 1780s. The building is now called Independence Hall in honor of the signing of the Declaration of Independence there in 1776. Historical Society of Pennsylvania.

knew firsthand the frustrations of thwarted executive power. A few elder statesmen attended, such as Benjamin Franklin and George Washington, but on the whole the delegates were young, like Madison and Hamilton.

The Virginia and New Jersey Plans

The convention worked in secrecy, which enabled the men to freely explore alternatives without fear that their honest opinions would come back to haunt them. The Virginia delegation first laid out a fifteen-point plan for a complete restructuring of the government. This **Virginia Plan** was a total repudiation of the principle of a confederation of states. Largely the work of Madison, the plan set out a three-branch government composed of a two-chamber legislature, a powerful executive, and a judiciary. It practically eliminated the voices of the smaller states by pegging representation in both houses of the congress to population. The theory was that government operated directly on people, not on states. Among the breathtaking powers assigned to the congress were the rights to veto state legislation and to coerce states militarily to obey national laws. To prevent the congress from having absolute power, the executive and judiciary could jointly veto its actions.

In mid-June, delegates from New Jersey, Connecticut, Delaware, and New Hampshire — all small states — unveiled an alternative proposal. The **New Jersey Plan**, as it was called, maintained the existing single-house congress of the Articles of Confederation in which each state had one vote. Acknowledging the need for an executive, it created a plural presidency to be shared by three men elected by the congress from among its membership. Where it sharply departed from the existing government was in the sweeping powers it gave to the new congress: the right to tax, regulate trade, and use force on unruly state governments. In favoring national power over states' rights, it aligned itself with the Virginia Plan. But the New Jersey Plan retained the confederation principle that the national government was to be an assembly of states, not of people.

For two weeks, delegates debated the two plans, focusing on the key issue of representation. The small-state delegates conceded that one house in a two-house legislature could be apportioned by population, but they would never agree that both houses could be. Madison was equally vehement about bypassing representation by state, which he viewed as the fundamental flaw in the Articles.

The debate seemed deadlocked, and for a while the convention was "on the verge of dissolution, scarce held together by the strength of a hair," according to one delegate. Only in mid-July did the so-called **Great Compromise** break the stalemate and produce the basic structural features of the emerging **United States Constitution**. Proponents of the competing plans agreed on a bicameral legislature. Representation in the lower house, the House of Representatives, would be apportioned by population, and representation in the upper house, the Senate, would come from all the states equally. Instead of one vote per state in the upper house, as in the New Jersey Plan, the compromise provided two senators who voted independently.

Representation by population turned out to be an ambiguous concept once it was subjected to rigorous discussion. Who counted? Were slaves, for example, people or property? As people, they would add weight to the southern delegations in the House of Representatives, but as property they would add to the tax burdens of those states. What emerged was the compromise known as the **three-fifths clause**: All free persons plus "three-fifths of all other Persons" constituted the numerical base for the apportionment of representatives.

Using "all other Persons" as a substitute for "slaves" indicates the discomfort delegates felt in acknowledging in the Constitution the existence of slavery. The words *slave* and *slavery* appear nowhere in the document, but slavery figured in two places besides the three-fifths clause. Government power over trade regulation naturally included the slave trade, which the Constitution euphemistically described as "the Migration or Importation of such Persons as any of the States now shall think proper to admit." Another provision contrived to guarantee the return of fugitive slaves using awkward, lawyer-like prose: "No person, held to Service or Labour in one State, under the Laws thereof, escaping into another, shall, in Consequence of any Law or Regulation therein, be discharged from such Service or Labour but shall be delivered up on Claim of the party to whom such Service or Labour may be due." Although slavery was nowhere named, it was nonetheless recognized, protected, and thereby perpetuated by the U.S. Constitution.

Democracy versus Republicanism

The delegates in Philadelphia made a distinction between *democracy* and *republicanism* new to the American political vocabulary. Pure democracy was now taken to be a dangerous thing. As a Massachusetts delegate put it, "The evils we experience flow from the excess of democracy." The delegates still favored republican institutions, but they created a government that gave direct voice to the people only in the House and that granted a check on that voice to the Senate, a body of men elected not by direct popular vote but by the state legislatures. Senators served for six years, with no limit on reelection; they were protected from the whims of democratic majorities, and their long terms fostered experience and maturity in office.

Similarly, the presidency evolved into a powerful office out of the reach of direct democracy. The delegates devised an electoral college whose only function was to elect the president and vice president. Each state's legislature would choose the electors, whose number was the sum of representatives and senators for the state, an interesting blending of the two principles of representation. The president thus would owe his office not to the Congress, the states, or the people, but to a temporary assemblage of distinguished citizens who could vote their own judgment on the candidates. His term of office was four years, but he could be reelected without limitation.

The framers had developed a far more complex form of federal government than that provided by the Articles of Confederation. To curb the excesses of democracy, they devised a government with limits and checks on all three of its branches. They set forth a powerful president who could veto legislation passed in Congress, but they gave Congress the power to override presidential vetoes. They set up a national judiciary to settle disputes between states and citizens of different states. They separated the branches of government not only by functions and by reciprocal checks but also by deliberately basing the election of each branch on different universes of voters — voting citizens (the House), state legislators (the Senate), and the electoral college (the presidency).

The convention carefully listed the powers of the president and of Congress. The president could initiate policy, propose legislation, and veto acts of Congress; he could command the military and direct foreign policy; and he could appoint the entire judiciary, subject to Senate approval. Congress held the purse strings: the power to levy taxes, to regulate trade, and to coin money and control the currency. States were expressly forbidden to issue paper money. Two more powers of Congress — to "provide for the common defence and general Welfare" of the country and "to make all laws which shall be necessary and proper" for carrying out its powers — provided elastic language that came closest to Madison's wish to grant sweeping powers to the new government.

While no one was entirely satisfied with every line of the Constitution, only three dissenters refused to sign the document. The Constitution specified a mechanism for ratification that avoided the dilemma faced earlier by the confederation government: Nine states, not all thirteen, had to ratify it, and special ratifying conventions elected only for that purpose, not state legislatures, would make the crucial decision.

> **REVIEW** Why did the government proposed by the constitutional convention employ multiple checks on each branch?

▶ Ratification of the Constitution

Had a popular vote been taken on the Constitution in the fall of 1787, it probably would have been rejected. In populous Virginia, Massachusetts, and New York, substantial majorities opposed a powerful new national government. North Carolina and Rhode Island refused to call ratifying conventions. Seven states were easy victories for the Constitution, but securing the approval of the nine required for ratification proved difficult. Pro-Constitution forces, called Federalists, had to strategize very shrewdly to defeat anti-Constitution forces, called Antifederalists.

The Federalists

Proponents of the Constitution moved into action swiftly. To silence the criticism that they had gone beyond their charge, they submitted the document to the congress. The congress withheld explicit approval but resolved to send the Constitution to the states for their consideration. The pro-Constitution forces shrewdly secured another advantage by calling themselves **Federalists**. By all logic, this label was more suitable for the backers of the confederation concept, because the Latin root of the word *federal* means "league." Their opponents thus became known as Antifederalists, a label that made them sound defensive and negative, lacking a program of their own.

To gain momentum, the Federalists targeted the states most likely to ratify quickly. Delaware provided unanimous ratification by early December, before the Antifederalists had even begun to campaign. Pennsylvania, New Jersey, and Georgia followed within a month. Delaware and New Jersey were small states surrounded by more powerful neighbors; a government that would regulate trade and set taxes according to population was an attractive proposition. Georgia sought the protection that a stronger national government would afford against hostile Indians and Spanish Florida to the south. "If a weak State with the Indians on its back and the Spaniards on its flank does not see the necessity of a General Government there must I think be wickedness or insanity in the way," said Federalist George Washington.

Another three easy victories came in Connecticut, Maryland, and South Carolina. As in Pennsylvania, merchants, lawyers, and urban artisans in general favored the new Constitution, as did large landowners and slaveholders. This tendency for the established political elite to be Federalist enhanced the prospects of victory, for Federalists already had power and influence disproportionate to their number. Antifederalists in these states tended to be rural, western, and noncommercial, men whose access to news was limited and whose participation in state government was tenuous.

Massachusetts was the first state to give the Federalists serious difficulty. The vote to select the ratification delegates decidedly favored the Antifederalists, whose strength lay in the western areas of the state, home to Shays's Rebellion. One rural delegate from Worcester County voiced widely shared suspicions: "These lawyers and men of learning and money men that talk so finely, and gloss over matters so smoothly, to make us poor illiterate people swallow down the pill, expect to get into Congress themselves; they expect to be the managers of the Constitution and get all the power and all the money into their own hands, and then they will swallow up all us little folks." Nevertheless, the Antifederalists' lead was slowly eroded by a vigorous newspaper campaign. In the end, the Federalists won in Massachusetts by a very slim margin and only with promises that amendments to the Constitution would be taken up in the first Congress.

By May 1788, eight states had ratified; only one more was needed. North Carolina and Rhode Island were hopeless for the Federalist cause, and New Hampshire seemed nearly as bleak. More worrisome was the failure to win over the largest and most economically critical states, Virginia and New York.

The Antifederalists

The **Antifederalists** were a composite group, united mainly in their desire to block the Constitution. Although much of their strength came from backcountry areas long suspicious of eastern elites, many Antifederalist leaders came from the same well-connected social background as Federalist leaders; economic class alone did not differentiate them. The Antifederalists also drew strength in states such as New York that were already on sure economic footing and could afford to remain independent. Probably the biggest appeal of the Antifederalists' position lay in the long-nurtured fear that distant power might infringe on people's liberties. The language of the earlier Revolutionary movement was not easily forgotten.

But by the time eight states had ratified the Constitution, the Antifederalists faced a far harder task than they had once imagined. First, they were no longer defending the status quo now that the momentum lay with the Federalists. Second, it was difficult to defend the confederation government with its admitted flaws. Even so, they remained genuinely fearful that the new government would be too distant from the people and could thus become corrupt or tyrannical. "The difficulty, if not impracticability, of exercising the equal and equitable powers of government by a single legislature over an extent of territory that reaches from the Mississippi to the western lakes, and from them to the Atlantic ocean, is an insuperable objection to the adoption of the new system," wrote one articulate Antifederalist in a compelling and much-read political pamphlet. The author, "A Columbia Patriot," was an alias for Mercy Otis Warren, a Massachusetts woman whose father, brother, and husband had all been active leaders in the Revolutionary movement in Boston.

The new government was indeed distant. In the proposed House of Representatives, the only directly democratic element of the Constitution, one member represented some 30,000 people. How could that member really know or communicate with his whole constituency, Antifederalists worried. One Antifederalist essayist contrasted the proposed model with the personal character of state-level representation: "The members of our state legislature are annually elected — they are subject to instructions — they are chosen within small circles — they are sent but a small distance from their respective homes. Their conduct is constantly known to their constituents. They frequently see, and are seen, by the men whose servants they are."

Silk Banner of the New York Society of Pewterers

As soon as nine states ratified the Constitution, the Federalists held spectacular victory celebrations meant to demonstrate national unity behind the new government. New York City's parade, coming three days before the state's own ratification vote in July 1788, involved five thousand participants marching under seventy-six occupational banners representing farmers, brewers, tobacconists, lawyers, and others. This banner was carried by the Society of Pewterers, metalsmiths who made household utensils. Despite the broad spectrum of male workers represented in the parade, many of whom could not vote, no working women participated. **Why?** © Collection of the New-York Historical Society.

Antifederalists also feared that representatives would always be elites and thus "ignorant of the sentiments of the middling and much more of the lower class of citizens, strangers to their ability, unacquainted with their wants, difficulties, and distress," a Maryland man worried. None of this would be a problem under a confederation system, according to the Antifederalists, because real power would continue to reside in the state governments.

The Federalists generally agreed that the elite would be favored for national elections. Indeed, Federalists wanted power to reside with intelligent, virtuous leaders like themselves. They did not envision a government constituted of every class of people. "Fools and knaves have voice enough in government already," quipped one Federalist, without being guaranteed representation in proportion to their total population. Alexander Hamilton claimed that mechanics and laborers preferred to have their social betters represent them. Antifederalists disagreed: "In reality, there will be no part of the people represented, but the rich. . . . It will literally be a government in the hands of the few to oppress and plunder the many."

Antifederalists fretted over many specific features of the Constitution. It prohibited state-issued paper money. It regulated the time and place of congressional elections, leading to fears that only one inconvenient polling place might be authorized, disfranchising rural voters. The most widespread objection was the Constitution's glaring omission of any guarantees of individual liberties in a bill of rights like those contained in many state constitutions.

Despite Federalist campaigns in the large states, it was a small state — New Hampshire — that provided the decisive ninth vote for ratification on June 21, 1788. Federalists there succeeded in getting the convention postponed from February to June and conducted an intense and successful lobbying effort on specific delegates in the interim.

The Big Holdouts: Virginia and New York

With nine states voting in favor, the Constitution was ensured passage, but four states still opposed ratification. A glance at a map demonstrated the necessity of pressing the Federalist case in the two largest, Virginia and New York. Although Virginia was home to Madison and Washington, an influential Antifederalist group led by Patrick Henry and George Mason made the outcome uncertain. The Federalists finally but barely won ratification in Virginia by proposing twenty specific amendments that the new government would promise to consider.

New York voters tilted toward the Anti-federalists out of a sense that a state so large and powerful need not relinquish so much authority to the new federal government. But New York was also home to some of the most persuasive Federalists. Starting in October 1787, Alexander Hamilton collaborated with James Madison and New York lawyer John Jay on a series of eighty-five essays on the political philosophy of the new Constitution. Published in New York newspapers and later republished as *The Federalist Papers*, the essays brilliantly set out the failures of the Articles of Confederation and offered an analysis of the complex nature of the Federalist position. In one of the most compelling essays, number 10, Madison challenged the Antifederalists' heartfelt conviction that republican government had to be small-scale. Madison argued that a large and diverse population was itself a guarantee of liberty. In a national government, no single faction could ever be large enough to subvert the freedom of other groups. "Extend the sphere, and you take in a greater variety of parties and interests; you make it less probable that a majority of the whole will have a common motive to invade the rights of other citizens," Madison asserted. He called it "a republican remedy for the diseases most incident to republican government."

At New York's ratifying convention, Anti-federalists predominated, but impassioned debate and lobbying — plus the dramatic news of Virginia's ratification — finally tipped the balance to the Federalists. Still, the Antifederalists' approval of the document was delivered with a list of twenty-four individual rights they hoped would be protected and thirty-three structural changes they hoped to see in the Constitution. New York's ratification ensured the legitimacy of the new government, yet it took another year and a half for Antifederalists in North Carolina to come around. Fiercely independent Rhode Island held out until May 1790, and even then it ratified by only a two-vote margin.

In less than twelve months, the U.S. Constitution was both written and ratified. (See appendix, page A-9.) An amazingly short time by twenty-first-century standards, it is even more remarkable for the late eighteenth century, with its horse-powered transportation and hand-printed communications. The Federalists had faced a formidable task, but by building momentum and ensuring consideration of a bill of rights, they did indeed carry the day.

> **REVIEW** Why did Antifederalists oppose the Constitution?

▶ Conclusion: The "Republican Remedy"

Thus ended one of the most intellectually tumultuous and creative periods in American history. American leaders experimented with ideas and drew up plans to embody their evolving and conflicting notions of how a society and a government ought to be formulated. There was widespread agreement that government should derive its power and authority from the people, but a narrow vision of "the people" prevailed. With limited exceptions — New Jersey, for example — free blacks and women were excluded from government. Indians, even when dubiously called "members" of a state, were never considered political participants, and neither were slaves. Even taking free white males as "the people," men disagreed fiercely over the degree of democracy — the amount of direct control of government by the people — that would be workable in American society.

The period began in 1775 with a confederation government that could barely be ratified because of its requirement of unanimity for approval. Amendments also required unanimity, which proved impossible to achieve on questions dealing with western lands, an impost, and the proper way to respond to unfair taxation in a republican state. The new Constitution offered a different approach to these problems by loosening the grip of impossible unanimity and by embracing the ideas of a heterogeneous public life and a carefully balanced government that together would prevent any one part of the public from tyrannizing another. The genius of James Madison was to anticipate that diversity of opinion was not only an unavoidable reality but also a hidden strength of the new society beginning to take shape. This is what he meant in *Federalist* essay number 10 when he spoke of the "republican remedy" for the troubles most likely to befall a government in which the people are the source of authority.

Despite Madison's optimism, political differences remained keen and worrisome to many. The Federalists still hoped for a society in which leaders of exceptional wisdom would discern the best path for public policy. They looked backward to a society of hierarchy, rank, and benevolent rule by an aristocracy of talent, but they created a government with forward-looking checks and balances as a guard against corruption, which they figured would most likely emanate from the people. The Antifederalists also looked backward, but to an old order of small-scale direct democracy and local control, in which virtuous people kept a close eye on potentially corruptible rulers. The Antifederalists feared a national government led by distant, self-interested leaders who needed to be held in check. In the 1790s, these two conceptions of republicanism and of leadership would be tested in real life. And to a degree, these competing visions of leadership, diversity, democracy, and corruption still animate American public life today.

Reviewing Chapter 8

REVIEW QUESTIONS

1. Why was the confederation government's authority so limited? (pp. 209–213)

2. How did states determine who would be allowed to vote? (pp. 213–218)

3. Why did farmers in western Massachusetts revolt against the state legislature? (pp. 218–227)

4. Why did the government proposed by the constitutional convention employ multiple checks on each branch? (pp. 227–231)

5. Why did Antifederalists oppose the Constitution? (pp. 231–235)

MAKING CONNECTIONS

1. Leaders in the new nation held that voting should be restricted to citizens who possessed independence of mind. What did they mean by "independence of mind," and why did they provide for this restriction? How did this principle limit voters in the early Republic?

2. Why did many Revolutionary leaders shaping the government of the new nation begin to find the principle of democracy troubling? How did they attempt to balance democracy with other concerns in the new government?

3. Twenty-first-century Americans see a profound tension between the Revolutionary ideals of liberty and equality and the persistence of American slavery. Did Americans in the late eighteenth century see a tension? How do the official documents cited in this chapter reflect their feelings on the topic of slavery? In your answer, be sure to discuss factors that might have shaped varied responses, such as region, race, and class.

4. The Northwest Territory was the confederation's greatest asset. Discuss the proposals to manage settlement of the new territory. How did they shape the nation's expansion? Which proposals succeeded, and which ones failed?

LINKING TO THE PAST

1. Compare and contrast the complaints against taxation connected with the Stamp Act in 1765 and those resulting from the congressional requisition of 1785. What were the principal arguments in each case? In either case, was it simply a matter of people refusing to pay to support government functions? Why do you think anti–Stamp Act activists like Samuel Adams took a negative view of the 1786 tax protests? (See chapter 6.)

2. Thomas Paine's pamphlet *Common Sense*, which sharply criticized the monarchy, was widely circulated and hailed by rebellious colonists in 1776. In light of the colonists' negative view toward monarchical power leading up to the Revolutionary War, how do you explain the powerful presidency that the victorious Americans set up in 1787? (See chapter 7.)

TIMELINE 1775–1804

1775 • Second Continental Congress begins to meet.

1776 • Declaration of Independence adopted.
• Virginia adopts state bill of rights.

1777 • Articles of Confederation sent to states.

1778 • State constitutions completed.

1780 • Pennsylvania institutes gradual emancipation.

1781 • Articles of Confederation ratified.
• Creation of executive departments.
• Slaves Mum Bett and Quok Walker successfully sue for freedom in Massachusetts.

1782 • Virginia relaxes state manumission law.

1783 • Newburgh Conspiracy exposed.
• Treaty of Paris signed, ending the Revolutionary War.
• Massachusetts extends suffrage to taxpaying free blacks.

1784 • Gradual emancipation laws passed in Rhode Island and Connecticut.
• Treaty of Fort Stanwix.

1785 • Treaty of Fort McIntosh.
• Congress issues requisition for $3 million to the states.

1786 • Shays's Rebellion begins.

1787 • Shays's Rebellion crushed.
• Northwest Ordinance.
• Delaware provides manumission law.
• Constitutional convention meets in Philadelphia.
• *The Federalist Papers* begin to appear in New York newspapers.

1788 • U.S. Constitution ratified.

1789 • Slavery ended in Massachusetts by judicial decision.

1790 • Maryland provides manumission law.

1799 • Gradual emancipation law passed in New York.

1804 • Gradual emancipation law passed in New Jersey.

▶ **FOR AN ONLINE BIBLIOGRAPHY, PRACTICE QUIZZES, WEB SITES, IMAGES, AND DOCUMENTS RELATED TO THIS CHAPTER,** see the Book Companion Site at **bedfordstmartins.com/roarkvalue**.

▶ **FOR DOCUMENTS RELATED TO THIS PERIOD,** see Michael Johnson, ed., *Reading the American Past*, Fifth Edition.

The New Nation Takes Form

1789–1800

ALEXANDER HAMILTON, THE NATION'S FIRST SECRETARY OF THE TREASURY, exercised vast influence over the economic and domestic policy of the new government. Heralded as a brilliant unifier of the pro-Constitution Federalists of 1788, Hamilton in his new role soon proved to be the most polarizing figure of the 1790s.

Determination marked his disadvantaged childhood. Hamilton grew up on a small West Indies island. His parents never married. His father, the impoverished fourth son of a Scottish lord, disappeared when Alexander was nine, and his mother, a woman with a checkered past, died two years later. Jeered as a "whore child," Hamilton developed a fierce ambition to make good. He clerked for a merchant who was so impressed with the lad that he sent him to the mainland colonies for an education. Hamilton started at King's College (now Columbia University) in 1773, but the war intruded. Political articles he wrote for a New York newspaper brought him to the attention of General George Washington, who made the nineteen-year-old his close aide and an officer. After the war, Hamilton practiced law in New York and participated in the constitutional convention in Philadelphia. His astute *Federalist* essays — he produced more than fifty in just a few months — helped secure the ratification of the Constitution.

Hamilton's private life was similarly upwardly mobile. Handsome and now well connected, he married Betsey Schuyler, daughter of a very wealthy New Yorker. Hamilton's magnetic charm attracted both men and women at dinner parties and social gatherings. Late-night socializing, however, never interfered with Hamilton's prodigious capacity for work.

Alexander Hamilton, by John Trumbull
Hamilton was confident, handsome, audacious, brilliant, and very hardworking. Ever slender, in marked contrast to the more corpulent leaders of his day, he posed for this portrait in 1792, at the age of thirty-seven and at the height of his power. CSFB Collection of Credit Suisse.

As secretary of the treasury, Hamilton quickly moved into high gear. "If a Government appears to be confident of its own powers, it is the surest way to inspire the same confidence in others," he once remarked. He immediately secured big loans from two banks and started to track tax revenues from trade, the government's main source of income. Most trade was with Britain, so Hamilton sought ways to protect Anglo-American relations. Next he tackled the country's unpaid Revolutionary War debt, writing in three months a forty-thousand-word report for Congress explaining how to fund the debt and pump millions of dollars into the U.S. economy. His bold plan for a national banking system aimed to enhance and control the money supply. Finally, he wrote a richly detailed analysis of ways to promote manufacturing via government subsidies and tariff policies.

Hamilton was both visionary and practical. No one could deny that he was a gifted man with remarkable political intuitions. Yet this magnetic man made enemies in the 1790s, as the "founding fathers" of the Revolution and Constitution became competitors and even bitter rivals. To some extent, jealousy over Hamilton's talents and his access to President Washington explains the chill, but serious differences in political philosophy drove the divisions deeper.

Personalities clashed. Hamilton's charm no longer worked with James Madison, now a representative in Congress and an opponent of all of Hamilton's plans. His charm had never worked with John Adams, the new vice president, who privately called him "the bastard brat of a Scotch pedlar" motivated by "disappointed Ambition and unbridled malice and revenge."

Years later, when asked why he had deserted Hamilton, Madison coolly replied, "Colonel Hamilton deserted me." Hamilton assumed that government was safest when in the hands of "the rich, the wise, and the good" — words he used to describe America's commercial elite. For Hamilton, economic and political power naturally belonged together, creating an energetic force for economic growth. By contrast, agrarian values ran deep with Jefferson and Madison, and they were suspicious of get-rich-quick speculators, financiers, and manufacturing development. Differing views of European powers also loomed large in the rivalries. Hamilton admired everything British, while Jefferson was enchanted by France, where he had lived in the 1780s. These loyalties governed foreign relations in the late 1790s, when the United States tangled with both overseas rivals.

The personal and political antagonisms of this first generation of American leaders left their mark on the young country. Leaders generally agreed on Indian policy in the new republic — peace when possible, war when necessary — but on little else. No one was prepared for the intense and passionate polarization over economic and foreign policy. The disagreements were articulated around particular events and policies: taxation and the public debt, a new farmers' rebellion in a western region, policies favoring commercial development, a treaty with Britain, a rebellion in Haiti, and the Quasi-War with France, which led to severe strictures on sedition and free speech. But at their heart, these disagreements sprang from opposing ideologies on the value of democracy, the nature of leadership, and the limits of federal power.

By 1800, the oppositional politics ripening between Hamiltonian and Jeffersonian politicians would begin to crystallize into political parties, the Federalists and the Republicans. To the citizens of that day, this was an unhappy development.

▶ The Search for Stability

After the struggles of the 1780s, the most urgent task in establishing the new government was to secure stability. Leaders sought ways to heal old divisions, and the first presidential election offered the means to do that in the person of George Washington, who enjoyed widespread veneration. People trusted him to exercise the untested and perhaps elastic powers of the presidency.

Congress had important work as well in initiating the new government. Congress quickly agreed on the Bill of Rights, which answered the concerns of many Antifederalists. In the cultural realm, the private virtue of women was mobilized to bolster the public virtue of male citizens and to enhance political stability. Republicanism was forcing a rethinking of women's relation to the state.

Washington Inaugurates the Government

The unanimous election of George Washington in February 1789 was quick work, the tallying of the 69 votes by the electoral college a mere formality. (By contrast, John Adams became vice president with just 34 electoral votes, with the remaining 35 votes split among a variety of candidates; Adams's pride was wounded.) Washington perfectly embodied the republican ideal of disinterested, public-spirited leadership. Indeed, he cultivated that image through astute ceremonies such as the dramatic surrender of his sword to the Continental Congress at the end of the war, symbolizing the subservience of military power to the law, a point he had made previously during the Newburgh Conspiracy (see chapter 8).

Once in office, Washington calculated his moves, knowing that every step set a precedent and that any misstep could be dangerous for the fragile government. Congress debated a title for Washington, ranging from "His Highness, the President of the United States of America and Protector of Their Liberties" to "His Majesty, the President"; Washington favored "His High Mightiness." But in the end, republican simplicity prevailed. The final title was simply "President of the United States of America," and the established form of address became "Mr. President," a subdued yet dignified title in a society where only property-owning adult white males could presume to be called "Mister."

Washington's genius in establishing the presidency lay in his capacity for implanting his own reputation for integrity into the office itself. He was not a brilliant thinker or a shrewd political strategist. He was not even a particularly congenial man. In the political language of the day, he was "virtuous," meaning that he took pains to elevate the public good over private interest and projected honesty and honor over ambition. He remained aloof, resolute, and dignified, to the point of appearing wooden at times. He encouraged pomp and ceremony to create respect for the office, traveling with six horses to pull his coach, hosting formal balls, and surrounding himself with uniformed servants. He even held weekly "levees," as European monarchs did, hour-long audiences granted to distinguished visitors (including women), at which Washington appeared attired in black velvet, with a feathered hat and a polished sword. The president and his guests bowed, avoiding the egalitarian familiarity of a handshake. But he always managed, perhaps just barely, to avoid the extreme of royal splendor.

Washington chose talented and experienced men to preside over the newly created Departments of War, Treasury, and State. For the Department of War, Washington selected General **Henry Knox**, former secretary of war in the confederation government. For the Treasury — an especially tough job in view of revenue conflicts during the confederation (see chapter 8) — the president appointed **Alexander Hamilton**, known for his general brilliance and financial astuteness. To lead the Department of State, the foreign policy arm of the executive branch, Washington chose **Thomas Jefferson**, a master of diplomatic relations and the current minister to France. For attorney general, Washington picked Edmund Randolph, a Virginian who had attended the constitutional convention but who had turned Antifederalist during ratification. For chief justice of the Supreme Court, Washington designated **John Jay**, a New York lawyer who, along with Madison and Hamilton, had vigorously defended the Constitution in *The Federalist Papers*.

Soon Washington began to hold regular meetings with these men, thereby establishing the precedent of a presidential cabinet. (Vice President John Adams was not included; his only official duty, to preside over the Senate, he found "a punishment." To his wife he complained, "My country has in its wisdom contrived for me the most insignificant office.") No one anticipated that two decades of party turbulence would emerge from the brilliant but explosive mix of Washington's first cabinet.

The Bill of Rights

An important piece of business for the First Congress, meeting in 1789, was the passage of the **Bill of Rights**. Seven states had ratified the Constitution on the condition that guarantees of individual liberties and limitations to federal power be swiftly incorporated. The Federalists of 1787 had thought an enumeration of rights unnecessary, but in 1789 Congressman James Madison understood that healing the divisions of the 1780s was of prime importance. He said, "It will be a desirable thing to extinguish from the bosom of every member of the community, any apprehensions that there are those among his countrymen who wish to deprive them of the liberty for which they valiantly fought and honorably bled."

Madison pulled much of his wording of rights directly from various state constitutions with bills of rights. He enumerated guarantees of freedom of speech, press, and religion; the right to petition and assemble; and the right to be free from unwarranted searches and seizures. One amendment asserted the right to keep and bear arms in support of a "well-regulated militia," to which Madison added, "but no person religiously scrupulous of bearing arms, shall be compelled to render military service in person." That provision for what a later century would call "conscientious objector" status failed to gain acceptance in Congress.

In September 1789, Congress approved a set of twelve amendments and sent them to the states for approval. The process of state ratification took another two years, but there was no serious doubt about the outcome. By 1791, ten amendments were eventually ratified. The First through Eighth Amendments dealt with individual liberties, and the Ninth and Tenth concerned the boundary between federal and state authority. (See the amendments to the U.S. Constitution in the appendix, page A-17.)

Still, not everyone was entirely satisfied. State ratifying conventions had submitted some eighty proposed amendments. Congress never considered proposals to change structural features of the new government, and Madison had no intention of reopening debates about the length of the president's term or the power to levy excise taxes. He also had no thought to use the Bill of Rights to address the status of enslaved people. But others capitalized on the First Amendment's right to petition to force the First Congress into a bitter debate over slavery.

Significantly, no one complained about one striking omission in the Bill of Rights: the right to vote. Only much later was voting seen as a fundamental liberty requiring protection by constitutional amendment — indeed, by four amendments. The Constitution deliberately left the definition of eligible voters to the states because of the existing wide variation in local voting practices. Most of these practices were based on property qualifications, but some touched on religion and, in one unusual case (New Jersey), on sex and race (see chapter 8).

The Republican Wife and Mother

The exclusion of women from political activity did not mean they had no civic role or responsibility. A flood of periodical articles in the 1790s by both male and female writers reevaluated courtship, marriage, and motherhood in light of republican ideals. Tyrannical power in the ruler, whether king or husband, was declared a thing of the past. Affection, not duty, bound wives to their husbands and citizens to their government. In republican marriages, the writers claimed, women had the capacity to reform the morals and manners of men. One male author promised women that "the solidity and stability of the liberties of your country rest with you; since Liberty is never sure, 'till Virtue reigns triumphant. . . . While you thus keep our country virtuous, you maintain its independence."

Until the 1790s, public virtue was strictly a masculine quality. But another sort of virtue enlarged in importance: sexual chastity, a private asset prized as a feminine quality. Essayists of the 1790s explicitly advised young women to use sexual virtue to increase public virtue in men. "Love and courtship . . . invest a lady with more authority than in any other situation that falls to the lot of human beings," one male essayist proclaimed. If women spurned selfish suitors, they could promote good morals more than any social institution could, essayists promised.

Republican ideals also cast motherhood in a new light. Throughout the 1790s, advocates for female education, still a controversial proposition, argued that education would produce better mothers, who in turn would produce better citizens, a concept historians call **republican motherhood**. Benjamin Rush, a Pennsylvania physician and educator, called for female education because "our ladies should be qualified . . . in instructing their sons in the principles of liberty and government." A woman speaker at a Fourth of July picnic in Connecticut in 1799 articulated family duty in service to the state to her all-female audience: "As mothers, wives, sisters, and daughters, we may all be important, [and] teach our little boys, the inestimable value of Freedom, how to blend and harmonize the natural and social rights of man, and as early impressions are indelible, thus assist our dear country, to be as glorious in maintaining, as it was great in gaining her immortal independence." A Massachusetts essayist named **Judith Sargent Murray** favored education that would remake women into self-confident, rational beings. Her first essay of 1790 was boldly titled "On the Equality of the Sexes," but a subsequent essay on education reassured readers that educated women would retain their "characteristic trait" of sweetness. Even Murray had to justify female education in the context of family duty.

This shift in understanding about women's relation to the state was subtle but profoundly important. Politics was still a masculine preserve, but now women's domestic obligations were infused with political meaning, and a few women became so bold as to claim an expanded scope for women's intellectual development as well. But nothing about this shift altered traditional gender relations. The analogy between marriage and civil society worked precisely because of the self-subordination inherent in the term *virtue*. Men should put the public good first, before selfish desires, just as women must put their husbands and families first, before themselves. Women might gain literacy and knowledge, but only in the service of improved domestic duty. In Federalist America, wives and citizens alike should feel affection for and trust in their rulers; neither should ever rebel.

> **REVIEW**   How did political leaders in the 1790s attempt to overcome the divisions of the 1780s?

▶ Hamilton's Economic Policies

The new government had the luck to be launched in flush economic times. Compared to the severe financial instability of the 1780s, the 1790s brimmed with opportunity, as seen in increased agricultural trade and improvements in transportation and banking. In 1790, the federal government moved from New York City to Philadelphia, a more central location with a substantial mercantile class. There, Alexander Hamilton, secretary of the treasury, embarked on his innovative plan to solidify the government's economic base. But controversy arose at every turn. Hamilton's plan to combine the large national debt with unpaid state debts produced a crisis in the First Congress. And his plan to raise revenues via taxation on whiskey brought on the country's first domestic rebellion.

Agriculture, Transportation, and Banking

Dramatic increases in international grain prices motivated American farmers to boost agricultural production for the export trade. Europe's rising population needed grain, and the French Revolutionary and Napoleonic Wars, which engulfed Europe after 1793 for a dozen years, severely compromised production there. From the Connecticut River valley to the Chesapeake, farmers planted more wheat, generating new jobs for millers, coopers, dockworkers, and ship and wagon builders.

Cotton production also underwent a boom, spurred by market demand and a mechanical invention. Limited amounts of smooth-seed cotton had long been grown in the coastal areas of the South, but this variety of cotton did not thrive in the drier inland regions. Greenseed cotton grew well inland, but its rough seeds stuck to the cotton fibers and were labor-intensive to remove. In 1793, Yale graduate Eli Whitney devised a machine called a gin that easily separated out the seeds; cotton production soared, giving a boost to transatlantic trade with Britain, whose factories eagerly processed the raw cotton into cloth.

A surge of road building further stimulated the economy. Before 1790, one bumpy road connected Maine to Georgia, but with the establishment of the U.S. Post Office in 1792, road mileage increased sixfold to facilitate the transport of mail. Private companies also built toll roads, such as the Lancaster Turnpike west of Philadelphia, the Boston-to-Albany turnpike, and a third road from Virginia to Tennessee. By 1800, a dense network of dirt, gravel, and plank

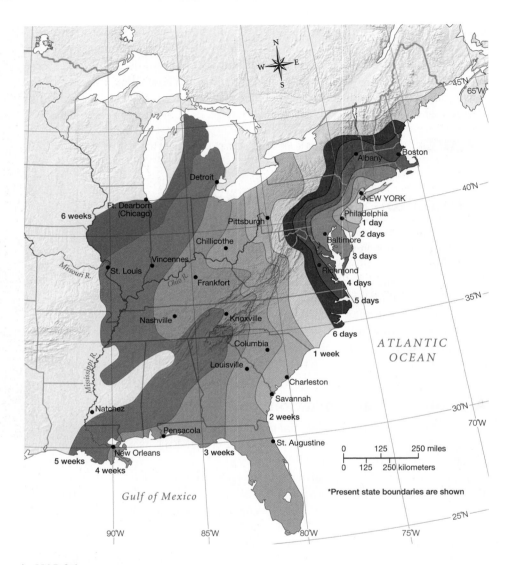

MAP 9.1

Travel Times from New York City in 1800

Notice that travel out of New York extends over a much greater distance in the first week than in subsequent weeks. River corridors in the West and East speeded up travel — but only if one were going downriver. Also notice that travel by sea (north and south along the coast) was much faster than land travel.

roadways connected towns in southern New England and the Middle Atlantic states, spurring commercial stage companies to regularize and speed up passenger traffic. A trip from New York to Boston took four days; from New York to Philadelphia, less than two (Map 9.1). In 1790, Boston had only three stagecoach companies; by 1800, there were twenty-four.

1790 Census Page

This page displays the final tally of the first federal census in 1790, mandated by the U.S. Constitution as the means to determine both representation in Congress and proportional taxation of the states. Notice the choice of five classifications for the count: free white males age sixteen or older, free white males under age sixteen, free white females, all other free persons, and slaves. To implement the Constitution's three-fifths clause (counting slaves as three-fifths of a person), slaves had to be counted separately from all free persons. Separating white males into two broad age groups at sixteen provided a measure of military strength, important to know in times of Indian (or other) wars.
U.S. Census Bureau.

The Return for SOUTH CAROLINA having been made since the foregoing Schedule was originally printed, the whole Enumeration is here given complete, except for the N. Weftern Territory, of which no Return has yet been publifhed.

DISTICTS	Free white Males of 16 years and upwards, including heads of families.	Free white Males under fixteen years.	Free white Females, including heads of families.	All other free perfons.	Slaves.	Total.
Vermont	22435	22328	40505	255	16	85539
N. Hampfhire	36086	34851	70160	630	158	141885
Maine	24384	24748	46870	538	NONE	96540
Maſſachuſetts	95453	87289	190582	5463	NONE	378787
Rhode Ifland	16019	15799	32652	3407	948	68825
Connecticut	60523	54403	117448	2808	2764	237946
New York	83700	78122	152320	4654	21324	340120
New Jerſey	45251	41416	83287	2762	11423	184139
Pennſylvania	110788	106948	206363	6537	3737	434373
Delaware	11783	12143	22384	3899	8887	59094
Maryland	55915	51339	101395	8043	103036	319728
Virginia	110936	116135	215046	12866	292627	747610
Kentucky	15154	17057	28922	114	12430	73677
N. Carolina	69988	77506	140710	4975	100572	393751
S. Carolina	35576	37722	66880	1801	107094	249073
Georgia	13103	14044	25739	398	29264	82548
	807094	791850	1541263	59150	694280	3893635

Total number of Inhabitants of the United States exclufive of S. Weftern and N. Territory.	Free white Males of 21 years and upwards.	Free Males under 21 years of age.	Free white Females.	All other perfons.	Slaves.	Total
S.W. territory	6271	10277	15365	361	3417	35691
N. Ditto	—	—	—	—	—	

A third development signaling economic resurgence was the growth of commercial banking. During the 1790s, the number of banks nationwide multiplied tenfold, from three to twenty-nine in 1800. Banks drew in money chiefly through the sale of stock. They then made loans in the form of banknotes, paper currency backed by the gold and silver that stockholders paid in. Because banks issued two or three times as much money in banknotes as they held in hard money, they were creating new money for the economy.

The U.S. population expanded along with economic development, propelled by large average family size and better than adequate food and land resources. As measured by the first two federal censuses in 1790 and 1800, the population grew from 3.9 million to 5.3 million, an increase of 35 percent.

The Public Debt and Taxes

The upturn in the economy, plus the new taxation powers of the government, suggested that the government might soon repay its wartime debt, amounting to more than $52 million owed to foreign and domestic creditors. But Hamilton had a different plan. He issued a *Report on Public Credit* in January 1790, recommending that the debt be funded — but not repaid immediately — at full value. This meant that old certificates of debt would be rolled over into new bonds, which would earn interest until they were retired several years later. There would still be a public debt, but it would be secure, giving its holders a direct financial stake in the new government. The bonds would circulate, injecting millions of dollars of new money into the economy. "A **national debt** if not excessive will be to us a national blessing; it will be a powerful cement of our union," Hamilton wrote to a financier. The debt was the "price of liberty," he further argued, and had to be honored, not repudiated. But it would not be paid off either: Hamilton's goal was to make the new country creditworthy, not debt-free.

Funding the debt in full was controversial because speculators had already bought up debt certificates cheaply, and Hamilton's report touched off further speculation. (Hamilton himself held no certificates, but his father-in-law held some with a face value of $60,000.) Philadelphia and New York speculators sent agents into backcountry regions looking for certificates of debt whose unwary owners were ignorant about the proposed face-value funding.

Hamilton compounded controversy with his proposal to add to the federal debt another $25 million that some state governments still owed to individuals. During the war, states had obtained supplies by issuing IOUs to farmers, merchants, and moneylenders. Some states, such as Virginia and New York, had paid off these debts entirely. Others, such as Massachusetts, had partially paid them off through heavy taxation of the people. About half the states had made little headway. Hamilton called for the federal government to assume these state debts and combine them with the federal debt, in effect consolidating federal power over the states.

Congressman James Madison strenuously objected to putting windfall profits in the pockets of speculators. He instead proposed a complex scheme to pay both the original holders of the federal debt and the speculators, each at fair fractions of the face value. Hamilton countered that tracking the history of traded certificates would be impossible, and further, each prior sale at a devalued price was the correct market price at that moment and could not be undone by the government. Madison also strongly objected to assumption of all the states' debts. A large debt was dangerous, Madison warned, especially because it would lead to high taxation. Secretary of State Jefferson also was fearful of Hamilton's proposals: "No man is more ardently intent to see the public debt soon and sacredly paid off than I am. This exactly marks the difference between Colonel Hamilton's views and mine, that I would wish the debt paid tomorrow; he wishes it never to be paid, but always to be a thing where with to corrupt and manage the legislature."

A solution to this impasse arrived when Jefferson invited Hamilton and Madison to dinner. Over good food and wine, Hamilton secured the reluctant Madison's promise to restrain his opposition. In return, Hamilton pledged to back efforts to locate the nation's new capital city in the South, along the Potomac River, an outcome that was sure to please Virginians. In early July 1790, Congress voted for the Potomac site, and in late July Congress passed the debt package, assumption and all.

The First Bank of the United States and the *Report on Manufactures*

The second and third major elements of Hamilton's economic plan were his proposal to create a national **Bank of the United States** and his program to encourage domestic manufacturing. Arguing that banks were the "nurseries of national wealth," Hamilton modeled his bank plan on European central banks, such as the Bank of England, a private corporation that used the government's money to invigorate the British economy. According to Hamilton's plan, the central bank was to be capitalized at $10 million, a sum larger than all the hard money in the entire nation. The federal government would hold 20 percent of the bank's stock, making the bank in effect the government's fiscal agent, holding its revenues derived from import duties, land sales, and various other taxes. The other 80 percent of the bank's capital would come from private investors, who could buy stock in the bank with either hard money (silver or gold) or the recently funded and thus sound federal securities. Because of its size and the privilege of being the only national bank, the central bank would help stabilize the economy by exerting prudent control over credit, interest rates, and the value of the currency.

Concerned that a few rich bankers might have undue influence over the economy, Madison tried but failed to stop the plan in Congress. Jefferson advised President Washington that the Constitution did not permit Congress to charter banks. Hamilton, however, pointed out that the Constitution gave Congress specific powers to regulate commerce and a broad right "to make all laws which shall be necessary and proper for carrying into execution the foregoing powers." Washington sided with Hamilton and signed the Bank of the United States into law in February 1791, with a charter allowing it to operate for twenty years.

When the bank's privately held stock went on sale in Philadelphia, Boston, and New York City in July, it sold out in a few hours, touching off an immediate mania of speculation in resale that lasted a month and drew in many hundreds of urban merchants and artisans. A discouraged Madison reported that in New York "the Coffee House is an eternal buzz with the gamblers," some of them self-interested congressmen intent on "public plunder." Stock prices shot upward and then plunged in mid-August, causing Jefferson to fret about the risk to morality inherent in gambling in stocks: "The spirit of gaming, once it has seized a subject, is incurable. The tailor who has made thousands in one day, tho' he has lost them the next, can never again be content with the slow and moderate earnings of his needle."

The third component of Hamilton's plan was issued in December 1791 in the *Report on Manufactures*, a proposal to encourage the production of American-made goods. Domestic manufacturing was in its infancy, and Hamilton aimed to mobilize the new powers of the federal government to grant subsidies to manufacturers and to impose moderate tariffs on those same products from overseas. Hamilton's plan targeted manufacturing of iron goods, arms and ammunition, coal, textiles, wood products, and glass. Among the blessings of manufacturing, he counted the new employment opportunities that would open to children and unmarried young women, who he assumed were under-utilized in agricultural societies. The *Report on Manufactures*, however, was never approved by Congress, and indeed never even voted on. Many confirmed agriculturalists in Congress feared that manufacturing was a curse rather than a blessing. Madison and Jefferson in particular were alarmed by stretching the "general welfare" clause of the Constitution to include public subsidies to private businesses.

The Whiskey Rebellion

Hamilton's plan to restore public credit required new taxation to pay the interest on the large national debt. In deference to the merchant class, Hamilton did not propose a general increase in import duties, nor did he propose land taxes, which would have fallen hardest on the nation's wealthiest landowners. Instead, he convinced Congress in 1791 to pass a 25 percent excise tax on whiskey, to be paid by farmers when they brought their grain to the distillery, then passed on to individual whiskey consumers in the form of higher prices. Members of Congress from eastern states favored the tax — especially New Englanders, where the favorite drink was rum. A New Hampshire representative observed that the country would be "drinking down the national debt," an idea he evidently found acceptable. More seriously, Virginia representative James Madison hoped that the tax might promote "sobriety and thereby prevent disease and untimely deaths."

Not surprisingly, the new excise tax proved unpopular with grain farmers in the western regions and whiskey drinkers everywhere. In 1791, farmers in Kentucky and the western parts of Pennsylvania, Virginia, Maryland, and the Carolinas forcefully conveyed to Congress their resentment of Hamilton's tax. One farmer complained that he had already paid half his grain to the local distillery for distilling his rye, and now the distiller was taking the new whiskey tax out of the farmer's remaining half. This "reduces the balance to less than one-third of the original quantity. If this is not an oppressive tax, I am at a loss to describe what is so," the farmer wrote. Congress responded with modest modifications to the tax in 1792, but even so, discontent was rampant.

Simple evasion of the law was the most common response. In some places, crowds threatened to tar and feather federal tax collectors, and distilleries underreported their production. Four counties in Pennsylvania established committees of correspondence and held assemblies to carry their message to Congress. Hamilton admitted to Congress that the revenue was far less than anticipated. But rather than abandon the law, he tightened up the prosecution of tax evaders.

In western Pennsylvania, Hamilton had one ally, a stubborn tax collector named John Neville who refused to quit even after a group of spirited farmers burned him in effigy. In May 1794, Neville filed charges against seventy-five farmers and distillers for tax evasion. His action touched off the **Whiskey Rebellion**. In July, he and a federal marshal were ambushed in Allegheny County by a group of forty men. Neville's house was then burned to the ground by a crowd estimated at five hundred, and one man in the crowd was killed. At the end of July, seven thousand Pennsylvania farmers planned a march — or perhaps an attack, some thought — on Pittsburgh to protest the hated tax.

In response, President Washington nationalized the Pennsylvania militia and set out, with Hamilton at his side, at the head of thirteen thousand soldiers. A worried Philadelphia newspaper criticized the show of force: "Shall Pennsylvania be converted into a human slaughter house because the dignity of the United States will not admit of conciliatory measures? Shall torrents of blood be spilled to support an odious excise system?" But in the end, no blood was spilled. By the time the army arrived in late September, the demonstrators had dispersed. No battles were fought, and no shots were exchanged. Twenty men were rounded up as rebels and charged with high treason, but only two were convicted, and both were soon pardoned by Washington.

Had the federal government overreacted? Thomas Jefferson thought so; he saw the event as a replay of Shays's Rebellion of 1786, when a protest against government taxation had been met with unreasonable government force (see chapter 8). The rebel farmers agreed; they felt entitled to protest oppressive taxation. Hamilton and Washington, however, thought that laws passed by a republican government must be obeyed. To them, the Whiskey Rebellion presented an opportunity for the new federal government to flex its muscles and stand up to civil disorder.

REVIEW Why were Hamilton's economic policies controversial?

▶ Conflict on America's Borders and Beyond

While the whiskey rebels challenged federal leadership from within the country, disorder threatened the United States from external sources as well. From 1789 onward, serious trouble brewed in four directions. To the southwest, the loosely confederated Creek Indians pushed back against the western thrust of the white southern population, which gave George Washington the opportunity to test the use of diplomacy and avoid costly war. To the northwest, a powerful confederation of Indian tribes in the Ohio Country went to formidable lengths to scare away white settlers, resulting in six years of brutal warfare. At the same time, conflicts between the major European powers forced Americans to take sides and nearly thrust the country into another war, this time across the Atlantic. And to the south, a Caribbean slave rebellion raised fears that racial war could arise in the United States. Despite these conflicts and the grave threats they posed to the young country, Washington won reelection to the presidency unanimously in the fall of 1792.

Creeks in the Southwest

An urgent task of the new government was to take charge of Indian affairs, ending the ambiguous divided authority between state and confederation government that had characterized the 1780s. Washington and his secretary of war, Henry Knox, hoped to secure peace with the Indians, partly out of a sense of fair play but also over worries about the expense of warfare. Some twenty thousand Indians affiliated with the Creeks occupied lands extending from Georgia into what is now Mississippi, and border skirmishes with land-hungry Georgians were becoming a frequent occurrence. Knox and Washington singled out one Creek chief, **Alexander McGillivray**, and sent a delegation to Georgia for preliminary treaty negotiations.

McGillivray, the son of a Scottish trader and a French-Creek mother, had an unusual history that prepared him to be a major cultural broker. His maternal line conferred a legitimate claim to Creek leadership; his paternal line afforded him access to the literacy and numeracy taught in American schools. Fluent in English and near fluent in Spanish, McGillivray spoke several Creek languages and had even studied Greek and Latin. In the 1770s, he worked for the British distributing gifts to various southern tribes; in the 1780s, he gained renown for brokering negotiations with the Spanish in Florida. The chief agreed to meet with Knox's delegates with some reluctance, since the Creeks' military strength at that point was quite sufficient to keep Georgia settlers at bay.

The American negotiators offered substantial terms to McGillivray, most notably a guarantee of the Creeks' extensive tribal lands and a promise to protect their borders from white settlers. In return, they asked him to cede a disputed tract of land where settlers already lived. But McGillivray sent the negotiators away, enjoying, as he wrote to a Spanish trader, the spectacle of the self-styled "masters of the new world" having "to bend and supplicate for peace at the feet of a people whom shortly before they despised."

A year later, Secretary Knox renewed efforts for a treaty. Georgia settlers and land speculators continued to push onto Creek land. Because of the war brewing north of the Ohio River with the much more belligerent tribes of the Northwest, the federal government had no military resources to spare. To coax McGillivray to the treaty table, Knox invited him to New York City to meet with the president himself. McGillivray arrived in a triumphal procession, joined by twenty-seven lesser chiefs and their entourages. The Creek leader was accorded the honors of a head of state.

The negotiations stretched out for a month in the capital city. In the end, the 1790 **Treaty of New York** incorporated Knox's original plan: Creek tribal lands were guaranteed, with a promise of boundary protection by federal troops against land-seeking settlers. The Creeks were assured of annual payments in money and trade goods, including "domestic animals and implements of husbandry" — words that hinted at a future time when the Creeks would become more agricultural and thus less in need of expansive hunting grounds. The Creeks promised to accept the United States alone as its trading partner, shutting out Spain. At the signing ceremony, Washington read the treaty aloud, with a translator repeating each article to the assembled chiefs. But both sides had made promises they could not keep. McGillivray thought that the Creeks' interests were best served by maintaining creative tension between the American and Spanish authorities, and by 1792, he had signed an agreement with the Spanish governor of New Orleans, in which each side offered mutual pledges to protect against encroachments by Georgia settlers. By the time Alexander McGillivray died in 1793, his purported leadership of the Creeks was in serious question, and the Treaty of New York joined the list of treaties never fully implemented. Its promise of federal border protection of Creek boundaries was unrealistic from the start, and its pledge of full respect for Creek sovereignty also was only a promise on paper.

At the very start of the new government, in dealing with the Creeks, Washington and Knox tried to find a different way to approach Indian affairs, one rooted more in British than in American experience. But in the end, the demographic imperative of explosive white population growth and westward-moving, land-seeking settlers, together with the economic imperative of land speculation, meant that confrontation with the native population was nearly inevitable. As Washington wrote in 1796, "I believe scarcely any thing short of a Chinese Wall, or line of Troops will restrain Land Jobbers, and the encroachment of Settlers, upon Indian Territory."

Ohio Indians in the Northwest

In the 1783 Treaty of Paris, Britain had yielded all land east of the Mississippi River to the United States without regard to the resident Indian population. The 1784 Treaty of Fort Stanwix (see chapter 8) had attempted to solve that omission by establishing terms between the new confederation government and native peoples, but the various key tribes of the Ohio Valley — the Shawnee, Delaware, and Miami — had not been involved in those negotiations. To confuse matters further, British troops still occupied half a dozen forts in the northwest, protecting an ongoing fur trade between British traders and Indians and thereby sustaining Indians' claims to that land.

The doubling of the American population from two million in 1770 to nearly four million in 1790 greatly intensified the pressure for western land. Several thousand settlers a year moved down the Ohio River in the mid-1780s. Most headed for Kentucky on the south bank of the river, but some eyed the forests to the north, in Indian country. By the late 1780s, government land sales in eastern Ohio had commenced, although actual settlement lagged.

Meanwhile, the U.S. Army entered the western half of Ohio, where white settlers did not dare to go. Fort Washington, built on the Ohio River in 1789 at the site of present-day Cincinnati, became the command post for three major invasions of Indian country (Map 9.2). General Josiah Harmar, under orders to subdue the Indians of western Ohio, marched with 1,400 men into Ohio's northwest region in the fall of 1790, burning Indian villages. His inexperienced troops were ambushed by Miami and Shawnee Indians led by their chiefs, **Little Turtle** and **Blue Jacket**. Harmar lost one-eighth of his soldiers.

Harmar's defeat spurred efforts to clear Ohio for permanent American settlement. General **Arthur St. Clair**, the military governor of the Northwest Territory, had pursued peaceful tactics in the 1780s, signing treaties with Indians for land in eastern Ohio — dubious treaties, as it happened, since the Indian negotiators were not authorized to yield land. In the wake of Harmar's bungled operation, St. Clair geared up for military action, and in the fall of 1791 he led two thousand men (accompanied by two hundred women camp followers) north from Fort Washington to claim Ohio territory from the Miami and Shawnee tribes. Along the route, St. Clair's men quickly built two forts, named for Hamilton and Jefferson. However, when the Indians attacked at daybreak on November 4 at the headwaters of the Wabash River, St. Clair's army was not protected by fortifications.

Before noon, 55 percent of the Americans were dead or wounded; only three of the women escaped alive. "The savages seemed not to fear anything we could do," wrote an officer afterward. "The ground was literally covered with the dead."

MAP 9.2
Western Expansion and Indian Land Cessions to 1810
By the first decade of the nineteenth century, intense Indian wars had resulted in significant cessions of land to the U.S. government by treaty.

The Indians captured valuable weaponry, scalped and dismembered the dying, and pursued fleeing survivors for miles. With more than nine hundred lives lost, this was the most stunning American loss in the history of the U.S.-Indian wars. Grisly tales of St. Clair's defeat became instantly infamous, increasing the level of terror that Americans brought to their confrontations with the Indians.

Washington doubled the U.S. military presence in Ohio and appointed a new commander, General Anthony Wayne of Pennsylvania, nicknamed "Mad Anthony" for his headstrong, hard-drinking style of leadership. About the Ohio natives, Wayne wrote, "I have always been of the opinion that we never should have a permanent peace with those Indians until they were made to experience our superiority." Throughout 1794, Wayne's army engaged in skirmishes with Shawnee, Delaware, and Miami Indians. Chief Little Turtle of the Miami tribe advised negotiation; in his view, Wayne's large army looked overpowering. But Blue Jacket of the Shawnees counseled continued warfare, and his view prevailed.

The decisive action came in August 1794 at the **battle of Fallen Timbers**, near the Maumee River where a recent tornado had felled many trees. The confederated Indians — mainly Ottawas, Potawatomis, Shawnees, and Delawares numbering around eight hundred — ambushed the Americans but were underarmed, and Wayne's troops made effective use of their guns and bayonets. The Indians withdrew and sought refuge at nearby Fort Miami, still held by the British, but their former allies locked the gate and refused protection. The surviving Indians fled to the woods, their ranks decimated.

Fallen Timbers was a major defeat for the Indians. The Americans had destroyed cornfields and villages on the march north, and with winter approaching, the Indians' confidence was sapped. They reentered negotiations in a much less powerful bargaining position. In 1795, about a thousand Indians representing nearly a dozen tribes met with Wayne and other American emissaries to work out the **Treaty of Greenville**. The Americans offered treaty goods (calico shirts, axes, knives, blankets, kettles, mirrors, ribbons, thimbles, and abundant wine and liquor casks) worth $25,000 and promised additional shipments every year. The government's idea was to create a dependency on American goods to keep the Indians friendly. In exchange, the Indians ceded most of Ohio to the Americans; only the northwest part of the territory was reserved solely for the Indians.

The treaty brought temporary peace to the region, but it did not restore a peaceful life to the Indians. The annual allowance from the United States too often came in the form of liquor. "More of us have died since the Treaty of Greenville than we lost by the years of war before, and it is all owing to the introduction of liquor among us," said Chief Little Turtle in 1800. "This liquor that they introduce into our country is more to be feared than the gun and tomahawk."

France and Britain

While Indian battles engaged the American military in the west, another war overseas to the east was also closely watched. Since 1789, revolution had been raging in France. At first, the general American reaction was positive, for it was flattering to think that the American Revolution had inspired imitation in France. As monarchy and privilege were overthrown in France, towns throughout America celebrated the victory of the French people with civic feasts and public festivities. Dozens of pro-French political clubs, called democratic or republican societies, sprang up around the country.

Treaty of Greenville, 1795
This painting of the 1790s purports to depict the signing of the Treaty of Greenville. An American officer kneels and writes—not a likely posture for drafting a treaty. One Indian gestures emphatically, as if to dictate terms, but in fact the treaty was completely favorable to the United States. Although Indians from a dozen Ohio tribes gathered at the signing ceremony, this picture shows unrealistically open spaces and very few Indians. Chicago Historical Society.

Many American women exhibited solidarity with revolutionary France by donning tricolor cockades, decorative knots of red, white, and blue ribbons. Pro-French headgear for committed women included an elaborate turban, leading one horrified Federalist newspaper editor to chastise the "fiery frenchified dames" thronging Philadelphia's streets. In Charleston, South Carolina, a pro-French pageant in 1793 united two women as partners, one representing France and the other America. The women repudiated their husbands "on account of ill treatment" and "conceived the design of living together in the strictest union and friendship," while a gun salute sealed the pledge. Most likely, this ceremony was not the country's first civil union but instead a richly metaphorical piece of street theater in which the spurned husbands represented the French and British monarchies. In addition to these purely symbolic actions, the growing exchange of political and intellectual ideas across the Atlantic helped plant the seeds of a woman's rights movement in America.

Anti–French Revolution sentiments also ran deep. Vice President John Adams, who lived in France in the 1780s, trembled to think of radicals in France or America. "Too many Frenchmen, after the example of too many Americans, pant for the equality of persons and property," Adams said. "The impracticability of this, God Almighty has decreed, and the advocates for liberty, who attempt it, will surely suffer for it."

Support for the French Revolution remained a matter of personal conviction until 1793, when Britain and France went to war and French versus British loyalty became a critical foreign policy debate. France had helped America substantially during the American Revolution, and the confederation government had signed an alliance in 1778 promising aid if France were ever under attack. Americans optimistic about the eventual outcome of the French Revolution wanted to deliver on that promise. But those shaken by the report of the guillotining of thousands of French people — including the king and queen — as well as those with strong commercial ties to Britain sought ways to stay neutral.

In May 1793, President Washington issued the Neutrality Proclamation, which contained friendly assurances to both sides, in an effort to stay out of European wars. Yet American ships continued to trade between the French West Indies and France. In late 1793 and early 1794, the British expressed their displeasure by capturing more than three hundred of these vessels near the West Indies. Clearly, something had to be done to assert American power.

President Washington sent John Jay, the chief justice of the Supreme Court and a man of strong pro-British sentiments, to England in 1794 to negotiate commercial relations in the British West Indies and secure compensation for the seizure of American ships. In addition, Jay was supposed to resolve several long-standing problems. Southern planters wanted reimbursement for the slaves lured away by the British army during the war, and western settlers wanted Britain to vacate the frontier forts still occupied because of their proximity to the Indian fur trade.

Jay returned from his diplomatic mission with a treaty that no one could love. First, the **Jay Treaty** failed to address the captured cargoes or the lost property in slaves. Second, it granted the British a lenient eighteen months to withdraw from the frontier forts, as well as continued rights in the fur trade. (This provision disheartened the Indians just then negotiating the Treaty of Greenville in Ohio. It was a significant factor in their decision to make peace.) Finally, the treaty called for repayment with interest of the debts that some American planters still owed to British firms dating from the Revolutionary War. In exchange for such generous terms, Jay secured limited trading rights in the West Indies and agreement that some issues — boundary disputes with Canada and the damage and loss claims of shipowners — would be decided later by arbitration commissions.

When newspapers published the terms of the treaty, powerful opposition emerged from Maine to Georgia. In Massachusetts, graffiti appeared on walls: "Damn John Jay! Damn everyone who won't damn John Jay! Damn everyone who won't stay up all night damning John Jay!" Bonfires in many places burned effigies of Jay and copies of the treaty. Nevertheless, the treaty passed the Senate in 1795 by a vote of 20 to 10. Some representatives in the House, led by Madison, tried to undermine the Senate's approval by insisting on a separate vote on the funding provisions of the treaty, on the grounds that the House controlled all spending bills. Finally, in 1796, the House approved funds to implement the various commissions mandated by the treaty, but by only a three-vote margin. The bitter vote in both houses of Congress divided along the same lines as the Hamilton-Jefferson split on economic policy.

The Haitian Revolution

In addition to the Indian troubles and the European wars across the Atlantic, yet another bloody conflict to the south polarized and even terrorized many Americans in the 1790s. The French colony of Saint Domingue, in the western third of the large Caribbean island of Hispaniola, became engulfed in revolution starting in 1791. Bloody war raged for more than a decade, resulting in 1804 in the birth of the Republic of Haiti, the first and only independent black state to arise out of a successful slave revolution.

The **Haitian Revolution** was a complex event involving many participants, including the diverse local population and, eventually, three European countries. Some 30,000 whites dominated the island in 1790, running sugar and coffee plantations with the enslaved labor of close to half a million blacks, two-thirds of them of African birth. The white French colonists were not the only plantation owners, however. About 28,000 free mixed-race people (*gens de couleur*) owned one-third of the island's plantations and nearly a quarter of the slave labor force. Despite their economic status, these mixed-race planters were barred from political power, but they aspired to it.

The French Revolution of 1789 was the immediate catalyst for rebellion in this already tense society. First, white colonists challenged the white royalist government in an effort to link Saint Domingue with the new revolutionary government in France. Next, the mixed-race planters rebelled in 1791, demanding equal civil rights with the whites. No sooner was this revolt viciously suppressed than another part of the island's population rose up; thousands of slaves armed with machetes and torches wreaked devastation and slaughter. In 1793, the civil war escalated to include French, Spanish, and British troops fighting the inhabitants and also one another. Led by former slave Toussaint L'Ouverture, slaves and free blacks in alliance with Spain occupied the northern regions of the island, leaving a thousand plantations in ruins and tens of thousands of people dead. Thousands of white and mixed-race planters, along with some of their slaves, fled to Spanish Louisiana and southern cities in the United States. Charleston alone accepted so many refugees that the city's population was one-sixth French in the early nineteenth century.

White Americans followed the revolution in fascinated horror through newspapers and refugees' accounts. A few sympathized with the impulse for liberty, but others feared that violent black insurrection might spread to the United States. White refugees were welcomed in Charleston, Norfolk, and Richmond, but French-speaking blacks, whether free or slave, were eventually barred from entry to all southern states except Virginia. Many black American slaves also fastened on news of the revolution, hearing about it from dockworkers, black sailors, and refugees and through oral networks in taverns and shops. The amazing news of the success of a first-ever massive revolution by slaves traveled quickly in this oral culture. Whites complained of behaviors that might prefigure plots and conspiracies, such

Toussaint L'Ouverture
This French engraving made around 1800 depicts the Haitian leader in full military dress and feathered hat commandingly issuing a document to French officers. Library of Congress.

as increased insolence and higher runaway rates among slaves.

The Haitian Revolution provoked naked fear of a race war in white southerners. Jefferson, agonizing over the contagion of liberty in 1797, wrote another Virginia slaveholder that "if something is not done, and soon done, we shall be the murderers of our own children . . . ; the revolutionary storm, now sweeping the globe, will be upon us, and happy if we make timely provision to give it an easy passage over our land. From the present state of things in Europe and America, the day which brings our combustion must be near at hand; and only a single spark is wanting to make that day to-morrow."

Jefferson's cataclysmic fears were not shared by New Englanders. Timothy Pickering of Massachusetts, in Washington's cabinet since 1795, chastised the inconsistent Jefferson for supporting French revolutionaries while condemning black Haitians fighting for freedom just because they had "a skin not colored like our own." Not that Pickering supported either type of violent revolutionary — he did not. But he and his political allies, soon to be called the Federalists, were far more willing to contemplate trade and diplomatic relations with the emerging black republic of Haiti.

REVIEW Why did the United States feel vulnerable to international threats in the 1790s?

▶ Federalists and Republicans

By the mid-1790s, polarization over the French Revolution, Haiti, the Jay Treaty, and Hamilton's economic plans had led to two distinct and consistent rival political groups: **Federalists** and **Republicans**. Politicians and newspapers adopted these labels, words that summarized conflicting political positions. Federalist leaders supported Britain in foreign policy and commercial interests at home, while Republicans rooted for liberty in France and worried about monarchical Federalists at home. The labels did not yet describe full-fledged political parties; such division was still thought to be a sign of failure of the experiment in government. Even so, Washington's decision not to seek a third term led to serious partisan electioneering in the presidential and congressional elections of 1796. Federalist John Adams won the presidency, but party strife accelerated over failed diplomacy in France, bringing the United States to the brink of war. Pro-war and antiwar antagonism created a major crisis over political free speech, militarism, and fears of sedition and treason.

The Election of 1796

Washington struggled to appear to be above party politics, and in his farewell address he stressed the need to maintain a "unity of government" reflecting a unified body politic. He also urged the country to "steer clear of permanent alliances with any portion of the foreign world." The leading contenders for his position, John Adams of Massachusetts and Thomas Jefferson of Virginia, in theory agreed with him, but around them raged a party contest split along pro-British versus pro-French lines.

Adams and Jefferson were not adept politicians in the modern sense, skilled in the arts of persuasion and intrigue. Bruised by his conflicts with Hamilton, Jefferson had resigned as secretary of state in 1793 and retreated to Monticello, his home in Virginia. Adams's job as vice president kept him closer to the political action, but his personality often put people off. He was temperamental, thin-skinned, and quick to take offense.

The leading Federalists informally caucused and chose Adams as their candidate, with Thomas Pinckney of South Carolina to run with him. The Republicans settled on Aaron Burr of New York to pair with Jefferson. The Constitution did not anticipate parties and tickets. Instead, each electoral college voter could cast two votes for any two candidates, but on only one ballot. The top vote-getter became president, and the next-highest assumed the vice presidency. (This procedural flaw was corrected by the Twelfth Amendment, adopted in 1804.) With only one ballot, careful maneuvering was required to make sure that the chief rivals for the presidency did not land in the top two spots.

Into that maneuverable moment stepped Alexander Hamilton. No longer in the cabinet, Hamilton had returned to his law practice in 1795, but he kept a firm hand on political developments. Hamilton did not trust Adams; he preferred Pinckney, and he tried to influence southern electors to switch from Jefferson to the slave-owning Pinckney by publishing a series of anonymous biting satires directed against Jefferson. But his plan failed: Adams was elected president with 71 electoral votes; Jefferson came in second with 68 and thus became vice president. Pinckney got 59 votes, while Burr trailed with 30.

Adams's inaugural speech pledged neutrality in foreign affairs and respect for the French people, based on his several years of residence there, which made Republicans hopeful. To please Federalists, Adams retained three cabinet members from Washington's administration — the secretaries of state, treasury, and war. But the three were Hamilton loyalists, passing off Hamilton's judgments and advice as their own to the unwitting Adams. Vice President Jefferson extended a concilia-tory hand to Adams when the two old friends met in Philadelphia, still the capital. They even took temporary lodging in the same boardinghouse, as if expecting to work closely together. But the Hamiltonian cabinet ruined the honeymoon. Jefferson's advice was spurned, and he withdrew from active counsel of the president.

The XYZ Affair

From the start, Adams's presidency was in crisis. France retaliated for the British-friendly Jay Treaty by abandoning its 1778 alliance with the United States. In 1796, it refused to recognize the U.S. minister sent by President Washington to France. Next, French privateers — armed private vessels — started detaining American ships carrying British goods; by March 1797, more than three hundred American vessels had been seized. To avenge these insults, Federalists started murmuring openly about war with France. Adams preferred negotiations and dispatched a three-man commission to France in the fall of 1797. But at the same time, the president recommended new expenditures for military defense. Negotiations, it appeared, would be backed by the muscle of military preparedness. Congress approved money for building three new naval frigates, for arming merchant ves-sels, and for reinforcing and improving defenses in coastal cities.

When the three American commissioners arrived in Paris, French officials would not receive them. Finally, the French minister of foreign affairs, Talleyrand, sent three French agents — unnamed and soon known to the American public as X, Y, and Z — to the American commissioners with the information that $250,000 might grease the wheels of diplomacy and that a $12 million loan to the French government would be the price of a peace treaty. Incensed, the commissioners brought news of the bribery attempt to the president.

Americans reacted to the **XYZ affair** with shock and anger. Even staunch pro-French Republicans began to reevaluate their allegiance. The Federalist-dominated Congress appropriated money for an army of ten thousand soldiers and repealed all prior treaties with France. In 1798, twenty naval warships launched the United States into its first undeclared war, called the **Quasi-War** by historians to underscore its uncertain legal status. The main scene of action was the Caribbean, where more than one hundred French ships were captured.

There was no home-front unity in this time of undeclared war; antagonism only intensified between Federalists and Republicans. Because there seemed to be very little chance of a land invasion by France, leading Republicans feared, with some justification, that the Federalists' real aim might be to raise the army to threaten domestic dissenters. Some claimed that Hamilton had masterminded the army buildup and was lobbying to be second in command, behind the aging ex-president Washington, presumed to be the man to lead the army. President Adams was increasingly mistrustful of members of his cabinet, but they backed the military buildup, and Adams was too weak politically to prevail. He was, moreover, begin-ning to suspect that his cabinet was more loyal to Hamilton than to the president.

Antagonism spiraled out of control between Federalists and Republicans. Republican newspapers heaped abuse on Adams. One denounced him as "a person without patriotism, without philosophy, and a mock monarch." Pro-French mobs roamed the streets of Philadelphia, the capital, and Adams, fearing for his personal safety, stocked weapons in his presidential quarters. Federalists, too, went on the offensive. In Newburyport, Massachusetts, they lit a huge bonfire and burned issues of the state's Republican newspapers. Officers in a New York militia unit drank a menacing toast on July 4, 1798: "One and but one party in the United States." A Federalist editor ominously declared that "he who is not for us is against us."

The Alien and Sedition Acts

With tempers so dangerously high and fears that political dissent was perhaps akin to treason, Federalist leaders moved to muffle the opposition. In mid-1798, Congress hammered out the Sedition Act, which not only made conspiracy and revolt illegal but also penalized speaking or writing anything that defamed the president or Congress. Criticizing government leaders became a criminal offense. One Federalist in Congress justified his vote for the law this way: "Let gentlemen look at certain papers printed in this city and elsewhere, and ask themselves whether an unwarrantable and dangerous combination does not exist to overturn and ruin the government by publishing the most shameless falsehoods against the representatives of the people." In all, twenty-five men, almost all Republican newspaper editors, were charged with sedition; twelve were convicted.

Congress also passed two Alien Acts. The first extended the waiting period for an alien to achieve citizenship from five to fourteen years and required all aliens to register with the federal government. The second empowered the president in time of war to deport or imprison without trial any foreigner suspected of being a danger to the United States. The clear intent of these laws was to harass French immigrants already in the United States and to discourage others from coming.

Republicans strongly opposed the **Alien and Sedition Acts** on the grounds that they were in conflict with the Bill of Rights, but they did not have the votes to revoke the acts in Congress, nor could the federal judiciary, dominated by Federalist judges, be counted on to challenge them. Jefferson and Madison turned to the state legislatures, the only other competing political arena, to press their opposition. Each man anonymously drafted a set of resolutions condemning the acts and had the legislatures of Virginia and Kentucky present them to the federal government in late fall 1798. The **Virginia and Kentucky Resolutions** put forth the decidedly novel argument that state legislatures have the right to judge the constitutionality of federal laws and even to nullify them. These were amazing assertions of state power, in view of Madison's role in 1787 in creating a federal government that superseded the states, and in view of Jefferson's position as the vice president. By their action, both men ran the risk of being charged with sedition. The resolutions made little dent in the Alien and Sedition Acts, but the idea of a state's right to nullify federal law did not disappear. It would resurface several times in decades to come, most notably in a major tariff dispute in 1832 and in the sectional arguments that led to the Civil War.

Amid all the war hysteria and sedition fears in 1798, President Adams regained his balance. He was uncharacteristically restrained in pursuing opponents under the Sedition Act, and he finally refused to declare war on France, as extreme Federalists

Cartoon of the Lyon-Griswold Fight in Congress
The political tensions of 1798 were not merely intellectual; two men brawled on the floor of Congress. Roger Griswold, a Connecticut Federalist, called Matthew Lyon, a Vermont Republican, a coward. Lyon responded with some well-aimed spit, the first departure from the gentleman's code of honor. Griswold responded by raising his cane to Lyon, whereupon Lyon grabbed nearby fire tongs to beat back his assailant. Madison wrote to Jefferson that the two should have dueled, the honorable way to avenge insults. But Lyon, a recent Scots-Irish immigrant, preferred rough-and-tumble fighting as the best response to insult. Library of Congress.

wished. No doubt he was beginning to realize how much he had been the dupe of Hamilton. He also shrewdly realized that France was not eager for war and that a peaceful settlement might be close at hand. In January 1799, a peace initiative from France arrived in the form of a letter assuring Adams that diplomatic channels were open again and that new peace commissioners would be welcomed in France.

Adams accepted this overture and appointed new negotiators. By late 1799, the Quasi-War with France had subsided, and in 1800 the negotiations resulted in a treaty declaring "a true and sincere friendship" between the United States and France. But Federalists were not pleased; Adams lost the support of a significant part of his own party and sealed his fate as the first one-term president of the United States.

The election of 1800 was openly organized along party lines. The self-designated national leaders of each group met to handpick their candidates for president and vice president. Adams's chief opponent was Thomas Jefferson. When the election was finally over, President Jefferson mounted the inaugural platform to announce,

"We are all republicans, we are all federalists," an appealing rhetoric of harmony appropriate to an inaugural address. But his formulation perpetuated a denial of the validity of party politics, a denial that ran deep in the founding generation of political leaders.

REVIEW Why did Congress pass the Alien and Sedition Acts in 1798?

▶ Conclusion: Parties Nonetheless

American political leaders began operating the new government in 1789 with great hopes of unifying the country and overcoming selfish factionalism. The enormous trust in President Washington was the central foundation for those hopes, and Washington did not disappoint, becoming a model Mr. President with a blend of integrity and authority. Stability was further aided by easy passage of the Bill of Rights (to appease Antifederalists) and by attention to cultivating a virtuous citizenry of upright men supported and rewarded by republican womanhood. Diplomatic attempts were made to secure a peace treaty with the Creeks in the southwest and to offer them protection. (Overtures to the Indians in the northwest were less successful.) Yet the hopes of the honeymoon period soon turned to worries and then fears as major political disagreements flared up.

At the core of the conflict was a group of talented men — Hamilton, Madison, Jefferson, and Adams — so recently allies but now opponents. They diverged over Hamilton's economic program, over relations with the British and the Jay Treaty, over the French and Haitian revolutions, and over preparedness for war abroad and free speech at home. Hamilton was perhaps the driving force in these conflicts, but the antagonism was not about mere personality. Parties were taking shape not around individuals, but around principles, such as ideas about what constituted enlightened leadership, how powerful the federal government should be, who was the best ally in Europe, and when oppositional political speech turned into treason. The Federalists were pro-British, pro-commerce, and ever alarmed about the potential excesses of democracy. The Republicans celebrated, up to a point, the radical republicanism of France and opposed the Sedition Act as an alarming example of an overbearing government cutting off freedom of speech.

When Jefferson in his inaugural address of 1800 offered his conciliatory assurance that Americans were at the same time "all republicans" and "all federalists," he probably mystified some listeners. Possibly, he meant to suggest that both groups shared two basic ideas — the value of republican government, in which power derived from the people, and the value of the unique federal system of shared governance structured by the Constitution. But by 1800, *Federalist* and *Republican* defined competing philosophies of government. To at least some of his listeners, Jefferson's assertion of harmony across budding party lines could only have seemed bizarre. For the next two decades, these two groups would battle each other, each fearing that the success of the other might bring about the demise of the country. And meanwhile, leaders continued to worry that partisan spirit itself was a bad thing.

Reviewing Chapter 9

REVIEW QUESTIONS

1. How did political leaders in the 1790s attempt to overcome the divisions of the 1780s? (pp. 241–245)

2. Why were Hamilton's economic policies controversial? (pp. 245–251)

3. Why did the United States feel vulnerable to international threats in the 1790s? (pp. 251–259)

4. Why did Congress pass the Alien and Sedition Acts in 1798? (pp. 259–264)

MAKING CONNECTIONS

1. Why did the Federalist alliance of the late 1780s fracture in the 1790s? Why was this development troubling to the nation? In your answer, cite specific ideological and political developments that hindered cooperation.

2. What provoked the Whiskey Rebellion? How did the government respond? In your answer, discuss the foundations and precedents of the conflict, as well as the significance of the government's response.

3. Americans held that virtue was pivotal to the success of their new nation. What did they mean by *virtue*? How did they hope to ensure that their citizens and their leaders possessed virtue?

4. The domestic politics of the new nation were profoundly influenced by conflicts beyond the nation's borders. Discuss how conflicts abroad contributed to domestic political developments in the 1790s.

LINKING TO THE PAST

1. Americans fought against the French in the Seven Years' War but welcomed them as allies during the Revolutionary War. Did either or both of those earlier experiences with France have any bearing on the sharp division in the 1790s between pro-French and anti-French political leaders in the United States? (See chapters 6 and 7.)

2. Shays's Rebellion appeared to some in 1786 to underscore the need for a stronger national government. Compare the Whiskey Rebellion to Shays's Rebellion. How were they similar, and how were they different? Did the Constitution of 1787 make a difference in the authorities' response to rebellion? (See chapter 8.)

TIMELINE 1789–1800

1789
- George Washington inaugurated first president.
- French Revolution begins.
- First Congress meets.
- Fort Washington erected in western Ohio.

1790
- Congress approves Hamilton's debt plan.
- Judith Sargent Murray publishes "On the Equality of the Sexes."
- National capital moved from New York City to Philadelphia.
- Shawnee and Miami Indians in Ohio defeat General Josiah Harmar.

1791
- States ratify Bill of Rights.
- Congress and president charter Bank of the United States.
- Ohio Indians defeat General Arthur St. Clair.
- Congress passes whiskey tax.
- Haitian Revolution begins.

- Hamilton issues *Report on Manufactures.*

1793
- Anglo-French Wars commence in Europe.
- Washington issues Neutrality Proclamation.
- Eli Whitney invents cotton gin.

1794
- Whiskey Rebellion.
- Battle of Fallen Timbers.

1795
- Treaty of Greenville.
- Jay Treaty.

1796
- Federalist John Adams elected second president.

1797
- XYZ affair.

1798
- Quasi-War with France erupts.
- Alien and Sedition Acts.
- Virginia and Kentucky Resolutions.

1800
- Republican Thomas Jefferson elected third president.

▶ **FOR AN ONLINE BIBLIOGRAPHY, PRACTICE QUIZZES, WEB SITES, IMAGES, AND DOCUMENTS RELATED TO THIS CHAPTER,** see the Book Companion Site at **bedfordstmartins.com/roarkvalue**.

▶ **FOR DOCUMENTS RELATED TO THIS PERIOD,** see Michael Johnson, ed., *Reading the American Past*, Fifth Edition.

10

Republicans in Power

1800–1824

THE NAME TECUMSEH TRANSLATES AS "SHOOTING STAR," A FITTING name for the Shawnee chief who reached meteoric heights of fame among Indians during Thomas Jefferson's presidency. From Canada to Georgia and west to the Mississippi, Tecumseh was accounted a charismatic leader, for which white Americans praised (and feared) him. Graceful, eloquent, compelling, astute: Tecumseh was all these and more, a gifted natural commander, equal parts politician and warrior.

The Ohio Country, where Tecumseh was born in 1768, was home to some dozen Indian tribes, including the Shawnee, recently displaced from the South. During the Revolutionary War, the region became a battleground with the "Big Knives," as the Shawnee people called the Americans. Tecumseh's childhood was marked by repeated violence and the loss of his father and two brothers in battle. The Revolution's end in 1783 brought no peace to Indian country. American settlers pushed west, and the youthful Tecumseh honed his warrior skills by ambushing pioneers flatboating down the Ohio River. He fought at the battle of Fallen Timbers, a major Indian defeat, but avoided the 1795 negotiations of the Treaty of Greenville, in which half a dozen dispirited tribes ceded much of Ohio to the Big Knives. In frustration, he watched as seven treaties between 1802 and 1805 whittled away more Indian land.

Some Indians, resigned and tired, looked for ways to accommodate, taking up farming, trade, and even intermarriage with the Big Knives. Others spent their treaty payments on alcohol. Tecumseh's younger brother Tenskwatawa led an embittered life of idleness and drink. But Tecumseh

267

rejected accommodation and instead campaigned for a return to ancient ways. Donning traditional animal-skin garb, he traveled around the Great Lakes region after 1805 persuading tribes to join his pan-Indian confederacy. The territorial governor of Indiana, William Henry Harrison, reported, "For four years he has been in constant motion. You see him today on the Wabash, and in a short time hear of him on the shores of Lake Erie or Michigan, or on the banks of the Mississippi, and wherever he goes he makes an impression favorable to his purpose."

Even Tecumseh's dissolute brother was born anew. After a near-death experience in 1805, Tenskwatawa revived and recounted a startling vision of meeting the Master of Life. Renaming himself the Prophet, he urged Indians everywhere to regard whites as children of the Evil Spirit, destined to be destroyed.

Tecumseh and the Prophet established a new village called Prophetstown, located in present-day Indiana, offering a potent blend of spiritual regeneration and political unity that attracted thousands of followers. Governor Harrison admired and feared Tecumseh, calling him "one of those uncommon geniuses which spring up occasionally to produce revolutions."

President Thomas Jefferson worried about an organized Indian confederacy and its potential for a renewed alliance with the British in Canada. Those worries became a reality during Jefferson's second term in office (1805–1809). Although his first term (1801–1805) brought notable successes, such as the Louisiana

Tecumseh
Several portraits of Tecumseh exist, but they all present a different visage, and none of them enjoys verified authenticity. This one perhaps comes closest to how Tecumseh actually looked. It is an 1848 engraving adapted from an earlier drawing that no longer exists, sketched by a French trader in Indiana named Pierre Le Dru in a live sitting with the Indian leader in 1808. The engraver has given Tecumseh a British army officer's uniform, showing that he fought on the British side in the War of 1812. Notice the head covering and the medallion around Tecumseh's neck, marking his Indian identity. Library of Congress.

Purchase and the Lewis and Clark expedition, his second term was consumed by the threat of war with either Britain or France, in a replay of
the late-1790s tensions. When war came in 1812, the enemy was Britain,
bolstered by a reenergized Indian-British alliance. Among the causes of
the war were insults over international shipping rights and the capture
of U.S. vessels. But the war also derived compelling strength from
Tecumseh's confederacy. Significant battles pitted U.S. soldiers against
Indians in the Great Lakes, Tennessee, and Florida.

In the end, the War of 1812 settled little between the United States
and Britain, but it was tragically conclusive for the Indians. Eight hundred
warriors led by Tecumseh helped defend Canada against U.S. attacks, but
the British did not reciprocate when the Indians were under threat.
Tecumseh died on Canadian soil at the battle of the Thames in the fall of
1813. No Indian leader with his star power would emerge again east of
the Mississippi.

The briefly unified Indian confederacy under Tecumseh had no counterpart in the young Republic's confederation of states, where widespread
unity behind a single leader proved impossible to achieve. Republicans did
battle with Federalists during the Jefferson and Madison administrations,
but then Federalists doomed their party by opposing the War of 1812. After
1815, they ceased to be a major force in political life. The next two presidents, James Monroe and John Quincy Adams, congratulated themselves on
the Federalists' demise and Republican unity, but in fact divisions within
their own party were extensive. Wives of politicians increasingly inserted
themselves into this dissonant mix, managing their husbands' politicking
and enabling them to appear above the fray and maintain the fiction of a
nonpartisan state. That it was a fiction became sharply apparent in the most
serious political crisis of this period, the Missouri Compromise of 1820.

▶ Jefferson's Presidency

The nerve-wracking election of 1800, decided in the House of Representatives,
stoked fears that party divisions would ruin the country. A panicky Federalist
newspaper in Connecticut predicted that a victory by **Thomas Jefferson** would
produce a bloody civil war and usher in an immoral reign of "murder, robbery,
rape, adultery and incest." Similar fears were expressed in the South, where a
frightful slave uprising seemed a possible outcome of Jefferson's victory. But
nothing nearly so dramatic occurred. Jefferson later called his election the
"revolution of 1800," referring to his repudiation of Federalist practices and his
cutbacks in military spending and taxes. While he cherished a republican simplicity in governance, he inevitably encountered events that required decisive

and sometimes expensive government action. One early example came when pirates repeatedly threatened American ships off the north coast of Africa.

Turbulent Times: Election and Rebellion

The result of the election of 1800 remained uncertain from polling times in the late fall to repeated roll call votes in the House of Representatives in February 1801. Federalist John Adams, never secure in his leadership of the Federalist Party, was no longer in the presidential race once it reached the House. Instead, the contest was between Jefferson and his running mate, Senator **Aaron Burr** of New York. Republican voters in the electoral college slipped up, giving Jefferson and Burr an equal number of votes, an outcome possible because of the single balloting to choose both president and vice president. (To fix this problem, the Twelfth Amendment to the Constitution, adopted in 1804, provided for distinct ballots for the two offices.) The vain and ambitious Burr declined to concede, so the sitting Federalist-dominated House of Representatives got to choose the president.

Each state delegation had one vote, and nine were needed to win. Some Federalists preferred Burr, believing that his character flaws made him susceptible to Federalist pressure. But the influential Alexander Hamilton, though no friend of Jefferson, recognized that the high-strung Burr would be more dangerous in the presidency. Jefferson was a "contemptible hypocrite" in Hamilton's opinion, but at least he was not corrupt. Jefferson received the votes of eight states on the first ballot. Thirty-six ballots and six days later, he got the critical ninth vote, as well as a tenth. This election demonstrated a remarkable feature of the new government: No matter how hard fought the campaign, the leadership of the nation could shift from one group to its rivals in a peaceful transfer of power effected by ballots, not bullets.

As the country struggled over its white leadership crisis, a twenty-four-year-old blacksmith named Gabriel, the slave of Thomas Prossor, plotted rebellion in Virginia. Inspired by the Haitian Revolution (see chapter 9), and perhaps directly informed of it by French slaves new to the Richmond area, Gabriel was said to be organizing a thousand slaves to march on the state capital of Richmond and take the governor, James Monroe, hostage. On the appointed day, however, a few nervous slaves went to the authorities with news of **Gabriel's rebellion**, and within days scores of implicated conspirators were jailed and brought to trial.

One of the jailed rebels compared himself to the most venerated icon of the early Republic: "I have nothing more to offer than what General Washington would have had to offer, had he been taken by the British and put to trial by them." Such talk invoking the specter of a black George Washington worried white Virginians, and in the fall of 1800 twenty-seven black men were hanged for allegedly contemplating rebellion. Finally, Jefferson advised Governor Monroe to halt the hangings. "The world at large will forever condemn us if we indulge a principle of revenge," Jefferson wrote.

Pistols from the Burr-Hamilton Duel
In 1804, Vice President Aaron Burr shot
and killed Alexander Hamilton with a
.54-caliber pistol. Hamilton had
long scorned Burr, and when
a newspaper published Hamilton's
disdain, Burr felt obliged to avenge
his honor. Dueling, fully accepted in the
South as an extralegal remedy for insult,
had recently been outlawed in northern states.
Burr was charged with a misdemeanor in New York, where
the challenge was issued, and with homicide in New Jersey,
where the duel was fought. After four months as a fugitive
in the South, Burr resumed his official duties in Washington.
He was never arrested. Courtesy of Chase Manhattan Archives.

The Jeffersonian Vision of Republican Simplicity

Once elected, Thomas Jefferson turned his attention to establishing his administration in clear contrast to the Federalists. For his inauguration, held in the
village called Washington City, he dressed in everyday clothing to strike a tone
of republican simplicity, and he walked to the Capitol for the modest swearing-in
ceremony. As president, he scaled back Federalist building plans for Washington
and cut the government budget.

Martha Washington and Abigail Adams had received the wives of government officials at weekly teas, thereby cementing social relations in the governing class. But Jefferson, a longtime widower, disdained female gatherings and
avoided the women of Washington City. He abandoned George Washington's
practice of holding weekly formal receptions, limiting these drop-in gatherings
to just two a year. His preferred social event was the small dinner party with
carefully chosen politicos, either all Republicans or all Federalists (and all male).
At these intimate dinners, the president exercised influence and strengthened
informal relationships that would help him govern.

Jefferson was no Antifederalist. He had supported the Constitution in 1788,
despite his concern about the unrestricted reelection allowed to the president. But
events of the 1790s had caused him to worry about the stretching of powers in
the executive branch. Jefferson had watched with distrust as Hamiltonian policies
refinanced the public debt, established a national bank, and secured commercial
ties with Britain (see chapter 9). These policies seemed to Jefferson to promote
the interests of money-hungry speculators and profiteers at the expense of the
rest of the country. Financial schemes that seemed merely to allow rich men to
become richer were corrupt and worthless, he believed, and their promotion by
the federal government was not authorized by the Constitution. In Jefferson's
vision, the source of true liberty in America was the independent farmer, someone
who owned and worked his land both for himself and for the market.

Jefferson set out to dismantle Federalist innovations. He reduced the size of the army by a third, preferring "a well-disciplined militia" for defense, and he cut back the navy to just half a dozen ships. With the consent of Congress, he abolished all federal taxes based on population or whiskey. Government revenue would now derive solely from customs duties and the sale of western land. This strategy benefited the South, where three-fifths of the slaves counted for representation but not for taxation now. By the end of his first term, Jefferson had deeply reduced Hamilton's cherished national debt.

A properly limited federal government, according to Jefferson, was responsible merely for running a postal system, maintaining the federal courts, staffing lighthouses, collecting customs duties, and conducting a census once every ten years. The president had one private secretary, a young man named Meriwether Lewis, to help with his correspondence, and Jefferson paid him out of his own pocket. The Department of State employed only 8 people: Secretary James Madison, 6 clerks, and a messenger. The Treasury Department was by far the largest unit, with 73 revenue commissioners, auditors, and clerks, plus 2 watchmen. The entire payroll of the executive branch amounted to a mere 130 people in 1801.

However, one large set of government workers lay beyond Jefferson's command. His predecessor, John Adams, had made 217 last-minute appointments of Federalists to various judicial and military posts. Jefferson refused to honor those "midnight judges" who had not yet been fully processed. One disappointed job seeker, William Marbury, sued the new secretary of state, James Madison, for failure to make good on the appointment. This action gave rise to a landmark Supreme Court case, **Marbury v. Madison**, decided in 1803. The Court ruled that although Marbury's commission was valid and the new president should have delivered it, the Court could not compel him to do so. What made the case significant was little noted at the time: The Court found that the grounds of Marbury's suit, resting in the Judiciary Act of 1789, were in conflict with the Constitution. For the first time, the Court acted to disallow a law on the grounds that it was unconstitutional.

Dangers Overseas: The Barbary Wars

Jefferson's desire to keep government and the military small met a severe test in the western Mediterranean Sea, where U.S. trading interests ran afoul of local Muslim states, leading to the first formal declaration of war against the United States by a foreign power. For well over a century, four Muslim states on the northern coast of Africa — Morocco, Algiers, Tunis, and Tripoli, called the Barbary States by Americans — controlled all Mediterranean shipping traffic by demanding large annual payments (called "tribute") for safe passage. Countries electing not to pay found their ships at risk for seizure, with cargoes plundered and crews captured and sold into slavery. By the mid-1790s, the United States was paying $50,000 a year. About a hundred American merchant ships annually traversed the Mediterranean, trading lumber, tobacco, sugar, and rum for regional delicacies such as raisins, figs, capers, and medicinal opium.

In May 1801, when the pasha (military head) of Tripoli failed to secure a large increase in his tribute, he declared war on the United States. Jefferson had long considered such payments extortion, and he sent four warships to the Mediterranean to protect U.S. shipping. From 1801 to 1803, U.S. frigates engaged in skirmishes with Barbary privateers.

Then, in late 1803, the USS *Philadelphia* ran aground near Tripoli's harbor. Its three-hundred-man crew was captured along with the ship. In retaliation, a U.S. naval ship commanded by Lieutenant Stephen Decatur sailed into the harbor after dark, guided by an Arabic-speaking pilot to fool harbor sentries. Decatur's crew set the *Philadelphia* on fire, rendering the ship useless to its hijackers and making Decatur an instant hero in America. A later foray into the harbor to try to blow up the entire Tripoli fleet with a bomb-laden boat failed when the explosives detonated prematurely, killing eleven Americans.

In 1804, William Eaton, an American officer stationed in Tunis, felt the humiliation of his country's ineffectiveness. He requested a thousand Marines to invade Tripoli, but Secretary of State James Madison rejected the plan and another scheme to ally with the pasha's exiled brother to effect regime change. On his own, Eaton contacted the brother, assembled a force of four hundred men (mostly Greek and Egyptian mercenaries plus his Marines), and marched them over five hundred miles of desert for a surprise attack on Derne, Tripoli's second-largest city. Amazingly, he succeeded. The pasha of Tripoli yielded, released — for a fee — the prisoners taken from the *Philadelphia*, and negotiated a treaty with the United States that terminated tribute. One significant clause of the treaty stipulated that the United States "has in itself no character of enmity against the Laws, Religion or Tranquility of Musselmen [Muslims]" and that "no pretext arising from Religious Opinions, shall ever produce an interruption of the Harmony existing between the two Nations." Peace with the other Barbary States came in a second treaty in 1812.

The **Barbary Wars** of 1801–1805 cost Jefferson's government more money than the tribute demanded. But the honor of the young country was thought to be at stake. At political gatherings, the slogan "Millions for defense, but not a cent for tribute" became a popular toast.

REVIEW How did Jefferson attempt to undo the Federalist innovations of earlier administrations?

▶ Opportunities and Challenges in the West

While Jefferson remained cautious about exercising federal power, he quickly learned that circumstances sometimes required him to enlarge the authority of the presidency. Shifting politics in Europe in 1803 opened an unexpected door to the spectacular purchase from France of the Louisiana Territory. To explore the largely unmarked boundaries of this huge acquisition, Jefferson sent four separate expeditions into the prairie and mountains. The powerful Osage of the

Arkansas River valley responded to overtures for an alliance and were soon lavishly welcomed by Jefferson in Washington City, but the even more powerful Comanche of the southern Great Plains stood their ground against all invaders. Meanwhile, the expedition by Lewis and Clark, the longest and northernmost trek of the four launched by Jefferson, mapped U.S. terrain all the way to the Pacific Ocean, giving a boost to expansionist aspirations.

The Louisiana Purchase

When the map of North America was redrawn in 1763, at the end of the Seven Years' War, a large expanse of the territory west of the Mississippi River shifted from France to Spain. Spain never controlled or settled the area centered on the Great Plains, which was already peopled by many Indian tribes, most notably the powerful and expansionist Comanche nation. New Orleans was Spain's principal stronghold in the region, a onetime French city strategically sited on the Mississippi River near its outlet to the Gulf of Mexico. Spain profited modestly from trade taxes it imposed on the small but growing flow of agricultural products shipped down the river from American farms in the western parts of Kentucky and Tennessee (to be sold at New Orleans or Caribbean destinations).

The biggest concern of the Spanish governor of New Orleans was that the sparse population of lower Louisiana was insufficient to ward off an anticipated westward movement of Americans. Spanish officials took steps to encourage European immigration, but only small numbers of Germans and French came. Up the river at St. Louis, the Spanish governor happily welcomed Native American refugees from the Northwest Territory who had been pushed out by what was termed a "plague of locusts" — American settlers — in the 1790s. Hoping that a Spanish-Indian alliance might be able to stop the expected demographic wave, he promised that the Spanish would "receive you in their homes as if you all belonged to our nation." Still, defending many hundreds of miles of the river against Americans on the move was a daunting prospect. "You can't put doors on open country," said an adviser to the Spanish king.

Thus, in 1800 Spain struck a secret deal to return this trans-Mississippi territory to France, in the hopes that a French Louisiana would provide a buffer zone between Spain's more valuable holdings in Mexico and the land-hungry Americans. The French emperor Napoleon accepted the transfer and agreed to Spain's condition that France could not sell Louisiana to anyone without Spain's permission.

From the U.S. perspective, Spain had proved a weak western neighbor, but France was another story. Jefferson was so alarmed by the rumored transfer that he instructed Robert R. Livingston, America's minister in France, to approach the French and offer to buy New Orleans. At first, the French denied they owned the city. But when Livingston hinted that the United States might seize it if buying was not an option, the French negotiator asked him to name his price for the entire Louisiana Territory from the Gulf of Mexico north to Canada. Livingston stalled, and the Frenchman made suggestions: $125 million? $60 million? Livingston shrewdly stalled some more and within days accepted the bargain price of $15 million (Map 10.1).

On the verge of war with Britain, France needed both money and friendly neutrality from the United States, and it got both from the quick sale of the Louisiana Territory. In addition, the recent and costly loss of Haiti as a colony made a French presence in New Orleans less feasible as well. But in selling Louisiana to the United States, France had broken its agreement with Spain, which protested that the sale was illegal.

Moreover, there was no consensus on the western border of this land transfer. Spain claimed that the border was about one hundred miles west of the Mississippi River, while in Jefferson's eyes it was some eight hundred miles farther west, defined by the crest of the Rocky Mountains. When Livingston pressured the French negotiator to clarify his country's understanding of the boundary, the negotiator replied, "I can give you no direction. You have made a noble bargain for yourself, and I suppose you will make the most of it."

Jefferson and most members of Congress were delighted with the **Louisiana Purchase**. In late 1803, the American army took formal control of the Louisiana Territory, and the United States nearly doubled in size — at least on paper. The Spanish inhabitants of New Orleans had relinquished the city to a few French officials just a month before the Americans arrived to claim it, and now many of the Spaniards left for Texas or West Florida (along the Gulf coast), lands still in Spanish hands. One departing Spanish officer expressed his loathing for the "ambitious, restless, lawless, conniving, changeable, and turbulent" Americans, writing, "I am so disgusted with hearing them that I can hardly wait to leave them behind me."

The Lewis and Clark Expedition

Jefferson quickly launched four government-financed expeditions up the river valleys of the new territory to establish relationships with Indian tribes and to determine Spanish influence and presence. The first set out in 1804 to explore the upper reaches of the Missouri River. Jefferson appointed twenty-eight-year-old Meriwether Lewis, his secretary, to head the expedition and instructed him to investigate Indian cultures, to collect plant and animal specimens, and to chart the geography of the West, with particular attention to locating the headwaters of the rivers "running southwardly" to Spain's settlements. The expedition was also charged with scouting locations for military posts, negotiating fur trade agreements, and identifying river routes to the West (see Map 10.1).

For his co-leader, Lewis chose Kentuckian William Clark, a veteran of the 1790s Indian wars. Together, they handpicked a crew of forty-five, including expert rivermen, gunsmiths, hunters, interpreters, a cook, and Clark's slave named York. The explorers left St. Louis in the spring of 1804, working their way northwest up the Missouri River. They camped for the winter at a Mandan village in what is now central North Dakota. The Mandan Indians were familiar

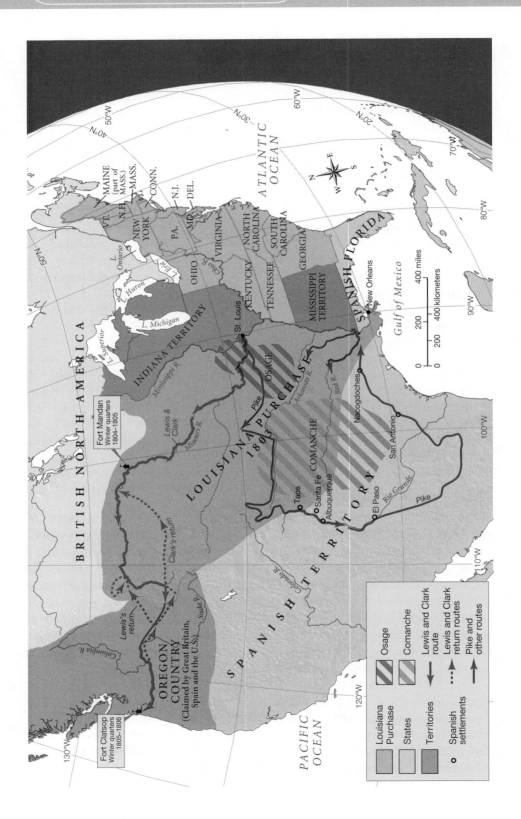

with British and French traders from Canada, but the black man York created a sensation. Reportedly, the Indians rubbed moistened fingers over the man's skin to see if the color was painted on.

The following spring, the explorers headed west, accompanied by a sixteen-year-old Shoshoni woman named **Sacajawea**. Kidnapped by Mandans at about age ten, she had been sold to a French trapper as a slave/wife. Hers was not a unique story among Indian women, and such women knew several languages, making them valuable translators and mediators. Further, Sacajawea and her new baby allowed the American expedition to appear peaceful to suspicious tribes. As Lewis wrote in his journal, "No woman ever accompanies a war party of Indians in this quarter."

The **Lewis and Clark expedition** reached the Pacific Ocean at the mouth of the Columbia River in November 1805. When the two leaders returned home the following year, they were greeted as national heroes. They had established favorable relations with dozens of Indian tribes; they had collected invaluable information on the peoples, soils, plants, animals, and geography of the West; and they had inspired a nation of restless explorers and solitary imitators.

Osage and Comanche Indians

The three additional U.S. expeditions set forth between 1804 and 1806 from the Mississippi River to probe the contested southwestern border of the Louisiana Purchase. The first exploring party left from Natchez, Mississippi, and ascended the Red River to the Ouachita River, ending at a hot springs in present-day Arkansas. Two years later, the second group of explorers followed the Red River west into eastern Texas, and the third embarked from St. Louis and traveled west, deep into the Rockies. This third group, led by Zebulon Pike, had gone too far, in the view of the Spaniards: Pike and his men were arrested, taken to northern Mexico, and soon released.

Of the scores of Indian tribes in this lower Great Plains region, two enjoyed reputations for territorial dominance. The **Osage** ruled the land between the Missouri and the lower Arkansas rivers, while the trading and raiding grounds of the **Comanche** stretched from the upper Arkansas River to the Rockies and south into Texas, a vast area called Comanchería. Both were formidable tribes that proved equal to the Spaniards. The Osage accomplished this through careful diplomacy and periodic shows of strength. The Comanche cemented their dominance by expert horsemanship; a brisk trade in guns, captives, and goods; and a constant readiness to employ strong-arm tactics and violence.

◀ **MAP 10.1**
Jefferson's Expeditions in the West, 1804–1806
The Louisiana Purchase of 1803 brought the U.S. a large territory without clear boundaries. Jefferson sent off four scientific expeditions to take stock of the land's possibilities and to assess the degree of potential antagonism from Indian and Spanish inhabitants.

Jefferson turned his attention to cultivating the Osage, whose attractive lands (in present-day southern Missouri) beckoned as farmland in America's future. He directed Meriwether Lewis, on his way west, to invite the Osage to Washington City. When the delegation of eleven Osage leaders arrived in 1804, Jefferson greeted them as heads of state, with elaborate ceremonies and generous gifts. He positioned the Osage as equals of the Americans: "The great spirit has given you strength & has given us strength, not that we might hurt one another, but to do each other all the good in our power." Jefferson's goal was to make the Osage a strong trading partner, but he also had firm notions about what items to offer for trade: hoes and ploughs for the men; spinning wheels and looms for the women. These highly gendered tools signified a departure from the native gender system in which women tended crops while men hunted game. As Jefferson saw it, such equipment would bring the Indians the blessings of an agricultural civilization. Diminished reliance on the hunt would reduce the amount of land that tribes needed to sustain their communities. Jefferson expressed his hope that "commerce is the great engine by which we are to coerce them, & not war."

For their part, the Osage wanted Jefferson primarily to provide protection against Indian refugees displaced by American settlers east of the Mississippi. Jefferson's Osage alliance soon proved to be quite expensive, with costs arising from ransoming prisoners, providing defense, brokering treaties, and giving gifts all around. In 1806, a second ceremonial visit to Washington and other eastern cities by a dozen Osage leaders cost the federal government $10,000.

These promising peace initiatives were short-lived. By 1808, intertribal warfare was on the rise, and the governor of the Louisiana Territory declared that the U.S. government no longer had an obligation to protect the Osage. Jefferson's presidency was waning, and soon the practice of whittling away Indian lands through coercive treaties, so familiar to men like Tecumseh, reasserted itself. A treaty in 1808, followed by others in 1818, 1825, and 1839, shrank the Osage lands, and by the 1860s they were forced onto a small region in present-day Oklahoma.

By contrast, the Comanche managed to resist attempts to dominate them. For nearly a century, several branches of the tribe extended control over other tribes and over the Spaniards, holding the latter in check in small settlements clustered around Santa Fe in New Mexico and a few locations in Texas. Maps drawn in Europe marking Spanish ownership of vast North American lands simply did not correspond to the reality on the ground. One sign of Comanche success was their demographic surge during the mid- to late eighteenth century, owing both to their ability to take captives and blend them into their tribe and to their superior command of food resources, especially buffalo.

In 1807, a Comanche delegation arrived at Natchitoches in Louisiana, where a newly appointed U.S. Indian agent entertained them lavishly to demonstrate American power and wealth. In a highly imaginative speech, the agent proclaimed an improbable solidarity with the Comanche: "It is now so long since our Ancestors came from beyond the great Water that we have no remembrance of it.

We ourselves are Natives of the Same land that you are, in other words white Indians, we therefore Should feel & live together like brothers & Good Neighbours." The Comanche welcomed the United States as a new trading partner and invited traders to travel into Comanchería to their market fairs. Into the late 1820s, this trade flourished on an extensive scale, with Americans selling weapons, cloth, and household metal goods in exchange for horses, mules, bison, and furs. And despite maps of the United States that showed the Red River just inside the southwestern border of the Louisiana Purchase, the land from the Red north to the Arkansas River, west of Arkansas, remained under Indian control and thus off-limits to settlement by white Americans until the late nineteenth century (see Map 10.1).

> **REVIEW** Why was Spain concerned that France sold the Louisiana Territory to the United States?

▶ Jefferson, the Madisons, and the War of 1812

Jefferson easily retained the presidency in the election of 1804, with his 162 electoral votes trouncing the 14 won by Federalist Charles Cotesworth Pinckney of South Carolina. Jefferson faced seriously escalating tensions with both France and Britain, leading him to try a novel tactic, an embargo, to stave off war. His Republican secretary of state, James Madison, followed Jefferson as president in 1808, again defeating Pinckney but by a much narrower margin.

Madison continued with a modified embargo, but he broke from Jefferson's all-male style of social networking by involving his gregarious wife, Dolley Madison, in serious politics. Under James Madison's leadership, the country declared war in 1812 on Britain and on Tecumseh's Indian confederacy. The two-year war cost the young nation its White House and its Capitol, but victory was proclaimed at the end nonetheless.

Impressment and Embargo

In 1803, France and Britain went to war, and both repeatedly warned the United States not to ship arms to the other. Britain acted on these threats in 1806, stopping U.S. ships to inspect cargoes for military aid to France and seizing suspected deserters from the British navy, along with many Americans. Ultimately, 2,500 U.S. sailors were "impressed" (taken by force) by the British, who needed them for their war with France. In retaliation against the **impressment** of American sailors, Jefferson convinced Congress to pass a nonimportation law banning a variety of British-made goods, such as leather products, window glass, and beer.

One incident made the usually cautious Jefferson nearly belligerent. In June 1807, the American ship *Chesapeake*, harboring some British deserters, was ordered to stop by the British frigate *Leopard*. The *Chesapeake* refused, and the *Leopard* opened fire, killing three Americans and capturing four alleged deserters — right at the mouth of the Chesapeake Bay, well within U.S. territorial waters. In response, Congress passed the **Embargo Act of 1807**, banning all importation of British goods into the country. Though a drastic measure, the embargo was meant to forestall war and make Britain suffer. All foreign ports were declared off-limits to American merchants to discourage illegal trading through secondary ports. Jefferson was convinced that Britain needed America's agricultural products far more than America needed British goods.

The Embargo Act of 1807 was a disaster. From 1790 to 1807, U.S. exports had increased fivefold, but the embargo brought commerce to a standstill. In New England, the heart of the shipping industry, unemployment rose. Grain plummeted in value, river traffic halted, tobacco rotted in the South, and cotton went unpicked. Protest petitions flooded Washington. The federal government suffered, too, for import duties were a significant source of revenue. Jefferson paid political costs as well and decided not to run for a third term. The Federalist Party, in danger of fading away after its weak showing in the election of 1804, began to revive.

James Madison was chosen to be the Republican candidate by party caucuses — informal political groups that orchestrated the selection of candidates for state and local elections. The Federalist caucuses again chose Pinckney, and in the election he secured 47 electoral votes, compared to 14 in 1804; Madison's total was 122. Support for the Federalists remained centered in New England, whose shipping industry suffered heavy losses in the embargo. The Republicans still held the balance of power nationwide.

Dolley Madison and Social Politics

As wife of the highest-ranking cabinet officer, **Dolley Madison** developed elaborate social networks during her first eight years in Washington. Hers constituted the top level of female politicking in the highly political city, since Jefferson had no First Lady. Although women could not vote and supposedly left politics to men, the female relatives of Washington politicians took on several overtly political functions that greased the wheels of the affairs of state. They networked through dinners, balls, receptions, and the intricate custom of "calling," in which men and women paid brief visits and left calling cards at each other's homes. Webs of friendship and influence in turn facilitated female political lobbying. It was not uncommon for women in this social set to write letters of recommendation for men seeking government work. Hostessing was no trivial or leisured business; it significantly influenced the federal government's patronage system.

When James Madison became president, Dolley Madison, called by some the "presidentress," struck a balance between queenliness and republican openness. She dressed the part in resplendent clothes, choosing a plumed velvet turban for her headdress at her husband's inauguration. She opened three elegant rooms in the executive mansion for a weekly open-house party called

***Dolley Madison,* by Gilbert Stuart**
The "presidentress" of the Madison administration sat for this official portrait in 1804.
She wears an empire-style dress, at the
height of French fashion in 1804 and a style
worn by many women at the coronation of
the emperor Napoleon in Paris. The hallmarks
of such a dress were a light fabric (muslin or
chiffon), short sleeves, a high waistline from
which the fabric fell straight to the ground,
and usually a low, open neckline, as shown
here. © White House Historical Association.

"Mrs. Madison's crush" or "squeeze."
In contrast to George and Martha
Washington's stiff, brief receptions,
the Madisons' parties went on for
hours, with scores or even hundreds
of guests milling about, talking, and
eating. Members of Congress, cabi-
net officers, distinguished guests, envoys from foreign countries, and their
womenfolk attended with regularity. The affable and generous Mrs. Madison
made her guests comfortable with small talk, but a female partygoer reported
that "Mr. Madison had no leisure for the ladies; every moment of his time is
engrossed by the crowd of male visitors who court his notice, and after passing
the first complimentary salutations, his attention is unavoidably withdrawn to
more important objects." His wife's weekly squeeze established informal channels of information and provided crucial political access, a key element of smooth
governance.

In 1810–1811, the Madisons' house acquired its present name, the White
House, probably in reference to its white-painted sandstone exterior. The many
guests at the weekly parties experienced simultaneously the splendor of the
executive mansion and the atmosphere of republicanism that made it accessible
to so many. Dolley Madison, ever an enormous political asset to her rather shy
husband, understood well the symbolic function of the White House to enhance
the power and legitimacy of the presidency.

Tecumseh and Tippecanoe

While the Madisons cemented alliances at home, difficulties with Britain and
France overseas and with Indians in the old Northwest continued to increase.
The Shawnee chief **Tecumseh** (see pages 267–269) actively solidified his confederacy, while the more northern tribes renewed their ties with supportive British
agents and fur traders in Canada, a potential source of food and weapons. If the

United States went to war with Britain, there would clearly be serious repercussions on the frontier.

Shifting demographics raised the stakes for both sides. The 1810 census counted some 230,000 Americans in Ohio only seven years after it achieved statehood. Another 40,000 Americans inhabited the territories of Indiana, Illinois, and Michigan. The Indian population of the entire region (the old Northwest Territory) was much smaller, probably about 70,000, a number unknown to the Americans but certainly gauged by Tecumseh during his extensive travels.

Up to 1805, Indiana's territorial governor, William Henry Harrison, had negotiated a series of treaties in a divide-and-conquer strategy aimed at extracting Indian lands for paltry payments. But with the rise to power of Tecumseh and his brother **Tenskwatawa**, the Prophet, Harrison's strategy faltered. A fundamental part of Tecumseh's message was the assertion that all Indian lands were held in common by all the tribes. "No tribe has the right to sell [these lands], even to each other, much less to strangers . . . ," Tecumseh said. "Sell a country! Why not sell the air, the great sea, as well as the earth? Didn't the Great Spirit make them all for the use of his children?" In 1809, while Tecumseh was away on a recruiting trip, Harrison assembled the leaders of the Potawatomi, Miami, and Delaware tribes to negotiate the Treaty of Fort Wayne. After promising (falsely) that this was the last cession of land the United States would seek, Harrison secured three million acres at about two cents per acre.

When he returned, Tecumseh was furious with both Harrison and the tribal leaders. Leaving his brother in charge at Prophetstown on the Tippecanoe River, the Shawnee chief left to seek alliances with tribes in the South. In November 1811, Harrison decided to attack Prophetstown with a thousand men. The two-hour battle resulted in the deaths of sixty-two Americans and forty Indians before the Prophet's forces fled the town, which Harrison's men set on fire. The **battle of Tippecanoe** was heralded as a glorious victory for the Americans, but Tecumseh was now more ready than ever to make war on the United States.

The War of 1812

The Indian conflicts in the old Northwest soon merged into the wider conflict with Britain, now known as the War of 1812. In 1809, Congress replaced Jefferson's stringent embargo with the Non-Intercourse Act, which prohibited trade only with Britain and France and their colonies, thus restoring trade with other European countries to alleviate somewhat the anguish of shippers, farmers, and planters. By 1811, the country was seriously divided and on the verge of war.

The new Congress seated in March 1811 contained several dozen young Republicans eager to avenge the insults from abroad. Thirty-four-year-old **Henry Clay** from Kentucky and twenty-nine-year-old John C. Calhoun from South Carolina became the center of a group informally known as the **War Hawks**. Mostly lawyers by profession, they came from the West and South and welcomed a war with Britain both to justify attacks on the Indians and to bring an end to impressment. Many were also expansionists, looking to occupy Florida and threaten Canada. Clay was elected Speaker of the House, an extraordinary honor for a newcomer. Calhoun won a seat on the Foreign Relations Committee. The War Hawks approved major defense expenditures, and the army soon quadrupled in size.

In June 1812, Congress declared war on Great Britain in a vote divided along sectional lines: New England and some Middle Atlantic states opposed the war, fearing its effect on commerce, while the South and West were strongly for it. Ironically, Britain had just announced that it would stop the search and seizure of American ships, but the war momentum would not be slowed. The Foreign Relations Committee issued an elaborate justification titled *Report on the Causes and Reasons for War*, written mainly by Calhoun and containing extravagant language about Britain's "lust for power," "unbounded tyranny," and "mad ambition." These were fighting words in a war that was in large measure about insult and honor.

The War Hawks proposed an invasion of Canada, confidently predicting victory in four weeks. Instead, the war lasted two and a half years, and Canada never fell. The northern invasion turned out to be a series of blunders that revealed America's grave unpreparedness for war against the unexpectedly powerful British and Indian forces. Detroit quickly fell, as did Fort Dearborn, site of the future Chicago (Map 10.2). By the fall of 1812, the outlook was grim.

Worse, the New England states dragged their feet in raising troops, and some New England merchants carried on illegal trade with Britain. While President Madison fumed about Federalist disloyalty, Bostonians drank East India tea in Liverpool cups. The fall presidential election pitted Madison against DeWitt Clinton of New York, nominally a Republican but able to attract the Federalist vote. Clinton picked up all of New England's electoral votes, with the exception of Vermont's, and also took New York, New Jersey, and part of Maryland. Madison won in the electoral college, 128 to 89, but his margin of victory was considerably smaller than in 1808.

In late 1812 and early 1813, the tide began to turn in the Americans' favor. First came some reassuring victories at sea. Then the Americans attacked York (now Toronto) and burned it in April 1813. A few months later, Commodore Oliver Hazard Perry defeated the British fleet at the western end of Lake Erie. Emboldened, General Harrison drove an army into Canada from Detroit and in October 1813 defeated the British and Indians at the battle of the Thames, where Tecumseh was killed.

Creek Indians in the South who had allied with Tecumseh's confederacy were also plunged into all-out war. Some 10,000 living in the Mississippi Territory put up a spirited fight against U.S. forces for ten months in 1813–1814. Even without Tecumseh's recruitment trip of 1811 or the War of 1812, the Creeks had grievances aplenty, sparked by American settlers moving into their territory. Using guns obtained from Spanish Florida, the Creeks mounted a strong defense. But the **Creek War** ended suddenly in March 1814 when a general named Andrew

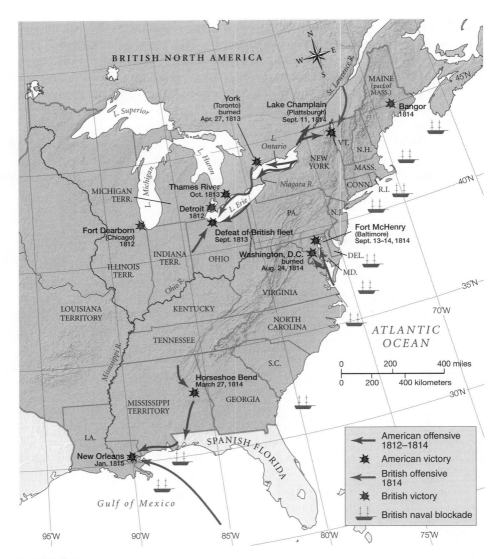

MAP 10.2
The War of 1812
During the War of 1812, battles were fought along the Canadian border and in the Chesapeake region. The most important American victory came in New Orleans two weeks after a peace agreement had been signed in England.

Jackson led 2,500 Tennessee militiamen in a bloody attack called the Battle of Horseshoe Bend. More than 550 Indians were killed, and several hundred more died trying to escape across a river. Later that year, General Jackson extracted from the defeated tribe a treaty relinquishing thousands of square miles of their land to the United States.

Washington City Burns: The British Offensive

In August 1814, British ships sailed into the Chesapeake Bay, landing 5,000 troops and throwing the capital into a panic. Families evacuated, banks hid their money, and government clerks carted away boxes of important papers. Dolley Madison, with dinner for guests cooking over the fire, fled with her husband's papers, leaving several struggling servants to rescue a portrait of George Washington. As the cook related, "When the British did arrive, they ate up the very dinner, and drank the wines, & c., that I had prepared for the President's party." Then they torched the White House. They also burned the Capitol, a newspaper office, and a well-stocked arsenal. Instead of trying to hold the city, the British headed north and attacked Baltimore, but a fierce defense by the Maryland militia thwarted that effort.

In another powerful offensive that same month, British troops marched from Canada into New York State, but a series of mistakes cost them a naval skirmish at Plattsburgh on Lake Champlain, and they retreated to Canada. Five months later, another large British army landed in lower Louisiana and, in early January 1815, encountered General Andrew Jackson and his militia just outside New Orleans. Jackson's forces dramatically carried the day. The British suffered between 2,000 and 3,000 casualties, the Americans fewer than 80. Jackson became an instant hero. The **battle of New Orleans** was the most glorious victory the Americans had experienced, allowing some Americans to boast that the United States had won a second war of independence from Britain. No one in the United States knew that negotiators in Europe had signed a peace agreement two weeks earlier.

The Treaty of Ghent, signed in December 1814, settled few of the surface issues that had led to war. Neither country could claim victory, and no land changed hands. Instead, the treaty reflected a mutual agreement to give up certain goals. The Americans dropped their plea for an end to impressments, which in any case subsided as soon as Britain and France ended their war in 1815. They also gave up any claim to Canada. The British agreed to stop all aid to the Indians. Nothing was said about shipping rights. The most concrete result was a plan for a commission to determine the exact boundary between the United States and Canada.

Antiwar Federalists in New England could not gloat over the war's ambiguous conclusion because of an ill-timed and seemingly unpatriotic move on their part. The region's leaders had convened a secret meeting in Hartford, Connecticut, in December 1814 to discuss dramatic measures to curb the South's power. They proposed abolishing the Constitution's three-fifths clause as a basis of representation; requiring a two-thirds vote instead of a simple majority for imposing embargoes, admitting states, or declaring war; limiting the president to one term; and prohibiting the election of successive presidents from the same state. The cumulative aim of these proposals was to reduce the South's political power and break Virginia's lock on the presidency. New England wanted to make sure that no sectional party could again lead the country into war against the clear interests of another. The Federalists at Hartford even discussed secession from the Union but rejected that path. Coming just as peace was achieved, however, the **Hartford Convention** looked very unpatriotic. The Federalist Party never recovered its grip, and within a few years it was reduced to a shadow of its former self, even in New England.

No one really won the War of 1812; however, Americans celebrated as though they had, with parades and fireworks. The war gave rise to a new spirit of nationalism. The paranoia over British tyranny evident in the 1812 declaration of war was laid to rest, replaced by pride in a more equal relationship with the old mother country. Indeed, in 1817 the two countries signed the Rush-Bagot disarmament treaty (named after its two negotiators), which limited each country to a total of four naval vessels, each with just a single cannon, to patrol the vast watery border between them. The Rush-Bagot treaty was perhaps the most successful disarmament treaty for a century to come.

The biggest winners in the War of 1812 were the young men, once called War Hawks, who took up the banner of the Republican Party and carried it in new, expansive directions. These young politicians favored trade, western expansion, internal improvements, and the energetic development of new economic markets. The biggest losers of the war were the Indians. Tecumseh was dead, his brother the Prophet was discredited, the prospects of an Indian confederacy were dashed, the Creeks' large homeland was seized, and the British protectors were gone.

REVIEW   Why did Congress declare war on Great Britain in 1812?

▶ Women's Status in the Early Republic

Dolley Madison's pioneering role as "presidentress" showed that at the pinnacles of power, elite women could assume an active presence in civic affairs. But, as with the 1790s cultural compromise that endorsed female education to make women into better wives and mothers (see chapter 9), Mrs. Madison and her female circle practiced politics to further their husbands' careers. There was little talk of the "rights of woman."

From 1800 to 1825, key institutions central to the shaping of women's lives — the legal system, marriage, and religion — proved fairly resistant to change. State legislatures and the courts maintained the legal dependency of married white women in a country whose defining characteristic for men was independence. Marriage laws for whites continued to support unequal power between men and women, while religious organizations reconsidered the role of women in church governance in the face of rising church membership rates for women. The most dramatic opportunity for women came with the flowering of female academies whose rigorous curricula fostered high-level literacy and rational thought. Even when advertised as institutions to prepare girls to be intelligent mothers, many academies built up their students' self-confidence and implanted expectations that their mental training would find a use beyond the kitchen and nursery.

Women and the Law

The Anglo-American view of women, embedded in English common law, was that wives had no independent legal or political personhood. The legal doctrine of *feme covert* (covered woman) held that a wife's civic life was completely subsumed by her husband's. A wife was obligated to obey her husband; her property was his, her domestic and sexual services were his, and even their children were legally his. Women had no right to keep their wages, to make contracts, or to sue or be sued.

State legislatures generally passed up the opportunity to rewrite the laws of domestic relations even though they redrafted other British laws in light of republican principles. Lawyers never paused to defend, much less to challenge, the assumption that unequal power relations lay at the heart of marriage.

The one aspect of family law that changed in the early Republic was divorce. Before the Revolution, only New England jurisdictions recognized a limited right to divorce; by 1820, every state except South Carolina did so. However, divorce was uncommon and in many states could be obtained only by petition to the state's legislature, a daunting obstacle for many ordinary people. A mutual wish to terminate a marriage was never sufficient grounds for a legal divorce. A New York judge affirmed that "it would be aiming a deadly blow at public morals to decree a dissolution of the marriage contract merely because the parties requested it.

"Divorces should never be allowed, except for the protection of the innocent party, and for the punishment of the guilty." States upheld the institution of marriage both to protect persons they thought of as naturally dependent (women and children) and to regulate the use and inheritance of property. (Unofficial self-divorce, desertion, and bigamy were remedies that ordinary people sometimes chose to get around the law, but all were socially unacceptable.) Legal enforcement of marriage as an unequal relationship played a major role in maintaining gender inequality in the nineteenth century.

Single adult women could own and convey property, make contracts, initiate lawsuits, and pay taxes. They could not vote (except in New Jersey before 1807), serve on juries, or practice law, so their civil status was limited. Single women's economic status was often limited as well, by custom as much as by law. Job prospects were few and low-paying. Unless they had inherited adequate property or could live with married siblings, single adult women in the early Republic very often were poor.

None of the legal institutions that structured white gender relations applied to black slaves. As property themselves, under the jurisdiction of slave owners, they could not freely consent to any contractual obligations, including marriage. The protective features of state-sponsored unions were thus denied to black men and women in slavery. But this also meant that slave unions did not establish unequal power relations between partners backed by the force of law, as did marriages among the free.

Women and Church Governance

In most Protestant denominations around 1800, white women made up the majority of congregants. Yet church leadership of most denominations rested in men's hands. There were some exceptions, however. In Baptist congregations in New England, women served along with men on church governance committees, deciding on the admission of new members, voting on hiring ministers, and even debating doctrinal points. Quakers, too, had a history of recognizing women's spiritual talents. Some were accorded the status of minister, capable of leading and speaking in Quaker meetings.

Between 1790 and 1820, a small and highly unusual set of women actively engaged in open preaching. Most were from Freewill Baptist groups centered in New England and upstate New York. Others came from small Methodist sects, and yet others rejected any formal religious affiliation. Probably fewer than a hundred such women existed, but several dozen traveled beyond their local communities, creating converts and controversy. They spoke from the heart, without prepared speeches, often exhibiting trances and claiming to exhort (counsel or warn) rather than to preach.

The best-known exhorting woman was **Jemima Wilkinson**, who called herself "the Publick Universal Friend." After a near-death experience from a high fever, Wilkinson proclaimed her body no longer female or male but the incarnation of the "Spirit of Light." She dressed in men's clothes, wore her hair in a masculine style, shunned gender-specific pronouns, and preached openly in Rhode Island and Philadelphia. In the early nineteenth century, Wilkinson established a town called New Jerusalem in western New York with some 250 followers. Her fame was sustained by periodic newspaper articles that fed public curiosity about her lifelong transvestism and her unfeminine forcefulness.

The decades from 1790 to the 1820s marked a period of unusual confusion, ferment, and creativity in American religion. New denominations blossomed, new styles of religiosity gripped adherents, and an extensive periodical press devoted to religion popularized all manner of theological and institutional innovations. In such a climate, the age-old tradition of gender subordination came into question here and there among the most radically democratic of the churches. But the presumption of male authority over women was deeply entrenched in American culture. Even denominations that had allowed women to participate in church governance began to pull back, and most churches reinstated patterns of hierarchy along gender lines.

Female Education

First in the North and then in the South, states and localities began investing in public schools to foster an educated citizenry deemed essential to the healthy functioning of a republic. Young girls attended district schools, sometimes along with boys or, in rural areas, more often in separate summer sessions. Basic literacy and numeracy formed the curriculum taught to white children aged roughly six to eleven. By 1830, girls had made rapid gains, in many places

Portrait of Emma Willard
Emma Willard's school in Troy, New York, offered young women a curriculum that approached the academic rigor of the elite men's colleges of the 1820s, including Latin, Greek, mathematics, and moral philosophy. A student named Elizabeth Cady, soon to be a leader of the midcentury woman's rights movement, recalled that Willard had a "profound self respect (a rare quality in a woman) which gave her a dignity truly regal," as can be seen in this portrait of the confident educator.

approaching male literacy rates. (Far fewer schools addressed the needs of free black children, whether male or female.)

More advanced female education came from a growing number of private academies. Judith Sargent Murray, the Massachusetts author who had called for equality of the sexes around 1790 (see chapter 9), predicted in 1800 that "a new era in female history" would emerge because "**female academies** are everywhere establishing." Some dozen female academies were established in the 1790s, and by 1830 that number had grown to nearly two hundred. Candidates for admission were primarily daughters of elite families as well as those of middling families with elite or intellectual aspirations, such as ministers' daughters.

The three-year curriculum included both ornamental arts and solid academics. The former strengthened female gentility: drawing, needlework, music, and French conversation. The academic subjects included English grammar, literature, history, the natural sciences, geography, and elocution (the art of effective public speaking). Academy catalogs show that, by the 1820s, the courses and reading lists at the top female academies equaled those at male colleges such as Harvard, Yale, Dartmouth, and Princeton. The girls at these academies studied Latin, rhetoric, logic, theology, moral philosophy, algebra, geometry, and even chemistry and physics.

Two of the best-known female academies were the Troy Female Seminary in New York, founded by Emma Willard in 1821, and the Hartford Seminary in Connecticut, founded by Catharine Beecher in 1822. Unlike theological seminaries that trained men for the clergy, Troy and Hartford prepared their female students to teach, on the grounds that women made better teachers than did men. Author Harriet Beecher Stowe, educated at her sister's school and then a teacher there, agreed: "If men have more knowledge they have less talent at communicating it. Nor have they the patience, the long-suffering, and gentleness necessary to superintend the formation of character."

The most immediate value of advanced female education lay in the self-cultivation and confidence it provided. Following the model of male colleges, female graduation exercises showcased speeches and recitations performed in front of a mixed-sex audience of family, friends, and local notables. Here, the young women's elocution studies paid off; they had learned the art of persuasion along with correct pronunciation and the skill of fluent speaking. Academies also took care to promote a pleasing female modesty. Female pedantry or intellectual immodesty triggered the stereotype of the "bluestocking," a British term of hostility for a too-learned woman doomed to fail in the marriage market.

By the mid-1820s, the total annual enrollment at the female academies and seminaries equaled enrollment at the near six dozen male colleges in the United States. Both groups accounted for only about 1 percent of their age cohorts in the country at large, indicating that advanced education was clearly limited to a privileged few. Among the men, this group disproportionately filled the future rosters of ministers, lawyers, judges, and political leaders. Most female graduates in time married and raised families, but first many of them became teachers at academies and district schools. A large number also became authors, contributing essays and poetry to newspapers, editing periodicals, and publishing novels. The new attention to the training of female minds laid the foundation for major changes in the gender system as girl students of the 1810s matured into adult women of the 1830s.

REVIEW   How did the civil status of American women and men differ in the early Republic?

▶ Monroe and Adams

With the elections of 1816 and 1820, Virginians continued their hold on the presidency. In 1816, **James Monroe** beat Federalist Rufus King of New York, garnering 183 electoral votes to King's 34. In 1820, the Republican Monroe was reelected with all but one electoral vote. The collapse of the Federalist Party ushered in an apparent period of one-party rule, but politics remained highly contentious. At the state level, increasing voter engagement sparked a drive for universal white male suffrage.

Many factors promoted increased partisanship. Monroe and his aloof wife, Elizabeth, sharply curtailed social gatherings at the White House, driving the hard work of social networking into competing channels. Ill feelings were stirred by a sectional crisis over the admission of Missouri to the Union, and foreign policy questions involving European claims to Latin America animated sharp disagreements as well. The election of 1824 brought forth an abundance of candidates, all claiming to be Republicans. The winner was John Quincy Adams in an election decided by the House of Representatives and, many believed, a backroom bargain. Put to the test of practical circumstances, the one-party political system failed and then fractured.

From Property to Democracy

Up to 1820, presidential elections occurred in the electoral college, at a remove from ordinary voters. The excitement generated by state elections, however, created an insistent pressure for greater democratization of presidential elections.

In the 1780s, twelve of the original thirteen states enacted property qualifications based on the time-honored theory that only male freeholders — landowners, as distinct from tenants or servants — had sufficient independence of mind to be entrusted with the vote. Of course, not everyone accepted that restricted idea of the people's role in government (see chapter 8). In the 1790s, Vermont became the first state to enfranchise all adult males, and four other states soon broadened suffrage considerably by allowing all male taxpayers to vote, a status that could be triggered simply by owning a cow, since local property taxes were an ever-present and generally nonburdensome reality. Between 1800 and 1830, greater democratization became a lively issue both in established states and in new states emerging in the West.

In the established states, lively newspaper exchanges and petition campaigns pushed state after state to hold constitutional conventions, where questions of suffrage, balloting procedures, apportionment, and representation were hotly debated. Both political philosophy and practical politics were entwined in these debates: Who are "the people" in a government founded on popular sovereignty, and whose party or interest group gains the most from expanded suffrage?

In new states, small populations together with yet smaller numbers of large property owners meant that few men could vote under typical restrictive property qualifications. Congress initially set a fifty-acre freehold as the threshold for voting, but in Illinois fewer than three hundred men met that test at the time of statehood. When Indiana, Illinois, and Mississippi became states, their constitutions granted suffrage to all

"We Owe Allegiance to No Crown"
John A. Woodside, a Philadelphia sign painter, made his living creating advertisements and ornamental pictures for hotels, taverns, and city fire engines. He specialized in promotional paintings conveying a booster spirit, especially heroic scenes on banners to be carried in parades. At some point in his decades-long career, which ran from about 1815 to 1850, he created this scene of a youthful sailor being crowned with a laurel wreath, the ancient Greek symbol of victory, by a breezy Miss Liberty (identified by the liberty cap she carries on a stick).

Painting on a patriotic motif by John A. Woodside of Philadelphia in the early 1800s.

taxpayers. Five additional new western states abandoned property and taxpayer qualifications altogether.

The most heated battles over suffrage occurred in eastern states, where expanding numbers of commercial men, renters, and mortgage holders of all classes contended with entrenched landed elites who, not surprisingly, favored the status quo. Still, by 1820, half a dozen states passed suffrage reform. Some stopped short of complete male suffrage, instead tying the vote to tax status or militia service. In the remainder of the states, the defenders of landed property qualifications managed to delay expanded suffrage for two more decades. But it was increasingly hard to persuade the disfranchised that landowners alone had a stake in government. Proponents of the status quo began to argue instead that the "industry and good habits" necessary to achieve a propertied status in life were what gave landowners the right character to vote. Opponents fired back blistering attacks. One delegate to New York's constitutional convention said, "More integrity and more patriotism are generally found in the labouring class of the community than in the higher orders." Owning land was no more predictive of wisdom and good character than it was of a person's height or strength, said another observer.

Both sides of the debate generally agreed that character mattered, and many ideas for ensuring an electorate of proper wisdom came up for discussion. The exclusion of paupers and felons convicted of "infamous crimes" found favor in legislation in many states. Literacy tests and raising the voting age to a figure in the thirties were debated but ultimately discarded. The exclusion of women required no discussion in the constitutional conventions, so firm was the legal power of *feme covert*. But in one exceptional moment, at the Virginia convention in 1829, a delegate wondered aloud why unmarried women over the age of twenty-one could not vote; he was quickly silenced with the argument that all women lacked the "free agency and intelligence" necessary for wise voting.

Free black men's enfranchisement was another story, generating much discussion at all the conventions. Under existing freehold qualifications, a small number of propertied black men could vote; universal or taxpayer suffrage would inevitably enfranchise many more. Many delegates at the various state conventions spoke against that extension, claiming that blacks as a race lacked prudence, independence, and knowledge. With the exception of New York, which retained the existing property qualification for black voters as it removed it for whites, the general pattern was one of expanded suffrage for whites and a total eclipse of suffrage for blacks.

The Missouri Compromise

The politics of race produced the most divisive issue during Monroe's term. In February 1819, Missouri — so recently the territory of the powerful Osage Indians — applied for statehood. Since 1815, four other states had joined the Union (Indiana, Mississippi, Illinois, and Alabama) following the blueprint laid out by the Northwest

Ordinance of 1787. But Missouri posed a problem. Although much of its area was on the same latitude as the free state of Illinois, its territorial population included ten thousand slaves brought there by southern planters.

Missouri's unusual combination of geography and demography led a New York congressman, James Tallmadge Jr., to propose two amendments to the statehood bill. The first stipulated that slaves born in Missouri after statehood would be free at age twenty-five, and the second declared that no new slaves could be imported into the state. Tallmadge's model was New York's gradual emancipation law of 1799 (see chapter 8). It did not strip slave owners of their current property, and it allowed them full use of the labor of newborn slaves well into their prime productive years. Still, southern congressmen objected because in the long run the amendments would make Missouri a free state, presumably no longer allied with southern economic and political interests. Just as southern economic power rested on slave labor, southern political power drew extra strength from the slave population because of the three-fifths rule. In 1820, the South owed seventeen of its seats in the House of Representatives to its slave population.

Tallmadge's amendments passed in the House by a close and sharply sectional vote of North against South. The ferocious debate led a Georgia representative to observe that the question had started "a fire which all the waters of the ocean could not extinguish. It can be extinguished only in blood." The Senate, with an even number of slave and free states, voted down the amendments, and Missouri statehood was postponed until the next congressional term.

In 1820, a compromise emerged. Maine, once part of Massachusetts, applied for statehood as a free state, balancing against Missouri as a slave state. The Senate further agreed that the southern boundary of Missouri — latitude 36°30' — extended west, would become the permanent line dividing slave from free states, guaranteeing the North a large area where slavery was banned (Map 10.3). The House also approved the **Missouri Compromise**, thanks to expert deal brokering by Kentucky's Henry Clay, who earned the nickname "the Great Pacificator" for his superb negotiating skills. The whole package passed because seventeen northern congressmen decided that minimizing sectional conflict was the best course and voted with the South.

President Monroe and former president Jefferson at first worried that the Missouri crisis would reinvigorate the Federalist Party as the party of the North. But even ex-Federalists agreed that the split between free and slave states was too dangerous a fault line to be permitted to become a shaper of national politics. When new parties did develop in the 1830s, they took pains to bridge geography, each party developing a presence in both North and South. Monroe and Jefferson also worried about the future of slavery. Both understood slavery to be deeply problematic, but, as Jefferson said, "we have the wolf by the ears, and we can neither hold him, nor safely let him go. Justice is in one scale, and self-preservation in the other."

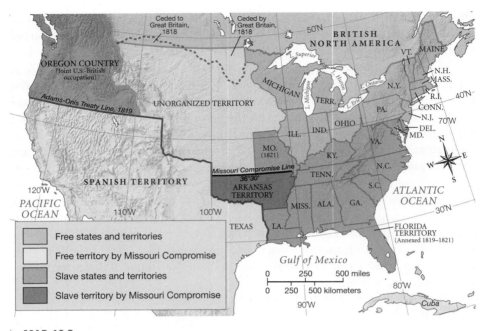

MAP 10.3
The Missouri Compromise, 1820
After a difficult battle in Congress, Missouri entered the Union in 1821 as part of a package of compromises. Maine was admitted as a free state to balance slavery in Missouri, and a line drawn at latitude 36°30′ put most of the rest of the Louisiana Territory off-limits to slavery in the future.

The Monroe Doctrine

As Congress struggled with the slavery issue, new foreign policy challenges also arose. In 1816, U.S. troops led by General Andrew Jackson invaded Spanish Florida in search of Seminole Indians harboring escaped slaves. Once there, Jackson declared himself the commander of northern Florida, demonstrating his power in 1818 by executing two British men who he claimed were dangerous enemies. In asserting rule over the territory, and surely in executing the two British subjects on Spanish land, Jackson had gone too far. Privately, President Monroe was distressed and pondered court-martialing Jackson, prevented only by Jackson's immense popularity as the hero of the battle of New Orleans. Instead, John Quincy Adams, the secretary of state, negotiated with Spain the Adams-Onís Treaty, which delivered all of Florida to the United States in 1819 and finally settled the disputed borders of the Louisiana Purchase. In exchange, the Americans agreed to abandon any claim to Texas or Cuba. Southerners viewed this as a large concession, having eyed both places as potential acquisitions for future slave states.

Spain at that moment was preoccupied with its colonies in South America. One after another, Chile, Colombia, Peru, and finally Mexico declared themselves independent in the early 1820s. To discourage Spain and other European countries from reconquering these colonies, Monroe in 1823 formulated a declaration of principles on South America, known in later years as the **Monroe Doctrine**. The president warned that "the American Continents, by the free and independent condition which they have assumed and maintain, are henceforth not to be considered as subjects for future colonization by any European power." Any attempt to interfere in the Western Hemisphere would be regarded as "the manifestation of an unfriendly disposition towards the United States." In exchange for noninterference by Europeans, Monroe pledged that the United States would stay out of European struggles. At that time, Monroe did not intend his statement to lay a foundation for U.S. intervention in South America. Indeed, the small American navy could not realistically defend Chile or Peru against a major power such as Spain or France. The doctrine was Monroe's idea of sound foreign policy, but it did not have the force of law.

The Election of 1824

Monroe's nonpartisan administration was the last of its kind, a throwback to eighteenth-century ideals, as was Monroe, with his powdered wig and knee breeches. Monroe's cabinet contained men of sharply different philosophies, all calling themselves Republicans. Secretary of State **John Quincy Adams** represented the urban Northeast; South Carolinian John C. Calhoun spoke for the planter aristocracy as secretary of war; and William H. Crawford of Georgia, secretary of the treasury, was a proponent of Jeffersonian states' rights and limited federal power. Even before the end of Monroe's first term, these men and others began to maneuver for the election of 1824.

Crucially helping them to maneuver were their wives, who accomplished some of the work of modern campaign managers by courting men — and women — of influence. The parties not thrown by Elizabeth Monroe were now given all over town by women whose husbands were jockeying for political favor. Louisa Catherine Adams had a weekly party for guests numbering in the hundreds.

The somber Adams lacked charm — "I am a man of reserved, cold, austere, and forbidding manners," he once wrote — but his abundantly charming (and hardworking) wife made up for that. She attended to the etiquette of social calls, sometimes making two dozen in a morning, and counted sixty-eight members of Congress as her regular guests. This was smart politics, in case the House of Representatives wound up deciding the 1824 election — which it did.

John Quincy Adams (as well as Louisa Catherine) was ambitious for the presidency, but so were others. Candidate Henry Clay, Speaker of the House and negotiator of the Treaty of Ghent with Britain in 1814, promoted a new "American System," a package of protective tariffs to encourage manufacturing and federal expenditures for internal improvements such as roads and canals. Treasurer William Crawford was a favorite of Republicans from Virginia and New York, even after he suffered an incapacitating stroke in mid-1824. Calhoun was another serious contender, having served in Congress and in several cabinets. A southern planter, he attracted northern support for his backing of internal improvements and protective tariffs.

The final candidate was an outsider and a latecomer: General **Andrew Jackson** of Tennessee. Jackson had far less national political experience than the others, but he enjoyed great celebrity from his military career. In 1824, on the anniversary of the battle of New Orleans, the Adamses threw a spectacular ball in his honor, hoping that some of Jackson's charisma would rub off on Adams, who was not yet thinking of Jackson as a rival for office. Not long after, Jackson's supporters put his name forward for the presidency, and voters in the West and South reacted with enthusiasm. Adams was dismayed, while Calhoun dropped out of the race and shifted his attention to winning the vice presidency.

Along with democratizing the vote, eighteen states (out of the full twenty-four) had put the power to choose members of the electoral college directly in the hands of voters, making the 1824 election the first one to have a popular vote tally for the presidency. Jackson proved by far to be the most popular candidate, winning 153,544 votes. Adams was second with 108,740, Clay won 47,136 votes, and the debilitated Crawford garnered 46,618. This was not a large turnout, probably amounting to just over a quarter of adult white males. Nevertheless, the election of 1824 marked a new departure in choosing presidents. Partisanship energized the electorate; apathy and a low voter turnout would not recur until the twentieth century.

In the electoral college, Jackson received 99 votes, Adams 84, Crawford 41, and Clay 37. Jackson lacked a majority, so the House of Representatives stepped in for the second time in U.S. history. Each congressional delegation had one vote; according to the Constitution's Twelfth Amendment, passed in 1804, only the top three candidates joined the runoff. Thus Henry Clay was out of the race and in a position to bestow his support on another candidate.

Jackson's supporters later characterized the election of 1824 as the "corrupt bargain." Clay backed Adams, and Adams won by one vote in the House in February 1825. Clay's support made sense on several levels. Despite strong mutual dislike, he and Adams agreed on issues such as federal support to build roads and canals. Moreover, Clay was uneasy with Jackson's volatile temperament and unstated political views and with Crawford's diminished capacity. What made Clay's decision look "corrupt" was that immediately after the election, Adams offered to appoint Clay secretary of state — and Clay accepted.

In fact, there probably was no concrete bargain; Adams's subsequent cabinet appointments demonstrated his lack of political astuteness. But Andrew Jackson felt that the election had been stolen from him, and he wrote bitterly that "the Judas of the West [Clay] has closed the contract and will receive the thirty pieces of silver."

The Adams Administration

John Quincy Adams, like his father, was a one-term president. His career had been built on diplomacy, not electoral politics, and despite his wife's deftness in the art of political influence, his own political horse sense was not well developed.

With his cabinet choices, he welcomed his opposition into his inner circle. He asked Crawford to stay on in the Treasury. He retained an openly pro-Jackson postmaster general even though that position controlled thousands of nationwide patronage appointments. He even asked Jackson to become secretary of war. With Calhoun as vice president (elected without opposition by the electoral college) and Clay at the State Department, the whole argumentative crew would have been thrust into the executive branch. Crawford and Jackson had the good sense to decline the appointments.

Adams had lofty ideas for federal action during his presidency, and the plan he put before Congress was so sweeping that it took Henry Clay aback. Adams called for federally built roads, canals, and harbors. He proposed a national university in Washington as well as government-sponsored scientific research. He wanted to build observatories to advance astronomical knowledge and to promote precision in timekeeping, and he backed a decimal-based system of weights and measures. In all these endeavors, Adams believed he was continuing the legacy of Jefferson and Madison, using the powers of government to advance knowledge. But his opponents feared he was too Hamiltonian, using federal power inappropriately to advance commercial interests.

Whether he was more truly Federalist or Republican was a moot point. Lacking the give-and-take political skills required to gain congressional support, Adams was unable to implement much of his program. He scorned the idea of courting voters to gain support and using the patronage system to enhance his power. He often made appointments (to posts such as customs collectors) to placate enemies rather than to reward friends. A story of a toast offered to the president may well have been mythical, but as humorous folklore it made the rounds during his term and came to summarize Adams's precarious hold on leadership. A dignitary raised a glass and said, "May he strike confusion to his foes," to which another voice scornfully chimed in, "as he has already done to his friends."

REVIEW How did the collapse of the Federalist Party influence the administrations of James Monroe and John Quincy Adams?

▶ Conclusion: Republican Simplicity Becomes Complex

The Jeffersonian Republicans at first tried to undo much of what the Federalists had created in the 1790s, but their promise of a simpler government gave way to the complexities of domestic and foreign issues. The sudden acquisition of the Louisiana Purchase promised land and opportunity to settlers but first required intricate federal-level dealings with powerful western Indians. British impressments of American sailors challenged Jefferson and Madison to stand up to the onetime mother country, culminating in the War of 1812. Fighting both the British and their Indian allies, the Americans engaged in two years of inconclusive battles, mostly on American soil. Their eventual triumph at the battle of New Orleans allowed them the illusion that they had fought a second war of independence.

The War of 1812 was the Indians' second lost war for independence. Tecumseh's vision of an unprecedentedly large confederacy of Indian tribes that would halt westward expansion by white Americans was cut short by the war and by his death. When Canada was under attack, the British valued its defense more than they valued their promises to help the Indians.

The war elevated to national prominence General Andrew Jackson, whose popularity with voters in the 1824 election surprised traditional politicians (and their politically astute wives) and threw the one-party rule of Republicans into a tailspin. New western states with more lenient voter qualifications and eastern states with reformed suffrage laws further eroded the old political elite. Appeals to the mass of white male voters would be the hallmark of all nineteenth-century elections after 1824. In such a system, John Quincy Adams and men like him were at a great disadvantage.

Ordinary American women, whether white or free black, had no place in government. Male legislatures maintained women's *feme covert* status, keeping wives dependent on husbands. A few women claimed greater personal autonomy through religion, while many others benefited from expanded female schooling in schools and academies. These increasingly substantial gains in education would blossom into a major transformation of gender starting in the 1830s and 1840s.

Amid the turmoil of the early Republic, two events in particular sparked developments that would prove momentous in later decades. The bitter debate over slavery that surrounded the Missouri Compromise accentuated the serious divisions between northern and southern states — divisions that would only widen in the decades to come. And Jefferson's long embargo and Madison's wartime trade stoppage gave a big boost to American manufacturing by removing competition with British factories. When peace returned in 1815, the years of independent development burst forth into a period of sustained economic growth that continued nearly unabated into the mid-nineteenth century.

Reviewing Chapter 10

REVIEW QUESTIONS

1. How did Jefferson attempt to undo the Federalist innovations of earlier administrations? (pp. 269–273)

2. Why was Spain concerned that France sold the Louisiana Territory to the United States? (pp. 273–279)

3. Why did Congress declare war on Great Britain in 1812? (pp. 279–286)

4. How did the civil status of American women and men differ in the early Republic? (pp. 286–290)

5. How did the collapse of the Federalist Party influence the administrations of James Monroe and John Quincy Adams? (pp. 290–297)

MAKING CONNECTIONS

1. When Jefferson assumed the presidency following the election of 1800, he expected to transform the national government. Describe his republican vision and his successes and failures in implementing it. Did subsequent Republican presidents advance the same objectives?

2. How did the United States expand and strengthen its control of territory in North America in the early nineteenth century? In your answer, discuss the roles of diplomacy, military action, and political leadership in contributing to this development.

3. Regional tensions emerged as a serious danger to the American political system in the early nineteenth century. Discuss specific conflicts that had regional dimensions. How did Americans resolve, or fail to resolve, these tensions?

4. Although the United States denied its female citizens equality in public life, some women were able to exert considerable influence. How did they do so? In your answer, discuss the legal, political, and educational status of women in the early Republic.

LINKING TO THE PAST

1. Compare the British-Indian alliance in the Revolutionary War with the British-Indian alliance in the War of 1812. Were there any reasons for men like Tecumseh to think that the alliance might work out better the second time? (See chapter 7.)

2. How do you think the Federalist supporters of the Constitution in 1787–1788 felt about the steady decline in states' property qualifications for male voters that occurred between 1800 and 1824? Did the democratization of voting necessarily undermine the Constitution's restrictions on direct democracy in the federal government? (See chapter 8.)

TIMELINE 1800–1825

1800
- Republicans Thomas Jefferson and Aaron Burr tie in electoral college.
- Fears of slave rebellion led by Gabriel in Virginia result in twenty-seven executions.

1801
- House of Representatives elects Thomas Jefferson president after thirty-six ballots.
- Pasha of Tripoli declares war on United States.

1803
- *Marbury v. Madison.*
- Britain and France each warn United States not to ship war-related goods to the other.
- United States purchases Louisiana Territory.

1804
- U.S. Marines and foreign mercenaries under William Eaton take Derne, Tripoli.
- President Jefferson meets with Osage leaders in Washington City.

1804–1806
- Lewis and Clark expedition travels from St. Louis to Pacific Ocean.

1807
- British attack and search *Chesapeake.*

- Embargo Act.
- United States establishes trade with Comanche Indians.

1808
- Republican James Madison elected president; Dolley Madison soon dubbed "presidentress."

1809
- Treaty of Fort Wayne.
- Non-Intercourse Act.

1811
- Battle of Tippecanoe.

1812
- United States declares war on Great Britain.

1813
- Tecumseh dies at battle of the Thames.

1814
- British attack Washington City.
- Treaty of Ghent.
- New England Federalists meet at Hartford Convention.

1815
- Battle of New Orleans.

1816
- Republican James Monroe elected president.

1819
- Adams-Onís Treaty.

1820
- Missouri Compromise.

1823
- Monroe Doctrine asserted.

1825
- John Quincy Adams elected president by House of Representatives.

▶ FOR AN ONLINE BIBLIOGRAPHY, PRACTICE QUIZZES, WEB SITES, IMAGES, AND DOCUMENTS RELATED TO THIS CHAPTER, see the Book Companion Site at **bedfordstmartins.com/roarkvalue**.

▶ FOR DOCUMENTS RELATED TO THIS PERIOD, see Michael Johnson, ed., *Reading the American Past*, Fifth Edition.

The Expanding Republic

1815–1840

IN 1837, LARGE AUDIENCES THROUGHOUT MASSACHUSETTS WITNESSED the astonishing spectacle of two sisters from a wealthy southern family delivering long, impassioned speeches about the evils of slavery. Sarah and Angelina Grimké showed no fear or hesitation. They were women on a mission, channeling a higher power to authorize their outspokenness. As Angelina, thirty-two, wrote to a friend after one event: "Whilst in the act of speaking I am favored to forget little 'I' entirely & to feel altogether hid behind the great cause I am pleading. Were it not for this feeling, I know not how I could face such audiences without embarrassment." In their seventy-nine speaking engagements, some forty thousand women — and men — came to hear them.

Not much in their family background predicted the sisters' radical break with tradition. And radical it was: The abolitionist movement was in its infancy in the 1830s, centered around Boston editor William Lloyd Garrison, who demanded an immediate end to slavery. Nearly as radical as Garrison, the Grimké sisters had crossed a gender line by speaking their own unscripted words of moral politics in front of mixed-sex audiences.

The Grimké sisters grew up in Charleston, South Carolina, in a prominent family whose wealth derived from slavery. With a dozen siblings, an invalid mother, and a busy father — he was chief justice of the State Supreme Court — the two sisters evaded familial surveillance enough to develop independent minds and explore alternative churches that opposed slavery. By the late 1820s, both sisters had moved to Philadelphia and joined the Quakers' Society of Friends.

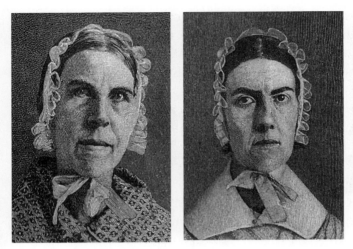

Grimké Sisters
Sarah M. and Angelina E. Grimké sat for these portraits probably sometime around 1840, when Sarah was 48 and Angelina was 35. Quaker women typically wore plain headdresses, but these day caps—sheer fabric with ruffles— are not very austere. Such caps were common indoor wear, to keep hair in place and protected, while outdoors, a large-brimmed sun-screening bonnet would go over the cap. Library of Congress.

Until 1835, they refrained from activism and remained aloof from Philadelphia's growing antislavery community. That year, the British abolitionist George Thompson lectured in town, inspiring Angelina to write to Garrison, describing herself as a white southern exile from slavery. When Garrison published her letter in his weekly paper, the *Liberator*, her rare voice of personal testimony caused a great stir. Angelina next wrote *An Appeal to the Christian Women of the South*, urging southern women to take political action against slavery; Charleston postmasters burned copies sent by mail. A year later, she issued *An Appeal to the Women of the Nominally Free States*, setting forth the ideas that would be articulated on her Massachusetts lecture tour.

The extended tour of Massachusetts caused a sensation and led to a doubling of membership in northern antislavery societies. Newspapers and state church leaders fiercely debated the Grimkés' position. And the issue of women's right to speak in public was open for full examination. The Grimké sisters defended their stand: "Whatever is morally right for a man to do is morally right for a woman to do," Angelina wrote. "I recognize no rights but human rights." Sarah produced a set of essays titled *Letters on the Equality of the Sexes* (1838), the first American treatise asserting women's equality with men.

The Grimké sisters' innovative radicalism was part of a vibrant, contested public life that came alive in the United States of the 1830s. This decade — often summed up as the Age of Jackson, in honor of the two-term president who left his distinctive mark on the period — was a time of rapid economic, political, and social change. Andrew Jackson's bold self-confidence mirrored the new confidence of American society in the years after 1815. An entrepreneurial spirit gripped the country, producing a market revolution of unprecedented scale. Old social hierarchies eroded; ordinary men dreamed of moving high up the ladder of success. Stunning advances in transportation and economic productivity fueled such dreams and propelled thousands to travel west or to cities. Urban growth and technological change fostered the diffusion of a distinctive and lively public culture, spread mainly through the increased circulation of newspapers and also by thousands of public lecturers, like the Grimké sisters, allowing popular opinions to coalesce and intensify.

Expanded communication transformed politics dramatically. Sharp disagreements over the best way to promote individual liberty, economic opportunity, and national prosperity in the new market economy defined key differences between presidential candidates in the election of 1828. By the early 1830s, these political differences were embedded in new political parties, which attracted increasing numbers of white male voters into their ranks. Religion became democratized as well. A nationwide evangelical revival brought its adherents the certainty that salvation was now available to all and that the moral perfection of society was within reach.

But perfection proved elusive. Steamboats blew up, banks and businesses periodically collapsed, alcoholism rates soared, Indians were killed or relocated farther west, and slavery continued to expand. The brash confidence that turned some people into rugged, self-promoting individuals inspired others to think about the human costs of rapid economic expansion and thus about reforming society in dramatic ways. The common denominator was a faith that people and societies could shape their own destinies.

▶ The Market Revolution

The return of peace in 1815 unleashed powerful forces that revolutionized the organization of the economy. Spectacular changes in transportation facilitated the movement of commodities, information, and people, while textile mills and other factories created many new jobs, especially for young unmarried women. Innovations in banking, legal practices, and tariff policies promoted swift economic growth.

This was not yet an industrial revolution, as was beginning in Britain, but rather a market revolution fueled by traditional sources — water, wood, beasts of burden, and human muscle. What was new was the accelerated pace of economic activity and the scale of the distribution of goods. Men and women were drawn out of old patterns of rural self-sufficiency into the wider realm of national market relations. At the same time, the nation's money supply enlarged considerably, leading to speculative investments in commerce, manufacturing, transportation, and land. The new nature and scale of production and consumption changed Americans' economic behavior, attitudes, and expectations. But in 1819 and again in 1837 and 1839, serious crashes of the economy punctured their optimistic expectations.

Improvements in Transportation

Before 1815, transportation in the United States was slow and expensive; it cost as much to ship a crate over thirty miles of domestic roads as it did to send it across the Atlantic Ocean. A stagecoach trip from Boston to New York took four days. But between 1815 and 1840, networks of roads, canals, steamboats, and finally railroads dramatically raised the speed and lowered the cost of travel.

Improved transportation moved goods into wider markets. It moved passengers, too, broadening their horizons and allowing young people as well as adults to take up new employment in cities or factory towns. Transportation also facilitated the flow of political information via the U.S. mail with its bargain postal rates for newspapers, periodicals, and books. Enhanced public transport was expensive and produced uneven economic benefits, so presidents from Jefferson to Monroe were reluctant to fund it with federal dollars. Only the National Road, begun in 1806, was government sponsored. By 1818, it linked Baltimore with Wheeling, in western Virginia. In all other cases, private investors pooled resources and chartered transport companies, receiving significant subsidies and monopoly rights from state governments. Turnpike and roadway mileage increased dramatically after 1815, reducing shipping costs. Stagecoach companies proliferated, and travel time on main routes was cut in half.

Water travel was similarly transformed. In 1807, Robert Fulton's steam-propelled boat, the *Clermont*, churned up the Hudson River from New York City to Albany, touching off a steamboat craze. By 1820, a dozen boats left New York City daily, and scores more operated on midwestern rivers and the Great Lakes. By the early 1830s, more than seven hundred steamboats were in operation on the Ohio and Mississippi rivers. A voyager on one of the first steamboats to go down the Mississippi reported that the Chickasaw Indians called the vessel a "fire canoe" and considered it "an omen of evil."

Indeed, steamboats were not benign advances. The urgency to cut travel time for competitive gain over rival steamboat companies — or to win impromptu races — led to overstoked furnaces, sudden boiler explosions, and terrible mass fatalities. An investigation of an accident near Cincinnati in 1838, in which 150 passengers were killed, charged: "Such disasters have their foundation in the present mammoth evil of our country, an inordinate love of gain. We are not satisfied with getting rich, but we must get rich in a day. We are not satisfied with traveling at a speed of ten miles an hour, but we must fly." By that year, nearly three thousand Americans had been killed in steamboat accidents, leading to initial federal attempts — at first unsuccessful — to regulate safety on ships used for interstate commerce. The environment also paid a huge price: Steamboats had to load fuel — "wood up" — every twenty miles or so, resulting in mass deforestation. By the 1830s, the banks of many main rivers were denuded of trees, and forests miles back from the rivers fell to the ax. Wood combustion transferred the carbon stored in trees into the atmosphere, creating America's first significant air pollution.

Canals were another major innovation of the transportation revolution. These shallow highways of water allowed passage for boats pulled by mules. Travel was slow — less than five miles per hour — but the low-friction water enabled one mule to pull a fifty-ton barge. Pennsylvania in 1815 and New York in 1817 commenced major state-sponsored canal enterprises. Pennsylvania's Schuylkill Canal stretched 108 miles west from Philadelphia when it was completed in 1826. Much more impressive was the **Erie Canal**, finished in 1825, covering 350 miles between Albany and Buffalo and linking the port of New York City with the entire Great Lakes region. Wheat and flour moved east, household goods and tools moved west, and passengers went in both directions. By the 1830s, the cost of shipping by canal fell to less than one-tenth of the cost of overland transport, and New York City quickly blossomed into the premier commercial city in the United States.

In the 1830s, private railroad companies began to give canals competition. The nation's first railroad, the Baltimore and Ohio, laid thirteen miles of track in 1829. During the 1830s, three thousand more miles of track materialized nationwide, the result of a speculative fever in railroad construction masterminded by bankers, locomotive manufacturers, and state legislators who provided subsidies, charters, and land rights-of-way. Rail lines in the 1830s were generally short, on the order of twenty to one hundred miles. They did not yet provide an efficient distribution system for goods, but passengers flocked to experience the marvelous speeds of fifteen to twenty miles per hour. Railroads and other advances in transportation made possible enormous change by unifying the country culturally and economically.

Factories, Workingwomen, and Wage Labor

Transportation advances promoted the expansion of manufacturing after 1815, creating an ever-expanding market for goods. The two leading industries, textiles and shoes, altered methods of production and labor relations. Textile production was greatly spurred by the development of water-driven machinery built near fast-coursing rivers. Shoe manufacturing, still using the power and skill of human hands, involved only a reorganization of production. Both industries pulled young women into wage-earning labor for the first time.

The earliest factory was built by English immigrant Samuel Slater in Pawtucket, Rhode Island, in the 1790s. It featured a mechanical spinning machine that produced thread and yarn. By 1815, nearly 170 spinning mills had been built along New England rivers. In British manufacturing cities, entire families worked in low-wage, health-threatening factories. By contrast, American factories targeted young women as employees; they were cheap to hire because of their limited employment options. Mill girls would "retire" to marriage, replaced by fresh recruits earning beginners' wages.

In 1821, a group of Boston entrepreneurs founded the town of Lowell on the Merrimack River, centralizing all aspects of cloth production: combing, shrinking, spinning, weaving, and dyeing. By 1836, the eight mills in Lowell employed more than five thousand young women, who lived in carefully managed company-owned boardinghouses. Corporation rules at the **Lowell mills** required church attendance and prohibited drinking and unsupervised courtship; dorms were locked at 10 P.M. A typical mill worker earned $2 to $3 for a seventy-hour week, more than

Mill Worker Tending a Power Loom, 1850
The young woman pictured here is tending a power loom in a textile mill. The mill worker's main task was to replace the spindle when it ran out of thread; she also had to be alert for sudden breaks in the warp, which required a fast shutdown of the loom and a quick repair of the thread. In the 1830s, women weavers generally tended two of these machines at a time. American Textile History Museum.

a seamstress or domestic servant could earn but less than a young man's wages. The job consisted of tending noisy power looms in rooms kept hot and humid, ideal for thread but not for people.

Despite the discomforts, young women embraced factory work as a means to earn spending money and build savings before marriage; several banks in town held the nest eggs of thousands of workers. Also welcome was the unprecedented, though still limited, personal freedom of living in an all-female social space, away from parents and domestic tasks. In the evening, the women could engage in self-improvement activities, such as writing for the company's periodical, the *Lowell Offering*, or attending lectures on literary, scientific, or even political topics. In 1837, 1,500 mill girls squeezed into Lowell's city hall to hear the Grimké sisters speak about the evils of slavery.

In the mid-1830s, worldwide growth and competition in the cotton market impelled mill owners to speed up work and decrease wages. The workers protested, emboldened by their communal living arrangement and by their relative independence as temporary employees. In 1834 and again in 1836, hundreds of women at Lowell went out on strike. All over New England, female mill workers led strikes and formed unions. In 1834, mill workers in Dover, New Hampshire, denounced their owners for trying to turn them into "slaves": "However freely the epithet of 'factory slaves' may be bestowed upon us, we will never deserve it by a base and cringing submission to proud wealth or haughty insolence." Their assertiveness surprised many, but ultimately the ease of replacing them undermined their bargaining power, and owners in the 1840s began to shift to immigrant families as their primary labor source.

The shoe manufacturing industry centered in eastern New England reorganized production and hired women, including wives, as shoebinders. Male shoemakers still cut the leather and made the soles in shops, but female shoebinders working from home now stitched the upper parts of the shoes. Working from home meant that wives could contribute to family income — unusual for most wives in that period — and still perform their domestic chores.

In the economically turbulent 1830s, shoebinder wages fell. Unlike mill workers, female shoebinders worked in isolation, a serious hindrance to organized protest. In Lynn, Massachusetts, a major shoemaking center, women used female church networks to organize resistance, communicating via religious newspapers. The Lynn shoebinders who demanded higher wages in 1834 built on a collective sense of themselves as women, even though they did not work together daily. "Equal rights should be extended to all — to the weaker sex as well as the stronger," they wrote in a document establishing the Female Society of Lynn.

In the end, the Lynn shoebinders' protests failed to achieve wage increases. At-home workers all over New England continued to accept low wages, and even in Lynn many women shied away from organized protest, preferring to situate their work in the context of family duty (helping their husbands to finish the shoes) instead of market relations.

Bankers and Lawyers

Entrepreneurs like the Lowell factory owners relied on innovations in the banking system to finance their ventures. Between 1814 and 1816, the number of state-chartered banks in the United States more than doubled from fewer than 90 to 208. By 1830, there were 330, and by 1840 hundreds more. Banks stimulated the economy by making loans to merchants and manufacturers and by enlarging the money supply. Borrowers were issued loans in the form of banknotes — certificates unique to each bank — that were used as money for all transactions. Neither federal nor state governments issued paper money, so banknotes became the country's currency.

In theory, a note could always be traded in at a bank for its hard-money equivalent in gold or silver, a transaction known as a "**specie payment**." A note from a solid local bank might be worth exactly what it was written for, but the face value of a note from a distant or questionable bank would be discounted. Buying and selling banknotes in this era required knowledge and caution. Not surprisingly, counterfeiting flourished.

Bankers exercised great power over the economy, deciding who would get loans and what the discount rates would be. The most powerful bankers sat on the board of directors for the **second Bank of the United States**, headquartered in Philadelphia and featuring eighteen branches throughout the country. The twenty-year charter of the first Bank of the United States had expired in 1811, and the second Bank of the United States opened for business in 1816 under another twenty-year charter. The rechartering of this bank would become a major issue in the 1832 presidential campaign.

Accompanying the market revolution was a revolution in commercial law, fashioned by politicians to enhance the prospects of private investment. In 1811, states started to rewrite their laws of incorporation (allowing the chartering of businesses by states), and the number of corporations expanded rapidly, from about twenty in 1800 to eighteen hundred by 1817. Incorporation protected individual investors from being held liable for corporate debts. State lawmakers also wrote laws of eminent domain, empowering states to buy land for roads and canals even from unwilling sellers. In such ways, entrepreneurial lawyers of the 1820s and 1830s created the legal foundation for an economy that favored ambitious individuals interested in maximizing their own wealth.

Not everyone applauded these developments. The skillful lawyer-turned-politician **Andrew Jackson** spoke for a large and mistrustful segment of the population when he warned about the potential abuses of power "which the moneyed interest derives from a paper currency which they are able to control, from the multitude of corporations with exclusive privileges which they have succeeded in obtaining in the different states, and which are employed altogether for their benefit." Jacksonians believed that ending government-granted privileges was the way to maximize individual liberty and economic opportunity.

Booms and Busts

One aspect of the economy that the lawyer-politicians could not control was the threat of financial collapse. The boom years from 1815 to 1818 exhibited a volatility that resulted in the first sharp, large-scale economic downturn in U.S. history. Americans called this downturn a "panic," and the pattern was repeated in the 1830s. Rapidly rising consumer demand stimulated price increases, and speculative investment opportunities offering the possibility of high payoffs abounded — in bank stocks, western land sales, urban real estate, and commodities markets. High inflation made some people wealthy but created hardships for workers on fixed incomes.

When the bubble burst in 1819, the overnight rich suddenly became the overnight poor. Some blamed the **panic of 1819** on the second Bank of the United States for failing to control state banks that had suspended specie payments in their eagerness to expand the economic bubble. By mid-1818, when the Bank of the United States called in its loans and insisted that the state banks do likewise, the contracting of the money supply sent tremors throughout the economy. The crunch was made worse by a financial crisis in Europe in the spring of 1819. Overseas, prices for American cotton, tobacco, and wheat plummeted by more than 50 percent. Thus, when the banks began to call in their outstanding loans, American debtors involved in the commodities trade could not come up with the money. Business and personal bankruptcies skyrocketed. The intricate web of credit and debt relationships meant that almost everyone with even a toehold in the new commercial economy was affected by the panic. Thousands of Americans lost their savings and property, and unemployment estimates suggest that half a million people lost their jobs.

Recovery took several years. Unemployment declined, but bitterness lingered, ready to be stirred up by politicians in the decades to come. The dangers of a system dependent on extensive credit were now clear. In one folksy formulation that circulated around 1820, a farmer compared credit to "a man pissing in his breeches on a cold day to keep his arse warm — very comfortable at first but I dare say . . . you know how it feels afterwards."

By the mid-1820s, the economy was back on track, driven by increases in productivity, consumer demand for goods, and international trade, as well as a restless and calculating people moving goods, human labor, and investment capital in expanding circles of commerce. Despite the panic of 1819, credit financing continued to fuel the system. With the growth of manufacturing and transportation networks, buyers and sellers operated in a much larger arena, using credit transactions on paper instead of moving actual (and scarce) hard money around. A merchant in Ohio who bought goods in New York City on credit hoped to repay the loan with interest when he sold the merchandise — often on credit — for a profit. Slave owners might obtain loans to purchase additional land or slaves, using currently owned slaves as collateral. A network of credit and debt relations grew dense by the 1830s in a system that encouraged speculation and risk taking. A pervasive optimism about continued growth supported the elaborate system, but a single business failure could produce many innocent victims. Well after the panic of 1819, an undercurrent of anxiety about rapid economic change continued to shape the political views of many Americans.

REVIEW   Why did the United States experience a market revolution after 1815?

▶ The Spread of Democracy

Just as the market revolution held out the promise, if not the reality, of economic opportunity for all who worked, the political transformation of the 1830s held out the promise of political opportunity for hundreds of thousands of new voters. During Andrew Jackson's presidency (1829–1837), the second American party system took shape. Not until 1836, however, would the parties have distinct names and consistent programs transcending the particular personalities running for office. Over those years, more men could and did vote, responding to new methods of arousing voter interest. In 1828, Jackson's charismatic personality defined his party, and his victory over incumbent president John Quincy Adams turned on questions of character. Once in office, Jackson championed ordinary citizens against the power elite — democracy versus aristocracy, in Jackson's terminology. A lasting contribution of the Jackson years was the notion that politicians needed to have the common touch in their dealings with voters.

Popular Politics and Partisan Identity

The election of 1828 was the first presidential contest in which the popular vote determined the outcome. In twenty-two out of twenty-four states, voters — not state legislatures — designated the number of electors committed to a particular candidate. More than a million voters participated, three times the number in

1824 and nearly half the free male population, reflecting the high stakes that voters perceived in the Adams-Jackson rematch. Throughout the 1830s, voter turnout continued to rise and reached 70 percent in some localities, partly because of the disappearance of property qualifications in all but three states and partly because of heightened political interest.

The 1828 election inaugurated new campaign styles. State-level candidates routinely gave speeches at rallies, picnics, and banquets. Adams and Jackson still declined such appearances as undignified, but **Henry Clay** of Kentucky, campaigning for Adams, earned the nickname "the Barbecue Orator." Campaign rhetoric became more informal and even blunt. The Jackson camp established many Hickory Clubs, trading on Jackson's popular nickname, "Old Hickory," from a common Tennessee tree suggesting resilience and toughness. (Jackson was the first presidential candidate to have an affectionate and widely used nickname.)

Partisan newspapers in ever-larger numbers defined issues and publicized political personalities as never before. Improved printing technology and rising literacy rates fueled a great expansion of newspapers of all kinds. Party leaders dispensed subsidies and other favors to secure the support of papers, even in remote towns and villages. In New York State, where party development was most advanced, a pro-Jackson group called the Bucktails controlled fifty weekly publications. Stories from the leading Jacksonian paper in Washington, D.C., were reprinted two days later in a Boston or Cincinnati paper, for example, as fast as the mail stage could carry them. Presidential campaigns were now coordinated in a national arena.

Politicians at first identified themselves as Jackson or Adams men, honoring the fiction of Republican Party unity. By 1832, however, the terminology had evolved to National Republicans, who favored federal action to promote commercial development, and Democratic Republicans, who promised to be responsive to the will of the majority. Between 1834 and 1836, National Republicans came to be called **Whigs**, while Jackson's party became simply the **Democrats**.

The Election of 1828 and the Character Issue

The campaign of 1828 was the first national election in which scandal and character questions reigned supreme. They became central issues because voters used them to comprehend the kind of public official each man would make. Character issues conveyed in shorthand larger questions about morality, honor, and discipline. Jackson and Adams presented two radically different styles of manhood.

John Quincy Adams was vilified by his opponents as an elitist, a bookish academic, and even a monarchist. Critics pointed to his White House billiard table and ivory chess set as symbols of his aristocratic degeneracy. They also attacked his "corrupt bargain" of 1824 — the alleged election deal between Adams and Henry Clay (see chapter 10). Adams's supporters returned fire with fire. They played on Jackson's fatherless childhood to portray him as the bastard son of a prostitute. Worse, the cloudy circumstances around his marriage to Rachel Donelson

Robards in 1791 gave rise to the story that Jackson was a seducer and an adulterer, having married a woman whose divorce from her first husband was not entirely legal. Pro-Adams newspapers howled that Jackson was sinful and impulsive, while portraying Adams as pious, learned, and virtuous.

Editors in favor of Adams played up Jackson's violent temper, as evidenced by his participation in many duels, brawls, and canings. Jackson's supporters used the same stories to project Old Hickory as a tough frontier hero who knew how to command obedience. As for learning, Jackson's rough frontier education gave him a "natural sense," wrote a Boston editor, that "can never be acquired by reading books — it can only be acquired, in perfection, by reading men." Jackson won a sweeping victory, with 56 percent of the popular vote and 178 electoral votes to Adams's 83 (Map 11.1). Old Hickory took most of the South and West and carried Pennsylvania and New York as well; Adams carried the remainder of the East. Jackson's vice president was **John C. Calhoun**, who had just served as vice president under Adams but had broken with Adams's policies.

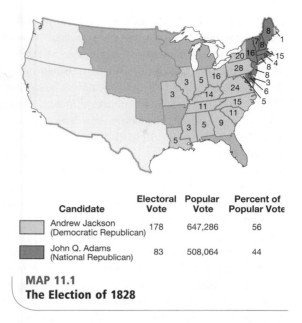

Candidate	Electoral Vote	Popular Vote	Percent of Popular Vote
Andrew Jackson (Democratic Republican)	178	647,286	56
John Q. Adams (National Republican)	83	508,064	44

MAP 11.1
The Election of 1828

After 1828, national politicians no longer deplored the existence of political parties. They were coming to see that parties mobilized and delivered voters, sharpened candidates' differences, and created party loyalty that surpassed loyalty to individual candidates and elections. Adams and Jackson clearly symbolized the competing ideas of the emerging parties: a moralistic, top-down party (the Whigs) ready to make major decisions to promote economic growth competing against a contentious, energetic party (the Democrats) ready to embrace liberty-loving individualism.

Jackson's Democratic Agenda

Before the inauguration in March 1829, Rachel Jackson died. Certain that the ugly campaign had hastened his wife's death, the president went into deep mourning, his depression worsened by constant pain from a bullet still lodged in his chest from an 1806 duel and by mercury poisoning from the medicines he took. Aged sixty-two, Jackson carried only 140 pounds on his six-foot-one frame. His adversaries doubted that he would make it to a second term. His supporters, however, went wild at the inauguration. Thousands cheered his ten-minute inaugural address, the shortest in history. An open reception at the White House turned into a near riot as well-wishers jammed the premises, used windows as doors, stood on furniture for a better view of the great man, and broke thousands of dollars' worth of china and glasses.

During his presidency, Jackson continued to offer unprecedented hospitality to the public. Twenty spittoons newly installed in the East Room of the White House accommodated the tobacco chewers among the throngs that arrived daily to see the president. The courteous Jackson, committed to his image as president of the "common man," held audiences with unannounced visitors throughout his two terms.

Past presidents had tried to lessen party conflict by including men of different factions in their cabinets, but Jackson would have only loyalists, a political tactic followed by most later presidents. For secretary of state, the key job, he tapped New Yorker Martin Van Buren, one of the shrewdest politicians of the day. Throughout the federal government, from postal clerks to ambassadors, Jackson replaced competent civil servants with party loyalists. "To the victor belong the spoils," said a Democratic senator from New York, expressing approval of patronage-driven appointments. Jackson's appointment practices became known as the **spoils system**; it was a concept the president strenuously defended.

Jackson's agenda quickly emerged. Fearing that intervention in the economy inevitably favored some groups at the expense of others, Jackson favored a Jeffersonian limited federal government. He therefore opposed federal support of transportation and grants of monopolies and charters that benefited wealthy investors. Like Jefferson, he anticipated the rapid settlement of the country's interior, where land sales would spread economic democracy to settlers. Thus, establishing a federal policy to remove the Indians from this area had high priority. Unlike Jefferson, Jackson exercised his presidential veto power over Congress. In 1830, he vetoed a highway project in Maysville, Kentucky — Henry Clay's home state — that Congress had backed. The Maysville Road veto articulated Jackson's principled stand that citizens' tax dollars could be spent only on projects of a "general, not local" character. In all, Jackson used the veto twelve times; all previous presidents combined had exercised that right a total of nine times.

> **REVIEW** Why did Andrew Jackson defeat John Quincy Adams so dramatically in the 1828 election?

▶ Jackson Defines the Democratic Party

In his two terms as president, Andrew Jackson worked to implement his vision of a politics of opportunity for all white men. To open land for white settlement, he favored the relocation of all eastern Indian tribes. He dramatically confronted John C. Calhoun and South Carolina when that state tried to nullify the tariff of 1828. Disapproving of all government-granted privilege, Jackson challenged what he called the "monster" Bank of the United States and took it down to defeat. In all this, he greatly enhanced the power of the presidency.

Andrew Jackson as "the Great Father"
In 1828, a new process of cheap commercial lithography found immediate application in a colorful presidential campaign aimed at capturing popular votes, and with it, a rich tradition of political cartoons was born. Jackson inspired at least five dozen satirical cartoons centering on caricatures of him. Strikingly, only one of them featured his Indian policy, controversial as it was, and only a single copy still exists. At some point, this cartoon was cropped at the bottom and top, and thus we do not have the cartoonist's caption or signature, both important for more fully understanding the artist's intent. Still, the sarcastic visual humor of Jackson cradling Indians packs an immediate punch. William L. Clements Library.

Indian Policy and the Trail of Tears

Probably nothing defined Jackson's presidency more than his efforts to solve what he saw as the Indian problem. Thousands of Indians lived in the South and the old Northwest, and many remained in New England and New York. In his first message to Congress in 1829, Jackson, who rose to fame fighting the Creek and Seminole tribes in the 1810s, declared that removing the Indians to territory west of the Mississippi was the only way to save them. White civilization destroyed Indian resources and thus doomed the Indians, he claimed: "That this fate surely awaits them if they remain within the limits of the states does not admit of a doubt. Humanity and national honor demand that every effort should be made to avert so great a calamity." Jackson never publicly wavered from this seemingly noble theme, returning to it in his next seven annual messages.

Prior administrations had experimented with different Indian policies. Starting in 1819, Congress funded missionary associations eager to "civilize" native peoples by converting them to Christianity and encouraging English literacy and agricultural practices. Missionaries also promoted white gender customs, but Indian women were reluctant to embrace practices that accorded them less power than their tribal systems did. The federal government had also pursued aggressive treaty making with many tribes, dealing with the Indians as foreign nations (see chapters 9 and 10).

Privately, Jackson thought it was "absurd" to treat the Indians as foreigners; he saw them as subjects of the United States. Jackson also did not approve of assimilation; that way lay extinction, he said. Removal was the answer. Congress backed Jackson's goal and passed the **Indian Removal Act of 1830**, appropriating

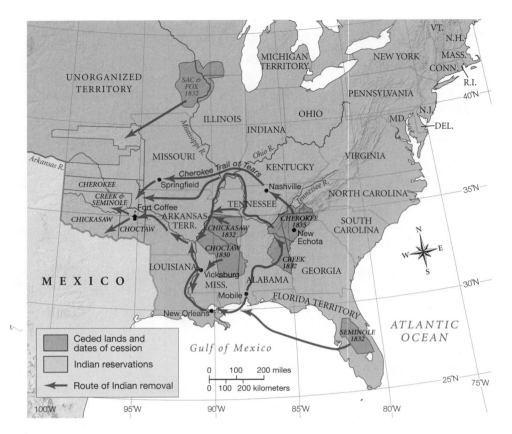

MAP 11.2

Indian Removal and the Trail of Tears

The federal government under President Andrew Jackson pursued a vigorous policy of Indian removal in the 1830s. Tribes were forcibly moved west to land known as Indian Territory (present-day Oklahoma). In 1838, as many as a quarter of the Cherokee Indians died on the route known as the Trail of Tears.

$500,000 to relocate eastern tribes west of the Mississippi. About 100 million acres of eastern land would be vacated for eventual white settlement under this act authorizing ethnic expulsion (Map 11.2).

Jackson's frequent claim that removal would save the Indians from extinction was in part formulated in response to the widespread controversy generated by the Indian Removal Act. Newspapers, public lecturers, and local clubs debated the expulsion law, and public opinion, especially in the North, was heated. "One would think that the guilt of African slavery was enough for the nation to bear, without the additional crime of injustice to the aborigines," one writer declared in 1829. In an unprecedented move, thousands of northern white women signed petitions opposing the removal policy. The right to petition for redress of grievances, part of the Constitution's First Amendment, had long been used by individual women acting on a personal cause — say, a military widow requesting her husband's pension. But mass petitioning by women was something new; it directly challenged the prevailing assumption that women could not be political actors. Between 1830 and 1832, women's petitions rolled into Washington, arguing specifically that the Cherokee Indians of Georgia were a sovereign people on the road to Christianity and entitled to stay on their land. Jackson ignored the petitions.

For the northern tribes, their numbers diminished by years of war, gradual removal was already well under way. But not all the Indians went quietly. In 1832 in western Illinois, Black Hawk, a leader of the Sauk and Fox Indians who had fought in alliance with Tecumseh in the War of 1812 (see chapter 10), resisted removal. Volunteer militias attacked and chased the Indians into southern Wisconsin, where, after several skirmishes and a deadly battle (later called the Black Hawk War), Black Hawk was captured and some four hundred of his people were massacred.

The large southern tribes — the Creek, Chickasaw, Choctaw, Seminole, and Cherokee — proved even more resistant to removal. The tribal leadership of the Cherokee in Georgia chose a unique path of resistance by taking their case to the U.S. Supreme Court. Georgia Cherokees had already taken several assimilationist steps. Spurred by dedicated missionaries, these leaders had incorporated written laws, including, in 1827, a constitution modeled on the U.S. Constitution. Two hundred of the wealthiest Cherokee men had intermarried with whites, adopting white styles of housing, dress, and cotton agriculture, including the ownership of slaves. They developed a written alphabet and published a newspaper and Christian prayer books in their language. These features helped make their cause attractive to the northern white women who petitioned the government on their behalf. Yet most of the seventeen thousand Cherokees maintained cultural continuity with past traditions.

In 1831, when Georgia announced its plans to seize all Cherokee property, the tribal leaders asked the U.S. Supreme Court to restrain Georgia. The Court held that the Cherokee people lacked standing to sue, not being citizens of either the United States or any foreign state. In the Court's view, tribes residing within U.S. boundaries were "domestic dependent nations," in effect wards of the state. A year later, they brought suit again, this time using an ally, a white missionary, as their stand-in plaintiff. In *Worcester v. Georgia* (1832), the Supreme Court upheld the territorial sovereignty of the Cherokee people, recognizing their existence as "a distinct community, occupying its own territory, in which the laws of Georgia can have no force." An angry President Jackson ignored the Court and pressed the Cherokee tribe to move west: "If they now refuse to accept the liberal terms offered, they can only be liable for whatever evils and difficulties may arise. I feel conscious of having done my duty to my red children."

The Cherokee tribe remained in Georgia for two more years without significant violence. Then, in 1835, a small, unauthorized faction of the acculturated leaders signed a treaty selling all the tribal lands to the state, which rapidly resold the land to whites. Chief John Ross, backed by several thousand Cherokees, petitioned the U.S. Congress to ignore the bogus treaty. "By the stipulations of this instrument," he wrote, "we are stripped of every attribute of freedom and eligibility for legal self-defense. Our property may be plundered before our eyes; violence may be committed on our persons; even our lives may be taken away. . . . We are denationalized; we are disfranchised."

As the Cherokees stubbornly held out, other tribes capitulated to Jackson's mandate and endured forcible relocation. Fifteen thousand Creek, twelve thousand Choctaw, five thousand Chickasaw, and several thousand Seminole Indians moved to Indian Territory (which became the state of Oklahoma in 1907). In his farewell address to the nation in 1837, Jackson assured white listeners of his faith in the humanitarian benefits of Indian removal: "This unhappy race . . . are now placed in a situation where we may well hope that they will share in the blessings of civilization and be saved from the degradation and destruction to which they were rapidly hastening while they remained in the states."

When the Cherokees refused to move by the voluntary evacuation deadline of May 1838, Jackson's successor, Martin Van Buren, sent federal troops to remove them. Under armed guard, the Cherokees embarked on a 1,200-mile journey west that came to be called the **Trail of Tears**. A newspaperman in Kentucky described the forced march: "Even aged females, apparently, nearly ready to drop into the grave, were traveling with heavy burdens attached to the back. . . . They buried fourteen to fifteen at every stopping place." Nearly a quarter of the Cherokees died en route from the hardship. Perhaps Jackson had genuinely believed that exile to the West was necessary to save Indian cultures from destruction. But for the forcibly removed tribes, the costs of relocation were high.

The Tariff of Abominations and Nullification

Jackson's Indian policy happened to harmonize with the principle of states' rights; the president supported Georgia's right to ignore the Supreme Court's decision in *Worcester v. Georgia*. But in another pressing question of states' rights, Jackson contested South Carolina's attempt to ignore federal tariff policy.

Federal tariffs as high as 33 percent on imports such as textiles and iron goods had been passed in 1816 and again in 1824 in an effort to shelter new American manufacturers from foreign competition. Some southern congressmen opposed the steep tariffs, fearing they would reduce overseas shipping and thereby hurt cotton exports. In 1828, Congress passed a revised tariff that came to be known as the **Tariff of Abominations**. A bundle of conflicting duties, some as high as 50 percent, the legislation contained provisions that pleased and angered every economic and sectional interest.

South Carolina in particular suffered from the Tariff of Abominations. Worldwide prices for cotton had declined in the late 1820s, and the falloff in shipping caused by the high tariffs further hurt the South. In 1828, a group of South Carolina politicians headed by John C. Calhoun advanced a doctrine called **nullification**. The Union, they argued, was a confederation of states that had yielded some but not all power to the federal government. When Congress overstepped its powers, states had the right to nullify Congress's acts. As precedents, they pointed to the Virginia and Kentucky Resolutions of 1798, intended to invalidate the Alien and Sedition Acts (see chapter 9). Congress had erred in using tariff policy to benefit specific industries, they claimed; tariffs should be used only to raise revenue.

On assuming the presidency in 1829, Jackson ignored the South Carolina statement of nullification and shut out Calhoun, his new vice president, from influence or power. Tariff revisions in early 1832 brought little relief to the South. Sensing futility, Calhoun resigned the vice presidency and became a senator to better serve his state. Finally, strained to their limit, South Carolina leaders took the radical step of declaring federal tariffs null and void in their state as of February 1, 1833. The constitutional crisis was out in the open.

Opting for a dramatic confrontation, Jackson sent armed ships to Charleston harbor and threatened to invade the state. He pushed through Congress the Force Bill, defining South Carolina's stance as treason and authorizing military action to collect federal tariffs. At the same time, Congress moved quickly to pass a revised tariff that was more acceptable to the South. The conciliating Senator Henry Clay rallied support for a moderate bill that gradually reduced tariffs down to the 1816 level. On March 1, 1833, Congress passed both the new tariff and the Force Bill. In response, South Carolina withdrew its nullification of the old tariff — and then nullified the Force Bill. It was a symbolic gesture, since Jackson's show of muscle was no longer necessary. Both sides were satisfied: Federal power had prevailed over an assertion of states' rights, and South Carolina got the lower tariff it wanted.

Yet the question of federal power versus states' rights was far from settled. The implied threat behind nullification was secession, a position articulated in 1832 by some South Carolinians whose concerns went beyond tariff policy. In the 1830s, the political moratorium on discussions of slavery agreed on at the time of the Missouri Compromise (see chapter 10) was coming unglued, and new northern voices opposed to slavery gained increasing attention. If and when a northern-dominated federal government decided to end slavery, the South Carolinians thought, the South should nullify such laws or else remove itself from the Union.

The Bank War and Economic Boom

Along with the tariff and nullification, President Jackson fought another political battle, over the Bank of the United States. After riding out the panic of 1819, the bank finally prospered. With twenty-nine branches, it handled the federal government's deposits, extended credit and loans, and issued banknotes — by 1830, the most stable currency in the country. Jackson, however, did not find the bank's functions sufficiently valuable to offset his criticism of the concept of a national bank: that it concentrated undue economic power in the hands of a few.

National Republican (Whig) senators Daniel Webster and Henry Clay decided to force the issue. They convinced the bank to apply for charter renewal in 1832, well before the fall election, even though the existing charter ran until 1836. They fully expected that Congress's renewal would force Jackson to follow through on his rhetoric with a veto, that the unpopular veto would cause Jackson to lose the election, and that the bank would survive on an override vote by a new Congress swept into power on the anti-Jackson tide.

At first, the plan seemed to work. The bank applied for rechartering, Congress voted to renew, and Jackson, angry over being manipulated, issued his veto. But it was a brilliantly written veto, full of fierce language about the privileges of the moneyed elite who oppressed the democratic masses in order to enrich themselves. "Many of our rich men have not been content with equal protection and equal benefits, but have besought us to make them richer by act of Congress," Jackson wrote.

Clay and his supporters found Jackson's economic ideas and his language of class antagonism so absurd that they distributed thousands of copies of the bank veto as campaign material for their own party. A confident Henry Clay headed his party's ticket for the presidency. But the plan backfired. Jackson's translation of the bank controversy into a language of class antagonism and egalitarian ideals resonated with many Americans. Old Hickory won the election easily, gaining 55 percent of the popular vote and 219 electoral votes to Clay's 49. Jackson's party still controlled Congress, so no override was possible. The second Bank of the United States would cease to exist after 1836. Distraught over the election, Clay condemned the "reign of Jackson," which he termed a "reign of corruption." "The dark cloud," he wrote, "has become more dense, more menacing, more alarming."

Confirming Clay's fears, Jackson took steps to destroy the bank sooner than 1836. Calling it a "monster," he ordered the sizable federal deposits to be removed from its vaults and redeposited into Democratic-inclined state banks. In retaliation, the Bank of the United States raised interest rates and called in loans. This action caused a brief decline in the economy in 1833 and actually enhanced Jackson's claim that the bank was too powerful for the good of the country.

Unleashed and unregulated, the economy went into high gear in 1834. Just at this moment, an excess of silver from Mexican mines made its way into American banks, giving bankers license to print ever more banknotes. From 1834 to 1837, inflation soared; prices of basic goods rose more than 50 percent. States quickly chartered hundreds of new private banks, each issuing its own banknotes. Entrepreneurs borrowed and invested money, and the webs of credit and debt relationships that were the hallmark of the American economy grew denser yet.

The market in western land sales also heated up. In 1834, about 4.5 million acres of the public domain had been sold, the highest annual volume since 1818. By 1836, the total reached an astonishing 20 million acres. Some of this was southern land in Mississippi and Louisiana, which slave owners rushed to bring under cultivation, but much more was in the North, where land offices were deluged with buyers. The Jackson administration worried that the purchasers were overwhelmingly eastern capitalist land speculators instead of independent farmers intending to settle on the land.

In one respect, the economy attained an admirable goal: The national debt disappeared, and from 1835 to 1837, for the only time in American history, the government had a monetary surplus. But much of that surplus consisted of questionable bank currencies — "bloated, diseased" currencies, in Jackson's vivid terminology. While the boom was on, however, few stopped to worry about the consequences if and when the bubble burst.

REVIEW Why did Jackson promote Indian removal?

▶ Cultural Shifts, Religion, and Reform

The growing economy, booming by the mid-1830s, transformed social and cultural life. For many families, especially in the commercialized Northeast, standards of living rose, consumption patterns changed, and the nature and location of work were altered. All this had a direct impact on the duties of men and women and on the training of youths for the economy of the future.

Along with economic change came an unprecedented revival of evangelical religion known as the Second Great Awakening. Just as universal male suffrage allowed all white men to vote, democratized religion offered salvation to all who embraced it. Among the most serious adherents of evangelical Protestantism were men and women of the new merchant classes, whose self-discipline in pursuing market ambitions meshed well with the message of self-discipline in pursuit of spiritual perfection. Not content with individual perfection, many of these people sought to perfect society as well, by defining excessive alcohol consumption, nonmarital sex, and slavery as three major evils of modern life in need of correction.

The Family and Separate Spheres

The centerpiece of new ideas about gender relations was the notion that husbands found their status and authority in the new world of work, leaving wives to tend the hearth and home. Sermons, advice books, periodicals, and novels reinforced the idea that men and women inhabited **separate spheres** and had separate duties. "To woman it belongs . . . to elevate the intellectual character of her household [and] to kindle the fires of mental activity in childhood," wrote Mrs. A. J. Graves in a popular book titled *Advice to American Women*. For men, by contrast, "the absorbing passion for gain, and the pressing demands of business, engross their whole attention." In particular, the home, now said to be the exclusive domain of women, was sentimentalized as the source of intimacy, love, and safety, a refuge from the cruel and competitive world of market relations.

Some new aspects of society gave substance to this formulation of separate spheres. Men's work was undergoing profound change after 1815 and increasingly brought cash to the household, especially in the manufacturing and urban Northeast. Farmers and tradesmen sold products in a market, and bankers, bookkeepers, shoemakers, and canal diggers earned regular salaries or wages. Furthermore, many men now worked away from the home, at an office or a store.

A woman's domestic role was more complicated than the cultural prescriptions indicated. Although the vast majority of married white women did not hold paying jobs, their homes required time-consuming labor. But the advice books treated housework as a loving familial duty, thus rendering it invisible in an economy that evaluated work by how much cash it generated. In reality, wives contributed directly to family income in many ways. Some took in boarders; others earned pay for shoebinding or needlework done at home. Wives in the poorest classes, including most free black wives, did not have the luxury of husbands earning adequate wages; for them, wage-paying work as servants or laundresses helped augment family income.

Idealized notions about the feminine home and the masculine workplace gained acceptance in the 1830s (and well beyond) because of the cultural ascendancy of the commercialized Northeast, with its domination of book and periodical publication. Men seeking manhood through work and pay could embrace competition and acquisitiveness, while women established femininity through dutiful service to home and family. This particular formulation of gender difference helped smooth the path for the first generation of Americans experiencing the market revolution, and both men and women of the middle classes benefited. Men were set free to pursue wealth, and women gained moral authority within the home. Beyond white families of the middle and upper classes, however, these new gender ideals had limited applicability. And new voices like those of the Grimké sisters challenged whether "virtue" and "duty" had separate masculine and feminine manifestations. Despite their apparent authority in printed material of the period, these gender ideals were never all-pervasive.

The Education and Training of Youths

The market economy required expanded opportunities for training youths of both sexes. By the 1830s, in both the North and the South, state-supported public school systems were the norm, designed to produce pupils of both sexes able, by age twelve to fourteen, to read, write, and participate in marketplace calculations. Literacy rates for white females climbed dramatically, rivaling the rates for white males for the first time. The fact that taxpayers paid for children's education created an incentive to seek an inexpensive teaching force. By the 1830s, school districts replaced male teachers with young females, for, as a Massachusetts report on education put it, "females can be educated cheaper, quicker, and better, and will teach cheaper after they are qualified." Many were trained in private female academies, now numbering in the hundreds (see chapter 10).

Advanced education continued to expand in the 1830s, with an additional two dozen colleges for men and several more female seminaries offering education on a par with the male colleges. Mount Holyoke Seminary in western Massachusetts, founded by educator Mary Lyon in 1837, developed a rigorous scientific curriculum, and Oberlin College in Ohio, founded by Presbyterians in 1835, became the first co-educational college when it opened its doors to women in 1837. Oberlin's goal was to train young men for the ministry and to prepare young women to be ministers' wives.

Still, only a very small percentage of young people attended institutions of higher learning. The vast majority of male youths left public school at age fourteen to apprentice in specific trades or to embark on business careers by seeking entry-level clerkships, abundant in the growing urban centers. Young women headed for mill towns or cities in unprecedented numbers, seeking work in the expanding service sector as seamstresses and domestic servants. Changes in patterns of youth employment meant that large numbers of youngsters escaped the watchful eyes of their parents. Moralists fretted about the dangers of unsupervised youths, and following the lead of the Lowell mill owners, some established apprentices' libraries and uplifting lecture series to keep young people honorably occupied. Advice books published by the hundreds instructed youths in the virtues of hard work and delayed gratification.

The Second Great Awakening

A newly invigorated version of Protestantism gained momentum in the 1820s and 1830s as the economy reshaped gender and age relations. The earliest manifestations of this fervent piety, which historians call the **Second Great Awakening**, appeared in 1801 in Kentucky, when a crowd of ten thousand people camped out on a hillside at Cane Ridge for a revival meeting that lasted several weeks. By the 1810s and 1820s, "camp meetings" had spread to the Atlantic seaboard states. The outdoor settings permitted huge attendance, intensifying the emotional impact of the revival.

The gatherings attracted women and men hungry for a more immediate access to spiritual peace, one not requiring years of soul-searching. One eyewitness reported that "some of the people were singing, others praying, some crying for mercy. . . . At one time I saw at least five hundred swept down in a moment as if a battery of a thousand guns had been opened upon them, and then immediately followed shrieks and shouts that rent the very heavens."

From 1800 to 1820, church membership doubled in the United States, much of it among the evangelical groups. Methodists, Baptists, and Presbyterians formed the core of the new movement; Episcopalians, Congregationalists, Unitarians, Dutch Reformed, Lutherans, and Catholics maintained strong skepticism about the emotional enthusiasm. Women more than men were attracted to the evangelical movement, and wives and mothers typically recruited husbands and sons to join them.

The leading exemplar of the Second Great Awakening was a lawyer turned minister named **Charles Grandison Finney**. Finney lived in western New York, where the completion of the Erie Canal in 1825 fundamentally altered the social and economic landscape overnight. Towns swelled with new inhabitants who brought remarkable prosperity along with other, less admirable side effects, such as prostitution, drinking, and gaming. Finney saw New York canal towns as especially ripe for evangelical awakening. In Rochester, he sustained a six-month revival through the winter of 1830–31, generating thousands of converts.

Finney's message was directed primarily at the business classes. He argued that a reign of Christian perfection loomed, one that required public-spirited outreach to the less-than-perfect to foster their salvation. Evangelicals promoted Sunday schools to bring piety to children; they battled to honor the Sabbath by ending mail delivery, stopping public transport, and closing shops on Sundays. Many women formed missionary societies that distributed millions of Bibles and religious tracts. Through such avenues, evangelical religion offered women expanded spheres of influence. Finney adopted the tactics of Jacksonian-era politicians — publicity, argumentation, rallies, and speeches — to sell his cause. His object, he said, was to get Americans to "vote in the Lord Jesus Christ as the governor of the Universe."

The Temperance Movement and the Campaign for Moral Reform

The evangelical disposition — a combination of faith, energy, self-discipline, and righteousness — animated vigorous campaigns to eliminate alcohol abuse and eradicate sexual sin. Millions of Americans took the temperance pledge to abstain from strong drink, and thousands became involved in efforts to end prostitution.

Alcohol consumption had risen steadily in the decades up to 1830, when the average person over age thirteen annually consumed an astonishing nine gallons of hard liquor plus thirty gallons of hard cider, beer, and wine. All classes imbibed. A lively saloon culture fostered masculine camaraderie along with extensive alcohol consumption among laborers, while in elite homes the after-dinner whiskey or sherry was commonplace. Colleges before 1820 routinely served students a pint of ale with meals, and the military included rum in the daily ration.

Organized opposition to drinking first surfaced in the 1810s among health and religious reformers. In 1826, Lyman Beecher, a Connecticut minister of an "awakened" church, founded the **American Temperance Society**, which warned that drinking led to poverty, idleness, crime, and family violence. Adopting the methods of evangelical ministers, temperance lecturers traveled the country expounding the damage of drink. By 1833, some six thousand local affiliates of the American Temperance Society boasted more than a million members. Middle-class drinking began a steep decline. One powerful tool of persuasion was the temperance pledge, which many business owners began to require of employees.

In 1836, leaders of the temperance movement regrouped into a new society, the American Temperance Union, which demanded total abstinence from its adherents. The intensified war against alcohol moved beyond individual moral suasion into the realm of politics as reformers sought to deny taverns liquor licenses. By 1845, temperance advocates had put an impressive dent in alcohol consumption, which diminished to one-quarter of the per capita consumption of 1830. In 1851, Maine became the first state to ban entirely the manufacture and sale of all alcoholic beverages.

More controversial than temperance was a social movement called "moral reform," which first aimed at public morals in general but quickly narrowed to

"Signing the Pledge"
This lithograph from the 1840s captures and celebrates a hard-won moment in the life of a hard-luck (but fictive) family. A temperance worker convinces the man of the household to give his solemn word to abstain from all alcohol, while his wife exhibits prayerful gratitude. What message does this picture send about the consequences of alcohol abuse? And about the possibilities of redemption? The temperance pledge was a major tool used by anti-alcohol advocates to curb drinking: Could it have really worked? Consider the power of religious oaths in a society infused with religious belief. The Granger Collection, NYC.

a campaign to eradicate sexual sin. In 1833, a group of Finneyite women started the New York Female Moral Reform Society. Its members insisted that uncontrolled male sexual expression posed a serious threat to society in general and to women in particular. The society's nationally distributed newspaper, the *Advocate of Moral Reform*, was the first major paper in the country that was written, edited, and typeset by women. In it, they condemned men who visited brothels or seduced innocent women. Within five years, more than four thousand auxiliary groups of women had sprung up, mostly in New England, New York, Pennsylvania, and Ohio.

In its analysis of the causes of licentiousness and its conviction that women had a duty to speak out about unspeakable things, the Moral Reform Society pushed the limits of what even the men in the evangelical movement could tolerate. Yet these women did not regard themselves as radicals. They were simply pursuing the logic of a gender system that defined home protection and morality as women's special sphere and a religious conviction that called for the eradication of sin.

Organizing against Slavery

More radical still was the movement in the 1830s to abolish the sin of slavery. The abolitionist movement had its roots in Great Britain in the late 1700s. Previously, the American Colonization Society, founded in 1817 by Maryland and Virginia planters, aimed to promote gradual individual emancipation of slaves followed by colonization in Africa. By the early 1820s, several thousand ex-slaves had been transported to Liberia on the West African coast. But not surprisingly, newly freed men and women often were not eager to emigrate; their African roots were three or more generations in the past. Colonization was too gradual (and expensive) to have much impact on American slavery.

Around 1830, northern challenges to slavery surfaced with increasing frequency and resolve, beginning in free black communities. In 1829, a Boston printer named David Walker published *An Appeal . . . to the Coloured Citizens of the World*, which condemned racism, invoked the egalitarian language of the Declaration of Independence, and hinted at racial violence if whites did not change their prejudiced ways. In 1830, at the inaugural National Negro Convention meeting in Philadelphia, forty blacks from nine states discussed the racism of American society and proposed emigration to Canada. In 1832 and 1833, a twenty-eight-year-old black woman named **Maria Stewart** delivered public lectures on slavery and racial prejudice to black audiences in Boston.

Although Stewart's arguments against slavery were welcomed, her voice — that of a woman — created problems even among her sympathetic audiences. Few American-born women had yet engaged in public speaking beyond theatrical performances or religious prophesying. Stewart was breaking a social taboo, an offense made more challenging by her statements suggesting that black women should rise above housework: "How long shall the fair daughters of Africa be compelled to bury their minds and talents beneath a load of iron pots and kettles?" She retired from the platform in 1833 but took up writing and published her lectures in a national publication called the *Liberator*, giving them much wider circulation.

The *Liberator*, founded in 1831 in Boston, took antislavery agitation to new heights. Its founder and editor, an uncompromising twenty-six-year-old white printer named **William Lloyd Garrison**, advocated immediate abolition: "On this subject, I do not wish to think, or speak, or write, with moderation. No! No! Tell a man whose house is on fire to give a moderate alarm; tell him to moderately rescue his wife from the hands of the ravisher; tell the mother to gradually extricate her babe from the fire into which it has fallen; — but urge me not to use moderation in a cause like the present." In 1832, Garrison's supporters started the New England Anti-Slavery Society.

Similar groups were organized in Philadelphia and New York in 1833. Soon a dozen antislavery newspapers and scores of antislavery lecturers were spreading the word and inspiring the formation of new local societies, which numbered thirteen hundred by 1837. Confined entirely to the North, their membership totaled a quarter of a million men and women.

Many white northerners, even those who opposed slavery as a blot on the country's ideals, were not prepared to embrace the abolitionist call for emancipation.

Controversy over Abolitionism

Mob violence erupted in northern cities with regularity when abolitionist speakers came to town. This 1837 poster from Poughkeepsie, New York, exemplifies the inflammatory language that kindled riots. The abolitionist speaker is framed as seditious, evil, and fanatical, while the citizens are called to the noble task of defending the Constitution and the Union.
Courtesy, American Antiquarian Society.

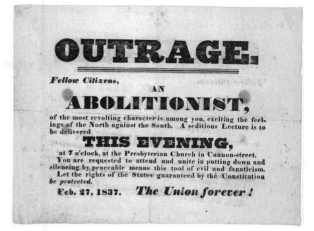

OUTRAGE.

Fellow Citizens,
AN
ABOLITIONIST,
of the most revolting character is among you, exciting the feelings of the North against the South. A seditious Lecture is to be delivered
THIS EVENING,
at 7 o'clock, at the Presbyterian Church in Cannon-street. You are requested to attend and unite in putting down and silencing by peaceable means this tool of evil and fanaticism. Let the rights of the States guaranteed by the Constitution be protected.
Feb. 27, 1837.   *The Union forever!*

From 1834 to 1838, there were more than a hundred eruptions of serious mob violence against abolitionists and free blacks. On one occasion, antislavery headquarters in Philadelphia and a black church and orphanage were burned to the ground. In another incident, Illinois abolitionist editor Elijah Lovejoy was killed by a rioting crowd attempting to destroy his printing press.

Women played a prominent role in abolition, just as they did in moral reform and evangelical religion. They formed women's auxiliaries and held fairs to sell handmade crafts to support male lecturers in the field. They circulated antislavery petitions, presented to the U.S. Congress with tens of thousands of their signatures. Up to 1835, women's petitions were framed as respectful memorials to Congress about the evils of slavery, but by mid-decade these petitions used urgent language to call for political action, instructing Congress to outlaw slavery in the District of Columbia (the only area under Congress's sole power). By such fervent tactics, antislavery women asserted their claim to be heard on political issues independently of their husbands and fathers.

Garrison particularly welcomed women's activity, despite the potential for danger. The 1837 Massachusetts speaking tour of the **Grimké sisters** (see pages 301–303) brought out respectful audiences of thousands but also drew intimidation from some quarters. The state leaders of the Congregational Church banned the sisters from speaking in their churches. They claimed that while a modest woman deserved deference and protection, an immodest woman presumptuously instructing men in public forfeited her privileges and invited male attack. "When she assumes the place and tone of man as a public reformer, our care and protection of her seem unnecessary; we put ourselves in self-defence against her . . . her character becomes unnatural." Serious violence occurred in 1838, when a mob attacked a female antislavery convention in Philadelphia. Rocks shattered windows as Angelina Grimké gave her speech, and after the women vacated the building, it was burned to the ground.

In the late 1830s, the cause of abolition divided the nation as no other issue did. Even among abolitionists, significant divisions emerged. The Grimké sisters, radicalized by the public reaction to their speaking tour, began to write and speak about woman's rights. Angelina Grimké compared the silencing of women to the silencing of slaves: "The denial of our duty to act, is a bold denial of our right to act; and if *we* have no right to act, then may we well be termed 'the white slaves of the North' — for, like our brethren in bonds, we must seal our lips in silence and despair." The Grimkés were opposed by moderate abolitionists who were unwilling to mix the new and controversial issue of woman's rights with their first cause, the rights of blacks. A few radical men, such as Garrison, embraced woman's rights fully, working to get women some leadership positions in the national antislavery group.

The many men and women active in reform movements in the 1830s found their initial inspiration in evangelical Protestantism's dual message: Salvation was open to all, and society needed to be perfected. Their activist mentality squared well with the interventionist tendencies of the party forming in opposition to Andrew Jackson's Democrats. Generally, reformers gravitated toward the Whig Party, the males as voters and the females as rallying supporters in the 1830s campaigns.

REVIEW How did evangelical Protestantism contribute to the social reform movements of the 1830s?

▶ Van Buren's One-Term Presidency

By the mid-1830s, a vibrant and tumultuous political culture occupied center stage in American life. A colorful military hero had left his stamp on the nation, but Andrew Jackson was too ill to stand for a third term. His vice president and handpicked successor, the northerner Martin Van Buren, inherited a strong Democratic organization, but he faced doubts from slave-owning Jacksonians and outright opposition from increasingly combative Whigs. Abolitionist tactics had pushed slavery into the political debate, but Van Buren managed to defuse that conflict somewhat and even use it to his advantage. What could not be forestalled, however, was the collapse of the economic boom so celebrated by both Democrats and Whigs. The shattering panic of 1837, followed by another panic in 1839, brought the country its worst economic depression yet.

The Politics of Slavery

Sophisticated party organization was the specialty of **Martin Van Buren**. Nicknamed "the Little Magician" for his consummate political skills, the New Yorker had built his career by pioneering many of the loyalty-enhancing techniques the Democrats used in the 1830s. First a senator and then governor, Van Buren became Jackson's secretary of state and then his running mate in 1832, replacing John C. Calhoun. His eight years in the volatile Jackson administration required the full measure of his political deftness as he sought repeatedly to save Jackson from both his enemies and his own obstinacy.

Jackson clearly favored Van Buren for the nomination in 1836, but starting in 1832, the major political parties had developed nominating conventions to choose their candidates. In 1835, Van Buren got the convention nod unanimously, to the dismay of his archrival, Calhoun, who then worked to discredit Van Buren among southern proslavery Democrats. Van Buren spent months assuring them that he was a "northern man with southern principles." This was not hard, since his Dutch family hailed from the Hudson River counties where New York slavery had once flourished, and his own family had owned at least one slave as late as the 1810s, although he chose not to broadcast that fact. (Slavery was only gradually phased out in New York starting in 1799.) Calhoun's partisans whipped up controversy over Van Buren's support of suffrage for New York's propertied free blacks at the 1821 state convention on suffrage. Van Buren's partisans countered by emphasizing that the Little Magician had argued that the mass of "poor, degraded blacks" were incapable of voting; he had merely favored retaining the existing stiff property qualifications for the handful of elite blacks who had always voted in New York, while simultaneously removing all such qualifications for white men.

Calhoun was able to stir up trouble for Van Buren because southerners were becoming increasingly alarmed by the rise of northern antislavery sentiment. When, in late 1835, abolitionists prepared to circulate in the South a million pamphlets condemning slavery, a mailbag of their literature was hijacked at the post office in Charleston, South Carolina, and ceremoniously burned along with effigies of leading abolitionists. President Jackson condemned the theft but issued approval for individual postmasters to exercise their own judgment about whether to allow incendiary materials to reach their destination. Abolitionists saw this as censorship of the mail.

The petitioning tactics of abolitionists escalated sectional tensions. As petitions demanding that Congress "purify" the District of Columbia by outlawing slavery grew into the hundreds, proslavery congressmen sought to short-circuit the appeals by passing a "gag rule" in 1836. The gag rule prohibited entering the documents into the public record on the grounds that what the abolitionists prayed for was unconstitutional and, further, an assault on the rights of white southerners, as one South Carolina representative put it. Abolitionists like the Grimké sisters considered the gag rule to be an abridgment of free speech. They also argued that, tabled or not, the petitions were effective. "The South already turns pale at the number sent," Angelina Grimké said in a speech exhorting more petitions to be circulated.

Van Buren shrewdly seized on both mail censorship and the gag rule to express his prosouthern sympathies. Abolitionists were "fanatics," he repeatedly claimed, possibly under the influence of "foreign agents" (British abolitionists). He dismissed the issue of abolition in the District of Columbia as "inexpedient" and promised that if he was elected president, he would not allow any interference in southern "domestic institutions."

Elections and Panics

Although the elections of 1824, 1828, and 1832 clearly bore the stamp of Jackson's personality, by 1836 the party apparatus was sufficiently developed to give Van Buren, a backroom politician, a shot at the presidency. Local and state committees existed throughout the country. Democratic candidates ran in every state election, succeeding even in the old Federalist stronghold of New England. More than four hundred newspapers self-identified as Democratic partisans.

The Whigs had also built state-level organizations and newspaper loyalty. They had no top contender with nationwide support, so three regional candidates opposed Van Buren. Senator Daniel Webster of Massachusetts could deliver New England, home to reformers, merchants, and manufacturers; Senator Hugh Lawson White of Tennessee attracted proslavery voters still suspicious of the northern Magician; and the aging General William Henry Harrison, now residing in Ohio and remembered for his Indian war heroics in 1811, pulled in the western anti-Indian vote. Not one of the three candidates had the ability to win the presidency, but together they came close to denying Van Buren a majority vote. Van Burenites called the three-Whig strategy a deliberate plot to derail the election and move it to the House of Representatives.

In the end, Van Buren won with 170 electoral votes, while the other three received a total of 113. The popular vote told a somewhat different story. Van Buren's narrow majorities, where he won, were far below those Jackson had commanded. Although Van Buren had pulled together a national Democratic Party with wins in both the North and the South, he had done it at the cost of committing northern Democrats to the proslavery agenda. And running three candidates had maximized the Whigs' success by drawing Whigs into office at the state level.

When Van Buren took office in March 1837, the financial markets were already quaking; by April, the country was plunged into crisis. The causes of the **panic of 1837** were multiple and far-ranging. Bad harvests in Europe and a large trade imbalance between Britain and the United States caused the Bank of England to start calling in loans to American merchants. Failures in various crop markets and a 30 percent downturn in international cotton prices fed the growing disaster. Cotton merchants in the South could no longer meet their obligations to New York creditors, whose firms began to fail — ninety-eight of them in March and April 1837 alone. Frightened citizens thronged the banks to try to get their money out, and businesses rushed to liquefy their remaining assets to pay off debts. Prices of stocks, bonds, and real estate fell 30 to 40 percent. The familiar events of the panic of 1819 unfolded again, with terrifying rapidity, and the credit market tumbled like a house of cards. Newspapers describing the economic free fall generally used the language of emotional states — excitement, anxiety, terror, panic. Such words focused on human reactions to the crisis rather than on the structural features of the economy that had interacted to amplify the downturn. The vocabulary for understanding the wider economy was still quite limited, making it hard to track the bigger picture of the workings of capitalism.

Instead, many observers looked to politics, religion, and character flaws to explain the crisis. Some Whig leaders were certain that Jackson's antibank and hard-money policies were responsible for the ruin. New Yorker Philip Hone, a wealthy Whig, called the Jackson administration "the most disastrous in the annals of the country" for its "wicked interference" in banking and monetary matters. Others framed the devastation as retribution for an immoral frenzy of speculation that had gripped the nation. A religious periodical in Boston hoped that Americans would now moderate their greed: "We were getting to think that there was no end to the wealth, and could be no check to the progress of our country; that economy was not needed, that prudence was weakness." In this view, the panic was a wakeup call, a blessing in disguise. Others identified the competitive, profit-maximizing capitalist system as the cause and looked to Britain and France for new socialist ideas calling for the common ownership of the means of production. American socialists, though few in number, were vocal and imaginative, and in the early 1840s several thousand developed utopian alternative communities (as discussed in chapter 12).

The panic of 1837 subsided by 1838, but in 1839 another run on the banks and ripples of business failures deflated the economy, creating a second panic. President Van Buren called a special session of Congress to consider creating an independent treasury system to perform some of the functions of the defunct Bank of the United States. Such a system, funded by government deposits, would deal only in hard money and would exert a powerful moderating influence on inflation and the credit market. But Van Buren encountered strong resistance in Congress, even among Democrats. The treasury system finally won approval in 1840, but by then Van Buren's chances of winning a second term in office were virtually nil.

In 1840, the Whigs settled on **William Henry Harrison** to oppose Van Buren. The campaign drew on voter involvement as no other presidential campaign ever had. The Whigs borrowed tricks from the Democrats: Harrison was touted as a common man born in a log cabin (in reality, he was born on a Virginia plantation), and raucous campaign parades featured toy log cabins held aloft. His Indian-fighting days, now thirty years behind him, were played up to give him a Jacksonian aura. Whigs staged festive rallies around the country, drumming up mass appeal with candlelight parades and song shows, and women participated in rallies as never before. Some 78 percent of eligible voters cast ballots — the highest percentage ever in American history.

Harrison took 53 percent of the popular vote and won a resounding 234 electoral college votes to Van Buren's 60. A Democratic editor lamented, "We have taught them how to conquer us!"

REVIEW How did slavery figure as a campaign issue in the election of 1836?

▶ Conclusion: The Age of Jackson or the Era of Reform?

Harrison's election closed a decade that had brought the common man and democracy to the forefront of American politics. Economic transformations loom large in explaining the fast-paced changes of the 1830s. Transportation advances put goods and people in circulation, augmenting urban growth and helping to create a national culture, and water-powered manufacturing began to change the face of wage labor. Trade and banking mushroomed, and western land once oc-cupied by Indians was auctioned off in a landslide of sales. Two periods of economic downturn — including the panic of 1819 and the panics of 1837 and 1839 — of-fered sobering lessons about speculative fever.

For many people, Andrew Jackson symbolized this age of opportunity. His fame as an aggressive general, Indian fighter, champion of the common man, and defender of slavery attracted growing numbers of voters to the emergent Democratic Party, which championed personal liberty, free competition, and egalitarian opportunity for all white men.

Jackson's constituency was challenged by a small but vocal segment of the population troubled by serious moral problems that Jacksonians preferred to ignore. Reformers drew sustenance from the message of the Second Great Awakening: that all men and women were free to choose salvation and that personal and societal sins could be overcome. Reformers targeted personal vices (illicit sex and intemperance) and social problems (prostitution, poverty, and slavery) and joined forces with evangelicals and wealthy lawyers and merchants (North and South) who appreciated a national bank and protective tariffs. The Whig Party was the party of activist moralism and state-sponsored entrepreneurship. Whig voters were, of course, male, but thousands of reform-minded women broke new ground by signing political petitions on the issues of Indian removal and slavery. A few exceptional women, like Sarah and Angelina Grimké, captured the national limelight by offering powerful testimony against slavery and in the process pio-neering new pathways for women to contribute a moral voice to politics.

National politics in the 1830s were more divisive than at any time since the 1790s. The new party system of Democrats and Whigs reached far deeper into the electorate than had the Federalists and Republicans. Stagecoaches and steamboats carried newspapers from the cities to the backwoods, politicizing voters and creating party loyalty. Politics acquired immediacy and excitement, causing nearly four out of five white men to cast ballots in 1840.

High rates of voter participation would continue into the 1840s and 1850s. Unprecedented urban growth, westward expansion, and early industrialism marked those decades, sustaining the Democrat-Whig split in the electorate. But critiques of slavery, concerns for free labor, and an emerging protest against women's second-class citizenship complicated the political scene of the 1840s, leading to third-party political movements. One of these third parties, called the Republican Party, would achieve dominance in 1860 with the election of an Illinois lawyer, Abraham Lincoln, to the presidency.

Reviewing Chapter 11

REVIEW QUESTIONS

1. Why did the United States experience a market revolution after 1815? (pp. 303–309)

2. Why did Andrew Jackson defeat John Quincy Adams so dramatically in the 1828 election? (pp. 309–312)

3. Why did Jackson promote Indian removal? (pp. 312–319)

4. How did evangelical Protestantism contribute to the social reform movements of the 1830s? (pp. 319–326)

5. How did slavery figure as a campaign issue in the election of 1836? (pp. 326–329)

MAKING CONNECTIONS

1. Describe the market revolution that began in the 1810s. How did it affect Americans' work and domestic lives? In your answer, be sure to consider how gender contributed to these developments.

2. Andrew Jackson's presidency coincided with important changes in American politics. Discuss how Jackson benefited from, and contributed to, the vibrant political culture of the 1830s. Cite specific national developments in your answer.

3. Describe Andrew Jackson's response to the "Indian problem" during his presidency. How did his policies revise or continue earlier federal policies toward Native Americans? How did Native Americans respond to Jackson's actions?

4. While a volatile economy buffeted the United States in the 1830s, some Americans looked to reform the nation. Discuss the objectives and strategies of two reform movements. What was the relationship of these reform movements to larger political and economic trends of the 1830s?

LINKING TO THE PAST

1. How were the economic circumstances and social anxieties that gave rise to the Second Great Awakening similar to, and different from, those that encouraged the First Great Awakening? (See chapter 5.)

2. Compare the development of political parties in the 1790s (Federalists and Republicans) with the second development of parties in the 1830s (Whigs and Democrats). Were the parties of the 1830s in any way the descendants of the two of the 1790s? Or were they completely different? (See chapter 9.)

TIMELINE 1807–1840

1807 • Robert Fulton's *Clermont* sets off steamboat craze.

1816 • Second Bank of the United States chartered.

1817 • American Colonization Society founded.

1818 • National Road links Baltimore to western Virginia.

1819 • Economic panic.

1821 • Mill town of Lowell, Massachusetts, founded.

1825 • Erie Canal completed in New York.

1826 • American Temperance Society founded.
• Schuylkill Canal completed in Pennsylvania.

1828 • Congress passes Tariff of Abominations.
• Democrat Andrew Jackson elected president.

1829 • David Walker's *Appeal . . . to the Coloured Citizens of the World* published.
• Baltimore and Ohio Railroad begun.

1830 • Indian Removal Act.
• Women's petitions for Indian rights begin.

1830–1831 • Charles Grandison Finney preaches in Rochester, New York.

1831 • William Lloyd Garrison starts *Liberator*.

1832 • Massacre of Sauk and Fox Indians led by Chief Black Hawk.
• *Worcester v. Georgia*.
• Jackson vetoes charter renewal of Bank of the United States.
• New England Anti-Slavery Society founded.

1833 • Nullification of federal tariffs declared in South Carolina.
• New York and Philadelphia antislavery societies founded.
• New York Female Moral Reform Society founded.

1834 • Female mill workers strike in Lowell, Massachusetts, and again in 1836.

1836 • Democrat Martin Van Buren elected president.
• American Temperance Union founded.

1837 • Economic panic.

1838 • Trail of Tears: Cherokees forced to relocate west.

1839 • Economic panic.

1840 • Whig William Henry Harrison elected president.

▶ FOR AN ONLINE BIBLIOGRAPHY, PRACTICE QUIZZES, WEB SITES, IMAGES, AND DOCUMENTS RELATED TO THIS CHAPTER, see the Book Companion Site at **bedfordstmartins.com/roarkvalue**.

▶ FOR DOCUMENTS RELATED TO THIS PERIOD, see Michael Johnson, ed., *Reading the American Past*, Fifth Edition.

12

The New West and the Free North

1840–1860

EARLY IN NOVEMBER 1842, ABRAHAM LINCOLN AND HIS NEW WIFE, Mary, moved into their first home in Springfield, Illinois, a rented room measuring eight by fourteen feet on the second floor of the Globe Tavern. The small, noisy room above the tavern and next door to a blacksmith shop was the nicest place that Abraham Lincoln had ever lived. It was the worst place that Mary Todd Lincoln had ever inhabited. She grew up in Lexington, Kentucky, attended by slaves in the elegant home of her father, a prosperous merchant, banker, and politician. In March 1861, nineteen years after their marriage, the Lincolns moved into what would prove to be their last home, the presidential mansion in Washington, D.C.

Abraham Lincoln climbed from the Globe Tavern to the White House by relentless work, unslaked ambition, and immense talent — traits he had honed since boyhood. Lincoln and many others celebrated his rise from humble origins as an example of the opportunities that beckoned in the free-labor economy of the North and West. They attributed his spectacular ascent to his individual qualities and tended to ignore the help he received from Mary and many others.

Born in a Kentucky log cabin in 1809, Lincoln grew up on small, struggling farms as his family migrated west. His father, Thomas Lincoln, who had been born in Virginia, never learned to read and, as his son recalled, "never did more in the way of writing than to bunglingly sign his own name." Lincoln's mother,

Lincoln's Springfield Home
After moving to Illinois and becoming a successful lawyer and politician in Springfield, Lincoln and his wife Mary moved in 1844 to the home shown here. Lincoln believed that the opportunities the free labor system offered to all Americans enabled him to achieve success in spite of his modest upbringing. © Bettmann/Corbis.

Nancy, could neither read nor write. In December 1816, Thomas Lincoln moved his young family from Kentucky to the Indiana wilderness. On the Indiana farmstead, Abraham learned the arts of agriculture practiced by families throughout the nation. Although only eight years old, he "had an axe put into his hands at once" and used it "almost constantly" for the next fifteen years, as he recalled later. When he could be spared from work, the boy attended school, less than a year in all. "There was absolutely nothing to excite ambition for education," Lincoln recollected. In contrast, Mary Todd received ten years of schooling in Lexington's best private academies for young women.

In 1830, Thomas Lincoln decided to move farther west. The Lincolns hitched up the family oxen and headed to central Illinois. The next spring, Thomas moved yet again, but this time Abraham stayed behind and set out on his own, a "friendless, uneducated, penniless boy," as he described himself.

By dogged striving, Abraham Lincoln gained an education and the respect of his Illinois neighbors, although a steady income eluded him for years. Mary Todd had many suitors, including Stephen A. Douglas, Lincoln's eventual political rival. After she married Lincoln, she said, "Intellectually my husband towers above Douglas . . . [and he] has no equal in the United States." The newlyweds received help from Mary's father, including eighty acres of land and a yearly allowance of about $1,100 for six years that helped them move out of their room above the Globe Tavern and into their own home. Abraham eventually built a thriving law practice in Springfield, Illinois, and served in the state legislature and then in Congress. Mary helped him in many ways, rearing their sons, tending their household, and integrating him into her wealthy and influential extended family in Illinois and Kentucky. Mary also shared Abraham's keen interest in politics and ambition for power. With Mary's support, Abraham's striving ultimately propelled them into the White House, where he became the first president born west of the Appalachian Mountains.

Like Lincoln, millions of Americans believed they could make something of themselves, whatever their origins, so long as they were willing to work. Individuals who refused to work — who were lazy, undisciplined, or foolish — had only themselves to blame if they failed. Work was a prerequisite for success, not a guarantee. This emphasis on work highlighted the individual efforts of men and tended to slight the many crucial contributions of women, family members, neighbors, and friends to the successes of men like Lincoln. In addition, the rewards of work were skewed toward white men and away from women and free African Americans. Nonetheless, the promise of such rewards spurred efforts that shaped the contours of America, pushing the boundaries of the nation ever westward to the Pacific Ocean. The nation's economic, political, and geographic expansion raised anew the question of whether slavery should also move west, the question that Lincoln and other Americans confronted again and again following the Mexican-American War, yet another outgrowth of the nation's ceaseless westward movement.

▶ Economic and Industrial Evolution

During the 1840s and 1850s, Americans experienced a profound economic transformation whose roots reached back to the beginning of the nineteenth century. Since 1800, the total output of the U.S. economy had multiplied twelvefold. Four fundamental changes in American society fueled this remarkable economic growth. First, millions of Americans moved from farms to towns and cities, Abraham Lincoln among them. Second, factory workers (primarily in towns and cities) increased to about 20 percent of the labor force by 1860. Third, a shift from water power to steam as a source of energy raised productivity, especially in factories and transportation. Railroads in particular harnessed steam power, speeding transport and cutting costs. Fourth, agricultural productivity nearly doubled during Lincoln's lifetime, spurring the nation's economic growth more than any other factor.

Historians often refer to this cascade of changes as an industrial revolution. However, these changes did not cause an abrupt discontinuity in America's economy or society, which remained overwhelmingly agricultural. Old methods of production continued alongside the new. The changes in the American economy during the 1840s and 1850s might better be termed "industrial evolution."

Agriculture and Land Policy

While cities, factories, and steam engines multiplied throughout the North and West, the foundation of the United States' economic growth lay in agriculture. A French traveler in the United States noted that Americans had "a general feeling of hatred against trees." Although the traveler exaggerated, his observation contained an important truth. Trees limited agricultural productivity because farmers had to spend a great deal of time and energy clearing land for planting. As farmers pushed westward in a quest for cheap land, they encountered the Midwest's comparatively treeless prairie, where they could spend less time with an ax and more time with a plow and hoe. Rich prairie soils yielded bumper crops, enticing farmers such as the Lincolns to migrate to the Midwest by the tens of thousands between 1830 and 1860. The populations of Indiana, Illinois, Michigan, Wisconsin, and Iowa exploded tenfold between 1830 and 1860, four times faster than the growth of the nation as a whole. Lincoln's home state of Illinois added more people during the 1850s than any other state in the Union.

Labor-saving improvements in farm implements also boosted agricultural productivity. Inventors tinkered to craft stronger, more efficient plows to furrow the earth with as little effort as possible. In 1837, **John Deere** made a strong, smooth steel plow that sliced through prairie soil so cleanly that farmers called it the "singing plow." Deere's company became the leading plow manufacturer in the Midwest, turning out more than ten thousand plows a year by the late 1850s. Humans and animals (rather than steam) provided the energy for plowing, but better plows permitted farmers to break more ground and plant more crops.

Improvements in wheat harvesting also increased farmers' productivity. In 1850, most farmers harvested wheat by hand, cutting two or three acres a day with backbreaking labor. In the 1840s, Cyrus McCormick and others experimented with designs for **mechanical reapers**, and by the 1850s a McCormick reaper that cost between $100 and $150 allowed a farmer to harvest twelve acres a day. Farmers had purchased about eighty thousand reapers by 1860, but most continued to cut their grain by hand. Still, improved reapers and plows, usually powered by horses or oxen, allowed farmers to cultivate more land, doubling the corn and wheat harvests between 1840 and 1860.

Federal land policy made possible the agricultural productivity that fueled the nation's economy. Up to 1860, the United States continued to be land-rich and labor-poor. Territorial acquisitions made the nation a great deal richer in land, adding more than a billion acres with the Louisiana Purchase (see chapter 10) and the annexation of Florida, Oregon, and vast territories following the Mexican-American War. The federal government made most of this land available for purchase to attract settlers and to generate revenue. Wily speculators found ways to claim large tracts of the most desirable plots and sell them to settlers at a generous markup. But millions of ordinary farmers bought federal land for just $1.25 an acre, or $50 for a forty-acre farm that could support a family. Millions of other farmers squatted on unclaimed federal land, carved out farms, and, if they still lacked funds to buy the land after a few years, usually moved farther west to squat on federal land elsewhere. By making land available to millions of Americans on relatively easy terms, the federal government achieved the goal of attracting settlers to the new territories in the West, which in due course joined the Union as new states. Above all, federal land policy facilitated the increase in agricultural productivity that underlay the nation's impressive economic growth.

Manufacturing and Mechanization

Changes in manufacturing arose from the nation's land-rich, labor-poor economy. European countries had land-poor, labor-rich economies; there, meager opportunities in agriculture kept factory laborers plentiful and wages low. In the United States, western expansion and government land policies buoyed agriculture, keeping millions of people on the farm — 80 percent of the nation's 31 million people lived in rural areas in 1860 — and thereby limiting the supply of workers for manufacturing and elevating wages. Because of this relative shortage of workers, American manufacturers searched constantly for ways to save labor.

Mechanization allowed manufacturers to produce more with less labor. In general, factory workers produced twice as much (per unit of labor) as agricultural workers. The practice of manufacturing and then assembling interchangeable parts spread from gun making to other industries and became known as the **American system**. Standardized parts produced by machine allowed manufacturers to employ unskilled workers, who were much cheaper and more readily available than highly trained craftsmen. A visitor to a Springfield, Massachusetts, gun factory in 1842 noted, for example, that standardized parts made the trained gunsmith's "skill of the eye and the hand, [previously] acquired by practice alone . . . no longer indispensable." Even in heavily mechanized industries, few factories had more than twenty or thirty employees.

Manufacturing and agriculture meshed into a dynamic national economy. New England led the nation in manufacturing, shipping goods such as guns, clocks, plows, and axes west and south, while southern and western states sent commodities such as wheat, pork, whiskey, tobacco, and cotton north and east. In the 1840s, mines in Pennsylvania, Ohio, and elsewhere began to produce millions of tons of coal for industrial fuel, accelerating the shift to steam power. Between 1840 and 1860, coal production multiplied eightfold, cutting prices in half and permitting coal-fired steam engines to power ever more factories, railroads, and ships. Even so, by 1860 coal accounted for less than a fifth of the nation's energy consumption while, in manufacturing, people and work animals provided thirty times more energy than steam did.

American manufacturers specialized in producing for the gigantic domestic market rather than for export. British goods dominated the international market and, on the whole, were cheaper and better than American-made products. U.S. manufacturers supported tariffs to minimize British competition, but their best protection from British competitors was to strive harder to please their American customers, most of them farmers. The burgeoning national economy was further fueled by the growth of the railroads, which served to link farmers and factories in new ways.

Railroads: Breaking the Bonds of Nature

A Swedish visitor in 1849 noticed that American schoolboys drew sketches of locomotives, always in motion, belching smoke. Railroads captured Americans' imagination because they seemed to break the bonds of nature. When canals and rivers froze in winter or became impassable during summer droughts, trains steamed ahead. When becalmed sailing ships went nowhere, locomotives kept on chugging, averaging more than twenty miles an hour during the 1850s. Above all, railroads gave cities not blessed with canals or navigable rivers a way to compete for rural trade.

In 1850, trains steamed along 9,000 miles of track, almost two-thirds of it in New England and the Middle Atlantic states. By 1860, several railroads spanned the Mississippi River, connecting frontier farmers to the nation's 30,000 miles of track, approximately as much as in all of the rest of the world combined (Map 12.1). In 1857, for example, France had 3,700 miles of track; England and Wales had 6,400 miles. The massive expansion of American railroads helped catapult the nation into position as the world's second-greatest industrial power, after Great Britain.

MAP 12.1
Railroads in 1860
Railroads were a crucial component of the revolutions in transportation and communications that transformed nineteenth-century America. The railroad system reflected the differences in the economies of the North and South.

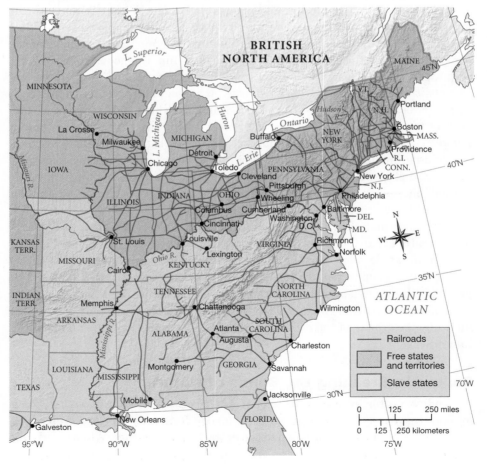

In addition to speeding transportation, railroads propelled the growth of other industries, such as iron and communications. Iron production grew five times faster than the population during the decades up to 1860, in part to meet railroads' demand. Railroads also stimulated the fledgling telegraph industry. In 1844, **Samuel F. B. Morse** persuasively demonstrated the potential of his telegraph by transmitting a series of dots and dashes that instantly conveyed an electronic message along forty miles of wire strung between Washington, D.C., and Baltimore. By 1861, more than fifty thousand miles of wire stretched across the continent to the Pacific Ocean, often alongside railroad tracks, making trains safer and more efficient and accelerating communications of all sorts.

In contrast to the government ownership of railroads common in other industrial nations, private corporations built and owned almost all American railroads. But the railroads received massive government aid, especially federal land grants. Up to 1850, the federal government had granted a total of seven million acres of federal land to various turnpike, highway, and canal projects. In 1850, Congress approved a precedent-setting grant to railroads of six square miles of federal land for each mile of track laid. By 1860, Congress had granted railroads more than twenty million acres of federal land, thereby underwriting construction costs and promoting the expansion of the rail network, the settlement of federal land, and the integration of the domestic market.

The railroad boom of the 1850s signaled the growing industrial might of the American economy. An Illinois farmer praised railroads' "cheap and easy conveyance of commodities to foreign markets." Like other industries, railroads succeeded because they served both farms and cities. But transportation was not revolutionized overnight. Most Americans in 1860 were still far more familiar with horses than with locomotives. And even by 1875, trains carried only about one-third of the mail; most of the rest still went by stagecoach or horseback.

The economy of the 1840s and 1850s linked an expanding, westward-moving population in farms and cities with muscles, animals, machines, steam, and railroads. Abraham Lincoln cut trees, planted corn, and split rails as a young man before he moved to Springfield, Illinois, and became a successful attorney who defended, among others, railroad corporations. His mobility — westward, from farm to city, from manual to mental labor, and upward — illustrated the direction of economic change and the opportunities that beckoned enterprising individuals.

> **REVIEW** Why did the United States become a leading industrial power in the nineteenth century?

▶ Free Labor: Promise and Reality

The nation's impressive economic performance did not reward all Americans equally. Native-born white men tended to do better than immigrants. With few exceptions, women were excluded from opportunities open to men. Tens of thousands of women worked as seamstresses, laundresses, domestic servants, factory hands, and teachers but had little opportunity to aspire to higher-paying jobs.

In the North and West, slavery was slowly eliminated in the half century after the American Revolution, but most free African Americans were relegated to dead-end jobs as laborers and servants. Discrimination against immigrants, women, and free blacks did not trouble most white men. With certain notable exceptions, they considered it proper and just.

The Free-Labor Ideal

During the 1840s and 1850s, leaders throughout the North and West emphasized a set of ideas that seemed to explain why the changes under way in their society benefited some people more than others. They referred again and again to the advantages of what they termed *free labor*. (The word *free* referred to laborers who were not slaves. It did not mean laborers who worked for nothing.) By the 1850s, free-labor ideas described a social and economic ideal that accounted for both the successes and the shortcomings of the economy and society taking shape in the North and West.

Spokesmen for the **free-labor ideal** celebrated hard work, self-reliance, and independence. They proclaimed that the door to success was open not just to those who inherited wealth or status but also to self-made men such as Abraham Lincoln. Free labor, Lincoln argued, was "the just and generous, and prosperous system, which opens the way for all — gives hope to all, and energy, and progress, and improvement of condition to all." Free labor permitted farmers and artisans to enjoy the products of their own labor, and it also benefited wageworkers. "The prudent, penniless beginner in the world," Lincoln asserted, "labors for wages awhile, saves a surplus with which to buy tools or land, for himself; then labors on his own account another while, and at length hires another new beginner to help him." Wage labor, he claimed, was the first rung on the ladder toward self-employment and eventually hiring others.

The free-labor ideal affirmed an egalitarian vision of human potential. Lincoln and other spokesmen stressed the importance of **universal education** to permit "heads and hands [to] cooperate as friends." Throughout the North and West, communities supported public schools to make the rudiments of learning available to young children. By 1860, many cities and towns had public schools that boasted that up to 80 percent of children ages seven to thirteen attended school at least for a few weeks each year. In rural areas, where the labor of children was more difficult to spare, schools typically enrolled no more than half the school-age children. Lessons included more than arithmetic, penmanship, and a smattering of other subjects. Textbooks and teachers — most of whom were young women — drummed into students the lessons of the free-labor system: self-reliance, discipline, and, above all else, hard work. "Remember that all the ignorance, degradation, and misery in the world is the result of indolence and vice," one textbook intoned. Both in and outside school, free-labor ideology emphasized labor as much as freedom.

Economic Inequality

The free-labor ideal made sense to many Americans, especially in the North and West, because it seemed to describe their own experiences. Lincoln frequently referred to his humble beginnings as a hired laborer and implicitly invited his listeners to consider how far he had come. In 1860, his assets of $17,000 easily placed him in the wealthiest 5 percent of the population. The opportunities presented by the expanding economy made a few men much, much richer. In 1860, the nation had about forty millionaires. Most Americans, however, measured success in more modest terms. The average wealth of adult white men in the North in 1860 barely topped $2,000. Nearly half of American men had no wealth at all; about 60 percent owned no land. Because property possessed by married women was normally considered to belong to their husbands, women typically had less wealth than men. Free African Americans had still less; 90 percent of them were propertyless.

Free-labor spokesmen considered these economic inequalities a natural outgrowth of freedom — the inevitable result of some individuals being both luckier and more able and willing to work. These inequalities also demonstrate the gap between the promise and the performance of the free-labor ideal. Economic growth permitted many men to move from being landless squatters to landowning farmers and from being hired laborers to independent, self-employed producers. But many more Americans remained behind, landless and working for wages. Even those who realized their aspirations often had a precarious hold on their independence. Bad debts, market volatility, crop failure, sickness, or death could quickly eliminate a family's gains.

Seeking out new opportunities in pursuit of free-labor ideals created restless social and geographic mobility. While fortunate people such as Abraham Lincoln rose far beyond their social origins, others shared the misfortune of a merchant who, an observer noted, "has been on the sinking list all his life." In search of better prospects, roughly two-thirds of the rural population moved every decade, and population turnover in cities was even greater. This constant coming and going weakened community ties to neighbors and friends and threw individuals even more on their own resources in times of trouble.

Immigrants and the Free-Labor Ladder

The risks and uncertainties of free labor did not deter millions of immigrants from entering the United States during the 1840s and 1850s. Almost 4.5 million immigrants arrived between 1840 and 1860, six times more than had come during the previous two decades. By 1860, foreign-born residents made up about one-eighth of the U.S. population, a fraction that held steady well into the twentieth century.

Nearly three-fourths of the immigrants who arrived in the United States between 1840 and 1860 came from either Germany or Ireland. The majority of the 1.4 million Germans who entered during these years were skilled tradesmen and their families. Roughly a quarter were farmers, some of whom settled in Texas. German butchers, bakers, beer makers, carpenters, shopkeepers, and machinists settled mostly in the Midwest, often congregating in cities. On the whole, German Americans were often Protestants and occupied the middle stratum of independent producers celebrated by free-labor spokesmen; relatively few worked as wage laborers or domestic servants.

Irish immigrants, in contrast, entered at the bottom of the free-labor ladder and struggled to climb up. Nearly 1.7 million Irish immigrants arrived between 1840 and 1860, nearly all of them desperately poor and often weakened by hunger and disease. Potato blight struck Ireland in 1845 and returned repeatedly in subsequent years, spreading a catastrophic famine throughout the island. Many of the lucky ones crowded into the holds of ships and set out for America, where they congregated in northeastern cities. As one immigrant group declared, "All we want is to get out of Ireland; we must be better anywhere than here." Death trailed after them. So many died crossing the Atlantic that ships from Ireland were often termed "coffin ships."

Roughly three out of four Irish immigrants worked as laborers or domestic servants. Irish men dug canals, loaded ships, laid railroad track, and did odd jobs while Irish women worked in the homes of others — cooking, washing and ironing, minding children, and cleaning house. Almost all Irish immigrants were Catholic, a fact that set them apart from the overwhelmingly Protestant native-born residents. Many natives regarded the Irish as hard-drinking, unruly, half-civilized folk. Such views lay behind the discrimination reflected in job announcements that commonly stated, "No Irish need apply." Despite such prejudices, native residents hired Irish immigrants because they accepted low pay and worked hard.

In America's labor-poor economy, Irish laborers could earn more in one day than in several weeks in Ireland, where opportunities were often scarce. In America, one immigrant explained in 1853, there was "plenty of work and plenty of wages plenty to eat and no land lords thats enough what more does a man want." But some immigrants wanted more, especially respect and decent working conditions. One immigrant complained that he was "a slave for the Americans as the generality of the Irish . . . are."

Such testimony illustrates that the free-labor system, whether for immigrants or native-born laborers, often did not live up to the optimistic vision outlined by Abraham Lincoln and others. Many wage laborers could not realistically aspire to become independent, self-sufficient property holders, despite the claims of free-labor proponents.

REVIEW How did the free-labor ideal account for economic inequality?

▶ The Westward Movement

The nation's swelling population, booming economy, and boundless confidence propelled a new era of rapid westward migration beginning in the 1840s. Until then, the overwhelming majority of Americans lived east of the Mississippi River. Native Americans inhabited the plains, deserts, and rugged coasts to the west. The British claimed the Oregon Country, and the Mexican flag flew over the vast expanse of the Southwest. But by 1850, the nation's limits pushed far beyond the boundaries of the 1803 Louisiana Purchase. The United States stretched to the Pacific and had more than doubled in size. By 1860, the great migration had carried four million Americans west of the Mississippi River.

Frontier settlers took the land and then, with the exception of the Mormons, lobbied their government to acquire the territory they had settled. The human cost of aggressive expansionism was high. The young Mexican nation lost a war and half of its territory. Two centuries of Indian wars east of the Mississippi ended during the 1830s, but the fierce struggle between native inhabitants and invaders continued for another half century in the West. Americans believed it was their destiny to conquer the continent.

Manifest Destiny

Most Americans believed that the superiority of their institutions and white culture bestowed on them a God-given right to spread their civilization across the continent. They imagined the West as a howling wilderness, empty and undeveloped. If they recognized Indians and Mexicans at all, they dismissed them as primitive drags on progress who would have to be redeemed, shoved aside, or exterminated. The West provided young men especially an arena in which to "show their manhood." The sense of uniqueness and mission was as old as the Puritans, but by the 1840s the conviction of superiority had been bolstered by the United States' amazing success. Most Americans believed that the West needed the civilizing power of the hammer and the plow, the ballot box and the pulpit, which had transformed the East.

In 1845, a New York political journal edited by John L. O'Sullivan coined the term *manifest destiny* as the latest justification for white settlers to take the land they coveted. O'Sullivan called on Americans to resist any foreign power — British, French, or Mexican — that attempted to thwart "the fulfillment of our manifest destiny to overspread the continent allotted by Providence for the free development of our yearly multiplying millions . . . [and] for the development of the great experiment of liberty and federative self-government entrusted to us." Almost overnight, the magic phrase *manifest destiny* swept the nation and provided an ideological shield for conquering the West.

As important as national pride and racial arrogance were to manifest destiny, economic gain made up its core. Land hunger drew hundreds of thousands of average Americans westward. Some politicians, moreover, had become convinced that national prosperity depended on capturing the rich trade of the Far East. To trade with Asia, the United States needed the Pacific coast ports that stretched from San Diego to Puget Sound. "The sun of civilization must shine across the sea: socially and commercially," Missouri senator Thomas Hart Benton declared. The United States and Asia must "talk together, and trade together. Commerce is a great civilizer." In the 1840s, American economic expansion came wrapped in the rhetoric of uplift and civilization.

Oregon and the Overland Trail

The Oregon Country — a vast region bounded on the west by the Pacific Ocean, on the east by the Rocky Mountains, on the south by the forty-second parallel, and on the north by Russian Alaska — caused the pulse of American expansionists to race. But the British also coveted the area. They argued that their claim lay with Sir Francis Drake's discovery of the Oregon coast in 1579. Americans countered with historic claims of their own. Unable to agree, the United States and Great Britain decided in 1818 on "joint occupation" that would leave Oregon "free and open" to settlement by both countries. A handful of American fur traders and "mountain men" roamed the region in the 1820s.

By the late 1830s, settlers began to trickle along the **Oregon Trail**, following a trail blazed by the mountain men. The first wagon trains headed west in 1841, and by 1843 about 1,000 emigrants a year set out from Independence, Missouri. By 1869, when the first transcontinental railroad was completed, approximately 350,000 migrants had traveled west to the Pacific in wagon trains.

Emigrants encountered the Plains Indians, a quarter of a million Native Americans scattered over the area between the Mississippi River and the Rocky Mountains. Some were farmers who lived peaceful, sedentary lives, but a majority — the Sioux, Cheyenne, Shoshoni, and Arapaho of the central plains and the Kiowa, Wichita, and Comanche of the southern plains — were horse-mounted, nomadic, nonagricultural peoples whose warriors symbolized the "savage Indian" in the minds of whites.

Horses, which had been brought to North America by Spaniards in the sixteenth century, permitted the Plains tribes to become highly mobile hunters of buffalo. They came to depend on buffalo for nearly everything — food, clothing, shelter, and fuel. Competition for buffalo led to war between the tribes. Young men were introduced to warfare early, learning to ride ponies at breakneck speed while firing off arrows and, later, rifles with astounding accuracy. "A Comanche on his feet is out of his element," observed western artist George Catlin, "but the moment he lays his hands upon his horse, his *face* even becomes handsome, and he gracefully flies away like a different being."

The Plains Indians struck fear in the hearts of whites on the wagon trains. But Native Americans had far more to fear from whites. Indians killed fewer than four hundred emigrants on the trail between 1840 and 1860, while whites brought alcohol and deadly epidemics of smallpox, measles, cholera, and scarlet fever. Moreover, white hunters slaughtered buffalo for the international hide market and sometimes just for sport. The buffalo still numbered some twelve million in 1860, but the herds were shrinking rapidly, intensifying conflict among the Plains tribes.

Emigrants insisted that the federal government provide them with more protection. The government constructed a chain of forts along the Oregon Trail. More important, it adopted a new Indian policy: "concentration." In 1851, the government called the Plains tribes to a conference at Fort Laramie, Wyoming. Some ten thousand Indians showed up, hopeful that something could be done to protect them from the ravages of the wagon trains. Instead, government negotiators at the **Fort Laramie conference** persuaded the chiefs to sign agreements that cleared a wide corridor for wagon trains by restricting Native Americans to specific areas that whites promised they would never violate. This policy of concentration became the seedbed for the subsequent policy of reservations. But whites would not keep out of Indian territory, and Indians would not easily give up their traditional ways of life. Struggle for control of the West meant warfare for decades to come.

Still, Indians threatened emigrants less than life on the trail did. The men, women, and children who headed west each spring could count on at least six months of grueling travel. With nearly two thousand miles to go and traveling no more than fifteen miles a day, the pioneers endured parching heat, drought, treacherous rivers, disease, physical and emotional exhaustion, and, if the snows closed the mountain passes before they got through, freezing and starvation. Women sometimes faced the dangers of trailside childbirth. It was said that a person could walk from Missouri to the Pacific stepping only on the graves of those who had died heading west. Such tribulations led one miserable woman, trying to keep her children dry in a rainstorm and to calm them as they listened to Indian shouts, to wonder "what had possessed my husband, anyway, that he should have thought of bringing us away out through this God forsaken country."

Pioneer Family on the Trail West

In 1860, W. G. Chamberlain photographed these unidentified travelers momentarily at rest by the upper Arkansas River in Colorado. We do not know their fates, but we can only hope that they fared better than the Sager family. Henry and Naomi Sager and their six children set out from St. Joseph, Missouri, in 1844. "Father," one of Henry and Naomi's daughters remembered, "was one of those restless men who are not content to remain in one place long at a time. [He] had been talking of going to Texas. But mother, hearing much said about the healthfulness of Oregon, preferred to go there." Still far from Oregon, Henry Sager died of fever. Twenty-six days later, Naomi died, leaving seven children, the last delivered on the trail. The Sager children, under the care of other families in the wagon train, pressed on. After traveling two thousand miles in seven months, the migrants arrived in Oregon, where Marcus and Narcissa Whitman, whose own daughter had drowned, adopted all seven of the Sager children. Denver Public Library, Western History Division # F3226.

Men usually found Oregon "one of the greatest countries in the world." From "the Cascade mountains to the Pacific, the whole country can be cultivated," exclaimed one eager settler. When women reached Oregon, they found that neighbors were scarce and things were in a "primitive state." One young wife arrived with only her husband, one stew kettle, and three knives. Necessity blurred the traditional division between men's and women's work. "I am maid of all traids," one busy woman remarked in 1853. Work seemed unending. "I am a very old woman," declared twenty-nine-year-old Sarah Everett. "My face is thin sunken and wrinkled, my hands bony withered and hard." Another settler observed, "A woman that can not endure almost as much as a horse has no business here." Yet despite the ordeal of the trail and the difficulties of starting from scratch, emigrants kept coming.

The Mormon Exodus

Not every wagon train heading west was bound for the Pacific Slope. One remarkable group of religious emigrants halted near the Great Salt Lake in what was then Mexican territory. The **Mormons** deliberately chose the remote site as a refuge. After years of persecution in the East, they fled west to find religious freedom and communal security.

In 1820, an upstate New York farm boy named **Joseph Smith Jr.** had begun to experience revelations that were followed, he said, by a visit from an angel who led him to golden tablets buried near his home. With the aid of magic stones, he translated the mysterious language on the tablets to produce *The Book of Mormon*, which he published in 1830. It told the story of an ancient Hebrew civilization in the New World and predicted the appearance of an American prophet who would reestablish Jesus Christ's undefiled kingdom in America. Converts, attracted to the promise of a pure faith in the midst of antebellum America's social turmoil and rampant materialism, flocked to the new Church of Jesus Christ of Latter-Day Saints (the Mormons).

Neighbors branded Mormons heretics and drove Smith and his followers from New York to Ohio, then to Missouri, and finally in 1839 to Nauvoo, Illinois, where they built a prosperous community. But a rift in the church developed after Smith sanctioned "plural marriage" (polygamy). Non-Mormons caught wind of the controversy and eventually arrested Smith and his brother. On June 27, 1844, a mob stormed the jail and shot both men dead.

The embattled church turned to an extraordinary new leader, **Brigham Young**, who oversaw a great exodus. In 1846, traveling in 3,700 wagons, 12,000 Mormons made their way to eastern Iowa, then the following year to their new home beside the Great Salt Lake. Young described the region as a barren waste, "the paradise of the lizard, the cricket and the rattlesnake." Within ten years, however, the Mormons developed an irrigation system that made the desert bloom. Under Young's stern leadership, the Mormons built a thriving community using cooperative labor, not the individualistic and competitive enterprise common among most emigrants.

In 1850, the Mormon kingdom was annexed to the United States as Utah Territory. The nation's attention focused on Utah in 1852 when Brigham Young announced that many Mormons practiced polygamy. Although only one Mormon man in five had more than one wife (Young had twenty-three), Young's statement caused a popular outcry that forced the U.S. government to establish its authority in Utah. In 1857, 2,500 U.S. troops invaded Salt Lake City in what was known as the Mormon War. The bloodless occupation illustrated that most Americans viewed the Mormons as a threat to American morality, law, and institutions. The invasion did not dislodge the Mormon Church from its central place in Utah, however, and for years to come, most Americans perceived the Mormon settlement as strange and suitably isolated.

The Mexican Borderlands

In the Mexican Southwest, westward-moving Anglo-American pioneers confronted northern-moving Spanish-speaking frontiersmen. On this frontier as elsewhere, national cultures, interests, and aspirations collided. Since 1821, when Mexico won its independence from Spain, the Mexican flag had flown over the vast expanse that stretched from the Gulf of Mexico to the Pacific and from the Oregon Country to Guatemala. But Mexico's northern provinces were sparsely populated, and the young nation was plagued by civil wars, economic crises, quarrels with the Roman Catholic Church, and devastating raids by the Comanche, Apache, and Kiowa. Mexico found it increasingly difficult to defend its borderlands, especially when faced with a northern neighbor convinced of its superiority and bent on territorial acquisition.

The American assault began quietly. In the 1820s, Anglo-American trappers, traders, and settlers drifted into Mexico's far northern provinces. Santa Fe, a remote outpost in the province of New Mexico, became a magnet for American enterprise. Each spring, American traders gathered at Independence, Missouri, for the long trek southwest along the Santa Fe Trail. They crammed their wagons with inexpensive American manufactured goods and returned home with Mexican silver, furs, and mules.

The Mexican province of Texas attracted a flood of Americans who had settlement, not long-distance trade, on their minds. Wanting to populate and develop its northern territory, the Mexican government granted the American **Stephen F. Austin** a huge tract of land along the Brazos River. In the 1820s, Austin became the first Anglo-American *empresario* (colonization agent) in Texas, offering land at only ten cents an acre. Thousands of Americans poured across the border. Most were Southerners who brought cotton and slaves with them.

By the 1830s, the settlers had established a thriving plantation economy in Texas. Americans numbered 35,000, while the *Tejano* (Spanish-speaking) population was less than 8,000. Few Anglo-American settlers were Roman Catholic, spoke Spanish, or cared about assimilating into Mexican culture. Afraid of losing Texas to the new arrivals, the Mexican government in 1830 banned further immigration to Texas from the United States and outlawed the introduction of additional slaves. The Anglo-Americans made it clear that they wanted to be rid of the "despotism of the sword and the priesthood" and to govern themselves. In Mexico City, however, General **Antonio López de Santa Anna** seized political power and set about restoring order to the northern frontier.

When the Texan settlers rebelled, Santa Anna ordered the Mexican army northward. In February 1836, the army arrived at the outskirts of San Antonio. Commanded by Colonel William B. Travis from Alabama, the rebels included the Tennessee frontiersman Davy Crockett and the Louisiana adventurer James Bowie, as well as a handful of Tejanos. They took refuge in a former Franciscan mission known as the Alamo. Santa Anna sent wave after wave of his 2,000-man army crashing against the walls until the attackers finally broke through and killed all 187 rebels. A few weeks later, outside the small town of Goliad, Mexican forces captured a garrison of Texans. Mexican firing squads executed almost 400 of the men as "pirates and outlaws." In April 1836, at San Jacinto, General Sam Houston's army adopted the massacre of Goliad as a battle cry and crushed Santa Anna's troops in a surprise attack. The Texans had succeeded in establishing the **Lone Star Republic**, and the following year the United States recognized the independence of Texas from Mexico.

Earlier, in 1824, in an effort to increase Mexican migration to the province of California, the Mexican government granted *ranchos* — huge estates devoted to cattle raising — to new settlers. *Rancheros* ruled over near-feudal empires worked by Indians whose condition sometimes approached that of slaves. Not satisfied, the rancheros coveted the vast lands controlled by the Franciscan missions. In 1834, they persuaded the Mexican government to confiscate the missions and make their lands available to new settlement, a development that accelerated the decline of the California Indians. Devastated by disease, the Indians, who had numbered approximately 300,000 when the Spanish arrived in 1769, had declined to half that number by 1846.

Despite the efforts of the Mexican government, California in 1840 had a population of only 7,000 Mexican settlers. Non-Mexican settlers numbered only 380, but among them were Americans who championed manifest destiny. They sought to woo American emigrants to California. In the 1840s, wagon after wagon left the Oregon Trail to head southwest on the California Trail. As the trickle of Americans became a river, Mexican officials grew alarmed. As a New York newspaper put it in 1845, "Let the tide of emigration flow toward California and the American population will soon be sufficiently numerous to play the Texas game." Only a few Americans in California wanted a war for independence, but many dreamed of living again under the U.S. flag.

The U.S. government made no secret of its desire to acquire California. In 1835, President Andrew Jackson tried unsuccessfully to purchase it. In 1846, American settlers in the Sacramento Valley took matters into their own hands. Prodded by John C. Frémont, a former army captain and explorer who had arrived with a party of sixty buckskin-clad frontiersmen spoiling for a fight, the Californians raised an independence movement known as the Bear Flag Revolt. By then, James K. Polk, a champion of aggressive expansion, sat in the White House.

REVIEW Why did westward migration expand dramatically in the mid-nineteenth century?

▶ Expansion and the Mexican-American War

Although emigrants acted as the advance guard of American empire, there was nothing automatic about the U.S. annexation of territory in the West. Acquiring territory required political action. In the 1840s, the politics of expansion became entangled with sectionalism and the slavery question. Texas, Oregon, and the Mexican borderlands also thrust the United States into dangerous diplomatic crises with Great Britain and Mexico.

Aggravation between Mexico and the United States escalated to open antagonism in 1845 when the United States annexed Texas. Absorbing territory still claimed by Mexico ruptured diplomatic relations between the two countries and set the stage for war. But it was President James K. Polk's insistence on having Mexico's other northern provinces that made war certain. The war was not as easy as Polk anticipated, but it ended in American victory and the acquisition of a new American West. One of the nation's new territories, California, proved immediately profitable; the discovery of gold prompted a massive wave of emigration to the western coast, a rush that nearly destroyed Native American and Californio society.

The Politics of Expansion

Texans had sought admission to the Union almost since winning their independence from Mexico in 1836. Almost constant border warfare between Mexico and the Republic of Texas in the decade following the revolution underscored the precarious nature of independence. It also made clear that annexing Texas to the United States risked precipitating war, for Mexico had never relinquished its claim to its lost province. But any suggestion of adding another slave state to the Union outraged most Northerners, who applauded westward expansion but imagined the expansion of liberty, not slavery.

President **John Tyler**, who became president in April 1841 when William Henry Harrison died one month after taking office, understood that Texas was a dangerous issue. Adding to the danger, Great Britain began sniffing around Texas, apparently contemplating adding the young republic to its growing empire. Tyler, an ardent expansionist, decided to risk annexing the Lone Star Republic. However, when he laid an annexation treaty before the Senate in 1844, howls of protest erupted across the North. Future Massachusetts senator Charles Sumner deplored the "insidious" plan to annex Texas and carve from it "great slaveholding states." The Senate soundly rejected the treaty, and it appeared that Tyler had succeeded only in inflaming sectional conflict.

The issue of Texas had not died down by the 1844 election. In an effort to appeal to northern voters, the Whig nominee for president, **Henry Clay**, came out against annexation of Texas. "Annexation and war with Mexico are identical," he declared. The Democrats chose Tennessean **James K. Polk**, a passionate expansionist who vigorously backed annexation. To make annexation palatable to Northerners, the Democrats shrewdly yoked Texas to Oregon, thus tapping the desire for expansion in the free states of the North as well as in the slave states of the South. The Democratic platform called for the "reannexation of Texas" and the "reoccupation of Oregon." The suggestion that the United States was merely reasserting existing rights was poor history but good politics.

When Clay finally recognized the popularity of expansion, he waffled, hinting that he might accept the annexation of Texas after all. His retreat succeeded only in alienating antislavery opinion in the North. James G. Birney, the candidate of the fledgling Liberty Party, picked up the votes of thousands of disillusioned Clay supporters. In the November election, Polk received 170 electoral votes and Clay 105. New York's 35 electoral votes proved critical to Clay's defeat. A shift of just one-third of Birney's 15,000 votes to Clay would have given Clay the state and the presidency.

In his inaugural address on March 4, 1845, Polk underscored his faith in America's manifest destiny. "This heaven-favored land," he proclaimed, enjoyed the "most admirable and wisest system of well-regulated self-government . . . ever devised by human minds." He asked, "Who shall assign limits to the achievements of free minds and free hands under the protection of this glorious Union?"

The nation did not have to wait for Polk's inauguration to see results from his victory. One month after the election, President Tyler announced that the triumph of the Democratic Party provided a mandate for the annexation of Texas "promptly and immediately." In February 1845, after a fierce debate between antislavery and proslavery forces, Congress approved a joint resolution offering the Republic of Texas admission to the United States. Texas entered as the fifteenth slave state.

Tyler delivered Texas, but Polk had promised Oregon, too. Westerners particularly demanded that the new president make good on the Democrats' pledge "Fifty-four Forty or Fight" — that is, all of Oregon, right up to Alaska (54°40′ was the southern latitude of Russian Alaska). But Polk was close to war with Mexico and could not afford a war with Britain over U.S. claims in Canada. He renewed an old offer to divide Oregon along the forty-ninth parallel. When Britain accepted the compromise, some Americans cried betrayal, but most celebrated the agreement that gave the nation an enormous territory peacefully. When the Senate finally approved the treaty in June 1846, the United States and Mexico were already at war.

The Mexican-American War, 1846–1848

From the day he entered the White House, Polk craved Mexico's remaining northern provinces: California and New Mexico, land that today makes up California, Nevada, Utah, most of New Mexico and Arizona, and parts of Wyoming and Colorado. Since the 1830s, Comanches, Kiowas, Apaches, and others had attacked Mexican ranches and towns, killing thousands, and the Polk administration invoked Mexico's inability to control its northern provinces to denigrate its claims to them. Polk hoped to buy the territory, but when the Mexicans refused to sell, he concluded that military force would be needed to realize the United States' manifest destiny.

MAP 12.2

The Mexican-American War, 1846–1848

American and Mexican soldiers skirmished across much of northern Mexico, but the major battles took place between the Rio Grande and Mexico City.

Polk had already ordered General **Zachary Taylor** to march his 4,000-man army 150 miles south from its position on the Nueces River, the southern boundary of Texas according to the Mexicans, to the banks of the Rio Grande, the boundary claimed by Texans (Map 12.2). Viewing the American advance as aggression, the Mexican general in Matamoros ordered Taylor back to the Nueces. Taylor refused, and on April 25, 1846, Mexican cavalry attacked a party of American soldiers, killing or wounding sixteen and capturing the rest. Even before news of the battle arrived in Washington, Polk had obtained his cabinet's approval of a war message.

On May 11, the president told Congress, "Mexico has passed the boundary of the United States, has invaded our territory, and shed American blood upon

Pass Congress

American soil." Thus "war exists, and, notwithstanding all our efforts to avoid it, exists by the act of Mexico herself." Congress passed a declaration of war and began raising an army. Despite years of saber rattling toward Mexico and Britain, the U.S. Army was pitifully small, only 8,600 soldiers. Faced with the nation's first foreign war, against a Mexican army that numbered more than 30,000, Polk called for volunteers. Eventually, more than 112,000 white Americans (40 percent of whom were immigrants; blacks were banned) joined the army to fight in Mexico.

Despite the flood of volunteers, the war divided the nation. Northern Whigs in particular condemned the war. The Massachusetts legislature claimed that the war was being fought for the "triple object of extending slavery, of strengthening the slave power, and of obtaining control of the free states." On January 12, 1848, a gangly freshman Whig representative from Illinois rose in the House of Representatives to deliver his first important speech in Congress. Before Abraham Lincoln sat down, he had questioned Polk's intelligence, honesty, and sanity. The president ignored the upstart representative, but antislavery, antiwar Whigs kept up the attack throughout the conflict. In their effort to undercut national support, they labeled it "Mr. Polk's War."

Since most Americans backed the war, it was not really Polk's war, but the president acted as if it were and directed the war personally. He planned a short war in which U.S. armies would occupy Mexico's northern provinces and defeat the Mexican army in a decisive battle or two, after which Mexico would sue for peace and the United States would keep the territory its armies occupied.

At first, Polk's strategy seemed to work. In May 1846, Zachary Taylor's troops drove south from the Rio Grande and routed the Mexican army, first at Palo Alto, then at Resaca de la Palma (see Map 12.2). "Old Rough and Ready," as Taylor was affectionately known among his adoring troops, became an instant war hero. Polk rewarded Taylor for his victories by making him commander of the Mexican campaign.

Taylor

A second prong of the campaign centered on Colonel Stephen Watts Kearny, who led a 1,700-man army from Missouri into New Mexico. Without firing a shot, U.S. forces took Santa Fe in August 1846. Kearny then marched into San Diego three months later, encountering a major Mexican rebellion against American rule. In January 1847, after several clashes and severe losses, the U.S. forces occupied Los Angeles. California and New Mexico were in American hands.

By then, Taylor had driven deep into the interior of Mexico. In September 1846, after house-to-house fighting, he took the city of Monterrey. Taylor then pushed his 5,000 troops southwest, where the Mexican hero of the Alamo, General Antonio López de Santa Anna, was concentrating an army of 21,000. On February 23, 1847, Santa Anna's troops attacked Taylor at Buena Vista. Superior American artillery and accurate musket fire won the day, but the Americans suffered heavy casualties, including Henry Clay Jr., the son of the man who had opposed Texas annexation for fear it would precipitate war. The Mexicans suffered even greater losses (some 3,400 dead, wounded, and missing, compared with 650 Americans). During the night, Santa Anna withdrew his battered army, much to the "profound disgust of the troops," one Mexican officer remembered. "They are filled with grief that they were going to lose the benefit of all the sacrifices that they had made; that the conquered field would be abandoned, and that the victory would be given to the enemy."

The series of uninterrupted victories in northern Mexico fed the American troops' sense of invincibility. "No American force has ever thought of being defeated by any amount of Mexican troops," one soldier declared. The Americans worried about other hazards, however. "I can assure you that fighting is the least dangerous & arduous part of a soldier's life," one young man declared. Letters home told of torturous marches across arid wastes alive with tarantulas, scorpions, and rattlesnakes. Others recounted dysentery, malaria, smallpox, cholera, and yellow fever. Of the 13,000 American soldiers who died (some 50,000 Mexicans perished), fewer than 2,000 fell to Mexican bullets and shells. Disease killed most of the others. Medicine was so primitive that, as one Tennessee man observed, "nearly all who take sick die."

Victory in Mexico

Although the Americans won battle after battle, President Polk's strategy misfired. Despite heavy losses on the battlefield, Mexico refused to trade land for peace. One American soldier captured the Mexican mood: "They cannot submit to be deprived of California after the loss of Texas, and nothing but the conquest of their Capital will force them to such a humiliation." Polk had arrived at the same conclusion. While Taylor occupied the north, General **Winfield Scott** would land an army on the Gulf coast of Mexico and march 250 miles inland to Mexico City. Polk's plan entailed enormous risk because Scott would have to cut himself off from supplies and lead his men deep into enemy country against a much larger army.

An amphibious landing on March 9, 1847, near Veracruz put some 10,000 American troops ashore. After a siege of two weeks and furious shelling, Veracruz surrendered. In April 1847, Scott's forces moved westward, following the path blazed more than three centuries earlier by Hernán Cortés to "the halls of Montezuma" (see chapter 2).

After the defeat at Buena Vista, Santa Anna had returned to Mexico City, where he rallied his ragged troops and marched them east to set a trap for Scott in the mountain pass at Cerro Gordo. Knifing through Mexican lines, the Americans almost captured Santa Anna, who fled the field on foot. So complete was the victory that Scott gloated to Taylor, "Mexico no longer has an army." But Santa Anna, ever resilient, again rallied the Mexican army. Some 30,000 troops took up defensive positions on the outskirts of Mexico City and began melting down church bells to cast new cannons.

In August 1847, Scott began his assault on the Mexican capital. The fighting proved the most brutal of the war. Santa Anna backed his army into the city, fighting each step of the way. At the battle of Churubusco, the Mexicans took 4,000 casualties in a single day and the Americans more than 1,000. At the castle of Chapultepec, American troops scaled the walls and fought the Mexican defenders hand to hand. After Chapultepec, Mexico City officials persuaded Santa

MAP 12.3
Territorial Expansion by 1860
Less than a century after its founding, the United States spread from the Atlantic seaboard to the Pacific coast. War, purchase, and diplomacy had gained a continent.

Anna to evacuate the city to save it from destruction, and on September 14, 1847, Scott rode in triumphantly.

On February 2, 1848, American and Mexican officials signed the **Treaty of Guadalupe Hidalgo** in Mexico City. Mexico agreed to give up all claims to Texas north of the Rio Grande and to cede the provinces of New Mexico and California — more than 500,000 square miles — to the United States (see Map 12.2). The United States agreed to pay Mexico $15 million and to assume $3.25 million in claims that American citizens had against Mexico. In March 1848, the Senate ratified the treaty. Polk had his Rio Grande border, his Pacific ports, and all the land that lay between.

The American triumph had enormous consequences. Less than three-quarters of a century after its founding, the United States had achieved its self-proclaimed manifest destiny to stretch from the Atlantic to the Pacific (Map 12.3). It would enter the industrial age with vast new natural resources and a two-ocean economy, while Mexico faced a sharply diminished economic future.

Golden California

Another consequence of the Mexican defeat was that California gold poured into American, not Mexican, pockets. In January 1848, just weeks before the formal transfer of territory, James Marshall discovered gold in the American River in the foothills of the Sierra Nevada. Marshall's discovery set off the **California gold rush**, one of the wildest mining stampedes in the world's history. Between 1849 and 1852, more than 250,000 "forty-niners," as the would-be miners were known, descended on the Golden State. In less than two years, Marshall's discovery transformed California from foreign territory to statehood.

Gold fever quickly spread around the world. A stream of men of various races and nationalities, all bent on getting rich, remade the quiet California world of Mexican ranches into a raucous, roaring mining and town economy. Only a few struck it rich, and life in the goldfields was nasty, brutish, and often short. Men faced miserable living conditions, sometimes sheltering in holes and brush lean-tos. They also faced cholera and scurvy, exorbitant prices for food (eggs cost a dollar apiece), deadly encounters with claim jumpers, and endless backbreaking labor. An individual with gold in his pocket could find only temporary relief in the saloons, card games, dogfights, gambling dens, and brothels that flourished in the mining camps.

By 1853, San Francisco had grown into a raw, booming city of 50,000 that depended as much on gold as did the mining camps inland. Like the towns that dotted the San Joaquin and Sacramento valleys, it suffered from overcrowding, fire, crime, and violence. But enterprising individuals had learned that there was money to be made tending to the needs of the miners. Hotels, saloons, restaurants, laundries, and stores of all kinds exchanged services and goods for miners' gold.

In 1851, the Committee of Vigilance determined to bring order to the city. Members pledged that "no thief, burglar, incendiary or assassin shall escape punishment, either by the quibbles of the law, the insecurity of prisons, the carelessness or corruption of the police, or a laxity of those who pretended to administer justice." Lynchings proved that the committee meant business. In time, merchants, tradesmen, and professionals made the city their home and brought their families from back east. Gunfights declined, but many years would pass before anyone pacified San Francisco.

Establishing civic order was made more difficult by California's diversity and Anglo bigotry. The Chinese attracted special scrutiny. By 1851, 25,000 Chinese lived in California, and their religion, language, dress, queues (long pigtails), eating habits, and recreational use of opium convinced many Anglos that they were not fit citizens of the Golden State. In 1850, the California legislature passed the Foreign Miners' Tax Law, which levied high taxes on non-Americans to drive them from the goldfields, except as hired laborers working on claims owned by Americans. The Chinese were segregated residentially and occupationally and made ineligible for citizenship. Along with blacks and Indians, Chinese were denied public education and the right to testify in court.

As early as 1852, opponents demanded a halt to Chinese immigration. Chinese leaders in San Francisco fought back. Admitting deep cultural differences, they insisted that "in the important matters we are good men. We honor our parents; we take care of our children; we are industrious and peaceable; we trade much;

Chinese Man
This daguerreotype of an unidentified Chinese man was made by Isaac Wallace Baker, a photographer who traveled through California's mining camps in his wagon studio. One of the earliest known portraits of an Asian in California, the portrait shows a proud man boldly displaying his queue (long braid). This was almost certainly an act of defiance, for Anglos ridiculed Chinese cultural traditions, and vigilantes chased down men who wore queues. Collection of the Oakland Museum of California, Gift of Anonymous Donor.

we are trusted for small and large sums; we pay our debts; and are honest, and of course must tell the truth." Their protestations offered little protection, however, and racial violence grew.

Anglo-American prospectors asserted their dominance over other groups, especially Native Americans and the Californios, Spanish and Mexican settlers who had lived in California for decades. Despite the U.S. government's pledge to protect Mexican and Spanish land titles after the cession of 1848, Americans took the land of the rancheros and through discriminatory legislation pushed Hispanic professionals, merchants, and artisans into the ranks of unskilled labor. Mariano Vallejo, a leading Californio, said of the forty-niners, "The good ones were few and the wicked many."

For Indians, the gold rush was catastrophic. Numbering about 150,000 in 1848, the Indian population of California fell to 25,000 by 1854. Starvation, disease, and a declining birthrate took a heavy toll. Indians also fell victim to wholesale murder. The nineteenth-century historian Hubert Howe Bancroft described white behavior toward Indians during the gold rush as "one of the last human hunts of civilization, and the basest and most brutal of them all." To survive, Indians moved to the most remote areas of the state and tried to stay out of the way.

The forty-niners created dazzling wealth: In 1852, 81 million ounces of gold, nearly half of the world's production, came from California. However, most forty-niners eventually took up farming, opened small businesses, or worked for wages for the corporations that took over the mining industry. Others looked beyond the land, for California's ports were connected to a vast trade network throughout the Pacific. Americans traded furs, hides, and lumber and engaged in whaling and the China trade in tea, silk, and porcelain. Still, as California's first congressional representative observed, the state was separated "by thousands of miles of plains, deserts, and almost impossible mountains" from the rest of the Union. Some dreamers imagined a railroad that would someday connect the Golden State with the thriving agriculture and industry of the East. Others imagined a country transformed not by transportation but by progressive individual and institutional reform.

REVIEW   Why was the annexation of Texas such a controversial policy?

▶ Reforming Self and Society

While manifest destiny, the Mexican-American War, and the California gold rush transformed the nation's boundaries, many Americans sought personal and social reform. The emphasis on self-discipline and individual effort at the core of the free-labor ideal led Americans to believe that insufficient self-control caused the major social problems of the era. Evangelical Protestants struggled to control individuals' propensity to sin. Temperance advocates exhorted drinkers to control their urge for alcohol. In the midst of the worldly disruptions of geographic expansion and economic change, about one-third of Americans belonged to a church in 1850. Although many — like Abraham Lincoln — remained outside churches, the influence of evangelical religion reached far beyond church members.

The evangelical temperament — a conviction of righteousness coupled with energy, self-discipline, and faith that the world could be improved — animated most reformers. However, a few activists pointed out that certain fundamental injustices lay beyond the reach of individual self-control. Transcendentalists and utopians believed that perfection could be attained only by rejecting the competitive, individualistic values of mainstream society. Woman's rights activists and abolitionists sought to reverse the subordination of women and to eliminate the enslavement of blacks by changing laws and social institutions as well as attitudes and customs. They confronted the daunting challenge of repudiating widespread assumptions about male supremacy and white supremacy and somehow challenging the entrenched institutions that reinforced those assumptions: the family and slavery.

The Pursuit of Perfection: Transcendentalists and Utopians

A group of New England writers who came to be known as transcendentalists believed that individuals should conform neither to the dictates of the materialistic world nor to the dogma of formal religion. Instead, people should look within themselves for truth and guidance. The leading transcendentalist, Ralph Waldo Emerson — an essayist, poet, and lecturer — proclaimed that the power of the solitary individual was nearly limitless. Henry David Thoreau, Margaret Fuller, and other transcendentalists agreed with Emerson that "if the single man plant himself indomitably on his instincts, and there abide, the huge world will come round to him." In many ways, the inward gaze and confident egoism of **transcendentalism** represented less an alternative to mainstream values than an exaggerated form of the rampant individualism of the age.

Unlike transcendentalists who sought to turn inward, a few reformers tried to change the world by organizing utopian communities as alternatives to prevailing social arrangements. Although these communities never attracted more than a few thousand people, the activities of their members demonstrated both dissatisfaction with the larger society and their efforts to realize their visions of perfection.

Some communities set out to become models of perfection whose success would point the way toward a better life for everyone. During the 1840s, more than two dozen communities organized themselves around the ideas of Charles Fourier, a French critic of contemporary society. Members of **Fourierist phalanxes**, as these communities were called, believed that individualism and competition were evils that denied the basic truth that "men . . . are brothers and not competitors." Phalanxes aspired to replace competition with harmonious cooperation based on communal ownership of property. But Fourierist communities failed to realize their lofty goals, and few survived more than two or three years.

The **Oneida community** went beyond the Fourierist notion of communalism. John Humphrey Noyes, the charismatic leader of Oneida, believed that American society's commitment to private property made people greedy and selfish. Noyes claimed that the root of private property lay in marriage, in men's conviction that their wives were their exclusive property. Drawing from a substantial inheritance, Noyes organized the Oneida community in New York in 1848 to abolish marital property rights through the practice of what he called "complex marriage." Sexual intercourse was not restricted to married couples but was permitted between any consenting man and woman in the community. Noyes also required all members to relinquish their economic property to the community, which developed a lucrative business manufacturing animal traps. Oneida's sexual and economic communalism attracted several hundred members, but most of their neighbors considered Oneidans adulterers, blasphemers, and worse. Yet the practices that set Oneida apart from its mainstream neighbors strengthened the community, and it survived long after the Civil War.

Woman's Rights Activists

Women participated in the many reform activities that grew out of evangelical churches. Women church members outnumbered men two to one and worked to put their religious ideas into practice by joining peace, temperance, antislavery, and other societies. Involvement in reform organizations gave a few women activists practical experience in such political arts as speaking in public, running a meeting, drafting resolutions, and circulating petitions. Along with such experience came confidence. The abolitionist Lydia Maria Child pointed out in 1841 that "those who urged women to become missionaries and form tract societies . . . have changed the household utensil to a living energetic being and they have no spell to turn it into a broom again."

In 1848, about three hundred reformers led by **Elizabeth Cady Stanton** and Lucretia Mott gathered at Seneca Falls, New York, for the first national woman's rights convention in the United States. As Stanton recalled, "The

BLOOMERISM—AN AMERICAN CUSTOM.

Bloomers and Woman's Emancipation

This 1851 British cartoon lampoons bloomers, the trouserlike garment worn beneath shortened skirts by two cigar-smoking American women. Bloomers were invented in the United States as an alternative to the uncomfortable, confining, and awkward dresses worn by fashionable women, suggested here by the clothing of the "respectable" women on the right. In the 1850s, Elizabeth Cady Stanton and other woman's rights activists wore bloomers and urged all American women to do likewise. Ridiculed as unfeminine by critics, American reformers eventually abandoned bloomers and focused on more important woman's rights issues. The "bloomerism" controversy illustrates the immense power of conventional notions of femininity confronted by woman's rights advocates. Miriam and Ira D. Wallach Division of Art, Prints, and Photographs, The New York Public Library. Astor, Lenox, and Tilden Foundations.

general discontent I felt with women's portion as wife, mother, housekeeper, physician, and spiritual guide, [and] the wearied anxious look of the majority of women impressed me with a strong feeling that some active measure should be taken to right the wrongs of society in general, and of women in particular." The **Seneca Falls Declaration of Sentiments** set an ambitious agenda to demand civil liberties for women and to right the wrongs of society. The declaration proclaimed that "the history of mankind is a history of repeated injuries and usurpations on the part of man toward woman, having in direct object the establishment of an absolute tyranny over her." In the style of the Declaration of Independence (see appendix, page A-1), the Seneca Falls declaration demanded that women "have immediate admission to all the rights and privileges which belong to them as citizens of the United States," particularly the "inalienable right to the elective franchise."

Nearly two dozen other woman's rights conventions assembled before 1860, repeatedly calling for suffrage and an end to discrimination against women. But women had difficulty receiving a respectful hearing, much less achieving legislative action. Even so, the Seneca Falls declaration served as a pathbreaking manifesto of dissent against male supremacy and of support for woman suffrage, and it inspired many women to challenge the barriers that limited their opportunities.

Stanton and other activists sought fair pay and expanded employment opportunities for women by appealing to free-labor ideology. Woman's rights advocate Paula Wright Davis urged Americans to stop discriminating against able and enterprising women: "Let [women] . . . open a Store, . . . plant and tend an Orchard, . . . learn any of the lighter mechanical Trades, . . . study for a Profession, . . . be called to the lecture-room, [and] . . . the Temperance rostrum . . . [and] let her be appointed [to serve in the Post Office]." Some women pioneered in these and many other occupations during the 1840s and 1850s. Woman's rights activists also succeeded in protecting married women's rights to their own wages and property in New York in 1860. But discrimination against women persisted, as most men believed that free-labor ideology required no compromise of male supremacy.

Abolitionists and the American Ideal

During the 1840s and 1850s, abolitionists continued to struggle to draw the nation's attention to the plight of slaves and the need for emancipation. Former slaves **Frederick Douglass**, Henry Bibb, and Sojourner Truth lectured to reform audiences throughout the North about the cruelties of slavery. Abolitionists published newspapers, held conventions, and petitioned Congress, but they never attracted a mass following among white Americans. Many white Northerners became convinced that slavery was wrong, but they still believed that blacks were inferior. Many other white Northerners shared the common view of white Southerners that slavery was necessary and even desirable. The westward extension of the nation during the 1840s offered abolitionists an opportunity to link their unpopular ideal to a goal that many white Northerners found much more attractive — limiting the geographic expansion of slavery, an issue that moved to the center of national politics during the 1850s (as discussed in chapter 14).

Black leaders rose to prominence in the abolitionist movement during the 1840s and 1850s. African Americans had actively opposed slavery for decades, but a new generation of leaders came to the forefront in these years. Frederick Douglass, Henry Highland Garnet, William Wells Brown, Martin R. Delany, and others became impatient with white abolitionists' appeals to the conscience of the white majority. In 1843, Garnet urged slaves to choose "Liberty or Death" and rise in insurrection against their masters, an idea that alienated almost all white people and carried little influence among slaves. To express their own uncompromising ideas, black abolitionists founded their own newspapers and held their own antislavery conventions, although they still cooperated with sympathetic whites.

The commitment of black abolitionists to battling slavery grew out of their own experiences with white supremacy. The 250,000 free African Americans in the North and West constituted less than 2 percent of the total population in 1860.

Abolitionist Meeting

This rare daguerreotype was made by Ezra Greenleaf Weld in August 1850 at an abolitionist meeting in Cazenovia, New York. Frederick Douglass, who had escaped from slavery in Maryland twelve years earlier, is seated on the platform next to the woman at the table. One of the nation's most brilliant and eloquent abolitionists, Douglass also supported equal rights for women. The man behind Douglass is Gerrit Smith, a wealthy and militant abolitionist whose funds supported many reform activities. Notice the two black women on either side of Smith and the white woman next to Douglass. Most white Americans considered such voluntary racial proximity scandalous and promiscuous. Collection of the J. Paul Getty Museum, Malibu, CA.

They confronted the humiliations of racial discrimination in nearly every arena of daily life. Only Maine, Massachusetts, New Hampshire, and Vermont permitted black men to vote; New York imposed a special property-holding requirement on black — but not white — voters, effectively excluding most black men from the franchise. The pervasive racial discrimination both handicapped and energized black abolitionists. Some cooperated with the efforts of the **American Colonization Society** to send freed slaves and other black Americans to Liberia in West Africa. Others sought to move to Canada, Haiti, or elsewhere. They were convinced that, as an African American from Michigan wrote, "it is impracticable, not to say impossible, for the whites and blacks to live together, and upon terms of social and civil equality, under the same government." Most black American leaders refused to embrace emigration and worked against racial prejudice in their own communities, organizing campaigns against segregation, particularly in transportation and education. Their most notable success came in 1855 when Massachusetts integrated its public schools. Elsewhere, white supremacy continued unabated.

Outside the public spotlight, free African Americans in the North and West contributed to the antislavery cause by quietly aiding fugitive slaves. **Harriet Tubman** escaped from slavery in Maryland in 1849 and repeatedly risked her freedom and her life to return to the South to escort slaves to freedom. When the opportunity arose, free blacks in the North provided fugitive slaves with food, a safe place to rest, and a helping hand. An outgrowth of the antislavery sentiment and opposition to white supremacy that unified nearly all African Americans in the North, this "**underground railroad**" ran mainly through black neighborhoods, black churches, and black homes.

REVIEW   Why were women especially prominent in many nineteenth-century reform efforts?

▶ Conclusion: Free Labor, Free Men

During the 1840s and 1850s, a cluster of interrelated developments — population growth, steam power, railroads, and the growing mechanization of agriculture and manufacturing — meant greater economic productivity, a burst of output from farms and factories, and prosperity for many. Diplomacy with Great Britain and war with Mexico handed the United States 1.2 million square miles and more than 1,000 miles of Pacific coastline. One prize of manifest destiny, California, almost immediately rewarded its new owners with tons of gold. To most Americans, new territory and vast riches were appropriate accompaniments to the nation's stunning economic progress and superior institutions.

To Northerners, industrial evolution confirmed the choice they had made to eliminate slavery and promote free labor as the key to independence, equality, and prosperity. Like Abraham Lincoln, millions of Americans could point to their personal experiences as evidence of the practical truth of the free-labor ideal. But millions of others had different stories to tell. They knew that in the free-labor system, poverty and wealth continued to rub shoulders. By 1860, more than half of the nation's free-labor workforce toiled for someone else. Free-labor enthusiasts denied that the problems were inherent in the country's social and economic systems. Instead, they argued, most social ills — including poverty and dependency — sprang from individual deficiencies. Consequently, many reformers focused on personal self-control and discipline, on avoiding sin and alcohol. Other reformers focused on woman's rights and the abolition of slavery. They challenged widespread conceptions of male supremacy and black inferiority, but neither group managed to overcome the prevailing free-labor ideology based on individualism, racial prejudice, and notions of male superiority.

By midcentury, half of the nation had prohibited slavery, and half permitted it. The North and the South were animated by different economic interests, cultural values, and political aims. Each celebrated its regional identity and increasingly disparaged that of the other. Not even the victory over Mexico could bridge the deepening divide between North and South.

Reviewing Chapter 12

REVIEW QUESTIONS

1. Why did the United States become a leading industrial power in the nineteenth century? (pp. 335–339)

2. How did the free-labor ideal account for economic inequality? (pp. 339–342)

3. Why did westward migration expand dramatically in the mid-nineteenth century? (pp. 342–348)

4. Why was the annexation of Texas such a controversial policy? (pp. 349–357)

5. Why were women especially prominent in many nineteenth-century reform efforts? (pp. 357–361)

MAKING CONNECTIONS

1. Varied political, economic, and technological factors promoted westward migration in the mid-nineteenth century. Considering these factors, discuss migration to two different regions (for instance, Texas, Oregon, Utah, or California). What drew migrants to the regions? How did the U.S. government contribute to their efforts?

2. How did the ideology of manifest destiny contribute to the mid-nineteenth-century drive for expansion? Discuss its implications for individual migrants and the nation. In your answer, consider how manifest destiny built on, or revised, earlier understandings of the nation's history and racial politics.

3. The Mexican-American War reshaped U.S. borders and more. Discuss the consequences of the war for national political and economic developments in subsequent decades. What resources did the new territory give the United States? How did debate over annexation revive older political disputes?

4. Some nineteenth-century reform movements drew on the free-labor ideal, while others challenged it. Discuss the free-labor ideal in relation to two reform movements (such as abolitionism and utopian communalism). How did the reform movements draw on the ideal to pursue specific reforms? How did these minority movements try to influence national developments?

LINKING TO THE PAST

1. In what ways were the North's economy, society, and political structure during the 1840s and 1850s shaped by the American Revolution and the Constitution? (See chapters 7 and 8.)

2. The nation's mighty push westward in the 1840s and 1850s extended a history of expansion that was as old as the nation itself. How was expansion to the West between 1840 and 1860 similar to and different from expansion between 1800 and 1820? (See chapter 10.)

TIMELINE 1830–1861

1830 • Joseph Smith Jr. publishes *The Book of Mormon*.

1836 • Battle of the Alamo.
• Texas declares independence from Mexico.

1837 • John Deere patents steel plow.

1840s • Practical mechanical reapers created.
• Fourierist phalanxes founded.

1841 • First wagon trains head west on Oregon Trail.
• Vice President John Tyler becomes president when William Henry Harrison dies.

1844 • Democrat James K. Polk elected president.
• Samuel F. B. Morse demonstrates telegraph.

1845 • Term *manifest destiny* coined.
• United States annexes Texas, which enters Union as slave state.
• Potato blight in Ireland spurs immigration to United States.

1846 • Bear Flag Revolt in California.
• Congress declares war on Mexico.

• United States and Great Britain agree to divide Oregon Country.

1847 • Mormons settle in Utah.

1848 • Treaty of Guadalupe Hidalgo.
• Oneida community organized in New York.
• First U.S. woman's rights convention takes place at Seneca Falls, New York.

1849 • California gold rush begins.

1850 • Mormon community annexed to United States as Utah Territory.
• Congress grants railroads six square miles of land for every mile of track laid.

1851 • Conference at Fort Laramie, Wyoming, marks the beginning of government policy of Indian concentration.

1855 • Massachusetts integrates public schools.

1857 • U.S. troops invade Salt Lake City in Mormon War.

1861 • California connected to rest of nation by telegraph.

▶ FOR AN ONLINE BIBLIOGRAPHY, PRACTICE QUIZZES, WEB SITES, IMAGES, AND DOCUMENTS RELATED TO THIS CHAPTER, see the Book Companion Site at **bedfordstmartins.com/roarkvalue**.

▶ FOR DOCUMENTS RELATED TO THIS PERIOD, see Michael Johnson, ed., *Reading the American Past*, Fifth Edition.

13

The Slave South

1820–1860

NAT TURNER WAS BORN A SLAVE IN SOUTHAMPTON COUNTY, VIRGINIA, in October 1800. People in his neighborhood claimed that he had always been different. His parents noticed special marks on his body, which they said were signs that he was "intended for some great purpose." His master said that he learned to read without being taught. As an adolescent, he adopted an austere lifestyle of Christian devotion and fasting. In his twenties, he received visits from the "Spirit," the same spirit, he believed, that had spoken to the ancient prophets. In time, Nat Turner began to interpret these things to mean that God had appointed him an instrument of divine vengeance for the sin of slaveholding.

In the early morning of August 22, 1831, he set out with six trusted friends — Hark, Henry, Sam, Nelson, Will, and Jack — to punish slave owners. Turner struck the first blow, an ax to the head of his master, Joseph Travis. The rebels killed all of the white men, women, and children they encountered. By noon, they had visited eleven farms and slaughtered fifty-seven whites. Along the way, they had added fifty or sixty men to their army. Word spread quickly, and soon the militia and hundreds of local whites gathered. By the next day, whites had captured or killed all of the rebels except Turner, who hid out for about ten weeks before being captured in nearby woods. Within a week, he was tried, convicted, and executed. By then, forty-five slaves had stood trial, twenty had been convicted and hanged, and another ten had been banished from Virginia. Frenzied whites had killed another hundred or more blacks — insurgents and innocent bystanders — in their counterattack against the rebellion.

Virginia's bewildered governor, John Floyd, struggled to understand why Turner's band of "assassins and murderers" assaulted the "unsuspecting and defenseless" citizens of "one of the fairest counties" of the state. White

Horrid Massacre in Virginia
No contemporary images of Nat Turner are known to exist. This woodcut simply imagines the rebellion as a nightmare in which black brutes took the lives of innocent whites. Although there was never another rebellion as large as Turner's, images of black violence continued to haunt white imaginations. Library of Congress.

Virginians prided themselves on having the "mildest" slavery in the South, but sixty black rebels on a rampage challenged the comforting theory of the contented slave. Nonetheless, whites found explanations that allowed them to feel safer. They placed the blame on outside agitators. In 1829, David Walker, a freeborn black man living in Boston, had published his *Appeal . . . to the Coloured Citizens of the World*, an invitation to slaves to rise up in bloody rebellion, and copies had fallen into the hands of Virginia slaves. Moreover, on January 1, 1831, in Boston, the Massachusetts abolitionist William Lloyd Garrison had published the first issue of the *Liberator*, his fiery newspaper (see chapter 11). White Virginians also dismissed the rebellion's leader, Nat Turner, as insane. "He is a complete fanatic, or plays his part admirably," wrote Thomas R. Gray, the lawyer who was assigned to defend Turner.

In the months following the insurrection, the Virginia legislature reaffirmed the state's determination to preserve black bondage by passing laws that strengthened the institution of slavery and further restricted free blacks. A professor at the College of William and Mary, Thomas R. Dew, published a vigorous defense of slavery that became the bible of Southerners' proslavery arguments. More than ever, the nation was divided along the Mason-Dixon line, the surveyors' mark that in colonial times had established the boundary between Maryland and Pennsylvania but half a century later divided the free North and the slave South.

Black slavery increasingly molded the South into a distinctive region. In the decades after 1820, Southerners, like Northerners, raced westward, but unlike Northerners who spread small farms, manufacturing, and free labor, Southerners spread slavery, cotton, and plantations. Geographic expansion meant that slavery became more vigorous and more profitable than ever, embraced more people, and increased the South's political power. Antebellum Southerners included diverse people who at times found themselves at odds with one another — not only slaves and free people but also women and men; Indians, Africans, and Europeans; and aristocrats and common folk. Nevertheless, beneath this diversity, a distinctively southern society and culture were forming. The South became a slave society, and most white Southerners were proud of it.

▶ The Growing Distinctiveness of the South

From the earliest settlements, inhabitants of the southern colonies had shared a great deal with northern colonists. Most whites in both sections were British and Protestant, spoke a common language, and shared an exuberant pride in their victorious revolution against British rule. The creation of the new nation under the Constitution in 1789 forged political ties that bound all Americans. The beginnings of a national economy fostered economic interdependence and communication across regional boundaries. White Americans everywhere celebrated the achievements of the prosperous young nation, and they looked forward to its seemingly boundless future.

Despite these national similarities, Southerners and Northerners grew increasingly different. The French political observer Alexis de Tocqueville believed he knew why. "I could easily prove," he asserted in 1831, "that almost all the differences which may be noticed between the character of the Americans in the Southern and Northern states have originated in slavery." Slavery made the South different, and it was the differences between the North and South, not the similarities, that increasingly shaped antebellum American history.

Cotton Kingdom, Slave Empire

In the first half of the nineteenth century, millions of Americans migrated west. In the South, the stampede began after the Creek War of 1813–1814, which divested the Creek Indians of 24 million acres and initiated the government campaign to remove Indian people living east of the Mississippi River to the West (see chapters 10 and 11). Hard-driving slaveholders seeking virgin acreage for new plantations, striving farmers looking for patches of cheap land for small farms, herders and drovers pushing their hogs and cattle toward fresh pastures — anyone who was restless and ambitious felt the pull of Indian land.

But more than anything it was cotton that propelled Southerners westward. South of the **Mason-Dixon line**, climate and geography were ideally suited for the cultivation of cotton. Cotton's requirements are minimal: two hundred frost-free days from planting to picking, and plentiful rain, conditions found in much of the South. By the 1830s, cotton fields stretched from the Atlantic seaboard to central Texas. Heavy migration led to statehood for Arkansas in 1836 and for Texas and Florida in 1845. Production soared from 300,000 bales in 1830 to nearly 5 million in 1860, when the South produced three-fourths of the world's supply. The South — especially that tier of states from South Carolina west to Texas called the Lower South — had become the **cotton kingdom** (Map 13.1).

The cotton kingdom was also a slave empire. The South's cotton boom rested on the backs of slaves, most of whom toiled in gangs under the direct supervision

MAP 13.1

Cotton Kingdom, Slave Empire: 1820 and 1860

As the production of cotton soared, the slave population increased dramatically. Slaves continued to toil in tobacco and rice fields, but in Alabama, Mississippi, and Texas, they increasingly worked on cotton plantations.

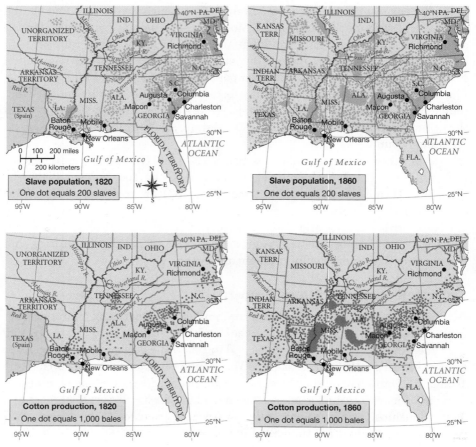

of whites. As cotton agriculture expanded westward, whites shipped more than a million enslaved men and women from the Atlantic coast across the continent in what has been called the "Second Middle Passage," a massive deportation that dwarfed the transatlantic slave trade to North America. Victims of this brutal domestic slave trade marched hundreds of miles southwest to new plantations in the Lower South. The earliest arrivals faced the hardest work, literally cutting plantations from forests. One observer noted that young male slaves in Alabama who were no more than nineteen or twenty looked twice their age. Cotton, slaves, and plantations moved west together.

The slave population grew enormously. Southern slaves numbered fewer than 700,000 in 1790, about 2 million in 1830, and almost 4 million by 1860. By 1860, the South contained more slaves than all the other slave societies in the New World combined. The extraordinary growth was not the result of the importation of slaves, which the federal government outlawed in 1808. Instead, the slave population grew through natural reproduction; by midcentury, most U.S. slaves were native-born Southerners. In comparison, Cuba and Brazil, slave societies that kept their slave trades open until the mid-nineteenth century, had more African-born slaves and thus stronger ties to Africa.

The South in Black and White

By 1860, one in every three Southerners was black (approximately 4 million blacks to 8 million whites). In the Lower South states of Mississippi and South Carolina, blacks constituted the majority. The contrast with the North was striking: In 1860, only one Northerner in seventy-six was black (about 250,000 blacks to 19 million whites).

The presence of large numbers of African Americans had profound consequences for the South. Southern culture — language, food, music, religion, and even accents — was in part shaped by blacks. But the most direct consequence of the South's biracialism was southern whites' commitment to white supremacy. Northern whites believed in racial superiority, too, but their dedication to white supremacy lacked the intensity and urgency increasingly felt by white Southerners who lived among millions of blacks who had every reason to hate them and to strike back, as Nat Turner had.

After 1820, attacks on slavery — from blacks and a handful of white Southerners opposed to slavery and from Northern abolitionists — jolted southern slaveholders into a distressing awareness that they lived in a dangerous world. As the only slave society embedded in an egalitarian, democratic republic, the South made extraordinary efforts to strengthen slavery. In the 1820s and 1830s, state legislatures constructed **slave codes** (laws) that required the total submission of slaves. As the Louisiana code stated, a slave "owes his master . . . a respect without bounds, and an absolute obedience." The laws also underlined the authority of all whites, not just masters. Any white could "correct" slaves who did not stay "in their place."

Intellectuals joined legislators in the campaign to strengthen slavery. The South's academics, writers, and clergy employed every imaginable defense. They argued that in the South slaves were legal property, and wasn't the protection of property the bedrock of American liberty? History also endorsed slavery, they claimed. Weren't the great civilizations — such as those of the Hebrews, Greeks, and Romans — slave societies? They claimed that the Bible, properly interpreted, also sanctioned slavery. Old Testament patriarchs owned slaves, they observed, and in the New Testament, Paul returned the runaway slave Onesimus to his master. Proslavery spokesmen played on the fears of Northerners and Southerners alike by charging that giving blacks equal rights would lead to the sexual mixing of the races, or **miscegenation**.

Another of slavery's champions, George Fitzhugh of Virginia, attacked the North's free-labor economy and society. He claimed that behind the North's grand slogans lay a heartless philosophy: "Every man for himself, and the devil take the hindmost." Gouging capitalists exploited wageworkers unmercifully, Fitzhugh declared, and he contrasted the North's vicious free-labor system with the humane relations that he said prevailed between masters and slaves because slaves were valuable capital that masters sought to protect.

But at the heart of the defense of slavery lay the claim of black inferiority. Black enslavement was both necessary and proper, slavery's defenders argued, because Africans were lesser beings. Rather than exploitative, slavery was a mass civilizing effort that lifted lowly blacks from barbarism and savagery, taught them disciplined work, and converted them to soul-saving Christianity. According to Virginian **Thomas R. Dew**, most slaves were grateful. He declared that "the slaves of a good master are his warmest, most constant, and most devoted friends."

Whites gradually moved away from defending slavery as a "necessary evil" — the halfhearted argument popular at the time of the American Revolution — and toward an aggressive defense of slavery as a "positive good." **John C. Calhoun**, an influential southern politician, declared that in the states where slavery had been abolished, "the condition of the African, instead of being improved, has become worse," while in the slave states, the Africans "have improved greatly in every respect."

Black slavery encouraged southern whites to unify around race rather than to divide by class. The grubbiest, most tobacco-stained white man could proudly proclaim his superiority to all blacks and his equality with the most refined southern patrician. Because of racial slavery, Georgia attorney Thomas R. R. Cobb observed, every white Southerner "feels that he belongs to an elevated class. It matters not that he is no slaveholder; he is not of the inferior race; he is a freeborn citizen." Consequently, the "poorest meets the richest as an equal; sits at his table with him; salutes him as a neighbor; meets him in every public assembly, and stands on the same social platform." In the South, Cobb boasted, "there is no war of classes."

In reality, slavery did not create perfect harmony among whites or ease every strain along class lines. But by providing every white Southerner membership in the ruling race, slavery helped whites bridge differences in wealth, education, and culture.

The Plantation Economy

As important as slavery was in unifying white Southerners, only about a quarter of the white population lived in slaveholding families. Most slaveholders owned fewer than five slaves. Only about 12 percent of slave owners owned twenty or more, the number of slaves that historians consider necessary to distinguish a **planter** from a farmer. Despite their small numbers, planters dominated the southern economy. In 1860, 52 percent of the South's slaves lived and worked on **plantations**. Plantation slaves produced more than 75 percent of the South's export crops, the backbone of the region's economy. Slavery was dying elsewhere in the New World (only Brazil and Cuba still defended slavery at midcentury), but slave plantations increasingly dominated southern agriculture.

The South's major cash crops — tobacco, sugar, rice, and cotton — grew on plantations (Map 13.2). Tobacco, the original plantation crop in North America, had shifted westward in the nineteenth century from the Chesapeake to Tennessee and Kentucky. Large-scale sugar production began in 1795, when Étienne de Boré built a modern sugar mill in what is today New Orleans, and sugar plantations

MAP 13.2
The Agricultural Economy of the South, 1860
Cotton dominated the South's agricultural economy, but the region grew a variety of crops and was largely self-sufficient in foodstuffs.

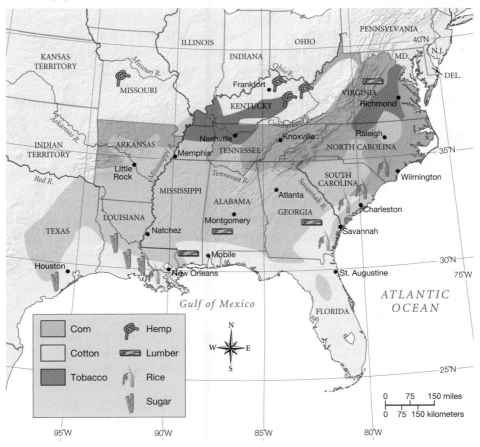

were confined almost entirely to Louisiana. Commercial rice production began in the seventeenth century, and like sugar, rice was confined to a small geographic area, a narrow strip of coast stretching from the Carolinas into Georgia.

Tobacco, sugar, and rice were labor-intensive crops that relied on large numbers of slaves to do the backbreaking work. Most phases of tobacco cultivation — planting, transporting, thinning, picking off caterpillars, cutting, drying, packing — required laborers to stoop or bend down. Work on sugarcane plantations was particularly physically demanding. During the harvest, slaves worked eighteen hours a day, and so hard was the slaves' task that one visitor concluded that "nothing but 'involuntary servitude' could go through the toil and suffering required to produce sugar." Working in water and mud in the heat of a Carolina summer regularly threatened slaves engaged in rice production with malaria, yellow fever, and other diseases.

But by the nineteenth century, cotton was king of the South's plantation crops. Cotton became commercially significant in the 1790s after the invention of a new cotton gin by Eli Whitney dramatically increased the production of raw cotton (see chapter 9). Cotton was relatively easy to grow and took little capital to get started — just enough to purchase land, seed, and simple tools. Thus, small farmers as well as planters grew cotton. But planters, whose fields were worked by gangs of slaves, produced three-quarters of the South's cotton, and cotton made planters rich.

Plantation slavery also enriched the nation. By 1840, cotton accounted for more than 60 percent of American exports. Most of the cotton was shipped to Great Britain, the world's largest manufacturer of cotton textiles. Much of the profit from the sale of cotton overseas returned to planters, but some went to northern middlemen who bought, sold, insured, warehoused, and shipped cotton to the mills in Great Britain and elsewhere. As one New York merchant observed, "Cotton has enriched all through whose hands it has passed." As middlemen invested their profits in the booming northern economy, industrial development received a burst of much-needed capital. Furthermore, southern plantations benefited northern industry by providing an important market for textiles, agricultural tools, and other manufactured goods.

The economies of the North and South steadily diverged. While the North developed a mixed economy — agriculture, commerce, and manufacturing — the South remained overwhelmingly agricultural. Year after year, planters funneled the profits they earned from land and slaves back into more land and more slaves. With its capital flowing into agriculture, the South did not develop many factories. By 1860, only 10 percent of the nation's industrial workers lived in the South. Some cotton mills sprang up, but the region that produced 100 percent of the nation's cotton manufactured less than 7 percent of its cotton textiles.

Without significant economic diversification, the South developed fewer cities than the North and West. In 1860, it was the least urban region in the country. Whereas nearly 37 percent of New England's population lived in cities, less than 12 percent of Southerners were urban dwellers. Southern cities were mostly port cities and were busy principally with exporting the agricultural products of plantations in the interior. Urban merchants provided agriculture

Steamboats and Cotton in New Orleans, circa 1858
Smokestacks of dozens of steamboats overlook hundreds of bales of cotton at the foot of Canal Street. This photograph by Jay Dearborn Edwards captures something of the magnitude of the cotton trade in the South's largest city and major port. A decade earlier, visitor Solon Robinson had expressed awe: "It must be seen to be believed; and even then, it will require an active mind to comprehend acres of cotton bales standing upon the levee. . . ." Amid the sea of cotton, few Southerners doubted that cotton was king. Historic New Orleans Collection.

with indispensable services, such as hauling, insuring, and selling cotton, rice, and sugar, but they were the tail on the plantation dog.

Because the South had so few cities and industrial jobs, it attracted small numbers of European immigrants. Seeking economic opportunity, not competition with slaves (whose labor would keep wages low), immigrants steered northward. In 1860, 13 percent of all Americans were born abroad. But in nine of the fifteen slave states, only 2 percent or less of the population was foreign-born.

Not every Southerner celebrated the region's commitment to cotton and slaves. Critics bemoaned what one called the "deplorable scarcity" of factories. Diversification, reformers promised, would make the South economically independent and more prosperous. State governments encouraged economic development by helping to create banking systems that supplied credit for a wide range of projects and by constructing railroads, but they failed to create some of the essential services modern economies required. By the mid-nineteenth century, for example, no southern legislature had created a statewide public school system. Planters failed to see any benefit in educating the children of small farmers, especially with their tax money. Despite the flurry of railroad building, the South's mileage in 1860 was less than half that of the North. Moreover, whereas railroads crisscrossed the North carrying manufactured goods and agricultural products, most railroads in the South were short stretches of track that ran from port cities back into farming areas in order to transport cotton.

Northerners claimed that slavery was a backward labor system, and compared with Northerners, Southerners invested less of their capital in industry, transportation, and public education. But planters' pockets were never fuller than in the 1850s. Planters' decisions to reinvest in agriculture ensured the momentum of the plantation economy and the political and social relationships rooted in it.

REVIEW   Why did the nineteenth-century southern economy remain primarily agricultural?

▶ Masters and Mistresses in the Big House

Nowhere was the contrast between northern and southern life more vivid than on the plantations of the South. Located on a patchwork of cleared fields and dense forests, a plantation typically included a "big house," where the plantation owner and his family lived, and a slave quarter. Scattered about were numerous outbuildings, each with a special function. Near the big house were the kitchen, storehouse, smokehouse (for curing and preserving meat), and hen coop. More distant were the barns, toolsheds, artisans' workshops, and overseer's house. Large plantations sometimes had an infirmary and a chapel for slaves. Depending on the crop, there was also a tobacco shed, a rice mill, a sugar refinery, or a cotton gin house. Lavish or plain, plantations everywhere had an underlying similarity.

The plantation was the home of masters, mistresses, and slaves. Slavery shaped the lives of all the plantation's inhabitants, from work to leisure activities, but it affected each differently. A hierarchy of rigid roles and duties governed relationships. Presiding was the master, who ruled his wife, children, and slaves, none of whom had many legal rights and all of whom were designated by the state as dependents under his dominion and protection.

Paternalism and Male Honor

Whereas smaller planters supervised the labor of their slaves themselves, larger planters hired **overseers** who went to the fields with the slaves, leaving the planters free to concentrate on marketing, finance, and the general affairs of the plantation. Planters also found time to escape to town to discuss cotton prices, to the courthouse and legislature to debate politics, and to the woods to hunt and fish.

Increasingly, planters characterized their mastery in terms of what they called "Christian guardianship" and what historians have called **paternalism**. The concept of paternalism denied that the form of slavery practiced in the South was brutal and exploitative. Instead, paternalism claimed that plantations joined master and slave together in an enterprise that benefited all. In exchange for the slaves' labor and obedience, masters provided basic care and necessary guidance for a childlike, dependent people. In 1814, Thomas Jefferson captured the essence of the advancing ideal: "We should endeavor, with those whom fortune has thrown on our hands, to feed & clothe them well, protect them from ill usage, require such reasonable labor only as is performed voluntarily by freemen, and be led by no repugnancies to abdicate them, and our duties to them." A South Carolina rice planter insisted, "I manage them as my children."

Paternalism was part propaganda and part self-delusion. But it was also economically shrewd. Masters increasingly recognized slaves as valuable assets, particularly after the nation closed its external slave trade in 1808 and the cotton boom simultaneously stimulated the demand for slaves. Planters realized that the expansion of the slave labor force could come only from natural reproduction. As one slave owner declared in 1849, "It behooves those who own them to make them last as long as possible." Another planter instructed his overseer to pay attention to "whatever tends to promote their health and render them prolific."

One consequence of this paternalism and economic self-interest was a small improvement in slaves' welfare. Diet improved, although nineteenth-century slaves still ate mainly fatty pork and cornmeal. Housing improved, although the cabins still had cracks large enough, slaves said, for cats to slip through. Clothing improved, although slaves seldom received much more than two crude outfits a year and perhaps a pair of cheap shoes. In the fields, workdays remained sunup to sundown, but planters often provided a rest period in the heat of the day. And most owners ceased the colonial practice of punishing slaves by branding and mutilation.

Paternalism should not be mistaken for "Ol' Massa's" kindness and goodwill. It encouraged better treatment because it made economic sense to provide at least minimal care for valuable slaves. Nor did paternalism require that planters put aside their whips. They could whip and still claim that they were only fulfilling their responsibilities as guardians of their naturally lazy and at times insubordinate black dependents. State laws gave masters nearly "uncontrolled authority over the body" of the slave, according to one North Carolina judge. Paternalism offered slaves some informal protection against the most brutal punishments, but whipping remained the planters' essential form of coercion.

Paternalism never won universal acceptance among planters, but by the nineteenth century it had become a kind of communal standard. With its notion that slavery imposed on masters a burden and a duty, paternalism provided slaveholders with a means of rationalizing their rule. But it also provided some slaves with leverage in controlling the conditions of their lives. Slaves learned to manipulate the slaveholder's need to see himself as a good master. To avoid a reputation as a cruel tyrant, planters sometimes negotiated with slaves, rather than just resorting to the whip. Masters sometimes granted slaves small garden plots in which they could work for themselves after working all day in the fields, or they gave slaves a few days off and a dance when they had gathered the last of the cotton.

Virginia statesman Edmund Randolph argued that slavery created in white southern

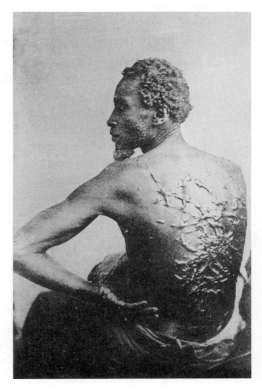

Gordon

This photograph of Gordon, a runaway slave from Baton Rouge, Louisiana, was taken on April 2, 1863. Frederick W. Mercer, an assistant surgeon with the Forty-seventh Massachusetts Regiment, examined four hundred other runaways and found many "to be as badly lacerated." Publication of Gordon's photograph in the popular *Harper's Weekly* made him a symbol of slavery's terrible brutality. Courtesy of the Massachusetts Historical Society.

men a "quick and acute sense of personal liberty" and a "disdain for every abridgement of personal independence." Indeed, prickly individualism and aggressive independence became crucial features of the southern concept of honor. Social standing, political advancement, and even self-esteem rested on an honorable reputation. Defending honor became a male passion. Andrew Jackson's mother reportedly told her son, "Never tell a lie, nor take what is not your own, nor sue anybody for slander or assault and battery. *Always settle them cases yourself.*" Among planters, such advice sometimes led to dueling, a ritual that had arrived from Europe in the eighteenth century. It died out in the North, but in the South, even after legislatures banned it, gentlemen continued to defend their honor with pistols at ten paces.

Southerners also expected an honorable gentleman to be a proper patriarch. Nowhere in America was masculine power more accentuated. Planters brooked no opposition from any of their dependents, black or white. The master's absolute dominion sometimes led to miscegenation. Laws prohibited interracial sex, but how many trips masters and their sons made to slave cabins is impossible to tell. As long as slavery gave white men extraordinary power, however, slave women were forced to submit to the sexual appetites of the men who owned them.

In time, as the children of one elite family married the children of another, ties of blood and kinship, as well as ideology and economic interest, linked planters to one another. Conscious of what they shared as slaveholders, planters worked together to defend their common interests. The values of the big house — slavery, honor, male domination — washed over the boundaries of plantations and flooded all of southern life.

The Southern Lady and Feminine Virtues

Like their northern counterparts, southern ladies were expected to possess the feminine virtues of piety, purity, chastity, and obedience within the context of marriage, motherhood, and domesticity. Countless toasts praised the southern lady as the perfect complement to her husband, the commanding patriarch. She was physically weak, "formed only for the less laborious occupations," and thus dependent on male protection. To gain this protection, she exhibited modesty and delicacy, possessed beauty and grace, and cultivated refinement and charm.

For women, this image of the southern lady was no blessing. **Chivalry** — the South's romantic ideal of male-female relationships — glorified the lady while it subordinated her. Chivalry's underlying assumptions about the weakness of women and the protective authority of men resembled the paternalistic defense of slavery.

Indeed, the most articulate spokesmen for slavery also vigorously defended the subordination of women. George Fitzhugh insisted that "a woman, like children, has but one right and that is the right to protection. The right to protection involves the obligation to obey. A husband, a lord and master, nature designed for every woman. . . . If she be obedient she stands little danger of maltreatment." Just as the slaveholder's mastery was written into law, so too were the paramount rights of husbands. Married women lost almost all their property rights to their husbands. Women throughout the nation found divorce difficult, but southern women found it almost impossible.

Daughters of planters confronted chivalry's demands at an early age. Their education aimed at fitting them to become southern ladies. At their private boarding schools, they read literature, learned languages, and studied the appropriate drawing-room arts. Elite women began courting at a young age and married early. Kate Carney exaggerated only slightly when she despaired in her diary: "Today, I am seventeen, getting quite old, and am not married." Yet marriage meant turning their fates over to their husbands and making enormous efforts to live up to their region's lofty ideal. One mother told her daughter: "A single life has fewer troubles; but then it is not the one for which our maker designed us."

Proslavery advocates claimed that slavery freed white women from drudgery. Surrounded "by her domestics," declared Thomas R. Dew, "she ceases to be a mere beast of burden" and "becomes the cheering and animating center of the family circle." In reality, however, having servants required the plantation mistress to work long hours. She managed the big house, directly supervising as many as a dozen slaves. But unlike her husband, the mistress had no overseer. All house servants answered directly to her. She assigned them tasks each morning, directed their work throughout the day, and punished them when she found fault. Southern ladies did not often lead lives of leisure.

Whereas masters used their status as slaveholders as a springboard into public affairs, mistresses' lives were circumscribed by the plantation. Masters left the plantation when they pleased, but mistresses needed chaperones to travel. When they could, they went to church, but women spent most days at home, where they often became lonely. In 1853, Mary Kendall wrote how much she enjoyed her sister's letter: "For about three weeks I did not have the pleasure of seeing one white female face, there being no white family except our own upon the plantation." Grand parties and balls occasionally broke the daily routine, but the burden of planning and supervising the preparation of the food and drink fell on the mistress.

As members of slaveholding families, mistresses lived privileged lives. But they also had significant grounds for discontent. No feature of plantation life generated more anguish among mistresses than miscegenation. Mary Boykin Chesnut of Camden, South Carolina, confided in her diary, "Ours is a monstrous system, a wrong and iniquity. Like the patriarchs of old, our men live all in one house with their wives and their concubines; and the mulattos one sees in every family partly resemble the white children. Any lady is ready to tell you who is the father of all the mulatto children in everybody's household but her own. Those, she seems to think drop from the clouds."

Most planters' wives, including Chesnut, accepted slavery. After all, the mistress's world rested on slave labor, just as the master's did. By acknowledging the realities of male power, mistresses enjoyed the rewards of their class and race. But these rewards came at a price. Still, the heaviest burdens of slavery fell not on those who lived in the big house, but on those who toiled to support them.

REVIEW   Why did the ideology of paternalism gain currency among planters in the nineteenth century?

▶ Slaves in the Quarter

On most plantations, only a few hundred yards separated the big house and the slave quarter. But the distance was great enough to provide slaves with some privacy. Out of eyesight and earshot of the big house, slaves drew together and built lives of their own. They created families, worshipped God, and developed an African American community and culture. Individually and collectively, slaves found subtle and not so subtle ways to resist their bondage.

Despite the rise of plantations, a substantial minority of slaves lived and worked elsewhere. Most labored on small farms, where they wielded a hoe alongside another slave or two and perhaps their master. But by 1860, almost half a million slaves (one in eight) did not work in agriculture at all. Some lived in towns and cities, where they worked in the homes and shops of their masters as domestics, day laborers, bakers, barbers, tailors, and more. Other slaves, far from urban centers, toiled as fishermen, lumbermen, railroad workers, and deckhands on riverboats. Slaves could also be found in most of the South's factories. Nevertheless, a majority of slaves (52 percent) counted plantations as their workplaces and homes.

Work

Ex-slave Albert Todd recalled, "Work was a religion that we were taught." Whites enslaved blacks for their labor, and all slaves who were capable of productive labor worked. Former slave Carrie Hudson recalled that children who were "knee high to a duck" were sent to the fields to carry water to thirsty workers or to protect ripening crops from hungry birds. Others helped in the slave nursery, caring for children even younger than themselves, or in the big house, where they swept floors or shooed flies in the dining room. When slave boys and girls reached the age of eleven or twelve, masters sent most of them to the fields, where they learned farmwork by laboring alongside their parents. After a lifetime of labor, old women left the fields to care for the small children and spin yarn, and old men moved on to mind livestock and clean stables.

The overwhelming majority of plantation slaves worked as field hands, and most grew cotton. Cotton had a long growing season, and work never stopped, from the clearing of the fields in January and February to the planting and cultivating in the spring and summer until the picking in the fall. Planters sometimes assigned men and women to separate gangs, the women working at lighter tasks and the men doing the heavy work of clearing and breaking the land. But women also did heavy work. "I had to work hard," Nancy Boudry remembered, and "plow and go and split wood just like a man." The backbreaking labor and the monotonous routines caused one ex-slave to observe that the "history of one day is the history of every day."

A few slaves (about one in ten) became house servants. Nearly all of those (nine out of ten) were women. They cooked, cleaned, babysat, washed clothes, and did the dozens of other tasks the master and mistress required. House servants enjoyed somewhat less physically demanding work than field hands, but they were constantly on call, with no time that was entirely their own. Since no servant could please constantly, most bore the brunt of white frustration and rage. Ex-slave Jacob Branch of Texas remembered, "My poor mama! Every washday old Missy give her a beating."

Isaac Jefferson
In this 1845 daguerreotype, seventy-year-old Isaac Jefferson proudly poses in the apron he wore while practicing his crafts as a tinsmith and nail maker. Slaves of Thomas Jefferson, Isaac, his wife, and their two children were deeded to Jefferson's daughter Mary when she married in 1797. Isaac worked at Jefferson's home, Monticello, until 1820, when he moved to Petersburg, Virginia. When work was slow on the home plantation, slave owners often would hire out their skilled artisans to neighbors who needed a carpenter, blacksmith, mason, or tinsmith. Special Collections Department, University of Virginia Library.

Even rarer than house servants were skilled artisans. In the cotton South, no more than one slave in twenty (almost all men) worked in a skilled trade. Most were blacksmiths and carpenters, but slaves also worked as masons, mechanics, millers, and shoemakers. Slave craftsmen took pride in their skills and often exhibited the independence of spirit that caused slaveholder James H. Hammond of South Carolina to declare in disgust that when a slave became a skilled artisan, "he is more than half freed." Skilled slave fathers took pride in teaching their crafts to their sons. "My pappy was one of the black smiths and worked in the shop," John Mathews remembered. "I had to help my pappy in the shop when I was a child and I learnt how to beat out the iron and make wagon tires, and make plows."

Rarest of all slave occupations was that of **slave driver**. Probably no more than one male slave in a hundred worked in this capacity. These men were well named, for their primary task was driving other slaves to work harder in the fields. In some drivers' hands, the whip never rested. Ex-slave Jane Johnson of South Carolina called her driver the "meanest man, white or black, I ever see." But other drivers showed all the restraint they could. "Ole Gabe didn't like that whippin' business," West Turner of Virginia remembered. "When Marsa was there, he would lay it on 'cause he had to. But when old Marsa wasn't lookin', he never would beat them slaves."

Normally, slaves worked from what they called "can to can't," from "can see" in the morning to "can't see" at night. Even with a break at noon for a meal and rest, it made for a long day. For slaves, Lewis Young recalled, "work, work, work, 'twas all they do."

Family and Religion

From dawn to dusk, slaves worked for the master, but at night, when the labor was done, and all day Sunday and usually Saturday afternoon, slaves were left largely to themselves. Bone tired perhaps, they nonetheless used the time to develop and enjoy what mattered most: family, religion, and community.

One of the most important consequences of slaves' limited autonomy was the preservation of the family. Though severely battered, the black family survived slavery. No laws recognized slave marriage, and therefore no master or slave was legally obligated to honor the bond. Nevertheless, plantation records show that slave marriages were often long-lasting. Young men and women in the quarter fell in love, married, and set up housekeeping in cabins of their own. The primary cause of the ending of slave marriages was death, just as it was in white families. But the second most frequent cause was the sale of the husband or wife, something no white family ever had to fear. Precise figures are unavailable, but during the massive deportation associated with the Second Middle Passage, sales destroyed hundreds of thousands of slave marriages.

In 1858, a South Carolina slave named Abream Scriven wrote a letter to his wife, who lived on a neighboring plantation. "My dear wife," he began, "I take the pleasure of writing you . . . with much regret to inform you I am Sold to man by the name of Peterson, a Treader and Stays in New Orleans." Scriven promised to send some things when he got to his new home in Louisiana, but he admitted that he was not sure how he would "get them to you and my children." He asked his wife to "give my love to my father and mother and tell them good Bye for me. And if we do not meet in this world I hope to meet in heaven. . . . My dear wife for you and my children my pen cannot express the griffe I feel to be parted from you all." He closed with words no master would have permitted in a slave's marriage vows: "I remain your truly husband until Death." The letter makes clear Scriven's love for his family; it also demonstrates slavery's massive assault on family life in the quarter.

Masters sometimes permitted slave families to work on their own. In the evenings and on Sundays, they tilled gardens, raised pigs and fowl, and chopped wood, selling the products in the market for a little pocket change. This "overwork," as it was called, allowed slaves to supplement their insufficient diets and even enjoy small luxuries. "Den each fam'ly have some chickens and sell dem and de eggs and maybe go huntin' and sell de hides and git some money," a former Alabama slave remembered. "Den us buy what am Sunday clothes with dat money, sech as hats and pants and shoes and dresses." Slave children remembered the extraordinary efforts their parents made to sustain their families. They held their parents in high esteem, grateful for the small bits of refuge from the rigors of slavery they provided.

Religion also provided slaves with a refuge and a reason for living. Evangelical Baptists and Methodists had great success in converting slaves from their African beliefs. By the mid-nineteenth century, perhaps as many as one-quarter of all slaves claimed church membership, and many of the rest would not have objected to being called Christians.

Planters promoted Christianity in the quarter because they believed that the slaves' salvation was part of the obligation of paternalism; they also hoped that religion would make slaves more obedient. South Carolina slaveholder **Charles Colcock Jones**, the leading missionary to the slaves, published his *Catechism for Colored Persons* in 1834. It instructed slaves "to count their Masters 'worthy of all honour,' as those whom God has placed over them in this world." But slaves laughed up their sleeves at such messages. "That old white preacher just was telling us slaves to be good to our masters," one ex-slave said with a chuckle. "We ain't cared a bit about that stuff he was telling us 'cause we wanted to sing, pray, and serve God in our own way."

Meeting in their cabins or secretly in the woods, slaves created an African American Christianity that served their needs, not the masters'. Laws prohibited teaching slaves to read, but a few could read enough to struggle with the Bible. They interpreted the Christian message themselves. Rather than obedience, their faith emphasized justice. Slaves believed that God kept score and that the accounts of this world would be settled in the next. "The idea of a revolution in the conditions of the whites and blacks is the corner-stone" of the slaves' religion, recalled one ex-slave. But the slaves' faith also spoke to their experiences in this world. In the Old Testament, they discovered Moses, who delivered his people from slavery, and in the New Testament, they found Jesus, who offered salvation to all. Jesus' message of equality provided a potent antidote to the planters' claim that blacks were an inferior people whom God condemned to slavery.

Christianity did not entirely drive out traditional African beliefs. Even slaves who were Christians sometimes continued to believe that conjurers, witches, and spirits possessed the power to injure and protect. Moreover, slaves' Christian music, preaching, and rituals reflected the influence of Africa, as did many of their secular activities, such as wood carving, quilt making, dancing, and storytelling. But by the mid-nineteenth century, black Christianity had assumed a central place in slaves' quest for freedom. In the words of one spiritual, "O my Lord delivered Daniel / O why not deliver me too?"

Resistance and Rebellion

Slaves did not suffer slavery passively. They were, as whites said, "troublesome property." Slaves understood that accommodation to what they could not change was the price of survival, but in a hundred ways they protested their bondage. Theoretically, the master was all-powerful and the slave powerless. But sustained by their families, religion, and community, slaves engaged in day-to-day resistance against their enslavers.

The spectrum of slave resistance ranged from mild to extreme. Telling a pointed story by the fireside in a slave cabin was probably the mildest form of protest. But when the weak got the better of the strong, as they did in tales of Br'er Rabbit and Br'er Fox (*Br'er* is a contraction of *Brother*), listeners could enjoy the thrill of a vicarious victory over their masters. Protest in the fields was riskier and included putting rocks in their cotton bags before having them weighed, feigning illness, and pretending to be so thickheaded that they could not understand the simplest instruction. Slaves broke so many hoes that owners outfitted the tools with oversized handles. Slaves so mistreated the work animals that masters switched from horses to mules, which could absorb more abuse. Although slaves worked hard in the master's fields, they also sabotaged his interests.

Running away was a common form of protest, but except along the borders with northern states and with Mexico, escape to freedom was almost impossible. Most runaways could hope only to escape for a few days. Seeking temporary respite from hard labor or avoiding punishment, they usually stayed close to their plantations, keeping to the deep woods or swamps and slipping back into the quarter at night to get food. "Lying out," as it was known, usually ended when the runaway, worn-out and ragged, gave up or was finally chased down by slave-hunting dogs.

Although resistance was common, outright rebellion — a violent assault on slavery by large numbers of slaves — was very rare. The scarcity of revolts in the South is not evidence of the slaves' contentedness, however. Rather, conditions gave rebels almost no chance of success. By 1860, whites in the South outnumbered blacks two to one and were heavily armed. Moreover, communication between plantations was difficult, and the South provided little protective wilderness into which rebels could retreat and defend themselves. Rebellion, as **Nat Turner**'s experience showed (see pages 365–367), was virtual suicide.

Despite steady resistance and occasional rebellion, slaves did not have the power to end their bondage. Slavery thwarted their hopes and aspirations. It broke some and crippled others. But slavery's destructive power had to contend with the resiliency of the human spirit. Slaves fought back physically, culturally, and spiritually. Not only did they survive bondage, but they also created in the quarter a vibrant African American culture that buoyed them up during long hours in the fields and brought them joy and hope in the few hours they had to themselves.

> **REVIEW** What types of resistance did slaves participate in, and why did slave resistance rarely take the form of rebellion?

▶ The Plain Folk

Most whites in the South did not own slaves, not even one. In 1860, more than six million of the South's eight million whites lived in slaveless households. Some slaveless whites lived in cities and worked as artisans, mechanics, and traders. Others lived in the country and worked as storekeepers, parsons, and schoolteachers. But most "plain folk" were small farmers. Perhaps three out of four were **yeomen**, small farmers who owned their own land. As in the North, farm ownership provided a family with an economic foundation, social respectability, and political standing. Unlike their northern counterparts, however, southern yeomen lived in a region whose economy and society were increasingly dominated by unfree labor.

In an important sense, the South had more than one white yeomanry. The huge southern landscape provided space enough for two yeoman societies, separated roughly along geographic lines. Yeomen throughout the South had much in common, but the life of a small farm family in the cotton belt — the flatlands that spread from South Carolina to east Texas — differed from the life of a family in the upcountry — the area of hills and mountains. And some rural slaveless whites were not yeomen; they owned no land at all and were sometimes desperately poor.

Plantation Belt Yeomen

Plantation belt yeomen lived within the orbit of the planter class. Small farms outnumbered plantations in the **plantation belt**, but they were dwarfed in importance. Small farmers grew mainly food crops, particularly corn, but they also devoted a portion of their land to cotton. With only family labor to draw on, they produced just a few 400-pound bales each year, whereas large planters measured their crop in hundreds of bales. The small farmers' cotton tied them to planters. Unable to afford cotton gins or baling presses of their own, they relied on slave owners to gin and bale their cotton. With no link to merchants in the port cities, plantation belt yeomen also turned to better-connected planters to ship and sell their cotton.

A network of relationships laced small farmers and planters together. Planters hired out surplus slaves to ambitious yeomen who wanted to expand cotton production. They sometimes chose overseers from among the sons of local farm families. Plantation mistresses occasionally nursed ailing neighbors. Family ties could span class lines, making planter and yeoman kin as well as neighbors. Yeomen helped police slaves by riding in slave patrols, which nightly scoured country roads to make certain that no slaves were moving about without permission. On Sundays, plantation dwellers and plain folk came together in church to worship and afterward lingered to gossip and to transact small business.

Plantation belt yeomen may have envied, and at times even resented, wealthy slaveholders, but small farmers learned to accommodate. Planters made accommodation easier by going out of their way to behave as good neighbors and avoid direct exploitation of slaveless whites in their community. As a consequence, rather than raging at the oppression of the planter regime, the typical plantation belt yeoman sought entry into it. He dreamed of adding acreage to his farm, buying a few slaves of his own, and retiring from exhausting field work.

Upcountry Yeomen

By contrast, the hills and mountains of the South resisted the spread of slavery and plantations. In the western parts of Virginia, North Carolina, and South Carolina; in northern Georgia and Alabama; and in eastern Tennessee and Kentucky, the higher elevation, colder climate, rugged terrain, and poor transportation made it difficult for commercial agriculture to make headway. As a result, yeomen dominated these isolated areas, and planters and slaves were scarce.

At the core of this **upcountry** society was the independent farm family working its own patch of land; raising hogs, cattle, and sheep; and seeking self-sufficiency and independence. Toward that end, all members of the family worked, their tasks depending on their sex and age. Husbands labored in the fields, and with their sons they cleared, plowed, planted, and cultivated primarily food crops — corn, wheat, beans, sweet potatoes, and perhaps some fruit. Women and their daughters labored in and about the cabin most of the year. One upcountry farmer remembered that his mother "worked in the house cooking, spinning, weaving [and doing] patchwork." Women also tended the vegetable garden, kept a cow and some chickens, preserved food, cleaned their homes, fed their families, and cared for their children. Male and female tasks were equally crucial to the farm's success, but as in other white southern households, the domestic sphere was subordinated to the will of the male patriarch.

The typical upcountry yeoman also grew a little cotton or tobacco, but food production was more important than cash crops. Not much currency changed hands in the upcountry. Barter was common. A yeoman might trade his small cotton or tobacco crop to a country store owner for a little salt, bullets, needles, and nails, or swap extra sweet potatoes for a plow from a blacksmith or for leather from a tanner. Networks of exchange and mutual assistance tied individual homesteads to the larger community. Farm families joined together in logrolling, house and barn raising, and cornhusking.

Even the hills had some plantations and slaves, but the few upcountry folks who owned slaves usually had only two or three. As a result, slaveholders had much less social and economic power, and yeomen had more. But the upcountry did not oppose slavery. As long as upcountry plain folk were free to lead their own lives, they defended slavery and white supremacy just as staunchly as other white Southerners.

Poor Whites

The majority of slaveless white Southerners were hardworking, landholding small farmers, but Northerners held a different image of this group. They believed that slavery had condemned most whites to poverty and backwardness. One antislavery advocate charged that the South harbored three classes: "the slaves on whom devolves all the regular industry, the slaveholders who reap all the fruits, and an idle and lawless rabble who live dispersed over vast plains little removed from absolute barbarism." Critics called this third class a variety of derogatory names: hillbillies, crackers, rednecks, and poor white trash. According to critics, poor whites were not just whites who were poor. They were also supposedly ignorant, diseased, and degenerate. Even slaves were known to chant, "I'd rather be a nigger an' plow ol' Beck / Than a white hillbilly with a long red neck."

Contrary to northern opinion, only about one in four nonslaveholding rural white men was landless and very poor. Some worked as tenants, renting land and struggling to make a go of it. Others survived by herding pigs and cattle. And still others worked for meager wages, ditching, mining, logging, and laying track for railroads. A Georgian remembered that his "father worked by the day when ever he could get work."

Some poor white men earned reputations for mayhem and violence. One visitor claimed that a "bowie-knife was a universal, and a pistol a not at all unusual companion." Edward Isham, an illiterate roustabout, spent about as much time fighting as he did working. When he wasn't engaged in ear-biting, eye-gouging free-for-alls, he was fighting with sticks, shovels, rocks, axes, tomahawks, knives, and guns. Working at what he could find, he took up with and abandoned many women, gambled, drank, stole, had run-ins with the law, and in 1860 murdered a respected slaveholder, for which he was hanged.

Unlike Isham, most poor white men did not engage in ferocious behavior but instead lived responsible lives. Although they sat at the bottom of the white pecking order, they were ambitious people eager to climb into the yeomanry. The Lipscomb family illustrates the possibility of upward mobility. In 1845, Smith and Sally Lipscomb and their children abandoned their worn-out land in South Carolina for Benton County, Alabama. "Benton is a mountainous country but ther is a heep of good levil land to tend in it," Smith wrote back to his brother. Alabama, Smith said, "will be better for the rising generation if not for ourselves but I think it will be the best for us all that live any length of time." Indeed, primitive living conditions made life precarious. All of the Lipscombs fell ill, but all recovered, and the entire family went to work.

Because they had no money to buy land, they squatted on seven unoccupied acres. With the help of neighbors, they built a 22-by-24-foot cabin, a detached kitchen, and two stables. From daylight to dark, Smith and his sons worked the land, and the first year they produced several bales of cotton and enough food for the table. The women worked just as hard in the cabin, and Sally contributed to the family's income by selling homemade shirts and socks. In time, the Lipscombs bought land and joined the Baptist church, completing their transformation to respectable yeomen.

Many poor whites succeeded in climbing the economic ladder, but in the 1850s upward mobility slowed. The cotton boom of that decade caused planters to expand their operations, driving the price of land beyond the reach of poor families. Whether they gained their own land or not, however, poor whites shared common cultural traits with yeoman farmers.

The Culture of the Plain Folk

Situated on scattered farms and in tiny villages, rural plain folk lived isolated lives. Bad roads and a lack of newspapers meant that life revolved around family, a handful of neighbors, the local church, and perhaps a country store. Work occupied most hours, but plain folk still found time for pleasure. "Dancing they are all fond of," a visitor to North Carolina discovered, "especially when they can get a fiddle, or bagpipe." They also loved their tobacco. Men smoked and chewed (and spat), while women dipped snuff. But the most popular pastimes of men and boys were fishing and hunting. A traveler in Mississippi recalled that his host sent "two of his sons, little fellows that looked almost too small to shoulder a gun," for food. "One went off towards the river and the other struck into the forest, and in a few hours we were feasting on delicious venison, trout and turtle."

Plain folk did not usually associate "book learning" with the basic needs of life. A northern woman visiting the South in the 1850s observed, "Education is not extended to the masses here as at the North." Private academies charged fees that yeomen could not afford, and public schools were scarce. Although most people managed to pick up the "three R's," approximately one southern white man

Camp Meeting, mid-19th Century

Camp meetings, or revivals, were a key feature of southern evangelical Christianity. Many preachers were itinerants who spoke wherever they could draw a crowd. Here an earnest clergyman preaches his message in an open field, with a tent in the background where coffee is being sold. The colorful individuals who surround the preacher include both the reverent and the not-so-reverent. Some of the audience is clearly skeptical, while others, like the two men sitting on the log, appear merely bemused. And still others have their backs to the preacher and pay no attention at all. Evangelical Christians, however, took their camp meetings, and their religion, seriously. Private Collection/Picture Research Consultants & Archives.

in five was illiterate in 1860, and the rate for white women was even higher. "People here prefer talking to reading," a Virginian remarked. Telling stories, reciting ballads, and singing hymns were important activities in yeoman culture.

Plain folk spent more hours in revival tents than in classrooms. Not all rural whites were religious, but many were, and the most characteristic feature of their evangelical Christian faith was the revival. Preachers spoke day and night to save souls. Revivalism crossed denominational lines, but Baptists and Methodists adopted it most readily and by midcentury had become the South's largest religious groups. By emphasizing free choice and individual worth, the plain folk's religion was hopeful and affirming. Hymns and spirituals provided guides to right and wrong — praising humility and steadfastness, condemning drunkenness and profanity. Above all, hymns spoke of the eventual release from worldly sorrows and the assurance of eternal salvation.

REVIEW Why did the lives of plantation belt yeomen and upcountry yeomen diverge?

▶ Black and Free: On the Middle Ground

All white Southerners — slaveholders and slaveless alike — considered themselves superior to all blacks, both slave and free. Not every black Southerner was a slave. In 1860, some 260,000 (approximately 6 percent) of the region's 4.1 million African Americans were free. What is surprising is not that their numbers were small but that they existed at all. "**Free black**" seemed increasingly a contradiction to most white Southerners. According to the emerging racial thinking, blacks were supposed to be slaves; only whites were supposed to be free. Blacks who were free stood out, and whites made them more and more targets of oppression. Free blacks stood precariously between slavery and full freedom, on what a free black artisan in Charleston characterized in 1848 as "a middle ground." But they made the most of their freedom, and a few found success despite the restrictions placed on them by white Southerners.

Precarious Freedom

The population of free blacks swelled after the Revolutionary War, when the natural rights philosophy of the Declaration of Independence and the egalitarian message of evangelical Protestantism joined to challenge slavery. A brief flurry of emancipation — the act of freeing from slavery — visited the Upper South, where the ideological assault on slavery coincided with a deep depression in the tobacco economy. By 1810, free blacks in the South numbered more than 100,000, a fact that worried white Southerners, who, because of the cotton boom, wanted more slaves, not more free blacks.

In the 1820s and 1830s, state legislatures acted to stem the growth of the free black population and to shrink the liberty of those blacks who had gained their freedom. New laws denied masters the right to free their slaves. Other laws humiliated and restricted free blacks by subjecting them to special taxes, prohibiting them from interstate travel, denying them the right to have schools and to participate in politics, and requiring them to carry "freedom papers" to prove they were not slaves. Increasingly, whites subjected free blacks to the same laws as slaves. Free blacks could not testify under oath in a court of law or serve on juries. Like slaves, they were liable to whipping and the treadmill, a wooden wheel with steps on which victims were made to walk until they dropped. Free blacks were forbidden to strike whites, even to defend themselves. "Free negroes belong to a degraded caste of society," a South Carolina judge said in 1848. "They are in no respect on a perfect equality with the white man. . . . They ought, by law, to be compelled to demean themselves as inferiors."

Laws confined most free African Americans to a constricted life of poverty and dependence. Typically, free blacks were rural, uneducated, unskilled agricultural laborers and domestic servants who had to scramble to survive. Opportunities of any kind — for work, education, or community — were slim. Planters believed that free blacks set a bad example for slaves, subverting the racial subordination that was the essence of slavery.

Whites feared that free blacks might cherish their race more than their status as free people and that as a consequence they would lead slaves in rebellion. In 1822, whites in Charleston accused **Denmark Vesey**, a free black carpenter, of conspiring with plantation slaves to slaughter Charleston's white inhabitants. The authorities rounded up scores of suspects, who, prodded by torture and the threat of death, implicated others in the plot "to riot in blood, outrage, and rapine." Although the city fathers never found any weapons and Vesey and most of the accused steadfastly denied the charges of conspiracy, officials hanged thirty-five black men, including Vesey, and banished another thirty-seven blacks from the state.

Achievement despite Restrictions

Despite increasingly harsh laws and stepped-up persecution, free African Americans made the most of the advantages their status offered. Unlike slaves, free blacks could legally marry. They could protect their families from arbitrary disruption and pass on their heritage of freedom to their children. Freedom also meant that they could choose occupations and own property. For most, however, these economic rights proved only theoretical, for a majority of the South's free blacks remained propertyless.

Still, some free blacks escaped the poverty and degradation whites thrust on them. Particularly in the cities of Charleston, Savannah, Mobile, and New Orleans, a small elite of free blacks emerged. Urban whites enforced restrictive laws only sporadically, allowing free blacks room to maneuver. The free black elite consisted overwhelmingly of light-skinned African Americans who worked at skilled trades, as tailors, carpenters, mechanics, and the like. The free black elite operated schools for their children and traveled in and out of their states, despite laws forbidding both activities. They worshipped with whites (in separate seating) in the finest churches and lived scattered about in white neighborhoods, not in ghettos. And like elite whites, some owned slaves. Blacks could own slaves because they had the right to own property, which in the South included human property. Of the 3,200 black slaveholders (barely 1 percent of the free black population), most owned only a few family members whom they could not legally free. Others owned slaves in large numbers and exploited them for labor.

One such free black slave owner was William Ellison of South Carolina. Born a slave in 1790, Ellison bought his freedom in 1816 and moved to a thriving plantation district about one hundred miles north of Charleston. He set up business as a cotton gin maker, a trade he had learned as a slave, and by 1835 he was prosperous enough to purchase the home of a former governor of the state. By the time of his death in 1861, he had become a cotton planter, with sixty-three slaves and an 800-acre plantation.

Most free blacks neither became slaveholders nor sought to raise a slave rebellion, as whites accused Denmark Vesey of doing. Rather, most free blacks simply tried to preserve their freedom, which was under increasing attack. Unlike blacks in the North whose freedom was secure, free blacks in the South clung to a precarious freedom by seeking to impress whites with their reliability, economic contributions, and good behavior.

REVIEW Why did many state legislatures pass laws restricting free blacks' rights in the 1820s and 1830s?

▶ The Politics of Slavery

By the mid-nineteenth century, all southern white men — planters and plain folk alike — and no southern black man, even those who were free, could vote. But even after the South's politics became democratic for the white male population, political power remained unevenly distributed. The nonslaveholding white majority wielded less political power than their numbers indicated. The slaveholding white minority wielded more. Self-conscious, cohesive, and with a well-developed sense of class interest, slaveholders busied themselves with party politics, campaigns, and officeholding and made demands of state governments. As a result, they received significant benefits. Nonslaveholding whites were concerned mainly with preserving their liberties and keeping their taxes low. Collectively, they asked government for little of an economic nature, and they received little.

Slaveholders sometimes worried about nonslaveholders' loyalty to slavery, but the majority of whites accepted the planters' argument that the existing social order served *all* Southerners' interests. Slavery rewarded every white man — no matter how poor — with membership in the South's white ruling race. It also provided the means by which nonslaveholders might someday advance into the ranks of the planters. White men in the South argued furiously about many things, but they agreed that they should take land from Indians, promote agriculture, uphold white supremacy and masculine privilege, and defend slavery from its enemies.

The Democratization of the Political Arena

The political reforms that swept the nation in the first half of the nineteenth century reached deeply into the South. Southern politics became democratic politics — for white men. Southerners eliminated the wealth and property requirements that had once restricted political participation. By the 1850s, every state had extended the right to vote to all adult white males. Most southern states also removed the property requirements for holding state offices. To be sure, undemocratic features lingered. Plantation districts still wielded disproportionate power in several state legislatures. Nevertheless, southern politics took place within an increasingly democratic political structure.

White male suffrage ushered in an era of vigorous electoral competition in the South. Eager voters rushed to the polls to exercise their new rights. High turnouts — often approaching 80 percent — became a hallmark of southern elections. Candidates crisscrossed their electoral districts, speaking to voters who demanded stirring oratory and also good entertainment — barbecues and bands, rum and races. In the South, it seemed, "everybody talked politics everywhere," even the "illiterate and shoeless."

As politics became aggressively democratic, it also grew fiercely partisan. From the 1830s to the 1850s, **Whigs** and **Democrats** battled for the electorate's favor. Both parties presented themselves as the plain white folk's best friend. All candidates declared their allegiance to republican equality and pledged themselves to defend the people's liberty. And each party sought to portray the other as a collection of rich, snobbish, selfish men who had antidemocratic designs up their silk sleeves.

The Whig and Democratic parties sought to serve the people differently, however. Southern Whigs tended, as Whigs did elsewhere in the nation, to favor government intervention in the economy, and Democrats tended to oppose it. Whigs backed state support of banks, railroads, and corporations, arguing that government aid would stimulate the economy, enlarge opportunity, and thus increase the general welfare. Democrats claimed that by granting favors to special economic interests, government intervention threatened individual liberty and restricted the common man's economic opportunity. Beginning with the panic of 1837 (see chapter 11), the parties clashed repeatedly on concrete economic and financial issues.

Planter Power

Whether Whig or Democrat, southern officeholders were likely to be slave owners. The power that slaveholders exerted over slaves did not translate directly into political authority over whites, however. In the nineteenth century, political power could be won only at the ballot box, and almost everywhere nonslaveholders were in the majority. Yet year after year, proud and noisily egalitarian common men elected wealthy slaveholders.

By 1860, the percentage of slave owners in state legislatures ranged from 41 percent in Missouri to nearly 86 percent in North Carolina. Legislators not only tended to own slaves; they also often owned large numbers. The percentage of planters (individuals with twenty or more slaves) in southern legislatures in 1860 ranged from 5.3 percent in Missouri to 55.4 percent in South Carolina. Even in North Carolina, where only 3 percent of the state's white families belonged to the planter class, more than 36 percent of state legislators were planters. The democratization of politics in the nineteenth century meant that more ordinary citizens participated in elections, but yeomen did not throw the planters out of office.

Upper-class dominance of southern politics reflected the elite's success in persuading the yeoman majority that what was good for slaveholders was also good for plain folk. In reality, the South had, on the whole, done well by common white men. Most had farms of their own. They participated as equals in a democratic political system. They enjoyed an elevated social status, above all blacks and in theory equal to all other whites. They commanded patriarchal authority over their households. And as long as slavery existed, they could dream of joining the planter class. Slaveless white men found much to celebrate in the slave South.

Most slaveholders took pains to win the plain folk's trust and to nurture their respect. One South Carolinian told his wealthy neighbor that he had a bright political future because he never thought himself "too good to sit down & talk to a poor man." Mary Boykin Chesnut complained about the fawning attention her husband, U.S. senator from South Carolina, showed to poor men, including one who had "mud sticking up through his toes." Smart candidates found ways to convince wary plain folk of their democratic convictions and egalitarian sentiments, whether they were genuine or not.

In 1846 when Walter L. Steele ran for a seat in the North Carolina legislature, he commented sarcastically to a friend that he was "busily engaged in proving to the people, the soundness of my political faith, and the purity of my personal character & playing fool to a considerable extent, as you know, all candidates are obliged to do." He detested pandering to the crowd, but he had learned to speak with "candied tongue."

Georgia politics illustrate how well planters protected their interests in state legislatures. In 1850, about half of the state's revenues came from taxes on slaves, the characteristic form of planter wealth. However, the tax rate on slaves was trifling, only about one-fifth the rate on land. Moreover, planters benefited from public spending far more than other groups did. Financing railroads — which carried cotton to market — was the largest state expenditure. The legislature also established low tax rates on land, the characteristic form of yeoman wealth, which meant that the typical yeoman's annual tax bill was small. Still, relative to their wealth, large slaveholders paid less than did other whites. Relative to their numbers, they got more in return. Slaveholding legislators protected planters' interests while giving the impression of protecting the small farmers' interests as well.

The South's elite defended slavery in other ways. In the 1830s, whites decided that slavery was too important to debate. "So interwoven is [slavery] with our interest, our manners, our climate and our very being," one man declared ominously in 1833, "that no change can ever possibly be effected without a civil commotion from which the heart of a patriot must turn with horror." To end free speech on the slavery question, powerful whites dismissed slavery's critics from college faculties, drove them from pulpits, and hounded them from political life. Sometimes antislavery Southerners fell victim to vigilantes and mob violence. One could defend slavery; one could even delicately suggest mild reforms. But no Southerner could any longer safely call slavery evil or advocate its destruction.

In the South, therefore, the rise of the common man occurred alongside the continuing, even growing, power of the planter class. Rather than pitting slaveholders against nonslaveholders, elections remained an effective means of binding the region's whites together. Elections affirmed the sovereignty of white men, whether planter or plain folk, and the subordination of African Americans. Those twin themes played well among white women as well. Though unable to vote, white women supported equality for whites and slavery for blacks. In the antebellum South, the politics of slavery helped knit together all of white society.

REVIEW   How did planters benefit from their control of state legislatures?

▶ Conclusion: A Slave Society

By the early nineteenth century, northern states had either abolished slavery or put it on the road to extinction, while southern states were building the largest slave society in the New World. Regional differences increased over time, not merely because the South became more and more dominated by slavery, but also because developments in the North rapidly propelled it in a very different direction.

One-third of the South's population was enslaved by 1860. Bondage saddled blacks with enormous physical and spiritual burdens: hard labor, harsh treatment, broken families, and, most important, the denial of freedom itself. Although degraded and exploited, they were not defeated. Out of African memories and New World realities, blacks created a life-affirming African American culture that sustained and strengthened them. Their families, religion, and community provided defenses to white racism and power. Defined as property, they refused to be reduced to things. Perceived as inferior beings, they rejected the notion that they were natural slaves.

Slavery was crucial to the South's distinctiveness and to the loyalty and regional identification of its whites. The South was not merely a society with slaves; it had become a slave society. Slavery shaped the region's economy, culture, social structure, and politics. Whites south of the Mason-Dixon line believed that racial slavery was necessary and just. By making all blacks a pariah class, all whites gained a measure of equality and harmony.

Many features of white southern life helped to confine class tensions: the wide availability of land, rapid economic mobility, the democratic nature of political life, the patriarchal power among all white men, and, most of all, slavery. All stress along class lines was not erased, however, and anxious slaveholders continued to worry that yeomen would defect from the proslavery consensus. But during the 1850s, white Southerners' near universal acceptance of slavery would increasingly unite them in political opposition to their northern neighbors.

Reviewing Chapter 13

REVIEW QUESTIONS

1. Why did the nineteenth-century southern economy remain primarily agricultural? (pp. 367–373)

2. Why did the ideology of paternalism gain currency among planters in the nineteenth century? (pp. 374–377)

3. What types of resistance did slaves participate in, and why did slave resistance rarely take the form of rebellion? (pp. 378–382)

4. Why did the lives of plantation belt yeomen and upcountry yeomen diverge? (pp. 382–386)

5. Why did many state legislatures pass laws restricting free blacks' rights in the 1820s and 1830s? (pp. 387–389)

6. How did planters benefit from their control of state legislatures? (pp. 389–391)

MAKING CONNECTIONS

1. By the mid-nineteenth century, the South had become a "cotton kingdom." How did cotton's profitability shape the region's antebellum development? In your answer, discuss the region's distinctive demographic and economic features.

2. How did southern white legislators and intellectuals attempt to strengthen the institution of slavery in the 1820s? What prompted them to undertake this work? In your answer, be sure to explore regional and national influences.

3. Although bondage restricted slaves' autonomy and left slaves vulnerable to extreme abuse, they resisted slavery. Discuss the variety of ways in which slaves attempted to lessen the harshness of slavery. What were the short- and long-term effects of their efforts?

4. Despite vigorous political competition in the South, by 1860 legislative power was largely concentrated in the hands of a regional minority — slaveholders. Why were slaveholders politically dominant? In your answer, be sure to consider how the region's biracialism contributed to its politics.

LINKING TO THE PAST

1. Compare and contrast Northerners' defense of free labor and white Southerners' defense of slave labor. (See chapter 12.)

2. How did President Andrew Jackson's Indian removal policies pave the way for the South's cotton empire? (See chapter 11.)

TIMELINE 1808–1860

1808
- External slave trade outlawed.

1810s–1850s
- Suffrage extended throughout South to all adult white males.

1813–1814
- Creek War opens Indian land to white settlement.

1820s–1830s
- Southern legislatures enact slave codes to strengthen slavery.
- Southern legislatures enact laws to restrict growth of free black population.
- Southern intellectuals fashion systematic defense of slavery.

1822
- Denmark Vesey executed for fomenting slave rebellion.

1829
- *Appeal . . . to the Coloured Citizens of the World* published.

1830
- Southern slaves number approximately two million.

1831
- Nat Turner's slave rebellion.
- First issue of the *Liberator* published.

1834
- *Catechism for Colored Persons* published.

1836
- Arkansas admitted to Union as slave state.

1840
- Cotton accounts for more than 60 percent of nation's exports.

1845
- Texas and Florida admitted to Union as slave states.

1860
- Southern slaves number nearly four million, one-third of South's population.

▶ FOR AN ONLINE BIBLIOGRAPHY, PRACTICE QUIZZES, WEB SITES, IMAGES, AND DOCUMENTS RELATED TO THIS CHAPTER, see the Book Companion Site at **bedfordstmartins.com/roarkvalue**.

▶ FOR DOCUMENTS RELATED TO THIS PERIOD, see Michael Johnson, ed., *Reading the American Past*, Fifth Edition.

14

The House Divided

1846–1861

OTHER THAN TWENTY CHILDREN, JOHN BROWN DID NOT HAVE MUCH to show for his life in 1859. Grizzled, gnarled, and fifty-nine years old, he had for decades lived like a nomad, hauling his large family back and forth across six states as he tried desperately to better himself. He turned his hand to farming, raising sheep, running a tannery, and selling wool, but failure dogged him. The world had given John Brown some hard licks — and yet it had not budged a conviction he had held since childhood: that slavery was wrong and ought to be destroyed. In the wake of the fighting that erupted over the future of slavery in Kansas in the 1850s, his beliefs turned violent. On May 24, 1856, he led an eight-man antislavery posse in the midnight slaughter of five allegedly proslavery men at Pottawatomie, Kansas. He told Mahala Doyle, whose husband and two oldest sons he killed, that if a man stood between him and what he thought right, he would take that man's life as calmly as he would eat breakfast.

After the killings, Brown slipped out of Kansas and reemerged in the East. More than ever, he was a man on fire for abolition. He spent thirty months begging money to support his vague plan for military operations against slavery. He captivated genteel easterners who were awed by his iron-willed determination and courage, but most could not accept violence. "These men are all talk," Brown declared. "What is needed is action — action!" But enough donated to the hypnotic-eyed Brown that he was able to gather a small band of antislavery warriors.

On the night of October 16, 1859, Brown took his war against slavery into the South. With only twenty-one men, including five African Americans,

John Brown
In this 1859 photograph, John Brown appears respectable, even statesmanlike, but contemporaries debated his mental state and moral character, and the debate still rages. Critics argue that he was a bloody terrorist, a religious fanatic who believed that he was touched by God for a great purpose, one for which he was willing to die. Admirers see a resolute and selfless hero, a rare white man who believed that black people were the equals of whites, and a shrewd political observer who recognized that only violence would end slavery in America. Library of Congress.

he invaded Harpers Ferry, Virginia. His band seized the town's armory and rifle works, but the invaders were immediately surrounded, first by local militia and then by Colonel Robert E. Lee, who commanded the U.S. troops in the area. When Brown refused to surrender, federal soldiers charged with bayonets. Although a few of Brown's raiders escaped, federal forces killed ten of his men (including two of his sons) and captured seven, among them Brown.

"When I strike, the bees will begin to swarm," Brown told Frederick Douglass a few months before the raid. As slaves rushed to Harpers Ferry, Brown said, he would arm them with the pikes he carried with him and with weapons stolen from the armory. They would then fight a war of liberation. Brown, however, neglected to inform the slaves when he had arrived in Harpers Ferry, and the few who knew of his arrival wanted nothing to do with his enterprise. "It was not a slave insurrection," Abraham Lincoln observed. "It was an attempt by white men to get up a revolt among slaves, in which the slaves refused to participate. In fact, it was so absurd that the slaves, with all their ignorance, saw plainly enough it could not succeed."

Although Brown's raid ended in utter defeat, white Southerners viewed it as proof of their growing suspicion that Northerners actively sought to incite slaves in bloody rebellion. For more than a decade, Northerners and Southerners had accused one another of hostile intentions, and by 1859 emotions were raw. Sectional tension was as old as the Constitution, but hostility had escalated with the outbreak of war with Mexico in May 1846 (see chapter 12). Only three months after the war began, national expansion and the slavery issue intersected when Representative David Wilmot introduced a bill to prohibit slavery in any territory that might be acquired as a result of the war.

After that, the problem of slavery in the territories became the principal wedge that divided the nation.

"Mexico is to us the forbidden fruit," South Carolina senator John C. Calhoun declared at the war's outset. "The penalty of eating it [is] to subject our institutions to political death." For a decade and a half, the slavery issue intertwined with the fate of former Mexican land, poisoning the national political debate. Slavery proved powerful enough to transform party politics into sectional politics. Rather than Whigs and Democrats confronting one another across party lines, Northerners and Southerners eyed one another hostilely across the Mason-Dixon line. Sectional politics encouraged the South's separatist impulses. Southern separatism, a fitful tendency before the Mexican-American War, gained strength with each confrontation. As the nation lurched from crisis to crisis, southern disaffection and alienation mounted, and support for compromise and conciliation eroded. The era began with a crisis of union and ended with the Union in even graver peril. As Abraham Lincoln predicted in 1858, "A house divided against itself cannot stand."

▶ The Bitter Fruits of War

Between 1846 and 1848, the nation grew by 1.2 million square miles, an incredible two-thirds. The gold rush of 1849 transformed the sleepy frontier of California into a booming, thriving economy (see chapter 12). The 1850s witnessed new "rushes," for gold in Colorado and silver in Nevada's Comstock Lode. People from around the world flocked to the West, where they produced a vibrant agriculture as well as tons of gold and silver. But it quickly became clear that Northerners and Southerners had very different visions of the West, particularly the place of slavery in its future.

History provided contradictory precedents for handling slavery in the territories. In 1787, the Northwest Ordinance banned slavery north of the Ohio River. In 1803, slavery was allowed to remain in the newly acquired Louisiana Territory. The Missouri Compromise of 1820 prohibited slavery in part of that territory but allowed it in the rest. In 1846, when the war with Mexico made likely the acquisition of new territory for the United States, politicians offered various plans. But when the war ended in 1848, Congress had made no headway in solving the issue of slavery in the land acquired from Mexico, called the Mexican cession. In 1850, Congress patched together a settlement, one that Americans hoped would be permanent.

The Wilmot Proviso and the Expansion of Slavery

In the years leading up to the Civil War, Americans focused not on slavery where it existed but on the possibility that slavery might expand into areas where it did not exist. Most Americans agreed that the Constitution left the issue of slavery to the individual states to decide. Northern states had done away with slavery, while southern states had retained it. But what about slavery in the nation's territories? The Constitution states that "Congress shall have power to . . . make all needful rules and regulations respecting the territory . . . belonging to the United States." The debate about slavery, then, turned toward Congress.

The spark for the national debate appeared in August 1846 when a Democratic representative from Pennsylvania, David Wilmot, proposed that Congress bar slavery from all lands acquired in the war with Mexico. The Mexicans had abolished slavery in their country, and Wilmot declared, "God forbid that we should be the means of planting this institution upon it."

Regardless of party affiliation, Northerners lined up behind the **Wilmot Proviso**. Many supported free soil, by which they meant territory in which slavery would be prohibited, because they wanted to preserve the West for **free labor**, for hardworking, self-reliant free men, not for slaveholders and slaves. But support also came from those who were simply anti-South. New slave territories would eventually mean new slave states, and Northerners opposed magnifying the political power of Southerners. Wilmot himself said his proposal would blunt "*the power* of slaveholders" in the national government.

Additional support for free soil came from Northerners who were hostile to blacks and wanted to reserve new land for whites. Wilmot himself blatantly encouraged racist support when he declared, "I would preserve for free white labor a fair country, a rich inheritance, where the sons of toil, of my own race and own color, can live without the disgrace which association with negro slavery brings upon free labor." It is no wonder that some called the Wilmot Proviso the "White Man's Proviso."

The thought that slavery might be excluded in the territories outraged white Southerners. Like Northerners, they regarded the West as a ladder for economic and social opportunity. They also believed that the exclusion of slavery was a slap in the face to veterans of the Mexican-American War, at least half of whom were Southerners. "When the war-worn soldier returns home," one Alabaman asked, "is he to be told that he cannot carry his property to the country won by his blood?"

Southern leaders also sought to maintain political parity with the North to protect the South's interests, especially slavery. The need seemed especially urgent in the 1840s, when the North's population and wealth were booming. James Henry Hammond of South Carolina predicted that ten new states would be carved from the acquired Mexican land. If free soil won, the North would "ride over us roughshod" in Congress, he claimed. "Our only safety is in *equality* of power."

The two sides squared off in the nation's capital. Because Northerners had a majority in the House, they easily passed the Wilmot Proviso. In the Senate, however, where slave states outnumbered free states fifteen to fourteen, Southerners defeated it in 1847. Senator **John C. Calhoun** of South Carolina boldly denied that Congress had the constitutional authority to exclude slavery from the nation's territories. He argued that because the territories were the "joint and common property" of all the states, Congress could not bar citizens of one state from migrating with their property (including slaves) to the territories. Whereas Wilmot demanded that Congress slam shut the door to slavery, Calhoun called on Congress to hold the door wide open.

In 1847, Senator **Lewis Cass** of Michigan offered a compromise through the doctrine of **popular sovereignty**, by which the people who settled the territories would decide for themselves slavery's fate. This solution, Cass argued, sat squarely in the American tradition of democracy and local self-government. It had the added attraction of removing the incendiary issue of the expansion of slavery from the nation's capital and lodging it in distant territorial legislatures, where it would excite fewer passions.

Popular sovereignty's most attractive feature was its ambiguity about the precise moment when settlers could determine slavery's fate. Northern advocates believed that the decision on slavery could be made as soon as the first territorial legislature assembled. With free-soil majorities likely because of the North's greater population, they would shut the door to slavery almost before the first slave arrived. Southern supporters believed that popular sovereignty guaranteed that slavery would be unrestricted throughout the entire territorial period. Only at the very end, when settlers in a territory drew up a constitution and applied for statehood, could they decide the issue of slavery. By then, slavery would have sunk deep roots. As long as the matter of timing remained vague, popular sovereignty gave hope to both sides.

When Congress ended its session in 1848, no plan had won a majority in both houses. Northerners who demanded no new slave territory anywhere, ever, and Southerners who demanded entry for their slave property into all territories, or else, staked out their extreme positions. Unresolved in Congress, the territorial question naturally became an issue in the presidential election of 1848.

The Election of 1848

When President Polk, worn-out and ailing, chose not to seek reelection, the Democratic convention nominated Lewis Cass of Michigan, the man most closely associated with popular sovereignty. The Whigs nominated a Mexican-American War hero, General **Zachary Taylor**. The Whigs declined to adopt a party platform, betting that the combination of a military hero and total silence on the slavery issue would unite their divided party. Taylor, who owned more than one hundred slaves on plantations in Mississippi and Louisiana, was hailed by Georgia politician Robert Toombs as a "Southern man, a slaveholder, a cotton planter."

Antislavery Whigs balked and looked for an alternative. Senator **Charles Sumner** called for a major political realignment, "one grand Northern party of Freedom." In the summer of 1848, antislavery Whigs and antislavery Democrats founded the **Free-Soil Party**, nominating a Democrat, Martin Van Buren, for president and a Whig, Charles Francis Adams, for vice president. The platform boldly proclaimed, "Free soil, free speech, free labor, and free men."

The November election dashed the hopes of the Free-Soilers. Although they succeeded in making slavery the campaign's central issue, they did not carry a single state. The major parties went through contortions to present their candidates favorably in both North and South, and their evasions succeeded. Taylor won the all-important electoral vote 163 to 127, carrying eight of the fifteen slave states and seven of the fifteen free states. (Wisconsin had entered the Union earlier in 1848 as the fifteenth free state.) Northern voters were not yet ready for Sumner's "one grand Northern party of Freedom," but the struggle over slavery in the territories had shaken the major parties badly.

Debate and Compromise

Southern slaveholder Zachary Taylor entered the White House in March 1849 and almost immediately shocked the nation by championing a free-soil solution to the Mexican cession. Believing that he could avoid further sectional strife if California and New Mexico skipped the territorial stage, the new president encouraged the settlers to apply for admission to the Union as states. Predominantly antislavery, the settlers began writing free-state constitutions. "For the first time," Mississippian Jefferson Davis lamented, "we are about permanently to destroy the balance of power between the sections."

Congress convened in December 1849, beginning one of the most contentious and most significant sessions in its history. President Taylor urged Congress to admit California as a free state immediately and to admit New Mexico, which lagged behind a few months, as soon as it applied. Southerners exploded. A North Carolinian declared that Southerners who would "consent to be thus degraded and enslaved, ought to be whipped through their fields by their own negroes."

Into this rancorous scene stepped Senator Henry Clay of Kentucky, the architect of Union-saving compromises in the Missouri and nullification crises (see chapters 10 and 11). Clay offered a series of resolutions meant to answer and balance "all questions in controversy between the free and slave states, growing out of the subject of slavery." Admit California as a free state, he proposed, but organize the rest of the Southwest without restrictions on slavery. Require Texas to abandon its claim to parts of New Mexico, but compensate it by assuming its preannexation debt. Abolish the domestic slave trade in Washington, D.C., but confirm slavery itself in the nation's capital. Reassert Congress's lack of authority to interfere with the interstate slave trade, and enact a more effective fugitive slave law.

Both antislavery advocates and "fire-eaters" (as radical Southerners who urged secession from the Union were called) savaged Clay's plan. Senator Salmon P. Chase of Ohio ridiculed it as "sentiment for the North, substance for the South." Senator Henry S. Foote of Mississippi denounced it as more offensive to the South than the speeches of abolitionists William Lloyd Garrison, Wendell Phillips, and Frederick Douglass combined. The most ominous response came from John C. Calhoun, who charged that unending northern agitation on the slavery question had "snapped" many of the "cords which bind these states together in one common union." He argued that the fragile political unity of North and South depended on continued equal representation in the Senate, which Clay's plan for a free California destroyed. "As things now stand," he said in February 1850, the South "cannot with safety remain in the Union."

After Clay and Calhoun had spoken, it was time for the third member of the "great triumvirate," Senator Daniel Webster of Massachusetts, to address the Senate.

Like Clay, Webster defended compromise. He told Northerners that the South had legitimate complaints, but he told Southerners that secession from the Union would mean civil war. He appealed for an end to reckless proposals and, to the dismay of many Northerners, mentioned by name the Wilmot Proviso. A legal ban on slavery in the territories was unnecessary, he said, because the harsh climate effectively prohibited the expansion of cotton and slaves into the new American Southwest. "I would not take pains uselessly to reaffirm an ordinance of nature, nor to reenact the will of God," Webster declared.

Free-soil forces recoiled from what they saw as Webster's desertion. Boston clergyman and abolitionist Theodore Parker could only conclude that "Southern men" must have offered Webster the presidency. Senator William H. Seward of New York responded that Webster's and Clay's compromise with slavery was "radically wrong and essentially vicious." He flatly rejected Calhoun's argument that Congress lacked the constitutional authority to exclude slavery from the territories. In any case, Seward said, in the most sensational moment in his address, there was a "higher law than the Constitution" — the law of God — to ensure freedom in all the public domain. Claiming that God was a Free-Soiler did nothing to cool the superheated political atmosphere.

In May 1850, the Senate considered a bill that joined Clay's resolutions into a single comprehensive package, known as the Omnibus Bill because it was a vehicle on which "every sort of passenger" could ride. Clay bet that a majority of Congress wanted compromise and that the members would vote for the package, even though it might contain provisions they disliked. But the omnibus strategy backfired. Free-Soilers and proslavery Southerners voted down the comprehensive plan.

Fortunately for those who favored a settlement, Senator **Stephen A. Douglas**, a rising Democratic star from Illinois, broke the bill into its parts and skillfully ushered each through Congress. The agreement Douglas won in September 1850 was very much the one Clay had proposed in January. California entered the Union as a free state. New Mexico and Utah became territories where slavery would be decided by popular sovereignty. Texas accepted its boundary with New Mexico and received $10 million from the federal government. Congress ended the slave trade in the District of Columbia but enacted a more stringent fugitive slave law. In September, Millard Fillmore, who had become president when Zachary Taylor died in July, signed into law each bill, collectively known as the **Compromise of 1850** (Map 14.1).

Actually, the Compromise of 1850 was not a true compromise at all. Douglas's parliamentary skill, not a spirit of conciliation, was responsible for the legislative success. Still, the nation breathed a sigh of relief, for the Compromise preserved the Union and peace for the moment. Some recognized, however, that the Compromise scarcely touched the deeper conflict over slavery. Free-Soiler Salmon Chase observed, "The question of slavery in the territories has been avoided. It has not been settled."

REVIEW Why did responses to the Wilmot Proviso split along sectional rather than party lines?

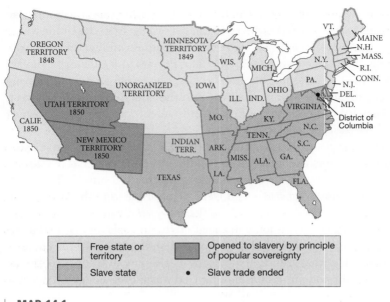

MAP 14.1
The Compromise of 1850
The patched-together sectional agreement was both clumsy and unstable. Few Americans —
in either North or South — supported all five parts of the Compromise.

▶ The Sectional Balance Undone

The Compromise of 1850 began to come apart almost immediately. The thread
that unraveled it was not slavery in the Southwest, the crux of the disagreement,
but runaway slaves in New England, a part of the settlement that had previously
received little attention. Instead of restoring calm, the Compromise brought the
horrors of slavery into the North.

Millions of Northerners who had never seen a runaway slave confronted
slavery in the early 1850s. Harriet Beecher Stowe's *Uncle Tom's Cabin*, a novel
that vividly depicts the brutality of the South's "peculiar institution," aroused
passions so deep that many found goodwill toward white Southerners nearly
impossible. But no groundswell of antislavery sentiment compelled Congress to
reopen the slavery controversy. Politicians did it themselves. Four years after
Congress stitched the sectional compromise together, it ripped the threads out.
With the Kansas-Nebraska Act, it again posed the question of slavery in the
territories, the deadliest of all sectional issues.

The Fugitive Slave Act

The issue of runaway slaves was as old as the Constitution, which contained a
provision for the return of any "person held to service or labor in one state" who
escaped to another. In 1793, a federal law gave muscle to the provision by

authorizing slave owners to enter other states to recapture their slave property. Proclaiming the 1793 law a license to kidnap free blacks, northern states in the 1830s began passing "personal liberty laws" that provided fugitives with some protection.

Some northern communities also formed vigilance committees to help runaways. Each year, a few hundred slaves escaped into free states and found friendly northern "conductors" who put them aboard the **underground railroad**, which was not a railroad at all but a series of secret "stations" (hideouts) on the way to Canada. Harriet Tubman, an escaped slave from Maryland, returned to the South more than a dozen times and guided more than three hundred slaves to freedom in this way.

Furious about northern interference, Southerners in 1850 insisted on the stricter fugitive slave law that was passed as part of the Compromise. According to the **Fugitive Slave Act**, to seize an alleged slave, a slaveholder simply had to appear before a commissioner and swear that the runaway was his. The commissioner earned $10 for every individual returned to slavery but only $5 for those set free. Most galling to Northerners, the law stipulated that all citizens were expected to assist officials in apprehending runaways.

Abolitionist Theodore Parker denounced the law as "a hateful statute of kidnappers." In Boston in February 1851, an angry crowd overpowered federal marshals and snatched a runaway named Shadrach from a courtroom, put him on the underground railroad, and whisked him off to Canada. Three years later, when another Boston crowd rushed the courthouse in a failed attempt to rescue Anthony Burns, who had recently fled slavery in Richmond, a guard was shot dead. Martha Russell, a writer for the antislavery journal *National Era*, was among the angry crowd that watched Burns being escorted to the ship that would return him to Virginia. "Did you ever feel every drop of blood in you boiling and seething, throbbing and burning, until it seemed you should suffocate?" she asked. "I have felt all this today. I have seen that poor slave, Anthony Burns, carried back to slavery!"

To white Southerners, it seemed that fanatics of the "higher law" creed had whipped Northerners into a frenzy of massive resistance. Actually, the overwhelming majority of fugitives claimed by slaveholders were reenslaved peacefully. But brutal enforcement of the unpopular law had a radicalizing effect in the North, particularly in New England. To Southerners it seemed that Northerners had betrayed the Compromise. "The continued existence of the United States as one nation," warned the *Southern Literary Messenger*, "depends upon the full and faithful execution of the Fugitive Slave Bill."

Uncle Tom's Cabin

The spectacle of shackled African Americans being herded south seared the conscience of every Northerner who witnessed such a scene. But even more Northerners were turned against slavery by a novel. **Harriet Beecher Stowe**, a white Northerner who had never set foot on a plantation, made the South's slaves into flesh-and-blood human beings almost more real than life.

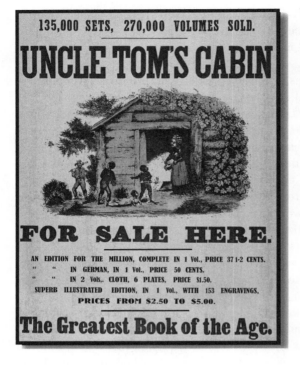

135,000 SETS, 270,000 VOLUMES SOLD.

UNCLE TOM'S CABIN

FOR SALE HERE.

AN EDITION FOR THE MILLION, COMPLETE IN 1 Vol., PRICE 37 1-2 CENTS.
"   "   IN GERMAN, IN 1 Vol., PRICE 50 CENTS.
"   "   IN 2 Vols,. CLOTH, 6 PLATES, PRICE $1.50.
SUPERB ILLUSTRATED EDITION, IN 1 Vol., WITH 153 ENGRAVINGS,
PRICES FROM $2.50 TO $5.00.

The Greatest Book of the Age.

Uncle Tom's Cabin Poster
After Congress passed the Fugitive Slave Act in 1850, Harriet Beecher Stowe's outraged sister-in-law told her, "Now Hattie, if I could use a pen as you can, I would write something that will make this whole nation feel what an accursed thing slavery is." This poster advertising the novel Stowe wrote calls it "The Greatest Book of the Age." The novel's vivid characters gripped readers' imaginations and fueled the growing antislavery crusade. The Granger Collection, NY.

A member of a famous clan of preachers, teachers, and reformers, Stowe despised the slave catchers and wrote to expose the sin of slavery. Published as a book in 1852, *Uncle Tom's Cabin, or Life among the Lowly* became a blockbuster hit, selling 300,000 copies in its first year and more than 2 million copies within ten years. Stowe's characters leaped from the page. Here was the gentle slave Uncle Tom, a Christian saint who forgave those who beat him to death; the courageous slave Eliza, who fled with her child across the frozen Ohio River; and the fiendish overseer Simon Legree, whose Louisiana plantation was a nightmare of torture and death.

Mother of seven children, Stowe aimed her most powerful blows at slavery's destructive impact on the family. Her character Eliza succeeds in keeping her son from being sold away, but other mothers are not so fortunate. When told that her infant has been sold, Lucy drowns herself. Driven half mad by the sale of a son and daughter, Cassy decides "never again [to] let a child live to grow up!" She gives her third child an opiate and watches as "he slept to death."

Northerners shed tears and sang praises to *Uncle Tom's Cabin*. The poet Henry Wadsworth Longfellow judged it "one of the greatest triumphs recorded in literary history." What Northerners accepted as truth, Southerners denounced as slander. The Virginian George F. Holmes proclaimed Stowe a member of the "Woman's Rights" and "Higher Law" schools and dismissed the novel as a work of "intense fanaticism." Although it is impossible to measure precisely the impact of a novel on public opinion, *Uncle Tom's Cabin* clearly helped to crystallize northern sentiment against slavery and to confirm white Southerners' suspicion that they no longer received any sympathy in the free states.

Other writers — ex-slaves who knew life in slave cabins firsthand — also produced stinging indictments of slavery. Solomon Northup's compelling *Twelve*

Years a Slave (1853) sold 27,000 copies in two years, and the powerful *Narrative of the Life of Frederick Douglass, as Told by Himself* (1845) eventually sold more than 30,000 copies. But no work touched the North's conscience as did the novel by a free white woman. A decade after its publication, when Stowe visited Abraham Lincoln at the White House, he reportedly said, "So you are the little woman who wrote the book that made this great war."

The Kansas-Nebraska Act

As the 1852 election approached, the Democrats and Whigs sought to close the sectional rifts that had opened within their parties. For their presidential nominee, the Democrats turned to Franklin Pierce of New Hampshire. Pierce's well-known sympathy with southern views on public issues caused his northern critics to include him among the "**doughfaces**," northern men malleable enough to champion southern causes. The Whigs were less successful in bridging differences. Adopting the formula that had worked in 1848, they chose another Mexican-American War hero, General Winfield Scott of Virginia. But the Whigs' northern and southern factions were hopelessly divided, and the party suffered a humiliating defeat. The Democrat Pierce carried twenty-seven states to Scott's four and won the electoral college vote 254 to 42 (see Map 14.2, page 407). In the afterglow of the Compromise of 1850, the Free-Soil Party lost almost half of the voters who had turned to it in the tumultuous political atmosphere of 1848.

Eager to leave the sectional controversy behind, the new president turned swiftly to foreign expansion. Manifest destiny remained robust. Pierce's major objective was Cuba, which was owned by Spain and in which slavery flourished, but antislavery Northerners blocked Cuba's acquisition to keep more slave territory from entering the Union.

Pierce's fortunes improved in Mexico. In 1853, diplomat James Gadsden negotiated a $10 million purchase of some 30,000 square miles of land in present-day Arizona and New Mexico. The **Gadsden Purchase** stemmed from the dream of a transcontinental railroad to California and Pierce's desire for a southern route through Mexican territory. The booming population of the Pacific coast made it obvious that the vast, loose-jointed Republic needed a railroad to bind it together. Talk of a railroad ignited rivalries in cities from New Orleans to Chicago as they maneuvered to become the eastern terminus. The desire for a transcontinental railroad evolved into a sectional contest, which by the 1850s inevitably involved slavery.

Illinois's Democratic senator Stephen A. Douglas badly wanted the transcontinental railroad for Chicago, and his chairmanship of the Senate Committee on Territories provided him with an opportunity. Any railroad that ran west from Chicago would pass through a region that Congress in 1830 had designated a "permanent" Indian reserve (see chapter 11). Douglas proposed giving this vast area between the Missouri River and the Rocky Mountains an Indian name, Nebraska, and then throwing the Indians out. Once the region achieved territorial status, whites could survey and sell the land, establish a civil government, and build a railroad.

Nebraska lay within the Louisiana Purchase and, according to the Missouri Compromise of 1820, was closed to slavery (see chapter 10). Since Douglas could not count on New England to back western economic development, he needed southern votes to pass his Nebraska legislation. But Southerners had no incentive to create another free territory or to help a northern city win the transcontinental railroad. Southerners, however, agreed to help if Congress organized Nebraska according to popular sovereignty. That meant giving slavery a chance in Nebraska Territory and reopening the dangerous issue of slavery expansion, which Douglas himself had helped to resolve only four years earlier.

In January 1854, Douglas introduced his bill to organize Nebraska Territory, leaving to the settlers themselves the decision about slavery. At southern insistence, and even though he knew it would "raise a hell of a storm," Douglas added an explicit repeal of the Missouri Compromise. Indeed, the Nebraska bill raised a storm of controversy. Free-Soilers branded Douglas's plan "a gross violation of a sacred pledge" and an "atrocious plot" to transform free land into a "dreary region of despotism, inhabited by masters and slaves."

Undaunted, Douglas skillfully shepherded the explosive bill through Congress in May 1854. Nine-tenths of the southern members (Whigs and Democrats) and half of the northern Democrats cast votes in favor of the bill. Like Douglas, most northern supporters believed that popular sovereignty would make Nebraska free territory. Ominously, however, half of the northern Democrats broke with their party and opposed the bill. In its final form, the **Kansas-Nebraska Act** divided the huge territory in two: Nebraska and Kansas. With this act, the government pushed the Plains Indians farther west, making way for farmers and railroads.

> **REVIEW** Why did the Fugitive Slave Act provoke such strong opposition in the North?

▶ Realignment of the Party System

The Kansas-Nebraska Act marked a fateful escalation of the sectional conflict. Douglas's measure had several consequences, none more crucial than the realignment of the nation's political parties. Since the rise of the Whig Party in the early 1830s, Whigs and Democrats had organized and channeled political conflict in the nation. This party system dampened sectionalism and strengthened the Union. To achieve national political power, the Whigs and Democrats had to retain their strength in both North and South. Strong northern and southern wings required that each party compromise and find positions acceptable to both wings.

The Kansas-Nebraska controversy shattered this stabilizing political system. In place of two national parties with bisectional strength, the mid-1850s witnessed the development of one party heavily dominated by one section and another party entirely limited to the other section. Rather than "national" parties, the country had what one critic disdainfully called "geographic" parties. Parties now sharpened ideological and policy differences between the sections and no longer muffled moral issues such as slavery. The new party system also thwarted political compromise and instead promoted political polarization that further jeopardized the Union.

The Old Parties: Whigs and Democrats

As early as the Mexican-American War, members of the Whig Party had clashed over the future of slavery in annexed Mexican lands. By 1852, the Whig Party could please its proslavery southern wing or its antislavery northern wing but not both. The Whigs' miserable showing in the election of 1852 made a despairing New York Whig ask, "Was there ever such a deluge since Noah's time?" It was clear that the Whigs were no longer a strong national party. By 1856, after more than two decades of contesting the Democrats, they were hardly a party at all (Map 14.2).

MAP 14.2
Political Realignment, 1848–1860

In 1848, slavery and sectionalism began taking their toll on the country's party system. The Whig Party was an early casualty. By 1860, national parties — those that contended for votes in both North and South — had been replaced by regional parties.

1848

Candidate	Electoral Vote	Popular Vote	Percent of Popular Vote
Zachary Taylor (Whig)	163	1,360,099	47.4
Lewis Cass (Democrat)	127	1,220,544	42.5
Martin Van Buren (Free-Soil)	0	291,263	10.1

1852

Candidate	Electoral Vote	Popular Vote	Percent of Popular Vote
Franklin Pierce (Democrat)	254	1,601,274	50.9
Winfield Scott (Whig)	42	1,386,580	44.1
John P. Hale (Free-Soil)	0	155,825	5.0

1856

Candidate	Electoral Vote	Popular Vote	Percent of Popular Vote
James Buchanan (Democrat)	174	1,838,169	45.3
John C. Frémont (Republican)	114	1,341,264	33.1
Millard Fillmore (American)	8	874,534	21.6

1860

Candidate	Electoral Vote	Popular Vote	Percent of Popular Vote
Abraham Lincoln (Republican)	180	1,866,452	39.9
John C. Breckinridge (Southern Democrat)	72	847,953	18.1
Stephen A. Douglas (Northern Democrat)	12	1,375,157	29.4
John Bell (Constitutional Union)	39	590,631	12.6

The collapse of the Whig Party left the Democrats as the country's only national party. Although the Democrats were not immune to the disruptive pressures of the territorial question, they discovered in popular sovereignty a doctrine that many Democrats could support. Even so, popular sovereignty very nearly undid the party. When Stephen Douglas applied the doctrine to the part of the Louisiana Purchase where slavery had been barred, he divided northern Democrats and destroyed the dominance of the Democratic Party in the free states. After 1854, even though the Democrats were a southern-dominated party, they remained a national political organization. Gains in the South more than balanced Democratic losses in the North. During the 1850s, Democrats elected two presidents and won majorities in Congress in almost every election.

The breakup of the Whigs and the disaffection of significant numbers of northern Democrats set many Americans politically adrift. As they searched for new political harbors, Americans found that the death of the old party system created a multitude of fresh political alternatives.

The New Parties: Know-Nothings and Republicans

Dozens of new political organizations vied for voters' attention. Out of the confusion, two emerged as true contenders. One grew out of the slavery controversy, a coalition of indignant antislavery Northerners. The other arose from an entirely different split in American society, between Roman Catholic immigrants and native Protestants.

The tidal wave of immigrants that broke over America from 1845 to 1855 produced a nasty backlash among Protestant Americans, who believed that the American Republic was about to drown in a sea of Roman Catholics from Ireland and Germany. Most immigrants became Democrats because they perceived that party as more tolerant of newcomers than were the Whigs. But in the 1850s, they met sharp political opposition when nativists (individuals who were anti-immigrant) began to organize, first into secret fraternal societies and then in 1854 into a political party. Recruits swore never to vote for either foreign-born or Roman Catholic candidates and not to reveal any information about the organization. When questioned, they said, "I know nothing." Officially, they were the American Party, but most Americans called them **Know-Nothings**.

The Know-Nothings exploded onto the political stage in 1854 and 1855 with a series of dazzling successes. They captured state legislatures in the Northeast, West, and South and claimed dozens of seats in Congress. Their greatest triumph came in Massachusetts, a favorite destination for Irish immigrants. Know-Nothings elected the Massachusetts governor, all of the state senators, all but two of the state representatives, and all of the congressmen. Members of the Democratic and Whig parties described the phenomenal success of the Know-Nothings as a "tornado," a "hurricane," and "a freak of political insanity." By 1855, an observer might reasonably have concluded that the Know-Nothings had emerged as the successor to the Whigs.

The Know-Nothings were not the only new party making noise, however. One of the new antislavery organizations provoked by the Kansas-Nebraska Act called itself the **Republican Party**. The Republicans attempted to unite all those who opposed the extension of slavery into any territory of the United States, including Whigs, Free-Soilers, anti-Nebraska Democrats, and even Know-Nothings.

The Republican creed tapped into the basic beliefs and values of Northerners. Slavery, the Republicans believed, degraded the dignity of white labor by associating work with blacks and servility. As evidence, they pointed to the South, where, one Republican claimed, three-quarters of whites "retire to the outskirts of civilization, where they live a semi-savage life, sinking deeper and more hopelessly into barbarism with every succeeding generation." Republicans warned that the insatiable slaveholders of the South, whom antislavery Northerners called the "Slave Power," were conspiring through their control of the Democratic Party to expand slavery, subvert liberty, and undermine the Constitution.

Only if slavery was restricted to the South, Republicans believed, could the system of free labor flourish elsewhere. In the North, one Republican declared in 1854, "every man holds his fortune in his own right arm; and his position in society, in life, is to be tested by his own individual character" (see chapter 12). Without slavery, western territories would provide vast economic opportunity for free men. Powerful images of liberty and opportunity attracted a wide range of Northerners to the Republican cause.

Women as well as men rushed to the new Republican Party. Indeed, three women helped found the party in Ripon, Wisconsin, in 1854. Although they could not vote before the Civil War and suffered from a raft of other legal handicaps, women nevertheless participated in partisan politics by writing campaign literature, marching in parades, giving speeches, and lobbying voters. Women's antislavery fervor attracted them to the Republican Party, and participation in party politics in turn nurtured the woman's rights movement. Susan B. Anthony, who attended Republican meetings throughout the 1850s, found that her political activity made her disfranchisement all the more galling. She and other women in the North worked on behalf of antislavery and to secure both woman suffrage and the right of married women to control their own property.

The Election of 1856

The election of 1856 revealed that the Republicans had become the Democrats' main challenger, and slavery in the territories, not nativism, was the election's principal issue. When the Know-Nothings insisted on a platform that endorsed the Kansas-Nebraska Act, most of the Northerners walked out, and the party came apart. The few Know-Nothings who remained nominated ex-president Millard Fillmore.

The Republicans adopted a platform that focused almost exclusively on "making every territory free." When they labeled slavery a "relic of barbarism," they signaled that they had written off the South. For president, they nominated the dashing soldier and California adventurer **John C. Frémont**, "Pathfinder of the West." Frémont lacked political credentials, but his wife, **Jessie Frémont**, the daughter of Senator Thomas Hart Benton of Missouri, knew the political map as well as her husband knew the western trails. Though careful to maintain a proper public

John and Jessie Frémont Poster
The election of 1856 marked the first time a candidate's wife appeared on campaign items. In this poster, Jessie Benton Frémont rides a spirited horse alongside her husband, John C. Frémont, the Republican Party's presidential nominee. Jessie helped plan her husband's campaign, coauthored his election biography, and drew northern women into political activity as never before. "What a shame that women can't vote!" declared abolitionist Lydia Maria Child. "We'd carry 'our Jessie' into the White House on our shoulders, wouldn't we." Critics of Jessie's violation of women's traditional sphere ridiculed both Frémonts. A San Francisco man pronounced Jessie "the better man of the two." Museum of American Political Life.

image, the vivacious young mother and antislavery zealot helped attract voters and draw women into politics.

The Democrats, successful in 1852 in bridging sectional differences by nominating a northern man with southern principles, chose another "doughface," James Buchanan of Pennsylvania. They took refuge in the ambiguity of popular sovereignty and portrayed the Republicans as extremists ("Black Republican Abolitionists") whose support for the Wilmot Proviso risked pushing the South out of the Union.

The Democratic strategy carried the day for Buchanan, but Frémont did astonishingly well. Buchanan won 174 electoral votes against Frémont's 114 and Fillmore's 8 (see Map 14.2, page 407). Campaigning under the banner "Free soil, Free men, Frémont," the Republican carried all but five of the states north of the Mason-Dixon line. The election made clear that the Whigs had disintegrated, the Know-Nothings would not ride nativism to national power, and the Democrats were badly strained. But the big news was what the press called the "glorious defeat" of the Republicans. Despite being a brand-new party and purely sectional, the Republicans had seriously challenged the Democrats for national power. Sectionalism had fashioned a new party system, one that spelled danger for the Republic. Indeed, war had already broken out between proslavery and antislavery forces in distant Kansas Territory.

REVIEW Why did the Whig Party disintegrate in the 1850s?

▶ Freedom under Siege

Events in Kansas Territory in the mid-1850s provided the young Republican organization with an enormous boost and help explain its strong showing in the election of 1856. Republicans organized around the premise that the slaveholding South provided a profound threat to "free soil, free labor, and free men," and now Kansas reeled with violence that Republicans argued was southern in origin. Kansas, Republicans claimed, opened a window to southern values and intentions. Republicans also pointed to the brutal beating by a Southerner of a respected northern senator on the floor of Congress. Even the Supreme Court, in the Republicans' view, reflected the South's drive toward tyranny and minority rule. Then, in 1858, the issues dividing North and South received an extraordinary airing in a senatorial contest in Illinois, when the nation's foremost Democrat debated a resourceful Republican.

"Bleeding Kansas"

Three days after the House of Representatives approved the Kansas-Nebraska Act in 1854, Senator William H. Seward of New York boldly challenged the South. "Come on then, Gentlemen of the Slave States," he cried, "since there is no escaping your challenge, I accept it in behalf of the cause of freedom. We will engage in competition for the virgin soil of Kansas, and God give the victory to the side which is stronger in numbers as it is in right." Because of Stephen Douglas, popular sovereignty would determine whether Kansas became slave or free. No one really expected New Mexico and Utah, with their harsh landscapes, to become slave states when Congress instituted popular sovereignty there in 1850, but many believed that Kansas could go either way. Free-state and slave-state settlers each sought a majority at the ballot box, claimed God's blessing, and kept their rifles ready.

In both North and South, emigrant aid societies sprang up to promote settlement from free states or slave states. The most famous, the New England Emigrant Aid Company, sponsored some 1,240 settlers in 1854 and 1855. Tiny rural communities from Virginia to Texas raised money to support proslavery settlers.

Missourians, already bordered on the east by the free state of Illinois and on the north by the free state of Iowa, especially thought it important to secure Kansas for slavery. Thousands of rough frontiersmen, egged on by Missouri senator David Rice Atchison, invaded Kansas. "There are eleven hundred coming over from Platte County to vote," Atchison reported, "and if that ain't enough we can send five thousand — enough to kill every God-damned abolitionist in the Territory." Not surprisingly, proslavery candidates swept the territorial elections in November 1854. When Kansas's first territorial legislature met, it enacted a raft of proslavery laws. Antislavery men, for example, were barred from holding office or serving on juries. Ever-pliant President Pierce endorsed the work of the fraudulently elected legislature. Free-soil Kansans did not. They elected their own legislature, which promptly banned both slaves and free blacks from the territory. Organized into two rival governments and armed to the teeth, Kansans verged on civil war.

Fighting broke out on the morning of May 21, 1856, when several hundred proslavery men raided the town of Lawrence, the center of free-state settlement. Only one man died, but the "Sack of Lawrence," as free-soil forces called it, inflamed northern opinion. Elsewhere in Kansas, news of events in Lawrence provoked **John Brown**, a free-soil settler, to announce that "it was better that a score of bad men should die than that one man who came here to make Kansas a Free State should be driven out" and to lead the posse that massacred five allegedly proslavery settlers along Pottawatomie Creek (see pages 395–397). After that, guerrilla war engulfed the territory.

Just as **"Bleeding Kansas"** gave the fledgling Republican Party fresh ammunition for its battle against the Slave Power, so too did an event that occurred in the national capital. In May 1856, Senator Charles Sumner of Massachusetts delivered a speech titled "The Crime against Kansas," which included a scalding personal attack on South Carolina senator Andrew P. Butler. Sumner described Butler as a "Don Quixote" who had taken as his mistress "the harlot, slavery."

Preston Brooks, a young South Carolina member of the House and a kinsman of Butler's, felt compelled to defend the honor of both his aged relative and his state. On May 22, Brooks entered the Senate, where he found Sumner working at his desk. He beat Sumner over the head with his cane until Sumner lay bleeding and unconscious on the floor. Brooks resigned his seat in the House, only to be promptly reelected. In the North, the southern hero became an archvillain. Like "Bleeding Kansas," "Bleeding Sumner" provided the Republican Party with a potent symbol of the South's "twisted and violent civilization."

The *Dred Scott* Decision

Political debate over slavery in the territories became so heated in part because the Constitution lacked precision on the issue. In 1857, in the case of *Dred Scott v. Sandford*, the Supreme Court announced its understanding of the meaning of the Constitution regarding slavery in the territories. The Court's decision demonstrated that it enjoyed no special immunity from the sectional and partisan passions that were convulsing the land.

In 1833, an army doctor bought the slave Dred Scott in St. Louis, Missouri, and took him as his personal servant to Fort Armstrong, Illinois, and then to Fort Snelling in Wisconsin Territory. Back in St. Louis in 1846, Scott, with the help of white friends, sued to prove that he and his family were legally entitled to their freedom. Scott based his claim on his travels and residences. He argued that living in Illinois, a free state, and Wisconsin, a free territory, had made his family free and that they remained free even after returning to Missouri, a slave state.

In 1857, the U.S. Supreme Court ruled in the case. Chief Justice **Roger B. Taney**, who hated Republicans and detested racial equality, wrote the Court's decision. First, the Court ruled in the ***Dred Scott* decision** that Scott could not legally claim violation of his constitutional rights because he was not a citizen of the United States. When the Constitution was written, Taney said, blacks "were regarded as beings of an inferior order . . . so far inferior, that they had no rights which the white man was bound to respect." Second, the laws of Dred Scott's home state, Missouri, determined his status, and thus his travels in free areas did not make him free. Third, Congress's power to make "all needful rules and regulations" for the territories did not include the right to prohibit slavery. The Court explicitly declared the Missouri Compromise unconstitutional, even though it had already been voided by the Kansas-Nebraska Act.

The Taney Court's extreme proslavery decision outraged Republicans. By denying the federal government the right to exclude slavery in the territories, it cut the legs out from under the Republican Party. Moreover, as the *New York Tribune* lamented, the decision cleared the way for "all our Territories . . . to be ripened into Slave States." Particularly frightening to African Americans in the North was the Court's declaration that free blacks were not citizens and had no rights.

The Republican rebuttal to the *Dred Scott* ruling relied heavily on the dissenting opinion of Justice Benjamin R. Curtis. Scott *was* a citizen of the United States, Curtis argued. At the time of the writing of the Constitution, free black men could vote in five states and participated in the ratification process. Scott *was* free. Because slavery was prohibited in Wisconsin, the "involuntary servitude of a slave, coming into the Territory with his master, should cease to exist." The Missouri Compromise

Portrait of Dred Scott, 1857
The *Dred Scott* case aroused enormous curiosity about the man suing for freedom. This portrait of Dred Scott was painted in 1857, the year of the Supreme Court's decision. Although the Court rejected his suit, he gained his freedom in May 1857 when a white man purchased and freed Scott and his family. Scott died of tuberculosis in September 1858. Collection of the New-York Historical Society.

was constitutional. The Founders had meant exactly what they said: Congress had the power to make "*all* needful rules and regulations" for the territories, including barring slavery.

In a seven-to-two decision, the Court rejected Curtis's arguments, thereby validating an extreme statement of the South's territorial rights. John C. Calhoun's claim that Congress had no authority to exclude slavery became the law of the land. White Southerners cheered, but the *Dred Scott* decision actually strengthened the young Republican Party. Indeed, that "outrageous" decision, one Republican argued, was "the best thing that could have happened," for it provided dramatic evidence of the Republicans' claim that a hostile "Slave Power" conspired against northern liberties.

Prairie Republican: Abraham Lincoln

By reigniting the sectional flames, the *Dred Scott* case provided Republican politicians with fresh challenges and fresh opportunities. **Abraham Lincoln** had long since put behind him his hardscrabble log-cabin beginnings in Kentucky and Indiana. He lived in a fine two-story house in Springfield, Illinois, and earned good money as a lawyer. The law provided Lincoln's living, but politics was his life. "His ambition was a little engine that knew no rest," observed his law partner William Herndon. Lincoln had served as a Whig in the Illinois state legislature and in the House of Representatives, but he had not held public office since 1849.

The disintegration of the Whig Party meant that Lincoln had no political home, but the Know-Nothings held no appeal. "How can anyone who abhors the oppression of negroes be in favor of degrading classes of white people?" he asked in 1855. "As a nation, we began by declaring that 'all men are created equal.' We now practically read it 'all men are created equal, except negroes.' When the Know-Nothings get control, it will read 'All men are created equal, except Negroes and foreigners and Catholics.'"

Convinced that slavery was a "monstrous injustice," a "great moral wrong," and an "unqualified evil to the negro, the white man, and the State," Lincoln gravitated toward the Republican Party. He condemned Douglas's Kansas-Nebraska Act of 1854 for giving slavery a new life and in 1856 joined the Republican Party. He accepted that the Constitution permitted slavery in those states where it existed, but he believed that Congress could contain its spread. Penned in, Lincoln believed, plantation slavery would wither, and in time Southerners would end slavery themselves.

Lincoln held what were, for his times, moderate racial views. Although he denounced slavery and defended black humanity, he also viewed black equality as impractical and unachievable. "Negroes have natural rights . . . as other men have," he said, "although they cannot enjoy them here." Insurmountable white prejudice made it impossible to extend full citizenship to blacks in America, he believed. Freeing blacks and allowing them to remain in this country would lead to a race war. In Lincoln's mind, social stability and black progress required that slavery end and that blacks leave the country.

Lincoln envisioned the western territories as "places for poor people to go to, and better their conditions." The "*free* labor system," he said, "opens the way for all — gives hope to all, and energy, and progress, and improvement of condition to all." But slavery's expansion threatened free men's basic right to succeed. The Kansas-Nebraska Act and the *Dred Scott* decision persuaded him that slaveholders were engaged in a dangerous conspiracy to nationalize slavery. The next step, Lincoln warned, would be "another Supreme Court decision, declaring that the Constitution of the United States does not permit a State to exclude slavery from its limits." Unless the citizens of Illinois woke up, he warned, the Supreme Court would make "Illinois a slave State."

In Lincoln's view, the nation could not "endure, permanently half slave and half free." Either opponents of slavery would arrest its spread and place it on the "course of ultimate extinction," or its advocates would see that it became legal in "*all* the States, *old* as well as *new* — *North* as well as *South.*" Lincoln's convictions that slavery was wrong and that Congress must stop its spread formed the core of the Republican ideology. Lincoln so impressed his fellow Republicans in Illinois that in 1858 they chose him to challenge the nation's premier Democrat, who was seeking reelection to the U.S. Senate.

The Lincoln-Douglas Debates

When Stephen Douglas learned that the Republican Abraham Lincoln would be his opponent for the Senate, he observed: "He is the strong man of the party — full of wit, facts, dates — and the best stump speaker, with his droll ways and dry jokes, in the West. He is as honest as he is shrewd, and if I beat him my victory will be hardly won."

Not only did Douglas have to contend with a formidable foe, but he also carried the weight of a burden not of his own making. The previous year, the nation's economy had experienced a sharp downturn. Prices had plummeted, thousands of businesses had failed, and many were unemployed. As a Democrat, Douglas had to go before the voters as a member of the party whose policies stood accused of causing the panic of 1857.

Douglas's response to another crisis in 1857, however, helped shore up his standing in Illinois. Proslavery forces in Kansas met in the town of Lecompton, drafted a proslavery constitution, and applied for statehood. Everyone knew that free-soilers outnumbered proslavery settlers, but President Buchanan instructed Congress to admit Kansas as the sixteenth slave state. Republicans denounced the "Lecompton swindle." Senator Douglas broke with the Democratic administration and denounced the **Lecompton constitution**; Congress killed the Lecompton bill. (When Kansans reconsidered the Lecompton constitution in an honest election, they rejected it six to one. Kansas entered the Union in 1861 as a free state.) By denouncing the fraudulent proslavery constitution, Douglas declared his independence from the South and, he hoped, made himself acceptable at home.

A relative unknown and a decided underdog in the Illinois election, Lincoln challenged Douglas to debate him face-to-face. The two met in seven communities for what would become a legendary series of debates. To the thousands who stood straining to see and hear, they must have seemed an odd pair. Douglas was five feet four inches tall, broad, and stocky; Lincoln was six feet four inches tall, angular, and lean. Douglas was in perpetual motion, darting across the platform, shouting, and jabbing the air; Lincoln stood still and spoke deliberately. Douglas wore the latest fashions and dazzled audiences with his flashy vests; Lincoln wore good suits but managed to look rumpled anyway.

The two men debated the crucial issues of the age — slavery and freedom. They showed the citizens of Illinois (and much of the nation because of widespread press coverage) the difference between an anti-Lecompton Democrat and a true Republican. Lincoln badgered Douglas with the question of whether he favored the spread of slavery. He tried to force Douglas into the damaging admission that the Supreme Court had repudiated Douglas's own territorial solution, popular sovereignty. At Freeport, Illinois, Douglas admitted that settlers could not now pass legislation barring slavery, but he argued that they could ban slavery just as effectively by not passing protective laws, such as those found in slave states. Southerners condemned Douglas's "Freeport Doctrine" and charged him with trying to steal the victory they had gained with the *Dred Scott* decision. Lincoln chastised his opponent for his "don't care" attitude about slavery, for "blowing out the moral lights around us."

Douglas worked the racial issue. He called Lincoln an abolitionist and an egalitarian enamored of "our colored brethren." Put on the defensive, Lincoln reaffirmed his faith in white rule: "I will say, then, that I am not, nor ever have been, in favor of bringing about in any way the social and political equality of the white and black race." But unlike Douglas, who told racist jokes, Lincoln was no negrophobe. He tried to steer the debate back to what he considered the true issue: the morality and future of slavery. "Slavery is wrong," Lincoln repeated, because "a man has the right to the fruits of his own labor."

As Douglas predicted, the election was hard-fought and closely contested. Until the adoption of the Seventeenth Amendment in 1911, citizens voted for state legislators, who in turn selected U.S. senators. Since Democrats won a slight majority in the Illinois legislature, the members returned Douglas to the Senate. But the **Lincoln-Douglas debates** thrust Lincoln, the prairie Republican, into the national spotlight.

> **REVIEW** Why did the *Dred Scott* decision strengthen northern suspicions of a "Slave Power" conspiracy?

▶ The Union Collapses

Lincoln's thesis that the "slavocracy" conspired to make slavery a national institution now seems exaggerated. But from the northern perspective, the Kansas-Nebraska Act, the Brooks-Sumner affair, the *Dred Scott* decision, and the Lecompton constitution amounted to irrefutable evidence of the South's aggressiveness. White Southerners, of course, saw things differently. They were the ones who were under siege, they declared. Signs were everywhere that the North planned to use its numerical advantage to attack slavery, and not just in the territories. Republicans had made it clear that they were unwilling to accept the *Dred Scott* ruling as the last word on the issue of slavery expansion. And John Brown's attempt to incite a slave insurrection in Virginia in 1859 proved that Northerners were unwilling to be bound by Christian decency and reverence for life.

Threats of secession increasingly laced the sectional debate. Talk of leaving the Union had been heard for years, but until the final crisis, Southerners had used secession as a ploy to gain concessions within the Union, not to destroy it. Then the 1850s delivered powerful blows to Southerners' confidence that they could remain in the Union and protect slavery. When the Republican Party won the White House in 1860, many Southerners concluded that they would have to leave.

The Aftermath of John Brown's Raid

For his attack on Harpers Ferry, John Brown stood trial for treason, murder, and incitement of slave insurrection. "To hang a fanatic is to make a martyr of him and fledge another brood of the same sort," cautioned one newspaper, but on December 2, 1859, Virginia executed Brown. In life, he was a ne'er-do-well, but, as the poet Stephen Vincent Benét observed, "he knew how to die." Brown told his wife that he was "determined to make the utmost possible out of a defeat." He told the court: "If it is deemed necessary that I should forfeit my life for the furtherance of the ends of justice, and mingle my blood further with the blood of . . . millions in this slave country whose rights are disregarded by wicked, cruel, and unjust enactments, I say, let it be done."

After Brown's execution, Americans across the land contemplated the meaning of his life and death. Northern denunciation of Brown as a dangerous fanatic gave way to grudging respect. Some even celebrated his "splendid martyrdom." Ralph Waldo Emerson likened Brown to Christ when he declared that Brown made "the gallows as glorious as the cross." Some abolitionists explicitly endorsed Brown's resort to violence. William Lloyd Garrison, who usually professed pacifism, announced, "I am prepared to say 'success to every slave insurrection at the South and in every country.'"

Most Northerners did not advocate bloody rebellion, however. Like Lincoln, they concluded that Brown's noble antislavery ideals could not "excuse violence, bloodshed, and treason." Still, when northern churches marked John Brown's hanging with tolling bells, hymns, and prayer vigils, white Southerners contemplated what they had in common with people who "regard John Brown as a martyr and a Christian hero, rather than a murderer and robber." Georgia senator Robert Toombs announced solemnly that Southerners must "never permit this Federal government to pass into the traitorous hands of the black Republican party." At that moment, the presidential election was only months away.

Republican Victory in 1860

Events between Brown's hanging and the presidential election only heightened sectional hostility. Across the South, whites feverishly searched for other John Browns and whipped and sometimes lynched those they suspected. A southern business convention meeting in Nashville shocked the nation (including many Southerners) by calling for the reopening of the African slave trade, closed since 1808 and considered an abomination almost everywhere in the Western world. Chief Justice Taney provoked new indignation when he ruled northern personal liberty laws unconstitutional and reaffirmed the Fugitive Slave Act. Then, the normally routine business of electing a Speaker of the House threatened to turn bloody as Democrats and Republicans battled over control of the office. After two months of acrimonious debate, one congressman observed that the "only persons who do not have a revolver and a knife are those who have two revolvers." A last-minute compromise may have averted a shootout.

When the Democrats converged on Charleston for their convention in April 1860, fire-eating Southerners denounced Stephen Douglas and demanded a platform that featured a federal slave code for the territories, a goal of extreme proslavery Southerners for years. Not only was Congress powerless to block slavery's spread, they argued, but it was obligated to offer slavery all "needful protection." But northern Democrats knew that northern voters would not stomach a federal slave code. When the delegates approved a platform with popular sovereignty, representatives from the entire Lower South and Arkansas stomped out of the convention. The remaining Democrats adjourned to meet a few weeks later in Baltimore, where they nominated Douglas for president.

Bolting southern Democrats immediately reconvened in Richmond, where they approved a platform with a federal slave code and nominated their own candidate for president: John C. Breckinridge of Kentucky, who was serving as vice president under Buchanan. Southern moderates, however, refused to support Breckinridge. They formed the **Constitutional Union Party** to provide voters with a Unionist choice. Instead of adopting a platform and confronting the slavery question, the Constitutional Union Party merely approved a vague resolution pledging "to recognize no political principle other than *the Constitution . . . the Union . . . and the Enforcement of the Laws.*" For president, they nominated former senator John Bell of Tennessee.

The Republicans smelled victory, but they estimated that they needed to carry nearly all the free states to win. To make their party more appealing, they expanded their platform beyond antislavery. They hoped that free homesteads, a protective tariff, a transcontinental railroad, and a guarantee of immigrant political rights would provide an economic and social agenda broad enough to unify the North. While reasserting their commitment to stop the spread of slavery, they also denounced John Brown's raid as "among the gravest of crimes" and confirmed the security of slavery in the South.

Republicans cast about for a moderate candidate to go with their evenhanded platform. The foremost Republican, William H. Seward, had made enemies with his radical "higher law" doctrine, which claimed that there was a higher moral law than the Constitution, and with his "irrepressible conflict" speech, in which he declared that North and South were fated to collide. Lincoln, however, since bursting onto the national scene in 1858 had demonstrated his clear purpose, good judgment, and solid Republican credentials. That, and his residence in Illinois, a

Abraham Lincoln
Lincoln actively sought the Republican presidential nomination in 1860. While in New York City to give a political address, he had his photograph taken by Mathew Brady. "While I was there I was taken to one of the places where they get up such things," Lincoln explained, sounding more innocent than he was, "and I suppose they got my shadow, and can multiply copies indefinitely." Multiply they did. Later, Lincoln credited his victory to his New York speech and to this dignified photograph by Brady. The Lincoln Museum, Fort Wayne, Indiana, #0-17.

crucial state, made him attractive to the party. On the third ballot, the delegates chose Lincoln. Defeated by Douglas in a state contest less than two years earlier, Lincoln now stood ready to take him on for the presidency.

The election of 1860 was like none other in American politics. It took place in the midst of the nation's severest crisis. Four major candidates crowded the presidential field. Rather than a four-cornered contest, however, the election broke into two contests, each with two candidates. In the North, Lincoln faced Douglas; in the South, Breckinridge confronted Bell. So outrageous did Southerners consider the Republican Party that they did not even permit Lincoln's name to appear on the ballot in ten of the fifteen slave states.

An unprecedented number of voters cast their ballots on November 6, 1860. Approximately 82 percent of eligible northern men and 70 percent of eligible southern men went to the polls. Lincoln swept all of the eighteen free states except New Jersey, which split its electoral votes between him and Douglas. Although Lincoln received only 39 percent of the popular vote, he won easily in the electoral college with 180 votes, 28 more than he needed for victory. Lincoln did not win because his opposition was splintered. Even if the votes of his three opponents had been combined, Lincoln still would have won. He won because his votes were concentrated in the free states, which contained a majority of electoral votes. Ominously, however, Breckinridge, running on a southern-rights platform, won the entire Lower South, plus Delaware, Maryland, and North Carolina.

Secession Winter

Across the country, telegraphs tapped out the news of Lincoln's victory. Antislavery advocate Charles Francis Adams of Massachusetts could hardly believe the results: "There is now scarcely a shadow of a doubt that the great revolution has actually taken place, and that the country has once and for all thrown off the domination of the Slaveholders." What Adams celebrated as liberation, anxious white Southerners feared was the onset of Republican tyranny. Throughout the South, they began debating what to do. Although Breckinridge had carried the South, a vote for "southern rights" was not necessarily a vote for secession. Besides, slightly more than half of the Southerners who had voted had cast ballots for Douglas and Bell, two stout defenders of the Union.

Southern Unionists tried to calm the fears that Lincoln's election triggered. Let the dust settle, they pleaded. Former congressman Alexander Stephens of Georgia asked what Lincoln had done to justify something as extreme as secession. Had he not promised to respect slavery where it existed? In Stephens's judgment, the fire-eater cure would be worse than the Republican disease. Secession might lead to war, which would loosen the hinges of southern society and possibly even open the door to slave insurrection. "Revolutions are much easier started than controlled," he warned. "I consider slavery much more secure in the Union than out of it."

Secessionists emphasized the dangers of delay. "Mr. Lincoln and his party assert that this doctrine of equality applies to the negro," former Georgia governor Howell Cobb declared, "and necessarily there can exist no such thing as property in our equals." Lincoln's election without a single electoral vote from the South meant that Southerners were no longer able to defend themselves within the Union, Cobb argued. Why wait, he asked, for Lincoln to appoint abolitionist judges, marshals, customs collectors, and postmasters to federal posts throughout the South? As for war, there would be none. The Union was a voluntary compact, and Lincoln would not coerce patriotism. If Northerners did resist with force, secessionists argued, one southern woodsman could whip five of Lincoln's greasy mechanics.

For all their differences, southern whites agreed that they had to defend slavery. John Smith Preston of South Carolina spoke for the overwhelming majority when he declared, "The South cannot exist without slavery." They disagreed about whether the mere presence of a Republican in the White House made it necessary to exercise what they considered a legitimate right to secede.

The debate about what to do was briefest in South Carolina; it seceded from the Union on December 20, 1860. By February 1861, the six other Lower South states marched in South Carolina's footsteps. In some states, the vote was close. In general, slaveholders spearheaded secession, while nonslaveholders in the Piedmont and mountain counties, where slaves were relatively few, displayed the greatest attachment to the Union. In February, representatives from South Carolina, Georgia, Florida, Alabama, Mississippi, Louisiana, and Texas met in Montgomery, Alabama, where they celebrated the birth of the **Confederate States of America**. Mississippi senator Jefferson Davis became president, and Alexander Stephens of Georgia, who had spoken so eloquently about the dangers of revolution, became vice president. In March 1861, Stephens declared that the Confederacy's "cornerstone" was "the great truth that the negro is not equal to the white man; that slavery, subordination to the superior race, is his natural and moral condition."

Lincoln's election had split the Union. Now secession split the South. Seven slave states seceded during the winter, but the eight slave states of the Upper South rejected secession, at least for the moment. The Upper South had a smaller stake in slavery. Barely half as many white families in the Upper South held slaves (21 percent) as in the Lower South (37 percent). Slaves represented twice as large a percentage of the population in the Lower South (48 percent) as in the Upper South (23 percent). Consequently, whites in the Upper South had fewer fears that Republican ascendancy meant economic catastrophe, social chaos, and racial war. Lincoln would need to do more than just be elected to provoke them into secession.

The nation had to wait until March 4, 1861, when Lincoln took office, to see what he would do. (Presidents-elect waited four months to take office until 1933, when the Twentieth Amendment to the Constitution shifted the inauguration to January 20.) After his election, Lincoln chose to stay in Springfield and to say nothing. "Lame-duck" president James Buchanan sat in Washington and did nothing. Buchanan demonstrated, William H. Seward said mockingly, that "it is the President's duty to enforce the laws, unless somebody opposes him." In Congress, efforts at cobbling together a peace-saving compromise came to nothing.

Lincoln began his inaugural address with reassurances to the South. He had "no lawful right" to interfere with slavery where it existed, he declared again, adding for emphasis that he had "no inclination to do so." Conciliatory about slavery, Lincoln proved inflexible about the Union. The Union, he declared, was "perpetual." Secession was "anarchy" and "legally void." The Constitution required him to execute the law "in all the States." The decision for civil war or peace rested in the South's hands, Lincoln said: "You can have no conflict, without being yourselves the aggressors. *You* have no oath registered in Heaven to destroy the government, while I shall have the most solemn one to 'preserve, protect, and defend' it." What Confederates in Charleston held in their hands at that very moment were the cords for firing the cannons aimed at the federal garrison at Fort Sumter.

REVIEW   Why did some southern states secede immediately after Lincoln's election?

▶ Conclusion: Slavery, Free Labor, and the Failure of Political Compromise

As their economies, societies, and cultures diverged in the nineteenth century, Northerners and Southerners expressed different concepts of the American promise and the place of slavery within it. Their differences crystallized into political form in 1846 when David Wilmot proposed banning slavery in any territory won in the Mexican-American War. "As if by magic," a Boston newspaper observed, "it brought to a head the great question that is about to divide the American people." Discovery of gold and other precious metals in the West added urgency to the controversy over slavery in the territories. Congress attempted to address the issue with the Compromise of 1850, but the Fugitive Slave Act and the publication of *Uncle Tom's Cabin* hardened northern sentiments against slavery and confirmed southern suspicions of northern ill will. The bloody violence that erupted in Kansas in 1856 and the incendiary *Dred Scott* decision in 1857 further eroded hope for a solution to this momentous question.

During the extended crisis of the Union that stretched from 1846 to 1861, the slavery question intertwined with national politics. The traditional Whig and Democratic parties struggled to hold together as new parties, most notably the Republican Party, emerged. Politicians fixed their attention on the expansion of slavery, but from the beginning the nation recognized that the controversy had less to do with slavery in the territories than with the future of slavery in America.

For more than seventy years, statesmen had found compromises that accepted slavery and preserved the Union. But as each section grew increasingly committed to its labor system and the promise it offered, Americans discovered that accommodation had limits. In 1859, John Brown's militant antislavery pushed white Southerners to the edge. In 1860, Lincoln's election convinced whites in the Lower South that slavery and the society they had built on it were at risk in the Union, and they seceded. In his inaugural address, Lincoln pleaded, "We are not enemies but friends. We must not be enemies." By then, however, seven southern states had ceased to sing what he called "the chorus of the Union." It remained to be seen whether disunion would mean war.

Reviewing Chapter 14

REVIEW QUESTIONS

1. Why did responses to the Wilmot Proviso split along sectional rather than party lines? (pp. 397–401)

2. Why did the Fugitive Slave Act provoke such strong opposition in the North? (pp. 402–406)

3. Why did the Whig Party disintegrate in the 1850s? (pp. 406–411)

4. Why did the *Dred Scott* decision strengthen northern suspicions of a "Slave Power" conspiracy? (pp. 411–416)

5. Why did some southern states secede immediately after Lincoln's election? (pp. 416–421)

MAKING CONNECTIONS

1. The process of compromise that had successfully contained tensions between slave and free states since the nation's founding collapsed with secession. Why did compromise fail at this moment? In your answer, address specific political conflicts and attempts to solve them between 1846 and 1861.

2. In the 1850s, many Americans supported popular sovereignty as the best solution to the explosive question of slavery in the western territories. Why was this solution so popular, and why did it ultimately prove inadequate? In your answer, be sure to address popular sovereignty's varied critics as well as its champions.

3. In the 1840s and 1850s, the United States witnessed the realignment of its long-standing two-party system. Why did the old system fall apart, what emerged to take its place, and how did this process contribute to the coming of the Civil War?

4. Abraham Lincoln believed that he had staked out a moderate position on the question of slavery, avoiding the extremes of immediate abolitionism and calls for the unlimited protection of slavery. Why, then, did some southern states determine that his election necessitated the radical act of secession?

LINKING TO THE PAST

1. How did social and economic developments in the South during the first half of the nineteenth century influence the decisions that southern politicians made in the 1840s and 1850s? (See chapter 13.)

2. How did the policies of the Republican Party reflect the free-labor ideals of the North? (See chapter 12.)

TIMELINE 1820–1861

1820 • Missouri Compromise.

1846 • Wilmot Proviso introduced in Congress.

1847 • Wilmot Proviso defeated in Senate.
• Compromise of "popular sovereignty" offered.

1848 • Free-Soil Party founded.
• Whig Zachary Taylor elected president.

1849 • California gold rush.

1850 • Taylor dies; Vice President Millard Fillmore becomes president.
• Compromise of 1850 becomes law.

1852 • *Uncle Tom's Cabin* published.
• Democrat Franklin Pierce elected president.

1853 • Gadsden Purchase.

1854 • American (Know-Nothing) Party emerges.
• Kansas-Nebraska Act.
• Republican Party founded.

1856 • "Bleeding Kansas."
• "Sack of Lawrence."
• Preston Brooks canes Charles Sumner.
• Pottawatomie massacre.
• Democrat James Buchanan elected president.

1857 • *Dred Scott* decision.
• Congress rejects Lecompton constitution.
• Panic of 1857.

1858 • Abraham Lincoln and Stephen A. Douglas debate slavery; Douglas wins Senate seat.

1859 • John Brown raids Harpers Ferry, Virginia.

1860 • Republican Abraham Lincoln elected president.
• South Carolina secedes from Union.

1861 • Six other Lower South states secede.
• Confederate States of America formed.
• Lincoln takes office.

▶**FOR AN ONLINE BIBLIOGRAPHY, PRACTICE QUIZZES, WEB SITES, IMAGES, AND DOCUMENTS RELATED TO THIS CHAPTER,** see the Book Companion Site at **bedfordstmartins.com/roarkvalue**.

▶**FOR DOCUMENTS RELATED TO THIS PERIOD,** see Michael Johnson, ed., *Reading the American Past*, Fifth Edition.

15

The Crucible of War

1861–1865

ON THE RAINY NIGHT OF SEPTEMBER 21, 1862, IN WILMINGTON, North Carolina, twenty-four-year-old William Gould and seven other runaway slaves crowded into a small boat on the Cape Fear River and quietly pushed away from the dock. They rowed hard throughout the night, reaching the Atlantic Ocean by dawn. They plunged into the swells and made for the Union navy patrolling offshore. At 10:30 that morning, the USS *Cambridge* took the men aboard.

Astonishingly, on the same day that Gould reached the federal ship, President Abraham Lincoln revealed his intention to issue a proclamation of emancipation freeing the slaves in the Confederate states. Because the proclamation would not take effect until January 1863, Gould was not legally free in the eyes of the U.S. government. But the U.S. Navy, suffering from a shortage of sailors, cared little about the formal status of runaway slaves. Within days, all eight runaways became sailors in the U.S. Navy.

William Gould could read and write, and he began making almost daily entries in his diary. In some ways, Gould's naval experience looked like that of a white sailor. He found duty on a ship in the blockading squadron both boring and exhilarating. Long days of tedious work were sometimes interrupted by a "period of daring exploit." When Gould's ship closed on a Confederate vessel, he declared that "we told them good morning in the shape of a shot." In a five-day period in 1862, the *Cambridge* helped capture four blockade runners and ran another aground.

But Gould's Civil War experience was shaped by his race. Like most black men in the Union military, he saw service as an opportunity to fight slavery.

The Crew of the USS *Hunchback*
African Americans served as sailors in the federal military long before they were permitted to become soldiers. Blacks initially served only as coal heavers, cooks, and stewards, but within a year some black sailors joined their ships' gun crews. The *Hunchback* was one of the Union's innovative ironclad ships. Although ironclads made wooden navies obsolete, they were far from invincible. During the assault on Charleston in 1863, five of the nine federal ironclads were partially or wholly disabled. National Archives.

From the beginning, Gould linked union and freedom, which he called "the holiest of all causes." Gould witnessed a number of ugly racial incidents on federal ships, however. "There was A malee [melee] on Deck between the white and colard [colored] men," he observed. Later, when a black regiment came aboard, "they were treated verry rough by the crew," he said. The white sailors "refused to let them eat off the mess pans and called them all kinds of names[;] . . . in all they was treated shamefully."

Still, Gould was proud of his service in the navy and monitored the progress of racial equality during the war. On shore leave in 1863, he cheered the "20th Regmt of U.S. (collard) Volunteers . . . pronounce[d] by all to be A splendid Regement." In March 1865, he celebrated the "passage of an amendment of the Con[sti]tution prohibiting slavery througho[ut] the United States." And a month later, he thrilled to the "Glad Tidings that the Stars and Stripe[s] had been planted over the Capital of the D—nd Confederacy by the invincible Grant." He added, we must not forget the "Mayrters to the cau[se] of Right and Equality."

Slaves like the eight runaways from Wilmington took the first steps toward making the war for union also a war for freedom. Early in the fighting, black abolitionist Frederick Douglass challenged the friends of freedom to *"be up and doing; — now is your time."* But for the first eighteen months of the war, federal soldiers fought solely to uphold the Constitution and preserve the nation. With the Emancipation Proclamation, however, the northern war effort took on a dual purpose: to save the Union and to free the slaves.

Even if the Civil War had not touched slavery, the conflict still would have transformed America. As the world's first modern war, it mobilized the entire populations of North and South, harnessed the productive capacities of both economies, and produced battles that fielded 200,000 soldiers and created casualties in the tens of thousands. The carnage lasted four years and cost the nation an estimated 620,000 lives, nearly as many as in all of its other wars combined. The war helped mold the modern American nation-state, and the federal government emerged with new power and responsibility over national life. The war encouraged industrialization. It tore families apart and pushed women into new work and roles. But because the war for union also became a war against slavery, the northern victory had truly revolutionary meaning.

Recalling the Civil War years, Frederick Douglass said, "It is something to couple one's name with great occasions." It *was* something — for William Gould and millions of other Americans. Poet Walt Whitman believed that the war was the "very centre, circumference, umbilicus" of his life. Whether they fought for the Confederacy or the Union, whether they labored behind the lines to supply Yankee or rebel soldiers, whether they prayed for the safe return of Northerners or Southerners, all Americans endured the crucible of war. But the war affected no group more than the 4 million African Americans who saw its beginning as slaves and emerged as free people.

▶ "And the War Came"

Abraham Lincoln faced the worst crisis in the history of the nation: disunion. He revealed his strategy on March 4, 1861, in his inaugural address, which was firm yet conciliatory. First, he sought to stop the contagion of secession by avoiding any act that would push the skittish Upper South (North Carolina, Virginia, Maryland, Delaware, Kentucky, Tennessee, Missouri, and Arkansas) out of the Union. Second, he sought to reassure the seceding Lower South (South Carolina, Georgia, Florida, Alabama, Mississippi, Louisiana, and Texas) that the Republicans would not abolish slavery. Lincoln believed that Unionists there would assert themselves and overturn the secession decision. Always, Lincoln denied the right of secession and upheld the Union.

His counterpart, Jefferson Davis, fully intended to establish the Confederate States of America as an independent republic. To achieve permanence, Davis had to sustain the secession fever that had carried the Lower South out of the Union. Even if the Lower South held firm, however, the Confederacy would remain weak without additional states. Davis watched for opportunities to add new stars to the Confederate flag.

Neither man sought war; both wanted to achieve their objectives peacefully. As Lincoln later observed, "Both parties deprecated war, but one of them would *make* war rather than let the nation survive, and the other would *accept* war rather than let it perish. And the war came."

Attack on Fort Sumter

Major Robert Anderson and some eighty U.S. soldiers occupied **Fort Sumter**, which was perched on a tiny island at the entrance to Charleston harbor in South Carolina. The fort with its American flag became a hated symbol of the nation that Southerners had abandoned, and they wanted federal troops out. Sumter was also a symbol to Northerners, a beacon affirming federal sovereignty in the seceded states.

Lincoln decided to hold Fort Sumter, but to do so, he had to provision it, for Anderson was running dangerously short of food. In the first week of April 1861, Lincoln authorized a peaceful expedition to bring supplies, but not military reinforcements, to the fort. The president understood that he risked war, but his plan honored his inaugural promises to defend federal property and to avoid using military force unless first attacked. Masterfully, Lincoln had shifted the fateful decision of war or peace to Jefferson Davis.

On April 9, Davis and his cabinet met to consider the situation in Charleston harbor. The territorial integrity of the Confederacy demanded the end of the federal presence, Davis argued. But his secretary of state, Robert Toombs of Georgia, pleaded against military action. "Mr. President," he declared, "at this time it is suicide, murder, and will lose us every friend at the North. You will wantonly strike a hornet's nest which extends from mountain to ocean, and legions now quiet will swarm out and sting us to death." But Davis sent word to Confederate troops in Charleston to take the fort before the relief expedition arrived. Thirty-three hours of bombardment on April 12 and 13 reduced the fort to rubble. Miraculously, not a single Union soldier died. On April 14, with the fort ablaze, Major Anderson offered his surrender and lowered the U.S. flag. The Confederates had Fort Sumter, but they also had war.

On April 15, when Lincoln called for 75,000 militiamen to serve for ninety days to put down the rebellion, several times that number rushed to defend the flag. Democrats responded as fervently as Republicans. Stephen A. Douglas, the recently defeated Democratic candidate for president, pledged his support. "There are only two sides to the question," he said. "Every man must be for the United States or against it. There can be no neutrals in this war, *only patriots — or traitors*." But the people of the Upper South found themselves torn.

The Upper South Chooses Sides

The Upper South faced a horrendous choice: either to fight against the Lower South or to fight against the Union. Many who only months earlier had rejected secession now embraced the Confederacy. To vote against southern independence was one thing, to fight fellow Southerners quite another. Thousands felt betrayed, believing that Lincoln had promised to achieve a peaceful reunion by waiting

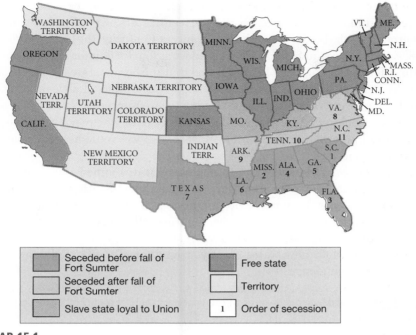

MAP 15.1

Secession, 1860–1861

After Lincoln's election, the fifteen slave states debated what to do. Seven states quickly left the Union, four left after the firing on Fort Sumter, and four remained loyal to the Union.

patiently for Unionists to retake power in the seceding states. It was a "politician's war," one man declared, but he conceded that "this is no time now to discuss the causes, but it is the duty of all who regard Southern institutions of value to side with the South, make common cause with the Confederate States and sink or swim with them."

One by one, the states of the Upper South jumped off the fence. Virginia, Arkansas, Tennessee, and North Carolina joined the Confederacy (Map 15.1). But in the border states of Delaware, Maryland, Kentucky, and Missouri, Unionism triumphed. Only in Delaware, where slaves accounted for less than 2 percent of the population, was the victory easy. In Maryland, Unionism needed a helping hand. Rather than allow the state to secede and make Washington, D.C., a federal island in a Confederate sea, Lincoln suspended the writ of habeas corpus, essentially setting aside constitutional guarantees that protect citizens from arbitrary arrest and detention, and he ordered U.S. troops into Baltimore. Maryland's legislature rejected secession.

The struggle turned violent in the West. In Missouri, Unionists won a narrow victory, but southern-sympathizing guerrilla bands roamed the state for the duration of the war, terrorizing civilians and soldiers alike. In Kentucky, Unionists also narrowly defeated secession, but the prosouthern minority claimed otherwise.

The Confederacy, not especially careful about counting votes, eagerly made Missouri and Kentucky the twelfth and thirteenth stars on the Confederate flag.

Throughout the border states, but especially in Kentucky, the Civil War divided families. Seven of Senator Henry Clay's grandsons fought: four for the Confederacy and three for the Union. Lincoln understood that the border states — particularly Kentucky — contained indispensable resources, population, and wealth and also controlled major rivers and railroads. "I think to lose Kentucky is nearly the same as to lose the whole game," Lincoln said. "Kentucky gone, we can not hold Missouri, nor, as I think, Maryland. These all against us, . . . we would as well consent to separation at once."

In the end, only eleven of the fifteen slave states joined the Confederate States of America. Moreover, the four seceding Upper South states contained significant numbers of people who felt little affection for the Confederacy. Dissatisfaction was so rife in the western counties of Virginia that in 1863 citizens there voted to create the separate state of West Virginia, loyal to the Union. Still, the acquisition of four new states greatly strengthened the Confederacy's drive for national independence.

> **REVIEW** Why did both the Union and the Confederacy consider control of the border states crucial?

▶ The Combatants

Only slaveholders had a direct economic stake in preserving slavery (estimated at some $3 billion in 1860), but most whites in the Confederacy defended the institution, the way of life built on it, and the Confederate nation. The degraded and subjugated status of blacks elevated the status of the poorest whites. "It matters not whether slaves be actually owned by many or by few," one Southerner declared. "It is enough that one simply belongs to the superior and ruling race, to secure consideration and respect." Moreover, Yankee "aggression" was no longer a mere threat; it was real and at the South's door. Southern whites equated the secession of 1861 with the declaration of independence from tyrannical British rule in 1776. As one Georgia woman said, Southerners wanted "nothing from the North but — to *be let alone.*"

For Northerners, rebel "treason" threatened to destroy the best government on earth. The South's failure to accept the democratic election of a president and its firing on the nation's flag challenged the rule of law, the authority of the Constitution, and the ability of the people to govern themselves. As an Indiana soldier told his wife, a "good government is the best thing on earth. Property is nothing without it, because it is not protected; a family is nothing without it, because they cannot be educated." Only a Union victory, Lincoln declared, would secure America's promise "to elevate the condition of man."

Northerners and Southerners rallied behind their separate flags, fully convinced that they were in the right and that God was on their side. But no one could argue that the Confederacy's resources and forces equaled the Union's. Yankees took heart from their superior power, but the rebels believed they had advantages that nullified every northern strength. Both sides mobilized swiftly in 1861, and each devised what it believed would be a winning military and diplomatic strategy.

How They Expected to Win

The balance sheet of northern and southern resources reveals enormous advantages for the Union. The twenty-three states remaining in the Union had a population of 22.3 million; the eleven Confederate states had a population of only 9.1 million, of whom 3.67 million (40 percent) were slaves. The North's economic advantages were even more overwhelming. Yet Southerners expected to win — for some good reasons — and they came very close to doing so.

Southerners knew they bucked the military odds, but hadn't the liberty-loving colonists in 1776 also done so? "Britain could not conquer three million," a Louisianan proclaimed, and "the world cannot conquer the South." How could anyone doubt the outcome of a contest between lean, hard, country-born rebel warriors defending family, property, and liberty, and soft, flabby, citified Yankee mechanics waging an unconstitutional war?

The South's confidence also rested on its belief that northern prosperity depended on the South's cotton. Without cotton, New England textile mills would stand idle. Without planters purchasing northern manufactured goods, northern factories would drown in their own unsold surpluses. And without the foreign exchange earned by the overseas sales of cotton, the financial structure of the entire Yankee nation would collapse. A Virginian spoke for most Confederates when he declared that in the South's ability to "withhold the benefits of our trade, we hold a power over the North more powerful than a powerful army in the field."

King Cotton diplomacy would also make Europe a powerful ally of the Confederacy, Southerners reasoned. After all, they said, Britain's economy (and, to a lesser degree, France's) also depended on cotton. Of the 900 million pounds of cotton Britain imported annually, more than 700 million pounds came from the American South. If the supply was interrupted, sheer economic need would make Britain (and perhaps France) a Confederate ally. And because the British navy ruled the seas, the North would find Britain a formidable foe.

Southerners' confidence may seem naive today, but even tough-minded European military observers picked the South to win. Offsetting the Union's power was the Confederacy's expanse. The North, Europeans predicted, could not conquer the vast territory (750,000 square miles) extending from the Potomac to the Rio Grande. To defeat the South, the Union would need to raise and equip a massive invading army and protect supply lines that would stretch farther than any in modern history.

Indeed, the South enjoyed major advantages, and the Confederacy devised a military strategy to exploit them. It recognized that a Union victory required the North to defeat and subjugate the South, but a Confederate victory required only that the South stay at home, blunt invasions, avoid battles that risked annihilating its army, and outlast the North's will to fight. When an opportunity presented itself, the South would strike the invaders. Like the American colonists, the South could win independence by not losing the war.

If the North did nothing, the South would by default establish itself as a sovereign nation. The Lincoln administration, therefore, adopted an offensive strategy that applied pressure at many points. Lincoln declared a naval blockade of the Confederacy to deny it the ability to sell cotton abroad, giving the South far fewer dollars to pay for war goods. Even before the North could mount an effective blockade, however, Jefferson Davis decided voluntarily to cease exporting cotton. He wanted to create a cotton "famine" that would enfeeble the northern economy and precipitate European intervention. But the cotton famine Davis created devastated the South, not the North, and kept Europe on the diplomatic sidelines. Lincoln also ordered the Union army into Virginia, at the same time planning a march through the Mississippi valley that would cut the Confederacy in two. Dubbed the **Anaconda Plan**, this ambitious strategy took advantage of the Union's superior resources.

Neither side could foresee the magnitude and duration of the war. Americans thought of war in terms of the Mexican-American War of the 1840s, a conflict that had cost relatively few lives and had inflicted only light damage on the countryside. On the eve of the fighting, they could not know that four ghastly years of bloodletting lay ahead.

Lincoln and Davis Mobilize

Mobilization required effective political leadership, and at first glance the South appeared to have the advantage. Jefferson Davis brought to the Confederate presidency a distinguished political career, including experience in the U.S. Senate. He was also a West Point graduate, a combat veteran and authentic hero of the Mexican-American War, and a former secretary of war. Dignified and ramrod straight, with "a jaw sawed in steel," Davis appeared to be everything a nation could want in a wartime leader.

By contrast, Abraham Lincoln brought to the White House one lackluster term in the House of Representatives and almost no administrative experience. His sole brush with anything military was as a captain in the militia in the Black Hawk War, a brief struggle in Illinois in 1832 in which whites expelled the last Indians from the state. Lincoln later joked about his service in the Black Hawk War as the time when he survived bloody encounters with mosquitoes and led raids on wild onion patches. The lanky, disheveled Illinois lawyer-politician looked anything but military or presidential in his bearing.

In fact, the hardworking Davis proved to be less than he appeared. He had no gift for military strategy yet intervened often in military affairs. He was an even less able political leader. Quarrelsome and proud, he had an acid tongue that made enemies the Confederacy could ill afford. The Confederacy's intimidating problems might have defeated an even more talented leader, however. For example, state sovereignty, which was enshrined in the Confederate constitution, made Davis's task of organizing a new nation and fighting a war difficult in the extreme.

With Lincoln the North got far more than met the eye. He proved himself a master politician and a superb leader. When forming his cabinet, Lincoln appointed the ablest men, no matter that they were often his chief rivals and critics. He appointed Salmon P. Chase secretary of the treasury, knowing that Chase had presidential ambitions. As secretary of state, he chose his chief opponent for the Republican nomination in 1860, William H. Seward. Despite his civilian background, Lincoln displayed an innate understanding of military strategy. No one was more crucial in mapping the Union war plan. Moreover, Lincoln's eloquent letters and speeches helped galvanize the northern people in defense of the nation he called "the last best hope of earth."

Lincoln and Davis began gathering their armies. Confederates had to build almost everything from scratch, and Northerners had to channel their superior numbers and industrial resources to the purposes of war. On the eve of the war, the federal army numbered only 16,000 men, most of them scattered over the West subjugating Indians. One-third of the officers followed the example of the Virginian Robert E. Lee, resigning their commissions and heading south. The U.S. Navy was in better shape. Forty-two ships were in service, and a large merchant marine would in time provide more ships and sailors for the Union cause. Possessing a much weaker navy, the South pinned its hopes on its armies.

The Confederacy made prodigious efforts to build new factories to produce tents, blankets, shoes, and its gray uniforms, but many rebel soldiers slept in the open air without blankets and were sometimes without shoes. Even when factories managed to produce what the soldiers needed, southern railroads — captured, destroyed, or left in disrepair — often could not deliver the goods. Food production proved less of a problem, but food sometimes rotted before it reached the soldiers. The one bright spot was the Confederacy's Ordnance Bureau, headed by Josiah Gorgas, a near miracle worker when it came to manufacturing gunpowder, cannons, and rifles. In April 1864, Gorgas proudly observed: "Where three years ago we were not making a gun, a pistol nor a sabre, no shot nor shell . . . we now make all these in quantities to meet the demands of our large armies."

Recruiting and supplying huge armies required enormous new revenues. At first, the Union and the Confederacy sold war bonds, which essentially were loans from patriotic citizens. In addition, both sides turned to taxes. The North raised one-fifth of its wartime revenue from taxes; the South raised only one-twentieth. Eventually, both began printing paper money. Inflation soared, but the Confederacy suffered more because it financed a greater part of its wartime costs through the printing press. Prices in the Union rose by about 80 percent during the war, while inflation in the Confederacy topped 9,000 percent.

Within months of the bombardment of Fort Sumter, both sides found men to fight and ways to supply them. But the underlying strength of the northern economy gave the Union the decided advantage. With their military and industrial muscles beginning to ripple, Northerners became itchy for action that would smash the rebellion. Horace Greeley's *New York Tribune* began to chant: "Forward to Richmond! Forward to Richmond!"

REVIEW Why did the South believe it could win the war despite numerical disadvantages?

▶ Battling It Out, 1861–1862

During the first year and a half of the war, armies fought major campaigns in both East and West. Because the rival capitals — Richmond and Washington, D.C. — were only ninety miles apart and each was threatened more than once with capture, the eastern campaign was especially dramatic. But the battles in the West proved more decisive. As Yankee and rebel armies pounded each other on land, the navies fought on the seas and on the rivers of the South. In Europe, Confederate and U.S. diplomats competed for advantage in the corridors of power. All the while, casualty lists on both sides reached appalling lengths.

Stalemate in the Eastern Theater

In the summer of 1861, Lincoln ordered the 35,000 Union troops assembling outside Washington to attack the 20,000 Confederates defending Manassas, a railroad junction in Virginia about thirty miles southwest of Washington. On July 21, the army forded Bull Run, a branch of the Potomac River, and engaged the southern forces (Map 15.2). But fast-moving southern reinforcements blunted the Union attack and then counterattacked. What began as an orderly Union retreat turned into a panicky stampede. Demoralized federal troops ran over shocked civilians as the soldiers raced back to Washington.

By Civil War standards, the casualties (wounded and dead) at the **battle of Bull Run** (or **Manassas**, as Southerners called the battle) were light, about 2,000 Confederates and 1,600 Federals. The significance of the battle lay in the lessons Northerners and Southerners drew from it. For Southerners, it confirmed the superiority of rebel fighting men and the inevitability of Confederate nationhood. Manassas was *"one of the decisive battles of the world,"* a Georgian proclaimed. It *"has* secured our independence." While victory fed southern pride, defeat sobered Northerners. It was a major setback, admitted the *New York Tribune*, but "let us go to work, then, with a will." Bull Run taught Lincoln that victory would be neither quick nor easy. Within four days of the disaster, the president authorized the enlistment of 1 million men for three years.

Lincoln also found a new general, the young **George B. McClellan**, whom he appointed commander of the newly named Army of the Potomac. Having graduated from West Point second in his class, the thirty-four-year-old McClellan believed that he was a great soldier and that Lincoln was a dunce, the "original Gorilla." A superb administrator and organizer, McClellan energetically whipped his dispirited soldiers into shape, but he was reluctant to send them into battle. For all his energy, McClellan lacked decisiveness. Lincoln wanted a general who

▶ **MAP 15.2**
The Civil War, 1861–1862
While most eyes were focused on the eastern theater, especially the ninety-mile stretch of land between Washington, D.C., and the Confederate capital of Richmond, Virginia, Union troops were winning strategic victories in the West.

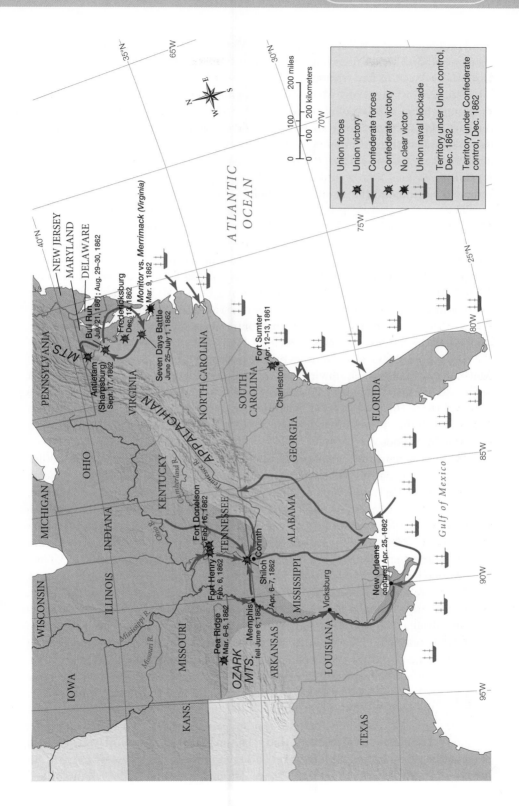

Legend:

- Union forces
- Union victory
- Confederate forces
- Confederate victory
- No clear victor
- Union naval blockade
- Territory under Union control, Dec. 1862
- Territory under Confederate control, Dec. 1862

Scale: 0   100   200 miles
0   100   200 kilometers

Map labels:

ATLANTIC OCEAN

Gulf of Mexico

NEW JERSEY
MARYLAND
DELAWARE
PENNSYLVANIA
OHIO
INDIANA
ILLINOIS
MICHIGAN
WISCONSIN
IOWA
MISSOURI
KANS.
ARKANSAS
TEXAS
LOUISIANA
MISSISSIPPI
ALABAMA
GEORGIA
FLORIDA
SOUTH CAROLINA
NORTH CAROLINA
VIRGINIA
KENTUCKY
TENNESSEE
APPALACHIAN MTS.
OZARK MTS.

Mississippi R.
Missouri R.
Ohio R.
Cumberland R.
Tennessee R.

Battles / events:

- Bull Run, July 21, 1861; Aug. 29–30, 1862
- Fredericksburg, Dec. 13, 1862
- *Monitor* vs. *Merrimack* (*Virginia*), Mar. 9, 1862
- Antietam (Sharpsburg), Sept. 17, 1862
- Seven Days Battle, June 25–July 1, 1862
- Fort Sumter, Apr. 12–13, 1861
- Charleston
- Fort Donelson, Feb. 16, 1862
- Fort Henry, Feb. 6, 1862
- Corinth
- Shiloh, Apr. 6–7, 1862
- Pea Ridge, Mar. 6–8, 1862
- Memphis, fell June 6, 1862
- Vicksburg
- New Orleans, captured Apr. 25, 1862

Coordinates: 40°N, 35°N, 30°N, 25°N, 65°W, 70°W, 75°W, 80°W, 85°W, 90°W, 95°W

would advance, take risks, and fight, but McClellan went into winter quarters. "If General McClellan does not want to use the army I would like to *borrow* it," Lincoln declared in frustration.

Finally, in May 1862, McClellan launched his long-awaited offensive. He transported his highly polished army, now 130,000 strong, to the mouth of the James River and began slowly moving up the Yorktown peninsula toward Richmond. When he was within six miles of the Confederate capital, General Joseph Johnston hit him like a hammer. In the assault, Johnston was wounded and was replaced by **Robert E. Lee**, who would become the South's most celebrated general. Lee named his command the Army of Northern Virginia.

The contrast between Lee and McClellan could hardly have been greater. McClellan brimmed with conceit and braggadocio; Lee was courteous and reserved. On the battlefield, McClellan grew timid and irresolute, and Lee became audaciously, even recklessly, aggressive. And Lee had at his side in the peninsula campaign military men of real talent: Thomas J. Jackson, nicknamed "Stonewall" for holding the line at Manassas, and James E. B. ("Jeb") Stuart, a dashing twenty-nine-year-old cavalry commander who rode circles around Yankee troops. Jackson ranks among the most brilliant commanders of the war, but in May 1863 he died at the battle of Chancellorsville.

Lee's assault initiated the Seven Days Battle (June 25–July 1) and began McClellan's march back down the peninsula. By the time McClellan reached safety, 30,000 men from both sides had died or been wounded. Although Southerners suffered twice the casualties of Northerners, Lee had saved Richmond. Lincoln wired McClellan to abandon the peninsula campaign and replaced him with General John Pope.

In August, north of Richmond, at the second battle of Bull Run, Lee's smaller army battered Pope's forces and sent them scurrying back to Washington. Lincoln ordered Pope to Minnesota to pacify the Indians and restored McClellan to command. Lincoln had not changed his mind about McClellan's capacity as a warrior, but he reluctantly acknowledged that "if he can't fight himself, he excels in making others ready to fight." Lee could fight, and he pushed his army across the Potomac and invaded Maryland. A victory on northern soil would dislodge Maryland from the Union, Lee reasoned, and might even cause Lincoln to sue for peace.

On September 17, 1862, McClellan's forces engaged Lee's army at Antietam Creek (see Map 15.2). Earlier, a Union soldier had found a copy of Lee's orders to his army dropped by a careless Confederate officer, so McClellan had a clear picture of Lee's position. While McClellan's characteristic caution cost him the opportunity to destroy the opposing army, he still did severe damage. With "solid shot . . . cracking skulls like eggshells," according to one observer, the armies went after each other. At Miller's Cornfield, the firing was so intense that "every stalk of corn in the . . . field was cut as closely as could have been done with a knife." By nightfall, 6,000 men lay dead or dying on the battlefield, and 17,000 more had been wounded. **The battle of Antietam** would be the bloodiest day of the war. Instead of being the war-winning fight Lee had anticipated when he came north, Antietam sent the battered Army of Northern Virginia limping back home. McClellan claimed to have saved the North, but Lincoln again removed him from command of the Army of the Potomac and appointed General Ambrose Burnside.

Though bloodied, Lee found an opportunity in December to punish the enemy at Fredericksburg, Virginia, where Burnside's 122,000 Union troops faced 78,500 Confederates dug in behind a stone wall on the heights above the Rappahannock River. Half a mile of open ground separated the armies. "A chicken could not live on that field when we open on it," a Confederate artillery officer predicted. Yet Burnside ordered a frontal assault. When the shooting ceased, the Federals counted nearly 13,000 casualties, the Confederates fewer than 5,000. The battle of Fredericksburg was one of the Union's worst defeats. As 1862 ended, the North seemed no nearer to ending the rebellion than it had been when the war began. Rather than checkmate, military struggle in the East had reached stalemate.

Union Victories in the Western Theater

While most eyes focused on events in the East, the decisive early encounters of the war were taking place between the Appalachian Mountains and the Ozarks (see Map 15.2). Confederates wanted Missouri and Kentucky, states they claimed but did not control. Federals wanted to split Arkansas, Louisiana, and Texas from the Confederacy by taking control of the Mississippi River and to occupy Tennessee, one of the Confederacy's main producers of food, mules, and iron — all vital resources.

Before Union forces could march on Tennessee, they needed to secure Missouri to the west. Union troops swept across Missouri to the border of Arkansas, where in March 1862 they encountered a 16,000-man Confederate army, which included three regiments of Indians from the so-called Five Civilized Tribes — the Choctaw, Chickasaw, Creek, Seminole, and Cherokee. Although Indians fought on both sides during the war, Native Americans who sided with the South hoped

Native American Recruits
Both the Union and the Confederacy enrolled Indian soldiers. Here, a Union recruiter swears in two recruits. The Confederates promised to assume the financial obligations of the old treaties with the United States, guarantee slavery, respect tribal independence, and permit the tribes to send delegates to Richmond. Cherokee chief John Ross, who signed with the Confederacy, likened his difficult choice to that of a man in a flood who sees a log floating by: "By refusing [the log] he is a doomed man. By seizing hold of it he has a chance for his life." Approximately 20,000 Indians fought in the Civil War, sometimes against each other. Wisconsin Historical Society.

that the Confederacy would grant them more independence than had the United States. The Union victory at the battle of Pea Ridge left Missouri free of Confederate troops, but Missouri was not free of Confederate fighters. Guerrilla bands led by the notorious William Clarke Quantrill and "Bloody Bill" Anderson burned, tortured, scalped, and murdered Union civilians and soldiers until the final year of the war.

Even farther west, Confederate armies sought to fulfill Jefferson Davis's vision of a slaveholding empire stretching all the way to the Pacific. Both sides recognized the immense value of the gold and silver mines of California, Nevada, and Colorado. And both sides bolstered their armies in the Southwest with Mexican Americans, some 2,500 fighting for the Confederacy and 1,000 joining Union forces. A quick strike by Texas troops took Santa Fe, New Mexico, in the winter of 1861–62. Then in March 1862, a band of Colorado miners ambushed and crushed southern forces at Glorieta Pass, outside Santa Fe. Confederate military failures in the far West meant that there would be no Confederate empire beyond Texas.

The principal western battles took place in Tennessee, where General **Ulysses S. Grant** emerged as the key northern commander. Grant had graduated from West Point and served bravely in Mexico. When the Civil War began, he was a thirty-nine-year-old dry-goods clerk in Galena, Illinois. Gentle at home, he became pugnacious on the battlefield. "The art of war is simple," he said. "Find out where your enemy is, get at him as soon as you can and strike him as hard as you can, and keep moving on." Grant's philosophy of war as attrition would take a huge toll in human life, but it played to the North's superiority in manpower. In his private's uniform and slouch hat, Grant did not look much like a general. But Lincoln, who did not look much like a president, learned his worth. Later, to critics who wanted the president to sack Grant because of his drinking, Lincoln would say, *"I can't spare this man. He fights."*

In February 1862, operating in tandem with U.S. Navy gunboats, Grant captured Fort Henry on the Tennessee River and Fort Donelson on the Cumberland (see Map 15.2). Defeat forced the Confederates to withdraw from all of Kentucky and most of Tennessee, but Grant followed.

On April 6, General Albert Sidney Johnston's army surprised Grant at Shiloh Church in Tennessee. Union troops were badly mauled the first day, but Grant remained cool and brought up reinforcements throughout the night. The next morning, the Union army counterattacked, driving the Confederates before it. The **battle of Shiloh** was terribly costly to both sides; there were 20,000 casualties, among them General Johnston. Grant later said that after Shiloh he "gave up all idea of saving the Union except by complete conquest."

Although no one knew it at the time, Shiloh ruined the Confederacy's bid to control the theater of operations in the West. The Yankees quickly captured the strategic town of Corinth, Mississippi; the river city of Memphis; and the South's largest city, New Orleans. By the end of 1862, the far West and most — but not all — of the Mississippi valley lay in Union hands. At the same time, the outcome of the struggle in another theater of war was also becoming clearer.

The Atlantic Theater

When the war began, the U.S. Navy's blockade fleet consisted of about three dozen ships to patrol more than 3,500 miles of southern coastline, and rebel merchant ships were able to slip in and out of southern ports nearly at will. Taking on cargoes in the Caribbean, sleek Confederate blockade runners brought in vital supplies — guns and medicine. But with the U.S. Navy commissioning a new blockader almost weekly, the naval fleet eventually numbered 150 ships on duty, and the Union navy dramatically improved its score.

Unable to build a conventional navy equal to the expanding U.S. fleet, the Confederates experimented with a radical new maritime design: the ironclad warship. At Norfolk, Virginia, the wooden hull of the frigate *Merrimack* was layered with two-inch-thick armor plate. Rechristened *Virginia*, the ship steamed out in March 1862 and sank two wooden federal ships, killing at least 240 Union sailors (see Map 15.2, page 435). When the *Virginia* returned to finish off the federal blockaders the next morning, it was challenged by the *Monitor*, a federal ironclad of even more radical design, topped with a revolving turret holding two eleven-inch guns. On March 9, the two ships hurled shells at each other for two hours, but when neither could penetrate the other's armor, the battle ended in a draw.

The Confederacy never found a way to break the **Union blockade** despite exploring many naval innovations, including a new underwater vessel — the submarine. Each month, the Union fleet tightened its noose. By 1863, the South had abandoned its embargo policy and desperately wanted to ship cotton to pay for imports of arms, shoes, and uniforms needed to fight the war. The growing effectiveness of the federal blockade, a southern naval officer observed, "shut the Confederacy out from the world, deprived it of supplies, weakened its military and naval strength." By 1865, the blockaders were intercepting about half of the southern ships attempting to break through. The Confederacy was sealed off, with devastating results.

International Diplomacy

What the Confederates could not achieve on the seas, they sought to achieve through international diplomacy. Confederates and Unionists both realized that the world was watching the struggle in North America. Nationalists everywhere understood that the American Civil War engaged issues central to their own nation-building efforts. The Confederates rested their claims to separate nationhood on the principles of self-determination and rightful rebellion against despotic power, and they desperately wanted Europe to intervene. The Lincoln administration explained why the Union had to be preserved and why Europe had to remain neutral. "The question," Lincoln noted, is "whether a constitutional republic, or a democracy — a government of the people, by the same people — can or cannot, maintain its territorial integrity, against its own domestic foes."

More practically, the Confederates based their hope for European support on King Cotton. In theory, cotton-starved European nations would have no choice but to break the Union blockade and recognize the Confederacy. Southern hopes were not unreasonable, for at the height of the "cotton famine" in 1862, when 2 million British workers were unemployed, Britain tilted toward recognition. Along with several other European nations, Britain granted the Confederacy "belligerent" status, which enabled it to buy goods and build ships in European ports. The British-built Confederate cruiser *Alabama* sank or captured sixty-four Union merchant ships before the USS *Kearsarge* sank it off the coast of France in 1864. But no country challenged the Union blockade or recognized the Confederate States of America as a nation, a bold act that probably would have drawn that country into war.

King Cotton diplomacy failed for several reasons. A bumper cotton crop in 1860 meant that the warehouses of British textile manufacturers bulged with surplus cotton throughout 1861. In 1862, when a cotton shortage did occur, European manufacturers found new sources in India, Egypt, and elsewhere. In addition, the development of a brisk trade between the Union and Britain — British war materiel for American grain and flour — helped offset the decline in textiles and encouraged Britain to remain neutral.

Europe's temptation to intervene disappeared for good in 1862. Union military successes in the West made Britain and France think twice about linking their fates to the struggling Confederacy. Moreover, in September 1862, Lincoln announced a new policy that made an alliance with the Confederacy an alliance with slavery — a commitment the French and British, who had outlawed slavery in their empires and looked forward to its eradication worldwide, were not willing to make. After 1862, the South's cause was linked irrevocably with slavery and reaction, and the Union's cause was linked with freedom and democracy. The Union, not the Confederacy, had won the diplomatic stakes.

REVIEW   Why did the Confederacy's bid for international support fail?

▶ Union *and* Freedom

For a year and a half, Lincoln insisted that the North fought strictly to save the Union and not to abolish slavery. Despite Lincoln's repeated pronouncements, however, the war for union became a war for African American freedom. Each month the conflict dragged on, it became clearer that the Confederate war machine depended heavily on slavery. Rebel armies used slaves to build fortifications, haul materiel, tend horses, and perform camp chores. On the home front, slaves labored in ironworks and shipyards, and they grew the food that fed both soldiers and civilians. Slavery undergirded the Confederacy as certainly as it had the Old South. As Frederick Douglass put it, slavery was "the stomach of this rebellion." Union military commanders and politicians alike gradually realized that to defeat the Confederacy, the North would have to destroy slavery. "I am a slow walker," Lincoln said, "but I never walk back."

From Slaves to Contraband

Lincoln detested human bondage, but as president he felt compelled to act prudently in the interests of the Union. He doubted his right under the Constitution to tamper with the "domestic institutions" of any state, even states in rebellion. An astute politician, Lincoln worked within the tight limits of public opinion. The issue of black freedom was particularly explosive in the loyal border states, where slaveholders threatened to jump into the arms of the Confederacy at even the hint of emancipation.

Black freedom also raised alarms in the free states. The Democratic Party gave notice that adding emancipation to the goal of union would make the war strictly a Republican affair. Moreover, many white Northerners were not about to risk their lives to satisfy what they considered abolitionist "fanaticism." "We Won't Fight to Free the Nigger," one popular banner read. They feared that emancipation would propel "two or three million semi-savages" northward, where they would crowd into white neighborhoods, compete for white jobs, and mix with white "sons and daughters." Thus, emancipation threatened to dislodge the loyal slave states from the Union, alienate the Democratic Party, deplete the armies, and perhaps even spark race warfare.

Yet proponents of emancipation pressed Lincoln as relentlessly as did the anti-emancipation forces. Abolitionists argued that by seceding, Southerners had forfeited their right to the protection of the Constitution and that Lincoln could — as the price of their treason — legally confiscate their property in slaves. When Lincoln refused, abolitionists scalded him. Frederick Douglass labeled him "the miserable tool of traitors and rebels."

The Republican-dominated Congress declined to leave slavery policy entirely in President Lincoln's hands. In August 1861, Congress approved the Confiscation Act, which allowed the seizure of any slave employed directly by the Confederate military. It also fulfilled the free-soil dream of prohibiting slavery in the territories and abolished slavery in Washington, D.C. Democrats and border-state representatives voted against even these mild measures, but Congress's attitude was clearly stiffening against slavery.

Slaves, not politicians, became the most insistent force for emancipation. By escaping their masters by the tens of thousands and running away to Union lines, they forced slavery on the North's wartime agenda. Runaways made Northerners answer a crucial question: Were the runaways now free, or were they still slaves who, according to the fugitive slave law, had to be returned to their masters? At first, Yankee military officers sent the fugitives back. But Union armies needed laborers. At Fort Monroe, Virginia, General Benjamin F. Butler refused to turn them over to their owners, calling them **contraband of war**, meaning "confiscated property," and put them to work. Congress made Butler's practice national policy in March 1862 when it forbade returning fugitive slaves to their masters. Slaves were still not legally free, but there was a tilt toward emancipation.

Lincoln's policy of noninterference with slavery gradually crumbled. To calm Northerners' racial fears, Lincoln offered colonization, the deportation of African Americans from the United States to Haiti, Panama, or elsewhere. In the summer of 1862, he told a delegation of black visitors that deep-seated racial prejudice among whites made it impossible for blacks to achieve equality in the United States. One African American responded, "This is our country as much as it is yours, and we will not leave." Congress voted a small amount of money to underwrite colonization, but after one miserable experiment on a small island in the Caribbean, practical limitations and stiff black opposition sank further efforts.

While Lincoln was developing his own antislavery initiatives, he snuffed out actions that he believed would jeopardize northern unity. He was particularly alert to Union commanders who tried to dictate slavery policy from the field. In August 1861, when John C. Frémont, former Republican presidential nominee and now commander of federal troops in Missouri, freed the slaves belonging to Missouri rebels, Lincoln forced the general to revoke his edict. The following May, when General David Hunter freed the slaves in Georgia, South Carolina, and Florida, Lincoln countermanded his order. Events moved so rapidly, however, that Lincoln found it impossible to control federal policy on slavery.

From Contraband to Free People

On August 22, 1862, Lincoln replied to an angry abolitionist who demanded that he attack slavery. "My paramount objective in this struggle *is* to save the Union," Lincoln said deliberately, "and is *not* either to save or destroy slavery. If I could save the Union without freeing *any* slave I would do it, and if I could save it by freeing *all* the slaves I would do it; and if I could save it by freeing some and leaving others alone I would also do that." Instead of simply restating his old position that union was the North's sole objective, Lincoln announced that slavery was no longer untouchable and that he would emancipate every slave if doing so would preserve the Union.

By the summer of 1862, events were tumbling rapidly toward emancipation. On July 17, Congress adopted the second Confiscation Act. The first had confiscated slaves employed by the Confederate military; the second declared all slaves of rebel masters "forever free of their servitude." In theory, this breathtaking measure freed most Confederate slaves, for slaveholders formed the backbone of the rebellion. Congress had traveled far since the war began.

Lincoln had, too. In July 1862, the president told two members of his cabinet that he had "about come to the conclusion that we must free the slaves or be ourselves subdued." A few days later, before the entire cabinet, he read a draft of a preliminary emancipation proclamation that promised to free *all* the slaves in the seceding states on January 1, 1863. Lincoln described emancipation as an "act of justice," but it was the lengthening casualty lists that finally brought him around. Emancipation, he declared, was "a military necessity, absolutely essential to the preservation of the Union." Only freeing the slaves would "strike at the heart of the rebellion." On September 22, Lincoln issued his preliminary **Emancipation Proclamation** promising freedom to slaves in areas still in rebellion on January 1, 1863.

The limitations of the proclamation — it exempted the loyal border states and the Union-occupied areas of the Confederacy — caused some to ridicule the act. The *Times* (London) observed cynically, "Where he has no power Mr. Lincoln will set the negroes free, where he retains power he will consider them as slaves." But Lincoln had no power to free slaves in loyal states, and invading Union armies would liberate slaves in the Confederacy as they advanced.

By presenting emancipation as a "military necessity," Lincoln hoped he had disarmed his conservative critics. Emancipation would deprive the Confederacy of valuable slave laborers, shorten the war, and thus save lives. Democrats, however, fumed that the "shrieking and howling abolitionist faction" had captured the White House and made it "a nigger war." Democrats made political hay out of Lincoln's action in the November 1862 elections, gaining thirty-four congressional seats. House Democrats quickly proposed a resolution branding emancipation "a high crime against the Constitution." The Republicans, who maintained narrow majorities in both houses of Congress, barely beat it back.

As promised, on New Year's Day 1863, Lincoln issued the final Emancipation Proclamation. Later in 1863 at Gettysburg, Pennsylvania, Lincoln famously confirmed the war's new purpose: "that this nation, under God, shall have a new birth of freedom — and that government of the people, by the people, for the people, shall not perish from the earth." In addition to freeing the slaves in the rebel states, the Emancipation Proclamation also committed the federal government to the fullest use of African Americans to defeat the Confederate enemy.

The War of Black Liberation

Even before Lincoln proclaimed emancipation a Union war aim, African Americans in the North had volunteered to fight. Military service, one black volunteer declared, would mean "the elevation of a downtrodden and despised race." But the War Department, doubtful of blacks' abilities and fearful of white reaction to serving side by side with them, refused to make black men soldiers. Instead, the army employed black men as manual laborers; black women sometimes found employment as laundresses and cooks. The navy, however, accepted blacks from the outset, including runaway slaves such as **William Gould** (see pages 425–427).

As Union casualty lists lengthened, Northerners gradually and reluctantly turned to African Americans to fill the army's blue uniforms. With the Militia Act of July 1862, Congress authorized enrolling blacks in "any military or naval service for which they may be found competent." After the Emancipation Proclamation, whites — like it or not — were fighting and dying for black freedom, and few insisted that blacks remain out of harm's way behind the lines. Indeed, whites insisted that blacks share the danger, especially after March 1863, when Congress resorted to the draft to fill the Union army.

The military was far from color-blind. The Union army established segregated black regiments, paid black soldiers $10 per month rather than the $13 it paid whites, refused blacks the opportunity to become commissioned officers, punished blacks as if they were slaves, and assigned blacks to labor battalions rather than to combat units. Still, when the war ended, 179,000 African American men had served in the Union army, approximately 10 percent of all soldiers. An astounding 71 percent of black men ages eighteen to forty-five in the free states wore Union blue, a participation rate that was substantially higher than that of white men. More than 130,000 black soldiers came from the slave states, perhaps 100,000 of them ex-slaves.

Black Men Working along the Wharf, 1860–1865
The black men seen here with picks and shovels working at the federal supply depot at City Point, Virginia, were likely fugitive slaves. Hundreds of thousands of able-bodied runaways cleared forests, built roads, erected bridges, constructed fortifications, and transported supplies for the U.S. army. They were overworked, paid irregularly, given inadequate food and clothing, and even physically assaulted, but they kept pouring into Union lines. Their labor became indispensable to the war effort, and as one Northerner remembered, "The truth was we never could get enough of them." Library of Congress.

In time, whites allowed blacks to put down their shovels and to shoulder rifles. At the battles of Port Hudson and Milliken's Bend on the Mississippi River and at Fort Wagner in Charleston harbor, black courage under fire finally dispelled notions that African Americans could not fight. More than 38,000 black soldiers died in the Civil War, a mortality rate that was higher than that of white troops. Blacks played a crucial role in the triumph of the Union and the destruction of slavery in the South.

REVIEW Why did the Union change policy in 1863 to allow black men to serve in the army?

▶ The South at War

Most white Southerners shifted their allegiance from the Union to the Confederacy easily, convinced that their new nation embodied the principles of the American Revolution. But by seceding, Southerners brought on themselves a firestorm of unimaginable fury. Monstrous losses on the battlefield nearly bled the Confederacy to death. Southerners on the home front also suffered, even at the hands of their own government. Efforts by the Davis administration in Richmond to centralize power in order to fight the war tested the loyalty of some men and women. Wartime economic changes hurt everyone, some more than others. By 1863, planters and yeomen who had stood together began to drift apart. Most disturbing of all, slaves became open participants in the destruction of slavery and the Confederacy.

Revolution from Above

As a Confederate general observed, Southerners were engaged in a total war "in which the whole population and the whole production . . . are to be put on a war footing, where every institution is to be made auxiliary to war." Jefferson Davis faced the task of building an army and navy from almost nothing, supplying them from factories that were scarce and anemic, and paying for it all from a treasury that did not exist. Finding eager soldiers proved easiest. Hundreds of officers defected from the U.S. Army, and hundreds of thousands of eager young rebels volunteered to follow them. Very quickly, the Confederacy developed formidable striking power.

The Confederacy's economy and finances proved tougher problems. Because of the Union blockade, the government had no choice but to build an industrial sector itself. Government-owned clothing and shoe factories, mines, arsenals, and powder works sprang up. The government also harnessed private companies, such as the huge Tredegar Iron Works in Richmond, to the war effort. Paying for the war became the most difficult task. A flood of paper money caused debilitating inflation. By 1863, people in Charleston paid ten times more for food than they had paid at the start of the war. By Christmas 1864, a Confederate soldier's monthly pay no longer bought a pair of socks. The Confederacy manufactured much more than most people imagined possible, but it never produced all that the South needed.

Richmond's war-making effort brought unprecedented government intrusion into the private lives of Confederate citizens. In April 1862, the Confederate Congress passed the first **conscription** (draft) law in American history. All able-bodied white males between the ages of eighteen and thirty-five (later seventeen and fifty) were liable to serve in the rebel army. The government adopted a policy of **impressment**, which allowed officials to confiscate food, horses, wagons, and whatever else they wanted from private citizens and to pay for them at below-market rates. After March 1863, the Confederacy legally impressed slaves, employing them as military laborers.

Richmond's centralizing efforts ran head-on into the South's traditional values of **states' rights** and unfettered individualism. Southerners lashed out at what Georgia governor Joseph E. Brown denounced as the "dangerous usurpation by Congress of the reserved right of the States." Richmond and the states struggled for control of money, supplies, and soldiers, with damaging consequences for the war effort. Despite the strain, popular commitment to the new nation endured.

Hardship Below

Hardships on the home front fell most heavily on the poor. Flour, which cost three or four cents a pound in 1861, cost thirty-five cents in 1863. The draft stripped yeoman farms of men, leaving the women and children to grow what they ate. Government agents took 10 percent of harvests as a "tax-in-kind" on agriculture. Like inflation, shortages afflicted the entire population, but the rich lost luxuries while the poor lost necessities. In the spring of 1863, **bread riots** broke out in a dozen cities and villages across the South. In Richmond, a mob of nearly a thousand hungry women broke into shops and took what they needed.

"Men cannot be expected to fight for the Government that permits their wives & children to starve," one Southerner observed. Although a few wealthy individuals shared their bounty and the Confederate and state governments made efforts at social welfare, every attempt fell short. In late 1864, one desperate farmwife told her husband, "I have always been proud of you, and since your connection with the Confederate army, I have been prouder of you than ever before. I would not have you do anything wrong for the world, but before God, Edward, unless you come home, we must die." When the war ended, one-third of the soldiers had already gone home. A Mississippi deserter explained, "We are poor men and are willing to defend our country but our families [come] first."

Yeomen perceived a profound inequality of sacrifice. They called it "a rich man's war and a poor man's fight." The draft law permitted a man who had money to hire a substitute to take his place. Moreover, the "**twenty-Negro law**" exempted one white man on every plantation with twenty or more slaves. The government intended this law to provide protection for white women and to see that slaves tended the crops, but yeomen perceived it as rich men evading military service. A Mississippian complained that stay-at-home planters sent their slaves into the fields to grow cotton while in plain view "poor soldiers' wives are plowing with *their own* hands to make a subsistence for themselves and children — while their husbands are suffering, bleeding and dying for their country." In fact, most slaveholders went off to war, but the extreme suffering of common folk and the relative immunity of planters increased class friction.

The Richmond government hoped that the crucible of war would mold a region into a nation. Officials actively promoted Confederate nationalism to "excite in our citizens an ardent and enduring attachment to our Government and its institutions." Patriotic songwriters, poets, authors, and artists extolled southern culture. Clergymen assured their congregations that God had blessed slavery and the new nation. Jefferson Davis claimed that the Confederacy was part of a divine plan and asked citizens to observe national days of fasting and prayer. Although these efforts failed to win over thousands of die-hard Unionists and the animosity between yeomen and planters increased, the Confederacy succeeded in inspiring loyalty and pride among the majority of whites. Still, the war threatened to rip the southern social fabric along its racial seam.

The Disintegration of Slavery

The legal destruction of slavery was the product of presidential proclamation, congressional legislation, and eventually constitutional amendment, but the practical destruction of slavery was the product of war, what Lincoln called war's "friction and abrasion." Slaves took advantage of the upheaval to reach for freedom. Some half a million of the South's 4 million slaves ran away to Union military lines. More than 100,000 runaways took up arms as federal soldiers and sailors and attacked slavery directly. Other men and women stayed in the slave quarter, where they staked their claim to more freedom.

War disrupted slavery in a dozen ways. Almost immediately, it called the master away, leaving the mistress to assume responsibility for the plantation. But mistresses could not maintain traditional standards of slave discipline in wartime, and the balance of power shifted. Slaves got to the fields late, worked indifferently, and quit early. Some slaveholders responded violently; most saw no alternative but to strike bargains — offering gifts or part of the crop — to keep slaves at home and at work. An Alabama woman complained that she "begged . . . what little is done." Slaveholders had believed that they "knew" their slaves, but they learned that they did not. When the war began, a North Carolina woman praised her slaves as "diligent and respectful." When it ended, she said, "As to the idea of a *faithful servant, it is all a fiction.*"

As military action sliced through the southern countryside, some slaveholders fled, leaving their slaves behind. Many more took their slaves with them, but flight meant additional chaos and offered slaves new opportunities to resist bondage. Whites' greatest fear — retaliatory violence — rarely occurred, however. Slaves who stayed home steadily undermined white mastery and expanded control over their own lives.

REVIEW How did wartime hardship in the South contribute to class friction?

▶ The North at War

Although little fighting took place on northern soil, Northerners could not avoid being touched by the war. Almost every family had a son, husband, father, or brother in uniform. A New Hampshire man reported in 1863 that "there is mourning all over the land, for there is scarcely a place but what some one has lost a friend or an acquaintance either in battle or the Hospital." Moreover, total war blurred the distinction between home front and battlefield. Men marched off to fight, but preserving the country was also women's work. For civilians as well as soldiers, for women as well as men, war was transforming.

The need to build and fuel the Union war machine boosted the economy. The Union sent nearly 2 million men into the military and still increased production in almost every area. But because the rewards and burdens of patriotism were distributed unevenly, the North experienced sharp, even violent, divisions. Workers confronted employers, whites confronted blacks, and Democrats confronted Republicans. Still, Northerners on the home front remained fervently attached to the Union.

The Government and the Economy

When the war began, the United States had no national banking system, no national currency, and no federal income tax. But the secession of eleven slave states cut the Democrats' strength in Congress in half and destroyed their capacity to resist Republican economic programs. The Legal Tender Act of February 1862 created a national currency, paper money that Northerners called "greenbacks." With the passage of the National Banking Act in February 1863, Congress established a system of national banks that by the 1870s had largely replaced the antebellum system of decentralized state banks. Congress also enacted a series of sweeping tax laws. By revolutionizing the country's banking, monetary, and tax structures, the Republicans generated enormous economic power.

The Republicans' wartime legislation also aimed at integrating the West more thoroughly into the Union. In May 1862, Congress approved the Homestead Act, which offered 160 acres of public land to settlers who would live and labor on it. The Homestead Act bolstered western loyalty and in time resulted in more than a million new farms. The Pacific Railroad Act in July 1862 provided massive federal assistance for building a transcontinental railroad that ran from Omaha to San Francisco when completed in 1869. Congress further bound East and West by subsidizing the Pony Express mail service and a transcontinental telegraph.

Two additional initiatives had long-term economic consequences. Congress created the Department of Agriculture and passed the Land-Grant College Act (also known as the Morrill Act after its sponsor, Representative Justin Morrill of Vermont), which set aside public land to support universities that emphasized "agriculture and mechanical arts." The Lincoln administration immeasurably strengthened the North's effort to win the war, but its ideas also permanently changed the nation.

Women and Work at Home and at War

More than a million farm men were called to the military, so farm women added men's chores to their own. "I met more women driving teams on the road and saw more at work in the fields than men," a visitor to Iowa reported in the fall of 1862. Rising production testified to their success in plowing, planting, and harvesting. Rapid mechanization assisted farm women in their new roles. Cyrus McCormick sold 165,000 of his reapers during the war years. The combination of high prices for farm products and increased production ensured that war and prosperity joined hands in the rural North.

A few industries, such as textiles (which depended on southern cotton), declined during the war, but many more grew. Huge profits prompted one Pennsylvania ironmaster to remark, "I am in no hurry for peace." With orders pouring in and a million nonfarmworkers at war, unemployment declined and wages often rose. The boom proved friendlier to owners than to workers, however. Inflation and taxes cut so deeply into workers' paychecks that their standard of living actually fell.

In cities, women stepped into jobs vacated by men, particularly in manufacturing, and also into essentially new occupations such as government secretaries and clerks. The number of women working for wages rose 40 percent during the war. As more and more women entered the workforce, employers cut wages. In 1864, New York seamstresses working fourteen-hour days earned only $1.54 a week. Urban workers resorted increasingly to strikes to wrench decent salaries from their employers, but their protests rarely succeeded. Nevertheless, tough times failed to undermine the patriotism of most workers.

Most middle-class white women stayed home and contributed to the war effort in traditional ways. They sewed, wrapped bandages, and sold homemade goods at local fairs to raise money to aid the soldiers. Other women expressed their patriotism in an untraditional way — as wartime nurses. Thousands of women on both sides defied prejudices about female delicacy and volunteered to nurse the wounded. Many northern female volunteers worked through the **U.S. Sanitary Commission**, a huge civilian organization that coordinated the efforts of seven thousand local women's groups to buy and distribute clothing, food, and medicine; recruit doctors and nurses; and bury the dead.

Some volunteers went on to become paid military nurses. **Dorothea Dix**, well known for her efforts to reform insane asylums, was named superintendent of female nurses in April 1861. Dix appointed some 3,000 nurses by 1863, when the power to select nurses was taken from her and given to army surgeons. Most nurses worked in hospitals behind the battle lines, but some, like **Clara Barton**, who later founded the American Red Cross, worked in battlefield units. Women who served in the war went on to lead the postwar movement to establish training schools for female nurses.

Politics and Dissent

At first, the bustle of economic and military mobilization seemed to silence politics, but bipartisan unity did not last. Within a year, Democrats were labeling the Republican administration a "reign of terror" and denouncing Republican policies — expanding federal power, subsidizing private business, emancipating the slaves — as unconstitutional, arguing that the "Constitution is as binding in war as in peace." In turn, Republicans were calling Democrats the party of "Dixie, Davis, and the Devil."

When the Republican-dominated Congress enacted the draft law in March 1863, Democrats had another grievance. The law required that all men between the ages of twenty and forty-five enroll and make themselves available for a lottery that would decide who went to war. What poor men found particularly galling were provisions that allowed a draftee to hire a substitute or simply to pay a $300 fee and get out of his military obligation. As in the South, common folk could be heard chanting, "A rich man's war and a poor man's fight."

Linking the draft and emancipation, Democrats argued that Republicans employed an unconstitutional means (the draft) to achieve an unconstitutional end (emancipation). In the summer of 1863, antidraft, antiblack mobs went on rampages in northern cities. In July in New York City, Democratic Irish workingmen—crowded into filthy tenements, gouged by inflation, enraged by the draft, and dead set against fighting to free blacks — erupted in four days of rioting. The **New York City draft riots** killed at least 105 people, most of them black, and left the Colored Orphan Asylum a smoking ruin.

Lincoln called Democratic opposition to the war "the fire in the rear" and believed that it was even more threatening to national survival than were Confederate armies. The antiwar wing of the Democratic Party, the Peace Democrats — whom some called "Copperheads," after the poisonous snake — found their chief spokesman in Ohio congressman **Clement Vallandigham**. He argued that the Confederacy could never be conquered and that Lincoln's attempt had "made this country one of the worst despotisms on earth." Vallandigham demanded: "Stop fighting. Make an armistice. . . . Withdraw your army from the seceding States."

In September 1862, in an effort to stifle opposition to the war, Lincoln placed under military arrest any person who discouraged enlistments, resisted the draft, or engaged in "disloyal" practices. Before the war ended, his administration imprisoned nearly 14,000 individuals, most in the border states. The administration's heavy-handed tactics suppressed free speech, but the campaign fell short of a reign of terror, for the majority of the prisoners were not northern Democratic opponents but Confederates, blockade runners, and citizens of foreign countries, and most of those arrested gained quick release. Still, Lincoln's net did capture Vallandigham, who was arrested, convicted of treason, and eventually banished. In May 1863, Union soldiers escorted the Ohioan to Confederate lines in Tennessee.

REVIEW Why was the U.S. Congress able to pass such a bold legislative agenda during the war?

▶ Grinding Out Victory, 1863–1865

In the early months of 1863, the Union's prospects looked bleak, and the Confederate cause stood at high tide. Then, in July 1863, the tide began to turn. The military man most responsible for this shift was Ulysses S. Grant. Elevated to supreme command, Grant knit together a powerful war machine that integrated a sophisticated command structure, modern technology, and complex logistics and supply systems. But the arithmetic of this plain man remained unchanged: Killing more of the enemy than he kills of you equaled "the complete overthrow of the rebellion."

The North ground out the victory battle by bloody battle. The balance tipped in the Union's favor in 1863, but Southerners were not deterred. The fighting escalated in the last two years of the war. As national elections approached in the fall of 1864, Lincoln expected a war-weary North to reject him. Instead, northern voters declared their willingness to continue the war in the defense of the ideals of union and freedom.

Vicksburg and Gettysburg

Vicksburg, Mississippi, situated on the eastern bank of the Mississippi River, stood between Union forces and complete control of the river. In May 1863, Union forces under Grant laid siege to the city in an effort to starve out the enemy. Civilian residents moved into caves to escape the incessant Union bombardment, and as the **siege of Vicksburg** dragged on, they ate mules and rats to survive. After six weeks, on July 4, 1863, nearly 30,000 rebels marched out of Vicksburg, stacked their arms, and surrendered unconditionally. A Yankee captain wrote home to his wife: "The backbone of the Rebellion is this day broken. The Confederacy is divided. . . . Vicksburg is ours. The Mississippi River is opened, and Gen. Grant is to be our next President."

On the same Fourth of July, word arrived that Union forces had crushed General Lee at Gettysburg, Pennsylvania (Map 15.3). Emboldened by his victory at Chancellorsville in May, Lee and his 75,000-man army had invaded Pennsylvania. On June 28, Union forces under General George G. Meade intercepted the Confederates at the small town of Gettysburg, where Union soldiers occupied the high ground. Three days of furious fighting involving 165,000 troops could not dislodge the Federals from the hills. Lee ached for a decisive victory, and on July 3 he ordered a major assault against the Union center on Cemetery Ridge. The dug-in Yankees enjoyed three-quarters of a mile of clear vision, and they raked the line of Confederate soldiers under General George E. Pickett with cannon and rifle fire. The **battle of Gettysburg** cost Lee more than one-third of his army — 28,000 casualties. "It's all my fault," he lamented. On the night of July 4, 1863, he marched his battered army back to Virginia.

The twin disasters at Vicksburg and Gettysburg proved to be the turning point of the war. The Confederacy could not replace the nearly 60,000 soldiers who were captured, wounded, or killed. Lee never launched another major offensive north of the Mason-Dixon line. It is hindsight, however, that permits us to see the pair of battles as decisive. At the time, the Confederacy still controlled the heartland of the South, and Lee still had a vicious sting. War-weariness threatened to erode the North's will to win before Union armies could destroy the Confederacy's ability to go on.

Grant Takes Command

In September 1863, Union general William Rosecrans placed his army in a dangerous situation in Chattanooga, Tennessee, where he had retreated after defeat at the battle of Chickamauga (see Map 15.3). Rebels surrounded the disorganized bluecoats and threatened to starve them into submission. Grant, now commander of Union forces between the Mississippi River and the Appalachians, arrived in Chattanooga in October. Within weeks, he opened an effective supply line, broke the siege, and routed the Confederate army. The victory at Chattanooga on November 25 opened the door to Georgia. It also confirmed Lincoln's estimation of Grant. In March 1864, the president asked Grant to come east to become the general in chief of all Union armies.

In Washington, General Grant implemented his grand strategy for a war of attrition. He ordered a series of simultaneous assaults from Virginia all the way to Louisiana. Two actions proved particularly significant. In one, General **William Tecumseh Sherman**, whom Grant appointed his successor to command the western armies, plunged southeast toward Atlanta. In the other, Grant, who took control of the Army of the Potomac, went head-to-head with Lee in Virginia for almost four straight weeks.

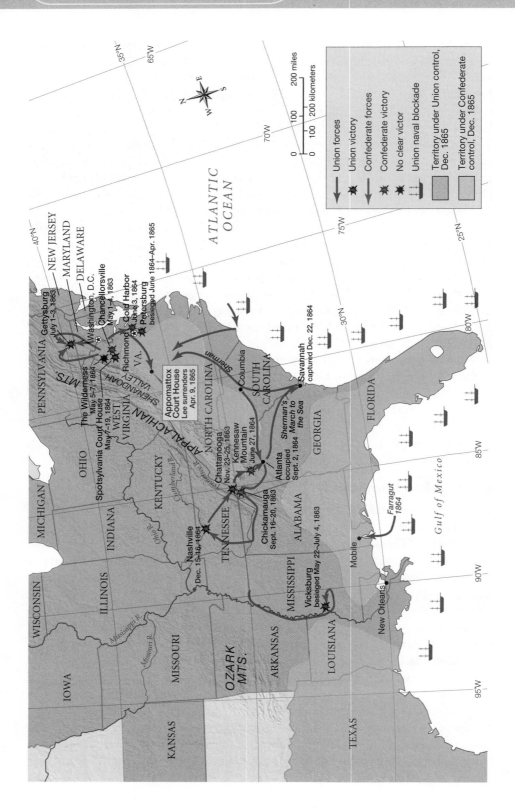

Map legend:

- Union forces
- Union victory
- Confederate forces
- Confederate victory
- No clear victor
- Union naval blockade
- Territory under Union control, Dec. 1865
- Territory under Confederate control, Dec. 1865

Scale: 0   100   200 miles
0   100   200 kilometers

Map labels:

ATLANTIC OCEAN

Gulf of Mexico

Gettysburg July 1–3, 1863
Washington, D.C.
Chancellorsville May 1–4, 1863
Cold Harbor June 3, 1864
Petersburg besieged June 1864–Apr. 1865
Richmond
The Wilderness May 5–7, 1864
Spotsylvania Court House May 7–19, 1864
Appomattox Court House Lee surrenders Apr. 9, 1865
SHENANDOAH VALLEY
Chattanooga Nov. 23–25, 1863
Kennesaw Mountain June 27, 1864
Atlanta occupied Sept. 2, 1864
Sherman's *March to the Sea* Dec. 2, 1864
Columbia
Savannah captured Dec. 22, 1864
Chickamauga Sept. 16–20, 1863
Nashville Dec. 15–16, 1864
Vicksburg besieged May 22–July 4, 1863
Farragut 1864
Mobile
New Orleans

Sherman
Cumberland R.
Tennessee R.
Ohio R.
Mississippi R.
Missouri R.

APPALACHIAN MTS.
OZARK MTS.

States:
MICHIGAN, WISCONSIN, IOWA, ILLINOIS, INDIANA, OHIO, PENNSYLVANIA, NEW JERSEY, MARYLAND, DELAWARE, WEST VIRGINIA, VIRGINIA, KENTUCKY, TENNESSEE, NORTH CAROLINA, SOUTH CAROLINA, GEORGIA, FLORIDA, ALABAMA, MISSISSIPPI, ARKANSAS, LOUISIANA, MISSOURI, KANSAS, TEXAS

40°N, 35°N, 30°N, 25°N
65°W, 70°W, 75°W, 80°W, 85°W, 90°W, 95°W

Wounded Men at Savage's Station
Misery did not end when the cannons ceased firing. The wounded men shown here were but a fraction of those injured or killed during General George McClellan's peninsula campaign in 1862.
Library of Congress.

Grant and Lee met in the first week of May 1864 in a dense tangle of scrub oaks and small pines. Often unable to see more than ten paces, the armies pounded away at each other until approximately 18,000 Yankees and 11,000 rebels had fallen. The savagery of the **battle of the Wilderness** did not compare with that at Spotsylvania Court House a few days later. Frenzied men fought hand to hand for eighteen hours in the rain. One veteran remembered men "piled upon each other in some places four layers deep, exhibiting every ghastly phase of mutilation." Spotsylvania cost Grant another 18,000 casualties and Lee 10,000, but the Yankee bulldog would not let go. Grant kept moving and tangled with Lee again at Cold Harbor, where he suffered 13,000 additional casualties to Lee's 5,000.

Twice as many Union soldiers as rebel soldiers died in four weeks of fighting in Virginia in May and June, but because Lee had only half as many troops as Grant, his losses were equivalent to Grant's. Grant knew that the South could not replace the losses. Moreover, the campaign carried Grant to the outskirts of Petersburg, just

◀ **MAP 15.3**
The Civil War, 1863–1865
Ulysses S. Grant's victory at Vicksburg divided the Confederacy at the Mississippi River. William Tecumseh Sherman's march from Chattanooga to Savannah divided it again. In northern Virginia, Robert E. Lee fought fiercely, but Grant's larger, better-supplied armies prevailed.

south of Richmond, where he abandoned the costly tactic of the frontal assault and began a siege that immobilized both armies and dragged on for nine months.

Simultaneously, Sherman invaded Georgia. Grant instructed Sherman to "get into the interior of the enemy's country as far as you can, inflicting all the damage you can against their War resources." In May, Sherman moved 100,000 men south against 65,000 rebels. Skillful maneuvering, constant skirmishing, and one pitched battle, at Kennesaw Mountain, brought Sherman to Atlanta, which fell on September 2.

Intending to "make Georgia howl," Sherman marched out of Atlanta on November 15 with 62,000 battle-hardened veterans, heading for Savannah, 285 miles away on the Atlantic coast. One veteran remembered, "[We] destroyed all we could not eat, stole their niggers, burned their cotton & gins, spilled their sorghum, burned & twisted their R. Roads and raised Hell generally." **Sherman's March to the Sea** aimed at destroying the will of the southern people. A few weeks earlier, General **Philip H. Sheridan** had carried out his own scorched-earth campaign in the Shenandoah Valley, complying with Grant's order to turn the valley into "a barren waste . . . so that crows flying over it for the balance of this season will have to carry their provender [food] with them." When Sherman's troops entered an undefended Savannah in mid-December, the general telegraphed Lincoln that he had "a Christmas gift" for him. A month earlier, Union voters had bestowed on the president an even greater gift.

The Election of 1864

In the summer of 1864, with Sherman temporarily checked outside Atlanta and Grant bogged down in the siege of Petersburg, the Democratic Party smelled victory in the fall elections. Rankled by a seemingly never-ending war, inflation, the draft, the attack on civil liberties, and the commitment to blacks, Northerners appeared ready for a change. Lincoln himself concluded, "It seems exceedingly probable that this administration will not be re-elected."

The Democrats were badly divided, however. Peace Democrats insisted on an armistice, while "war" Democrats supported the conflict but opposed Republican means of fighting it. The party tried to paper over the chasm by nominating a war candidate, General George McClellan, but adopting a peace platform that demanded that "immediate efforts be made for a cessation of hostilities." Republicans denounced the peace plank as a cut-and-run plan that "virtually proposed to surrender the country to the rebels in arms against us."

The capture of Atlanta in September turned the political tide in favor of the Republicans. Lincoln received 55 percent of the popular vote, but his electoral margin was a whopping 212 to McClellan's 21. Lincoln's party won a resounding victory, one that gave him a mandate to continue the war until slavery and the Confederacy were dead.

The Confederacy Collapses

As 1865 dawned, military disaster littered the Confederate landscape. With the destruction of John B. Hood's army at Nashville in December 1864, the interior of the Confederacy lay in Yankee hands (see Map 15.3). Sherman's troops, rest-

Robert E. Lee and Friends, by Mathew Brady, 1865

One week after his surrender at Appomattox Court House, Robert E. Lee sat for this portrait by Mathew Brady, the country's foremost photographer. Lee is joined by his eldest son, Major General George Washington Custis Lee (left), and a longtime aide, Lieutenant Colonel Walter H. Taylor (right). Lee's sober, weary expression reflects four hard years of war and his final defeat. Already a matchless hero among white Southerners, Lee was well on his way toward saintly immortality. In 1868, one woman described Lee as "bathed in the white light which falls directly upon him from the smile of an approving and sustaining God." Library of Congress.

ing momentarily in Savannah, eyed South Carolina hungrily. Farther north, Grant had Lee's army pinned down in Petersburg, a few miles from Richmond.

In the final days, some Confederates turned their backs on the rebellion. News from the battlefield made it difficult not to conclude that the Yankees had beaten them. Soldiers' wives begged their husbands to return home to keep their families from starving, and the stream of deserters grew dramatically. In most cases, when white Southerners lost the will to continue, it was not because they lost faith in independence but because they had been battered into submission. Despite the deep divisions within the Confederacy, white Southerners had demonstrated a remarkable endurance for their cause. Half of the 900,000 Confederate soldiers had been killed or wounded, and ragged, hungry women and children had sacrificed throughout one of the bloodiest wars then known to history.

The end came with a rush. On February 1, 1865, Sherman's troops stormed out of Savannah into South Carolina, the "cradle of the Confederacy." In Virginia, Lee abandoned Petersburg on April 2, and Richmond fell on April 3. Grant pursued Lee until he surrendered on April 9, 1865, at Appomattox Court House, Virginia. Grant offered generous peace terms. He allowed Lee's men to return home and to keep their horses to help "put in a crop to carry themselves and their families through the next winter." With Lee gone, the remaining Confederate armies lost hope and gave up within two weeks. After four years, the war was over.

No one was more relieved than Lincoln, but his celebration was restrained. He told his cabinet that his postwar burdens would weigh almost as heavily as those of wartime. Seeking a distraction, Lincoln attended Ford's Theatre on the evening of Good Friday, April 14, 1865. John Wilkes Booth, an actor with southern sympathies, slipped into the president's box and shot Lincoln in the head.

He died at 7:22 the following morning. Vice President Andrew Johnson became president. The man who had led the nation through the war would not lead it during the postwar search for a just peace.

> **REVIEW** Why were the siege of Vicksburg and the battle of Gettysburg crucial to the outcome of the war?

▶ Conclusion: The Second American Revolution

A transformed nation emerged from the crucible of war. Antebellum America was decentralized politically and loosely integrated economically. To bend the resources of the country to a Union victory, Congress enacted legislation that reshaped the nation's political and economic character. It created a national currency and banking system and turned to free land, a transcontinental railroad, and miles of telegraph lines to bind the West to the rest of the nation. Congress also established the sovereignty of the federal government and permanently increased its power. To most citizens before the war, Washington meant the post office and little more. During the war, the federal government drafted, taxed, and judged Americans in unprecedented ways. The massive changes brought about by the war — the creation of a national government, a national economy, and a national spirit — led one historian to call the American Civil War the "Second American Revolution."

The Civil War also had a profound effect on individual lives. When the war began in 1861, millions of men dropped their hoes, hammers, and pencils; put on blue or gray uniforms; and fought and suffered for what they passionately believed was right. The war disrupted families, leaving women at home with additional responsibilities and giving others wartime work in factories, offices, and hospitals. It offered blacks new and more effective ways to resist slavery and agitate for equality.

The war devastated the South. Three-fourths of southern white men of military age served in the Confederate army, and half of them were wounded or killed or died of disease. The war destroyed two-fifths of the South's livestock, wrecked half of the farm machinery, and blackened dozens of cities and towns. The immediate impact of the war on the North was more paradoxical. The struggle cost the North a heavy price: 360,000 lives. But rather than devastating the land, the war set the countryside and cities humming with business activity. The radical shift in power from South to North signaled a new direction in American development: the long decline of agriculture and the rise of industrial capitalism.

Most revolutionary of all, the war ended slavery. Ironically, the South's war to preserve slavery destroyed it. Nearly 200,000 black men, including ex-slave William Gould, dedicated their wartime service to its eradication. Because slavery was both a labor and a racial system, the institution was entangled in almost every aspect of southern life. Slavery's uprooting inevitably meant fundamental change. But the full meaning of abolition remained unclear in 1865. Determining the new economic, political, and social status of nearly 4 million ex-slaves would be the principal task of reconstruction.

Reviewing Chapter 15

REVIEW QUESTIONS

1. Why did both the Union and the Confederacy consider control of the border states crucial? (pp. 427–430)

2. Why did the South believe it could win the war despite numerical disadvantages? (pp. 430–433)

3. Why did the Confederacy's bid for international support fail? (pp. 434–440)

4. Why did the Union change policy in 1863 to allow black men to serve in the army? (pp. 440–444)

5. How did wartime hardship in the South contribute to class friction? (pp. 444–447)

6. Why was the U.S. Congress able to pass such a bold legislative agenda during the war? (pp. 447–450)

7. Why were the siege of Vicksburg and the battle of Gettysburg crucial to the outcome of the war? (pp. 450–456)

MAKING CONNECTIONS

1. Despite loathing slavery, Lincoln embraced emancipation as a war objective late and with great caution. Why? In your answer, trace the progression of Lincoln's position, considering how legal, political, military, and moral concerns influenced his policies.

2. The Emancipation Proclamation did not accomplish the destruction of slavery on its own. How did a war over union bring about the end of slavery? In your answer, consider the direct actions of slaves and Union policymakers as well as indirect factors within the Confederacy.

3. In addition to restoring the Union and destroying slavery, what other significant changes did the war produce on the home front and in the nation's capital? In your answer, discuss economic, governmental, and social developments, being attentive to regional variations.

4. Brilliant military strategy alone did not determine the outcome of the war; victory also depended on generating revenue, materiel mobilization, diplomacy, and politics. In light of these considerations, explain why the Confederacy believed it would succeed and why it ultimately failed.

LINKING TO THE PAST

1. Why were white slaveholders surprised by the wartime behavior of slaves? (See chapter 13.)

2. In what ways did the Lincoln administration's wartime policies fulfill the prewar aspirations of Northerners? (See chapters 12 and 14.)

TIMELINE 1861–1865

1861
- **April** Attack on Fort Sumter.
- **April–May** Four Upper South states join Confederacy.
- **July** Union forces routed in first battle of Bull Run (Manassas).
- **August** First Confiscation Act.

1862
- **February** Grant captures Fort Henry and Fort Donelson.
- **March** Confederates defeated at battle of Glorieta Pass.
- **March** Union victory at battle of Pea Ridge.
- **April** Battle of Shiloh in Tennessee ends Confederate bid to control Mississippi valley.
- **April** Confederate Congress authorizes draft.
- **May** Homestead Act.
- **May–July** Union forces defeated during Virginia peninsula campaign.
- **July** Second Confiscation Act.
- **July** Militia Act.
- **September** Battle of Antietam stops Lee's advance into Maryland.

1863
- **January** Emancipation Proclamation becomes law.
- **February** National Banking Act.
- **March** Congress authorizes draft.
- **July** Fall of Vicksburg to Union forces.
- **July** Lee defeated at battle of Gettysburg.
- **July** New York City draft riots.

1864
- **March** Grant appointed Union general in chief.
- **May–June** Wilderness campaign.
- **September** Fall of Atlanta to Sherman.
- **November** Lincoln reelected.
- **December** Fall of Savannah to Sherman.

1865
- **April 2–3** Fall of Petersburg and Richmond.
- **April 9** Lee surrenders to Grant.
- **April 15** Lincoln dies from bullet wound; Vice President Andrew Johnson becomes president.

▶ FOR AN ONLINE BIBLIOGRAPHY, PRACTICE QUIZZES, WEB SITES, IMAGES, AND DOCUMENTS RELATED TO THIS CHAPTER, see the Book Companion Site at **bedfordstmartins.com/roarkvalue**.

▶ FOR DOCUMENTS RELATED TO THIS PERIOD, see Michael Johnson, ed., *Reading the American Past*, Fifth Edition.

16

Reconstruction

1863–1877

IN 1856, JOHN RAPIER, A FREE BLACK BARBER IN FLORENCE, ALABAMA, urged his four freeborn sons to flee the increasingly repressive and dangerous South. Searching for a color-blind society, the brothers scattered around the world. James T. Rapier chose Canada, where he went to live with his uncle in a largely black community and studied Greek and Latin in a log schoolhouse. After his conversion at a Methodist revival, James wrote to his father: "I have not thrown a card in 3 years[,] touched a woman in 2 years[,] smoked nor drunk any Liquor in going on 2 years." He vowed, "I will endeavor to do my part in solving the problems [of African Americans] in my native land."

The Union victory in the Civil War gave James Rapier the opportunity to redeem his pledge. In 1865, after more than eight years of exile, the twenty-seven-year-old Rapier returned to Alabama, where he presided over the first political gathering of former slaves in the state. Alabama freedmen produced a petition that called on the federal government to thoroughly reconstruct the South, to guarantee suffrage, free schools, and equal rights for all men, regardless of color.

Rapier soon discovered that Alabama's whites found it agonizingly difficult to accept defeat and black freedom. They responded to the revolutionary changes under the banner "White Man — Right or Wrong — Still the White Man!" In 1868, when Rapier and other Alabama blacks vigorously supported the Republican presidential candidate, former Union general Ulysses S. Grant, the recently organized Ku Klux Klan went on a bloody rampage of whipping, burning, and shooting. A mob of 150 outraged whites scoured Rapier's neighborhood seeking four black politicians they claimed were trying to "Africanize Alabama." They caught and hanged three, but the "nigger carpet-bagger from Canada" escaped. Rapier considered fleeing the state, but he decided to stay and fight.

James T. Rapier

Black suffrage sent fourteen African American congressmen to Washington, D.C., during Reconstruction, among them James T. Rapier of Alabama. Temporarily at least, he and his black colleagues helped shape post-emancipation society. In 1874, when Rapier spoke on behalf of a civil rights bill, he described the humiliation of being denied service at inns all along his route from Montgomery to Washington. Elsewhere in the world, he said, class and religion were invoked to defend discrimination. In Europe, "they have princes, dukes, lords"; in India, "brahmans or priests, who rank above the sudras or laborers." But in America, "our distinction is color." Alabama Department of Archives and History.

By the early 1870s, Rapier had emerged as Alabama's most prominent black leader. Demanding that the federal government end the violence against ex-slaves, guarantee their civil rights, and give them land, he won election in 1872 to the House of Representatives, where he joined six other black congressmen. Defeated for reelection in 1874 in a campaign marked by white violence and ballot-box stuffing, Rapier turned to cotton farming, generously giving thousands of dollars of his profits to black schools and churches.

But persistent black poverty and unrelenting racial violence convinced Rapier that blacks could never achieve equality and prosperity in the South. He purchased land in Kansas and urged Alabama's blacks to escape with him. In 1883, however, before he could leave Alabama, Rapier died of tuberculosis at the age of forty-five.

In 1865, Union general Carl Schurz had foreseen many of the troubles Rapier would encounter in the postwar South. Schurz concluded that the Civil War was "a revolution but half accomplished." Northern victory had freed the slaves, he observed, but it had not changed former slaveholders' minds about blacks' unfitness for freedom. Left to themselves, whites would "introduce some new system of forced labor, not perhaps exactly slavery in its old form but something similar to it." To defend their freedom, Schurz concluded, blacks would need federal protection, land of their own, and voting rights. Until whites "cut loose from the past, it will be a dangerous experiment to put Southern society upon its own legs."

As Schurz discovered, the end of the war did not mean peace. The United States was one of only two societies in the New World in which slavery ended in a bloody war. (The other was Haiti.) Not surprisingly, racial turmoil continued in the South after the armies quit fighting in 1865. The nation entered one of its most chaotic and conflicted eras — Reconstruction, a violent period that would define the defeated South's status within the Union and the meaning of freedom for ex-slaves.

The place of the South within the nation and the extent of black freedom were determined not only in Washington, D.C., where the federal government played an active role, but also in the state legislatures and county seats of the South, where blacks eagerly participated in the process. Moreover, on farms and plantations from Virginia to Texas, ex-slaves struggled to become free workers while ex-slaveholders clung to the Old South. A small band of white women joined in the struggle for racial equality, and soon their crusade broadened to include gender equality. Their attempts to secure voting rights for women were thwarted, however.

Reconstruction witnessed a gigantic struggle to determine the consequences of Confederate defeat and emancipation. In the end, white Southerners prevailed. Their New South was a different South from the one to which most whites wished to return but also vastly unlike the one of which James Rapier dreamed.

▶ Wartime Reconstruction

Reconstruction did not wait for the end of war. As the odds of a northern victory increased, thinking about reunification quickened. Immediately, a question arose: Who had authority to devise a plan for reconstructing the Union? President Abraham Lincoln firmly believed that reconstruction was a matter of executive responsibility. Congress just as firmly asserted its jurisdiction. Fueling the argument were significant differences about the terms of reconstruction. Lincoln's primary aim was the restoration of national unity, which he sought through a program of speedy, forgiving political reconciliation. Congress feared that the president's program meant restoring the old southern ruling class to power. It wanted assurances of white loyalty and guarantees of black rights.

In their eagerness to formulate a plan for political reunification, neither Lincoln nor Congress gave much attention to the South's land and labor problems. But as the war rapidly eroded slavery and traditional plantation agriculture, Yankee military commanders in the Union-occupied areas of the Confederacy had no choice but to oversee the emergence of a new labor system.

"To Bind Up the Nation's Wounds"

On March 4, 1865, in his second inaugural address, President Lincoln surveyed the history of the war and then looked ahead to peace. "With malice toward none; with charity for all; with firmness in the right, as God gives us to see the right,"

Lincoln said, "let us strive on to finish the work we are in; to bind up the nation's wounds . . . to do all which may achieve and cherish a just, and a lasting peace." Lincoln had contemplated reunion for nearly two years. While deep compassion for the enemy guided his thinking about peace, his plan for reconstruction aimed primarily at shortening the war and ending slavery.

Lincoln's Proclamation of Amnesty and Reconstruction in December 1863 set out his terms. He offered a full pardon, restoring property (except slaves) and political rights, to rebels willing to renounce secession and to accept emancipation. His offer excluded only high-ranking Confederate military and political officers and a few other groups. When 10 percent of a state's voting population had taken an oath of allegiance, the state could organize a new government and be readmitted into the Union. Lincoln's plan did not require ex-rebels to extend social or political rights to ex-slaves, nor did it anticipate a program of long-term federal assistance to freedmen. Clearly, the president looked forward to the rapid, forgiving restoration of the broken Union.

Lincoln's easy terms enraged abolitionists such as Wendell Phillips of Boston, who charged that the president "makes the negro's freedom a mere sham." He "is willing that the negro should be free but seeks nothing else for him." He compared Lincoln to the most passive of the Civil War generals: "What McClellan was on the battlefield — 'Do as little hurt as possible!' — Lincoln is in civil affairs — 'Make as little change as possible!'" Phillips and other northern radicals called instead for a thorough overhaul of southern society. Their ideas proved to be too drastic for most Republicans during the war years, but Congress agreed that Lincoln's plan was inadequate.

In July 1864, Congress put forward a plan of its own. Congressman Henry Winter Davis of Maryland and Senator Benjamin Wade of Ohio jointly sponsored a bill that demanded that at least half of the voters in a conquered rebel state take the oath of allegiance before reconstruction could begin. The **Wade-Davis bill** also banned all ex-Confederates from participating in the drafting of new state constitutions. Finally, the bill guaranteed the equality of freedmen before the law. Congress's reconstruction would be neither as quick nor as forgiving as Lincoln's. When Lincoln refused to sign the bill and let it die, Wade and Davis charged the president with usurpation of power. They warned Lincoln to confine himself to "his executive duties — to obey and execute, not make the laws — to suppress by arms armed rebellion, and leave political organization to Congress."

Undeterred, Lincoln continued to nurture the formation of loyal state governments under his own plan. Four states — Louisiana, Arkansas, Tennessee, and Virginia — fulfilled the president's requirements, but Congress refused to seat representatives from the "Lincoln states." In his last public address in April 1865, Lincoln defended his plan but for the first time expressed publicly his endorsement of suffrage for southern blacks, at least "the very intelligent, and . . . those who serve our cause as soldiers." The announcement demonstrated that Lincoln's thinking about reconstruction was still evolving. Four days later, he was dead.

Land and Labor

Of all the problems raised by the North's victory in the war, none proved more critical than the South's transition from slavery to free labor. As federal armies invaded and occupied the Confederacy, hundreds of thousands of slaves became free workers. In addition, Union armies controlled vast territories in the South where legal title to land had become unclear. The Confiscation Acts passed during the war punished "traitors" by taking away their property. The question of what to do with federally occupied land and how to organize labor on it engaged former slaves, former slaveholders, Union military commanders, and federal government officials long before the war ended.

In the Mississippi valley, occupying federal troops announced a new labor code. It required slaveholders to sign contracts with ex-slaves and to pay wages. It obligated employers to provide food, housing, and medical care. It outlawed whipping, but it reserved to the army the right to discipline blacks who refused to work. The code required black laborers to enter into contracts, work diligently, and remain subordinate and obedient. Military leaders clearly had no intention of promoting a social or economic revolution. Instead, they sought to restore plantation agriculture with wage labor. The effort resulted in a hybrid system that one contemporary called "compulsory free labor," something that satisfied no one.

Planters complained because the new system fell short of slavery. Blacks could not be "transformed by proclamation," a Louisiana sugar planter declared. Yet under the new system, blacks "are expected to perform their new obligations without coercion, & without the fear of punishment which is essential to stimulate the idle and correct the vicious." Without the right to whip, he argued, the new labor system did not have a chance. Either Union soldiers must *compel* the negroes to work," planters insisted, or the planters themselves must "be authorized and sustained in using force."

African Americans found the new regime too reminiscent of slavery to be called free labor. Its chief deficiency, they believed, was the failure to provide them with land of their own. Freedmen believed they had a moral right to land because they and their ancestors had worked it without compensation for more than two centuries. "What's the use of being free if you don't own land enough to be buried in?" one man asked. Several wartime developments led freedmen to believe that the federal government planned to undergird black freedom with landownership.

In January 1865, General William Tecumseh Sherman set aside part of the coast south of Charleston for black settlement. He devised the plan to relieve himself of the burden of thousands of impoverished blacks who trailed desperately behind his army. By June 1865, some 40,000 freedmen sat on 400,000 acres of "Sherman land." In addition, in March 1865, Congress passed a bill establishing the Bureau of Refugees, Freedmen, and Abandoned Lands. The **Freedmen's Bureau**, as it was called, distributed food and clothing to destitute Southerners and eased the transition of blacks from slaves to free persons. Congress also authorized the agency to divide abandoned and confiscated land into 40-acre plots, to rent them to freedmen, and eventually to sell them "with such title as the United States can convey." By June 1865, the bureau had situated nearly

10,000 black families on a half million acres abandoned by fleeing planters. Other ex-slaves eagerly anticipated farms of their own.

Despite the flurry of activity, wartime reconstruction failed to produce agreement about whether the president or Congress had the authority to devise policy or what proper policy should be.

The African American Quest for Autonomy

Ex-slaves never had any doubt about what they wanted from freedom. They had only to contemplate what they had been denied as slaves. Slaves had to remain on their plantations; freedom allowed blacks to see what was on the other side of the hill. Slaves had to be at work in the fields by dawn; freedom permitted blacks to sleep through a sunrise. Freedmen also tested the etiquette of racial subordination. "Lizzie's maid passed me today when I was coming from church *without speaking to me*," huffed one plantation mistress.

To whites, emancipation looked like pure anarchy. Blacks, they said, had reverted to their natural condition: lazy, irresponsible, and wild. Without the discipline of slavery, whites predicted, blacks would go the way of "the Indian and the buffalo." Actually, former slaves were experimenting with freedom, but they could not long afford to roam the countryside, neglect work, and casually provoke whites. Soon, most were back at work in whites' kitchens and fields.

But other items on ex-slaves' agenda of freedom endured. They continued to dream of land and economic independence. "The way we can best take care of ourselves is to have land," one former slave declared in 1865, "and turn it and till it by our own labor." Freedmen also wanted to learn to read and write. Many black soldiers had become literate in the Union army, and they understood the value of the pen and book. "I wishes the Childern all in School," one black veteran asserted. "It is beter for them then to be their Surveing a mistes [mistress]."

The restoration of broken families was another persistent black aspiration. Thousands of freedmen took to the roads in 1865 to look for kin who had been sold away or to free those who were being held illegally as slaves. A black soldier from Missouri wrote his daughters that he was coming for them. "I will have you if it cost me my life," he declared. "Your Miss Kitty said that I tried to steal you," he told them. "But I'll let her know that god never intended for a man to steal his own flesh and blood." And he swore that "if she meets me with ten thousand soldiers, she [will] meet her enemy."

Independent worship was another continuing aspiration. African Americans greeted freedom with a mass exodus from white churches, where they had been required to worship when slaves. Some joined the newly established southern branches of all-black northern churches, such as the African Methodist Episcopal Church. Others formed black versions of the major southern denominations, Baptists and Methodists. Freedmen interpreted the events of the Civil War and reconstruction as Christian people. One black woman thanked Lincoln for the Emancipation Proclamation, declaring, "When you are dead and in Heaven, in a thousand years that action of yours will make the Angels sing your praises I know it."

REVIEW Why did Congress object to Lincoln's wartime plan for reconstruction?

▶ Presidential Reconstruction

Abraham Lincoln died on April 15, 1865, just hours after John Wilkes Booth shot him at a Washington, D.C., theater. Chief Justice Salmon P. Chase immediately administered the oath of office to Vice President **Andrew Johnson** of Tennessee. Congress had adjourned in March and would not reconvene until December. Throughout the summer and fall, the "accidental president" made critical decisions about the future of the South without congressional advice. With dizzying speed, he drew up and executed a plan of reconstruction.

Congress returned to the capital in December to find that, as far as the president and former Confederates were concerned, reconstruction was completed. Most Republicans, however, thought Johnson's puny demands of ex-rebels made a mockery of the sacrifice of Union soldiers. Instead of honoring the dead by insisting on "a new birth of freedom," as Lincoln had promised in his 1863 speech at Gettysburg, Johnson had acted as midwife to the rebirth of the Old South and the stillbirth of black liberty. They proceeded to dismantle Johnson's program and substitute a program of their own.

Johnson's Program of Reconciliation

Born in 1808 in Raleigh, North Carolina, Andrew Johnson was the son of illiterate parents. Self-educated and ambitious, Johnson moved to Tennessee, where he worked as a tailor, accumulated a fortune in land, acquired five slaves, and built a career in politics championing the South's common white people and assailing its "illegitimate, swaggering, bastard, scrub aristocracy." The only senator from a Confederate state to remain loyal to the Union, Johnson held the planter class responsible for secession. Less than two weeks before he became president, he announced what he would do to planters if he ever had the chance: "I would arrest them — I would try them — I would convict them and I would hang them."

Despite such statements, Johnson was no friend of the Republicans. A Democrat all his life, Johnson occupied the White House only because the Republican Party in 1864 had needed a vice presidential candidate who would appeal to loyal, Union-supporting Democrats. Johnson vigorously defended states' rights (but not secession) and opposed Republican efforts to expand the power of the federal government. A steadfast supporter of slavery, Johnson had owned slaves until 1862, when Tennessee rebels, angry at his Unionism, confiscated them. When he grudgingly accepted emancipation, it was more because he hated planters than sympathized with slaves. "Damn the negroes," he said. "I am fighting those traitorous aristocrats, their masters." At a time when the nation confronted the future of black Americans, the new president harbored unshakable racist convictions. Africans, Johnson said, were "inferior to the white man in point of intellect — better calculated in physical structure to undergo drudgery and hardship."

Like Lincoln, Johnson stressed the rapid restoration of civil government in the South. Like Lincoln, he promised to pardon most, but not all, ex-rebels. Johnson recognized the state governments created by Lincoln but set out his own requirements for restoring the other rebel states to the Union. All that the citizens of a state had to do was to renounce the right of secession, deny that the debts of the Confederacy were legal and binding, and ratify the Thirteenth Amendment abolishing slavery, which became part of the Constitution in December 1865.

Johnson's eagerness to restore relations with southern states and his lack of sympathy for blacks also led him to return to pardoned ex-Confederates all confiscated and abandoned land, even if it was in the hands of freedmen. Reformers were shocked. They had expected the president's hatred of planters to mean the permanent confiscation of the South's plantations and the distribution of the land to loyal freedmen. Instead, his instructions canceled the promising beginnings made by General Sherman and the Freedmen's Bureau to settle blacks on land of their own. As one freedman observed, "Things was hurt by Mr. Lincoln getting killed."

White Southern Resistance and Black Codes

In the summer of 1865, delegates across the South gathered to draw up the new state constitutions required by Johnson's plan of reconstruction. Rather than take their medicine, delegates choked on even the president's mild requirements. Refusing to renounce secession, the South Carolina and Georgia conventions merely "repudiated" their secession ordinances, preserving in principle their right to secede. South Carolina and Mississippi refused to disown their Confederate war debts. Mississippi rejected the Thirteenth Amendment outright, and Alabama rejected it in part. Despite these defiant acts, Johnson did nothing. White Southerners began to think that by standing up for themselves they — not victorious Northerners — would shape reconstruction.

In the fall of 1865, newly elected southern legislators across the South adopted a series of laws known as **black codes**, which made a travesty of black freedom. The codes sought to keep ex-slaves subordinate to whites by subjecting them to every sort of discrimination. Several states made it illegal for blacks to own a gun. Mississippi made insulting gestures and language by blacks a criminal offense. The codes barred blacks from jury duty. Not a single southern state granted any black the right to vote.

At the core of the black codes, however, lay the matter of labor. Faced with the death of slavery, legislators sought to hustle freedmen back to the plantations. Whites were almost universally opposed to black landownership. Whitelaw Reid, a northern visitor to the South, found that the "man who should sell small tracts to them would be in actual personal danger." South Carolina attempted to limit blacks to either farmwork or domestic service by requiring them to pay annual taxes of $10 to $100 to work in any other occupation. Mississippi declared that blacks who did not possess written evidence of employment could be declared vagrants and be subject to involuntary plantation labor. Under so-called apprenticeship laws, courts bound thousands of black children — orphans and others whose parents they deemed unable to support them — to work for planter "guardians."

Johnson refused to intervene. A staunch defender of states' rights, he believed that the citizens of every state should be free to write their own constitutions and laws. Moreover, Johnson was as eager as other white Southerners to restore white supremacy and black subordination. As he remarked in 1865, "White men alone must manage the South."

But Johnson also followed the path that he believed offered him the greatest political return. A conservative Tennessee Democrat at the head of a northern Republican Party, he began to look southward for political allies. Despite tough talk about punishing traitors, he personally pardoned fourteen thousand wealthy or high-ranking ex-Confederates. By pardoning powerful whites, by accepting governments even when they failed to satisfy his minimal demands, and by acquiescing in the black codes, he won useful southern friends.

In the fall elections of 1865, white Southerners dramatically expressed their mood. To represent them in Congress, they chose former Confederates. Of the eighty senators and representatives they sent to Washington, fifteen had served in the Confederate army, ten of them as generals. Another sixteen had served in civil and judicial posts in the Confederacy. Nine others had served in the Confederate Congress. One — Alexander Stephens — had been vice president of the Confederacy. As one Georgian remarked, "It looked as though Richmond had moved to Washington."

Expansion of Federal Authority and Black Rights

Southerners had blundered monumentally. They had assumed that what Andrew Johnson was willing to accept, Republicans would accept as well. But southern intransigence compelled even moderates to conclude that ex-rebels were a "generation of vipers," still untrustworthy and dangerous. So angry were Republicans with the rebels that the federal government refused to supply artificial limbs to disabled Southerners, as they did for Union veterans.

The black codes became a symbol of southern intentions to "restore all of slavery but its name." Northerners were hardly saints when it came to racial justice, but black freedom had become a hallowed war aim. "We tell the white men of Mississippi," the *Chicago Tribune* roared, "that the men of the North will convert the State of Mississippi into a frog pond before they will allow such laws to disgrace one foot of the soil in which the bones of our soldiers sleep and over which the flag of freedom waves."

The moderate majority of the Republican Party wanted only assurance that slavery and treason were dead. They did not champion black equality, the confiscation of plantations, or black voting, as did the radical minority within the party. But southern obstinacy had succeeded in forging unity (at least temporarily) among Republican factions. In December 1865, exercising Congress's right to determine the qualifications of its members, Republicans refused to seat the southern representatives elected in the fall elections. Rather than accept Johnson's claim that the "work of restoration" was done, Congress challenged his executive power.

Republican senator Lyman Trumbull declared that the president's policy meant that an ex-slave would "be tyrannized over, abused, and virtually reenslaved without some legislation by the nation for his protection." Early in 1866, the moderates produced two bills that strengthened the federal shield. The first, the Freedmen's Bureau bill, prolonged the life of the agency established by the previous Congress. It had distributed food, supervised labor contracts, and sponsored schools for freedmen. Arguing that the Constitution never contemplated a "system for the support of indigent persons," President

Andrew Johnson vetoed the bill. Congress failed by a narrow margin to over-ride the president's veto.

The moderates designed their second measure, what would become the **Civil Rights Act of 1866**, to nullify the black codes by affirming African Americans' rights to "full and equal benefit of all laws and proceedings for the security of person and property as is enjoyed by white citizens." The act boldly required the end of racial discrimination in state laws and represented an extraordinary ex-pansion of black rights and federal authority. The president argued that the civil rights bill amounted to "unconstitutional invasion of states' rights" and vetoed it. In essence, he denied that the federal government possessed the authority to protect the civil rights of blacks.

In April 1866, an incensed Republican Party again pushed the civil rights bill through Congress and overrode the presidential veto. In July, it passed another Freedmen's Bureau bill and overrode Johnson's veto. For the first time in American history, Congress had overridden presidential vetoes of major legislation. As a worried South Carolinian observed, Johnson had succeeded in uniting the Republicans and probably touched off "a fight this fall such as has never been seen."

REVIEW How did the North respond to the passage of black codes in the southern states?

▶ Congressional Reconstruction

By the summer of 1866, President Andrew Johnson and Congress had dropped their gloves and stood toe-to-toe in a bare-knuckle contest unprecedented in American history. Johnson made it clear that he would not budge on either con-stitutional issues or policy. Moderate Republicans responded by amending the Constitution. But the obstinacy of Johnson and white Southerners pushed Republican moderates ever closer to the radicals and to acceptance of additional federal in-tervention in the South. Congress also voted to impeach the president for the first time since the nation was formed. In time, Congress debated whether to make voting rights color-blind, while women sought to make voting sex-blind as well.

The Fourteenth Amendment and Escalating Violence

In June 1866, Congress passed the **Fourteenth Amendment** to the Constitution, and two years later it gained the necessary ratification of three-fourths of the states. The most important provisions of this complex amendment made all native-born or naturalized persons American citizens and prohibited states from abridging the "privileges and immunities" of citizens, depriving them of "life, liberty, or property without due process of law," and denying them "equal protec-tion of the laws." By making blacks national citizens, the amendment provided a national guarantee of equality before the law. In essence, it protected blacks against violation by southern state governments.

The Fourteenth Amendment also dealt with voting rights. It gave Congress the right to reduce the congressional representation of states that withheld suffrage from some of its adult male population. In other words, white Southerners could either allow black men to vote or see their representation in Washington slashed. Whatever happened, Republicans stood to benefit from the Fourteenth Amendment. If southern whites granted voting rights to freedmen, Republicans would gain valuable black votes. If whites refused, the representation of southern Democrats would plunge.

The Fourteenth Amendment's suffrage provisions ignored the small band of politicized women who had emerged from the war demanding "the ballot for the two disenfranchised classes, negroes and women." Founding the **American Equal Rights Association** in 1866, **Susan B. Anthony** and **Elizabeth Cady Stanton** lobbied for "a government by the people, and the whole people; for the people and the whole people." They felt betrayed when their old antislavery allies refused to work for their goals. "It was the Negro's hour," Frederick Douglass explained. Senator Charles Sumner suggested that woman suffrage could be "the great question of the future."

The Fourteenth Amendment provided for punishment of any state that excluded voters on the basis of race but not on the basis of sex. The amendment also introduced the word *male* into the Constitution when it referred to a citizen's right to vote. Stanton predicted that "if that word 'male' be inserted, it will take us a century at least to get it out."

Tennessee approved the Fourteenth Amendment in July, and Congress promptly welcomed the state's representatives and senators back. Had President Johnson counseled other southern states to ratify this relatively mild amendment and warned them that they faced the fury of an outraged Republican Party if they refused, they might have listened. Instead, Johnson advised Southerners to reject the Fourteenth Amendment and to rely on him to trounce the Republicans in the fall congressional elections.

Johnson had decided to make the Fourteenth Amendment the overriding issue of the 1866 elections and to gather its white opponents into a new conservative party, the National Union Party. The

Elizabeth Cady Stanton and Susan B. Anthony, 1870
Outspoken suffragists Elizabeth Cady Stanton (left) and Susan B. Anthony (right) were veteran reformers who advocated, among other things, better working conditions for labor, married women's property rights, liberalization of divorce laws, and women's admission into colleges and trade schools. Their passion for other causes led some conservatives to oppose women's political rights because they equated the suffragist cause with radicalism in general. Women could not easily overcome such views, and the long struggle for the vote eventually drew millions of women into public life.
©Bettmann/Corbis.

president's strategy suffered a setback when whites in several southern cities went on rampages against blacks. When a mob in New Orleans assaulted delegates to a black suffrage convention, thirty-four blacks died. In Memphis, white mobs killed at least forty-six people. The slaughter shocked Northerners and renewed skepticism about Johnson's claim that southern whites could be trusted. "Who doubts that the Freedmen's Bureau ought to be abolished forthwith," a New Yorker observed sarcastically, "and the blacks remitted to the paternal care of their old masters, who 'understand the nigger, you know, a great deal better than the Yankees can.'"

The 1866 elections resulted in an overwhelming Republican victory. Johnson had bet that Northerners would not support federal protection of black rights and that a racist backlash would blast the Republican Party. But the war was still fresh in northern minds, and as one Republican explained, southern whites "with all their intelligence were traitors, the blacks with all their ignorance were loyal."

Radical Reconstruction and Military Rule

When Johnson continued to urge Southerners to reject the Fourteenth Amendment, every southern state except Tennessee voted it down. "The last one of the sinful ten," thundered Representative James A. Garfield of Ohio, "has flung back into our teeth the magnanimous offer of a generous nation." After the South rejected the moderates' program, the radicals seized the initiative.

Each act of defiance by southern whites had boosted the standing of the radicals within the Republican Party. Except for freedmen themselves, no one did more to make freedom the "mighty moral question of the age." Radicals such as Massachusetts senator Charles Sumner and Pennsylvania representative Thaddeus Stevens did not speak with a single voice, but they united in demanding civil and political equality. Southern states were "like clay in the hands of the potter," Stevens declared in January 1867, and he called on Congress to begin reconstruction all over again.

In March 1867, Congress overturned the Johnson state governments and initiated military rule of the South. The **Military Reconstruction Act** (and three subsequent acts) divided the ten unreconstructed Confederate states into five military districts. Congress placed a Union general in charge of each district and instructed him to "suppress insurrection, disorder, and violence" and to begin political reform. After the military had completed voter registration, which would include black men, voters in each state would elect delegates to conventions that would draw up new state constitutions. Each constitution would guarantee black suffrage. When the voters of each state had approved the constitution and the state legislature had ratified the Fourteenth Amendment, the state could submit its work to Congress. If Congress approved, the state's senators and representatives could be seated, and political reunification would be accomplished.

Radicals proclaimed the provision for black suffrage "a prodigious triumph," for it extended far beyond the limited suffrage provisions of the Fourteenth Amendment. Republicans now believed that only the voting power of ex-slaves could bring about a permanent revolution in the South. When combined with the disfranchisement of thousands of ex-rebels, it promised to cripple any neo-Confederate resurgence and guarantee Republican state governments in the South.

Despite its bold suffrage provision, the Military Reconstruction Act of 1867 disappointed those who also advocated the confiscation of southern plantations and their redistribution to ex-slaves. Thaddeus Stevens agreed with the freedman who said, "Give us our own land and we take care of ourselves, but without land, the old masters can hire us or starve us, as they please." But most Republicans believed they had provided blacks with what they needed: equal legal rights and the ballot. If blacks were to get land, they would have to gain it themselves.

Declaring that he would rather sever his right arm than sign such a formula for "anarchy and chaos," Andrew Johnson vetoed the Military Reconstruction Act. Congress overrode his veto the very same day, dramatizing the shift in power from the executive to the legislative branch of government. With the passage of the Reconstruction Acts of 1867, congressional reconstruction was virtually completed. Congress left whites owning most of the South's land but, in a departure that justified the term "radical reconstruction," had given black men the ballot. In 1867, the nation began an unprecedented experiment in interracial democracy — at least in the South, for Congress's plan did not touch the North. But before the spotlight swung away from Washington to the South, the president and Congress had one more scene to play.

Impeaching a President

Despite his defeats, Andrew Johnson had no intention of yielding control of reconstruction. In a dozen ways, he sabotaged Congress's will and encouraged southern whites to resist. He issued a flood of pardons, waged war against the Freedmen's Bureau, and replaced Union generals eager to enforce Congress's Reconstruction Acts with conservative officers eager to defeat them. Johnson claimed that he was merely defending the "violated Constitution." At bottom, however, the president subverted congressional reconstruction to protect southern whites from what he considered the horrors of "Negro domination."

When Congress realized that overriding Johnson's vetoes did not ensure that it got its way, it looked for other ways to exert its will. According to the Constitution, the House of Representatives can impeach and the Senate can try any federal official for "treason, bribery, or other high crimes and misdemeanors." Radicals argued that Johnson's abuse of constitutional powers and his failure to fulfill constitutional obligations to enforce the law were impeachable offenses. But moderates interpreted the constitutional provision to mean violation of criminal statutes. As long as Johnson refrained from breaking the law, impeachment (the process of formal charges of wrongdoing against the president or other federal official) remained stalled.

Then, in August 1867, Johnson suspended Secretary of War Edwin M. Stanton from office. The Tenure of Office Act, which had been passed earlier in the year, demanded the approval of the Senate for the removal of any government official who had been appointed with Senate approval. As required by the act, the president requested the Senate to consent to Stanton's dismissal. When the Senate balked, Johnson removed Stanton anyway. "Is the President crazy, or only drunk?" asked a dumbfounded Republican moderate. "I'm afraid his doings will make us all favor impeachment."

News of Johnson's open defiance of the law convinced every Republican in the House to vote for a resolution impeaching the president. Supreme Court chief justice Salmon Chase presided over the Senate trial, which lasted from March until May 1868. Chase refused to allow Johnson's opponents to raise broad issues of misuse of power and forced them to argue their case exclusively on the narrow legal grounds of Johnson's removal of Stanton. Johnson's lawyers argued that the president had not committed a criminal offense, that the Tenure of Office Act was unconstitutional, and that in any case it did not apply to Stanton, who had been appointed by Lincoln. When the critical vote came, thirty-five senators voted guilty and nineteen not guilty. The impeachment forces fell one vote short of the two-thirds needed to convict.

After his trial, Johnson called a truce, and for the remaining ten months of his term, congressional reconstruction proceeded unhindered by presidential interference. Without interference from Johnson, Congress revisited the suffrage issue.

The Fifteenth Amendment and Women's Demands

In February 1869, Republicans passed the **Fifteenth Amendment** to the Constitution, which prohibited states from depriving any citizen of the right to vote because of "race, color, or previous condition of servitude." The Reconstruction Acts of 1867 already required black suffrage in the South; the Fifteenth Amendment extended black voting nationwide. Partisan advantage played an important role in the amendment's passage. Gains by northern Democrats in the 1868 elections worried Republicans, and black voters now represented the balance of power in several northern states. By giving the ballot to northern blacks, Republicans could lessen their own political vulnerability. As one Republican congressman observed, "Party expediency and exact justice coincide for once."

Some Republicans, however, found the final wording of the Fifteenth Amendment "lame and halting." Rather than absolutely guaranteeing the right to vote, the amendment merely prohibited exclusion on grounds of race. The distinction would prove to be significant. In time, white Southerners would devise tests of literacy and property and other apparently nonracial measures that would effectively disfranchise blacks yet not violate the Fifteenth Amendment. But an amendment that fully guaranteed the right to vote courted defeat outside the South. Rising antiforeign sentiment — against the Chinese in California and European immigrants in the Northeast — caused states to resist giving up total control of suffrage requirements. In March 1870, after three-fourths of the states had ratified it, the Fifteenth Amendment became part of the Constitution. Republicans generally breathed a sigh of relief, confident that black suffrage was "the last great point that remained to be settled of the issues of the war."

Woman suffrage advocates, however, were sorely disappointed with the Fifteenth Amendment's failure to extend voting rights to women. The amendment denied states the right to forbid suffrage only on the basis of race. Elizabeth Cady Stanton and Susan B. Anthony condemned the Republicans' "negro first" strategy and pointed out that women remained "the only class of citizens wholly unrepresented in the government." Stanton wondered aloud why ignorant black men should legislate for educated and cultured white women. Increasingly, activist women concluded that woman "must not put her trust in man." The Fifteenth Amendment severed the early feminist movement from its abolitionist roots. Over the next several decades, feminists established an independent suffrage crusade that drew millions of women into political life.

Republicans took enough satisfaction in the Fifteenth Amendment to promptly scratch the "Negro question" from the agenda of national politics. Even that steadfast crusader for equality Wendell Phillips concluded that the black man now held "sufficient shield in his own hands. . . . Whatever he suffers will be largely now, and in future, his own fault." Northerners had no idea of the violent struggles that lay ahead.

REVIEW Why did Johnson urge the southern states to reject the Fourteenth Amendment?

▶ The Struggle in the South

Northerners believed they had discharged their responsibilities with the Reconstruction Acts and the amendments to the Constitution, but Southerners knew that the battle had just begun. Black suffrage established the foundation for the rise of the Republican Party in the South. Gathering together outsiders and outcasts, southern Republicans won elections, wrote new state constitutions, and formed new state governments.

Challenging the established class for political control was dangerous business. Equally dangerous were the confrontations that took place on southern farms and plantations, where blacks sought to give economic meaning to their newly won legal and political equality. Ex-masters had their own ideas about the labor system that should replace slavery. Freedom remained contested territory, and Southerners fought pitched battles with one another to determine the contours of their new world.

Freedmen, Yankees, and Yeomen

African Americans made up the majority of southern Republicans. After gaining voting rights in 1867, nearly all eligible black men registered to vote as Republicans, grateful to the party that had freed them and granted them the franchise. "It is the hardest thing in the world to keep a negro away from the polls," observed an Alabama white man. Black women, like white women, remained disfranchised, but they mobilized along with black men. In the 1868 presidential election, they bravely wore buttons supporting the Republican candidate, Ulysses S. Grant. Southern blacks did not all have identical political priorities, but they united in their desire for education and equal treatment before the law.

Northern whites who made the South their home after the war were a second element of the South's Republican Party. Conservative white Southerners called them **carpetbaggers**, men so poor that they could stuff all their earthly belongings in a single carpet-sided suitcase and swoop southward like buzzards to "fatten on our misfortunes." But most Northerners who moved south were young men who looked upon the South as they did the West — as a promising place to make a living. Northerners in the southern Republican Party consistently supported programs that encouraged vigorous economic development along the lines of the northern free-labor model.

Southern whites made up the third element of the South's Republican Party. Approximately one out of four white Southerners voted Republican. The other three condemned the one who did as a traitor to his region and his race and called him a **scalawag**, a term for runty horses and low-down, good-for-nothing rascals. Yeoman farmers accounted for the majority of southern white Republicans. Some were Unionists who emerged from the war with bitter memories of Confederate persecution. Others were small farmers who wanted to end state governments' favoritism toward plantation owners. Yeomen supported initiatives for public schools and for expanding economic opportunity in the South.

The South's Republican Party, then, was made up of freedmen, Yankees, and yeomen — an improbable coalition. The mix of races, regions, and classes inevitably meant friction as each group maneuvered to define the party. But Reconstruction represents an extraordinary moment in American politics: Blacks and whites joined together in the Republican Party to pursue political change. Formally, of course, only men participated in politics — casting ballots and holding offices — but white and black women also played a part in the political struggle by joining in parades and rallies, attending stump speeches, and even campaigning.

Reconstruction politics was not for cowards. Most whites in the South condemned southern Republicans as illegitimate and felt justified in doing whatever they could to stamp them out. Violence against blacks — the "white terror" — took brutal institutional form in 1866 with the formation in Tennessee of the

Ku Klux Klan Rider in Tennessee about 1868
The white robes that we associate with the Ku Klux Klan are a twentieth-century phenomenon. During Reconstruction, Klansmen wore robes of various designs and colors. Hooded horses added another element to the Klan's terror. Tennessee State Museum Collection.

Ku Klux Klan, a social club of Confederate veterans that quickly developed into a paramilitary organization supporting Democrats. The Klan went on a rampage of whipping, hanging, shooting, burning, and throat-cutting to defeat Republicans and restore white supremacy. Rapid demobilization of the Union army after the war left only twenty thousand troops to patrol the entire South. Without effective military protection, southern Republicans had to take care of themselves.

Republican Rule

In the fall of 1867, southern states held elections for delegates to state constitutional conventions, as required by the Reconstruction Acts. About 40 percent of the white electorate stayed home because they had been disfranchised or because they had decided to boycott politics. Republicans won three-fourths of the seats. About 15 percent of the Republican delegates to the conventions were Northerners who had moved south, 25 percent were African Americans, and 60 percent were white Southerners. As a British visitor observed, the delegate elections reflected "the mighty revolution that had taken place in America." But Democrats described the state conventions as zoos of "baboons, monkeys, mules . . . and other jackasses." In fact, the conventions brought together serious, purposeful men who hammered out the legal framework for a new order.

The reconstruction constitutions introduced two broad categories of changes in the South: those that reduced aristocratic privilege and increased democratic equality and those that expanded the state's responsibility for the general welfare. In the first category, the constitutions adopted universal male suffrage, abolished property qualifications for holding office, and made more offices elective and fewer appointed. In the second category, they enacted prison reform; made the state responsible for caring for orphans, the insane, and the deaf and mute; and exempted debtors' homes from seizure.

To Democrats, however, the new state constitutions looked like wild revolution. They were blind to the fact that no constitution confiscated and redistributed land, as virtually every former slave wished, or disfranchised ex-rebels wholesale, as most southern Unionists advocated. And Democrats were convinced that the new constitutions initiated "Negro domination" in politics. In fact, although four out of five Republican voters were black men, more than four out of five Republican officeholders were white. Southerners sent fourteen black congressmen and two black senators to Washington, but only 6 percent of Southerners in Congress during Reconstruction were black. The sixteen black men in Congress included exceptional men, such as Representative **James T. Rapier** of Alabama (see pages 459–461) and Mississippi senator Blanche K. Bruce, who was born a slave in Virginia and became a local school superintendent in Mississippi, a position that paved his way to the Senate. No state legislature experienced "Negro rule," despite black majorities in the populations of some states.

Southern voters ratified the new constitutions and swept Republicans into power. When the former Confederate states ratified the Fourteenth Amendment, Congress readmitted them. Southern Republicans then turned to a staggering array of problems. Wartime destruction — burned cities, shattered bridges,

Students at a Freedmen's School in Virginia, ca. 1870s
"The people are hungry and thirsty after knowledge," a former slave observed immediately after the Civil War. African American leader Booker T. Washington remembered "a whole race trying to go to school." The students at this Virginia school stand in front of their log-cabin classroom reading; for people long forbidden to learn to read and write, literacy symbolized freedom. Literacy also allowed those who were deeply religious to experience the joy of reading the Bible for themselves and those who were merely practical to understand labor contracts and participate knowledgeably in politics.
Valentine Museum, Cook Collection.

broken levees, devastated railroads — littered the landscape. The South's share of the nation's wealth had fallen from 30 percent to only 12 percent. Manufacturing, always a small contributor to the southern economy, limped along at a fraction of prewar levels, and once-powerful agricultural production remained anemic. Without the efforts of the Freedmen's Bureau, black and white Southerners would have starved. Making matters worse, racial harassment and reactionary violence dogged Southerners who sought reform. In this desperate context, Republicans struggled to breathe life into the region.

Activity focused on three areas — education, civil rights, and economic development. Every state inaugurated a system of public education. Before the Civil War, whites had deliberately kept slaves illiterate, and planter-dominated governments rarely spent tax money to educate the children of yeomen. By 1875, half of Mississippi's and South Carolina's eligible children (the majority of whom were black) were attending school. Although schools were underfunded, literacy rates rose sharply. Public schools were racially segregated, but education remained for many blacks a tangible, deeply satisfying benefit of freedom and Republican rule.

State legislatures also attacked racial discrimination and defended civil rights. Republicans especially resisted efforts to segregate blacks from whites in public transportation. Mississippi levied fines of up to $1,000 and three years in jail for owners of railroads and steamboats that pushed blacks into "smoking cars" or to lower decks. Well-off blacks took particular aim at hotels and theaters that denied "full and equal rights." But passing color-blind laws was one thing; enforcing them was another. A Mississippian complained: "Education amounts to nothing, good behavior counts for nothing, even money cannot buy for a colored man or woman decent treatment and the comforts that white people claim and can obtain." Despite the laws, segregation — later called Jim Crow — developed at white insistence and became a feature of southern life long before the end of the Reconstruction era.

Republican governments also launched ambitious programs of economic development. They envisioned a South of diversified agriculture, roaring factories, and booming towns. State legislatures chartered scores of banks and industrial companies, appropriated funds to fix ruined levees and drain swamps, and went on a railroad-building binge. These efforts fell far short of solving the South's economic troubles, however. In addition, Republican spending to stimulate economic growth meant rising taxes and enormous debt that siphoned funds from schools and other programs.

The southern Republicans' record, then, was mixed. To their credit, the biracial party adopted an ambitious agenda to change the South, even though money was scarce, the Democrats continued their harassment, and factionalism threatened the Republican Party from within. However, corruption infected Republican governments in the South. Public morality reached new lows everywhere in the nation after the Civil War, and the chaos of the postwar South proved fertile soil for bribery, fraud, and influence peddling. Despite shortcomings, however, the Republican Party made headway in its efforts to purge the South of aristocratic privilege and racist oppression. Republican governments had less success in overthrowing the long-established white oppression of black farm laborers in the rural South.

White Landlords, Black Sharecroppers

Ex-slaves who wished to escape slave labor and ex-masters who wanted to reinstitute old ways clashed repeatedly. Except for having to pay subsistence wages, planters had not been required to offer many concessions to emancipation. They continued to believe that African Americans would not work without coercion. Whites moved quickly to restore the antebellum (pre–Civil War) world of work gangs, white overseers, field labor for black women and children, clustered cabins, minimal personal freedom, and even whipping whenever they could get away with it.

Ex-slaves resisted every effort to turn back the clock. They argued that if any class could be described as "lazy," it was the planters, who, as one former slave noted, "lived in idleness all their lives on stolen labor." Ex-slaves believed that land of their own would anchor their economic independence and end planters' interference in their personal lives. They could then, for example, make their own decisions about whether women and children would labor in the fields. Indeed, within months after the war, perhaps one-third of black women abandoned field labor to work on chores in their own cabins just as poor white women did. Hundreds of thousands of black children enrolled in school. But without their own land, ex-slaves had little choice but to work on plantations, and they feared that their return to the planters' fields would undermine their independence.

Freedmen resisted efforts by ex-masters to restore slavelike conditions on plantations. Instead of working for wages, David Golightly Harris of South Carolina observed, "the negroes all seem disposed to rent land," which increased their independence from whites. By rejecting wage labor, by striking, and by abandoning the most reactionary employers, blacks sought to force concessions. Out of this tug-of-war between white landlords and black laborers emerged a new system of southern agriculture.

Sharecropping was a compromise that offered something to both ex-masters and ex-slaves but satisfied neither. Under the new system, planters divided their cotton plantations into small farms that freedmen rented, paying with a share of each year's crop, usually half. Sharecropping gave blacks more freedom than the system of wages and labor gangs and released them from day-to-day supervision by whites. Black families abandoned the old slave quarters and scattered over plantations, building separate cabins for themselves on the patches of land they rented (Map 16.1). Black families now decided who would work, for how

MAP 16.1

A Southern Plantation in 1860 and 1881

These maps of the Barrow plantation in Georgia illustrate some of the ways in which ex-slaves expressed their freedom. Freedmen and freedwomen deserted the clustered living quarters behind the master's house, scattered over the plantation, built family cabins, and farmed rented land. The former Barrow slaves also worked together to build a school and a church.

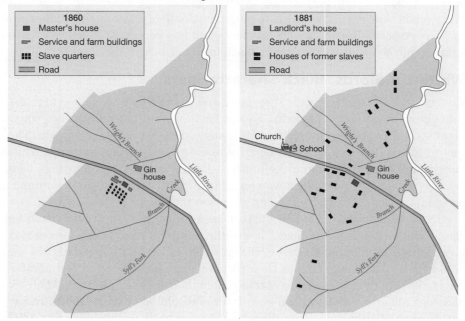

long, and how hard. Black women negotiated with ex-mistresses about work the white women wanted done in the big house. Still, most black families remained dependent on white landlords, who had the power to evict them at the end of each growing season. For planters, sharecropping offered a way to resume agricultural production, but it did not allow them to restore the old slave plantation.

Sharecropping introduced a new figure — the country merchant — into the agricultural equation. Landlords supplied sharecroppers with land, mules, seeds, and tools, but blacks also needed credit to obtain essential food and clothing before they harvested their crops. Thousands of small crossroads stores sprang up to offer credit. Under an arrangement called a **crop lien**, a merchant would advance goods to a sharecropper in exchange for a *lien*, or legal claim, on the farmer's future crop. Some merchants charged exorbitant rates of interest, as much as 60 percent, on the goods they sold. At the end of the growing season, after the landlord had taken half of the farmer's crop for rent, the merchant took most of the rest. Sometimes, the farmer's debt to the merchant exceeded the income he received from his remaining half of the crop, and the farmer would have no choice but to borrow more from the merchant and begin the cycle all over again.

An experiment at first, sharecropping spread quickly and soon dominated the cotton South. Lien merchants forced tenants to plant cotton, which was easy to sell, instead of food crops. The result was excessive production of cotton and falling cotton prices, developments that cost thousands of small white farmers their land and pushed them into the great army of sharecroppers. The new share-cropping system of agriculture took shape just as the political power of Republicans in the South began to buckle under Democratic pressure.

REVIEW   What brought the elements of the South's Republican coalition together?

▶ Reconstruction Collapses

By 1870, after a decade of war and reconstruction, Northerners wanted to put "the southern problem" behind them. Increasingly, practical, business-minded men came to the forefront of the Republican Party, replacing the band of reformers and idealists who had been prominent in the 1860s. While northern commitment to defend black freedom eroded, southern commitment to white supremacy inten-sified. Without northern protection, southern Republicans were no match for the Democrats' economic coercion, political fraud, and bloody violence. One by one, Republican state governments fell in the South. The election of 1876 both confirmed and completed the collapse of reconstruction.

Grant's Troubled Presidency

In 1868, the Republican Party's presidential nomination went to **Ulysses S. Grant**, the North's favorite general. Hero of the Civil War and a supporter of congres-sional reconstruction, Grant was the obvious choice. His Democratic opponent, Horatio Seymour of New York, ran on a platform that blasted congressional re-construction as "a flagrant usurpation of power . . . unconstitutional, revolutionary, and void." The Republicans answered by **"waving the bloody shirt"** — that is, they reminded voters that the Democrats were "the party of rebellion." During the campaign, the Ku Klux Klan erupted in a reign of terror across the South, murdering hundreds of Republicans. Fear of violence cost Grant votes, but he gained a narrow 309,000-vote margin in the popular vote and a substantial victory (214 votes to 80) in the electoral college.

Grant was not as good a president as he was a general. The talents he had demonstrated on the battlefield — decisiveness, clarity, and resolution — were less obvious in the White House. He hoped to forge a policy that secured both justice for blacks and sectional reconciliation, but he took office at a time when a majority of white Northerners had grown weary of the "Southern Question" and were increasingly willing to let southern whites manage their own affairs. Moreover, Grant surrounded himself with fumbling kinfolk and old friends from his army days. He made a string of dubious appointments that led to a series of damaging scandals. Charges of corruption tainted his vice president, Schuyler Colfax, and brought down two of his cabinet officers. Though never personally implicated in any scandal, Grant was aggravatingly naive and blind to the rot that filled his administration. Republican congressman James A. Garfield declared: "His imperturbability is amazing. I am in doubt whether to call it greatness or stupidity."

In 1872, anti-Grant Republicans bolted and launched the Liberal Party. To clean up the graft and corruption, Liberals proposed ending the spoils system, by which victorious parties rewarded loyal workers with public office, and replacing it with a nonpartisan civil service commission that would oversee competitive examinations for appointment to office (as discussed in chapter 18). Liberals also demanded that the federal government remove its troops from the South and restore "home rule" (southern white control). Democrats liked the Liberals' southern policy and endorsed the Liberal presidential candidate, Horace Greeley, the longtime editor of the *New York Tribune*. The nation, however, still felt enormous affection for the man who had saved the Union and reelected Grant with 56 percent of the popular vote.

Grant's ambitions for his administration extended beyond reconstruction, but not even foreign affairs could escape the problems of the South. Grant coveted Santo Domingo (present-day Dominican Republic) in the Caribbean and argued that the acquisition of this tropical land would permit the United States to expand its trade and would also provide a new home for the South's blacks, who were so desperately harassed by the Klan. Aggressive foreign policy had not originated with the Grant administration. Lincoln's and Johnson's secretary of state, William H. Seward, had thwarted French efforts to set up a puppet empire under Maximilian in Mexico, and his purchase of Alaska ("Seward's Ice Box") from Russia in 1867 for only $7 million fired Grant's imperialist ambition. But in the end, Grant could not convince Congress to approve the treaty annexing Santo Domingo. The South preoccupied Congress and undermined Grant's initiatives.

Northern Resolve Withers

Although Grant genuinely wanted to see blacks' civil and political rights protected, he understood that most Northerners had grown weary of reconstruction and were increasingly willing to let southern whites manage their own affairs. Citizens wanted to shift their attention to other issues, especially after the nation slipped into a devastating economic depression in 1873. More than eighteen thousand businesses collapsed, leaving more than a million workers on the streets. Northern businessmen wanted to invest in the South but believed that recurrent federal intrusion was itself a major cause of instability in the region. Republican leaders began to question the wisdom of their party's alliance with the South's lower classes — its small farmers and sharecroppers. One member of Grant's administration proposed allying with the "thinking and influential native southerners . . . the intelligent, well-to-do, and controlling class."

Congress, too, wanted to leave reconstruction behind, but southern Republicans made that difficult. When the South's Republicans begged for federal protection from Klan violence, Congress enacted three laws in 1870 and 1871 that were intended to break the back of white terrorism. The severest of the three, the **Ku Klux Klan Act** (1871), made interference with voting rights a felony. Federal marshals arrested thousands of Klansmen and came close to destroying the Klan, but they did not end all terrorism against blacks. Congress also passed the **Civil Rights Act of 1875**, which boldly outlawed racial discrimination in transportation, public accommodations, and juries. But federal authorities never enforced the law aggressively, and segregated facilities remained the rule throughout the South.

By the early 1870s, the Republican Party had lost its leading champions of African American rights to death or defeat at the polls. Other Republicans concluded that the quest for black equality was mistaken or hopelessly naive. In May 1872, Congress restored the right of officeholding to all but three hundred ex-rebels. Many Republicans had come to believe that traditional white leaders offered the best hope for honesty, order, and prosperity in the South.

Underlying the North's abandonment of reconstruction was unyielding racial prejudice. Northerners had learned to accept black freedom during the war, but deep-seated prejudice prevented many from accepting black equality. Even the actions they took on behalf of blacks often served partisan political advantage. Northerners generally supported Indiana senator Thomas A. Hendricks's harsh declaration that "this is a white man's Government, made by the white man for the white man."

The U.S. Supreme Court also did its part to undermine reconstruction. The Court issued a series of decisions that significantly weakened the federal government's ability to protect black Southerners. In the *Slaughterhouse* **cases** (1873), the Court distinguished between national and state citizenship and ruled that the Fourteenth Amendment protected only those rights that stemmed from the federal government, such as voting in federal elections and interstate travel. Since the Court decided that most rights derived from the states, it sharply curtailed the federal government's authority to defend black citizens. Even more devastating, the *United States v. Cruikshank* ruling (1876) said that the reconstruction amendments gave Congress the power to legislate against discrimination only by states, not by individuals. The "suppression of ordinary crime," such as assault, remained a state responsibility. The Supreme Court did not declare reconstruction unconstitutional but eroded its legal foundation.

The mood of the North found political expression in the election of 1874, when for the first time in eighteen years the Democrats gained control of the House of Representatives. As one Republican observed, the people had grown tired of the "negro question, with all its complications, and the reconstruction of Southern States, with all its interminable embroilments." Reconstruction had come apart. The people were tired of it. Grant grew increasingly unwilling to enforce it. Congress gradually abandoned it. And the Supreme Court denied the constitutionality of significant parts of it. Rather than defend reconstruction from its southern enemies, Northerners steadily backed away from the challenge. By the early 1870s, southern Republicans faced the forces of reaction largely on their own.

White Supremacy Triumphs

Reconstruction was a massive humiliation to most white Southerners. Republican rule meant intolerable insults: Black militiamen patrolled town streets, black laborers negotiated contracts with former masters, black maids stood up to former mistresses, black voters cast ballots, and black legislators such as James T. Rapier enacted laws. Whites resisted the consequences of their defeat in the Civil War by making it clear that military failure did not discredit their "civilization." They expressed their devotion to all that was good in the South — racial hierarchy, honor, vigorous masculinity — by making an idol of Robert E. Lee, the embodiment of the southern gentleman. They celebrated the "great Confederate cause," or **Lost Cause**, by extolling the deeds of their soldiers, "the noblest band of men who ever fought or ever took pen to record." Southern women took the lead in erecting monuments to the Confederate dead and, with pageantry, oratory, and flowers, in keeping alive the memory of the Lost Cause throughout the old Confederacy.

But the most important way white Southerners responded to the humiliation of reconstruction was their assault on Republican governments in the South, which attracted more hatred than did any other political regimes in American history. The northern retreat from reconstruction permitted southern Democrats to harness white rage to politics. Taking the name **Redeemers**, Democrats in the South promised to replace "bayonet rule" (a few federal troops continued to be stationed in the South) with "home rule." They branded Republican governments a carnival of extravagance, waste, and fraud and promised that honest, thrifty Democrats would supplant the irresponsible tax-and-spend Republicans. Above all, Redeemers swore to save southern civilization from a descent into "African barbarism." As one man put it, "We must render this either a white man's government, or convert the land into a Negro man's cemetery."

Southern Democrats adopted a multipronged strategy to overthrow Republican governments. First, they sought to polarize the parties around color. They went about gathering all the South's white voters into the Democratic Party, leaving the Republicans to depend on blacks, who made up a minority of the population in almost every southern state. To dislodge whites from the Republican Party, Democrats fanned the flames of racial prejudice. A South Carolina Democrat crowed that his party appealed to the "proud Caucasian race, whose sovereignty on earth God has proclaimed." Local newspapers published the names of whites who kept company with blacks, and neighbors ostracized offenders. One victim proclaimed,

"No white man can live in the South in the future and act with any other than the Democratic party unless he is willing and prepared to live a life of social isolation."

Democrats also exploited the severe economic plight of small white farmers by blaming it on Republican financial policy. Government spending soared during reconstruction, and small farmers saw their tax burden skyrocket. "This is tax time," a South Carolinian reported. "We are nearly all on our head about them. They are so high & so little money to pay with" that farmers were "selling every egg and chicken they can get." In 1871, Mississippi reported that one-seventh of the state's land — 3.3 million acres — had been forfeited for nonpayment of taxes. The small farmers' economic distress had a racial dimension. Because few freedmen succeeded in acquiring land, they rarely paid taxes. In Georgia in 1874, blacks made up 45 percent of the population but paid only 2 percent of the taxes. From the perspective of a small white farmer, Republican rule meant that he was paying more taxes and paying them to aid blacks.

If racial pride, social isolation, and financial hardship proved insufficient to drive yeomen from the Republican Party, Democrats turned to terrorism. "Night riders" targeted white Republicans as well as blacks for murder and assassination. Whether white or black, a "dead Radical is very harmless," South Carolina Democratic leader Martin Gary told his followers.

But the primary victims of white violence were black Republicans, especially local leaders. Emanuel Fortune, whom the Klan drove from Jackson County, Florida, declared: "The object of it is to kill out the leading men of the republican party."

"Of Course He Wants to Vote the Democratic Ticket"
This Republican cartoon from the October 21, 1876, issue of *Harper's Weekly* comments sarcastically on the possibility of honest elections in the South. The caption reads: "You're free as air, ain't you? Say you are or I'll blow yer black head off." The cartoon demonstrates not only some Northerners' concern that violence would deliver the election to the Democrats but also the perception that white Southerners were crude, drunken, ignorant brutes. The Granger Collection, NYC.

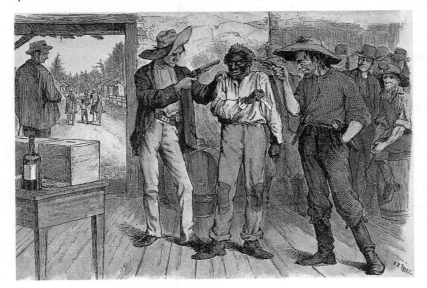

But violence targeted all black voters, not just leaders. And it escalated to an unprecedented ferocity on Easter Sunday in 1873 in tiny Colfax, Louisiana. The black majority in the area had made Colfax a Republican stronghold until 1872, when Democrats turned to intimidation and fraud to win the local election. Republicans refused to accept the result and eventually occupied the courthouse in the middle of the town. After three weeks, 165 white men attacked. They overran the Republicans' defenses and set the courthouse on fire. When the blacks tried to surrender, the whites murdered them. At least 81 black men were slaughtered that day. Although the federal government indicted the attackers, the Supreme Court ruled that it did not have the right to prosecute. And since local whites would not prosecute neighbors who killed blacks, the defendants in the **Colfax massacre** went free.

Even before adopting the all-out white supremacist tactics of the 1870s, Democrats had taken control of the governments of Virginia, Tennessee, and North Carolina. The new campaign brought fresh gains. The Redeemers retook Georgia in 1871, Texas in 1873, and Arkansas and Alabama in 1874. Mississippi became a scene of open, unrelenting, and often savage intimidation of black voters and their few remaining white allies. As the state election approached in 1876, Governor Adelbert Ames appealed to Washington for federal troops to control the violence, only to hear from the attorney general that the "whole public are tired of these annual autumnal outbreaks in the South." Abandoned, Mississippi Republicans succumbed to the Democratic onslaught in the fall elections. By 1876, only three Republican state governments survived in the South (Map 16.2).

An Election and a Compromise

The centennial year of 1876 witnessed one of the most tumultuous elections in American history. Its chaos and confusion provided a fitting conclusion to the experiment known as reconstruction. The election took place in November, but not until March 2 of the following year did the nation know who would be inaugurated president on March 4. The Democrats nominated New York's governor, **Samuel J. Tilden**, who immediately targeted the corruption of the Grant administration and the "despotism" of Republican reconstruction. The Republicans put forward **Rutherford B. Hayes**, governor of Ohio. Privately, Hayes considered "bayonet rule" a mistake but concluded that waving the bloody shirt — reminding voters that the Democrats were the "party of rebellion" — remained the Republicans' best political strategy.

On election day, Tilden tallied 4,288,590 votes to Hayes's 4,036,000. But in the all-important electoral college, Tilden fell one vote short of the majority required for victory. The electoral votes of three states — South Carolina, Louisiana, and Florida, the only remaining Republican governments in the South — remained in doubt because both Republicans and Democrats in those states claimed victory. To win, Tilden needed only one of the nineteen contested votes. Hayes had to have all of them.

Congress had to decide who had actually won the elections in the three southern states and thus who would be president. The Constitution provided no guidance for this situation. Moreover, Democrats controlled the House, and Republicans controlled the Senate. Congress created a special electoral commission to arbitrate the disputed returns. All of the commissioners voted their party

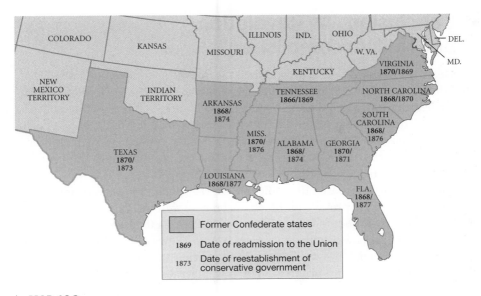

MAP 16.2
The Reconstruction of the South
Myth has it that Republican rule of the former Confederacy was not only harsh but long. In most states, however, conservative southern whites stormed back into power in months or just a few years. By the election of 1876, Republican governments could be found in only three states, and they soon fell.

affiliation, giving every state to the Republican Hayes and putting him over the top in electoral votes.

Some outraged Democrats vowed to resist Hayes's victory. Rumors flew of an impending coup and renewed civil war. But the impasse was broken when negotiations behind the scenes resulted in an informal understanding known as the **Compromise of 1877**. In exchange for a Democratic promise not to block Hayes's inauguration and to deal fairly with the freedmen, Hayes vowed to refrain from using the army to uphold the remaining Republican regimes in the South and to provide the South with substantial federal subsidies for railroads. Two days later, the nation celebrated Hayes's peaceful inauguration.

Stubborn Tilden supporters bemoaned the "stolen election" and damned "His Fraudulency," Rutherford B. Hayes. Old-guard radicals such as William Lloyd Garrison denounced Hayes's bargain as a "policy of compromise, of credulity, of weakness, of subserviency, of surrender." But the nation as a whole celebrated, for the country had weathered a grave crisis. The last three Republican state governments in the South fell quickly once Hayes abandoned them and withdrew the U.S. Army. Reconstruction came to an end.

REVIEW   How did the Supreme Court undermine the Fourteenth and Fifteenth Amendments?

▶ Conclusion: "A Revolution But Half Accomplished"

In 1865, when General Carl Schurz visited the South, he discovered "a revolution but half accomplished." White Southerners resisted the passage from slavery to free labor, from white racial despotism to equal justice, and from white political monopoly to biracial democracy. The old elite wanted to get "things back as near to slavery as possible," Schurz reported, while African Americans such as James T. Rapier and some whites were eager to exploit the revolutionary implications of defeat and emancipation.

The northern-dominated Republican Congress pushed the revolution along. Although it refused to provide for blacks' economic welfare, Congress employed constitutional amendments to require ex-Confederates to accept legal equality and share political power with black men. Congress was not willing to extend such power to women, however. Conservative southern whites fought ferociously to recover their power and privilege. When Democrats regained control of politics, whites used both state power and private violence to wipe out many of the gains of Reconstruction, leading one observer to conclude that the North had won the war but the South had won the peace.

The Redeemer counterrevolution, however, did not mean a return to slavery. Northern victory in the Civil War ensured that ex-slaves no longer faced the auction block and could send their children to school, worship in their own churches, and work independently on their own rented farms. Sharecropping, with all its hardships, provided more autonomy and economic welfare than bondage had. It was limited freedom, to be sure, but it was not slavery.

The Civil War and emancipation set in motion the most profound upheaval in the nation's history, and nothing reactionary whites did entirely erased its revolutionary impact. War destroyed the largest slave society in the New World. The world of masters and slaves succumbed to that of landlords and sharecroppers, a world in which white racial dominance continued, though with greater freedom for blacks. War also gave birth to a modern nation-state, and Washington increased its role in national affairs. When the South returned to the Union, it did so as a junior partner. The victorious North set the nation's compass toward the expansion of industrial capitalism and the final conquest of the West.

Despite massive changes, however, the Civil War remained only a "half accomplished" revolution. By not fulfilling the promises the nation seemed to hold out to black Americans at war's end, Reconstruction represents a tragedy of enormous proportions. The failure to protect blacks and guarantee their rights had enduring consequences. Almost a century after Reconstruction, the nation would embark on what one observer called a "second reconstruction." The solid achievements of the Thirteenth, Fourteenth, and Fifteenth Amendments to the Constitution would provide a legal foundation for the renewed commitment. It is worth remembering, though, that it was only the failure of the first reconstruction that made the modern civil rights movement necessary.

Reviewing Chapter 16

REVIEW QUESTIONS

1. Why did Congress object to Lincoln's wartime plan for reconstruction? (pp. 461–464)

2. How did the North respond to the passage of black codes in the southern states? (pp. 465–468)

3. Why did Johnson urge the southern states to reject the Fourteenth Amendment? (pp. 468–473)

4. What brought the elements of the South's Republican coalition together? (pp. 473–479)

5. How did the Supreme Court undermine the Fourteenth and Fifteenth Amendments? (pp. 479–485)

MAKING CONNECTIONS

1. Reconstruction succeeded in advancing black civil rights but failed to secure them over the long term. Why and how did the federal government retreat from defending African Americans' civil rights in the 1870s? In your answer, cite specific actions by Congress and the Supreme Court.

2. Why was distributing plantation land to former slaves such a controversial policy? In your answer, discuss why landownership was important to freedmen and why Congress rejected redistribution as a general policy.

3. At the end of the Civil War, it remained to be seen exactly how emancipation would transform the South. How did emancipation change political and labor organization in the region? In your answer, discuss how ex-slaves exercised their new freedoms and how white Southerners attempted to limit them.

4. The Republican Party shaped Reconstruction through its control of Congress and state legislatures in the South. How did the identification of the Republican Party with Reconstruction policy affect the party's political fortunes in the 1870s? In your answer, be sure to address developments on the federal and state levels.

LINKING TO THE PAST

1. In what ways did the attitudes and actions of President Johnson increase northern resolve to reconstruct the South and the South's resolve to resist reconstruction?

2. White women, abolitionists, and blacks all had hopes for a brighter future that were in some ways dashed during the turmoil of reconstruction. What specific goals of these groups slipped away? What political allies abandoned their causes, and why?

TIMELINE 1863–1877

1863 • Proclamation of Amnesty and Reconstruction.

1864 • Lincoln refuses to sign Wade-Davis bill.

1865 • Freedmen's Bureau established.
• President Abraham Lincoln shot; dies on April 15; succeeded by Andrew Johnson.
• Black codes enacted.
• Thirteenth Amendment becomes part of Constitution.

1866 • Congress approves Fourteenth Amendment.
• Civil Rights Act.
• American Equal Rights Association founded.
• Ku Klux Klan founded.

1867 • Military Reconstruction Act.
• Tenure of Office Act.

1868 • Impeachment trial of President Johnson.
• Republican Ulysses S. Grant elected president.

1869 • Congress approves Fifteenth Amendment.

1871 • Ku Klux Klan Act.

1872 • Liberal Party formed.
• President Grant reelected.

1873 • Economic depression sets in for remainder of decade.
• *Slaughterhouse* cases.
• Colfax massacre.

1874 • Democrats win majority in House of Representatives.

1875 • Civil Rights Act.

1876 • *United States v. Cruikshank.*

1877 • Republican Rutherford B. Hayes assumes presidency; Reconstruction era ends.

▶ **FOR AN ONLINE BIBLIOGRAPHY, PRACTICE QUIZZES, WEB SITES, IMAGES, AND DOCUMENTS RELATED TO THIS CHAPTER,** see the Book Companion Site at **bedfordstmartins.com/roarkvalue**.

▶ **FOR DOCUMENTS RELATED TO THIS PERIOD,** see Michael Johnson, ed., *Reading the American Past*, Fifth Edition.

17

The Contested West

1865–1900

TO CELEBRATE THE FOUR HUNDREDTH ANNIVERSARY OF COLUMBUS'S voyage to the New World, Chicago hosted the World's Columbian Exposition in 1893. Architects and landscapers created a magical White City on the shores of Lake Michigan, complete with a Midway Plaisance where the first Ferris wheel awed and delighted the four million fairgoers.

Among the organizations vying to hold meetings in the White City was the American Historical Association, whose members — dedicated to the advancement of historical studies — gathered on a warm July evening to hear Frederick Jackson Turner deliver his landmark essay "The Significance of the Frontier in American History." Turner began by noting that the 1890 census could no longer discern a clear frontier line. His tone was elegiac: "The existence of an area of free land, its continuous recession, and the advance of settlement westward," he observed, "explained American development."

Of course, *west* has always been a comparative term in American history. Until the gold rush focused attention on California, the West for settlers lay beyond the Appalachians and east of the Mississippi in lands drained by the Ohio River, a part of the country now known as the Old Northwest. But by the second half of the nineteenth century, with the end of the Mexican-American War, the West now stretched from Canada to Mexico, from the Mississippi River to the Pacific Ocean.

Turner, who had originally studied the old frontier east of the Mississippi, viewed the West as a process as much as a place. The availability of land provided a "safety valve," releasing social tensions and providing opportunities for social mobility that worked to Americanize Americans. The West

demanded strength and nerve, fostered invention and adaptation, and produced self-confident, individualistic Americans. Turner's theory underscored
the exceptionalism of America's history, highlighting its difference from the
rest of the world. His "frontier thesis" would earn him a professorship at
Harvard and a permanent place in American history.

Yet the historians who applauded Turner in Chicago had short memories.
That afternoon, they had crossed the midway to attend Buffalo Bill Cody's
Wild West extravaganza, which featured exhibitions of riding, shooting, and
roping and presented dramatic reenactments of great moments in western
lore. Part circus, part theater, the show included 100 cowboys, 97 Indians, 180
horses, and 18 American bison. The troupe performed the "Attack on the
Settler's Cabin" and their own version of "Custer's Last Stand," ending with
Buffalo Bill galloping to the rescue through a cloud of dust only to mouth the
words "Too late." The historians cheering in the stands that July afternoon no
doubt dismissed Buffalo Bill's history as amateur, but he made a point that

Buffalo Bill Poster
Buffalo Bill Cody used colorful posters to publicize his Wild West show during the 1880s and 1890s.
One of his most popular features was the reenactment of Custer's Last Stand, which he performed
for Queen Victoria in London and at the World's Columbian Exposition in Chicago. Sitting Bull,
who fought at the Battle of the Little Big Horn, toured with the company in 1885 and traveled to
England with the show. Cody's romantic depictions of western history helped create the myth of
the Old West. Buffalo Bill Historical Center, Cody, Wyoming.

Turner's thesis ignored: The West was neither free nor open. The story of the country was a story of fierce and violent contest for land and resources.

In the decades following the Civil War, the United States pursued empire in the American West in Indian wars that lasted until 1890. Pushed off their land and onto reservations, Native Americans resisted as they faced waves of miners and settlers and the transformation of the environment by railroads, mines, barbed wire, and mechanized agriculture. The pastoral agrarianism Turner celebrated in his frontier thesis belied the urban, industrial West already emerging on the Comstock Lode in Nevada and in the commercial farms of California.

Buffalo Bill's mythic West, with its heroic cowboys and noble savages, obscured the complex reality of the West as a fiercely contested terrain. Competing groups of Anglos, Hispanics, former slaves, Chinese, and a host of others arrived seeking the promise of land and riches, while the Indians who inhabited the vast territory struggled to preserve their sovereignty and their cultural identity. And, with its emphasis on the rugged individualism of white men pioneering the frontier, Turner's vision of the West overlooked racial diversity and failed to acknowledge the role of women in community building.

Yet in the waning decade of the nineteenth century, as history blurred with nostalgia, Turner's evocation of the frontier as a crucible for American identity hit a nerve in a population facing rapid changes. A major depression started in May 1893, even before the Columbian Exposition opened its doors. Americans already worried about the economy, immigration, and urban industrialism found in Turner's message a new cause for concern. Would America continue to be America now that the frontier was closed? As they struggled with the question, it became clear that the West did not exist out of place and time. Nor was it particularly exceptional. The problems confronting the United States at the turn of the twentieth century — the exploitation of land and labor, the consolidation of capital, and vicious ethnic and racial rivalries — all played themselves out under western skies.

▶ Conquest and Empire in the West

While the European powers expanded their authority and wealth through imperialism and colonialism, establishing far-flung empires in Asia, Africa, and South America, the United States focused its attention on the West. As posited by **Frederick Jackson Turner**, American exceptionalism stressed how the history of the United States differed from that of European nations, citing America's western frontier as a case in point. Yet recent historians have argued that the process by which the United States expanded its borders in the nineteenth century can best be understood in the global context of imperialism and colonialism — language applied to

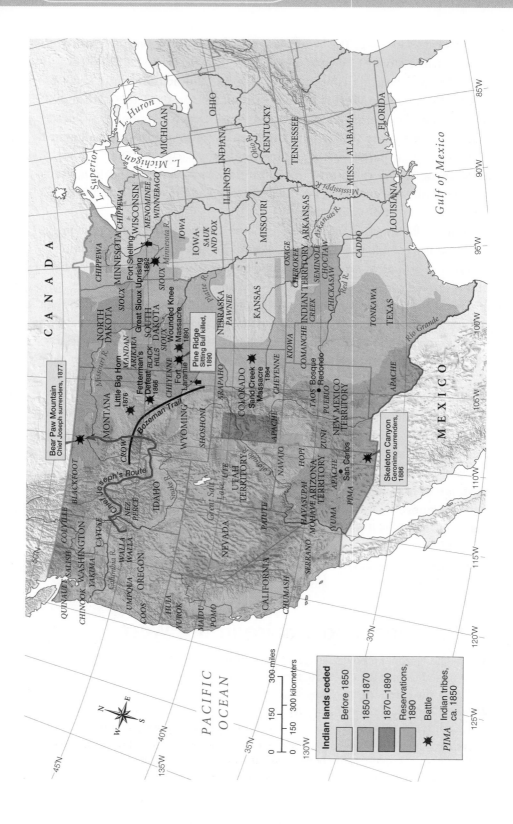

CANADA

C A N A D A

Bear Paw Mountain
Chief Joseph surrenders, 1877

Skeleton Canyon
Geronimo surrenders,
1886

Pine Ridge
Sitting Bull killed,
1890

Bozeman Trail

Chief Joseph's Route

Little Big Horn
1876

Fetterman's
Defeat
1866

Fort
Laramie

Wounded Knee
Massacre
1890

Great Sioux Uprising
1862

Fort Snelling

Sand Creek
Massacre
1864

Bosque
Redondo

San Carlos

States, Territories, and Tribes

QUINAULT, CHINOOK, SALISH, COLVILLE, CAYUSE, YAKIMA, WALLA WALLA, UMPQUA, COOS, HUPA, YUROK, MAIDU, POMO, CHUMASH, SERRANO, MOHAVE, YUMA, PIMA, HAVASUPAI, HOPI, ZUNI, PUEBLO, NAVAJO, APACHE, PAIUTE, UTE, SHOSHONI, CROW, BLACKFOOT, NEZ PERCE, MANDAN, ARIKARA, SIOUX, CHEYENNE, ARAPAHO, PAWNEE, IOWA, SAUK AND FOX, WINNEBAGO, MENOMINEE, CHIPPEWA, OSAGE, CHEROKEE, CREEK, SEMINOLE, CHICKASAW, CHOCTAW, CADDO, KIOWA, COMANCHE, TONKAWA

WASHINGTON, OREGON, CALIFORNIA, NEVADA, IDAHO, MONTANA, WYOMING, UTAH TERRITORY, ARIZONA TERRITORY, NEW MEXICO TERRITORY, COLORADO, NORTH DAKOTA, SOUTH DAKOTA, NEBRASKA, KANSAS, OKLAHOMA INDIAN TERRITORY, TEXAS, MINNESOTA, IOWA, MISSOURI, ARKANSAS, WISCONSIN, MICHIGAN, ILLINOIS, INDIANA, OHIO, KENTUCKY, TENNESSEE, MISSISSIPPI, ALABAMA, LOUISIANA, FLORIDA, TAOS

MEXICO

PACIFIC OCEAN

Gulf of Mexico

L. Superior, L. Huron, L. Michigan

Black Hills

Missouri R., Platte R., Minnesota R., Mississippi R., Ohio R., Arkansas R., Red R., Rio Grande, Columbia R., Snake R., Colorado R., Great Salt Lake

Legend

Indian lands ceded
- Before 1850
- 1850–1870
- 1870–1890
- Reservations, 1890
- ★ Battle
- PIMA Indian tribes, ca. 1850

0   150   300 miles
0   150   300 kilometers

N W E S

European powers in this period that makes explicit how expansion in the American West involved the conquest, displacement, and rule over native peoples.

The federal government, through chicanery and conquest, pushed the Indians off their lands (Map 17.1) and onto designated Indian territories or reservations. The Indian wars that followed the Civil War depleted the Native American population and handed the lion's share of Indian land over to white settlers. The decimation of the bison herds inevitably pushed the Plains Indians onto reservations, where they lived as wards of the state. Through the lens of colonialism, we can see how the United States, with its commitment to an imperialist, expansionist ideology, colonized the West.

Indian Removal and the Reservation System

Beginning in the early days of the Republic, the government advocated a policy of **Indian removal**. With plenty of land open in the West, the army removed eastern tribes — often against their will — to territory west of the Mississippi. In the 1830s, President Andrew Jackson pushed the Five Civilized Tribes — the Cherokee, Choctaw, Chickasaw, Creek, and Seminole peoples — off their land in the southern United States. Jackson's Indian removal forced thousands of men, women, and children to leave their homes in Georgia and Tennessee and walk hundreds of miles west. So many died of hunger, exhaustion, and disease along the way that the Cherokees called their path "the trail on which we cried." At the end of this trail of tears stood land set aside as Indian Territory (present-day Oklahoma). Here, the government promised, the Indians could remain "as long as grass shall grow." But hunger for western land soon negated that promise.

Manifest destiny — the belief that the United States had a "God-given" right to aggressively spread the values of white civilization and expand the nation from ocean to ocean — dictated U.S. policy. In the name of manifest destiny, Americans forced the removal of the Five Civilized Tribes to Oklahoma; colonized Texas and won its independence from Mexico in 1836; conquered California, Arizona, New Mexico, and parts of Utah and Colorado in the Mexican-American War of 1846–1848; and invaded Oregon in the mid-1840s.

By midcentury, western land no longer seemed inexhaustible, and instead of removing Indians to the west, the government sought to take control of Indian lands and promised in return to pay annuities and put the Indians on lands reserved for their use — **reservations**. In 1851, some ten thousand Plains Indians came together at Fort Laramie in Wyoming to negotiate a treaty that ceded a wide swath of their land to allow passage of wagon trains headed west. In return, the government promised that the rest of the Indian land would remain inviolate.

◀ **MAP 17.1**
The Loss of Indian Lands, 1850–1890
By 1890, western Indians were isolated on small, scattered reservations. Native Americans had struggled to retain their land in major battles, from the Santee Uprising in Minnesota in 1862 to the massacre at Wounded Knee, South Dakota, in 1890.

The Indians who "touched the pen" to the 1851 **Treaty of Fort Laramie** hoped to preserve their culture in the face of the white onslaught, which had already decimated their population and despoiled their environment. White invaders cut down trees, miners polluted streams, and hunters killed off bison and small game. Whites brought alcohol, guns, and something even more deadly — disease. Smallpox was the biggest killer of Native Americans in the West. Epidemics spread from Mexico up to Canada. Between 1780 and 1870, the population of the Plains tribes declined by half. Cholera, diphtheria, measles, scarlet fever, and other contagious diseases also took their toll. "If I could see this thing, if I knew where it came from, I would go there and fight it," a Cheyenne warrior anguished. Disease shifted the balance of power on the plains from Woodland agrarian tribes like the Mandan and Hidatsa (who died at the rate of 79 percent) to the Lakota (Western) Sioux, who fled the contagion of villages to take up life as equestrian (horse-riding) nomads on the western plains. As the Sioux pushed west, they displaced weaker tribes.

In the Southwest, the Navajo people, like the Cherokee, endured a forced march called the "Long Walk" from their homeland to the desolate Bosque Redondo Reservation in New Mexico in 1864. "This ground we were brought on, it is not productive," complained the Navajo leader Barboncito. "We plant but it does not yield. All the stock we brought here have nearly all died."

Poverty and starvation stalked the reservations. Confined by armed force, the Indians eked out an existence on stingy government rations. These once proud peoples found themselves dependent on government handouts and the assistance of Indian agents who, in the words of Paiute Sarah Winnemucca, did "nothing but fill their pockets." Winnemucca launched a lecture campaign in the United States and Europe denouncing the government's reservation policy.

Styled as stepping-stones on the road to "civilization," Indian reservations closely resembled colonial societies where native populations, ruled by outside bureaucrats, saw their culture assaulted, their religious practices outlawed, their children sent away to school, and their way of life attacked in the name of progress and civilization. Self-styled "friends of the Indians," many of them easterners with little experience in the West, maintained that reservations would provide a classroom of civilization where Indians could be taught to speak English, to worship a Christian god, to give up hunting for farming, and to reject tribal ways.

To Americans raised on theories of racial superiority, the Indians constituted, in the words of one Colorado militia major, "an obstacle to civilization . . . [and] should be exterminated." This attitude pervaded the military, and the cavalry annihilated entire villages with ruthless efficiency. In November 1864 at the Sand Creek massacre in Colorado Territory, Colonel John M. Chivington and his Colorado militia descended on a village of Cheyenne, mostly women and children. Their leader, Black Kettle, raised a white flag and an American flag to signal surrender, but the charging cavalry ignored his signal and butchered 270 Indians. Chivington watched as his men scalped and mutilated their victims and later justified the killing of Indian children with the terse remark, "Nits make lice." The city of Denver treated Chivington and his men as heroes, but a congressional inquiry castigated the soldiers for their "fiendish malignity" and condemned the "savage cruelty" of the massacre.

The Decimation of the Great Bison Herds

In the centuries following the arrival of the first European settlers, the great herds of buffalo (American bison), once numbering as many as thirty million, fell into serious decline. A host of environmental and human factors contributed to the destruction of the bison. The dynamic ecology of the Great Plains, with its droughts, fires, and blizzards, combined with the ecological imperialism of humans (Indian buffalo-robe traders as well as whites and their cattle), put increasing pressure on the bison. By the 1850s, a combination of drought and commerce had driven the great herds onto the far western plains.

After the Civil War, the accelerating pace of industrial expansion brought about the near extinction of the bison. Industrial demand for heavy leather belting used in machinery and the development of larger, more accurate rifles combined to hasten the slaughter of the bison. At the same time, the nation's growing transcontinental rail system cut the range in two and divided the herds. For the Sioux and other nomadic tribes of the plains, the buffalo constituted a way of life — a source of food, fuel, and shelter and a central part of their religion and rituals. To the railroads, the bison were a nuisance, at best a cheap source of meat for their workers and a target for sport. "It will not be long before all the buffaloes are extinct near and between the railroads," Ohio senator John Sherman predicted in 1868.

In the end, the army took credit for the conquest of the Plains Indians, but victory came about largely as a result of the decimation of the great bison herds. General Philip Sheridan acknowledged as much when he applauded white hide hunters for "destroying the Indians' commissary." With their food supply gone, Indians had to choose between starvation and the reservation. "A cold wind blew across the prairie when the last buffalo fell," the great Sioux leader **Sitting Bull** lamented, "a death wind for my people."

On the southern plains in 1867, more than five thousand warring Comanches, Kiowas, and Southern Arapahos gathered at Medicine Lodge Creek in Kansas to negotiate a treaty. Satak, or Sitting Bear, a prominent Kiowa chief and medicine man, explained why the Indians sought peace: "In the far-distant past . . . the world seemed large enough for both the red man and the white man." But, he observed, "its broad plains seem now to contract, and the white man grows jealous of his red brother." To preserve their land from white encroachment, the Indians signed the Treaty of Medicine Lodge, agreeing to move to a reservation. Yet they continued to leave the reservation's confines to hunt during the summer months. After 1870, hide hunters poured into the region, and within a decade they had nearly exterminated the southern bison herds. Luther Standing Bear recounted the sight and stench: "I saw the bodies of hundreds of dead buffalo lying about, just wasting, and the odor was terrible. . . . They were letting our food lie on the plains to rot." With the buffalo gone, the Indians faced starvation and reluctantly moved to the reservations.

Indian Wars and the Collapse of Comanchería

The Indian wars in the West marked the last resistance of a Native American population devastated by disease and demoralized by the removal policy pursued by the federal government. More accurately called "settlers' wars" (since they began with "peaceful settlers," often miners, overrunning Native American land), the wars flared up again only a few years after the signing of the Fort Laramie treaty. The Dakota Sioux in Minnesota went to war in 1862. For years, under the leadership of Chief Little Crow, the Dakota, also known as the Santee, had pursued a policy of accommodation, ceding land in return for the promise of annuities. But with his people on the verge of starvation (the local Indian agent told the hungry Dakota, "Go and eat grass"), Little Crow reluctantly led his angry warriors in a desperate campaign against the intruders, killing more than 1,000 settlers. American troops quelled what was called the Great Sioux Uprising (also called the Santee Uprising) and marched 1,700 Sioux to Fort Snelling, where 400 Indians were put on trial for murder and 38 died in the largest mass execution in American history.

After the Civil War, President Ulysses S. Grant faced the prospect of protracted Indian war on the Great Plains. Reluctant to spend more money and sacrifice more lives in battle, Grant adopted a "peace policy" designed to segregate and control the Indians while opening up land to white settlers. This policy won the support of both friends of the Indians, who feared for their survival, and Indian haters, who coveted their land and wished to confine them to the least desirable areas in the West. General William Tecumseh Sherman summed up the new Indian policy succinctly: "Remove all to a safe place and then reduce them to a helpless condition." The army herded the Indians onto reservations (see Map 17.1), where the U.S. Bureau of Indian Affairs supposedly ministered to their needs. But peace in the West remained elusive.

The great Indian empire of **Comanchería**, which in the eighteenth century stretched from the Canadian plains to Mexico, by 1865 numbered fewer than five thousand Comanches, who ranged from west Texas north to Oklahoma. Through decades of dealings with the Spanish and French, the Comanches had built a complex empire based on trade in horses, hides, guns, and captives. Expert equestrians, the Comanches inaugurated the horse-centered way of life that eventually came to characterize the Plains Indians.

In 1871, Grant's peace policy in the West gave way to all-out warfare as the U.S. Army dispatched three thousand soldiers to wipe out the remains of the Comanche empire. Comanchería had been greatly reduced, but Comanche raiding parties took a toll in lives and livestock and virtually obliterated white settlements in west Texas. To defeat the Indians, the army adopted the tactics General William Sherman had used in his march through Confederate Georgia during the Civil War. At the decisive battle of Palo Duro Canyon in 1874, only three Comanche warriors died in battle, but U.S. soldiers took the Indians' camp, burning more than two hundred tepees, hundreds of robes and blankets, and thousands of pounds of winter supplies and shooting more than a thousand horses. Coupled with the decimation of the bison, the army's scorched-earth policy led to the final collapse of the Comanche people — more an economic than a military defeat. Crippled by poverty, malnutrition, and the loss of their trading-raiding economy, the surviving Indians of Comanchería, now numbering fewer than 1,500, reluctantly retreated to the reservation at Fort Sill.

The Fight for the Black Hills

On the northern plains, the fever for gold fueled the conflict between Indians and Euro-Americans. In 1866, the Cheyenne united with the Sioux in Wyoming to protect their hunting grounds in the Powder River valley, which were threatened by the construction of the Bozeman Trail connecting Fort Laramie with the goldfields in Montana. Captain William Fetterman, who had boasted that with eighty men he could ride through the Sioux nation, was killed along with all of his troops in an Indian attack. The Sioux's impressive victories led to the second **Treaty of Fort Laramie** in 1868, in which the United States agreed to abandon the Bozeman Trail and guaranteed the Indians control of the **Black Hills**, land sacred to the Lakota Sioux.

The second Treaty of Fort Laramie was full of contradictions — in one breath promising to preserve Indian land and in the next forcing the tribes to relinquish all territory outside their reservations. A controversial provision of the treaty guaranteed the Indians access to their traditional hunting grounds "so long as the buffalo may range thereon in such numbers as to justify the chase." With the bison facing extermination, the provision was ominous. Yet the government's fork-tongued promises induced some of the tribes to accept the treaty. The great Sioux chief Red Cloud led many of his people onto the reservation. Red Cloud soon regretted his decision. "Think of it!" he told a visitor to the Pine Ridge Reservation. "I, who used to own . . . country so extensive that I could not ride through it in a week . . . must tell Washington when I am hungry. I must beg for that which I own." Several Sioux chiefs, among them **Crazy Horse** of the Oglala band and Sitting Bull of the Hunkpapa, refused to sign the treaty. Crazy Horse said that he wanted no part of the "piecemeal penning" of his people.

In 1874, the discovery of gold in the Black Hills of the Dakotas led the government to break its promise to Red Cloud. Miners began pouring into the region, and the Northern Pacific Railroad made plans to lay track. Lieutenant Colonel **George Armstrong Custer**, whose troopers found gold in the area, trumpeted news of the strike. At first, the government offered to purchase the Black Hills. But to the Lakota Sioux, the Black Hills were sacred — "the heart of everything that is." They refused to sell. The army responded by issuing an ultimatum ordering all Lakota Sioux and Northern Cheyenne bands onto the Pine Ridge Reservation and threatening to hunt down those who refused.

In the summer of 1876, the army launched a three-pronged attack led by Custer, General **George Crook**, and Colonel John Gibbon. Crazy Horse stopped Crook at the Battle of the Rosebud. Custer, leading the second prong of the army's offensive, divided his troops and ordered an attack. On June 25, he spotted signs of the Indians' camp. Crying "Hurrah Boys, we've got them," he led 265 men of the Seventh Cavalry into the largest Indian camp ever assembled on the Great Plains, more than 8,000 Indians. Nomadic bands of Sioux, Cheyenne, and Arapaho had come together for a summer buffalo hunt and camped along the banks of the Greasy Grass River (whites called it the Little Big Horn). Indian warriors led by Sitting Bull and Crazy Horse set upon Custer and his men and quickly annihilated them. "It took us about as long as a hungry man to eat his dinner," the Cheyenne chief Two Moons recalled. Gibbon arrived two days later to discover the carnage.

"Custer's Last Stand," as the **Battle of the Little Big Horn** was styled in myth, turned out to be the last stand for the Sioux. The Indians' nomadic way of life meant they could not remain a combined force for long. The bands that had massed at the Little Big Horn scattered, and the army hunted them down. "Wherever we went," wrote the Oglala holy man Black Elk, "the soldiers came to kill us." In 1877, Crazy Horse was captured and killed. Four years later, in 1881, Sitting Bull surrendered. The government took the Black Hills and confined the Lakota to the Great Sioux Reservation. The Sioux never accepted the loss of the Black Hills. In 1923, they filed suit, demanding the return of the land illegally taken from them. After a protracted court battle lasting nearly sixty years, the U.S. Supreme Court ruled in 1980 that the government had illegally abrogated the Treaty of Fort Laramie and upheld an award of $122.5 million in compensation to the tribes. The Sioux refused the settlement and continue to press for the return of the Black Hills.

> **REVIEW** How did the slaughter of the bison contribute to the Plains Indians' removal to reservations?

▶ Forced Assimilation and Resistance Strategies

More than two hundred years of contact with whites utterly transformed Native American societies. The indigenous peoples Christopher Columbus had mistakenly dubbed "Indians" included more than five hundred distinct tribal entities with different languages, myths, religions, and physical appearance. According to the census of 1900, the Indian population in the continental United States stood at 250,000 (admittedly an undercount), down from estimates as high as 15 million at the time of first contact with Europeans. Not only had the population been decimated by war, disease, and the obliteration of the bison, but Indian lands had shrunk so much that by 1890 Euro-Americans controlled 97.5 percent of the territory formerly occupied by Native Americans.

Imperialistic attitudes of whites toward Indians continued to evolve in the late nineteenth century. To "civilize" the Indians, the U.S. government sought to force assimilation on their children. Reservations, once designed as stepping-stones to civilization, became increasingly unpopular among whites who coveted Indian land. A new policy of allotment gained favor. It promised to put Indians on parcels of land, forcing them into farming, and then to redistribute the rest of the land to settlers. In the face of this ongoing assault on their way of life, Indians actively resisted, contested, and adapted to colonial rule.

Indian Schools and the War against Indian Culture

Indian schools constituted the cultural battleground of the Indian wars in the West, their avowed purpose being "to destroy the Indian in him and save the man." In 1877, Congress appropriated funds for Indian education, reasoning that "it was less expensive to educate Indians than to kill them." Virginia's Hampton Institute, created in 1868 to school newly freed slaves, accepted its first Indian students in 1878. Although many Indian schools operated on the reservations, authorities much preferred boarding facilities that isolated students from the "contamination" of tribal values.

Many Native American parents resisted sending their children away. When all else failed, the military kidnapped the children and sent them off to school. An agent at the Mescalero Apache Agency in Arizona Territory reported in 1886 that "it became necessary to visit the camps unexpectedly with a detachment of police, and seize such children as were proper and take them away to school, willing or unwilling." The parents put up a struggle. "Some hurried their children off to the mountains or hid them away in camp, and the police had to chase and capture them like so many wild rabbits," the agent observed. "This unusual proceeding created quite an outcry. The men were sullen and muttering, the women loud in their lamentations and the children almost out of their wits with fright." Once at school, the children were stripped and scrubbed, their clothing and belongings were confiscated, and their hair was hacked off and doused with kerosene to kill lice. Issued stiff new uniforms, shoes, and what one boy recalled as the "torture" of woolen long underwear, the children often lost not only their possessions but also their names: Hehakaavita (Yellow Elk) became Thomas Goodwood; Polingaysi Qoyawayma became Elizabeth White.

The curriculum featured agricultural and manual arts for boys and domestic skills for girls, training designed to make Indians "willing workers" who would no longer be a burden to the government. The **Carlisle Indian School** in Pennsylvania, founded in 1879, became the model for later institutions. To encourage assimilation, Carlisle pioneered the "outing system" — sending students to live with white families during summer vacations. The policy reflected the school's slogan: "To civilize the Indian, get him into civilization. To keep him civilized, let him stay."

Merrill Gates, a member of the Board of Indian Commissioners, summed up the goal of Indian education: "To get the Indian out of the blanket and into trousers, — and trousers with a pocket in them, *and with a pocket that aches to be filled with dollars!*" Gates's faith in the "civilizing" power of the dollar reflected the unabashed materialism of the Gilded Age. But the cultural annihilation that Gates cheerfully predicted did not prove so easy.

The Dawes Act and Indian Land Allotment

In the 1880s, the practice of rounding up Indians and herding them onto reservations lost momentum in favor of allotment — a new policy designed to encourage assimilation through farming and the ownership of private property. Americans vowing to avenge Custer urged the government to get tough with the Indians. Reservations, they argued, took up too much good land that white settlers could put to better use. At the same time, people sympathetic to the Indians were appalled at the desperate poverty on the reservations and feared for the Indians' survival. Helen Hunt Jackson, in her classic work *A Century of Dishonor* (1881), convinced many readers that the Indians had been treated unfairly. "Our Indian policy," the *New York Times* concluded, "is usually spoliation behind the mask of benevolence."

The Indian Rights Association, a group of mainly white easterners formed in 1882, campaigned for the dismantling of the reservations, now viewed as obstacles to progress. To "cease to treat the Indian as a red man and treat him as a man" meant putting an end to tribal communalism and fostering individualism. "Selfishness," declared Senator Henry Dawes of Massachusetts, "is at the bottom of civilization." Dawes called for "allotment in severalty" — the institution of private property.

In 1887, Congress passed the **Dawes Allotment Act**, dividing up reservations and allotting parcels of land to individual Indians as private property. Each unmarried Indian man and woman as well as married men and children (married women were excluded) became eligible to receive 160 acres of land from reservation property. Indians who took allotments earned U.S. citizenship. To protect Indians from land speculators, the government held most of the allotted land in trust, and the Indians could not sell it for twenty-five years. Since Indian land far surpassed the acreage needed for allotments, the government reserved the right to sell the "surplus" to white settlers.

The Dawes Act effectively reduced Indian land from 138 million acres to a scant 48 million. The legislation, in the words of one critic, worked "to despoil the Indians of their lands and to make them vagabonds on the face of the earth." The Dawes Act completed the dispossession of the western Indian peoples and dealt a crippling blow to traditional tribal culture. Amended in 1891 and again in 1906, it remained in effect until 1934, when the United States restored the right of Native Americans to own land communally (as discussed in chapter 24).

Indian Resistance and Survival

Faced with the extinction of their entire way of life, different groups of Indians responded in different ways in the waning decades of the nineteenth century. In the 1870s, Comanche and Kiowa raiding parties frustrated the U.S. Army by using the reservation at Fort Sill as an asylum, knowing that troops could not pursue them onto reservation land. They brazenly used the reservations as a seasonal supply base during the winter months, taking the meager annuities doled out by the Indian agents, only to resume their nomadic ways when spring came. Soon other tribes followed their lead.

Some tribes, including the Crow, Arikara, Pawnee, and Shoshoni, chose to fight alongside the army against their old enemies, the Sioux. The Crow chief Plenty Coups explained why he allied with the United States: "Not because we loved the white man . . . or because we hated the Sioux . . . but because we plainly saw that this course was the only one which might save our beautiful country for us." The Crow and Shoshoni got to stay in their homelands and avoided the fate of other tribes shipped to reservations far away.

Indians who refused to stay on reservations risked being hunted down — a clear indication that reservations were intended to keep Indians in, not to keep whites out, as the friends of the Indians had intended. The Nez Percé war of 1877 is perhaps the most harrowing example of the army's policy. In 1863, the government dictated a treaty drastically reducing Nez Percé land. Most of the chiefs refused to sign the treaty and did not move to the reservation. In 1877, the army issued an ultimatum — come in to the reservation or be hunted down. Some eight hundred Nez Percé people, many of them women and children, fled across the mountains of Idaho, Wyoming, and Montana, heading for the safety of Canada. At the end of their 1,300-mile trek, 50 miles from freedom, they stopped to rest in the snow. The army's Indian scouts spotted their tepees, and the soldiers attacked. Yellow Wolf recalled their plight: "Children crying with cold. No fire. There could be no light. Everywhere the crying, the death wail." After a five-day siege, the Nez Percé leader, **Chief Joseph**, surrendered. His speech, reported by a white soldier, would become famous. "I am tired of fighting," he said as he surrendered his rifle. "Our chiefs are killed. It is cold and we have no blankets. The little children are freezing to death. . . . I am tired. My heart is sick and sad. From where the sun now stands, I will fight no more forever."

In the Southwest, the Apaches resorted to armed resistance. They roamed the Sonoran Desert of southern Arizona and northern Mexico, perfecting a hit-and-run guerrilla warfare that terrorized

Chief Joseph

Chief Joseph came to symbolize the heroic resistance of the Nez Percé. General Nelson Miles promised the Nez Percé that they could return to their homeland if they surrendered. But he betrayed them, as he would betray the Apache people seven years later. The Nez Percé were shipped off to Indian Territory (Oklahoma). In 1879, Chief Joseph traveled to Washington, D.C., to speak for his people. "Let me be a free man," he pleaded, "free to choose my own teachers, free to follow the religion of my fathers, free to think and talk and act for myself — and I will obey every law." National Anthropological Archives, Smithsonian Institution, Washington, D.C. (#2906).

white settlers and bedeviled the army in the 1870s and 1880s. General George Crook combined a policy of dogged pursuit with judicious diplomacy. Crook relied on Indian scouts to track the raiding parties, recruiting nearly two hundred, including Apaches, Navajos, and Paiutes. By 1882, Crook had succeeded in persuading most of the Apaches to settle on the San Carlos Reservation in Arizona Territory. A desolate piece of desert inhabited by scorpions and rattlesnakes, San Carlos, in the words of one Apache, was "the worst place in all the great territory stolen from the Apaches."

Geronimo, a respected shaman (medicine man) of the Chiricahua Apache, refused to stay at San Carlos and repeatedly led raiding parties in the early 1880s. His warriors attacked ranches to obtain ammunition and horses. Among Geronimo's band was **Lozen**, a woman who rode with the warriors, armed with a rifle and a cartridge belt. The sister of a great chief who described her as being as "strong as a man, braver than most, and cunning in strategy," Lozen never married and remained a warrior in Geronimo's band even after her brother's death. In the spring of 1885, Geronimo and his followers, including Lozen, went on a ten-month offensive, moving from the Apache sanctuary in the Sierra Madre to raid and burn ranches and towns on both sides of the Mexican border. General Crook caught up with Geronimo in the fall and persuaded him to return to San Carlos, only to have him slip away on the way back to the reservation. Chagrined, Crook resigned his post. General **Nelson Miles**, Crook's replacement, adopted a policy of hunt and destroy.

Geronimo's band of thirty-three Apaches, including women and children, managed to elude Miles's troops for more than five months. In the end, this small band fought two thousand soldiers to a stalemate. After months of pursuit, Lieutenant Leonard Wood, a member of Miles's spit-and-polish cavalry, discarded his horse and most of his clothes until he was reduced to wearing nothing "but a pair of canton flannel drawers, and an old blue blouse, a pair of moccasins and a hat without a crown."

Eventually, Miles's scouts cornered Geronimo in 1886 at Skeleton Canyon. Caught between Mexican regulars and the U.S. Army, Geronimo agreed to march north with the soldiers and negotiate a settlement. "We have not slept for six months," he admitted, "and we are worn out." Although fewer than three dozen Apaches had been considered "hostile," when General Miles induced them to surrender, the government rounded up nearly five hundred Apaches, including the scouts who had helped track Geronimo, and sent them as prisoners to Florida. By 1889, more than a quarter of them had died, some as a result of illnesses contracted in the damp lowland climate and some by suicide. Their plight roused public opinion, and in 1892 they were moved to Fort Sill in Oklahoma and later to New Mexico.

Geronimo lived to become something of a celebrity. He appeared at the St. Louis Exposition in 1904, and he rode in President Theodore Roosevelt's inaugural parade in 1905. In a newspaper interview, he confessed, "I want to go to my old home before I die. . . . Want to go back to the mountains again. I asked the Great White Father to allow me to go back, but he said no." None of the Apaches were permitted to return to Arizona; when Geronimo died in 1909, he was buried in Oklahoma.

On the plains, many tribes turned to a nonviolent form of resistance — a compelling new religion called the **Ghost Dance**. The Paiute shaman Wovoka, drawing on a cult that had developed in the 1870s, combined elements of Christianity and traditional Indian religion to found the Ghost Dance religion in 1889. Wovoka claimed that he had received a vision in which the Great Spirit spoke through him to all Indians, prophesying that if they would unite in the Ghost Dance ritual, whites would be destroyed in an apocalypse. The shaman promised that Indian warriors slain in battle would return to life and that buffalo once again would roam the land unimpeded. This religion, born of despair and with a message of hope, spread like wildfire over the plains. The Ghost Dance was performed in Idaho, Montana, Utah, Wyoming, Colorado, Nebraska, Kansas, the Dakotas, and Indian Territory by tribes as diverse as the Sioux, Arapaho, Cheyenne, Pawnee, and Shoshoni. Dancers often went into hypnotic trances, dancing until they dropped from exhaustion.

The Ghost Dance was nonviolent, but it frightened whites, especially when the Sioux taught that wearing a white ghost shirt made Indians immune to soldiers' bullets. Soon whites began to fear an uprising. "Indians are dancing in the snow and are wild and crazy," wrote the Bureau of Indian Affairs agent at the Pine Ridge Reservation in South Dakota. Frantic, he pleaded for reinforcements. "We are at the mercy of these dancers. We need protection, and we need it now." President Benjamin Harrison dispatched several thousand federal troops to Sioux country to handle any outbreak.

In December 1890, when Sitting Bull joined the Ghost Dance, he was killed by Indian police as they tried to arrest him at his cabin on the Standing Rock Reservation. His people, fleeing the scene, joined with a larger group of Miniconjou Sioux, who were apprehended by the Seventh Cavalry, Custer's old regiment, near Wounded Knee Creek, South Dakota. As the Indians laid down their arms, a soldier attempted to take a rifle from a deaf Miniconjou man, and the gun went off. The soldiers opened fire. In the ensuing melee, Indian men, women, and children were mowed down in minutes by the army's brutally efficient Hotchkiss rapid-fire guns. Caught in the crossfire, one Indian recounted, "I saw my friends sinking about me, and heard the whine of many bullets." In a matter of minutes, eighty-three Indian men lay dead. The cavalry then hunted down women and children attempting to flee into the bluffs and canyons. The next day, more than two hundred Sioux lay dead or dying in the snow.

Settler Jules Sandoz surveyed the scene the day after the massacre at **Wounded Knee**. "Here in ten minutes an entire community was as the buffalo that bleached on the plains," he wrote. "There was something loose in the world that hated joy and happiness as it hated brightness and color, reducing everything to drab agony and gray." It had taken Euro-Americans 250 years to wrest control of the eastern half of the United States from the Indians. It took them less than 40 years to take the western half. The subjugation of the American Indians marked the first chapter in a national mission of empire that would presage overseas imperialistic adventures in Asia, Latin America, the Caribbean, and the Pacific islands.

REVIEW In what ways did different Indian groups defy and resist colonial rule?

▶ Gold Fever and the Mining West

Mining stood at the center of the United States' quest for empire in the West. The California gold rush of 1849 touched off the frenzy. The four decades following witnessed equally frenetic rushes for gold and other metals, most notably on the **Comstock Lode** in Nevada and later in New Mexico, Colorado, the Dakotas, Montana, Idaho, Arizona, and Utah. Each rush built on the last, producing new mining technologies and innovations in financing as hordes of miners, eager to strike it rich, moved from one boomtown to the next. Mining in the West, however, was a story not only of boom and bust but also of community building and the development of territories into states.

At first glance, the mining West may seem much different from the East, but by the 1870s the term *urban industrialism* described Virginia City, Nevada, as accurately as it did Pittsburgh or Cleveland. A close look at mining on the Comstock Lode indicates some of the patterns and paradoxes of western mining. The diversity of peoples drawn to the West by the promise of mining riches and land made the region the most cosmopolitan in the nation, as well as the most contested. And a look at territorial government uncovers striking parallels with the corruption and cupidity in politics east of the Mississippi.

Mining on the Comstock Lode

By 1859, refugees from California's played-out goldfields flocked to the Washoe basin in Nevada. There prospectors found the gold they sought mired in blackish sand they called "that blasted blue stuff." Eventually, an enterprising miner had the stuff assayed, and it turned out that the Washoe miners had stumbled on the richest vein of silver ore on the continent — the legendary Comstock Lode, named for prospector Henry Comstock.

To exploit even potentially valuable silver claims required capital and expensive technology well beyond the means of the prospector. An active San Francisco stock market sprang up to finance operations on the Comstock. Shrewd businessmen soon recognized that the easiest way to get rich was not to mine at all but to sell their claims or to form mining companies and sell shares of stock. The most unscrupulous mined the wallets of gullible investors by selling shares in bogus mines. Speculation, misrepresentation, and outright thievery ran rampant. In twenty years, more than $300 million poured from the earth in Nevada alone. A little stayed in Virginia City, but a great deal more went to speculators in California, some of whom got rich without ever leaving San Francisco.

The promise of gold and silver drew thousands to the mines of the West, the honest as well as the unprincipled. As author Mark Twain observed in Virginia City's *Territorial Enterprise*, "All the peoples of the earth had representative adventures in the Silverland." Irish, Chinese, Germans, English, Scots, Welsh, Canadians, Mexicans, Italians, Scandinavians, French, Swiss, Chileans, and other South and Central Americans came to share in the bonanza. With them came a sprinkling of Russians, Poles, Greeks, Japanese, Spaniards, Hungarians,

Portuguese, Turks, Pacific Islanders, and Moroccans, as well as other North Americans, African Americans, and American Indians. This polyglot population, typical of mining boomtowns, made Virginia City in the 1870s more cosmopolitan than New York or Boston. In the part of Utah Territory that eventually became Nevada, as many as 30 percent of the people came from outside the United States, compared to 25 percent in New York and 21 percent in Massachusetts.

Irish immigrants formed the largest ethnic group in the mining district. In Virginia City, fully one-third of the population claimed at least one parent from Ireland. Irish and Irish American women constituted the largest group of women on the Comstock. As servants, boardinghouse owners, and washerwomen, they made up a significant part of the workforce. By contrast, the Chinese community, numbering 642 in 1870, remained overwhelmingly male. Virulent anti-Chinese sentiment barred the men from work in the mines, but despite the violent anti-Asian rhetoric, the mining community came to depend on Chinese labor. Many boardinghouses and affluent homes employed a Chinese cook or servant along with an Irish parlor maid.

As was so often the case in the West, where Euro-American ambitions clashed with Native American ways, the discovery of precious metals on the Comstock spelled disaster for the Indians. No sooner had the miners struck pay dirt than they demanded that army troops "hunt Indians" and establish forts to protect transportation to and from the diggings. This sudden and dramatic intrusion left Nevada's native tribes — the Northern Paiute and Bannock Shoshoni — exiles in their own land. At first they resisted, but over time they made peace with the in-vaders and developed resourceful strategies to adapt and preserve their culture and identity despite the havoc wreaked by western mining and settlement.

In 1873, Comstock miners uncovered a new vein of ore, a veritable cavern of gold and silver. This "Big Bonanza" speeded the transition from small-scale in-dustry to corporate oligopoly, creating a radically new social and economic envi-ronment. The Comstock became a laboratory for new mining technology. Huge stamping mills pulverized rock with pistonlike hammers driven by steam engines. Enormous Cornish pumps sucked water from the mine shafts, and huge ventila-tors circulated air in the underground chambers. No backwoods mining camp, Virginia City was an industrial center with more than 1,200 stamping mills working on average a ton of ore every day. Almost 400 men worked in milling, nearly 300 labored in manufacturing industries, and roughly 3,000 toiled in the mines. The Gould and Curry mine covered sixty acres. Most of the miners who came to the Comstock ended up as laborers for the big companies.

New technology eliminated some of the dangers of mining but often created new ones. In the hard-rock mines of the West, accidents in the 1870s disabled one out of every thirty miners and killed one in eighty. Ross Moudy, who worked as a miner in Cripple Creek, Colorado, recalled how a stockholder visiting the mine nearly fell to his death. The terrified visitor told the miner next to him that "instead of being paid $3 a day, they ought to have all the gold they could take out." Moudy's biggest worry was carbon dioxide, which often filled the tunnels because of poor ventilation. "Many times," he confessed, "I have been carried out unconscious." Those who avoided accidents still breathed air so dangerous that respiratory diseases eventually disabled them. After a year on the job, Moudy joined a labor union "because I saw it would help me to keep in work and for protection in case of accident or sickness." The union provided good sick benefits and hired nurses, "so if one is alone and sick he is sure to be taken care of." On the Comstock Lode, because of the difficulty of obtaining skilled labor, the richness of the ore, and the need for a stable workforce, labor unions formed early and held considerable bargaining power. Comstock miners commanded $4 a day, the highest wage in the mining West.

The mining towns of the "Wild West" are often portrayed as lawless outposts, filled with saloons and rough gambling dens and populated almost exclusively by men, except for the occasional dance-hall floozy. The truth is more complex, as Virginia City's development attests. An established urban community built to serve an industrial giant, Virginia City in its first decade boasted churches, schools, theaters, an opera house, and hundreds of families. By 1870, women composed 30 percent of the population, and 75 percent of the women listed their occupation in the census as housekeeper. Mary McNair Mathews, a widow from Buffalo, New York, who lived on the Comstock in the 1870s, worked as a teacher, nurse, seamstress, laundress, and lodging-house operator. She later published a book on her adventures.

By 1875, Virginia City boasted a population of 25,000 people, making it one of the largest cities between St. Louis and San Francisco. A must-see stop on the way west, the "Queen of the Comstock" hosted American presidents as well as legions of lesser dignitaries. No rough outpost of the Wild West, Virginia City represented, in the words of a recent chronicler, "the distilled essence of America's newly established course — urban, industrial, acquisitive, and materialistic, on the move, 'a living polyglot' of cultures that collided and converged."

The Diverse Peoples of the West

The West of the late nineteenth century was indeed a polyglot place, as much so as the big cities of the East. The sheer number of peoples who mingled in the West produced a complex blend of racism and prejudice. One historian has noted, not entirely facetiously, that there were at least eight oppressed "races" in the West — Indians, Latinos, Chinese, Japanese, blacks, Mormons, strikers, and radicals.

African Americans who ventured out to the territories faced hostile settlers determined to keep the West "for whites only." In response, they formed all-black communities such as Nicodemas, Kansas. That settlement, founded by thirty black Kentuckians in 1877, grew to a community of seven hundred by 1880. Isolated and often separated by great distances, small black settlements grew up throughout the West, in Nevada, Utah, and the Pacific Northwest, as well as in Kansas. Black soldiers who served in the West during the Indian wars often stayed on as settlers. Called **buffalo soldiers** because Native Americans thought their hair resembled that of the bison, these black troops numbered up to 25,000. In the face of discrimination, poor treatment, and harsh conditions, the buffalo soldiers served with distinction and boasted the lowest desertion rate in the army.

Hispanic peoples had lived in Texas and the Southwest since Juan de Oñate led pioneer settlers up the Rio Grande in 1598. Hispanics had occupied the Pacific coast since San Diego was founded in 1769. Overnight, they were reduced to a "minority" after the United States annexed Texas in 1845 and took land stretching to California after the Mexican-American War ended in 1848. At first, the Hispanic owners of large *ranchos* in California, New Mexico, and Texas greeted conquest as an economic opportunity — new markets for their livestock and buyers for their lands. But racial prejudice soon ended their optimism. Californios (Mexican residents of California), who had been granted American citizenship by the Treaty of Guadalupe Hidalgo (1848), faced discrimination by Anglos who sought to keep them out of California's mines and commerce. Whites illegally squatted on *rancho* land while protracted litigation over Spanish and Mexican land grants forced the Californios into court. Although the U.S. Supreme Court eventually validated most of their claims, it took so long — seventeen years on average — that many Californios sold their property to pay taxes and legal bills. The city of Oakland, California, sits on what was once a 19,000-acre ranch owned by the Peralta family, who lost the land to Anglos.

Swindles, chicanery, and intimidation dispossessed scores of Californios. Many ended up segregated in urban barrios (neighborhoods) in their own homeland. Their percentage of California's population declined from 82 percent in 1850 to 19 percent in 1880 as Anglos migrated to the state. In New Mexico and Texas, Mexicans remained a majority of the population but became increasingly impoverished as Anglos dominated business and took the best jobs. Skirmishes between Hispanics and whites in northern New Mexico over the fencing of the open range lasted for decades. Groups of Hispanics with names such as *Las Manos Negras* (the Black Hands) cut fences and burned barns. In Texas, violence along the Rio Grande pitted Tejanos (Mexican residents of Texas) against the Texas Rangers, who saw their role as "keeping Mexicans in their place."

Even more than the Mexicans, the Chinese suffered brutal treatment at the hands of employers and other laborers. Drawn by the promise of gold, more than 20,000 Chinese had joined the rush to California by 1852. Miners determined to keep "California for Americans" succeeded in passing prohibitive foreign license laws to keep the Chinese out of the mines. But Chinese immigration continued. In the 1860s, when white workers moved on to find riches in the bonanza mines of Nevada, Chinese laborers took jobs abandoned by the whites. Railroad magnate Charles Crocker hired Chinese gangs to work on the Central Pacific, reasoning that "the race that built the Great Wall" could lay tracks across the treacherous Sierra Nevada. Some 12,000 Chinese, representing 90 percent of Crocker's workforce, completed America's first transcontinental railroad in 1869.

By 1870, more than 63,000 Chinese immigrants lived in America, 77 percent of them in California. A 1790 federal statute that limited naturalization to "white persons" was modified after the Civil War to extend naturalization to blacks ("persons of African descent"). But the Chinese and other Asians continued to be denied access to citizenship. As perpetual aliens, they constituted a reserve army of transnational laborers that many saw as a threat to American labor. For the most part, the Chinese did not displace white workers but instead found work as railroad laborers, cooks, servants, and farmhands while white workers sought

Chinese Workers
Chinese section hands, wearing their distinctive conical hats, are shown here in 1898 shoveling dirt for the North Pacific Coast Railroad in Corte Madera, California. Charles Crocker was the first railroad executive to hire Chinese laborers to work on the Central Pacific railroad in the 1860s, reasoning that the race that built the Great Wall could build tracks through the Sierra Nevada. California Historical Society, FN-25345.

out more lucrative fields. In the 1870s, when California and the rest of the nation weathered a major economic depression, the Chinese became easy scapegoats. California workingmen rioted and fought to keep Chinese workers out of the state, claiming they were "coolie labor" — involuntary contract laborers recruited by business interests determined to keep wages at rock bottom.

In 1876, the Workingmen's Party formed to fight for Chinese exclusion. Racial and cultural animosities stood at the heart of anti-Chinese agitation. Denis Kearney, the fiery San Francisco leader of the movement, made clear this racist bent when he urged legislation to "expel every one of the moon-eyed lepers." Nor was California alone in its anti-immigrant nativism. As the country confronted growing ethnic and racial diversity with the rising tide of global immigration in the decades following the Civil War, many questioned the principle of racial equality at the same time they argued against the assimilation of "nonwhite" groups. In this climate, Congress passed the **Chinese Exclusion Act** in 1882, effectively barring Chinese immigration and setting a precedent for further immigration restrictions.

The Chinese Exclusion Act led to a sharp drop in the Chinese population — from 105,465 in 1880 to 89,863 in 1900 — because Chinese immigrants, overwhelmingly male, did not have families to sustain their population. Eventually, Japanese immigrants, including women as well as men, replaced the Chinese, particularly in agriculture. As "nonwhite" immigrants, they could not become naturalized citizens, but their children born in the United States claimed the rights of citizenship. Japanese parents, seeking to own land, purchased it in their children's names. Although anti-Asian prejudice remained strong in California and elsewhere in the West, Asian immigrants formed an important part of the economic fabric of the western United States.

The Mormons, who had fled west to Utah Territory in 1844 to avoid religious persecution, established Salt Lake City, a thriving metropolis of more than 150,000 residents by 1882. To counter criticism of the Mormon practice of polygamy (church leader Brigham Young had twenty-seven wives), the Utah territorial legislature gave women the right to vote in 1870, the first universal woman suffrage act in the nation. (Wyoming had granted suffrage to white women in 1869.) Although woman's rights advocates argued that the newly enfranchised women would "do away with the horrible institution of polygamy," it remained in force. Not until 1890 did the church hierarchy yield to pressure and renounce polygamy. The fierce controversy over polygamy postponed statehood for Utah until 1896.

Territorial Government

The federal government practiced a policy of benign neglect when it came to territorial government in the West. The president appointed a governor, a secretary, and two to four judges, along with an attorney and a marshal. In Nevada Territory, that meant that a handful of officials governed an area the size of New England. Originally a part of the larger Utah Territory, Nevada, propelled by mining interests, moved on the fast track to statehood, entering the Union in 1864, long before its population or its development merited statehood.

More typical were the territories extant in 1870 — New Mexico, Utah, Washington, Colorado, Dakota, Arizona, Idaho, Montana, and Wyoming. These areas remained territories for inordinately long periods ranging from twenty-three to sixty-two years. While awaiting statehood, they were subject to territorial governors who were underpaid, often unqualified, and largely ignored in Washington. Most territorial governors won their posts because of party loyalty and had little knowledge of the areas they served, little notions of their duties, and limited ability to perform them.

In theory, territorial governors received adequate salaries, as high as $3,500 in an era when the average workingman earned less than $500 a year. In practice, the funds rarely arrived in a timely fashion, and more than one governor found that he had to pay government expenses out of his own pocket. As one cynic observed, "Only the rich or those having 'no visible means of support,' can afford to accept office." John C. Frémont, the governor of Arizona Territory, complained he was so poor that he could not inspect the Grand Canyon because he didn't have money to keep a horse.

Territorial governors with fewer scruples accepted money from special interests — mine owners and big ranchers. Nearly all territorial appointees tried to make ends meet by maintaining business connections with the East or by taking advantage of investment opportunities in the West. Distance and the lack of funds made it difficult to summon officers from Washington to investigate charges of corruption. Officials who ventured west to look into such charges often felt intimidated by gun-packing westerners. One judge sent to New Mexico Territory in 1871 reported that he "stayed three days, made up his mind that it would be dangerous to do any investigating, . . . and returned to his home without any action." Underfunded and overlooked, victims of political cronyism, and prey to special interests, territorial governments were rife with conflicts of interest and corruption, mirroring the self-serving political and economic values of the country as a whole in the rush for riches that followed the Civil War.

REVIEW How did industrial technology change mining in Nevada?

▶ Land Fever

In the three decades following 1870, more land was settled than in all the previous history of the country. Americans by the hundreds of thousands packed up and moved west, goaded if not by the hope of striking gold, then by the promise of owning land. The agrarian West shared with the mining West a persistent restlessness, an equally pervasive addiction to speculation, and a penchant for exploiting natural resources and labor.

Two factors stimulated the land rush in the trans-Mississippi West. The **Homestead Act of 1862** promised 160 acres free to any citizen or prospective citizen, male or female, who settled on the land for five years. Even more important, **transcontinental railroads** opened up new areas and actively recruited settlers. After the completion of the first transcontinental railroad in 1869, homesteaders abandoned the covered wagon, and by the 1880s they could choose from four competing rail lines and make the trip west in a matter of days.

Although the country was rich in land and resources, not all who wanted to own land achieved their goal. During the transition from the family farm to large commercial farming, small farms gave way to vast spreads worked by migrant labor or paid farmworkers. Just as industry corporatized and consolidated in the East, the period from 1870 to 1900 witnessed corporate consolidation in mining, ranching, and agriculture.

Moving West: Homesteaders and Speculators

A Missouri homesteader remembered packing as her family pulled up stakes and headed west to Oklahoma in 1890. "We were going to God's Country," she wrote. "You had to work hard on that rocky country in Missouri. I was glad to be leaving it. . . . We were going to a new land and get rich."

People who ventured west searching for "God's Country" faced hardship, loneliness, and deprivation. To carve a farm from the raw prairie of Iowa, the plains of Nebraska, or the forests of the Pacific Northwest took more than fortitude and backbreaking toil. It took luck. Blizzards, tornadoes, grasshoppers, hailstorms, drought, prairie fires, accidental death, and disease were only a few of the catastrophes that could befall even the best farmer. Homesteaders on free land still needed as much as $1,000 for a house, a team of farm animals, a well, fencing, and seed. Poor farmers called "sodbusters" did without even these basics, living in dugouts carved into hillsides and using muscle instead of machinery.

"Father made a dugout and covered it with willows and grass," one Kansas girl recounted. When it rained, the dugout flooded, and "we carried the water out in

Norwegian Immigrant and Sod House
Norwegian immigrant Beret Olesdater sits in front of her sod house in Lac qui Parle, Minnesota, in 1896. On the plains, where trees were scarce and lumber was often prohibitively expensive, settlers built with the materials at hand. The dugout was the most primitive dwelling, carved into a hillside. Huts cut from blocks of sod, like the one pictured here, marked a step up. Life for women on the plains proved especially lonely and hard. © Minnesota Historical Society/Corbis.

buckets, then waded around in the mud until it dried." Rain wasn't the only problem. "Sometimes the bull snakes would get in the roof and now and then one would lose his hold and fall down on the bed. . . . Mother would grab the hoe . . . and after the fight was over Mr. Bull Snake was dragged outside." The sod house, a step up from the dugout, had walls cut from blocks of sod and a roof of sod, lumber, or tin.

For women on the frontier, obtaining simple daily necessities such as water and fuel meant backbreaking labor. Out on the plains, where water was scarce, women often had to trudge to the nearest creek or spring. "A yoke was made to place across [Mother's] shoulders, so as to carry at each end a bucket of water," one daughter recollected, "and then water was brought a half mile from spring to house." Gathering fuel was another heavy chore. Without ready sources of coal or firewood, settlers on the plains turned to what substitutes they could scavenge — twigs, tufts of grass, corncobs, sunflower stalks. But by far the most prevalent fuel was "chips" — chunks of dried cattle and buffalo dung, found in abundance on the plains.

Despite the hardships, some homesteaders succeeded in building comfortable lives. The sod hut made way for a more substantial house; the log cabin yielded to a white clapboard home with a porch and a rocking chair. For others, the promise of the West failed to materialize. Already by the 1870s, much of the best land had been taken. Too often, homesteaders found that only the least desirable tracts were left — poor land, far from markets, transportation, and society. "There is plenty of land for sale in California," one migrant complained in 1870, but "the majority of the available lands are held by speculators, at prices far beyond the reach of a poor

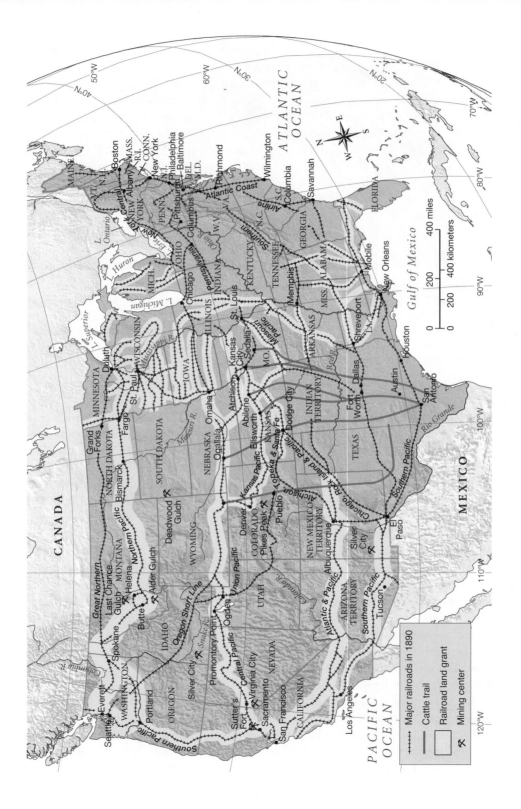

man." The railroads, flush from land grants provided by the state and federal governments, owned huge swaths of land in the West and actively recruited settlers. Altogether, the land grants totaled approximately 180 million acres — an area almost one-tenth the size of the United States (Map 17.2). Of the 2.5 million farms established between 1860 and 1900, homesteading accounted for only one in five; the vast majority of farmland sold for a profit.

As land grew scarce on the prairie in the 1870s, farmers began to push farther west, moving into western Kansas, Nebraska, and eastern Colorado — the region called the **Great American Desert** by settlers who had passed over it on their way to California and Oregon. Many agricultural experts warned that the semi-arid land (where less than twenty inches of rain fell annually) would not support a farm on the 160 acres allotted to homesteaders. But their words of caution were drowned out by the extravagant claims of western promoters, many employed by the railroads to sell off their land grants. "Rain follows the plow" became the slogan of western boosters, who insisted that cultivation would alter the climate of the region and bring more rainfall. Instead, drought followed the plow. Droughts were a cyclical fact of life on the Great Plains. Plowed up, the dry topsoil blew away in the wind. A period of relatively good rainfall in the early 1880s encouraged farming; then a protracted drought in the late 1880s and early 1890s sent starving farmers reeling back from the plains. Thousands left, some in wagons carrying the slogan "In God we trusted, in Kansas we busted."

Fever for fertile land set off a series of spectacular land runs in Oklahoma. When two million acres of land in former Indian Territory opened for settlement in 1889, thousands of homesteaders massed on the border. At the opening pistol shot, "with a shout and a yell the swift riders shot out, then followed the light buggies or wagons," a reporter wrote. "Above all, a great cloud of dust hover[ed] like smoke over a battlefield." By nightfall, Oklahoma boasted two tent cities with more than ten thousand residents. In the last frenzied land rush on Oklahoma's Cherokee strip in 1893, several settlers were killed in the stampede, and nervous men guarded their claims with rifles. As public land grew scarce, the hunger for land grew fiercer for both farmers and ranchers.

Ranchers and Cowboys

Cattle ranchers followed the railroads onto the plains, establishing a cattle kingdom from Texas to Wyoming between 1865 and 1885. Cowboys drove huge herds, as many as three thousand head of cattle that grazed on public lands as they

◀ **MAP 17.2**
Federal Land Grants to Railroads and the Development of the West, 1850–1900
Generous federal land grants meant that railroads could sell the desirable land next to the track at a profit or hold it for speculation. Railroads received more than 180 million acres, an area as large as Texas. Built well ahead of demand, the western railroads courted settlers, often onto land not fit for farming.

followed cattle tracks like the Chisholm Trail from Texas to railheads in Kansas. More than 1.5 million Texas longhorns went to market before the range began to close in the 1880s.

Barbed wire revolutionized the cattle business and sounded the death knell for the open range. In 1874, Joseph F. Glidden, an Illinois sheriff, invented and patented barbed wire. Gambler and promoter John "Bet a Million" Gates made his fortune by corralling a herd of Texas longhorns in downtown San Antonio, proving the merit of the flimsy-looking wire he went on to market profitably. As the largest ranches in Texas began to fence, nasty fights broke out between big ranchers and "fence cutters," who resented the end of the free range. One old-timer observed, "Those persons, Mexicans and Americans, without land but who had cattle were put out of business by fencing." Fencing forced small-time ranchers who owned land but could not afford to buy barbed wire or sink wells to sell out for the best price they could get. The displaced ranchers, many of them Mexicans, ended up as wageworkers on the huge spreads owned by Anglos or by European syndicates.

On the range, the cowboy gave way to the cattle king and, like the miner, became a wage laborer. Many cowboys were African Americans (as many as five thousand in Texas alone). Writers of western literature chose to ignore the presence of black cowboys like Deadwood Dick (Nat Love), who was portrayed as a white man in the dime novels of the era.

By 1886, cattle overcrowded the range. Severe blizzards during the winter of 1886–87 decimated the herds. "A whole generation of cowmen," wrote one chronicler, "went dead broke." Fencing worsened the situation. During blizzards, cattle stayed alive by keeping on the move. But when they ran up against barbed wire fences, they froze to death. In the aftermath of the "Great Die Up," new labor-intensive forms of cattle ranching replaced the open-range model.

Tenants, Sharecroppers, and Migrants

In the post–Civil War period, as agriculture became a big business tied by the railroads to national and global markets, an increasing number of laborers worked land that they would never own. In the southern United States, farmers labored under particularly heavy burdens. The Civil War wiped out much of the region's capital, which had been invested in slaves, and crippled the plantation economy. Newly freed slaves rarely obtained land of their own and often ended up as farm laborers. "The colored folks stayed with the old boss man and farmed and worked on the plantations," a black Alabama sharecropper observed bitterly. "They were still slaves, but they were free slaves." Some freedpeople did manage to pull together enough resources to go west. In 1879, more than fifteen thousand black **Exodusters** moved from Mississippi and Louisiana to take up land in Kansas.

California's Mexican cowboys, or *vaqueros*, commanded decent wages throughout the Southwest. Skilled horsemen, the vaqueros boasted that five of them could do the work of thirty Anglo cowboys. The vocabulary of ranching, with words such as *rodeo*, *lasso*, and *lariat*, testified to the centrality of the vaqueros' place in the cattle industry. But by 1880, as the coming of the railroads ended the long cattle drives and as large feedlots began to replace the open range, the value of their skills declined. Many vaqueros ended up as migrant laborers, often on land their families had once owned. Similarly, in Texas, Tejanos found themselves displaced. After the heyday of cattle ranching ended in the late 1880s, cotton production rose in the southeastern regions of the state. Ranchers turned their pastures into sharecroppers' plots and hired displaced cowboys, most of them Mexicans, as seasonal laborers for as little as seventy-five cents a day, thereby creating a growing army of agricultural wageworkers.

Land monopoly and large-scale farming fostered tenancy and migratory labor on the West Coast. By the 1870s, less than 1 percent of California's population owned half the state's available agricultural land. The rigid economics of large-scale commercial agriculture and the seasonal nature of the crops spawned a ragged army of migratory agricultural laborers. Derisively labeled "blanket men" or "bindle stiffs," these transients worked the fields in the growing season and wintered in the flophouses of San Francisco. Most farm laborers were Chinese immigrants. After passage of the Chinese Exclusion Act of 1882, Mexicans, Filipinos, and Japanese immigrants filled the demand for migratory workers.

Commercial Farming and Industrial Cowboys

In the late nineteenth century, the population of the United States remained overwhelmingly rural. The 1870 census showed that nearly 80 percent of the nation's people lived on farms and in villages of fewer than 8,000 inhabitants. By 1900, the figure had dropped to 66 percent. At the same time, the number of farms rose. Rapid growth in the West increased the number of the nation's farms from 2 million in 1860 to more than 5.7 million in 1900.

Despite the hardships individual farmers experienced, new technology and farming techniques revolutionized American farm life. Mechanized farm machinery halved the time and labor cost of production and made it possible to cultivate vast tracts of land. Meanwhile, urbanization provided farmers with expanding markets for their produce, and railroads carried crops to markets thousands of miles away. Even before the start of the twentieth century, American agriculture had entered the era of what would come to be called agribusiness — farming as a big business — with the advent of huge commercial farms.

As farming moved onto the prairies and plains, mechanization took command. Steel plows, reapers, mowers, harrows, seed drills, combines, and threshers replaced human muscle. Horse-drawn implements gave way to steam-powered machinery. By 1880, a single combine could do the work of twenty men, vastly increasing the acreage a farmer could cultivate. Mechanization spurred the growth of bonanza wheat farms, some more than 100,000 acres, in California and the Red River Valley of North Dakota and Minnesota. This agricultural revolution meant that Americans raised more than four times the corn, five times the hay, and seven times the wheat and oats they had before the Civil War.

Loggers in Washington, 1890
Loggers pose on and beside one huge felled tree. The loggers worked in all-male crews with a "faller" cutting down the tree, "buckers" cutting it into manageable pieces, and "whistle punks" relaying information. By 1890, loggers using only axes and handsaws had harvested over one billion board feet of timber in the state of Washington alone. The massive deforestation continued and picked up speed as steam power replaced brawn and horse-power. Loggers lived a hard, dirty life in remote migratory camps, working long hours and sometimes wearing the same clothes for months on end. ©Bettmann/Corbis.

Like cotton farmers in the South, western grain and livestock farmers increasingly depended on foreign markets for their livelihood. A fall in global market prices meant that a farmer's entire harvest went to pay off debts. In the depression that followed the panic of 1893, many heavily mortgaged farmers lost their land to creditors. As a Texas cotton farmer complained, "By the time the World Gets their Liveing out of the Farmer as we have to Feed the World, we the Farmer has nothing Left but a Bear Hard Liveing." Commercial farming, along with mining, represented another way in which the West developed its own brand of industrialism. The far West's industrial economy sprang initially from California gold and the vast territory that came under American control following the Mexican-American War. In the ensuing rush on land and resources, environmental factors interacted with economic and social forces to produce enterprises as vast in scale and scope as anything found in the East.

Two Alsatian immigrants, Henry Miller and Charles Lux, pioneered the West's mix of agriculture and industrialism. Beginning as meat wholesalers, Miller and Lux quickly expanded their business to encompass cattle, land, and land reclamation projects such as dams and irrigation systems. With a labor force of migrant workers, a highly coordinated corporate system, and large sums of investment capital, the firm of **Miller & Lux** became one of America's industrial behemoths. Eventually, these "industrial cowboys" grazed a herd of 100,000 cattle on 1.25 million acres of company land in California, Oregon, and Nevada and employed more than 1,200 migrant laborers on their corporate ranches. Miller & Lux dealt with the labor problem by offering free meals to migratory workers, thus keeping wages low while winning goodwill among an army of unemployed who competed for the work. When the company's Chinese cooks rebelled at washing the dishes resulting from the free meals, the migrant laborers were forced to eat after the ranch hands and use their dirty plates. By the 1890s, more than eight hundred migrants a year followed what came to be known as the "Dirty Plate Route" on Miller & Lux ranches throughout California.

Since the days of Thomas Jefferson, agrarian life had been linked with the highest ideals of a democratic society. Now agrarianism itself had been transformed. The farmer was no longer a self-sufficient yeoman but often a businessman or a wage laborer tied to a global market. And even as farm production soared, industrialization outstripped it. More and more farmers left the fields for urban factories or found work in the "factories in the fields" of the new industrialized agribusiness. Now that the future seemed to lie not with the small farmer but with industrial enterprises, was democracy itself at risk? This question would ignite a farmers' revolt in the 1880s and dominate political debate in the 1890s.

> **REVIEW**   Why did many homesteaders find it difficult to acquire good land in the West?

▶ Conclusion: The West in the Gilded Age

In 1871, author Mark Twain published *Roughing It*, a chronicle of his days spent in mining towns in California and Nevada. There he found corrupt politics, vulgar display, and mania for speculation, the same cupidity he later skewered in *The Gilded Age* (1873), his biting satire of greed and corruption in the nation's capital. Far from being an antidote to the meretricious values of the East — an innocent idyll out of place and time — the American West, with its get-rich-quick ethos and its addiction to gambling and speculation, helped set the tone for the Gilded Age.

Twain's view countered that of Frederick Jackson Turner and perhaps better suited a West that witnessed the overbuilding of railroads, the consolidation of business in mining and ranching; the rise of commercial farming; corruption and a penchant for government handouts; racial animosity, whether in the form of Indian wars or Chinese exclusion; the exploitation of labor and natural resources, which led to the decimation of the great bison herds, the pollution of rivers with mining wastes, and the overgrazing of the plains; and the beginnings of an imperial policy that would provide a template for U.S. adventures abroad. Turner, intent on promoting what was unique about the frontier, failed to note that the same issues that came to dominate debate east of the Mississippi — the growing power of big business, the exploitation of land and labor, corruption in politics, and ethnic and racial tensions exacerbated by colonial expansion and unparalleled immigration — took center stage in the West at the end of the nineteenth century.

Reviewing Chapter 17

REVIEW QUESTIONS

1. How did the slaughter of the bison contribute to the Plains Indians' removal to reservations? (pp. 491–498)

2. In what ways did different Indian groups defy and resist colonial rule? (pp. 498–503)

3. How did industrial technology change mining in Nevada? (pp. 504–510)

4. Why did many homesteaders find it difficult to acquire good land in the West? (pp. 510–517)

MAKING CONNECTIONS

1. Westward migration brought settlers into conflict with Native Americans. What was the U.S. government's policy toward Indians in the West, and how did it evolve over time? How did the Indians resist and survive white encroachment? In your answer, discuss the cultural and military features of the conflict.

2. The economic and industrial developments characteristic of the East after the Civil War also made their mark on the West. How did innovations in business and technology transform mining and agriculture in the West? In your answer, be sure to consider effects on production and the consequences for the lives of miners and agricultural laborers.

3. Settlers from all over the world came to the American West seeking their fortunes but found that opportunity was not equally available to all. In competition for work and land, why did Anglo-American settlers usually have the upper hand? How did legal developments contribute to this circumstance?

4. Railroads had a profound impact on the development of the western United States. What role did railroads play in western settlement, industrialization, and agriculture? How did railroads affect Indian populations in the West?

LINKING TO THE PAST

1. In what ways were the goals of migrants to the West similar to those of the northerners who moved to the South after the Civil War? How did they differ? (See chapter 16.)

2. How did the racism of the West compare with the racist attitudes against African Americans in the Reconstruction South? (See chapter 16.)

TIMELINE 1851–1900

1851 • First Treaty of Fort Laramie.

1862 • Homestead Act.
• Great Sioux Uprising (Santee Uprising).

1864 • Sand Creek massacre.

1867 • Treaty of Medicine Lodge.

1868 • Second Treaty of Fort Laramie.

1869 • First transcontinental railroad completed.

1870 • Hunters begin to decimate bison herds.

1873 • "Big Bonanza" discovered on Comstock Lode.

1874 • Discovery of gold in Black Hills.

1876 • Battle of the Little Big Horn.

1877 • Chief Joseph surrenders.
• Crazy Horse arrested and killed.

1878 • Indian students enroll at Hampton Institute in Virginia.

1879 • Carlisle Indian School opens in Pennsylvania.
• More than fifteen thousand Exodusters move to Kansas.

1881 • Sitting Bull surrenders.

1882 • Chinese Exclusion Act.
• Indian Rights Association formed.

1886 • Geronimo surrenders.

1886–1888 • Severe blizzards decimate cattle herds.

1887 • Dawes Allotment Act.

1889 • Rise of Ghost Dance.
• Two million acres in Oklahoma opened for settlement.

1890 • Sitting Bull killed.
• Massacre at Wounded Knee, South Dakota.

1893 • Last land rush takes place in Oklahoma Territory.
• Frederick Jackson Turner presents "frontier thesis."

1900 • Census finds 66 percent of population lives in rural areas, compared to 80 percent in 1870.

▶ **FOR AN ONLINE BIBLIOGRAPHY, PRACTICE QUIZZES, WEB SITES, IMAGES, AND DOCUMENTS RELATED TO THIS CHAPTER,** see the Book Companion Site at **bedfordstmartins.com/roarkvalue**.

▶ **FOR DOCUMENTS RELATED TO THIS PERIOD,** see Michael Johnson, ed., *Reading the American Past*, Fifth Edition.

Business and Politics in the Gilded Age

1865–1900

ONE NIGHT OVER DINNER, AUTHORS MARK TWAIN AND CHARLES DUDLEY
Warner teased their wives about the sentimental novels they read. When the
two women challenged them to write something better, they set to work.
Warner supplied the melodrama, while Twain "hurled in the facts." The result
was a runaway best seller, a savage satire of the "get-rich-quick" era that
would forever carry the book's title, *The Gilded Age* (1873).

Twain left no one unscathed in the novel — political hacks, Washington
lobbyists, Wall Street financiers, small-town boosters, and the "great putty-
hearted public" that tolerated the plunder. Underneath the glitter of the
Gilded Age lurked vulgarity, crass materialism, and political corruption. Twain
had witnessed the crooked partnership of business and politics in the administration of Ulysses S. Grant. Here he describes how a lobbyist finagled to get a
bill through Congress:

> Why the matter is simple enough. A Congressional appropriation costs
> money. . . . A majority of the House Committee, say $10,000 apiece — $40,000;
> a majority of the Senate Committee, the same each — say $40,000; a little
> extra to one or two chairmen of one or two such committees, say $10,000
> each — $20,000; and there's $100,000 of the money gone, to begin with.
> Then, seven male lobbyists, at $3,000 each — $21,000; one female lobbyist,
> $3,000; a high moral Congressman or Senator here and there — the high
> moral ones cost more, because they give tone to a measure — say ten of
> these at $3,000 each, is $30,000; then a lot of small fry country members who

Mark Twain
Popular author Mark Twain (Samuel Langhorne Clemens) wrote acerbically about the excesses of the Gilded Age in his novel of that name written with Charles Dudley Warner and published in 1873. No one knew the meretricious lure of the era better than Twain, who succumbed to a get-rich-quick scheme that led him to the brink of bankruptcy. Newberry Library.

won't vote for anything whatever without pay — say twenty at $500 apiece, is $10,000 altogether; lot of jimcracks for Congressmen's wives and children — those go a long way — you can't spend too much money in that line — well, those things cost in a lump, say $10,000 — along there somewhere; — and then comes your printed documents. . . . [W]ell, never mind the details, the total in clean numbers foots up $118,254.42 thus far!

In Twain's satire, Congress is for sale to the highest bidder. The corrupt interplay of business and politics raised serious questions about the health of American democracy.

The Gilded Age seemed to tarnish all who touched it. No one would learn that better than Twain, who, even as he attacked it as an "era of incredible rottenness," fell prey to its enticements. Born Samuel Langhorne Clemens, he grew up in a rough Mississippi River town, where he became a riverboat pilot. Taking the pen name Mark Twain, he gained fame chronicling western mining booms. In 1866, he came east to launch a career as an author, public speaker, and itinerant humorist. Twain played to packed houses, but his work was judged too vulgar for the genteel tastes of the time because he wrote about common people using common language. His masterpiece, *The Adventures of Huckleberry Finn*, was banned in Boston when it appeared in 1884.

Huck Finn's creator eventually stormed the citadels of polite society, hobnobbing with the wealthy and living in increasingly lavish style. Succumbing to the money fever of his age, Twain plunged into a scheme in the hope of making millions. By the 1890s, he faced bankruptcy and began a dogged climb out of debt.

Twain's tale was common in an age when the promise of wealth led as many to ruin as to riches. In the Gilded Age, fortunes were made and lost with dizzying frequency. Those who pursued riches, whether in the mines of the West or in the stock market, found many rocks in their path. Wall Street panics in 1873 and 1893 periodically interrupted the boom times and plunged the country into economic depression. But with railroad overbuilding and industry expanding on every level, the mood of the country remained buoyant.

The rise of industrialism in the United States and the interplay of business and politics strike the key themes in the Gilded Age. From 1870 to 1890, the transition from a rural, agricultural economy to urban industrialism, global in its reach, transformed American society. The growth of old industries and the creation of new ones, along with the rise of big business, signaled the coming of age of industrial capitalism. Economic issues increasingly shaped party politics, although old divisions engendered by sectionalism and slavery by no means disappeared. Meanwhile, new concerns over lynchings, temperance, and suffrage propelled women into more active roles in society.

Perhaps nowhere were the hopes and fears that industrialism inspired more evident than in the public's attitude toward the business moguls of the day. Men like Andrew Carnegie, John D. Rockefeller, and J. P. Morgan sparked the popular imagination as the heroes and villains in the high drama of industrialization. And as concern grew over the power of big business and the growing chasm between rich and poor, many Americans looked to the government for solutions.

▶ Old Industries Transformed, New Industries Born

In the years following the Civil War, the American economy underwent a transformation. Where once wealth had been measured in tangible assets — property, livestock, buildings — the economy now ran on money and the new devices of business — paper currency, securities, and anonymous corporate entities. Wall Street, the heart of the country's financial system, increasingly affected Main Street. The scale and scope of American industry expanded dramatically. Old industries like iron transformed into modern industries typified by the behemoth U.S. Steel. Discovery and invention stimulated new industries, from oil refining to electric light and power. The expansion of the nation's rail system in the decades after the Civil War played the key role in the transformation of the American economy.

Jay Gould, Andrew Carnegie, John D. Rockefeller, and other business leaders pioneered new strategies to seize markets and consolidate power in the rising

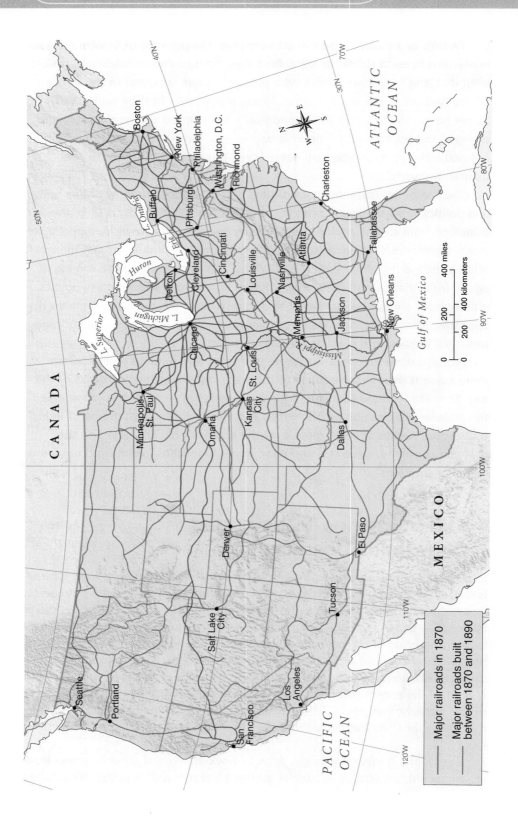

Major railroads in 1870

Major railroads built between 1870 and 1890

railroad, steel, and oil industries. Always with an eye to the main chance, these business tycoons set the tone in the get-rich-quick era of freewheeling capitalism that came to be called the **Gilded Age**.

Railroads: America's First Big Business

The military conquest of America's inland empire and the dispossession of Native Americans (see chapter 17) relied on an elaborate new railroad system, which allowed businesses to expand on a nationwide scale. The first transcontinental railroad, completed in 1869, linked new markets in the West to the nation's eastern and midwestern farms and cities. Between 1870 and 1880, overbuilding doubled the amount of track in the country and it nearly doubled again in the following decade. By 1900, the nation boasted more than 193,000 miles of railroad track — more than in all of Europe and Russia combined (Map 18.1). The railroads had become America's first big business. Privately owned but publicly financed by enormous land grants from the federal government and the states, the railroads epitomized the insidious nexus of business and politics in the Gilded Age.

To understand how the railroads came to dominate American life, there is no better place to start than with the career of **Jay Gould**, who pioneered the expansion of America's railway system and became the era's most notorious speculator. Jason "Jay" Gould bought his first railroad before he turned twenty-five. It was only sixty-two miles long, in bad repair, and on the brink of failure, but within two years he sold it at a profit of $130,000.

Gould, by his own admission, knew little about railroads and cared less about their operation. The secretive Gould operated in the stock market like a shark, looking for vulnerable railroads, buying enough stock to take control, and threatening to undercut his competitors until they bought him out at a high profit. The railroads that fell into his hands fared badly and often went bankrupt. Gould's genius lay not in providing transportation, but in cleverly buying and selling railroad stock on Wall Street, the nerve center of the new economy.

The New York Stock Exchange, dating back to 1792, expanded as the volume of stock increased sixfold between 1869 and 1901. Where on one sleepy day in 1830 only thirty-one stocks traded, by 1886 more than a million shares a day changed hands. As the scale and complexity of the financial system increased, the line between investment and speculation blurred, causing many Americans to question if the concern with paper profits fueled the boom and bust cycles that led to panic and depression, putting hardworking Americans

◀ **MAP 18.1**
Railroad Expansion, 1870–1890
Railroad mileage nearly quadrupled between 1870 and 1890, with the greatest growth occurring in the trans-Mississippi West. The western railroads — the Great Northern, Northern Pacific, Southern Pacific, and Atlantic and Pacific — were completed in the 1880s. Fueled by speculation and built ahead of demand, the western railroads made fortunes for individual speculators. But they rarely paid for themselves and often left disaster in their wake. At the same time, they fed a culture of insider dealing and political corruption.

out of jobs. Yet however crass their motives, millionaire speculators like Jay Gould built America's rail system. In the 1880s, Gould moved to put together a second transcontinental railroad. His competitors had little choice but to adopt his strategy of expansion and consolidation, which in turn encouraged overbuilding and stimulated a national market.

The dramatic growth of the railroads created the country's first big business. Before the Civil War, even the largest textile mill in New England employed no more than 800 workers. By contrast, the Pennsylvania Railroad by the 1870s boasted a payroll of more than 55,000 workers. Capitalized at more than $400 million, the Pennsylvania Railroad constituted the largest private enterprise in the world.

The big business of railroads bestowed enormous riches on a handful of tycoons. Both Gould and his competitor "Commodore" Cornelius Vanderbilt amassed fortunes estimated at $100 million. Such staggering wealth eclipsed that of upper-class Americans from previous generations and left a legacy of lavish spending for an elite crop of ultrarich heirs.

The Republican Party, firmly entrenched in Washington, worked closely with business interests, subsidizing the transcontinental railroad system with land grants of a staggering 100 million acres of public land and $64 million in tax incentives and direct aid. States and local communities joined the railroad boom, knowing that only those towns and villages along the tracks would grow and flourish. The combined federal and state land giveaway amounted to more than 180 million acres, an area larger than Texas.

A revolution in communication accompanied and supported the growth of the railroads. The telegraph, developed by Samuel F. B. Morse, marched across the continent alongside the railroad. By transmitting coded messages along electrical wire, the telegraph formed the "nervous system" of the new industrial order. Telegraph service quickly replaced Pony Express mail carriers in the West and transformed business by providing instantaneous communication. Again Jay Gould took the lead. In 1879, through stock manipulation, he seized control of Western Union, the company that monopolized the telegraph industry. By the end of the century, the telegraph carried 63 million messages a year and made it possible to move money around the world. Financiers in London and New York could follow the markets on ticker tape and transfer funds by wire.

The railroads soon fell on hard times. Already by the 1870s, lack of planning led to overbuilding. Across the nation, railroads competed fiercely for business. A manufacturer in an area served by competing railroads could get substantially reduced shipping rates in return for promises of steady business. Because railroad owners lost money through this kind of competition, they tried to set up agreements, or "pools," to end cutthroat competition by dividing up territory and setting rates. But these informal gentlemen's agreements invariably failed because men like Jay Gould, intent on undercutting all competitors, refused to play by the rules.

Novelist Charles Dudley Warner described how the rail speculators operated:

> [They fasten upon] some railway that is prosperous, pays dividends, pays a liberal interest on its bonds, and has a surplus. They contrive to buy, no matter at what the cost, a controlling interest in it. . . . Then they absorb its surplus; let it run down so that it

pays no dividends and by-and-by cannot even pay its interest; then they squeeze the bondholders, who may be glad to accept anything that is offered out of the wreck, and perhaps then they throw the property into the hands of a receiver, or consolidate it with some other road at a value enormously greater than it cost them in stealing it. Having in one way or another sucked it dry, they look around for another road.

The public's alarm at the control wielded by the new railroad magnates and the tactics they employed provided a barometer of attitudes toward big business itself. When Gould died in 1892, the press described him as "the world's richest man." Rival Cornelius Vanderbilt judged Gould "the smartest man in America." But to the public, he was, as he himself admitted shortly before his death, "the most hated man in America."

Andrew Carnegie, Steel, and Vertical Integration

If Jay Gould was the man Americans loved to hate, **Andrew Carnegie** became one of America's heroes. Unlike Gould, for whom speculation was the game and wealth the goal, Carnegie turned his back on speculation and worked to build something enduring — Carnegie Steel, the biggest steel business in the world during the Gilded Age.

The growth of the steel industry proceeded directly from railroad building. The first railroads ran on iron rails, which cracked and broke with alarming frequency. Steel, both stronger and more flexible than iron, remained too expensive for use in rails until Englishman Henry Bessemer developed a way to make steel more cheaply from pig iron. Andrew Carnegie, among the first to champion the new "King Steel," came to dominate the emerging industry.

Carnegie, a Scottish immigrant, landed in New York in 1848 at the age of twelve. He rose from a job cleaning bobbins in a textile factory to become one of the richest men in America. Before he died, he gave away more than $300 million, most notably to public libraries. His generosity, combined with his own rise from poverty, burnished his public image.

When Carnegie was a teenager, his skill as a telegraph operator caught the attention of Tom Scott, superintendent of the Pennsylvania Railroad. Scott hired Carnegie, soon promoted him, and lent him the money for his first foray into Wall Street investment. As a result of this crony capitalism, Carnegie became a millionaire before his thirtieth birthday. At that point, Carnegie turned away from speculation and struck out on his own to reshape the iron and steel industry. "My preference was always manufacturing," he wrote. "I wished to make something tangible." By applying the lessons of cost accounting and efficiency that he had learned from twelve years with the Pennsylvania Railroad, Carnegie turned steel into the nation's first manufacturing big business.

In 1872, Andrew Carnegie acquired one hundred acres in Braddock, Pennsylvania, on the outskirts of Pittsburgh, convenient to two railroad lines and fronted by the Monongahela River, a natural highway to Pittsburgh and the Ohio River and to the coal and iron mines farther north. There Carnegie built the largest, most up-to-date Bessemer steel plant in the world. At that time, steelmakers produced about 70 tons a week. Within two decades, Carnegie's blast furnaces poured out an incredible 10,000 tons a week. He soon cut the cost of making rails by more than half, from $58 to $25 a ton. His formula for success was simple: "Cut the prices, scoop the market, run the mills full; watch the costs and profits will take care of themselves."

To guarantee the lowest costs and the maximum output, Carnegie pioneered a system of business organization called **vertical integration**. All aspects of the business were under Carnegie's control — from the mining of iron ore, to its transport on the Great Lakes, to the production of steel. Vertical integration, in the words of one observer, meant that "from the moment these crude stuffs were dug out of the earth until they flowed in a stream of liquid steel in the ladles, there was never a price, profit, or royalty paid to any outsider."

Always Carnegie kept his eyes on the account books, looking for ways to cut costs. The great productivity Carnegie encouraged came at a high price. He deliberately pitted his managers against one another, firing the losers and rewarding the winners with a share in the company. Workers achieved the output Carnegie demanded by enduring low wages, dangerous working conditions, and twelve-hour days six days a week. One worker, commenting on the contradiction between Carnegie's generous philanthropy in endowing public libraries and his tightfisted labor policy, observed, "After working twelve hours, how can a man go to a library?"

By 1900, Andrew Carnegie had become the best-known manufacturer in the nation, and the age of iron had yielded to an age of steel. Steel from Carnegie's mills supported the elevated trains in New York and Chicago, formed the skeleton of the Washington Monument, supported the first steel bridge to span the Mississippi, and girded America's first skyscrapers. Carnegie steel armored the naval fleet that helped make the United States a world military power. As a captain of industry, Carnegie's only rival was the titan of the oil industry, John D. Rockefeller.

John D. Rockefeller, Standard Oil, and the Trust

Edwin Drake's discovery of oil in Pennsylvania in 1859 sent thousands rushing to the oil fields in search of "black gold." In the days before the automobile and gasoline, crude oil was refined into lubricating oil for machinery and kerosene for lamps, the major source of lighting in nineteenth-century houses before the invention of gas lamps and electric lighting. The amount of capital needed to buy or build an oil refinery in the 1860s and 1870s remained relatively low — less than $25,000, or roughly what it cost to lay one mile of railroad track. With start-up costs so low, the new petroleum industry experienced riotous competition among many small refineries. Ultimately, **John D. Rockefeller** and his Standard Oil Company succeeded in controlling nine-tenths of the oil-refining business.

Rockefeller grew up the son of a shrewd Yankee who peddled quack cures for cancer. Under his father's rough tutelage, he learned how to drive a hard bargain. "I trade with the boys and skin 'em and just beat 'em every time I can," "Big Bill" Rockefeller boasted. "I want to make 'em sharp." John D. learned his lessons well. In 1865, at the age of twenty-five, he controlled the largest oil refinery in Cleveland. Like a growing number of business owners, Rockefeller abandoned partnership or single proprietorship to embrace the corporation as the business structure best suited to maximize profit and minimize personal liability. In 1870, he incorporated his oil business, founding the Standard Oil Company, a behemoth so huge that it served as the precursor not only of today's ExxonMobil but also of Amoco, Chevron, Sunoco, and ConocoPhillips.

As the largest refiner in Cleveland, Rockefeller demanded secret rebates from the railroads in exchange for his steady business. Rebates enabled Rockefeller to drive out his competitors through predatory pricing. The railroads, facing the pressures of cutthroat competition, needed Rockefeller's business so badly that they gave him a share of the rates that his competitors paid. A Pennsylvania Railroad official later confessed that Rockefeller extracted such huge rebates that the railroad, which could not risk losing his business, sometimes ended up paying him to transport Standard's oil. Secret deals, predatory pricing, and rebates enabled Rockefeller to undercut his competitors and pressure competing refiners to sell out or face ruin.

To gain legal standing for Standard Oil's secret deals, Rockefeller in 1882 pioneered a new form of corporate structure — the **trust**. The trust differed markedly from Carnegie's vertical approach in steel. Instead of attempting to control all aspects of the oil business, from the well to the consumer, Rockefeller used horizontal integration to control the refining process. Several trustees held stock in various refinery companies "in trust" for Standard's stockholders. This elaborate stock swap allowed the trustees to coordinate policy among the refineries, giving Rockefeller a virtual monopoly on the oil-refining business. The Standard Oil trust, valued at more than $70 million, paved the way for trusts in sugar, whiskey, matches, and many other products.

When the federal government responded to public pressure to outlaw the trust as a violation of free trade, Standard Oil changed tactics and reorganized as a holding company. Instead of stockholders in competing companies acting through trustees to set prices and determine territories, the holding company simply brought competing companies under one central administration. No longer technically separate businesses, they could act in concert without violating antitrust laws that forbade companies from forming "combinations in restraint of trade." As Standard Oil's empire grew, Rockefeller ended the independence of the refinery operators and closed inefficient plants. Next he moved to control sources of crude oil and took charge of the transportation and marketing of petroleum products. By the 1890s, Standard Oil ruled more than 90 percent of the oil business, employed 100,000 people, and was the biggest, richest, most feared, and most admired business organization in the world.

John D. Rockefeller enjoyed enormous success in business, but he was not well liked by the public. Before he died in 1937 at the age of ninety-eight, Rockefeller had become the country's first billionaire. But despite his modest habits, his pious Baptist faith, and his many charitable gifts, he never shared in the public affection that Carnegie enjoyed. Editor and journalist Ida M. Tarbell's "History of the Standard Oil Company," which ran for three years (1902–1905) in serial form in *McClure's Magazine*, largely shaped the public's harsh view of Rockefeller.

Ida M. Tarbell had grown up in the Pennsylvania oil region, and her father had owned one of the small refineries gobbled up by Standard Oil. Her devastatingly thorough history chronicled the methods Rockefeller had used to take over the oil industry. Publicly, Rockefeller refused to respond to her allegations, although in private he dubbed her "Miss Tarbarrel." "If I step on that worm I will call attention to it," he explained. "If I ignore it, it will disappear." Yet by the time Tarbell finished publishing her story, Rockefeller slept with a loaded revolver by his bed in fear of would-be assassins. Standard Oil and the man who created it had become the symbol of heartless monopoly.

New Inventions: The Telephone and Electricity

The second half of the nineteenth century was an age of invention. Men like Thomas Alva Edison and Alexander Graham Bell became folk heroes. But no matter how dramatic the inventors or the inventions, the new electric and telephone industries pioneered by Edison and Bell soon eclipsed their inventors and fell under the control of bankers and industrialists.

Alexander Graham Bell came to America from Scotland at the age of twenty-four with a passion to find a way to teach the deaf to speak (his wife and mother were deaf). Instead, he developed a way to transmit voice over wire — the telephone. Bell's invention astounded the world when he demonstrated it at the Philadelphia Centennial Exposition in 1876. Dumbfounded by the display, the emperor of Brazil cried out, "My God, it talks!"

In 1880, Bell's company, American Bell, pioneered "long lines" (long-distance telephone service), creating American Telephone and Telegraph (AT&T) as a subsidiary. In 1900, AT&T became the parent company of the system as a whole, controlling Western Electric, which manufactured and installed the equipment, and coordinating the Bell regional divisions. This complicated organizational structure meant that Americans could communicate not only locally but also across the country. And unlike a telegraph message, which had to be written out and taken to a telegraph station, sent over the wire, and then delivered by hand to the recipient, the telephone connected both parties immediately and privately. Bell's invention proved a boon to business, contributing to speed and efficiency. The number of telephones soared, reaching 310,000 in 1895 and more than 1.5 million in 1900.

Even more than Alexander Graham Bell, inventor **Thomas Alva Edison** embodied the old-fashioned virtues of Yankee ingenuity and rugged individualism that Americans most admired. A self-educated dynamo, he worked twenty hours a day in his laboratory in Menlo Park, New Jersey, vowing to turn out "a minor invention every ten days and a big thing every six months or so." He almost made good on his promise. At the height of his career, he averaged a patent every eleven days and invented such "big things" as the phonograph, the motion picture camera, and the filament for the incandescent lightbulb.

Edison, in competition with George W. Westinghouse, pioneered the use of electricity as an energy source. By the late nineteenth century, electricity had become a part of American urban life. It powered trolley cars and lighted factories, homes, and office buildings. Indeed, electricity became so prevalent in urban life

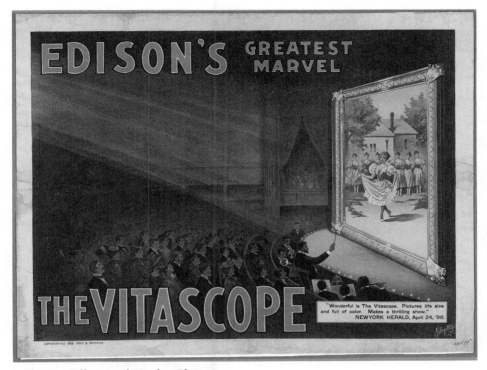

Thomas Edison and Moving Pictures

Edison's "greatest marvel," the Vitascope, was actually not his own invention. Edison was slow to develop a projection system, but the market for a machine that would project films for large audiences led him to acquire the Vitascope, pictured here in a postcard, from Thomas Armat and C. Francis Jenkins. The first theatrical exhibition took place in New York City in 1896. The Vitascope became a popular attraction in variety and vaudeville theaters, where rapt audiences like the one pictured here dressed up and enjoyed moving pictures accompanied by a live orchestra. Library of Congress.

that it symbolized the city, whose bright lights contrasted with rural America, left largely in the dark because private enterprise judged it not profitable enough to run electric lines to outlying farms and ranches.

While Americans thrilled to the new electric cities and the changes wrought by inventors, the day of the inventor quietly yielded to the heyday of the corporation. In 1892, the electric industry consolidated. Reflecting a nationwide trend in business, Edison General Electric dropped the name of its inventor, becoming simply General Electric (GE). For years, an embittered Edison refused to set foot inside a GE building. General Electric could afford to overlook the slight. A prime example of the trend toward business consolidation taking place in the 1890s, GE soon dominated the market.

REVIEW What devices did John D. Rockefeller use to gain control of 90 percent of the oil-refining business by 1890?

▶ From Competition to Consolidation

Even as Rockefeller and Carnegie built their empires, the era of the "robber barons," as they were dubbed by their detractors, was drawing to a close. Increasingly, businesses replaced partnerships and sole proprietorships with the anonymous corporate structure that would come to dominate the twentieth century. At the same time, mergers led to the creation of huge new corporations.

Banks and financiers played a key role in this consolidation, so much so that the decades at the turn of the twentieth century can be characterized as a period of **finance capitalism** — investment sponsored by banks and bankers. When the depression that followed the panic of 1893 bankrupted many businesses, bankers stepped in to bring order and to reorganize major industries. During these years, a new social philosophy based on the theories of naturalist Charles Darwin helped to justify consolidation and to inhibit state or federal regulation of business. A conservative Supreme Court further frustrated attempts to control business by consistently declaring unconstitutional legislation designed to regulate railroads or to outlaw trusts and monopolies.

J. P. Morgan and Finance Capitalism

John Pierpont Morgan, the preeminent finance capitalist of the late nineteenth century, loathed competition and sought whenever possible to eliminate it by substituting consolidation and central control. Morgan's passion for order made him the architect of business mergers. The son of a prominent banker, **J. P. Morgan** inherited along with his wealth the stern business code of the old-fashioned merchant bankers, men who valued character and reputation. Aloof and silent, Morgan looked down on the climbers and the speculators with a haughtiness that led his rivals to call him "Jupiter," after the ruler of the Roman gods. At the turn of the twentieth century, he dominated American banking, exerting an influence so powerful that his critics charged he controlled a vast "money trust" even more insidious than Rockefeller's Standard Oil.

Morgan acted as a power broker in the reorganization of the railroads and the creation of industrial giants such as General Electric and U.S. Steel. When the railroads fell on hard times in the 1890s, he used his access to capital to rescue embattled, wrecked, and ruined companies. Morgan quickly took over the struggling railroads and moved to eliminate competition by creating what he called "a community of interest" among the managers he handpicked. By the time he finished "Morganizing" the railroads, a handful of directors controlled two-thirds of the nation's track.

Banker control of the railroads helped to coordinate the industry. But reorganization came at a high price. To keep investors happy and to guarantee huge profits from the sale of stock, Morgan heavily "watered" the stock of the railroads, issuing more shares than the assets of the company warranted. J. P. Morgan & Co. made millions of dollars from commissions and from blocks of stock acquired through reorganization. The flagrant overcapitalization created by the watered stock hurt the railroads in the long run, saddling them with enormous debt.

Equally harmful was the management style of the Morgan directors. Bankers, not railroad men, they aimed at short-term profit and discouraged the continued technological and organizational innovation needed to run the railroads effectively.

In 1898, Morgan moved into the steel industry, directly challenging Andrew Carnegie. Morgan supervised the mergers of several smaller steel companies, which soon expanded from the manufacture of finished goods to compete head-to-head with Carnegie in steel production. The pugnacious Carnegie cabled his partners in the summer of 1900: "Action essential: crisis has arrived . . . have no fear as to the result; victory certain." The press trumpeted news of the impending fight between the feisty Scot and the haughty Wall Street banker, but what the papers called the "battle of the giants" in the end proved little more than the wily maneuvering of two businessmen so adept that even today it is difficult to say who won. For all his belligerence, the sixty-six-year-old Carnegie yearned to retire to Skibo Castle, his home in Scotland. He may well have welcomed Morgan's bid for power. Morgan, who disdained haggling, agreed to pay Carnegie's asking price, $480 million (the equivalent of about $10 billion in today's currency). According to legend, when Carnegie later teased Morgan, saying that he should have asked $100 million more, Morgan replied, "You would have got it if you had."

Morgan's acquisition of Carnegie Steel signaled the passing of the old entrepreneurial order personified by Andrew Carnegie and the arrival of a new, anonymous corporate world. The banker quickly moved to pull together Carnegie's chief competitors to form a huge new corporation, United States Steel, known today as USX. Created in 1901 and capitalized at $1.4 billion, U.S. Steel was the

Homestead Steelworks
The Homestead steelworks, outside Pittsburgh, is pictured shortly after J. P. Morgan bought out Andrew Carnegie and created U.S. Steel, the precursor of today's USX. Try to count the smokestacks in the picture. Air pollution on this scale posed a threat to the health of citizens and made for a dismal landscape. Workers complained that trees would not grow in Homestead. Hagley Museum & Library.

largest corporation in the world. Yet for all its size, it did not hold a monopoly in the steel industry. Significant small competitors, such as Bethlehem Steel, remained independent, creating a competitive system called an oligopoly, in which several companies control production. The smaller manufacturers simply followed the lead of U.S. Steel in setting prices and dividing the market so that each company held a comfortable share. Although oligopoly did not entirely eliminate competition, it did effectively blunt it.

When J. P. Morgan died in 1913, his estate totaled $68 million, not counting an estimated $50 million in art treasures. Andrew Carnegie, who gave away more than $300 million before his death six years later, is said to have quipped, "And to think he was not a rich man!" But Carnegie's gibe missed the mark. The quest for power, not wealth, had motivated J. P. Morgan, and his power could best be measured not in the millions he owned but in the billions he controlled. Even more than Carnegie or Rockefeller, Morgan left his stamp on the twentieth century and formed the model for corporate consolidation that economists and social scientists soon justified with a new social theory known as social Darwinism.

Social Darwinism, Laissez-Faire, and the Supreme Court

John D. Rockefeller Jr., the son of the founder of Standard Oil, once remarked to his Baptist Bible class that the Standard Oil Company, like the American Beauty rose, resulted from "pruning the early buds that grew up around it." The elimination of smaller, inefficient units, he said, was "merely the working out of a law of nature and a law of God." The comparison of the business world to the natural world gave rise to a theory of society paralleling the relatively new notion of evolution formulated by the British naturalist Charles Darwin. In his monumental work *On the Origin of Species* (1859), Darwin theorized that in the struggle for survival, adaptation to the environment triggered among species a natural selection process that led to evolution. Herbert Spencer in Britain and William Graham Sumner in the United States developed the theory of **social Darwinism**. The social Darwinists concluded that societal progress came about as a result of relentless competition in which the strong survived and the weak died out.

In social terms, the idea of the "survival of the fittest," coined by Herbert Spencer, had profound significance, as Sumner, a professor of political economy at Yale University, made clear in his book *What Social Classes Owe to Each Other* (1883). "The drunkard in the gutter is just where he ought to be, according to the fitness and tendency of things," Sumner insisted. Conversely, "millionaires are the product of natural selection," and although "they get high wages and live in luxury," Sumner claimed, "the bargain is a good one for society."

Social Darwinists equated wealth and power with "fitness" and believed that the unfit should be allowed to die off to advance the progress of humanity. Any efforts by the rich to aid the poor would only tamper with the rigid laws of nature and slow down evolution. Social Darwinism acted to curb social reform while at the same time glorifying great wealth. In an age when Rockefeller and Carnegie amassed hundreds of millions of dollars (billions in today's currency) and the average worker earned $500 a year, social Darwinism justified economic inequality.

Andrew Carnegie softened some of the harshness of social Darwinism in his essay "The Gospel of Wealth," published in 1889. The millionaire, Carnegie wrote, acted as a "mere trustee and agent for his poorer brethren, bringing to their service his superior wisdom, experience, and ability to administer, doing for them better than they could or would do for themselves." Carnegie preached philanthropy and urged the rich to "live unostentatious lives" and "administer surplus wealth for the good of the people." His **gospel of wealth** earned much praise but won few converts. Most millionaires followed the lead of J. P. Morgan, who contributed to charity but hoarded private treasures in his marble library.

Social Darwinism nicely suited an age in which the gross inequalities accompanying industrialization seemed to cry out for action. Assuaging the nation's conscience, social Darwinism justified neglect of the poor in the name of "race progress." With so many of the poor coming from different races and ethnicities, social Darwinism fueled racism. A new "scientific racism" purported to prove "Anglo-Saxons" superior to all other groups. Social Darwinism buttressed the status quo and reassured comfortable, white Americans that all was as it should be. Even the gospel of wealth, which mitigated the harshest dictates of social Darwinism, insisted that Americans lived in the best of all possible worlds and that the rich were the natural rulers.

With its emphasis on the free play of competition and the survival of the fittest, social Darwinism encouraged the economic theory of **laissez-faire** (French for "let it alone"). Business argued that government should not meddle in economic affairs, except to protect private property. A conservative Supreme Court agreed. During the 1880s and 1890s, the Court increasingly reinterpreted the Constitution to protect business from taxation, regulation, labor organization, and antitrust legislation.

In a series of landmark decisions, the Court used the Fourteenth Amendment, originally intended to protect freed slaves from state laws violating their rights, to protect corporations. Defining corporations as "persons," the Court reiterated the amendment's language, that no state can "deprive any person of life, liberty, or property, without due process of law." In 1886 in *Santa Clara County v. Southern Pacific Railroad*, the Court reasoned that legislation designed to regulate the railroad deprived the corporation of "due process." Using the same reasoning, the Court struck down state laws regulating railroad rates, declared income tax unconstitutional, and judged labor unions a "conspiracy in restraint of trade." The Court's elevation of the rights of property over other rights stemmed from the conservatism of its justices. According to Justice Stephen J. Field, the Constitution "allows no impediments to the acquisition of property." Field, born into a wealthy New England family, spoke with the bias of the privileged class to whom property rights were sacrosanct. Imbued with this ideology, the Court refused to impede corporate consolidation and did nothing to curb the excesses of big business or promote the humane treatment of workers. Only in the arena of politics did Americans tackle the issues raised by corporate capitalism.

REVIEW Why did the ideas of social Darwinism appeal to many Americans in the late nineteenth century?

▶ Politics and Culture

For many Americans, politics provided a source of identity, a means of livelihood, and a ready form of entertainment. No wonder voter turnout averaged a hefty 77 percent (compared to 57 percent in the 2008 presidential election). A variety of factors contributed to the complicated interplay of politics and culture. Patronage provided an economic incentive for voter participation, but ethnicity, religion, sectional loyalty, race, and gender all influenced the political life of the period.

Political Participation and Party Loyalty

Patronage proved a strong motivation for party loyalty among many voters. Political parties in power doled out federal, state, and local government jobs to their loyal supporters. With hundreds of thousands of jobs to be filled, the choice of party affiliation could mean the difference between a paycheck and an empty pocket. Money greased the wheels of this system of patronage, dubbed the **spoils system** from the adage "to the victor go the spoils." With their livelihoods tied to their party identity, government employees in particular had an incentive to vote in great numbers.

Political affiliation provided a powerful sense of group identity for many voters proud of their loyalty to the Democrats or the Republicans. Democrats, who traced the party's roots back to Thomas Jefferson, called theirs "the party of the fathers." The Republican Party, founded in the 1850s, still claimed strong loyalties in the North as a result of its alignment with the Union during the Civil War. Republicans proved particularly adept at evoking Civil War loyalty, using a tactic called "waving the bloody shirt" — reminding voters which side they had fought for in the Civil War. Noting the power of old sectional loyalties, one of the party faithful observed, "Iowa will go Democratic when Hell goes Methodist."

Religion and ethnicity also played a significant role in politics. In the North, Protestants from the old-line denominations, particularly Presbyterians and Methodists, flocked to the Republican Party, which championed a series of moral reforms, including local laws requiring businesses to close in observance of the Sabbath. In the burgeoning cities, the Democratic Party courted immigrants and working-class Catholic and Jewish voters, charging, rightly, that Republican moral crusades often masked attacks on immigrant culture.

Sectionalism and the New South

After the end of Reconstruction, most white voters in the former Confederate states remained loyal Democrats, voting for Democratic candidates in every presidential election for the next seventy years. Labeling the Republican Party the agent of "Negro rule," Democrats urged white southerners to "vote the way you shot." Yet the so-called solid South proved far from solid on the state and local levels. The economic plight of the South led to shifting political alliances and to third-party movements that challenged Democratic attempts to define politics along race lines and maintain the Democratic Party as the white man's party.

The South's economy, devastated by the war, foundered at the same time the North experienced an unprecedented industrial boom. Soon an influential group of southerners called for a **New South** modeled on the industrial North. Henry Grady, the ebullient young editor of the *Atlanta Constitution*, used his paper's influence (it boasted the largest circulation of any weekly in the country) to extol the virtues of a new industrial South. Part bully, part booster, Grady exhorted the South to use its natural advantages — cheap labor and abundant natural resources — to go head-to-head in competition with northern industry.

Grady's message fell on receptive ears. Many southerners, men and women, black and white, joined the national migration from farm to city, leaving the old plantations to molder and decay. With the end of military rule in 1877, southern Democrats took back state governments, calling themselves "Redeemers." Yet rather than restore the economy of the old planter class, they embraced northern promoters who promised prosperity and profits.

The railroads came first, opening up the region for industrial development. Southern railroad mileage grew fourfold from 1865 to 1890. The number of cotton spindles also soared as textile mill owners abandoned New England in search of the cheap labor and proximity to raw materials promised in the South. By 1900, the South had become the nation's leading producer of cloth, and more than 100,000 southerners, many of them women and children, worked in the region's textile mills.

The New South prided itself most on its iron and steel industry, which grew up in the area surrounding Birmingham, Alabama. During this period, the smokestack replaced the white-pillared plantation as the symbol of the New South. Andrew Carnegie toured the region in 1889 and observed, "The South is Pennsylvania's most formidable industrial enemy." But southern industry remained controlled by northern investors, who had no intention of letting the South beat the North at its own game. Elaborate mechanisms rigged the price of southern steel, inflating it, as one northern insider confessed, "for the purpose of protecting the Pittsburgh mills and in turn the Pittsburgh steel users." Similarly, in the lumber and mining industries, investors in the North and abroad, not southerners, reaped the lion's share of the profits.

In only one industry did the South truly dominate — tobacco. Capitalizing on the invention of a machine for rolling cigarettes, the American Tobacco Company, founded by the Duke family of North Carolina, eventually dominated the industry. As cigarettes replaced chewing tobacco in popularity at the turn of the twentieth century, a booming market developed for Duke's "ready mades." Soon the company sold 400,000 cigarettes a day.

In practical terms, the industrialized New South proved an illusion. Much of the South remained agricultural, caught in the grip of the insidious crop lien system (see chapter 16). White southern farmers, desperate to get out of debt, sometimes joined with African Americans to pursue their goals politically. Between 1865 and 1900, voters in every state south of the Mason-Dixon line experimented with political alliances that crossed the color line and threatened the status quo.

Gender, Race, and Politics

Gender — society's notion of what constitutes acceptable masculine or feminine behavior — influenced politics throughout the nineteenth century. From the early days of the Republic, citizenship had been defined in male terms. Citizenship and its prerogatives (voting and officeholding) served as a badge of manliness and rested on its corollary, patriarchy — the power and authority men exerted over their wives and families. With the advent of universal (white) male suffrage in the early nineteenth century, gender eclipsed class as the defining feature of citizenship; men's dominance over women provided the common thread that knit all white men together politically. The concept of **separate spheres** dictated political participation for men only. Once the public sphere of political participation became equated with manhood, women found themselves increasingly restricted to the private sphere of home and hearth.

Women were not alone in their limited access to the public sphere. Though Reconstruction legislation had guaranteed their freedom, blacks continued to face discrimination, especially in the New South. Segregation, commonly practiced under the rubric of **Jim Crow** laws (as discussed in chapter 21), prevented ex-slaves from riding in the same train cars as whites, from eating in the same restaurants, or from using the same toilet facilities.

Amid the turmoil of the post-Reconstruction South, some groups struck cross-racial alliances in search of political might. In Virginia, the "Readjusters," a coalition of blacks and whites determined to "readjust" (lower) the state debt and spend more money on public education, captured state offices from 1879 to 1883. Groups like the Readjusters rested on the belief that universal political rights (voting, officeholding, patronage) could be extended to black males in the public sphere while maintaining racial segregation in the private sphere. Democrats, for their part, fought back by trying to convince voters that black voting would inevitably lead to miscegenation (racial mixing). Black male political power and sexual power, they warned, went hand in hand. Ultimately, their arguments prevailed, and many whites returned to the Democratic fold to protect "white womanhood" and with it white supremacy.

The notion that black men threatened white southern womanhood reached its most vicious form in the practice of lynching — the killing and mutilation of black men by white mobs. By 1892, the practice had become so prevalent that a courageous black editor, **Ida B. Wells**, launched an antilynching movement. That year, a white mob lynched a friend of Wells's whose grocery store competed too successfully with a white-owned store. Wells shrewdly concluded that lynching served "as an excuse to get rid of Negroes who were acquiring wealth and property and thus keep the race terrorized." She began to collect data on lynching and discovered that in the decade between 1882 and 1892 lynching rose in the South by an overwhelming 200 percent, with more than 241 black people killed. The vast increase in lynching testified to the retreat of the federal government following Reconstruction and to white southerners' determination to maintain supremacy through terrorism and intimidation.

Ida B. Wells

Ida B. Wells began her antilynching campaign in 1892 after a friend's murder led her to examine the problem of lynching in the South. She spread her message in lectures and pamphlets like this one, distributed for fifteen cents. Wells brought the horror of lynching to a national and international audience and mobilized other African American women to undertake social action under the auspices of the National Association of Colored Women. She later became a founding member of the National Association for the Advancement of Colored People (NAACP). Manuscript, Archives and Rare Books Division, Schomburg Center for Research in Black Culture, The New York Public Library, Astor, Lenox, and Tilden Foundations.

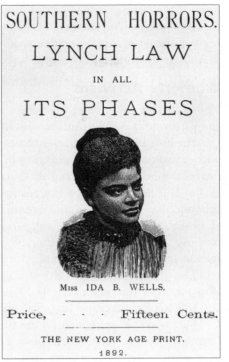

SOUTHERN HORRORS.
LYNCH LAW
IN ALL
ITS PHASES

Miss IDA B. WELLS.

Price, · · · Fifteen Cents.

THE NEW YORK AGE PRINT.
1892.

In the face of this carnage, Wells struck back. As the first salvo in her attack, she put to rest the "old threadbare lie that Negro men assault white women." As she pointed out, violations of black women by white men, which were much more frequent than black attacks on white women, went unnoticed and unpunished. Wells articulated lynching as a problem of race and gender. She insisted that the myth of black attacks on white southern women masked the reality that mob violence had more to do with economics and the shifting social structure of the South than with rape. She demonstrated in a sophisticated way how the southern patriarchal system, having lost its control over blacks with the end of slavery, used its control over white women to circumscribe the liberty of black men.

Wells's strong stance immediately resulted in reprisal. While she was traveling in the North, vandals ransacked her office in Tennessee and destroyed her printing equipment. Yet the warning that she would be killed on sight if she ever returned to Memphis only stiffened her resolve. As she wrote in her autobiography, *Crusade for Justice* (1928), "Having lost my paper, had a price put on my life and been made an exile . . . , I felt that I owed it to myself and to my race to tell the whole truth now that I was where I could do so freely." As a reporter, first for the *New York Age* and later for the *Chicago Inter-Ocean*, she used every opportunity to hammer home her message. Beginning in 1894 and continuing for decades, antilynching bills were introduced in Congress, only to be defeated by southern opposition.

Lynching did not end during Ida B. Wells's lifetime, but Wells's forceful voice brought the issue to national and international prominence. At her funeral in 1931, black leader W. E. B. Du Bois eulogized Wells as the woman who "began the awakening of the conscience of the nation." Wells's determined campaign against lynching provided just one example of women's political activism during the Gilded Age. The suffrage and temperance movements, along with the growing popularity of women's clubs, dramatized how women refused to be relegated to a separate sphere that kept them out of politics.

Women's Activism

No one better recognized the potency of the gendered notion of political rights than Elizabeth Cady Stanton, who lamented the introduction of the word *male* into the Fourteenth Amendment (see chapter 16). The explicit linking of manhood with citizenship and voting rights in the Constitution marked a major setback for reformers who supported the vote for women. In 1869, Stanton along with Susan B. Anthony formed the National Woman Suffrage Association, the first independent woman's rights organization in the United States (discussed in chapter 20). Women found ways to act politically long before they voted and cleverly used their moral authority as wives and mothers to move from the domestic sphere into the realm of politics.

The extraordinary activity of women's clubs in the period following the Civil War provides just one example. Women's clubs proliferated from the 1860s to the 1890s, often in response to the exclusionary policies of men's organizations. In 1868, newspaper reporter Jane Cunningham Croly (pen name Jennie June) founded the Sorosis Club in New York City after the New York Press Club denied entry to women journalists wishing to attend a banquet honoring the British author Charles Dickens. In 1890, Croly brought state and local clubs together under the umbrella of the **General Federation of Women's Clubs** (GFWC). Not wanting to alienate southern women, the GFWC barred black women's clubs from joining, despite their vehement objections. Women's clubs soon abandoned literary pursuits to devote themselves to "civic usefulness," endorsing an end to child labor, supporting the eight-hour workday, and helping pass pure food and drug legislation.

The temperance movement (the movement to end drunkenness) attracted by far the largest number of organized women in the late nineteenth century. By the late 1860s and the 1870s, the liquor business was flourishing, with about one saloon for every fifty males over the age of fifteen. During the winter of 1873–74, temperance women adopted a radical new tactic. Armed with Bibles and singing hymns, they marched on taverns and saloons and refused to leave until the proprietors signed a pledge to quit selling liquor. Known as the Woman's Crusade, the movement spread like a prairie fire through small towns in Ohio, Indiana, Michigan, and Illinois and soon moved east into New York, New England, and Pennsylvania. Before it was over, more than 100,000 women had marched in more than 450 cities and towns.

The women's tactics may have been new, but the temperance movement dated back to the 1820s. Originally, the movement was led by Protestant men who organized clubs to pledge voluntary abstinence from liquor. By the 1850s, temperance advocates won significant victories when states, starting with Maine, passed laws to prohibit the sale of liquor (known as "Maine laws"). The Woman's

Crusade dramatically brought the issue of temperance back into the national spotlight and led to the formation of a new organization, the **Woman's Christian Temperance Union** (WCTU) in 1874. Composed entirely of women, the WCTU advocated total abstinence from alcohol.

Temperance provided women with a respectable outlet for their increasing resentment of women's inferior status and their growing recognition of women's capabilities. In its first five years, the WCTU relied on education and moral suasion, but when Frances Willard became president in 1879, she politicized the organization (as discussed in chapter 20). When the women of the WCTU joined with the Prohibition Party (formed in 1869 by a group of evangelical clergymen), one wag observed, "Politics is a man's game, an' women, childhern, and prohyibitionists do well to keep out iv it." By sharing power with women, the Prohibitionist men violated the old political rules and risked attacks on their honor and manhood.

Even though they could not yet vote, women found ways to affect the political process. Like men, they displayed strong party loyalties and rallied around traditional Republican and Democratic candidates. Third parties courted women, recognizing that their volunteer labor and support could be key assets in party building. Nevertheless, despite growing political awareness among women, politics, particularly presidential politics, remained an exclusively male prerogative.

REVIEW How did race and gender influence politics?

▶ Presidential Politics

The presidents of the Gilded Age, from Rutherford B. Hayes (1877–1881) to William McKinley (1897–1901), are largely forgotten men, primarily because so little was expected of them. In wartime, Lincoln had expanded the power of the presidency, but following the war, even as the nation addressed western expansion, economic transformation, and nascent urban industrialism, the power of the presidency waned. The dominant creed of laissez-faire, coupled with the dictates of social Darwinism, warned the president and the government to leave business alone. Still, presidents in the Gilded Age grappled with corruption and party strife and struggled toward the creation of new political ethics designed to replace patronage with a civil service system that promised to award jobs on the basis of merit, not party loyalty.

Corruption and Party Strife

The political corruption and party factionalism that characterized the administration of Ulysses S. Grant (1869–1877) (see chapter 16) continued to trouble the nation in the 1880s. The spoils system — awarding jobs for political purposes — remained the driving force in party politics at all levels of government in the Gilded Age. Pro-business Republicans generally held a firm grip on the White House, while Democrats had better luck in Congress. Both parties relied on patronage to cement party loyalty. Corruption was rampant, with senators and representatives, and sometimes members of the executive branch, on the payrolls of business interests. The notion of "conflict of interest" did not exist; nor did a standard of accepted ethical behavior. Reformers eager to end corruption and the replace the spoils system with a merit-based civil service system faced an uphill battle.

A small but determined group of reformers championed a new ethics that would preclude politicians from getting rich from public office. The selection of U.S. senators particularly concerned them. Under the Constitution, senators were selected by state legislatures, not directly elected by the voters. Powerful business interests often contrived to control state legislatures and through them U.S. senators. As journalist Henry Demarest Lloyd quipped, Standard Oil "had done everything to the Pennsylvania legislature except to refine it." Nothing prevented a senator from collecting a paycheck from any of the great corporations. So many did so that political cartoonists often portrayed senators as huge money bags labeled with the names of the corporations they served. In this climate, a constitutional amendment calling for the direct election of senators faced stiff opposition from entrenched interests.

Republican president **Rutherford B. Hayes**, whose disputed election in 1876 signaled the end of Reconstruction in the South, tried to steer a middle course between spoilsmen and reformers. Although the Democratic press ridiculed him as "Rutherfraud" because he had not been popularly elected (see chapter 16), Hayes proved a hardworking, well-informed executive who wanted peace, prosperity, and an end to party strife. Yet the Republican Party remained divided into factions led by strong party bosses who boasted that they could make or break any president.

Foremost among the Republican bosses in the Senate stood Roscoe Conkling of New York, a master spoilsman who ridiculed civil service as "snivel service." He and his followers, called the "Stalwarts," represented the Grant faction of the party. Conkling's archrival, Senator James G. Blaine of Maine, led the "Half Breeds." Not as openly corrupt as the Grant wing of the party, the Half Breeds and their champion were nevertheless tainted with charges of corruption. A third group, called the "Mugwumps," consisted primarily of reform-minded Republicans from Massachusetts and New York who deplored the spoils system and advocated **civil service reform**. The name "Mugwump" came from the Algonquian word for "chief," but critics used the term derisively, punning that the Mugwumps straddled the fence on issues of party loyalty, "with their mug on one side and wump on the other."

President Hayes's middle course pleased no one, and he soon managed to alienate all factions of his party. No one was surprised when he announced that he would not seek reelection in 1880. To avoid choosing among its factions, the Republican Party in 1880 nominated a dark-horse candidate, Representative **James A. Garfield** of Ohio. To foster party unity, they picked Stalwart Chester A. Arthur as the vice presidential candidate. The Democrats made an attempt to overcome sectionalism and establish a national party by selecting as their presidential standard-bearer an old Union general, Winfield Scott Hancock.

But as one observer noted, "It is a peculiarly constituted party that sends rebel brigadiers to Congress because of their rebellion, and then nominates a Union General as its candidate for president because of his loyalty." Hancock garnered only lukewarm support, receiving just 155 electoral votes to Garfield's 214, although the popular vote was less lopsided.

Garfield's Assassination and Civil Service Reform

"My God," Garfield swore after only a few months in office, "what is there in this place that a man should ever want to get into it?" Garfield, like Hayes, faced the difficult task of remaining independent while pacifying the party bosses and placating the reformers. As the federal bureaucracy grew to nearly 150,000 jobs, thousands of office seekers swarmed to the nation's capital, each clamoring for a position. In the days before Secret Service protection, the White House door stood open to all comers. Garfield took a fatalistic view. "Assassination," he told a friend, "can no more be guarded against than death by lightning, and it is best not to worry about either."

On July 2, 1881, less than four months after taking office, Garfield was shot. His assailant, Charles Guiteau, though clearly insane, turned out to be a disappointed office seeker who claimed to be motivated by political partisanship. He told the police officer who arrested him, "I did it; I will go to jail for it; Arthur is president, and I am a Stalwart." Throughout the hot summer, the country kept a deathwatch as Garfield lingered. When he died in September, Chester A. Arthur became president. The press almost universally condemned Republican factionalism for creating the political climate that produced Guiteau and led to the second political assassination in a generation.

Stalwart Roscoe Conkling saw his hopes for the White House dashed. Attacks on the spoils system increased, and the public joined the chorus calling for reform. Both parties claimed credit for passage of the Pendleton Civil Service Act of 1883, which established a permanent Civil Service Commission consisting of three members appointed by the president. Some fourteen thousand jobs came under a merit system that required examinations for office and made it impossible to remove jobholders for political reasons. The new law also prohibited federal jobholders from contributing to political campaigns, thus drying up the major source of the party bosses' revenue. Soon, business interests stepped in to replace officeholders as the nation's chief political contributors. Ironically, civil service reform thus gave business an even greater influence in political life.

Reform and Scandal: The Campaign of 1884

With Conkling's downfall, James G. Blaine assumed leadership of the Republican Party and at long last captured the presidential nomination in 1884. A magnetic Irish American, Blaine inspired such devotion that his supporters called themselves Blainiacs. But Mugwumps like editor Carl Schurz insisted that Blaine "wallowed in spoils like a rhinoceros in an African pool." They bolted the party and embraced the Democrats' presidential nominee, the stolid **Grover Cleveland**, reform governor of New York. The burly, beer-drinking Cleveland distinguished

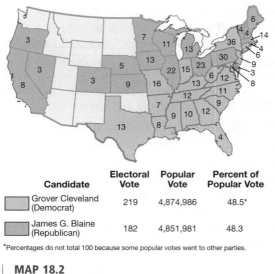

Candidate	Electoral Vote	Popular Vote	Percent of Popular Vote
Grover Cleveland (Democrat)	219	4,874,986	48.5*
James G. Blaine (Republican)	182	4,851,981	48.3

*Percentages do not total 100 because some popular votes went to other parties.

MAP 18.2
The Election of 1884

himself from an entire generation of politicians by the simple motto "A public office is a public trust." First as mayor of Buffalo and later as governor of New York, he built a reputation for honesty, economy, and administrative efficiency. The Democrats, who had not won the presidency since 1856, had high hopes for his candidacy, especially after the Mugwumps threw their support to Cleveland. As the Mugwumps insisted, "The paramount issue this year is moral rather than political."

The Mugwumps soon regretted their words. The 1884 contest degenerated so far into scandal and nasty mudslinging that one disgusted journalist styled it "the vilest campaign ever waged." In July, Cleveland's hometown paper, the *Buffalo Telegraph*, dropped the bombshell that the candidate had fathered an illegitimate child in an affair with a local widow. Cleveland, a bachelor, stoically accepted responsibility for the child. Crushed by the scandal, the Mugwumps lost much of their enthusiasm. At public rallies, Blaine's partisans taunted Cleveland, chanting, "Ma, Ma, where's my Pa?" Silent but fuming, Cleveland waged his campaign in the traditional fashion by staying home.

Blaine set a new campaign style by launching a whirlwind national tour. On a last-minute stop in New York City, the exhausted candidate committed a misstep that may have cost him the election. He overlooked a remark by a supporter, a local clergyman who cast a slur on Catholic voters by styling the Democrats as the party of "Rum, Romanism, and Rebellion." Linking drinking (rum) and Catholicism (Romanism) offended Irish Catholic voters, whom Blaine had counted on to desert the Democratic Party and support him because of his Irish background.

With less than a week to go until the election, Blaine had no chance to recover from the negative publicity. He lost New York State by fewer than 1,200 votes and with it the election. In the final tally, Cleveland defeated Blaine by a scant 23,005 votes nationwide but won with 219 electoral votes to Blaine's 182 (Map 18.2), ending twenty-four years of Republican control of the presidency. Cleveland's followers had the last word. To the chorus of "Ma, Ma, where's my Pa?" they retorted, "Going to the White House, ha, ha, ha."

REVIEW How did the question of civil service reform contribute to divisions within the Republican Party?

▶ Economic Issues and Party Realignment

Four years later, in the election of 1888, fickle voters turned Cleveland out, electing Republican Benjamin Harrison, the grandson of President William Henry Harrison. Then, in the only instance in American history when a president once defeated at the polls returned to office, the voters brought Cleveland back in the election of 1892. What factors account for such a surprising turnaround? The 1880s witnessed a remarkable political realignment as a set of economic concerns replaced appeals to Civil War sectional loyalties. The tariff, federal regulation of the railroads and trusts, and the campaign for free silver restructured American politics. A Wall Street panic in 1893 set off a major depression that further fed political unrest.

The Tariff and the Politics of Protection

The tariff became a potent political issue in the 1880s. The concept of a protective tariff to raise the price of imported goods and stimulate American industry dated back to Alexander Hamilton in the founding days of the Republic. The Republicans turned the tariff to political ends in 1861 by enacting a measure that both raised revenues for the Civil War and rewarded their industrial supporters, who wanted protection from foreign competition. After the war, the pro-business Republicans continued to revise and enlarge the tariff. Manufactured goods such as steel and textiles, and some agricultural products, including sugar and wool, benefited from protection. Most farm products, notably wheat and cotton, did not. By the 1880s, the tariff produced more than $2.1 billion in revenue. Not only did the high tariff pay off the nation's Civil War debt and fund pensions for Union soldiers, but it also created a huge surplus that sat idly in the Treasury's vaults while the government argued about how (or even whether) to spend it.

To many Americans, particularly southern and midwestern farmers who sold their crops in a world market but had to buy goods priced artificially high because of the protective tariff, the answer was simple: Reduce the tariff. Advocates of free trade and moderates agitated for tariff reform. But those who benefited from the tariff — industrialists insisting that America's "infant industries" needed protection and some westerners producing protected raw materials such as wool, hides, and lumber — firmly opposed lowering the tariff. Many argued that workers, too, benefited from high tariffs that protected American wages by giving American products an edge over imported goods.

The Republican Party seized on the tariff question to forge a new national coalition. "Fold up the bloody shirt and lay it away," Blaine advised a colleague in 1880. "It's of no use to us. You want to shift the main issue to protection." By encouraging an alliance among industrialists, labor, and western producers of raw materials — groups seen to benefit from the tariff—Blaine hoped to solidify the North, Midwest, and West against the solidly Democratic South. Although the tactic failed for Blaine in the presidential election of 1884, it worked for the Republicans four years later.

Cleveland, who had straddled the tariff issue in the election of 1884, startled the nation in 1887 by calling for tariff reform. Cleveland attacked the tariff as a tax levied on American consumers by powerful industries. And he pointed out that high tariffs impeded the expansion of American markets abroad at a time when American industries needed to expand if they were to keep growing. The Republicans countered by arguing that "tariff tinkering" would only unsettle prosperous industries, drive down wages, and shrink the farmers' home market. Republican Benjamin Harrison, who supported the high tariff, ousted Cleveland from the White House in 1888, carrying all the western and northern states except Connecticut and New Jersey.

Back in power, the Republicans brazenly passed the highest tariff in the nation's history in 1890. The new tariff, sponsored by Republican representative William McKinley of Ohio and signed into law by Harrison, stirred up a hornet's nest of protest across the United States. The American people had elected Harrison to preserve protection but not to enact a higher tariff. Democrats condemned the **McKinley tariff** and labeled the Republican Congress that passed it the "Billion Dollar Congress" for its carnival of spending, which depleted the nation's surplus by enacting a series of pork barrel programs shamelessly designed to bring federal money to congressmen's own constituents. In the congressional election of 1890, angry voters swept the hapless Republicans, including tariff sponsor McKinley, out of office. Two years later, Harrison himself was defeated. Grover Cleveland, whose call for tariff revision had cost him the election in 1888, triumphantly returned to the White House vowing to lower the tariff. Such were the changes in the political winds whipped up by the tariff issue.

Controversy over the tariff masked deeper divisions in American society. Conflict between workers and farmers on the one side and bankers and corporate giants on the other erupted throughout the 1880s and came to a head in the 1890s. Both sides in the tariff debate spoke to concern over class conflict when they insisted that their respective plans, whether McKinley's high tariff or Cleveland's tariff reform, would bring prosperity and harmony. For their part, many working people shared the sentiment voiced by one labor leader that the tariff was "only a scheme devised by the old parties to throw dust in the eyes of laboring men."

Railroads, Trusts, and the Federal Government

American voters may have divided on the tariff, but increasingly they agreed on the need for federal regulation of the railroads and federal legislation to curb the power of the "trusts" (a term loosely applied to all large business combinations). As early as the 1870s, angry farmers in the Midwest who suffered from the unfair shipping practices of the railroads organized to fight for railroad regulation. The Patrons of Husbandry, or the Grange, founded in 1867 as a social and educational organization for farmers, soon became an independent political movement. By electing Grangers to state office, farmers made it possible for several midwestern states to pass laws in the 1870s and 1880s regulating the railroads. At first, the Supreme Court ruled in favor of state regulation (*Munn v. Illinois*, 1877). But in

1886, the Court reversed itself, ruling that because railroads crossed state boundaries, they fell outside state jurisdiction (*Wabash v. Illinois*). With more than three-fourths of railroads crossing state lines, the Supreme Court's decision effectively quashed the states' attempts at railroad regulation.

Anger at the *Wabash* decision finally led to the first federal law regulating the railroads, the Interstate Commerce Act, passed in 1887 during Cleveland's first administration. The act established the nation's first federal regulatory agency, the **Interstate Commerce Commission (ICC)**, to oversee the railroad industry. In its early years, the ICC was never strong enough to pose a serious threat to the railroads. For example, it could not end rebates to big shippers. In its early decades, the ICC proved more important as a precedent than effective as a watchdog.

Concern over the growing power of the trusts led Congress to pass the **Sherman Antitrust Act** in 1890. The act outlawed pools and trusts, ruling that businesses could no longer enter into agreements to restrict competition. It did nothing to restrict huge holding companies such as Standard Oil, however, and proved to be a weak sword against the trusts. In the following decade, the government successfully struck down only six trusts but used the law four times against labor by outlawing unions as a "conspiracy in restraint of trade." In 1895, the conservative Supreme Court dealt the antitrust law a crippling blow in *United States v. E. C. Knight Company*. In its decision, the Court ruled that "manufacture" did not constitute "trade." This semantic quibble drastically narrowed the law, in this case allowing the American Sugar Refining Company, which had bought out a number of other sugar companies (including E. C. Knight) and controlled 98 percent of the production of sugar, to continue its virtual monopoly.

Both the ICC and the Sherman Antitrust Act testified to the nation's concern about corporate abuses of power and to a growing willingness to use federal measures to intervene on behalf of the public interest. As corporate capitalism became more and more powerful, public pressure toward government intervention grew. Yet not until the twentieth century would more active presidents sharpen and use these weapons effectively against the large corporations.

The Fight for Free Silver

While the tariff and regulation of the trusts gained many backers, the silver issue stirred passions like no other issue of the day. On one side stood those who believed that gold constituted the only honest money. Although other forms of currency circulated, notably paper money such as banknotes and greenbacks, the government's support of the gold standard meant that anyone could redeem paper money for gold. Many who supported the gold standard were eastern creditors who did not wish to be paid in devalued dollars. On the opposite side stood a coalition of western silver barons and poor farmers from the West and South who called for **free silver**. The mining interests, who had seen the silver bonanza in the West drive down the price of the precious metal, wanted the government to buy silver and mint silver dollars. Farmers from the West and South who had suffered from deflation during the 1870s and 1880s hoped that increasing the

U.S. Currency
Gold remained the nation's standard currency, but silver supporters, including farmers and western mining interests, demanded the minting of silver dollars and the issuance of silver certificates like the one above. The American Numismatic Association; Picture Research Consultants & Archives.

money supply with silver dollars, thus causing inflation, would give them some debt relief by enabling them to pay off their creditors with cheaper dollars.

During the depression following the panic of 1873, critics of hard money organized the Greenback Labor Party, an alliance of farmers and urban wage laborers. The Greenbackers favored issuing paper currency not tied to the gold supply, citing the precedent of the greenbacks issued during the Civil War. The government had the right to define what constituted legal tender, the Greenbackers reasoned: "Paper is equally money, when . . . issued according to law." They proposed that the nation's currency be based on its wealth — land, labor, and capital — and not simply on its reserves of gold. The Greenback Labor Party captured more than a million votes and elected fourteen members to Congress in 1878. Although conservatives considered the Greenbackers dangerous cranks, their views eventually prevailed in the 1930s, when the country abandoned the gold standard.

After the Greenback Labor Party collapsed, proponents of free silver came to dominate the monetary debate in the 1890s. Advocates of free silver pointed out that until 1873 the country had enjoyed a system of bimetallism — the minting of both silver and gold into coins. In that year, at the behest of those who favored gold, the Republican Congress had voted to stop buying and minting silver, an act silver supporters denounced as the "crime of '73." By sharply contracting the money supply at a time when the nation's economy was burgeoning, the Republicans had enriched bankers and investors at the expense of cotton and wheat farmers and industrial wageworkers. In 1878 and again in 1890, with the Sherman Silver Purchase Act, Congress took steps to ease the tight money policy and appease advocates of silver by passing legislation requiring the government to buy silver and issue silver certificates. Though good for the mining interests, the laws did little to promote the inflation desired by farmers. Soon monetary reformers began to call for "the free and unlimited coinage of silver," a plan whereby nearly all the silver mined in the West would be minted into coins circulated at the rate of sixteen ounces of silver — equal in value to one ounce of gold.

By the 1890s, the silver issue crossed party lines. The Democrats hoped to use it to achieve a union between western and southern voters. Unfortunately for them, Democratic president Grover Cleveland remained a staunch conservative in money matters and supported the gold standard as vehemently as any Republican. After a panic on Wall Street in the spring of 1893, Cleveland called a special session of Congress and bullied the legislature into repealing the Silver Purchase Act because he believed it threatened economic confidence. Repeal proved disastrous for Cleveland, not only economically but also politically. It did nothing to bring prosperity and dangerously divided the country. Angry farmers, furious at the president's harsh monetary policy, warned Cleveland not to travel west of the Mississippi River if he valued his life.

Panic and Depression

President Cleveland had scarcely begun his second term in office in 1893 when the country faced the worst depression it had yet seen. In the face of economic disaster, Cleveland clung to the economic orthodoxy of the gold standard. In the winter of 1894–95, the president walked the floor of the White House, sleepless over the prospect that the United States might go bankrupt. Individuals and investors, rushing to trade in their banknotes for gold, strained the country's monetary system. The Treasury's gold reserves dipped so low that unless they could be buttressed, the unthinkable might happen: The U.S. Treasury might not be able to meet its obligations.

At this juncture, J. P. Morgan stepped in and suggested a plan. A group of bankers would purchase $65 million in U.S. government bonds, paying in gold. Cleveland knew that such a scheme would unleash a thunder of protest, yet to save the gold standard, the president had no choice but to accept Morgan's help. A storm of controversy erupted over the deal. The press claimed that Cleveland had lined his own pockets and rumored that Morgan had made $8.9 million. Neither allegation was true. Cleveland had not profited a penny, and Morgan made far less than the millions his critics claimed.

But if President Cleveland's action managed to salvage the gold standard, it did not save the country from hardship. The winter of 1894–95 was one of the worst times in American history. People faced unemployment, cold, and hunger. A firm believer in limited government, Cleveland insisted that nothing could be done to help: "I do not believe that the power and duty of the General Government ought to be extended to the relief of individual suffering which is in no manner properly related to the public service or benefit." Nor did it occur to Cleveland that his great faith in the gold standard prolonged the depression, favored creditors over debtors, and caused immense hardship for millions of Americans.

REVIEW   Why were Americans split on the question of the tariff and currency?

▶ Conclusion: Business Dominates an Era

The gold deal between J. P. Morgan and Grover Cleveland underscored a dangerous reality: The federal government was so weak that its solvency depended on a private banker. This lopsided power relationship signaled the dominance of business in the era Mark Twain satirically but accurately characterized as the Gilded Age. Perhaps no other era in American history spawned greed, corruption, and vulgarity on so grand a scale — an era when speculators like Jay Gould not only built but wrecked railroads to turn paper profits; an era when the get-rich-quick ethic of the western prospector infused the whole continent; and an era when business boasted openly of buying politicians, who in turn lined their pockets at the public's expense.

Nevertheless, the Gilded Age was not without its share of solid achievements, many inextricably linked to its empire in the West (see chapter 17). Where dusty roads and cattle trails once sprawled across the continent, steel rails now bound the country together, creating a national market that enabled America to make the leap into the industrial age. Factories and refineries poured out American steel and oil at unprecedented rates. Businessmen like Carnegie, Rockefeller, and Morgan developed new strategies to consolidate American industry. New inventions, including the telephone and electric light and power, changed Americans' everyday lives. By the end of the nineteenth century, the country had achieved industrial maturity. It boasted the largest, most innovative, most productive economy in the world. No other era in the nation's history witnessed such a transformation.

Yet the changes that came with these developments worried many Americans and gave rise to the era's political turmoil. Race and gender profoundly influenced American politics, leading to new political alliances. Fearless activist Ida B. Wells fought racism in its most brutal form — lynching. Women's organizations championed causes, notably suffrage and temperance, and challenged prevailing views of woman's proper sphere. Reformers fought corruption by instituting civil service. And new issues — the tariff, the regulation of the trusts, and currency reform — restructured the nation's politics.

The Gilded Age witnessed a nation transformed. Fueled by expanding industry, cities grew exponentially, not only with new inhabitants from around the globe but also with new bridges, subways, and skyscrapers. The frenzied growth of urban America brought wealth and opportunity, but also the exploitation of labor, racism toward newcomers, and social upheaval that lent a new urgency to calls for social reform.

Reviewing Chapter 18

REVIEW QUESTIONS

1. What devices did John D. Rockefeller use to gain control of 90 percent of the oil-refining business by 1890? (pp. 523–531)

2. Why did the ideas of social Darwinism appeal to many Americans in the late nineteenth century? (pp. 532–535)

3. How did race and gender influence politics? (pp. 536–541)

4. How did the question of civil service reform contribute to divisions within the Republican Party? (pp. 541–544)

5. Why were Americans split on the question of the tariff and currency? (pp. 545–549)

MAKING CONNECTIONS

1. How did the railroads contribute to the growth of American industry? In your answer, discuss the drawbacks and benefits of these developments.

2. Late-nineteenth-century industrialization depended on developments in technology and business strategy. What were some of the key innovations in both arenas? How did they facilitate the maturation of American industry?

3. By the 1870s, several new concerns had displaced slavery as the defining question of American politics. What were these new issues, and how did they shape new regional, economic, and racial alliances and rivalries? In your answer, consider the part that political parties played in this process.

4. Energetic political activity characterized Gilded Age America, both within and beyond formal party politics. How did the activism of women denied the vote contribute to the era's electoral politics? In your answer, be sure to cite specific examples of political action.

5. The U.S. Congress and the Supreme Court facilitated the concentration of power in the hands of private business concerns during the Gilded Age. Citing specific policies and court decisions, discuss how government helped augment the power of big business in the late nineteenth century.

LINKING TO THE PAST

1. In what ways did the military conquest of the trans-Mississippi West, with its dislocation of Native Americans, play a significant role in the industrial boom of the Gilded Age? (See chapter 17.)

2. In what ways did the rampant get-rich-quick mentality of western miners and land speculators help set the tone for the Gilded Age? Is the West the herald of the Gilded Age, or must we look to New York and Washington? (See chapter 17.)

TIMELINE 1869–1901

1869 • First transcontinental railroad completed.
• National Woman Suffrage Association founded.

1870 • John D. Rockefeller incorporates Standard Oil Company.

1872 • Andrew Carnegie builds the largest, most up-to-date Bessemer steel plant in the world.

1873 • Wall Street panic leads to major economic depression.

1874 • Woman's Christian Temperance Union (WCTU) founded.

1876 • Alexander Graham Bell demonstrates telephone.

1877 • Republican Rutherford B. Hayes sworn in as president.
• "Redeemers" come to power in South.
• *Munn v. Illinois*.

1880 • Republican James A. Garfield elected president.

1881 • Garfield assassinated; Vice President Chester A. Arthur becomes president.

1882 • John D. Rockefeller develops the trust.

1883 • Pendleton Civil Service Act.

1884 • Democrat Grover Cleveland elected president.

1886 • *Wabash v. Illinois*.

1887 • Interstate Commerce Act.

1888 • Republican Benjamin Harrison elected president.

1890 • McKinley tariff.
• General Federation of Women's Clubs (GFWC) founded.
• Sherman Antitrust Act.

1892 • Ida B. Wells launches antilynching campaign.

1893 • Wall Street panic touches off national depression.

1895 • J. P. Morgan bails out U.S. Treasury.

1901 • U.S. Steel incorporated and capitalized at $1.4 billion.

▶ **FOR AN ONLINE BIBLIOGRAPHY, PRACTICE QUIZZES, WEB SITES, IMAGES, AND DOCUMENTS RELATED TO THIS CHAPTER,** see the Book Companion Site at **bedfordstmartins.com/roarkvalue**.

▶ **FOR DOCUMENTS RELATED TO THIS PERIOD,** see Michael Johnson, ed., *Reading the American Past*, Fifth Edition.

19

The City and Its Workers

1870–1900

"A TOWN THAT CRAWLED NOW STANDS ERECT, AND WE WHOSE BACKS were bent above the hearths know how it got its spine," boasted a steelworker surveying New York City. Where once wooden buildings stood rooted in the mire of unpaved streets, cities of stone and steel sprang up in the last decades of the nineteenth century. The labor of millions of workers, many of them immigrants, laid the foundations for urban America.

No symbol better represented the new urban landscape than the Brooklyn Bridge, opened in May 1883. The great bridge soared over the East River in a single mile-long span. Begun in 1869, the bridge was the dream of builder John Roebling, who died in a freak accident almost as soon as construction began.

Building the Brooklyn Bridge took fourteen years and cost the lives of twenty-seven men. Nearly three hundred workers labored around the clock in three shifts, six days a week, most for $2 a day. To sink the foundation deep into the riverbed, common laborers tunneled down through mud and debris, working in reinforced wooden boxes called caissons, which were open at the bottom and pressurized to keep the water from flooding in. Before long, the workers experienced a mysterious malady they called "bends" because it left them doubled over in pain after they came to the surface. Scientists later discovered that nitrogen bubbles trapped in the bloodstream caused the condition and that it could be prevented if the men came up slowly to allow for decompression.

The first death occurred when the caissons reached a depth of seventy-one feet. On April 22, 1872, a heavyset German immigrant named John Meyers complained that he did not feel well and headed home to his boardinghouse.

Before he could reach his bed, he collapsed and died. Eight days later, another man dropped dead, and the entire workforce in the caissons went out on strike. Conditions had become so hazardous and terrifying that the workers demanded a higher wage for fewer hours of work.

One worker, Frank Harris, remembered the men's fear of working in the caissons. As a scrawny sixteen-year-old from Ireland, Harris started to work a few days after landing in America. He described his experience:

> The six of us were working naked to the waist in the small iron chamber with the temperature of about 80 degrees Fahrenheit: In five minutes the sweat was pouring from us, and all the while we were standing in icy water that was only kept from rising by the terrific pressure. No wonder the headaches were blinding.

By the fifth day, Harris experienced terrible shooting pains in his ears, and fearing he might go deaf, he quit. Like Harris, many immigrant workers walked off the job, often as many as a hundred a week. But a ready supply of immigrants meant that the work never slowed or stopped; new workers eagerly entered the caissons, where they could earn in a day more than they made in a week in Ireland or Italy.

Irish workers.

Workers in the Caissons
In 1870 *Frank Leslie's Illustrated Weekly* ran an article on the construction of the Brooklyn Bridge. Illustrations show the workers inside the caissons below the East River. Crews entered through a cylindrical airlock that took them down more than seventy feet. There in the wooden caissons they worked with pick and shovel to break up the big boulders and haul the rock away. "What with the flaming lights, the deep shadows, the confusing noise of hammer, drills, and chains, the half-naked forms flitting about," wrote one reporter, the scene resembled hell. The hot, dangerous work fell primarily to Irish immigrant workers. Library of Congress.

Washington Roebling, who took over as chief engineer after his father's death, routinely worked twelve to fourteen hours six days a week. Soon he, too, fell victim to the bends and ended up an invalid, directing the completion of the bridge through a telescope from his window in Brooklyn Heights. His wife, Emily Warren Roebling, acted as site superintendent and general engineer of the project. At the dedication of the bridge, Roebling turned to his wife and said, "I want the world to know that you, too, are one of the Builders of the Bridge."

At the end of the nineteenth century, the Brooklyn Bridge stood as a symbol of many things: the industrial might of the United States; the labor of the nation's immigrants; the ingenuity and genius of its engineers and inventors; the rise of iron and steel; and, most of all, the ascendancy of urban America. Poised on the brink of the twentieth century, the nation was shifting inexorably from a rural, agricultural society to an urban, industrial nation. In the burgeoning cities, tensions would erupt into conflict as workers squared off to fight for their rights to organize into labor unions and to demand safer working conditions, shorter hours, and better pay. And the explosive growth of the cities would foster political corruption as unscrupulous bosses and entrepreneurs cashed in on the building boom. Immigrants, political bosses, middle-class managers, poor laborers, and the very rich populated the nation's cities, crowding the streets, laboring in the stores and factories, and taking their leisure at the new ballparks, amusement parks, dance halls, and municipal parks that dotted the urban landscape. As the new century dawned, the city and its workers moved to center stage in American life.

▶ The Rise of the City

"We cannot all live in cities, yet nearly all seem determined to do so," New York editor Horace Greeley complained. The last three decades of the nineteenth century witnessed an urban explosion. Cities and towns grew more than twice as rapidly as the total population. Among the fastest-growing cities, Chicago expanded at a meteoric rate, doubling its population each decade. The number of cities with more than 100,000 inhabitants jumped from eighteen in 1870 to thirty-eight in 1900. Most of the nation's largest cities were east of the Mississippi, although St. Louis and San Francisco both ranked among the top ten urban areas. By 1900, the United States boasted three cities with more than a million inhabitants — New York, Chicago, and Philadelphia.

Patterns of **global migration** contributed to the rise of the city. In the port cities of the East Coast, more than fourteen million people arrived, many from southern and eastern Europe, and huddled together in dense urban ghettos. The

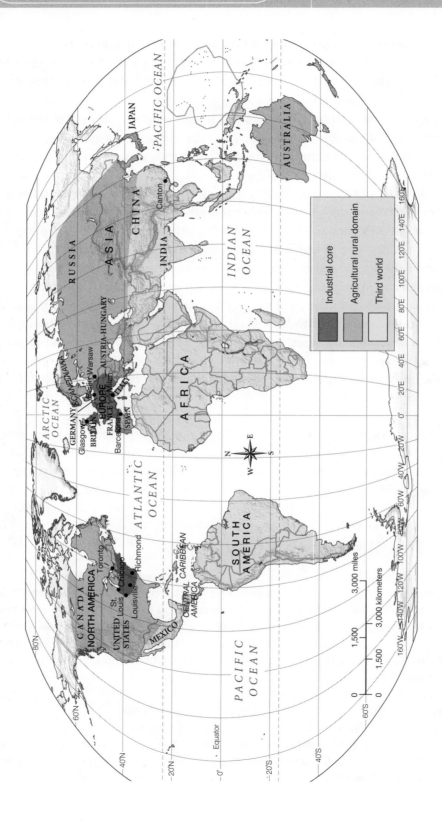

word *slum* entered the American vocabulary along with a growing concern over the rising tide of newcomers. In the city, the widening gap between rich and poor became more visible, exacerbated by changes in the city landscape brought about by advances in transportation and technology.

The Urban Explosion: A Global Migration

The United States grew up in the country and moved to the city, or so it seemed by the end of the nineteenth century. Between 1870 and 1900, eleven million people moved into cities. Burgeoning industrial centers such as Pittsburgh, Chicago, New York, and Cleveland acted as giant magnets, attracting workers from the countryside. But rural Americans were by no means the only ones migrating to cities. Worldwide in scope, the movement from rural areas to urban industrial centers attracted millions of immigrants to American shores in the waning decades of the nineteenth century.

By the 1870s, the world could be conceptualized as three interconnected geographic regions (Map 19.1). At the center stood an industrial core bounded by Chicago and St. Louis in the west; Toronto, Glasgow, and Berlin in the north; Warsaw in the east; and Milan, Barcelona, Richmond, and Louisville in the south. Surrounding this industrial core lay a vast agricultural domain encompassing Canada, much of Scandinavia, Russia and Poland, Hungary, Greece, Italy and Sicily, southern Spain, the South and the western plains of America, central and northern Mexico, the hinterlands of northern China, and the southern islands of Japan. Capitalist development in the late nineteenth century shattered traditional patterns of economic activity in this rural periphery. As old patterns broke down, these rural areas exported, along with other raw materials, new recruits for the industrial labor force.

Beyond this second circle lay an even larger third world including the Caribbean, Central and South America, the Middle East, Africa, India, and most of Asia. Ties between this part of the world and the industrial core strengthened in the late nineteenth century, but most of the people living there stayed put. They worked on plantations and railroads, and in mines and ports, as part of a huge export network managed by foreign powers that staked out spheres of influence and colonies in this vast region.

In the 1870s, railroad expansion and low steamship fares gave the world's peoples a newfound mobility, enabling industrialists to draw on a global population for cheap labor. When Andrew Carnegie opened his first steel mill in 1872,

◀ **MAP 19.1**
Economic Regions of the World, 1890s
The global nature of the world economy at the turn of the twentieth century is indicated by three interconnected geographic regions. At the center stands the industrial core — western Europe and the northeastern United States. The second region — the agricultural periphery — supplied immigrant laborers to the industries in the core. Beyond these two regions lay a vast area tied economically to the industrial core by colonialism.

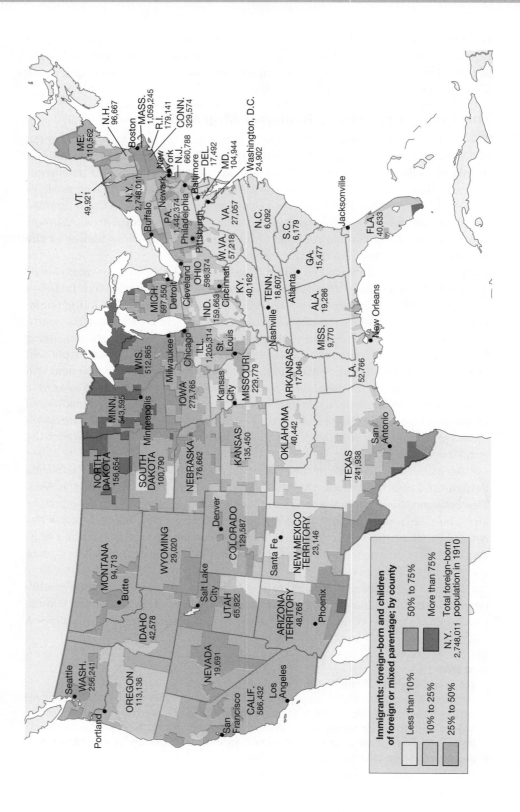

N.H. 96,667
MASS. 1,059,245
Boston
R.I. 179,141
CONN. 329,574
ME. 110,562
New York
Newark, N.J. 660,788
DEL. 17,492
VT. 49,921
MD. 104,944
N.Y. 2,748,011
Buffalo
Washington, D.C. 24,902
PA. 1,442,374
Philadelphia
Baltimore
Pittsburgh
VA. 27,057
W.VA. 57,218
N.C. 6,092
Jacksonville
S.C. 6,179
FLA. 40,633
MICH. 597,550
Detroit
Cleveland
OHIO 598,374
IND. 159,663
Cincinnati
KY. 40,162
GA. 15,477
Atlanta
ALA. 19,286
New Orleans
WIS. 512,865
Milwaukee
Chicago
ILL. 1,205,314
St. Louis
TENN. 18,607
Nashville
MISS. 9,770
IOWA 273,765
Kansas City
MISSOURI 229,779
ARKANSAS 17,046
LA. 52,766
MINN. 543,595
Minneapolis
San Antonio
NORTH DAKOTA 156,654
SOUTH DAKOTA 100,790
NEBRASKA 176,662
KANSAS 135,450
OKLAHOMA 40,442
TEXAS 241,938
Denver
COLORADO 129,587
NEW MEXICO TERRITORY 23,146
MONTANA 94,713
WYOMING 29,020
Santa Fe
Butte
Salt Lake City
IDAHO 42,578
UTAH 65,822
ARIZONA TERRITORY 48,765
Phoenix
Seattle
WASH. 256,241
NEVADA 19,691
Los Angeles
Portland
OREGON 113,136
San Francisco
CALIF. 586,432

Immigrants: foreign-born and children
of foreign or mixed parentage; by county

Less than 10%
10% to 25%
25% to 50%
50% to 75%
More than 75%

N.Y. 2,748,011   Total foreign-born population in 1910

his superintendent hired workers he called "buckwheats" — young American boys just off the farm. By the 1890s, however, Carnegie's workforce was liberally sprinkled with other rural boys, Hungarians and Slavs who had migrated to the United States, willing to work for low wages.

Altogether, more than 25 million immigrants came to the United States between 1850 and 1920. They came from all directions: east from Asia, south from Canada, north from Latin America, and west from Europe (Map 19.2). Part of a worldwide migration, immigrants traveled to South America and Australia as well as to the United States. Yet more than 70 percent of all European immigrants chose North America as their destination.

The largest number of immigrants to the United States came from the British Isles and from German-speaking lands. The vast majority of immigrants were white; Asians accounted for fewer than one million immigrants, and other people of color numbered even fewer. Yet ingrained racial prejudices increasingly influenced the country's perception of immigration patterns. One of the classic formulations of the history of European immigration divided immigrants into two distinct waves that have been called the "old" and the "new" immigration. According to this theory, before 1880 the majority of immigrants came from northern and western Europe, with Germans, Irish, English, and Scandinavians making up approximately 85 percent of the newcomers. After 1880, the pattern shifted, with more and more ships carrying passengers from southern and eastern Europe. Italians, Hungarians, eastern European Jews, Turks, Armenians, Poles, Russians, and other Slavic peoples accounted for more than 80 percent of all immigrants by 1896. Implicit in the distinction was an invidious comparison between "old" pioneer settlers and "new" unskilled laborers. Yet this sweeping generalization spoke more to perception than to reality. In fact, many of the earlier immigrants from Ireland, Germany, and Scandinavia came not as settlers or farmers, but as wageworkers, and they were met with much the same disdain as the Italians and Slavs who followed them.

The "new" immigration resulted from a number of factors. Improved economic conditions in western Europe coupled with increased immigration to Australia and Canada slowed the flow of immigrants coming into the United States from northern and western Europe. At the same time, economic depression in southern Italy, the persecution of Jews in eastern Europe, and a general desire to avoid conscription into the Russian army led many people from southern and eastern Europe to move to the United States. The need of America's industries for cheap, unskilled labor during prosperous years also stimulated immigration.

Steamship companies courted immigrants — a highly profitable, self-loading cargo. By the 1880s, the price of a ticket from Liverpool had dropped to less than $25.

◀ MAP 19.2
The Impact of Immigration, to 1910
Immigration flowed in all directions — south from Canada, north from Mexico and Latin America, east from Asia, and west from Europe.

Would-be immigrants eager for information about the United States relied on letters from friends and relatives, advertisements, and word of mouth — sources that were not always dependable or truthful. Even photographs proved deceptive: Workers dressed in their Sunday best looked more prosperous than they actually were to relatives in the old country, where only the very wealthy wore white collars or silk dresses. No wonder people left for the United States believing, as one Italian immigrant observed, "that if they were ever fortunate enough to reach America, they would fall into a pile of manure and get up brushing the diamonds out of their hair."

Most of the newcomers stayed in the nation's cities. By 1900, almost two-thirds of the country's immigrant population resided in cities, many of the immigrants too poor to move on. (The average laborer immigrating to the United States carried only about $21.50.) Although the foreign-born population rarely outnumbered the native-born population, taken together immigrants and their American-born children did constitute a majority in some areas, particularly in the nation's largest cities: Philadelphia, 55 percent; Boston, 66 percent; Chicago, 75 percent; and New York City, an amazing 80 percent in 1900.

Not all the newcomers came to stay. Perhaps eight million European immigrants — most of them young men — worked for a year or a season and then returned to their homelands. Immigration officers called these immigrants, many of them Italians, "birds of passage" because they followed a regular pattern of migration to and from the United States. By 1900, almost 75 percent of the new immigrants were young, single men.

Women generally had less access to funds for travel and faced tighter family control. Because the traditional sexual division of labor relied on women's unpaid domestic labor and care of the very young and the very old, women most often came to the United States as wives, mothers, or daughters, not as single wage laborers. Only among the Irish did women immigrants outnumber men by a small margin from 1871 to 1891.

Jews from eastern Europe most often came with their families and came to stay. Beginning in the 1880s, a wave of violent **pogroms**, or persecutions, in Russia and Poland prompted the departure of more than a million Jews in the next two decades. Most of the Jewish immigrants settled in the port cities of the East, creating distinct ethnic enclaves, like Hester Street in the heart of New York City's Lower East Side, which rang with the calls of pushcart peddlers and vendors hawking their wares, from pickles to feather beds.

Racism and the Cry for Immigration Restriction

Ethnic diversity and racism played a role in dividing skilled workers (those with a craft or specialized ability) from the globe-hopping proletariat of unskilled workers (those who supplied muscle or tended machines). As industrialists mechanized to replace skilled workers with lower-paid unskilled labor, they drew on recent immigrants, particularly those from southern and eastern Europe, who had come to the United States in the hope of bettering their lives. Skilled workers, frequently members of older immigrant groups, criticized the newcomers. One Irish worker complained, "There should be a law . . . to keep all the Italians from comin' in and takin' the bread out of the mouths of honest people."

The Irish worker's resentment brings into focus the impact of racism on America's immigrant laborers. Throughout the nineteenth century and into the twentieth, members of the educated elite as well as the uneducated viewed ethnic and even religious differences as racial characteristics, referring to the Polish or the Jewish "race." Americans judged "new" immigrants of southern and eastern European "races" as inferior. Each wave of newcomers was deemed somehow inferior to the established residents. The Irish who criticized the Italians so harshly had themselves been stigmatized as a lesser "race" a generation earlier.

Immigrants not only brought their own religious and racial prejudices to the United States but also absorbed the popular prejudices of American culture. Social Darwinism, with its strongly racist overtones, decreed that whites stood at the top of the evolutionary ladder. But who was "white"? Skin color supposedly served as a marker for the "new" immigrants — "swarthy" Italians; dark-haired, olive-skinned Jews. But even blond, blue-eyed Poles were not considered white. The social construction of "race" is nowhere more apparent than in the testimony of an Irish dockworker who boasted that he hired only "white men," a category that he insisted excluded "Poles and Italians." For the new immigrants, Americanization and assimilation would prove inextricably part of becoming "white."

For African Americans, the cities of the North promised not just economic opportunity but an escape from institutionalized segregation and persecution. Throughout the South, Jim Crow laws — restrictions that segregated blacks — became common in the decades following Reconstruction. Intimidation and lynching terrorized blacks. "To die from the bite of frost is far more glorious than at the hands of a mob," proclaimed the *Defender*, Chicago's largest African American newspaper. In the 1890s, many blacks moved north, settling for the most part in the growing cities. Racism relegated them to poor jobs and substandard living conditions, but by 1900 New York, Philadelphia, and Chicago had the largest black communities in the nation. Although the most significant African American migration out of the South would occur during and after World War I, the great exodus was already under way.

On the West Coast, Asian immigrants became scapegoats of the changing economy. After California's gold rush, many Chinese who had come to work "on the gold mountain" found jobs on the country's transcontinental railroads. When the railroad work ended, they took work other groups shunned, including domestic service. But hard times in the 1870s made them a target for disgruntled workers. Prohibited from owning land, the Chinese migrated to the cities. In 1870, San Francisco housed a Chinese population estimated at 12,022, and it continued to grow until passage of the Chinese Exclusion Act in 1882 (see chapter 17). For the first time in the nation's history, U.S. law excluded an immigrant group on the basis of race.

Huang Zunxian came to San Francisco in 1882 as Chinese consul general. Disillusioned with the anti-Chinese violence he saw all around him, he wrote a series of angry poems that took Americans to task for their hypocrisy. One of them read:

> They have sealed the gates tightly
> Door after door with guards beating alarms.
> Anyone with a yellow-colored face
> Is beaten even if guiltless.
> The American eagle strides the heavens soaring
> With half of the globe clutched in his claw.
> Although the Chinese arrived later,
> Couldn't you leave them a little space?

Despite the Chinese Exclusion Act, some Chinese managed to come to America using a loophole that allowed relatives to join their families. By contrast, the nation's small Japanese community of about 3,000 expanded rapidly after 1890, until pressures to keep out all Asians led in 1910 to the creation of an immigration station at Angel Island in San Francisco Bay. Asian immigrants were detained there, sometimes for months, and many were deported as "undesirable." Their sad stories can be read in the graffiti on the barracks walls.

On the East Coast, the volume of immigration from Europe in the last two decades of the century proved unprecedented. In 1888 alone, more than half a million Europeans landed in America, 75 percent of them in New York City. The Statue of Liberty, a gift from the people of France erected in 1886, stood sentinel in the harbor. The verse inscribed at Liberty's base was penned by a young Jewish woman named Emma Lazarus:

> Give me your tired, your poor,
> Your huddled masses yearning to breathe free,
> The wretched refuse of your teeming shore,
> Send these, the homeless, tempest-tost to me,
> I lift my lamp beside the golden door!

The tide of immigrants to New York City soon swamped the immigration office at Castle Garden in lower Manhattan. After the federal government took over immigration in 1890, it built a facility on **Ellis Island** in New York harbor, opened in 1892. After a fire gutted the wooden building, an imposing new brick edifice replaced it in 1900. Its overcrowded halls became the gateway to the United States for millions.

To many Americans, the "new" immigrants seemed uneducated, backward, and uncouth — impossible to assimilate. "These people are not Americans," editorialized the popular journal *Public Opinion*, "they are the very scum and offal of Europe." Terence V. Powderly, head of the broadly inclusive Knights of Labor, complained that the newcomers "herded together like animals and lived like beasts." Blue-blooded Yankees led by Senator Henry Cabot Lodge of Massachusetts formed an unlikely alliance with leaders of organized labor — who feared that immigrants would drive down wages — to press for immigration restrictions. Lodge and his supporters championed a literacy test as a requirement for immigration, knowing that the vast majority of Italian and Slavic peasants could neither read nor write. In 1896, Congress approved a literacy test for immigrants, but President Grover Cleveland promptly vetoed it. "It is said," the president reminded Congress, "that the quality of recent immigration is undesirable. The time is quite within recent memory when the same thing was said of immigrants, who, with their descendants, are now numbered among our best citizens." Cleveland's veto forestalled immigration restriction but did not stop anti-immigrant forces from seeking to close the gates. They would continue to press for restrictions until they achieved their goal in the 1920s (as discussed in chapter 23).

The Social Geography of the City

During the Gilded Age, cities experienced demographic and technological changes that greatly altered the social geography of the city. Cleveland, Ohio, provides a good example. In the 1870s, Cleveland was a small city in both population and area. Oil magnate John D. Rockefeller could, and often did, walk from his large brick house on Euclid Avenue to his office downtown. On his way, he passed the small homes of his clerks and other middle-class families. Behind these homes ran miles of alleys crowded with the dwellings of Cleveland's working class. Farther out, on the shores of Lake Erie, close to the factories and foundries, clustered the shanties of the city's poorest laborers.

Within two decades, the Cleveland that Rockefeller knew no longer existed. The coming of mass transit transformed the walking city. In its place emerged a central business district surrounded by concentric rings of residences organized by ethnicity and income. First the horse car in the 1870s and then the electric streetcar in the 1880s made it possible for those who could afford the five-cent fare to work downtown and flee after work to the "cool green rim" of the city, with its single-family homes, lawns, gardens, and trees. Social segregation — the separation of rich and poor, and of ethnic and old-stock Americans — was one of the major social changes engendered by the rise of the industrial metropolis, evident not only in Cleveland but in cities across the nation.

Race and ethnicity affected the way cities evolved. Newcomers to the nation's cities faced hostility and not surprisingly sought out their kin and country folk as they struggled to survive. Distinct ethnic neighborhoods often formed around a synagogue or church. African Americans typically experienced the greatest residential segregation, but every large city had its ethnic enclaves — Little Italy, Chinatown, Bohemia Flats, Germantown — where English was rarely spoken.

Poverty, crowding, dirt, and disease constituted the daily reality of New York City's immigrant poor — a plight documented by photojournalist **Jacob Riis** in his best-selling book *How the Other Half Lives* (1890). By taking his camera into the hovels of the poor, Riis opened the nation's eyes to conditions in the city's slums. Riis invited his readers into a Bottle Street tenement:

One, two, three beds are there, if the old boxes and heaps of foul straw can be called by that name; a broken stove with a crazy pipe from which the smoke leaks at every joint; a table of rough boards propped up on boxes, piles of rubbish in the corner. The closeness and smell are appalling.

While Riis's audience shivered at his revelations about the "other half," many middle-class Americans worried equally about the excesses of the wealthy. They feared the class antagonism fueled by the growing chasm between rich and poor so visible in the nation's cities, and shared Riis's view that "the real danger to society comes not only from the tenements, but from the ill-spent wealth which reared them."

The excesses of the Gilded Age's newly minted millionaires were nowhere more visible than in the lifestyle of the Vanderbilts. "Commodore" Cornelius Vanderbilt, an uncouth ferryman who built the New York Central Railroad, died in 1877, leaving his son $90 million. William Vanderbilt doubled that sum, and his two sons proceeded to spend lavishly on Fifth Avenue mansions and "cottages" in Newport, Rhode Island, that sought to rival the palaces of Europe. In 1883, Alva (Mrs. William) Vanderbilt launched herself into New York society by throwing a costume party so opulent that not even old New York society, which turned up its nose at the nouveau riche, could resist an invitation. Dressed as a Venetian princess, the hostess greeted her twelve hundred guests. But her sister-in-law Alice Vanderbilt stole the show by appearing as that miraculous new invention, the electric light, resplendent in a white satin evening dress studded with diamonds. The *New York World* speculated that Alva Vanderbilt's party cost more than a quarter of a million dollars (more than $4 million today).

Such ostentatious displays of wealth became especially alarming when they were coupled with disdain for the well-being of ordinary people. When a reporter in 1882 asked William Vanderbilt whether he considered the public good when running his railroads, he shot back, "The public be damned." The fear that America had become a plutocracy — a society ruled by the rich — gained credence from the fact that the wealthiest 1 percent of the population owned more than half the real and personal property in the country. As the new century dawned, reformers would form a progressive movement to address the problems of urban industrialism and the substandard living and working conditions it produced.

REVIEW Why did American cities experience explosive growth in the late nineteenth century?

▶ At Work in Industrial America

The number of industrial wageworkers in the United States exploded in the second half of the nineteenth century, more than tripling from 5.3 million in 1860 to 17.4 million in 1900. More than half of the country's men, women, and children made up the laboring class that performed manual work for wages.

These workers toiled in a variety of settings. Many skilled workers and artisans still earned a living in small workshops. But with the rise of corporate capitalism, large factories, mills, and mines increasingly dotted the landscape. Sweatshops and outwork — the contracting of piecework, including finishing garments by hand, to be performed in the home — provided work experiences different from those of factory operatives and industrial workers. Pick-and-shovel labor, whether on the railroads or in the building trades, constituted yet another kind of work. Managers, as well as women "typewriters" and salesclerks, formed a new white-collar segment of America's workforce.

America's Diverse Workers

Common laborers formed the backbone of the American labor force. They built the railroads and subways, tunneled under New York's East River to anchor the Brooklyn Bridge, and helped lay the foundation of industrial America. These "human machines" stood at the bottom of the country's economic ladder and generally came from the most recent immigrant groups. Initially, the Irish wielded the picks and shovels that built American cities, but by the turn of the century, as the Irish bettered their lot, Slavs and Italians took up their tools.

At the opposite end of labor's hierarchy stood skilled craftsmen like iron puddler James J. Davis, a Welsh immigrant who worked in the Pennsylvania mills. Using brains along with brawn, puddlers took up the melted pig iron in the heat of the furnace and, with long, heavy "spoons" (poles), formed the cooling metal into 200-pound balls, relying on eye and intuition to make each ball uniform. Davis likened his work to baking bread: "I am like some frantic baker in the inferno. . . . My spoon weighs twenty-five pounds, my porridge is pasty iron, and the heat of my kitchen is so great that if my body was not hardened to it the ordeal would drop me in my tracks."

Possessing such a skill meant earning good wages. Davis made up to $7 a day, when there was work. But most industry and manufacturing work in the nineteenth century remained seasonal; few workers could count on year-round pay. In addition, two major depressions only twenty years apart, beginning in 1873 and 1893, spelled unemployment and hardship. In an era before unemployment insurance, workers' compensation, or old-age pensions, even the best worker could not guarantee security for his family. "The fear of ending in the poor-house is one of the terrors that dog a man through life," Davis confessed.

Skilled workers like Davis wielded power on the shop floor. Employers attempted to limit workers' control by replacing people with machines, breaking down skilled work into ever-smaller tasks that could be performed by unskilled factory operatives. New England's textile mills provide a classic example of the effects of mechanized factory labor in the nineteenth century. Mary, a weaver at the mills in Fall River, Massachusetts, went to work in the 1880s at the age of twelve. By then, mechanization of the looms had reduced the job of the weaver to watching for breaks in the thread. "At first the noise is fierce, and you have to breathe the cotton all the time, but you get used to it," Mary told a reporter from *Independent* magazine. "When the bobbin flies out and a girl gets hurt, you can't hear her shout — not if she just screams, you can't. She's got to wait, 'till you see her. . . . Lots of us is deaf."

During the 1880s, the number of foreign-born mill workers almost doubled. At Fall River, Mary and her Scots-Irish family resented the new immigrants. "The Polaks learn weavin' quick," she remarked, using a common derogatory term to identify a rival group. "They just as soon live on nothin' and work like that. But it won't do 'em much good for all they'll make out of it." Employers encouraged racial and ethnic antagonism because it inhibited labor organization.

The majority of factory operatives in the textile mills were young, unmarried women like Mary. They worked from six in the morning to six at night six days a week, and they took home about $1 a day. The seasonal nature of the work also drove wages down. "Like as not your mill will 'shut down' three months," and "some weeks you only get two or three days' work," Mary recounted. After twenty years of working in the mill, Mary's family had not been able to scrape together enough money to buy a house: "We saved some, but something always comes."

Mechanization transformed the garment industry as well. With the introduction of the foot-pedaled sewing machine in the 1850s and the use of mechanical cloth-cutting knives in the 1870s, independent tailors were replaced with workers hired by contractors to sew pieces of cloth into suits and dresses. Working in **sweatshops**, small rooms hired for the season or even in the contractor's own tenement, women and children formed an important segment of garment workers. Discriminated against in the marketplace, where they earned less than men, women generally worked for wages for only eight to ten years, until they married.

Sadie Frowne, a sixteen-year-old Polish Jew, went to work in a Brooklyn sweatshop in the 1890s. Frowne sewed for eleven hours a day in a 20-by-14-foot room containing fourteen machines. "The machines go like mad all day, because the faster you work the more money you get," she recalled. Paid by the piece, she earned about $4.50 a week and, by rigid economy, tried to save $2. Young and single, Frowne typified the woman wage earner in the late nineteenth century. In 1890, the average workingwoman was twenty-two and had been working since the age of fifteen, laboring twelve hours a day six days a week and earning less than $6 a week. Only marriage delivered women from dead-end jobs. No wonder single working women scrimped to buy ribbons and finery to make themselves attractive to young men.

The Family Economy: Women and Children

In 1900, the typical male worker in manufacturing earned $435 a year, about $12,000 in today's dollars. Many working-class families, whether native-born or immigrant, lived in or near poverty, their economic survival dependent on the contributions of all family members, regardless of sex or age. "Father," asked one young immigrant girl, "does everybody in America live like this? Go to work early, come home late, eat and go to Sleep? And the next day again work, eat, and sleep?" Most workers did. The **family economy** meant that everyone needed to contribute to maintain even the most meager household. Children dutifully turned over their wages to their fathers and kept only a tiny portion for themselves. One

Bootblacks

The faces and hands of the two bootblacks shown here with a third boy on a New York City street in 1896 testify to their grimy trade. Boys as young as six years old found work on city streets as bootblacks and newsboys. Often they worked for contractors who took a cut of their meager earnings. When families could no longer afford to feed their children, boys often headed out on their own at a young age. For these child workers, even free education was a luxury they could not afford. Alice Austin photo, Staten Island Historical Society.

statistician estimated that in 1900 as many as 64 percent of working-class families relied on income other than the husband's wages to make ends meet. The paid and unpaid work of women and children proved essential for family survival, let alone economic advancement.

In the cities, boys as young as six years old plied their trades as bootblacks and newsboys. Often working under an adult contractor, these children earned as little as fifty cents a day. Many of them were homeless — orphaned or cast off by their families. "We wuz six, and we ain't got no father," a child of twelve told reporter Jacob Riis. "Some of us had to go."

Child labor increased decade by decade after 1870. The percentage of children under fifteen engaged in paid labor did not drop until after World War I. The 1900 census estimated that 1,750,178 children ages ten to fifteen were employed, an increase of more than a million over thirty years. Children in this age range constituted more than 18 percent of the industrial labor force. Many younger children not counted by the census worked beside their older siblings in mills, in factories, and on the streets.

In the late nineteenth century, the number of women workers also rose sharply, with their most common occupations changing slowly from domestic service to factory work and then to office work. In 1870, the census listed 1.5 million women working for wages in nonagricultural occupations. By 1890, the number had more than doubled, with 3.7 million women working for pay. Women's working patterns varied considerably according to race and ethnicity. White married women, even among the working class, rarely worked for wages outside the home. In 1890, only 3 percent were employed. Nevertheless, working-class married women found ways to contribute to the family economy. In many Italian families, for example, piece-work such as making artificial flowers allowed married women to contribute to the family economy without leaving their homes. Black women, married and unmarried, worked for wages in much greater numbers. The 1890 census showed that 25 percent of married African American women were employed, often as domestics in the houses of white families.

White-Collar Workers: Managers, "Typewriters," and Salesclerks

In the late nineteenth century, business expansion and consolidation led to a managerial revolution, creating a new class of white-collar workers who worked in offices and stores. As skilled workers saw their crafts replaced by mechanization, some moved into management positions. "The middle class is becoming a salaried class," a writer for the *Independent* magazine observed, "and is rapidly losing the economic and moral independence of former days." As large business organizations consolidated, corporate development separated management from ownership, and the job of directing the firm became the province of salaried executives and managers, the majority of whom were white men drawn from the 8 percent of Americans who held high school diplomas.

Until late in the century, when engineering schools began to supply recruits, many skilled workers moved from the shop floor to positions of considerable responsibility. William "Billy" Jones, the son of a Welsh immigrant, was one such worker. Beginning as an apprentice at the age of ten, Jones rose through the ranks to become plant superintendent at Andrew Carnegie's Pittsburgh steelworks in 1872. By all accounts, Jones was the best steel man in the industry, and Carnegie rewarded him with a "hell of a big salary," $25,000 — the same salary as the president of the United States. Most middle managers averaged far less, $1,100 a year being counted as a good salary. Senior executives, generally recruited from the college-educated elite, took home $4,000 or more, and a company's general manager could earn as much as $15,000 a year, approximately 30 times what the average worker earned. (Today's top CEOs on average earn 550 times more than the average worker receives.) At the top of the economic pyramid, the great industrialists amassed fortunes that rank John D. Rockefeller, Andrew Carnegie, and Cornelius Vanderbilt among the top ten richest men in American history, easily outpacing today's billionaires.

The new white-collar workforce also included women **"typewriters"** and salesclerks. In the decades after the Civil War, as businesses became larger and more far-flung, the need for more elaborate and exact records, as well as the greater volume of correspondence, led to the hiring of more office workers. Mechanization transformed business as it had industry and manufacturing. The adding machine, the cash register, and the typewriter came into general use in the 1880s. Employers seeking literate workers soon turned to nimble-fingered women. Educated men had many other career choices, but for middle-class white women, secretarial work constituted one of the very few areas where they could put their literacy to use for wages.

Sylvie Thygeson was typical of the young women who went to work as secretaries. Thygeson grew up in an Illinois prairie town and went to work as a country schoolteacher after graduating high school in 1884. Realizing that teaching school did not pay a living wage, she mastered typing and stenography and found work as a secretary to help support her family. According to her account, she made "a fabulous sum of money" (possibly $25 a month). Nevertheless, she gave up her job after a few years when she met and married her husband.

Clerical Worker
A stenographer takes dictation in an 1890s office. Notice that the apron, a symbol of feminine domesticity, has accompanied women into the workplace. In the 1880s, with the invention of the typewriter, many women put their literacy skills to use in the nation's offices. Brown Brothers.

Called "typewriters," women workers like Thygeson were seen as indistinguishable from the machines they operated. Far from viewing their jobs as dehumanizing, women typewriters took pride in their work and relished the economic independence it afforded them. But the entry of women into the workplace challenged traditional gender roles. Society distinguished between "ladies" (who stayed at home) and "working girls" (by definition lower-class women and a term often used for prostitutes). When white middle-class women entered offices as court reporters, typewriters, and stenographers, issues of class and gender clashed. Could a "lady" work? And if she did, did her economic independence threaten men and marriage? Some of this ambivalence can be seen in a poem published in 1896 in the Boston *Courier*. The poet waxes eloquent on his attraction to the "typewriter":

> The click of the keys, as her fingers fly,
>> And the ring of the silvery bell,
> I hardly hear, though I sit quite near,
>> Enchained by her magic spell.

After several verses, however, he ruefully abandons his ardor in the face of her modesty and professional manner. And, more telling, he acknowledges that the independent working woman may not need him at all.

> So, to her of my love I shall never speak,
>> Twould be vain I can clearly see.
> Why, she gets sixteen dollars a week.
>> And what does she want of me?

As Sylvie Thygeson's story shows, most women chose marriage and the home over the office, despite concerns to the contrary. But by the 1890s, secretarial work was the overwhelming choice of native-born, single white women, who constituted more than 90 percent of the female clerical force. Not only considered more genteel than factory work or domestic labor, office work also meant more money for shorter hours. In 1883, Boston's clerical workers on average made more than $6 a week, compared with less than $5 for women working in manufacturing.

As a new consumer culture came to dominate American urban life in the late nineteenth century, department stores offered another employment opportunity for women in the cities. Boasting ornate facades, large plate-glass display windows, and marble and brass fixtures, stores such as Macy's in New York, Wanamaker's in Philadelphia, and Marshall Field in Chicago stood as monuments to the material promise of the era. Within these palaces of consumption, cash girls, stock clerks, and wrappers earned as little as $3 a week, while at the top of the scale, buyers like Belle Cushman of the fancy goods department at Macy's earned $25 a week, an unusually high salary for a woman in the 1870s. Salesclerks counted themselves a cut above factory workers. Their work was neither dirty nor dangerous, and even when they earned less than factory workers, they felt a sense of superiority.

> **REVIEW** How did business expansion and consolidation change workers' occupations in the late nineteenth century?

▶ Workers Organize

By the late nineteenth century, industrial workers were losing ground in the workplace. In the fierce competition to reduce prices and cut costs, industrialists, led by Andrew Carnegie, invested heavily in new machinery that replaced skilled workers with unskilled labor. The erosion of skills and the redefinition of labor as mere "machine tending" left the worker with a growing sense of individual helplessness that served as a spur to collective action. In 1877, in the midst of a depression that left many workers destitute, labor flexed its muscle in the Great Railroad Strike and showed the power of collective action. This and other strikes underscored the tensions produced by rapid industrialization.

In the 1870s and 1880s, labor organizations grew, and the Knights of Labor and the American Federation of Labor attracted workers. Convinced of the inequity of the wage-labor system, labor organizers spoke eloquently of abolishing class privileges and monopoly. Their rhetoric as well as the violence often associated with strikes frightened many middle-class Americans and caused them to equate the labor movement with the specter of class war and anarchism.

The Great Railroad Strike of 1877

Economic depression following the panic of 1873 threw as many as three million people out of work. Those who were lucky enough to keep their jobs watched as pay cuts eroded their wages until they could no longer feed their families. In the summer of 1877, the Baltimore and Ohio (B&O) Railroad announced a 10 percent wage cut at the same time it declared a 10 percent dividend to its stockholders. Angry brakemen in West Virginia, whose wages had already fallen from $70 to $30 a month, walked out on strike. One B&O worker described the hardship that drove him to take such desperate action: "We eat our hard bread and tainted meat two days old on the sooty cars up the road, and when we come home, find our wives complaining that they cannot even buy hominy and molasses for food."

The West Virginia brakemen's strike touched off the **Great Railroad Strike** of 1877, a nationwide uprising that spread rapidly to Pittsburgh and Chicago, St. Louis and San Francisco. Within a few days, nearly 100,000 railroad workers walked off the job. The spark of rebellion soon led an estimated 500,000 laborers to join the train workers. In Reading, Pennsylvania, militiamen refused to fire on the strikers, saying, "We may be militiamen, but we are workmen first." Rail traffic ground to a halt; the nation lay paralyzed.

Destruction from the Great Railroad Strike of 1877

Pictures of the devastation caused in Pittsburgh during the strike shocked many Americans. When militiamen fired on striking workers, killing more than twenty strikers, the mob retaliated by destroying a two-mile area along the track, reducing it to a smoldering rubble. Property damage totaled $2 million. Curious pedestrians came out to view the destruction. Carnegie Library of Pittsburgh.

Violence erupted as the strike spread. In Pittsburgh, strikers clashed with militia brought in from Philadelphia, who arrogantly boasted they would clean up "the workingmen's town." Charging with bayonets leveled, the troops opened fire on the crowds, killing twenty people. Angry workers retaliated by reducing an area two miles long beside the tracks to smoldering rubble. Before the day ended, twenty more workers had been shot, and the railroad had sustained millions of dollars' worth of property damage. Nothing like the Pittsburgh riots had ever happened in American history. Armed workers had chased the Philadelphia militia out of town. Now business pressured the federal government to step in.

Within eight days, the governors of nine states, acting at the prompting of the railroad owners and managers, defined the strike as an "insurrection" and called for federal troops. President Rutherford B. Hayes, after hesitating briefly, called out the army. By the time the troops arrived, the violence had run its course. Federal troops did not shoot a single striker in 1877. But they struck a blow against labor by acting as strikebreakers — opening rail traffic, protecting nonstriking train crews (known by the derogatory term "scabs"), and maintaining peace along the line. In three weeks, the strike was over.

Although many middle-class Americans initially sympathized with the conditions that led to the strike, they condemned the strikers for the violence and property damage that occurred. The *New York Times* editorialized about the "dangerous classes," and the *Independent* magazine offered the following advice on how to deal with "rioters": "If the club of a policeman, knocking out the brains of the rioter, will answer then well and good; but if it does not promptly meet the exigency, then bullets and bayonets . . . constitutes [*sic*] the one remedy and one duty of the hour."

"The strikes have been put down by force," President Hayes noted in his diary on August 5. "But now for the real remedy. Can't something be done by education of the strikers, by judicious control of the capitalists, by wise general policy to end or diminish the evil? The railroad strikers, as a rule, are good men, sober, intelligent, and industrious." While Hayes acknowledged the workers' grievances, most businessmen and industrialists did not and fought the idea of labor unions, arguing that workers and employers entered into contracts as individuals and denying the right of unions to bargain collectively for their workers. For their part, workers quickly recognized that they held little power individually and flocked to join unions. As labor leader Samuel Gompers noted, the nation's first national strike dramatized the frustration and unity of the workers and served as an alarm bell to labor "that sounded a ringing message of hope to us all."

The Knights of Labor and the American Federation of Labor

The **Knights of Labor**, the first mass organization of America's working class, proved the chief beneficiary of labor's newfound consciousness. The Noble and Holy Order of the Knights of Labor had been founded in 1869 by Uriah Stephens, a Philadelphia garment cutter. A secret society of workers, the Knights envisioned a "universal brotherhood" of all workers, from common laborers to master craftsmen.

The organization's secrecy and ritual served to bind Knights together at the same time that it discouraged company spies and protected members from reprisals.

Although the Knights played no active role in the 1877 railroad strike, membership swelled as a result of the growing interest in labor organizing that followed the strike. In 1878, the Knights abandoned secrecy and launched an ambitious campaign to organize workers, attempting to bridge the boundaries of ethnicity, gender, ideology, race, and occupation in a badly fragmented society. **Leonora Barry** served as general investigator for women's work from 1886 to 1890, helping the Knights recruit teachers, waitresses, housewives, and domestics along with factory and sweatshop workers. Women composed perhaps 20 percent of the membership. The Knights also made good on its vow to include African Americans, organizing more than 95,000 black workers. That the Knights of Labor often fell short of its goals to unify the working class proved less surprising than the scope of its efforts.

Under the direction of Grand Master Workman **Terence V. Powderly**, the Knights became the dominant force in labor during the 1880s. The organization advocated a kind of workers' democracy that embraced reforms including public ownership of the railroads, an income tax, equal pay for women workers, and the abolition of child labor. A loose mix of ideology, unionism, culture, fraternalism, and mysticism, the Knights called for one big union to create a cooperative commonwealth that would supplant the wage system and remove class distinctions. Only the "parasitic" members of society — gamblers, stockbrokers, lawyers, bankers, and liquor dealers — were denied membership.

In theory, the Knights of Labor opposed strikes. Powderly championed arbitration and preferred to use boycotts. But in practice, much of the organization's appeal came from the Knights' sweeping victory against railroad tycoon Jay Gould in the Great Southwest Strike of 1885. Despite the reservations of its leadership, the Knights became a militant labor organization that won passionate support from working people with the slogan "An injury to one is the concern of all."

The Knights of Labor was not without rivals. Many skilled workers belonged to craft unions organized by trade. Among the largest and richest of these unions stood the Amalgamated Association of Iron and Steel Workers, founded in 1876 and counting twenty thousand skilled workers as members. Trade unionists spurned the broad reform goals of the Knights and focused on workplace issues. **Samuel Gompers**, a cigar maker born in London of Dutch Jewish ancestry, promoted what he called "pure and simple" unionism. Gompers founded the Organized Trades and Labor Unions in 1881 and reorganized it in 1886 into the **American Federation of Labor** (AFL), which coordinated the activities of craft unions throughout the United States. His plan was simple: organize skilled workers such as machinists and locomotive engineers — those with the most bargaining power — and use strikes to gain immediate objectives such as higher pay and better working conditions. Gompers at first drew few converts. The AFL had only 138,000 members in 1886, compared with 730,000 for the Knights of Labor. But events soon brought down the Knights, and Gompers's brand of unionism came to prevail.

Haymarket and the Specter of Labor Radicalism

While the AFL and the Knights of Labor competed for members, more radical labor groups, including socialists and anarchists, believed that reform was futile and called instead for social revolution. Both the socialists and the anarchists, sensitive to criticism that they preferred revolution in theory to improvements here and now, rallied around the popular issue of the eight-hour day.

Since the 1840s, labor had sought to end the twelve-hour workday, which was standard in industry and manufacturing. By the mid-1880s, it seemed clear to many workers that labor shared too little in the new prosperity of the decade, and pressure mounted for the eight-hour day. Labor championed the popular issue and launched major rallies in cities across the nation. Supporters of the movement set May 1, 1886, as the date for a nationwide general strike in support of the eight-hour workday.

All factions of the nascent labor movement came together in Chicago on May Day for what was billed as the largest demonstration to date. A group of labor radicals led by anarchist Albert Parsons, a *Mayflower* descendant, and August Spies, a German socialist, spearheaded the eight-hour movement in Chicago. Chicago's Knights of Labor rallied to the cause even though Terence Powderly and the union's national leadership, worried about the increasing activism of the rank and file, refused to endorse the movement for shorter hours. Samuel Gompers was on hand, too, to lead the city's trade unionists, although he privately urged the AFL assemblies not to participate in the general strike.

Gompers's skilled workers were labor's elite. Many still worked in small shops where negotiations between workers and employers took place in an environment tempered by personal relationships. Well dressed in their frock coats and starched shirts, the AFL's skilled workers stood in sharp contrast to the dispossessed workers out on strike across town at Chicago's huge McCormick reaper works. There strikers watched helplessly as the company brought in strikebreakers to take their jobs and marched the "scabs" to work under the protection of the Chicago police and security guards supplied by the Pinkerton Detective Agency. Cyrus McCormick Jr., son of the inventor of the mechanical reaper, viewed labor organization as a threat to his power as well as to his profits; he was determined to smash the union.

During the May Day rally, 45,000 workers paraded peacefully down Michigan Avenue in support of the eight-hour day, many singing the song that had become the movement's anthem:

> We want to feel the sunshine;
> We want to smell the flowers,
> We're sure that God has willed it,
> And we mean to have eight hours.
> Eight hours for work, eight hours for rest,
> eight hours for what we will!

Trouble came two days later, when strikers attacked strikebreakers outside the McCormick works and police opened fire, killing or wounding six men. Angry radicals rushed out a circular urging workers to "arm yourselves and appear in full force" at a rally in Haymarket Square.

On the evening of May 4, the turnout at Haymarket was disappointing. No more than two or three thousand gathered in the drizzle to hear Spies, Parsons, and the other speakers. Mayor Carter Harrison, known as a friend of labor, mingled conspicuously in the crowd, pronounced the meeting peaceable, and went home to bed. Sometime later, police captain John "Blackjack" Bonfield, who had made his reputation cracking skulls, marched his men into the crowd, by now fewer than three hundred people, and demanded that it disperse. Suddenly, someone threw a bomb into the police ranks. After a moment of stunned silence, the police drew their revolvers. "Fire and kill all you can," shouted a police lieutenant. When the melee ended, seven policemen and an unknown number of other people lay dead. An additional sixty policemen and thirty or forty civilians suffered injuries.

News of the "Haymarket riot" provoked a nationwide convulsion of fear, followed by blind rage directed at anarchists, labor unions, strikers, immigrants, and the working class in general. Eight men, including Parsons and Spies, went on trial in Chicago, although witnesses testified that none of them had thrown the bomb. "Convict these men," thundered the state's attorney, Julius S. Grinnell, "make examples of them, hang them, and you save our institutions." Although the state could not link any of the defendants to the **Haymarket bombing**, the jury nevertheless found them all guilty. Four were executed, one committed suicide, and three received prison sentences. On the gallows, Spies spoke for the Haymarket martyrs: "The time will come when our silence will be more powerful than the voices you throttle today."

The bomb blast at Haymarket had lasting repercussions. To commemorate the death of the Haymarket martyrs, labor made May 1 an annual international celebration of the worker. But the Haymarket bomb, in the eyes of one observer, proved "a godsend to all enemies of the labor movement." It effectively scotched the eight-hour-day movement and dealt a blow to the Knights of Labor, already wracked by internal divisions. With the labor movement everywhere under attack, many skilled workers turned to the American Federation of Labor. Gompers's narrow economic strategy made sense at the time and enabled one segment of the workforce — the skilled — to organize effectively and achieve tangible gains. But the nation's unskilled workers remained untouched by the AFL's brand of trade unionism. The vast majority of America's workers would have to wait another forty years before a mainstream labor union, the Congress of Industrial Organizations (CIO), moved to organize the unskilled (as discussed in chapter 24).

REVIEW Why did the fortunes of the Knights of Labor rise in the late 1870s and decline in the 1890s?

▶ At Home and at Play

The growth of urban industrialism not only dramatically altered the workplace but also transformed home and family life and gave rise to new forms of commercialized leisure. Industrialization redefined the very concepts of work and home. Increasingly, men went out to work for wages, while most white married women stayed home, either working in the home without pay — cleaning, cooking, and rearing children — or supervising paid domestic servants who did the housework.

Domesticity and "Domestics"

The separation of the workplace and the home that marked the shift to industrial society redefined the home as a "haven in the heartless world," presided over by a wife and mother who made the household her separate sphere. The growing separation of workplace and home led to a new ideology, one that sentimentalized the home and women's role in it. The cultural ideology that dictated woman's place in the home began to develop in the early 1800s and has been called the **cult of domesticity**, a phrase used to prescribe an ideal of middle-class, white womanhood that dominated the period from 1820 to the end of the nineteenth century.

The cult of domesticity and the elaboration of the middle-class home led to a major change in patterns of hiring household help. The live-in servants, or **domestics**, became a fixture in the North, replacing the hired girl of the previous century. In American cities by 1870, 15 to 30 percent of all households included live-in domestic servants, more than 90 percent of them women. Earlier in the mid-nineteenth century, native-born women increasingly took up other work and left domestic service to immigrants. In the East, the maid was so often Irish that "Bridget" became a generic term for female domestics. (The South continued to rely on black female labor, first slave and later free.)

Servants by all accounts resented the long hours and lack of privacy. "She is liable to be rung up at all hours," one study of domestics reported. "Her very meals are not secure from interruption, and even her sleep is not sacred." No wonder tension between domestic servants and their female employers proved endemic. Domestic service became the occupation of last resort, a "hard and lonely life" in the words of one female servant.

For women of the white middle class, domestics were a boon, freeing them from household drudgery and giving them more time to spend with their children or to pursue club work or reform. Thus, while domestic service supported the cult of domesticity, it created for those women who could afford it opportunities that expanded their horizons outside the home in areas such as women's clubs and the temperance and suffrage movements.

Such benefits of middle-class respectability contrasted sharply with the austerity of the working-class home. Reformer Margaret Byington recounted her visit with the family of a Slavic worker in Homestead, the Carnegie mill town outside Pittsburgh. The family lived in a two-room dwelling, and Byington found the young mother doing the family laundry in a big washtub set on a chair in the middle of the downstairs room, struggling to keep her two babies from tumbling into the scalding water. Further describing the congested home, Byington noted the room's single large bed and "the inevitable cook stove upon which in the place of honor was simmering the evening's soup. Upstairs in a second room, a boarder and the man of the house were asleep. Soon they would get up and turn their beds over to two more boarders, who were out at work." In the eyes of Byington and many middle-class reformers, the Slavs' crowded tenement, with its lack of privacy, scarcely qualified as a "home."

Cheap Amusements

Growing class divisions manifested themselves in patterns of leisure as well as in work and home life. The poor and working class took their leisure, when they had any, not in the crowded tenements that housed their families, but increasingly in the cities' new dance halls, music houses, ballparks, and amusement arcades, which by the 1890s formed a familiar part of the urban landscape.

The growing anonymity of urban industrial society posed a challenge to traditional rituals of courtship. Young workingwomen no longer met prospective husbands only through their families. Fleeing crowded tenements, the young sought each other's company in dance halls and other commercial retreats. Scorning proper introductions, working-class youths "picked up" partners at dance halls, where drinking was part of the evening's entertainment. Young workingwomen, who rarely could afford more than trolley fare when they went out, counted on being "treated" by men, a transaction that often implied sexual payback. Young women's need to negotiate sexual encounters if they wished to participate in commercial amusements blurred the line between respectability and promiscuity and made the dance halls a favorite target of reformers who feared they lured teenaged girls into prostitution.

For men, baseball became a national pastime in the 1870s — then, as now, one force in urban life capable of uniting a city across class lines. Cincinnati mounted the first entirely paid team, the Red Stockings, in 1869. Soon professional teams proliferated in cities across the nation, and Mark Twain hailed baseball as "the very symbol, the outward and visible expression, of the drive and push and rush and struggle of the raging, tearing, booming nineteenth century."

The increasing commercialization of entertainment in the late-nineteenth-century city was best seen at **Coney Island**. A two-mile stretch of sand nine miles from Manhattan by trolley or steamship, Coney Island in the 1870s and 1880s attracted visitors to its beaches, dance pavilions, and penny arcades, where they consumed treats ranging from oysters to saltwater taffy. In the 1890s, Coney Island was transformed into the site of some of the largest and most elaborate amusement parks in the country. Promoter George Tilyou built Steeplechase Park in 1897, advertising "10 hours of fun for 10 cents." With its mechanical thrills and fun-house laughs, the amusement park encouraged behavior that one schoolteacher aptly described as "everyone with the brakes off." By 1900, as many as a million New Yorkers flocked to Coney Island on any given weekend, making the amusement park the unofficial capital of a new mass culture.

REVIEW   How did urban industrialism shape the world of leisure?

▶ City Growth and City Government

Private enterprise, not planners, built the cities of the United States. Boosters, builders, businessmen, and politicians all had a hand in creating the modern metropolis. With a few notable exceptions, such as Washington, D.C., and Savannah, Georgia, there was no such thing as a comprehensive city plan. Cities simply mushroomed, formed by the dictates of profit and the exigencies of local politics. With the rise of the city came the need for public facilities, transportation, and services that would tax the imaginations of America's architects and engineers and set the scene for the rough-and-tumble of big-city government, politics, and politicians.

Building Cities of Stone and Steel

Skyscrapers and mighty bridges dominated the imagination and the urban landscape. Less imposing but no less significant were the paved streets, the parks and public libraries, and the subways and sewers. In the late nineteenth century, Americans rushed to embrace new technology of all kinds, making their cities the most modern in the world.

Structural steel made enormous advances in building possible. A decade after the completion of the **Brooklyn Bridge** (see pages 553–555), engineers used the new technology to construct the Williamsburg Bridge just to the north. More prosaic and utilitarian than its neighbor, the new bridge was never as acclaimed, but it was longer by four feet and completed in half the time. It became the model for future building as the age of steel supplanted the age of stone and iron.

Chicago, not New York, gave birth to the modern skyscraper. Rising from the ashes of the Great Fire of 1871, which destroyed three square miles and left eighteen thousand people homeless, Chicago offered a generation of skilled

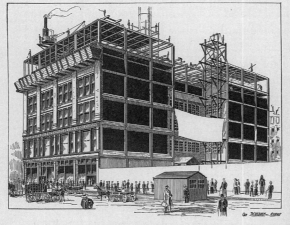

VIEW OF CONSTRUCTION OF "THE FAIR" BUILDING, CHICAGO.
Illustrating Paper by W. L. B. Jenney, Architect, published in this number.

Chicago Skyscraper Going Up
With the advent of structural steel, skyscrapers like this one in progress in Chicago in 1891 became prominent features of the American urban landscape. This architect's rendering of the Fair Building, a department store designed by William Le Baron Jenney, shows a modern skyscraper whose foundations supported the structural steel skeleton so that the walls could simply "hang" on the outside of the building, because they no longer had to support the structure.
Newberry Library (*Inland Architect*, Nov. 1891).

architects and engineers the chance to experiment. Commercial architecture became an art form at the hands of a skilled group of architects who together constituted the "Chicago school." Men of genius such as Louis Sullivan gave Chicago some of the world's finest commercial buildings. Employing the dictum "Form follows function," they built startlingly modern structures. A fitting symbol of modern America, the skyscraper expressed the domination of corporate power.

Alongside the skyscrapers rose new residential apartments for the rich and the middle class. The "French flat" — apartments with the latest plumbing and electricity — gained popularity in the 1880s as affluent city dwellers overcame their distaste for multifamily housing (which carried the stigma of the tenement) and gave in to "flat fever." "Housekeeping isn't fun," cried one New York woman. "Give us flats!" In 1883 alone, more than one thousand new apartments went up in Chicago.

Across the United States, municipal governments undertook public works on a scale never before seen. They paved streets, built sewers and water mains, replaced gas lamps with electric lights, ran trolley tracks on the old horsecar lines, and dug underground to build subways, tearing down the unsightly elevated tracks that had clogged city streets. In San Francisco, Andrew Smith Hallidie mastered the city's hills, building a system of cable cars in 1873. Boston completed the nation's first subway system in 1897, and New York and Philadelphia soon followed.

Cities became more beautiful with the creation of urban public parks to complement the new buildings that quickly filled city lots. Much of the credit for America's greatest parks goes to one man — landscape architect **Frederick Law Olmsted**. The indefatigable Olmsted designed parks in Atlanta, Boston, Brooklyn, Hartford, Detroit, Chicago, and Louisville, as well as the grounds for the U.S. Capitol. But he is best remembered for the creation of New York City's Central Park. Completed in 1873, it became the first landscaped public park in the United States. Olmsted and his partner, Calvert Vaux, directed the planting of more than five million trees, shrubs, and vines to transform the eight hundred acres between 59th and 110th streets into an oasis for urban dwellers. "We want a place," he wrote, where people "may stroll for an hour, seeing, hearing, and feeling nothing of the bustle and jar of the streets."

American cities did not overlook the mind in their efforts at improvement. They created a comprehensive free public school system that educated everyone from the children of the middle class to the sons and daughters of immigrant workers. Yet the exploding urban population strained the system and led to crowded and inadequate facilities. In 1899, more than 544,000 pupils attended school in New York's five boroughs. Municipalities across the United States provided free secondary school education for all who wished to attend, even though only 8 percent of Americans completed high school.

To educate those who couldn't go to school, American cities created the most extensive free public library system in the world. In 1895, the Boston Public Library opened its bronze doors under the inscription "Free to All." Designed in the style of a Renaissance palazzo, with more than 700,000 books on the shelves ready to be checked out, the library earned the description "a palace of the people."

Despite the Boston Public Library's legend "Free to All," the poor did not share equally in the advantages of city life. The parks, the libraries, and even the subways and sewers benefited some city dwellers more than others. Few library cards were held by Boston's laborers, who worked six days a week and found the library closed on Sunday. And in the 1890s, there was nothing central about New York's Central Park. It was a four-mile walk from the tenements of Hester Street to the park's entrance at 59th Street and Fifth Avenue. Then, as now, the comfortable majority, not the indigent minority, reaped a disproportionate share of the benefits in the nation's big cities.

Any story of the American city, it seems, must be a tale of two cities — or, given the cities' great diversity, a tale of many cities within each metropolis. At the turn of the twentieth century, a central paradox emerged: The enduring monuments of America's cities — the bridges, skyscrapers, parks, and libraries — stood as the undeniable achievements of the same system of municipal government that reformers dismissed as boss-ridden, criminal, and corrupt.

City Government and the "Bosses"

The physical growth of the cities required the expansion of public services and the creation of entirely new facilities: streets, subways, elevated trains, bridges, docks, sewers, and public utilities. There was work to be done and money to be made. The professional politician — the colorful big-city boss — became a phenomenon of urban growth and **bossism** a national phenomenon. Though corrupt and often criminal, the boss saw to the building of the city and provided needed social services for the new residents. Yet not even the big-city boss could be said to rule the unruly city. The governing of America's cities resembled more a tug-of-war than boss rule.

The most notorious of all the city bosses was **William Marcy "Boss" Tweed** of New York. At midcentury, Boss Tweed's Democratic Party "machine" held sway. A machine was really no more than a political party organized at the grassroots level. Its purpose was to win elections and reward its followers, often with jobs on the city's payroll. New York's citywide Democratic machine, **Tammany Hall**, commanded an army of party functionaries. At the bottom were district captains. In return for votes, they provided services for their constituents, everything from a scuttle of coal in the winter to housing for an evicted family. At the top were powerful ward bosses who distributed lucrative franchises for subways and streetcars. They formed a shadow government more powerful than the city's elected officials.

As chairman of the Tammany general committee, Tweed kept the Democratic Party together and ran the city through the use of bribery and graft. "As long as I count the votes," he shamelessly boasted, "what are you going to do about it?" The excesses of the Tweed ring soon led to a clamor for reform and cries of "Throw the rascals out." Cartoonist Thomas Nast pilloried Tweed in the pages of *Harper's Weekly*. His cartoons, easily understood even by those who could not read, did the boss more harm than hundreds of outraged editorials. Tweed's rule ended in 1871. Eventually, he was tried and convicted and later died in jail.

New York was not the only city to experience bossism and corruption. The British visitor James Bryce concluded in 1888, "There is no denying that the government of cities is the one conspicuous failure of the United States." More than 80 percent of the nation's thirty largest cities experienced some form of boss rule in the decades around the turn of the twentieth century. However, infighting among powerful ward bosses often meant that no single boss enjoyed exclusive power in the big cities.

Urban reformers and proponents of good government (derisively called "goo goos" by their rivals) challenged machine rule and sometimes succeeded in electing reform mayors. But the reformers rarely managed to stay in office for long. Their detractors called them "mornin' glories," observing that they "looked lovely in the mornin' and withered up in a short time." The bosses enjoyed continued success largely because the urban political machine helped the cities' immigrants and poor, who remained the bosses' staunchest allies. "What tells in holding your district," a Tammany ward boss observed, "is to go right down among the poor and help them in the different ways they need help. It's philanthropy, but it's politics, too — mighty good politics." Saloons were the epicenter of ward politics. They played a crucial role in workers' lives and often served informally as political headquarters, as well as employment agencies and union halls.

A few reform mayors managed to achieve success and longevity by following the bosses' model. **Hazen S. Pingree** of Detroit exemplified the successful reform mayor. A businessman who went into politics in the 1890s, Pingree, like most good-government candidates, promised to root out dishonesty and inefficiency. But when the depression of 1893 struck, Pingree emerged as a champion of the working class and the poor. He hired the unemployed to build schools, parks, and public baths. By providing jobs and needed services, he built a powerful political organization based on working-class support. Detroit's voters kept him in the mayor's office for four terms and then helped elect him governor twice.

The big-city boss, through the skillful orchestration of rewards, exerted powerful leverage and lined up support for his party from a broad range of constituents, from the urban poor to wealthy industrialists. In 1902, when journalist **Lincoln Steffens** began "The Shame of the Cities," a series of articles exposing city corruption, he found that business leaders who fastidiously refused to mingle socially with the bosses nevertheless struck deals with them. "He is a self-righteous fraud, this big businessman," Steffens concluded. "I found him buying boodlers [bribers] in St. Louis, defending grafters in Minneapolis, originating corruption in Pittsburgh, sharing with bosses in Philadelphia, deploring reform in Chicago, and beating good government with corruption funds in New York."

The complexity of big-city government, apparent in the many levels of corruption that Steffens uncovered, pointed to one conclusion: For all the color and flamboyance of the big-city boss, he was simply one of many actors in the drama of municipal government. Old-stock aristocrats, new professionals, saloonkeepers, pushcart peddlers, and politicians all fought for their interests in the hurly-burly of city government. They didn't much like each other, and they sometimes fought savagely. But they learned to live with one another. Compromise and accommodation — not boss rule — best characterized big-city government by the turn of the twentieth century, although the cities' reputation for corruption left an indelible mark on the consciousness of the American public.

White City or City of Sin?

Americans have always been of two minds about the city. They like to boast of its skyscrapers and bridges, its culture and sophistication, and they pride themselves on its bigness and bustle. At the same time, they fear it as the city of sin, the home of immigrant slums, the center of vice and crime. Nowhere did the divided view of the American city take form more graphically than in Chicago in 1893. In that year, Chicago hosted the **World's Columbian Exposition**, the grandest world's fair in the nation's history. The fairground on Lake Michigan offered a lesson in what Americans on the eve of the twentieth century imagined a city might be. Only five miles down the shore from downtown Chicago, the White City, as the fairground became known, seemed light-years away from Chicago, with its stockyards, slums, and bustling terminals. Frederick Law Olmsted and architect Daniel Burnham supervised the transformation of a swampy wasteland into a pristine paradise of lagoons, fountains, wooded islands, gardens, and imposing buildings.

"Sell the cookstove if necessaray and come," novelist Hamlin Garland wrote to his parents on the farm. And come they did, in spite of the panic and depression that broke out only weeks after the fair opened in May 1893. In six months, fairgoers purchased more than 27 million tickets, turning a profit of nearly a half million dollars for promoters. Visitors from home and abroad strolled the elaborate grounds and visited the exhibits — everything from a model of the Brooklyn Bridge carved in soap to the latest goods and inventions. Half carnival, half culture, the great fair offered something for everyone. On the Midway Plaisance, crowds thrilled to the massive wheel built by Mr. Ferris and watched agog as Little Egypt danced the hootchy-kootchy.

In October, the fair closed its doors in the midst of the worst depression the country had yet seen. During the winter of 1894, Chicago's unemployed and homeless took over the grounds, vandalized the buildings, and frightened the city's comfortable citizens out of their wits. When reporters asked Daniel Burnham what should be done with the moldering remains of the White City, he responded, "It should be torched." And it was. In July 1894, in a clash between federal troops and striking railway workers, incendiaries set fires that leveled the fairgrounds.

In the end, the White City remained what it had always been, a dreamscape. Buildings that looked like marble were actually constructed of staff, a plaster substance that began to crumble even before fire destroyed the fairgrounds. Perhaps it was not so strange, after all, that the legacy of the White City could be found on Coney Island, where two new amusement parks, Luna and Dreamland, sought to combine, albeit in a more tawdry form, the beauty of the White City and the thrill of the Midway Plaisance. More enduring than the White City itself was what it represented: the emergent industrial might of the United States, at home and abroad, with its inventions, manufactured goods, and growing consumer culture.

> **REVIEW** How did municipal governments respond to the challenges of urban expansion?

▶ Conclusion: Who Built the Cities?

As much as the great industrialists and financiers, as much as eminent engineers like John and Washington Roebling, common workers, most of them immigrants, built the nation's cities. The unprecedented growth of urban, industrial America resulted from the labor of millions of men, women, and children who toiled in workshops and factories, in sweatshops and mines, on railroads and construction sites across America.

America's cities in the late nineteenth century teemed with life. Immigrants and blue bloods, poor laborers and millionaires, middle-class managers and corporate moguls, secretaries, salesgirls, sweatshop laborers, and society matrons lived in the cities and contributed to their growth. Town houses and tenements jostled for space with skyscrapers and great department stores, while parks, ball fields, amusement arcades, and public libraries provided the city masses with recreation and entertainment.

Municipal governments, straining to build the new cities, experienced the rough-and-tumble of machine politics as bosses and their constituents looked to profit from city growth. Reformers deplored the graft and corruption that accompanied the rise of the cities. But they were rarely able to oust the party bosses for long because they failed to understand the services the political machines provided for their largely immigrant and poor constituents; nor did reformers account for the ties between city politicians and wealthy businessmen who sought to benefit from franchises and contracts.

For America's workers, urban industrialism along with the rise of big business and corporate consolidation drastically changed the workplace. Industrialists replaced skilled workers with new machines that could be operated by cheaper unskilled labor. And during hard times, employers did not hesitate to cut workers' already meager wages. As the Great Railroad Strike of 1877 demonstrated, when labor united, it could bring the nation to attention. Organization held out the best hope for the workers; first the Knights of Labor and later the American Federation of Labor won converts among the nation's working class.

The rise of urban industrialism challenged the American promise, which for decades had been dominated by Jeffersonian agrarian ideals. Could such a promise exist in the changing world of cities, tenements, immigrants, and huge corporations? In the great depression that came in the 1890s, mounting anger and frustration would lead farmers and workers to join forces and create a grassroots movement to fight for change under the banner of a new People's Party.

Reviewing Chapter 19

REVIEW QUESTIONS

1. Why did American cities experience explosive growth in the late nineteenth century? (pp. 555–564)

2. How did business expansion and consolidation change workers' occupations in the late nineteenth century? (pp. 564–570)

3. Why did the fortunes of the Knights of Labor rise in the late 1870s and decline in the 1890s? (pp. 570–575)

4. How did urban industrialism shape the world of leisure? (pp. 575–577)

5. How did municipal governments respond to the challenges of urban expansion? (pp. 578–583)

MAKING CONNECTIONS

1. Americans expressed both wonder and concern at the nation's mushrooming cities. Why did cities provoke such divergent responses? In your answer, discuss the dramatic demographic, environmental, and political developments associated with urbanization.

2. Why did patterns of immigration to the United States in the late nineteenth century change? How did Americans respond to the immigrants who arrived late in the century? In your answer, consider how industrial capitalism, nationally and globally, contributed to these developments.

3. How did urban industrialization affect Americans' lives outside of work? Describe the impact of late-nineteenth-century economic developments on home life and leisure. In your answer, consider how class, race, gender, and ethnicity contributed to diverse urban experiences.

4. When workers began to embrace organization in the late 1870s, what did they hope to accomplish? Were they successful? Why or why not? In your answer, discuss both general conditions and specific events that shaped these developments.

LINKING TO THE PAST

1. Compare the lives of migrant workers and industrial cowboys in the West to workers in the nation's cities. What are the major similarities? (See chapter 17.)

2. You have already looked at the development of America's industries in the nineteenth century from the vantage point of moguls such as Andrew Carnegie and John D. Rockefeller. How does your view of industrialism change when the focus is shifted to the nation's workers? (See chapter 18.)

TIMELINE 1869–1897

1869
- Knights of Labor founded.
- Cincinnati mounts first paid baseball team, the Red Stockings.

1871
- Boss Tweed's rule in New York ends.
- Chicago's Great Fire.

1873
- Panic on Wall Street touches off depression.
- San Francisco's cable car system opens.

1877
- Great Railroad Strike.

1880s
- Immigration from southern and eastern Europe rises.

1882
- Chinese Exclusion Act.

1883
- Brooklyn Bridge opens.

1886
- American Federation of Labor (AFL) founded.
- Haymarket bombing.

1890s
- African American migration from the South begins.

1890
- Jacob Riis publishes *How the Other Half Lives*.

1892
- Ellis Island opens in New York harbor to process immigrants.

1893
- World's Columbian Exposition.
- Panic on Wall Street touches off major economic depression.

1895
- Boston Public Library opens.

1896
- President Grover Cleveland vetoes immigrant literacy test.

1897
- Steeplechase Park opens on Coney Island.
- Nation's first subway system opens in Boston.

▶ FOR AN ONLINE BIBLIOGRAPHY, PRACTICE QUIZZES, WEB SITES, IMAGES, AND DOCUMENTS RELATED TO THIS CHAPTER, see the Book Companion Site at **bedfordstmartins.com/roarkvalue**.

▶ FOR DOCUMENTS RELATED TO THIS PERIOD, see Michael Johnson, ed., *Reading the American Past*, Fifth Edition.

Dissent, Depression, and War

1890–1900

FRANCES WILLARD TRAVELED TO ST. LOUIS IN FEBRUARY 1892 WITH HIGH
hopes. Political change was in the air, and Willard was there to help fashion a
new reform party, one that she hoped would embrace her two passions —
temperance and woman suffrage. As head of the Woman's Christian
Temperance Union, an organization with members in every state and territory
in the nation, Willard wielded considerable clout. At her invitation, twenty-
eight of the country's leading reformers had already met in Chicago to draft a
set of principles to bring to St. Louis. Always expedient, Willard had settled for
a statement condemning the saloon rather than an endorsement for a stronger
measure to prohibit the sale of alcohol. But at the convention, she hoped to
press the case for woman suffrage and prohibition. Willard knew it would not
be easy, but in the heady atmosphere of 1892 she determined to try. No
American woman before her had played such a central role in a political movement. At the height of her political power, Willard took her place among the
leaders on the podium in St. Louis.

Exposition Music Hall presented a colorful spectacle. "The banners of the
different states rose above the delegates throughout the hall, fluttering like
the flags over an army encamped," wrote one reporter. The fiery orator
Ignatius Donnelly attacked the money kings of Wall Street. Mary Elizabeth
Lease, a veteran campaigner from Kansas known for exhorting farmers to

586

Frances Willard
Frances Willard, the forward-thinking leader of the Woman's Christian Temperance Union, learned to ride a bicycle at age fifty-three. The bicycle became hugely popular in the 1890s, even though traditionalists fulminated that it was unladylike for women to straddle a bike and immodest for them to wear the divided skirts that allowed them to pedal. Shown here in 1895, Willard declared bicycling a "harmless pleasure" that encouraged "clear heads and steady hands." Willard brought her progressive ideas to the People's Party 1892 convention, where she shared a place on the platform with the new party's leaders. Photo: Courtesy of the Frances E. Willard Memorial Library and Archives (WCTU).

"raise less corn and more hell," added her powerful voice to the cause. Terence V. Powderly, head of the Knights of Labor, called on workers to join hands with farmers against the "nonproducing classes." Frances Willard urged the crowd to outlaw the liquor traffic and give the vote to women. Between speeches, the crowd sang labor songs like "Hurrah for the Toiler" and "All Hail the Power of Laboring Men."

Over the next few days, delegates hammered out a series of demands, breathtaking in their scope. They tackled the tough questions of the day — the regulation of business, the need for banking and currency reform, the right of labor to organize and bargain collectively, and the role of the federal government in regulating business, curbing monopoly, and guaranteeing democracy. But the new party determined to stick to economic issues and resisted endorsing either temperance or woman suffrage. As a member of the platform committee, Willard fought for both and complained of the "crooked methods . . . employed to scuttle these planks." Outmaneuvered in committee, she brought the issues to the floor of the convention, only to go down to defeat by a vote of 352 to 238.

Despite Willard's disappointment, the convention ended its work amid a chorus of cheers. According to one eyewitness, "Hats, paper, handkerchiefs, etc., were thrown into the air; . . . cheer after cheer thundered and reverberated through the vast hall reaching the outside of the building where thousands who had been waiting the outcome joined in the applause till for blocks in every direction the exultation made the din indescribable."

What was all the shouting about? The cheering crowd was celebrating the birth of a new political party, officially named the People's Party. Fed up with the Democrats and Republicans, a broad coalition of groups came together in St. Louis to fight for change. They resolved to reconvene in Omaha in July to nominate candidates for the upcoming presidential election. Defeated but not willing to abandon the new party, Willard resolved to work for the nomination of a presidential candidate committed to temperance and suffrage.

The St. Louis gathering marked an early milestone in one of the most turbulent decades in U.S. history. Unrest, agitation, agrarian revolt, labor strikes, a severe financial panic and depression, and a war of expansion shook the 1890s. As the decade opened, Americans dissatisfied with the two major political parties were already flocking to organizations including the Farmers' Alliance, the American Federation of Labor, and the Woman's Christian Temperance Union, and they worked together to create the political alliance that gave birth to the People's (or Populist) Party. In a decade of unrest and uncertainty, the People's Party countered laissez-faire economics by insisting that the federal government play a more active role to ensure greater economic equity in industrial America.

This challenge to the status quo culminated in 1896 in one of the most hotly contested presidential elections in the nation's history. At the close of the tumultuous decade, the Spanish-American War helped to bring the country together, with Americans rallying to support the troops. But disagreement over American imperialism and overseas expansion raised questions about the nation's role on the world stage as the United States stood poised to enter the twentieth century.

▶ The Farmers' Revolt

Hard times in the 1880s and 1890s created a groundswell of agrarian revolt. A bitter farmer wrote from Minnesota, "I settled on this Land in good Faith Built House and Barn. Broken up Part of the Land. Spent years of hard Labor in grubbing fencing and Improving." About to lose his farm to foreclosure, he lamented, "Are they going to drive us out like trespassers . . . and give us away to the Corporations?"

Crop prices for the nation's six million farmers fell decade after decade, even as their share of the world market grew. In parts of Kansas, wheat sold for so little that angry farmers burned their crops for fuel rather than take them to market. At the same time, consumer prices soared. Farmers couldn't make ends meet. In Kansas alone, almost half the farms had fallen into the hands of the banks by 1894 through foreclosure.

The Farmers' Alliance

At the heart of the farmers' problems stood a banking system dominated by eastern commercial banks committed to the gold standard, a railroad rate system that was capricious and unfair, and rampant speculation that drove up the price of land. In the West, farmers rankled under a system that allowed railroads to charge them exorbitant freight rates while granting rebates to large shippers (see chapter 18). In the South, lack of currency and credit drove farmers to the stopgap credit system of the crop lien, turning the entire region into "a vast pawn shop." Determined to do something, farmers banded together to fight for change.

Farm protest was not new. In the 1870s, farmers had supported the Grange and the Greenback Labor Party. As the farmers' situation grew more desperate, they organized, forming regional alliances. The first **Farmers' Alliance** came together in Lampasas County, Texas, to fight "landsharks and horse thieves." During the 1880s, the movement spread rapidly. In frontier farmhouses in Texas, in log cabins in the backwoods of Arkansas, and in the rural parishes of Louisiana, separate groups of farmers formed similar alliances for self-help.

As the movement grew, farmers' groups consolidated into two regional alliances: the Northwestern Farmers' Alliance, active in Kansas, Nebraska, and other midwestern Granger states; and the more radical Southern Farmers' Alliance. In the 1880s, traveling lecturers preached the Alliance message. Worn-out men and careworn women did not need to be convinced that something was wrong. By 1887, the Southern Farmers' Alliance had grown to more than 200,000 members, and by 1890 it counted more than 3 million members.

Radical in its inclusiveness, the Southern Alliance reached out to African Americans, women, and industrial workers. Through cooperation with the **Colored Farmers' Alliance**, an African American group founded in Texas in the 1880s, blacks and whites attempted to make common cause. As Georgia's Tom Watson, a Southern Alliance stalwart, pointed out, "The colored tenant is in the same boat as the white tenant, . . . and . . . the accident of color can make no difference in the interests of farmers, croppers, and laborers."

The political culture of the Alliance encouraged the inclusion of women and children and used the family as its defining symbol. Women rallied to the Alliance banner along with their menfolk, drawn to meetings that combined picnic, parade, revival, country fair, and political convention. "I am going to work for prohibition, the Alliance, and for Jesus as long as I live," swore one woman.

In wagon trains, men and women in the thousands thronged to Alliance meetings to listen to speeches and to debate and discuss the issues of the day. The Alliance leaders aimed to do more than exhort their followers; they aimed to educate them. The Farmers' Alliance produced and distributed "a perfect avalanche of literature" — speeches, newspapers, books, and tracts — full of damning details about the political collusion between business and politics, along with detailed analyses of the securities and commodities markets, the tariff and international trade, and credit and currency. Alliance lecturers reached out to the illiterate, often speaking for hours under the broiling sun to educate their rapt audiences on the fine points of economics and politics.

At the heart of the Alliance movement stood a series of farmers' cooperatives. By "bulking" their cotton — that is, selling it together — farmers could negotiate a better price. And by setting up trade stores and exchanges, they sought to escape the grasp of the merchant/creditor. Through the cooperatives, the Farmers' Alliance promised to change the way farmers lived. "We are going to get out of debt and be free and independent people once more," exulted one Georgia farmer.

Cooperatives sprang up throughout the South and West. But the Alliance faced insurmountable difficulties in running successful cooperatives. Opposition by merchants, bankers, wholesalers, and manufacturers made it impossible for the cooperatives to get credit. As the cooperative movement died, the Farmers' Alliance moved toward direct political action. Confounded by the failure of the Democrats and Republicans to break with commercial interests and support the farmers, Alliance leaders moved, often reluctantly, toward the formation of a third party.

The Populist Movement

In the earliest days of the Alliance movement, a leader of the Southern Farmers' Alliance insisted, "The Alliance is a strictly white man's nonpolitical, secret business association." But by 1892, it was none of those things. Advocates of a third party carried the day at the convention of laborers, farmers, and common folk in 1892 in St. Louis, where the Farmers' Alliance gave birth to the **People's Party** and launched the Populist movement. "There is something at the back of all this turmoil more than the failure of crops or the scarcity of ready cash," a journalist observed in 1892.

The same spirit of religious revival that animated the Farmers' Alliance infused the People's Party. The Populists built on the work of the Alliance to mount a critique of industrial society and a call for action. Convinced that the money and banking systems worked to the advantage of the wealthy few, they demanded economic democracy. To help farmers get the credit they needed at reasonable rates, southern farmers hit on the ingenious idea of a **subtreasury** — a plan that would allow farmers to store their nonperishable crops until prices rose and to receive commodity credit from the federal government to obtain needed supplies. The subtreasury promised to get rid of the crop lien system once and for all. Although the idea would be enacted piecemeal in progressive and New Deal legislation in the twentieth century, conservatives in the 1890s dismissed it as far-fetched "corn tassel communism."

To the western farmer, the Populists promised land reform, championing a plan that would claim excessive land granted to railroads or sold to foreign investors. The Populists' boldest proposal called for government ownership of the railroads and the telegraph system to put an end to discriminatory rates. Citing examples of how the powerful railroads had corrupted the political system, the Populists did not shrink from advocating what their opponents branded state socialism.

The Populists also demanded currency reform. Farmers in all sections rallied to the cry for cheaper currency, calling for free silver and greenbacks — attempts to increase the nation's tight money supply and thus make credit easier to obtain. And to empower the common people, the Populist platform called for the direct election of senators (then chosen by state legislatures) and for other electoral reforms, including the secret ballot and the right to initiate legislation, to recall elected officials, and to submit issues to the people by means of a referendum. Because the Populists shared common cause with labor against corporate interests, they also supported the eight-hour workday and an end to contract labor.

The sweeping array of Populist reforms enacted in the Populist platform changed the agenda of politics for decades to come. More than just a response to hard times, Populism presented an alternative vision of American economic democracy.

REVIEW   Why did American farmers organize alliances in the late nineteenth century?

▶ The Labor Wars

While farmers united to fight for change, industrial laborers fought their own battles in a series of bloody strikes so fiercely waged on both sides that historians have called them the "labor wars." Industrial workers felt increasingly threatened as businesses combined into huge corporations, and in the 1890s labor took a stand. At issue was the right of workers to organize and to speak through unions to bargain collectively and fight for better working conditions, higher wages, shorter hours, and greater worker control in the face of increased mechanization.

Three major conflicts of the period — the lockout of steelworkers in Homestead, Pennsylvania, in 1892; the miners' strike in Cripple Creek, Colorado, in 1894; and the Pullman strike in Illinois that same year — raised fundamental questions about the rights of labor and the sanctity of private property.

The Homestead Lockout

In 1892, steelworkers in Pennsylvania squared off against Andrew Carnegie in a decisive struggle over the right to organize in the Homestead steel mills. Carnegie was unusual among industrialists as a self-styled friend of labor. In 1886, he had written, "The right of the workingmen to combine and to form trade unions is no less sacred than the right of the manufacturer to enter into associations and conferences with his fellows."

Yet as much as he cherished his liberal beliefs, Carnegie cherished his profits more. In 1892, Carnegie resolved to crush the Amalgamated Iron and Steel

Workers, one of the largest and richest craft unions in the American Federation of Labor (AFL). When the Amalgamated attempted to renew its contract at Carnegie's Homestead mill, its leaders were told that since "the vast majority of our employees are Non union, the Firm has decided that the minority must give place to the majority." While it was true that only 800 skilled workers belonged to the elite Amalgamated, the union had long enjoyed the support of the plant's 3,000 non-union workers. Slavs, who did much of the unskilled work, made common cause with the Welsh, Scottish, and Irish skilled workers who belonged to the union. Never before had the Amalgamated been denied a contract.

Carnegie preferred not to be directly involved in the union busting that lay on the horizon, so that spring he sailed to Scotland and left **Henry Clay Frick**, the toughest antilabor man in the industry, in charge of the Homestead plant. By summer, a strike looked inevitable. Frick prepared by erecting a fifteen-foot fence around the plant and topping it with barbed wire. Workers aptly dubbed it "Fort Frick." To defend his fort and protect strikebreakers, Frick hired 316 mercenaries from the Pinkerton National Detective Agency at the rate of $5 per day, more than double the wage of the average Homestead worker.

The Pinkerton Agency, founded before the Civil War, came into its own in the 1880s as a private security force for hire. Pinkerton agents were a motley crew, recruited from all levels of society, from urban thugs to college boys. The "Pinks" earned the hatred of workers by protecting strikebreakers and acting as company spies.

On June 28, the **Homestead lockout** began when Frick locked the workers out of the mills and prepared to bring in strikebreakers, whom the workers derogatorily referred to as "scabs." Hugh O'Donnell, the young Irishman who led the union, vowed to prevent scabs from entering the plant. On July 6 at 4 a.m., a lookout spotted two barges moving up the Monongahela River in the fog. Frick was attempting to smuggle Pinkertons into Homestead.

Workers sounded the alarm, and within minutes a crowd of more than a thousand, hastily armed with rifles, hoes, and fence posts, rushed to the riverbank to meet the enemy. When the Pinkertons attempted to come ashore, gunfire broke out, and more than a dozen Pinkertons and some thirty strikers fell, killed or wounded. The Pinkertons retreated to the barges. For twelve hours, the workers, joined by their family members, threw everything they had at the barges, from fireworks to dynamite. Finally, the Pinkertons hoisted a white flag and arranged with O'Donnell to surrender. With three workers dead and scores wounded, the crowd, numbering perhaps ten thousand, was in no mood for conciliation. As the hated "Pinks" came up the hill, they were forced to run a gantlet of screaming, cursing men, women, and children. When a young guard dropped to his knees, weeping for mercy, a woman used her umbrella to poke out his eye. One Pinkerton had been killed in the siege on the barges. In the grim rout that followed their surrender, not one avoided injury.

The "battle of Fort Frick" ended in a dubious victory for the workers. They took control of the plant and elected a council to run the community. At first, public opinion favored their cause. Newspapers urged Frick to negotiate or submit to arbitration. A congressman castigated Carnegie for "skulking in his castle in Scotland." Populists, meeting in St. Louis, condemned the use of "hireling armies."

The action of the Homestead workers struck at the heart of the capitalist system, pitting the workers' right to their jobs against the rights of private property. The workers' insistence that "we are not destroying the property of the company — merely protecting our rights" did not prove as compelling to the courts and the state as the property rights of the mill owners. Four days after the confrontation, Pennsylvania's governor, who sympathized with the workers, nonetheless yielded to pressure from Frick and ordered eight thousand National Guard troops into Homestead to protect Carnegie's property. The strikers, thinking they had nothing to fear from the militia, welcomed the troops with a brass band. But they soon understood the reality. The troops' ninety-five-day occupation not only protected Carnegie's property but also enabled Frick to reopen the mills and bring in strikebreakers. "We have been deceived," one worker complained bitterly. "We have stood idly by and let the town be occupied by soldiers who come here, not as our protectors, but as the protectors of non-union men. . . . If we undertake to resist the seizure of our jobs, we will be shot down like dogs."

Then, in a misguided effort to ignite a general uprising, **Alexander Berkman**, a Russian immigrant and anarchist, attempted to assassinate Frick. Berkman bungled his attempt. Shot twice and stabbed with a dagger, Frick survived and showed considerable courage, allowing a doctor to remove the bullets but refusing to leave his desk until the day's work was completed. "I do not think that I shall die," Frick remarked coolly, "but whether I do or not, the Company will pursue the same policy and it will win." After the assassination attempt, public opinion turned against the workers. Berkman was quickly tried and sentenced to prison. Although the Amalgamated and the AFL denounced his action, the incident linked anarchism and unionism, already associated in the public mind as a result of the Haymarket bombing in 1886 (see chapter 19). Hugh O'Donnell later wrote, "The bullet from Berkman's pistol, failing in its foul intent, went straight through the heart of the Homestead strike."

In the end, the workers capitulated. The Homestead mill reopened in November, and the men returned to work, except for the union leaders, now blacklisted in every steel mill in the country. With the owners firmly in charge, the company slashed wages, reinstated the twelve-hour day, and eliminated five hundred jobs.

In the drama of events at Homestead, the significance of what occurred often remained obscured: The workers at Homestead had been taught a lesson. They would never again, in the words of the National Guard commander, "believe the works are their's [sic] quite as much as Carnegie's." Another forty-five years would pass before steelworkers, unskilled as well as skilled, successfully unionized. In the meantime, Carnegie's production tripled, even in the midst of a depression. "Ashamed to tell you profits these days," Carnegie wrote a friend in 1899. And no wonder: Carnegie's profits had grown from $4 million in 1892 to $40 million in 1900.

The Cripple Creek Miners' Strike of 1894

Less than a year after the Homestead lockout, a panic on Wall Street in the spring of 1893 touched off a bitter economic depression. In the West, silver mines fell on hard times, leading to the **Cripple Creek miners' strike of 1894**. When mine owners moved to lengthen the workday from eight to ten hours, the newly formed Western Federation of Miners (WFM) vowed to hold the line in Cripple Creek, Colorado. In February 1894, the WFM threatened to strike all mines working more than eight-hour shifts. The mine owners divided: Some quickly settled with the WFM; others continued to demand ten hours, provoking a strike.

The striking miners received help from many quarters. Working miners paid $15 a month to a strike fund, and miners in neighboring districts sent substantial contributions. The miners enjoyed the support and assistance of local businesses and grocers, who provided credit to the strikers. With these advantages, the Cripple Creek strikers could afford to hold out for their demands.

Even more significant, Governor Davis H. Waite, a Populist elected in 1892, had strong ties to the miners and refused to use the power of the state against the strikers. Governor Waite asked the strikers to lay down their arms and demanded that the mine owners disperse their hired deputies. The miners agreed to arbitration and selected Waite as their sole arbitrator. By May, the recalcitrant mine owners capitulated, and the union won an eight-hour day.

Governor Waite's intervention demonstrated the pivotal power of the state in the nation's labor wars. Having a Populist in power made a difference. A decade later, in 1904, with Waite out of office, mine owners relied on state troops to take back control of the mines, defeating the WFM and blacklisting all of its members. In retrospect, the Cripple Creek miners' strike of 1894 proved the exception to the rule of state intervention on the side of private property. More typical was the outcome of another strike in 1894 in Pullman, Illinois.

Eugene V. Debs and the Pullman Strike

The economic depression that began in 1893 swelled the ranks of the unemployed to three million, almost half of the working population. "A fearful crisis is upon us," wrote a labor publication. Nowhere were workers more demoralized than in the model town of Pullman, on the outskirts of Chicago.

In the wake of the Great Railroad Strike of 1877, **George M. Pullman**, the builder of Pullman railroad cars, had moved his plant and workers away from the "snares of the great city." In 1880, he purchased 4,300 acres nine miles south of Chicago and built a model town. The town of Pullman boasted parks, fountains, playgrounds, an auditorium, a library, a hotel, shops, and markets, along with 1,800 units of housing. Noticeably absent was a saloon.

The housing in Pullman was clearly superior to that in neighboring areas, but workers paid a high price to live in the model town. George M. Pullman expected a 6 percent return on his investment. As a result, Pullman's rents ran 10 to 20 percent higher than housing costs in nearby communities. And a family in

A Pullman Craftsworker

Pullman Palace cars were known for their luxurious details. Here, a painter working in the 1890s applies elaborate decoration to the exterior of a Pullman car. In the foreground is an intricately carved door, an example of fine hand-detailing. The Pullman workers' strike in 1894 stemmed in part from the company's efforts to undermine the status of craftsworkers by reducing them to low-paid piecework. Control of the workplace, as much as issues related to wages and hours, fueled the labor wars of the 1890s. Chicago Historical Society.

Pullman could never own its own home. George Pullman refused to "sell an acre under any circumstances." As long as he controlled the town absolutely, he held the powerful whip of eviction over his employees and could quickly get rid of "troublemakers." Although observers at first praised the beauty and orderliness of the town, critics by the 1890s compared Pullman's model town to a "gilded cage" for workers.

The depression brought hard times to Pullman. Workers saw their wages slashed five times between May and December 1893, with cuts totaling at least 28 percent. At the same time, Pullman refused to lower the rents in his model town, insisting that "the renting of the dwellings and the employment of workmen at Pullman are in no way tied together." When workers went to the bank to cash their paychecks, they found that the rent had been taken out. One worker discovered only forty-seven cents in his pay envelope for two weeks' work. When the bank teller asked him whether he wanted to apply it to his back rent, he retorted, "If Mr. Pullman needs that forty-seven cents worse than I do, let him have it." At the same time, Pullman continued to pay his stockholders an 8 percent dividend, and the company accumulated a $25 million surplus.

At the heart of the labor problems at Pullman lay not only economic inequity but also the company's attempt to control the work process, substituting piecework for day wages and undermining skilled craftsworkers. The Pullman workers rebelled. During the spring of 1894, Pullman's desperate workers, seeking help, flocked to the ranks of the **American Railway Union** (ARU), led by the charis- matic **Eugene V. Debs**. The ARU, unlike the skilled craft unions of the AFL, pledged to organize all railway workers — from engineers to engine wipers. "It has been my life's desire," wrote Debs, "to unify railroad employees and to eliminate the aristocracy of labor, which unfortunately exists, and organize them so all will be on an equality." The ARU's belief in industrial democracy, however, was not matched by a commitment to racial equality; by a narrow margin, union members voted to exclude African American workers.

George Pullman responded to union organization at his plant by firing three of the union's leaders the day after they led a delegation to protest wage cuts. Angry men and women walked off the job in disgust. What began as a spontane- ous protest in May 1894 quickly blossomed into a strike that involved more than 90 percent of Pullman's 3,300 workers. "We do not know what the outcome will be, and in fact we do not much care," one worker confessed. "We do know that we are working for less wages than will maintain ourselves and families in the necessaries of life, and on that proposition we refuse to work any longer." Pullman countered by shutting down the plant.

In June, the Pullman strikers appealed to the ARU to come to their aid. Debs hesitated to commit his fledgling union to a major strike in the midst of a depression. He pleaded with the workers to find another solution. But when George Pullman adamantly refused arbitration, the ARU membership voted to boycott all Pullman cars. Beginning on June 29, switchmen across the United States refused to handle any train that carried Pullman cars.

The conflict escalated quickly. The General Managers Association (GMA), an organization of managers from twenty-four different railroads, acted in concert to quash the **Pullman boycott**. Determined to kill the ARU, they recruited strikebreakers and fired all the protesting switchmen. Their tactics set off a chain reaction. Entire train crews walked off the job in a show of solidarity with the Pullman workers. In a matter of days, the boycott/strike spread to more than fifteen railroads and affected twenty-seven states and territories. By July 2, rail lines from New York to California lay paralyzed. Even the GMA was forced to concede that the railroads had been "fought to a standstill."

The boycott remained surprisingly peaceful. In contrast to the Great Railroad Strike of 1877, no major riots broke out, and no serious property damage occurred. Debs, in a whirlwind of activity, fired off telegrams to all parts of the country advising his followers to avoid violence and respect law and order. But the na- tion's newspapers, fed press releases by the GMA, distorted the issues and mis- represented the strike. Across the country, papers ran headlines like "Wild Riot in Chicago" and "Mob Is in Control."

In Washington, Attorney General Richard B. Olney, a lawyer with strong ties to the railroads, determined to put down the strike. In his way stood the governor of Illinois, John Peter Altgeld, who, observing that the boycott remained peaceful, refused to call out troops. To get around Altgeld, Olney convinced President Grover Cleveland that federal troops had to intervene to protect the mails. To further cripple the boycott, two conservative Chicago judges issued an injunction so sweeping that it prohibited Debs from speaking in public. By issuing the injunction, the court made the boycott a crime punishable by a jail sentence for contempt of court, a civil process that did not require a jury trial. Even the conservative *Chicago Tribune* judged the injunction "a menace to liberty . . . a weapon ever ready for the capitalist." Furious, Debs risked jail by refusing to honor it.

Olney's strategy worked. President Grover Cleveland called out the army. On July 5, nearly 8,000 troops marched into Chicago. The GMA was jubilant. "It has now become a fight between the United States Government and the American Railway Union," a spokesman observed, "and we shall leave them to fight it out." Violence immediately erupted. In one day, troops killed 25 workers and wounded more than 60. In the face of bullets and bayonets, the strikers held firm. "Troops cannot move trains," Debs reminded his followers, a fact that was borne out as the railroads remained paralyzed despite the military intervention. But if the army could not put down the boycott, the injunction could and did. Debs was arrested and imprisoned for contempt of court. With its leader in jail, its headquarters raided and ransacked, and its members demoralized, the ARU was defeated along with the boycott. Pullman reopened his factory, hiring new workers to replace many of the strikers and leaving 1,600 workers without jobs.

In the aftermath of the strike, a special commission investigated the events at Pullman, taking testimony from 107 witnesses, from the lowliest workers to George M. Pullman himself. Stubborn and self-righteous, Pullman spoke for the business orthodoxy of his era, steadfastly affirming the right of business to safeguard its interests through confederacies such as the GMA and at the same time denying labor's right to organize. "If we were to receive these men as representatives of the union," he stated, "they could probably force us to pay any wages which they saw fit."

From his jail cell, Eugene Debs reviewed the events of the Pullman strike. With the courts and the government ready to side with industrialists in the interest of defending private property, Debs realized that labor had little recourse. Strikes seemed futile, and unions remained helpless; workers would have to take control of the state itself. Debs went into jail a trade unionist and came out six months later a socialist. At first, he turned to the Populist Party, but after its demise he formed the Socialist Party in 1900 and ran for president on its ticket five times. Debs's dissatisfaction with the status quo was shared by another group even more alienated from the political process — women.

REVIEW What tactics led to the defeat of the strikers in the 1890s? Where were they able to succeed and why?

▶ Women's Activism

"Do everything," **Frances Willard** urged her followers in 1881 (see pages 586–588). The new president of the Woman's Christian Temperance Union (WCTU) meant what she said. The WCTU followed a trajectory that was common for women in the late nineteenth century. As women organized to deal with issues that touched their homes and families, they moved into politics, lending new urgency to the cause of woman suffrage. Urban industrialism dislocated women's lives no less than men's. Like men, women sought political change and organized to promote issues central to their lives, campaigning for temperance and woman suffrage.

Frances Willard and the Woman's Christian Temperance Union

A visionary leader, Frances Willard spoke for a group left almost entirely out of the U.S. electoral process. In 1890, only one state, Wyoming, allowed women to vote in national elections. But lack of the franchise did not mean that women were apolitical. The WCTU demonstrated the breadth of women's political activity in the late nineteenth century.

Women supported the temperance movement because they felt particularly vulnerable to the effects of drunkenness. Dependent on men's wages, women and children suffered when money went for drink. The drunken, abusive husband epitomized the evils of a nation in which women remained second-class citizens. The WCTU, composed entirely of women, viewed all women's interests as essentially the same and therefore did not hesitate to use the singular *woman* to emphasize gender solidarity. Although mostly white and middle-class, WCTU members resolved to speak for their entire sex.

When Frances Willard became president in 1879, she radically changed the direction of the organization. Social action replaced prayer as women's answer to the threat of drunkenness. Viewing alcoholism as a disease rather than a sin and poverty as a cause rather than a result of drink, the WCTU became involved in labor issues, joining with the Knights of Labor to press for better working conditions for women workers. Describing workers in a textile mill, a WCTU member wrote in the organization's *Union Signal* magazine, "It is dreadful to see these girls, stripped almost to the skin . . . and running like racehorses from the beginning to the end of the day." She concluded, "The hard slavish work is drawing the girls into the saloon."

Willard capitalized on the cult of domesticity as a shrewd political tactic to move women into public life and gain power to ameliorate social problems. Using "home protection" as her watchword, she argued as early as 1884 that women needed the vote to protect home and family. By the 1890s, the WCTU's grassroots network of local unions had spread to all but the most isolated rural areas of the country. Strong and rich, with more than 200,000 dues-paying members, the WCTU was a formidable group.

Willard worked to create a broad reform coalition in the 1890s, embracing the Knights of Labor, the People's Party, and the Prohibition Party. Until her death in 1898, she led, if not a woman's rights movement, then the first organized mass movement of women united around a women's issue. By 1900, thanks largely to the WCTU, women could claim a generation of experience in political action — speaking, lobbying, organizing, drafting legislation, and running private charitable institu-tions. As Willard observed, "All this work has tended more toward the liberation of women than it has toward the extinction of the saloon."

Elizabeth Cady Stanton, Susan B. Anthony, and the Movement for Woman Suffrage

Unlike the WCTU, the organized movement for woman suffrage remained small and relatively weak in the late nineteenth century. The U.S. woman's rights movement was begun by **Elizabeth Cady Stanton** at the first woman's rights convention in the United States, at Seneca Falls, New York, in 1848. Women's rights advocates split in 1867 over whether the Fourteenth and Fifteenth Amendments, which granted voting rights to African American males, should have extended the vote to women as well. Stanton and her ally, **Susan B. Anthony**, launched the National Woman Suffrage Association in 1869, demanding the vote for women (see chapter 18). A more conservative group, the American Woman Suffrage Association (AWSA), formed the same year. Composed of men as well as women, the AWSA believed that women should vote in local but not national elections.

By 1890, the split had healed, and the newly united **National American Woman Suffrage Association** (NAWSA) launched campaigns on the state level to gain the vote for women. Twenty years had made a great change. Woman suffrage, though not yet generally supported, was no longer considered a crackpot idea. Thanks to the WCTU's support of the "home protec-tion" ballot, suffrage had become accepted as a means to an end even when it was not embraced as a woman's natural right. The NAWSA honored Elizabeth Cady Stanton by electing her its first president, but Susan B. Anthony, who took the helm in 1892, emerged as the leading figure in the new united organization.

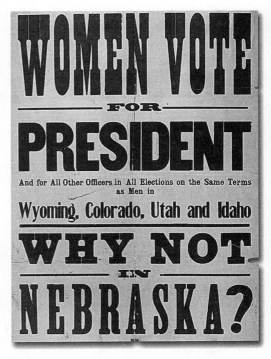

Campaigning for Woman Suffrage
In 1896, women voted in only four states — Wyoming, Colorado, Idaho, and Utah. The West led the way in the campaign for woman suffrage, with Wyoming Territory granting women the vote as early as 1869. Sparse population meant that only sixteen votes were needed in the state's territorial legislature to obtain passage of woman suffrage. The poster calls on Nebraska to join its western neighbors in the suffrage column.
Nebraska State Historical Society.

Stanton and Anthony, both in their seventies, were coming to the end of their public careers. Since the days of the Seneca Falls woman's rights convention, they had worked for reforms for their sex, including property rights, custody rights, and the right to education and gainful employment. But the prize of woman suffrage still eluded them. Suffragists won victories in Colorado in 1893 and Idaho in 1896. One more state joined the suffrage column in 1896 when Utah entered the Union. But women suffered a bitter defeat in a California referendum on woman suffrage that same year. Never losing faith, Susan B. Anthony remarked in her last public appearance, in 1906, "Failure is impossible." It would take until 1920 for all women to gain the vote with the ratification of the Nineteenth Amendment, but the unification of the two woman suffrage groups in 1890 signaled a new era in women's fight for the vote, just as Frances Willard's place on the platform in 1892 in St. Louis symbolized women's growing role in politics and reform.

REVIEW   How did women's temperance activism contribute to the cause of woman suffrage?

▶ Depression Politics

The depression that began in the spring of 1893 and lasted for more than four years put nearly half of the labor force out of work, a higher percentage than during the Great Depression of the 1930s (as discussed in chapters 23 and 24). The human cost of the depression was staggering. "I Take my pen in hand to let you know that we are Starving to death," a Kansas farm woman wrote to the governor in 1894. "Last cent gone," wrote a young widow in her diary. "Children went to work without their breakfasts." The burden of feeding and sheltering the unemployed and their families fell to private charity, city government, and some of the stronger trade unions. Following the harsh dictates of social Darwinism and laissez-faire, the majority of America's elected officials believed that it was inappropriate for the government to intervene. But the scope of the depression made it impossible for local agencies to supply sufficient relief, and increasingly Americans called on the federal government to take action. Armies of the unemployed marched on Washington to demand relief, and the Populist Party experienced a surge of support as the election of 1896 approached.

Coxey's Army

Masses of unemployed Americans marched to Washington, D.C., in the spring of 1894 to call attention to their plight and to urge Congress to enact a public works program to end unemployment. Jacob S. Coxey of Massilon, Ohio, led the most publicized contingent. Convinced that men could be put to work building badly needed roads for the nation, Coxey proposed a scheme to finance public works through non-interest-bearing bonds. "What I am after," he maintained, "is to try to put this country in a condition so that no man who wants work shall be obliged to remain idle." His plan won support from the AFL and the Populists.

Starting out from Ohio with one hundred men, **Coxey's army**, as it was dubbed, swelled as it marched east through the spring snows of the Alleghenies. In Pennsylvania, Coxey recruited several hundred from the ranks of those left unemployed by the Homestead lockout. Called by Coxey the Commonweal of Christ, the army advanced to the tune of "Marching through Georgia":

> We are not tramps nor vagabonds,
>   that's shirking honest toil,
> But miners, clerks, skilled artisans,
>   and tillers of the soil
> Now forced to beg our brother worms
>   to give us leave to toil,
> While we are marching with Coxey.
> Hurrah! hurrah! for the unemployed's appeal
> Hurrah! hurrah! for the marching commonweal!

Coxey's Army

A contingent of Coxey's army stops to rest on its way to Washington, D.C. A "petition in boots," Coxey's followers were well dressed, as evidenced by the men in this photo wearing white shirts, vests, neckties, and bowler hats. Music was an important component of the march, including the anthem "Marching with Coxey," sung to the tune of "Marching through Georgia." Band members are pictured on the right with their instruments. Despite their peaceful pose, the marchers stirred the fears of many conservative Americans, who predicted an uprising of the unemployed. Instead, Coxey and a contingent of his marchers were arrested and jailed for "walking on the grass" when they reached the nation's capital. Ohio Historical Society.

On May 1, Coxey's army arrived in Washington. When Coxey defiantly marched his men onto the Capitol grounds, police set upon the demonstrators with nightsticks, cracking skulls and arresting Coxey and his lieutenants. Coxey went to jail for twenty days and was fined $5 for "walking on the grass."

Those who had trembled for the safety of the Republic heaved a sigh of relief after Coxey's arrest, hoping that it would halt the march on Washington. But other armies of the unemployed, totaling possibly as many as five thousand people, were still on their way. Too poor to pay for railway tickets, they rode the rails as "freeloaders." The more daring contingents commandeered entire trains, stirring fears of revolution. Journalists who covered the march did little to quiet the nation's fears. They delighted in military terminology, describing themselves as "war correspondents." To boost newspaper sales, they gave to the episode a tone of urgency and heightened the sense of a nation imperiled.

By August, the leaderless, tattered armies dissolved. Although the "On to Washington" movement proved ineffective in forcing federal relief legislation, Coxey's army dramatized the plight of the unemployed and acted, in the words of one participant, as a "living, moving object lesson." Like the Populists, Coxey's army called into question the underlying values of the new industrial order and demonstrated how ordinary citizens turned to means outside the regular party system to influence politics in the 1890s.

The People's Party and the Election of 1896

Even before the depression of 1893 gave added impetus to their cause, the Populists had railed against the status quo. "We meet in the midst of a nation brought to the verge of moral, political, and material ruin," Ignatius Donnelly had declared in his keynote address at the creation of the People's Party in St. Louis in 1892. "The fruits of the toil of millions are boldly stolen to build up colossal fortunes for a few. . . . From the same prolific womb of governmental injustice we breed the two great classes — tramps and millionaires."

The fiery rhetoric frightened many who saw in the People's Party a call not to reform but to revolution. Throughout the country, the press denounced the Populists as "cranks, lunatics, and idiots." When one self-righteous editor dismissed them as "calamity howlers," Populist governor Lorenzo Lewelling of Kansas shot back, "If that is so I want to continue to howl until those conditions are improved."

The People's Party captured more than a million votes in the presidential election of 1892, a respectable showing for a new party. But increasingly, sectional and racial animosities threatened its unity. In the South, the Populists' willingness to form common cause with black farmers made them anathema. Realizing that race prejudice obscured the common economic interests of black and white farmers, **Tom Watson** of Georgia openly courted African Americans, appearing on platforms with black speakers and promising "to wipe out the color line." When angry Georgia whites threatened to lynch a black Populist preacher, Watson rallied two thousand gun-toting Populists to the man's defense. Although many

Populists remained racist in their attitudes toward African Americans, the spectacle of white Georgians riding through the night to protect a black man from lynching was symbolic of the enormous changes the Populist Party promised in the South.

As the presidential election of 1896 approached, the depression intensified cries for reform not only from the Populists but also throughout the electorate. Depression worsened the tight money problem caused by the deflationary pressures of the gold standard. Once again, proponents of free silver stirred rebellion in the ranks of both the Democratic and the Republican parties. When the Republicans nominated Ohio governor **William McKinley** on a platform pledging the preservation of the gold standard, western advocates of free silver representing miners and farmers walked out of the convention. Open rebellion also split the Democratic Party as vast segments in the West and South repudiated President Grover Cleveland because of his support for gold. In South Carolina, Benjamin Tillman won his race for Congress by promising, "Send me to Washington and I'll stick my pitchfork into [Cleveland's] old ribs!"

The spirit of revolt animated the Democratic National Convention in Chicago in the summer of 1896. **William Jennings Bryan** of Nebraska, the thirty-six-year-old "boy orator from the Platte," whipped the convention into a frenzy with his passionate call for free silver. In his speech in favor of the silver plank in the party's platform, Bryan masterfully cataloged the grievances of farmers and laborers, closing his dramatic speech with a ringing exhortation: "Do not crucify mankind upon a cross of gold." Pandemonium broke loose as delegates stampeded to nominate Bryan, the youngest candidate ever to run for the presidency.

The juggernaut of free silver rolled out of Chicago and on to St. Louis, where the People's Party met a week after the Democrats adjourned. Smelling victory, many western Populists urged the party to ally with the Democrats and endorse Bryan. A major obstacle in the path of fusion, however, was Bryan's running mate, Arthur M. Sewall. A Maine railway director and bank president, Sewall, who had been placed on the ticket to appease conservative Democrats, embodied everything the Populists detested.

Populism's regional constituencies remained as divided over tactics as they were uniform in their call for change. Western Populists, including a strong coalition of farmers and miners in states such as Idaho and Colorado, championed free silver. In these largely Republican states, Populists had joined forces with Democrats in previous elections and saw no problem with becoming "Popocrats" once Bryan led the Democratic ticket on a free silver platform. Similarly in the Midwest, a Republican stronghold, Populists who had used fusion with the Democrats as a tactic to win elections had little trouble backing Bryan. But in the South, where Democrats had resorted to fraud and violence to steal elections from the Populists in 1892 and 1894, support for a Democratic ticket proved especially hard to swallow. Die-hard southern Populists wanted no part of fusion.

All of these tactical differences emerged as the Populists met in St. Louis in 1896 to nominate a candidate for president. To show that they remained true to their principles, delegates first voted to support all the planks of the 1892 platform, added to it a call for public works projects for the unemployed, and only narrowly defeated a plank for woman suffrage. To deal with the problem of fusion, the convention selected the vice presidential candidate first. The nomination of Tom Watson undercut opposition to Bryan's candidacy. And although Bryan quickly sent a telegram to protest that he would not drop Sewall as his running mate, mysteriously his message never reached the convention floor. Fusion triumphed. Watson's vice presidential nomination paved the way for the selection of Bryan by a lopsided vote. The Populists did not know it, but their cheers for Bryan signaled not a chorus of victory but the death knell for the People's Party.

Few contests in the nation's history have been as fiercely fought and as full of emotion as the presidential election of 1896. On one side stood Republican William McKinley, backed by the wealthy industrialist and party boss Mark Hanna. Hanna played on the business community's fears of Populism to raise a Republican war chest more than double the amount of any previous campaign. On the other side, William Jennings Bryan, with few assets beyond his silver tongue, struggled to make up in energy and eloquence what his party lacked in campaign funds, crisscrossing the country in a whirlwind tour, traveling more than eighteen thousand miles and delivering more than six hundred speeches in three months. According to his own reckoning, he visited twenty-seven states and spoke to more than five million Americans.

As election day approached, the silver states of the Rocky Mountains lined up solidly for Bryan. The Northeast stood solidly for McKinley. Much of the South, with the exception of the border states, abandoned the Populists and returned to the Democratic "party of the fathers," leaving Tom Watson to lament that "[Populists] play Jonah while [Democrats] play the whale." The Midwest hung in the balance. Bryan intensified his campaign in Illinois, Michigan, Ohio, and Indiana. But midwestern farmers proved less receptive than western voters to the blandishments of free silver.

In the cities, Democrats charged the Republicans with mass intimidation. "Men, vote as you please," the head of New York's Steinway Piano Company reportedly announced to his workers on the eve of the election, "but if Bryan is elected tomorrow the whistle will not blow Wednesday morning." Intimidation alone did not explain the failure of urban labor to rally to Bryan. Republicans repeatedly warned workers that if the Democrats won, the inflated silver dollar would be worth only fifty cents. However much farmers and laborers might insist that they were united as producers against the nonproducing bosses, it was equally true that inflation did not offer the boon to urban laborers that it did to western farmers.

On election day, four out of five voters went to the polls in an unprecedented turnout. In the critical midwestern states, as many as 95 percent of the eligible voters cast their ballots. In the end, the election hinged on between 100 and 1,000 votes in several key states, including Wisconsin, Iowa, and Minnesota. Although McKinley won twenty-three states to Bryan's twenty-two, the electoral vote showed a lopsided 271 to 176 in McKinley's favor.

The biggest losers in 1896 turned out to be the Populists. On the national level, they polled fewer than 300,000 votes, a million less than in 1894. In the clamor to support Bryan, Populists in the South, determined to beat McKinley at any cost, swallowed their differences and drifted back to the Democratic Party. The People's Party was crushed, and with it the agrarian revolt.

But if Populism proved unsuccessful at the polls, it nevertheless set the domestic political agenda for the United States in the next decades, highlighting issues such as railroad regulation, banking and currency reform, electoral reforms, and an enlarged role for the federal government in the economy. Meanwhile, as the decade ended, the bugle call to arms turned America's attention to foreign affairs and effectively drowned out the trumpet of reform. The struggle for social justice gave way to a war for empire as the United States asserted its power on the world stage.

> **REVIEW** Why was the People's Party unable to translate national support into victory in the 1896 election?

▶ The United States and the World

Throughout much of the second half of the nineteenth century, U.S. interest in foreign policy took a backseat to territorial expansion in the American West. The United States stood aloof while Great Britain, France, Germany, Spain, Belgium, and an increasingly powerful Japan competed for empires in Asia, Africa, Latin America, and the Pacific. Between 1870 and 1900, European nations colonized more than 20 percent of the world's landmass and 10 percent of the world's population.

At the turn of the twentieth century, the United States pursued a foreign policy consisting of two currents — isolationism and expansionism. Although the determination to remain detached from European politics had been a hallmark of U.S. foreign policy since the nation's founding, Americans simultaneously believed in manifest destiny — the "obvious" right to expand the nation from ocean to ocean. With its own inland empire secured, the United States looked outward. Determined to protect its sphere of influence in the Western Hemisphere and to expand its trading in Asia, the nation moved away from isolationism and toward a more active role on the world stage. The push for commercial expansion joined with a sense of Christian mission and led both to the strengthening of the Monroe Doctrine in the Western Hemisphere and to a more assertive policy in Asia. All of these trends were in evidence during the Spanish-American War and the debates that followed.

Markets and Missionaries

The depression of the 1890s provided a powerful impetus to American commercial expansion. As markets weakened at home, American businesses looked abroad for profits. As early as 1890, Captain Alfred Thayer Mahan, leader of a growing group of American expansionists, prophesied, "Whether they will or not, Americans must now begin to look outward. The growing production of the country requires it." As the depression deepened, one diplomat warned that Americans "must turn [their] eyes abroad, or they will soon look inward upon discontent."

Exports constituted a small but significant percentage of the profits of American business in the 1890s. And where American interests led, businessmen expected the government's power and influence to follow to protect their investments. Companies like Standard Oil actively sought to use the U.S. government as their agent, often putting foreign service employees on the payroll. "Our ambassadors and ministers and consuls," wrote John D. Rockefeller appreciatively, "have aided to push our way into new markets and to the utmost corners of the world." Whether "our" referred to the United States or to Standard Oil remained ambiguous; in practice, the distinction was of little importance in late-nineteenth-century foreign policy.

America's foreign policy often appeared little more than a sidelight to business development. In Hawai'i (first called the Sandwich Islands), American sugar interests fomented a rebellion in 1893, toppling the increasingly independent Queen Lili'uokalani. They pushed Congress to annex the islands, which would allow planters to avoid the high McKinley tariff on sugar. When President Cleveland learned that Hawai'ians opposed annexation, he withdrew the proposal from

Queen Lili'uokalani (1838–1917)
An accomplished woman who straddled two cultures, Lydia Kamakaeha Dominis, or Queen Lili'uokalani, spoke English as easily as her native Hawai'ian and was fluent in French and German as well. She traveled widely in Europe and the United States. Despite President Cleveland's belief that the monarchy should be restored, Lili'uokalani never regained her throne. In 1898, she published *Hawai'i's Story by Hawai'i's Queen,* outlining her version of the events that had led to her downfall. In 1993, on the one hundredth anniversary of the revolution that deposed her, Congress passed and President Bill Clinton signed a resolution offering an apology to native Hawai'ians for the overthrow of their queen. Courtesy of the Lili'uokalani Trust.

Congress. But expansionists still coveted the islands and continued to look for an excuse to push through annexation.

However compelling the economic arguments about overseas markets proved, business interests alone did not account for the new expansionism that seized the nation during the 1890s. As Mahan confessed, "Even when material interests are the original exciting cause, it is the sentiment to which they give rise, the moral tone which emotion takes that constitutes the greater force." Much of that moral tone was set by American missionaries intent on spreading the gospel of Christianity to the "heathen." No area on the globe constituted a greater challenge than China.

An 1858 agreement, the Tianjin (Tientsin) treaty admitted foreign missionaries to China. Although Christians converted only 100,000 in a population of 400 million, the Chinese nevertheless resented the interference of missionaries in village life. Opposition to foreign missionaries took the form of antiforeign secret societies, most notably the Boxers, whose Chinese name translated to "Righteous Harmonious Fist." No simple boxing club, the Boxers in 1899 began to hunt down and kill Chinese Christians and missionaries in northwestern Shandong (Shan-tung) Province. With the tacit support of China's Dowager Empress, the Boxers became bolder. Under the slogan "Uphold the Ch'ing Dynasty, Exterminate the Foreigners," they marched on the cities. Their rampage eventually led to the massacre of some 30,000 Chinese converts and 250 foreign nuns, priests, and missionaries along with their families. In August 1900, 2,500 U.S. troops joined an international force sent to rescue the foreigners and put down the uprising in the Chinese capital of Beijing (Peking). The European powers imposed the humiliating Boxer Protocol in 1901, giving themselves the right to maintain military forces in Beijing and requiring the Chinese government to pay an exorbitant indemnity of $333 million for the loss of life and property resulting from the **Boxer uprising**.

In the aftermath of the uprising, missionaries voiced no concern at the paradox of bringing Christianity to China at gunpoint. "It is worth any cost in money, worth any cost in bloodshed," argued one bishop, "if we can make millions of Chinese true and intelligent Christians." Merchants and missionaries alike shared such moralistic reasoning. Indeed, they worked hand in hand; trade and Christianity marched into Asia together. "Missionaries," admitted the American clergyman Charles Denby, "are the pioneers of trade and commerce. . . . The missionary, inspired by holy zeal, goes everywhere and by degrees foreign commerce and trade follow."

The Monroe Doctrine and the Open Door Policy

The emergence of the United States as a world power pitted the nation against other colonial powers, particularly Germany and Japan, which posed a threat to the twin pillars of America's expansionist foreign policy — one dating back to President James Monroe in the 1820s, the other formalized in 1900 under President William McKinley. The first, the **Monroe Doctrine**, came to be interpreted as establishing the Western Hemisphere as an American "sphere of influence" and warned European powers to stay away or risk war. The second, the Open Door, dealt with maintaining market access to China.

American diplomacy actively worked to buttress the Monroe Doctrine, with its assertion of American hegemony (domination) in the Western Hemisphere. In the 1880s, Republican secretary of state James G. Blaine promoted hemispheric peace and trade through Pan-American cooperation but at the same time used American troops to intervene in Latin American border disputes. In 1895, President Cleveland risked war with Great Britain to enforce the Monroe Doctrine when a conflict developed between Venezuela and British Guiana. After American saber rattling, the British backed down and accepted U.S. mediation in the area despite their territorial claims in Guiana.

In Central America, American business triumphed in a bloodless takeover that saw French and British interests routed by behemoths such as the United Fruit Company of Boston. United Fruit virtually dominated the Central American nations of Costa Rica and Guatemala, while an importer from New Orleans turned Honduras into a "banana republic" (a country run by U.S. business interests). Thus, by 1895, the United States, through business as well as diplomacy, had successfully achieved hegemony in Latin America and the Caribbean, forcing even the British to concur with the secretary of state that "the infinite resources [of the United States] combined with its isolated position render it master of the situation and practically invulnerable as against any or all other powers."

At the same time that American foreign policy warned European powers to stay out of the Western Hemisphere, the United States competed for trade in the Eastern Hemisphere. As American interests in China grew, the United States became more aggressive in defending its presence in Asia and the Pacific. The United States risked war with Germany in 1889 to guarantee the U.S. Navy access to Pago Pago in the Samoan Islands, a port for refueling on the way to Asia. Germany, seeking dominance over the islands, challenged the United States by sending warships to the region. But before fighting broke out, a great typhoon destroyed the German and American ships. Acceding to the will of nature, the potential combatants later divided the islands amicably in the 1899 Treaty of Berlin.

The biggest prize in Asia remained the China market. In the 1890s, China, weakened by years of internal warfare, was beginning to be partitioned into spheres of influence by Britain, Japan, Germany, France, and Russia. Concerned about the integrity of China and no less about American trade, Secretary of State John Hay in 1899–1900 wrote a series of notes calling for an "open door" policy that would ensure trade access to all and maintain Chinese sovereignty. The notes — sent to Britain, Germany, and Russia and later to France, Japan, and Italy — were greeted by the major powers with polite evasion. Nevertheless, Hay skillfully managed to maneuver the major powers into doing his bidding, and in 1900 he boldly announced the Open Door as international policy. The United States, by insisting on the **Open Door policy**, managed to secure access to Chinese markets, expanding its economic power while avoiding the problems of maintaining a far-flung colonial empire on the Asian mainland. But as the

Spanish-American War soon demonstrated, Americans found it hard to resist the temptations of overseas empire.

"A Splendid Little War"

The **Spanish-American War** began as a humanitarian effort to free Cuba from Spain's colonial grasp and ended with the United States itself acquiring territory overseas and fighting a dirty guerrilla war with Filipino nationalists who, like the Cubans, sought independence. Behind the contradiction stood the twin pillars of American foreign policy: The Monroe Doctrine made Spain's presence in Cuba unacceptable, and U.S. determination to keep open the door to Asia made the Philippines attractive as a stepping-stone to China. Precedent for the nation's imperial adventures also came from the recent Indian wars in the American West, which provided a template for the subjugation of native peoples in the name of civilization.

Looking back on the Spanish-American War of 1898, Secretary of State John Hay judged it "a splendid little war; begun with the highest motives, carried on with magnificent intelligence and spirit, favored by that fortune which loves the brave." At the close of a decade marred by bitter depression, social unrest, and political upheaval, the war offered Americans a chance to wave the flag and march in unison. War fever proved as infectious as the tune of a John Philip Sousa march. Few argued the merits of the conflict until it was over and the time came to divide the spoils.

The war began with moral outrage over the treatment of Cuban revolutionaries, who had launched a fight for independence against the Spanish colonial regime in 1895. In an attempt to isolate the guerrillas, the Spanish general Valeriano Weyler herded Cubans into crowded and unsanitary concentration camps, where thousands died of hunger, disease, and exposure. Starvation soon spread to the cities. Tens of thousands of Cubans died, and countless others were left without food, clothing, or shelter. By 1898, fully a quarter of the island's population had perished in the Cuban revolution.

As the Cuban rebellion dragged on, pressure for American intervention mounted. American newspapers fueled public outrage at Spain. A fierce circulation war raged in New York City between William Randolph Hearst's *Journal* and Joseph Pulitzer's *World*. Their competition provoked what came to be called **yellow journalism**, named for the colored ink used in a popular comic strip. Practitioners of yellow journalism pandered to the public's appetite for sensationalism. The Cuban war provided a wealth of dramatic copy. Newspapers fed the American people a daily diet of "Butcher" Weyler and Spanish atrocities. Hearst sent artist Frederic Remington to document the horror, and when Remington wired home, "There is no trouble here. There will be no war," Hearst shot back, "You furnish the pictures and I'll furnish the war."

American interests in Cuba were, in the words of the U.S. minister to Spain, more than "merely theoretical or sentimental." American business had more than $50 million invested in Cuban sugar, and American trade with Cuba, a brisk $100 million a year before the rebellion, had dropped to near zero.

Nevertheless, the business community balked, wary of a war with Spain. When industrialist Mark Hanna, the Republican kingmaker and senator from Ohio, urged restraint, a hotheaded **Theodore Roosevelt** exploded, "We will have this war for the freedom of Cuba, Senator Hanna, in spite of the timidity of commercial interests."

To expansionists like Roosevelt, more than Cuban independence was at stake. War with Spain opened up the prospect of expansion into Asia as well, since Spain controlled not only Cuba and Puerto Rico but also Guam and the Philippine Islands. Appointed assistant secretary of the navy in April 1897, Roosevelt took the helm in the absence of his boss and audaciously ordered the U.S. fleet to Manila in the Philippines. In the event of conflict with Spain, Roosevelt would have the navy in a position to capture the islands and gain an entry point to China.

President McKinley slowly moved toward intervention. In a show of American force, he dispatched the battleship *Maine* to Cuba. On the night of February 15, 1898, a mysterious explosion destroyed the *Maine*, killing 267 crew members. The source of the explosion remained unclear, but inflammatory stories in the press enraged Americans, who immediately blamed the Spanish government. Rallying to the cry "Remember the *Maine*," Congress declared war on Spain in April. In a surge of patriotism, more than a million men rushed to enlist. War brought with it a unity of purpose and national harmony that ended a decade of political dissent and strife. "In April, everywhere over this good fair land, flags were flying," wrote Kansas editor William Allen White. "At the stations, crowds gathered to hurrah for the soldiers, and to throw hats into the air, and to unfurl flags."

Soon they had something to cheer about. Five days after McKinley signed the war resolution, a U.S. Navy squadron commanded by Admiral George Dewey destroyed the Spanish fleet in Manila Bay (Map 20.1). Dewey's stunning victory caught the United States by surprise. Although naval strategists including Theodore Roosevelt had been orchestrating the move for some time, few Americans had ever heard of the Philippines. Even McKinley confessed that he could not immediately locate the archipelago on the map. He nevertheless recognized the strategic importance of the Philippines and dispatched U.S. troops to secure the islands.

The war in Cuba ended almost as quickly as it began. The first troops landed on June 22, and after a handful of battles the Spanish forces surrendered on July 17. The war lasted just long enough to elevate Theodore Roosevelt to the status of bona fide war hero. Roosevelt resigned his navy post and formed the Rough Riders, a regiment composed of a sprinkling of Ivy League polo players and a number of western cowboys. Roosevelt admired horsemanship and had gained the cowboys' respect during his stint as a cattle rancher in the Dakotas. While the troops languished in Tampa awaiting their orders, Roosevelt and his men staged rodeos for the press, with the likes of New York socialite William Tiffany busting broncos in competition with Dakota cowboy Jim "Dead Shot" Simpson. When the Rough Riders shipped out to Cuba, journalists fought for a berth with the colorful regiment. The Rough Riders' charge up Kettle Hill and Roosevelt's role in the decisive battle of San Juan Hill made front-page news. Overnight, Roosevelt became the most famous man in America. By the time he

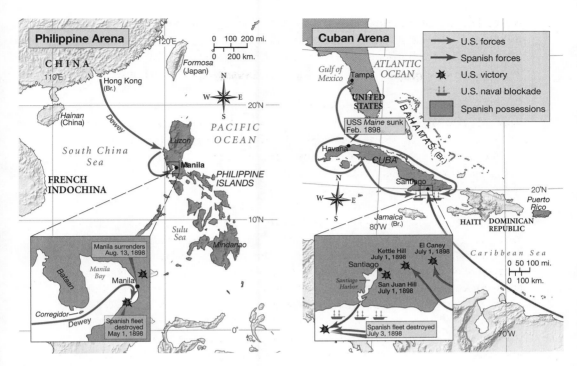

MAP 20.1
The Spanish-American War, 1898
The Spanish-American War was fought in two theaters, the Philippine Islands and Cuba. Five days after President William McKinley called for a declaration of war, Admiral George Dewey captured Manila without the loss of a single American sailor. The war lasted only eight months. Troops landed in Cuba in mid-June and by mid-July had taken Santiago and Havana and destroyed the Spanish fleet.

sailed home from Cuba, a coalition of independent Republicans was already plotting his political future.

The Debate over American Imperialism

After a few brief campaigns in Cuba and Puerto Rico brought the Spanish-American War to an end, the American people woke up in possession of an empire that stretched halfway around the globe. As part of the spoils of war, the United States acquired Cuba, Puerto Rico, Guam, and the Philippines. Yielding to pressure from American sugar growers, President McKinley expanded the empire further, annexing Hawai'i in July 1898.

Contemptuous of the Cubans, whom General William Shafter declared "no more fit for self-government than gun-powder is for hell," the U.S. government directed the writing of a new Cuban constitution in 1900 and refused to give up military control of the island until the Cubans accepted the so-called Platt Amendment — a series of provisions that granted the United States the right to intervene to protect Cuba's "independence," as well as the power to oversee Cuban

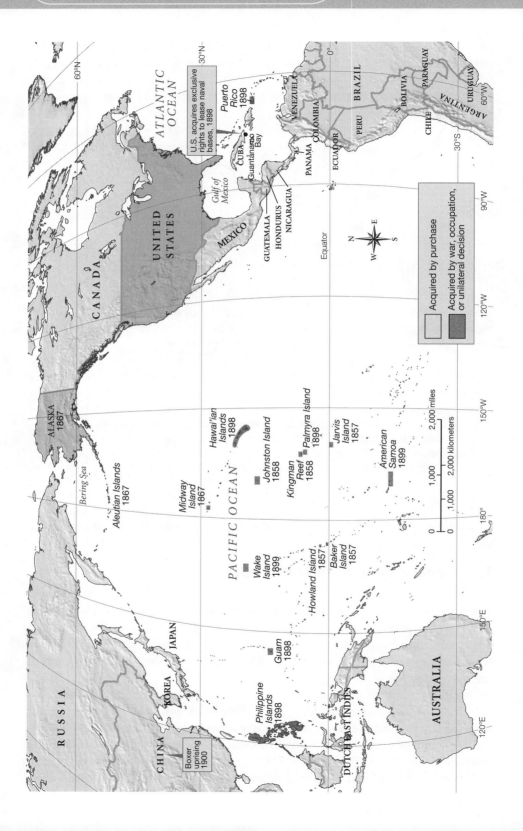

U.S. acquires exclusive rights to lease naval bases, 1898

Acquired by purchase

Acquired by war, occupation, or unilateral decision

ATLANTIC OCEAN

PACIFIC OCEAN

CANADA

UNITED STATES

MEXICO

Gulf of Mexico

CUBA

Guantánamo Bay

Puerto Rico 1898

GUATEMALA
HONDURUS
NICARAGUA

PANAMA

ECUADOR

VENEZUELA

COLOMBIA

BRAZIL

PERU

BOLIVIA

PARAGUAY

CHILE

ARGENTINA

URUGUAY

Equator

ALASKA 1867

Bering Sea

Aleutian Islands 1867

Midway Island 1867

Hawai'ian Islands 1898

Johnston Island 1858

Kingman Reef 1858

Palmyra Island 1898

Jarvis Island 1857

American Samoa 1899

Wake Island 1899

Howland Island 1857

Baker Island 1857

RUSSIA

JAPAN

KOREA

CHINA

Boxer uprising 1900

Guam 1898

Philippine Islands 1898

DUTCH EAST INDIES

AUSTRALIA

0   1,000   2,000 miles
0   1,000   2,000 kilometers

30°N
60°N
30°S
0°
60°W
90°W
120°W
150°W
180°
150°E
120°E

debt so that European creditors would not find an excuse for intervention. For good measure, the United States gave itself a ninety-nine-year lease on a naval base at Guantánamo. In return, McKinley promised to implement an extensive sanitation program to clean up the island, making it more attractive to American investors.

In the formal Treaty of Paris (1898), Spain ceded the Philippines to the United States along with the former Spanish colonies of Puerto Rico and Guam (Map 20.2). Empire did not come cheap. When Spain initially balked at these terms, the United States agreed to pay an indemnity of $20 million for the islands. Nor was the cost measured in money alone. Filipino revolutionaries under **Emilio Aguinaldo**, who had greeted U.S. troops as liberators, bitterly fought the new masters. It would take seven years and 4,000 American dead — almost ten times the number killed in Cuba — not to mention an estimated 20,000 Filipino casualties, to defeat Aguinaldo and secure American control of the Philippines, America's coveted stepping-stone to China.

At home, a vocal minority, mostly Democrats and former Populists, resisted the country's foray into overseas empire, judging it unwise, immoral, and unconstitutional. William Jennings Bryan, who enlisted in the army but never saw action, concluded that American expansionism only distracted the nation from problems at home. Pointing to the central paradox of the war, Representative Bourke Cockran of New York admonished, "We who have been the destroyers of oppression are asked now to become its agents." Mark Twain, lending his bitter eloquence to the cause of anti-imperialism, lamented that the United States had become "yet another Civilized Power, with its banner of the Prince of Peace in one hand and its loot-basket and its butcher-knife in the other."

The anti-imperialists were soon drowned out by cries for empire. As Senator Knute Nelson of Minnesota assured his colleagues, "We come as ministering angels, not as despots." Fresh from the conquest of Native Americans in the West, the nation largely embraced the heady mixture of racism and missionary zeal that fueled American adventurism abroad. The *Washington Post* trumpeted, "The taste of empire is in the mouth of the people," thrilled at the prospect of "an imperial policy, the Republic renascent, taking her place with the armed nations."

REVIEW   Why did the United States largely abandon its isolationist foreign policy in the 1890s?

◀ **MAP 20.2**
U.S. Overseas Expansion through 1900
The United States extended its interests abroad with a series of territorial acquisitions. Although Cuba was granted independence, the Platt Amendment kept the new nation firmly under U.S. control. In the wake of the Spanish-American War, the United States woke up to find that it held an empire extending halfway around the globe.

▶ Conclusion: Rallying around the Flag

A decade of domestic strife ended amid the blare of martial music and the waving of flags. The Spanish-American War drowned out the calls for social reform that had fueled the Populist politics of the 1890s. During that decade, angry farmers facing hard times looked to the Farmers' Alliance to fight for their vision of economic democracy, workers staged bloody battles across the country to assert their rights, and women attacked drunkenness and the conditions that fostered it and mounted a suffrage movement to secure their basic political rights. In St. Louis in 1892, Frances Willard joined with other disaffected Americans to form a new People's Party to fight for change.

The bitter depression that began in 1893 led to increased labor strife. The Pullman boycott brutally dramatized the power of property and the conservatism of the laissez-faire state. Even the miners' victory in Cripple Creek, Colorado, in 1894 proved short-lived. But workers' willingness to confront capitalism on the streets of Chicago, Homestead, Cripple Creek, and a host of other sites across America eloquently testified to labor's growing determination, unity, and strength.

As the depression deepened, the sight of Coxey's army of unemployed marching on Washington to demand federal intervention in the economy signaled a growing shift in the public mind against the stand-pat politics of laissez-faire personified by President William McKinley. The call for the government to take action to better the lives of workers, farmers, and the dispossessed manifested itself in the fiercely fought presidential campaign of William Jennings Bryan in 1896. With the outbreak of the Spanish-American War in 1898, the decade ended on a harmonious note with patriotic Americans rallying around the flag. Few questioned America's foray into overseas empire. The United States took its place on the world stage, buttressing its hemispheric domination with the Monroe Doctrine and employing the Open Door policy, which promised access to the riches of China. But even though Americans basked in patriotism and contemplated empire, old grievances had not been laid to rest. The People's Party had been beaten, but the Populist spirit lived on in the demands for greater government involvement in the economy, expanded opportunities for direct democracy, and a more equitable balance of profits and power between the people and the big corporations. This reform agenda would be taken up by a new generation of progressive reformers in the first decades of the twentieth century.

Reviewing Chapter 20

REVIEW QUESTIONS

1. Why did American farmers organize alliances in the late nineteenth
century? (pp. 588–591)

2. What tactics led to the defeat of the
strikers in the 1890s? Where were
they able to succeed and why?
(pp. 591–597)

3. How did women's temperance activism contribute to the cause of
woman suffrage? (pp. 597–600)

4. Why was the People's Party unable
to translate national support into
victory in the 1896 election?
(pp. 600–605)

5. Why did the United States largely
abandon its isolationist foreign
policy in the 1890s? (pp. 605–613)

MAKING CONNECTIONS

1. In the late nineteenth century,
Americans clashed over the disparity of power brought about by industrial capitalism. Why did many
farmers and urban workers look to
the government to help advance
their vision of economic justice? In
your answer, discuss specific reforms working-class Americans
pursued and the strategies they
employed.

2. In the 1890s, workers mounted
labor protests and strikes. What
circumstances gave rise to these actions? How did they differ from earlier strikes, such as the Great
Railroad Strike of 1877? In your
answer, discuss specific actions,

being sure to consider how local
and national circumstances contributed to their ultimate resolution.

3. How did women's activism in the
late nineteenth century help advance the cause of woman suffrage?
In your answer, discuss specific
gains made in the late nineteenth
century, as well as shifts in reformers' strategies.

4. Given the farmers' unrest in the
1890s, why did the Populist Party
fail to defeat Republican William
McKinley in the election of 1896?
What coalitions failed to come
together?

LINKING TO THE PAST

1. How did the conquest of Native
Americans in the West foreshadow
U.S. expansion abroad? In what
ways did the assumptions of racial
superiority evident in U.S. Indian
policy affect the treatment of Cubans
and Filipinos? (See chapter 17.)

2. Why in the midst of burgeoning
growth did the United States experience a major depression in the
1890s? Draw on your knowledge of
the development of U.S.
industries such as the railroads.
(See chapter 18.)

TIMELINE 1884–1901

1884 • Frances Willard, head of Woman's Christian Temperance Union, calls for woman suffrage.

1890 • National American Woman Suffrage Association (NAWSA) formed.
• Wyoming only state allowing women to vote in national elections.
• Southern Farmers' Alliance numbers three million members.

1892 • People's (Populist) Party founded.
• Homestead lockout.

1893 • Stock market crash touches off severe economic depression.
• President Grover Cleveland nixes attempt to annex Hawai'i.

1894 • Miners' strike in Cripple Creek, Colorado.
• Coxey's army marches to Washington, D.C.
• Federal troops and court injunction crush Pullman boycott.

1895 • President Grover Cleveland enforces Monroe Doctrine in border dispute between British Guiana and Venezuela.

1896 • Democrats and Populists support William Jennings Bryan for president.
• Republican William McKinley elected president.

1898 • U.S. battleship *Maine* explodes in Havana harbor.
• Congress declares war on Spain.
• Admiral George Dewey destroys Spanish fleet in Manila Bay, the Philippines.
• U.S. troops defeat Spanish forces in Cuba.
• Treaty of Paris ends war with Spain and cedes Philippines, Puerto Rico, and Guam to the United States.
• United States annexes Hawai'i.

1899– 1900 • Secretary of State John Hay enunciates Open Door policy in China.
• Boxer uprising in China.

1901 • Boxer Protocol imposed on Chinese government.

▶ FOR AN ONLINE BIBLIOGRAPHY, PRACTICE QUIZZES, WEB SITES, IMAGES, AND DOCUMENTS RELATED TO THIS CHAPTER, see the Book Companion Site at **bedfordstmartins.com/roarkvalue**.

▶ FOR DOCUMENTS RELATED TO THIS PERIOD, see Michael Johnson, ed., *Reading the American Past*, Fifth Edition.

Progressivism from the Grass Roots to the White House

1890–1916

IN THE SUMMER OF 1889, JANE ADDAMS LEASED TWO FLOORS OF A
dilapidated mansion on Chicago's West Side. Her Italian and Russian Jewish
neighbors must have scratched their heads, wondering why this well-dressed
woman, who surely could afford a better house in a better neighborhood,
chose to live on South Halsted Street. Yet the house, built by Charles Hull,
precisely suited Addams's needs.

Personal action marked the first step in Addams's search for solutions to
the social problems created by urban industrialism. Her object was twofold:
She wanted to help her immigrant neighbors, and she wanted to offer an
opportunity for educated women like herself to find meaningful work.
Addams's emphasis on the reciprocal relationship between the social classes
made Hull House different from other philanthropic enterprises. She wished
to do things with, not just for, Chicago's poor.

In the next decade, Hull House expanded from two rented floors in the
old brick mansion wedged between a saloon and an undertaker to some thirteen buildings housing a remarkable variety of activities. Addams converted
the basement bathroom into public baths, opened a restaurant for workingwomen too tired to cook after their long shifts, and sponsored a nursery and

Jane Addams

Jane Addams was twenty-nine years old when she founded Hull House on South Halsted Street in Chicago. She and her college roommate, Ellen Gates Starr, established America's premier social settlement. Her desire to live among the poor and her insistence that settlement house work benefited educated women such as herself as well as her immigrant neighbors separated her from the charity workers who had come before her and marked the distance from philanthropy to progressive reform. Jane Addams ca. 1892. Photographed by Max Platz. Jane Addams Hull-House Photographic Collections JAMC_0000_0005_0014. University of Illinois at Chicago Library, Special Collections.

kindergarten. Hull House offered classes, lectures, art exhibits, musical instruction, and college extension courses. It boasted a gymnasium, a theater, a manual training workshop, a labor museum, and the first public playground in Chicago.

From the first, Hull House attracted an extraordinary set of reformers. Some stayed for decades, as did Julia Lathrop before she went to Washington, D.C., in 1912 to head the Children's Bureau. Others, like Gerard Swope, who later became president of the General Electric Company, came for only a short time. Hull House residents pioneered the scientific investigation of urban ills. Armed with statistics, they launched campaigns to improve housing, end child labor, fund playgrounds, mediate between labor and management, and lobby for laws to protect workers.

Addams quickly learned that it was impossible to deal with urban problems without becoming involved in political action. Her determination to clean up the garbage on Halsted Street led her into politics. Piles of decaying garbage overflowed the street's wooden trash bins, breeding flies and disease. Investigation revealed that the local ward boss got a kickback from a contractor who didn't bother to provide adequate service. To end the graft, Addams got herself appointed garbage inspector. Out on the streets at six in the morning, she rode atop the garbage wagon to make sure it made its rounds. Eventually, her struggle to aid the urban poor led her not only to city hall but on to the state capitol and to Washington, D.C., as well.

Under Jane Addams's leadership, Hull House became a "spearhead for reform," part of a broader movement that contemporaries called progressivism. The transition from personal action to political activism that Addams personified became one of the hallmarks of this reform period, which lasted from the 1890s to World War I.

By the 1890s, many Americans recognized that the laissez-faire approach of government toward business no longer worked. The classical liberalism of the nation's Founders, which opposed the tyranny of centralized government, had not foreseen the enormous private wealth and power of the Gilded Age's business giants. As the gap between rich and poor widened in the 1890s, progressive reformers began demanding government intervention to guarantee a more equitable society. The willingness to use the government to promote change and to counterbalance the power of private interests redefined liberalism in the twentieth century.

Faith in activism in both the political and the private realms united an otherwise diverse group of progressive reformers. A sense of Christian mission inspired some. Others, fearing social upheaval, sought to remove some of the worst evils of urban industrialism — tenements, child labor, and harsh working conditions. A belief in technical expertise and scientific management infused progressivism and made the cult of efficiency part and parcel of the movement.

Progressives shared a growing concern about the power of wealthy individuals and corporations and a strong dislike of the trusts, but they were not immune to the prejudices of the era. Although they pressed for direct democracy, many progressives sought to restrict the rights of African Americans, Asians, and even the women who formed the backbone of the movement.

All of these elements — uplift and efficiency, social justice and social control, direct democracy and discrimination — came together in the Progressive Era both at the grassroots level in the cities and states and in the presidencies of Theodore Roosevelt and Woodrow Wilson.

▶ Grassroots Progressivism

Much of progressive reform began at the grassroots level and percolated upward into local, state, and eventually national politics as reformers attacked the social problems fostered by urban industrialism. Although **progressivism** flourished in many different settings across the country, urban problems inspired the progressives' greatest efforts. In their zeal to "civilize the city," reformers founded settlement houses, professed a new Christian social gospel, and campaigned against vice and crime in the name of "social purity." Allying with the working class, they sought to better the lot of sweatshop garment workers and to end child labor. Their reform efforts often began on the local level but ended up being debated in state legislatures and in the U.S. Congress.

Civilizing the City

Progressives attacked the problems of the city on many fronts. The settlement house movement attempted to bridge the distance between the classes. The social gospel called for churches to play a new role in social reformation. And the social purity movement campaigned to clean up vice, particularly prostitution.

The **settlement house** movement, which began in England, came to the United States in 1886 with the opening of the University Settlement House in New York City. The needs of poor urban neighborhoods provided the impetus for these social settlements. In 1893, Lillian Wald, a nurse attending medical school in New York, went to care for a woman living in a dilapidated tenement. The experience led Wald to leave medical school and recruit several other nurses to move to New York City's Lower East Side "to live in the neighborhood as nurses, identify ourselves with it socially, and . . . contribute to it our citizenship." Wald's Henry Street settlement expanded in 1895, pioneering public health nursing. Although Wald herself was Jewish, she insisted that the settlement remain independent of religious ties, making it different from the avowedly religious settlements in England.

Women, particularly college-educated women like **Jane Addams** and Lillian Wald, formed the backbone of the settlement house movement and stood in the vanguard of the progressive movement. Settlement houses gave college-educated women eager to use their knowledge a place to put their talents to work in the service of society and to champion progressive reform. Largely because of women's efforts, settlements like Hull House grew in number from six in 1891 to more than four hundred in 1911. In the process, settlement house women created a new profession — social work — and stimulated the new reform movement of progressivism.

For their part, churches confronted urban social problems by enunciating a new **social gospel**, one that saw its mission as not simply to reform individuals but to reform society. The social gospel offered a powerful corrective to social Darwinism and the gospel of wealth, which fostered the belief that riches somehow signaled divine favor (see chapter 18). Washington Gladden, a prominent social gospel minister, challenged that view when he urged Congregationalists to turn down a gift from John D. Rockefeller, arguing that it was "tainted money." In place of the gospel of wealth, progressive clergy exhorted their congregations to put Christ's teachings to work in their daily lives. Charles M. Sheldon's popular book *In His Steps* (1898) called on men and women to Christianize capitalism by asking the question "What would Jesus do?"

Ministers also played an active role in the **social purity movement**, the campaign to attack vice. The Reverend Charles H. Parkhurst shocked his Madison Square congregation in the 1890s by donning a disguise and touring New York City's brothels to uncover the links between political corruption and urban vice. Armed with eyewitness accounts and affidavits, he demanded reform. To end the "social evil," as reformers delicately referred to prostitution, the social purity movement brought together ministers who wished to stamp out sin, doctors concerned about the spread of venereal disease, and women reformers determined to fight the double standard that made premarital and extramarital sex acceptable for men but demanded chastity of women. Advanced progressive reformers linked prostitution to poverty and championed higher wages for women. "Is it any wonder," asked the Chicago vice commission, "that a tempted girl who receives only six dollars per week working with her hands sells her body for twenty-five dollars per week when she learns there is a demand for it and men are willing to pay the price?"

Attacks on alcohol went hand in hand with the push for social purity. In the early twentieth century, the Anti-Saloon League, formed in 1895 under the leadership of Protestant clergy, added to the efforts of the Woman's Christian Temperance Union in campaigning to end the sale of liquor. Reformers pointed to links between drinking, prostitution, wife and child abuse, unemployment, and industrial accidents. The powerful liquor lobby fought back, spending liberally in election campaigns, fueling the charge that liquor corrupted the political process.

An element of nativism (dislike of foreigners) ran through the movement for prohibition, as it did in a number of progressive reforms. The Irish, the Italians, and the Germans were among the groups stigmatized by temperance reformers for their drinking. Even though most workers toiled six days a week and had only Sunday for recreation and relaxation, some progressives campaigned on the local level to enforce the Sunday closing of taverns, stores, and other commercial establishments. To further deny the working class access to alcohol, these progressives pushed for state legislation to outlaw the sale of liquor. By 1912, seven states were "dry."

Progressives' efforts to civilize the city demonstrated their willingness to take action; their belief that environment, not heredity alone, determined human behavior; and their optimism that conditions could be corrected through government action without radically altering America's economy or institutions. All of these attitudes characterized the progressive movement.

Progressives and the Working Class

Day-to-day contact with their neighbors made settlement house workers particularly sympathetic to labor unions. When Mary Kenney O'Sullivan complained that her bookbinders' union met in a dirty, noisy saloon, Jane Addams invited the union to meet at Hull House. And during the Pullman strike in 1894, Hull House residents organized strike relief. "Hull-House has been so unionized," grumbled one Chicago businessman, "that it has lost its usefulness and become a detriment and harm to the community." But to the working class, the support of middle-class reformers marked a significant gain.

Attempts to forge a cross-class alliance became institutionalized in 1903 with the creation of the **Women's Trade Union League** (WTUL). The WTUL brought together women workers and middle-class "allies." Its goal was to organize workingwomen into unions under the auspices of the American Federation of Labor (AFL). However, as one workingwoman confided, "The men think that the girls should not get as good work as the men and should not make half as much money as a man." Samuel Gompers, president of the AFL, endorsed the principle of equal pay for equal work, shrewdly observing that it would help male workers more than women, since many employers hired women precisely because they could be paid less.

Although the alliance between workingwomen, primarily immigrants and daughters of immigrants, and their middle-class allies was not without tension, the WTUL helped workingwomen achieve significant gains. Its most notable success came in 1909 in the "uprising of the twenty thousand," when hundreds of women employees of the Triangle Shirtwaist Company in New York City went on strike to protest low wages, dangerous working conditions, and management's refusal to recognize their union, the International Ladies' Garment Workers Union. In support, an estimated twenty thousand garment workers, most of them teenage girls and many of them Jewish and Italian immigrants, stayed out on strike through the winter, picketing in the bitter cold. By the time the strike ended in February 1910, the workers had won important demands in many shops. The solidarity shown by the women workers proved to be the strike's greatest achievement. As Clara Lemlich, one of the strike's leaders, exclaimed, "They used to say that you couldn't even organize women. They wouldn't come to union meetings. They were 'temporary' workers. Well we showed them!"

The WTUL made enormous contributions to the strike. It provided volunteers for the picket lines, posted more than $29,000 in bail, protested police brutality, organized a parade of ten thousand strikers, took part in the arbitration conference, appealed for funds, and generated publicity for the strike. Under the leadership of the WTUL, women from every class of society, from J. P. Morgan's daughter Anne to socialists on New York's Lower East Side, joined the strikers in a dramatic display of cross-class alliance.

But for all its success, the uprising of the twenty thousand failed fundamentally to change conditions for women workers, as the tragic Triangle fire dramatized in 1911. A little over a year after the shirtwaist makers' strike ended, fire alarms sounded at the Triangle Shirtwaist factory. The ramshackle building, full of lint and combustible cloth, burned to rubble in half an hour. A WTUL member described the scene below on the street: "Two young girls whom I knew to be working in the vicinity came rushing toward me, tears were running from their eyes and they were white and shaking as they caught me by the arm. 'Oh,' shrieked one of them, 'they are jumping. Jumping from ten stories up! They are going through the air like bundles of clothes.'"

The terrified Triangle workers had little choice but to jump. Flames blocked one exit, and the other door had been locked to prevent workers from pilfering. The flimsy, rusted fire escape collapsed under the weight of fleeing workers, killing dozens. Trapped, 54 workers on the top floors jumped to their deaths. Of 500 workers, 146 died and scores of others were injured. The owners of the Triangle firm went to trial for negligence, but they avoided conviction when authorities determined that the fire had been started by a careless smoker. The Triangle Shirtwaist Company reopened in another firetrap within a matter of weeks.

Outrage and a sense of futility overwhelmed Rose Schneiderman, a leading
WTUL organizer, who made a bitter speech at the memorial service for the dead
Triangle workers. "I would be a traitor to those poor burned bodies if I came here
to talk good fellowship," she told her audience. "We have tried you good people
of the public and we have found you wanting. . . . I know from my experience it
is up to the working people to save themselves . . . by a strong working class
movement." The Triangle fire severely tested the bonds of the cross-class alliance.
Schneiderman and other WTUL leaders determined that organizing and striking
were no longer enough, particularly when the AFL paid so little attention to
women workers. Increasingly, the WTUL turned its efforts to lobbying for protective legislation — laws that would limit hours and regulate women's working
conditions.

Advocates of protective legislation won a major victory in 1908 when the U.S.
Supreme Court, in *Muller v. Oregon*, reversed its previous rulings and upheld
an Oregon law that limited to ten the hours women could work in a day. A mass
of sociological evidence put together by Florence Kelley of the National Consumers'
League and Josephine Goldmark of the WTUL demonstrated the ill effects of
long hours on the health and safety of women. The data convinced the Court that
long hours endangered women and therefore the entire human race. The Court's
ruling set a precedent, but one that separated the well-being of women workers
from that of men by arguing that women's reproductive role justified special
treatment. Later generations of women fighting for equality would question the
effectiveness of this strategy and argue that it ultimately closed good jobs to
women. The WTUL, however, greeted protective legislation as a first step in the
attempt to ensure the safety of all workers.

The **National Consumers' League** (NCL), like the WTUL, fostered cross-
class alliance. When Florence Kelley took over the leadership of the NCL in 1899,
she urged middle-class women to boycott stores and exert pressure for decent
wages and working conditions for women employees, primarily saleswomen. The
league published a "white list" of stores that met its standards. Like the WTUL,
the NCL increasingly promoted protective legislation to better working conditions
for women. Frustrated by the reluctance of the private sector to respond to the
need for reform, progressives turned to government at all levels. Aware that
European governments had assumed a social role, providing regulation of industries and benefits to workers, American progressives wanted their own state and
federal governments to help level the playing field between workers and industrialists. Critics would later charge that the progressives assumed too easily that
government regulation could best solve social problems.

Reform also fueled the fight for woman suffrage. For women like Jane Addams
and Florence Kelley, involvement in social reform led inevitably to support for
woman suffrage. These new suffragists emphasized the reforms that could be
accomplished if women had the vote. Addams insisted that in an urban, industrial
society, a good housekeeper could not be sure the food she fed her family or the
water and milk they drank were pure unless she became involved in politics and

wielded the ballot — and not just the broom — to protect her family. The concept of **municipal housekeeping** encouraged women to put their talents to work in the service of society.

> **REVIEW** What types of people were drawn to the progressive movement, and what motivated them?

▶ Progressivism: Theory and Practice

Progressive reformers developed a theoretical basis for their activist approach by countering social Darwinism with a dynamic new reform Darwinism. The progressives emphasized action and experimentation. Dismissing the view that humans should leave progress to the dictates of natural selection, progressive reform Darwinists argued that human intelligence could shape change and improve society. In their zeal for action, progressives often showed an unchecked admiration for speed and efficiency that promoted scientific management and a new cult of efficiency. These varied strands of progressive theory found practical application in state and local politics, where reformers challenged traditional laissez-faire government.

Reform Darwinism and Social Engineering

The active, interventionist approach of the progressives directly challenged social Darwinism, with its insistence that the world operated on the principle of survival of the fittest and that human beings stood powerless in the face of the law of natural selection. Without abandoning the evolutionary framework of Darwinism, a new group of sociologists argued that evolution could be advanced more rapidly if men and women used their intellects to alter the environment. Sociologist Lester Frank Ward put it clearly in his book *Dynamic Sociology* (1883). "I insist that the time must soon come," he wrote, "when control of blind natural forces in society must give way to human foresight." Dubbed **reform Darwinism**, the new sociological theory condemned the laissez-faire approach, insisting that the liberal state should play a more active role in solving social problems.

Efficiency and *expertise* became watchwords in the progressive vocabulary. In *Drift and Mastery* (1914), journalist and critic Walter Lippmann called for skilled "technocrats" to use scientific techniques to control social change, substituting social engineering for aimless drift. Progressive reformers' emphasis on expertise inevitably fostered a kind of elitism. Unlike the Populists, who advocated a greater voice for the masses, progressives, for all their interest in social justice, insisted that experts be put in charge.

At its extreme, the application of expertise and social engineering took the form of **scientific management**, whose mechanized routine alienated the working class. Frederick Winslow Taylor pioneered "systematized shop management." After dropping out of Harvard, Taylor went to work as a machinist at Midvale Steel in Philadelphia in the 1880s. Obsessed with making humans and machines produce more and faster, he earned a master's of engineering degree in 1885 and went back to Midvale to restructure the workplace. With a stopwatch in his hand, he meticulously timed workers and attempted to break down their work into its simplest components, one repetitious action after another, on the theory that productivity would increase if tasks could be simplified. An advocate of piecework, quotas, and pay incentives for productivity, Taylor insisted that unions were unnecessary. As a consulting engineer, he spread his gospel of efficiency and won many converts among corporate managers. Workers hated the monotony of systematized shop management and argued that it led to the speedup — pushing workers to produce more in less time and for less pay. But many progressives applauded the increased productivity and efficiency of Taylor's system.

Progressive Government: City and State

The politicians who became premier progressives were generally the followers, not the leaders, in a movement already well advanced at the grassroots level. Yet they left their stamp on the movement. Tom Johnson made Cleveland a model of progressive reform, Robert M. La Follette turned Wisconsin into a laboratory for progressivism, and Hiram Johnson ended the domination of the Southern Pacific Railroad in California politics.

Progressivism burst forth at every level of government in 1900, but nowhere more forcefully than in Cleveland with the election of Democrat **Thomas Loftin Johnson** as mayor. A self-made millionaire by age forty, Johnson moved to Cleveland in 1899, where he began his career in politics. During his mayoral campaign, he pledged to reduce the streetcar fare from five cents to three cents. His election touched off a seven-year war between Johnson and the streetcar moguls, who argued that they couldn't meet costs with the lower fare. To get his three-cent fare, Johnson had the city buy the streetcar system, a tactic of municipal ownership progressives called "gas and water socialism." Under Johnson's administration, Cleveland became, in the words of journalist Lincoln Steffens, the "best governed city in America." Reelected four times, Johnson fought for fair taxation and championed greater democracy through the use of the initiative, referendum, and recall — devices that allowed voters to have a direct say in legislative and judicial matters.

In Wisconsin, Republican **Robert M. La Follette** converted to the progressive cause early in the 1900s. An astute politician, La Follette capitalized on the grassroots movement for reform to launch his long political career as governor (1901–1905) and U.S. senator (1906–1925). A graduate of the University of Wisconsin, La Follette brought scientists and professors into his administration and used the university, just down the street from the statehouse in Madison, as a resource in drafting legislation.

As governor, La Follette lowered railroad rates, raised railroad taxes, improved education, preached conservation, established factory regulation and workers' compensation, instituted the first direct primary in the country, and inaugurated the first state income tax. Under his leadership, Wisconsin earned the title "laboratory of democracy." A fiery orator, "Fighting Bob" La Follette united his supporters around issues that transcended party loyalties.

This emphasis on reform characterized progressivism, which attracted followers from both major parties. Democrats like Tom Johnson and Republicans like Robert La Follette could lay equal claim to the label "progressive." Democrats and Republicans alike crossed party lines to work for reform.

West of the Rockies, progressivism arrived somewhat later and found a champion in Republican **Hiram Johnson** of California, who served as governor from 1911 to 1917 and later as a U.S. senator. Since the 1870s, California politics had been dominated by the Southern Pacific Railroad, a corporation so rapacious that novelist Frank Norris styled it *The Octopus* (1901). Johnson ran for governor in 1910 on the promise to "kick the Southern Pacific out of politics." With the support of the reform wing of the Republican Party and the promise "to return the government to the people," he handily won. As governor, he introduced the direct primary; supported the initiative, referendum, and recall; strengthened the state's railroad commission; supported conservation; and signed an employer's liability law.

REVIEW   How did progressives justify their demand for more activist government?

▶ Progressivism Finds a President: Theodore Roosevelt

On September 6, 1901, President William McKinley was shot by Leon Czolgosz, an anarchist, while attending the Pan-American Exposition in Buffalo, New York. Eight days later, McKinley died. When news of his assassination reached his friend and political mentor Mark Hanna, Hanna is said to have growled, "Now that damned cowboy is president." He was speaking of Vice President Theodore Roosevelt, the colorful hero of the battle of San Juan Hill, who had indeed punched cattle in the Dakotas in the 1880s.

In the first hours of his presidency, Roosevelt reassured the shocked nation that he intended "to continue absolutely unbroken" the policies of McKinley. But Roosevelt was as different from McKinley as the twentieth century was from the nineteenth. An activist and a moralist, imbued with the progressive spirit, Roosevelt would turn the White House into a "bully pulpit," advocating conservation and antitrust reforms and championing the nation's emergence as a world power. In the process, Roosevelt would work to shift the nation's center of power from Wall Street to Washington.

After serving nearly two full terms as president, Roosevelt left office at the height of his powers. Any man would have found it difficult to follow in his footsteps, but his handpicked successor, William Howard Taft, proved hopelessly ill suited to the task. Taft's presidency was marked by a progressive stalemate, a bitter break with Roosevelt, and a schism in the Republican Party.

The Square Deal

At age forty-two, Theodore Roosevelt became the youngest man ever to move into the White House. A patrician by birth and an activist by temperament, Roosevelt

Theodore Roosevelt
Aptly described by a contemporary observer as "a steam engine in trousers," Theodore Roosevelt, at forty-two, was the youngest president ever to occupy the White House. He brought to the office energy, intellect, and activism in equal measure. Roosevelt boasted that he used the presidency as a "bully pulpit" — a forum from which he advocated reforms ranging from trust-busting to conservation. Library of Congress.

brought to the job enormous talent and energy. By the time he graduated from Harvard, he was already an accomplished naturalist, an enthusiastic historian, and a naval strategist. He could have chosen from any of those promising careers; instead, he chose politics, not a bad choice for a man who relished competition and craved power.

Roosevelt was shrewd enough to realize that the path to power did not lie in the good government leagues formed by his well-bred friends. "If it is the muckers that govern," he wrote, "then I want to see if I cannot hold my own with them." So he apprenticed himself early on to the local Republican ward boss Thomas C. Platt, who held court in a grimy, smoke-filled club above a Manhattan saloon. Roosevelt's rise in politics was swift and sure. He went from the New York assembly at the age of twenty-three to the presidency in less than twenty years, with time out as a cowboy in the Dakotas, police commissioner of New York City, assistant secretary of the navy, colonel of the Rough Riders, and governor of New York. Elected governor in 1898 as a moderate reformer, Roosevelt soon clashed with Platt, who finagled to get him "kicked upstairs" as a candidate for the vice presidency in 1900. As vice president, the party bosses reasoned, Roosevelt could do little harm. But one bullet proved the error of their logic.

As president, Roosevelt would harness his explosive energy to strengthen the power of the federal government, putting business on notice that it could no longer count on a laissez-faire government to give it free rein. In Roosevelt's eyes, self-interested capitalists like John D. Rockefeller, whose Standard Oil trust monopolized the refinery business, constituted "the most dangerous members of the criminal class — the criminals of great wealth." The "absolutely vital question" facing the country, Roosevelt wrote to a friend in 1901, was "whether or not the government has the power to control the trusts." The Sherman Antitrust Act of 1890 had been badly weakened by a conservative Supreme

Court and by attorneys general more willing to use it against labor unions than against monopolies. To determine whether the law had any teeth left, Roosevelt, in one of his first acts as president, ordered his attorney general to begin a secret antitrust investigation of the Northern Securities Company.

He picked a good target. Northern Securities had resulted from one of the most controversial mergers of the era. Two railroad magnates had fought a ruinous rate war that precipitated a panic on Wall Street, bankrupting thousands of small investors. To bring peace to the warring factions, financier J. P. Morgan stepped in and created the Northern Securities Company in 1901, linking three competing railroads under one management. This new behemoth monopolized railroad traffic in the Northwest. Small investors still smarting from their losses, farmers worried about freight rates, and the public in general saw in Northern Securities the symbol of corporate highhandedness.

In February 1902, just five months after Roosevelt took office, Wall Street rocked with the news that the government had filed an antitrust suit against Northern Securities. As one newspaper editor sarcastically observed, "Wall Street is paralyzed at the thought that a President of the United States would sink so low as to try to enforce the law." An indignant J. P. Morgan demanded to know why he had not been consulted. "If we have done anything wrong," he told the attorney general, "send your man to my man and they can fix it up." Roosevelt, amused, later noted that Morgan "could not help regarding me as a big rival operator." Roosevelt's thunderbolt put Wall Street on notice that the new president expected to be treated as an equal and was willing to use government as a weapon to curb business excesses. Perhaps sensing the new mood, the Supreme Court, in a significant turnaround, upheld the Sherman Act and called for the dissolution of Northern Securities in 1904.

"Hurrah for Teddy the Trustbuster," cheered the papers. Roosevelt went on to use the Sherman Act against forty-three trusts, including such giants as American Tobacco, Du Pont, and Standard Oil. Always the moralist, he insisted on a "rule of reason." He would punish "bad" trusts (those that broke the law) and leave "good" ones alone. In practice, he preferred regulation to antitrust suits. In 1903, he pressured Congress to pass the Elkins Act, outlawing railroad rebates. And he created the new cabinet-level Department of Commerce and Labor with the subsidiary Bureau of Corporations to act as a corporate watchdog.

Observing Roosevelt in action, journalist Joseph Pulitzer remarked, "He has subjugated Wall Street." Pulitzer exaggerated, but Roosevelt had masterfully asserted the moral and political authority of the executive, underscoring, in his words, the "duty of the President to act upon the theory that he is the steward of the people." In his handling of the anthracite coal strike in 1902, Roosevelt again demonstrated his willingness to assert the authority of the presidency, this time to mediate between labor and management.

In May, 147,000 coal miners in Pennsylvania went on strike. The United Mine Workers (UMW) demanded a reduction in the workday from twelve to ten hours, an equitable system of weighing each miner's output, and a 10 percent

Breaker Boys
Child labor in America's mines and mills was common at the turn of the twentieth century, despite state laws that tried to restrict it. Here, "breaker boys," some as young as seven years old, pick over coal in a Pennsylvania mine. Their unsmiling faces bear witness to the difficulty and danger of their work. A committee investigating child labor found more than ten thousand children illegally employed in the Pennsylvania coalfields.
Brown Brothers.

wage increase, along with recognition of the union. When asked about the appalling conditions in the mines that led to the strike, George Baer, the mine operators' spokesman, scoffed, "The miners don't suffer, why they can't even speak English." Buttressed by social Darwinism, Baer observed that "God in his infinite wisdom" had placed "the rights and interests of the laboring man" in the hands of the capitalists, not "the labor agitators."

The strike dragged on through the summer and into the fall. Hoarding and profiteering drove the price of coal from $2.50 to $6.00 a ton. As winter approached, coal shortages touched off near riots in the nation's big cities. At this juncture, Roosevelt stepped in to mediate, inviting representatives from both sides to meet in Washington in October. His unprecedented intervention served notice that government counted itself an independent force in business and labor disputes. At the same time, it gave unionism a boost by granting the UMW a place at the table.

At the meeting, Baer and the mine owners refused to talk with the union representative — a move that angered the attorney general and insulted the president. The meeting ended in an impasse. Beside himself with rage over the "woodenheaded obstinacy and stupidity" of management, Roosevelt threatened to seize the mines and run them with federal troops. It was a powerful bluff, one that called into question not only the supremacy of private property but also the rule of law. But the specter of federal troops being used to operate the mines quickly brought management around. In the end, the miners won a reduction in hours and a wage increase, but the owners succeeded in preventing formal recognition of the UMW.

Taken together, Roosevelt's actions in the Northern Securities case and the anthracite coal strike marked a dramatic departure from the presidential passivity of the Gilded Age. Roosevelt's actions demonstrated conclusively that government intended to act as a countervailing force to the power of the big corporations. Pleased with his role in the anthracite strike, Roosevelt announced that all he had tried to do was give labor and capital a square deal.

The phrase **Square Deal** became Roosevelt's campaign slogan in the 1904 election. But to win the presidency in his own right, Roosevelt needed to wrest control of the Republican Party from kingmaker and party boss Mark Hanna. Roosevelt adroitly used patronage to win supporters and weaken Hanna's power. Hanna died of typhoid fever in 1904, leaving Roosevelt the undisputed leader of the party.

In the presidential election of 1904, Roosevelt easily defeated the Democrats, who abandoned their former candidate, William Jennings Bryan, to support Judge Alton B. Parker, a "safe" choice they hoped would lure business votes away from Roosevelt. In the months before the election, the president prudently toned down his criticism of big business. Wealthy Republicans like J. P. Morgan may have grumbled privately, branding Roosevelt a class traitor, but they remained loyal to the party. Roosevelt swept into office with the largest popular majority — 57.9 percent — any candidate had polled up to that time.

Roosevelt the Reformer

"Tomorrow I shall come into my office in my own right," Roosevelt is said to have remarked on the eve of his election. "Then watch out for me!" Roosevelt's stunning victory gave him a mandate for reform. He would need all the popularity and political savvy he could muster, however, to guide his reform measures through Congress. The Senate remained controlled by a staunchly conservative Republican "old guard," with many senators on the payrolls of the corporations Roosevelt sought to curb. Roosevelt's pet project remained railroad regulation. The Elkins Act prohibiting rebates had not worked. No one could stop big shippers like Standard Oil from wringing concessions from the railroads. Roosevelt determined that the only solution lay in giving the Interstate Commerce Commission (ICC) real power to set rates and prevent discriminatory practices. But the right to determine the price of goods or services was an age-old prerogative of private enterprise, and one that business had no intention of yielding to government.

To ensure passage of the **Hepburn Act**, which would increase the power of the ICC, Roosevelt worked skillfully behind the scenes. In its final form, the Hepburn Act, passed in May 1906, gave the ICC the power to set rates subject to court review. Committed progressives like La Follette judged the law a defeat for reform. Die-hard conservatives branded it a "piece of populism." Both sides exaggerated. The law left the courts too much power and failed to provide adequate means for the ICC to determine rates, but its passage proved a landmark in federal control of private industry. For the first time, a government commission had the power to investigate private business records and to set rates.

Always an apt reader of the public temper, Roosevelt witnessed a growing appetite for reform. Revelations of corporate and political wrongdoing and social injustice filled the papers and boosted the sales of popular magazines. Roosevelt, who wielded publicity like a weapon in his pursuit of reform, counted many of the new investigative journalists, including Jacob Riis, among his friends. But he warned them against going too far, citing the allegorical character in *Pilgrim's Progress* who was so busy raking muck that he took no notice of higher things. Roosevelt's criticism gave the American vocabulary a new word, *muckraker,* which journalists soon appropriated as a title of honor.

Muckraking, as Roosevelt well knew, provided enormous help in securing progressive legislation. In the spring of 1906, publicity generated by the muckrakers about poisons in patent medicines goaded the Senate, with Roosevelt's backing, into passing a pure food and drug bill. Opponents in the House of Representatives hoped to keep the legislation locked up in committee. There it would have died, were it not for the publication of Upton Sinclair's novel *The Jungle* (1906), with its sensational account of filthy conditions in meatpacking plants. A massive public outcry led to the passage of the **Pure Food and Drug Act** and the Meat Inspection Act in 1906.

In the waning years of his administration, Roosevelt allied with the more progressive elements of the Republican Party. In speech after speech, he attacked "malefactors of great wealth." Styling himself a "radical," he claimed credit for leading the "ultra conservative" party of McKinley to a position of "progressive conservatism and conservative radicalism."

When an economic panic developed in the fall of 1907, business interests quickly blamed the president. The panic of 1907 proved severe but short. Once again, J. P. Morgan stepped in to avert disaster, this time switching funds from one bank to another to prop up weak institutions. For his services, he claimed the Tennessee Coal and Iron Company, an independent steel business that had long been coveted by the U.S. Steel Corporation. Morgan dispatched his lieutenants to Washington, where they told Roosevelt that the sale of the company would aid the economy "but little benefit" U.S. Steel. Willing to take the word of a gentleman, Roosevelt tacitly agreed not to institute antitrust proceedings against U.S. Steel over the acquisition. Roosevelt later learned that Morgan had been less than candid. U.S. Steel acquired Tennessee Coal and Iron for a price well below market value, doing away with a competitor and undercutting the economy of the Southeast. Roosevelt's promise not to institute antitrust proceedings against U.S. Steel would give rise to the charge that he acted as a tool of the Morgan interests.

The charge of collusion between business and government underscored the extent to which corporate leaders like Morgan found federal regulation preferable to unbridled competition or harsher state measures. During the Progressive Era, enlightened business leaders cooperated with government in the hope of avoiding antitrust prosecution. Convinced that regulation and not trust-busting offered the best way to deal with big business, Roosevelt never acknowledged that his regulatory policies fostered an alliance between business and government that today is called corporate liberalism.

Roosevelt and Conservation

In the area of conservation, Roosevelt proved indisputably ahead of his time. When he took office, some 43 million acres of forestland remained as government reserves. He more than quadrupled that number to 194 million acres. To conserve natural resources, he fought western cattle barons, lumber kings, mining interests, and powerful leaders in Congress, including Speaker of the House Joseph Cannon, who vowed to spend "not one cent for scenery."

As the first president to have lived and worked in the West, Roosevelt came to the White House convinced of the need for better management of the nation's rivers and forests and the preservation of wildlife and wilderness. During his presidency, he placed the nation's conservation policy in the hands of scientifically trained experts like his chief forester, Gifford Pinchot. Pinchot preached conservation — the efficient use of natural resources. Willing to permit grazing, lumbering, and the development of hydroelectric power, conservationists fought private interests only when they felt business acted irresponsibly or threatened to monopolize water and electric power. Preservationists like John Muir, founder of the Sierra Club, believed that the wilderness needed to be protected. Roosevelt, who hiked Yosemite with Muir, understood the need for both preservation and conservation.

Roosevelt's multifaceted personality encompassed many contradictions. A fervent Darwinian naturalist and an (overly) enthusiastic game hunter, a conservationist who built big dams and a preservationist who saved the redwoods, Roosevelt aimed to have it both ways. And he did.

One of Roosevelt's first acts as president was to establish a pelican refuge in Florida. An avid bird-watcher since his youth, he added 50 more bird reservations from Florida to Alaska during his presidency. The passage of the Antiquities Act in 1906 gave the president unchecked power to protect archaeological, scientific, and environmentally significant federal lands instead of "dilly dallying" with a "tortoise-paced Congress." Roosevelt wielded his power with relish, creating 18 national monuments, 6 national parks, and 150 national forests. He prided himself on saving the Grand Canyon from miners and developers. At the same time, he supported the Newlands Reclamation Act (1902), much criticized by today's ecologists, as a measure to irrigate the West by building large dams and reservoirs in the "conquest" of the desert ecosystem and the promotion of population growth.

In 1907, Congress attempted to put the brakes on Roosevelt's conservation program by passing a law limiting his power to create forest reserves in six western states. In the days leading up to the law's enactment, Roosevelt feverishly created twenty-one new reserves and enlarged eleven more, saving 16 million acres from development. Once again, Roosevelt had outwitted his adversaries. "Opponents of the forest service turned handsprings in their wrath," he wrote, "but the threats . . . were really only a tribute to the efficiency of our action." Worried that private utilities were gobbling up waterpower sites and creating a monopoly of hydroelectric power, he connived with Pinchot to withdraw 2,565 power sites from private use by designating them "ranger stations." Firm in his commitment to wild America, Roosevelt proved willing to stretch the law when it served his ends. His legacy is more than 234 million acres of American wilderness saved for posterity (Map 21.1).

The Big Stick

Roosevelt's activism extended to his foreign policy, where he worked to buttress the nation's newly won place among world leaders. A fierce proponent of America's interests abroad, he believed that Congress was inept in foreign affairs, and he relied on executive power to pursue a vigorous foreign policy, sometimes stretching the powers of the presidency beyond legal limits. In his relations with the European powers, he relied on military strength and diplomacy, a combination he aptly described with the aphorism "Speak softly but carry a big stick." In the Caribbean, Roosevelt jealously guarded the U.S. sphere of influence defined in the Monroe Doctrine. His proprietary attitude toward the Western Hemisphere became evident in the case of the Panama Canal. Roosevelt had long been a supporter of a canal linking the Caribbean and the Pacific. By enabling ships to move quickly from the Atlantic to the Pacific, a canal would trim 8,000 miles from a coast-to-coast voyage and effectively double the U.S. Navy's power.

Having decided on a route across the Panamanian isthmus (a narrow strip of land connecting North and South America), then part of Colombia, Roosevelt in 1902 offered the Colombian government a one-time sum of $10 million and an annual rent of $250,000. When the government in Bogotá refused to accept the offer, Roosevelt became incensed at what he called the "homicidal corruptionists" in Colombia for trying to "blackmail" the United States. At the prompting of a group of New York investors, the Panamanians staged an uprising in 1903, and with unseemly haste the U.S. government recognized the new government within twenty-four hours. The Panamanians promptly accepted the $10 million, and the building got under way. The canal would take eleven years and $375 million to complete; it opened in 1914.

In the wake of the Panama affair, a confrontation with Germany over Venezuela, and yet another default on a European debt, this time in the Dominican Republic, Roosevelt announced in 1904 what became known as the **Roosevelt Corollary** to the Monroe Doctrine. Couched in the moralistic rhetoric typical of Roosevelt, the corollary declared that the United States would not intervene in Latin America as long as nations there conducted their affairs with "decency." But the United States would step in if any Latin American nation proved guilty of "brutal wrongdoing." The Roosevelt Corollary in effect made the United States the policeman of the Western Hemisphere and served notice to the European powers to keep out.

In Asia, Roosevelt inherited the Open Door policy initiated by Secretary of State John Hay in 1899, designed to ensure U.S. commercial entry into China.

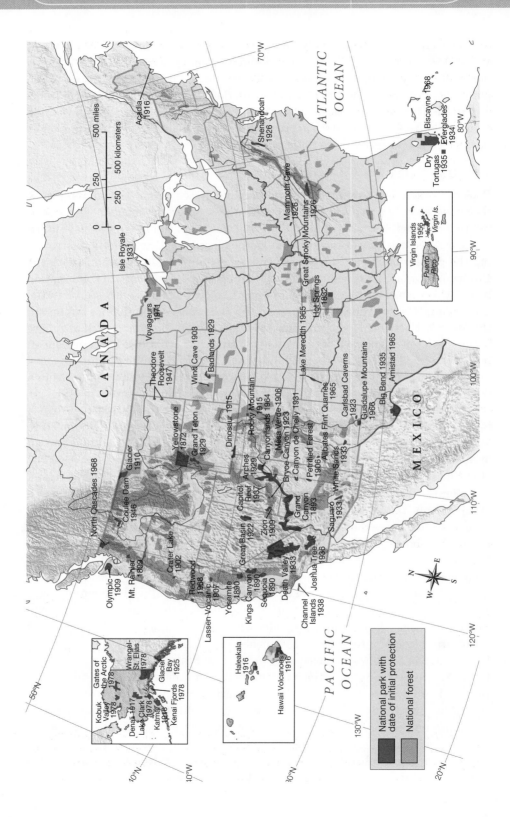

ATLANTIC OCEAN

PACIFIC OCEAN

CANADA

MEXICO

500 miles
500 kilometers
0   250   500
0   250

Acadia 1916
Shenandoah 1926
Mammoth Cave 1926
Great Smoky Mountains 1926
Biscayne 1968
Everglades 1934
Dry Tortugas 1935
Isle Royale 1931
Voyageurs 1971
Theodore Roosevelt 1947
Wind Cave 1903
Badlands 1929
Hot Springs 1832
Lake Meredith 1965
Guadalupe Mountains 1966
Big Bend 1935
Amistad 1965
Yellowstone 1872
Grand Teton 1929
Dinosaur 1915
Rocky Mountain 1915
Canyonlands 1964
Mesa Verde 1906
Canyon de Chelly 1931
Petrified Forest 1906
Albates Flint Quarries 1965
Carlsbad Caverns 1923
North Cascades 1968
Glacier 1910
Coulee Dam 1946
Arches 1929
Capitol Reef 1937
Bryce Canyon 1923
Grand Canyon 1893
White Sands 1933
Crater Lake 1902
Great Basin 1922
Zion 1909
Saguaro 1933
Olympic 1909
Mt. Rainier 1899
Redwood 1968
Yosemite 1890
Kings Canyon 1890
Sequoia 1890
Death Valley 1933
Joshua Tree 1936
Channel Islands 1938
Lassen Volcanic 1907

Virgin Islands 1956
Puerto Rico
Virgin Is.

Gates of the Arctic 1978
Kobuk Valley 1978
Wrangel-St. Elias 1978
Glacier Bay 1925
Denali 1917
Lake Clark 1978
Katmai 1918
Kenai Fjords 1978

Haleakala 1916
Hawaii Volcanoes 1916

National park with date of initial protection
National forest

N E S W

70°W
80°W
90°W
100°W
110°W
120°W
130°W
50°N
40°N
30°N
20°N

As Britain, France, Russia, Japan, and Germany raced to secure Chinese trade and territory, Roosevelt was tempted to use force to enter the fray and gain economic or possibly territorial concessions. As a result of victory in the Spanish-American War, the United States already enjoyed a foothold in the Philippines. Realizing that Americans would not support an aggressive Asian policy, Roosevelt sensibly held back.

In his relations with Europe, Roosevelt sought to establish the United States, fresh from its victory over Spain, as a rising force in world affairs. When tensions flared between France and Germany in Morocco in 1905, Roosevelt mediated at a conference in Algeciras, Spain, where he worked to maintain a balance of power that helped neutralize German ambitions. His skillful mediation gained him a reputation as an astute player on the world stage and demonstrated the nation's new presence in world affairs.

Roosevelt earned the Nobel Peace Prize in 1906 for his role in negotiating an end to the Russo-Japanese War, which had broken out when the Japanese invaded Chinese Manchuria, threatening Russia's sphere of influence in the area. Once again, Roosevelt sought to maintain a balance of power, in this case working to curb Japanese expansionism. Roosevelt admired the Japanese, judging them "the most dashing fighters in the world," but he did not want Japan to become too strong in Asia.

When good relations with Japan were jeopardized by discriminatory legislation in California calling for segregated public schools for Asians, Roosevelt smoothed over the incident and negotiated the "Gentlemen's Agreement" in 1907, which allowed the Japanese to save face by voluntarily restricting immigration to the United States. To demonstrate America's naval power and to counter Japan's growing bellicosity, Roosevelt dispatched the Great White Fleet, sixteen of the navy's most up-to-date battleships, on a "goodwill mission" around the world. U.S. relations with Japan improved, and in the 1908 Root-Takahira agreement the two nations pledged to maintain the Open Door and support the status quo in the Pacific. Roosevelt's show of American force constituted a classic example of his dictum "Speak softly but carry a big stick."

The Troubled Presidency of William Howard Taft

Roosevelt had promised on the eve of his election in 1904 that he would not seek another term. So he retired from the presidency in 1909 at age fifty and removed himself from the political scene by going on safari in Africa. He turned the White House over to **William Howard Taft**, a lawyer who had served as governor-general

◀ **MAP 21.1**
National Parks and Forests
The national park system in the West began with Yellowstone in 1872. Grand Canyon, Yosemite, Kings Canyon, and Sequoia followed in the 1890s. During his presidency, Theodore Roosevelt added six parks — Crater Lake, Wind Cave, Petrified Forest, Lassen Volcanic, Mesa Verde, and Zion.

of the Philippines. In the presidential election of 1908, Taft soundly defeated the perennial Democratic candidate, William Jennings Bryan, in the electoral college. But Taft's popular majority amounted to only half of Roosevelt's record win in 1904.

A genial man with a talent for law, Taft had no experience in elective office, no feel for politics, and no nerve for controversy. His ambitious wife coveted the office and urged him to seek it. He would have been better off listening to his mother, who warned, "Roosevelt is a good fighter and enjoys it, but the malice of politics would make you miserable." Her words proved prophetic.

Once in office, Taft proved a perfect tool in the hands of Republicans who yearned for a return to the days of a less active executive. A lawyer by training and instinct, Taft believed that it was up to the courts, not the president, to arbitrate social issues. Roosevelt had carried presidential power to a new level, often flouting the separation of powers and showing thinly veiled contempt for Congress and the courts. A legalist, Taft found it difficult to condone Roosevelt's actions. Wary of the progressive insurgents in Congress, Taft relied increasingly on conservatives in the Republican Party. As a progressive senator lamented, "Taft is a ponderous and amiable man completely surrounded by men who know exactly what they want."

Taft's troubles began on the eve of his inaugural, when he called a special session of Congress to deal with the tariff, which had grown inordinately high under Republican rule. Roosevelt had been too politically astute to tackle the troublesome tariff issue, even though he knew that rates needed to be lowered. Taft blundered into the fray. The House of Representatives passed a modest downward revision, but the conservative Senate struck down the tax and added more than eight hundred crippling amendments to the tariff. The Payne-Aldrich bill that emerged actually raised the tariff, benefiting big business and the trusts at the expense of consumers. As if paralyzed, Taft neither fought for changes nor vetoed the measure. On a tour of the Midwest in 1909, he was greeted with jeers when he claimed, "I think the Payne bill is the best bill that the Republican Party ever passed." In the eyes of a growing number of Americans, Taft's praise of the tariff made him either a fool or a liar.

Taft's legalism soon got him into hot water in the area of conservation. He undid Roosevelt's work to preserve hydroelectric power sites when he learned that they had been improperly designated as ranger stations. And when Gifford Pinchot publicly denounced Taft's secretary of the interior as a tool of western land-grabbers, Taft fired Pinchot, touching off a storm of controversy that damaged Taft and alienated Roosevelt.

When Roosevelt returned to the United States in June 1910, he received a hero's welcome and attracted a stream of visitors and reporters seeking his advice and opinions. Hurt, Taft kept his distance. By late summer, Roosevelt had taken sides with the progressive insurgents in his party. "Taft is utterly hopeless as a leader," Roosevelt confided to his son as he set out on a speaking tour of the West. Reading the mood of the country, Roosevelt began to sound more and more like a candidate.

With the Republican Party divided, the Democrats swept the congressional elections of 1910. Branding the Payne-Aldrich tariff "the mother of trusts," they captured a majority in the House of Representatives and won several key governorships. The revitalized Democratic Party could look to new leaders, among them the progressive governor of New Jersey, Woodrow Wilson.

The new Democratic majority in the House, working with progressive Republicans in the Senate, achieved a number of key reforms, including legislation to regulate mine and railroad safety, to create the Children's Bureau in the Department of Labor, and to establish an eight-hour day for federal workers. Two significant constitutional amendments — the Sixteenth Amendment, which provided for a modest graduated income tax, and the Seventeenth Amendment, which called for the direct election of senators (formerly chosen by state legislatures) — went to the states, where they would win ratification in 1913. While Congress rode the high tide of progressive reform, Taft sat on the sidelines.

In foreign policy, Taft continued Roosevelt's policy of extending U.S. influence abroad, but here, too, Taft had a difficult time following in Roosevelt's footsteps. His policy of **dollar diplomacy** championed commercial goals rather than the strategic aims Roosevelt had pursued. Taft naively assumed he could substitute "dollars for bullets." In the Caribbean, he provoked anti-American feeling by attempting to force commercial treaties on Nicaragua and Honduras and by dispatching U.S. Marines to Nicaragua and the Dominican Republic in 1912 pursuant to the Roosevelt Corollary. In Asia, he openly avowed his intent to promote "active intervention to secure for . . . our capitalists opportunity for profitable investment." Lacking Roosevelt's understanding of power politics, Taft never recognized that an aggressive commercial policy could not exist without the willingness to use military might to back it up.

Taft faced the limits of dollar diplomacy when revolution broke out in Mexico in 1911. Under pressure to protect American investments, which amounted to more than $4 billion, he mobilized troops along the border. In the end, however, with no popular support for a war with Mexico, he had to fall back on diplomatic pressure to salvage American interests.

Taft hoped to encourage world peace through the use of a world court and arbitration. He unsuccessfully sponsored a series of arbitration treaties that Roosevelt, who prized national honor more than international law, vehemently opposed as weak and cowardly. By 1910, Roosevelt had become a vocal critic of Taft's foreign policy, which he dismissed as "maudlin folly." The final breach between Taft and Roosevelt came in 1911, when Taft's attorney general filed an antitrust suit against U.S. Steel. In its brief against the corporation, the government cited Roosevelt's agreement with the Morgan interests in the 1907 acquisition of Tennessee Coal and Iron. The incident greatly embarrassed Roosevelt. Thoroughly enraged, he lambasted Taft's "archaic" antitrust policy and hinted that he might be persuaded to run for president again.

REVIEW In what ways did Roosevelt's domestic policies respond to progressive demands?

▶ Woodrow Wilson and Progressivism at High Tide

Progressives' disillusionment with Taft resulted in a split in the Republican Party and the creation of a new Progressive Party led by Theodore Roosevelt. In the election of 1912, four candidates, including Socialist Eugene V. Debs, styled themselves "progressives." Democrat **Woodrow Wilson**, with a minority of the popular vote, won the election. Born in Virginia and raised in Georgia, he became the first southerner to be elected president since 1844 and only the second Democrat to occupy the White House since Reconstruction. A believer in states' rights, Wilson nevertheless promised legislation to break the hold of the trusts.

This lean, ascetic scholar was, as one biographer conceded, a man whose "political convictions were never as fixed as his ambition." Although he owed his governorship to the Democratic machine, he quickly turned his back on the bosses and, with his eye on the presidency, put New Jersey in the vanguard of progressivism. He brought to the White House a gift for oratory, a stern will, and a set of fixed beliefs. Wilson proved rarely able to compromise. His tendency to turn differences of opinion into personal hatreds would impair his leadership and damage his presidency. Fortunately for Wilson, he came to power with a Democratic Congress eager to do his bidding.

Progressive Insurgency and the Election of 1912

Convinced that Taft was "hopelessly inept," Roosevelt announced his candidacy for the Republican nomination with the colorful phrase "My hat is in the ring." But for all his popularity, Roosevelt no longer controlled the party machinery. Taft, with uncharacteristic strength, refused to step aside. As he bitterly told a journalist, "Even a rat in a corner will fight." Roosevelt took advantage of newly passed primary election laws and ran in thirteen states, winning 278 delegates to Taft's 48. But at the Chicago convention, Taft's bosses refused to seat the Roosevelt delegates. Fistfights broke out on the convention floor as Taft won nomination on the first ballot. Crying robbery, Roosevelt's supporters bolted the party.

Seven weeks later, in the same Chicago auditorium, the hastily organized Progressive Party met to nominate Roosevelt. Amid a thunder of applause, Jane Addams seconded Roosevelt's nomination. Full of reforming zeal, the delegates chose Roosevelt and Hiram Johnson to head the new party and approved the most ambitious platform since that of the Populists. Planks called for woman suffrage, presidential primaries, conservation of natural resources, an end to child labor, workers' compensation, a minimum wage that would include women workers, social security, and a federal income tax.

Roosevelt arrived in Chicago to accept the nomination and announced that he felt "as fit as a bull moose," giving the new party a nickname and a mascot. But for all the excitement and the cheering, the new Progressive Party was doomed, and the candidate knew it. The people may have supported the party, but the politicians, even progressives such as La Follette, stayed within the

Republican fold. "I am under no illusion about it," Roosevelt confessed to a friend. "It is a forlorn hope." But he had gone too far to turn back. He led the Bull Moose Party into the fray, exhorting his followers in ringing biblical tones, "We shall not falter, we stand at Armageddon and do battle for the Lord."

The Democrats, delighted at the split in the Republican ranks, smelled victory. Their convention turned into a bitter fight for the nomination. After forty-six ballots, Woodrow Wilson became the party's nominee. Wilson's career in politics was nothing short of meteoric. He was elected governor of New Jersey in 1910, and after only eighteen months in office the former professor of political science and president of Princeton University found himself running for president of the United States.

Voters in 1912 could choose among four candidates who claimed to be progressives. Taft, Roosevelt, and Wilson each embraced the label, and even the Socialist candidate, Eugene V. Debs, styled himself a progressive. That the term *progressive* could stretch to cover these diverse candidates underscored major disagreements in progressive thinking about the relationship between business and government. Taft, in spite of his trust-busting, was generally viewed as the candidate of the old guard. The real contest for the presidency was between Roosevelt and Wilson and the two political philosophies summed up in their respective campaign slogans: "**The New Nationalism**" and "**The New Freedom**."

The New Nationalism expressed Roosevelt's belief in federal planning and regulation. He accepted the inevitability of big business but demanded that government act as "a steward of the people" to regulate the giant corporations. Wilson, schooled in the Democratic principles of limited government and states' rights, set a markedly different course with his New Freedom. Wilson promised to use antitrust legislation to get rid of big corporations and to give small businesses and farmers better opportunities in the marketplace.

The energy and enthusiasm of the Bull Moosers made the race seem closer than it was. In the end, the Republican vote split, while the Democrats remained united. No candidate claimed a majority in the race. Wilson captured a bare 42 percent of the popular vote. Roosevelt and his Bull Moose Party won 27 percent, an unprecedented tally for a new party. Taft came in third with 23 percent. The Socialist Party, led by Debs, captured 6 percent. In the electoral college, however, Wilson won a decisive 435 votes, with 88 going to Roosevelt and only 8 to Taft (Map 21.2). The Republican Party moved in a conservative direction, while the Progressive Party essentially collapsed after Roosevelt's defeat. It had always been, in the words of one astute observer, "a house divided against itself and already mortgaged."

Wilson's Reforms: Tariff, Banking, and the Trusts

Although he endorsed states' rights and opposed big government in his campaign, Wilson was prepared to work on the base built by Roosevelt to strengthen presidential power, exerting leadership to achieve banking reform and working through his party in Congress to accomplish the Democratic agenda. Before he was finished,

Candidate	Electoral Vote	Popular Vote	Percent of Popular Vote
Woodrow Wilson (Democrat)	435	6,293,454	41.9
Theodore Roosevelt (Progressive)	88	4,119,538	27.4
William H. Taft (Republican)	8	3,484,980	23.2
Eugene V. Debs (Socialist)	0	900,672	6.1

MAP 21.2
The Election of 1912

Wilson presided over progressivism at high tide and lent his support not only to the platform of the Democratic Party but also to many of the Progressive Party's social reforms.

In March 1913, Wilson showed off his oratorical ability by becoming the first president since John Adams to go to Capitol Hill and speak directly to Congress. With the Democratic Party firmly in control, he called for tariff reform. "The object of the tariff," Wilson told Congress, "must be effective competition." The Democratic House of Representatives hastily passed the Underwood tariff, which lowered rates by 15 percent. To compensate for lost revenue, the House approved a moderate federal income tax. In the Senate, lobbyists for industries quietly went to work to get the tariff raised, but Wilson rallied public opinion by attacking the "industrious and insidious lobby." In the harsh glare of publicity, the Senate passed the Underwood tariff, which earned praise as "the most honest tariff since the Civil War."

Wilson next turned his attention to banking. The panic of 1907 dramatically testified to the failure of the banking system. That year, Roosevelt, like President Grover Cleveland before him, had to turn to J. P. Morgan to avoid economic catastrophe. But by the time Wilson came to office, Morgan's legendary power had come under close scrutiny. In 1913, a Senate committee investigated the "money trust," calling J. P. Morgan himself to testify. The committee uncovered an alarming concentration of banking power. J. P. Morgan and Company and its affiliates held 341 directorships in 112 corporations, controlling assets of more than $22 billion ($500 billion in today's dollars). The sensational findings created a mandate for banking reform.

The **Federal Reserve Act** of 1913 marked the most significant piece of domestic legislation of Wilson's presidency. It established a national banking system composed of twelve regional banks, privately controlled but regulated and supervised by the Federal Reserve Board, appointed by the president. It gave the United States its first efficient banking and currency system and, at the same time, provided for a greater degree of government control over banking. The new system made currency more elastic and credit adequate for the needs of business and agriculture. It did not, however, attempt to take control of the boom and bust cycles in the U.S. economy, which would produce the Great Depression of the 1930s (as discussed in chapters 23 and 24).

Wilson, flush with success, tackled the trust issue next. When Congress reconvened in January 1914, he supported the introduction and passage of the Clayton Antitrust Act to outlaw "unfair competition" — practices such as price discrimination and interlocking directorates (directors from one corporation sitting on the board of another). By spelling out unfair practices, Wilson hoped to guide business activity back to healthy competition without resorting to regulation. In the midst of the successful fight for the Clayton Act, Wilson changed course and threw his support behind the creation of the **Federal Trade Commission** (FTC), precisely the kind of federal regulatory agency that Roosevelt had advocated in his New Nationalism platform. The FTC, created in 1914, had not only wide investigatory powers but also the authority to prosecute corporations for "unfair trade practices" and to enforce its judgments by issuing "cease and desist" orders. Despite his campaign promises, Wilson's antitrust program worked to regulate rather than to break up big business.

By the fall of 1914, Wilson had exhausted the stock of ideas that made up the New Freedom. He alarmed progressives by declaring that the progressive movement had fulfilled its mission and that the country needed "a time of healing." Disgruntled progressives also disapproved of Wilson's conservative appointments. Having fought provisions in the Federal Reserve Act that would give bankers control, Wilson promptly named a banker as the first chief of the Federal Reserve Board. Appointments to the new FTC also went to conservative businessmen. The progressive penchant for expertise helps explain Wilson's choices. Believing that experts in the field could best understand the complex issues at stake, Wilson appointed bankers to oversee the banks and businessmen to regulate business.

Wilson, Reluctant Progressive

As Wilson repeatedly obstructed or obstinately refused to endorse further progressive reforms, progressives watched in dismay. He failed to support labor's demand for an end to court injunctions against labor unions. He twice threatened to veto legislation providing farm credits for nonperishable crops. He refused to support child labor legislation or woman suffrage. Wilson used the rhetoric of the New Freedom to justify his actions, claiming that his administration would condone "special privileges to none." But, in fact, his stance often reflected the interests of his small-business constituency.

In the face of Wilson's obstinacy, reform might have ended in 1913 had not politics intruded. In the congressional elections of 1914, the Republican Party, no longer split by Roosevelt's Bull Moose faction, won substantial gains. Democratic strategists, with their eyes on the 1916 presidential race, recognized that Wilson needed to pick up support in the Midwest and the West by capturing votes from former Bull Moose progressives. Wilson responded belatedly by lending his support to reform in the months leading up to the election of 1916. In a sharp about-face, he cultivated union labor, farmers, and social reformers. To please labor, he appointed progressive Louis Brandeis to the Supreme Court. To woo farmers, he threw his support behind legislation to obtain rural credits. And he won praise from labor by supporting workers' compensation and the Keating-Owen child labor law (1916), which outlawed the regular employment of children younger than sixteen. When a railroad strike threatened in the months before the election, Wilson practically ordered Congress to establish an eight-hour day on the railroads. He had moved a long way from his position in 1912 to embrace many of the social reforms championed by Theodore Roosevelt. As Wilson boasted, the Democrats had "opened their hearts to the demands of social justice" and had "come very near to carrying out the platform of the Progressive Party." Wilson's shift toward reform, along with his claim that he had kept the United States out of the war in Europe (as discussed in chapter 22), helped him win reelection in 1916.

REVIEW   How and why did Wilson's reform program evolve during his first term?

▶ The Limits of Progressive Reform

While progressivism called for a more active role for the liberal state, at heart it was a movement that sought reforms designed to preserve American institutions and stem the tide of more radical change. Its basic conservatism can be seen by comparing it with the more radical movements of socialism, radical labor, and birth control — and by looking at the groups progressive reform left behind, including women and African Americans.

Radical Alternatives

The year 1900 marked the birth of the Social Democratic Party in America, later called simply the **Socialist Party**. Like the progressives, the socialists were middle-class and native-born. They had broken with the older, more militant Socialist Labor Party precisely because of its dogmatic approach and immigrant constituency. The new group of socialists proved eager to appeal to a broad mass of disaffected Americans.

The Socialist Party chose as its presidential standard-bearer Eugene V. Debs, whose experience in the Pullman strike of 1894 (see chapter 20) convinced him that "there is no hope for the toiling masses of my countrymen, except by the pathways mapped out by Socialism." Debs would run for president five times, in every election (except 1916) from 1900 to 1920. The socialism Debs advocated preached cooperation over competition and urged men and women to liberate themselves from "the barbarism of private ownership and wage slavery." In the 1912 election, Debs indicted both old parties as "Tweedledee and Tweedledum," each dedicated to the preservation of capitalism and the continuation of the wage system. Only through socialism, he argued, could democracy exist. Styling the Socialist Party the "revolutionary party of the working class," he urged voters to rally to his standard. Debs's best showing came in 1912, when his 6 percent of the popular vote totaled more than 900,000 votes.

Farther to the left than the socialists stood the **Industrial Workers of the World** (IWW), nicknamed the Wobblies. In 1905, Debs, along with Western Federation of Miners leader William Dudley "Big Bill" Haywood, created the IWW, "one big union" dedicated to organizing the most destitute segment of the workforce, the unskilled workers disdained by Samuel Gompers's AFL: western miners, migrant farmworkers, lumbermen, and immigrant textile workers. Haywood, a craggy-faced miner with one eye (he had lost the other in a childhood accident), was a charismatic leader and a proletarian intellectual. Seeing workers on the lowest rung of the social ladder as the victims of violent repression, the IWW advocated direct action, sabotage, and the general strike — tactics designed to trigger a workers' uprising. The IWW never had more than 10,000 members at any one time, although possibly as many as 100,000 workers belonged to the union at one time or another in the early twentieth century. Nevertheless, the IWW's influence on the country extended far beyond its numbers (as discussed in chapter 22).

In contrast to political radicals like Debs and Haywood, **Margaret Sanger** promoted birth control as a movement for social change. Sanger, a nurse who had worked among the poor on New York's Lower East Side, coined the term *birth control* in 1915 and launched a movement with broad social implications. Sanger and her followers saw birth control not only as a sexual and medical reform but also as a means to alter social and political power relationships and to alleviate human misery.

The desire for family limitation was widespread, and in this sense birth control was nothing new. The birthrate in the United States had been falling consistently throughout the nineteenth century. The average number of children per family dropped from 7.0 in 1800 to 3.6 by 1900. But the open advocacy of *contraception*, the use of artificial means to prevent pregnancy, struck many people as both new and shocking. And it was illegal. Anthony Comstock, New York City's commissioner of vice, promoted laws in the 1870s making it a felony not only to sell contraceptive devices like condoms and cervical caps but also to publish information on how to prevent pregnancy.

When Margaret Sanger used her militant feminist newspaper, the *Woman Rebel*, to promote birth control, the Post Office confiscated Sanger's publication and brought charges of obscenity against her. Facing arrest, she fled to Europe, only to return in 1916 as something of a national celebrity. In her absence, birth control had become linked with free speech and had been taken up as a liberal cause. Under public pressure, the government dropped the charges against Sanger, who undertook a nationwide tour to publicize the birth control cause.

Sanger then turned to direct action, opening the nation's first birth control clinic in the Brownsville section of Brooklyn in October 1916. Located in the heart of a Jewish and Italian immigrant neighborhood, the clinic attracted 464 clients. On the tenth day, police shut down the clinic and threw Sanger in jail. By then, she had become a national figure, and the cause she championed had gained legitimacy, if not legality. After World War I, the birth control movement would become much less radical as Sanger turned to medical doctors for support and mouthed popular racist genetic theories. But in its infancy, the movement Sanger led was part of a radical vision for reforming the world that made common cause with the socialists and the IWW in challenging the limits of progressive reform.

Progressivism for White Men Only

The day before President Woodrow Wilson's inauguration in March 1913, the largest mass march to that date in the nation's history took place as more than five thousand demonstrators took to the streets in Washington to demand the vote for women. A rowdy crowd on hand to celebrate the Democrats' triumph attacked the marchers. Men spat at the suffragists and threw lighted cigarettes and matches at their clothing. "If my wife were where you are," a burly cop told one suffragist, "I'd break her head." But for all the marching, Wilson pointedly ignored woman suffrage in his inaugural address the next day.

The march served as a reminder that the political gains of progressivism were not spread equally throughout the population. As the twentieth century dawned, women still could not vote in most states, although they had won major victories

Woman Suffrage Parade

Here women gather for the suffrage parade in Washington, D.C., in 1913. A mass march was a novel tactic for the time, and some worried that women would not be physically up to it. Ambulances stood by to tend to those who fainted along the way. The marching women proved neither faint nor fainthearted. They had to fend off angry crowds who attacked them and tried to break up the parade. Wisconsin Historical Society (WHi-3782).

in the West. Increasingly, however, woman suffrage had become an international movement. In Great Britain, Emmeline Pankhurst and her daughters Cristabel and Sylvia promoted a new, militant suffragism. They seized the spotlight in a series of marches, mass meetings, and acts of civil disobedience that sometimes escalated into riots, violence, and arson.

Alice Paul, a Quaker social worker who had visited England and participated in suffrage activism there, returned to the United States in 1910 in time to plan the mass march on the eve of Wilson's inauguration and to lobby for a federal amendment to give women the vote. Paul's dramatic tactics alienated many in the National American Woman Suffrage Association. In 1916, Paul founded the militant National Woman's Party, which became the radical voice of the suffrage movement, advocating direct action such as mass marches and civil disobedience.

Women weren't the only group left out in progressive reform. Progressivism, as it was practiced in the West and South, was tainted with racism and sought to limit the rights of African and Asian Americans. Anti-Asian bigotry in the West led to a renewal of the Chinese Exclusion Act in 1902. At first, California governor Hiram Johnson stood against the strong anti-Asian prejudice of his state. But in 1913, he caved in to popular pressure and signed the Alien Land Law, which barred Japanese immigrants from purchasing land in California. The law was largely symbolic — ineffectual in practice because Japanese children born in the United States were U.S. citizens and property could be purchased in their names.

South of the Mason-Dixon line, the progressives' racism targeted African Americans. Progressives preached the disfranchisement of black voters as a "reform." During the bitter electoral fights that had pitted Populists against Democrats in the 1890s, the party of white supremacy held its power by votes purchased or coerced from African Americans. Southern progressives proposed to "reform" the electoral system by eliminating black voters. Beginning in 1890 with Mississippi, southern states curtailed the African American vote through devices such as poll taxes (fees required for voting) and literacy tests. The racist intent of southern voting legislation became especially clear after 1900 when states resorted to the grandfather clause, a legal provision that allowed men who failed a literacy test to vote if their grandfathers had cast a ballot. Grandfathering thus permitted illiterate southern white men to vote while excluding illiterate blacks.

The Progressive Era also witnessed the rise of Jim Crow laws to segregate public facilities. The new railroads precipitated segregation in the South where it had rarely existed before, at least on paper. Soon, separate railcars, separate waiting rooms, separate bathrooms, and separate dining facilities for blacks sprang up across the South. In courtrooms in Mississippi, blacks were required to swear on a separate Bible.

In the face of this growing repression, **Booker T. Washington**, the preeminent black leader of the day, urged caution and restraint. A former slave, Washington had opened the Tuskegee Institute in Alabama in 1881 to teach vocational skills to African Americans. He emphasized education and economic progress for his race and urged African Americans to put aside issues of political and social equality. In an 1895 speech in Atlanta that came to be known as the **Atlanta Compromise**, he stated, "In all things that are purely social we can be as separate as the fingers, yet one as the hand in all things essential to mutual progress." Washington's accommodationist policy appealed to whites and elevated "the wizard of Tuskegee" to the role of national spokesman for African Americans.

The year after Washington proclaimed the Atlanta Compromise, the Supreme Court upheld the legality of racial segregation, affirming in ***Plessy v. Ferguson*** (1896) the constitutionality of the doctrine of "separate but equal." Blacks could be segregated in separate schools, restrooms, and other facilities as long as the facilities were "equal" to those provided for whites. Of course, facilities for blacks rarely proved equal. In the North, where racism of a different sort led to a clamor for legislation to restrict immigration, support for African American equality found few advocates. And with anti-Asian bigotry strong in the West, the doctrine of "white supremacy" found increasing support in all sections of the country.

When Theodore Roosevelt invited Booker T. Washington to dine at the White House in 1901, a storm of racist criticism erupted. One southern editor fumed that the White House "had been painted black." But Roosevelt summoned Washington to talk politics and patronage, not African American rights. Roosevelt's unquestioned racial prejudice became clear in the Brownsville incident in 1906, when he dishonorably discharged an entire battalion of 167 black soldiers because he suspected (although there was no proof) that they were shielding the murderer of a white saloonkeeper killed in a shoot-out in the Texas town.

W. E. B. Du Bois

W. E. B. Du Bois grew up in Great Barrington, Massachusetts, and in 1895 he became the first African American to earn a doctorate from Harvard. Throughout his life, he urged African Americans not only to focus on their own education and economic prospects but also to work politically for racial equality. In *The Souls of Black Folk* (1903), he wrote that he wished "to make it possible for a man to be both a Negro and an American, without being cursed and spit upon by his fellows, without having the doors of Opportunity closed roughly in his face." Special Collections Department, W. E. B. Du Bois Library, University of Massachusetts Amherst.

Woodrow Wilson brought to the White House southern attitudes toward race and racial segregation. He instituted segregation in the federal workforce, especially the Post Office, and approved segregated drinking fountains and restrooms in the nation's capital. When critics attacked the policy, Wilson insisted that segregation was "in the interest of the Negro."

In 1906, a major race riot in Atlanta called into question Booker T. Washington's strategy of uplift and accommodation. For three days in September, the streets of Atlanta ran red with blood as angry white mobs chased and cornered any blacks they happened upon, pulling passengers from streetcars and invading black neighborhoods to kill and loot. An estimated 250 African Americans died in the riots — members of Atlanta's black middle class along with the poor and derelict. Professor William Crogman of Clark College noted the central irony of the riot: "Here we have worked and prayed and tried to make good men and women of our colored population," he observed, "and at our very doorstep the whites kill these good men." In Dark Town, a working-class neighborhood, blacks fought back to defend their homes, shooting into the white mob and driving off the attackers. In the aftermath of the riot, the city's leaders, black and white, managed to quash any nascent black unity by falling back on the old strategy of allying "the best white people and the best colored people." Yet the riot caused many African Americans to question Washington's strategy of gradualism and accommodation.

Foremost among Washington's critics stood **W. E. B. Du Bois**, a Harvard graduate who urged African Americans to fight for civil rights and racial justice. In *The Souls of Black Folk* (1903), Du Bois attacked the "Tuskegee Machine," comparing Washington to a political boss who used his influence to silence his critics and reward his followers. Du Bois founded the Niagara movement in 1905, calling for universal male suffrage, civil rights, and leadership composed of a black intellectual elite. The Atlanta riot only bolstered his resolve. In 1909, the Niagara movement helped found the **National Association for the Advancement of Colored People** (NAACP), a coalition of blacks and whites that sought legal and political rights for African Americans through the courts. In the decades that followed, the NAACP came to represent the future for African Americans, while Booker T. Washington, who died in 1915, represented the past.

REVIEW How did race, class, and gender shape the limits of progressive reform?

▶ Conclusion: The Transformation of the Liberal State

Progressivism was never a radical movement. Its goal remained to reform the existing system — by government intervention if necessary — but without uprooting any of the traditional American political, economic, or social institutions. As Theodore Roosevelt, the bellwether of the movement, insisted, "The only true conservative is the man who resolutely sets his face toward the future." Roosevelt was such a man, and progressivism was such a movement. But although progressivism was never radical, neither was it the laissez-faire liberalism of the previous century. Progressives' willingness to use the power of government to regulate business and achieve a measure of social justice redefined liberalism in the twentieth century, tying it to the expanded power of the state.

Progressivism contained many paradoxes. A diverse coalition of individuals and interests, the progressive movement began at the grass roots but left as its legacy a stronger presidency and unprecedented federal involvement in the economy and social welfare. A movement that believed in social justice, progressivism often promoted social control. And while progressives called for greater democracy, they fostered elitism with their worship of experts and efficiency and often failed to champion equality for women and minorities.

Whatever its inconsistencies and limitations, progressivism took action to deal with the problems posed by urban industrialism. Progressivism saw grass-roots activists address social problems on the local and state levels and search for national solutions. By increasing the power of the presidency and expanding the power of the state, progressives worked to bring about greater social justice and to achieve a better balance between government and business. Jane Addams and Theodore Roosevelt could lay equal claim to the movement that redefined liberalism and launched the liberal state of the twentieth century. War on a global scale would provide progressivism with yet another challenge even before it had completed its ambitious agenda.

Reviewing Chapter 21

REVIEW QUESTIONS

1. What types of people were drawn to the progressive movement, and what motivated them? (pp. 619–624)

2. How did progressives justify their demand for more activist government? (pp. 624–626)

3. In what ways did Roosevelt's domestic policies respond to progressive demands? (pp. 626–637)

4. How and why did Wilson's reform program evolve during his first term? (pp. 638–642)

5. How did race, class, and gender shape the limits of progressive reform? (pp. 642–647)

MAKING CONNECTIONS

1. Diverse approaches to reform came under the umbrella of progressivism. Discuss the work of three progressive reformers working at the grassroots or local government level. What do your examples reveal about progressivism? What characteristics connected their reform efforts? What separated them?

2. Theodore Roosevelt's foreign policy was summed up in the dictum "Speak softly but carry a big stick." Using two examples, describe how this policy worked. By contrast, why did Taft's policy of dollar diplomacy fail?

3. Opponents on the campaign stump, Theodore Roosevelt and Woodrow Wilson shared a commitment to domestic reform. Compare their legislative programs, including the evolution of their policies over time and their ability to respond to shifting political circumstances. What do their policies reveal about their understandings of the roles of the executive and the federal government?

4. What contemporary movements lay beyond the limits of progressive reform? Why did progressive reform coincide with the restriction of minority rights? In your answer, discuss how radical movements provide insights into the character of progressivism itself.

LINKING TO THE PAST

1. In what ways did Populism and progressivism differ? In what ways were they similar? (See chapter 20.)

2. During the Gilded Age, industrial capitalism concentrated power in the hands of corporations. How did Theodore Roosevelt respond to this problem? How did his approach differ from that of the Gilded Age presidents? Was his strategy effective? (See chapter 18.)

TIMELINE 1889–1916

1889 • Jane Addams opens Hull House.

1895 • Booker T. Washington enunciates Atlanta Compromise.

1896 • *Plessy v. Ferguson.*

1900 • Socialist Party founded.

1901 • William McKinley assassinated; Theodore Roosevelt becomes president.

1902 • Antitrust lawsuit filed against Northern Securities Company.
• Roosevelt mediates anthracite coal strike.

1903 • Women's Trade Union League (WTUL) founded.
• United States begins construction of Panama Canal.
• Elkins Act.

1904 • Roosevelt Corollary to Monroe Doctrine.

1905 • Industrial Workers of the World (IWW) founded.
• W. E. B. Du Bois founds Niagara movement.

1906 • Pure Food and Drug Act and Meat Inspection Act.
• Atlanta race riot.
• Hepburn Act.

1907 • Panic on Wall Street.
• Roosevelt signs "Gentlemen's Agreement" with Japan restricting immigration.

1908 • *Muller v. Oregon.*
• Republican William Howard Taft elected president.

1909 • Garment workers' strike in New York City.
• National Association for the Advancement of Colored People (NAACP) formed.

1910 • Hiram Johnson elected governor of California.

1911 • Triangle fire in New York City.
• Taft launches antitrust suit against U.S. Steel.

1912 • Roosevelt runs for president on Progressive Party ticket.
• Democrat Woodrow Wilson elected president.

1913 • Suffragists march in Washington, D.C.
• Federal Reserve Act.

1914 • Federal Trade Commission (FTC) created.
• Clayton Antitrust Act.

1916 • Alice Paul launches National Woman's Party.
• Margaret Sanger opens first U.S. birth control clinic.
• Keating-Owen child labor law.

▶ **FOR AN ONLINE BIBLIOGRAPHY, PRACTICE QUIZZES, WEB SITES, IMAGES, AND DOCUMENTS RELATED TO THIS CHAPTER,** see the Book Companion Site at **bedfordstmartins.com/roarkvalue.**

▶ **FOR DOCUMENTS RELATED TO THIS PERIOD,** see Michael Johnson, ed., *Reading the American Past,* Fifth Edition.

22

World War I: The Progressive Crusade at Home and Abroad

1914–1920

GEORGE "BROWNIE" BROWNE WAS ONE OF 2 MILLION SOLDIERS WHO crossed the Atlantic during World War I to serve in the American Expeditionary Force (AEF) in France. The twenty-three-year-old civil engineer from Waterbury, Connecticut, volunteered in July 1917, three months after the United States entered the war, serving with the 117th Engineers Regiment, 42nd Division. Two-thirds of the "doughboys" (American soldiers in Europe) saw action during the war, and few white troops saw more than Brownie did.

When Brownie and the 42nd arrived at the front in northeastern France, veteran French troops provided advanced instruction in the techniques of trench warfare. They taught Brownie's regiment of engineers how to build and maintain trenches, barbed-wire entanglements, and artillery and machine-gun positions. Although his sector of the front was deemed "quiet," Brownie came under German artillery, machine-gun, and rifle fire each day. Still, in February 1918, he wrote Martha Johnson, his girlfriend back home, "the longer I'm here the more spirit I have to 'stick it out' for the good of humanity and the U.S. which is the same thing."

Training ended abruptly in the spring of 1918 when the Germans launched a massive offensive, and the 42nd entered the trenches in the

George "Brownie" Browne
Mobilizing an army was easy compared with preparing men for battle. Training at Fort Slocum, New York, Brownie complained about the Army's red tape, bad food, shortage of equipment, inexperienced officers, lack of sleep, and physical exhaustion. Writing to his girlfriend just before evening taps in August 1917, Brownie said, "Believe me I *am* tired." Despite the hardships, however, Brownie enjoyed the camaraderie of the camp and was, as this photograph reveals, a happy soldier. When his unit arrived at Saint-Nazaire in October 1917, Brownie was proud to be one of the first doughboys to set foot in France. Courtesy of Janet W. Hansen.

Champagne region. The German bombardment made the night "as light as daytime, and the ground . . . was a mass of flames and whistling steel from the bursting shells." Wave after wave of German soldiers rushed forward. One doughboy from the 42nd remembered, "The destruction was terrible and the advancing waves were torn and split apart. The great gaps [in the line of soldiers] were filled, only to be again torn and shattered by the direct artillery fire." Another said, "Dead bodies were all around me. Americans, French, Hun [Germans] in all phases and positions of death." A third declared that soon "the odor was something fierce. We had to put on our gas masks to keep from getting sick." In Champagne, the engineers became infantry. After helping to stop the German advance during eight days of combat, the 42nd suffered nearly 6,500 dead, wounded, and missing, 20 percent of the division.

Brownie came through the campaign unscathed, but he had not had a bath in four weeks, was covered with "cooties" (body lice), and was bone tired. After only ten days' rest, however, his unit joined in the first major American offensive, an attack against German defenses at Saint-Mihiel. To maintain secrecy, the 42nd marched sixty miles in six rainy nights. Widespread misery and confusion prompted one doughboy to remark,

"Now I know why they call us the A.E.F. It means 'Ass End First.'" At 1:00 a.m. on September 12, 3,000 American artillery launched more than a million rounds against German positions. This time the engineers preceded the advancing infantry, cutting through or blasting any barbed wire that remained. The battle cost the 42nd another 1,200 casualties, but Brownie was not among them.

At the end of September, the 42nd shifted to the Meuse-Argonne region, where it participated in the most brutal American fighting of the war. And it was there that Brownie's war ended. While the engineers were clearing paths through the barbed wire for the infantry, the Germans fired thousands of poison gas shells. The gas, "so thick you could cut it with a knife," felled Brownie. When the war ended on November 11, 1918, he was recovering from his respiratory wounds at a camp behind the lines. Discharged from the army in February 1919, Brownie returned home, where he and Martha married. Like the rest of the country, they were eager to get on with their lives.

President Woodrow Wilson had never expected to lead the United States into the Great War, as the Europeans called it. When war erupted in 1914, he declared America's absolute neutrality. But trade and principle entangled the United States in Europe's troubles and gradually drew the nation into the conflict. Wilson claimed that America's participation would serve grand purposes and uplift both the United States and the entire world.

At home, the war helped progressives finally achieve their goals of national prohibition and woman suffrage, but it also promoted a vicious attack on Americans' civil liberties. While George Browne and the other doughboys were helping to win the war in Europe, hyperpatriotism meant intolerance, repression, and vigilante violence at home. In 1919, Wilson sailed for Europe to secure a just peace. Unable to dictate terms to the victors, Wilson accepted disappointing compromises. Upon his return to the United States, he met a crushing defeat that marked the end of Wilsonian internationalism. Crackdowns on dissenters, immigrants, racial and ethnic minorities, and unions signaled the end of the Progressive Era at home.

▶ Woodrow Wilson and the World

Shortly after winning election to the presidency in 1912, **Woodrow Wilson** confided to a friend: "It would be an irony of fate if my administration had to deal with foreign affairs." Indeed, Wilson had focused his life and career on domestic concerns, seldom venturing far from home and traveling abroad only on brief vacations. As president of Princeton University and then governor of New Jersey, he had remained rooted in local affairs. In his campaign for the presidency, Wilson spoke passionately about domestic reform but hardly mentioned foreign affairs.

Wilson, however, could not avoid the world and the rising tide of militarism, nationalism, and violence that beat against American shores. Economic interests compelled the nation outward. Moreover, Wilson was drawn abroad by his own progressive political principles. He believed that the United States had a moral duty to champion national self-determination, peaceful free trade, and political democracy. "We have no selfish ends to serve," he proclaimed. "We desire no conquest, no dominion. . . . We are but one of the champions of the rights of mankind." Yet as president, Wilson revealed that he was as ready as any American president to apply military solutions to problems of foreign policy.

Taming the Americas

When he took office, Wilson sought to distinguish his foreign policy from that of his Republican predecessors. To Wilson, Theodore Roosevelt's "big stick" and William Howard Taft's "dollar diplomacy" appeared crude flexing of military and economic muscle. To signal a new direction, Wilson appointed **William Jennings Bryan** as secretary of state. A pacifist on religious grounds, Bryan immediately turned his attention to making agreements with thirty nations for the peaceful settlement of disputes.

But Wilson and Bryan, like Roosevelt and Taft, also believed that the Monroe Doctrine gave the United States special rights and responsibilities in the Western Hemisphere. Issued in 1823 to warn Europeans not to attempt to colonize the Americas again, the doctrine had become a cloak for U.S. domination. Thus, when it appeared that unrest might undermine American interests in Nicaragua, Haiti, and the Dominican Republic, Wilson authorized U.S. military intervention, paving the way for U.S. banks and corporations to assert financial control. All the while, Wilson believed that U.S. actions were promoting order and democracy. "I am going to teach the South American Republics to elect good men!" he declared.

Wilson's most serious involvement in Latin America came in Mexico, where revolution broke out in 1910. When General Victoriano Huerta seized power by violent means three years later, most European nations promptly recognized Mexico's new government, but Wilson refused, declaring that he would not support a "government of butchers." In April 1914, Wilson sent 800 Marines to seize the port of Veracruz to prevent the unloading of a large shipment of arms for Huerta, who was by then involved in a civil war of his own. Huerta fled to Spain, and the United States welcomed a more compliant government.

Wilson could not tame Mexico that easily, however. A rebellion erupted among desperately poor farmers who believed that the new government of Venustiano Carranza, aided by U.S. business interests, had betrayed the revolution's promise to help the common people. In January 1916, the rebel army, commanded by **Francisco "Pancho" Villa**, seized a train carrying gold to Texas from an American-owned mine in Mexico and killed the 17 American engineers aboard. In March, a band of some 400 to 500 of Villa's men crossed the border for a predawn raid on Columbus, New Mexico. They stayed for less than two hours, but they burned

Francisco "Pancho" Villa
The dashing Mexican revolutionary Pancho Villa gallops along a column of his soldiers in 1914. After Villa's raid into New Mexico in 1916 to punish Americans for aiding his revolutionary rivals, General John J. Pershing dove across the border, pursued Villa for three hundred miles into Mexico, and then returned home almost a year later empty-handed. Brown Brothers.

much of the town and killed 18 Americans. Wilson promptly dispatched 12,000 troops, led by Major General John J. Pershing. The wily Villa avoided capture, and in January 1917 Wilson recalled Pershing so that the general might prepare the army for the possibility of fighting in the Great War.

The European Crisis

Before 1914, Europe had enjoyed decades of peace, but just beneath the surface lay the potentially destructive forces of nationalism and imperialism. The consolidation of the German and Italian states into unified nations and the similar ambition of Russia to create a Pan-Slavic union initiated new rivalries throughout Europe. As the conviction spread that colonial possessions were a mark of national greatness, competition expanded onto the world stage. Most ominously, Germany under Kaiser **Wilhelm II** meant to challenge Great Britain's world supremacy by creating industrial muscle at home, an empire abroad, and a mighty navy. The German challenge threatened the balance of power and thus the peace.

European nations sought to avoid an explosion by developing a complex web of military and diplomatic alliances. By 1914, Germany, Austria-Hungary, and Italy (the **Triple Alliance**) stood opposed to Great Britain, France, and Russia (the **Triple Entente**, also known as "the Allies"). But in their effort to prevent war

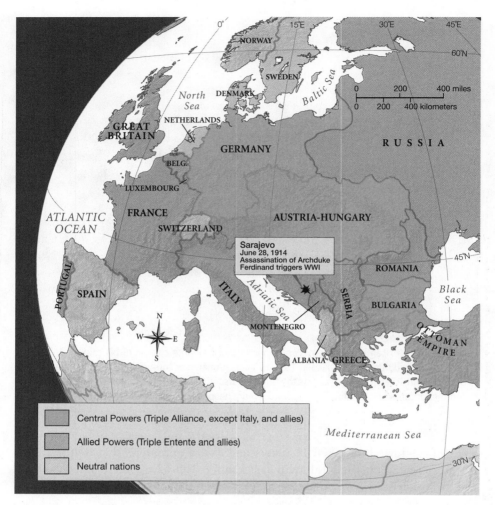

MAP 22.1

European Alliances after the Outbreak of World War I

With Germany and Austria-Hungary wedged between their Entente rivals and all parties fully armed, Europe was poised for war when Archduke Franz Ferdinand of Austria-Hungary was assassinated in Sarajevo in June 1914.

through a balance of power, Europeans had actually magnified the possibility of large-scale conflict by creating trip wires along the boundaries of two heavily armed power blocs (Map 22.1). Treaties, some of them secret, obligated members of the alliances to come to the aid of another member if attacked.

The fatal sequence began on June 28, 1914, in the Bosnian city of Sarajevo, when a Bosnian Serb terrorist assassinated **Archduke Franz Ferdinand**, heir to the Austro-Hungarian throne. On July 18, Austria-Hungary declared war on Serbia, holding it accountable for the killing. The elaborate alliance system meant that the war could not remain local. Russia announced that it would back the

Serbs. Compelled by treaty to support Austria-Hungary, Germany on August 3 attacked Russia and France. In response, Great Britain, upholding its pact with France, declared war on Germany on August 4. Within weeks, Europe was engulfed in war. The conflict became a world war when Japan, seeing an opportunity to rid itself of European competition in China, joined the cause against Germany. The evenly matched alliances would fight a disastrous war lasting more than four years, at a cost of 8.5 million soldiers' lives — an entire generation of young men. A war that started with a solitary murder proved impossible to stop. Indeed, Britain's foreign secretary, Edward Grey, announced sadly: "The lamps are going out all over Europe. We shall not see them lit again in our lifetime."

The Ordeal of American Neutrality

Woodrow Wilson promptly announced that the war was purely a European matter. Because it engaged no vital American interest and involved no significant principle, he said, the United States would remain neutral and continue normal relations with the warring nations. America had traditionally insisted that "free ships made free goods" — that neutral nations were entitled to trade safely with all nations at war. But more was involved than lofty principle. In the year before Europe went to war, the U.S. economy had slipped into a recession that wartime disruption of European trade could drastically worsen.

Although Wilson proclaimed neutrality, his sympathies, like those of many Americans, lay with Great Britain and France. Americans gratefully remembered crucial French assistance in the American Revolution and shared with the British a language, a culture, and a commitment to liberty. Germany, by contrast, was a monarchy with strong militaristic traditions. The British portrayed the German ruler, Kaiser Wilhelm II, as personally responsible for the war's atrocities, and before long American newspapers were labeling him "the Mad Dog of Europe" and "the Beast of Berlin." Still, Wilson insisted on neutrality, in part because he feared the conflict's effects on the United States as a nation of immigrants, millions of whom had only recently come from countries now at war. As he told the German ambassador, "We definitely have to be neutral, since otherwise our mixed populations would wage war on each other."

Britain's powerful fleet controlled the seas and quickly set up an economic blockade of Germany. The United States vigorously protested, but Britain refused to give up its naval advantage. The blockade actually had little economic impact on the United States. Between 1914 and the spring of 1917, while trade with Germany evaporated, war-related exports to Britain — food, clothing, steel, and munitions — escalated by some 400 percent, enough to pull the American economy out of its prewar slump. Although the British blockade violated American neutrality, the Wilson administration gradually acquiesced, thus beginning the fateful process of alienation from Germany.

Germany retaliated with a submarine blockade of British ports. This terrifying new form of combat by *Unterseebooten*, or **U-boats**, threatened traditional rules of war. Unlike surface warships that could harmlessly stop freighters and prevent them from entering a war zone, submarines relied on sinking their quarry.

And once they sank a ship, the tiny U-boats could not possibly pick up survivors. Britain portrayed the submarine as an outlaw weapon that violated notions of "civilized" warfare. Nevertheless, in February 1915, Germany announced that it intended to sink on sight enemy ships en route to the British Isles. On May 7, 1915, a German U-boat torpedoed the British passenger liner *Lusitania*, killing 1,198 passengers, 128 of them U.S. citizens.

American newspapers featured drawings of drowning women and children, and some demanded war. Calmer voices pointed out that Germany had warned prospective passengers and that the *Lusitania* carried millions of rounds of ammunition and so was a legitimate target. Secretary of State Bryan resisted the hysteria and declared that a ship carrying war materiel "should not rely on passengers to protect her from attack — it would be like putting women and children in front of an army." He counseled Wilson to warn American citizens that they traveled on ships of belligerent countries at their own risk.

Wilson sought a middle course that would retain his commitment to peace and neutrality without condoning German attacks on passenger ships. On May 10, 1915, he rejected American intervention, declaring that "there is such a thing as a man being too proud to fight." But Wilson also rejected Bryan's position. Any further destruction of ships, Wilson announced, would be regarded as "deliberately unfriendly" and might lead the United States to break off diplomatic relations with Germany. Wilson essentially demanded that Germany abandon unrestricted submarine warfare. Bryan resigned, predicting that the president had placed the United States on a collision course with Germany. Wilson's replacement for Bryan, **Robert Lansing**, was far from neutral. He believed that Germany's antidemocratic character and goal of "world dominance" meant that it "must not be permitted to win this war or even to break even."

After Germany apologized for the civilian deaths on the *Lusitania*, tensions subsided. But in 1916, to ensure continued U.S. neutrality, Germany went further, promising no more submarine attacks without warning and without provisions for the safety of civilians. Wilson's supporters celebrated the success of his middle-of-the-road strategy that steered a course between belligerence and pacifism.

Wilson's diplomacy proved helpful in his bid for reelection in 1916. In the contest against Republican Charles Evans Hughes, the Democratic Party ran Wilson under the slogan "He kept us out of war." Wilson felt uneasy with the claim, recognizing that any "little German lieutenant can push us into the war at any time by some calculated outrage." But the Democrats' case for Wilson's neutrality appealed to enough of those in favor of peace to eke out a majority. Wilson won, but only by the razor-thin margins of 600,000 popular and 23 electoral votes.

The United States Enters the War

Step-by-step, the United States backed away from "absolute neutrality" and more forthrightly sided with the Allies (the Triple Entente). The consequence of protesting the German blockade of Great Britain but accepting the British blockade of Germany was that by 1916 the United States was supplying the Allies with 40 percent of their war materiel. When France and Britain ran short of money to pay for U.S. goods and asked for loans, Wilson argued that "loans by American bankers to any foreign government which is at war are inconsistent with the true spirit of neutrality." But rather than jeopardize America's wartime prosperity, Wilson relaxed his objections, and billions of dollars in loans kept American goods flowing to Britain and France.

In January 1917, Germany decided that it could no longer afford to allow neutral shipping to reach Great Britain while Britain's blockade gradually starved Germany. It announced that its navy would resume unrestricted submarine warfare and sink without warning any ship, enemy or neutral, found in the waters off Great Britain. Germany understood that the decision would probably bring the United States into the war but gambled that the submarines would strangle the British economy and allow German armies to win a military victory in France before American troops arrived in Europe.

Resisting demands for war, Wilson continued to hope for a negotiated peace and only broke off diplomatic relations with Germany. Then on February 25, 1917, British authorities informed Wilson of a secret telegram sent by the German foreign secretary, Arthur Zimmermann, to the German minister in Mexico. It promised that in the event of war between Germany and the United States, Germany would see that Mexico regained its "lost provinces" of Texas, New Mexico, and Arizona if Mexico would declare war against the United States. Wilson angrily responded to the **Zimmermann telegram** by asking Congress to approve a policy of "armed neutrality" that would allow merchant ships to fight back against any attackers. Germany's overture to Mexico convinced Wilson that the war was, indeed, a defense of democracy against German aggression.

In March, German submarines sank five American vessels off Britain, killing 66 Americans. On April 2, the president asked Congress to issue a declaration of war. He accused Germany of "warfare against all mankind." Still, he called for a "war without hate" and insisted that the destruction of Germany was not the goal of the United States. Rather, America fought to "vindicate the principles of peace and justice." He promised a world made "safe for democracy." On April 6, 1917, by majorities of 373 to 50 in the House and 82 to 6 in the Senate, Congress voted to declare war. Among those voting no was Representative Jeannette Rankin of Montana, the first woman elected to Congress.

Wilson feared what war would do at home. He said despairingly, "Once lead this people into war, and they'll forget there ever was such a thing as tolerance. To fight you must be brutal and ruthless, and the spirit of ruthless brutality will infect Congress, the courts, the policeman on the beat, the man in the street."

REVIEW Why did President Wilson fail to maintain U.S. neutrality during World War I?

▶ "Over There"

American soldiers sailed for France with songwriter George M. Cohan's rousing "Over There" ringing in their ears:

> Over there, over there
> Send the word, send the word over there,
> That the Yanks are coming, the Yanks are coming
> The drums rum-tumming ev'rywhere.

America's military venture in Europe was by far the largest the nation had ever undertaken on foreign soil. Filled with a sense of democratic mission and trained to be morally upright as well as fiercely effective, some doughboys, such as George Browne, found the adventure exhilarating and maintained their idealism to the end. The majority, however, saw little that was gallant in rats, lice, and poison gas and — despite the progressives' hopes — little to elevate the human soul in a landscape of utter destruction and death. Most were dedicated simply to defeating the "Huns" and returning home.

The Call to Arms

When America entered the war, Britain and France were nearly exhausted after almost three years of conflict. Millions of soldiers had perished; food and morale were dangerously low. Another Allied power, Russia, was in turmoil. In March 1917, a revolution had forced Czar Nicholas II to abdicate, and eight months later, in a separate peace with Germany, the **Bolshevik** revolutionary government withdrew Russia from the war. Peace with Russia allowed Germany to withdraw hundreds of thousands of its soldiers from the eastern front and to deploy them against the Allies on the western front in France.

On May 18, 1917, to meet the demand for fighting men, Wilson signed a sweeping **Selective Service Act**, authorizing a draft of all young men into the armed forces. Conscription helped transform a tiny volunteer armed force of 80,000 men into a vast army and navy. Although almost 350,000 inductees either failed to report or claimed conscientious objector status, draft boards eventually inducted 2.8 million men into the armed services, in addition to the 2 million, including George Browne, who volunteered.

Among the 4.8 million men under arms, 370,000 were black Americans. Although African Americans remained understandably skeptical about President Wilson's war for democracy, most followed W. E. B. Du Bois's advice to "close ranks" and to temporarily "forget our special grievances" until the nation had won the war. During training, black recruits suffered the same prejudices that they encountered in civilian life. Rigidly segregated, they faced crude abuse and miserable conditions, and they were usually assigned to labor battalions, where they shouldered shovels more often than rifles.

Training camps sought to transform raw white recruits into fighting men. Progressives in the government were also determined that the camps turn out soldiers with the highest moral and civic values. Secretary of War Newton D. Baker

"Men Wanted for the United States Army"
The exuberant soldiers swarming over this truck were so thrilled with their task of recruiting new men that they managed to display the flag backward. Their urgency reflects the fact that when America declared war on Germany in April 1917, its army numbered only 127,000, roughly the size of Chile's army. Unwilling to trust voluntary enlistments, Wilson called for a draft, and within months nearly 10 million American men had registered for the draft. When the war ended, 2 million men had volunteered for military service, and 2.8 million had been drafted. Brown Brothers.

created the Commission on Training Camp Activities, staffed by YMCA workers and veterans of the settlement house and playground movements. Military training included games, singing, and college extension courses. The army asked soldiers to stop thinking about sex, explaining that a "man who is thinking below the belt is not efficient." The Military Draft Act of 1917 prohibited prostitution and alcohol near training camps.

Wilson's choice to command the **American Expeditionary Force (AEF)** on the battlefields of France, Major General **John "Black Jack" Pershing**, was as morally upright as he was militarily uncompromising. "The standards for the American Army will be those of West Point," the ramrod-straight Pershing announced early in the war. "The upright bearing, attention to detail, uncomplaining obedience to instruction required of the cadet will be required of every officer and soldier of our armies in France." Described by one observer as "lean, clean, keen," he gave progressives perfect confidence.

The War in France

At the front, the AEF discovered a desperate situation. The war had degenerated into a stalemate of armies defensively dug into hundreds of miles of trenches that stretched across France. Huddling in the mud among the corpses and rats, soldiers were separated from the enemy by only a few hundred yards of "no-man's-land." When ordered "over the top," troops raced desperately toward the enemy's trenches, only to be entangled in barbed wire, enveloped in poison gas, and mowed down by machine guns. In three days of fighting at the battle of the Somme in 1916, French and British forces lost 600,000 dead and wounded and the Germans 500,000. The deadliest battle of the war allowed the Allies to advance their trenches only a few meaningless miles across devastated land.

Still, U.S. troops saw almost no combat in 1917. The major exception was the 92nd Division of black troops. When Pershing received an urgent call for troops from the French, he sent the 92nd to the front because he did not want to lose command over the white troops he valued more. In the 191 days they spent in battle — longer than any other American outfit — the 369th Regiment of the 92nd Division won more medals than any other American combat unit. Black soldiers recognized the irony of having to serve with the French to gain respect. Pershing told the French that their failure to draw the color line risked "spoiling the Negroes." German propagandists raised some painful questions. In a leaflet that aviators dropped among black troops, the Germans reminded them of their second-class citizenship and asked, "Why, then, fight the Germans, only for the benefit of the Wall Street robbers and to protect the millions they have loaned to the British, French, and Italians?"

White troops continued to train and used their free time to explore places that most of them otherwise could never have hoped to see. True to the crusader image, American officials allowed only morally uplifting tourism. Paris's temptations were off limits, and French premier Georges Clemenceau's offer to supply U.S. troops with licensed prostitutes was declined with the half-serious remark that if Wilson found out, he would stop the war.

Sightseeing and training ended abruptly in March 1918. When the Brest-Litovsk treaty signed that month by Germany and the Bolsheviks officially took Russia out of the war, the Germans launched a massive offensive aimed at French ports on the Atlantic. After 6,000 cannons unleashed the heaviest barrage in history, a million German soldiers smashed a hole in the Allied lines at a cost of 250,000 casualties on each side. Pershing, who believed the right moment for U.S. action had finally come, visited Ferdinand Foch, head of the French army, to ask for the "great honor" of becoming "engaged in the greatest battle in history." Foch agreed to Pershing's terms of a separate American command and in May assigned the Americans to the central sector.

In May and June, at Cantigny and then at Château-Thierry, the eager but green Americans checked the German advance with a series of dashing assaults.

Then they headed toward the forest stronghold of Belleau Wood, moving against streams of retreating Allied soldiers who cried defeat: "La guerre est finie!" (The war is over!) A French officer commanded the Americans to retreat with them, but the American commander replied sharply, "Retreat, hell. We just got here." After charging through a wheat field against withering machine-gun fire, the Marines plunged into hand-to-hand combat. Victory came hard, but a German report praised the enemy's spirit, noting that "the Americans' nerves are not yet worn out." Indeed, it was German morale that was on the verge of cracking.

In the summer of 1918, the Allies launched a massive counteroffensive that would end the war. A quarter of a million U.S. troops joined in the rout of German forces along the Marne River. In September, more than a million Americans took part in the assault that threw the Germans back from positions along the Meuse River. In four brutal days during the Meuse-Argonne offensive, the AEF sustained 45,000 casualties. Pershing had predicted that German defenses would crack in thirty-six hours; six weeks later, the Germans gave way. In November, a revolt against the German government sent Kaiser Wilhelm II fleeing to Holland. On November 11, 1918, a delegation from the newly established German republic met with the French high command to sign an armistice that brought the fighting to an end.

The adventure of the AEF was brief, bloody, and victorious. When Germany had resumed unrestricted U-boat warfare in 1917, it had been gambling that it could defeat Britain and France before the Americans could raise and train an army and ship it to France. The German military had miscalculated badly. Of the 2 million American troops in Europe, 1.4 million saw some action. By the end, 112,000 AEF soldiers perished from wounds and disease, while another 230,000 Americans, including George Browne, suffered casualties but survived. Only the Civil War, which lasted much longer, had been more costly in American lives. European nations, however, suffered much greater losses: 2.2 million Germans, 1.9 million Russians, 1.4 million French, and 900,000 Britons. Where they had fought, the landscape was as blasted and barren as the moon.

REVIEW   How did the American Expeditionary Force contribute to the defeat of Germany?

▶ The Crusade for Democracy at Home

Many progressives hoped that the war would improve the quality of American life as well as free Europe from tyranny and militarism. Mobilization helped propel the crusades for woman suffrage and prohibition to success. Progressives enthusiastically channeled industrial and agricultural production into the war effort. Labor shortages caused by workers entering the military provided new opportunities for women in the booming wartime economy. With labor at a premium, unionized workers gained higher pay and shorter hours. To instill loyalty in Americans whose ancestry was rooted in the belligerent nations, Wilson launched a campaign to foster patriotism. The campaign included the creation of a government agency to promote official propaganda, indoctrination in the schools, and parades, rallies, and films. But fanning patriotism led to suppressing dissent. When the government launched a harsh assault on civil liberties, mobs gained license to attack those whom they considered disloyal. As Wilson feared, the progressive ideals of rational progress and free expression took a beating at home when the nation undertook its foreign crusade for democracy.

The Progressive Stake in the War

The idea of the war as an agent of national improvement stirred the old zeal of the progressive movement. The influential philosopher-educator John Dewey urged Americans to embrace the "social possibilities of war." The Wilson administration realized that the federal government would have to assert greater control to mobilize the nation's human and physical resources. The nation's capital soon bristled with agencies charged with managing the war effort. Bernard Baruch headed the War Industries Board, created to stimulate and direct industrial production. A wealthy Wall Street stockbroker and a reform Democrat, Baruch brought industrial management and labor together into a team that produced everything from boots to bullets and made U.S. troops the best-equipped soldiers in the world.

Herbert Hoover, a self-made millionaire engineer, headed the Food Administration. He led remarkably successful "Hooverizing" campaigns for "meatless" Mondays and "wheatless" Wednesdays and other ways of conserving resources. Guaranteed high prices, the American heartland not only supplied the needs of U.S. citizens and armed forces but also became the breadbasket of America's allies.

Wartime agencies multiplied: The Railroad Administration directed railroad traffic, the Fuel Administration coordinated the coal industry and other fuel suppliers, the Shipping Board organized the merchant marine, and the National War Labor Policies Board resolved labor disputes. Their successes gave progressives reason to believe that the war promoted harmony between business and labor. Some progressives, however, stubbornly refused to accept the argument that war and reform marched together. Wisconsin senator Robert La Follette attacked the war unrelentingly, claiming that Wilson's promises of peace and democracy were a case of "the blind leading the blind" at home and abroad.

Industrial leaders found that wartime agencies enforced efficiency, which helped corporate profits triple. Some working people also had cause to celebrate. Mobilization meant high prices for farmers and plentiful jobs at high wages in the new war industries. Because increased industrial production required peaceful labor relations, the National War Labor Policies Board enacted the eight-hour day, a living minimum wage, and collective bargaining rights in some industries. Wages rose sharply during the war (as did prices), and the American Federation of Labor (AFL) saw its membership soar from 2.7 million to more than 5 million.

The war also provided a huge boost to the stalled moral crusade to ban alcohol. By 1917, prohibitionists had convinced nineteen states to go dry. Liquor's opponents now argued that banning alcohol would make the cause of democracy powerful and pure. At the same time, shutting down the distilleries would save millions of bushels of grain that could feed the United States and its allies. "Shall the many have food or the few drink?" the drys asked. Prohibitionists added a patriotic twist by arguing that closing breweries with German names such as Schlitz, Pabst, and Anheuser-Busch would deal a blow to the German cause. In December 1917, Congress passed the **Eighteenth Amendment**, which banned the manufacture, transportation, and sale of alcohol. After swift ratification by the states, the amendment went into effect on January 1, 1920.

Women, War, and the Battle for Suffrage

Women had made real strides during the Progressive Era, and war presented new opportunities. More than 25,000 women served in France. About half were nurses. The others drove ambulances; ran canteens for the Salvation Army, Red Cross, and YMCA; worked with French civilians in devastated areas; and acted as telephone operators and war correspondents. Like men who joined the war effort, they believed that they were taking part in a great national venture. "I am more than willing to live as a soldier and know of the hardships I would have to undergo," one canteen worker declared when applying to go overseas, "but I want to help my country. . . . I want . . . to do the *real* work." And like men, women struggled against disillusionment in France. One woman explained: "Over in America, we thought we knew something about the war . . . but when you get here the difference is [like the one between] studying the laws of electricity and being struck by lightning."

At home, long-standing barriers against hiring women fell when millions of workingmen became soldiers and few new immigrant workers crossed the Atlantic. Tens of thousands of women found work in defense plants as welders, metalworkers, and heavy machine operators — jobs traditionally reserved for men — and with the railroads. A black woman, a domestic before the war, celebrated her job as a laborer in a railroad yard: "We are making more money at this than any work we can get, and we do not have to work as hard as at housework which requires us to be on duty from six o'clock in the morning until nine or ten at night, with might[y] little time off and at very poor wages." Other women found white-collar work. Between 1910 and 1920, the number of women clerks doubled. Before the war ended, more than a million women had found work in war industries.

The most dramatic advance for women came in the political arena. Since the Seneca Falls convention of 1848, where women voiced their first formal demand for the ballot, the struggle for woman suffrage had inched forward. Adopting a state-by-state approach, suffragists had achieved some success, but before 1910 only four sparsely populated western states had adopted woman suffrage (Map 22.2). Elsewhere, voting rights for women met strong hostility and defeat. After 1910, suffrage leaders added a federal campaign to amend the Constitution, targeting Congress and the president, to the traditional state-by-state strategy for suffrage.

The radical wing of the suffragists, led by the indomitable Alice Paul, picketed the White House, where the marchers unfurled banners that proclaimed "America Is Not a Democracy. Twenty Million Women Are Denied the Right to Vote." They

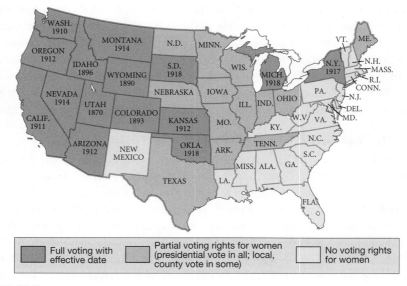

■ Full voting with effective date	■ Partial voting rights for women (presidential vote in all; local, county vote in some)
	□ No voting rights for women

MAP 22.2
Women's Voting Rights before the Nineteenth Amendment
The long campaign for women's voting rights reversed the pioneer epic that moved from east to west. From its first successes in the new democratic West, suffrage rolled eastward toward the entrenched, male-dominated public life of the Northeast and South.

chained themselves to fences and went to jail, where many engaged in hunger strikes. "They seem bent on making their cause as obnoxious as possible," Woodrow Wilson declared. His wife, Edith, detested the idea of "masculinized" voting women. But membership in the mainstream organization, the National American Woman Suffrage Association (NAWSA), led by Carrie Chapman Catt, soared to some two million. The NAWSA even accepted African American women into its ranks, though not on an equal basis. Seeing the handwriting on the wall, the Republican and Progressive parties endorsed woman suffrage in 1916.

In 1918, Wilson gave his support to suffrage, calling the amendment "vital to the winning of the war." He conceded that it would be wrong not to reward the wartime "partnership of suffering and sacrifice" with a "partnership of privilege and right." By linking their cause to the wartime emphasis on national unity, the advocates of woman suffrage finally triumphed. In 1919, Congress passed the **Nineteenth Amendment**, granting women the vote, and by August 1920 the required two-thirds of the states had ratified it. But rather than being the end of the long road to women's full equality, as some suffragists contended, woman suffrage proved to be only the beginning.

Rally around the Flag — or Else

When Congress committed the nation to war, most peace advocates rallied around the flag. The Carnegie Endowment for International Peace adopted new stationery with the heading "Peace through Victory" and issued a resolution saying that "the most effectual means of promoting peace is to prosecute the war against the Imperial German Government."

Only a handful of reformers resisted the tide of patriotism. A group of professional women, led by settlement house leader Jane Addams and economics professor Emily Greene Balch, denounced what Addams described as "the pathetic belief in the regenerative results of war." The Women's Peace Party, which emerged in 1915, and its foreign affiliates in the Women's International League for Peace and Freedom led the struggle to persuade governments to negotiate peace and spare dissenters from harsh punishment. After America entered the conflict, advocates for peace were routinely labeled cowards and traitors, their efforts crushed by the steamroller of conformity.

To suppress criticism of the war, Wilson stirred up patriotic fervor. In 1917, the president created the **Committee on Public Information** under the direction of George Creel, a journalist, who became the nation's cheerleader for war. He sent "Four-Minute Men," a squad of 75,000 volunteers, around the country to give brief pep talks that celebrated successes on the battlefields and in the factories. Posters, pamphlets, and cartoons depicted brave American soldiers and sailors defending freedom and democracy against the evil "Huns."

America rallied around Creel's campaign. The film industry cranked out melodramas about battle-line and home-front heroes and taught audiences to hiss at the German kaiser. A musical, *The Kaiser: The Beast of Berlin*, opened on Broadway in 1918. Faculties of colleges and universities generated war propaganda in the guise of scholarship. When Professor James McKeen Cattell of Columbia University urged that America seek peace with Germany short of victory, university president Nicholas Murray Butler fired him on the grounds that "what had been folly is now treason."

A firestorm of anti-German passion erupted. Across the nation, "100% American" campaigns enlisted ordinary people to sniff out disloyalty. German, the most widely taught foreign language in 1914, practically disappeared from the nation's schools. Targeting German-born Americans, the *Saturday Evening Post* declared that it was time to rid the country of "the scum of the melting pot." Rabid anti-German action reached its extreme with the lynching of Robert Prager, a baker in Collinsville, Illinois. In the eyes of the mob, it was enough that Prager was German-born and had socialist leanings, even though he had not opposed American participation in the war. Persuaded by the defense lawyer who praised what he called a "patriotic murder," the jury at the trial of the killers took only twenty-five minutes to acquit.

As hysteria increased, the campaign reached absurd levels. In Montana, a school board barred a history text that had good things to say about medieval Germany. Menus across the nation changed German toast to French toast and sauerkraut to liberty cabbage. In Milwaukee, vigilantes mounted a machine gun outside the Pabst Theater to prevent the staging of Schiller's *Wilhelm Tell*, a powerful protest against tyranny. One vigilant citizen claimed to see a periscope in the Great Lakes, and the fiancée of one of the war's leading critics, caught dancing on the dunes of Cape Cod, was held on suspicion of signaling to German submarines.

The Wilson administration's zeal in suppressing dissent contrasted sharply with its war aims of defending democracy. In the name of self-defense, the Espionage Act (June 1917), the Trading with the Enemy Act (October 1917), and the Sedition Act (May 1918) gave the government sweeping powers to punish any opinion or activity it considered "disloyal, profane, scurrilous, or abusive." When Postmaster General Albert Burleson blocked mailing privileges for dissenting publications, dozens of journals were forced to close down. Of the 1,500 individuals eventually charged with sedition, all but a dozen had merely spoken words the government found objectionable. One of them was Eugene V. Debs, the leader of the Socialist Party, who was convicted under the Espionage Act for speeches condemning the war as a capitalist plot and sent to the Atlanta penitentiary.

The president hoped that national commitment to the war would silence partisan politics, but his Republican rivals used the war as a weapon against the Democrats. The trick was to oppose Wilson's conduct of the war but not the war itself. Republicans outshouted Wilson on the nation's need to mobilize for war but then complained that Wilson's War Industries Board was a tyrannical agency that crushed free enterprise. Such attacks appealed to widely diverse business, labor, and patriotic groups. As the war progressed, Republicans gathered power against the Democrats, who had narrowly reelected Wilson in 1916.

In 1918, Republicans gained a narrow majority in both the House and the Senate. The end of Democratic control of Congress not only halted further domestic reform but also meant that the United States would advance toward military victory in Europe with political power divided between a Democratic president and a Republican Congress likely to challenge Wilson's plans for international cooperation.

REVIEW   How did progressive ideals fare during wartime?

▶ A Compromised Peace

Wilson decided to reaffirm his noble war ideals by announcing his peace aims before the end of hostilities. He hoped the victorious Allies would adopt his plan for international democracy, but he was sorely disappointed. The leaders of Britain, France, and Italy (which had joined the Allies in 1915 in hopes of postwar gains) understood that Wilson's principles jeopardized their own postwar plans for the acquisition of enemy territory, new colonial empires, and reparations. Wilson also faced strong opposition at home from those who feared that his enthusiasm for international cooperation would undermine American sovereignty.

Wilson's Fourteen Points

On January 8, 1918, President Wilson revealed to Congress his **Fourteen Points**, his blueprint for a new democratic world order. The first five points affirmed basic liberal ideals: an end to secret treaties; freedom of the seas; removal of economic barriers to free trade; reduction of weapons of war; and recognition of the rights of colonized peoples. The next eight points supported the right to self-determination of European peoples who had been dominated by Germany or its allies. Wilson's fourteenth point called for a "general association of nations" — a **League of Nations** — to provide "mutual guarantees of political independence and territorial integrity to great and small states alike." A League of Nations reflected Wilson's lifelong dream of a "parliament of man." Only such an organization of "peace-loving nations," he believed, could justify the war and secure a lasting peace.

Citizens of the United States and of every Allied country greeted the Fourteen Points enthusiastically. Wilson felt confident that he could prevail against undemocratic and selfish forces at the peace table. During the final year of the war, he pressured the Allies to accept the Fourteen Points as the basis of the postwar settlement.

The Paris Peace Conference

From January 18 to June 28, 1919, the eyes of the world focused on Paris. There, powerful men wrestled with difficult problems. Although no other American president had ever gone to Europe while in office, Wilson, inspired by his mission, decided to head the U.S. delegation. He said he owed it to the American soldiers. "It is now my duty," he announced, "to play my full part in making good what they gave their life's blood to obtain." A dubious British diplomat retorted that Wilson was drawn to Paris "as a debutante is entranced by the prospect of her first ball." The decision to leave the country at a time when his political opponents challenged his leadership was risky enough, but his stubborn refusal to include prominent Republicans in the delegation proved foolhardy and eventually cost him his dream of a new world order with the United States at its center.

After four terrible years of war, the common people of Europe almost worshipped Wilson, believing that he would create a safer, more decent world. When the peace conference convened at Louis XIV's magnificent palace at Versailles, however, Wilson encountered a different reception. Representing the Allies were the decidedly unidealistic David Lloyd George, prime minister of Britain; Georges Clemenceau, premier of France; and Vittorio Orlando, former prime minister of Italy. To the Allied leaders, Wilson appeared a naive and impractical moralist. His desire to gather former enemies within a new international democratic order showed how little he understood hard European realities. Clemenceau claimed that Wilson "believed you could do everything by formulas" and "empty theory." Disparaging the Fourteen Points, he added, "God himself was content with ten commandments."

The Allies wanted to fasten blame for the war on Germany, totally disarm it, and make it pay so dearly that it would never threaten its neighbors again. The French demanded retribution in the form of territory containing Germany's richest mineral resources. The British made it clear that they were not about to give up the powerful weapon of naval blockade for the vague principle of freedom of the seas.

The Allies forced Wilson to make drastic compromises. In return for France's moderating its territorial claims, he agreed to support Article 231 of the peace treaty, assigning war guilt to Germany. Though saved from permanently losing Rhineland territory to the French, Germany was outraged at being singled out as the instigator of the war and being saddled with more than $33 billion in damages. Many Germans felt that their nation had been betrayed. After agreeing to an armistice in the belief that peace terms would be based in Wilson's generous Fourteen Points, they faced hardship and humiliation instead.

Wilson had better success in establishing the principle of self-determination. But from the beginning, Secretary of State Robert Lansing knew that the president's concept of self-determination was "simply loaded with dynamite." Lansing wondered, "What unit has he in mind? Does he mean a race, a territorial area, or a community?" Even Wilson was vague about what self-determination actually meant. "When I gave utterance to those words," he admitted, "I said them without the knowledge that nationalities existed, which are coming to us day after day." Lansing suspected that the notion "will raise hopes which can never be realized. It will, I fear, cost thousands of lives. In the end it is bound to be discredited, to be called the dream of an idealist who failed to realize the danger until it was too late."

Yet partly on the basis of self-determination, the conference redrew the map of Europe and parts of the rest of the world. Portions of Austria-Hungary were ceded to Italy, Poland, and Romania, and the remainder was reassembled into Austria, Hungary, Czechoslovakia, and Yugoslavia — independent republics whose boundaries were drawn with attention to concentrations of major ethnic groups. More arbitrarily, the Ottoman empire was carved up into small mandates (including Palestine) run by local leaders but under the control of France and Great Britain. The conference reserved the mandate system for those regions it deemed insufficiently "civilized" to have full independence. Thus, the reconstructed nations — each beset with ethnic and nationalist rivalries — faced the challenge of making a new democratic government work (Map 22.3). Many of today's bitterest disputes — in the Balkans and Iraq, between Greece and Turkey, between Arabs and Jews — have roots in the decisions made in Paris in 1919.

Wilson hoped that self-determination would also dictate the fate of Germany's colonies in Asia and Africa. But the Allies, who had taken over the colonies during the war, allowed the League of Nations only a mandate to administer them. Technically, the mandate system rejected imperialism, but in reality it allowed the Allies to maintain control. Thus, while denying Germany its colonies, the Allies retained and added to their own far-flung territories.

The cause of democratic equality suffered another setback when the peace conference rejected Japan's call for a statement of racial equality in the treaty. Wilson's belief in the superiority of whites, as well as his apprehension about how white Americans would respond to such a declaration, led him to oppose the clause. To soothe hurt feelings, Wilson agreed to grant Japan a mandate over the Shantung Peninsula in northern China, which had formerly been controlled by Germany. The gesture mollified Japan's moderate leaders, but the military

MAP 22.3
Europe after World War I
The post–World War I settlement redrew boundaries to create new nations based on ethnic groupings. Within defeated Germany and Russia, this outcome left bitter peoples who resolved to recover the territory taken from them.

faction preparing to take over the country used bitterness toward racist Western colonialism to build support for expanding Japanese power throughout Asia.

Closest to Wilson's heart was finding a new way to manage international relations. In Wilson's view, war had discredited the old strategy of balance of power. Instead, he proposed a League of Nations that would provide collective security. The league would establish rules of international conduct and resolve conflicts between nations through rational and peaceful means. When the Allies agreed to the league, Wilson was overjoyed. He believed that the league would rectify the errors his colleagues had forced on him in Paris. The league would solidify and extend the noble work he had begun.

To some Europeans and Americans, the **Versailles treaty** came as a bitter disappointment. Wilson's admirers were shocked that the president dealt in compromise like any other politician. But without Wilson's presence, the treaty that was signed on June 28, 1919, surely would have been more vindictive. Wilson returned home in July 1919 consoled that, despite his frustrations, he had gained what he most wanted — a League of Nations. In Wilson's judgment, "We have completed in the least time possible the greatest work that four men have ever done."

The Fight for the Treaty

The tumultuous reception Wilson received when he arrived home persuaded him, probably correctly, that the American people supported the treaty. When the president submitted the treaty to the Senate in July 1919, he warned that failure to ratify it would "break the heart of the world." By then, however, criticism of the treaty was mounting, especially from Americans convinced that their countries of ethnic origin had not been given fair treatment. Irish Americans, Italian Americans, and German Americans launched especially sharp attacks. Others worried that the president's concessions at Versailles had jeopardized the treaty's capacity to provide a generous plan for rebuilding Europe and to guarantee world peace.

Some of the most potent critics were found in the Senate. Bolstered by a slight Republican majority in Congress, a group of Republican "irreconcilables," which included such powerful isolationist senators as Hiram Johnson of California and William Borah of Idaho, condemned the treaty for entangling the United States in world affairs. A larger group of Republicans did not object to American participation in world politics but feared that membership in the League of Nations would jeopardize the nation's ability to act independently. No Republican, in any case, was eager to hand Wilson and the Democrats a foreign policy victory with the 1920 presidential election little more than a year away.

At the center of Republican opposition was Wilson's archenemy, Senator **Henry Cabot Lodge** of Massachusetts. Lodge's hostility was in part personal. "I never thought I could hate a man as much as I hate Wilson," he once admitted. But Lodge also raised cogent objections to the treaty and the league. Lodge was no isolationist, but he thought that much of the Fourteen Points was a "general bleat about virtue being better than vice." Lodge expected the United States' economic and military power to propel the nation into a major role in world affairs. But he insisted that membership in the League of Nations, which would require collective action to maintain peace, threatened the nation's independence in foreign relations.

Lodge used his position as chairman of the Senate Foreign Relations Committee to air every sort of complaint. Out of the committee hearings came several amendments, or "reservations," that sought to limit the consequences of American membership in the league. For example, several reservations required approval of both the House and the Senate before the United States could participate in league-sponsored economic sanctions or military action.

It gradually became clear that ratification of the treaty depended on acceptance of the Lodge reservations. Democratic senators, who overwhelmingly supported the treaty, urged Wilson to accept Lodge's terms, arguing that they left the essentials of the treaty intact. Wilson, however, insisted that the reservations cut "the very heart out of the treaty." He expressed personal hatred as well. "*Lodge* reservations?" he thundered. "Never! I'll never consent to adopt any policy with which that impossible name is so prominently identified."

Wilson decided to take his case directly to the people. On September 3, 1919, still exhausted from the peace conference and against the objections of his doctors, he set out by train on the most ambitious speaking tour ever undertaken by a president. On September 25 in Pueblo, Colorado, Wilson collapsed and had to return to Washington. There, he suffered a massive stroke that partially paralyzed him. From his bedroom, Wilson sent messages instructing Democrats in the Senate to hold firm against any and all reservations. Wilson commanded enough loyalty to ensure a vote against the Lodge reservations. But when the treaty without reservations came before the Senate in March 1920, the combined opposition of the Republican irreconcilables and reservationists left Wilson six votes short of the two-thirds majority needed for passage. Wilson told his doctor, "The Devil is a busy man."

The nations of Europe organized the League of Nations at Geneva, Switzerland. Although Woodrow Wilson received the Nobel Peace Prize in 1920 for his central role in creating the league, the United States never became a member. In refusing to accept relatively minor compromises with Senate moderates, Wilson lost his treaty and American membership in the league. Whether American membership could have prevented the world war that would begin in Europe in 1939 is highly unlikely, but the United States' failure to join certainly weakened the league from the start. Woodrow Wilson and Henry Cabot Lodge both died in 1924, never seeing international order or security, never knowing the whirlwind of resentment and violence that would eventually follow the Great War's failure to make the world safe for democracy.

REVIEW   Why did the Senate fail to ratify the Versailles treaty?

▶ Democracy at Risk

The defeat of Wilson's plan for international democracy proved the crowning blow to progressives who had hoped that the war could boost reform at home. When the war ended, Americans wanted to demobilize swiftly. In the process, servicemen, defense workers, and farmers lost their war-related jobs. The volatile combination — of unemployed veterans returning home, a stalled economy, and leftover wartime patriotism looking for a new cause — threatened to explode. Wartime anti-German passion was quickly followed by antiradicalism, a fevered campaign that ensnared unionists, socialists, dissenters, and African Americans and Mexicans who had committed no offense but to seek to escape rural poverty.

The 1920 election marked the end of Wilson's two terms in the White House and his crusades.

Economic Hardship and Labor Upheaval

Americans greeted peace with a demand that the United States return to a peacetime economy. The government abruptly abandoned its wartime economic controls and canceled war contracts worth millions of dollars. In a matter of months, 3 million soldiers mustered out of the military and flooded the job market just as war production ceased. Unemployment soared. At the same time, consumers went on a postwar spending spree that drove inflation skyward. In 1919, prices rose 75 percent over prewar levels, and in 1920 prices rose another 28 percent.

Most of the gains workers had made during the war evaporated. Freed from government controls, business turned against the eight-hour day and attacked labor unions. With inflation eating up their paychecks, workers fought back. The

Returning Veterans and Work

After the triumphal parades ended, attention turned to the question of what the heroes would do at home. The U.S. Employment Service had little to offer veterans and unions were unprepared to cope with the massive numbers of former soldiers who needed retraining. As workplace conditions deteriorated, the largest number of strikes in the nation's history broke out in 1919. Library of Congress.

year 1919 witnessed nearly 3,600 strikes involving 4 million workers. The most spectacular strike occurred in February 1919 in Seattle, where shipyard workers had been put out of work by demobilization. When a coalition of the radical Industrial Workers of the World (IWW, called Wobblies) and the moderate American Federation of Labor called a general strike, the largest work stoppage in American history shut down the city. Newspapers claimed that the walkout was "a Bolshevik effort to start a revolution." The suppression of the **Seattle general strike** by city officials cost the AFL many of its wartime gains and contributed to the destruction of the IWW soon afterward.

A strike by Boston policemen in the fall of 1919 underscored postwar hostility toward labor militancy. Although the police had received no raise since before the war and were paid less than pick-and-shovel laborers, they won little sympathy. Once the officers stopped walking their beats, looters sacked the city. Massachusetts governor Calvin Coolidge called in the National Guard to restore order and broke the **Boston police strike**. The public, yearning for peace and security in the wake of war, welcomed Coolidge's anti-union assurance that "there is no right to strike against the public safety by anybody, anywhere, any time."

Labor strife climaxed in the grim **steel strike of 1919**. Faced with the industry's plan to revert to seven-day weeks, twelve-hour days, and weekly wages of about $20, Samuel Gompers, head of the AFL, called for a strike. In September, 350,000 workers in fifteen states walked out. The steel industry hired 30,000 strikebreakers (many of them African Americans) and convinced the public that the strikers were radicals bent on subverting democracy and capitalism. In January 1920, after 18 striking workers were killed, the strike collapsed. That devastating defeat initiated a sharp decline in the fortunes of the labor movement, a trend that would continue for almost twenty years.

The Red Scare

Suppression of labor strikes was one response to the widespread fear of internal subversion that swept the nation in 1919. The **Red scare** ("Red" referred to the color of the Bolshevik flag) far outstripped even the assault on civil liberties during the war. It had homegrown causes: the postwar recession, labor unrest, terrorist acts, and the difficulties of reintegrating millions of returning veterans. But unsettling events abroad also added to Americans' anxieties.

Two epidemics swept the globe in 1918. One was Spanish influenza, which brought on a lethal accumulation of fluid in the lungs. A nurse near the front lines in France observed that victims "run a high temperature, so high that we can't believe it's true. . . . It is accompanied by vomiting and dysentery. When they die, as about half of them do, they turn a ghastly dark gray and are taken out at once and cremated." Before the flu virus had run its course, 40 million people had died worldwide, including some 700,000 Americans.

The other epidemic was Russian bolshevism, which seemed to most Americans at the time equally contagious and deadly. Bolshevism became even more menacing in March 1919, when the new Soviet leaders created the Comintern, a worldwide association of Communists intent on fomenting revolution in capitalist countries.

A Communist revolution in the United States was extremely unlikely, but edgy Americans, faced with a flurry of terrorist acts, believed otherwise. Dozens of prominent individuals had received bombs through the mail. On September 16, 1920, a wagon filled with dynamite and iron exploded on Wall Street, killing 38 and maiming 143 others. Authorities never caught the terrorists, and the successful attack on America's financial capital fed the nation's fear, anger, and uncertainty.

Even before the Wall Street bombing, the government had initiated a hunt for domestic revolutionaries. Led by Attorney General **A. Mitchell Palmer**, the campaign targeted men and women who harbored ideas that Palmer believed could lead to violence, even though the individuals may not have done anything illegal. In January 1920, Palmer ordered a series of raids that netted 6,000 alleged subversives. Finding no revolutionary conspiracies, Palmer nevertheless ordered 500 noncitizen suspects deported. His action came in the wake of a campaign against the most notorious radical alien, Russian-born **Emma Goldman**. Before the war, Goldman's passionate support of labor strikes, women's rights, and birth control had made her a symbol of radicalism. Finally, after a stay in prison for denouncing military conscription, she was ordered deported by J. Edgar Hoover, the eager director of the Justice Department's Radical Division. In December 1919, as Goldman and 250 others boarded a ship for exile in Russia, she turned defiantly to thumb her nose at a jeering crowd.

The effort to rid the country of alien radicals was matched by efforts to crush troublesome citizens. Law enforcement officials and vigilante groups joined hands against so-called Reds. In November 1919 in the rugged lumber town of Centralia, Washington, a menacing crowd gathered in front of the IWW hall. Nervous Wobblies inside opened fire, killing three people. Three IWW members were arrested and later convicted of murder, but another, ex-soldier Wesley Everett, was carried off by the mob, which castrated him, hung him from a bridge, and then riddled his body with bullets. His death was officially ruled a suicide.

Public institutions joined the attack on civil liberties. Local libraries removed dissenting books. Schools fired unorthodox teachers. Police shut down radical newspapers. State legislatures refused to seat elected representatives who professed socialist ideas. And in 1919, Congress removed its lone socialist representative, Victor Berger, on the pretext that he was a threat to national safety.

That same year, the Supreme Court provided a formula for restricting free speech. In upholding the conviction of socialist Charles Schenck for publishing a pamphlet urging resistance to the draft during wartime (**Schenck v. United States**), the Court established a "clear and present danger" test. Such utterances as Schenck's during a time of national peril, Justice Oliver Wendell Holmes wrote, were equivalent to shouting "Fire!" in a crowded theater. But Schenck's pamphlet had little power to provoke a public firmly opposed to its message.

In 1920, the assault on civil liberties provoked the creation of the **American Civil Liberties Union (ACLU)**, which was dedicated to defending the individual rights that the Constitution guaranteed. One of the ACLU's founders, Roger Baldwin, declared, "So long as we have enough people in this country willing to fight for their rights, we'll be called a democracy." The ACLU championed the targets of Attorney General Palmer's campaign — politically radical immigrants, trade unionists, socialists and Communists, and antiwar activists who still languished in jail.

But in the end, the Red scare collapsed because of its excesses. In particular, the antiradical campaign lost credibility after Palmer warned in the spring of 1920 that radicals were planning to celebrate the Bolshevik Revolution with a nation-wide wave of violence on May 1, international workers' day. Officials called out state militias, mobilized bomb squads, and even placed machine-gun nests at major city intersections. When May 1 came and went without a single disturbance, the public mood turned from fear to scorn.

The Great Migrations of African Americans and Mexicans

Before the Red scare lost steam, the government raised alarms about the loyalty of African Americans. A Justice Department investigation concluded that Reds were fomenting racial unrest among blacks. Although the report was wrong about Bolshevik influence, it was correct in noticing a new stirring among African Americans, an assertiveness born of participation in the war effort and the massive migration out of the South.

In 1900, nine of every ten blacks still lived in the South, where poverty, disfranchisement, segregation, and violence dominated their lives. A majority of black men continued to toil in agriculture as dirt-poor tenants or sharecroppers or worked for wages of 60 cents a day. Black women worked in the homes of whites as domestics for $2 a week. Whites remained committed to keeping blacks down. "If we own a good farm or horse, or cow, or bird-dog, or yoke of oxen," a black sharecropper in Mississippi observed in 1913, "we are harassed until we are bound to sell, give away, or run away, before we can have any peace in our lives."

The First World War provided African Americans with the opportunity to escape the South's cotton fields and kitchens. War channeled almost 5 million American workers into military service and caused the number of European immigrants to fall from more than a million in 1914 to 31,000 in 1918. Deprived of their traditional sources of laborers just as production demands were increasing, northern industrialists turned to black labor. Young black men, who made up the bulk of the early migrants, found work in steel mills, shipyards, munitions plants, railroad yards, automobile factories, and mines. From 1915 to 1920, a half million blacks (approximately 10 percent of the South's black population) boarded trains bound for Philadelphia, Detroit, Cleveland, Chicago, St. Louis, and other industrial cities.

Thousands of migrants wrote home to tell family and friends about their experiences in the North. One man announced proudly that he had recently been promoted to "first assistant to the head carpenter." He added, "I should have been here twenty years ago. I just begin to feel like a man. . . . My children are going to the same school with the whites and I don't have to [h]umble to no one. I have registered — will vote the next election and there ain't any 'yes sir' — it's all yes and no and Sam and Bill."

But the North was not the promised land. Black men stood on the lowest rungs of the labor ladder. Jobs of any kind proved scarce for black women, and

African Americans Migrate North Wearing their Sunday best and carrying the rest of what they owned in two suitcases, this southern family waits to board a northern-bound train in 1912. Once in the North, black men could expect to find work in mills, shipyards, and factories, but black women often continued working as domestic servants as they had in the South. Photographs and Prints Division, Schomburg Center for Research in Black Culture, New York Public Library, Astor, Lenox, and Tilden Foundations.

most worked as domestic servants as they did in the South. The existing black middle class sometimes shunned the less educated, less sophisticated rural southerners crowding into northern cities. Many whites, fearful of losing jobs and status, lashed out against the new migrants. Savage race riots ripped through two dozen northern cities. The worst occurred in July 1917 when a mob of whites invaded a section of East St. Louis, Illinois, crowded with blacks who had been recruited to help break a strike. The mob murdered at least 39 people and left most of the black district in flames. In 1918, the nation witnessed 96 lynchings of blacks, some of them decorated war veterans still in uniform.

Still, most black migrants stayed in the North and encouraged friends and family to follow. By 1940, more than one million blacks had left the South, profoundly changing their own lives and the course of the nation's history. Black enclaves such as Harlem in New York and the South Side of Chicago, "cities within cities," emerged in the North. These assertive communities provided a foundation for black protest and political organization in the years ahead.

At nearly the same moment that black Americans streamed into northern cities, another migration was under way in the American Southwest. Between 1910 and 1920, the Mexican-born population in the United States soared from 222,000 to 478,000. Mexican immigration resulted from developments on both sides of the border. In Mexico, dictator Porfirio Díaz initiated land policies that decimated poor farmers. When the Mexicans revolted against Díaz in 1910, initiating a ten-year civil war, the trickle of migration became a flood. North of the border, the Chinese Exclusion Act of 1882 and later the disruption of World War I cut off the supply of cheap foreign labor and caused western employers in the expanding rail, mining, construction, and agricultural industries to look south to Mexico for workers.

As a result of Americans' racial stereotyping of Mexicans — a U.S. government economist described them as "docile, patient, usually orderly in camp, fairly intelligent under competent supervision, obedient and cheap" — Mexicans were considered excellent prospects for manual labor but not for citizenship. Employers tried to dampen racial fears by stressing that the immigrants were only temporary residents, not a lasting threat. In 1917, when anti-immigration advocates convinced Congress to do something about foreigners coming into the United States, the restrictive legislation bowed to southwestern industry and exempted Mexicans. By 1920, ethnic Mexicans made up about three-fourths of California's farm laborers. They were also crucial to the Texas economy, accounting for three-fourths of laborers in the cotton fields and in construction there.

Like immigrants from Europe and black migrants from the South, Mexicans in the American Southwest dreamed of a better life. And like the others, they found both opportunity and disappointment. Wages were better than in Mexico, but life in the fields, mines, and factories was hard, and living conditions — in boxcars, labor camps, or urban barrios — often were dismal. Signs warning "No Mexicans Allowed" increased rather than declined. Mexican women nurtured families, but many also worked picking cotton or as domestics. Among Mexican Americans, some of whom had lived in the Southwest for a century or more, *los recién llegados* (the recent arrivals) encountered mixed reactions. One Mexican American expressed this ambivalence: "We are all Mexicans anyway because the gueros [Anglos] treat us all alike." But he also called for immigration quotas because the recent arrivals drove down wages and incited white prejudice that affected all ethnic Mexicans.

Despite friction, large-scale immigration into the Southwest meant a resurgence of the Mexican cultural presence, which became the basis for greater solidarity and political action for the ethnic Mexican population. In 1929 in Texas, Mexican Americans formed the League of United Latin American Citizens.

Postwar Politics and the Election of 1920

A thousand miles away in Washington, D.C., President Woodrow Wilson, bedridden and paralyzed, stubbornly ignored the mountain of domestic troubles — labor strikes, the Red Scare, race riots, immigration backlash — and insisted that the 1920 election would be a "solemn referendum" on the League of Nations. Dutifully, the Democratic nominees for president, James M. Cox of Ohio, and for vice president, Franklin Delano Roosevelt of New York, campaigned on Wilson's international ideals. The Republican Party chose the handsome, gregarious Warren Gamaliel Harding, senator from Ohio. Harding's rise in Ohio politics was a tribute to his amiability, not his mastery of the issues.

Harding found the winning formula when he declared that "America's present need is not heroics, but healing; not nostrums [questionable remedies] but normalcy." But what was "normalcy"? Harding explained: "By 'normalcy' I don't mean the old order but a regular steady order of things. I mean normal procedure, the natural way, without excess." Eager to put wartime crusades and postwar strife behind them, voters responded by giving Harding the largest presidential victory ever: 60.5 percent of the popular vote and 404 out of 531 electoral votes. Once in office, Harding and his wife, Florence, threw open the White House gates, which had been closed since the declaration of war in 1917. Their welcome brought throngs of visitors and lifted the national pall, signaling a new, more easygoing era.

REVIEW How did the Red scare contribute to the erosion of civil liberties after the war?

▶ Conclusion: Troubled Crusade

America's experience in World War I was exceptional. For much of the world, the Great War produced great destruction, endless blackened fields, thousands of ruined factories, and millions of casualties. But in the United States, war and prosperity marched hand in hand. America emerged from the war with the strongest economy in the world and a position of international preeminence.

Still, the nation paid a heavy price both at home and abroad. American soldiers like George Browne encountered unprecedented horrors — submarines, poison gas, machine guns — and more than 100,000 died. On Memorial Day 1919, at the Argonne Cemetery, where 14,200 Americans lie, General John J. Pershing said, "It is . . . for us to uphold the conception of duty, honor and country for which they fought and for which they died. It is for the living to carry forward their purpose and make fruitful their sacrifice." Rather than redeeming their sacrifice as Pershing intoned and Wilson promised, however, the peace that followed the armistice tarnished it. The flawed treaty forced a humiliating peace on Germany and contributed to the rise of Adolf Hitler and a second world war even more catastrophic than the first.

At home, rather than permanently improving working conditions, advancing public health, and spreading educational opportunity, as progressives had hoped, the war threatened to undermine the achievements of the previous two decades. Moreover, rather than promoting democracy in the United States, the war bred fear, intolerance, and repression that led to a crackdown on dissent and a demand for conformity. Reformers could count only woman suffrage as a permanent victory and prohibition as, ultimately, a temporary one.

Woodrow Wilson had promised more than anyone could deliver. Progressive hopes of extending democracy and liberal reform nationally and internationally were dashed. In 1920, a bruised and disillusioned society stumbled into a new decade. The era coming to an end had called on Americans to crusade and sacrifice. The new era promised peace, prosperity, and a good time.

Reviewing Chapter 22

REVIEW QUESTIONS

1. Why did President Wilson fail to maintain U.S. neutrality during World War I? (pp. 653–659)

2. How did the American Expeditionary Force contribute to the defeat of Germany? (pp. 660–663)

3. How did progressive ideals fare during wartime? (pp. 663–668)

4. Why did the Senate fail to ratify the Versailles treaty? (pp. 668–673)

5. How did the Red scare contribute to the erosion of civil liberties after the war? (pp. 673–680)

MAKING CONNECTIONS

1. Why did the United States at first resist intervening in World War I? Why did it later retreat from this policy and send troops? In your answer, discuss whether these decisions revised or reinforced earlier U.S. foreign policy.

2. Some reformers were optimistic that World War I would advance progressive ideals at home. Discuss specific wartime domestic developments that displayed progressivism's influence. How did the war contribute to these developments? Did they endure in peacetime? Why or why not?

3. A conservative reaction in American politics followed peace, most vividly in the labor upheaval and Red scare that swept the nation. What factors drove these developments? How did they shape the postwar political spectrum?

4. During World War I, the nation witnessed important demographic changes. What drove African American and Mexican migration north? How did the war facilitate these changes? In your answer, explain the significance of these developments to the migrants and the nation.

LINKING TO THE PAST

1. How did America's experience in World War I compare with its experience during the Spanish-American War, its previous war abroad? Discuss the decision to go to war in each case, the military aspects, and the outcome. (See chapter 20.)

2. How did the experience of America's workers during World War I compare with their experience in the previous three decades? Consider the composition of the workforce, wages, conditions, and labor's efforts to organize. (See chapters 20 and 21.)

TIMELINE 1914–1920

1914
- **April** U.S. Marines occupy Veracruz, Mexico.
- **June 28** Assassination of Archduke Franz Ferdinand.
- **July 18** Austria-Hungary declares war on Serbia.
- **August 3** Germany attacks Russia and France.
- **August 4** Great Britain declares war on Germany.

1915
- *Lusitania* sunk.
- Women's Peace Party formed.
- Italy joins Allies.

1916
- Pancho Villa attacks Americans in Mexico and New Mexico.
- Wilson reelected.

1917
- Zimmermann telegram intercepted.
- **April 6** United States declares war on Germany.
- Committee on Public Information created.
- Selective Service Act.
- Espionage Act and Trading with the Enemy Act.
- East St. Louis, Illinois, race riot.

1918
- **January 8** President Wilson gives Fourteen Points speech.
- **March** Russia arranges separate peace with Germany.
- **May** Sedition Act.
- **May–June** U.S. Marines see first major combat at Cantigny and Château-Thierry.
- **November 11** Armistice signed ending World War I.

1919
- **January** Paris peace conference begins.
- **June** Treaty of Versailles signed.
- **September** Wilson undertakes speaking tour.
- Wave of labor strikes.

1920
- American Civil Liberties Union founded.
- **January** Prohibition begins.
- **January** Palmer raids.
- **March** Senate votes against ratification of Treaty of Versailles.
- **August** Nineteenth Amendment ratified.
- **November** Republican Warren G. Harding elected president.

▶ **FOR AN ONLINE BIBLIOGRAPHY, PRACTICE QUIZZES, WEB SITES, IMAGES, AND DOCUMENTS RELATED TO THIS CHAPTER,** see the Book Companion Site at **bedfordstmartins.com/roarkvalue**.

▶ **FOR DOCUMENTS RELATED TO THIS PERIOD,** see Michael Johnson, ed., *Reading the American Past*, Fifth Edition.

23

From New Era to Great Depression

1920–1932

AMERICANS IN THE 1920S CHEERED HENRY FORD AS AN AUTHENTIC American hero. When the decade began, he had already produced six million automobiles; by 1927, the figure reached fifteen million. In 1920, one car rolled off the Ford assembly line every minute; in 1925, one appeared every ten seconds. In 1920, a Ford car cost $845; in 1928, the price was less than $300, within range of most of the country's skilled workingmen. Henry Ford put America on wheels, and in the eyes of most Americans he was an honest man who made an honest car: basic, inexpensive, and reliable. He became the greatest example of free enterprise's promise and achievement. But like the age in which he lived, Henry Ford was many-sided, more complex and more contradictory than this simple image suggests.

Born in 1863 on a farm in Dearborn, Michigan, Ford hated the drudgery of farmwork and loved tinkering with machines. At sixteen, he fled rural life for Detroit, where he became a journeyman machinist and experimented with internal combustion engines. In 1893, he put together one of the first successful gasoline-driven carriages in the United States. His ambition, he said, was to "make something in quantity." The product he chose reflected American restlessness, the desire to be on the move. "Everybody wants to be someplace he ain't," Ford declared. "As soon as he gets there he wants to go right back." In 1903, with $28,000 from a few backers, Ford gathered twelve workers in a 250-by-50-foot shed and created the Ford Motor Company.

Ford's early cars were custom-made one at a time. By 1914, his cars were being built along a continuously moving assembly line: Workers bolted on parts brought to them by cranes and conveyor belts. Ford made only one kind

Henry Ford, 1921
A dapper Henry Ford inspects a new Model T in Buffalo, New York, in 1921, while curious onlookers inspect him. Henry Ford was a man of genius whose compelling vision of modern mass production led the way in the 1920s, but he was also cranky, pinched, and mean-spirited. He hated Jews and Catholics, bankers and doctors, and liquor and tobacco, and his millions allowed him to act on his prejudices. Still, his name became synonymous with American success. From the Collections of The Henry Ford.

of car, the Model T, which became synonymous with mass production. A boxlike black vehicle, it was cheap, easy to drive, and simple to repair. The Model T dominated the market. Throughout the rapid expansion of the automotive industry, the Ford Motor Company remained the industry leader, peaking in 1925, when it outsold all its rivals combined.

Nobody entertained grander or more contradictory visions of the new America he had helped to create than Henry Ford himself. When he began his rise, progressive critics condemned the industrial giants of the nineteenth century as "robber barons" who lived in luxury while reducing their workers to wage slaves. Ford, however, identified with the common folk and saw himself as the benefactor of Americans yearning to be free and mobile.

Ford's automobile plants made him a billionaire, but their highly regimented assembly lines reduced Ford workers to near robots. On the cutting edge of modern technology, Ford nevertheless remained nostalgic about rural values. He sought to revive the past in Greenfield Village, a museum outside Detroit, where he relocated buildings from a bygone era, including his parents' farmhouse. His museum contrasted sharply with the roaring Ford plant farther along the Detroit River at River Rouge. The African American and immigrant workers who worked at the plant found no place in Greenfield Village. Yet all would be well, Ford insisted, if Americans remained true to their agrarian past and somehow managed to be modern and scientific at the same time.

Tension between traditional values and modern conditions lay at the heart of the conflicted 1920s. For the first time, more Americans lived in urban than in rural areas, yet Americans remained nostalgic about farms and small towns. Although the nation generally prospered, the new wealth widened the gap between rich and poor. While millions admired urban America's sophisticated new style and consumer products, others condemned postwar society for its vulgar materialism. A great outpouring of artistic talent led, ironically, to incessant critiques of America's artistic barrenness. The Ku Klux Klan and other champions of an idealized older America resorted to violence as well as words when they chastised the era's "new woman," "New Negro," and surging immigrant populations.

The public, disillusioned with the outcome of World War I, turned away from the Christian moralism and idealism of the Progressive Era. In the 1920s, Ford and businessmen like him replaced political reformers such as Theodore Roosevelt and Woodrow Wilson as the models of progress. The U.S. Chamber of Commerce crowed, "The American businessman is the most influential person in the nation." Social justice gave way to individual advancement. At the center of it all, President Calvin Coolidge spoke in praise of those in power when he declared, "The business of America is business." The fortunes of the era rose, then crashed, according to the values and practices of the business community.

▶ The New Era

The 1920s were a time of contradiction and ambivalence. Once Woodrow Wilson left the White House, the energy flowed away from government activism and civic reform and toward private economic endeavor. The rise of a freewheeling economy and a heightened sense of individualism caused Secretary of Commerce Herbert Hoover to declare that America had entered a "New Era," one of many labels used to describe the complex 1920s. Some terms focus on the decade's high-spirited energy and cultural changes: Roaring Twenties, Jazz Age, Flaming Youth, Age of the Flapper. Others echo the rising importance of money—Dollar Decade, Golden Twenties, Prosperity Decade—or reflect the sinister side of gangster profiteering—Lawless Decade. Still others emphasize the lonely confusion of the Lost Generation and the stress and anxiety of the Aspirin Age.

America in the twenties was many things, but there was no getting around the truth of Calvin Coolidge's insight: The business of America *was* business. Politicians and diplomats proclaimed business the heart of American civilization. Average men and women bought into the idea that business and its wonderful products were what made America great, as they snatched up the flood of new consumer items American factories sent forth.

A Business Government

Republicans controlled the White House from 1921 to 1933. The first of the three Republican presidents was **Warren Gamaliel Harding**, the Ohio senator who in his 1920 campaign called for a "return to normalcy," by which he meant the end of public crusades and a return to private pursuits. Harding promised a government run by the best minds, and he appointed a few men of real stature to his cabinet. Herbert Hoover, the energetic and ambitious former head of the wartime Food Administration, became secretary of commerce. However, wealth also counted: Andrew Mellon, one of the richest men in America, became secretary of the treasury. And friendship counted, too. Harding handed out jobs to members of his old "Ohio gang," whose only qualification was their friendship. This curious combination of merit and cronyism made for a disjointed administration in which a few men debated national needs, while other men looked for ways to advance their own interests.

When Harding was elected in 1920 in a landslide over Democratic opponent James Cox, the unemployment rate hit 20 percent, the highest ever up to that point. Farmers fared the worst; their bankruptcy rate increased tenfold. Harding pushed measures to regain national prosperity — high tariffs to protect American businesses (the Fordney-McCumber tariff in 1922 raised duties to unprecedented levels), price supports for agriculture, and the dismantling of wartime government control over industry in favor of unregulated private business. "Never before, here or anywhere else," the U.S. Chamber of Commerce said proudly, "has a government been so completely fused with business."

Harding's policies to boost American enterprise made him very popular, but ultimately his small-town congeniality and trusting ways did him in. Some of his friends in the Ohio gang were up to their necks in lawbreaking. Three of Harding's appointees would go to jail. Interior Secretary Albert Fall was convicted of accepting bribes of more than $400,000 for leasing oil reserves on public land in Teapot Dome, Wyoming, and "**Teapot Dome**" became a synonym for political corruption.

Baffled about how to deal with "my Goddamned friends," Harding in the summer of 1923 took a trip to Alaska to escape his troubles. But the president found no rest, and his health declined. In the early morning of August 2, Vice President **Calvin Coolidge** was awakened at his family's farmhouse in Vermont with the news that Harding had died of a heart attack. By the flickering light of an oil lamp, Coolidge's father, a justice of the peace, swore his son in as president.

This rustic drama calmed a nation confronting the death of a president and continuing scandal in Washington. Coolidge was a modest man of integrity who had once expressed his belief that "the man who builds a factory builds a temple, the man who works there worships there." Reverence for free enterprise meant that Coolidge continued and extended Harding's policies of promoting business and limiting government. With Coolidge's approval, Secretary of the Treasury Andrew Mellon reduced the government's control over the economy and cut taxes for corporations and wealthy individuals. New rules for the Federal Trade Commission severely limited its power to regulate business. Secretary of Commerce Herbert Hoover limited government authority by encouraging trade associations that would keep business honest and efficient through voluntary cooperation.

Coolidge found a staunch ally in the Supreme Court. For many years, the Court had opposed federal regulation of hours, wages, and working conditions on the grounds that such legislation was the proper concern of the states. With Coolidge, the Court also found ways to curtail a state's ability to regulate business. It ruled against closed shops — businesses where only union members could be employed — while confirming the right of owners to form exclusive trade associations. In 1923, the Court declared unconstitutional the District of Columbia's minimum-wage law for women, asserting that the law interfered with the freedom of employer and employee to make labor contracts. The Court and the president attacked government intrusion in the free market, even when the prohibition of government regulation threatened the welfare of workers.

The election of 1924 confirmed the defeat of the progressive principle that the state should take a leading role in ensuring the general welfare. To oppose Coolidge, the Democrats nominated John W. Davis, a corporate lawyer whose conservative views differed little from Republican principles. Only the Progressive Party and its presidential nominee, Senator Robert La Follette of Wisconsin, offered a genuine alternative. When La Follette championed labor unions, regulation of business, and protection of civil liberties, Republicans coined the slogan "Coolidge or Chaos." Turning their backs on what they considered labor radicalism and reckless reform, voters chose Coolidge in a landslide. Coolidge was right when he declared, "This is a business country, and it wants a business government." What was true of the government's relationship to business at home was also true abroad.

Promoting Prosperity and Peace Abroad

After orchestrating the Senate's successful effort to block U.S. membership in the League of Nations, Henry Cabot Lodge boasted, "We have torn Wilsonism up by the roots." But repudiation of Wilsonian internationalism and rejection of collective security through the League of Nations did not mean that the United States retreated into isolationism. The United States emerged from World War I with its economy intact and enjoyed a decade of stunning growth. Economic involvement in the world and the continuing chaos in Europe made withdrawal impossible. New York replaced London as the center of world finance, and the United States became the world's chief creditor.

One of the Republicans' most ambitious foreign policy initiatives was the Washington Disarmament Conference, which convened to establish a global balance of naval power. Secretary of State Charles Evans Hughes shaped the **Five-Power Naval Treaty of 1922** committing Britain, France, Japan, Italy, and the United States to a proportional reduction of naval forces. The treaty led to the scrapping of more than two million tons of warships, by far the world's greatest success in disarmament. Americans celebrated President Harding for safeguarding the peace while remaining outside the League of Nations. By fostering international peace, he also helped make the world a safer place for American trade.

A second major effort on behalf of world peace came in 1928, when Secretary of State Frank Kellogg joined French foreign minister Aristide Briand to produce the **Kellogg-Briand pact**. Nearly fifty nations signed the solemn pledge to renounce war and settle international disputes peacefully. Most Americans considered the nation's signature an affirmation of its commitment to peace rather than to Wilson's foolish notion of a progressive, uplifting war.

But Republican administrations preferred private-sector diplomacy to state action. With the blessing of the White House, a team of American financiers led by Chicago banker Charles Dawes swung into action when Germany suspended its war reparation payments in 1923. Impoverished, Germany was staggering under the massive bill of $33 billion presented by the victorious Allies in the Versailles treaty. When Germany failed to meet its annual payment, France occupied Germany's industrial Ruhr Valley, creating the worst international crisis since the war. In 1924, American corporate leaders produced the **Dawes Plan**, which halved Germany's annual reparation payments, initiated fresh American loans to Germany, and caused the French to retreat from the Ruhr. Although the United States failed to join the league, it continued to exercise significant economic and diplomatic influence abroad. These Republican successes overseas helped fuel prosperity at home.

Automobiles, Mass Production, and Assembly-Line Progress

The automobile industry emerged as the largest single manufacturing industry in the nation. Aided by the federal government's decision to spend more on roads than on anything else, cars, trucks, and buses surged past railroads as the primary haulers of passengers and freight. **Henry Ford** shrewdly located his company in Detroit, knowing that key materials for his automobiles were manufactured in nearby states. Keystone of the American economy, the automobile industry not only employed hundreds of thousands of workers directly but also brought whole industries into being — filling stations, garages, fast-food restaurants, and "guest cottages" (motels). The need for tires, glass, steel, highways, oil, and refined gasoline for automobiles provided millions of related jobs. By 1929, one American in four found employment directly or indirectly in the automobile industry. "Give us our daily bread" was no longer addressed to the Almighty, one commentator quipped, but to Detroit.

Automobiles altered the face of America. Cars changed where people lived, what work they did, how they spent their leisure, even how they thought. Hundreds of small towns decayed because the automobile enabled rural people to bypass them in favor of more distant cities and towns. Urban streetcars began to disappear as workers moved to the suburbs and commuted to work along crowded highways. In Los Angeles, which boasted of the nation's most extensive system of electronic trolleys, almost a thousand miles of track suffered a slow death at the hands of the automobile. Nothing shaped modern America more than the automobile, and efficient mass production made the automobile revolution possible.

Mass production by the assembly-line technique had become standard in almost every factory, from automobiles to meatpacking to cigarettes. To improve efficiency, corporations reduced assembly-line work to the simplest, most repetitive tasks. They also established specialized divisions — purchasing, production, marketing, and employee relations — each with its own team of professionally trained managers. Changes on the assembly line and in management, along with technological advances, significantly boosted overall efficiency. Between 1922 and 1929, productivity in manufacturing increased 32 percent. Average wages, however, increased only 8 percent. As assembly lines became standard, workers lost many of the skills in which they had once taken pride, but corporations reaped great profits from these changes.

Industries also developed programs for workers that came to be called **welfare capitalism**. Some businesses improved safety and sanitation inside factories and instituted paid vacations and pension plans. Welfare capitalism encouraged loyalty to the company and discouraged traditional labor unions. Not wanting to relive the chaotic strikes of 1919, industrialists sought to eliminate reasons for workers to join unions. One labor organizer in the steel industry bemoaned the success of welfare capitalism. "So many workmen here had been lulled to sleep by the company union, the welfare plans, the social organizations fostered by the employer," he declared, "that they had come to look upon the employer as their protector, and had believed vigorous trade union organization unnecessary for their welfare."

Consumer Culture

Mass production fueled corporate profits and national economic prosperity. During the 1920s, per capita income increased by a third, the cost of living stayed the same, and unemployment remained low. But the rewards of the economic boom were not evenly distributed. Americans who labored with their hands inched ahead, while white-collar workers enjoyed significantly more spending money and more leisure time to spend it. Mass production of a broad range of new products — automobiles, radios, refrigerators, electric irons, washing machines — produced a consumer goods revolution.

In this new era of abundance, more people than ever conceived of the American dream in terms of the things they could acquire. In *Middletown* (1929), a study of the inhabitants of Muncie, Indiana, sociologists Robert and Helen Lynd revealed how the business boom and business values of the 1920s affected average Americans. Muncie was, above all, "a culture in which everything hinges on money." Moreover, faced with technological and organizational change beyond their comprehension, many citizens had lost confidence in their ability to play an effective role in civic affairs. More and more they became passive consumers, deferring to the supposed expertise of leaders in politics and economics.

The pied piper of these disturbing changes was the rapidly expanding business of advertising, which stimulated the desire for new products and hammered away at the traditional values of thrift and saving. Newspapers, magazines, radios, and billboards told Americans what they had to have in order to be popular, secure, and successful. Advertising linked material goods to the fulfillment of every spiritual and emotional need. Americans increasingly defined and measured their social status, and indeed their personal worth, on the yardstick of material possessions. Happiness itself rode on owning a car and choosing the right cigarettes and toothpaste.

By the 1920s, the United States had achieved the physical capacity to satisfy Americans' material wants. The economic problem shifted from production to consumption: Who would buy the goods flying off American assembly lines? One solution was to expand America's markets in foreign countries, and government and business joined in that effort. Another solution to the problem of consumption was to expand the market at home.

Henry Ford realized early on that "mass production requires mass consumption." He understood that automobile workers not only produced cars but would also buy them if they made enough money. "One's own employees ought to be one's own best customers," Ford said. In 1914, he raised wages in his factories to $5 a day, more than twice the going rate. High wages made for workers who were more loyal and more exploitable, and high wages returned as profits when workers bought Fords.

Not all industrialists were as farseeing as Ford. Because the wages of many workers barely edged upward, many people's incomes were too puny to satisfy the growing desire for consumer goods. Business supplied the solution: Americans could realize their dreams through credit. Installment buying — a little money down, a payment each month — allowed people to purchase expensive items they could not otherwise afford or to purchase items before saving the necessary money. As one newspaper announced, "The first responsibility of an American to his country is no longer that of a citizen, but of a consumer." During the 1920s, America's motto became spend, not save. Old values — "Use it up, wear it out, make it do or do without" — seemed about as pertinent as a horse and buggy. American culture had shifted.

(**REVIEW**) How did the spread of the automobile transform the United States?

▶ The Roaring Twenties

By the beginning of the decade, psychoanalyst **Sigmund Freud** had become a household name. Most Americans knew little of the complexity of his pioneering work in the psychology of the unconscious, but people realized that Freud offered a way of looking at the world that was radically different. In the twenties, much to Freud's disgust, the American media turned his ideas about the sexual origins of behavior on its head. If it is wrong to deny that we are sexual beings, some reasoned, then the key to health and fulfillment must lie in following impulse freely. Those who doubted this reasoning were simply "repressed." The new ethic of personal freedom excited many Americans to seek pleasure without guilt in a whirl of activity that earned the decade the name "Roaring Twenties." Prohibition made lawbreakers of millions of otherwise decent folk. Flappers and "new women" challenged traditional gender boundaries. Other Americans enjoyed the Roaring Twenties through the words and images of vastly expanded mass communication. Motion pictures, radio, and magazines marketed celebrities. In the freedom of America's big cities, particularly New York, a burst of creativity produced the "New Negro," who confounded and disturbed white Americans. The "Lost Generation" of writers, profoundly disillusioned with mainstream America's cultural direction, fled the country.

Prohibition

Republicans generally sought to curb the powers of government, but the twenties witnessed a great exception to this rule when the federal government implemented one of the last reforms of the Progressive Era: the Eighteenth Amendment, which banned the manufacture and sale of alcohol and took effect in January 1920 (see chapter 22). Drying up the rivers of liquor that Americans consumed, supporters of **prohibition** claimed, would eliminate crime, boost production, and lift the nation's morality. Instead, prohibition initiated a fourteen-year orgy of lawbreaking unparalleled in the nation's history.

Charged with enforcing prohibition, the Treasury Department faced a staggering task. Although it smashed more than 172,000 illegal stills in 1925 alone, there were never enough Treasury agents. Moreover, loopholes in the law almost guaranteed failure. Sacramental wine was permitted, allowing fake clergy to party with bogus congregations. Farmers were allowed to ferment their own "fruit juices." Doctors and dentists could prescribe liquor for medicinal purposes. America's wettest city was probably Detroit, known widely as "the city on a still." Detroit was home to more than 20,000 illegal drinking establishments, making the alcohol business the city's second-largest industry, behind automobile manufacturing.

In 1929, a Treasury agent in Indiana reported intense local resistance to enforcement of prohibition. "Conditions in most important cities very bad," he declared. "Lax and corrupt public officials great handicap . . . prevalence of drinking among minor boys and the . . . middle or better classes of adults." The "speakeasy," an illegal nightclub, became a common feature of the urban landscape. Speakeasies' dance floors led to the sexual integration of the formerly all-male drinking culture, changing American social life forever. One liquor dealer, trading on common knowledge that whiskey still flowed in the White House, distributed cards advertising himself as the "President's Bootlegger."

Eventually, serious criminals took over the liquor trade. Alphonse "Big Al" Capone became the era's most notorious gang lord by establishing in Chicago a bootlegging empire that the government estimated brought in $95 million a year, when a chicken dinner cost 5 cents. During the first four years of prohibition, Chicago witnessed more than two hundred gang-related killings as rival mobs struggled for control of the lucrative liquor trade. The most notorious event came on St. Valentine's Day 1929, when Capone's Italian-dominated mob machine-gunned seven members of a rival Irish gang. Federal authorities finally sent Capone to prison for income tax evasion. Capone never denied being a bootlegger. "I violate the Prohibition law — sure," he told a reporter. "Who doesn't? The only difference is, I take more chances than the man who drinks a cocktail before dinner."

While prohibition did cut down on drinking and alcohol-related illnesses, Americans overwhelmingly favored the repeal of the Eighteenth Amendment. In 1931, a panel of distinguished experts reported that prohibition, which supporters had defended as "a great social and economic experiment," had failed. The social and political costs of prohibition outweighed the benefits. Prohibition fueled criminal activity, corrupted the police, demoralized the judiciary, and caused ordinary citizens to disrespect the law. In 1933, the nation ended prohibition with the Twenty-first Amendment, making the Eighteenth Amendment the only constitutional amendment to be repealed.

The New Woman

Of all the changes in American life in the 1920s, none sparked more heated debate than the alternatives offered to the traditional roles of women. Increasing numbers of women worked and went to college, defying older gender hierarchies and norms. Even mainstream magazines such as the *Saturday Evening Post* began publishing stories about young, college-educated women who drank gin cocktails, smoked cigarettes, and wore skimpy dresses and dangly necklaces. Before the Great War, the **new woman** dwelt in New York City's bohemian Greenwich Village, but afterward the mass media brought her into middle-class America's living rooms.

When the Nineteenth Amendment, ratified in 1920, granted women the vote, feminists felt liberated and expected women to reshape the political landscape. A Kansas woman declared, "I went to bed last night a *slave*[;] I awoke this morning a *free woman*." Women began pressuring Congress to pass laws that especially concerned women, including measures to protect women in factories and grant federal aid to schools. Black women lobbied particularly for federal courts to assume jurisdiction over the crime of lynching. But women's only significant national legislative success came in 1921 when Congress enacted the Sheppard-Towner Act, which extended federal assistance to states seeking to reduce high infant mortality rates. Rather than the beginning of women's political success, the act marked the high tide of women's influence in the 1920s.

A number of factors helped thwart women's political influence. Male domination of both political parties, the rarity of female candidates, and lack of experience in voting, especially among recent immigrants, kept many women away from the polls. In some places, male-run election machines actually disfranchised women, despite the Nineteenth Amendment. In the South, poll taxes, literacy tests, and outright terrorism continued to decimate the vote of African Americans, men and women alike.

Most important, rather than forming a solid voting bloc, feminists divided. Some argued for women's right to special protection; others demanded equal protection. The radical National Woman's Party fought for an **Equal Rights Amendment** that stated flatly: "Men and women shall have equal rights throughout the United States." The more moderate League of Women Voters feared that the amendment's wording threatened state laws that provided women special protection, such as preventing them from working on certain machines. Put before Congress in 1923, the Equal Rights Amendment went down to defeat, and radical women were forced to work for the causes of birth control, legal equality for minorities, and the end of child labor through other means.

Economically, more women worked for pay — approximately one in four by 1930 — but they clustered in "women's jobs." The proportion of women working in manufacturing fell, while the number of women working as secretaries, stenographers, and typists skyrocketed. Women almost monopolized the occupations of librarian, nurse, elementary school teacher, and telephone operator. Women also represented 40 percent of salesclerks by 1930. More female white-collar workers meant that fewer women were interested in protective legislation for women; new women wanted salaries and opportunities equal to men's.

Increased earnings gave working women more buying power in the new consumer culture. A stereotype soon emerged of the **flapper**, so called because of the short-lived fad of wearing unbuckled galoshes. The flapper had short "bobbed" hair and wore lipstick and rouge. She spent freely on the latest styles — dresses with short skirts and drop waists, no sleeves, and no petticoats — and she danced all night to wild jazz.

The new woman both reflected and propelled the modern birth control movement. Margaret Sanger, the crusading pioneer for contraception

"The Girls' Rebellion"
The August 1924 cover of *Redbook*, a popular women's magazine, portrays the kind of postadolescent girl who was making respectable families frantic. Flappers scandalized their middle-class parents by flouting the old moral code. This young woman sports the "badges of flapperhood," including what one critic called an "intoxication of rouge." The cover promises a story inside about girls gone wild. Fictionalized, emotion-packed stories such as this brought the new woman into every woman's home. Picture Research Consultants & Archives.

during the Progressive Era (see chapter 21), restated her principal conviction in 1920: "No woman can call herself free until she can choose consciously whether she will or will not be a mother." By shifting strategy in the twenties, Sanger courted the conservative American Medical Association; linked birth control with the eugenics movement, which advocated limiting reproduction among "undesirable" groups; and thus made contraception a respectable subject for discussion.

Flapper style and values spread from coast to coast through films, novels, magazines, and advertisements. New women challenged American convictions about separate spheres for women and men, the double standard of sexual conduct, and Victorian ideas of proper female appearance and behavior. Although only a minority of American women became flappers, all women, even those who remained at home, felt the great changes of the era.

The New Negro

The 1920s witnessed the emergence not only of the "new woman" but also of the "New Negro." Both new identities riled conservatives and reactionaries. African Americans who challenged the caste system that confined dark-skinned Americans to the lowest levels of society confronted whites who insisted that race relations would not change. Cheers for black soldiers quickly faded after their return from World War I, and African Americans soon faced grim days of economic hardship and race riots (see chapter 22).

The prominent African American intellectual W. E. B. Du Bois and the National Association for the Advancement of Colored People (NAACP) aggressively pursued the passage of a federal antilynching law to counter mob violence against blacks in the South. Many poor blacks, however, disillusioned with mainstream politics, turned for new leadership to a Jamaican-born visionary named **Marcus Garvey**. Garvey urged African Americans to rediscover the heritage of Africa, take pride in their own achievements, and maintain racial purity by avoiding miscegenation. In 1917, Garvey launched the Universal Negro Improvement Association (UNIA) to help African Americans gain economic and political independence entirely outside white society. In 1919, the UNIA created its own shipping company, the Black Star Line, to support the "Back to Africa" movement among black Americans. But the business was an economic failure, and in 1927 the federal government pinned charges of illegal practices on Garvey and deported him to Jamaica. Nevertheless, the issues Garvey raised about racial pride, black identity, and the search for equality persisted, and his legacy remains at the center of black nationalist thought.

Still, most African Americans maintained hope in the American promise. In New York City, hope and talent came together. Poor blacks from the South, as well as sophisticated immigrants from the West Indies, poured into Harlem in uptown Manhattan. New York City's black population jumped 115 percent (from 152,000 to 327,000) in the 1920s, while its white population increased only 20 percent. Similar demographic changes occurred on a smaller scale throughout the North. Overcrowding and unsanitary housing accompanied this black population explosion, but so too did a new self-consciousness and self-confidence that fed into artistic accomplishment.

In Harlem, an extraordinary mix of black artists, sculptors, novelists, musicians, and poets deliberately set out to create a distinctive African American culture that drew on their identities as Americans and Africans. As scholar Alain Locke put it in 1925, they introduced to the world the "**New Negro**," who rose from the ashes of slavery and segregation to proclaim African Americans' creative genius.

The emergence of the New Negro came to be known as the **Harlem Renaissance**. Building on the independence and pride displayed by black soldiers during the war, black artists sought to defeat the fresh onslaught of racial discrimination and violence with poems, paintings, and plays. "We younger Negro artists . . . intend to express our individual dark-skinned selves without fear or shame," poet Langston Hughes said of the Harlem Renaissance. "If white people are pleased, we are glad. If they are not, it doesn't matter. We know we are beautiful. And ugly, too."

The Harlem Renaissance produced dazzling talent. Black writer James Weldon Johnson, who in 1903 had written the Negro national anthem, "Lift Every Voice,"

Duke Ellington at the Cotton Club

Duke Ellington, at the piano, presides over the floor show at the Cotton Club in Harlem, where black performers played for white audiences. The chorus girls—who were all supposed to be "tall, tan, and terrific"—dance in the "jungle style" that whites expected. During the years from 1927 to 1931 that his orchestra was the house band at the Cotton Club, Ellington recorded more than one hundred of his compositions, establishing him as America's greatest jazz composer and bandleader. The Frank Driggs Collection.

wrote *God's Trombones* (1927), in which he expressed the wisdom and beauty of black folktales from the South. The poetry of Langston Hughes, Claude McKay, and Countee Cullen celebrated the vitality of life in Harlem. Zora Neale Hurston's novel *Their Eyes Were Watching God* (1937) explored the complex passions of black people in a southern community. Black painters, led by Aaron Douglas, linked African art, which had recently inspired European modernist artists, to the concept of the New Negro.

Despite such vibrancy, Harlem for most whites remained a separate black ghetto known only for its lively nightlife. Fashionable whites crowded into Harlem's segregated nightclubs, the most famous of which was the Cotton Club, where they believed they could hear "real" jazz, a relatively new musical form, in its "natural" surroundings. The vigor of the Harlem Renaissance left a powerful legacy for black Americans, but the creative burst did little in the short run to dissolve the prejudice of white society.

Entertainment for the Masses

By the late 1920s, jazz had captured the nation, and jazz giants such as Louis Armstrong, Jelly Roll Morton, Duke Ellington, and Bessie Smith performed for huge audiences. Jazz was only one of the entertainment choices of Americans in the 1920s. Popular culture, like consumer goods, was mass-produced and mass-consumed. The proliferation of movies, radios, music, and sports meant that Americans found plenty to do, and in doing the same things, they helped create a national culture.

Nothing offered escapist delights like the movies. Hollywood, California, discovered the successful formula of combining opulence, sex, and adventure. By 1929, the movies were drawing more than 80 million people in a single week, as many as lived in the entire country. Admission was cheap, and blacks as well as whites attended, although they entered theaters through different entrances and sat separately. Rudolph Valentino, described as "catnip to women," and Clara Bow, the "It Girl" (everyone knew what *it* was), became household names. Most loved of all was the comic Charlie Chaplin, whose famous character, the wistful Little Tramp, showed an endearing inability to cope with the rules and complexities of modern life.

Americans also found heroes in sports. Baseball, professionalized since 1869 and segregated into white and black leagues, solidified its place as the national pastime in the 1920s. It remained essentially a game played by and for the working class. In George Herman "Babe" Ruth, baseball had the most cherished free spirit of the time. "The Sultan of Swat" mixed his record-setting home runs with rowdy escapades, demonstrating to fans that sports offered a way to break out of the ordinariness of everyday life. By "his sheer exuberance," one sportswriter declared, Ruth "has lightened the cares of the world."

The public also fell in love with a young boxer from the grim mining districts of Colorado. As a teenager, Jack Dempsey had made his living hanging around saloons betting he could beat anyone in the house. When he took the heavyweight crown just after World War I, he was revered as the people's champ, an American equalizer who was a stand-in for the average American who felt increasingly confined by bureaucracy and machine-made culture. In Philadelphia in 1926, a crowd of 125,000 fans saw challenger Gene Tunney pummel and defeat the people's champ.

Football, essentially a college sport, held greater sway with the upper classes. The most famous coach, Knute Rockne of Notre Dame, celebrated football for its life lessons of hard work and teamwork. Let the professors make learning as interesting and significant as football, Rockne advised, and the problem of getting young people to learn would disappear. But in keeping with the times, football moved toward a more commercial spectacle. Harold "Red" Grange, "the Galloping Ghost," led the way by going from stardom at the University of Illinois to the Chicago Bears in the new professional football league.

The decade's hero worship reached its zenith in the celebration of **Charles Lindbergh**, a young pilot who set out on May 20, 1927, from Long Island in his single-engine plane, *The Spirit of St. Louis*, to become the first person to fly non-stop across the Atlantic. Newspapers tagged Lindbergh "the Lone Eagle" — the perfect hero for an age that celebrated individual accomplishment. "Charles Lindbergh," one journalist proclaimed, "is the stuff out of which have been made the pioneers that opened up the wilderness. His are the qualities which we, as a people, must nourish." Lindbergh realized, however, that technical and organizational complexity was fast reducing chances for solitary achievement. Consequently, he titled his book about the flight *We* (1927) to include the machine that had made it all possible.

Another machine — the radio — became important to mass culture. The nation's first licensed radio station, KDKA in Pittsburgh, began broadcasting in 1920, and soon American airwaves buzzed with news, sermons, soap operas, sports, comedy, and music. For the first time, Americans on the West Coast laughed at the latest jokes from New York, and citizens everywhere listened to the voices of political candidates without leaving home. Because they could now reach prospective customers in their own homes, advertisers bankrolled radio's rapid growth. Between 1922 and 1929, the number of radio stations in the United States increased from 30 to 606. In just seven years, homes with radios jumped from 60,000 to a staggering 10.25 million.

Radio added to the spread of popular music, especially jazz. Jazz — with its energy and freedom — provided the sound track for a new, distinct social class of youths. As the traditional bonds of community, religion, and family loosened, the young felt less pressure to imitate their elders and more freedom to develop their own culture. An increasing number of college students helped the "rah-rah" style of college life become a fad promoted in movies, songs, and advertisements. The collegiate set was the vanguard of the decade's "flaming youth."

The Lost Generation

Some writers and artists felt alienated from America's mass-culture society, which they found shallow, anti-intellectual, and materialistic. Adoration of silly movie stars disgusted them. Moreover, they believed that business culture blighted

American life. To their minds, Henry Ford made a poor hero. Young, white, and mostly college educated, these expatriates, as they came to be called, felt embittered by the war and renounced the progressives who had promoted it as a crusade. For them, Europe — not Hollywood or Harlem — seemed the place to seek their renaissance.

The American-born writer Gertrude Stein, long established in Paris, remarked famously as the young exiles gathered around her, "They are the lost generation." Most of the expatriates, however, believed to the contrary that they had finally found themselves. The **Lost Generation** helped launch the most creative period in American art and literature in the twentieth century. The novelist whose spare, clean style best exemplified the expatriate efforts to make art mirror basic reality was Ernest Hemingway. Hemingway's experience in the Great War convinced him that the world in which he was raised, with its Christian moralism and belief in progress, was bankrupt. Admirers found the terse language and hard lessons of his novel *The Sun Also Rises* (1926) to be perfect expressions of a world stripped of illusions.

Many writers who remained in America were exiles in spirit. Before the war, intellectuals had eagerly joined progressive reform movements. Afterward, they were more likely critics of American cultural vulgarity. Novelist Sinclair Lewis in *Main Street* (1920) and *Babbitt* (1922) satirized his native Midwest as a cultural wasteland. Humorists such as James Thurber created outlandish characters to poke fun at American stupidity and inhibitions. And southern writers, led by William Faulkner, explored the South's grim class and race heritage. Worries about alienation surfaced as well. Although F. Scott Fitzgerald gained fame as the chronicler of flaming youth, he spoke sadly in *This Side of Paradise* (1920) of a disillusioned generation "grown up to find all Gods dead, all wars fought, all faiths in man shaken."

> **REVIEW** How did the new freedoms of the 1920s challenge older conceptions of gender and race?

▶ Resistance to Change

Large areas of the country did not share in the wealth of the 1920s. By the end of the decade, 40 percent of the nation's farmers were landless, and 90 percent of rural homes lacked indoor plumbing, gas, or electricity. Rural America's wariness and distrust of urban America turned to despair in the 1920s when the census reported that the majority of the population had shifted to the city (Map 23.1). Urban domination over the nation's political and cultural life and sharply rising economic disparity drove rural Americans in often ugly, reactionary directions.

Cities seemed to stand for everything rural areas stood against. Rural America imagined itself as solidly Anglo-Saxon (despite the presence of millions of African Americans in the South and Mexican Americans, Native Americans, and Asian Americans in the West), and the cities seemed to be filled with undesirable immigrants. Rural America was the home of old-time Protestant religion, and the

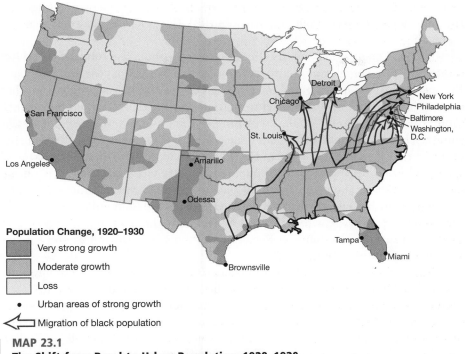

MAP 23.1
The Shift from Rural to Urban Population, 1920–1930
The movement of whites and Hispanics toward urban and agricultural opportunity made Florida, the West, and the Southwest the regions of fastest population growth. By contrast, large numbers of blacks left the rural South to find a better life in the North. Because almost all migrating blacks went from the countryside to cities in distant parts of the nation, while white and Hispanic migrants tended to move shorter distances toward familiar places, the population shift brought more drastic overall change to blacks than to whites and Hispanics.

cities teemed with Catholics, Jews, liberal Protestants, and atheists. Rural America championed old-fashioned moral standards — abstinence and self-denial — while the cities spawned every imaginable vice. In the 1920s, frustrated rural people sought to recapture their country by helping to push through prohibition, dam the flow of immigrants, revive the Ku Klux Klan, defend the Bible as literal truth, and defeat an urban Roman Catholic for president.

Rejecting the Undesirables

Before the war, when about a million immigrants arrived each year, some Americans warned that unassimilable foreigners were smothering the nation. War against Germany and its allies expanded nativist and antiradical sentiment. After the war, large-scale immigration resumed (another 800,000 immigrants arrived in 1921) at a moment when industrialists no longer needed new factory laborers. Returning veterans, as well as African American and Mexican migration, had relieved labor shortages. Moreover, union leaders feared that millions of poor immigrants would undercut their efforts to organize American workers.

Rural America's God-fearing Protestants were particularly alarmed that most of the immigrants were Catholic or Jewish. In 1921, Congress responded by severely restricting immigration.

In 1924, Congress very nearly slammed the door shut. The **Johnson-Reed Act** limited the number of immigrants to no more than 161,000 a year and gave each European nation a quota based on 2 percent of the number of people from that country in America in 1890. The act revealed the fear and bigotry that fueled anti-immigration legislation. While it cut immigration by more than 80 percent, it squeezed some nationalities far more than others. Backers of Johnson-Reed openly declared that America had become the "garbage can and the dumping ground of the world," and they manipulated quotas to ensure entry only to "good" immigrants. By basing quotas on the 1890 census, in which western Europeans predominated, the law effectively reversed the trend toward immigration from southern and eastern Europe, which by 1914 had amounted to 75 percent of the yearly total. For example, the Johnson-Reed Act allowed Great Britain 62,458 entries, but Russia could send only 1,992.

The 1924 law reaffirmed the 1880s legislation barring Chinese immigrants and added Japanese and other Asians to the list of the excluded. But it left open immigration from the Western Hemisphere. Farmers in the Southwest demanded continued access to cheap agricultural labor, and during the 1920s some 500,000 Mexicans crossed the border. In addition, Congress in 1924 passed the Indian Citizenship Act, which extended suffrage and citizenship to all American Indians. Indian veterans of World World I had already been made citizens, but now Congress deemed every Indian worthy of participating in American democracy.

Rural Americans, who had most likely never laid eyes on a Polish packinghouse worker, a Slovak coal miner, an Armenian sewing machine operator, or a Chinese laundry worker, strongly supported the Johnson-Reed Act, as did industrialists and labor leaders. The immigration restriction laws of the 1920s provided the framework for immigration policy until the 1960s. These laws marked the end of an era — the denial of the Statue of Liberty's open-arms welcome to Europe's "huddled masses yearning to breathe free."

Antiforeign hysteria climaxed in the trial of two anarchist immigrants from Italy, **Nicola Sacco and Bartolomeo Vanzetti.** Arrested in 1920 for robbery and murder in South Braintree, Massachusetts, the men were sentenced to death by a judge who openly referred to them as "anarchist bastards." In response to doubts about the fairness of the verdict, a blue-ribbon review committee found the trial judge guilty of a "grave breach of official decorum" but refused to recommend a motion for retrial. Massachusetts's execution of Sacco and Vanzetti on August 23, 1927, provoked international outrage. Fifty thousand American mourners followed the caskets in the rain, convinced that the men had died because they were immigrants and radicals, not because they were murderers.

The Rebirth of the Ku Klux Klan

The nation's sour antiforeign mood struck a responsive chord in members of the **Ku Klux Klan.** The Klan first appeared in the South during Reconstruction to thwart black freedom and expired with the reestablishment of white supremacy (see chapter 16). In 1915, the Klan was reborn at Stone Mountain, Georgia, but when the new Klan extended its targets beyond black Americans, it quickly spread beyond the South. Under a banner proclaiming "100 percent Americanism," the Klan promised to defend family, morality, and traditional American values against the threats posed by blacks, immigrants, radicals, feminists, Catholics, and Jews.

Building on the frustrations of rural America, the Klan attracted three million to four million members — women as well as men. By the mid-1920s, the Klan had spread throughout the nation, almost controlling Indiana and influencing politics in Illinois, California, Oregon, Texas, Louisiana, Oklahoma, and Kansas. In 1926, Klan imperial wizard Hiram Wesley Evans described the assault of modernity: "One by one all our traditional moral standards went by the boards or were so disregarded that they ceased to be binding," he explained. "The sacredness of our Sabbath, of our homes, of chastity, and finally even of our right to teach our own children in schools [represented] fundamental facts and truth torn away from us." The Klan's uniforms and rituals offered a certain counterfeit dignity to old-stock, Protestant, white Americans who felt passed over, and the hoods allowed members to beat and intimidate their victims with little fear of consequences.

Eventually, social changes, along with lawless excess, crippled the Klan. Immigration restrictions eased the worry about invading foreigners, and sensational wrongdoing by Klan leaders cost it the support of traditional moralists. Grand Dragon David Stephenson of Indiana, for example, went to jail for the kidnapping and rape of a woman who subsequently committed suicide. Yet the social grievances, economic problems, and religious anxieties of the countryside and small towns remained, ready to be ignited.

The Scopes Trial

In 1925 in a Tennessee courtroom, old-time religion and the new spirit of science went head-to-head. The confrontation occurred after several southern states passed legislation against the teaching of Charles Darwin's theory of evolution in the public schools. Fundamentalist Protestants insisted that the Bible's creation story be taught as the literal truth. Scientists and civil liberties organizations clamored for a challenge to the law, and John Scopes, a young biology teacher in Dayton, Tennessee, offered to test his state's ban on teaching evolution. When Scopes came to trial, Clarence Darrow, a brilliant defense lawyer from Chicago, volunteered to defend him. Darrow, an avowed agnostic, took on the prosecution's fundamentalist William Jennings Bryan. Bryan, a three-time Democratic nominee for president and a symbol of rural America, was eager to defeat the proposition that humans had evolved from apes.

The **Scopes trial** quickly degenerated into a media circus. The first trial to be covered live on radio, it attracted a nationwide audience. Most of the reporters from big-city newspapers were hostile to Bryan, none more so than the cynical H. L. Mencken, who painted Bryan as a sort of Darwinian missing link ("a sweating anthropoid" and a "gaping primate"). When, under relentless questioning by

Darrow, Bryan declared on the witness stand that he did indeed believe that the world had been created in six days and that Jonah had lived in the belly of a whale, his humiliation in the eyes of most urban observers was complete. Nevertheless, the Tennessee court upheld the law and punished Scopes with a $100 fine. Although fundamentalism won the battle, it lost the war. Mencken had the last word in a merciless obituary for Bryan, who died just a week after the trial ended. Portraying the "monkey trial" as a battle between the country and the city, Mencken flayed Bryan as a "charlatan, a mountebank, a zany without shame or dignity," motivated solely by "hatred of the city men who had laughed at him for so long."

As Mencken's acid prose indicated, Bryan's humiliation was not purely a victory of reason and science. It also revealed the disdain urban people felt for country people and the values they clung to. The Ku Klux Klan revival and the Scopes trial dramatized and inflamed divisions between city and country, intellectuals and the uneducated, the privileged and the poor, the scoffers and the faithful.

Al Smith and the Election of 1928

The presidential election of 1928 brought many of the developments of the 1920s — prohibition, immigration, religion, and the clash of rural and urban values — into sharp focus. Republicans emphasized the economic success of their party's pro-business government and turned to Herbert Hoover, the energetic secretary of commerce and leading public symbol of 1920s prosperity. But because both parties generally agreed that the American economy was basically sound, the campaign turned on social issues that divided Americans.

The Democrats nominated four-time governor of New York **Alfred E. Smith**. Smith adopted "The Sidewalks of New York" as a campaign theme song and seemed to represent all that rural Americans feared and resented. A child of immigrants, Smith got his start in politics with the help of Tammany Hall, New York City's Irish-dominated political machine and to many the epitome of big-city corruption. He denounced immigration quotas, signed New York State's anti-Klan bill, and opposed prohibition, believing that it was a nativist attack on immigrant customs. When Smith supposedly asked reporters in 1922, "Wouldn't you like to have your foot on the rail and blow the foam off some suds?" prohibition forces dubbed him "Alcohol Al."

Smith's greatest vulnerability in the heartland, however, was his religion. He was the first Catholic to run for president. A Methodist bishop in Virginia denounced Roman Catholicism as "the Mother of ignorance, superstition, intolerance and sin" and begged Protestants not to vote for a candidate who represented "the kind of dirty people that you find today on the sidewalks of New York." The magazine *Baptist and Commoner* argued that Smith's election would mean "granting the Pope the right to dictate to this government what it should do."

Hoover, who neatly combined the images of morality, efficiency, service, and prosperity, won the election by a landslide. He received nearly 58 percent of the vote and gained 444 electoral votes to Smith's 87. The Republicans' most notable success came in the previously solid Democratic South, where Smith's religion,

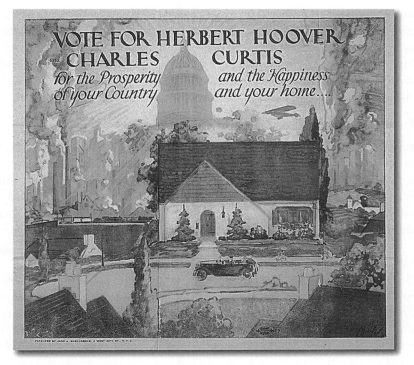

Hoover Campaign Poster
This poster effectively illustrates Herbert Hoover's 1928 campaign message: Republican administrations in the 1920s had produced middle-class prosperity, complete with a house in the suburbs and the latest automobile. To remind voters that Hoover as secretary of commerce had promoted industry that made the suburban dream possible, the poster portrays smoking chimneys at a discreet distance. The poster gives no hint that this positive message would give way to outright religious bigotry in the campaign against Democrat (and Catholic) Al Smith. Collection of Janice L. and David J. Frent.

views on prohibition, and big-city persona allowed them to take four states. The only bright spot for Democrats was the nation's cities, which voted Democratic, indicating the rising strength of ethnic minorities, including Smith's fellow Catholics.

REVIEW Why did the relationship between urban and rural America deteriorate in the 1920s?

▶ The Great Crash

At his inauguration in 1929, Herbert Hoover told the American people, "Given a chance to go forward with the policies of the last eight years, we shall soon with the help of God be in sight of the day when poverty will be banished from this nation." Those words came back to haunt Hoover, for within eight months the Roaring Twenties came to a crashing halt. The prosperity Hoover touted collapsed with the stock market, and the nation ended nearly three decades of barely interrupted economic growth. Like much of the world, the United States fell into the most serious economic depression of all time. Hoover and his reputation were among the first casualties, along with the reverence for business that had been the hallmark of the New Era.

Herbert Hoover: The Great Engineer

When **Herbert Hoover** became president in 1929, he seemed the perfect choice to lead a prosperous business nation. He personified America's rags-to-riches ideal, having risen from poor Iowa orphan to one of the world's most celebrated mining engineers by the time he was thirty. His success in managing efforts to feed civilian victims of the fighting during World War I won him acclaim as "the Great Humanitarian" and led Woodrow Wilson to name him head of the Food Administration once the United States entered the war. Hoover's reputation soared even higher as secretary of commerce in the Harding and Coolidge administrations.

Hoover belonged to the progressive wing of the Republican Party, and as early as 1909 he declared, "The time when the employer could ride roughshod over his labor[ers] is disappearing with the doctrine of 'laissez-faire' on which it is founded." He urged a limited business-government partnership that would manage the sweeping changes Americans experienced. When Hoover entered the White House, he brought a reform agenda: "We want to see a nation built of home owners and farm owners. We want to see their savings protected. We want to see them in steady jobs. We want to see more and more of them insured against death and accident, unemployment and old age. We want them all secure."

But Hoover also had ideological and political liabilities. Principles that appeared strengths in the prosperous 1920s — individual self-reliance, industrial self-management, and a limited federal government — became straitjackets when economic catastrophe struck. Moreover, Hoover had never held an elected public office, had a poor political touch, and was too thin-skinned to be an effective politician. Even so, most Americans considered him "a sort of superman" able to solve any problem. Prophetically, he confided to a friend his fear that "if some unprecedented calamity should come upon the nation . . . I would be sacrificed to the unreasoning disappointment of a people who expected too much." The distorted national economy set the stage for the calamity Hoover so feared.

The Distorted Economy

In the spring of 1929, the United States enjoyed a fragile prosperity. Although America had become the world's leading economy, it had done little to help rebuild Europe's shattered economy after World War I. Instead, the Republican administrations demanded that Allied nations repay their war loans, creating a tangled web of debts and reparations that sapped Europe's economic vitality. Moreover, to boost American business, the United States enacted tariffs that prevented other nations from selling their goods to Americans. Fewer sales meant that foreign nations had less money to buy American goods, which were pouring out in record abundance. American banks propped up the nation's export trade by extending credit to foreign customers, and fresh debt piled onto existing debt in an absurd pyramid.

American prosperity was real enough, but the domestic economy was also in trouble. Wealth was badly distributed. Farmers continued to suffer from low prices and chronic indebtedness; the average income of families working the land amounted to only $240 per year. The wages of industrial workers, though rising during the decade, failed to keep up with productivity and corporate profits. Overall, nearly two-thirds of all American families lived on less than the $2,000 per year that economists estimated would "supply only basic necessities." Statistics captured the grim reality. The wealthiest 1 percent of the population received 15 percent of the nation's income — the same amount received by the poorest 42 percent. The Coolidge administration worsened the deepening inequality by cutting taxes on the wealthy.

By 1929, the inequality of wealth produced a serious problem in consumption. The rich spent lavishly, but they could absorb only a tiny fraction of the nation's output. Ordinary folk, on whom the system ultimately depended, were unable to take up the slack. For a time, the new device of installment buying — buying on credit — kept consumer demand up. By the end of the decade, four out of five cars and two out of three radios were bought on credit.

Signs of economic trouble began to appear at mid-decade. New construction slowed down. Automobile sales faltered. Companies began cutting back production and laying off workers. Between 1921 and 1928, as investment and loan opportunities faded, five thousand banks failed, wiping out the life savings of hundreds of thousands of people. Still, the boom seemed to roar on, muffling the sounds of economic distress just beneath the surface.

The Crash of 1929

Even as the international and domestic economies faltered, Americans remained remarkably upbeat. Hoping for even bigger slices of the economic pie, Americans speculated wildly in the stock market on Wall Street. Between 1924 and 1929, the values of stocks listed on the New York Stock Exchange increased by more than 400 percent. In September 1929, General Electric traded at $396 a share, three times the price of a year earlier. Buying stocks on margin — that is, putting up only part of the money at the time of purchase — accelerated. Many people got rich this way, but those who bought on credit could finance their loans only if their stocks increased in value. Speculators could not imagine that the market might fall and that they would be forced to meet their margin loans with cash they did not have. A Yale economist assured doubters that stock prices had reached "a permanently high plateau."

Finally, in the autumn of 1929, the market hesitated. Investors nervously began to sell their overvalued stocks. The dip quickly became a panic on October 24, the day that came to be known as Black Thursday. Brokers jammed the stock exchange desperately trying to unload shares. The giants of finance gathered in the offices of J. P. Morgan Jr., son of the nineteenth-century Wall Street lion, to plot ways of restoring confidence. They injected $100 million of their assets to bolster the market and issued brave declarations of faith. But more panic selling came on **Black Tuesday**, October 29, the day the market suffered a greater fall than ever before. In the next six months, the stock market lost six-sevenths of its total value.

It was once thought that the crash alone caused the Great Depression. It did not. In 1929, the national and international economies were already riddled with severe problems. But the dramatic losses in the stock market crash and the fear of risking what was left acted as a great brake on economic activity. The collapse on Wall Street shattered the New Era's confidence that America would enjoy perpetually expanding prosperity.

Hoover and the Limits of Individualism

At first, Americans expressed relief that Herbert Hoover resided in the White House when the bubble broke. Unlike some conservatives who believed that the government should do nothing during economic downturns, Hoover believed that "we should use the powers of government to cushion the situation." Not surprisingly for a man who had been such an active secretary of commerce, Hoover acted quickly to arrest the decline.

In November 1929, to keep the stock market collapse from ravaging the entire economy, Hoover called a White House conference of business and labor leaders and urged them to join in a voluntary plan for recovery: Businesses would maintain production and keep their workers on the job; labor would accept existing wages, hours, and conditions. Within a few months, however, the bargain fell apart. As demand for their products declined, industrialists cut production, sliced wages, and laid off workers. Poorly paid or unemployed workers could not buy much, and their decreased spending led to further cuts in production and further loss of jobs. Thus began the terrible spiral of economic decline.

To deal with the problems of rural America, Hoover got Congress to pass the Agricultural Marketing Act in 1929. The act created the **Farm Board**, which used its budget of $500 million to buy up agricultural surpluses and thus, it was hoped, raise prices. But prices declined. To help end the decline, Hoover joined conservatives in urging protective tariffs on agricultural goods, and the **Hawley-Smoot tariff** of 1930 established the highest rates in history. The same year, Congress also authorized $420 million for public works projects to give the unemployed jobs and create more purchasing power. In three years, the Hoover administration nearly doubled federal public works expenditures.

But with each year of Hoover's term, the economy weakened. Tariffs did not end the suffering of farmers because foreign nations retaliated with increased tariffs of their own that crippled American farmers' ability to sell abroad. In 1932, Hoover hoped to help hard-pressed industry with the **Reconstruction Finance Corporation (RFC)**, a federal agency empowered to lend government funds to endangered banks and corporations. The theory was **trickle-down economics**: Pump money into the economy at the top, and in the long run the people at the bottom would benefit. Or as one wag put it, "Feed the sparrows by feeding the horses." In the end, very little of what critics of the RFC called a "millionaires' dole" trickled down to the poor.

And the poor multiplied. Hundreds of thousands of workers lost their jobs each month. By 1932, an astounding one-quarter of the American workforce — some thirteen million people — were unemployed. There was no direct federal assistance, and state services and private charities were swamped. The depression that began in 1929 devastated much of the world, but no other industrialized nation provided such feeble support to the jobless. Cries grew louder for the federal government to give hurting people relief.

Hoover was no do-nothing president, but there were limits to his activism. He intended a limited role for the federal government in fighting the economic disaster. He compared direct federal aid to the needy to the "dole" in Britain, which he thought destroyed the moral fiber of the chronically unemployed. "Prosperity cannot be restored by raids upon the public Treasury," he declared. Besides, he said, the poor could rely on the charitable spirit of their neighbors to protect them "from hunger and cold." In 1931, he allowed the Red Cross to distribute government-owned agricultural surpluses to the hungry. In 1932, he relaxed his principles further to offer small federal loans, not gifts, to the states to help them in their relief efforts. But Hoover's circumscribed notions of legitimate government action proved vastly inadequate to address the problems of restarting the economy and ending human suffering.

REVIEW Why did the American economy collapse in 1929?

▶ Life in the Depression

In 1930, suffering on a massive scale set in. Despair settled over the land. Men and women hollow-eyed with hunger grew increasingly bewildered and angry in the face of cruel contradictions. They saw agricultural surpluses pile up in the countryside and knew that their children were going to bed hungry. They saw factories standing idle and knew that they and millions of others were willing to work. The gap between the American people and leaders who failed to resolve these contradictions widened as the depression deepened. By 1932, America's economic problems had created a dangerous social and political crisis.

The Human Toll

Statistics only hint at the human tragedy of the Great Depression. When Herbert Hoover took office in 1929, the American economy stood at its peak. When he left in 1933, it had reached its twentieth-century low (Figure 23.1). In 1929, national income was $88 billion. By 1933, it had declined to $40 billion. In 1929, unemployment was 3.1 percent, or 1.5 million workers. By 1933, unemployment stood at 25 percent, almost 13 million workers. In Cleveland, Ohio, 50 percent of the workforce was jobless, and in Toledo, 80 percent. The nation's steel industry operated at only 12 percent of capacity. By 1932, more than 9,000 banks had shut their doors, wiping out some 9 million savings accounts.

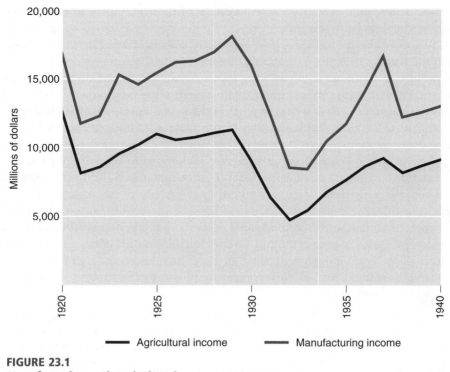

FIGURE 23.1
Manufacturing and Agricultural Income, 1920–1940
After economic collapse, recovery in the 1930s began under New Deal auspices. The sharp declines in 1937–1938, when federal spending was reduced, indicated that New Deal stimuli were still needed to restore manufacturing and agricultural income.

Jobless, homeless victims wandered in search of work, and the tramp, or hobo, became one of the most visible figures of the decade. Riding the rails or hitchhiking, a million vagabonds moved southward and westward looking for seasonal agricultural work. Other unemployed men and women, sick or less hopeful, huddled in doorways, overcome, one man remembered, by "helpless despair and submission." Scavengers haunted alleys behind restaurants in search of food. One writer told of an elderly woman who always took off her glasses to avoid seeing the maggots crawling over the garbage she ate. The Children's Bureau announced that one in five schoolchildren did not get enough to eat. "I don't want to steal," a Pennsylvania man wrote to the governor in 1931, "but I won't let my wife and boy cry for something to eat. . . . How long is this going to keep up? I cannot stand it any longer."

Rural poverty was most acute. Tenant farmers and sharecroppers, mainly in the South, came to symbolize how poverty crushed the human spirit. Eight and a half million people, three million of them black, crowded into cabins without plumbing, electricity, or running water. They subsisted — just barely — on salt pork, cornmeal, molasses, beans, peas, and whatever they could hunt or fish.

All the diseases of dietary and vitamin deficiencies wracked them. When economist John Maynard Keynes was asked whether anything like this degradation had existed before, he replied, "Yes, it was called the Dark Ages and it lasted four hundred years."

There was no federal assistance to meet this human catastrophe. Instead, Hoover relied on a patchwork of strapped charities and destitute state and local agencies. For a family of four without any income, the best the city of Philadelphia could do was provide $5.50 per week. That was not enough to live on but was still comparatively generous. New York City provided only $2.39 per week. Detroit, devastated by the auto industry's failure, allotted 60 cents a week before the city ran out of money altogether, joining a hundred other cities in 1932 that appropriated no money at all for the indigent.

The deepening crisis roused old fears and caused some Americans to look for scapegoats. Among the most thoroughly scapegoated were Mexican Americans. During the 1920s, cheap agricultural labor from Mexico flowed legally across the

Deportation to Mexico

A crowd gathered at the train depot in Miami, Arizona, to say good-bye to friends and family who were being pushed to leave depression-wracked America. Scenes like this one were repeated throughout the Southwest. In 1931, Los Angeles County chartered trains to carry Mexicans and Mexican Americans out of the country, arguing that the $15,000 expense "would be recovered within six weeks in saving on charity." But contrary to popular belief, immigrants did not put undue pressure on social services. Moreover, some of the deportees were American citizens who had never been south of the border. Arizona State University Library.

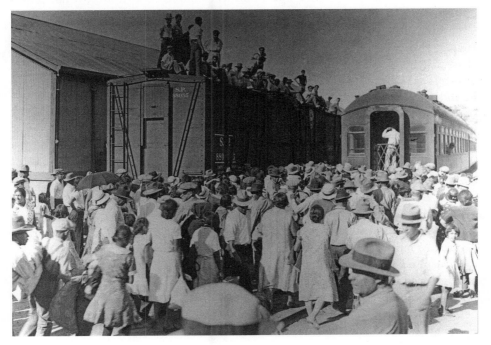

U.S. border, welcomed by the large farmers. In the 1930s, however, the public denounced the newcomers as dangerous aliens who took jobs from Americans. Government officials, most prominently those in Los Angeles County, targeted Mexican residents for deportation regardless of citizenship status. As many as half a million Mexicans and Mexican Americans were deported or fled to Mexico.

The depression deeply affected the American family. Young people postponed marriage; between 1929 and 1932, marriages declined by 31 percent. When they did marry, they produced few children. For the first time in American history, the birthrate was on the verge of dropping below the death rate. Moreover, white women, who generally worked in low-paying service areas, did not lose their jobs as often as men who worked in steel, automobile, and other heavy industries. Idle husbands suffered a loss of self-esteem. "Before the depression," one unemployed man reported, "I wore the pants in this family, and rightly so." Jobless, he lost "self-respect" and also "the respect of my children, and I am afraid that I am losing my wife." Another unemployed father said, "A man is not a man without work." Employers discriminated against married women workers, but necessity continued to drive women into the marketplace. As a result, by 1940 some 25 percent more women were employed for wages than in 1930.

Denial and Escape

President Hoover had no idea of how to reach out to the suffering nation. To express his optimism about economic recovery, he maintained formal dress and manners in the White House and continued to keep a retinue of valets and wait-ers to attend him. All he did was to repeat that economic recovery was on its way. Contradicting the president's optimism were makeshift shantytowns, called "**Hoovervilles**," that sprang up on the edges of America's cities. Newspapers used as cover by those sleeping on the streets were "Hoover blankets." An empty pocket turned inside out was a "Hoover flag," and jackrabbits caught for food were "Hoover hogs." Bitter jokes circulated about the increasingly unpopular president. One told of Hoover asking for a nickel to telephone a friend. Flipping him a dime, an aide said, "Here, call them both."

While Hoover practiced denial, other Americans sought refuge from reality at the movies. Throughout the depression, between 60 million and 75 million people (nearly two-thirds of the nation) scraped together enough change to fill the movie palaces every week. Box office hits such as *Forty-second Street* and *Gold Diggers of 1933* capitalized on the hope that prosperity lay just around the corner. But a few filmmakers grappled with realities rather than escape them. *The Public Enemy* (1931) taught hard lessons about gangsters' ill-gotten gains. Indeed, under the new production code of 1930, designed to protect public morals, all movies had to find some way to show that crime did not pay.

Despite Hollywood's efforts to keep Americans on the right side of the law, crime increased. Out in the countryside, the plight of people who had lost their farms to bank foreclosures led to the romantic idea that bank robbers were only getting back what banks had stolen from the poor. Woody Guthrie, the populist folksinger from Oklahoma, captured the public's tolerance for outlaws in his tribute to a murderous bank robber with a choirboy face, "The Ballad of Pretty Boy Floyd":

> Yes, as through this world I ramble,
> I see lots of funny men,
> Some will rob you with a six-gun,
> Some will rob you with a pen.
> But as through your life you'll travel,
> Wherever you may roam,
> You won't never see an outlaw drive
> A family from their home.

Working-Class Militancy

It was the nation's working class that bore the brunt of the economic collapse. In Chicago, workingwomen received less than twenty-five cents an hour. Sawmill workers in the West got a nickel. By 1931, William Green, head of the American Federation of Labor (AFL), had turned militant. "I warn the people who are exploiting the workers," he shouted, "that they can drive them only so far before they will turn on them and destroy them. They are taking no account of the history of nations in which governments have been overturned. Revolutions grow out of the depths of hunger."

The American people were slow to anger, but on March 7, 1932, several thousand unemployed autoworkers massed at the gates of Henry Ford's River Rouge factory in Dearborn, Michigan, to demand work. Pelted with rocks, Ford's private security forces responded with gunfire, killing four demonstrators. Forty thousand outraged citizens turned out for the unemployed men's funerals.

Farmers mounted uprisings of their own. When Congress refused to guarantee farm prices that would at least equal the cost of production, several thousand farmers created the National Farmers' Holiday Association in 1932, so named because its members planned to take a "holiday" from shipping crops to market. When some farmers persisted, militants barricaded roads and dumped thousands of gallons of milk in ditches. Farm militants also resorted to what they called "penny sales." When banks foreclosed and put farms up for auction, neighbors warned others not to bid, bought the foreclosed property for a few pennies, and returned it to the bankrupt owners. Under this kind of pressure, some states suspended debts or reduced mortgages. In California in 1933, when landowners cut their laborers' already substandard wages, more than 50,000 farmworkers, most of them Mexicans, went on strike. Militancy won farmers little in the way of long-term solutions, but one individual observed that "the biggest and finest crop of revolutions you ever saw is sprouting all over the country right now."

Even those who had proved their patriotism by serving in World War I rose up in protest against the government. In June and July 1932, tens of thousands of unemployed veterans traveled to Washington, D.C., to petition Congress for the immediate payment of the pension (known as a "bonus") that Congress had promised them in 1924. The throng included, according to a Washington reporter, "truck drivers and blacksmiths, steel workers and coal miners, stenographers and common laborers," in all "a fair cross section" of the nation. President Hoover feared that the veterans would spark a riot and ordered the U.S. Army to evict the **Bonus Marchers** from their camp on the outskirts of the city. Tanks decimated the squatters' encampments while five hundred soldiers wielding bayonets and tear gas sent the ragtag protesters fleeing. The mayhem, which was captured on newsreels, appalled the nation and further undermined public support for the beleaguered Hoover. "So all the misery and suffering had finally come to this," reported one journalist, "soldiers marching with their guns against American citizens."

Such scenes during the Great Depression — the massive failure of capitalism — brought socialism back to life in the United States and catapulted the Communist Party to its greatest size and influence in American history. Some 100,000 Americans — workers, intellectuals, college students — joined the Communist Party in the belief that only an overthrow of the capitalist system could save the victims of the depression. In 1931, the party, through its National Miners Union, moved into Harlan County, Kentucky, to support a strike by brutalized coal miners. The mine owners unleashed thugs against the strikers and eventually beat the miners down. But the Communist Party gained a reputation as the most dedicated and fearless champion of the union cause.

The left also led the fight against racism. While both major parties refused to challenge segregation in the South, the Socialist Party, led by Norman Thomas, attacked the system of sharecropping that left many African Americans in near servitude. The Communist Party also took action. When nine young black men in Scottsboro, Alabama (the **Scottsboro Boys**), were arrested on trumped-up rape charges in 1931, a team of lawyers sent by the party saved the defendants from the electric chair.

Radicals on the left often sparked action, but protests by moderate workers and farmers occurred on a far greater scale. Breadlines, soup kitchens, foreclosures, unemployment, government violence, and cold despair drove patriotic men and women to question American capitalism. "I am as conservative as any man could be," a Wisconsin farmer explained, "but any economic system that has in its power to set me and my wife in the streets, at my age — what can I see but red?"

REVIEW   How did the depression reshape American politics?

▶ Conclusion: Dazzle and Despair

In the aftermath of World War I, America turned its back on progressive crusades and embraced conservative Republican politics, the growing influence of corporate leaders, and business values. Changes in the nation's economy — Henry Ford's automobile revolution, advertising, mass production — propelled fundamental change throughout society. Living standards rose, economic opportunity increased, and Americans threw themselves into private pleasures — gobbling up the latest household goods and fashions, attending baseball and football games and boxing matches, gathering around the radio, and going to the movies. As big cities came to dominate American life, the culture of youth and flappers became the leading edge of what one observer called a "revolution in manners and morals." At home in Harlem and abroad in Paris, American literature, art, and music flourished.

For many Americans, however, none of the glamour and vitality had much meaning. Instead of seeking thrills at speakeasies, plunging into speculation on Wall Street, or escaping abroad, the vast majority struggled to earn a decent living. Blue-collar America did not participate fully in white-collar prosperity. Rural America was almost entirely left out of the Roaring Twenties. Country folk, deeply suspicious and profoundly discontented, championed prohibition, revived the Klan, attacked immigration, and defended old-time Protestant religion.

Just as the dazzle of the Roaring Twenties hid deep divisions in society, extravagant prosperity masked structural flaws in the economy. The crash of 1929 and the depression that followed starkly revealed the economy's crises of international trade and consumption. Hard times swept high living off the front pages of the nation's newspapers. Different images emerged: hoboes hopping freight trains, strikers confronting police, malnourished sharecroppers staring blankly into the distance, empty apartment buildings alongside cardboard shantytowns, and mountains of food rotting in the sun while guards with shotguns chased away the hungry.

The depression hurt everyone, but the poor were hurt most. As farmers and workers sank into aching hardship, businessmen rallied around Herbert Hoover to proclaim that private enterprise would get the country moving again. But things fell apart, and Hoover faced increasingly radical opposition. Membership in the Socialist and Communist parties surged, and more and more Americans contemplated desperate measures. By 1932, the depression had nearly brought the nation to its knees. America faced its greatest crisis since the Civil War, and citizens demanded new leaders who would save them from the "Hoover Depression."

Reviewing Chapter 23

REVIEW QUESTIONS

1. How did the spread of the automobile transform the United States? (pp. 685–690)

2. How did the new freedoms of the 1920s challenge older conceptions of gender and race? (pp. 690–698)

3. Why did the relationship between urban and rural America deteriorate in the 1920s? (pp. 698–703)

4. Why did the American economy collapse in 1929? (pp. 703–707)

5. How did the depression reshape American politics? (pp. 707–712)

MAKING CONNECTIONS

1. In the 1920s, Americans' wariness of the concentration of power in the hands of industrial capitalists gave way to unrestrained confidence in American business. What drove this shift in popular opinion? How did it influence Republicans' approach to governance and the development of the American economy in the 1920s?

2. Americans' encounters with the wealth and increased personal freedom characteristic of the 1920s varied greatly. Discuss the impact such variation had on Americans' responses to new circumstances. Why did some embrace the era's changes, while others resisted them? Ground your answer in a discussion of specific political, legal, or cultural conflicts.

3. How did shifting government policy contribute to both the boom of the 1920s and the bust of 1929? In your answer, consider the part domestic and international policy played in these developments, including taxation, tariffs, and international banking.

4. The Great Depression plunged the nation into a profound crisis with staggering personal and national costs. How did Americans attempt to lessen the impact of these circumstances? In your answer, discuss and compare the responses of individual Americans and the federal government.

LINKING TO THE PAST

1. How did America's experience in World War I — both at home and abroad — help shape the 1920s? (See chapter 22.)

2. How did attitudes toward government in the Progressive Era differ from those in the 1920s? (See chapter 21.)

TIMELINE 1920–1932

1920
- Eighteenth Amendment goes into effect.
- Nineteenth Amendment ratified.
- Republican Warren G. Harding elected president.

1921
- Sheppard-Towner Act.
- Congress restricts immigration.

1922
- Fordney-McCumber tariff.
- Five-Power Naval Treaty.

1923
- Equal Rights Amendment defeated in Congress.
- Harding dies; Vice President Calvin Coolidge becomes president.

1924
- Dawes Plan.
- Coolidge elected president.
- Johnson-Reed Act.
- Indian Citizenship Act.

1925
- Scopes trial.

1927
- Charles Lindbergh flies nonstop across the Atlantic.
- Nicola Sacco and Bartolomeo Vanzetti executed.

1928
- Kellogg-Briand pact.
- Republican Herbert Hoover elected president.

1929
- St. Valentine's Day murders.
- Agricultural Marketing Act.
- Publication of *Middletown*.
- Stock market collapses.

1930
- Congress authorizes $420 million for public works projects.
- Hawley-Smoot tariff.

1931
- Scottsboro Boys arrested.
- Harlan County, Kentucky, coal strike.

1932
- River Rouge factory demonstration.
- Reconstruction Finance Corporation established.
- National Farmers' Holiday Association formed.

▶ **FOR AN ONLINE BIBLIOGRAPHY, PRACTICE QUIZZES, WEB SITES, IMAGES, AND DOCUMENTS RELATED TO THIS CHAPTER,** see the Book Companion Site at **bedfordstmartins.com/roarkvalue**.

▶ **FOR DOCUMENTS RELATED TO THIS PERIOD,** see Michael Johnson, ed., *Reading the American Past*, Fifth Edition.

The New Deal Experiment

1932–1939

IN EARLY MARCH 1936, FLORENCE OWENS PILED HER SEVEN CHILDREN, ages one to fourteen, into an old Hudson. Owens and her family had been picking beets in the Imperial Valley of southern California, near the Mexican border, but the harvest was over now. Owens headed north toward Watsonville, where she hoped to find work picking lettuce. About halfway there, near the small town of Nipomo, her car broke down. She coasted into a labor camp of more than two thousand migrant workers who were hungry, out of work, and stuck, lacking the money to look for work elsewhere. They had been attracted by growers' advertisements of work in the pea fields, only to find the crop ruined by a heavy frost. Owens set up a lean-to shelter and prepared food for her family while two of her sons worked on the car. They ate half-frozen peas from the field and small birds the children killed. Owens recalled later, "I started to cook dinner for my kids, and all the little kids around the camp came in. 'Can I have a bite? Can I have a bite?' And they was hungry, them people was."

Florence Owens was born in 1903 in Oklahoma, or what was then Indian Territory. Both of Florence's parents were Cherokee. When she was a baby, her father abandoned her mother, who soon remarried a Choctaw man, and the young family moved to a small farm near Tahlequah, Oklahoma, where Florence grew up. When she was seventeen, Florence married Cleo Owens, a farmer who, after a few years, moved his growing family to California, where he worked in sawmills. Cleo died of tuberculosis in 1931, leaving Florence a widow with six young children.

Florence began to work as a farm laborer in California's Central Valley to support herself and her children. She picked cotton, earning about $2 a day. "I'd leave home before daylight and come in after dark," she explained. "We just existed! Anyway, we survived, let's put it that way." To survive, she worked nights as a waitress, making "50-cents a day and the leftovers." Sometimes, she remembered, "I'd carry home two water buckets full" of leftovers to feed her children.

Like tens of thousands of other migrant laborers, Owens followed the crops, planting, cultivating, and harvesting as jobs opened up in the fields along the West Coast from California to Oregon and Washington. Joining Owens and other migrants — many of whom were Mexicans and Filipinos — were Okie refugees from the Dust Bowl, the large swath of Great Plains states that suffered drought, failed crops, and foreclosed mortgages during the 1930s. As one Okie told a government official in California about the Dust Bowl, "Back there we like to starve to death"; working as a migrant laborer, tough as it was, he said, "beats starvin to death."

Florence Owens and Children
This classic photograph of migrant farm laborer Florence Owens and her children, known as *Migrant Mother*, was taken in 1936 in the labor camp of a pea field in California by New Deal photographer Dorothea Lange. The photo depicts the privations common among working people during the depression, but it also evokes a mother's leadership, dignity, and affection, qualities that helped shelter her family from poverty and joblessness. The photo suggests the depression's cruel assault on most Americans' first safety net — their families — a reality that the New Deal sought to remedy with its proposals for relief, recovery, and reform. Library of Congress.

Soon after Florence Owens fed her children at the pea pickers' camp, a car pulled up, and a woman with a camera got out and began to take photographs of Owens. The woman was Dorothea Lange, a photographer employed by a New Deal agency to document conditions among farmworkers in California. Lange snapped six photos of Owens, moving closer each time until, with the last shot, she filled the frame with Owens and three of her children. After about ten minutes, Lange climbed back in her car and headed to Berkeley. Owens and her family, their car now repaired, drove off to the lettuce fields of Watsonville.

Within days, Lange's last photograph of Owens was published in San Francisco, and news of the near-famine conditions in the pea pickers' camp reached Washington, D.C. Federal officials rushed twenty thousand pounds of food to the camp, but Owens and her children were long gone when it arrived. The photograph of Owens, however, subsequently known as *Migrant Mother*, became an icon of the desperation among Americans that President Franklin Roosevelt's New Deal sought to alleviate. *Migrant Mother* became Dorothea Lange's most famous photograph, but Florence Owens continued to work in the fields, "ragged, hungry, and broke," as a San Francisco newspaper noted. One of Owens's daughters recalled, "That photo never gave mother or us kids any relief."

Unlike Owens, her children, and other migrant workers, many Americans received government help from Roosevelt's New Deal initiatives to provide relief for the needy, to speed economic recovery, and to reform basic economic and governmental institutions. Roosevelt's New Deal elicited bitter opposition from critics on the right and the left and failed to satisfy fully its own goals of relief, recovery, and reform. But within the Democratic Party, the New Deal energized a powerful political coalition that helped millions of Americans withstand the privations of the Great Depression. In the process, the federal government became a major presence in the daily lives of most American citizens.

▶ Franklin D. Roosevelt: A Patrician in Government

Unlike the millions of impoverished Americans, Franklin Roosevelt came from a wealthy and privileged background that contributed to his optimism, self-confidence, and vitality. He constantly drew on these personal qualities in his political career to bridge the economic, social, and cultural chasm that separated him from the struggles of ordinary people like Florence Owens. During the twelve years he served as president (1933–1945), many elites came to hate him as a traitor to his class, while millions more Americans, especially the hardworking poor and dispossessed, revered him because he cared about them and their problems.

The Making of a Politician

Born in 1882, **Franklin Delano Roosevelt** grew up on his father's leafy estate at Hyde Park on the Hudson River, north of New York City. Roosevelt was steeped at home and school in high-minded doctrines of public service and Christian duty to help the poor and weak. He prepared for a career in politics, hoping to follow in the political footsteps of his fifth cousin, Theodore Roosevelt. In 1905, Franklin married his distant cousin, Eleanor Roosevelt. Theodore Roosevelt — the current president of the United States — gave the bride away, an indication of Franklin's gilt-edged connections.

Unlike his cousin Teddy, Franklin Roosevelt sought his political fortune in the Democratic Party. He served in Woodrow Wilson's administration as assistant secretary of the navy, fueling a lifelong interest in maritime matters. In 1920, he catapulted to the second spot on the national Democratic ticket as the vice presidential candidate of presidential nominee James M. Cox. Although Cox lost the election (see chapter 22), Roosevelt's energetic campaigning convinced Democratic leaders that he had a bright future in national politics.

In the summer of 1921, at the age of thirty-nine, Roosevelt caught polio, which paralyzed both his legs. For the rest of his life, he wore heavy steel braces, and he could walk a few steps only by leaning on another person. Tireless physical therapy helped him regain his vitality and intense desire for high political office. But he recaptured his political momentum mostly from a sitting position, although he carefully avoided being photographed in the wheelchair he used routinely.

After his polio attack, Roosevelt frequented a polio therapy facility at Warm Springs, Georgia. There, he combined the health benefits of the soothing waters with political overtures to southern Democrats, which helped make him a rare political creature: a New Yorker from the Democratic Party's urban and immigrant wing with whom whites from the Democratic Party's entrenched southern wing felt comfortable.

By 1928, Roosevelt had recovered sufficiently to campaign to become governor of New York, and he squeaked out a victory. As governor of the nation's most populous state, Roosevelt showcased his leadership and his suitability for a presidential campaign of his own. His activist policies as governor became a dress rehearsal for his presidency.

As the Great Depression spread hard times throughout the nation, Governor Roosevelt believed that government should intervene to protect citizens from economic hardships rather than wait for the law of supply and demand to improve the economy. According to the laissez-faire views of many conservatives — especially Republicans, but also numerous Democrats — the depression simply represented market forces separating strong survivors from weak losers. Unlike Roosevelt, conservatives believed that government help for the needy sapped individual initiative and impeded the self-correcting forces of the market by rewarding people for losing the economic struggle to survive. Roosevelt lacked a full-fledged counterargument to these conservative claims, but he sympathized with the plight of poor people. "To these unfortunate citizens," he proclaimed, "aid must be extended by governments, not as a matter of charity but as a matter of social duty. . . . [No one should go] unfed, unclothed, or unsheltered."

The highlight of Roosevelt's efforts to relieve the economic woes of New Yorkers was the Temporary Emergency Relief Administration, created in 1931. It provided an unprecedented $20 million in aid for the poor, earning him the gratitude of needy New Yorkers and the attention of national politicians.

To his supporters, Roosevelt seemed to be a leader determined to attack the economic crisis without deviating from democracy — unlike the fascist parties gaining strength in Europe — or from capitalism — unlike the Communists in power in the Soviet Union. Roosevelt's ideas about precisely how to revive the economy were vague. A prominent journalist described Roosevelt in 1931 as "a kind of amiable boy scout . . . a pleasant man who, without any important qualifications for the office, would very much like to be president." Such sneering comments did not sway his many supporters who appreciated his energy and activism. His conviction that government should do something to help Americans climb out of the economic abyss propelled him into the front ranks of the national Democratic Party.

The Election of 1932

Democrats knew that Herbert Hoover's unpopularity gave them a historic opportunity to recapture the White House in 1932. Since Abraham Lincoln's election, Republicans had occupied the White House three-fourths of the time, a trend Democrats hoped to reverse. Democrats, however, had to overcome warring factions that divided the party by region, religion, culture, and commitment to the status quo. Southern Democrats chaired powerful committees in Congress thanks to their continual reelection in a one-party South devoted to white supremacy. This southern, native-born, white, rural, Protestant, conservative wing of the Democratic Party found little common ground with the northern, immigrant, urban, disproportionately Catholic, liberal wing. Rural and native-born drys (supporters of prohibition) clashed with urban and foreign-born wets (opponents of prohibition). Eastern-establishment Democratic dignitaries shared few goals with angry farmers and factory workers. Still, this unruly coalition managed to agree on Franklin Roosevelt as its presidential candidate.

In his acceptance speech, Roosevelt vowed to help "the forgotten man at the bottom of the pyramid" with "bold, persistent experimentation." Highlighting his differences with Hoover and the Republicans, he pledged "a new deal for the American people." Few details about what Roosevelt meant by "a new deal" emerged in the presidential campaign. He declared that "the people of America want more than anything else . . . two things: work . . . with all the moral and spiritual values that go with work . . . and a reasonable measure of security . . . for themselves and for their wives and children." Although Roosevelt never explained exactly how the federal government could provide either work or security, voters decided that whatever his new deal might be, it was better than reelecting Hoover.

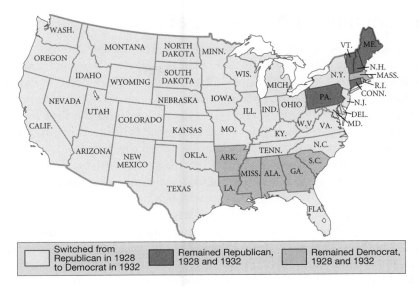

MAP 24.1

Electoral Shift, 1928–1932

The Democratic victory in 1932 signaled the rise of a New Deal coalition within which women and minorities, many of them new voters, made the Democrats the majority party for the first time in the twentieth century.

Roosevelt won the 1932 presidential election in a historic landslide. He received 57 percent of the nation's votes, the first time a Democrat had won a majority of the popular vote since 1852. He amassed 472 electoral votes to Hoover's 59, carrying state after state that had voted Republican for years (Map 24.1). Roosevelt's coattails swept Democrats into control of Congress by large margins. The popular mandate for change was loud and clear.

Roosevelt's victory represented the emergence of what came to be known as the **New Deal coalition**. Attracting support from farmers, factory workers, immigrants, city folk, African Americans, women, and progressive intellectuals, Roosevelt launched a realignment of the nation's political loyalties. The New Deal coalition dominated American politics throughout Roosevelt's presidency and remained powerful long after his death in 1945. United less by ideology or support for specific policies, voters in the New Deal coalition instead expressed faith in Roosevelt's promise of a government that would, somehow, change things for the better. Nobody, including Roosevelt, knew exactly what the New Deal would change or whether the changes would revive the nation's ailing economy and improve Americans' lives. But Roosevelt and many others knew that the future of American capitalism and democracy was at stake.

REVIEW Why did Franklin D. Roosevelt win the 1932 presidential election by such a large margin?

▶ Launching the New Deal

At noon on March 4, 1933, Americans gathered around their radios to hear the inaugural address of the newly elected president. Roosevelt began by asserting his "firm belief that the only thing we have to fear is fear itself — nameless, unreasoning, unjustified terror which paralyzes needed efforts to convert retreat into advance." He promised "direct, vigorous action," and the first months of his administration, termed "the Hundred Days," fulfilled that promise in a whirlwind of government initiatives that launched the New Deal.

Roosevelt and his advisers had three interrelated objectives: to provide relief to the destitute, especially the one out of four Americans who were unemployed; to foster the economic recovery of farms and businesses, thereby creating jobs and reducing the need for relief; and to reform the government and economy in ways that would reduce the risk of devastating consequences in future economic slumps. The New Deal never fully achieved these goals of relief, recovery, and reform. But by aiming for them, Roosevelt's experimental programs enormously expanded government's role in the nation's economy and society.

The New Dealers

To design and implement the New Deal, Roosevelt needed ideas and people. He convened a "Brains Trust" of economists and other leaders to offer suggestions and advice about the problems facing the nation. Among the most important reformers to join the Roosevelt administration were two veterans of Roosevelt's New York governorship: **Harry Hopkins** and **Frances Perkins**. Hopkins, a social worker, administered New Deal relief efforts and served as one of the president's loyal confidants. Perkins, who had extensive experience trying to improve working conditions in shops and factories, served as secretary of labor, making her the first woman cabinet member in American history.

No New Dealers were more important than the president and his wife, Eleanor. The gregarious president radiated charm and good cheer, giving the New Deal's bureaucratic regulations a benevolent human face. **Eleanor Roosevelt** became the New Deal's unofficial ambassador. She served, she said, as "the eyes and ears of the New Deal," traveling throughout the nation meeting Americans of all colors and creeds in church basements, town halls, and front parlors. A North Carolina women's rights activist recalled, "One of my great pleasures was meeting Mrs. Roosevelt. . . . [S]he was so free of prejudice . . . and she was always willing to take a stand, and there were stands to take about blacks and women."

As Roosevelt's programs swung into action, the millions of beneficiaries of the New Deal became grassroots New Dealers who expressed their appreciation by voting Democratic on election day. In this way, the New Deal created a durable political coalition of Democrats that reelected Roosevelt in 1936, 1940, and 1944.

As Roosevelt and his advisers developed plans to meet the economic emergency, their watchwords were *action*, *experiment*, and *improvise*. Without a sharply defined template for how to provide relief, recovery, and reform, they moved from ideas to policies as quickly as possible, hoping to identify ways to help people and to boost the economy. Four guiding ideas shaped their policies.

First, Roosevelt and his advisers sought capitalist solutions to the economic crisis. They believed that the depression had resulted from basic imbalances in the nation's capitalist economy — imbalances they wanted to correct. They had no desire to eliminate private property or impose socialist programs, such as public ownership of productive resources. Instead, they hoped to save the capitalist economy by remedying its flaws.

Second, Roosevelt's Brains Trust persuaded him that the greatest flaw of America's capitalist economy was **underconsumption**, the root cause of the current economic paralysis. Underconsumption, New Dealers argued, resulted from the gigantic productive success of capitalism. Factories and farms produced more than they could sell to consumers, causing factories to lay off workers and farmers to lose money on bumper crops. Workers without wages and farmers without profits shrank consumption and choked the economy. Somehow, the balance between consumption and production needed to be restored.

Third, New Dealers believed that the immense size and economic power of American corporations needed to be counterbalanced by government and by organization among workers and small producers. Unlike progressive trustbusters, New Dealers did not seek to splinter big businesses. Huge businesses had developed for good economic reasons and were here to stay. Roosevelt and his advisers hoped to counterbalance big economic institutions with government programs focused on protecting individuals and the public interest.

Fourth, New Dealers felt that government must somehow moderate the imbalance of wealth created by American capitalism. Wealth concentrated in a few hands reduced consumption by most Americans and thereby contributed to the current economic gridlock. In the long run, government needed to find a way to permit ordinary working people to share more fully in the fruits of the economy. In the short term, New Dealers sought to lend a helping hand to poor people who suffered from the maldistribution of wealth.

Banking and Finance Reform

Roosevelt wasted no time making good on his inaugural pledge for "action now." As he took the oath of office on March 4, the nation's banking system was on the brink of collapse. Roosevelt immediately declared a four-day "bank holiday" to devise a plan to shore up banks and restore depositors' confidence. Working round the clock, New Dealers drafted the Emergency Banking Act, which gave the secretary of the treasury the power to decide which banks could be safely reopened and to release funds from the Reconstruction Finance Corporation to bolster banks' assets. To secure the confidence of depositors, Congress passed the Glass-Steagall Banking Act, setting up the **Federal Deposit Insurance Corporation (FDIC)**, which guaranteed bank customers that the federal government would reimburse them for deposits if their banks failed. In addition, the act required the separation of commercial banks (which accept deposits and make loans to individuals and small businesses) and investment banks (which make speculative investments with their funds), in an effort to insulate the finances of Main Street America from the risky speculations of Wall Street wheeler-dealers.

Fireside Chat
President Roosevelt explained New Deal programs to ordinary Americans in his frequent radio broadcasts. People throughout the nation, like the man shown here, listened to Roosevelt's fireside chats in the quiet of their homes. The chats reassured many Americans that Washington cared about their suffering and was trying to relieve it. One New Yorker wrote the president that he felt Roosevelt had "walked into my home, sat down, and in plain and forceful language explained to me how he was tackling the job I and my fellow citizens gave him." Franklin D. Roosevelt Library.

On Sunday night, March 12, while the banks were still closed, Roosevelt broadcast the first of a series of **fireside chats**. Speaking in a friendly, informal manner, he explained the new banking legislation that, he said, made it "safer to keep your money in a reopened bank than under the mattress." With such plain talk, Roosevelt translated complex matters into common sense. This and subsequent fireside chats forged a direct connection — via radio waves — between Roosevelt and millions of Americans, a connection felt by a man from Paris, Texas, who wrote to Roosevelt, "You are the one & only President that ever helped a Working Class of People. . . . Please help us some way I Pray to God for relief."

The banking legislation and fireside chat worked. Within a few days, most of the nation's major banks reopened, and they remained solvent as reassured depositors switched funds from their mattresses to their bank accounts. Some radical critics of the New Deal believed that Roosevelt should have nationalized the banks and made them a cornerstone of economic planning by the federal government.

Instead, these first New Deal measures propped up the private banking system with federal funds and subjected banks to federal regulation and oversight.

In his inaugural address, Roosevelt criticized financiers for their greed and incompetence. To prevent the fraud, corruption, and insider trading that had tainted Wall Street and contributed to the crash of 1929, Roosevelt pressed Congress to regulate the stock market. Legislation in 1934 created the **Securities and Exchange Commission (SEC)** to oversee financial markets by licensing investment dealers, monitoring all stock transactions, and requiring corporate officers to make full disclosures about their companies. To head the SEC, Roosevelt named an abrasive and ambitious Wall Street financier, Joseph P. Kennedy, who had a somewhat shady reputation for stock manipulation. When critics complained about his selection, Roosevelt replied, "Set a thief to catch a thief." Under Kennedy's leadership, the SEC helped a cleaned-up and regulated Wall Street to recover slowly, although the stock market stayed well below its frothy heights during the 1920s.

Relief and Conservation Programs

Patching the nation's financial structure provided little relief for the hungry and unemployed. A poor man from Nebraska asked Eleanor Roosevelt "if the folk who was borned here in America . . . are this Forgotten Man, the President had in mind, [and] if we are this Forgotten Man then we are still Forgotten." Since its founding, the federal government had never assumed responsibility for needy people, except in moments of natural disaster or emergencies such as the Civil War. Instead, churches, private charities, county and municipal governments, and occasionally states assumed the burden of poor relief, usually with meager payments. The depression necessitated unprecedented federal relief efforts, according to Harry Hopkins and other New Dealers. As one New Yorker who still had a job wrote the government, "We work, ten hours a day for six days. In the grime and dirt of a nation [for] . . . low pay [making us] . . . slaves — slaves of the depression!"

Hopkins galvanized support for the **Federal Emergency Relief Administration (FERA)**, established in May 1933, which supported four million to five million households with $20 or $30 a month. FERA also created jobs for the unemployed on thousands of public works projects, organized by Hopkins into the Civil Works Administration (CWA), which put paychecks worth more than $800 million into the hands of previously jobless workers. Earning wages between 40 and 60 cents an hour, laborers renovated schools, dug sewers, and rebuilt roads and bridges. FERA extended the scope of relief to include health and education, funding literacy classes and providing vaccinations for millions.

The most popular work relief program was the **Civilian Conservation Corps (CCC)**, established in March 1933. It offered unemployed young men a chance to earn wages while working to conserve natural resources, a long-standing interest of Roosevelt. Women were excluded from working in the CCC until Eleanor Roosevelt demanded that a token number of young women be hired. One of the young men who enlisted in the CCC, Blackie Gold, had been out of work and had to "beg for coal, [and] buy bread that's two, three days old" to support his large family. After he joined the CCC, Gold earned $30 a month and was required to send all but $5 of it home to his family. By the end of the program in 1942, the three million CCC workers had checked soil erosion, tamed rivers, and planted more than two billion trees. CCC workers left a legacy of vast new recreation areas, along with roads that made those areas accessible to millions of Americans. Just as important, the CCC, CWA, and other work relief efforts replaced the stigma of welfare with the dignity of jobs. As one woman said about her husband's work relief job, "We aren't on relief anymore. My husband is working for the Government."

The New Deal also sought to harness natural resources for hydroelectric power. Continuing a project begun under Hoover, the New Deal completed the colossal Hoover Dam across the Colorado River in Nevada, providing not only electricity but also flood control and irrigation water for Arizona and southern California. Building the dam also provided badly needed jobs and wages for thousands of unemployed workers.

The New Deal's most ambitious and controversial natural resources development project was the **Tennessee Valley Authority (TVA)**, created in May 1933 to build dams along the Tennessee River to supply impoverished rural communities with cheap electricity (Map 24.2). The TVA planned model towns for power station

MAP 24.2
The Tennessee Valley Authority
The New Deal created the Tennessee Valley Authority to modernize a vast impoverished region with hydroelectric power dams and, at the same time, to reclaim eroded land and preserve old folkways.

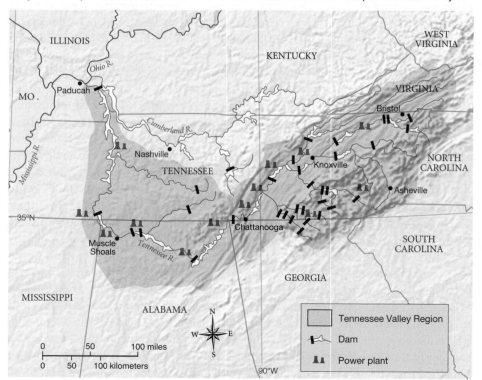

workers and new homes for the farmers who would benefit from electricity and flood control. The most ambitious example of New Deal enthusiasm for planning, the TVA set out to demonstrate that a partnership between the federal government and local residents could overcome the barriers of state governments and private enterprises to make efficient use of abundant natural resources and break the ancient cycle of poverty. The TVA never fully realized these utopian ends, but it improved the lives of millions in the region with electric power, flood protection, soil reclamation, and jobs.

New sources of hydroelectric power helped the New Deal bring the wonders of electricity to country folk, fulfilling an old progressive dream. When Roosevelt became president, 90 percent of rural Americans lacked electricity. Private electric companies refused to build transmission lines into the sparsely settled countryside when they had a profitable market in more accessible and densely populated urban areas. Beginning in 1935, the **Rural Electrification Administration (REA)** made low-cost loans available to local cooperatives for power plants and transmission lines to serve rural communities. Within ten years, the REA delivered electricity to nine out of ten farms, giving rural Americans access for the first time to modern conveniences that urban people had enjoyed for decades.

Agricultural Initiatives

Farmers had been mired in a depression since the end of World War I. New Dealers diagnosed the farmers' plight as a classic case of overproduction and underconsumption. Following age-old practices, farmers tried to compensate for low crop prices by growing more crops, hoping to boost their earnings by selling larger quantities. Instead, producing more crops pushed prices lower still. Farm income sank from a disastrously low $6 billion in 1929 to a catastrophically low $2 billion in 1932. Income among farm families plunged to $167 a year, barely one-tenth of the national average.

New Dealers sought to cut agricultural production, thereby raising crop prices and farmers' income. With more money in their pockets, farm families — who made up one-third of all Americans — would then buy more goods and lift consumption in the entire economy. To reduce production, the **Agricultural Adjustment Act (AAA)** authorized the "domestic allotment plan," which paid farmers *not* to grow crops. Individual farmers who agreed not to plant crops on a portion of their fields (their "allotment") would receive a government payment compensating them for the crops they did not plant. Since crops were already in the ground by the time the act was passed in May 1933, drastic measures were necessary to reduce production immediately. While millions of Americans like Florence Owens and her children went to bed hungry, farmers slaughtered countless cattle, hogs, sheep, and other livestock and destroyed untold acres of crops to qualify for their allotment payments.

With the formation of the Commodity Credit Corporation, the federal government allowed farmers to hold their harvested crops off the market and wait for a higher price. In the meantime, the government stored the crop and gave farmers a "commodity loan" based on a favorable price. In effect, commodity loans addressed the problem of underconsumption by making the federal government a major consumer of agricultural goods and reducing farmers' vulnerability to low prices. New Dealers also sponsored the Farm Credit Act (FCA) to provide long-term credit on mortgaged farm property, allowing debt-ridden farmers to avoid foreclosures that were driving thousands off their land.

Crop allotments, commodity loans, and mortgage credit made farmers major beneficiaries of the New Deal. Crop prices rose impressively, farm income jumped 50 percent by 1936, and FCA loans financed 40 percent of farm mortgage debt by the end of the decade. These gains were distributed fairly equally among farmers in the corn, hog, and wheat region of the Midwest. In the South's cotton belt, however, landlords controlled the distribution of New Deal agricultural benefits and shamelessly rewarded themselves while denying benefits to many sharecroppers and tenant farmers — blacks and whites — by taking the land they worked out of production and assigning it to the allotment program. When that happened, tenants and sharecroppers got booted off the land they worked, and their privation worsened. As the president of the Oklahoma Tenant Farmers' Union explained, large farmers who got "Triple-A" payments often used the money to buy tractors and then "forced their tenants and [share]croppers off the land," causing these "Americans to be starved and dispossessed of their homes in our land of plenty."

Industrial Recovery

Unlike farmers, industrialists cut production with the onset of the depression. Between 1929 and 1933, industrial production fell more than 40 percent in an effort to balance low demand with low supply and thereby maintain prices. But falling industrial production meant that millions of working people lost their jobs. Unlike farmers, most working people lived in towns and cities and needed jobs to eat. Mass unemployment also reduced consumer demand for industrial products, contributing to a downward spiral in both production and jobs, with no end in sight. Industries responded by reducing wages for employees who still had jobs, further reducing demand — a trend made worse by competition among industrial producers. New Dealers struggled to find a way to break this cycle of unemployment and underconsumption — a way consistent with corporate profits and capitalism.

The New Deal's National Industrial Recovery Act opted for a government-sponsored form of industrial self-government through the **National Recovery Administration (NRA)**, established in June 1933. The NRA encouraged industrialists in every part of the economy to agree on rules, known as codes, to define fair working conditions, to set prices, and to minimize competition. The idea behind codes was to stabilize existing industries and maintain their workforces while avoiding what both industrialists and New Dealers termed "destructive competition," which forced employers to cut wages and jobs. Industry after industry wrote elaborate codes addressing detailed features of production, pricing, and competition. In exchange for the relaxation of federal antitrust regulations that prohibited such business agreements, the participating businesses promised to recognize the right of working people to organize and engage in collective bargaining. To encourage consumers to patronize businesses participating in NRA codes, the New Deal mounted a public relations campaign that displayed the NRA's Blue Eagle in shop windows and on billboards throughout the nation.

New Dealers hoped that NRA codes would yield businesses with a social conscience, ensuring fair treatment of workers and consumers and promotion of the general economic welfare. Instead, NRA codes tended to strengthen conventional business practices. Large corporations wrote codes that served primarily their own interests rather than the needs of workers or the welfare of the national economy. The failure of codes to cover domestic workers or agricultural laborers like Florence Owens led one woman to complain to Roosevelt that the NRA "never mentioned the robbery of the Housewives" by the privations caused by the depression.

Many business leaders criticized NRA codes as heavy-handed government regulation of private enterprise. Some even claimed that the NRA was a homegrown version of Benito Mussolini's fascism, then taking shape in Italy. In reality, however, compliance with NRA codes was voluntary, and government enforcement efforts were weak to nonexistent. The NRA did little to reduce unemployment, raise consumption, or relieve the depression. In effect, it represented a peace offering to business leaders by Roosevelt and his advisers, conveying the message that the New Deal did not intend to wage war against profits or private enterprise. The peace offering failed, however. Most corporate leaders became active and often bitter opponents of Roosevelt and the New Deal.

REVIEW How did the New Dealers try to steer the nation toward recovery from the Great Depression?

▶ Challenges to the New Deal

The first New Deal initiatives engendered fierce criticism and political opposition. From the right, Republicans and business people charged that New Deal programs were too radical, undermining private property, economic stability, and democracy. Critics on the left faulted the New Deal for its failure to allay the human suffering caused by the depression and for its timidity in attacking corporate power and greed.

Resistance to Business Reform

New Deal programs rescued capitalism, but business leaders lambasted Roosevelt, even though their economic prospects improved more than those of most other Americans during the depression. Republicans and business leaders denounced New Deal efforts to regulate or reform what they considered their private enterprises. Although concentrated corporate power avoided reform, business leaders still conducted stridently anti–New Deal campaigns that expressed their resentment and fear of regulations, taxes, and unions. One opponent called the president "Stalin Delano Roosevelt" and insisted that the New Deal was really a "Raw Deal."

By 1935, two major business organizations, the National Association of Manufacturers and the Chamber of Commerce, had become openly anti–New Deal.

Their critiques were amplified by the American Liberty League, founded in 1934, which blamed the New Deal for betraying basic constitutional guarantees of freedom and individualism. To them, the AAA was a "trend toward fascist control of agriculture," relief programs marked "the end of democracy," and the NRA was a plunge into the "quicksand of visionary experimentation." Although the Liberty League's membership never exceeded 125,000, its well-financed publicity campaign widened the rift between Roosevelt and business people.

Economists who favored rational planning in the public interest and labor leaders who sought to influence wages and working conditions by organizing unions attacked the New Deal from the left. In their view, the NRA stifled enterprise by permitting monopolistic practices. They pointed out that industrial trade associations twisted NRA codes to suit their aims, thwarted competition, and engaged in price gouging. Labor leaders especially resented the NRA's willingness to allow businesses to form company-controlled unions while blocking workers from organizing genuine grassroots unions to bargain for themselves.

The Supreme Court stepped into this cross fire of criticisms in May 1935 and declared that the NRA unconstitutionally conferred powers reserved to Congress on an administrative agency staffed by government appointees. The NRA codes soon lost the little authority they had. The failure of the NRA demonstrated the depth of many Americans' resistance to economic planning and the stubborn refusal of business leaders to yield to government regulations or reforms.

Casualties in the Countryside

The AAA weathered critical battering by champions of the old order better than the NRA. Allotment checks for keeping land fallow and crop prices high created loyalty among farmers with enough acreage to participate. As a white farmer in North Carolina declared, "I stand for the New Deal and Roosevelt . . . , the AAA . . . and crop control." Agricultural processors and distributors, however, criticized the AAA. They objected that the program reduced the volume of crop production — the only source of their profits — while they paid a tax on processed crops that funded the very program that disadvantaged them. In 1936, the Supreme Court agreed with their contention that they were victims of an illegal attempt to tax one group (processors and distributors) to enrich another (farmers). Down but not out, the AAA rebounded from the Supreme Court ruling by eliminating the offending tax and funding allotment payments from general government revenues.

Protests stirred, however, among those who did not qualify for allotments. The Southern Farm Tenants Union argued passionately that the AAA enriched large farmers while it impoverished small farmers who rented rather than owned their land. One black sharecropper explained why only $75 a year from New Deal agricultural subsidies trickled down to her: "De landlord is landlord, de politicians is landlord, de judge is landlord, de shurf [sheriff] is landlord, ever'body is landlord, en we [sharecroppers] ain' got nothin'!" Such testimony showed that the AAA, like the NRA, tended to help most those who least needed help. Roosevelt's

Evicted Sharecroppers
An unintended consequence of the New Deal's Agricultural Adjustment Administration's plan to maintain farm prices by reducing acreage in production was the eviction of tenant farmers when the land they worked was left idle. These African American sharecroppers were part of a squatters camp that stretched for 150 miles along the western floodplain of the Mississippi River in southeastern Missouri in January 1939. They protested AAA policies that caused cotton farmers to evict them from their homes. Homeless and jobless, camping out with all their earthly belongings, these families were among the many rural laborers whose lives were made worse by New Deal agricultural policies. © Bettmann/Corbis.

political dependence on southern Democrats caused him to avoid confronting such economic and racial inequities in the South's entrenched order.

Displaced tenants often joined the army of migrant workers like Florence Owens who straggled across rural America during the 1930s, some to flee Great Plains dust storms. Many migrants came from Mexico to work Texas cotton, Michigan beans, Idaho sugar beets, and California crops of all kinds. But since the number of people willing to take agricultural jobs usually exceeded the number of jobs available, wages fell and native-born white migrants fought to reserve even these low-wage jobs for themselves. Hundreds of thousands of "Okies" streamed out of the **Dust Bowl** of Oklahoma, Kansas, Texas, and Colorado, where chronic drought and harmful agricultural practices blasted crops and hopes. Parched, poor, and windblown, Okies — like the Joad family immortalized in John Steinbeck's novel *The Grapes of Wrath* (1939) — migrated to the lush fields and orchards of California, congregating in labor camps and hoping to find work and a future. But migrant laborers seldom found steady or secure work. As one Okie said, "When they need us they call us migrants, and when we've picked their crop, we're bums and we got to get out."

Politics on the Fringes

Politically, the New Deal's staunchest opponents were in the Republican Party — organized, well heeled, mainstream, and determined to challenge Roosevelt at every turn. But the New Deal also faced challenges from the political fringes, fueled by the hardship of the depression and the hope for a cure-all.

Socialists and Communists accused the New Deal of being the handmaiden of business elites and of rescuing capitalism from its self-inflicted crisis. Socialist author **Upton Sinclair** ran for governor of California in 1934 on a plan he called "End Poverty in California." Sinclair demanded that the state take ownership of idle factories and unused land and give them to cooperatives of working people, a first step toward what he envisioned as a "Cooperative Commonwealth" that would put the needs of people above profits. Sinclair lost the election, ending the most serious socialist electoral challenge to the New Deal.

Some intellectuals and artists sought to advance the cause of more radical change by joining left-wing organizations, including the American Communist Party. At its high point in the 1930s, the party had about thirty thousand members, the large majority of them immigrants, especially Scandinavians in the upper Midwest and eastern European Jews in major eastern and midwestern cities. Individual Communists worked to organize labor unions, protect the civil rights of black people, and help the destitute, but the party preached the overthrow of "bourgeois democracy" and the destruction of capitalism in favor of Soviet-style communism. Party spokesmen termed the NRA a "fascist slave program" and likened Roosevelt and the New Deal to Hitler and the Nazis. Such talk attracted few followers among the nation's millions of poor and unemployed. They wanted jobs and economic security within American capitalism and democracy, not violent revolution to establish a dictatorship of the Communist Party.

More powerful radical challenges to the New Deal sprouted from homegrown roots. Many Americans felt overlooked by New Deal programs that concentrated on finance, agriculture, and industry but did little to produce jobs or aid the poor. The merciless reality of the depression also continued to erode the security of people who still had jobs but worried constantly that they, too, might be pushed into the legions of the unemployed and penniless.

A Catholic priest in Detroit named **Charles Coughlin** spoke to and for many worried Americans in his weekly radio broadcasts, which reached a nationwide audience of 40 million. Father Coughlin expressed outrage at the suffering and inequities that he blamed on Communists, bankers, and "predatory capitalists" who, he claimed, appealing to widespread anti-Semitic sentiments, were mostly Jews. In 1932, Coughlin applauded Roosevelt's election and declared, "The New Deal is Christ's deal." But Coughlin became frustrated by Roosevelt's refusal to grant him influence, turned against the New Deal, and in 1935 founded the

National Union for Social Justice, or Union Party, to challenge Roosevelt in the 1936 presidential election.

Dr. **Francis Townsend**, of Long Beach, California, also criticized the timidity of the New Deal. Angry that many of his retired patients lived in misery, Townsend proposed in 1934 the creation of the Old Age Revolving Pension, which would pay every American over age sixty a pension of $200 a month. To receive the pension, senior citizens had to agree to spend the entire amount within thirty days, thereby stimulating the economy.

Townsend organized pension clubs with more than two million paying members and petitioned the federal government to enact his scheme. When the major political parties rebuffed his impractical plan, Townsend merged his forces with Coughlin's Union Party in time for the 1936 election.

A more formidable challenge to the New Deal came from the powerful southern wing of the Democratic Party. **Huey Long**, son of a backcountry Louisiana farmer, was elected governor of the state in 1928 with his slogan "Every man a king, but no one wears a crown." Unlike nearly all other southern white politicians who harped on white supremacy, Long championed the poor over the rich, country people over city folk, and the humble over elites. As governor, "the Kingfish" — as he liked to call himself — delivered on his promises to provide jobs and build roads, schools, and hospitals, but he also behaved ruthlessly to achieve his goals. Journalists routinely referred to him as the "dictator of Louisiana." Swaggering and bullying to get his way, Long delighted his supporters, who elected him to the U.S. Senate in 1932. Senator Long introduced a sweeping "soak the rich" tax bill that would outlaw personal incomes of more than $1 million and inheritances of more than $5 million. When the Senate rejected his proposal, Long decided to run for president, mobilizing more than five million Americans behind his "Share Our Wealth" plan. Like Townsend's scheme, Long's program promised far more than it could deliver. The Share Our Wealth campaign died when Long was assassinated in 1935, but his constituency and the wide appeal of a more equitable distribution of wealth persisted.

The challenges to the New Deal from both Republicans and more radical groups stirred Democrats to solidify their winning coalition. In the midterm congressional elections of 1934 — normally a time when a president loses support — voters gave New Dealers a landslide victory. Democrats increased their majority in the House of Representatives and gained a two-thirds majority in the Senate.

REVIEW Why did groups at both ends of the political spectrum criticize the New Deal?

▶ Toward a Welfare State

The popular mandate for the New Deal revealed by the congressional elections persuaded Roosevelt to press ahead with bold new efforts to achieve relief, recovery, and reform. Despite the initiatives of the Hundred Days, the depression still strangled the economy. Rumbles of discontent from Father Coughlin, Huey Long, and their supporters showed that New Deal programs had fallen far short of their goals. In 1935, Roosevelt capitalized on his congressional majorities to enact major new programs that signaled the emergence of an American welfare state.

Taken together, these New Deal efforts stretched a safety net under the lives of ordinary Americans. Although many citizens remained unprotected, New Deal programs helped millions with jobs, relief, and government support. Knitting together the safety net was the idea that when individual Americans suffered because of forces beyond their control, the federal government bore responsibility to support and protect them. The safety net of welfare programs tied the political loyalty of working people to the New Deal and the Democratic Party. As a North Carolina mill worker said, "Mr. Roosevelt is the only man we ever had in the White House who would understand that my boss is a sonofabitch."

Relief for the Unemployed

First and foremost, Americans still needed jobs. Since the private economy left eight million people jobless by 1935, Roosevelt and his advisers launched a massive work relief program. Roosevelt believed that direct government handouts crippled recipients with "spiritual and moral disintegration . . . destructive to the human spirit." Jobs, by contrast, bolstered individuals' "self-respect, . . . self-confidence, . . . courage, and determination." With a congressional appropriation of nearly $5 billion — more than all government revenues in 1934 — the New Deal created the **Works Progress Administration (WPA)** to give unemployed Americans government-funded jobs on public works projects. The WPA put millions of jobless citizens to work on roads, bridges, parks, public buildings, and more. In addition, Congress passed — over Roosevelt's veto — the bonus long sought by the Bonus Marchers (see chapter 23), giving veterans an average of $580 and further stimulating the economy.

By 1936, WPA funds provided jobs for 7 percent of the nation's labor force. In effect, the WPA made the federal government the employer of last resort, creating useful jobs when the capitalist economy failed to do so. In hiring, WPA officials tended to discriminate in favor of white men and against women and racial minorities. But by the time the WPA ended in 1943 — because mobilization for World War II created full employment — it had made major contributions to both relief and recovery. Overall, WPA jobs put thirteen million men and women to work and gave them paychecks worth $10 billion.

About three out of four WPA jobs involved construction and renovation of the nation's physical infrastructure. WPA workers built 572,000 miles of roads, 78,000 bridges, 67,000 miles of city streets, 40,000 public buildings, 8,000 parks, 350 airports, and much else. In addition, the WPA gave jobs to thousands of artists, musicians, actors, journalists, poets, and novelists. The WPA also organized sewing rooms for jobless women, giving them work and wages and allowing them to produce more than 100 million pieces of clothing that were donated to the needy. The WPA reached the most isolated corners of the nation, funding librarians and nurses on horseback to deliver books and health care to remote cabins in Appalachia. Throughout the nation, WPA projects displayed tangible evidence of the New Deal's commitment to public welfare.

Grand Coulee Dam

The New Deal's Works Progress Administration helped pay for these and other workers to construct the giant Grand Coulee Dam on the Columbia River in eastern Washington state. Like other WPA projects, the Grand Coulee Dam gave employment to thousands of Americans and harnessed natural resources for what officials considered the public good. Once completed in 1942, the dam provided electricity for major war industries in Oregon and Washington, including uranium processing for the wartime Manhattan Project that resulted in the atomic bomb. Library of Congress.

Empowering Labor

During the Great Depression, factory workers who managed to keep their jobs worried constantly about being laid off while their wages and working hours were cut. When workers tried to organize labor unions to protect themselves, municipal and state governments usually sided with employers. Since the Gilded Age, state and federal governments had been far more effective at busting unions than at busting trusts. The New Deal dramatically reversed the federal government's stance toward unions. With legislation and political support, the New Deal encouraged an unprecedented wave of union organizing among the nation's working people. When the head of the United Mine Workers, John L. Lewis, told coal miners that "the President wants you to join a union," he exaggerated only a little. New Dealers believed that unions would counterbalance the organized might of big corporations by defending working people, maintaining wages, and replacing the bloody violence that often accompanied strikes with economic peace and commercial stability.

Violent battles on the nation's streets and docks showed the determination of militant labor leaders to organize unions that would protect jobs as well as wages. In 1934, striking workers in Toledo, Minneapolis, San Francisco, and elsewhere were beaten and shot by police and the National Guard. In Congress, labor leaders lobbied for the National Labor Relations Act, a bill sponsored by Senator Robert Wagner of New York that authorized the federal government to intervene in labor disputes and supervise the organization of labor unions. Justly considered a "Magna Carta for labor," the **Wagner Act**, as it came to be called, guaranteed industrial workers the right to organize unions, putting the might of federal law behind the appeals of labor leaders. The Wagner Act created the National Labor Relations Board to sponsor and oversee elections for union representation. If the majority of workers at a company voted for a union, the union became the sole bargaining agent for the entire workplace, and the employer was required to negotiate with the elected union leaders. Roosevelt signed the Wagner Act in July 1935, for the first time providing federal support for labor organization — the most important New Deal reform of the industrial order.

The achievements that flowed from the Wagner Act and renewed labor militancy were impressive. When Roosevelt became president in 1933, union membership — composed almost entirely of skilled workers in trade unions affiliated with the American Federation of Labor (AFL) — stood at three million, down by half since the end of World War I. With the support of the Wagner Act, union membership expanded almost fivefold, to fourteen million, by the time of Roosevelt's death in 1945. By then, 30 percent of the workforce was unionized, the highest union representation in American history.

Most of the new union members were factory workers and unskilled laborers, many of them immigrants, women, and African Americans. For decades, established AFL unions had no desire to organize factory and unskilled workers, who struggled along without unions. In 1935, under the aggressive leadership of the mine workers' John L. Lewis and the head of the Amalgamated Clothing Workers, Sidney Hillman, a coalition of unskilled workers formed the **Committee for Industrial Organization** (CIO; later the Congress of Industrial Organizations). The CIO, helped by the Wagner Act, mobilized organizing drives in major industries. The exceptional courage and organizing skill of labor militants earned the CIO the leadership role in the campaign to organize the bitterly anti-union automobile and steel industries.

The bloody struggle by the CIO-affiliated United Auto Workers (UAW) to organize workers at General Motors climaxed in January 1937. Striking workers occupied the main assembly plant in Flint, Michigan, in a **sit-down strike** that slashed the plant's production of 15,000 cars a week to a mere 150. Stymied, General Motors eventually surrendered and agreed to make the UAW the sole bargaining agent for all the company's workers and to refrain from interfering with union activity. Having subdued the auto industry's leading producer, the UAW expanded its campaign until, after much violence, the entire industry was unionized when the Ford Motor Company capitulated in 1941.

The CIO hoped to ride organizing success in auto plants to victory in the steel mills. But after unionizing the industry giant U.S. Steel, the CIO ran up against ruthless opposition from smaller steel firms. Following a police attack that killed ten strikers at Republic Steel outside Chicago in May 1937, the battered steelworkers halted their organizing campaign. In steel and other major industries, such as the stridently anti-union southern textile mills, organizing efforts stalled until after 1941, when military mobilization created labor short-ages that gave workers greater bargaining power.

Social Security and Tax Reform

The single most important feature of the New Deal's emerging welfare state was **Social Security**. An ambitious, far-reaching, and permanent reform, Social Security was designed to provide a modest income to relieve the poverty of elderly people. Only about 15 percent of older Americans had private pension plans, and during the depression corporations and banks often failed to pay the meager pensions they had promised. Corporations routinely fired or demoted employees to avoid or reduce pension payments. Prompted by the popular but impractical panaceas of Dr. Townsend, Father Coughlin, and Huey Long, Roosevelt became the first president to advocate protection for the elderly. He told Congress that "it is our plain duty to provide for that security upon which welfare depends . . . and undertake the great task of furthering the security of the citizen and his family through social insurance."

The political struggle for Social Security highlighted class differences among Americans. Support for the measure came from a coalition of advocacy groups for the elderly and the poor, traditional progressives, leftists, social workers, and labor unions. Arrayed against them were economic conservatives, including the American Liberty League, the National Association of Manufacturers, the Chamber of Commerce, and the American Medical Association. Enact the Social Security system, these conservatives and their representatives in the Republican Party warned, and the government will ruin private property, destroy initiative, and reduce proud individuals to spineless loafers.

The large New Deal majority in Congress passed the Social Security Act in August 1935. The act provided that contributions from workers and their employ-ers would fund pensions for the elderly, giving contributing workers a personal stake in the system and making it politically invulnerable. When eligible work-ers reached retirement age, they were not subject to a means test to prove that they were needy. Instead, they had earned benefits based on their contributions and years of work. Social Security also created unemployment insurance that provided modest benefits for workers who lost their jobs.

Not all workers benefited from the Social Security Act. It excluded domestic and agricultural workers like Florence Owens, thereby making ineligible about half of all African Americans and more than half of all employed women — about five million people in all. In addition, the law excluded workers employed by religious and nonprofit organizations, such as schools and hospitals, rendering ineligible even more working women and minorities.

In a bow to traditional beliefs about local governments' responsibility for public assistance, Social Security issued multimillion-dollar grants to the states to help support dependent children, public health services, and the blind. After the Supreme Court in 1937 upheld Social Security, the program was expanded to include benefits for dependent survivors of deceased recipients. Although the first Social Security check (for $41.30) was not issued until 1940, the system gave millions of working people the assurance that when they became too old to work, they would receive a modest income from the federal government. This safety net protected many ordinary working people from fears of a penniless and insecure old age.

Fervent opposition to Social Security struck New Dealers as evidence that the rich had learned little from the depression. Roosevelt had long felt contempt for the moneyed elite who ignored the suffering of the poor. He looked for a way to redistribute wealth that would weaken conservative opposition, advance the cause of social equity, and defuse political challenges from Huey Long and Father Coughlin. In June 1935, as the Social Security Act was being debated, Roosevelt delivered a message to Congress outlining comprehensive tax reform. Charging that large fortunes put "great and undesirable concentration of control in [the hands of] relatively few individuals," Roosevelt urged a graduated tax on corporations, an inheritance tax, and an increase in maximum personal income taxes. Congress endorsed Roosevelt's basic principle by taxing those with higher incomes at a somewhat higher rate.

Neglected Americans and the New Deal

The patchwork of New Deal reforms erected a two-tier welfare state. In the top tier, organized workers in major industries were the greatest beneficiaries of New Deal initiatives. In the bottom tier, millions of neglected Americans — women, children, and old folks, along with the unorganized, unskilled, uneducated, and unemployed — often fell through the New Deal safety net. Many working people remained more or less untouched by New Deal benefits. The average unemployment rate for the 1930s stayed high — 17 percent. Workers in industries that resisted unions received little help from the Wagner Act or the WPA. Tens of thousands of women in southern textile mills, for example, commonly received wages of less than ten cents an hour and were fired if they protested. Domestic workers — almost all of them women — and agricultural workers — many of them African, Hispanic, or Asian Americans — were neither unionized nor eligible for Social Security.

The New Deal neglected few citizens more than African Americans. About half of black Americans in cities were jobless, more than double the unemployment rate among whites. In the rural South, where the vast majority of African Americans lived, conditions were worse, given the New Deal agricultural policies such as the AAA that favored landowners, who often pushed blacks off the land they farmed. Only 11 of more than 10,000 WPA supervisors in the South were black, even though African Americans accounted for a third of the region's population. Disfranchisement by intimidation and legal subterfuge prevented southern blacks from protesting their plight at the ballot box. Protesters risked vicious retaliation from local whites. After years of decline, lynching increased during the 1930s. In 1935, a riot in Harlem focused on white-owned businesses, dramatizing blacks' resentment and despair. Bitter critics charged that the New Deal's NRA stood for "Negro Run Around" or "Negroes Ruined Again."

Roosevelt responded to such criticisms with great caution, since New Deal reforms required the political support of powerful conservative, segregationist, southern white Democrats who would be alienated by programs that aided blacks. A white Georgia relief worker expressed the common view that "any Nigger who gets over $8 a week is a spoiled Nigger, that's all." Stymied by the political clout of entrenched white racism, New Dealers still tried to attract political support from black leaders. Roosevelt's overtures to African Americans prompted northern black voters in the 1934 congressional elections to shift from the Republican to the Democratic Party, helping elect New Deal Democrats.

Eleanor Roosevelt sponsored the appointment of **Mary McLeod Bethune** — the energetic cofounder of the National Council of Negro Women — as head of the Division of Negro Affairs in the National Youth Administration. The highest-ranking black official in Roosevelt's administration, Bethune used her position to guide a small number of black professionals and civil rights activists to posts within New Deal agencies. Nicknamed the "Black Cabinet," these men and women composed the first sizable representation of African Americans in white-collar posts in the federal government, and they ultimately helped about one in four African Americans get access to New Deal relief programs.

Despite these gains, by 1940 African Americans still suffered severe handicaps. Most of the thirteen million black workers toiled at low-paying menial jobs, unprotected by the New Deal safety net. Making a mockery of the "separate but equal" doctrine, segregated black schools had less money and worse facilities than white schools, and only 1 percent of black students earned college degrees. In southern states, there were no black police officers or judges and hardly any black lawyers. Vigilante violence against blacks went unpunished. For these problems of black Americans, the New Deal offered few remedies.

Hispanic Americans fared no better. About a million Mexican Americans lived in the United States in the 1930s, most of them first- or second-generation immigrants who worked crops throughout the West. During the depression, field workers saw their low wages plunge lower still to about a dime an hour. Ten thousand Mexican American pecan shellers in San Antonio, Texas, earned only a nickel an hour. To preserve scarce jobs for U.S. citizens, the federal government choked off immigration from Mexico, while state and local officials prohibited the employment of aliens on work relief projects and deported tens of thousands of Mexican Americans, many with their American-born children. Local white administrators of many New Deal programs throughout the West discriminated against Hispanics and other people of color. A New Deal study concluded that "the Mexican is . . . segregated from the rest of the community as effectively as the Negro . . . [by] poverty and low wages."

Asian Americans had similar experiences. Asian immigrants were still excluded from U.S. citizenship and in many states were not permitted to own land. By 1930, more than half of Japanese Americans had been born in the United States, but they were still liable to discrimination. One young Asian American expressed the frustration felt by many others: "I am a fruit-stand worker. I would much rather it were doctor or lawyer . . . but my aspirations

[were] frustrated long ago by circumstances. . . . I am only what I am, a professional carrot washer."

Native Americans also suffered neglect from New Deal agencies. As a group, they remained the poorest of the poor. Since the Dawes Act of 1887 (see chapter 17), the federal government had encouraged Native Americans to assimilate — to abandon their Indian identities and adopt the cultural norms of the majority society. Under the leadership of the New Deal's commissioner of Indian affairs, John Collier, the New Deal's **Indian Reorganization Act (IRA)** of 1934 largely reversed that policy. Collier claimed that "the most interesting and important fact about Indians" was that they "do not expect much, often they expect nothing at all; yet they are able to be happy." Given such views, the IRA provided little economic aid to Native Americans, but it did restore their right to own land communally and to have greater control over their own affairs, including a vote on whether they should live under the IRA, as more than two-thirds opted to do. The IRA brought little immediate benefit to Native Americans and remained a divisive issue for decades, but it provided an important foundation for Indians' economic, cultural, and political resurgence a generation later.

Voicing common experiences among Americans neglected by the New Deal, singer and songwriter Woody Guthrie traveled the nation for eight years during the 1930s and heard other rambling men tell him "the story of their life": "how the home went to pieces, how . . . the crops got to where they wouldn't bring nothing, work in factories would kill a dog . . . and — always, always [you] have to fight and argue and cuss and swear . . . to try to get a nickel more out of the rich bosses."

REVIEW   What features of a welfare state did the New Deal create and why?

▶ The New Deal from Victory to Deadlock

To accelerate the sputtering economic recovery, Roosevelt shifted the emphasis of the New Deal in the mid-1930s. Instead of seeking cooperation from conservative business leaders, he decided to rely on the growing New Deal coalition to enact reforms over the strident opposition of the Supreme Court, Republicans, and corporate interests.

Added to New Deal strength in farm states and big cities were some new allies on the left. Throughout Roosevelt's first term, socialists and Communists denounced the slow pace of change and accused the New Deal of failing to serve the interests of the workers who produced the nation's wealth. But in 1935, the Soviet Union, worried about the threat of fascism in Europe, instructed Communists throughout the world to join hands with non-Communist progressives in a "Popular Front" to advance the fortunes of the working class. With varying degrees of enthusiasm, many radicals switched from opposing the New Deal to supporting its relief programs and encouragement of labor unions.

Roosevelt's conservative opponents reacted to the massing of New Deal force by intensifying their opposition to the welfare state. To Roosevelt, the situation seemed part of a historic drama that dated to the nation's origins, pitting a Hamiltonian faction of wealth and privilege against the heirs of Jefferson, who like Roosevelt, favored a more equitable distribution of wealth and opportunity.

The Election of 1936

Roosevelt believed that the presidential election of 1936 would test his leadership and progressive ideals. The depression still had a stranglehold on the economy. Nearly eight million Americans remained jobless, and millions more were stuck in poverty. Conservative leaders believed that the New Deal's failure to lift the nation out of the depression indicated that Americans were ready for a change. Left-wing critics insisted that the New Deal had missed the opportunity to displace capitalism with a socialist economy and that voters would embrace candidates who recommended more radical remedies.

Republicans turned to the Kansas heartland to select Governor Alfred (Alf) Landon as their presidential nominee. A moderate who had supported some New Deal measures, Landon stressed mainstream Republican proposals to achieve a balanced federal budget and to ease the perils of illness and old age with old-fashioned neighborliness instead of faceless government bureaucracies such as Social Security.

Roosevelt believed that the growing coalition of New Deal supporters would help him liberate the nation from a long era of privilege and wealth for a few and "economic slavery" for the rest. Roosevelt assailed his "old enemies . . . business and financial monopoly, speculation, reckless banking, [and] class antagonism," and proclaimed, "Never before in all our history have these forces been so united against one candidate. . . . They are unanimous in their hate for me — and I welcome their hatred."

Roosevelt triumphed spectacularly. He won 60.8 percent of the popular vote, making it the widest margin of victory in a presidential election to date. Third parties — including the Socialist and Communist parties — fell pitifully short of the support they expected and never again mounted a significant challenge to the New Deal. Congressional results were equally lopsided, with Democrats outnumbering Republicans more than three to one in both houses. In his inaugural address, Roosevelt pledged to use his mandate to help all citizens achieve a decent standard of living. He announced, "I see one third of a nation ill-housed, ill-clad, [and] ill-nourished," and he promised to devote his second term to alleviating their hardship.

Court Packing

In the afterglow of his reelection triumph, Roosevelt pondered how to remove the remaining obstacles to New Deal reforms. He decided to target the Supreme Court. Laden with conservative justices appointed by Republican presidents, the Court had invalidated eleven New Deal measures as unconstitutional interferences with free enterprise. Now, Social Security, the Wagner Act, the Securities and Exchange Commission, and other New Deal innovations were about to be considered by the justices.

To ensure that the Supreme Court's "horse and buggy" notions did not dismantle the New Deal, Roosevelt proposed a **court-packing plan** that added one new justice for each existing judge who had served for ten years and was over the age of seventy. In effect, the proposed law would give Roosevelt the power to pack the Court with up to six New Dealers who could outvote the elderly, conservative, Republican justices.

But the president had not reckoned with Americans' deeply rooted deference to the independent authority of the Supreme Court. More than two-thirds of Americans believed that the Court should be free from political interference. Even New Deal supporters were disturbed by the court-packing scheme. The suggestion that individuals over age seventy had diminished mental capacity offended many elderly members of Congress, and the Senate defeated the bill in 1937.

Although Roosevelt's court-packing plan failed, Supreme Court justices got the message. After the furor abated, Chief Justice Charles Evans Hughes and fellow moderate Owen Roberts changed their views enough to keep the Court from invalidating the Wagner Act and Social Security. Then the most conservative of the elderly justices — the "four horsemen of reaction," one New Dealer called them — retired. Roosevelt eventually named eight justices to the Court — more than any other president — ultimately giving New Deal laws safe passage through the Court.

Reaction and Recession

Emboldened by their defeat of the court-packing plan, Republicans and southern Democrats rallied around their common conservatism to obstruct additional reforms. Former president Herbert Hoover proclaimed that the New Deal was the "repudiation of Democracy" and that "the Republican Party alone [was] the guardian of . . . the charter of freedom." Democrats' arguments over whether the New Deal needed to be expanded — and if so, how — undermined the consensus among reformers and sparked antagonism between Congress and the White House. The ominous rise of belligerent regimes in Germany, Italy, Japan, and elsewhere slowed reform as some Americans began to worry more about defending the nation than changing it.

Roosevelt himself favored slowing the pace of the New Deal. He believed that existing New Deal measures had steadily boosted the economy and largely eliminated the depression crisis. In fact, the gross national product in 1937 briefly equaled the 1929 level before dropping lower for the rest of the decade. Unemployment declined to 14 percent in 1937 but quickly spiked upward and stayed higher until 1940. Roosevelt's unwarranted optimism about the economic recovery persuaded him that additional deficit spending by the federal government was no longer necessary.

Roosevelt's optimism failed to consider the stubborn realities of unemployment and poverty, and the reduction in deficit spending reversed the improving economy. Even at the high-water mark of recovery in the summer of 1937, seven million people lacked jobs. In the next few months, national income and production slipped so steeply that almost two-thirds of the economic gains since 1933 were lost by June 1938. Farm prices dropped 20 percent, and unemployment rose by more than two million.

This economic reversal hurt the New Deal politically. Conservatives argued that this recession proved that New Deal measures produced only an illusion of progress. The way to weather the recession was to tax and spend less and wait for the natural laws of supply and demand to restore prosperity. Many New Dealers insisted instead that the continuing depression demanded that Roosevelt revive federal spending and redouble efforts to stimulate the economy. In 1938, Congress heeded such pleas and enacted a massive new program of federal spending.

The recession scare of 1937–1938 taught the president the lesson that economic growth had to be carefully nurtured. The English economist John Maynard Keynes, in a theory that became known as **Keynesian economics**, argued in his influential work *The General Theory of Employment, Interest, and Money* (1936) that only government intervention could pump enough money into the economy to restore prosperity. Roosevelt never had the inclination or time to master Keynesian theory. But in a commonsense way, he understood that escape from the depression required a plan for large-scale spending to alleviate distress and stimulate economic growth.

The Last of the New Deal Reforms

From the moment he was sworn in, Roosevelt sought to expand the powers of the presidency. He believed that the president needed more authority to meet emergencies such as the depression and to administer the sprawling federal bureaucracy. In September 1938, Congress passed the Administrative Reorganization Act, which gave Roosevelt (and future presidents) new influence over the bureaucracy. Combined with a Democratic majority in Congress, a now-friendly Supreme Court, and the revival of deficit spending, the newly empowered White House seemed to be in a good position to move ahead with a revitalized New Deal.

Resistance to further reform was also on the rise, however. Conservatives argued that the New Deal had pressed government centralization too far. Even the New Deal's friends became weary of one emergency program after another while economic woes continued to shadow New Deal achievements. By the midpoint of Roosevelt's second term, restive members of Congress balked at new initiatives. Clearly, the New Deal was losing momentum, but enough support remained for one last burst of reform.

Agriculture still had strong claims on New Deal attention in the face of drought, declining crop prices, and impoverished sharecroppers and tenants. In 1937, the Agriculture Department created the Farm Security Administration (FSA) to provide housing and loans to help tenant farmers become independent. A black tenant farmer in North Carolina who received an FSA loan told a New Deal interviewer, "I wake up in the night sometimes and think I must be half-dead and gone to heaven." But relatively few tenants received loans, because the

FSA was starved for funds and ran up against major farm organizations intent on serving their own interests. For those who owned farms, the New Deal offered renewed prosperity with a second Agricultural Adjustment Act (AAA) in 1938. To moderate price swings by regulating supply, the plan combined production quotas on five staple crops — cotton, tobacco, wheat, corn, and rice — with storage loans through its Commodity Credit Corporation. The most prosperous farmers benefited most, but the act's Federal Surplus Commodities Corporation added an element of charity by issuing food stamps so that the poor could obtain surplus food. The AAA of 1938 brought stability to American agriculture and ample food to most — but not all — tables.

Advocates for the urban poor also made modest gains after decades of neglect. New York senator Robert Wagner convinced Congress to pass the **National Housing Act** in 1937. By 1941, some 160,000 residences had been made available to poor people at affordable rents. The program did not come close to meeting the need for affordable housing, but for the first time the federal government took an active role in providing decent urban housing.

Distributing Surplus Food to the Needy

When bountiful harvests produced surplus crops that would depress prices if they were sent to market, the New Deal arranged to distribute some of them to needy Americans. Here, farmworkers in east-central Arizona near the New Mexico border line up to receive a ration of potatoes authorized by the New Deal agent checking the box of index cards. Surplus commodity distribution represented New Dealers' attempt to provide relief for the hungry with crops that otherwise would rot or need to be destroyed in order to limit supply and thereby maintain agricultural prices. Library of Congress.

The last major piece of New Deal labor legislation, the **Fair Labor Standards Act** of June 1938, reiterated the New Deal pledge to provide workers with a decent standard of living. After lengthy haggling and compromise that revealed the waning strength of the New Deal, Congress finally agreed to intervene in the long-sacrosanct realm of worker contracts. The new law set wage and hours standards and at long last curbed the use of child labor. The minimum-wage level was modest — twenty-five cents an hour for a maximum of forty-four hours a week. To critics of the minimum wage law who said it was "government interference," one New Dealer responded, "It was. It interfered with the fellow running that pecan shelling plant . . . [and] told him he couldn't pay that little widow seven cents an hour." To attract enough conservative votes, the act exempted merchant seamen, fishermen, domestic help, and farm laborers — relegating most women and African Americans to lower wages. Enforcement of the minimum-wage standards was weak and haphazard. Nevertheless, the Fair Labor Standards Act slowly advanced Roosevelt's inaugural promise to improve the living standards of the poorest Americans.

The final New Deal reform effort failed to make much headway against the hidebound system of racial injustice. Although Roosevelt denounced lynching as murder, he would not jeopardize his vital base of southern political support by demanding antilynching legislation, and Congress voted down attempts to make lynching a federal crime. Laws to eliminate the poll tax — used to deny blacks the opportunity to vote — encountered the same overwhelming resistance. The New Deal refused to confront racial injustice with the same vigor it brought to bear on economic hardship.

By the end of 1938, the New Deal had lost steam and encountered stiff opposition. In the congressional elections of 1938, Republicans made gains that gave them more congressional influence than they had enjoyed since 1932. New Dealers could claim unprecedented achievements since 1933, but nobody needed reminding that those achievements had not ended the depression. In his annual message to Congress in January 1939, Roosevelt signaled a halt to New Deal reforms by speaking about preserving the progress already achieved rather than extending it. Roosevelt pointed to the ominous threats posed by fascist aggressors in Germany and Japan, and he proposed defense expenditures that surpassed New Deal appropriations for relief and economic recovery.

REVIEW Why did political support for New Deal reforms decline?

▶ Conclusion: Achievements and Limitations of the New Deal

The New Deal reflected Roosevelt's confidence, optimism, and energetic pragmatism. A growing majority of Americans agreed with Roosevelt that the federal government should help those in need, thereby strengthening the political coalition that propelled the New Deal. Through programs that sought relief, recovery, and reform, the New Deal vastly expanded the size and influence of the federal government and changed the way many Americans viewed Washington. New Dealers achieved significant victories, such as Social Security, labor's right to organize, and guarantees that farm prices would be maintained through controls on production and marketing. New Deal measures marked the emergence of a welfare state, but the New Deal's limited, two-tier character left many needy Americans like Florence Owens and her children with little aid.

Full-scale relief, recovery, and reform eluded New Deal programs. Even though millions of Americans benefited from New Deal initiatives, both relief and recovery were limited and temporary. In 1940, the depression still plagued the economy. Perhaps the most impressive achievement of the New Deal was what did not happen. Although authoritarian governments and anticapitalist policies were common outside the United States during the 1930s, they were shunned by the New Deal. The greatest economic crisis the nation had ever faced did not cause Americans to abandon democracy, as happened in Germany, where Adolf Hitler seized dictatorial power. Nor did the nation turn to radical alternatives such as socialism or communism.

Republicans and other conservatives claimed that the New Deal amounted to a form of socialism that threatened democracy and capitalism. But rather than attack capitalism, Franklin Roosevelt sought to save it. And he succeeded. That success also marked the limits of the New Deal's achievements. Franklin Roosevelt believed that a shift of authority toward the federal government would allow capitalist enterprises to be balanced by the nation's democratic tradition. The New Deal stopped far short of challenging capitalism either by undermining private property or by imposing strict national planning.

New Dealers repeatedly described their programs as a kind of warfare against the depression of the 1930s. In the next decade, the Roosevelt administration had to turn from the economic crisis at home to participate in a worldwide conflagration to defeat the enemies of democracy abroad.

Nonetheless, many New Deal reforms continued for decades to structure the basic institutions of banking, the stock market, union organizations, agricultural markets, Social Security, minimum-wage standards, and more. Opponents of these measures and of the basic New Deal notion of an activist government remained powerful, especially in the Republican Party. They claimed that government was the problem, not the solution — a slogan that Republicans championed during and after the 1980s and that led, with the cooperation of some Democrats, to the dismantling of a number of New Deal programs, including the regulation of banking. The deregulation of financial institutions was in large part responsible for the economic collapse that began in 2008.

Reviewing Chapter 24

REVIEW QUESTIONS

1. Why did Franklin D. Roosevelt win the 1932 presidential election by such a large margin? (pp. 718–721)

2. How did the New Dealers try to steer the nation toward recovery from the Great Depression? (pp. 722–729)

3. Why did groups at both ends of the political spectrum criticize the New Deal? (pp. 729–733)

4. What features of a welfare state did the New Deal create and why? (pp. 733–740)

5. Why did political support for New Deal reforms decline? (pp. 740–745)

MAKING CONNECTIONS

1. Franklin Roosevelt's landslide victory in 1932 changed the political landscape. How did Roosevelt build an effective interregional political coalition for the Democratic Party? How did the challenges of balancing interests within the coalition shape the policies of the New Deal? In your answer, discuss the character of the coalition and specific reforms.

2. New Dealers experimented with varied solutions to the economic disorder of the 1930s. Compare reform efforts targeting rural and industrial America. Were they effective? Why or why not? What do they reveal about how the Roosevelt administration understood the underlying causes of the Great Depression?

3. Although the New Deal enjoyed astonishing popularity, some Americans were consistently critical of Roosevelt's reforms. Why? In your answer, discuss three opponents of the New Deal, being attentive to changes over time in their opinions. Were they able to influence the New Deal? If so, how?

4. Although the New Deal extended help to many Americans, all did not benefit equally from the era's reforms. Who remained outside the reach of New Deal assistance? Why? In your answer, consider how politics shaped the limits of reform, both in constituents' ability to demand assistance and in the federal government's response to their demands.

LINKING TO THE PAST

1. To what degree did the New Deal reflect a continuation of the progressive movement of the late nineteenth and early twentieth centuries? In what ways was the New Deal a departure from progressive ideals? In general, how new was the New Deal? (See chapters 21 and 22.)

2. How did the New Deal coalition compare to the long-standing political coalition that had elected Republicans to the presidency since 1920? What accounted for the differences and similarities? (See chapter 23.)

TIMELINE 1933–1938

1933 • Democrat Franklin D. Roosevelt becomes president.
  • **March–June** Legislation of the Hundred Days establishes the New Deal.
  • Roosevelt closes the nation's banks for a four-day "bank holiday."
  • Federal Emergency Relief Administration (FERA) established.

1934 • Securities and Exchange Commission (SEC) created.
  • Upton Sinclair loses bid for governorship of California.
  • American Liberty League founded.
  • Dr. Francis Townsend devises Old Age Revolving Pension scheme.
  • Indian Reorganization Act.

1935 • Legislation creates Works Progress Administration (WPA).
  • Wagner Act.
  • Committee for Industrial Organization (CIO) founded.

  • Social Security Act.
  • Father Charles Coughlin begins National Union for Social Justice.

1936 • John Maynard Keynes publishes *The General Theory of Employment, Interest, and Money.*
  • Franklin Roosevelt elected to a second term by a landslide.

1937 • United Auto Workers stages successful sit-down strike at General Motors plant in Flint, Michigan.
  • Roosevelt's court-packing legislation defeated in the Senate.
  • Economic recession slows recovery from depression.

1938 • Second Agricultural Adjustment Act and Fair Labor Standards Act.
  • Congress rejects administration's antilynching bill.
  • Administrative Reorganization Act.

▶ FOR AN ONLINE BIBLIOGRAPHY, PRACTICE QUIZZES, WEB SITES, IMAGES, AND DOCUMENTS RELATED TO THIS CHAPTER, see the Book Companion Site at **bedfordstmartins.com/roarkvalue**.

▶ FOR DOCUMENTS RELATED TO THIS PERIOD, see Michael Johnson, ed., *Reading the American Past*, Fifth Edition.

The United States and the Second World War

1939–1945

ON A SUN-DRENCHED FLORIDA AFTERNOON IN JANUARY 1927,
twelve-year-old Paul Tibbets cinched on a leather helmet and clambered
into the front seat of the open cockpit of a biplane for his first airplane
ride. While the pilot sitting behind him brought the plane in low over the
Hialeah racetrack in Miami, Tibbets pitched Baby Ruth candy bars tethered
to small paper parachutes to racing fans in the grandstands below. After
two more candy-bar drops over the racetrack, the pilot raced to the beach,
and Tibbets tossed out the remaining candy bars and watched the bathers
scramble for chocolate from heaven. After this stunt, sales of Baby Ruths
soared, and Tibbets was hooked on flying.

In 1937, Tibbets joined the Army Air Corps and became a military pilot.
Shortly after the Japanese attack on Pearl Harbor in December 1941, Tibbets
led a squadron of airplanes flying antisubmarine patrol against German
U-boats lurking along the East Coast. When the heavily armored B-17 Flying
Fortress bombers began to come off American assembly lines early in 1942,
he took a squadron of the new planes from the United States to England.
On August 17, 1942, he led the first American daytime bombing raid on
German-occupied Europe, releasing 1,100 pounds of bombs from his B-17,
nicknamed *Butcher Shop*, on railroad yards in northern France, the first of
some 700,000 tons of explosives dropped by American bombers during the
air war in Europe.

After numerous raids over Europe, Tibbets was reassigned to the North African campaign, where his duties included ferrying the American commander, General Dwight D. Eisenhower, into the battle zone. After eight months of combat missions, Tibbets returned to the United States and was ordered to test the new B-29 Super Fortress being built in Wichita, Kansas. The B-29 was much bigger than the B-17 and could fly higher and faster, making it ideal for the campaign against Japan. Tibbets's mastery of the B-29 caused him to be singled out in September 1944 to command a top-secret unit training for a special mission.

The mission was to be ready to drop on Japan a bomb so powerful that it might end the war. No such bomb yet existed, but American scientists and engineers were working around the clock to build one. Tibbets kept this secret from his men but took them and his B-29s to Utah to develop a way to drop such a powerful weapon without getting blown up by it. In May 1945, Tibbets and his men went to Tinian Island in the Pacific, where they trained for their secret mission by flying raids over Japanese cities and dropping ordinary bombs. The atomic bomb arrived on Tinian on July 26, just ten days after a successful test explosion in the New Mexico desert. Nicknamed "Little Boy," the bomb packed the equivalent of 40 million pounds of TNT, or 200,000 of the 200-pound bombs Tibbets and other American airmen had dropped on Europe.

At 2:30 a.m. on August 6, 1945, Tibbets, his crew, and their atomic payload took off in the B-29 bomber *Enola Gay*, named for Tibbets's mother, and headed for Japan. Less than seven hours later, over the city of Hiroshima,

Colonel Paul Tibbets
Before taking off to drop the world's first atomic bomb on Hiroshima, Tibbets posed on the tarmac next to his customized B-29 Super Fortress bomber, named *Enola Gay* in honor of his mother. A crew of eleven handpicked airmen accompanied Tibbets on the top-secret mission. After the war, President Harry S. Truman invited Tibbets to the White House and told him, "Don't you ever lose any sleep over the fact that you planned and carried out that mission. It was my decision. You had no choice."
© Bettmann/Corbis.

Tibbets and his men released Little Boy from the *Enola Gay's* bomb bay. The plane bucked upward after dropping the 4.5-ton explosive, while Tibbets struggled to maintain control as the shock wave from the explosion blasted past and a purple cloud mushroomed nearly ten miles into the air. Three days later, airmen from Tibbets's command dropped a second atomic bomb on Nagasaki, and within five days Japan surrendered.

Paul Tibbets's experiences traced an arc followed by millions of Americans during World War II, from the innocence of bombarding Miami with candy bars to the deadly nuclear firestorms that rained down on Japan. Like Tibbets, Americans joined their allies to fight the Axis powers in Europe and Asia. Like his *Enola Gay* crewmen — who hailed from New York, Texas, California, New Jersey, New Mexico, Maryland, North Carolina, Pennsylvania, Michigan, and Nevada — Americans from all regions united to defeat the fascist aggressors. American industries mobilized to produce advanced bombers — like the ones Tibbets piloted — along with enough other military equipment to supply the American armed forces and their allies. At enormous cost in human life and suffering, the war resulted in employment and prosperity to most Americans at home, ending the depression, providing new opportunities for women, and ushering the nation into the postwar world as a triumphant economic and — on the wings of Tibbets's *Enola Gay* — atomic superpower.

▶ Peacetime Dilemmas

The First World War left a dangerous and ultimately deadly legacy. The victors — especially Britain, France, and the United States — sought to avoid future wars at almost any cost. The defeated nation, Germany, aspired to reassert its power and avenge its losses by means of renewed warfare. Italy and Japan felt humiliated by the Versailles peace settlement and saw war as a legitimate way to increase their global power. Japan invaded the northern Chinese province of Manchuria in 1931 with ambitions to expand throughout Asia. Italy, led by the fascist **Benito Mussolini** since 1922, hungered for an empire in Africa. In Germany, National Socialist **Adolf Hitler** rose to power in 1933 in a quest to dominate Europe and the world. These aggressive, militaristic, antidemocratic regimes seemed a smaller threat to most people in the United States during the 1930s than did the economic crisis at home. Shielded from external threats by the Atlantic and Pacific oceans, Americans hoped to avoid entanglement in foreign woes and to concentrate on climbing out of the nation's economic abyss.

Roosevelt and Reluctant Isolation

Like most Americans during the 1930s, Franklin Roosevelt believed that the nation's highest priority was to attack the domestic causes and consequences of the depression. But unlike most Americans, Roosevelt had long advocated an active role for the United States in international affairs. After World War I, Roosevelt embraced Woodrow Wilson's vision that the United States should take the lead in making the world "safe for democracy," and he continued to advocate American membership in the League of Nations during the isolationist 1920s.

The depression forced Roosevelt to retreat from his previous internationalism. He came to believe that energetic involvement in foreign affairs diverted resources and political support from domestic recovery. Once in office, Roosevelt sought to combine domestic economic recovery with a low-profile foreign policy that encouraged free trade and disarmament.

Roosevelt's pursuit of international amity was constrained by economic circumstances and American popular opinion. After an opinion poll demonstrated popular support for recognizing the Soviet Union — an international pariah since the Bolshevik Revolution in 1917 — Roosevelt established formal diplomatic relations in 1933. But when the League of Nations condemned Japanese and German aggression, Roosevelt did not support the league's attempts to keep the peace because he feared jeopardizing isolationists' support for New Deal measures in Congress. America watched from the sidelines when Japan withdrew from the league and ignored the limitations on its navy imposed after World War I. The United States also looked the other way when Hitler rearmed Germany and recalled its representative to the league in 1933, declaring that the international organization sought to thwart Germany's national ambitions. Roosevelt worried that German and Japanese violations of league sanctions and the Versailles settlement threatened world peace. But he reassured Americans that the nation would not "use its armed forces for the settlement of any [international] dispute anywhere."

The Good Neighbor Policy

In his 1933 inaugural address, Franklin Roosevelt announced that the United States would pursue "the policy of the good neighbor" in international relations. A few weeks later, he emphasized that this policy applied specifically to Latin America, where U.S. military forces had often intervened in local affairs. In December 1933, Secretary of State Cordell Hull formalized the good neighbor pledge that no nation had the right to intervene in the internal or external affairs of another.

The **good neighbor policy** did not indicate a U.S. retreat from empire in Latin America. Instead, it declared that the United States would not depend on military force to exercise its influence in the region. When Mexico nationalized American oil holdings and revolution boiled over in Nicaragua, Guatemala, and Cuba during the 1930s, Roosevelt refrained from sending troops to defend the interests of American corporations. In 1934, Roosevelt even withdrew American Marines from Haiti, which they had occupied since 1916. While nonintervention honored the principle of national self-determination, it also permitted the rise of dictators, such as Anastasio Somoza in Nicaragua and Fulgencio Batista in Cuba, who exploited and terrorized their nations with private support from U.S. businesses and the hands-off policy of Roosevelt's administration.

Military nonintervention also did not prevent the United States from exerting its economic influence in Latin America. In 1934, Congress passed the Reciprocal Trade Agreements Act, which gave the president the power to reduce tariffs on goods imported into the United States from nations that agreed to lower their own tariffs on U.S. exports. By 1940, twenty-two nations had agreed to reciprocal tariff reductions, helping to double U.S. exports to Latin America and contributing to the New Deal's goal of boosting the domestic economy through free trade. Although the economic power of the United States continued to overshadow that of its neighbors, the nonintervention policy planted seeds of friendship and hemispheric solidarity.

The Price of Noninvolvement

In Europe, fascist governments in Italy and Germany threatened military aggression. Italian dictator Benito Mussolini proclaimed, "War is to the man what maternity is to the woman. . . . Peace [is] . . . depressing and a negation of all the fundamental virtues of man." Hitler rebuilt Germany's military strength, openly defying the terms of the Versailles peace treaty. Britain and France only made verbal protests. Emboldened, Hitler plotted to avenge defeat in World War I by recapturing territories with German inhabitants, all the while accusing Jews of polluting the purity of the Aryan master race. The virulent anti-Semitism of Hitler and his Nazi Party unified non-Jewish Germans and attracted sympathizers among many other Europeans, even in France and Britain, thereby weakening support for those who opposed Hitler or defended Jews.

In Japan, a stridently militaristic government planned to follow the invasion of Manchuria in 1931 with conquests extending throughout Southeast Asia. The Manchurian invasion bogged down in a long and vicious war when Chinese Nationalists rallied around their leader, **Jiang Jieshi (Chiang Kai-shek)**, to fight against the Japanese. Preparations for new Japanese conquests continued, however. In 1936, Japan openly violated naval limitation treaties it had agreed to and began to build a battle-ready fleet to achieve naval superiority in the Pacific.

In the United States, the hostilities in Asia and Europe reinforced isolationist sentiments. Popular disillusionment with the failure of Woodrow Wilson's idealistic goals caused many Americans to question the nation's participation in World War I. In 1933, Gerald Nye, a Republican from North Dakota, chaired a Senate committee that investigated why the United States had gone to war in 1917. The Nye committee concluded that greedy "merchants of death" — American weapons makers, bankers, and financiers — dragged the nation into the war to line their own pockets. The Nye committee persuaded many Americans that war profiteers might once again push the nation into a world war. International tensions and the Nye committee report prompted Congress to pass a series of **neutrality acts** between 1935 and 1937 designed to avoid entanglement in foreign wars. The neutrality acts prohibited making loans and selling arms to nations at war.

By 1937, the growing conflicts overseas caused some Americans to call for a total embargo on all trade with warring countries. Roosevelt and Congress worried that such an embargo would hurt the nation's economy by reducing production and boosting unemployment. The Neutrality Act of 1937 attempted to reconcile the nation's desire for both peace and foreign trade with a "cash-and-carry" policy that required warring nations to pay cash for nonmilitary goods and to transport them in their own ships. This policy supported foreign trade and thereby benefited the nation's economy, but it also helped foreign aggressors by supplying them with goods and thereby undermining peace.

The desire for peace in France, Britain, and the United States led Germany, Italy, and Japan to launch offensives on the assumption that the Western democracies lacked the will to oppose them. In March 1936, Nazi troops marched into the industry-rich Rhineland on Germany's western border, in blatant violation of the Treaty of Versailles. One month later, Italian armies completed their conquest of Ethiopia, projecting fascist power into Africa. In December 1937, Japanese invaders captured Nanjing (Nanking) and celebrated their triumph in the "Rape of Nanking," a deadly rampage of murder, rape, and plunder that killed 200,000 Chinese civilians.

In Spain, a bitter civil war broke out in July 1936 when the Nationalists, fascist rebels led by General Francisco Franco, attacked the democratically elected Republican government. Both Germany and Italy reinforced Franco with soldiers, weapons, and aircraft, while the Soviet Union provided much less aid to the Republican Loyalists. The **Spanish civil war** seemed to many observers a dress rehearsal for a coming worldwide conflict, but it did not cause European democracies or the U.S. government to help the Loyalists, despite sympathy for their cause. More than 3,000 individual Americans enlisted in the Russian-sponsored Abraham Lincoln Brigade to fight on the Republican side. But, abandoned by the Western nations, the Republican Loyalists and their allies were defeated in 1939, and Franco built a fascist bulwark in southwestern Europe.

Hostilities in Europe, Africa, and Asia alarmed Roosevelt and some Americans. The president sought to persuade most Americans to moderate their isolationism and find a way to support the victims of fascist aggression. Speaking in Chicago in October 1937, Roosevelt declared that the "epidemic of world lawlessness is spreading" and warned that "mere isolation or neutrality" offered no remedy. Instead, he proposed that the United States "quarantine" aggressor nations and stop the spread of war's contagion.

Roosevelt's speech ignited a storm of protest from isolationists. Critics accused the president of seeking to replace "Americanism" with "internationalism." Disappointed by the strength of isolationism and the absence of congressional support for his quarantine policy, Roosevelt remarked, "It's a terrible thing to look over your shoulder when you are trying to lead and find no one there." The popularity of isolationist sentiment convinced Roosevelt that he needed to maneuver carefully if the United States were to help prevent fascist aggressors from conquering Europe and Asia, leaving the United States an isolated and imperiled island of democracy.

REVIEW   Why did isolationism during the 1930s concern Roosevelt?

▶ The Onset of War

Between 1939 and 1941, fascist victories overseas eventually eroded American isolationism. Continuing German and Japanese aggression caused more and more Americans to believe that it was time for the nation to take a stand. At first, taking a stand was limited to providing material support to the enemies of Germany and Japan, principally Britain, China, and the Soviet Union. But Japan's surprise attack on Pearl Harbor eliminated that restraint, and the nation began to mobilize for an all-out assault on foreign foes.

Nazi Aggression and War in Europe

Under the spell of isolationism, Americans passively watched Hitler's relentless campaign to dominate Europe. In 1938, Hitler bullied Austria into accepting incorporation — *Anschluss* — into the Third Reich, the Nazis' name for Germany. Next, Hitler turned his attention to the German-speaking Sudetenland, granted to Czechoslovakia by the World War I peace settlement. Hoping to avoid war, British prime minister Neville Chamberlain went to Munich, Germany, in September 1938 and offered Hitler terms of **appeasement** that would give the Sudetenland to Germany if Hitler agreed to leave the rest of Czechoslovakia alone. Hitler accepted Chamberlain's offer and promised that he would make no more territorial claims in Europe. But he never intended to honor his promise. In March 1939, the German army boldly marched into Czechoslovakia and conquered it without firing a shot.

In April 1939, Hitler demanded that Poland return the German territory it had been awarded after World War I. Recognizing that appeasement had failed, Britain and France assured Poland that they would go to war with Germany if Hitler launched an attack across the Polish border. In turn, Hitler negotiated with his bitter enemy, Soviet premier **Joseph Stalin**, offering him concessions in order to prevent the Soviet Union from joining Britain and France in opposing a German attack on Poland. Despite the enduring hatred between fascist Germany and the Communist Soviet Union, the two powers signed the Nazi-Soviet treaty of non-aggression in August 1939, exposing Poland to an onslaught by both the German Wehrmacht (army) and the Soviet Red Army.

At dawn on September 1, 1939, Hitler unleashed his *blitzkrieg* (literally, "lightning war") on Poland. "Act brutally!" Hitler exhorted his generals. "Send [every] man, woman, and child of Polish descent and language to their deaths, pitilessly and remorselessly." The attack triggered Soviet attacks on eastern Poland and declarations of war from France and Britain two days later, igniting a conflagration that raced around the globe. In September 1939, Germany seemed invincible, causing many people to fear that all of Europe would soon share Poland's fate.

After the Nazis overran Poland, Hitler paused for a few months before launching a westward blitzkrieg. In April 1940, German forces smashed through Denmark and Norway. In May, Germany invaded the Netherlands, Belgium, Luxembourg,

Nazi Invasion of Poland
Adolf Hitler relished the early success of the German army's *blitzkrieg* against Poland in 1939. This photo shows Hitler reviewing a victory parade of his soldiers in Warsaw. Nazi insignia hanging from every lamp post declare the German conquest of Poland. After the conquest, Germans systematically murdered hundreds of thousands of Polish civilians and confined even more to slave labor camps. Notably, the photo shows no Poles celebrating Hitler's victory. Photo by Hugo Jaeger/Timepix/Time Life Pictures/ Getty Images.

and France. The French believed that their Maginot Line, a concrete fortification built after World War I, would halt the German attack. But the Maginot Line proved little more than a detour for Hitler's mechanized divisions, which wheeled around it and raced south toward Paris.

The speed of the German attack trapped more than 300,000 British and French soldiers, who retreated to the port of Dunkirk, where an improvised armada of British vessels hurriedly ferried them to safety across the English Channel. By mid-June 1940, France had surrendered the largest army in the world, signed an armistice that gave Germany control of the entire French coastline and nearly two-thirds of the countryside, and installed a collaborationist government at Vichy in southern France. With an empire that stretched across Europe from Poland to France, Hitler seemed poised to attack Britain.

The new British prime minister, **Winston Churchill**, vowed that Britain, unlike France, would never surrender to Hitler. "We shall fight on the seas and oceans [and] . . . in the air," he proclaimed, "whatever the cost may be, we shall fight on the beaches, . . . and in the fields and in the streets." Churchill's defiance stiffened British resolve for a defense against Hitler's attack, which began in mid-June 1940 when wave after wave of German bombers targeted British military installations and cities, killing tens of thousands of civilians. The undermanned and outgunned Royal Air Force fought as doggedly as Churchill had predicted and finally won the **Battle of Britain** by November, clearing German bombers from British skies and handing Hitler his first defeat. Churchill praised the valiant British pilots, declaring that "never . . . was so much owed by so many to so few." Advance knowledge of German plans aided British pilots. The British made use of the new technology of radar and also learned to decipher Germany's top-secret military codes. Battered and exhausted by German attacks, Britain needed American help to continue to fight, as Churchill repeatedly wrote Roosevelt in private.

From Neutrality to the Arsenal of Democracy

When Hitler attacked Poland, Roosevelt issued an official proclamation of American neutrality. Most Americans condemned German aggression and favored Britain and France, but isolationism remained powerful. Roosevelt feared that if Congress did not repeal the arms embargo mandated by the Neutrality Act of 1937, France and Britain would soon succumb to the Nazi onslaught. After heated debate, Congress voted in November 1939 to revise the neutrality legislation and allow belligerent nations to buy arms, as well as nonmilitary supplies, on a cash-and-carry basis.

In practice, the revised neutrality law permitted Britain and France to purchase American war materiel and carry it across the Atlantic in their own ships, thereby shielding American vessels from attack by German submarines lurking in the Atlantic. Roosevelt wrote a friend, "What worries me is that public opinion . . . is patting itself on the back every morning and thanking God for the Atlantic Ocean (and the Pacific Ocean)" and underestimating "the serious implications" of the European war "for our own future." Roosevelt searched for a way to aid Britain short of entering a formal alliance or declaring war against Germany. Churchill pleaded for American destroyers, aircraft, and munitions, but he had no money to buy them under the prevailing cash-and-carry neutrality law. By late summer in 1940, as the Battle of Britain raged, Roosevelt concocted a scheme to deliver fifty old destroyers to Britain in exchange for American access to British bases in the Western Hemisphere. Claiming the constitutional power to strengthen America's defenses by swapping destroyers for bases, Roosevelt took the first steps toward building a firm Anglo-American alliance against Hitler.

While German Luftwaffe (air force) pilots bombed Britain, Roosevelt decided to run for an unprecedented third term as president in 1940. He hoped to woo voters away from their complacent isolationism to back the nation's international interests as well as New Deal reforms. But the presidential election, which Roosevelt won handily, provided no clear mandate for American involvement in the European war. The Republican candidate, Wendell Willkie, a former Democrat who generally favored New Deal measures and Roosevelt's foreign policy, attacked Roosevelt as a warmonger. Willkie's accusations caused the president to promise voters, "Your boys are not going to be sent into any foreign wars," a pledge counterbalanced by his repeated warnings about the threats to America posed by Nazi aggression.

Once reelected, Roosevelt maneuvered to support Britain in every way short of war. In a fireside chat shortly after Christmas 1940, he proclaimed that it was incumbent on the United States to become "the great arsenal of democracy" and send "every ounce and every ton of munitions and supplies that we can possibly spare to help the defenders who are in the front lines."

In January 1941, Roosevelt proposed the **Lend-Lease Act**, which allowed the British to obtain arms from the United States without paying cash but with the promise to reimburse the United States when the war ended. The purpose of Lend-Lease, Roosevelt proclaimed, was to defend democracy and human rights throughout the world, specifically the Four Freedoms: "freedom of speech and expression . . . freedom of every person to worship God in his own way . . . freedom from want . . . [and] freedom from fear." The Lend-Lease Act passed in March 1941 and started a flow of support to Britain that totaled more than $50 billion during the war, far more than all federal expenditures combined since Roosevelt had become president in 1933.

Stymied in his plans for an invasion of England, Hitler turned his massive army eastward and on June 22, 1941, sprang a surprise attack on the Soviet Union, his ally in the 1939 Nazi-Soviet nonaggression pact. Neither Roosevelt nor Churchill had any love for Joseph Stalin or communism, but they both welcomed the Soviet Union to the anti-Nazi cause. Both Western leaders understood that Hitler's attack on Russia would provide relief for the hard-pressed British. Roosevelt quickly persuaded Congress to extend Lend-Lease to the Soviet Union, beginning the shipment of millions of tons of trucks, jeeps, and other equipment that, in all, supplied about 10 percent of Russian war materiel.

As Hitler's Wehrmacht raced across the Russian plains and Nazi U-boats tried to choke off supplies to Britain and the Soviet Union, Roosevelt met with Churchill aboard a ship near Newfoundland to cement the Anglo-American alliance. In August 1941, the two leaders issued the **Atlantic Charter**, pledging the two nations to freedom of the seas and free trade as well as the right of national self-determination.

Japan Attacks America

Although the likelihood of war with Germany preoccupied Roosevelt, Hitler exercised a measure of restraint in directly provoking America. Japanese ambitions in Asia clashed more openly with American interests and commitments, especially in China and the Philippines. And unlike Hitler, the Japanese high command planned to attack the United States if necessary to pursue Japan's aspirations to rule an Asian empire it termed the Greater East Asia Co-Prosperity Sphere. Appealing to widespread Asian bitterness toward such white colonial powers as the British in India and Burma, the French in Indochina (now Vietnam), and the Dutch in the East Indies (now Indonesia), the Japanese campaigned to preserve "Asia for the Asians." Japan's invasion of China — which had lasted for ten years by 1941 — proved that its true goal was Asia for the Japanese. Japan coveted the raw materials available from China and Southeast Asia and ignored American demands to stop its campaign of aggression.

In 1940, Japan signaled a new phase of its imperial designs by entering a defensive alliance with Germany and Italy — the Tripartite Pact. To thwart Japanese plans to invade the Dutch East Indies, in July 1941 Roosevelt announced a trade embargo that denied Japan access to oil, scrap iron, and other goods essential for its war machines. Roosevelt hoped the embargo would strengthen factions within Japan that opposed the militarists and sought to restore relations with the United States.

Instead, the American embargo played into the hands of Japanese militarists headed by General Hideki Tojo, who seized control of the government in October 1941 and persuaded other leaders, including Emperor Hirohito, that swift destruction of American naval bases in the Pacific would leave Japan free to follow its destiny. On December 7, 1941, 183 attack aircraft lifted off six Japanese carriers and attacked the U.S. Pacific Fleet at **Pearl Harbor** on the Hawai'ian island of Oahu. The devastating surprise attack sank or disabled eighteen ships, including all of the fleet's battleships; killed more than 2,400 Americans; and wounded more than 1,000, almost crippling U.S. war-making capacity in the Pacific. Luckily for the United States, Japanese pilots failed to destroy the vital machine shops and oil storage facilities at Pearl Harbor, and none of the nation's aircraft carriers happened to be in port at the time of the attack.

The Japanese scored a stunning tactical victory at Pearl Harbor, but in the long run the attack proved a colossal blunder. The victory made many Japanese commanders overconfident about their military prowess. Worse for the Japanese, Americans instantly united in their desire to fight and avenge the attack, which Roosevelt termed "dastardly and unprovoked." The president vowed that "this form of treachery shall never endanger us again." On December 8, Congress endorsed the president's call for a declaration of war. Neither Hitler nor Mussolini knew about the Japanese attack in advance, but they both declared war against America on December 11, bringing the United States into all-out war with the Axis powers in both Europe and Asia.

REVIEW How did Roosevelt attempt to balance American isolationism with the increasingly ominous international scene of the late 1930s?

▶ Mobilizing for War

The time had come, Roosevelt announced, for the prescriptions of "Dr. New Deal" to be replaced by the stronger medicines of "Dr. Win-the-War." Military and civilian leaders rushed to secure the nation against possible attacks, causing Americans of Japanese descent to be stigmatized and sent to internment camps. Roosevelt and his advisers lost no time enlisting millions of Americans in the armed forces to bring the isolationist-era military to fighting strength for a two-front war. The war emergency also required economic mobilization unparalleled in the nation's history. As Dr. Win-the-War, Roosevelt set aside the New Deal goal of reform and plunged headlong into transforming the American economy into the world's greatest military machine, thereby achieving full employment and economic recovery, goals that had eluded the New Deal.

Home-Front Security

Shortly after declaring war against the United States, Hitler dispatched German submarines to hunt American ships along the Atlantic coast from Maine to Florida, where Paul Tibbets and other American pilots tried to destroy them. The U-boats had devastating success for about eight months, sinking hundreds of U.S. ships and threatening to disrupt the Lend-Lease lifeline to Britain and the Soviet Union. But by mid-1942, the U.S. Navy had chased German submarines away from the East Coast and into the mid-Atlantic, reducing the direct threat to the nation.

Within the continental United States, Americans remained sheltered from the chaos and destruction the war was bringing to hundreds of millions in Europe and Asia. Nevertheless, the government worried constantly about espionage and internal subversion. The campaign for patriotic vigilance focused on German and Japanese foes, but Americans of Japanese descent became targets of official and popular persecution because of Pearl Harbor and long-standing racial prejudice against people of Asian descent.

About 320,000 people of Japanese descent lived in U.S. territory in 1941, two-thirds of them in Hawai'i, where they largely escaped such wartime persecution because they were essential and valued members of society. On the mainland, however, Japanese Americans were a tiny minority — even along the West Coast, where most of them worked on farms and in small businesses — subject to frenzied wartime suspicions and persecution. Although an official military survey concluded that Japanese Americans posed no danger, popular hostility fueled a campaign to round up all mainland Japanese Americans — two-thirds of them U.S. citizens. "A Jap's a Jap. . . . It makes no difference whether he is an American citizen or not," one official declared.

On February 19, 1942, Roosevelt issued Executive Order 9066, which authorized sending all Americans of Japanese descent to ten makeshift **internment camps** — euphemistically termed "relocation centers" — located in remote areas of the West (Map 25.1). Allowed little time to secure or sell their property, Japanese Americans lost homes and businesses worth about $400 million and lived out the war penned in by barbed wire and armed guards. Although several thousand Japanese Americans served with distinction in the U.S. armed forces and no case of subversion by a Japanese American was ever uncovered, the Supreme Court, in its 1944 *Korematsu* decision, upheld Executive Order 9066's blatant violation of constitutional rights as justified by "military necessity."

Building a Citizen Army

In 1940, Roosevelt encouraged Congress to pass the **Selective Service Act** to register men of military age who would be subject to a draft if the need arose. More than 6,000 local draft boards registered more than 30 million men and, when war came, rapidly inducted them into military service. In all, more than

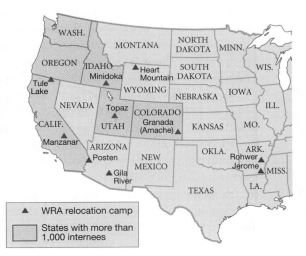

MAP 25.1

Western Relocation Authority Centers

Responding to prejudice and fear of sabotage, President Roosevelt authorized the roundup and relocation of all Americans of Japanese descent in 1942. Taken from their homes in the cities and fertile farmland of the far West, more than 120,000 Japanese Americans were confined in desolate camps scattered as far east as the Mississippi River.

16 million men and women served in uniform during the war, two-thirds of them draftees, mostly young men. Women were barred from combat duty, but they worked at nearly every noncombatant task, eroding traditional barriers to women's military service.

The Selective Service Act prohibited discrimination "on account of race or color," and almost a million African American men and women donned uniforms, as did half a million Mexican Americans, 25,000 Native Americans, and 13,000 Chinese Americans. The racial insults and discrimination suffered by all people of color made some soldiers ask, as a Mexican American GI did on his way to the European front, "Why fight for America when you have not been treated as an American?" Only black Americans were trained in segregated camps, confined in segregated barracks, and assigned to segregated units. Most black Americans were consigned to manual labor, and relatively few served in combat until late in 1944, when the need for military manpower in Europe intensified. Then, as General George Patton told black soldiers in a tank unit in Normandy, "I don't care what color you are, so long as you go up there and kill those Kraut sonsabitches."

Homosexuals also served in the armed forces, although in much smaller numbers than black Americans. Allowed to serve as long as their sexual preferences remained covert, gay Americans, like other minorities, sought to demonstrate their worth under fire. "I was superpatriotic," a gay combat veteran recalled. Another gay GI remarked, "Who in the hell is going to worry about [homosexuality]" in the midst of the life-or-death realities of war?

Conversion to a War Economy

In 1940, the American economy remained mired in the depression. Nearly one worker in seven was still without a job, factories operated far below their productive capacity, and the total federal budget was under $10 billion. Shortly after the attack on Pearl Harbor, Roosevelt announced the goal of converting the economy to produce "overwhelming . . . , crushing superiority of equipment in any theater of the world war." Factories were converted from making passenger cars to assembling tanks and airplanes, and production soared to record levels. By the end of the war, jobs exceeded workers, plants operated at full capacity, and the federal budget topped $100 billion.

To organize and oversee this tidal wave of military production, Roosevelt called upon business leaders to come to Washington and, for the token payment of a dollar a year, head new government agencies such as the **War Production Board**, which, among other things, set production priorities and pushed for maximum output. Contracts flowed to large corporations, often on a basis that guaranteed their profits. During the first half of 1942, the government issued contracts worth more than the entire gross national product in 1941.

Booming wartime employment swelled union membership. To speed production, the government asked unions to pledge not to strike. Despite the relentless pace of work, union members kept their no-strike pledge, with the important exception of members of the United Mine Workers, who walked out of the coal mines in 1943, demanding a pay hike and earning the enmity of many Americans.

Overall, conversion to war production achieved Roosevelt's ambitious goal of "crushing superiority" in military goods. At a total cost of $304 billion during the war, the nation produced an avalanche of military equipment, more than double the combined production of Germany, Japan, and Italy. This outpouring of military goods supplied not only U.S. forces but also America's allies, giving tangible meaning to Roosevelt's pledge to make America the "arsenal of democracy."

REVIEW How did the Roosevelt administration mobilize the human and industrial resources necessary to fight a two-front war?

▶ Fighting Back

The United States confronted a daunting military challenge in December 1941. The attack on Pearl Harbor destroyed much of its Pacific Fleet, crippling the nation's ability to defend against Japan's offensive throughout the southern Pacific. In the Atlantic, Hitler's U-boats sank American ships, while German armies occupied most of western Europe and relentlessly advanced eastward into the Soviet Union. Roosevelt and his military advisers believed that defeating Germany took top priority. To achieve that victory required preventing Hitler from defeating America's allies, Britain and the Soviet Union. If they fell, Hitler would command all the resources of Europe in a probable assault on the United States. To fight back effectively against Germany and Japan, the United States had to coordinate military and political strategy with its allies and muster all its human and economic assets. But in 1941, nobody knew whether that would be enough.

Turning the Tide in the Pacific

In the Pacific theater, Japan's leading military strategist, Admiral Isoroku Yamamoto, believed that if his forces did not quickly conquer and secure the territories they targeted, Japan would eventually lose the war as a result of America's far greater resources. Swiftly, the Japanese assaulted American airfields in the Philippines and captured U.S. outposts on Guam and Wake Island. After capturing Singapore and Burma, Japan sought to complete its domination of the southern Pacific with an attack on the American stronghold in the Philippines.

The Japanese unleashed a withering assault against the Philippines in January 1942 (see Map 25.3, page 774). American defenders surrendered to the Japanese in May. The Japanese victors sent captured American and Filipino soldiers on the infamous Bataan Death March to a concentration camp, causing thousands to die. By the summer of 1942, the Japanese war machine had conquered the Dutch East Indies and was poised to strike Australia and New Zealand.

In the spring of 1942, U.S. forces launched a major two-pronged counter-offensive that military officials hoped would reverse the Japanese advance. Forces led by General **Douglas MacArthur**, commander of the U.S. armed forces in the Pacific the-ater, moved north from Australia and eventually attacked the Japanese in the Philippines. Far more decisively, Admiral **Chester W. Nimitz** sailed his battle fleet west from

Japanese Pilot's Flag
Japanese pilots often carried small flags covered with admonitions to fight hard and well. This flag belonged to a pilot named Imano, whose relatives sent him aloft with an inscription that read, "Let your divine plane soar in the sky. We who are left behind pray only for your certain success in sinking an enemy ship." Notably, the inscription emphasized harming Japan's enemies rather than returning home safely. © U.S. Naval Academy Museum/ photo by Richard D. Bond Jr.

Hawai'i to retake Japanese-held islands in the southern and mid-Pacific. On May 7–8, 1942, in the Coral Sea just north of Australia, the American fleet and carrier-based warplanes defeated a Japanese armada that was sailing around the coast of New Guinea.

Nimitz then learned from an intelligence intercept that the Japanese were massing an invasion force aimed at Midway Island, an outpost guarding the Hawai'ian Islands. Nimitz maneuvered his carriers and cruisers into the Central Pacific to surprise the Japanese. In a furious battle that raged on June 3–6, American ships and planes delivered a devastating blow to the Japanese navy.

The **Battle of Midway** reversed the balance of naval power in the Pacific and put the Japanese at a disadvantage for the rest of the war. Japan managed to build only six more large aircraft carriers during the war, while the United States launched dozens, proving the wisdom of Yamamoto's prediction. But the Japanese still occupied and defended the many places they had conquered.

The Campaign in Europe

After Pearl Harbor, Hitler's eastern-front armies marched ever deeper into the Soviet Union while his western-front forces prepared to invade Britain. As in World War I, the Germans attempted to starve the British into submission by destroying their seaborne lifeline. In 1941 and 1942, they sank Allied ships faster than new ones could be built. Overall, the U-boat campaign sank 4,700 merchant vessels and nearly 200 warships and killed 40,000 Allied seamen.

Until mid-1943, the outcome of the war in the Atlantic remained in doubt. Then, newly invented radar detectors and production of sufficient destroyer escorts for merchant vessels allowed the Allies to prey upon the lurking U-boats. After suffering a 75 percent casualty rate among U-boat crews, Hitler withdrew German submarines from the North Atlantic in late May 1943, allowing thousands of American supply ships to cross the Atlantic unimpeded. Winning the battle of the Atlantic allowed the United States to continue to supply its British and Soviet allies for the duration of the war and to reduce the imminent threat of a German invasion of Britain.

The most important strategic questions confronting the United States and its allies were when and where to open a second front against the Nazis. Stalin demanded that America and Britain mount an immediate and massive assault across the English Channel into western France to force Hitler to divert his armies from the eastern front and relieve the pressure on the Soviet Union. Churchill and Roosevelt instead delayed opening a second front, allowing the Germans and the Soviets to slug it out. This drawn-out conflict weakened both the Nazis and the Communists and made an eventual Allied attack on western France more likely to succeed. Churchill and Roosevelt promised Stalin that they would open a second front, but they decided to strike first in North Africa, a region of long-standing British influence that could help secure Allied control of the Mediterranean.

In October and November 1942, British forces at El-Alamein in Egypt halted German general Erwin Rommel's drive to capture the Suez Canal, Britain's lifeline to the oil of the Middle East and to British colonies in India and South Asia (see Map 25.2, page 772). In November, an American army under General **Dwight D. Eisenhower** landed far to the west, in French Morocco. Propelled by American tank units commanded by General **George Patton**, the Allied armies defeated the Germans in North Africa in May 1943. The North African campaign killed and captured 350,000 Axis soldiers, pushed the Germans out of Africa, made the Mediterranean safe for Allied shipping, and opened the door for an Allied invasion of Italy.

In January 1943, while the North African campaign was still under way, Roosevelt and Churchill met in Casablanca and announced that they would accept nothing less than the "unconditional surrender" of the Axis powers, ruling out peace negotiations. They concluded that while continuing to amass forces for the cross-Channel invasion of France, they should capitalize on their success in North Africa and strike against Italy, consigning the Soviet Union to bear the brunt of the Nazi war machine for another year.

On July 10, 1943, combined American and British amphibious forces landed 160,000 troops in Sicily. The badly equipped Italian defenders quickly withdrew to the mainland. Soon afterward, Mussolini was deposed in Italy, ending the reign of Italian fascism. Quickly, the Allies invaded the mainland, and the Italian government surrendered unconditionally. The Germans responded by rushing reinforcements to Italy and seizing control of Rome, turning the Allies' Italian campaign into a series of battles to liberate Italy from German occupation.

German troops dug into strong fortifications and fought to defend every inch of Italy's rugged terrain. Only after a long, deadly, and frustrating campaign up the Italian peninsula did the Allies finally liberate Rome in June 1944. Allied forces continued to push into northern Italy against stubborn German defenses for the remainder of the war, making the Italian campaign the war's deadliest for American infantrymen. One soldier wrote that his buddies "died like butchered swine."

Stalin denounced the Allies' Italian campaign because it left "the Soviet Army, which is fighting not only for its country, but also for its Allies, to do the job alone, almost single-handed." The Italian campaign exacted a high cost from the Americans and British, bringing the Nazis no closer to surrender and consuming men and materiel that might have been reserved for a second front in France.

> **REVIEW**   How did the United States seek to counter the Japanese in the Pacific and the Germans in Europe?

▶ The Wartime Home Front

The war effort mobilized Americans as never before. Factories churned out ever more bombs, bullets, tanks, ships, and airplanes, which workers rushed to assemble, leaving their farms and small towns and congregating in cities. Women took jobs with wrenches and welding torches, boosting the nation's workforce and fraying traditional notions that a woman's place was in the home rather than on the assembly line. Despite rationing and shortages, unprecedented government expenditures for war production brought prosperity to many Americans after years of depression-era poverty. Although Americans in uniform risked their lives on battlefields in Europe and Asia, Americans on the U.S. mainland enjoyed complete immunity from foreign attack — in sharp contrast to their Soviet and British allies. The wartime ideology of human rights provided justification for the many sacrifices Americans were required to make in support of the military effort. It also established a standard of basic human equality that became a potent weapon in the campaign for equal rights at home and in condemning the atrocities of the Holocaust perpetrated by the Nazis.

Women and Families, Guns and Butter

Millions of American women gladly took their places on assembly lines in defense industries. At the start of the war, about a quarter of adult women worked outside the home, most as teachers, nurses, social workers, and domestic servants. Few women worked in factories, except for textile mills and sewing industries, because employers and male workers often discriminated against them. But wartime mobilization of the economy and the siphoning of millions of men into the armed forces left factories begging for women workers.

Government advertisements urged women to take industrial jobs by assuring them that their household chores had prepared them for work on the "Victory Line." One billboard proclaimed,

Riveting Rosies
American women flocked to war industries, and manufacturers welcomed them in jobs previously restricted to men. Here Dora Miles and Dorothy Johnson rivet an airplane frame in a plant in Long Beach, California. The tool in Miles's hands drove a rivet into the metal and another tool (not shown) held by Johnson smashed the end of the rivet snug against the airframe, securing it. War industries employed an unprecedented number of African American women and men who often worked alongside whites, as shown here. Library of Congress.

"If you've sewed on buttons, or made buttonholes, on a [sewing] machine, you can learn to do spot welding on airplane parts." Millions of women responded. Advertisers often referred to a woman who worked in a war industry as **"Rosie the Riveter,"** a wartime term that became popular. By the end of the war, women working outside the home numbered 18 million, 50 percent more than in 1939. Contributing to the war effort also paid off in wages. A Kentucky woman remembered her job at a munitions plant, where she earned "the fabulous sum of $32 a week. To us it was an absolute miracle." Although men were paid an average of $54 for comparable wartime work, women accepted the pay differential and welcomed their chance to earn wages and help win the war at the same time.

The majority of married women remained at home, occupied with domestic chores and child care. But they, too, supported the war effort, planting Victory Gardens to provide homegrown vegetables, saving tin cans and newspapers for recycling into war materiel, and hoarding pennies and nickels to buy war bonds. Many families scrimped to cope with the 30 percent inflation during the war, but families supported by men and women in manufacturing industries enjoyed wages that grew twice as fast as inflation.

The war influenced how all families spent their earnings. Buying a new washing machine or car was out of the question, since factories that formerly built them now made military goods. Many other consumer goods — such as tires, gasoline, shoes, and meat — were rationed at home to meet military needs overseas. But most Americans had more money in their pockets than ever before, and they readily found things to buy, including movie tickets, cosmetics, and music recordings.

The wartime prosperity and abundance enjoyed by most Americans contrasted with the experiences of their hard-pressed allies. Personal consumption fell by 22 percent in Britain, and food output plummeted to just one-third of prewar levels in the Soviet Union, creating widespread hunger and even starvation. Few went hungry in the United States. New Deal restraints on agricultural production were lifted, and farm output grew by 25 percent each year during the war, providing a cornucopia of food to be exported to the Allies.

The Double V Campaign

Fighting against Nazi Germany and its ideology of Aryan racial supremacy, Americans were confronted with the extensive racial prejudice in their own country. The *Pittsburgh Courier*, a leading black newspaper, asserted that the wartime emergency called for a **Double V campaign** seeking "victory over our enemies at home and victory over our enemies on the battlefields abroad." It was time, the *Courier* proclaimed, "to persuade, embarrass, compel and shame our government and our nation . . . into a more enlightened attitude."

In 1941, black organizations demanded that the federal government require companies receiving defense contracts to integrate their workforces. **A. Philip Randolph**, head of the Brotherhood of Sleeping Car Porters, promised that 100,000 African American marchers would descend on Washington if the president did not eliminate discrimination in defense industries. Roosevelt decided to risk offending his white allies in the South and in unions and issued Executive Order 8802 in mid-1941. It authorized the **Committee on Fair Employment Practices** to investigate and prevent racial discrimination in employment. Civil rights champions hailed the act, and Randolph triumphantly called off the march.

Progress came slowly, however. In 1940, nine out of ten black Americans lived below the federal poverty line, and those who worked earned an average of just 39 percent of whites' wages. In search of better jobs and living conditions, 5.5 million black Americans migrated from the South to centers of industrial production in the North and West, making a majority of African Americans city dwellers for the first time in U.S. history. Many discovered that unskilled jobs were available but that unions and employers often barred blacks from skilled trades. At least eighteen major unions explicitly prohibited black members. Severe labor shortages and government fair employment standards opened assembly-line jobs in defense plants to African Americans, causing black unemployment to drop by 80 percent during the war. But more jobs did not mean equal pay for blacks. The average income of black families rose during the war, but by the end of the conflict it still stood at only half of what white families earned.

Blacks' migration to defense jobs intensified racial antagonisms, which boiled over in the hot summer of 1943, when 242 race riots erupted in 47 cities. In the "zoot suit riots" in Los Angeles, hundreds of white servicemen, claiming they were punishing draft dodgers, chased and beat young Mexican American men who dressed in distinctive broad-shouldered, peg-legged zoot suits. The worst mayhem occurred in Detroit, where a long-simmering conflict between whites and blacks over racially segregated housing ignited into a race war. Whites with clubs smashed through black neighborhoods, and blacks retaliated by destroying and looting white-owned businesses. In two days of violence, twenty-five blacks and nine whites were killed, and scores more were injured.

Racial violence created the impetus for the Double V campaign, officially supported by the National Association for the Advancement of Colored People (NAACP), which asserted black Americans' demands for the rights and privileges enjoyed by all other Americans — demands reinforced by the Allies' wartime ideology of freedom and democracy. While the NAACP focused on court challenges to segregation, a new organization founded in 1942, the Congress of Racial Equality, organized picketing and sit-ins against racially segregated restaurants and theaters. The Double V campaign greatly expanded membership in the NAACP but achieved only limited success against racial discrimination during the war.

Wartime Politics and the 1944 Election

Americans rallied around the war effort in unprecedented unity. Despite the consensus on war aims, the strains and stresses of the nation's massive wartime mobilization made it difficult for Roosevelt to maintain his political coalition. Whites often resented blacks who migrated to northern cities, took jobs, and made themselves at home. Many Americans complained about government price controls and the rationing of scarce goods while the war dragged on. Republicans seized the opportunity to roll back New Deal reforms. A conservative coalition of Republicans and southern Democrats succeeded in abolishing several New Deal agencies in 1942 and 1943, including the Works Progress Administration and the Civilian Conservation Corps.

In June 1944, Congress recognized the sacrifices made by millions of veterans, unanimously passing the landmark **GI Bill of Rights**, which gave GIs government funds for education, housing, and health care and provided loans to help them start businesses and buy homes. The GI Bill put the financial resources of the federal government behind the abstract goals of freedom and democracy for which veterans were fighting, and it empowered millions of GIs to better themselves and their families after the war.

After twelve turbulent years in the White House, Roosevelt was exhausted and gravely ill with heart disease, but he was determined to remain president until the war ended. His poor health made the selection of a vice presidential candidate unusually important. Convinced that many Americans had soured on liberal reform, Roosevelt chose Senator **Harry S. Truman** of Missouri as his running mate. A reliable party man from a southern border state, Truman satisfied urban Democratic leaders while not worrying white southerners who were nervous about challenges to racial segregation.

The Republicans, confident of a strong conservative upsurge in the nation, nominated as their presidential candidate the governor of New York, Thomas E. Dewey, who had made his reputation as a tough crime fighter. In the 1944 presidential campaign, Roosevelt's failing health alarmed many observers, but his frailty was outweighed by Americans' unwillingness to change presidents in the midst of the war and by Dewey's failure to persuade most voters that the New Deal was a creeping socialist menace. Voters gave Roosevelt a 53.5 percent majority, his narrowest presidential victory, ensuring his continued leadership as Dr. Win-the-War.

Reaction to the Holocaust

Since the 1930s, the Nazis had persecuted Jews in Germany and every German-occupied territory, causing many Jews to seek asylum beyond Hitler's reach. Roosevelt sympathized with the refugees' pleas for help, but he did not want to jeopardize his foreign policy or offend American voters. After Hitler's Anschluss in 1938, thousands of Austrian Jews sought to immigrate to the United States, but 82 percent of Americans opposed admitting them, and they were turned away. Roosevelt tried to persuade countries in Latin America and Africa to accept Jewish refugees, but only the Dominican Republic agreed to do so, eventually providing refuge for about 800 people.

In 1942, numerous reports reached the United States that Hitler was sending Jews, Gypsies, religious and political dissenters, homosexuals, and others to concentration camps, where old people, children, and others deemed too weak to work were systematically slaughtered and cremated, while the able-bodied were put to work at slave labor until they died of starvation and abuse. Despite such reports,

U.S. officials refused to grant asylum to Jewish refugees. Most Americans, including top officials, believed that reports of the killing camps were exaggerated. Only 152,000 of Europe's millions of Jews managed to gain refuge in the United States prior to America's entry into the war. Afterward, the number of refugees admitted dropped steadily, to just 2,400 by 1944.

Desperate to stem the killing, the World Jewish Congress appealed to the Allies to bomb the death camps and the railroad tracks leading to them in order to hamper the killing and block further shipments of victims. Intent on achieving military victory as soon as possible, the Allies repeatedly turned down such bombing requests, arguing that the air forces could not spare resources from their military missions.

The nightmare of the **Holocaust** was all too real. When Russian troops arrived at Auschwitz in Poland in January 1945, they found emaciated prisoners, skeletal corpses, gas chambers, pits filled with human ashes, and loot the Nazis had stripped from the dead, including hair, gold fillings, and false teeth. At last, the truth about the Holocaust began to be known beyond the Germans who had perpetrated and tolerated these atrocities and the men, women, and children who had succumbed to the genocide. By then, it was too late for the 11 million civilian victims — mostly Jews — of the Nazis' crimes against humanity.

REVIEW How did the war influence American society?

▶ Toward Unconditional Surrender

By February 1943, Soviet defenders had finally defeated the massive German offensive against **Stalingrad**, turning the tide of the war in Europe. After gargantuan sacrifices in fighting that had lasted for eighteen months and killed more than 95 percent of the Russian soldiers and noncommissioned officers engaged at Stalingrad, the Red Army forced Hitler's Wehrmacht to turn back toward the west. Stalin continued to urge Britain and the United States to open a second front in France, but that offensive was postponed for more than a year after the victory at Stalingrad. In the Pacific, the Allies had halted the expansion of the Japanese empire but now had the deadly task of dislodging Japanese defenders from the far-flung outposts they still occupied. Allied military planners devised a strategy to annihilate Axis resistance by taking advantage of America's industrial superiority.

From Bombing Raids to Berlin

While the Allied campaigns in North Africa and Italy were under way, British and American pilots flew bombing missions from England to German-occupied territories and to Germany itself as an airborne substitute for the delayed second front on the ground. During night raids, British bombers targeted general areas, hoping to hit civilians, create terror, and undermine morale. Beginning with Paul Tibbets's flight in August 1942, American pilots flew heavily armored B-17s from English airfields in daytime raids on industrial targets vital for the German war machine.

German air defenses took a fearsome toll on Allied pilots and aircraft. In 1943, two-thirds of American airmen did not survive to complete their twenty-five-mission tours of duty. In all, 85,000 American airmen were killed in the skies over Europe. Many others were shot down and held as prisoners of war. In February 1944, the arrival of America's durable and deadly P-51 Mustang fighter gave Allied bombers superior protection. The Mustangs slowly began to sweep the Luftwaffe from the skies, allowing bombers to penetrate deep into Germany and pound civilian and military targets around the clock.

In November 1943, Churchill, Roosevelt, and Stalin met in Teheran to discuss wartime strategy and the second front. Roosevelt conceded to Stalin that the Soviet Union would exercise de facto control of the eastern European countries that the Red Army occupied as it rolled back the still-potent German Wehrmacht. Stalin agreed to enter the war against Japan once Germany finally surrendered, in effect promising to open a second front in the Pacific theater. Roosevelt and Churchill promised that they would at last launch a massive second-front assault in northern France, code-named Overlord, scheduled for May 1944.

General Eisenhower was assigned overall command of Allied forces and stockpiled mountains of military supplies in England. German defenders, directed by General Erwin Rommel, fortified the cliffs and mined the beaches of north-western France. But the huge deployment of Hitler's armies in the east, which were trying to halt the Red Army's westward offensive, left too few German troops to stop the millions of Allied soldiers waiting to attack. More decisive, years of Allied air raids had decimated the German Luftwaffe, which could send aloft only 300 fighter planes against 12,000 Allied aircraft.

After frustrating delays caused by stormy weather, Eisenhower launched the largest amphibious assault in world history on **D Day**, June 6, 1944 (Map 25.2). Rough seas and deadly fire from German machine guns slowed the assault, but Allied soldiers finally succeeded in securing the beachhead. As naval officer Tracy Sugarman recalled, "What I thought were piles of cordwood [on the beach] I later learned were the bodies of 2,500 men killed by withering fire from the Nazi gun emplacements." An officer told his men, "The only people on this beach are the dead and those that are going to die — now let's get the hell out of here." And they did, finally surmounting the cliffs that loomed over the beach and destroying the German defenses. Sugarman reported that he and the other GIs who made the landing "were exhausted and we were exultant. We had survived D Day!"

Within a week, a flood of soldiers, tanks, and other military equipment swamped the Normandy beaches and propelled Allied forces toward Germany. On August 25, the Allies liberated Paris from four years of Nazi occupation. As the giant pincers of the Allied and Soviet armies closed on Germany in December 1944, Hitler ordered a counterattack to capture the Allies' essential supply port at Antwerp, Belgium. In the Battle of the Bulge (December 16, 1944, to January 31, 1945), as the Allies termed it, German forces drove fifty-five miles into Allied lines before being stopped at Bastogne. More than 70,000 Allied soldiers were killed,

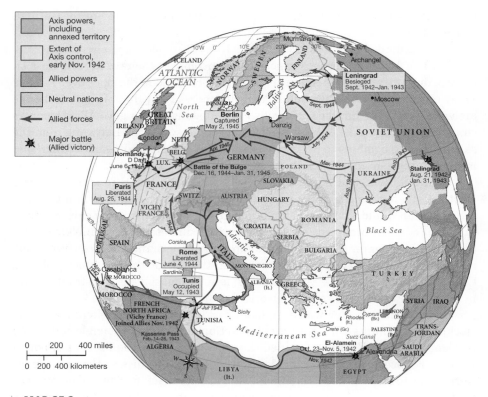

MAP 25.2
The European Theater of World War II, 1942–1945
The Russian reversal of the German offensive at Stalingrad and Leningrad, combined with Allied landings in North Africa and Normandy, trapped Germany in a closing vise of Allied armies on all sides.

including more Americans than in any other battle of the war. The Nazis lost more than 100,000 men and hundreds of tanks, fatally depleting Hitler's reserves.

In February 1945, while Allied armies relentlessly pushed German forces backward, Churchill, Stalin, and Roosevelt met secretly at the **Yalta Conference** (named for the Russian resort town where it was held) to discuss their plans for the postwar world. Seriously ill and noticeably frail, Roosevelt managed to secure Stalin's promise to permit votes of self-determination in the eastern European countries occupied by the Red Army. The Allies pledged to support Jiang Jieshi (Chiang Kai-shek) as the leader of China. The Soviet Union obtained a role in the postwar governments of Korea and Manchuria in exchange for entering the war against Japan after the defeat of Germany.

The "Big Three" also agreed on the creation of a new international peacekeeping organization, the **United Nations (UN)**. All nations would have a place in the UN General Assembly, but the Security Council would wield decisive power, and its permanent representatives from the Allied powers — China, France, Great Britain, the Soviet Union, and the United States — would possess a veto over

UN actions. The Senate ratified the United Nations Charter in July 1945 by a vote of 89 to 2, reflecting the triumph of internationalism during the nation's mobilization for war.

While Allied armies sped toward Berlin, Allied warplanes dropped more bombs after D Day than in all the previous European bombing raids combined. By April 11, Allied armies sweeping in from the west reached the banks of the Elbe River, the agreed-upon rendezvous with the Red Army, and paused while the Soviets smashed into Berlin. In three weeks of vicious house-to-house fighting, the Red Army captured Berlin on May 2. Hitler committed suicide on April 30, and the provisional German government surrendered unconditionally on May 7. The war in Europe was finally over, with the sacrifice of 135,576 American soldiers, nearly 250,000 British troops, and 9 million Russian combatants.

Roosevelt did not live to witness the end of the war. On April 12, while resting in Warm Springs, Georgia, he suffered a fatal stroke. Americans grieved for the man who had led them through years of depression and world war, and they worried about his untested successor, Vice President Harry Truman.

The Defeat of Japan

After the punishing defeats in the Coral Sea and at Midway, Japan had to fend off Allied naval and air attacks. In 1943, British and American forces, along with Indian and Chinese allies, launched an offensive against Japanese outposts in southern Asia, pushing through Burma and into China, where Jiang's armies continued to resist conquest. In the Pacific, Americans and their allies attacked Japanese strongholds by sea, air, and land, moving island by island toward the Japanese homeland (Map 25.3).

The island-hopping campaign began in August 1942, when American Marines landed on Guadalcanal in the southern Pacific. For the next six months, a savage battle raged for control of the strategic area. Finally, during the night of February 8, 1943, Japanese forces withdrew. The terrible losses on both sides indicated to the Marines how costly it would be to defeat Japan. After the battle, Joseph Steinbacher, a twenty-one-year-old from Alabama, sailed from San Francisco to New Guinea, where, he recalled, "all the cannon fodder waited to be assigned" to replace the killed and wounded.

In mid-1943, Allied forces launched offensives in New Guinea and the Solomon Islands that gradually secured the South Pacific. In the Central Pacific, amphibious forces conquered the Gilbert and Marshall islands, which served as forward bases for air assaults on the Japanese home islands. As the Allies attacked island after island, Japanese soldiers were ordered to refuse to surrender no matter how hopeless their plight. The fierce Japanese resistance spurred remorseless Allied bombing attacks on Japanese-occupied islands, followed by amphibious landings by Marines and grinding, inch-by-inch combat to root Japanese fighters out of bunkers and caves.

While the island-hopping campaign kept pressure on Japanese forces, the Allies invaded the Philippines in the fall of 1944. In the four-day **Battle of Leyte Gulf**, one of the greatest naval battles in world history, the American fleet crushed

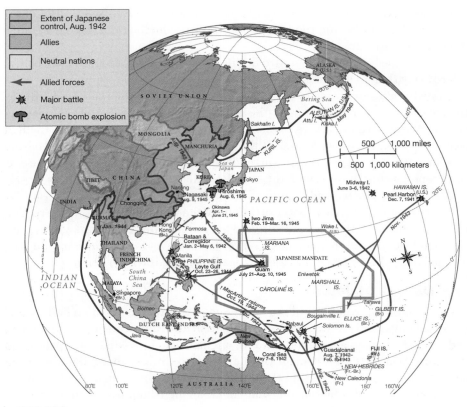

MAP 25.3
The Pacific Theater of World War II, 1941–1945
To drive the Japanese from their far-flung empire, the Allies launched two combined naval and military offensives — one to recapture the Philippines and then attack Japanese forces in China, the other to hop from island to island in the Central Pacific toward the Japanese mainland.

the Japanese armada, clearing the way for Allied victory in the Philippines. While the Philippine campaign was under way, American forces captured two crucial islands — Iwo Jima and Okinawa — from which they planned to launch an attack on the Japanese homeland. To defend Okinawa, Japanese leaders ordered thousands of suicide pilots, known as *kamikaze*, to crash their bomb-laden planes into Allied ships. But instead of destroying the American fleet, they demolished the last vestige of the Japanese air force. By June 1945, the Japanese were nearly defenseless on the sea and in the air. Still, their leaders prepared to fight to the death for their homeland.

Joseph Steinbacher and other GIs who had suffered "horrendous" casualties in the Philippines were now told by their commanding officer, "Men, in a few short months we are going to invade [Japan]. . . . We will be going in on the first wave and are expecting ninety percent casualties the first day. . . . For the few of us left alive the war will be over." Steinbacher later recalled his mental attitude at that moment: "I know that I am now a walking dead man and will not have a snowball's chance in hell of making it through the last great battle to conquer the home islands of Japan."

Atomic Warfare

In mid-July 1945, as Allied forces prepared for the final assault on Japan, American scientists tested a secret weapon at an isolated desert site near Los Alamos, New Mexico. In 1942, Roosevelt had authorized the top-secret **Manhattan Project** to find a way to convert nuclear energy into a superbomb before the Germans added such a weapon to their arsenal. More than 100,000 Americans, led by scientists, engineers, and military officers at Los Alamos, worked frantically to win the race for an atomic bomb. Germany surrendered two and a half months before the test on July 16, 1945, when scientists first witnessed an atomic explosion that sent a mushroom cloud of debris eight miles into the atmosphere. After watching the successful test of the bomb, J. Robert Oppenheimer, the head scientist at Los Alamos, remarked soberly, "Lots of boys not grown up yet will owe their life to it."

President Truman heard about the successful bomb test when he was in Potsdam, Germany, negotiating with Stalin about postwar issues. Truman realized that the atomic bomb could hasten the end of the war with Japan, perhaps before the Russians could attack the Japanese, as Stalin had pledged at Yalta. Within a few months after the defeat of Germany, Truman also recognized that the bomb gave the United States a devastating atomic monopoly that could be used to counter Soviet ambitions and advance American interests in the postwar world.

Truman saw no reason not to use the atomic bomb against Japan if doing so would save American lives. Despite numerous defeats, Japan still had more than 6 million reserves at home for a last-ditch defense against the anticipated Allied assault, which U.S. military advisers estimated would kill at least 250,000 Americans. But first he issued an ultimatum: Japan must surrender unconditionally or face utter ruin. When the Japanese failed to respond by the deadline, Truman ordered that an atomic bomb be dropped on a Japanese city not already heavily damaged by American raids. The bomb that Colonel Paul Tibbets and his crew released over **Hiroshima** on August 6 leveled the city and incinerated about 100,000 people. Three days later, after the Japanese government still refused to surrender, the second atomic bomb killed nearly as many civilians at **Nagasaki**. Robert Oppenheimer celebrated the bombings with other Los Alamos scientists responsible for creating the weapons by declaring that "his only regret was that we hadn't developed the bomb in time to have used it against the Germans."

With American assurance that the emperor could retain his throne after the Allies took over, Japan surrendered on August 14. On a troop ship departing from Europe for what would have been the final assault on Japan, an American soldier spoke for millions of others when he heard the wonderful news that the killing was over: "We are going to grow to adulthood after all."

While all Americans welcomed peace, Robert Oppenheimer and others worried about the consequences of unleashing atomic power. Shortly after the war, Oppenheimer warned: "We have made a thing, a most terrible weapon that has

Hiroshima

This photo shows part of Hiroshima shortly after the atomic bomb dropped from the *Enola Gay*, leveling the densely populated city. The destructive force unleashed by the atomic bomb included not only the heat and blast of the explosion itself but also the deadly radiation that maimed and killed Japanese civilians for years afterward. National Archives.

altered abruptly and profoundly the nature of the world . . . a thing that by all the standards of the world we grew up in is an evil thing." Almost every American, including Oppenheimer, believed that the "evil thing" had brought peace in 1945, but nobody knew what it would bring in the future, although everybody knew it would inevitably shape the world to come, as in fact it did.

REVIEW Why did Truman elect to use the atomic bomb against Japan?

▶ Conclusion: Allied Victory and America's Emergence as a Superpower

Shortly after Pearl Harbor, Hitler pronounced America "a decayed country . . . half Judaized, and the other half Negrified"; a country "where everything is built on the dollar" and bound to fall apart. American mobilization for World War II disproved Hitler's arrogant prophecy, as Paul Tibbets's historic flight dramatized. At a cost of 405,399 American lives, the nation united with its allies to crush the Axis aggressors into unconditional surrender. Almost all Americans believed they had won a "good war" against totalitarian evil. The Allies saved Asia and Europe from enslavement and finally halted the Nazis' genocidal campaign against Jews and many others whom the Nazis considered inferior. To secure human rights and protect the world against future wars, the Roosevelt administration took the lead in creating the United Nations.

Wartime production lifted the nation out of the Great Depression. The gross national product soared to four times what it had been when Roosevelt became president in 1933. Jobs in defense industries eliminated chronic unemployment, provided wages for millions of women workers and African American migrants from southern farms, and boosted Americans' prosperity. Ahead stretched the challenge of maintaining that prosperity while reintegrating millions of uniformed men and women.

By the end of the war, the United States had emerged as a global superpower. Wartime mobilization made the American economy the strongest in the world, buttressed by the military clout of the nation's nuclear monopoly. Although the war left much of the world a rubble-strewn wasteland, the American mainland had enjoyed immunity from attack. The Japanese occupation of China had left 50 million people without homes and millions more dead, maimed, and orphaned. The German offensive against the Soviet Union had killed more than 20 million Russian soldiers and civilians. Germany and Japan lay in ruins, their economies and societies as shattered as their military forces. But in the gruesome balance sheet of war, the Axis powers had inflicted far more grief, misery, and destruction on the global victims of their aggression than they had suffered in return.

As the dominant Western nation in the postwar world, the United States asserted its leadership in the reconstruction of Europe while occupying Japan and overseeing its economic and political recovery. America soon confronted new challenges in the tense aftermath of the war, as the Soviets seized political control of eastern Europe, a Communist revolution swept China, and national liberation movements emerged in the colonial empires of Britain and France. The forces unleashed by World War II would shape the United States and the rest of the world for decades to come. Before the ashes of World War II had cooled, America's wartime alliance with the Soviet Union fractured, igniting a Cold War between the superpowers. To resist global communism, the United States became, in effect, the policeman of the free world, repudiating the pre–World War II legacy of isolationism.

Reviewing Chapter 25

REVIEW QUESTIONS

1. Why did isolationism during the 1930s concern Roosevelt? (pp. 751–754)

2. How did Roosevelt attempt to balance American isolationism with the increasingly ominous international scene of the late 1930s? (pp. 755–759)

3. How did the Roosevelt administration mobilize the human and industrial resources necessary to fight a two-front war? (pp. 759–762)

4. How did the United States seek to counter the Japanese in the Pacific and the Germans in Europe? (pp. 762–765)

5. How did the war influence American society? (pp. 765–770)

6. Why did Truman elect to use the atomic bomb against Japan? (pp. 770–776)

MAKING CONNECTIONS

1. Did isolationism bolster or undermine national security and national economic interests? Discuss Roosevelt's evolving answer to this question as revealed in his administration's policies toward Europe. In your answer, consider how other constraints (such as politics, history, and ethics) affected administration policies.

2. World War II brought new prosperity to many Americans. Who benefited most from the wartime economy? What financial limitations did various members of society face, and why?

3. Japan's attack on Pearl Harbor plunged the United States into war with the Axis powers. How did the United States recover from this attack to play a decisive role in the Allies' victory? Discuss three American military or diplomatic actions and their contribution to the defeat of the Axis powers.

4. As the United States battled racist regimes abroad, the realities of discrimination at home came sharply into focus. How did minorities' contributions to the war effort as soldiers and laborers draw attention to these problems? What were the political implications of these developments? In your answer, consider both grassroots political action and federal policy.

LINKING TO THE PAST

1. How did America's involvement in World War II differ from its participation in World War I? Consider diplomacy, allies and enemies, wartime military and economic policies, and social and cultural changes. (See chapter 22.)

2. Why did World War II succeed in creating the full economic recovery that remained elusive during the New Deal? Consider specifically the scope and limits of New Deal economic reforms and how they changed, if at all, during World War II. (See chapter 24.)

TIMELINE 1935–1945

1935–1937
- Congress passes neutrality acts.

1936
- Nazi Germany occupies Rhineland.
- Italian armies conquer Ethiopia.
- Spanish civil war begins.

1937
- Japanese troops capture Nanjing.
- Roosevelt introduces his quarantine policy.

1938
- Hitler annexes Austria.

1939
- German troops occupy Czechoslovakia.
- Nazi-Soviet nonaggression pact.
- **September 1.** Germany's attack on Poland begins World War II.

1940
- Germany invades Denmark, Norway, France, Belgium, Luxembourg, and the Netherlands.
- British and French evacuate from Dunkirk.
- Vichy government installed in France.
- Battle of Britain.
- Tripartite Pact signed by Japan, Germany, and Italy.

1941
- Lend-Lease Act.
- **June.** Germany invades Soviet Union.
- **August.** Atlantic Charter issued.
- **December 7.** Japanese attack Pearl Harbor.

1942
- Roosevelt authorizes internment of Japanese Americans.
- Japan captures Philippines.
- Congress of Racial Equality founded.
- Battles of Coral Sea and Midway.
- Roosevelt authorizes Manhattan Project.
- **November.** U.S. forces invade North Africa.

1943
- Allied leaders demand unconditional surrender of Axis powers.
- Race riots in 47 cities.
- U.S. and British forces invade Sicily.

1944
- **June 6.** D Day.

1945
- **February.** Yalta Conference.
- **April 12.** Roosevelt dies; Vice President Harry Truman becomes president.
- **May 7.** Germany surrenders.
- **July.** United States joins United Nations.
- **August 6, 9.** United States drops atomic bombs on Hiroshima and Nagasaki.
- **August 14.** Japan surrenders, ending World War II.

▶ **FOR AN ONLINE BIBLIOGRAPHY, PRACTICE QUIZZES, WEB SITES, IMAGES, AND DOCUMENTS RELATED TO THIS CHAPTER,** see the Book Companion Site at **bedfordstmartins.com/roarkvalue**.

▶ **FOR DOCUMENTS RELATED TO THIS PERIOD,** see Michael Johnson, ed., *Reading the American Past*, Fifth Edition.

26

Cold War Politics in the Truman Years

1945–1953

HEADS TURNED WHEN CONGRESSWOMAN HELEN GAHAGAN DOUGLAS walked through the U.S. Capitol. When she served there from 1945 to 1951, she had no more than 10 female colleagues in the 435-member House of Representatives. Not only did she stand out as a woman in a thoroughly male institution, but she also drew attention as a strikingly attractive former Broadway star and opera singer. She served in Congress when the fate of the New Deal was up for grabs and the nation charted a dramatic new course in foreign policy.

Born in 1900, Helen Gahagan grew up in Brooklyn, New York. Drawn to the theater as a child, she defied her father and left Barnard College for the stage after her sophomore year. She quickly won fame on Broadway, starring in show after show until she fell in love with one of her leading men, Melvyn Douglas. They married in 1931, and she followed him to Hollywood, where he hoped to advance his movie career. During the 1930s, she bore two children and continued to appear onstage, but her career was on the wane.

Helen Gahagan Douglas admired Franklin D. Roosevelt's leadership during the depression, and both she and her husband were drawn into Hollywood's liberal political circles. The Douglases were shaken by the anti-Semitism and militarism that they witnessed on a visit to Germany in 1937, and they subsequently joined the Anti-Nazi League in California. But it was the plight of poor migrant farmworkers moving to California from Oklahoma and other states that pushed Helen Douglas into politics. Visiting migrant camps, she saw "faces stamped with poverty and despair," a "human calamity" that prompted her to head the John Steinbeck Committee to Aid Migratory Workers.

Helen Gahagan Douglas at the Democratic National Convention
Long accustomed as an actress to appearing before an audience, the congresswoman from California was a popular campaigner for the Democrats and a featured speaker at Democratic National Conventions. Her appeal, shown in this photo from the 1948 convention, sparked interest in her for higher office. *The Washington Post* called it the "first genuine boom in history for a woman for vice-president," but she made it clear that she was not in the running. © Bettmann/Corbis.

Douglas's work on behalf of migrant farmworkers connected her to the White House. She testified before Congress and became a friend of Eleanor Roosevelt and a campaigner for the president in 1940. In California, she rose fast in party politics, becoming vice chair of the state Democratic Party and head of the Women's Division. In 1944, she won election to Congress, representing not the posh Hollywood district where she lived, but the multiracial population of the Fourteenth Congressional District in downtown Los Angeles, which cemented her dedication to progressive politics.

Like many liberals devoted to Roosevelt, Douglas was devastated by his death and unsure of his successor, Harry S. Truman. "Who was Harry Truman anyway?" she asked. A compromise choice for the vice presidency, this "accidental president" lacked the charisma and political skills with which Roosevelt had transformed foreign and domestic policy, won four presidential elections, and forged a Democratic Party coalition that dominated national politics. Truman faced a resurgent Republican Party, which had gained strength in Congress, as well as revolts from within his own party. Besides confronting domestic problems that the New Deal had not solved — how to avoid another depression without the war to fuel the economy — Truman faced new international challenges that threatened to undermine the nation's security.

By 1947, a new term described the intense rivalry that had emerged between the United States and the Soviet Union: Cold War. Truman and his advisers became convinced that the Soviet Union posed a major threat to the United States, and they gradually shaped a policy to contain Soviet power wherever it threatened to spread. As a member of the House Foreign Affairs Committee, Douglas urged cooperation with the Soviet Union, and she initially opposed aid to Greece and Turkey, the first step in the new containment policy. Yet thereafter, Douglas was Truman's loyal ally, supporting the Marshall Plan, the creation of the North Atlantic Treaty Organization, and the war in Korea. The containment policy achieved its goals in Europe, but communism spread in Asia, and at home a wave of anti-Communist hysteria — a second Red scare — harmed many Americans and stifled dissent and debate.

Douglas's earlier links with leftist groups and her advocacy of civil rights, women's rights, and social welfare programs made her and other liberals easy targets for conservative politicians seeking to capitalize on anti-Communist fervor. When she ran for the U.S. Senate in 1950, she faced Republican Richard M. Nixon, who had gained national attention as a member of the House Un-American Activities Committee, which sought to expose Communists in government. Nixon's campaign labeled Douglas as "pink right down to her underwear" and telephoned thousands of homes with the anonymous message, "I think you should know Helen Douglas is a Communist." Nixon won a decisive victory but throughout his life carried the appellation Douglas gave him, "Tricky Dick." Douglas's political career ended in defeat, just as much of Truman's domestic agenda fell victim to the Red scare.

▶ From the Grand Alliance to Containment

With Japan's surrender in August 1945, Americans besieged the government for the return of their loved ones. Baby booties arrived at the White House with a note, "Please send my daddy home." Americans wanted to dismantle the large military establishment and expected the Allies, led by the United States and working within the United Nations, to cooperate in the management of international peace. Postwar realities quickly dashed these hopes. New threats arose as the wartime alliance forged by the United States, Great Britain, and the Soviet Union crumbled, and the United States began to focus on strategies for containing the spread of Soviet power around the globe.

The Cold War Begins

"The guys who came out of World War II were idealistic," reported Harold Russell, a young paratrooper who had lost both hands in a training accident. "We felt the day had come when the wars were all over." Public opinion polls echoed the veterans' confidence in the promise of peace. But these hopes were quickly dashed. Once the Allies had overcome a common enemy, the prewar mistrust and antagonism between the Soviet Union and the West resurfaced over their very different visions of the postwar world.

The Western Allies' delay in opening a second front in Western Europe aroused Soviet suspicions during the war. The Soviet Union made supreme wartime sacrifices, losing more than twenty million citizens and vast portions of its agricultural and industrial capacity. Soviet leader **Joseph Stalin** wanted to make Germany pay for Soviet economic reconstruction and to expand Soviet influence in the world. Above all, he wanted friendly governments on the Soviet Union's borders in Eastern Europe, especially in Poland, through which German troops had marched to attack Russia twice in the past twenty-five years. A ruthless dictator, Stalin also wanted to maintain his own power.

In contrast to the Soviet devastation, enemy fire had never touched the mainland of the United States, and its 405,000 dead amounted to just 2 percent of the Soviet loss. With a vastly expanded economy and a monopoly on atomic weapons, the United States was the most powerful nation on the planet. That sheer power, along with U.S. economic interests, policymakers' views about how the recent war might have been avoided, and a belief in the superiority of American institutions and intentions, all affected how American leaders approached the Soviet Union.

Fearing a return of the depression, U.S. officials believed that a healthy economy depended on opportunities abroad. American companies needed access to raw materials, markets for their goods, and security for their investments overseas. These needs could be met best in countries with similar economic and political systems, not in those where government controls interfered with the free flow of products and dollars. As President **Harry S. Truman** put it in 1947, "The American system can survive in America only if it becomes a world system." Yet leaders and citizens alike regarded their foreign policy not as a self-interested campaign to guarantee economic interests, but as the means to preserve national security and bring freedom, democracy, and capitalism to the rest of the world. Laura Briggs, a woman from Jerome, Idaho, spoke for many Americans who believed "it was our destiny to prove that we were the children of God and that our way was right for the world."

Recent history also shaped postwar foreign policy. Americans believed that World War II might have been avoided had Britain and France resisted rather than appeased Hitler's initial aggression. Navy Secretary James V. Forrestal argued against trying to "buy [the Soviets'] understanding and sympathy. We tried that

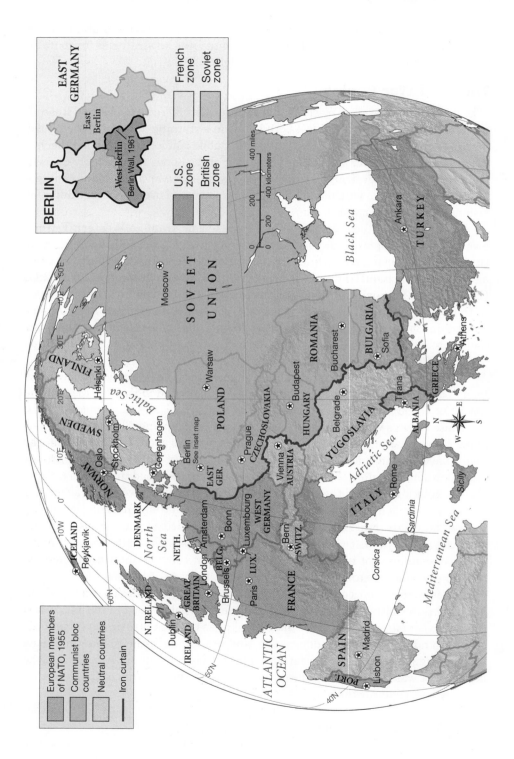

BERLIN

EAST GERMANY

East Berlin

West Berlin

Berlin Wall, 1961

French zone

Soviet zone

U.S. zone

British zone

400 miles

400 kilometers

200

200

0

0

European members of NATO, 1955

Communist bloc countries

Neutral countries

Iron curtain

SOVIET UNION

Moscow

FINLAND

Helsinki

SWEDEN

Stockholm

NORWAY

Oslo

Baltic Sea

Copenhagen

DENMARK

North Sea

NETH.

Amsterdam

London

GREAT BRITAIN

BELG.

Brussels

N. IRELAND

IRELAND

Dublin

ICELAND

Reykjavik

ATLANTIC OCEAN

Paris

LUX.

Luxembourg

FRANCE

WEST GERMANY

Bonn

Berlin
See inset map

EAST GER.

Prague

CZECHOSLOVAKIA

Vienna

AUSTRIA

Bern

SWITZ.

ITALY

Rome

Corsica

Sardinia

Sicily

SPAIN

Madrid

PORT.

Lisbon

Mediterranean Sea

Warsaw

POLAND

Budapest

HUNGARY

Belgrade

YUGOSLAVIA

Adriatic Sea

ROMANIA

Bucharest

BULGARIA

Sofia

Tirana

ALBANIA

GREECE

Athens

Black Sea

Ankara

TURKEY

10W

0

10E

20E

30E

40E 50E

60N

50N

40N

once with Hitler." This "appeasement" analogy would be invoked repeatedly when the United States faced challenges to the international status quo.

The man with ultimate responsibility for U.S. policy was a keen student of history but came to the White House with little international experience. Harry S. Truman anticipated Soviet-American cooperation, as long as the Soviet Union conformed to U.S. plans for the postwar world and restrained its expansionist impulses. Proud of his ability to make quick decisions, Truman determined to be firm with the Soviets, knowing well that America's nuclear monopoly gave him the upper hand.

Soviet and American interests clashed first in Eastern Europe. Stalin insisted that the Allies' wartime agreements gave him a free hand in the countries defeated or liberated by the Red Army, just as the United States was unilaterally reconstructing governments in Italy and Japan. The Soviet dictator used harsh methods to install Communist governments in neighboring Poland and Bulgaria. Elsewhere, the Soviets initially tolerated non-Communist governments in Hungary and Czechoslovakia. In the spring of 1946, Stalin responded to pressure from the West and removed troops from Iran on the Soviet Union's southwest border, allowing U.S. access to the rich oil fields there.

Stalin considered U.S. officials hypocritical in demanding democratic elections in Eastern Europe while supporting dictatorships friendly to U.S. interests in Latin America. The United States clung to its sphere of influence while opposing Soviet efforts to create its own. But the Western Allies were unwilling to match tough words with military force against the largest army in the world. They issued sharp protests but failed to prevent the Soviet Union from establishing satellite countries throughout Eastern Europe.

In 1946, the wartime Allies contended over Germany's future. Both sides wanted to demilitarize Germany, but U.S. policymakers sought rapid industrial revival there to foster European economic recovery and thus America's own long-term prosperity. By contrast, the Soviet Union wanted Germany weak both militarily and economically, and Stalin demanded heavy reparations from Germany to help rebuild the devastated Soviet economy. Unable to settle their differences, the Allies divided Germany. The Soviet Union installed a puppet Communist government in the eastern section, and Britain, France, and the United States began to unify their occupation zones, a process that eventually established the Federal Republic of Germany — West Germany — in 1949 (Map 26.1).

The war of words escalated early in 1946. Boasting of the superiority of the Soviet system, Stalin told a Moscow audience in February that capitalism inevitably produced war. One month later, Truman accompanied Winston Churchill to Westminster College in Fulton, Missouri, where the former prime minister

◀ **MAP 26.1**

The Division of Europe after World War II

The "iron curtain," a term coined by Winston Churchill to refer to the Soviet grip on Eastern and central Europe, divided the continent for nearly fifty years. Communist governments controlled the countries along the Soviet Union's western border. The only exception was Finland, which remained neutral.

denounced Soviet interference in Eastern and central Europe. "From Stettin in the Baltic to Trieste in the Adriatic, an **iron curtain** has descended across the Continent," Churchill said. Stalin saw Churchill's proposal for joint British-American action to combat Soviet aggression as "a call to war against the USSR."

In February 1946, **George F. Kennan**, a career diplomat and expert on Russia, wrote a comprehensive rationale for hard-line foreign policy. Downplaying the influence of Communist ideology in Soviet policy, he instead stressed the Soviets' insecurity and Stalin's need to maintain authority at home. These factors, he believed, prompted Stalin to exaggerate threats from abroad and motivated the Soviet government to try to "fill every nook and cranny available to it in the basin of world power." Kennan believed that the Soviet Union would retreat from its expansionist efforts if the United States would respond with "unalterable counterforce." He predicted that this approach, which came to be called **containment**, would eventually end in "either the breakup or the gradual mellowing of Soviet power." Kennan later expressed dismay when his ideas were used to justify what he considered indiscriminate American interventions wherever communism seemed likely to arise. Nonetheless, his analysis marked a critical turning point in the development of the **Cold War**, providing a compelling rationale for wielding U.S. power throughout the world.

Not all public figures accepted the toughening line. In September 1946, Secretary of Commerce Henry A. Wallace urged greater understanding of the Soviets' concerns about their nation's security, insisting that "we have no more business in the political affairs of Eastern Europe than Russia has in the political affairs of Latin America." State Department officials were furious at this challenge to the hardening of U.S. policy, and Truman fired Wallace.

The Truman Doctrine and the Marshall Plan

In 1947, the United States began to implement the doctrine of containment that would guide foreign policy for the next four decades. It was not an easy transition; Americans approved taking a hard line against the Soviet Union, but they wanted to keep their soldiers and tax dollars at home. In addition to selling containment to the public, Truman had to gain the support of a Republican-controlled Congress, which included a forceful bloc opposed to a strong U.S. presence in Europe.

Crises in two Mediterranean countries triggered the implementation of containment. In February 1947, Britain informed the United States that its crippled economy could no longer sustain military assistance either to Greece, where the autocratic government faced a leftist uprising, or to Turkey, which was trying to resist Soviet pressures. Truman promptly sought congressional authority to send the two countries military and economic missions, along with $400 million in aid. Meeting with congressional leaders, Undersecretary of State Dean Acheson predicted that if Greece and Turkey fell, communism would soon consume three-fourths of the world. After a stunned silence, Michigan senator Arthur Vandenberg, the Republican foreign policy leader and a recent convert from isolationism, warned that to get approval, Truman would have to "scare hell out of the country."

Truman did just that. Outlining what would later be called the "domino theory," he warned that if Greece fell to the rebels, "confusion and disorder might well spread throughout the entire Middle East" and then create instability in Europe. Failure to act, he said, "may endanger the peace of the world — and shall surely endanger the welfare of the nation." According to what came to be called the **Truman Doctrine**, the United States would not only resist Soviet military power but also "support free peoples who are resisting attempted sub-jugation by armed minorities or by outside pressures." The president failed to convince Helen Gahagan Douglas and some of her colleagues in Congress, who wanted the United States to work through the United Nations before acting unilaterally and who opposed propping up the authoritarian Greek government. But the administration won the day, setting a precedent for forty years of Cold War interventions that would aid any kind of government if the only alternative appeared to be communism. Said one World War II veteran in response to the Truman Doctrine, "I told my wife to dust off my uniform."

A much larger assistance program for Europe followed aid to Greece and Turkey. In May 1947, Acheson described a war-ravaged Western Europe, with "factories destroyed, fields impoverished, transportation systems wrecked, populations scattered and on the borderline of starvation." American citizens were sending generous amounts of private aid, but most Europeans were surviving on diets of 1,500 calories a day. Acheson insisted that Europe needed large-scale assistance to keep desperate citizens from turning to socialism or communism.

When British Foreign Secretary Ernest Bevin heard Secretary of State George C. Marshall propose the European Recovery Program, Bevin compared it to "a lifeline to a sinking man." Congress approved the measure, which came to be called the **Marshall Plan**, in March 1948, and over the next five years the United States spent $13 billion ($117 billion in 2010 dollars) to restore the economies of sixteen Western European nations. Marshall invited all European nations and the Soviet Union to cooperate in a request for aid, but as administration officials expected, the Soviets objected to the American terms of free trade and financial disclosure and ordered their Eastern European satellites likewise to reject the offer.

Humanitarian impulses as well as the goal of keeping Western Europe free of communism drove the adoption of this enormous aid program, one of the out-standing achievements of U.S. postwar foreign policy. But the Marshall Plan also helped boost the U.S. economy because the participating European nations spent most of the dollars to buy American products and Europe's economic recovery created new markets and opportunities for American investment. In addition, by insisting that the recipient nations work together, the Marshall Plan marked the first step toward the European Union.

While Congress had been debating the Marshall Plan, in February 1948 the Soviets staged a brutal coup and installed a Communist regime in Czechoslovakia, the last democracy left in Eastern Europe. Next, Stalin threatened Western access to Berlin. That former capital of Germany lay within Soviet-controlled

The Berlin Airlift
After the Soviet Union block-
aded land routes into West
Berlin in June 1948, the Western
allies used airplanes to deliver
food, fuel, and other necessities to Germans living there.
At the peak of the airlift, U.S.
or British planes landed every
three minutes twenty-four
hours a day. These children
may have been watching
for Air Force pilot Gail S.
Halvorsen, who, after meeting
hungry schoolchildren, began
to drop candy and gum as his
plane approached the landing
strip. The vulnerability of Germans like these helped to ease
hostile feelings that Americans
and other Europeans felt toward their former enemies.
Charles Fenno Jacobs/Hulton Archive/
Getty Images.

East Germany, but all four Allies jointly occupied Berlin, dividing it into separate administrative units. As the Western Allies moved to organize West Germany as a separate nation, the Soviets retaliated by blocking roads and rail lines between West Germany and the Western-held sections of Berlin, cutting off food, fuel, and other essentials to two million inhabitants.

"We stay in Berlin, period," Truman vowed. To avoid a confrontation with Soviet troops, for nearly a year U.S. and British pilots airlifted 2.3 million tons of goods to sustain the West Berliners. Stalin hesitated to shoot down these cargo planes, and in 1949 he lifted the blockade. The city was then divided into East Berlin, under Soviet control, and West Berlin, which became part of West Germany.

For many Americans, the **Berlin airlift** confirmed the wisdom of containment: When challenged, the Russians backed down, as George Kennan had predicted.

Building a National Security State

During the Truman years, advocates of the new containment policy fashioned a six-pronged defense strategy: (1) development of atomic weapons, (2) strengthening of traditional military power, (3) military alliances with other nations, (4) military and economic aid to friendly nations, (5) an espionage network and secret means to subvert Communist expansion, and (6) a propaganda offensive to win popular admiration for the United States around the world.

In September 1949, the United States lost its nuclear monopoly when the Soviet Union detonated its own atomic bomb. To keep the United States ahead, in January 1950 Truman approved the development of a **hydrogen bomb**, equivalent to five hundred atomic bombs. He rejected the counterarguments of several scientists who had worked on the atomic bomb and of George Kennan, who warned of an endless arms race. The "super bomb" was ready by 1954, but the U.S. advantage was brief. In November 1955, the Soviets exploded their own hydrogen bomb.

From the 1950s through the 1980s, deterrence formed the basis of American nuclear strategy. To deter the Soviet Union from attacking, the United States strove to maintain a nuclear force more powerful than the Soviets'. Because the Russians pursued a similar policy, the superpowers became locked in an ever-escalating nuclear weapons race. Albert Einstein, whose mathematical discoveries had laid the foundations for nuclear weapons, commented grimly on the enormous destructive force the superpowers now possessed. The war that came after World War III, he warned, would "be fought with sticks and stones."

Implementing the second component of its containment strategy, the United States beefed up its conventional military power to deter Soviet threats that might not warrant nuclear retaliation. The National Security Act of 1947 streamlined defense planning by uniting the military branches under a single secretary of defense and creating the National Security Council (NSC) to advise the president. During the Berlin crisis in 1948, Congress hiked military appropriations and enacted a peacetime draft. In addition, Congress granted permanent status to the women's military branches, though it limited their numbers and rank and banned them from combat. General Dwight D. Eisenhower had recognized the contributions women could make in such traditionally female jobs as office work and nursing, and he assured Congress that "after an enlistment or two women will ordinarily — and thank God — they will get married." With 1.5 million men and women in uniform in 1950, the military strength of the United States had quadrupled since the 1930s, and defense expenditures claimed one-third of the federal budget.

Collective security, the third prong of containment strategy, marked a sharp reversal of the nation's traditional foreign policy. In 1949, the United States joined Canada and Western European nations in its first peacetime military alliance, the **North Atlantic Treaty Organization (NATO)**, designed to counter a Soviet threat to Western Europe (see Map 26.1). For the first time in its history, the United States pledged to go to war if one of its allies was attacked.

The fourth element of defense strategy involved foreign assistance programs to strengthen friendly countries, such as aid to Greece and Turkey and the Marshall Plan. In addition, in 1949 Congress approved $1 billion of military aid to its NATO allies, and the government began economic assistance to nations in other parts of the world.

The fifth ingredient of containment improved the government's espionage capacities and ability to thwart communism through covert activities. The National Security Act of 1947 created the **Central Intelligence Agency (CIA)** not only to gather information but also to perform any activities "related to intelligence affecting the national security" that the NSC might authorize. Such functions included propaganda, sabotage, economic warfare, and support for "anti-communist elements in threatened countries of the free world." In 1948, secret CIA operations helped defeat Italy's Communist Party. Subsequently, CIA agents would intervene even more actively, helping to topple legitimate foreign governments and violating the rights of U.S. citizens.

Finally, the U.S. government sought, through cultural exchanges and propaganda, to win "hearts and minds" throughout the world. The government expanded the Voice of America, created during World War II to broadcast U.S. propaganda abroad. In addition, the State Department sent books, exhibits, jazz musicians, and other performers to foreign countries as "cultural ambassadors."

By 1950, the United States had abandoned age-old tenets of foreign policy. Isolationism and neutrality had given way to a peacetime military alliance and efforts to control events far beyond U.S. borders. Short of war, the United States could not stop the descent of the iron curtain, but it aggressively and successfully promoted economic recovery and a military shield for the rest of Europe.

Superpower Rivalry around the Globe

Efforts to implement containment moved beyond Europe. In Africa, Asia, and the Middle East, World War II accelerated a tide of national liberation movements against war-weakened imperial powers. By 1960, forty countries, with more than a quarter of the world's people, had won their independence. These nations, along with Latin America, came to be referred to collectively as the third world, a term denoting countries outside the Western (first world) and Soviet (second world) orbits that had not yet developed industrial economies.

Like Woodrow Wilson during World War I, Roosevelt and Truman promoted the ideal of self-determination. The United States granted independence to the Philippines in 1946, applauded the British withdrawal from India, and encouraged France to give up its control of Indochina. At the same time, both the United States and the Soviet Union cultivated governments in emerging nations that were friendly to their own interests. As the Cold War intensified, however, the ideal of self-determination gave way to American leaders' concern about the nature of the new governments supplanting the old empires. Policymakers wanted to preserve opportunities for American trade, and U.S. corporations coveted the vast oil reserves in the Middle East. The United States viewed its own Revolution as the best model for independence movements and expected newly emerging nations to create institutions in the American democratic and capitalist image.

Yet leaders of many liberation movements, impressed with Russia's rapid economic growth, adopted socialist or Communist ideas. Although few of these movements had formal ties with the Soviet Union, American leaders saw them as a threatening extension of Soviet power. Seeking to hold communism at bay by fostering economic development and political stability, the Truman administration initiated the Point IV Program in 1949, providing technical aid to developing nations.

Civil war raged in China, where the Communists, led by **Mao Zedong** (Mao Tse-tung), fought the official Nationalist government under Jiang Jieshi

(Chiang Kai-shek) as it sought to recover from the Japanese occupation. While the Communists gained support among the peasants for their land reforms and valiant stand against the Japanese, Jiang's corrupt and incompetent government alienated much of the population. Failing to promote negotiations between Jiang and Mao, the United States provided almost $3 billion in aid to the Nationalists during the civil war. Yet, recognizing the ineptness of Jiang's government, Truman and his advisers refused to divert further resources from Europe to China.

In October 1949, Mao established the People's Republic of China (PRC), and the Nationalists fled to the island of Taiwan. Fearing a U.S.-supported invasion to recapture China for the Nationalists, Mao signed a mutual defense treaty with the Soviet Union in which each nation pledged to defend the other in case of attack. The United States refused to recognize the PRC, blocked its admission to the United Nations, and supported the Nationalist government in Taiwan. Only a massive U.S. military commitment could have stopped the Chinese Communists, yet some Republicans charged that Truman and "pro-Communists in the State Department" had "lost" China. China became a political albatross for the Democrats, who resolved never again to be vulnerable to charges of being soft on communism.

With China in turmoil, the administration reconsidered its plans for postwar Japan. U.S. policy shifted to helping Japan rapidly reindustrialize and secure access to natural resources and markets in Asia. In a short time, the Japanese economy was flourishing, and the official military occupation ended when the two nations signed a peace treaty and a mutual security pact in September 1951. Like West Germany, Japan now sat squarely within the American orbit, ready to serve as an economic hub in a vital area.

The one place where Cold War considerations did not control American policy was Palestine. In 1943, then-senator Harry Truman spoke passionately about Nazi Germany's annihilation of the Jews, asserting, "This is not a Jewish problem, it is an American problem — and we must . . . face it squarely and honorably." As president, he made good on his words. Jews had been migrating to Palestine, their biblical homeland, since the nineteenth century, resulting in tension and hostilities with the Palestinian Arabs. After World War II, as hundreds of thousands of European Jews sought refuge and the creation of a national homeland in Palestine, fighting escalated into brutal terrorism on both sides.

Truman's foreign policy experts sought American-Arab friendship as a barrier against Soviet influence in the Middle East and as a means to secure access to Arabian oil. Uncharacteristically defying his advisers, the president responded instead to pleas from Jewish organizations, his moral commitment to Holocaust survivors, and his interest in the American Jewish vote for the 1948 election. When Jews in Palestine declared the state of Israel in May 1948, Truman quickly recognized the new country and made its defense the cornerstone of U.S. policy in the Middle East.

REVIEW Why did relations between the United States and the Soviet Union deteriorate after World War II?

▶ Truman and the Fair Deal at Home

Referring to the Civil War general who coined the phrase "War is hell," Truman said in December 1945, "Sherman was wrong. I'm telling you I find peace is hell." Challenged by crises abroad, Truman also faced shortages, strikes, inflation, and other problems as the economy shifted to peacetime production. At the same time, he tried to expand New Deal reform with his own **Fair Deal** agenda of initiatives in civil rights, housing, education, and health care — efforts hindered by the wave of anti-Communist hysteria sweeping the country. In sharp contrast to his success with Congress in foreign policy, Truman achieved but a modest slice of his domestic agenda.

Reconverting to a Peacetime Economy

Despite scarcities and deprivations during World War II, most Americans had enjoyed a higher standard of living than ever before. Economic experts as well as ordinary citizens worried about sustaining that standard and providing jobs for millions of returning soldiers. Truman wasted no time unveiling his plan, asking Congress to enact a twenty-one-point program of social and economic reforms. He wanted to maintain the government's power to regulate the economy while it adjusted to peacetime production, and he sought government programs to provide basic essentials such as housing and health care to those in need, programs that had been on the drawing board during the New Deal. "Not even President Roosevelt ever asked for as much at one sitting," exploded Republican leader Joseph W. Martin Jr.

Congress approved one of Truman's key proposals — full-employment legislation — but even that was watered down. The Employment Act of 1946 invested the federal government with the responsibility "to promote maximum employment, production, and purchasing power," thereby formalizing what had been implicit in Roosevelt's antidepression measures — government's responsibility for maintaining a healthy economy. The law created the Council of Economic Advisors to assist the president, but it authorized no new powers to translate the government's obligation into effective action.

Inflation, not unemployment, turned out to be the most severe problem in the early postwar years. Consumers had $30 billion in wartime savings to spend, but shortages of meat, automobiles, housing, and other items persisted. Until industry could convert fully to civilian production and make more goods available, consumer demand would continue to drive up prices. With a basket of groceries on her arm to dramatize rising costs, Helen Gahagan Douglas urged Congress to support Truman's efforts to maintain price and rent controls. Those efforts fell, however, to pressures from business groups and others determined to trim government powers.

Labor relations were another thorn in Truman's side. Organized labor survived the war stronger than ever, its 14.5 million members making up 35 percent of the civilian workforce. Yet union members feared the erosion of wartime gains and launched an intense struggle to preserve them. Turning to the weapon they had set aside during the war, 5 million workers went out on strike in 1946, affecting nearly every major industry. Workers saw corporate executives profiting at their expense. Shortly before voting to strike, a former Marine and his coworkers calculated that a lavish party given by a company executive had cost more than they would earn in a whole year at the steel mill. "That sort of stuff made us realize, hell we had to bite the bullet. . . . The bosses sure didn't give a damn for us." Although most Americans approved of unions in principle, they became fed up with strikes, blamed unions for shortages and rising prices, and called for government restrictions on organized labor. When the wave of strikes subsided, workers had won wage increases of about 20 percent, but the loss of overtime pay along with rising prices left their purchasing power only slightly higher than in 1942.

Women workers fared even worse. Polls indicated that as many as 68 to 85 percent wanted to keep their wartime jobs, but most who remained in the work-force had to settle for relatively low-paying jobs in light industry or the service sector. Displaced from her shipyard work, Marie Schreiber took a cashier's job, lamenting, "You were back to women's wages, you know . . . practically in half." With the backing of women's organizations and union women, Congresswoman Douglas sponsored bills to require equal pay for equal work, to provide child care for employed mothers, and to create a government commission to study the sta-tus of women. But at a time when women were viewed primarily as wives and mothers and a strong current of opinion resisted further expansion of federal powers, these initiatives got nowhere.

Women's Postwar Future

This photograph headed a *New York Times Magazine* article in June 1946. The article discussed the needs of women workers, stressing their right to work and to receive equal pay, but it also assumed that women would all but vanish from heavy manufacturing. Ellen Kaiper Collection, Oakland.

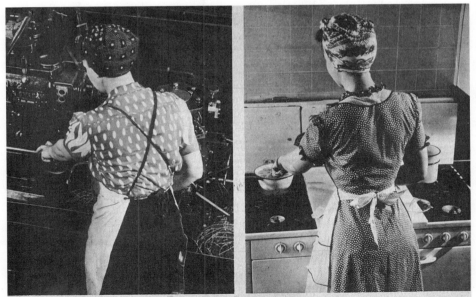

Sisters under the apron—Yesterday's war worker becomes today's housewife.

What's Become of Rosie the Riveter?

By 1947, the economy had stabilized, avoiding the postwar depression that so many had feared. Wartime profits enabled businesses to expand. Consumers could now spend their wartime savings on houses, cars, and appliances that had lain beyond their reach during the depression and war. Defense spending and foreign aid that enabled war-stricken countries to purchase American products also stimulated the economy. A soaring birthrate further sustained consumer demand. Although prosperity was far from universal, the United States entered into a remarkable economic boom that lasted through the 1960s (as discussed in chapter 27).

Another economic boost came from the only large welfare measure passed after the New Deal. The **Servicemen's Readjustment Act (GI Bill)**, enacted in 1944, offered 16 million veterans job training and education; unemployment compensation while they looked for jobs; and low-interest loans to purchase homes, farms, and small businesses. By 1948, some 1.3 million veterans had bought houses with government loans. Helping 2.2 million ex-soldiers attend college, the subsidies sparked a boom in higher education. A drugstore clerk before his military service, Don Condren was able to get an engineering degree and buy his first house. "I think the GI Bill gave the whole country an upward boost economically," he said.

Condren overlooked the disparate ways in which the GI Bill operated. As wives and daughters of veterans, women did benefit indirectly from the GI subsidies. Yet because women had filled just a small proportion of military slots during the war, most women did not qualify for the employment and educational preferences available to some 15 million men. As a result, while women's enrollments increased after the war, their share of college degrees plunged below the prewar level.

Like key New Deal programs such as unemployment insurance and aid to mothers with dependent children, GI programs were administered at the state and local levels, which especially in the South routinely discriminated against African Americans. Southern universities remained segregated, and the small historically black colleges could not accommodate all who wanted to attend. Black veterans who sought jobs for which the military had trained them were shuttled into menial labor. One decorated veteran said that the GI Bill "draws no color line," yet "my color bars me from most decent jobs, and if, instead of accepting menial work, I collect my $20 a week readjustment allowance, I am classified as a 'lazy nigger.'" Thousands of black veterans did benefit from the GI Bill, but it did not help all ex-soldiers equally.

Blacks and Mexican Americans Push for Their Civil Rights

"I spent four years in the army to free a bunch of Frenchmen and Dutchmen," an African American corporal declared, "and I'm hanged if I'm going to let the Alabama version of the Germans kick me around when I get home." Black veterans as well as civilians resolved that the return to peace would not be a return to the racial injustices of prewar America. Their political clout had grown with the migration of two million African Americans to northern and western cities, where they could vote and participate in ongoing struggles to end discrimination in housing and education. Pursuing civil rights through the courts and Congress, the National Association for the Advancement of Colored People (NAACP) counted half a million members.

In the postwar years, individual African Americans broke through the color barrier, achieving several "firsts." Jackie Robinson integrated major league baseball, playing for the Brooklyn Dodgers and braving abuse from fans and players to win the Rookie of the Year Award in 1947. In 1950, Ralph J. Bunche received the Nobel Peace Prize for his United Nations work, and Gwendolyn Brooks won the Pulitzer Prize for poetry. Charlie "Bird" Parker, Ella Fitzgerald, and a host of other black musicians were hugely popular across racial lines.

Still, for most African Americans little had changed, especially in the South, where most blacks still lived and where violence greeted their attempts to assert their rights. Armed white men turned back Medgar Evers (who would become a key civil rights leader in the 1960s) and four other veterans trying to vote in Mississippi. A mob lynched Isaac Nixon for voting in Georgia, and an all-white jury acquitted the men accused of his murder. In the South, political leaders and local vigilantes routinely intimidated potential black voters with threats of violence and warnings that they could lose their livelihoods.

The Cold War heightened American leaders' sensitivity to racial issues, as the superpowers vied for the allegiance of newly independent nations with non-white populations. Soviet propaganda repeatedly highlighted racial injustice in the United States. Republican senator Henry Cabot Lodge called race relations "our Achilles' heel before the world," while Secretary of State Dean Acheson noted that systematic segregation and discrimination endangered "our moral leadership of the free and democratic nations of the world."

"My very stomach turned over when I learned that Negro soldiers just back from overseas were being dumped out of army trucks in Mississippi and beaten," wrote Truman. Despite his need for southern white votes, Truman spoke more boldly on civil rights than any previous president had, thus appealing more to northern black and liberal voters. In 1946, he created the President's Committee on Civil Rights, and in February 1948 he asked Congress to enact the committee's recommendations. The first president to address the NAACP, Truman asserted that all Americans should have equal rights to housing, education, employment, and the ballot.

As with much of his domestic program, the president failed to act aggressively on his bold words. Congress rejected Truman's proposals for national civil rights legislation, although some northern and western states did pass laws against discrimination in employment and public accommodations. Running for reelection in 1948, Truman issued an executive order to desegregate the armed services, but it lay unimplemented until the Korean War, when the cost of segregation to military efficiency became apparent. Army officers gradually integrated their ranks, and by 1953, 95 percent of all African Americans served in mixed units. Despite the gap between Truman's words and what his administration actually accomplished, desegregation of the military and the administration's support of civil rights cases in the Supreme Court contributed to far-reaching changes, while his Committee on Civil Rights set an agenda for years to come.

Although discussion of race and civil rights usually focused on African Americans, Mexican Americans endured similar injustices. In 1929, they had formed the League

Dr. Héctor P. García

Héctor García, shown here with patients, came from Mexico to the United States as a small boy and, like all of his five siblings, became a doctor. While leading the G.I. Forum and advocating for Mexican-American rights, García treated all who needed his medical care regardless of whether they could pay for it. An associate referred to García, who also became active in politics, as "a man who in the space of one week delivers 20 babies, 20 speeches, and 20 thousand votes." He was appointed as an alternate U.S. Ambassador to the United Nations and served on the U.S. Commission on Civil Rights. Héctor P. García Papers, Special Collections & Archives, Texas A&M. University, Corpus Christi, Bell Library.

of United Latin-American Citizens (LULAC) to combat discrimination and segregation in the Southwest. Like black soldiers after World War II, Mexican American veterans believed, as one of them insisted, that "we had earned our credentials as American citizens. We had paid our dues." Problems with getting their veterans' benefits spurred the formation of a new organization in 1948 in Corpus Christi, Texas — the **American GI Forum**. Dr. **Héctor Peréz García**, president of the local LULAC chapter and a combat surgeon who had received the Bronze Star, led the GI Forum, which became a key national organization for battling discrimination against Latinos and electing sympathetic officials.

"Education is our freedom," read the GI Forum's motto, yet Mexican American children were routinely segregated in public schools. In 1945, with the help of LULAC, parents filed a class action suit in southern California, challenging several school districts that barred their children from white schools. In the resulting decision, *Mendez v. Westminster* (1947), a federal court for the first time struck down school segregation. NAACP lawyer Thurgood Marshall filed a supporting brief in the case, which foreshadowed the landmark *Brown* decision in

1954 (as discussed in chapter 27). Efforts to gain equal education, along with challenges to discrimination in employment and campaigns for political representation, demonstrated a growing mobilization of Mexican Americans in the Southwest.

The Fair Deal Flounders

Republicans capitalized on public frustrations with strikes and shortages in the 1946 congressional election, accusing the administration of "confusion, corruption, and communism." Helen Gahagan Douglas hung on to her seat, but the Republicans captured control of Congress for the first time in fourteen years. Many had campaigned against New Deal "bureaucracy" and "radicalism" in 1946, and in the Eightieth Congress they succeeded in weakening some reform programs and enacting tax cuts favoring higher-income groups.

Organized labor took the most severe blow when Congress passed the **Taft-Hartley Act** over Truman's veto in 1947. Called a "slave labor" law by unions, the measure reduced the power of organized labor and made it more difficult to organize workers. For example, states could now pass "right-to-work" laws, which banned the practice of requiring all workers to join a union once a majority had voted for it. Many states, especially in the South and West, rushed to enact such laws, encouraging industries to relocate there. Taft-Hartley maintained the New Deal principle of government protection for collective bargaining, but it put the government more squarely between labor and management.

In the 1948 elections, Truman faced not only a resurgent Republican Party headed by New York governor Thomas E. Dewey but also two revolts within his own party. On the left, Henry A. Wallace, whose foreign policy views had cost him his cabinet seat, led the new Progressive Party. On the right, South Carolina governor J. Strom Thurmond headed the States' Rights Party — the Dixiecrats — formed by southern Democrats who had walked out of the 1948 Democratic Party convention when it passed a liberal civil rights plank.

Almost alone in believing he could win, Truman crisscrossed the country by train, answering supporters' cries of "Give 'em hell, Harry." So bleak were Truman's prospects that on election night the *Chicago Daily Tribune* printed its next day's issue with the headline "Dewey Defeats Truman." But even though the Dixiecrats won four southern states, Truman took 303 electoral votes to Dewey's 189, and his party regained control of Congress. His unexpected victory attested to the broad support for his foreign policy and the enduring popularity of New Deal reform.

While the major New Deal programs survived Republican attacks, Truman failed to enact his Fair Deal agenda. Congress made modest improvements in Social Security and raised the minimum wage, but it passed only one significant reform measure. Enacted with significant Republican support, the **Housing Act of 1949** authorized 810,000 units of government-constructed housing over the next six years and represented a landmark commitment by the government to address the housing needs of the poor. Yet it fell far short of actual need — just 61,000 units had been built when Truman left office — and slum clearance frequently displaced the poor without providing decent alternatives.

With southern Democrats posing a primary obstacle, Congress rejected Truman's proposals for civil rights, a powerful medical lobby blocked plans for a universal health care program based on the Social Security model, and conflicts over race and religion thwarted federal aid to education. Truman's efforts to revise immigration policy were mixed. The McCarran-Walter Act of 1952 ended the outright ban on immigration and citizenship for Japanese and other Asians, but it also authorized the government to bar suspected Communists and homosexuals and maintained the discriminatory quota system established in the 1920s. The president denounced that provision as "unworthy of our traditions and our ideals," but Congress overrode his veto.

Truman's concentration on foreign policy rather than domestic proposals contributed to the failure of his Fair Deal. Moreover, by late 1950, the Korean War embroiled the president in controversy and depleted his power as a legislative leader (see pages 800–805). Truman's failure to make good on his domestic proposals and expand the framework of the welfare state begun by Roosevelt set the United States apart from most European nations. By the 1950s, most other industrial democracies had in place comprehensive health, housing, and employment security programs to underwrite the material well-being of their populations.

The Domestic Chill: McCarthyism

Truman's domestic program also suffered from a wave of anticommunism that weakened liberal and leftist forces. "Red-baiting" (attempts to discredit individuals or ideas by associating them with communism) and official retaliation against leftist critics of the government had flourished during the Red scare at the end of World War I (see chapter 22). A second Red scare followed World War II, born of partisan political maneuvering, the collapse of the Soviet-American alliance, setbacks in U.S. foreign policy, and disclosures of Soviet espionage in the United States, Canada, and Great Britain.

Republicans who had attacked the New Deal as a plot of radicals now jumped on such Cold War events as the Soviet takeover of Eastern Europe and the Communist triumph in China to accuse Democrats of fostering internal subversion. Wisconsin senator **Joseph R. McCarthy** avowed that "the Communists within our borders have been more responsible for the success of Communism abroad than Soviet Russia." McCarthy's charges — such as the allegation that retired general George C. Marshall belonged to a Communist conspiracy — were reckless and often ludicrous, but the press covered him avidly, and McCarthyism became a term synonymous with the anti-Communist crusade.

Revelations of Soviet espionage gave some credibility to fears of internal communism. For example, a number of ex-Communists, including Whittaker Chambers and Elizabeth Bentley, testified that they and others had provided secret documents to the Soviets. Chambers asserted that Alger Hiss, a former New Dealer who had served in the wartime State Department, had belonged to a secret Communist cell. Although Hiss denied the charges and prominent Democrats defended him, in 1950 a jury convicted him of lying to congressional investigators about his connections with Chambers, and he spent four years in prison. Most alarming of all, in 1950 a British physicist working on the atomic bomb project confessed that he was a spy and implicated several Americans, including Ethel and Julius Rosenberg. The Rosenbergs pleaded not guilty but were convicted of conspiracy to commit espionage and electrocuted in 1953, the only Americans to be executed for treason during the Red scare.

Records opened in the 1990s showed that the Soviet Union did receive secret documents from Americans that probably hastened its development of nuclear weapons by a year or two. Yet the vast majority of individuals hunted down in the Red scare had done nothing more than at one time joining the Communist Party, associating with Communists, or supporting radical causes. And most of those activities had taken place long before the Cold War had made the Soviet Union an enemy. Investigators often cared little for such distinctions, however.

The hunt for subversives was conducted by both Congress and the executive branch. Stung by charges of communism in the 1946 midterm elections, Truman issued Executive Order 9835 in March 1947, establishing loyalty review boards to investigate every federal employee. "A nightmare from which there [was] no awakening" was how State Department employee Esther Brunauer described it when she and her husband, a chemist in the navy, both lost their jobs because he had joined a Communist youth organization in the 1920s and associated with suspected radicals. Government investigators routinely violated the Bill of Rights by allowing anonymous informers to make charges and by placing the burden of proof on the accused. More than two thousand civil service employees lost their jobs, and another ten thousand resigned as **Truman's loyalty program** continued into the mid-1950s. Hundreds of homosexuals resigned or were fired over charges of "sexual perversion," which anti-Communist crusaders said could subject them to blackmail. Years later, Truman admitted that the loyalty program had been a mistake.

Congressional committees, such as the **House Un-American Activities Committee (HUAC)**, also investigated individuals' past and present political associations. When those under scrutiny refused to name names, investigators charged that silence was tantamount to confession, and these "unfriendly witnesses" lost their jobs and suffered public ostracism. In 1947, HUAC investigated radical activity in Hollywood. Singer Frank Sinatra protested, wondering if someone called for "a square deal for the underdog, will they call you a Commie? . . . Are they going to scare us into silence?" Some actors and directors cooperated, but ten refused, citing their First Amendment rights. The "Hollywood Ten" served jail sentences for contempt of Congress — a punishment that Helen Gahagan Douglas fought — and then found themselves blacklisted in the movie industry.

The Truman administration went after the Communist Party directly, prosecuting its leaders under the Smith Act of 1940, which made it a crime to "advocate the overthrow and destruction of the Government of the United States by force and violence." Although civil libertarians argued that the guilty verdicts violated First Amendment rights of freedom of speech, press, and association, the Supreme Court ruled in 1951 (*Dennis v. United States*) that the Communist threat overrode constitutional guarantees.

The domestic Cold War spread beyond the nation's capital. State and local governments investigated citizens, demanded loyalty oaths, fired employees suspected of disloyalty, banned books from public libraries, and more. College professors and public school teachers lost their jobs in New York, California, and elsewhere. Because the Communist Party had helped organize unions and championed racial justice, labor and civil rights activists fell prey to McCarthyism as well. African American activist Jack O'Dell remembered that segregationists pinned the tag of Communist on "anybody who supported the right of blacks to have civil rights."

McCarthyism caused untold harm to thousands of innocent individuals. Anti-Communist crusaders humiliated and discredited law-abiding citizens, hounded them from their jobs, and in some cases even sent them to prison. Throughout the nearly ten years of the second Red scare, fundamental constitutional rights of freedom of speech and association were violated, the expression of dissenting ideas was stifled, and unpopular causes were removed from public contemplation.

REVIEW Why did Truman have limited success in implementing his domestic agenda?

▶ The Cold War Becomes Hot: Korea

The Cold War erupted into a shooting war in June 1950 when troops from Communist North Korea invaded South Korea. For the first time, Americans went into battle to implement containment. Confirming the global reach of the Truman Doctrine, U.S. involvement in Korea also marked the militarization of American foreign policy. The United States, in concert with the United Nations, ultimately held the line in Korea, but at a great cost in lives, dollars, and domestic unity.

Korea and the Military Implementation of Containment

The war grew out of the artificial division of Korea after World War II. Having expelled the Japanese, who had controlled Korea since 1904, the United States and the Soviet Union created two occupation zones separated by the thirty-eighth parallel (Map 26.2). With Moscow and Washington unable to agree on a unification plan, the United Nations sponsored elections in South Korea in July 1948. The American-favored candidate, Syngman Rhee, was elected president, and the United States withdrew most of its troops. In the fall of 1948, the Soviets established the People's Republic of North Korea under Kim Il-sung and also withdrew. Although doubting that Rhee's repressive government could sustain popular support, U.S. officials appreciated his staunch anticommunism and provided small amounts of economic and military aid to South Korea.

Insurgencies of workers and peasants against factory owners, landlords, and the Rhee government claimed 100,000 lives between 1946 and mid-1950, and skirmishes between North and South Korean troops at the thirty-eighth parallel began in 1948. Then, in June 1950, 90,000 North Koreans swept into South Korea. Truman's advisers assumed that the Soviet Union or China had instigated the

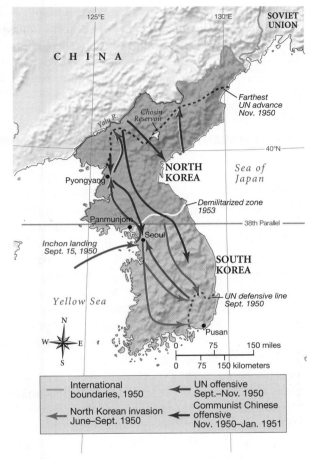

Map 26.2 The Korean War, 1950–1953
Although each side had plunged deep into enemy territory, the war ended in 1953 with the dividing line between North and South Korea nearly where it had been before the fighting began.

attack, but later revelations pinned the initiative on Kim Il-sung, who won only reluctant acquiescence from China and Russia. Truman wasted little time deciding to intervene, viewing Korea as "the Greece of the Far East." With the Soviet Union boycotting the UN Security Council to protest the council's refusal to seat a representative from the People's Republic of China, the United States obtained UN sponsorship of a collective effort to repel the attack. Authorized to appoint a commander for the UN force, Truman named General **Douglas MacArthur**, World War II hero and head of the postwar occupation of Japan.

Sixteen nations, including many NATO allies, sent troops to Korea, but the United States furnished most of the personnel and weapons, deploying almost 1.8 million troops and dictating military strategy. By dispatching troops without asking Congress for a declaration of war, Truman violated the spirit if not the letter of the Constitution and contributed to the expansion of executive power that would characterize the Cold War. Congress did appropriate funds to fight the **Korean War**, but the absence of a congressional declaration of war enabled the president's political opponents to call it "Truman's war" when the military situation worsened.

The first American soldiers rushed to Korea unprepared and ill equipped. One regimental commander grumbled that troops had "spent a lot of time listening to lectures on the differences between communism and Americanism and not enough time crawling on their bellies on maneuvers [or learning] how to clear a machine gun when it jams." U.S. forces suffered severe defeats in the first three months of the war. The North Koreans took the capital of Seoul and drove deep into South Korea, forcing UN troops to retreat to Pusan. Then, in September 1950, General MacArthur launched a bold counteroffensive at Inchon, 180 miles behind North Korean lines. The attack succeeded, and by October UN and South Korean forces had retaken Seoul and pushed the North Koreans back to the thirty-eighth parallel. These victories posed the momentous decision of whether to invade North Korea and seek to unify the country.

From Containment to Rollback to Containment

"Troops could not be expected . . . to march up to a surveyor's line and stop," remarked Secretary of State Dean Acheson, reflecting popular and official support for transforming the military objective from containment to elimination of the enemy and unification of Korea. Thus, for the only time during the Cold War, the United States tried to roll back communism by force. With UN approval, on September 27, 1950, Truman authorized MacArthur to cross the thirty-eighth parallel. Concerned about possible intervention by China or the Soviet Union, the president directed him to keep UN troops away from the Korean-Chinese border. Disregarding the order, MacArthur sent UN forces to within forty miles of China, whereupon 300,000 Chinese soldiers crossed the Yalu River into Korea. With Chinese help, the North Koreans recaptured Seoul.

After three months of grueling battle, UN forces fought their way back to the thirty-eighth parallel. At that point, Truman decided to seek a negotiated settlement. MacArthur was furious when the goal of the war reverted to containment, which to him represented defeat. In comments to the press and letters to sympathetic members of Congress, the general challenged both the president's authority to conduct foreign policy and the principle of civilian control of the military. Fed up with MacArthur's insubordination, Truman relieved him of command in April 1951. Many Americans, however, sided with MacArthur. "Quite an explosion. . . . Letters of abuse by the dozens," Truman recorded in his diary. The adulation for MacArthur reflected Americans' frustration with containment. Why should Americans die simply to preserve the status quo? Why not destroy the enemy once and for all? In siding with MacArthur, Americans assumed that the United States was all-powerful and that stalemate in Korea resulted from the government's ineptitude or willingness to shelter subversives.

When Congress investigated MacArthur's dismissal, all of the top military leaders supported the president. According to the chairman of the Joint Chiefs of Staff, MacArthur wanted to wage "the wrong war, at the wrong place, at the wrong time, with the wrong enemy." Yet Truman never recovered from the political fallout. Nor was he able to end the war. Negotiations began in July 1951, but peace talks dragged on for two more years while twelve thousand more U.S. soldiers died.

Korea, Communism, and the 1952 Election

Popular discontent with President Truman's war boosted Republican candidates in the 1952 election. The Republicans' presidential nominee, General **Dwight D. Eisenhower**, had emerged from World War II with immense popularity. Reared in modest circumstances in Abilene, Kansas, Eisenhower attended West Point and rose steadily through the army ranks. As supreme commander in Europe, he won widespread acclaim for leading the Allied armies to victory over Germany. After the war, he served as army chief of staff, and in 1950 Truman appointed Eisenhower the first supreme commander of NATO forces.

Both Republicans and Democrats had courted Eisenhower for the presidency in 1948. Although Eisenhower believed that professional soldiers should stay out of politics, he found compelling reasons to run in 1952. He largely agreed with Democratic foreign policy, but he deplored the Democrats' propensity to solve domestic problems with costly new federal programs. He equally disliked the foreign policy views of the leading Republican presidential contender, Senator Robert A. Taft, an opponent of NATO, who sought to cut defense spending and limit the nation's involvement abroad. Eisenhower decided to run both to stop Taft and the conservative wing of the Republican Party and to turn the Democrats out of the White House.

Eisenhower defeated Taft for the nomination, but the old guard prevailed on the party platform. It excoriated containment as "negative, futile, and immoral" and charged the Truman administration with shielding "traitors to the Nation in high places." By choosing thirty-nine-year-old Senator **Richard M. Nixon** for his running mate, Eisenhower helped to appease the right wing of the party and ensured that anticommunism would be a major theme of the campaign.

Richard Milhous Nixon grew up in southern California, worked his way through college and law school, served in the navy, and briefly practiced law. In 1946, he helped the Republicans recapture Congress by defeating a liberal incumbent for a seat in the House of Representatives. Nixon quickly made a name for himself as a member of HUAC (see page 799) and a key anti-Communist, moving to the Senate with his victory over Helen Gahagan Douglas in 1950.

With his public approval ratings plummeting, Truman decided not to run for reelection. The Democrats nominated Adlai E. Stevenson, the popular governor of Illinois, who was acceptable to both liberals and southerners. Stevenson could not escape the domestic fallout from the Korean War, however; nor could he match the widespread appeal of Eisenhower. The Republican campaign stumbled just once, over the last item of its "Korea, Communism, and Corruption" policy. When the press reported that Nixon had accepted money from a private political fund supported by wealthy Californians, Democrats jumped to the attack, even though such gifts were common and legal. While Eisenhower deliberated about whether to dump Nixon from the ticket, Nixon saved himself by making an emotional nationwide appeal on the new medium of television. He disclosed his finances and documented his modest standard of living. Conceding that the family pet, Checkers, might be considered an illegal gift, Nixon refused to break his daughters' hearts by returning the cocker spaniel. The overwhelmingly positive response to the "Checkers speech" kept Nixon on the ticket.

Shortly before the election, Eisenhower announced dramatically, "I shall go to Korea," and voters registered their confidence in his ability to end the war.

The 1952 Republican Ticket
At the Republican convention in 1952, presidential nominee Dwight D. Eisenhower stands with his wife, Mamie (right); his running mate, Richard Nixon; and Nixon's wife, Patricia (left), at the start of their campaign. © Bettmann/Corbis.

Cutting sharply into traditional Democratic territory, Eisenhower won several southern states and garnered 55 percent of the popular vote overall. His coattails carried a narrow Republican majority to Congress.

An Armistice and the War's Costs

Eisenhower made good on his pledge to end the Korean War. In July 1953, the two sides reached an armistice that left Korea divided, again roughly at the thirty-eighth parallel, with North and South separated by a two-and-a-half-mile-wide demilitarized zone (see Map 26.2). The war took the lives of 36,000 Americans and wounded more than 100,000. Nick Tosques, one of thousands of U.S. soldiers taken as prisoners of war, spent more than two years in a POW camp. "They interrogated us every day," he recalled. "Pretty soon I was telling them anything, just to keep from getting hit." South Korea lost more than 1 million people to war-related causes, and more than 1.8 million North Koreans and Chinese were killed or wounded.

The Truman administration judged the war a success for containment, since the United States had backed up its promise to help nations that were resisting communism. Both Truman and Eisenhower managed to contain what amounted to a world war — involving twenty nations altogether — within a single country and to avoid the use of nuclear weapons.

The Korean War had an enormous effect on defense policy and spending. In April 1950, two months before the war began, the National Security Council completed a top-secret report, known as **NSC 68**, on the United States' military strength. It warned that the survival of the nation required a massive military buildup and a tripling of the defense budget. Truman took no immediate action on these recommendations, but the Korean War brought about nearly all of the military expansion called for in NSC 68, vastly increasing U.S. capacity to act as a global power. Military spending shot up from $14 billion in 1950 to $50 billion in 1953 and remained above $40 billion thereafter. By 1952, defense spending claimed nearly 70 percent of the federal budget, and the size of the armed forces had tripled.

To General Matthew Ridgway, MacArthur's successor as commander of the UN forces, Korea taught the lesson that U.S. forces should never again fight a land war in Asia. Eisenhower concurred. Nevertheless, the Korean War induced the Truman administration to expand its role in Asia by increasing aid to the French, who were fighting to hang on to their colonial empire in Indochina. As U.S. Marines retreated from a battle against Chinese soldiers in 1950, they sang, prophetically, "We're Harry's police force on call, / So put back your pack on, / The next step is Saigon, / Cheer up, me lads, bless 'em all."

REVIEW   How did the Korean War shape American foreign policy in the 1950s?

▶ Conclusion: The Cold War's Costs and Consequences

Arguing that the United Nations rather than unilateral American intervention should be the means of resolving foreign crises, Helen Gahagan Douglas opposed the implementation of containment with aid to Greece and Turkey in 1947, and she initially resisted designating the Soviet Union as an enemy. By 1948, however, Douglas had gotten behind Truman's decision to fight communism throughout the world, which marked the most momentous foreign policy initiative in the nation's history.

More than any development in the postwar world, the Cold War defined American politics and society for decades to come. It transformed the federal government, shifting its priorities from domestic to external affairs, greatly expanding its budget, and substantially increasing the power of the president. Military spending helped transform the nation itself, as defense contracts encouraged economic and population booms in the West and Southwest. The nuclear arms race put the people of the world at risk, consumed resources that might have been used to improve living standards, and skewed the economy toward dependence on military projects.

In sharp contrast to foreign policy, the domestic policies of the postwar years reflected continuity with the past. Most of the New Deal reforms remained in place despite Republicans' promises to turn back the clock. Helen Gahagan Douglas had come to Congress hoping to expand the New Deal, to help find "a way by which all people can live out their lives in dignity and decency."

She avidly supported Truman's proposals for new programs in education, health, and civil rights, but a majority of her colleagues did not. Consequently, the poor and minorities suffered even while a majority of Americans enjoyed a higher standard of living in an economy boosted by Cold War spending and the reconstruction of Western Europe and Japan.

Another high cost of the early Cold War years was the anti-Communist hysteria that swept the nation, denying Douglas a Senate seat and more generally stifling debate and narrowing the range of ideas acceptable for political discussion. Partisan politics and Truman's warnings about the Communist menace fueled McCarthyism, but the obsession with subversion also fed on popular frustrations over the failure of containment to produce clear-cut victories. Convulsing the nation in bitter disunity, McCarthyism reflected a loss of confidence in American power. The Korean War, which ended in stalemate rather than the defeat of communism, exacerbated feelings of frustration. It would be a major challenge of the Eisenhower administration to restore national unity and confidence.

Reviewing Chapter 26

REVIEW QUESTIONS

1. Why did relations between the United States and the Soviet Union deteriorate after World War II? (pp. 782–791)

2. Why did Truman have limited success in implementing his domestic agenda? (pp. 792–800)

3. How did the Korean War shape American foreign policy in the 1950s? (pp. 800–805)

MAKING CONNECTIONS

1. What was the containment policy, and how successful was it up to 1953? In your answer, discuss both the supporters and the critics of the policy.

2. How did returning American servicemen change postwar domestic life in the areas of education and civil rights? In your answer, discuss how wartime experiences influenced their demands.

3. Why did anti-Communist hysteria sweep the country in the early 1950s? How did it shape domestic politics? In your answer, be sure to consider the influence of developments abroad and at home.

LINKING TO THE PAST

1. What events and decisions during World War II contributed to the rise of the Cold War in the late 1940s? (See chapter 25.)

2. What did the anti-Communist hysteria of the late 1940s and the 1950s have in common with the Red scare that followed World War I, and how did these two phenomena differ? (See chapter 22.)

TIMELINE 1945–1953

1945
- Roosevelt dies; Vice President Harry S. Truman becomes president.

1946
- Postwar labor unrest.
- President's Committee on Civil Rights created.
- George F. Kennan drafts a containment policy.
- United States grants independence to Philippines.
- Employment Act.
- Republicans gain control of Congress.

1947
- National Security Act: National Security Council (NSC) and Central Intelligence Agency (CIA) created.
- Truman asks for aid to Greece and Turkey and announces Truman Doctrine.
- Truman establishes loyalty program.
- *Mendez v. Westminster* invalidates segregation of Mexican Americans in California schools.

1948
- Congress approves Marshall Plan.
- Women become permanent part of armed services.
- Truman orders desegregation of armed services.
- American GI Forum founded.
- United States recognizes state of Israel.
- Truman elected president.

1948–1949
- Berlin crisis and airlift.

1949
- Communists take over mainland China; Nationalists retreat to Taiwan.
- North Atlantic Treaty Organization (NATO) formed.
- Soviet Union explodes atomic bomb.

1950
- Senator Joseph McCarthy begins to accuse U.S. government of harboring Communists.
- Truman approves development of hydrogen bomb.
- United States sends troops to South Korea.

1951
- Truman relieves General Douglas MacArthur of command in Korea.
- United States ends occupation of Japan and signs peace treaty and mutual security pact.

1952
- Republican Dwight D. Eisenhower elected president.

1953
- Armistice halts Korean War.

▶ FOR AN ONLINE BIBLIOGRAPHY, PRACTICE QUIZZES, WEB SITES, IMAGES, AND DOCUMENTS RELATED TO THIS CHAPTER, see the Book Companion Site at **bedfordstmartins.com/roarkvalue**.

▶ FOR DOCUMENTS RELATED TO THIS PERIOD, see Michael Johnson, ed., *Reading the American Past*, Fifth Edition.

The Politics and Culture of Abundance

1952–1960

TRAILED BY REPORTERS, U.S. VICE PRESIDENT RICHARD M. NIXON LED
Soviet premier Nikita Khrushchev through the American National Exhibition
in Moscow in July 1959. The display of American consumer goods followed
an exhibition of Soviet products in New York, part of a cultural exchange
between the two superpowers that reflected a slight thaw in the Cold War
after Khrushchev replaced Stalin. In Moscow, both Khrushchev and Nixon
seized on the propaganda potential of the moment. As they made their way
through the display, their verbal sparring turned into a slugfest of words
and gestures that reporters dubbed the kitchen debate.

Showing off a new color television set, Nixon said the Soviet Union
"may be ahead of us . . . in the thrust of your rockets for . . . outer space,"
but he insisted to Khrushchev that the United States outstripped the Soviets
in consumer goods. Nixon linked capitalism with democracy, asserting that
the array of products represented "what freedom means to us . . . our right
to choose." Moreover, "any steelworker could buy this house," Nixon
boasted, as they walked through a model of a six-room ranch-style home.
Khrushchev retorted that in the Soviet Union "you are entitled to housing,"
whereas in the United States the homeless slept on pavements.

While the two men inspected household appliances, Nixon declared,
"These are designed to make things easier for our women." Khrushchev
responded that his country did not have "the capitalist attitude toward

809

The Kitchen Debate
Soviet premier Nikita Khrushchev (left) and Vice President Richard M. Nixon (center) debate the relative merits of their nations' economies at the American National Exhibition held in Moscow in 1959. "You are a lawyer for capitalism and I am a lawyer for communism," Khrushchev told Nixon as each tried to outdo the other. Howard Sochurek/TimePix/Getty.

women" and appreciated women's contributions to the economy, not their domesticity. The Soviet leader found many of the items on display interesting, but he said, "they are not needed in life. . . . They are merely gadgets." In reply, Nixon insisted, "Isn't it far better to be talking about washing machines than machines of war?" Khrushchev agreed, yet Cold War tensions surfaced when he later blustered, "We too are giants. You want to threaten — we will answer threats with threats."

The Eisenhower administration (1953–1961) in fact had begun with threats to the Soviet Union. During the 1952 campaign, Republicans had vowed to roll back communism and liberate "enslaved" peoples under Soviet rule. In practice, however, President Dwight D. Eisenhower settled for a containment policy much like that of his predecessor, Harry S. Truman, though Eisenhower relied more on nuclear weapons and on secret actions by the Central Intelligence Agency (CIA) against left-leaning governments. Yet as Nixon's visit to Moscow demonstrated, Eisenhower seized on political changes in the Soviet Union to reduce tensions in Soviet-American relations.

Continuity with the Truman administration also characterized domestic policy. Although Eisenhower favored corporations with tax cuts and opposed strong federal efforts in health care, education, and race relations, he did not propose to roll back New Deal programs. He even extended the reach of the federal government with a massive highway program, and he remained immensely popular through his two terms in office.

Although poverty clung stubbornly to some 20 percent of the population, the Moscow display testified to the unheard-of material gains savored by most Americans in the postwar era. Cold War weapons production spurred the economy, whose vitality stimulated suburban development, contributed to the burgeoning population and enterprise in the West and Southwest (the Sun Belt), and enabled millions of Americans to buy a host of new products.

As new homes, television sets, and household appliances transformed living patterns, Americans took part in a consumer culture that celebrated marriage, family, and traditional gender roles, even as more and more married women took jobs outside the home. Also challenging dominant norms were an emerging youth culture and dissenting writers known as the Beats.

The Cold War and the economic boom helped African Americans mount the most dramatic challenge of the 1950s, a struggle against the system of segregation and disfranchisement that had replaced slavery. Large numbers of African Americans took direct action against the institutions of injustice, developing the organizations, leadership, and strategies to mount a civil rights movement of unprecedented size and influence.

▶ Eisenhower and the Politics of the "Middle Way"

Moderation was the guiding principle of Eisenhower's domestic agenda and leadership style. In 1953, he pledged a "middle way between untrammeled freedom of the individual and the demands for the welfare of the whole Nation," promising that his administration would "avoid government by bureaucracy as carefully as it avoids neglect of the helpless." On the one hand, Eisenhower generally resisted expanding the federal government's power, he acted reluctantly when the Supreme Court ordered schools to desegregate, and his administration terminated the federal trusteeship of dozens of Indian tribes.

On the other hand, as a moderate Republican, Eisenhower supported the continuation, and in some cases the expansion, of New Deal programs. He signed key legislation establishing a national highway system and enlarged the federal bureaucracy with a new Department of Health, Education, and Welfare. Nicknamed "Ike," the confident war hero remained popular, but he was not able to lift the Republican Party to national dominance.

Modern Republicanism

In contrast to the old guard conservatives in his party who criticized containment and wanted to repeal much of the New Deal, **Dwight D. Eisenhower** preached "modern Republicanism." This meant resisting additional federal intervention in economic and social life, but it did not mean turning the clock back to the 1920s. "Should any political party attempt to abolish social security and eliminate labor laws and farm programs," he wrote to his brother in 1954, "you would not hear of that party again in our political history." Democratic control of Congress after the elections of 1954 further contributed to Eisenhower's moderate approach, which overall maintained the course charted by Roosevelt and Truman.

The new president attempted to distance himself from the anti-Communist fervor that had plagued the Truman administration, even as he intensified Truman's loyalty program, allowing federal executives to dismiss thousands of employees on grounds of loyalty, security, or "suitability." Reflecting his inclination to avoid controversial issues, Eisenhower refused to denounce Senator Joseph McCarthy publicly. In 1954, McCarthy began to destroy himself when he went after the army. As he hurled reckless charges of communism against military personnel during weeks of televised hearings, public opinion turned against him. When the army's lawyer demanded of McCarthy, "Have you left no sense of decency?" those in the hearing room applauded. A Senate vote to condemn McCarthy in December 1954 marked the end of his influence, but not the end of searching out radicals.

Eisenhower sometimes echoed the conservative Republicans' conviction that government was best left to the states and economic decisions to private business. "If all Americans want is security, they can go to prison," he commented about social welfare in 1949. Yet the welfare state grew somewhat during his administration, and Eisenhower signed laws bringing ten million more workers into Social Security, increasing the minimum wage, and continuing the federal government's modest role in financing public housing. He created a new Department of Health, Education, and Welfare, appointing as its head former Women's Army Corps commander Oveta Culp Hobby, the second woman to hold a cabinet post. And when the spread of polio neared epidemic proportions and terrified parents, Eisenhower obtained funds from Congress to distribute a vaccine, even though conservatives wanted to leave that responsibility to the states.

Eisenhower's greatest domestic initiative was the **Interstate Highway and Defense System Act of 1956** (Map 27.1), which involved the federal government in activities previously left to the states and localities. Promoted as essential to national defense and an impetus to economic growth, the act authorized the construction of a national highway system, with the federal government paying most of the costs through increased fuel and vehicle taxes. The new highways accelerated the mobility of Americans and the movement of goods and spurred suburban expansion, shopping malls, and growth in the fast-food and motel industries. The trucking, construction, and automobile industries had lobbied hard for the law and benefited substantially from it. Eventually, the monumental highway project exacted unforeseen costs in the form of air pollution, energy consumption, declining railroads and mass transportation, and decay of central cities.

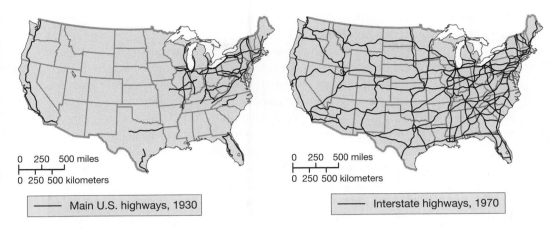

MAP 27.1
The Interstate Highway System, 1930 and 1970
Built with federal funds authorized in the Interstate Highway and Defense System Act of 1956, superhighways soon crisscrossed the nation. Trucking, construction, gasoline, and travel were among the industries that prospered, but railroads suffered from the subsidized competition.

In other areas, Eisenhower restrained federal activity in favor of state governments and private enterprise. His large tax cuts directed most benefits to business and the wealthy, he resisted federal aid to primary and secondary education, and he avoided strong White House leadership on behalf of civil rights. Eisenhower opposed national health insurance, preferring the growing practice of private insurance through employment. Moreover, whereas Democrats sought to keep nuclear power in government hands, Eisenhower signed legislation authorizing the private manufacture and sale of nuclear energy. The first commercial nuclear power plant in the United States opened in 1958 in Shippingport, Pennsylvania, northwest of Pittsburgh.

Termination and Relocation of Native Americans

Eisenhower's efforts to limit the federal government were consistent with a new direction in Indian policy, which reversed the emphasis on strengthening tribal governments and preserving Indian culture that had been established in the 1930s (see chapter 24). After World War II, when some 25,000 Indians had left their homes for military service and another 40,000 for work in defense industries, policymakers began to favor assimilating Native Americans and ending their special relationships with the government.

To some officials, who reflected the Cold War emphasis on conformity to dominant American values, the communal practices of Indians resembled socialism and stifled individual initiative. Eisenhower's commissioner of Indian affairs, Glenn Emmons, did not believe that tribal lands could produce income sufficient to lift Indians from poverty, but he also revealed the ethnocentrism of policymakers when he insisted that Indians wanted to "work and live like Americans." Moreover, government treaties with Indian nations protected Indian rights to water, land, minerals, and other resources that were increasingly attractive to state governments and private entrepreneurs.

By 1960, the government had implemented a three-part program of compensation, termination, and relocation. In 1946, Congress established the Indian Claims Commission to discharge outstanding claims by Native Americans for land taken by the government. When it closed in 1978, the commission had settled 285 cases, with compensation exceeding $800 million. Yet the awards were based on land values at the time the land was taken and did not include interest.

The second policy, termination, also originated in the Truman administration, during which Commissioner Dillon S. Myer asserted that his Bureau of Indian Affairs should do "nothing for Indians which Indians can do for themselves." Beginning in 1953, Eisenhower signed bills transferring jurisdiction over tribal land to state and local governments and ending the trusteeship relationship between Indians and the federal government. The loss of federal hospitals, schools, and other special arrangements devastated Indian tribes. As had happened after passage of the Dawes Act in 1887 (see chapter 17), some corporate interests and individuals took advantage of the opportunity to purchase Indian land cheaply. For many Indians, termination was "like the strike of doom." The government abandoned termination in the 1960s after some 13,000 Indians and more than one million acres of their land had been affected. Several tribes, including the Menominee and the Klamath, fought successfully to reverse termination and to secure restoration of their tribal status.

The **Indian Relocation Program**, the third piece of Native American policy, began in 1948 and involved more than 100,000 Native Americans by 1973. The government encouraged Indians to move to cities, where relocation centers were supposed to help with housing, job training, and medical care. Even though government officials made it difficult to return home by sending Indians far away from their reservations, about one-third returned to the reservation.

Most who stayed in cities faced racism, lack of adequately paying jobs for which they had skills, poor housing, and the loss of their traditional culture. "I wish we had never left home," said one woman whose husband was out of work and drinking heavily. "It's dirty and noisy, and people all around, crowded. . . . It seems like I never see the sky or trees." Moreover, Native Americans who relocated to cities found them to be on the decline, as urban wealth began to shift to the suburbs throughout the 1950s and 1960s. Like African Americans who migrated to cities in great numbers in the 1950s, Indians found declining opportunities for economic progress (see page 825).

Reflecting long-standing disagreements among Indians themselves, some who overcame these obstacles applauded the program. But most urban Indians remained in or near poverty, and even many who had welcomed relocation began to worry that "we would lose our identity as Indian people, lose our culture and our [way] of living." Within two decades, a national pan-Indian movement emerged to resist assimilation and to demand much more for Indians (as discussed in chapter 28). The new militancy and connections across tribal lines that arose were a by-product of the urbanization of Native Americans.

The 1956 Election and the Second Term

Not all citizens were living the American dream, but with the nation at peace and the economy booming, Eisenhower easily defeated Adlai Stevenson in 1956, doubling his victory margin of 1952. Yet Democrats kept control of Congress, and in the midterm elections two years later, they all but wiped out the Republican Party, gaining a 64–34 majority in the Senate and a 282–135 advantage in the House. Although Ike captured voters' hearts, a majority of Americans remained wedded to the programs and policies of the Democrats.

Eisenhower faced more serious leadership challenges in his second term. When the economy plunged into a recession in late 1957, he fought with Congress over the budget and vetoed bills to expand housing, urban development, and public works projects. The president and Congress did reach agreement in two key areas: enacting the first, though largely symbolic, civil rights legislation in a century and extending the federal government's role in education, largely in the interest of national security (as discussed on pages 820–821 and 826–827).

In the end, the first Republican administration after the New Deal left the size and functions of the federal government intact, though it tipped policy some-what more in favor of corporate interests. Unparalleled prosperity graced the Eisenhower years, and inflation was kept low. The economy weathered two recessions without testing the president's aversion to substantial federal intervention. Eisenhower celebrated what he called the "wide diffusion of wealth and incomes" across the United States. Yet neglected amid the remarkable abundance were some forty million Americans who lived below the poverty level. Rural deprivation was particularly pronounced, as was poverty among African Americans and other minorities, who failed to benefit from the massive defense spending that fueled the economy as a whole.

REVIEW   How did Eisenhower's domestic policies reflect his moderate political vision?

▶ Liberation Rhetoric and the Practice of Containment

At his 1953 inauguration, Eisenhower warned that "forces of good and evil are massed and armed and opposed as rarely before in history." Like Truman, he saw communism as a threat to the nation's security and economic interests and wanted to maintain the United States' position as the most powerful country in the world. Eisenhower's foreign policy differed from Truman's, however, in three areas: its rhetoric, its means, and — after Stalin's death in 1953 — its movement toward accommodation with the Soviet Union.

Republican rhetoric, voiced most prominently by Secretary of State John Foster Dulles, deplored containment as "negative, futile, and immoral" because it accepted the existing Soviet sphere of control. Yet despite promises to roll back Soviet power, the Eisenhower administration continued the containment policy.

The United States intervened at the margins of Communist power — in Asia, the Middle East, and Latin America — but not at its core in Europe. Eisenhower assigned nuclear weapons and CIA secret operations larger roles in defense strategy, and he took steps to ease tensions between the two superpowers.

The "New Look" in Foreign Policy

To meet his goals of balancing the budget and cutting taxes, Eisenhower was determined to control military expenditures. Moreover, he feared that massive defense spending would threaten the nation's economic strength. As he declared in 1953, "Every gun that is made, every warship launched, every rocket fired signifies, in the final sense, a theft from those who hunger and are not fed, those who are cold and not clothed."

Reflecting Americans' confidence in technology and their opposition to a large peacetime army, Eisenhower's defense strategy concentrated U.S. military strength in nuclear weapons and the planes and missiles to deliver them. Instead of maintaining large ground forces of its own, the United States would give friendly nations American weapons and back them up with an ominous nuclear arsenal, providing, according to the secretary of defense, "more bang for the buck." This was Eisenhower's "New Look" in foreign policy. Secretary of State Dulles believed that America's

Missiles in the Nuclear Arms Race

After World War II, both the United States and the Soviet Union dug for information about rocketry from German installations and German scientists and engineers, who were leaders in the development of missiles. By the 1950s, both nations were arming missiles with nuclear weapons. In 1957, the United States began building intercontinental ballistic missiles (ICBMs) that could hit the Soviet Union from a launching site in the American Midwest. Shown here are missiles being manufactured by Boeing, a leading corporation in the aerospace industry, housed in Seattle, Washington. Photo by B. Anthony Stewart/National Geographic/Getty Images.

willingness to "go to the brink" of war with its intimidating nuclear weapons — a strategy called brinksmanship — would block any Soviet efforts to expand.

Throughout the 1950s, the United States far outpaced the Soviet Union in nuclear warheads and delivery missiles, yet its superiority did not ensure security. Nuclear weapons could not stop a Soviet nuclear attack. In response to one, however, they could inflict enormous destruction. This certainty of "massive retaliation" was meant to deter the Soviets from launching an attack. Because the Soviet Union could respond similarly to an American first strike, this nuclear standoff became known as **mutually assured destruction,** or **MAD**. Leaders of both nations pursued an ever-escalating arms race.

Nuclear weapons could not roll back the iron curtain. When a revolt against the Soviet-controlled government began in Hungary in 1956, Dulles's liberation rhetoric proved to be empty. As Soviet tanks arrived to crush the revolt, a radio plea from freedom fighters cried, "SOS! They just brought us a rumor that the American troops will be here within one or two hours." But help did not come. Eisenhower was unwilling to risk U.S. soldiers and possible nuclear war, and Soviet troops soon suppressed the insurrection, killing or wounding thousands of Hungarians.

Applying Containment to Vietnam

A major challenge to the containment policy came in Southeast Asia. During World War II, Ho Chi Minh, a Vietnamese nationalist who also embraced communism, had founded a coalition called the Vietminh to fight both the occupying Japanese forces and the French colonial rulers. In 1945, the Vietminh declared Vietnam's independence from France, and when France fought to maintain its colony, the area plunged into war. After the Communists won control of China, the Truman administration quietly began to provide aid to the French and recognized their puppet government in the southern part of Vietnam (see chapter 29, Map 29.2). American principles of national self-determination took a backseat to the battle against communism.

Eisenhower viewed communism in Vietnam much as Truman had regarded it in Greece and Turkey, a view that became known as the **domino theory**. "You have a row of dominoes," Eisenhower explained, and "you knock over the first one, and what will happen to the last one is the certainty that it will go over very quickly." A Communist victory in Southeast Asia, he warned, could trigger the fall of Japan, Taiwan, and the Philippines. By 1954, the United States was contributing 75 percent of the cost of France's war, but Eisenhower resisted a larger role. When the French asked for troops and airplanes from the United States to avert almost certain defeat at Dien Bien Phu, Eisenhower, conscious of U.S. losses in the Korean War (see chapter 26), said no.

Dien Bien Phu fell in May 1954 and with it the French colony of Vietnam. Two months later in Geneva, France signed a truce. The **Geneva accords** temporarily partitioned Vietnam at the seventeenth parallel, separating the Vietminh in the north from the puppet government established by the French in the south. Within two years, the Vietnamese people were to vote in elections for a unified government. Some officials warned against U.S. involvement in Vietnam. Defense Secretary Charles Wilson saw "nothing but grief in store for us if we remained in that area." Eisenhower and Dulles nonetheless moved to prop up the dominoes with a new alliance. In September 1954, the United States joined with Britain, France, Australia, New Zealand, Thailand, Pakistan, and the Philippines in the Southeast Asia Treaty Organization, committed to the defense of Cambodia, Laos, and South Vietnam. Shortly thereafter, Eisenhower began to send weapons and military advisers to South Vietnam and put the CIA to work infiltrating and destabilizing North Vietnam. Fearing a Communist victory in the elections mandated by the Geneva accords, the United States supported South Vietnamese prime minister Ngo Dinh Diem's refusal to hold the vote.

Between 1955 and 1961, the United States provided $800 million to the South Vietnamese army (the Army of the Republic of Vietnam, or ARVN). Yet the ARVN proved grossly unprepared for the guerrilla warfare that began in the late 1950s. With military assistance from Ho Chi Minh's government in Hanoi, Vietminh rebels in the south stepped up their guerrilla attacks on the Diem government. The insurgents gained support from the largely Buddhist peasants, who were outraged by the repressive regime of the Catholic, Westernized Diem. Unwilling to abandon containment, Eisenhower left his successor with the deteriorating situation and a firm commitment to defend South Vietnam against communism.

Interventions in Latin America and the Middle East

While supporting friendly governments in Asia, the Eisenhower administration worked secretly to topple unfriendly ones in Latin America and the Middle East. Officials saw internal civil wars in terms of the Cold War conflict between the superpowers and tended to view nationalist uprisings as Communist threats to democracy. They acted against governments that not only seemed too leftist but also threatened U.S. economic interests. The Eisenhower administration took this course of action out of sight of Congress and the public, making the CIA an important arm of foreign policy.

The government of Guatemala, under the popularly elected reformist president Jacobo Arbenz, was not Soviet controlled, but it accepted support from the local Communist Party (see chapter 29, Map 29.1). In 1953, Arbenz moved to help landless, poverty-stricken peasants by nationalizing uncultivated land owned by the United Fruit Company, a U.S. corporation whose annual profits were twice the size of the Guatemalan government's budget. United Fruit refused Arbenz's offer to compensate the company at the value of the land it had declared for tax purposes. Then, in response to the nationalization program, the CIA organized and supported an opposition army that overthrew the elected government and installed a military dictatorship in 1954. United Fruit kept its land, and Guatemala descended into a series of destructive civil wars that lasted through the 1990s.

In 1959, the desire for political and economic autonomy erupted into the **Cuban revolution**, led by **Fidel Castro**. At the time, a CIA agent promised "to take care of Castro just like we took care of Arbenz." American companies had long controlled major Cuban resources, and decisions made in Washington directly influenced the lives of the Cuban people. The 1959 uprising drove out the U.S.-supported dictator Fulgencio Batista and led the CIA to warn Eisenhower that "Communists and other extreme radicals appear to have penetrated the Castro movement." When the United States denied Castro's requests for loans, he turned to the Soviet Union. And when U.S. companies refused Castro's offer to purchase them at their assessed value, he began to nationalize their property. Many anti-Castro Cubans fled to the United States and reported his atrocities, including the execution of hundreds of Batista's supporters. Before leaving office, Eisenhower broke off diplomatic relations with Cuba and authorized the CIA to train Cuban exiles for an invasion.

In the Middle East, the CIA intervened to oust an elected government, support an unpopular dictatorship, and maintain Western access to Iranian oil (see chapter 30, Map 30.2). In 1951, the Iranian parliament, led by **Mohammed Mossadegh**, the nationalist prime minister, nationalized the country's oil fields and refineries. Most of the oil operations had been held by a British company for decades, and Iran received less than 20 percent of the profits from its own resources. The British strongly objected to the takeover and eventually sought help from the United States.

Advisers convinced Eisenhower that Mossadegh, whom *Time* magazine had called "the Iranian George Washington," left Iran vulnerable to communism, and the president wanted to keep oil-rich areas "under the control of people who are friendly." With his authorization, CIA agents instigated a coup by bribing army officers and financing demonstrations against the government. In August 1953, Iranian army officers captured the prime minister and reestablished the authority of the shah of Iran, Mohammad Reza Pahlavi, known for favoring Western interests and the Iranian wealthy classes. Iran renegotiated its oil concessions, giving U.S. companies a 40 percent share. Resentment over this use of force would poison U.S.-Iranian relations into the twenty-first century.

Elsewhere in the Middle East, the Eisenhower administration continued Truman's support of Israel but also sought to foster friendships with Arab nations to secure access to oil and build a bulwark against communism. Yet U.S. officials demanded that smaller nations take the American side in the Cold War, even when those nations preferred to remain nonaligned, with the opportunity for assistance from both Western and Communist nations. In 1955, as part of the U.S. effort to win Arab allies, Secretary of State Dulles began talks with Egypt about American support to build the Aswan Dam on the Nile River. The following year, Egypt's leader, **Gamal Abdel Nasser**, sought arms from Communist Czechoslovakia, formed a military alliance with other Arab nations, and recognized the People's Republic of China. Unwilling to tolerate such independence, Dulles called off the deal for the dam.

On July 26, 1956, Nasser responded by seizing the Suez Canal, then owned by Britain and France but scheduled to revert to Egypt within seven years. In response to the seizure, Israel, whose forces had been skirmishing with Egyptian troops along their common border since 1948, attacked Egypt, with military help from Britain and France. Eisenhower opposed the intervention, recognizing that the Egyptians had claimed their own territory and that Nasser "embodie[d] the emotional demands of the people . . . for independence." He put economic pressure on Britain and France while calling on the United Nations to arrange a truce. The French and British soon pulled back, forcing Israel to retreat.

Despite staying out of the **Suez crisis**, Eisenhower made it clear that the United States would actively combat communism in the Middle East. In March 1957, Congress passed a joint resolution approving aid to any Middle Eastern nation "requesting assistance against armed aggression from any country controlled by international communism." The president invoked this **Eisenhower Doctrine** to send aid to Jordan in 1957 and troops to Lebanon in 1958 to counter anti-Western pressures on those governments.

The Nuclear Arms Race

While Eisenhower moved against perceived Communist inroads abroad, he also sought to reduce superpower tensions. After Stalin's death in 1953, a more moderate leadership under **Nikita Khrushchev** emerged. Like Eisenhower, who remarked privately that the arms race would lead "at worst to atomic warfare, at best to robbing every people and nation on earth of the fruits of their own toil," Khrushchev wanted to reduce defense spending and the threat of nuclear devastation. Eisenhower and Khrushchev met in Geneva in 1955 at the first summit conference since the end of World War II. Although the meeting produced no new agreements, it symbolized what Eisenhower called "a new spirit of conciliation and cooperation."

In August 1957, the Soviets test-fired their first intercontinental ballistic missile (ICBM) and two months later beat the United States into space by launching *Sputnik*, the first artificial satellite to circle the earth. The United States launched a successful satellite of its own in January 1958, but *Sputnik* raised fears that the United States lagged behind the Soviets not only in missile development and space exploration but also in science and education. In response, Eisenhower established the National Aeronautics and Space Administration (NASA), approving a huge budget increase for space research and development. Also in 1958, Congress passed the National Defense Education Act, providing support for instruction at all levels in math, foreign languages, and science and technology. Eisenhower assured the public that the United States possessed nuclear superiority. In fact, during his presidency, the stockpile of nuclear weapons more than quadrupled; the United States had installed ICBMs at home and in Britain and was prepared to deploy more in Italy and Turkey. The first Polaris submarine carrying nuclear missiles was launched in November 1960. Yet these weapons could not guarantee security because both superpowers possessed sufficient nuclear capacity to devastate each other. Most Americans did not follow Civil Defense Administration recommendations to construct home bomb shelters, but they did realize how precarious nuclear weapons had made their lives.

In the midst of the arms race, the superpowers continued to talk. In 1959, Khrushchev visited the United States, and Nixon went to the Soviet Union, where he engaged in the famous kitchen debate. By 1960, the two sides were close to a ban on nuclear testing. But just before a planned summit in Paris, a Soviet missile shot down an American U-2 spy plane over Soviet territory. The State Department first denied that U.S. planes had been violating Soviet airspace, but the Soviets produced the pilot and the photos taken on his flight. Eisenhower and Khrushchev met briefly in Paris, but the U-2 incident dashed all prospects for a nuclear arms agreement.

As Eisenhower left office, he warned about the growing influence of the **military-industrial complex** in American government and life. Eisenhower had struggled against persistent pressures from defense contractors who, in tandem with the military, sought more dollars for newer, more powerful weapons systems. In his farewell address, he warned that the "conjunction of an immense military establishment and a large arms industry . . . exercised a total influence . . . in every city, every state house, every office of the federal government." The Cold War had created a warfare state.

REVIEW Where and how did Eisenhower practice containment?

▶ New Work and Living Patterns in an Economy of Abundance

Stimulated in part by Cold War spending, economic productivity increased enormously in the 1950s. A multitude of new items came on the market, and consumption became the order of the day. Millions of Americans enjoyed new homes in the suburbs, and higher education enrollments skyrocketed. Although every section of the nation enjoyed the new abundance, the West and Southwest — the **Sun Belt** — especially boomed in production, commerce, and population.

Work itself was changing. Fewer people labored on farms, service sector employment overtook manufacturing jobs, and women's employment grew. These economic shifts disadvantaged some Americans, and they did little to help the forty million who lived in poverty. Most Americans, however, enjoyed a higher standard of living, prompting economist John Kenneth Galbraith to call the United States "the affluent society."

Technology Transforms Agriculture and Industry

Between 1940 and 1960, agricultural output mushroomed even while the number of farmworkers declined by almost one-third. Farmers achieved nearly miraculous productivity through greater crop specialization, intensive use of fertilizers, and, above all, mechanization. A single mechanical cotton picker, for example, replaced fifty people and cut the cost of harvesting a bale of cotton from $40 to $5.

The decline of family farms and the growth of large commercial farming, or agribusiness, were both causes and consequences of mechanization. Benefiting handsomely from federal price supports begun in the New Deal, larger farmers could afford technological improvements, whereas smaller producers lacked capital to invest in the machinery necessary to compete. Consequently, average farm size more than doubled between 1940 and 1964, and the number of farms fell by more than 40 percent.

Many small farmers who hung on constituted a core of rural poverty often overlooked in the celebration of affluence. Southern landowners replaced sharecroppers and tenants with machines, forcing them off the land. Hundreds of thousands of African Americans joined an exodus to cities, where racial discrimination and a lack of jobs for which they could qualify mired many in urban poverty. A Mississippi mother whose family had worked on a plantation since slavery reported that most of her relatives headed for Chicago when they realized that "it was going to be machines now that harvest the crops." Worrying that "it might be worse up there" for her children, she agonized, "I'm afraid to leave and I'm afraid to stay."

Industrial production was also transformed by new technologies. Between 1945 and 1960, for example, the number of labor-hours needed to manufacture a car fell by 50 percent. Technology transformed industries such as electronics, chemicals, and air transportation and promoted the growth of television, plastics, computers, and other newer industries. American businesses enjoyed access to cheap oil, ample markets abroad, and little foreign competition. Moreover, even with Eisenhower's conservative fiscal policies, government spending reached $80 billion annually and created new jobs.

Labor unions enjoyed their greatest success during the 1950s, and real earnings for production workers shot up 40 percent. The merger in 1955 of the American Federation of Labor (AFL) and the Congress of Industrial Organizations (CIO) improved labor's bargaining position. As one worker put it, "We saw continual improvement in wages, fringe benefits like holidays, vacation, medical plans . . . all sorts of things that provided more security for people." In most industrial nations, government programs underwrote their citizens' security, but the United States developed a mixed system in which company-funded programs won by unions through collective bargaining played a much larger role in providing for retirement, health care, and the like. This system, often called a private welfare state, resulted in wide disparities among workers, severely disadvantaging those not represented by unions and those with irregular employment.

While the absolute number of organized workers continued to grow, union membership peaked at 27.1 percent of the labor force in 1957. Technological advances eliminated jobs in heavy industry, reducing the number of workers in the steel, copper, and aluminum industries by 17 percent. "You are going to have trouble collecting union dues from all of these machines," commented a Ford manager to union leader Walter Reuther. Moreover, the economy as a whole was shifting from production to service as more workers distributed goods, performed services, provided education, and carried out government work. Unions made some headway in these fields, especially among government employees, but most service industries resisted unionization.

The growing clerical and service occupations swelled the demand for female workers. By the end of the 1950s, 35 percent of all women over age sixteen worked outside the home, and women held nearly one-third of all jobs. The vast majority of them worked in offices, light manufacturing, domestic service, teaching, and nursing; because these occupations were occupied primarily by women, wages were relatively low. In 1960, the average female full-time worker earned just 60 percent of the average male worker's wages. At the bottom of the employment ladder, black women took home only 42 percent of what white men earned.

Burgeoning Suburbs and Declining Cities

Although suburbs had existed since the nineteenth century, nothing symbolized the affluent society more than their tremendous expansion in the 1950s. Eleven million new homes went up in the suburbs, and by 1960 one in four Americans lived there. As Nixon boasted to Khrushchev during the **kitchen debate** (see pages 809–811), the suburbs were accessible to families with modest incomes. Builder William J. Levitt adapted the factory assembly-line process to home building, planning nearly identical units so that individual construction workers could move from house to house and perform the same single operation in each one. In 1949, families could purchase mass-produced houses in his 17,000-home development, called Levittown, on Long Island, New York, for just under $8,000 each. Developments similar to Levittown, as well as more luxurious ones, quickly went up throughout the country. The government underwrote home ownership by guaranteeing low-interest mortgages through the Federal Housing Administration and the Veterans Administration and by making interest on mortgages tax deductible. Thousands of miles of government-funded interstate highway running through urban areas indirectly subsidized suburban development.

The growing suburbs helped polarize society, especially along racial lines. Each Levittown homeowner signed a contract pledging not to rent or sell to a non-Caucasian. The Supreme Court declared such covenants unenforceable in 1948, but suburban America remained dramatically segregated. Social critic Lewis Mumford blasted the suburbs as "a multitude of uniform, unidentifiable houses in a treeless communal wasteland, inhabited by people of the same class, the same income, the same age group." By the 1960s, suburbs also came under attack for bulldozing the natural environment, creating groundwater contamination, and disrupting wildlife patterns.

Although some African Americans joined the suburban migration, most moved to cities in search of economic opportunity, increasing their numbers in most cities by 50 percent during the 1950s. These migrants, however, came to cities that were already in decline, losing not only population but also commerce and industry to the suburbs or to southern and western states. Shoppers gradually chose new suburban malls over downtown department stores. Many of the new jobs lay beyond the reach of the recent black arrivals to the inner cities.

The Rise of the Sun Belt

No regions experienced the postwar economic and population booms more intensely than the West and Southwest (Map 27.2). Architect Frank Lloyd Wright quipped, "Everything loose will land in Los Angeles." California overtook New York as the most populous state. Sports franchises followed fans: In 1958, the Brooklyn Dodgers moved to Los Angeles, joined by the Minneapolis Lakers three years later.

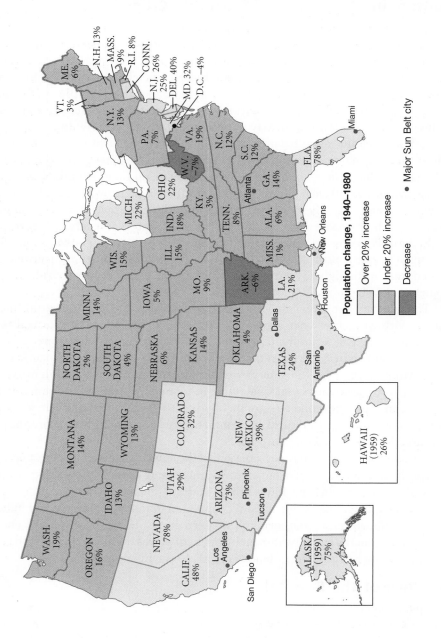

Population change, 1940–1980

☐ Over 20% increase
▨ Under 20% increase
▦ Decrease
● Major Sun Belt city

A pleasant natural environment drew new residents to the West and Southwest, but no magnet proved stronger than the promise of economic opportunity. As railroads had fueled western growth in the nineteenth century, so the automobile and airplane spurred the post–World War II surge. The technology of air-conditioning facilitated industrial development and by 1960 cooled nearly eight million homes in the so-called Sun Belt, which stretched from Florida to California.

So important was the defense industry to the South and West that the area was later referred to as the "Gun Belt." The aerospace industry boomed in Seattle–Tacoma, Los Angeles, and Dallas–Fort Worth, and military bases helped underwrite prosperity in cities such as San Diego and San Antonio. Although defense dollars benefited other regions, the Sun Belt captured the lion's share of Cold War spending. By the 1960s, nearly one of every three California workers held a defense-related job.

The surging populations and industries soon threatened the environment. Providing sufficient water and power to cities and to agribusiness meant building dams and reservoirs on free-flowing rivers. Native Americans lost fishing sites on the Columbia River, and dams on the Upper Missouri displaced nine hundred Indian families. Sprawling urban and suburban settlement without efficient public transportation contributed to blankets of smog over Los Angeles and other cities.

The high-technology basis of postwar economic development drew well-educated, highly skilled workers to the West, but the economic promise also attracted the poor. "We see opportunity all around us here. . . . We smell freedom here, and maybe soon we can taste it," commented a black mother in California. Between 1945 and 1960, more than one-third of the African Americans who left the South moved west.

The Mexican American population also grew, especially in California and Texas. To supply California's vast agribusiness industry, the government continued the *bracero* program begun during World War II, under which Mexican laborers were permitted to enter the United States to work for a limited period. Until the program ended in 1964, more than 100,000 Mexicans entered the United States each year to labor in the fields — and many of them stayed, legally or illegally. But permanent Mexican immigration was not as welcome as Mexicans' low-wage labor. In 1954, the government launched a series of raids called "Operation Wetback," resulting in the deportation of more than three million Mexicans. Even Mexicans with legal status felt unwelcome and vulnerable to incidents of mistaken identity.

At the same time, Mexican American citizens gained a victory in their ongoing struggle for civil rights in **Hernandez v. Texas**. When a Texas jury convicted Pete Hernandez of murder, lawyers from the American GI Forum and the League of United Latin-American Citizens (see chapter 26) appealed on the grounds that persons of Mexican origin had been routinely excluded from jury service. In 1954,

◀ **MAP 27.2**
The Rise of the Sun Belt, 1940–1980
The growth of defense industries, a non-unionized labor force, and the spread of air-conditioning all helped spur economic development and population growth in the West and South, which made the Sun Belt the fastest-growing region of the country between 1940 and 1980.

Rounding Up Undocumented Migrants Not all Mexican Americans who wanted to work in the United States were accommodated by the *bracero* program. In 1953, Los Angeles police arrested these men, who did not have legal documents and were hiding in a freight train. Some Americans used the crude term "wetback" to refer to illegal Mexican immigrants because many of them swam across the Rio Grande, which forms part of the border between the United States and Mexico. © Bettmann/Corbis.

the Supreme Court decided its first Mexican American civil rights case of the post–World War II era, ruling unanimously that Mexican Americans constituted a distinct group and that their systematic exclusion from juries violated the Fourteenth Amendment guarantee of equal protection. Legal scholar Ian Haney-López called the *Hernandez* ruling "huge for the Mexican American community. They now had the highest court in the land saying it's unconstitutional to treat Mexicans as if they're an inferior race."

Free of the discrimination faced by minorities, white Americans enjoyed the fullest prosperity in the West. In April 1950, when California developers opened Lakewood, a large housing development in Los Angeles County, thirty thousand people lined up to buy houses at prices ranging from $71,000 to $89,000 in 2010 dollars. Many of the new homeowners were veterans, blue-collar, and lower-level white-collar workers whose defense-based jobs at aerospace corporations enabled them to fulfill the American dream of the 1950s. A huge shopping mall, Lakewood Center, offered myriad products of the consumer culture, and the workers' children lived within commuting distance of community colleges and six state universities.

The Democratization of Higher Education

California's university system exemplified a spectacular transformation of higher education. Between 1940 and 1960, college enrollments in the United States more than doubled. More than 40 percent of young Americans attended college by the mid-1960s, up from 15 percent in the 1940s. Prosperity enabled more families to keep their children in school longer, and the federal government subsidized the education of more than two million veterans. The Cold War also sent millions of federal dollars to universities for defense-related research. And state governments vastly expanded the number of public colleges and universities, while municipalities began to build two-year community colleges.

All Americans did not benefit equally from the democratization of higher education. Although their college enrollments surged from 37,000 in 1941 to 90,000 in 1961, African Americans constituted only about 5 percent of all college students. Black men and women attended college in nearly equal numbers, but for a time the educational gap between white men and women grew, even while the number of women attending college increased. In 1940, women had earned 40 percent of undergraduate degrees, but as veterans flocked to college campuses, women's proportion fell to 25 percent in 1950 and rebounded to only 33 percent by 1960. The large veteran enrollments moved colleges to relax rules that had forbidden students to marry. Unlike men, however, women tended to drop out of college after marriage and to take jobs so their husbands could stay in school. Reflecting gender norms of the 1950s, most college women agreed that "it is natural for a woman to be satisfied with her husband's success and not crave personal achievement."

> **REVIEW** How did technology contribute to changes in the economy, suburbanization, and the growth of the Sun Belt?

▶ The Culture of Abundance

Prosperity in the 1950s intensified the transformation of the nation into a consumer society, changing the way Americans lived and converting the traditional work ethic into an ethic of consumption. People married at earlier ages, the birthrate soared, and dominant values celebrated family life and traditional gender roles. Religious observance expanded even as Americans sought satisfaction in material possessions. Television entered the homes of most Americans, both reflecting and helping to promote a consumer culture. Undercurrents of rebellion, especially among young people, and women's increasing employment defied some of the dominant norms but did not greatly disrupt the complacency of the 1950s.

Consumption Rules the Day

Journalist Robert Samuelson remembered that in the 1950s "you were a daily witness to the marvels of affluence . . . a seemingly endless array of new gadgets and machines." Scorned by Khrushchev during the kitchen debate as unnecessary contrivances, consumer items flooded American society. Although the purchase and display of consumer goods was not new (see chapter 23), by the 1950s consumption had become a reigning value, vital for economic prosperity and essential to individuals' identity and status. In place of the traditional emphasis on work and savings, the consumer culture encouraged satisfaction and happiness through the purchase and use of new products.

The consumer culture rested on a firm material base. Between 1950 and 1960, both the gross national product (the value of all goods and services produced) and median family income grew by 25 percent in constant dollars. Economists claimed that 60 percent of Americans enjoyed middle-class incomes in 1960. Referring to the popular ranch-style houses in the new suburbs, *House Beautiful* magazine boasted, "Our houses are all on one level, like our class structure." Though ignoring the one in five Americans who still lived in poverty, the statement did reflect the increasing ability of people to consume products that made class differences less visible. By 1960, four out of every five families owned a television set, nearly all had a refrigerator, and most owned at least one car. The number of shopping centers quadrupled between 1957 and 1963.

Several forces spurred this unparalleled abundance. A population surge — from 152 million in 1950 to 180 million in 1960 — expanded the demand for products and boosted industries ranging from housing to baby goods. Consumer borrowing also fueled the economic boom, as people increasingly made purchases on install-ment plans and began to use credit cards. In what *Life* magazine referred to as a "revolution in consumer purchasing," Americans now enjoyed their possessions while they paid for them instead of saving their money for future purchases.

Although the sheer need to support themselves and their families explained most women's employment, a desire to secure some of the new abundance sent growing numbers of women to work. In fact, married women's employment rose more than that of any other group in the 1950s. As one woman remarked, "My Joe can't put five kids through college . . . and the washer had to be replaced, and Ann was ashamed to bring friends home because the living room furniture was such a mess, so I went to work." The standards for family happiness imposed by the consumer culture increasingly required a second income.

The Revival of Domesticity and Religion

Despite married women's growing employment, a dominant ideology celebrated traditional family life and conventional gender roles. Both popular culture and public figures defined the ideal family as a male breadwinner, a full-time homemaker, and three or four children. The emphasis on home and family life reflected in part the desire for security amid anxieties about the Cold War and the nuclear menace.

Writer and feminist **Betty Friedan** gave a name to the idealization of women's domestic roles in her 1963 book *The Feminine Mystique*. Friedan criticized scholars, advertisers, and public officials for promulgating a set of ideas based on the assumption that biological differences dictated different roles for men and women. According to this feminine mystique, women should find fulfillment in devotion to their homes, families, and serving others. Not many women directly challenged these ideas, but Edith Stern, a college-educated writer, maintained that "many arguments about the joys of housewifery have been advanced, largely by those who have never had to work at it."

Although the glorification of domesticity clashed with women's increasing employment, many Americans' lives did embody the family ideal. Postwar prosper-ity enabled people to marry earlier and to have more children. The American birthrate soared between 1945 and 1960, peaking in 1957 with 4.3 million births and producing the **baby boom** generation. Experts encouraged mothers to devote even more attention to child rearing, while they also urged fathers to cultivate family "togetherness" by spending more time with their children.

The 1950s also witnessed a surge of interest in religion. From 1940 to 1960, membership in churches and synagogues rose from 50 to 63 percent of all Americans.

Polls reported that 95 percent of the population believed in God. Evangelism took on new life, most notably in the nationwide crusades of Baptist minister **Billy Graham**. Congress linked religion more closely to the state by adding "under God" to the pledge of allegiance and by requiring that "In God We Trust" be printed on all currency.

Religion helped to calm anxieties in the nuclear age, while ministers such as Graham made the Cold War a holy war, labeling communism "a great sinister anti-Christian movement masterminded by Satan." Some critics questioned the depth of the religious revival, attributing the growth in church membership to a desire for conformity and a need for social outlets. One commentator, for example, noted that 53 percent of Americans could not name any book of the Christian Bible's New Testament.

Television Transforms Culture and Politics

Just as family life and religion offered a respite from Cold War anxieties, so too did the new medium of television. By 1960, close to 90 percent of American homes boasted a television set, and the average viewer spent more than five hours each day in front of the screen. Audiences were especially attracted to situation comedies, which projected the family ideal and the feminine mystique into millions of homes. On TV, married women did not have paying jobs, and they deferred to their husbands, though they often got the upper hand through subtle manipulation. In the most popular television show of the early 1950s, *I Love Lucy*, the husband-and-wife team of Lucille Ball and Desi Arnaz played the couple Lucy and Ricky Ricardo. Ricky would not let Lucy get a job, and many plots depicted her zany attempts to get around him.

Television also began to affect politics. Eisenhower's 1952 presidential campaign used TV ads for the first time, although he was not happy that "an old soldier should come to this." By 1960, television played a key role in election campaigns. Reflecting on his narrow victory in 1960, president-elect John F. Kennedy remarked, "We wouldn't have had a prayer without that gadget."

Television transformed politics in other ways. Money played a much larger role in elections because candidates needed to pay for expensive TV spots. The ability to appeal directly to voters in their living rooms put a premium on personal attractiveness and encouraged candidates to build their own campaign organizations, relying less on political parties. The declining strength of parties and the growing power of money in elections were not new trends, but TV helped accelerate them.

Unlike government-financed television in Europe, American TV was paid for by private enterprise. What NBC called a "selling machine in every living room" became the major vehicle for hawking the products of the affluent society and creating a consumer culture. In the mid-1950s, advertisers spent $10 billion to push their goods on TV, and they did not hesitate to interfere with shows that might jeopardize the sale of their products. The cigarette company that sponsored the *Camel News Caravan* banned any news film clips showing "No Smoking" signs. Television programs also tantalized viewers with things to buy. On *Queen for a Day*, for example, the women with the most pitiful personal stories won fur coats, vacuum cleaners, and other merchandise.

In 1961, Newton Minow, chairman of the Federal Communications Commission, called television a "vast wasteland." While acknowledging some of TV's great achievements, particularly documentaries and drama, Minow depicted it as "a procession of game shows, . . . formula comedies about totally unbelievable families, blood and thunder, mayhem, violence, sadism, murder . . . and cartoons." But viewers kept tuning in. In little more than a decade, television came to dominate Americans' leisure time, influence their consumption patterns, and shape their perceptions of the nation's leadership.

Countercurrents

Pockets of dissent underlay the complacency of the 1950s. Some intellectuals took exception to the materialism and conformity of the era. In *The Lonely Crowd* (1950), sociologist David Riesman lamented a shift from the "inner-directed" to the "other-directed" individual, as Americans replaced independent thinking with an eagerness to adapt to external standards of behavior and belief. Sharing that distaste for the importance of "belonging," William H. Whyte Jr., in his popular book *The Organization Man* (1956), blamed the modern corporation for making employees tailor themselves to the group. Vance Packard's 1959 best seller, *The Status Seekers*, decried "the vigorous merchandising of goods as status-symbols" and argued that "class lines . . . appear to be hardening."

Implicit in much of the critique of consumer culture was concern about the loss of traditional masculinity. Consumption itself was associated with women and their presumed greater susceptibility to manipulation. Men, required to conform to get ahead, moved farther away from the nineteenth-century masculine ideals of individualism and aggressiveness. Moreover, the increase in married women's employment compromised the male ideal of breadwinner.

Into this gender confusion came *Playboy*, which began publication in 1953 and quickly gained a circulation of one million. The new magazine idealized masculine independence in the form of bachelorhood and assaulted the reigning middle-class norms of domesticity and respectability. By associating the sophisticated bachelor with good wine, music, furnishings, and the like, the magazine made consumption more masculine while promoting sexual freedom, at least for men.

In fact, new research on Americans' sexual behavior disclosed that it often departed from the postwar family ideal. Two books published by **Alfred Kinsey** and other researchers at Indiana University — *Sexual Behavior in the Human Male* (1948) and *Sexual Behavior in the Human Female* (1953) — uncovered a surprising range of sexual conduct. In a large survey, Kinsey found that 85 percent of the men and 50 percent of the women had had sex before marriage, half of the husbands and a quarter of the wives had engaged in adultery, and one-third of the men and one-seventh of the women reported homosexual experiences. Although Kinsey's sampling procedures later cast doubt on his ability to generalize across the population, the books became best sellers. They also drew a firestorm of outrage, especially because Kinsey insisted on the natural variability of human sexuality and refused to make moral judgments.

Less direct challenges to mainstream standards appeared in the everyday behavior of young Americans. "Roll over Beethoven and tell Tchaikovsky the news!"

Elvis Presley
Elvis Presley began recording in 1954, and within two years — by the age of 21 — he was a national star, appearing frequently on television and scoring his first number one single hit, "Heartbreak Hotel." He drew adoring teenage crowds wherever he performed, including this appearance in his hometown of Tupelo, Mississippi, in 1956. His fans' parents were not so enthralled, complaining about his "grunt and groin antics" and "unnecessary bump and grind routine." Elvis Presley Enterprises, Inc.

belted out Chuck Berry in his 1956 hit record celebrating **rock and roll**, a new form of music that combined country sounds and black rhythm and blues. White teenagers lionized Elvis Presley, who shocked their parents with his tight pants, hip-rolling gestures, and sensuous rock-and-roll music. "Before there was Elvis . . . I started going crazy for 'race music,'" recalled a white man of his teenage years. "That got me into trouble with my parents and the schools." His recollection underscored African Americans' contributions to rock and roll, as well as the rebellion expressed by white youths' attraction to black music.

The most blatant revolt against conventionality came from the self-proclaimed **Beat generation**, a small group of primarily male literary figures based in New York City and San Francisco. Rejecting nearly everything in mainstream culture — patriotism, consumerism, technology, conventional family life, discipline — the Beats celebrated spontaneity and absolute personal freedom, including drug consumption and freewheeling sex. In his landmark poem *Howl* (1956), Allen Ginsberg denounced the social forces that "frightened me out of my natural ecstasy!" Jack Kerouac, who gave the Beat generation its name, published the best-selling novel *On the Road* (1957), whose energetic, stream-of-consciousness, bebop-style prose narrated the impetuous cross-country travels of two young men. "The only people for me," he wrote, "are the mad ones . . . the ones who never yawn or say a commonplace thing, but burn, burn, burn like fabulous yellow roman candles exploding like spiders across the stars." The Beats' lifestyles shocked "square" Americans, but they would provide a model for a much larger movement of youthful dissidents in the 1960s.

Bold new styles in the visual arts also showed the 1950s to be more than a decade of bland conventionality. In New York City, an artistic revolution known as "action painting" or "abstract expressionism" flowered, rejecting the idea that painting should represent recognizable forms. Jackson Pollock and other abstract expressionists, emphasizing spontaneity, poured, dripped, and threw paint on canvases or substituted sticks and other implements for brushes. The new form of painting so captivated and redirected the Western art world that New York replaced Paris as its center.

> **REVIEW** Why did American consumption expand so dramatically in the 1950s, and what aspects of society and culture did it influence?

▶ The Emergence of a Civil Rights Movement

Building on the civil rights initiatives begun during World War II, African Americans posed the most dramatic challenge to the status quo of the 1950s as they sought to overcome the political, economic, and social barriers that had replaced the literal bonds of slavery. Every southern state mandated rigid segregation in public settings ranging from hospitals and schools to drinking fountains and restrooms. Voting laws and practices in the South disfranchised the vast majority of African Americans; employment discrimination kept them at the bottom of the economic ladder throughout the country; and schools, restaurants, and other public spaces were often as segregated, though not usually by law, in the North as they were in the South.

Although black protest was as old as American racism, in the 1950s grassroots movements arose that attracted national attention and the support of white liberals. Pressed by civil rights groups, the Supreme Court delivered significant institutional reforms, but the most important changes of all occurred among blacks themselves. Ordinary African Americans in substantial numbers sought their own liberation, building a movement that would transform race relations in the United States.

African Americans Challenge the Supreme Court and the President

Several factors spurred black protest in the 1950s. Between 1940 and 1960, more than three million African Americans moved from the South into areas where they had a political voice. Black leaders made sure that foreign policy officials realized how racist practices at home tarnished the U.S. image abroad and handicapped the United States in its competition with the Soviet Union. The very system of segregation meant that African Americans controlled certain organizational resources, such as churches, colleges, and newspapers, where leadership skills could be honed, networks developed, and information spread.

The legal strategy of the major civil rights organization, the National Association for the Advancement of Colored People (NAACP), reached its crowning achievement with the Supreme Court decision in **Brown v. Board of Education** in 1954. *Brown* consolidated five separate suits that reflected the growing determination of black Americans to fight for their rights. Oliver Brown, a World War II veteran in Topeka, Kansas, filed suit because his daughter had to pass by a white school just seven blocks from their home to attend a black school more than a mile away. In Virginia, sixteen-year-old Barbara Johns initiated a student strike over wretched conditions in her black high school, leading to another of the suits joined in *Brown*. The NAACP's lead lawyer, future Supreme Court justice Thurgood Marshall, urged the Court to overturn the "separate but equal" precedent established in *Plessy v. Ferguson* in 1896 (see chapter 21). A unanimous Court, headed by Chief Justice Earl Warren, declared, "Separate educational facilities are inherently unequal" and thus violated the Fourteenth Amendment.

Ultimate responsibility for enforcement of the decision lay with President Eisenhower, but he refused to endorse *Brown*. He also kept silent in 1955 when whites murdered Emmett Till, a fourteen-year-old black boy who had allegedly whistled at a white woman in Mississippi. Reflecting his own prejudice, his preference for limited federal intervention in the states, and a leadership style that favored consensus and gradual progress, Eisenhower kept his distance from civil rights issues. Such inaction fortified southern resistance to school desegregation and contributed to the gravest constitutional crisis since the Civil War.

The crisis came in Little Rock, Arkansas, in September 1957, when Governor Orval Faubus sent Arkansas National Guard troops to block the enrollment of nine black students in Little Rock's Central High School. Later, he allowed them to enter but withdrew the National Guard, leaving the students to face an angry white mob. "During those years when we desperately needed approval from our peers," Melba Patillo Beals remembered, "we were victims of the most harsh rejection imaginable." As television cameras transmitted the ugly scene, Eisenhower was forced to send regular army troops to Little Rock, the first federal military intervention in the South since Reconstruction. Paratroopers escorted the "**Little Rock Nine**" into the school, but forty-four teachers who had supported them lost their jobs. Despite Eisenhower's explanation that he had acted to preserve the law, not to promote integration, southern leaders were outraged. Other southern cities avoided integration by closing public schools and using tax dollars to support private ones. Seven years after *Brown*, only 6.4 percent of southern black students attended integrated schools.

School segregation outside the South was not usually sanctioned by law, but northern school districts separated black and white students through manipulation of neighborhood boundaries and through other devices. Even before *Brown*, black parents in dozens of northern cities challenged the assignment of their children to inferior "colored" schools. While their boycotts reaped some successes, the structure of residential segregation, often supported by official action, made school segregation a severe disadvantage for African Americans in the North as well as in the South.

Although Eisenhower rejected an aggressive approach to racial issues, he did order the integration of public facilities in Washington, D.C., and on military bases, and he supported the first federal civil rights legislation since Reconstruction. Yet southern members of Congress made sure that the Civil Rights Acts of 1957 and 1960 were little more than symbolic. Baseball star Jackie Robinson spoke for many African Americans when he wired Eisenhower in 1957, "We disagree that half a loaf is better than none. Have waited this long for a bill with meaning — can wait a little longer." Eisenhower appointed the first black professional to the White House staff, E. Frederick Morrow, but Morrow confided in his diary, "I feel ridiculous . . . trying to defend the administration's record on civil rights."

Montgomery and Mass Protest

What set the civil rights movement of the 1950s and 1960s apart from earlier acts of black protest was its widespread presence in the South, the large number of people involved, their willingness to confront white institutions directly, and the use of nonviolent protest and civil disobedience to bring about change. The Congress of Racial Equality and other groups had experimented with these tactics in the 1940s, organizing, for example, to integrate movie theaters in Cincinnati, restaurants in Chicago, swimming pools in New Jersey, and a public playground in Washington, D.C. In the South, African Americans boycotted the segregated bus system in Baton Rouge, Louisiana, in 1953, but the first sustained protest to claim national attention began in Montgomery, Alabama, on December 1, 1955.

That day, police arrested **Rosa Parks** for violating a local segregation ordinance. Riding a crowded bus home from her job as a seamstress in a department store, she refused to give up her seat so that a white man could sit down. "People always say that I didn't give up my seat because I was tired, but that isn't true," Parks recalled. "I was not tired physically. . . . I was not old. . . . I was forty-two. No, the only tired I was, was tired of giving in." The bus driver called the police, who promptly arrested her.

Parks had long been active in the local NAACP, headed by E. D. Nixon. They had already talked about challenging bus segregation. So had the Women's Political Council (WPC), composed of black professional women and led by Jo Ann Robinson, an English professor at Alabama State, who had once been humiliated by a bus driver when she accidentally sat in the white section. Such local individuals and organizations, long committed to improving conditions for African Americans, laid critical foundations for the black freedom struggle throughout the South.

When word came that Parks would fight her arrest, WPC leaders mobilized teachers and students to distribute fliers calling for blacks to stay off the buses. E. D. Nixon called a mass meeting at the Holt Street Baptist Church, where those assembled founded the Montgomery Improvement Association (MIA) to organize a bus boycott. The MIA arranged volunteer car pools and marshaled more than 90 percent of the black community to sustain the yearlong **Montgomery bus boycott**.

Elected to head the MIA was twenty-six-year-old **Martin Luther King Jr.**, a young Baptist pastor with a doctorate in theology from Boston University. As a seminary student in 1950, he had been denied service in a New Jersey restaurant and refused to leave until the owner chased him and his friends out with a gun. A captivating speaker, King addressed mass meetings at churches throughout the bus boycott, inspiring blacks' courage and commitment by linking racial justice to Christianity. He promised, "If you will protest courageously and yet with dignity and Christian love . . . historians will have to pause and say, 'There lived a great people — a black people — who injected a new meaning and dignity into the veins of civilization.'"

Montgomery blacks summoned their courage and determination in abundance. An older woman insisted, "I'm not walking for myself, I'm walking for my children and my grandchildren." Boycotters walked miles or carpooled to get to work, contributed their meager financial resources, and stood up with dignity to intimidation and police harassment. Jo Ann Robinson,

Martin Luther King, Jr.
The twenty-six-year-old Martin Luther King, Jr. had been in Montgomery, Alabama, for less than two years when he was selected in 1955 to lead the city-wide bus boycott, which had been started by more-seasoned community leaders. Here he is shown greeting members of his Dexter Avenue Baptist Church congregation near the Montgomery State Capitol. King's philosophy of nonviolent resistance to injustice derived in part from his study of the principles of the Indian nationalist leader Mahatma Gandhi, and in 1964, he became the youngest person to be awarded the Nobel Peace Prize. Dan Weiner, Courtesy Sandra Weiner.

a cautious driver, got seventeen tickets in the space of two months. Authorities arrested several leaders, and whites firebombed King's house. Yet the movement persisted until November 1956, when the Supreme Court declared unconstitutional Alabama's laws requiring bus segregation. African Americans had demonstrated that they could sustain a lengthy protest and would not be intimidated.

King's face on the cover of *Time* magazine in February 1957 marked his rapid rise to national and international fame. In January, black clergy from across the South had chosen King to head the **Southern Christian Leadership Conference (SCLC),** newly established to coordinate local protests against segregation and disfranchisement. The prominence of King and other ministers obscured the substantial numbers and critical importance of black women in the movement. In fact, the SCLC owed much of its success to Ella Baker, a seasoned activist who came from New York to manage its office in Atlanta. King's prominence and the media's focus on the South also hid the national scope of racial injustice and the struggles for racial equality in the North that both encouraged and benefited from the black freedom struggle in the South.

> **REVIEW**   What were the goals and strategies of civil rights activists in the 1950s?

▶ Conclusion: Peace and Prosperity Mask Unmet Challenges

At the American National Exhibition in Moscow in 1959, the consumer goods that Nixon proudly displayed to Khrushchev and the Cold War competition that crackled through their dialogue reflected two dominant themes of the 1950s: the prosperity of the U.S. economy and the superpowers' success in keeping their antagonism within the bounds of peace. The tremendous economic growth of the 1950s, which raised the standard of living for most Americans, resulted in part from the Cold War: One of every ten American jobs depended directly on defense spending.

Affluence changed the very landscape of the United States. Suburban housing developments sprang up, interstate highways began to cut up cities and connect the country, farms declined in number but grew in size, and population and industry moved south and west. Daily habits and even the values of ordinary people shifted as the economy became more service oriented and the appearance of a host of new products intensified the growth of a consumer culture that had begun decades earlier.

The prosperity, however, masked a number of developments and problems that Americans would face head-on in later years: rising resistance to racial injustice, a 20 percent poverty rate, married women's movement into the labor force, and the emergence of a self-conscious youth generation. Although the federal government's defense spending and housing, highway, and education subsidies helped to sustain the economic boom, in general Eisenhower tried to curb domestic programs and let private enterprise have its way. His administration maintained the welfare state inherited from the New Deal but resisted the expansion of federal programs.

In global affairs, Eisenhower exercised restraint on large issues, recognizing the limits of U.S. power. In the name of deterrence, he promoted the development of more destructive atomic weapons, but he withstood pressures for even larger defense budgets. Nonetheless, Eisenhower shared Truman's fundamental assumption that the United States must fight communism everywhere, and when movements in Iran, Guatemala, Cuba, and Vietnam seemed too radical, too friendly to communism, or too inimical to American economic interests, he tried to undermine them, often with secret operations and severe consequences for native populations.

Although Eisenhower presided over eight years of peace and prosperity, his foreign policy inspired anti-Americanism, established dangerous precedents for the expansion of executive power, and forged commitments and interventions that future generations would deem unwise. As Eisenhower's successors took on the struggle against communism and grappled with the domestic challenges of race, poverty, and urban decay that he had avoided, the tranquility and consensus of the 1950s would give way to the turbulence and conflict of the 1960s.

Reviewing Chapter 27

REVIEW QUESTIONS

1. How did Eisenhower's domestic policies reflect his moderate political vision? (pp. 811–815)

2. Where and how did Eisenhower practice containment? (pp. 815–821)

3. How did technology contribute to changes in the economy, suburbanization, and the growth of the Sun Belt? (pp. 821–827)

4. Why did American consumption expand so dramatically in the 1950s, and what aspects of society and culture did it influence? (pp. 827–832)

5. What were the goals and strategies of civil rights activists in the 1950s? (pp. 832–836)

MAKING CONNECTIONS

1. Eisenhower was the first Republican president since the New Deal had transformed the role of the federal government. How did his "modern Republicanism" address Roosevelt's legacy? How did the shape and character of government change or not change during Eisenhower's administration?

2. The 1950s brought significant changes to the everyday lives of many Americans. Discuss the economic and demographic changes that contributed to the growth of suburbs and the Sun Belt. In your answer, consider both Americans who participated in these trends and those who did not.

3. What actual developments in American society in the 1950s were at odds with prevailing norms and values?

4. During the 1950s, actions by the federal government and the courts had a significant impact on African Americans, Native Americans, and Mexican Americans. Discuss how new policies and court actions came about and how laws affected these groups for better and for worse.

LINKING TO THE PAST

1. How did the policies of termination and relocation differ from the New Deal's policy toward Indians? (See chapter 24.)

2. What developments stemming from World War II influenced U.S. foreign policy in such areas as Vietnam and Latin America? (See chapter 25.)

TIMELINE 1952–1960

1952 • Republican Dwight D. Eisenhower elected president.

1953 • Termination of special status of Native Americans and relocation of thousands off reservations.
• CIA engineers coup against government of Iran.

1954 • CIA stages coup against government of Guatemala.
• France signs Geneva accords, withdrawing from Vietnam.
• United States begins aid to South Vietnam.
• Government launches Operation Wetback.
• *Hernandez v. Texas*.
• *Brown v. Board of Education*.
• Senate condemns Senator Joseph McCarthy.

1955 • Eisenhower and Khrushchev meet in Geneva.

1955–1956 • Montgomery, Alabama, bus boycott.

1956 • Interstate Highway and Defense System Act.
• Eisenhower reelected by landslide to second term.
• *Howl* published.

1957 • Southern Christian Leadership Conference (SCLC) founded.
• Soviets launch *Sputnik*.
• Labor union membership peaks at 27.1 percent of labor force.
• Civil Rights Act of 1957.
• *On the Road* published.

1958 • National Aeronautics and Space Administration (NASA) established.
• National Defense Education Act.

1959 • Kitchen debate between Nixon and Khrushchev.

1960 • Soviets shoot down U.S. U-2 spy plane.
• One-quarter of Americans live in suburbs.
• Thirty-five percent of women work outside the home.

▶ **FOR AN ONLINE BIBLIOGRAPHY, PRACTICE QUIZZES, WEB SITES, IMAGES, AND DOCUMENTS RELATED TO THIS CHAPTER,** see the Book Companion Site at **bedfordstmartins.com/roarkvalue**.

▶ **FOR DOCUMENTS RELATED TO THIS PERIOD,** see Michael Johnson, ed., *Reading the American Past*, Fifth Edition.

Reform, Rebellion, and Reaction

1960–1974

ON AUGUST 31, 1962, FANNIE LOU HAMER BOARDED A BUS CARRYING eighteen African Americans from Ruleville, Mississippi, to the county seat in Indianola, where they intended to register to vote. Blacks accounted for more than 60 percent of Sunflower County's population but only 1.2 percent of registered voters. Before civil rights activists arrived in Ruleville to start a voter registration drive, Hamer recalled, "I didn't know that a Negro could register and vote." Her forty-five years of poverty, exploitation, and political disfranchisement typified the lives of most blacks in the rural South. The daughter of sharecroppers, Hamer began work in the cotton fields at age six, attending school in a one-room shack from December to March and only until she was twelve. After marrying Perry Hamer, she moved onto a plantation, where she worked in the fields, did domestic work for the owner, and recorded the cotton that sharecroppers harvested.

At the Indianola County courthouse, Hamer and her companions had to pass through a hostile, white, gun-carrying crowd. Using a common practice to deny blacks the vote, the registrar tested Hamer on an obscure section of the state constitution. She failed the test but resolved to try again. When the plantation owner ordered Hamer to withdraw her registration application or get off his land, she left the plantation. Ten days later, bullets flew into the home of friends who had taken her in. Refusing to be intimidated, she registered to vote on her third attempt, attended a civil rights leadership training conference, and began to mobilize others to vote. In 1963, she and other activists were arrested in Winona, Mississippi, and brutally beaten. Hamer went from jail to the hospital, where her sister could not recognize her battered face.

Mississippi Freedom Democratic Party Rally
Fannie Lou Hamer (left foreground) and other activists sing at a rally outside the Democratic National Convention hall in 1964, supporting the Mississippi Freedom Democratic Party (MFDP) in its challenge to the all-white delegation sent by the regular state Democratic Party. Next to Hamer is Eleanor Holmes Norton, a civil rights lawyer, and Ella Baker (far right), who helped organize the Southern Christian Leadership Conference and later managed MFDP headquarters in Washington, D.C. In the rear is SNCC leader, Stokely Carmichael (in the straw hat). © George Ballis/Take Stock/The Image Works.

Fannie Lou Hamer's courage and determination made her a prominent figure in the black freedom struggle. Such activists shook the nation's conscience, provided a protest model for other groups, and pushed the government to enact not only civil rights legislation but also a host of other liberal policies. Although the federal government often tried to curb civil rights protest, the two Democratic presidents of the 1960s favored using government to ameliorate social and economic problems. After John F. Kennedy was assassinated in November 1963, Lyndon B. Johnson launched the Great Society — a multitude of efforts to promote racial justice, education, medical care, urban development, environmental and economic health, and more. Those who struggled for racial justice lost property and sometimes their lives, but by the end of the decade American law had caught up with the American ideal of equality.

Yet strong civil rights legislation and pathbreaking Supreme Court decisions could not alone mitigate the deplorable economic conditions of African Americans nationwide, on which Hamer and others increasingly focused after 1965. Nor were liberal politicians reliable supporters, as Hamer found out in 1964 when President Johnson and his allies rebuffed black Mississippi Democrats' efforts to be represented at the Democratic National Convention. "We followed all the laws," she said, only to find that "the white man is not going to give up his power to us. . . . We have to take [it] for ourselves." By 1966, a minority of African American activists were demanding black power; the movement soon splintered, and white support sharply declined. The war in Vietnam stifled liberal reform, while a growing conservative movement, protesting that the Great Society went too far, condemned the challenge to American traditions and institutions mounted by blacks, students, and others.

Though disillusioned and often frustrated, Fannie Lou Hamer remained an activist until her death in 1977, participating in new social movements stimulated by the black freedom struggle. In 1969, she supported students at Mississippi Valley State College who demanded black studies courses and a voice in campus decisions. In 1972, she attended the first conference of the National Women's Political Caucus, established to achieve greater representation for women in government. The caucus was part of a diverse feminist movement that transformed women's legal status as well as everyday relationships between women and men.

Feminists and other groups, including ethnic minorities, environmentalists, and gays and lesbians, carried the tide of reform into the 1970s. They pushed Richard M. Nixon's Republican administration to sustain the liberalism of the 1960s, with its emphasis on a strong government role in regulating the economy, guaranteeing the welfare and rights of all individuals, and improving the quality of life. Despite its conservative rhetoric, the Nixon administration implemented school desegregation and affirmative action and adopted pathbreaking measures in environmental regulation, equality for women, and justice for Native Americans. The years between 1960 and 1974 witnessed the greatest efforts to reconcile America's promise with reality since the New Deal.

▶ Liberalism at High Tide

At the Democratic National Convention in 1960, John F. Kennedy announced "a New Frontier" that would confront "unsolved problems of peace and war, unconquered pockets of ignorance and prejudice, unanswered questions of poverty and surplus." Four years later, Lyndon B. Johnson invoked the ideal of a "Great Society, [which] rests on abundance and liberty for all [and] demands an end to poverty and racial injustice." Acting under the liberal faith that government should use its power to solve social and economic problems, end injustice, and promote the welfare of all citizens, the Democratic administrations of the 1960s won legislation on civil rights, poverty, education, medical care, housing, consumer safeguards, and environmental protection. These measures, along with path-breaking Supreme Court decisions, advanced the unfulfilled agendas of the New Deal and Fair Deal, responded to demands for rights from African Americans and other groups, and addressed problems arising from rapid economic growth.

The Unrealized Promise of Kennedy's New Frontier

John F. Kennedy grew up in privilege, the child of an Irish Catholic businessman who served as ambassador to Great Britain and nourished political ambitions for his sons. Helped by a distinguished World War II navy record, Kennedy won election to the House of Representatives in 1946 and the Senate in 1952. With a powerful political machine, his family's fortune, and a dynamic personal appeal, Kennedy won the Democratic presidential nomination in 1960. He stunned many Democrats by choosing as his running mate Lyndon B. Johnson of Texas, a rival for the presidential nomination whom liberals disparaged as a typical southern conservative.

Kennedy defeated his Republican opponent, Vice President Richard M. Nixon, in an excruciatingly close election. African American voters contributed to his victory, helping to offset the 52 percent of the white vote cast for Nixon and contributing to Kennedy's 118,550-vote margin overall. Lyndon Johnson helped carry most of the South, and a rise in unemployment in 1960 also favored the Democrats. Finally, Kennedy benefited from the nation's first televised presidential debates, at which he appeared cool and confident beside a nervous and pale Nixon.

The Kennedy administration projected energy, idealism, and glamour, although Kennedy was in most ways a cautious, pragmatic politician. The first president to hold televised press conferences, Kennedy charmed the audience with his grace and wit. Journalists kept from the public Kennedy's serious health problems and extramarital affairs, instead projecting warm images of a vigorous president with his chic and cultured wife, Jacqueline.

At his inauguration, the forty-three-year-old Kennedy called on Americans to serve the common good. "Ask not what your country can do for you," he implored, "ask what you can do for your country." Although Kennedy's idealism inspired many, he failed to redeem campaign promises to expand the welfare state with federal education and health care programs. Moreover, he resisted leadership on behalf of racial justice until civil rights activists gave him no choice and he issued a dramatic call for a comprehensive civil rights bill, marking a turning point in his domestic agenda.

Moved by the desperate conditions he observed while campaigning in Appalachia, Kennedy pushed poverty onto the national agenda. In 1962, he read Michael Harrington's *The Other America*, which described the poverty that left more than one in five Americans "maimed in body and spirit, existing at levels beneath those necessary for human decency." By 1962, Kennedy had won support for a $2 billion urban renewal program that offered incentives to businesses to locate in economically depressed areas and a training program for the unemployed. In the summer of 1963, he asked aides to plan a full-scale attack on poverty. Kennedy had promised to make economic growth a key objective. "A rising tide lifts all boats" expressed his belief that economic growth could eradicate poverty. To that end, he asked Congress to pass an enormous tax cut in 1963, arguing that reducing taxes would infuse money into the economy and thus increase demand, boost production, and reduce unemployment. Passed in February 1964, the law contributed to an economic boom, as unemployment dropped to 4.1 percent and the gross national product shot up by 7 to 9 percent annually between 1964 and 1966. Some liberal critics of the tax cut, however, pointed out that it favored the well-off and that economic growth alone would not eliminate poverty. They argued instead for increased spending on social programs.

Kennedy's antipoverty, civil rights, and economic initiatives had not reached fruition when an assassin's bullets struck him down on November 22, 1963. Within minutes of the shooting — which occurred as Kennedy's motorcade passed through Dallas, Texas — radio and television broadcast the unfolding horror to the nation. Millions watched as *Air Force One* returned to Washington bearing the president's coffin, his widow in a bloodstained suit, and the new president, Lyndon Baines Johnson.

Stunned Americans struggled to understand what had happened. Soon after the assassination, police arrested Lee Harvey Oswald and concluded that he had fired the shots from a nearby building. Two days later, while officers were transferring Oswald from one jail to another, a local nightclub operator, Jack Ruby, killed him. Suspicions arose that Ruby murdered Oswald to cover up a conspiracy by ultraconservatives who hated Kennedy, or by Communists who supported Castro's Cuba (as discussed in chapter 29). To get at the truth, President Johnson appointed a commission headed by Chief Justice Earl Warren, which concluded that both Oswald and Ruby had acted alone. Although some contested the lone-killer explanation, most scholars agreed that no conspiracy had existed.

Debate continued over how to assess Kennedy's domestic record. It had been unremarkable in his first two years, but his proposals on taxes, civil rights, and poverty in 1963 suggested an important shift. Whether Kennedy could have persuaded Congress to enact them remained in question. In the words of journalist James Reston, "What was killed was not only the president but the promise. . . . He never reached his meridian: We saw him only as a rising sun."

Johnson Fulfills the Kennedy Promise

Lyndon B. Johnson assumed the presidency with a wealth of political experience. A self-made man from Texas's Hill Country, he had won election in 1937 to the House of Representatives and in 1948 to the Senate, where, after 1955, he served skillfully as Senate majority leader. Although his Texas base required caution on civil rights and issues affecting oil and other big businesses, Johnson's presidential aspirations led him to take more liberal stands. His own modest upbringing in an impoverished area, his admiration for Franklin Roosevelt, and his fierce ambition to outdo the New Deal president all spurred his commitment to reform in order to build what he called a **Great Society**. Equally compelling were external pressures generated by the black freedom struggle and the host of movements it helped inspire.

Johnson's coarse wit and vanity repulsed those who preferred the sophisticated Kennedy style. Lacking his predecessor's charm and eloquence, Johnson excelled behind the scenes, where he could entice, maneuver, or threaten legislators to support his objectives. His persuasive power, known as the "Johnson treatment," became legendary. In his ability to achieve consensus around his goals, Johnson had few peers in American history.

Johnson entreated Congress to act so that "John Fitzgerald Kennedy did not live or die in vain." He signed Kennedy's tax cut bill in February 1964. More remarkable was passage of the **Civil Rights Act of 1964**, which Kennedy had proposed in response to black protest. The strongest such measure since Reconstruction, the law required every ounce of Johnson's political skill to pry sufficient votes from Republicans to balance the "nays" of southern Democrats. Senate Republican leader Everett Dirksen's aide reported that Johnson "never left him alone for thirty minutes."

Antipoverty legislation followed fast on the heels of the Civil Rights Act. Just two months after Johnson announced "an unconditional war on poverty" in his January 1964 State of the Union message, the administration rushed a draft bill to Congress, which responded with equal haste in August. The Economic Opportunity Act of 1964 authorized ten new programs, allocating $800 million — about 1 percent of the federal budget — for the first year. Many provisions targeted children and youths, including Head Start for preschoolers, work-study grants for college students, and the Job Corps for unemployed young people. The Volunteers in Service to America (VISTA) program paid modest wages to volunteers working with the disadvantaged, and a legal services program provided lawyers for the poor.

The most novel and controversial part of the law, the Community Action Program (CAP), required "maximum feasible participation" of the poor themselves in antipoverty projects. Poor people began to organize community action programs to take control of their neighborhoods and to make welfare agencies, school boards, police departments, and housing authorities more accountable to the people they served. When mayors complained that activists were challenging local governments and "fostering class struggle," Johnson backed off from pushing genuine representation for the poor. Nonetheless, CAP gave people usually excluded from government an opportunity to act on their own behalf and develop leadership skills. To a Mississippi sharecropper, the local CAP literacy program "meant more to me than I can express," providing him basic skills and self-respect.

Policymaking for a Great Society

As the 1964 election approached, Johnson projected stability and security in the midst of a booming economy. Few voters wanted to risk the dramatic change promised by his Republican opponent, Arizona senator Barry M. Goldwater, who attacked the welfare state and suggested using nuclear weapons if necessary to crush communism in Vietnam. Although Goldwater captured five southern states, Johnson achieved a record-breaking landslide of 61 percent of the popular vote, and Democrats won resounding majorities in the House (295–140) and Senate (68–32). Still, Goldwater's campaign aroused considerable grassroots support, and a movement on the right grew alongside the more visible left-wing and liberal movements (as discussed in chapter 30).

"I want to see a whole bunch of coonskins on the wall," Johnson told his aides, using a hunting analogy to stress his ambitious legislative goals for what he called the "Great Society." The large Democratic majorities in Congress, his own political skills, and pressure from the black freedom struggle enabled Johnson to succeed mightily. He persuaded Congress to act on discrimination, poverty, education, medical care, housing, consumer and environmental protection, and more. Reporters called the legislation of the Eighty-ninth Congress (1965–1966) "a political miracle."

The Economic Opportunity Act of 1964 was the opening shot in the **War on Poverty**. Congress doubled the program's funding in 1965, enacted new economic development measures for depressed regions, and authorized more than $1 billion to improve the nation's slums. Direct aid included a new food stamp program, giving poor people greater choice in obtaining food, and rent supplements that provided alternatives to public housing projects for some poor families. Moreover, a movement of welfare mothers, the National Welfare Rights Organization, assisted by antipoverty lawyers, pushed administrators of Aid to Families with Dependent Children (AFDC) to ease restrictions on welfare recipients. The number of families receiving assistance jumped from less than one million in 1960 to three million by 1972, benefiting 90 percent of those eligible.

Central to Johnson's War on Poverty were efforts to equip the poor with the skills necessary to find jobs. A former schoolteacher, Johnson saw federal support for public education as a natural extension of the New Deal; it had been on the Democratic Party agenda for two decades. His Elementary and Secondary Education Act of 1965 marked a turning point by involving the federal government in K–12 education. The measure sent federal dollars to local school districts based on

A Tribute to Johnson for Medicare
George Niedermeyer, who lived in Hollywood, Florida, and received a Social Security pension, painted pieces of wood and glued them together to create this thank-you to President Johnson for establishing Medicare. Niedermeyer entrusted his congressional representative, Claude Pepper, known for his support of the interests of the elderly, to deliver the four-foot-tall tribute to Johnson in 1967. LBJ Library, photo by Henry Groskinsky.

the number of poor children they enrolled, and it provided equipment and supplies to private and parochial schools serving the poor. That same year, Congress passed the Higher Education Act, vastly expanding federal assistance to colleges and universities for buildings, programs, scholarships, and loans.

The federal government's responsibility for health care marked an even more significant watershed. Faced with a powerful medical lobby that opposed national health insurance as "socialized medicine," Johnson pared down Truman's proposal for government-sponsored universal care. Instead, he focused on the elderly, who constituted a large portion of the nation's poor. Congress responded with the **Medicare** program, providing the elderly with universal compulsory medical insurance financed largely through Social Security taxes. A separate program, **Medicaid**, authorized federal grants to supplement state-paid medical care for poor people. By the twenty-first century, these two programs covered 87 million Americans, nearly 30 percent of the population.

Whereas programs such as Medicare fulfilled New Deal and Fair Deal promises, the Great Society's civil rights legislation represented a break with tradition and an expansion of liberalism. Racial minorities were neglected or discriminated against in many New Deal programs, and Truman's civil rights proposals bore few results. By contrast, the Civil Rights Act of 1964 made discrimination in employment, education, and public accommodations illegal. The **Voting Rights Act of 1965** banned literacy tests like the one that had stymied Fannie Lou Hamer and authorized federal intervention to ensure access to the voting booth.

Another form of bias fell with the **Immigration and Nationality Act of 1965**, which abolished the fifty-year-old quota system based on national origins that discriminated against immigrants from areas outside northern and western Europe (see chapter 23). The law maintained caps on the total number of immigrants and for the first time limited those from the Western Hemisphere; preference was now given to immediate relatives of U.S. citizens and to those with desirable skills. Massachusetts senator Edward Kennedy predicted that "our cities will not be flooded with a million citizens annually," but the measure's unanticipated consequences did nearly that, triggering a surge of immigration near the end of the century (as discussed in chapter 31).

Great Society benefits reached well beyond victims of discrimination and the poor. Medicare, for example, covered the elderly, regardless of income. A groundswell of consumer activism fueled by Ralph Nader's exposé of the auto industry, *Unsafe at Any Speed* (1965), won legislation making cars safer and raising standards for the food, drug, and cosmetics industries.

Johnson himself insisted that the Great Society meet "not just the needs of the body but the desire for beauty and hunger for community." In 1965, he sent Congress the first presidential message on the environment, obtaining measures to control water and air pollution and to preserve the natural beauty of the American landscape. First Lady "Lady Bird" Johnson made beautification of the environment her primary public project. In addition, the National Arts and Humanities Act of 1965 funded artists, musicians, writers, and scholars and brought their work to public audiences.

The flood of reform legislation dwindled after 1966, when Democratic majorities in Congress diminished and a backlash against government programs arose. Some Americans expressed their opposition with buttons reading "I fight poverty — I work." The Vietnam War dealt the largest blow to Johnson's ambitions, diverting his attention, spawning an antiwar movement that crippled his leadership, and devouring tax dollars that might have been used for reform (as discussed in chapter 29).

Against these odds, in 1968 Johnson pried out of Congress one more civil rights law, which banned discrimination in housing and jury service (see page 855). He also signed the National Housing Act of 1968, which authorized an enormous increase in low-income housing — 1.7 million units over three years — and, by leaving construction and ownership in private hands, a new way of providing it.

Assessing the Great Society

Measured by statistics, the reduction in poverty in the 1960s was considerable. The number of poor Americans fell from more than 20 percent of the population in 1959 to around 13 percent in 1968. Those who in Johnson's words "live on the outskirts of hope" gained more control of their circumstances and a sense of their right to a fairer share of America's bounty. To Rosemary Bray, what turned her family of longtime welfare recipients into taxpaying workers "was the promise of the civil rights movement and the war on poverty." A Mexican American who learned to be a sheet metal worker through a jobs program reported, "[My children] will finish high school and maybe go to college. . . . I see my family and I know the chains are broken."

Certain groups fared better than others. Many of the aged and many male-headed families rose out of poverty, while impoverishment among female-headed families actually increased. Whites escaped poverty at a faster rate than racial and ethnic minorities. Great Society programs contributed to a burgeoning black middle class, and the proportion of African Americans who were poor fell by 10 percentage points between 1966 and 1974. Still, one out of three remained poverty-stricken.

Conservative critics charged that Great Society programs discouraged initiative and sustained a "cycle of poverty" across generations by giving the poor "handouts." Liberal critics claimed that focusing on training and education wrongly placed the cause of poverty on the poor themselves rather than on an economic system that could not provide enough adequately paying jobs. Most government training programs prepared graduates for low-skilled labor and could not guarantee employment. In contrast to the New Deal, the Great Society avoided structural reform of the economy and spurned public works projects as a means of providing jobs for the disadvantaged.

Who reaped the greatest advantages from Great Society programs? Programs such as Medicare and those addressing consumer safety and environmental reform benefited Americans across the board. Funds for economically depressed areas built highways, benefiting the construction industry. Real estate developers, investors, and moderate-income families benefited most from the National Housing Act of 1968. Urban renewal often relied on slum clearance programs, which displaced the poor and caused blacks to refer to it as "Negro removal." Physicians' fees and hospital costs soared after the enactment of Medicare and Medicaid, resulting in advantages for both health care providers and the elderly and poor.

Some critics argued that ending poverty required a redistribution of income — raising taxes and using those funds to create jobs, overhaul welfare systems, and rebuild slums. Great Society programs did invest more heavily in the public sector, but they were funded from economic growth rather than from new taxes on the rich or middle class. There was no significant redistribution of income, despite large increases in subsidies for food stamps, housing, medical care, and AFDC. Economic prosperity allowed spending for the poor to rise and improved the lives of millions, but that spending never approached the amounts necessary to claim victory in the War on Poverty. Between 1965 and 1968, the Office of Economic Opportunity spent an average of $40 to $65 each year for each poor person in the country.

The Judicial Revolution

A key element of liberalism's ascendancy emerged in the Supreme Court under Chief Justice Earl Warren (1953–1969). In contrast to the federal courts of the Progressive Era and New Deal, which blocked reform, the **Warren Court** often moved out in front of Congress and public opinion. Expanding the Constitution's promise of equality and individual rights, the Court's decisions supported an activist government to prevent injustice and provided new protections to disadvantaged groups and accused criminals.

Following the pathbreaking *Brown v. Board of Education* school desegregation decision of 1954 (see chapter 27), the Court struck down southern states' educational plans to avoid integration and defended civil rights activists' rights to freedom of assembly and speech. In addition, a unanimous Court in *Loving v. Virginia* (1967) struck down state laws banning interracial marriage. The justices' declaration that marriage was one of the "basic civil rights of man" would later be repeated by gay men and lesbians seeking the right to marry.

Chief Justice Warren considered *Baker v. Carr* (1963) his most important decision. The case grew out of a complaint that Tennessee electoral districts were drawn so inequitably that sparsely populated rural districts had far more representatives than densely populated urban areas. Using the Fourteenth Amendment guarantee of "equal protection of the laws," *Baker* established the principle of "one person, one vote" for both state legislatures and the House of Representatives. As states redrew electoral districts, legislatures became more responsive to metropolitan interests.

The Warren Court also reformed the criminal justice system, overturning a series of convictions on the grounds that the accused had been deprived of "life, liberty, or property, without due process of law," guaranteed in the Fourteenth Amendment. In decisions that dramatically altered law enforcement practices and the treatment of individuals accused of crimes, the Court declared that states, as well as the federal government, were subject to the Bill of Rights.

Gideon v. Wainwright (1963) ruled that when an accused criminal could not afford to hire a lawyer, the state had to provide one. In 1966, *Miranda v. Arizona* required police officers to inform suspects of their rights upon arrest. The Court also overturned convictions based on evidence obtained by unlawful arrest, by electronic surveillance, or without a search warrant. Critics accused the justices of "handcuffing the police" and letting criminals go free; liberals argued that these rulings promoted equal treatment in the criminal justice system.

The Court's decisions on religion provoked even greater outrage. *Abington School District v. Schempp* (1963) ruled that requiring Bible reading and prayer in the schools violated the First Amendment principle of separation of church and state. Later judgments banned official prayer in public schools even if students were not required to participate. These decisions left students free to pray on their own, but an infuriated Alabama legislator complained, "They put Negroes in the schools and now they've driven God out." The Court's supporters, however, declared that the religion cases protected the rights of non-Christians and atheists.

Critics of the Court, part of a larger backlash mounting against Great Society liberalism, worked to pass laws or constitutional amendments that would upset despised decisions, and billboards demanded, "Impeach Earl Warren." Nonetheless, the Court's major decisions withstood the test of time.

> **REVIEW** How did the Kennedy and Johnson administrations exemplify a liberal vision of the federal government?

▶ The Second Reconstruction

As much as Supreme Court decisions, the black freedom struggle distinguished the liberalism of the 1960s from that of the New Deal. Before the Great Society reforms — and, in fact, contributing to them — African Americans had mobilized a movement that struck down legal separation and discrimination in the South. Whereas the first Reconstruction reflected the power of northern Republicans in the aftermath of the Civil War, the second Reconstruction depended heavily on the courage and determination of black people themselves. Sheyann Webb, one of the thousands of marchers in the 1965 Selma, Alabama, campaign for voting rights, recalled, "We were just people, ordinary people, and we did it."

Civil rights activism that focused on the South and on voting and other legal rights won widespread acceptance. But when African Americans stepped up protest against racial injustice in the rest of the country and challenged the economic deprivation that equal rights left untouched, a strong backlash developed, and Martin Luther King's vision faced challenges from other black activists.

The Flowering of the Black Freedom Struggle

The Montgomery bus boycott of 1955–1956 gave racial issues national visibility and produced a leader in **Martin Luther King Jr.** In the 1960s, protest expanded dramatically, mobilizing blacks into direct confrontation with the people and institutions that segregated and discriminated against them: retail establishments, public parks and libraries, buses and depots, voting registrars, and police forces.

Massive direct action in the South began in February 1960, when four African American college students in Greensboro, North Carolina, requested service at the whites-only Woolworth's lunch counter. Within days, hundreds of young people joined them, and others launched sit-ins in thirty-one southern cities.

From Southern Christian Leadership Conference headquarters, Ella Baker telephoned her young contacts at black colleges: "What are you going to do? It's time to move." Baker organized a meeting of student activists in April 1960 and supported their decision to form a new organization, the **Student Nonviolent Coordinating Committee (SNCC)**, pronounced "snick." Embracing civil disobedience and the nonviolence principles of Martin Luther King Jr., activists would confront their oppressors and stand up for their rights, but they would not respond if attacked. In the words of SNCC leader James Lawson, "Nonviolence nurtures the atmosphere in which reconciliation and justice become actual possibilities." SNCC, however, rejected the top-down leadership of King and the established civil rights organizations, adopting a decentralized structure that fostered decision making and the development of leadership at the grassroots level.

The activists' optimism and commitment to nonviolence soon underwent severe tests. Although some cities quietly met student demands, more typically activists encountered violence. Hostile whites poured food over demonstrators, burned them with cigarettes, called them "niggers," and pelted them with rocks. Local police attacked protesters with dogs, clubs, fire hoses, and tear gas; they arrested more than 3,600 demonstrators in the year following the Greensboro sit-in.

Another wave of protest occurred in May 1961, when the Congress of Racial Equality (CORE) organized Freedom Rides to integrate interstate transportation in the South. When a group of six whites and seven blacks reached Alabama, whites bombed their bus and beat them with baseball bats so fiercely that an observer "couldn't see their faces through the blood." CORE rebuffed President Kennedy's pleas to call off the rides. But after a huge mob attacked the riders in Montgomery, Alabama, Attorney General Robert Kennedy dispatched federal marshals to restore order. Although violence against the riders abated, Freedom Riders arriving in Jackson, Mississippi, were promptly arrested, and several hundred spent weeks in jail. All told, more than four hundred blacks and whites participated in the Freedom Rides, which typified the black freedom struggle: administration efforts to stop the protests, officials' reluctance to intervene to protect demonstrators, and the steely courage of civil rights activists in the face of violence.

Encouraged by Kennedy administration officials who preferred voter registration to civil disobedience, SNCC and other groups began the Voter Education Project in the summer of 1961. They, too, met violence. Whites bombed black churches, threw tenant farmers out of their homes, and beat and jailed activists such as **Fannie Lou Hamer** (see pages 840–842). In June 1963, a white man gunned down Mississippi NAACP leader Medgar Evers in front of his house in Jackson. Similar violence met

King's 1963 campaign in Birmingham, Alabama, to integrate public facilities and open jobs to blacks. The police attacked demonstrators with dogs, cattle prods, and fire hoses — brutalities that television broadcast around the world.

The largest demonstration drew 250,000 blacks and whites to the nation's capital in August 1963 in the **March on Washington for Jobs and Freedom**, inspired by the strategy of A. Philip Randolph in 1941 (see chapter 25). Its chief architect was Bayard Rustin, a radical Christian and pacifist, who had helped Martin Luther King develop the principles and practice of nonviolence. Speaking from the Lincoln Memorial, King put his indelible stamp on the day, drawing on all the passion and skills that made him the greatest orator of his day. "I have a dream," he repeated again and again, imagining the day "when all of God's children . . . will be able to join hands and sing . . . 'Free at last, free at last; thank God Almighty, we are free at last.'"

The euphoria of the March on Washington faded as activists returned to face continued violence in the South. In 1964, the **Mississippi Freedom Summer Project** mobilized more than a thousand northern black and white college students to conduct voter registration drives. Resistance was fierce, intensified by the sight of white activist women working alongside black men. By the end of the summer, only twelve hundred new voters had been allowed to register. Southern whites had killed several activists, beaten eighty, arrested more than a thousand, and burned thirty-five black churches. Hidden resistance came from the federal government

The Selma March for Voting Rights

In 1963, the Student Nonviolent Coordinating Committee began a campaign for voting rights in Selma, Alabama, where white officials had registered only 335 of the 15,000 eligible African Americans. In March 1965, demonstrators began a fifty-four-mile march from Selma to Montgomery, the state capital, to insist that blacks be registered. In this photograph, young African Americans march with nuns, priests, and other supporters. What do you think motivated the marchers to carry the American flag? Steve Shapiro/TimePix/Getty.

itself, as the FBI spied on King and other leaders and expanded its activities to "expose, disrupt, misdirect, discredit, or otherwise neutralize" black protest.

Still, the movement persisted. In March 1965, Alabama state troopers used such violent force to turn back a voting rights march from Selma to the state capitol in Montgomery that the incident earned the name "Bloody Sunday" and compelled President Johnson to call up the Alabama National Guard to protect the marchers. Battered and hospitalized on Bloody Sunday, John Lewis, chairman of SNCC (and later a congressman from Georgia), managed to make the final stretch of the **Selma march** to the capitol. Calling the Voting Rights Act, which passed that October, "every bit as momentous as the Emancipation Proclamation," he said, "we all felt we'd had a part in it."

The Response in Washington

Civil rights leaders would have to wear sneakers, Lyndon Johnson said, if they were going to keep up with him. But both Kennedy and Johnson, reluctant to alienate southern voters and their congressional representatives, tended to move only when events gave them little choice. Kennedy sent federal marshals to protect the Freedom Riders, dispatched troops to enable air force veteran James H. Meredith to enroll in the all-white University of Mississippi in 1962, and called up the Alabama National Guard during the Birmingham demonstrations. But, aware of the political costs of deploying federal force, he told activists pleading for more protection that law enforcement was a local matter.

In June 1963, Kennedy finally made good on his promise to seek strong antidiscrimination legislation. Pointing to the injustice suffered by blacks, Kennedy asked white Americans, "Who among us would then be content with the counsels of patience and delay?" Johnson took up Kennedy's commitment with passion, as scenes of violence against peaceful demonstrators appalled television viewers across the nation. The resulting public support, the "Johnson treatment," and the president's appeal to memories of the martyred Kennedy all produced the most important civil rights law since Reconstruction.

The Civil Rights Act of 1964 guaranteed access for all Americans to public accommodations, public education, employment, and voting. It sounded the death knell for the South's system of segregation, outlawed job discrimination that was rampant throughout the nation, and extended constitutional protections to Indians on reservations. Title VII of the measure, banning discrimination in employment, not only attacked racial discrimination but also outlawed discrimination against women. Because Title VII applied to every aspect of employment, including wages, hiring, and promotion, it represented a giant step toward equal employment opportunity for white women as well as for racial minorities.

Responding to black voter registration drives in the South, Johnson demanded legislation to remove "every remaining obstacle to the right and the opportunity to vote." In August 1965, he signed the Voting Rights Act, empowering the federal government to intervene directly to enable African Americans to register and vote, thereby launching a major transformation in southern politics. Black voting rates shot up dramatically (Map 28.1). In turn, the number of African Americans

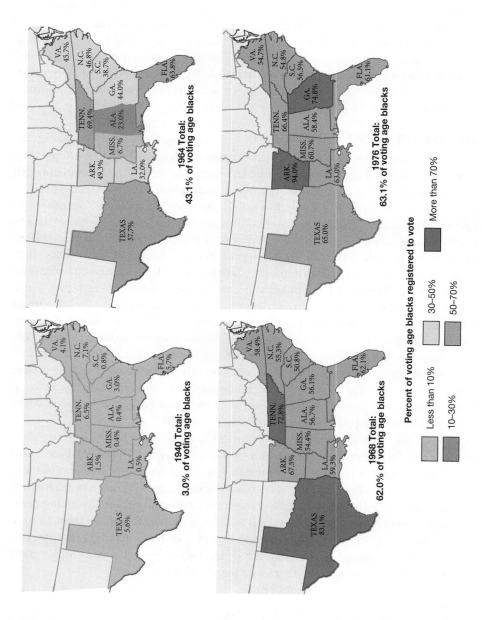

VA. 45.7%
N.C. 46.8%
S.C. 38.7%
FLA. 63.8%
GA. 44.0%
TENN. 69.4%
ALA. 23.0%
MISS. 6.7%
ARK. 49.3%
LA. 32.0%
TEXAS 57.7%

1964 Total:
43.1% of voting age blacks

VA. 54.7%
N.C. 54.8%
S.C. 56.5%
FLA. 61.1%
GA. 74.8%
TENN. 66.4%
ALA. 58.4%
MISS. 60.7%
ARK. 94.0%
LA. 63.0%
TEXAS 65.0%

1976 Total:
63.1% of voting age blacks

VA. 4.1%
N.C. 7.1%
S.C. 0.8%
FLA. 5.7%
GA. 3.0%
TENN. 6.5%
ALA. 0.4%
MISS. 0.4%
ARK. 1.5%
LA. 0.5%
TEXAS 5.6%

1940 Total:
3.0% of voting age blacks

VA. 58.4%
N.C. 55.3%
S.C. 50.8%
FLA. 62.1%
GA. 56.1%
TENN. 72.8%
ALA. 56.7%
MISS. 54.4%
ARK. 67.5%
LA. 59.3%
TEXAS 83.1%

1968 Total:
62.0% of voting age blacks

Percent of voting age blacks registered to vote

Less than 10%

10–30%

30–50%

50–70%

More than 70%

holding political office in the South increased from a handful in 1964 to more than a thousand by 1972. Such gains translated into tangible benefits as black officials upgraded public facilities, police protection, and other basic services for their constituents. When Unita Blackwell became the first black female mayor in Mississippi, a resident of her town recalled, "She brought in the water tower.... Sewage, too. There wasn't nothing but those little outdoor houses."

Johnson also declared the need to realize "not just equality as a right and theory, but equality as fact and result." To this end, he issued an executive order in 1965 to require employers holding government contracts (affecting about one-third of the labor force) to take affirmative action to ensure equal opportunity. Extended to cover women in 1967, the affirmative action program was called "reverse discrimination" by people who incorrectly thought that it required quotas and the hiring of unqualified candidates. In fact, it required employers to counter the effects of centuries of oppression by acting forcefully to align their labor force with the available pool of qualified candidates. Most corporations came to see affirmative action as a good employment practice.

In 1968, Johnson maneuvered one final bill through Congress. While those in other regions often applauded the gains made by the black freedom struggle in the South, they were just as likely to resist claims for racial justice in their own locations. In 1963, for example, California voters rejected a law passed by the legislature banning discrimination in housing; a majority of voters were more concerned with their right to do as they pleased with their property than with the rights of minorities to be free of discrimination. And when Martin Luther King Jr. launched a campaign against de facto segregation in Chicago in 1966, thousands of whites jeered and threw stones at demonstrators. Johnson's efforts to get a federal open-housing law succeeded only in the wake of King's assassination in 1968. The **Civil Rights Act of 1968** banned racial discrimination in housing and jury selection and authorized federal intervention when states failed to protect civil rights workers from violence.

Black Power and Urban Rebellions

By 1966, black protest was visible throughout the nation, demanding not just legal equality but also economic justice and no longer holding nonviolence as a basic principle. These developments were not entirely new. African Americans had waged campaigns for decent jobs, housing, and education outside the South since the 1930s. Moreover, some African Americans had always armed themselves in self-defense, and even in the early 1960s many activists doubted that their passive suffering would change the hearts of racists. Still, the black freedom struggle began to appear more threatening to the white majority.

◀ **MAP 28.1**
The Rise of the African American Vote, 1940–1976
Voting rates of southern blacks increased gradually in the 1940s and 1950s but shot up dramatically in the deep South after the Voting Rights Act of 1965 provided for federal agents to enforce African Americans' right to vote.

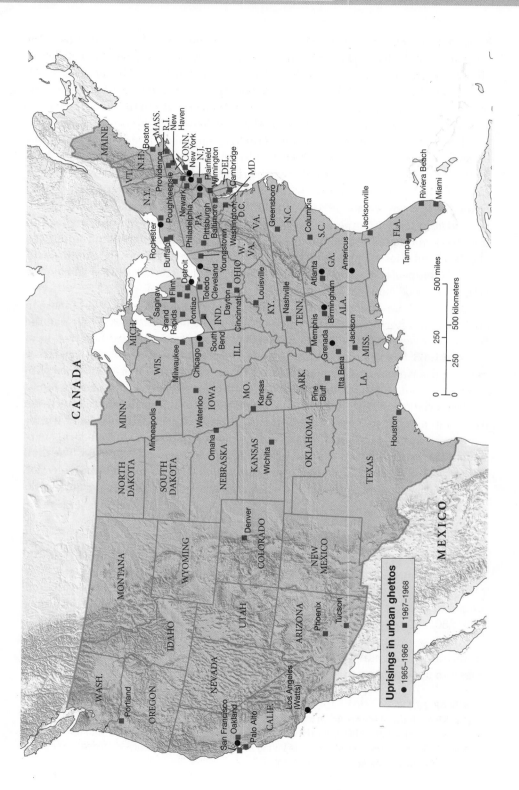

Uprisings in urban ghettos
● 1965–1966   ■ 1967–1968

The new emphases resulted from a combination of heightened activism and unrealized promise. Legal equality could not quickly improve the material conditions of blacks, and black rage at oppressive conditions erupted in waves of urban uprisings from 1965 to 1968 (Map 28.2). In a situation where virtually all-white police forces patrolled black neighborhoods, incidents between police and local blacks typically sparked rioting and resulted in looting, destruction of property, injuries, and deaths. The worst looting and property damage occurred in the Watts district of Los Angeles in August 1965, Newark and Detroit in July 1967, and the nation's capital in April 1968, but violence visited hundreds of cities. The Detroit riots ended in 43 deaths (30 at the hands of law enforcement officers, with most of the victims black), 7,000 arrests, and 1,300 destroyed buildings.

Rioting and looting seemed to many young blacks the only means available to protest the poverty, lack of opportunity, and official insensitivity they experienced daily. "Since the riot, we're not niggers anymore. We're black men," reported a New Jersey activist. In Los Angeles, an observer said to a reporter, "I don't understand all this talk about 'looting.' They rob us every day. They rob us on the rent, on the food, on the job. They rob our kids on education." Most whites, however, saw the riots as criminal activity, plain and simple, blaming them on radicals who were challenging the principles of King.

Malcolm X was one of those who resisted an emphasis on integration and passive resistance. In 1952, he joined the Nation of Islam, whose adherents called themselves Black Muslims and drew on the long tradition of black nationalism. Calling for black pride and autonomy, separation from the "corrupt [white] society," and self-defense against white violence, Malcolm X attracted a large following, especially in urban ghettos.

At a June 1966 rally in Greenwood, Mississippi, SNCC chairman **Stokely Carmichael** gave the ideas espoused by Malcolm X a new name when he shouted, "We want black power." Those words quickly became the rallying cry in SNCC and CORE, and the **black power movement** riveted national attention in the late 1960s. Carmichael called integration "a subterfuge for the maintenance of white supremacy" and rejected assimilation because it implied white superiority. African Americans were encouraged to develop independent businesses and control their own schools, communities, and political organizations. The phrase "Black is beautiful" emphasized pride in African American culture and connections to dark-skinned

◀ **MAP 28.2**
Urban Uprisings, 1965–1968
When a white police officer in the Watts district of Los Angeles struck a twenty-one-year-old African American, whom he had just pulled over for driving drunk, one onlooker shouted, "We've got no rights at all — it's just like Selma." The altercation escalated into a five-day uprising, during which young blacks set fires, looted, and attacked police and firefighters. When National Guardsmen and police finally quelled the riot, 34 people were dead, 900 blacks had been injured and 4,000 arrested, hundreds of families had lost their homes, and scores of businesses had been wiped out. Similar violence, though usually not on such a large scale, erupted in dozens of cities across the nation during the next three summers, as this map indicates.

people around the world, who were claiming their independence from colonial domination. According to black power advocates, nonviolence brought only more beatings and killings. After police killed an unarmed black teenager in San Francisco in 1966, Huey Newton and Bobby Seale organized the Black Panther Party for Self-Defense to combat police brutality.

The press paid inordinate attention to black radicals, and the civil rights movement encountered a severe white backlash. Although the urban riots of the mid-1960s erupted spontaneously, triggered by specific incidents of alleged police mistreatment, horrified whites blamed black power militants. By 1966, 85 percent of the white population — up from 34 percent two years earlier — thought that African Americans were pressing for too much too quickly.

Agreeing with black power advocates about the need for "a radical reconstruction of society," Martin Luther King Jr. expanded the scope of the struggle. In 1965, he mounted a drive for better jobs, schools, and housing in Chicago. Yet he clung to nonviolence and integration as the means to this end. In April 1968, the thirty-nine-year-old leader went to Memphis to support striking municipal sanitation workers. There, on April 4, he was murdered by an escaped white convict.

Although black power organizations captured the headlines, they failed to gain the massive support from African Americans that King and other leaders had attracted. Nor could they alleviate the poverty and racism entrenched in the urban North and West. Black radicals were harassed by the FBI and jailed; some encounters left both black militants and police dead. Yet black power's emphasis on racial pride and its critique of American institutions resonated loudly and helped shape the protest activities of other groups.

REVIEW   How and why did the civil rights movement change in the mid-1960s?

▶ A Multitude of Movements

The civil rights movement's undeniable moral claims helped make protest more respectable, while its successes encouraged other groups with grievances. Native Americans, Latinos, college students, women, gay men and lesbians, and others drew on the black freedom struggle for inspiration and models of activism. Many of these groups engaged in direct-action protests, expressed their own cultural nationalism, and challenged dominant institutions and values. Like participants in the black freedom struggle, they met strong resistance, and their accomplishments fell far below their aims. Still, their grievances gained attention in the political arena, and they expanded justice and opportunity for many of their constituents.

Native American Protest

The cry "red power" reflected the influence of black radicalism on young Native Americans, whose activism took on fresh militancy and goals in the 1960s. The termination and relocation programs of the 1940s and 1950s, contrary to their intent, stirred a sense of Indian identity across tribal lines and a determination to preserve traditional culture. Native Americans demonstrated and occupied land and public buildings, claiming rights to natural resources and territory they had owned collectively before European settlement.

In 1969, Native American militants captured world attention when several dozen seized Alcatraz Island, an abandoned federal prison in San Francisco Bay, claiming their right of "first discovery" of this land. They held the island for nineteen months, using the occupation to publicize injustices against Indians, promote pan-Indian cooperation, and celebrate traditional cultures. One of the organizers, Dr. LaNada Boyer, the first Native American to attend the University of California, Berkeley, said of Alcatraz, "We were able to reestablish our identity as Indian people, as a culture, as political entities."

In Minneapolis in 1968, two Chippewa Indians, Dennis Banks and George Mitchell, founded the **American Indian Movement (AIM)** to attack problems in cities, where about 300,000 Indians lived. AIM sought to protect Indians from police harassment, secure antipoverty funds, and establish "survival schools" to teach Indian history and values. The movement's appeal quickly spread and filled many Indians with a new sense of purpose. AIM members did not have "that hangdog reservation look I was used to," Lakota activist and author Mary Crow Dog wrote, and their visit to her South Dakota reservation "loosened a sort of earthquake inside me."

AIM leaders helped organize the "Trail of Broken Treaties" caravan to the nation's capital in 1972, when activists occupied the Bureau of Indian Affairs to express their outrage at the bureau's policies and bureaucratic interference in Indians' lives. In 1973, a much longer siege occurred on the Lakota Sioux reservation in South Dakota. Conflicts there between AIM militants and older tribal leaders led AIM to take over for seventy-two days the village of Wounded Knee, where U.S. troops had massacred more than one hundred Sioux Indians in 1890 (see chapter 17).

Although these dramatic occupations failed to achieve their specific goals, Indians won the end of relocation and termination policies, greater tribal sovereignty and control over community services, protection of Indian religious practices, and a measure of respect and pride. A number of laws and court decisions restored rights to ancestral lands and compensated tribes for land seized in violation of treaties.

Latino Struggles for Justice

The fastest-growing minority group in the 1960s was Latino, or Hispanic American, an extraordinarily varied population encompassing people of Mexican, Puerto Rican, Caribbean, and other Latin American origins. (The term *Latino* stresses their common bonds as a minority group in the United States. The older, less political term *Hispanic* also includes people with origins in Spain.) People of Puerto Rican and Caribbean descent flocked to East Coast cities, but more than half of the nation's Latino population — including some six million Mexican Americans — lived in the Southwest. In addition, thousands illegally crossed the border between Mexico and the United States yearly in search of economic opportunity. Political organization of Mexican Americans dated back to the League of United Latin-American Citizens (LULAC), founded in 1929, which fought segregation and discrimination through litigation (see chapter 26). In the 1960s, however, young Mexican Americans increasingly rejected traditional politics in favor of direct action. One symbol of this generational challenge was young activists' adoption of the term *Chicano* (from *mejicano*, the Spanish word for "Mexican").

Chicano protest drew national attention to California, where **Cesar Chavez** and **Dolores Huerta** organized a movement to improve the wretched conditions of migrant agricultural workers. As a child moving from farm to farm with his family, living in soggy tents and exploited by labor contractors, Chavez changed schools frequently and encountered indifference and discrimination. One teacher, he recalled, "hung a sign on me that said, 'I am a clown, I speak Spanish.'" After serving in World War II, Chavez began to organize voter registration drives among Mexican Americans.

In contrast to Chavez, Dolores Huerta grew up in an integrated urban neighborhood where she avoided the farmworkers' grinding poverty but witnessed subtle forms of discrimination. Once, a high school teacher challenged her authorship of an essay because it was so well written. Believing that a labor union was the key to progress, she and Chavez founded the United Farm Workers (UFW) in 1962. Although Chavez headed the union until his death in 1993, Huerta was indispensable to its vitality.

Cesar Chavez and Dolores Huerta

Under posters showing Senator Robert Kennedy and Mahatma Gandhi, Chavez and Huerta confer in 1968 during the United Farm Workers' five-year struggle with grape growers for better wages and working conditions and union recognition. Chavez, like Martin Luther King, had studied the ideas of Gandhi, who used civil disobedience and nonviolence to gain independence for India. People across the country supported the UFW's grape boycott, including Robert Kennedy. Huerta left her teaching job to organize workers, saying, "I thought I could do more by organizing farm workers than by trying to teach their hungry children." Arthur Schatz/TimePix/Getty Images.

To gain leverage for striking workers, the UFW mounted a nationwide boycott of California grapes, which drew support from millions of Americans and helped win a wage increase for the workers in 1970. Although the UFW struggled and lost membership during the 1970s, it helped politicize Mexican Americans and improve farmworkers' lives.

Other Chicanos mobilized to force the Equal Employment Opportunity Commission (EEOC), the enforcement agency of Title VII of the Civil Rights Act of 1964, to act against job discrimination against Mexican Americans. LULAC, the American GI Forum (see chapter 26), and other groups picketed government offices. President Johnson responded in 1967 by appointing Vicente T. Ximenes as the first Mexican American EEOC commissioner and by creating a special committee on Mexican American affairs.

Claiming "brown power," Chicanos organized to end discrimination in education, gain political power, and combat police brutality. In Denver, Rodolfo "Corky" Gonzales set up "freedom schools" where Chicano children studied the Spanish language and Mexican American history. The nationalist strains of Chicano protest were evident in La Raza Unida (the United Race), a political party founded in 1970 in Texas and based on cultural pride and brotherhood. Along with blacks and Native Americans, Chicanos continued to be disproportionately represented among the poor, but they gradually won more political offices, more effective enforcement of antidiscrimination legislation, and greater respect for their culture.

Student Rebellion, the New Left, and the Counterculture

Although materially and legally more secure than their African American, Indian, and Latino counterparts, white youths also expressed dissent, supporting the black freedom struggle and launching student protests, the antiwar movement, and the new feminist movement. Challenging establishment institutions and traditional values, young activists helped change higher education, the family, the national government, and other key institutions. They were part of a larger international phenomenon, as student movements arose in Mexico, Germany, Turkey, Czechoslovakia, Japan, and other nations around the globe.

The central organization of white student protest was **Students for a Democratic Society (SDS)**, formed in 1960. In 1962, the organizers wrote in their statement of purpose, "We are people of this generation, bred in at least modest comfort, housed now in universities, looking uncomfortably at the world we inherit." The idealistic students criticized the complacency of their elders, the remoteness of decision makers from those affected by their actions, and the powerlessness and alienation generated by a bureaucratic society. SDS aimed to mobilize a "New Left" around the goals of civil rights, peace, and universal economic security. Other forms of student activism soon followed.

The first large-scale white student protest arose at the University of California, Berkeley, in 1964, when university officials banned students from setting up tables to recruit support for various causes. Led by whites returning from civil rights work in the South, the students claimed the right to freedom of expression and political action. Members of the "free speech" movement occupied the administration building, and more than seven hundred students were arrested before the California Board of Regents overturned the new restrictions.

Hundreds of student rallies and building occupations followed on campuses across the country, especially after 1965, when opposition to the Vietnam War mounted and students protested against universities' ties with the military (as discussed in chapter 29). Students also changed the collegiate environment. Women at the University of Chicago, for example, charged in 1969 that all universities "discriminate against women, impede their full intellectual development, deny them places on the faculty, exploit talented women and mistreat women students." At Howard University, African American students called for a "Black Awareness Research Institute," demanding that academic departments "place more emphasis on how these disciplines may be used to effect the liberation of black people." Across the country, students won curricular reforms such as black studies and women's studies programs, more financial aid for minority and poor students, independence from paternalistic rules, and a larger voice in campus decision making.

Student protest bewildered and angered older Americans, even more so when it blended into a cultural revolution against nearly every conventional standard of behavior. Drawing on the ideas of the Beats of the 1950s (see chapter 27), the "hippies," as they were called, rejected mainstream values such as materialism, order, and sexual control. Seeking personal rather than political change, they advocated "Do your own thing" and drew attention with their long hair, wildly colorful clothing, and use of marijuana, LSD, and other illegal drugs. Across the country, thousands of radicals established communes in cities or on farms, where they renounced private property and shared everything, often including sexual partners.

Rock and folk music defined both the counterculture and the political left. English groups such as the Beatles and the Rolling Stones and homegrown performers such as Bob Dylan, Janis Joplin, and the Grateful Dead took American youth by storm. Music during the 1960s often carried insurgent political and social messages that reflected radical youth culture. "Eve of Destruction," a top hit of 1965, reminded young men at a time when the voting age was twenty-one, "You're old enough to kill but not for votin'." The Woodstock Music Festival epitomized the centrality of music to the youth rebellion. Woodstock featured the greatest rock and folk musicians of the era and drew 400,000 young people to a farm in Bethel, New York, in 1969.

Hippies faded away in the 1970s, but many elements of the counterculture — rock music, jeans, and long hair, as well as new social attitudes — filtered into the mainstream. More tolerant approaches to sexual behaviors spawned what came to be called the "sexual revolution," with help from the birth control pill, which became available in the 1960s. Self-fulfillment became a dominant concern of many Americans, and questioning of authority became more widespread.

Gay Men and Lesbians Organize

More permissive sexual norms did not stretch easily to include tolerance of homosexuality. Gay men and lesbians escaped discrimination and ridicule only by concealing their very identities. Those who couldn't or wouldn't found themselves fired from jobs, arrested for their sexual activities, deprived of their children, or accused of being "perverted." While most kept their sexuality hidden, in the 1950s some gays and lesbians began to organize.

Some of the first gay activism challenged the government's aggressive efforts to keep homosexuals out of the civil service. In October 1965, a picket line formed outside the White House with signs calling discrimination against homosexuals "as immoral as discrimination against Negroes and Jews." Not until ten years later, however, did the Civil Service Commission formally end its antigay policy.

The spark that ignited a larger movement was struck in 1969 when police raided a gay bar, the Stonewall Inn, in New York City's Greenwich Village, and gay men and lesbians fought back. "Suddenly, they were not submissive anymore," a police officer remarked. Energized by the defiance shown at the **Stonewall riots**, gay men and lesbians organized a host of new groups, such as the Gay Liberation Front. A more reformist organization, the National Gay and Lesbian Task Force, was founded in 1973 to ensure that gay issues received sustained national attention.

The gay rights movement struggled much longer and harder to win recognition than did other social movements. In 1972, Ann Arbor, Michigan, passed the first antidiscrimination ordinance, and two years later Elaine Noble's election to the Massachusetts legislature marked the first time an openly gay candidate won state office. In 1973, gay activists persuaded the American Psychiatric Association to withdraw its designation of homosexuality as a mental disease. It would take decades for these initial gains to improve conditions for most homosexuals, but by the mid-1970s gay men and lesbians had established a movement through which they could claim equal rights and express pride in their identities.

REVIEW How did the black freedom struggle influence other reform movements of the 1960s and 1970s?

► The New Wave of Feminism

On August 26, 1970, fifty years after women won the right to vote, tens of thousands of women across the country — from radical women in jeans to conservatively dressed suburbanites, peace activists, and politicians — took to the streets. They carried signs reading "Sisterhood Is Powerful" and "Don't Cook Dinner — Starve a Rat Today." Some of the banners opposed the war in Vietnam, others demanded racial justice, but women's own liberation stood at the forefront.

Becoming visible by the late 1960s, the women's movement reached its high tide in the 1970s and persisted into the twenty-first century. By that time, despite a powerful countermovement, women had experienced tremendous transformations in their legal status, public opportunities, and personal and sexual relationships, and popular expectations about appropriate gender roles had shifted dramatically.

A Multifaceted Movement Emerges

Beginning in the 1940s, large demographic changes laid the preconditions for a resurgence of feminism. As more and more women took jobs, the importance of their paid work to the economy and their families belied the idea of women as dependent, domestic beings and awakened many women workers, especially labor union women, to the inferior conditions of their employment. The democratization of higher education brought more women to college campuses, where their aspirations exceeded the confines of domesticity and of routine, subordinate jobs.

Policy initiatives in the early 1960s reflected both these larger transformations and the efforts of women's rights activists. In 1961, Assistant Secretary of Labor Esther Peterson persuaded President Kennedy to create the President's Commission on the Status of Women (PCSW). In 1963, the commission reported widespread discrimination against women and recommended remedies, although it did not challenge women's domestic roles. Counterparts of the PCSW sprang up in every state, filled with women eager for action. One of the commission's concerns was addressed even before it issued its report, when Congress passed the Equal Pay Act of 1963, making it illegal to pay women less than men for the same work.

Like other movements, the rise of feminism owed much to the black freedom struggle. Women gained protection from employment discrimination through Title VII of the Civil Rights Act of 1964 and the extension of affirmative action to women by piggybacking onto civil rights measures. They soon grew impatient when the government failed to take these new policies seriously. Outraged by the government's slowness in enforcing Title VII, Betty Friedan, civil rights activist Pauli Murray, several union women, and others founded the **National Organization for Women (NOW)** in 1966.

Simultaneously, a more radical feminism grew among civil rights and New Left activists. In 1965, two white women, Mary King and Casey Hayden, wrote that their work in SNCC had awakened them to sex discrimination. Although most black women did not consider themselves to be marginalized in the movement, King and Hayden presented their ideas to white male radicals in the New Left, who responded with indifference or ridicule. By contrast, their message invigorated other white women who shared their frustration with subordinate roles. Many women walked out of New Left organizations and created an independent women's liberation movement composed of small groups across the nation.

Women's liberation began to gain public attention, especially when dozens of women picketed the Miss America beauty pageant in 1968, protesting against being forced "to compete for male approval [and] enslaved by ludicrous 'beauty' standards." Women began to speak publicly about personal experiences that had always been

Women's Strike for Equality
On the fiftieth anniversary of the Nineteenth Amendment granting woman suffrage, Betty Friedan and others organized a nationwide Women's Strike for Equality. While the numbers who participated were relatively small, in New York City more than ten thousand women marched down Fifth Avenue, in defiance of police who tried to keep them on the sidewalks. The three central demands of the protest were equal opportunity in employment and education, child care, and abortion rights. During what were still the early days of second-wave feminism, ABC News showed a U.S. senator calling the demonstrators "a small band of bra-less bubble heads."
Getty John Olson/Time & Life Pictures/Getty Images.

shrouded in secrecy, such as rape and abortion. Throughout the country, women joined consciousness-raising groups, where they discovered that what they had considered "personal" problems reflected an entrenched system of discrimination against and devaluation of women.

Radical feminists, who called their movement "women's liberation," differed from feminists in NOW and other more mainstream groups in several ways. NOW focused on equal treatment for women in the public sphere; women's liberation emphasized ending women's subordination in family and other personal relationships. Groups such as NOW wanted to integrate women into existing institutions; radical groups insisted that women's liberation required a total transformation of economic, political, and social institutions. Differences between these two strands of feminism blurred in the 1970s, as NOW and other mainstream groups embraced many of the issues raised by radicals.

Although NOW elected a black president, Aileen Hernandez, in 1970, the new feminism's leadership and constituency were predominantly white and middle-class. Women of color criticized white feminists for their inadequate attention to the disproportionate poverty experienced by minority women and to the additional layers of discrimination based on race or ethnicity. One black woman said, "My mother took care of rich white kids. I didn't think they were oppressed." To black women, who were much more frequently compelled to work in the lowest-paying jobs for their families' survival, employment did not necessarily look like liberation.

In addition to struggling with vast differences among women, feminism also contended with the refusal of the mass media to take women's grievances seriously. When the House of Representatives passed an equal rights amendment to the U.S. Constitution in 1970, the *New York Times* criticized it in an editorial titled "The Henpecked House." After Gloria Steinem founded *Ms: The New Magazine for Women* in 1972, feminists had their own mass-circulation periodical controlled by women and featuring articles on a broad range of feminist issues.

Ms. reported on a movement that was exceedingly multifaceted. Most African American women worked through their own groups, such as the older National Council of Negro Women and the National Black Feminist Organization, founded in 1973. Similarly, in the early 1970s, Native American women and Mexican American women founded national organizations, and Asian American women formed local movements. Labor union women, who had long struggled for workplace gender justice, organized the National Coalition of Labor Union Women in 1974. Lesbians established collectives throughout the country, as well as their own caucuses in organizations such as NOW. Welfare mothers formed the National Welfare Rights Organization, and religious women mobilized in the National Council of Churches of Christ to "place the question of women's liberation in the main stream of the church's concern." Other new groups focused on single issues such as health, abortion rights, education, and violence against women. In addition, U.S. feminists interacted with women abroad, joining a movement that crossed national boundaries.

Common threads underlay the great diversity of organizations, issues, and activities. Above all, feminism represented the belief that women were barred from, unequally treated in, or poorly served by the male-dominated public arena, encompassing politics, medicine, law, education, culture, and religion. Many feminists also sought equality in the private sphere, challenging traditional norms that identified women primarily as wives and mothers or sex objects, subservient to men.

Feminist Gains Spark a Countermovement

Although more an effect than a cause of women's rising employment, feminism lifted female aspirations and helped lower barriers to posts monopolized by men. Between 1970 and 2000, women's share of law degrees shot up from 5 percent to nearly 50 percent, and their proportion of medical degrees from less than 10 percent to more than 35 percent. Women gained political offices very slowly; yet by 2010, they constituted about 17 percent of Congress and more than 20 percent of all state executives and legislators.

Feminists encountered frustrations along with achievements. Despite some inroads into male-dominated occupations, women still tended to concentrate in low-paying, traditionally female jobs, and their earnings lagged below men's well into the twenty-first century. Employed women continued to bear primary responsibility for their homes and families, thereby working a "double day."

Although public opinion polls registered support for most feminist goals, by the mid-1970s feminism faced a powerful countermovement, organized around opposition to a central goal of the women's movement: an **Equal Rights Amendment (ERA)** that would outlaw differential treatment of men and women under all state and federal laws. After Congress passed the ERA in 1972, Phyllis Schlafly, a conservative activist in the Republican Party, mobilized thousands of women at the grassroots level who feared that the ERA would devalue their own God-given roles as wives and mothers. These women, marching on state capitols, persuaded some male legislators to block ratification. When the time limit ran out in 1982, only thirty-five states had ratified the amendment, three short of the necessary three-fourths majority.

Powerful opposition likewise arose to feminists' quest for the right to abortion. "Without the full capacity to limit her own reproduction," abortion rights activist Lucinda Cisler insisted, "a woman's other 'freedoms' are tantalizing mockeries that cannot be exercised." In 1973, the Supreme Court issued the landmark *Roe v. Wade* decision, ruling that the Constitution protects the right to abortion, which states cannot prohibit in the early stages of pregnancy. This decision galvanized many Americans who believed that human life begins with conception and equated abortion with murder. Like ERA opponents, with whom they often overlapped, activists in the right-to-life movement mobilized thousands of women who believed that abortion disparaged motherhood and that feminism threatened their traditional roles. Beginning in 1977, abortion foes successfully pressured Congress to restrict the right to abortion by prohibiting coverage under Medicaid and other government-financed health programs, and the Supreme Court allowed states to impose additional obstacles.

Despite resistance, feminists won other lasting gains. **Title IX** of the Education Amendments Act of 1972 banned sex discrimination in all aspects of education, such as admissions, athletics, and hiring. Congress also outlawed sex discrimination in credit in 1974, opened U.S. military academies to women in 1976, and prohibited discrimination against pregnant workers in 1978. Moreover, the Supreme Court struck down laws that treated men and women differently in Social Security, welfare and military benefits, and workers' compensation.

At the state and local levels, women saw reforms in areas that radical feminists had first introduced. They won laws forcing police departments and the legal system to treat rape victims more justly and humanely. Activists also pushed domestic violence onto the public agenda, obtaining government financing for shelters for battered women as well as laws ensuring both greater protection for victims of domestic violence and more effective prosecution of abusers.

REVIEW   What were the key goals of feminist reformers, and why did a countermovement arise to resist them?

▶ Liberal Reform in the Nixon Administration

Opposition to civil rights measures, Great Society reforms, and protest groups — along with frustrations surrounding the war in Vietnam (as discussed in chapter 29) — delivered the White House to Republican **Richard M. Nixon** in 1968. Nixon attacked the Great Society for "pouring billions of dollars into programs that have failed," and he promised to represent the "forgotten Americans, the non-shouters, the non-demonstrators." Yet despite Nixon's desire to capitalize on the backlash against civil rights and the Great Society, his administration either promoted or accepted substantially greater federal assistance to the poor, new protections for minorities and women, major environmental regulations, and financial policies deviating sharply from traditional Republican economics.

Extending the Welfare State and Regulating the Economy

A number of factors shaped the liberal policies of the Nixon administration. Not only did the Democrats continue to control Congress, but Nixon also saw political advantages in accepting some liberal programs. Nor could he entirely ignore grassroots movements, and several of his advisers were sympathetic to particular concerns, such as environmentalism and Native American rights. Serious economic problems also compelled new approaches, and although Nixon's real passion lay in foreign policy, he knew that his domestic record would in part determine whether he enjoyed history's approving gaze.

Under Nixon, government assistance programs grew. Congress resisted his attempts to eliminate the Office of Economic Opportunity. Key programs such as Medicaid, Head Start, and Legal Services remained intact. Social Security benefits increased and were now required to rise with the cost of living; subsidies for low-income housing tripled; a new billion-dollar program provided Pell grants for low-income students to attend college; and the food stamp program expanded to benefit 12.5 million recipients. Noting the disparity between what Nixon said and what he did, his speechwriter, the archconservative Pat Buchanan, grumbled, "Vigorously did we inveigh against the Great Society, enthusiastically did we fund it."

Nixon also acted contrary to his antigovernment rhetoric when economic crises and energy shortages induced him to increase the federal government's power in the marketplace. By 1970, both inflation and unemployment had surpassed 6 percent, an unprecedented combination dubbed "stagflation." Domestic troubles were compounded by the decline of American dominance in the international economy. With the productive capacity of Japan and Western Europe fully recovered from World War II, foreign cars, electronic equipment, and other products now competed favorably with American goods. In 1971, for the first time in decades, the United States imported more than it exported. Because the amount of dollars in foreign hands exceeded U.S. gold reserves, the nation could no longer back up its currency with gold.

In 1971, Nixon abandoned the convertibility of dollars into gold and devalued the dollar to increase exports. To protect domestic manufacturers, he imposed a 10 percent surcharge on most imports, and he froze wages and prices, thus enabling the government to stimulate the economy without fueling inflation. In the short run, these policies worked, and Nixon was resoundingly reelected in 1972. Yet by 1974, unemployment had crept back up and inflation soared, leaving to Nixon's successor the most severe economic crisis since the 1930s.

Skyrocketing energy prices intensified stagflation. Throughout the post–World War II economic boom, the nation's abundant oil deposits and access to cheap Middle Eastern oil had encouraged the building of large cars and skyscrapers with no concern for fuel efficiency. By the 1970s, the United States was consuming one-third of the world's fuel resources.

In the fall of 1973, the United States faced its first energy crisis. Arab nations, furious at the administration's support of Israel during the Yom Kippur War (as discussed in chapter 29), cut off oil shipments to the United States. Long lines formed at gas stations, where prices had nearly doubled, and many homes were cold. In response, Nixon authorized temporary emergency measures allocating petroleum and establishing a national 55-mile-per-hour speed limit to save gasoline. The energy crisis eased, but the nation had yet to come to grips with its seemingly unquenchable demand for fuel and dependence on foreign oil.

Responding to Environmental Concerns

The oil crisis dovetailed with a rising environmental movement, which was pushing the government to conserve energy and protect nature and human beings from the hazards of rapid economic growth. Like the conservation movement born in the Progressive Era (see chapter 21), the new environmentalists sought to preserve natural areas for recreational and aesthetic purposes and to conserve natural resources for future use. Especially in the West, the post–World War II explosion of economic growth and mushrooming population, with the resulting demands for electricity and water, made such efforts seem even more critical. Environmental groups began mobilizing in the 1950s to stop the construction of dams that would disrupt national parks and wilderness areas.

The new environmentalists, however, went beyond conservationism to attack the ravaging effects of industrial development and technological advances on human life and health. To the leaders of a new organization, Friends of the Earth, unlimited economic growth was "no longer healthy, but a cancer."

Biologist Rachel Carson drew national attention in 1962 with her best seller *Silent Spring*, which described the harmful effects of toxic chemicals such as the pesticide DDT. The Sierra Club and other older conservation organizations expanded their agendas, and a host of new groups arose. Millions of Americans expressed environmental concerns on the first observation of Earth Day in April 1970.

Responding to these concerns, Nixon built on the efforts begun in the Johnson administration. He called "clean air, clean water, open spaces . . . the birthright of every American" and urged Congress to "end the plunder of America's natural heritage." In 1970, he created the **Environmental Protection Agency (EPA)** to conduct research, enforce environmental laws, and reduce human health and environmental risks from pollutants. He also signed the Occupational Safety and Health Act, protecting workers against job-related accidents and disease, and the Clean Air Act of 1970, setting national standards for air quality and restricting factory and automobile emissions of carbon dioxide and other pollutants. Environmentalists claimed that Nixon failed to do enough, pointing particularly to his veto — for budgetary reasons — of the Clean Water Act of 1972, which Congress overrode. Yet his environmental initiatives surpassed those of previous administrations.

Expanding Social Justice

Nixon's 1968 campaign had exploited hostility to black protest and new civil rights policies to appeal to southern Democrats and white workers, but his administration had to answer to the courts and to Congress. In 1968, fourteen years after the *Brown* decision, school desegregation had barely touched the South. Like Eisenhower, Nixon was reluctant to use federal power to compel integration, but the Supreme Court overruled the administration's efforts to delay court-ordered desegregation and compelled it to enforce the law. By the time Nixon left office, fewer than one in ten southern black children attended totally segregated schools.

Nixon also began to implement affirmative action among federal contractors and unions and awarded more government contracts and loans to minority businesses. Congress took the initiative in other areas. In 1970, it extended the Voting Rights Act of 1965, and in 1972 it strengthened the Civil Rights Act of 1964 by enlarging the powers of the Equal Employment Opportunity Commission. In 1971, Congress also responded to the massive youth movement with the Twenty-sixth Amendment to the Constitution, which reduced the voting age to eighteen.

Women as well as minority groups benefited from the implementation of affirmative action and the strengthened EEOC, but several measures of the Nixon administration also specifically attacked sex discrimination. The president privately expressed patronizing attitudes about women. "Thank God we don't have any in the Cabinet," he told aides. Yet again, he confronted a growing movement that included Republican feminists. Nixon vetoed a comprehensive child care bill and publicly opposed abortion, but he signed the pathbreaking Title IX, guaranteeing equality in all aspects of education, and allowed his Labor Department to push affirmative action.

President Nixon gave more public support for justice to Native Americans than to any other protest group. While not bowing to radical demands, the administration dealt cautiously with extreme protests, such as the occupation of the Bureau of Indian Affairs in Washington, D.C. Nixon signed measures recognizing claims of Alaskan and New Mexican Indians and set in motion legislation restoring tribal lands and granting Indians more control over their schools and other service institutions.

REVIEW Why and how did Republican president Richard Nixon expand the liberal reforms of previous administrations?

▶ Conclusion: Achievements and Limitations of Liberalism

Senate majority leader Mike Mansfield was not alone in concluding that Lyndon Johnson "has done more than FDR ever did, or ever thought of doing." Building on initiatives from John F. Kennedy's New Frontier, the Great Society expanded the New Deal's focus on economic security, refashioning liberalism to embrace individual rights and to extend material well-being to groups left out of or discriminated against in New Deal programs. Yet opposition to Johnson's leadership grew so strong that by 1968 his liberal vision lay in ruins. "How," he asked, "was it possible that all these people could be so ungrateful to me after I have given them so much?"

Fannie Lou Hamer could have responded by pointing out how slowly the government acted when efforts to win African Americans' rights met with violence. In addition, Hamer's failed attempts to use Johnson's antipoverty programs to help poor blacks in Mississippi resulted in part from internal problems, but those failures also reflected some of the more general shortcomings of the War on Poverty. Hastily planned and inadequately funded, antipoverty programs focused more on remediating individual shortcomings than on reforms that would ensure adequately paying jobs for all. Because Johnson launched an all-out war in Vietnam and refused to ask for sacrifices from prosperous Americans, the Great Society never commanded the resources necessary for victory over poverty.

Furthermore, black aspirations exceeded white Americans' commitment to genuine equality. When the civil rights movement attacked racial barriers long entrenched throughout the nation and sought equality in fact as well as in law, it faced a powerful backlash. By the end of the 1960s, the revolution in the legal status of African Americans was complete, but the black freedom struggle had lost momentum, and African Americans remained, with Native Americans and Chicanos, at the bottom of the economic ladder.

Johnson's critics overlooked the Great Society's more successful and lasting elements. Medicare and Medicaid continue to provide access to health care for the elderly and the poor. Federal aid for education and housing became permanent elements of national policy. Moreover, Richard Nixon's otherwise conservative administration implemented school desegregation in the South and affirmative action, initiated substantial environmental reforms, and secured new rights for Native Americans and women. Women especially benefited from the decline of discrimination, and significant numbers of African Americans and other minority groups began to enter the middle class.

Yet the perceived shortcomings of government programs contributed to social turmoil and fueled the resurgence of conservative politics. Young radicals launched direct confrontations with the government and universities, calling for both domestic reform and an end to the war in Vietnam. The combination of racial conflict and youth activism escalated into widespread political discord and social disorder. The Vietnam War polarized American society as much as did racial issues or the behavior of young people, and it devoured resources that might have been used for social reform even as it undermined faith in presidential leadership.

Reviewing Chapter 28

REVIEW QUESTIONS

1. How did the Kennedy and Johnson administrations exemplify a liberal vision of the federal government? (pp. 842–850)

2. How and why did the civil rights movement change in the mid-1960s? (pp. 850–858)

3. How did the black freedom struggle influence other reform movements of the 1960s and 1970s? (pp. 858–863)

4. What were the key goals of feminist reformers, and why did a counter-movement arise to resist them? (pp. 863–868)

5. Why and how did Republican president Richard Nixon expand the liberal reforms of previous administrations? (pp. 868–871)

MAKING CONNECTIONS

1. In what ways did Lyndon Johnson's Great Society build on the initiatives of John F. Kennedy? Why were Johnson's reforms so much more far-reaching?

2. During the 1960s, African Americans made substantial gains in asserting their freedoms and rights. What specific gains did the civil rights movement achieve? Were there limits to its success? What part did government play in this process?

3. Women participated in various ways in the feminism that emerged in the 1960s. How can we explain the rise of this movement? What assumptions and goals were held in common in this diverse movement?

4. Most of the reform movements of the 1960s sought equality as one of their key priorities, but significant differences existed among Americans in general about what equality meant. Should equality be limited to equal treatment under the law, or should it extend to economic welfare, education, sexual relations, and other aspects of life? Examining two reform movements, discuss how different ideas of equality contributed to the accomplishments and disappointments of each movement.

LINKING TO THE PAST

1. Both Franklin Roosevelt's New Deal and Lyndon Johnson's Great Society attacked poverty. How was Johnson's approach different from Roosevelt's? Which was more successful, and what contributed to the relative successes and failures of each approach? (See chapter 24.)

2. What changes that had been taking place in the United States since 1940 laid a foundation for the rise of a feminist movement in the 1960s? (See chapters 25 and 26.)

TIMELINE 1960–1973

1960
- Democrat John F. Kennedy elected president.
- Student Nonviolent Coordinating Committee (SNCC) established.
- Students for a Democratic Society (SDS) founded.

1961
- Congress of Racial Equality (CORE) sponsors Freedom Rides.

1962
- United Farm Workers (UFW) founded.

1963
- President's Commission on the Status of Women issues report.
- Equal Pay Act.
- *Baker v. Carr.*
- *Abington School District v. Schempp.*
- March on Washington for Jobs and Freedom.
- President Kennedy assassinated; Lyndon B. Johnson becomes president.

1964
- Civil Rights Act.
- Mississippi Freedom Summer Project.
- Economic Opportunity Act.
- Major tax cuts enacted.

1965
- Voting Rights Act.

1965–1966
- Congress passes most of Johnson's Great Society domestic programs.

1965–1968
- Riots in major cities.

1966
- Black Panther Party for Self-Defense founded.
- *Miranda v. Arizona.*
- National Organization for Women (NOW) founded.

1967
- *Loving v. Virginia.*

1968
- Martin Luther King Jr. assassinated.
- American Indian Movement (AIM) founded.
- Republican Richard M. Nixon elected president.

1969
- Stonewall riots.

1970
- First Earth Day celebrated.
- Environmental Protection Agency (EPA) established.
- Clean Air Act.

1971
- Constitutional amendment lowers voting age to eighteen.

1972
- Title IX of Education Amendments Act.
- Congress passes Equal Rights Amendment; sends it to states for ratification.
- American Indians' "Trail of Broken Treaties" caravan to Washington, D.C.

1973
- *Roe v. Wade.*

▶ **FOR AN ONLINE BIBLIOGRAPHY, PRACTICE QUIZZES, WEB SITES, IMAGES, AND DOCUMENTS RELATED TO THIS CHAPTER,** see the Book Companion Site at **bedfordstmartins.com/roarkvalue**.

▶ **FOR DOCUMENTS RELATED TO THIS PERIOD,** see Michael Johnson, ed., *Reading the American Past*, Fifth Edition.

Vietnam and the End of the Cold War Consensus

1961–1975

LIEUTENANT FREDERICK DOWNS GREW UP ON A FARM IN INDIANA, played football in high school, and finished three years of college before enlisting in the army at the age of twenty-two. Leaving a ten-month-old daughter behind, he graduated from officer candidate school at Fort Benning, Georgia, and arrived in Vietnam in September 1967, prepared to lead an infantry platoon. He and his fellow soldiers went to Vietnam, "cocky and sure of our destiny, gung ho, invincible."

That confidence was tempered by the conditions he found in Vietnam. Unlike most of America's previous wars, there was no fixed battle front; helicopters ferried fighting units all over South Vietnam, as U.S. and South Vietnamese troops attempted to defeat the South Vietnamese rebels and their North Vietnamese allies. In a civil conflict characterized by guerrilla warfare, Downs led his men out on search-and-destroy missions in areas where they struggled to distinguish civilians from combatants and burned down villages just because they might be used by the enemy. He had faith that his country could win the war, but he found its ally, the South Vietnamese army, to be lazy and ineffective. "Maybe the people in Nam are worth saving, but their army isn't worth shit," he wrote in his memoir. Downs won several medals for bravery, but his one-year stint in Vietnam was cut short when a land mine blew off his left arm and wedged shrapnel into his legs and back.

Lieutenant Frederick Downs, Jr., in 1967
Frederick Downs—shown here before he lost his arm in Vietnam—returned from the war with a shoulder full of medals and spent the rest of his life helping other soldiers. After earning a masters degree in business administration, he worked for the Veterans Administration and eventually became director of its prosthetics and sensory aids program. In the 1980s, Downs visited Vietnam several times. As he got to know the former enemy as individuals, he lost the hatred he had once harbored, feeling "only sorrow at the ways of man." Collection of Frederick Downs.

Downs's service in Vietnam came at the height of a U.S. engagement that began with the Cold War commitments made in the 1940s and 1950s by Presidents Harry S. Truman and Dwight D. Eisenhower. John F. Kennedy wholeheartedly took on those commitments, promising more flexible and vigorous efforts to thwart communism. The most memorable words of his 1961 inaugural address declared that the United States would "pay any price, bear any burden, meet any hardship, support any friend, oppose any foe to assure the survival and the success of liberty."

Vietnam became the foremost test of John F. Kennedy's anticommunism. He sent increasing amounts of American arms and personnel to sustain the South Vietnamese government, but it was Lyndon B. Johnson who dramatically escalated that commitment in 1965 and turned a civil war among the Vietnamese into America's war. At peak strength in 1968, 543,000 U.S. military personnel served in Vietnam; all told, some 2.6 million saw duty there. Yet this massive intervention not only failed to defeat North Vietnam but also created intense discord at home, "poisoning the soul of America," as Downs put it. It cost President Johnson another term in office and contributed to the downfall of his Republican successor, Richard M. Nixon. Some Americans supported the government's goal in Vietnam and decried only its failure to pursue it effectively. Others believed that preserving a non-Communist South Vietnam was neither in the best interests of the United States nor within its capacity or moral right to achieve. Back home in college after months of surgery, Downs encountered a man who asked about the hook descending from his sleeve. When he said that he had lost his arm in Vietnam, the man shot back, "Serves you right."

This internal conflict was just one of the war's great costs. Like Downs, more than 150,000 soldiers suffered severe wounds, and more than 58,000 lost their lives. Martin Luther King Jr. mourned "the promises of the Great Society . . . shot down on the battlefield of Vietnam." In addition to derailing domestic reform, the war depleted the federal budget, disrupted the economy, kindled internal conflict, and led to the violation of protesters' rights, leaving a lasting mark on the nation.

Even while fighting communism in Vietnam and, on a much smaller scale, in other third world countries, American leaders moved to ease Cold War tensions with the major Communist powers. After a dramatic standoff with the Soviet Union during the Cuban missile crisis, the United States began to cooperate with its Cold War enemy to limit the spread of nuclear weapons. In addition, Nixon's historic visit to China in 1972 marked the abandonment of the policy of isolating China and paved the way for normal diplomatic relations by the end of the 1970s.

▶ New Frontiers in Foreign Policy

John F. Kennedy moved quickly to pursue containment more aggressively and with more flexible means. In contrast to the Eisenhower administration's emphasis on nuclear weapons, Kennedy expanded not only the nation's nuclear capacity but also its ability to fight conventional battles and to engage in guerrilla warfare. To ensure U.S. superiority over the Soviet Union in every domain, Kennedy accelerated the nation's space exploration program and increased attention to the third world. When the Soviets tried to establish a nuclear outpost in the Western Hemisphere in Cuba in 1962, he took the United States to the brink of war. Less dramatically but no less resolutely, Kennedy sent increasing amounts of American arms and personnel to save the South Vietnamese government from Communist insurgents.

Meeting the "Hour of Maximum Danger"

Underlying Kennedy's foreign policy was an assumption that the United States had "gone soft — physically, mentally, spiritually soft," as he put it in 1960. Calling the Eisenhower era "years of drift and impotency," he associated that administration with femininity when he mocked Nixon's celebration of American consumer goods

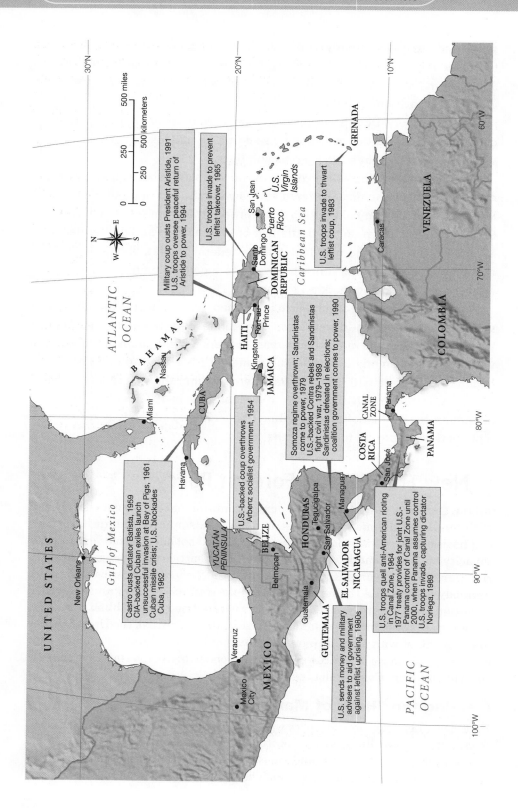

Military coup ousts President Aristide, 1991
U.S. troops oversee peaceful return of
Aristide to power, 1994

U.S. troops invade to prevent
leftist takeover, 1965

U.S. troops invade to thwart
leftist coup, 1983

Castro ousts dictator Batista, 1959
CIA-backed Cuban exiles launch
unsuccessful invasion at Bay of Pigs, 1961
Cuban missile crisis; U.S. blockades
Cuba, 1962

U.S.-backed coup overthrows
Arbenz socialist government, 1954

Somoza regime overthrown; Sandinistas
come to power, 1979
U.S.-backed Contra rebels and Sandinistas
fight civil war, 1979–1989
Sandinistas defeated in elections;
coalition government comes to power, 1990

U.S. troops quell anti-American rioting
in Canal Zone, 1964
1977 treaty provides for joint U.S.-
Panama control of Canal Zone until
2000, when Panama assumes control
of Canal Zone; U.S. troops invade,
capturing dictator Noriega, 1989

U.S. sends money and military
advisers to aid government
against leftist uprising, 1980s

ATLANTIC
OCEAN

Caribbean Sea

PACIFIC
OCEAN

Gulf of Mexico

UNITED STATES

MEXICO

YUCATÁN
PENINSULA

BAHAMAS

CUBA

JAMAICA

HAITI

DOMINICAN
REPUBLIC

Puerto
Rico

U.S.
Virgin
Islands

GRENADA

VENEZUELA

COLOMBIA

PANAMA

CANAL
ZONE

COSTA
RICA

NICARAGUA

EL SALVADOR

HONDURAS

BELIZE

GUATEMALA

New Orleans

Miami

Havana

Nassau

Mexico
City

Veracruz

Guatemala

Belmopan

Tegucigalpa

San Salvador

Managua

San José

Panama

Kingston

Port-au-
Prince

Santo
Domingo

San Juan

Caracas

500 miles

500 kilometers

0   250   500

0   250   500

N
E
W
S

in the kitchen debate with **Nikita Khrushchev.** "I would rather take my television black and white and have the largest rockets in the world," Kennedy declared. Criticizing the Eisenhower administration for relying too heavily on nuclear weapons, Kennedy built up conventional ground forces to provide a flexible response to Communist expansion. He also charged that limits on defense spending had caused the United States to fall behind even in nuclear capability. In January 1961, Kennedy warned that the nation faced a grave peril: "Each day the crises multiply. . . . Each day we draw nearer the hour of maximum danger."

Kennedy exaggerated the threat to national security; the United States remained ahead of the Soviets in nuclear capacity. Yet several developments in 1961 heightened the sense of crisis and provided a rationalization for his military buildup. Shortly before Kennedy's inauguration, Khrushchev publicly encouraged "wars of national liberation," thereby aligning the Soviet Union with independence movements in the third world that were often anti-Western. His statement reflected in part the Soviet competition with China for the allegiance of emerging nations, but U.S. officials saw in his words a threat to the status quo of containment.

Cuba, just ninety miles off the Florida coast, posed the most immediate threat to the United States. The revolution led by **Fidel Castro** had already moved Cuba into the Soviet orbit, and Eisenhower's Central Intelligence Agency (CIA) had been planning an invasion of the island by Cuban exiles living in Florida. Kennedy ordered the invasion to proceed even though his military advisers gave it only a fair chance of success.

On April 17, 1961, about 1,400 anti-Castro exiles trained and armed by the CIA landed at the **Bay of Pigs** on the south shore of Cuba (Map 29.1). Contrary to U.S. expectations, no popular uprising materialized to support the anti-Castro brigade. Kennedy refused to provide direct military support, and the invaders quickly fell to Castro's forces. The disaster humiliated Kennedy and the United States, posing a stark contrast to the president's inaugural promise of a new, more effective foreign policy. The attempted invasion evoked memories of Yankee imperialism among Latin Americans and aligned Cuba even more closely with the Soviet Union.

Days before the Bay of Pigs invasion, the Soviet Union delivered a psychological blow when a Soviet astronaut became the first human being to orbit the earth. In May 1961, Kennedy called for a huge new commitment to the space program, with the goal of sending a man to the moon by 1970. Congress authorized the **Apollo program** and boosted appropriations for space exploration. John H. Glenn orbited the earth in 1962, and the United States beat the Soviets to the moon, landing two astronauts there in 1969.

Early in his presidency, Kennedy determined to show American toughness to Khrushchev. But when the two met in June 1961 in Vienna, Austria, Khrushchev

◀ **MAP 29.1**
U.S. Involvement in Latin America and the Caribbean, 1954–1994
During the Cold War, the United States frequently intervened in Central American and Caribbean countries to suppress Communist or leftist movements.

was belligerent and shook the president's confidence. The stunned Kennedy reported privately, "He just beat [the] hell out of me. . . . If he thinks I'm inexperienced and have no guts . . . we won't get anywhere with him." Khrushchev demanded an agreement recognizing the existence of two Germanys and made veiled threats about America's occupation rights in and access to West Berlin.

Khrushchev was concerned about the massive exodus of East Germans into West Berlin, a major embarrassment for the Communists. To stop this flow, in August 1961 East Germany shocked the world by erecting a wall between East and West Berlin. With the **Berlin Wall** stemming the tide of migration and Kennedy insisting that West Berlin was "the great testing place of Western courage and will," Khrushchev backed off from his threats. But not until 1972 did the super-powers recognize East and West Germany as separate nations and guarantee Western access to West Berlin.

Kennedy used the Berlin crisis to add $3.2 billion to the defense budget. He increased draft calls and mobilized the reserves and National Guard, adding 300,000 troops to the military. This buildup of conventional forces provided for a "flexible response," offering "a wider choice than humiliation or all-out nuclear action." Still, Kennedy also pushed for the development of new nuclear weapons and delivery systems, more than doubling the nation's nuclear force within three years.

New Approaches to the Third World

Complementing Kennedy's hard-line policy toward the Soviet Union were fresh approaches to the nationalist movements that had multiplied since the end of World War II. In 1960 alone, seventeen African nations gained their independence. Much more than his predecessors, Kennedy publicly supported third world aspirations, believing that the United States could win the hearts and minds of people in developing nations by helping to fulfill hopes for autonomy and democracy.

To that end, Kennedy created the Alliance for Progress in 1961, pledging $20 billion in Latin American aid over the next decade. Like the Marshall Plan (see chapter 26), the Alliance for Progress was designed to thwart communism and hold nations within the American sphere by fostering economic development. Yet by 1969, the United States had provided only half of the promised $20 billion, much of which went to military projects or corrupt ruling elites.

Kennedy launched his most dramatic third world initiative in 1961 with an idea borrowed from Senator Hubert H. Humphrey: the **Peace Corps**. The program recruited young people to work in developing countries, attracting many who had been moved by Kennedy's appeal for idealism and sacrifice in his inaugural address. One volunteer's service eased his guilt at having been "born between clean sheets when others were issued into the dust with a birthright of hunger." After studying a country's language and culture, Peace Corps volunteers went to work directly with its people, opening schools, providing basic health care, and assisting with agriculture and small economic enterprises. By the mid-1970s, more than 60,000 volunteers had served in Latin America, Africa, and Asia. Peace Corps projects were generally welcomed, but they did not address the receiving countries' larger economic and political structures.

Kennedy also used direct military means to bring political stability to the third world. He rapidly expanded the elite special forces corps established under Eisenhower to aid groups fighting against Communist-leaning movements. These counterinsurgency forces, including the army's Green Berets and the navy's SEALs, were trained to wage guerrilla warfare and equipped with the latest technology. They would get their first test in Vietnam.

The Arms Race and the Nuclear Brink

The final piece of Kennedy's defense strategy was to strengthen American nuclear dominance. He upped the number of nuclear weapons based in Europe from 2,500 to 7,200 and multiplied fivefold the supply of intercontinental ballistic missiles (ICBMs). Concerned that this buildup would enable the United States to launch a first strike and wipe out Soviet missile sites before they could respond, the Soviet Union stepped up its own ICBM program. Thus began the most intense arms race in history.

The superpowers came perilously close to using their weapons during the **Cuban missile crisis** in 1962. Khrushchev decided to install nuclear missiles in Cuba to protect Castro's regime from further U.S. attempts at intervention and to balance the U.S. missiles aimed at the Soviet Union from Britain, Italy, and Turkey. The thirteen-day crisis began on October 16, when the CIA showed Kennedy aerial photographs of missile launching sites under construction. Considering this an intolerable threat to the United States, the president decided to react. On October 22, he announced to a television audience that the military was on full alert and that the navy would turn back any Soviet vessel suspected of carrying offensive missiles to Cuba. Kennedy warned that any attack launched from Cuba would trigger a full nuclear assault against the Soviet Union.

Projecting the appearance of toughness was paramount to President Kennedy. Conceding that the missiles did not "alter the strategic balance in fact," one of his aides insisted that "that balance would have been substantially altered in appearance; and in matters of national will and world leadership such appearances contribute to reality." Kennedy also worried that "Communism and Castroism are going to be spread [in Latin America] as governments frightened by this new evidence of power [fall]."

But if Kennedy risked nuclear war for appearances, both he and Khrushchev also exercised caution. Kennedy refused advice from the military to bomb the missile sites. On October 24, Russian ships carrying nuclear warheads toward Cuba suddenly turned back. When one ship crossed the blockade line, Kennedy ordered the navy to follow the ship rather than attempt to stop it.

While Americans experienced the Cold War's most dangerous days, Kennedy and Khrushchev negotiated an agreement. The Soviets removed the missiles and pledged not to introduce new offensive weapons into Cuba. The United States promised not to invade the island. Secretly, Kennedy also agreed to remove U.S. missiles from Turkey. The Cuban crisis contributed to Khrushchev's fall from power two years later, while Kennedy emerged triumphant. "I cut his balls off," Kennedy rejoiced in private. The image of an inexperienced president fumbling

MISSILE SHELTER TENT

TRACKED PRIME MOVERS

OXIDIZER TANK TRAILERS

FUEL TANK TRAILERS

Preparing for the Worst during the Cuban Missile Crisis
The thirteen-day Cuban Missile Crisis was one of the most tense and dangerous periods of the Cold War. Aerial photographs like this one taken by the U.S. Navy on October 23, 1962 confirmed the Soviet Union's military presence within range of the United States and brought home the very real threat of nuclear war. © Bettmann/Corbis.

the Bay of Pigs invasion gave way to that of a strong leader bearing the United States through its "hour of maximum danger."

Having proved his toughness, Kennedy worked with Khrushchev to prevent future confrontations by installing a special "hot line" to speed top-level communication. In a major speech at American University in June 1963, Kennedy called for a reexamination of Cold War assumptions, asking Americans "not to see conflict as inevitable." Acknowledging the superpowers' differences, Kennedy stressed what they had in common: "We all breathe the same air. We all cherish our children's future and we are all mortal." In August 1963, the United States, the Soviet Union, and Great Britain signed a limited nuclear test ban treaty, reducing the threat of radioactive fallout from nuclear testing and raising hopes for further superpower accord.

A Growing War in Vietnam

In his American University speech, Kennedy criticized the idea of "a Pax Americana enforced on the world by American weapons of war," but in 1961 he began to increase the flow of those weapons into South Vietnam. Kennedy's strong anticommunism and attachment to a vigorous foreign policy prepared him to expand the commitment in Vietnam that he had inherited from Eisenhower. Convinced that China and the Soviet Union were behind the efforts of North Vietnamese leader **Ho Chi Minh** to unify Vietnam under communism, Kennedy's key military adviser,

MAP 29.2
The Vietnam War, 1964–1975
The United States sent 2.6 million soldiers to Vietnam and spent more than $150 billion on the longest war in American history, but it was unable to prevent the unification of Vietnam under a Communist government.

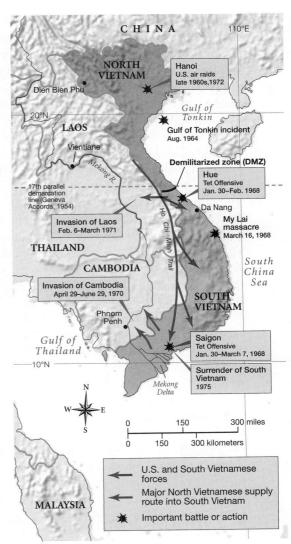

General Maxwell Taylor, argued that holding firm in Vietnam would show the Soviets and Chinese that wars of national liberation were "costly, dangerous, and doomed to failure."

By the time Kennedy took office, more than $1 billion in aid and seven hundred U.S. military advisers had failed to stabilize South Vietnam. Two major obstacles stood in the way. First, the South Vietnamese insurgents — whom Americans called Vietcong, short for *Vietnam Cong-san* ("Vietnamese Communists") — were an indigenous force whose initiative came from within, not from the Soviet Union or China. Because the Saigon government refused to hold elections, the rebels saw no choice but to take up arms. Increasingly, Ho Chi Minh's Communist government in North Vietnam supplied them with weapons and soldiers.

Second, the South Vietnamese government refused to satisfy the demands of the insurgents, but the **Army of the Republic of Vietnam (ARVN)** could not defeat them militarily. Ngo Dinh Diem, South Vietnam's premier from 1954 to 1963, chose self-serving military leaders for their personal loyalty rather than for their effectiveness. Many South Vietnamese, the majority of whom were Buddhists, saw the Catholic Diem as a corrupt and brutal tool of the West. Even Secretary of State Dean Rusk called him "an oriental despot."

The growing intervention by North Vietnam made matters worse. In 1960, the Hanoi government established the **National Liberation Front (NLF)**, composed of South Vietnamese rebels but directed by the northern army. In addition, Hanoi constructed a network of infiltration routes, called the Ho Chi Minh Trail, in neighboring Laos and Cambodia, through which it sent people and supplies to help liberate the South (Map 29.2). Violence escalated between 1960 and 1963, bringing the Saigon government close to collapse.

Kennedy responded to the deteriorating situation with measured steps. Some advisers called for using any force necessary to save South Vietnam from communism. Others questioned whether such a victory was either necessary or possible. Taking the middle ground, Kennedy gradually escalated the U.S. commitment. By the spring of 1963, military aid had doubled, and the 9,000 Americans serving in Vietnam as military advisers occasionally participated in actual combat. The South Vietnamese government promised reform but never made good on its promises.

Reflecting racist attitudes of American superiority over nonwhite populations, officials assumed that U.S. technology and sheer power could win in Vietnam. Yet advanced weapons were ill suited to the guerrilla warfare practiced by the enemy, whose surprise attacks were designed to weaken support for the South Vietnamese government. In addition, U.S. weapons and strategy harmed the very people they were intended to save. Thousands of peasants were uprooted and resettled in "strategic hamlets," supposedly secure from the Communists. Those left in the countryside fell victim to bombs — containing the highly flammable substance napalm — dropped by the South Vietnamese air force to quell the Vietcong. In January 1962, U.S. planes began to spray herbicides such as **Agent Orange** to destroy the Vietcong's jungle hideouts and food supply.

With tacit permission from Washington, South Vietnamese military leaders executed a coup against Diem and his brother, who headed the secret police, in November 1963. Kennedy expressed shock when the two were murdered but indicated no change in policy. In a speech to be given on the day he was assassinated, Kennedy referred specifically to Southeast Asia and warned, "We dare not weary of the task." At his death, 16,700 Americans were stationed in Vietnam, and 100 had died there.

> **REVIEW** Why did Kennedy believe that engagement in Vietnam was crucial to his foreign policy?

▶ Lyndon Johnson's War against Communism

The Cold War assumptions that had shaped Kennedy's foreign policy underlay his successor's approach to Southeast Asia and Latin America. Retaining Kennedy's key advisers — Secretary of State Rusk, Secretary of Defense Robert McNamara, and National Security Adviser McGeorge Bundy — **Lyndon B. Johnson** continued the massive buildup of nuclear weapons and conventional and counterinsurgency forces. In 1965, Johnson made the fateful decisions to order U.S. troops into combat in Vietnam and to initiate sustained bombing of the North. That same year, Johnson sent U.S. Marines to the Dominican Republic to crush a leftist rebellion.

An All-Out Commitment in Vietnam

The president who wanted to make his mark on domestic policy was compelled to deal with the commitments his predecessors had made in Vietnam. Some advisers, politicians, and international leaders raised questions about the wisdom of a greater commitment there, viewing the situation as a civil war rather than Communist aggression. Most U.S. allies did not consider Vietnam crucial to containing communism and were not prepared to share the military burden in more than token ways. Senate majority leader Mike Mansfield wondered whether Vietnam could be won with a "limited expenditure of American lives and resources somewhere commensurate with our national interests." Johnson expressed his own doubt privately: "I don't think it's worth fighting for and I don't think we can get out."

Believing that the nation's reputation as a staunch defender against communism was on the line, the president expanded the United States' military involvement. Moreover, like Kennedy, he remembered how Truman had suffered politically when the Communists took over China. Johnson wanted to prevent Republicans from charging that Democrats were weak on national security, and he believed that conceding defeat in Vietnam would undermine his ability to achieve his Great Society.

Johnson understood the ineffectiveness of his South Vietnamese allies and agonized over sending young men into combat. Yet he continued to dispatch more military advisers, weapons, and economic aid and, in August 1964, seized an opportunity to increase the pressure on North Vietnam. While spying in the Gulf of Tonkin, off the coast of North Vietnam, two U.S. destroyers reported that North Vietnamese gunboats had fired on them (see Map 29.2). Johnson quickly ordered air strikes on North Vietnamese torpedo bases and oil storage facilities. Concealing the uncertainty about whether the second attack had even occurred and the provocative U.S. operations along the North Vietnamese coast, he won from Congress the **Gulf of Tonkin Resolution**, authorizing him to take "all necessary measures to repel any armed attacks against the forces of the United States and to prevent further aggression."

The president's tough stance only two months before the 1964 election helped counter the charges made by his opponent, Arizona senator Barry Goldwater, that he was "soft on communism." Yet Johnson also presented himself as the peace candidate, assuring Americans that "we are not going to send American boys nine or ten thousand miles away from home to do what Asian boys ought to be doing for themselves."

Johnson might have used the political capital from his overwhelming reelection victory to disengage from Vietnam. Instead he widened the war, rejecting peace overtures from North Vietnam, because it insisted on American withdrawal and a coalition government in South Vietnam as steps toward ultimate unification of the country. In February 1965, Johnson authorized **Operation Rolling Thunder**, a strategy of gradually intensified bombing of North Vietnam. Less than a month later, Johnson ordered the first U.S. combat troops to South Vietnam, and in July he shifted U.S. troops from defensive to offensive operations, dispatching 50,000 more soldiers. Although the administration downplayed the import of these decisions, they marked a critical turning point. Now it was genuinely America's war.

Preventing Another Castro in Latin America

Closer to home, Johnson faced persistent problems in Latin America. Thirteen times during the 1960s, military coups toppled Latin American governments, and local insurgencies grew apace. The administration's response varied from case to case but centered on the determination to prevent any more Castro-type revolutions.

In 1964, riots erupted in the Panama Canal Zone, which the United States had seized and made a U.S. territory early in the century (see chapter 21). Instigated by Panamanians who viewed the United States as a colonial power, the riots left four U.S. soldiers and more than twenty Panamanians dead. Johnson sent troops to quell the disturbance, but he also initiated negotiations that eventually returned the canal to Panamanian authority in 2000.

Elsewhere, Johnson's Latin American policy generated new cries of "Yankee imperialism." In 1961, voters in the Dominican Republic ousted a longtime dictator and elected a constitutional government headed by reformist Juan Bosch, who was overthrown by a military coup two years later. In 1965, when Bosch supporters launched an uprising against the military government, Johnson sent more than 20,000 soldiers to quell what he perceived to be a leftist revolt and to take control of the island. A truce was arranged, and in 1966 Dominicans voted in a constitutional government under a moderate rightist.

This first outright show of Yankee force in Latin America in four decades damaged the administration at home and abroad. Although Johnson had justified intervention as necessary to prevent "another Cuba," no Communists were found among the rebels, and U.S. intervention kept the reform-oriented Boschists from returning to power. Moreover, the president had not consulted the Dominicans or the Organization of American States (OAS), to which the United States had promised it would respect national sovereignty in Latin America.

The Americanized War

The military success in the Dominican Republic no doubt encouraged the president to press on in Vietnam. From 1965 to early 1968, the United States gradually escalated the war. While increasing numbers of U.S. troops fought the National Liberation Front in South Vietnam, Operation Rolling Thunder sought to break the will and capacity of the North Vietnamese to support the insurgents. Johnson carefully calibrated the attacks, boasting, "They can't even bomb an outhouse without my approval."

Some military officials chafed at the restrictions placed on the air war, but Johnson remembered what had happened in Korea and that "China is there on the [North Vietnamese] border with 700 million men." The administration banned strikes near that border and on sites where Chinese or Soviet advisers might be present, determined to avoid provoking intervention by either China or the Soviet Union, both of which now possessed nuclear weapons. To contain both domestic and international criticism of the war, Johnson also prohibited bombing targets where high civilian casualties might result.

Despite restrictions, U.S. pilots dropped 643,000 tons of bombs on North Vietnam and more than twice that amount in the South, a total surpassing all the explosives the United States dropped in World War II. Yet the bombing was no match for the determination and ingenuity of the North Vietnamese. Their sheer effort compensated for the destruction of transportation lines, industry sites, and power plants. For example, when bombs struck a rail line, civilians rushed in with bicycles to unload a train's cargo, carry it beyond the break, and load it onto a second train. In South Vietnam, the massive U.S. bombing campaign destroyed villages and fields, alienating the very population that the Americans had come to save.

On the ground, General William Westmoreland's strategy of attrition was designed to seek out and kill the Vietcong and North Vietnamese regular army. With no fixed battle front, officials calculated progress not in territory seized but in "body counts" and "kill ratios" — the number of enemies killed relative to the cost in American and ARVN lives. According to Lieutenant Frederick Downs, "To win a battle, we had to kill them. For them to win, all they had to do was survive." He realized that "we would fight and bleed to take ground," and the enemy would withdraw "after they had exacted their toll"; but then U.S. forces would leave, and the Vietcong could come back whenever they liked. The Americans, Downs said, "never owned anything except the ground they stood on."

Those Who Served

Teenagers fought the Vietnam War, in contrast to World War II, in which the average soldier was twenty-six years old. All the men in Lieutenant Downs's platoon were between the ages of eighteen and twenty-one, and the average age for all soldiers was nineteen. Until a constitutional amendment dropped the voting age from twenty-one to eighteen in 1971, most could not even vote for the officials who sent them to war. Men of all classes had fought in World War II, but in Vietnam the poor and working class constituted about 80 percent of the troops. More privileged youths avoided the draft by using college deferments or family connections to get into the National Guard. Sent from Plainville, Kansas, to Vietnam in 1965, Mike Clodfelter could not recall "a single middle-class son of the town's businessmen, lawyers, doctors, or ranchers from my high school graduating class who experienced the Armageddon of our generation."

Much more than World War II, Vietnam was a men's war. Because the United States did not undergo full mobilization for Vietnam, officials did not seek women's sacrifices for the war effort. Still, between 7,500 and 10,000 women served in Vietnam, the vast majority of them nurses. Some women were exposed to enemy fire, and eight lost their lives. Many more struggled with their helplessness in the face of the dead and maimed bodies they tended. "When you finally saved a life," said Peggy DuVall, "you wondered what kind of life you had saved."

Early in the war, African Americans constituted 31 percent of combat troops, often choosing the military over the meager opportunities in the civilian economy.

Special forces ranger Arthur E. Woodley Jr. recalled, "I was just what my country needed. A black patriot. . . . The only way I could possibly make it out of the ghetto was to be the best soldier I possibly could." Death rates among black soldiers were disproportionately high until 1966, when the military adjusted personnel assignments to achieve a better racial balance.

The young troops faced extremely difficult conditions. Frederick Downs's platoon fought in thick jungles filled with leeches, in rain and oppressive heat, always vulnerable to sniper bullets and land mines. He remembered that "the terror of an explosion never failed to send a shiver through our guts." Soldiers in previous wars had served "for the duration," but in Vietnam a soldier served a one-year tour of duty. A commander called it "the worst personnel policy in history," because men had less incentive to fight near the end of their tours, wanting merely to stay alive and whole.

The U.S. military inflicted great losses on the enemy, yet the war remained a stalemate. Dispatched to an area thick with Vietcong sympathizers, Downs wondered how to win the people's hearts and minds: "How could we compete with countrymen who could speak to them, live with them, were related to them?" He remained convinced that his country was doing the right thing yet recognized that "all Vietnamese had a common desire — to see us go home."

The South Vietnamese government was an enormous obstacle to victory, even though in 1965 it settled into a period of stability when it was headed by two military leaders. Graft and corruption continued to flourish in the government. In the intensified fighting and with the inability to distinguish friend from foe, ARVN and American troops killed and wounded thousands of South Vietnamese civilians and destroyed their villages. By 1968, nearly 30 percent of the population had become refugees. The failure to stabilize South Vietnam even as the U.S. military presence expanded enormously created grave challenges for the administration at home.

REVIEW Why did massive amounts of airpower and ground troops fail to bring U.S. victory in Vietnam?

▶ A Nation Polarized

Soon President Johnson was fighting a war on two fronts. Domestic opposition to the war swelled after 1965 as daily television broadcasts made it the first "living-room war." In March 1968, torn between his domestic critics and the military's clamor for more troops, Johnson announced a halt to the bombing, a new effort at negotiations, and his decision not to pursue reelection. Throughout 1968, demonstrations, violence, and assassinations convulsed the increasingly polarized nation. Vietnam took center stage in the election, and voters narrowly favored the Republican candidate, former vice president Richard Nixon, who promised to achieve "peace with honor."

The Widening War at Home

Johnson's authorization of Operation Rolling Thunder expanded the previously quiet doubts and criticism into a mass movement against the war. In April 1965, Students for a Democratic Society (SDS) recruited 20,000 people for the first major demonstration against the war in Washington, D.C. SDS chapters sprang up on more than three hundred college campuses. Thousands of students protested against Reserve Officers Training Corps (ROTC) programs, CIA recruiters, military research projects, and manufacturers of war materiel. Martin Luther King Jr. deployed his moral authority, rebuking the U.S. government in 1967 as "the greatest purveyor of violence in the world today." Environmentalists attacked the use of chemical weapons, such as the deadly Agent Orange.

Antiwar sentiment entered society's mainstream. The *New York Times* began questioning the war in 1965, and by 1968 media critics included the *Wall Street Journal, Life* magazine, and popular TV anchorman Walter Cronkite. Clergy, business people, scientists, and physicians formed their own groups to pressure Johnson to stop the bombing and start negotiations. Prominent Democratic senators, including J. William Fulbright, George McGovern, and Mike Mansfield, urged Johnson to substitute negotiation for force.

Opposition to the war took diverse forms: letters to officials, teach-ins on college campuses, mass marches, student strikes, withholding of federal taxes, draft card and flag burnings, and attempts to stop trains carrying troops. Although the peace movement never claimed a majority of the population, it focused media attention on the

Mothers against the War
Founded in 1961 to work for nuclear disarmament, Women Strike for Peace (WSP) began to "alert the public to the dangers and horrors of the war in Vietnam" in 1963. Identifying themselves as "concerned housewives" and mothers, members mobilized around the slogan "Not Our Sons, Not Your Sons, Not Their Sons." In February 1967, WSP held the first antiwar protest at the Pentagon. More than 2,000 women, some shown here, banged their shoes on Pentagon doors, which were locked as they approached. What characteristics of the war did these women focus on? How were their objections to the war similar to and different from those of other protesters? © Bettmann/Corbis.

war and severely limited the administration's options. The twenty-year-old consensus around Cold War foreign policy had broken down.

Many would not fight in the war. The World Boxing Association stripped Muhammad Ali of his world heavyweight title when he refused to serve in what he called a "white man's war." More than 170,000 men who opposed the war on moral or religious grounds gained conscientious objector status and performed nonmilitary duties at home or in Vietnam. About 60,000 fled the country to escape the draft, and more than 200,000 were accused of failing to register or of committing other draft offenses.

Opponents of the war held diverse views. Those who saw the conflict in moral terms wanted total withdrawal, insisting that their country had no right to interfere in a civil war and stressing the suffering of the Vietnamese people. A larger segment of antiwar sentiment reflected practical considerations — the belief that the war could not be won at a bearable cost. Those activists wanted Johnson to stop bombing North Vietnam and seek negotiations.

Working-class people were no more antiwar than other groups, but they recognized the class dimensions of the war and the antiwar movement. A firefighter whose son had died in Vietnam said bitterly, "It's people like us who give up our sons for the country. The businesspeople, they run the country and make money from it. The college types . . . go to Washington and tell the government what to do. . . . But their sons don't end up in the swamps over there, in Vietnam." The antiwar movement outraged millions of Americans who supported the war. Some members of the generation who had fought against Hitler could not understand younger men's refusal to support their government. They expressed their anger at war protesters with bumper stickers that read "America: Love It or Leave It."

By 1967, the administration realized that "discontent with the war is now wide and deep." President Johnson used various means to silence critics. He equated opposition to the war with communism and assistance to the enemy. To avoid focusing attention on the war's costs, he eschewed measures to control inflation and delayed asking for a tax increase to pay for the war. Not until June 1968 did Congress pass a 10 percent income tax surcharge. Great Society programs suffered, and the surcharge failed to check inflation.

The administration deceived the public by making optimistic statements and concealing officials' ever-graver doubts about the possibility of success in Vietnam. Johnson ordered the CIA to spy on peace advocates, and without the president's specific authorization, the FBI infiltrated the peace movement, disrupted its work, and spread false information about activists. Even the resort to illegal measures failed to subdue the opposition.

The Tet Offensive and Johnson's Move toward Peace

The year 1968 was marked by violent confrontations around the world. Protests against governments erupted from Mexico City to Paris to Tokyo, usually led by students in collaboration with workers. American society also became increasingly polarized. On one side, the so-called hawks charged that the United States was fighting with one hand tied behind its back and called for intensification of the war. The doves wanted de-escalation or withdrawal. As U.S. troop strength neared half a million and military deaths approached 20,000 by the end of 1967, most people were torn between weariness with the war and a desire to fulfill the U.S. commitment. As one woman said, "I want to get out but I don't want to give up."

Grave doubts penetrated the administration itself in 1967. Secretary of Defense **Robert McNamara**, a principal architect of U.S. involvement, now believed that the North Vietnamese "won't quit no matter how much bombing we do." He feared for the image of the United States, "the world's greatest super-power, killing or seriously injuring 1,000 noncombatants a week, while trying to pound a tiny, backward nation into submission on an issue whose merits are hotly disputed." McNamara did not publicly oppose the war, but in early 1968 he left the administration.

A critical turning point came with the **Tet Offensive**. On January 30, 1968, the North Vietnamese and Vietcong launched attacks on key cities, every major American base in South Vietnam, and the U.S. Embassy in Saigon. This was the biggest surprise of the war, and not simply because both sides had customarily observed a truce during Tet, the Vietnamese New Year holiday. The offensive displayed the Communists' vitality and refusal to be intimidated by the presence of half a million American soldiers. Militarily, the enemy suffered a defeat, losing ten times as many soldiers as ARVN and U.S. forces. Psychologically, however, Tet was devastating to the United States.

The Tet Offensive underscored the credibility gap between official statements and the war's actual progress. TV anchorman Walter Cronkite wondered, "What the hell is going on? I thought we were winning the war." The attacks created a million more South Vietnamese refugees as well as widespread destruction. Explaining how he had defended a village, a U.S. Army official said, "We had to destroy the town to save it." The statement epitomized for more and more Americans the brutality and senselessness of the war. Public approval of Johnson's handling of it dropped to 26 percent.

In the aftermath of Tet, Johnson conferred with advisers in the Defense Department and an unofficial group of foreign policy experts who had been key architects of Cold War policies for two decades. Dean Acheson, Truman's secretary of state, summarized their conclusion: "We can no longer do the job we set out to do in the time we have left and we must begin to take steps to disengage."

On March 31, 1968, Lyndon Johnson announced in a televised speech that the United States would sharply curtail its bombing of North Vietnam and that he was prepared to begin peace talks. He added the stunning declaration that he would not run for reelection. The gradual escalation of the war was over, and military strategy shifted from "Americanization" to "Vietnamization" of the war. But this was not a shift in policy. The goal remained a non-Communist South Vietnam; the United States would simply rely more heavily on the South Vietnamese to achieve it.

Negotiations began in Paris in May 1968. The United States would not agree to recognition of the Hanoi government's National Liberation Front, to a coalition government, or to American withdrawal. The North Vietnamese would agree to nothing less. Although the talks continued, so did the fighting.

Meanwhile, violence escalated at home. Protests occurred on two hundred college campuses in the spring of 1968, and as many as one million students participated in nationwide strikes. In the bloodiest action, students occupied buildings at Columbia University in New York City, making demands connected to the university's war-related research and to its treatment of African Americans. When negotiations failed, university officials called in the city police, who cleared the buildings, injuring scores of demonstrators and arresting hundreds. An ensuing student strike prematurely ended the academic year.

The Tumultuous Election of 1968

Disorder and violence also entered the election process. In June, two months after the murder of Martin Luther King Jr. and the riots that followed, another assassination shook the nation. Antiwar candidate Senator Robert F. Kennedy, campaigning in California for the Democratic Party's presidential nomination, was shot by a Palestinian Arab refugee who was outraged by Kennedy's support for Israel.

In August, protesters battled the police in Chicago, where the Democratic Party had convened to nominate its presidential ticket. Several thousand demonstrators came to the city, some to support the peace candidate Senator Eugene McCarthy, others to cause disruption. The Youth International Party (Yippies), a splinter group of SDS, urged protesters to demonstrate their hatred of the establishment by provoking the police and creating chaos. On August 25, when demonstrators jeered at orders to disperse, police attacked them with tear gas and clubs. Street battles continued for three days, culminating in a police riot on the night of August 28. Taunted by the crowd, the police used Mace and nightsticks, clubbing not only those who had come to provoke violence but also reporters, peaceful demonstrators, and convention delegates.

Although the bloodshed in Chicago horrified those who saw it on television, it had little effect on the convention's outcome. An assassin had ended Robert Kennedy's promising campaign in June, and Vice President **Hubert H. Humphrey** trounced the remaining antiwar candidate, McCarthy, by nearly three to one for the Democratic nomination.

In contrast to the turmoil around the Democratic convention, the Republican convention met peacefully and nominated former vice president Richard Nixon on the first ballot. For his running mate, Nixon chose Maryland governor Spiro T. Agnew, hoping to gather southern support. A strong third candidate entered the electoral scene when the American Independent Party nominated former Alabama governor and staunch segregationist **George C. Wallace**. Wallace appealed to Americans' dissatisfaction with the reforms and rebellions of the 1960s and their outrage at the assaults on traditional values. Nixon guardedly played on resentments that fueled the Wallace campaign, calling for "law and order" and attacking liberal Supreme Court decisions, busing for school desegregation, and protesters.

Nixon and Humphrey differed little on the central issue of Vietnam. Nixon promised "an honorable end" to the war but did not indicate how he would do it.

Humphrey had strong reservations about U.S. policy in Vietnam, yet as vice president he was tied to Johnson's policies. With nearly 13 percent of the total popular vote, the American Independent Party produced the strongest third-party finish since 1924. Nixon edged out Humphrey by just half a million popular votes but garnered 301 electoral college votes to Humphrey's 191 and Wallace's 46. The Democrats maintained control of Congress.

The 1968 election revealed deep cracks in the coalition that had kept the Democrats in power for most of the previous thirty years. Johnson's liberal policies on race shattered a century of Democratic Party dominance in the South, which delivered all its electoral votes to Wallace and Nixon. Elsewhere, large numbers of blue-collar workers broke with labor's traditional support for the Democratic Party to vote for Wallace or Nixon, as did other groups that associated the Democrats with racial turmoil, poverty programs, changing sexual mores, and failure to turn the tide in Vietnam. These resentments would soon be mobilized into a resurging right in American politics (as discussed in chapter 30).

REVIEW How did the Vietnam War shape the election of 1968?

▶ Nixon, Détente, and the Search for Peace in Vietnam

Richard M. Nixon took office with ambitious foreign policy goals, hoping to make his mark on history by applying his broad understanding of international relations to a changing world. Diverging from Republican orthodoxy, he made dramatic overtures to the Soviet Union and China. Yet anticommunism remained central to U.S. policy. In Latin America, Africa, and the Middle East, Nixon backed repressive regimes when the alternatives suggested victories for the left. Relying even more than his predecessor on public deception, secrecy, and silencing opponents, Nixon aggressively pursued the war in Vietnam. He expanded the conflict into Cambodia and Laos and ferociously bombed North Vietnam. Yet in the end, he was forced to settle for peace without victory.

Moving toward Détente with the Soviet Union and China

In Nixon's view, the "rigid and bipolar world of the 1940s and 1950s" was giving way to "the fluidity of a new era of multilateral diplomacy." America's European allies were seeking to ease East-West tensions. Moreover, Nixon and his national security adviser **Henry A. Kissinger** recognized the increasing conflict between the Soviet Union and China and believed they could exploit the situation. This Soviet-Chinese hostility, according to Nixon, "served our purpose best if we maintained closer relations with each side than they did with each other." In addition, these two nations might be used to help the United States extricate itself from Vietnam.

Following two years of secret negotiations, in February 1972 Nixon became the nation's first president to set foot on Chinese soil — an astonishing act by a

Nixon in China
"This was the week that changed the world," proclaimed President Nixon in February 1972, emphasizing the stunning turnaround in relations with America's former enemy, the People's Republic of China. Nixon's trip was meticulously planned to dramatize the event on television and, aside from criticism from some conservatives, won overwhelming support from Americans. The Great Wall of China forms the setting for this photograph of Nixon and his wife, Pat. Nixon Presidential Materials Project, National Archives and Record Administration.

man whose career had rested on fervent anticommunism. In fact, his anti-Communist credentials enabled him to conduct this shift in U.S.-Chinese relations with no significant domestic repercussions. Although his visit was largely symbolic, cultural and scientific exchanges followed, and American manufacturers began to find markets in China — small steps in the process of globalization that would take giant strides in the 1990s (as discussed in chapter 31). China had been admitted to the United Nations in 1971, and in 1979 the United States and China would establish formal diplomatic relations.

As Nixon and Kissinger had hoped, the warming of U.S.-Chinese relations furthered their strategy of **détente**, their term for easing conflict with the Soviet Union. Détente did not mean abandoning containment but instead meant focusing on issues of common concern, such as arms control and trade. Containment would be achieved not only by military threat but also by ensuring that the Soviets and Chinese had stakes in a stable international order. Nixon's goal was "a stronger healthy United States, Europe, Soviet Union, China, Japan, each balancing the other."

Arms control, trade, and stability in Europe were three areas where the United States and the Soviet Union had common interests. In May 1972, Nixon visited Moscow, signing several agreements on trade and cooperation in science and space. Most significantly, Soviet and U.S. leaders concluded arms limitation treaties that had grown out of the **Strategic Arms Limitation Talks (SALT)** begun in 1969, agreeing to limit antiballistic missiles (ABMs) to two each. Giving up pursuit of a defense against nuclear weapons was a crucial move, because it prevented either nation from building so secure an ABM defense against a nuclear attack that it would risk a first strike.

Although the policy of détente made little progress after 1974, U.S., Soviet, and European leaders signed a historic agreement in 1975 in Helsinki, Finland, that formally recognized the post–World War II boundaries in Europe. The **Helsinki accords** were controversial because they acknowledged Soviet domination over Eastern Europe — a condition that had triggered the Cold War thirty years earlier. Yet they also contained a clause committing the signing countries to recognize "the universal significance of human rights and fundamental freedoms." Dissidents in the Soviet Union and its Eastern European satellites used this official promise of rights to challenge the Soviet dictatorship and help force its overthrow fifteen years later.

Shoring Up U.S. Interests around the World

Nixon promised in 1973 that "the time has passed when America will make every other nation's conflict our own . . . or presume to tell the people of other nations how to manage their own affairs." Yet in Vietnam and elsewhere, Nixon and Kissinger continued to view left-wing movements as threats to U.S. interests and actively resisted social revolutions that might lead to communism.

Consequently, the Nixon administration helped to overthrow **Salvador Allende**, a self-proclaimed Marxist who was elected president of Chile in 1970. Since 1964, the CIA and U.S. corporations concerned about nationalization of their Chilean properties had assisted Allende's opponents. After Allende became president, Nixon ordered the CIA director to destabilize his government by making the Chilean economy "scream." In 1973, the CIA helped the Chilean military engineer a coup, killing Allende and establishing a brutal dictatorship under General Augusto Pinochet. Representative government did not return until 1990.

In other parts of the world, too, the Nixon administration stood by repressive regimes. In southern Africa, it eased pressures on white minority governments that tyrannized blacks. In the Middle East, the United States sent massive arms shipments to support the shah of Iran's harsh regime because Iran had enormous petroleum reserves and seemed a stable anti-Communist ally. Unnoticed by most Americans, the administration cemented a relationship that turned many Iranians against the United States and would ignite a new crisis when the shah was overthrown in 1979 (as discussed in chapter 30).

Like his predecessors, Nixon pursued a delicate balance between defending Israel's security and seeking the goodwill of Arab nations strategically and economically important to the United States. Conflict between Israel and the Arab nations had escalated into the **Six-Day War** in 1967, when Israel attacked Egypt after that nation had massed troops on the Israeli border and cut off sea passage to Israel's southern port. Although Syria and Jordan joined the war on Egypt's side, Israel won a stunning victory, seizing territory that amounted to twice its original size. Israeli forces took control of the Sinai Peninsula and the Gaza Strip from Egypt, the Golan Heights from Syria, and the West Bank, where hundreds of thousands of Palestinians lived, from Jordan.

That decisive victory did not quell Middle Eastern turmoil. In October 1973, on the Jewish holiday Yom Kippur, Egypt and Syria surprised Israel with a full-scale attack. When the Nixon administration sided with Israel in the **Yom Kippur War**, Arab nations retaliated with an oil embargo that created severe shortages in the United States. After Israel repulsed the attack, Kissinger attempted to mediate between Israel and the Arab nations, but with very limited success. The Arab countries refused to recognize Israel's right to exist, Israel began to settle its citizens in the West Bank and other territories occupied during the Six-Day War, and no solution could be found for the Palestinian refugees who had been displaced by the creation of Israel in the late 1940s (see chapter 26). The simmering conflict contributed to anti-American sentiment among Arabs who viewed the United States as Israel's supporter.

Vietnam Becomes Nixon's War

"I'm not going to end up like LBJ, holed up in the White House afraid to show my face on the street," the new president asserted. "I'm going to stop that war. Fast." Nixon gradually withdrew U.S. ground troops, but he was no more willing than Eisenhower, Kennedy, or Johnson to be the president who allowed South Vietnam to fall to the Communists. That goal was tied to the larger objective of maintaining American credibility. Regardless of the wisdom of the initial intervention, Kissinger asserted, "the commitment of 500,000 Americans has settled the importance of Vietnam. For what is involved now is confidence in American promises."

From 1969 to 1972, Nixon and Kissinger pursued a four-pronged approach. First, they tried to strengthen the South Vietnamese military and government. Second, to disarm the antiwar movement at home, Nixon gradually replaced U.S. forces with South Vietnamese soldiers and American technology and bombs. Third, the United States negotiated with both North Vietnam and the Soviet Union. Fourth, the military applied intensive bombing to persuade Hanoi to accept American terms at the bargaining table.

As part of the Vietnamization of the war, ARVN forces grew to more than a million, and the South Vietnamese air force became the fourth largest in the world. The United States also promoted land reform, village elections, and the building of schools, hospitals, and transportation facilities. Meanwhile, U.S. forces withdrew, decreasing from 543,000 in 1968 to 140,000 by the end of 1971, a move that critics called merely "changing the color of the corpses." Even with the reduction of U.S. forces, however, more than 20,000 Americans perished in Vietnam between 1969 and 1973.

In the spring of 1969, Nixon began a ferocious air war in Cambodia, carefully hiding it from Congress and the public for more than a year. Seeking to knock out North Vietnamese sanctuaries in Cambodia, Americans dropped more than

100,000 tons of bombs but succeeded only in sending the North Vietnamese to other hiding places. Echoing Johnson, Kissinger believed that a "fourth-rate power like North Vietnam" had to have a "breaking point," but the massive bombing failed to find it.

To support a new, pro-Western Cambodian government installed through a military coup in 1970 and "to show the enemy that we were still serious about our commitment in Vietnam," Nixon ordered a joint U.S.-ARVN invasion of Cambodia in April 1970. That order made Vietnam "Nixon's war" and provoked outrage at home. Nixon made a belligerent speech defending his move and emphasizing the importance of U.S. credibility: "If when the chips are down, the world's most powerful nation acts like a pitiful helpless giant, the forces of totalitarianism and anarchy will threaten free nations" everywhere.

Upon reading a draft of the speech, a cabinet member predicted, "This will make the students puke." They did more than that. In response, more than 100,000 people protested in Washington, D.C., and students boycotted classes on hundreds of campuses. At **Kent State University** in Ohio, National Guard troops were dispatched after protesting students burned an old ROTC building. Then, at a rally there on May 4, when some students threw rocks at the troops, they fired at the students, killing four and wounding ten others. "They're starting to treat their own children like they treat us," commented a black woman in Harlem. In a confrontation at **Jackson State College** in Mississippi on May 14, police shot into a dormitory, killing two black students. And in August, police in Los Angeles used tear gas and clubs against Chicano antiwar protesters.

Congressional reaction to the invasion of Cambodia revealed increasing concern about abuses of presidential power. In the name of national security, presidents since Franklin Roosevelt had conducted foreign policy without the consent or sometimes even the knowledge of Congress — for example, Eisenhower in Iran and Johnson in the Dominican Republic. But in their determination to win the war in Vietnam, Johnson and Nixon had taken extreme measures to deceive the public and silence their critics. The bombing and invasion of Cambodia infuriated enough legislators that the Senate voted to terminate the Gulf of Tonkin Resolution, which had given the president virtually a blank check in Vietnam, and to cut off funds for the Cambodian operation. The House refused to go along, but by the end of June 1970 Nixon had pulled all U.S. troops out of Cambodia.

The Cambodian invasion failed to break the will of North Vietnam, but it set in motion a terrible tragedy for the Cambodian people. The North Vietnamese moved farther into Cambodia and strengthened the Khmer Rouge, Communist insurgents attempting to overthrow the U.S.-supported government of Lon Nol. A brutal civil war raged until 1975, when the Khmer Rouge triumphed and imposed a savage rule, slaughtering millions of Cambodians and giving the name "killing fields" to the land of a historically peaceful people.

In 1971, Vietnam veterans became a visible part of the peace movement, the first men in U.S. history to protest a war in which they had fought. They held a public investigation of "war crimes" in Vietnam, rallied in front of the Capitol, and cast away their war medals. In May 1971, veterans numbered among the 40,000 protesters who engaged in civil disobedience in an effort to shut down Washington. Officials made more than 12,000 arrests, which courts later ruled violations of protesters' rights.

After the spring of 1971, there were fewer massive antiwar demonstrations, but protest continued. Public attention focused on the court-martial of Lieutenant William Calley, which began in November 1970. During the trial, Americans learned that in March 1968 Calley's company had systematically killed every inhabitant of the hamlet of **My Lai**, even though the soldiers had encountered no enemy forces and the four hundred villagers were nearly all old men, women, and children. The military covered up the atrocity for more than a year before a journalist exposed it. Eventually, twelve officers and enlisted men were charged with murder or assault, but only Calley was convicted.

Administration policy suffered another blow in June 1971 when the *New York Times* published the **Pentagon Papers**, secret government documents consisting mostly of an internal study of the war begun in 1967. Nixon sent government lawyers to court to stop further publication, in part out of fear that other information would be leaked. The Supreme Court, however, ruled that the attempt to stop publication was a "flagrant, indefensible" violation of the First Amendment. Subsequent circulation of the *Pentagon Papers*, which revealed considerable pessimism among officials even as they made rosy promises, heightened disillusionment with the war by casting doubts on the government's credibility. More than 60 percent of Americans polled in 1971 considered it a mistake to have sent American troops to Vietnam; 58 percent believed the war to be immoral.

Military morale sank in the last years of the war. Having been exposed to the antiwar movement at home, many of the remaining soldiers had less faith in the war than their predecessors had had. Racial tensions among soldiers mounted, many soldiers sought escape in illegal drugs, and enlisted men committed hundreds of "fraggings," attacks on officers. In a 1971 report, "The Collapse of the Armed Forces," a retired Marine Corps colonel described the lack of discipline: "Our army that now remains in Vietnam [is] near mutinous."

The Peace Accords

Nixon and Kissinger continued to believe that intensive firepower could bring the North Vietnamese to their knees. In March 1972, responding to a strong North Vietnamese offensive, the United States resumed sustained bombing of the North, mined Haiphong and other harbors for the first time, and announced a naval blockade. With peace talks stalled, in December Nixon ordered the most devastating bombing of North Vietnam yet, producing worldwide condemnation. The intense bombing, which Kissinger called "jugular diplomacy," was costly to both sides, but it brought renewed negotiations. On January 27, 1973, representatives of the United States, North Vietnam, South Vietnam, and the Vietcong (now called the People's Revolutionary Government) signed a formal peace accord in Paris. The agreement required removal of all U.S. troops and

Evacuating South Vietnam
As Communist troops rolled south toward Saigon in the spring of 1975, desperate South Vietnamese attempted to flee along with the departing Americans. These South Vietnamese, carrying little or nothing, attempt to scale the wall of the U.S. Embassy to reach evacuation helicopters. Thousands of Vietnamese who wanted to be evacuated were left behind. Even though space for evacuees was desperately limited, South Vietnamese president Nguyen Van Thieu fled to Taiwan on a U.S. plane, taking with him fifteen tons of baggage. AP Images

military advisers from South Vietnam but allowed North Vietnamese forces to remain. Both sides agreed to return prisoners of war. Nixon called the agreement "peace with honor," but in fact it allowed only a face-saving withdrawal for the United States.

Fighting resumed immediately among the Vietnamese. Nixon's efforts to support the South Vietnamese government, and indeed his ability to govern at all, were increasingly eroded by what came to be known as the Watergate scandal (as discussed in chapter 30). Nixon had been forced to give up his office by 1975, when North Vietnam launched a new offensive. On April 30, it occupied Saigon and renamed it Ho Chi Minh City to honor the Communist leader. The Americans hastily evacuated, along with 150,000 of their South Vietnamese allies.

Confusion, humiliation, and tragedy marked the rushed departure. The United States lacked sufficient transportation capabilities and time to evacuate all the South Vietnamese who had supported the South Vietnamese government and were desperate to leave. Former lieutenant Philip Caputo, who had returned to South Vietnam as a journalist, reported that his departing helicopter "took some ground fire from South Vietnamese soldiers who probably felt that the Americans had betrayed them."

During the four years it took Nixon to end the war, he had expanded the conflict into Cambodia and Laos and launched massive bombing campaigns. Although increasing numbers of legislators criticized the war, Congress never denied the president the funds to fight it. Only after the peace accords did the legislative branch try to reassert its constitutional authority in the making of war. The War Powers Act of 1973 required the president to secure congressional approval for any substantial, long-term deployment of troops abroad. The new law, however, did little to dispel the distrust of and disillusionment with the government that resulted from Americans' realization that their leaders had not told the truth about Vietnam.

The Legacy of Defeat

The disorder that had accompanied antiwar protests and bitter divisions among Americans were other legacies of the war. Vietnam diverted money from domestic programs and sounded the death knell for Johnson's Great Society. It created federal budget deficits and triggered inflation that contributed to ongoing economic crises throughout the 1970s (as discussed in chapter 30).

Four presidents had declared that the survival of South Vietnam was essential for U.S. containment policy, but their dire predictions that a Communist victory in South Vietnam would set the dominoes cascading did not materialize. Although Vietnam, Laos, and Cambodia all fell within the Communist camp in the spring of 1975, the rest of Southeast Asia did not. When China and Vietnam reverted to their historically hostile relationship, the myth of a monolithic Communist power overrunning Asia evaporated.

The long pursuit of victory in Vietnam complicated the United States' relations with other nations, as even its staunchest ally, Britain, doubted the wisdom of the war. The spectacle of terrifying American power used against a small Asian country alienated many in the third world and compromised efforts to win the hearts and minds of people in developing nations.

The cruelest legacy of Vietnam fell on those who had served. "The general public just wanted to ignore us," remembered Frederick Downs, while opponents of the war "wanted to argue with us until we felt guilty about what we had done over there." The failure of the United States to win the war, its unpopularity at home, and its character as a guerrilla war denied veterans the traditional soldiers' homecoming. Veterans themselves expressed different reactions to the defeat. Many believed in the war's purposes and felt betrayed by the government for not letting them win it. Other veterans blamed the government for sacrificing the nation's youth in an immoral, unnecessary, or useless war, expressing their sense of the war's futility by referring to their dead comrades as having been "wasted." Some veterans belonging to minority groups had more reason to doubt the nobility of their purpose. A Native American soldier assigned to resettle Vietnamese civilians found it to be "just like when they moved us to the rez [reservation]. We shouldn't have done that."

Because the Vietnam War was a civil war involving guerrilla tactics, combat was especially brutal. The terrors of conventional warfare were multiplied, and so were the motivations to commit atrocities. The 1968 massacre at My Lai was only the most widely publicized war crime. To demonstrate the immorality of the war, peace advocates stressed the atrocities, contributing to a distorted image of the Vietnam veteran as dehumanized and violent. "Antiwar types considered us to be psychopathic killers," Downs maintained.

Most veterans came home to public neglect. Government benefits were less generous to Vietnam veterans than they had been to those of the previous two wars. While two-thirds of Vietnam veterans said that they would serve again, and while most veterans readjusted well to civilian life, some suffered long after the war ended. The Veterans Administration estimated that nearly one-sixth of the veterans suffered from post-traumatic stress disorder, with its symptoms of recurring nightmares, feelings of guilt and shame, violence, drug and alcohol abuse, and suicidal tendencies. Thirty years after performing army intelligence work in Saigon, Doris Allen "still hit the floor sometimes when [she heard] loud bangs." Many of those who had served in Vietnam began to produce children with deformities and fell ill themselves with cancer, severe skin disorders, and other ailments. Veterans claimed a link between those illnesses and Agent Orange, which had exposed many to the deadly poison dioxin in Vietnam. Not until 1991 did Congress provide assistance to veterans with diseases linked to the poison.

By then, the climate had changed. The war began to enter the realm of popular culture, with novels, TV shows, and hit movies depicting a broad range of military experience — from soldiers reduced to brutality, to men and women serving with courage and integrity. The incorporation of the Vietnam War into the collective experience was symbolized most dramatically in the Vietnam Veterans Memorial unveiled in Washington, D.C., in November 1982. Designed by Yale architecture student Maya Lin, the black, V-shaped wall inscribed with the names of 58,200 men and women lost in the war became one of the most popular sites in the nation's capital. In an article describing the memorial's dedication, a Vietnam combat veteran spoke to and for his former comrades: "Welcome home. The war is over."

REVIEW What strategies did Nixon implement to bring American involvement in Vietnam to a close?

▶ Conclusion: An Unwinnable War

Lieutenant Frederick Downs fought in America's longest war. The United States spent more than $150 billion (more than $800 billion in 2011 dollars) and sent 2.6 million young men and women to Vietnam. Of those, 58,200 never returned, and 150,000, like Downs, suffered serious injury. The war shattered consensus at home, increased presidential power at the expense of congressional authority and public accountability, weakened the economy, and contributed to the downfall of two presidents.

Even as Nixon and Kissinger took steps to ease Cold War tensions with the major Communist powers — the Soviet Union and China — they also acted vigorously throughout the third world to install or prop up anti-Communist governments. They embraced their predecessors' commitment to South Vietnam as a necessary Cold War engagement: To do otherwise would threaten American credibility and make the United States appear weak. Defeat in Vietnam did not make the United States the "pitiful helpless giant" predicted by Nixon, but it did mark a relative decline of U.S. power and the impossibility of containment on a global scale.

One of the constraints on U.S. power was the tenacity of revolutionary movements determined to achieve national independence. Overestimating the effectiveness of American technological superiority, U.S. officials badly underestimated the sacrifices that the enemy was willing to make and failed to realize how easily the United States could be perceived as a colonial intruder. Simply put, Americans were not well prepared for a guerrilla war. "It's a hell of a thing," Downs discovered, "to try to fight a war with all these goddamn civilians around."

A second constraint on Eisenhower, Kennedy, Johnson, and Nixon was their resolve to avoid a major confrontation with the Soviet Union or China. For Johnson, who conducted the largest escalation of the war, caution was critical so as not to provoke direct intervention by the Communist superpowers. After China exploded its first atomic bomb in 1964, the potential heightened for the Vietnam conflict to escalate into worldwide disaster.

Third, in Vietnam the United States sought to prop up an extremely weak ally engaged in a civil war. The South Vietnamese government failed to win the support of its people, and the intense devastation the war brought to civilians only made things worse. Short of taking over the South Vietnamese government and military, the United States could do little to strengthen South Vietnam's ability to resist communism.

Finally, domestic opposition to the war, which by 1968 had spread to mainstream America, constrained the options of Johnson and Nixon. As the war dragged on, with increasing American casualties and growing evidence of the damage being inflicted on innocent Vietnamese, more and more civilians wearied of the conflict. Even some who had fought in the war joined the peace movement, sending their military ribbons and bitter letters of protest to the White House. In 1973, Nixon and Kissinger bowed to the resolution of the enemy and the limitations of U.S. power. As the war wound down, passions surrounding it contributed to a rising conservative movement that would substantially alter the post–World War II political order.

Reviewing Chapter 29

REVIEW QUESTIONS

1. Why did Kennedy believe that engagement in Vietnam was crucial to his foreign policy? (pp. 877–884)

2. Why did massive amounts of airpower and ground troops fail to bring U.S. victory in Vietnam? (pp. 884–888)

3. How did the Vietnam War shape the election of 1968? (pp. 888–893)

4. What strategies did Nixon implement to bring American involvement in Vietnam to a close? (pp. 893–901)

MAKING CONNECTIONS

1. Cuba featured prominently in the most dramatic foreign policy actions of the Kennedy administration. Citing specific events, discuss why Cuba was an area of great concern to the administration. How did Cuba figure into Kennedy's Cold War policies? Were his actions regarding Cuba effective?

2. Explain the Gulf of Tonkin incident and its significance to American foreign policy. How did President Lyndon Johnson respond to the incident? What considerations, domestic and international, contributed to his course of action?

3. The United States' engagement in Vietnam divided the nation. Discuss the range of American responses to the war. How did they change over time? How did the war shape domestic politics in the 1960s and early 1970s?

4. What was détente, and how did it affect the United States' Cold War foreign policy? What were its achievements and limitations? In your answer, discuss how Nixon's approach to communism built on and departed from the approaches of the previous two administrations.

LINKING TO THE PAST

1. What commitments were made in the Truman and Eisenhower administrations that resulted in the United States' full-scale involvement in Vietnam? (See chapters 26 and 27.)

2. Compare public sentiment during America's involvement in World War II to that during its involvement in Vietnam. What policies, events, attitudes, and technological advancements contributed to the differences? (See chapter 25.)

TIMELINE 1961–1975

1961 • Bay of Pigs invasion.
 • Berlin Wall erected.
 • Kennedy administration increases military aid to South Vietnam.
 • Alliance for Progress established.
 • Peace Corps created.

1962 • Cuban missile crisis.

1963 • Limited nuclear test ban treaty signed.
 • President Kennedy assassinated; Lyndon B. Johnson becomes president.

1964 • Anti-American rioting brings U.S. troops to Panama Canal Zone.
 • Gulf of Tonkin Resolution.

1965 • First major demonstration against Vietnam War.
 • Operation Rolling Thunder begins.
 • Johnson orders first combat troops to Vietnam.
 • U.S. troops invade Dominican Republic.

1967 • Arab-Israeli Six-Day War.

1968 • Demonstrations against Vietnam War increase.
 • Tet Offensive.

 • Johnson decides not to seek second term.
 • Police and protesters clash near Democratic convention in Chicago.
 • Republican Richard Nixon elected president.

1969 • American astronauts land on moon.

1970 • Nixon orders invasion of Cambodia.
 • Students killed during protests at Kent State and Jackson State.

1971 • *New York Times* publishes *Pentagon Papers.*

1972 • Nixon becomes first U.S. president to visit China.
 • Nixon visits Moscow to sign arms limitation treaties with Soviets.

1973 • Paris Peace Accords.
 • War Powers Act.
 • CIA-backed military coup in Chile.
 • Arab oil embargo following Yom Kippur War.

1975 • North Vietnam takes over South Vietnam, ending the war.
 • Helsinki accords.

▶ FOR AN ONLINE BIBLIOGRAPHY, PRACTICE QUIZZES, WEB SITES, IMAGES, AND DOCUMENTS RELATED TO THIS CHAPTER, see the Book Companion Site at **bedfordstmartins.com/roarkvalue**.

▶ FOR DOCUMENTS RELATED TO THIS PERIOD, see Michael Johnson, ed., *Reading the American Past*, Fifth Edition.

30

America Moves to the Right

1969–1989

PHYLLIS SCHLAFLY CALLED IT "ONE OF THE MOST EXCITING DAYS OF my life" when she heard conservative Republican Barry Goldwater address the National Federation of Republican Women in 1963. Like Goldwater, Schlafly opposed the moderate stance of the Eisenhower administration and current Republican leadership. Both Schlafly and Goldwater wanted the United States to do more than just contain communism — they wanted to eliminate that threat entirely. They also wanted to cut back the federal government, especially its role in providing social welfare and enforcing civil rights. Goldwater's loss to Lyndon Johnson in 1964 did not diminish Schlafly's conservative commitment. She assailed the policy innovations and turmoil of the 1960s, adding new issues to the conservative agenda and cultivating a grassroots movement that would redefine the Republican Party and American politics into the twenty-first century.

Phyllis Stewart was born in St. Louis in 1924, attended Catholic schools, and worked her way through Washington University testing ammunition at a World War II defense plant. She earned a master's degree in government from Radcliffe College in 1945 and went to work at the American Enterprise Institute, where she imbibed the think tank's conservatism. Returning to the Midwest, she married Fred Schlafly, an Alton, Illinois, attorney whose anticommunism and antigovernment passions equaled hers. The mother of six children, Schlafly claimed, "I don't think there's anything as much fun as taking care of a baby," and she asserted that she would "rather scrub bathroom floors" than write political articles.

The

Phyllis Schlafly Report

VOL. 5, NO. 10, SECTION 2   Box 618, ALTON, ILLINOIS 62002   MAY, 1972

The Fraud Called The Equal Rights Amendment

If there ever was an example of how a tiny minority can cram its views down the throats of the majority, it is the Equal Rights Amendment, called ERA. A noisy claque of women's lib agitators rammed ERA through Congress, intimidating the men into voting for it so they would not be labeled "anti-woman."

The ERA passed Congress with big majorities on March 22, 1972 and was sent to the states for ratification. When it is ratified by 38 states, it will become the law of the land. Within two hours of Senate passage, Hawaii ratified it. New Hampshire and Nebraska, both anxious to be second, rushed their approval the next day. Then in steady succession came Iowa, Idaho, Delaware, Kansas, Texas, Maryland, Tennessee, Alaska, Rhode Island, and New Jersey. As this goes to press, 13 states have ratified it and others are on the verge of doing so.

Three states have rejected it: Oklahoma, Vermont and Connecticut.

What is ERA? The Equal Rights Amendment reads: "Equality of rights under the law shall not be denied or abridged by the United States or by any state on account of sex."

Does that sound good? Don't kid yourself. This innocuous-sounding amendment will take away far more important rights than it will ever give. This was made abundantly clear by the debate in Congress. Senator Sam Ervin (D., N.C.) called it "the most drastic measure in Senate history." He proved this by putting into the *Congressional Record* an article from the *Yale Law Journal* of April 1971.

The importance of this *Yale Law Journal* article is that both the proponents and the opponents of ERA agree that it is an accurate analysis of the consequences of ERA. Congresswoman Martha Griffiths, a leading proponent of ERA, sent a copy of this article to every member of Congress, stating that "It will ... understand the purposes and effec... Rights Amendment.... The arti...

ERA will work in mo...

the most important of all women's rights.

"In all states husbands are primarily liable for the support of their wives and children.... The child support sections of the criminal nonsupport laws ... could not be sustained where only the male is liable for support." (*YLJ*, pp. 944-945)

"The Equal Rights Amendment would bar a state from imposing greater liability for support on a husband than on a wife merely because of his sex." (*YLJ*, p. 945)

"Like the duty of support during marriage and the obligation to pay alimony in the case of separation or divorce, nonsupport would have to be eliminated as a ground for divorce against husbands only...." (*YLJ*, p. 951)

"The Equal Rights Amendment would not require that alimony be abolished but only that it be available equally to husbands and wives." (*YLJ*, p. 952)

2. ERA will wipe out the laws which protect only women against sex crimes such as rape.

"Courts faced with criminal laws which do not apply equally to men and women would be likely to invalidate the laws rather than extending or rewriting them to apply to women and men alike." (*YLJ*, p. 966)

"Seduction laws, statutory rape laws, laws prohibiting obscene language in the presence of women, prostitution and 'manifest danger' laws ... The Equal Rights Amendment would not permit such laws, which base their sex discriminatory classification on social stereotypes." (*YLJ*, p. 954)

"The statutory rape laws, which punish men for having sexual intercourse with any wom... nder an age specified by law ... suffer from ... fect under the ...ual Rights Amendmen...

"To ...ngling ou...

...ect...

Yet while insisting that caring for home and family was women's most important career, Schlafly spent much of her time on the road — writing, speaking, leading Republican women's organizations, and testifying before legislative committees. She ran twice for Congress but lost in her heavily Democratic district in Illinois. Her book, *A Choice Not an Echo*, pushed Barry Goldwater for president and sold more than three million copies. In 1967, she began publishing *The Phyllis Schlafly Report*, a monthly newsletter about current political issues. Throughout the 1950s and 1960s, Schlafly called for stronger efforts to combat communism at home and abroad, a more powerful military, and a less active government in domestic affairs — all traditional conservative goals.

In the 1970s, Schlafly began to address new issues, including feminism and the Equal Rights Amendment, abortion, gay rights, busing for racial integration, and religion in the schools. Her positions resonated with many Americans who were fed up with the expansion of government, the Supreme Court decisions, the protest movements, the challenges to authority, and the loosening of moral standards that seemed to define the 1960s. And the votes of those Americans began to reshape politics — in Richard Nixon's victories in 1968 and 1972; in the presidency of Jimmy Carter, whose policies stood to the right of his Democratic predecessors; and in the conservative Ronald Reagan's capture of the Republican Party, the presidency, and the political agenda in 1980.

Although Richard Nixon did not embrace the entire conservative agenda, he sought to make the Republicans the dominant party by appealing to disaffected blue-collar and southern white Democrats. The Watergate revelations forced Nixon to resign the presidency in 1974, and his Republican successor, Gerald Ford, occupied the Oval Office for little more than two years, but the shift of the political spectrum to the right continued even when Democrat Jimmy Carter captured the White House in 1976.

Antigovernment sentiment grew out of the deceptions of the Johnson administration, Nixon's abuse of presidential powers, and the inability of Presidents Ford and Carter to resolve domestic and foreign crises. As Americans saw their incomes shrink from an unprecedented combination of unemployment and inflation — called stagflation — their confidence in government and willingness to pay taxes eroded.

In 1980, Phyllis Schlafly's earlier call for "a choice not an echo" was realized when Ronald Reagan won the presidency. Cutting taxes and government regulations, attacking social programs, expanding the nation's military capacity, and pressuring the Soviet Union and communism in the third world, Reagan addressed the hopes of traditional conservatives. Like Schlafly, he also championed the concerns of Christian conservatives, who opposed abortion and sexual permissiveness and supported a larger role for religion in public life.

Reagan's goals encountered resistance from feminists, civil rights groups, environmentalists, and others who fought to keep what they had won in the 1960s and 1970s. Although Reagan failed to enact the entire conservative agenda, enormously increased the national debt, and engaged in illegal activities to thwart communism in Latin America, his popularity helped send his vice president, George H. W. Bush, to the White House at the end of his second term. And Reagan's determined optimism and spirited leadership contributed to a revival in national pride and confidence.

▶ Nixon, Conservatism, and Constitutional Crisis

As we saw in chapter 28, Nixon acquiesced in continuing most Great Society programs and even approved pathbreaking environmental and minority and women's rights measures. Yet his public rhetoric and some of his actions signaled the country's rightward move. Whereas Kennedy had appealed to Americans to contribute to the common good, Nixon invited Americans to "let each of us ask — not just what will government do for me, but what can I do for myself?" His words invoked individualism and reliance on private enterprise rather than on government.

These preferences would grow stronger in the nation during the 1970s and beyond, as a new strand of conservatism joined the older movement that focused on anticommunism, a strong national defense, and a limited federal role in domestic affairs. New conservatives, whom **Phyllis Schlafly** helped mobilize, wanted to restore what they considered traditional moral values by increasing the presence of Christianity in public life.

Nixon won a resounding victory in the 1972 election. Two years later, however, his abuse of power and efforts to cover up crimes committed by subordinates, revealed in the so-called Watergate scandal, forced the first presidential resignation in history. His handpicked successor, Gerald Ford, faced the aftermath of Watergate and severe economic problems, which returned the White House to the Democrats in 1976. Nonetheless, the rising conservative tide challenged the Democratic administration that followed.

Emergence of a Grassroots Movement

Hidden beneath Lyndon Johnson's landslide victory over Arizona senator Barry Goldwater in 1964 lay a rising conservative movement. Defining his purpose as "enlarging freedom at home and safeguarding it from the forces of tyranny abroad," Goldwater echoed the ideas of conservative intellectuals who argued that government intrusions into economic life hindered prosperity, stifled personal responsibility, and interfered with individuals' rights to determine their own values. Conservatives assailed big government in domestic affairs but demanded a strong military to eradicate "Godless communism."

Behind Goldwater's nomination was a growing grassroots movement. Vigorous especially in the South and West, it included middle-class suburban women and men, members of the rabidly anti-Communist John Birch Society, and college students in the new Young Americans for Freedom (YAF). They did not give up when Goldwater lost the election. In California, newly energized conservatives helped Ronald Reagan defeat the incumbent liberal governor, Edmund Brown, in 1966. Linking Brown with the Watts riot and student disruptions at the University of California at Berkeley (see chapter 28), Reagan exploited popular fears about rising taxes, student rebellion, and black demands for justice.

Grassroots conservatism was not limited to the West and South, but a number of Sun Belt characteristics made it especially strong in places such as Orange County, California; Dallas, Texas; and Scottsdale, Arizona. Such predominantly white areas contained relatively homogeneous, skilled, and economically comfortable populations, as well as military bases and defense production facilities. The West harbored a long-standing tradition of Protestant morality, individualism, and opposition to interference by a remote federal government. That tradition continued with the growing conservative movement, even though it was hardly consistent with the Sun Belt's economic dependence on defense spending and on huge federal projects providing water and power for the burgeoning population and its economy.

The South, which also benefited from military bases and the space program, shared the West's antipathy toward the federal government. Hostility to racial change, however, was much more central to the South's conservatism. After signing the Civil Rights Act of 1964, President Lyndon Johnson remarked privately, "I think we just delivered the South to the Republican Party." Indeed, Barry Goldwater carried five southern states in 1964.

Grassroots movements proliferated around what conservatives believed marked the "moral decline" of their nation. For example, in 1962 Mel and Norma Gabler succeeded in getting the Texas board of education to drop books that they found not in conformity with "the Christian-Judeo morals, values, and standards as given to us by God through . . . the Bible." Sex education roused the ire of Eleanor Howe in Anaheim, California, who felt that "nothing [in the sex education curriculum] depicted my values. . . . It wasn't so much the information. It was the shift in values." The Supreme Court's liberal decisions on issues such as

The Tax Revolt
Neighbors gather on the lawn of Los Angeles homeowner Mark Slade to rally for Proposition 13, an initiative campaign launched by conservative activist Howard Jarvis in 1978. Many homeowners rallied to Jarvis's antitax movement because rising land values and new assessments had increased their property taxes sharply, as their signs indicate. After Californians passed Proposition 13 by a large majority, tax revolts spread across the nation. Some thirty-seven states cut property taxes, and twenty-eight reduced income taxes. The tax issue helped the Republican Party end nearly half a century of Democratic dominance. Korody/Sygma/Corbis.

school prayer, obscenity, and abortion also galvanized conservatives to restore "traditional values" to the nation.

In the 1970s, grassroots protests against taxes grew alongside concerns about morality. As Americans struggled with inflation and unemployment, many found themselves paying higher taxes, especially higher property taxes as the value of their homes increased. In 1978, Californians revolted in a popular referendum, reducing property taxes by more than one-half and limiting the state legislature's ability to raise taxes. Howard Jarvis, leader of the antitax movement, insisted, "You will have to take control of the government again, or else it is going to control you." What a newspaper called a "primal scream by the People against Big Government" spread to similar antitax crusades in other states.

Nixon Courts the Right

In his 1968 presidential campaign, Richard Nixon exploited hostility to black protest and new civil rights policies, wooing white southerners and a considerable number of northern voters away from the Democratic Party. As president, he used this "southern strategy" to make further inroads into traditional Democratic strongholds in the 1972 election.

The Nixon administration reluctantly enforced court orders to achieve high degrees of integration in southern schools, but it resisted efforts to deal with seg-regation outside the South. In northern and western cities, where segregation resulted from discrimination in housing and in the drawing of school district boundaries, half of all African American children attended nearly all-black schools. After courts began to order the transfer of students between schools in white and black neighborhoods to achieve desegregation, busing became "political dynamite," according to a Gallup poll. "We've had all we can take of judicial interference with local schools," Phyllis Schlafly railed in 1972.

Children had been riding buses to school for decades, but busing for racial integration provoked fury. Violence erupted in Boston in 1974 when a district judge found that school officials had maintained what amounted to a dual system based on race and ordered busing "if necessary to achieve a unitary school system." When black students began to attend the formerly all-white South Boston High School, white students boycotted classes, and angry whites threw rocks at black students getting off buses. The whites most affected by busing came from working-class families who remained in cities abandoned by the more affluent and whose children often rode buses to predominantly black, overcrowded schools with deficient facilities. Clarence McDonough decried the liberal officials who bused his "kid half way around Boston so that a bunch of politicians can end up their careers with a clear conscience." African Americans themselves were conflicted about sending their children on long rides to schools where white teachers might not welcome or respect them.

White parents eventually became more accepting of integration, especially after the creation of magnet schools and other new mechanisms for desegregation offered more choice. Nonetheless, integration propelled white flight to the suburbs. By 1987, the number of white students in Boston public schools was just one-third of what it had been in 1974. Nixon failed to persuade Congress to end court-ordered busing, but after he had appointed four new justices, the Supreme Court imposed strict limits on the use of that tool to achieve racial balance.

Nixon's judicial appointments also reflected the southern strategy. He criticized the Supreme Court under Chief Justice Earl Warren for being "unprecedentedly politically active . . . using their interpretation of the law to remake American society according to their own social, political, and ideological precepts." When Warren resigned in 1969, Nixon replaced him with **Warren E. Burger**, a federal appeals court judge who was a strict constructionist—someone inclined to interpret the Constitution narrowly and to limit government intervention on behalf of individual rights. The Burger Court proved more sympathetic than the Warren Court to the president's agenda, restricting somewhat the protections of individual rights established by the previous Court, but continuing to uphold many of the liberal programs of the 1960s. For example, the Court limited the range of affirmative action in *Regents of the University of California v. Bakke* (1978), but it allowed universities to consider race as one factor in admission decisions if they avoided strict quotas.

Nixon's southern strategy and other repercussions of the civil rights revolution of the 1960s ended the Democratic hold on the "solid South." In 1964, South Carolina senator Strom Thurmond, leader of the Dixiecrat challenge to Truman in 1948 (see chapter 26), changed his party affiliation to Republican. North Carolina senator Jesse Helms followed suit in 1971, and politicians throughout the South began to realize that the future for Democratic candidates had darkened there. By 2005, Republicans held the majority of southern seats in Congress and governorships in seven southern states.

In addition to exploiting racial fears, Nixon aligned himself with those anxious about women's changing roles and new demands. In 1971, he vetoed a bill providing federal funds for day care centers with a message that combined the old and new conservatism. Parents should purchase child care services "in the private, open market," he insisted, not rely on government. He appealed to social conservatives by warning about the measure's "family-weakening implications." In response to the movement to liberalize abortion laws, Nixon sided with "defenders of the right to life of the unborn." He did not comment publicly on *Roe v. Wade* (1973), which legalized abortion, but his earlier stance against abortion anticipated the Republican Party's eventual embrace of this as a key issue.

The Election of 1972

Nixon's ability to attract Democrats and appeal to concerns about Vietnam, race, law and order, and traditional morality heightened his prospects for reelection in 1972. Although the war in Vietnam continued, antiwar protests diminished with the decrease in American ground forces and casualties. Nixon's economic initiatives had temporarily checked inflation and unemployment (see chapter 28), and his attacks on busing and antiwar protesters had won increasing support from the right.

A large field of contenders vied for the Democratic nomination, including New York congresswoman **Shirley Chisholm**, the first African American to make a serious bid for the presidency. South Dakota senator George S. McGovern came to the Democratic convention as the clear leader, and the new makeup of the convention delegates made his position even stronger. After the bitter 1968 convention in Chicago (see chapter 29), the Democrats reformed their rules, requiring delegations to represent the proportions of minorities, women, and young people in their states. These newcomers displaced many regular Democrats — officeholders, labor leaders, and representatives of older ethnic groups. One labor leader grumbled that "the Democratic party was taken over by the kooks," referring to the considerable numbers of young people and women who were to the left of party regulars. Though easily nominated, McGovern struggled against Nixon from the outset. Republicans portrayed him as a left-wing extremist, and his support for busing, a generous welfare program, and immediate withdrawal from Vietnam alienated conservative Democrats.

Nixon achieved a landslide victory, winning 60.7 percent of the popular vote and every state except Massachusetts. Although the Democrats maintained control of Congress, Nixon won majorities among traditional Democrats — southerners, Catholics, urbanites, and blue-collar workers. The president, however, had little time to savor his triumph, as revelations began to emerge about crimes committed to ensure the victory.

Watergate

During the early-morning hours of June 17, 1972, five men working for Nixon's reelection campaign crept into Democratic Party headquarters in the Watergate complex in Washington, D.C. Intending to repair a bugging device installed in an earlier break-in, they were discovered and arrested. Nixon and his aides then tried to cover up the intruders' connection to administration officials, setting in motion the most serious constitutional crisis since the Civil War. Reporters dubbed the scandal **Watergate**.

Over the next two years, Americans learned that Nixon and his associates had engaged in other abuses, such as accepting illegal contributions and unlawfully attempting to silence critics of the administration. Nixon was not the first president to lie to the public or to misuse power. Every president since Franklin D. Roosevelt had enlarged the powers of his office in the name of national security. This expansion of executive powers, often called the "imperial presidency," weakened the traditional checks and balances on the executive branch and opened the door to abuses. No president, however, had dared go as far as Nixon, who saw opposition to his policies as a personal attack and was willing to violate the Constitution to stop it.

Upon the arrest of the Watergate burglars, Nixon publicly denied any connection to them, while plotting secretly to have the CIA keep the FBI from investigating the crime. In April 1973, after investigations by a grand jury and the Senate suggested that White House aides had been involved in the cover-up effort, Nixon accepted official responsibility for Watergate but denied any knowledge of the break-in or cover-up. He also announced the resignations of three White House aides and the attorney general. In May, he authorized the appointment of an independent special prosecutor, Archibald Cox, to conduct an investigation.

Meanwhile, sensational revelations exploded in testimony before the Senate investigating committee, headed by Democrat Samuel J. Ervin of North Carolina. White House counsel John Dean described projects to harass "enemies" through tax audits and other illegal means and implicated the president in efforts to cover up the Watergate break-in. Another White House aide struck the most damaging blow when he disclosed that all conversations in the Oval Office were taped. Both Cox and the Ervin committee immediately asked for the tapes related to Watergate. When Nixon refused, citing executive privilege and separation of powers, Cox and Ervin won a unanimous decision from the Supreme Court ordering him to release the tapes.

Additional disclosures exposed Nixon's misuse of federal funds and tax evasion. In August 1973, Vice President Spiro Agnew resigned after an investigation revealed that he had taken bribes while governor of Maryland. Although Nixon's choice of House minority leader Gerald Ford of Michigan to succeed Agnew won widespread approval, Agnew's resignation further tarnished the administration, and Nixon's popular support plummeted to 27 percent.

In February 1974, the House of Representatives voted to begin an impeachment investigation. Upon reading passages from the White House tapes, House Republican leader Hugh Scott of Pennsylvania abandoned his support of the president, calling the transcripts a "deplorable, shabby, disgusting, and immoral performance by all." The transcripts revealed Nixon's orders to aides in March 1973: "I don't give a shit what happens. I want you all to stonewall it, let them plead the Fifth Amendment, cover up or anything else, if it'll save it — save the plan."

In July 1974, the House Judiciary Committee voted to impeach the president on three counts: obstruction of justice, abuse of power, and contempt of Congress. Seven or eight Republicans on the committee sided with the majority, and it seemed certain that the House would follow suit. Georgia state legislator and civil rights activist Julian Bond commented, "The prisons of Georgia are full of people who stole $5 or $10, and this man tried to steal the Constitution."

To avoid impeachment, Nixon announced his resignation to a national television audience on August 8, 1974. Acknowledging some incorrect judgments, he insisted that he had always tried to do what was best for the nation. The next morning, Nixon ended a rambling, emotional farewell to his staff with some advice: "Always give your best, never get discouraged, never get petty; always remember, others may hate you, but those who hate you don't win unless you hate them, and then you destroy yourself." Had he practiced that advice, he might have saved his presidency.

The Ford Presidency and the 1976 Election

Gerald R. Ford, who had represented Michigan in the House of Representatives since 1948, had built a reputation as a middle-of-the-road party loyalist known for his integrity, humility, and dedication to public office. "I'm a Ford, not a

Lincoln," he acknowledged. Most of official Washington and the American public looked favorably on his succession as president.

Upon taking office, Ford announced, "Our long national nightmare is over." But he shocked many Americans one month later by granting Nixon a pardon "for all offenses against the United States which he . . . has committed or may have committed or taken part in" during his presidency. Prompted by Ford's concern for Nixon's physical and mental health and by his hope to get the country beyond Watergate, this sweeping pardon saved Nixon from nearly certain indictment and trial, and it provoked a tremendous outcry from Congress and the public. Democrats made impressive gains in the November congressional elections, while Ford's action gave Nixon a new political life. Having gained a pardon without having to admit that he had violated the law, Nixon rebuilt his image over the next two decades into that of an elder statesman. Thirty of his associates ultimately pleaded guilty to or were convicted of crimes related to Watergate.

Congress's efforts to guard against the types of abuses revealed in the Watergate investigations had only limited effects. The **Federal Election Campaign Act of 1974** established public financing of presidential campaigns and imposed some restrictions on contributions to help prevent the selling of political favors. Yet politicians found other ways of raising money — for example, through political action committees (PACs), to which individuals could contribute more than they could to candidates. Moreover, in the 1976 case *Buckley v. Valeo*, the Supreme Court struck down limitations on campaign spending as violations of freedom of speech. Ever-larger campaign donations flowed to candidates from interest groups, corporations, labor unions, and wealthy individuals.

Special congressional investigating committees discovered a host of illegal FBI and CIA activities stretching back to the 1950s, including harassment of political dissenters and plots to assassinate Fidel Castro and other foreign leaders. In response to these revelations, President Ford established new controls on covert operations, and Congress created permanent committees to oversee the intelligence agencies. Yet these measures did little to diminish the public's cynicism about their government.

Disillusionment grew as the Ford administration struggled with serious economic problems: a low growth rate, high unemployment, a foreign trade deficit, and soaring energy prices. Ford carried these burdens into the election campaign of 1976, while contending with a major challenge from the Republican right. Blasting Nixon's and Ford's foreign policy of détente for causing the "loss of U.S. military supremacy," California governor Reagan came close to capturing the nomination.

The Democrats nominated **James Earl "Jimmy" Carter Jr.**, former governor of Georgia. A graduate of the U.S. Naval Academy, Carter spent seven years as a nuclear engineer in the navy before returning to Plains, Georgia, to run the family peanut farming business. Carter prided himself on his knowledge of policy issues, but people responded most to his promise of honesty and decency in government. He stressed his faith as a "born-again Christian" and his distance from the government in Washington. Although he selected liberal senator **Walter F. Mondale** of Minnesota as his running mate, Carter's nomination nonetheless marked a rightward turn in the party.

Carter had considerable appeal as a candidate who carried his own bags, lived modestly, and taught a Bible class at his Baptist church. He also benefited from Ford's failure to solve the country's economic problems, which helped him win the traditional Democratic coalition of blacks, organized labor, and ethnic groups and even recapture some of the white southerners who had voted for Nixon in 1972. Still, Carter received just 50 percent of the popular vote to Ford's 48 percent, although Democrats retained substantial margins in Congress.

REVIEW How did Nixon's policies reflect the increasing influence of conservatives on the Republican Party?

▶ The "Outsider" Presidency of Jimmy Carter

Carter promised a government that was "competent" as well as "decent, open, fair, and compassionate." He also warned Americans "that even our great Nation has its recognized limits, and that we can neither answer all questions nor solve all problems." Carter's humility and personal integrity helped revive trust in the presidency, but he faltered in the face of domestic and foreign crises.

Energy shortages and stagflation worsened, exposing Carter's deficiencies in working with Congress and rallying the public to his objectives. His administration achieved notable advances in environmental and energy policies, and he oversaw foreign policy successes concerning the Panama Canal, China, and the Middle East. Yet near the end of his term, Soviet-American relations deteriorated, new crises emerged in the Middle East, and the economy plummeted, all costing him a second term.

Retreat from Liberalism

Jimmy Carter vowed "to help the poor and aged, to improve education, and to provide jobs," but at the same time "not to waste money." When these goals conflicted, reform took second place to budget balancing. Carter's approach pleased increasing numbers of Americans unhappy about their tax dollars being used to benefit the disadvantaged while stagflation eroded their own standard of living. But his fiscal stringency frustrated liberal Democrats pushing for major welfare reform and a national health insurance program. Carter himself said, "In many cases I feel more at home with the conservative Democratic and Republican members of Congress than I do with the others."

Carter did fulfill liberals' desire to make government more inclusive. He appointed Andrew Young, former congressman and assistant to Martin Luther King Jr., as the first African American ambassador to the United Nations; and he named four women, including the first two black women, as cabinet heads. Moreover,

Carter began to transform the federal judiciary. He appointed forty women to federal judgeships, five times as many as had all his predecessors combined. He also increased the numbers of African American and Latino and Latina judges and named the first Latino ambassador to Mexico.

In contrast to his appointments, a number of factors hindered Carter's ability to transform his goals into policy. His outsider status helped him win the election but left him without strong ties to party leaders in Congress. Democrats complained of inadequate consultation and Carter's tendency to flood them with comprehensive proposals without devising a strategy to get them enacted. In addition, Carter refused to offer simple solutions to the American people, who were impatient for quick action against the forces that were squeezing their pocketbooks.

Even if he had possessed Lyndon Johnson's political skills, Carter might not have done much better. The economic problems he inherited — unemployment, inflation, and sluggish economic growth — confounded economic doctrine. Usually, rising prices accompanied a humming economy with a strong demand for labor. Now, however, stagflation burdened the economy with both steep inflation and high unemployment.

Carter first targeted unemployment. Although liberals complained that his programs did not do enough, Carter signed bills pumping $14 billion into the economy through public works and public service jobs programs and cutting taxes by $34 billion. Unemployment receded, but then inflation surged. Working people, wrote one journalist, "winced and ached" as their paychecks bought less and less, "hollowing their hopes and dreams, their plans for a house or their children's college education." To curb inflation, Carter curtailed federal spending, and the Federal Reserve Board tightened the money supply. Not only did these measures fail to halt inflation, which surpassed 13 percent in 1980, but they also contributed to rising unemployment, reversing the gains made in Carter's first two years.

Carter's commitment to holding down the federal budget frustrated Democrats pushing for comprehensive welfare reform, national health insurance, and a substantial jobs program that would make government the employer of last resort. His refusal to propose a comprehensive national health insurance plan, long a key Democratic Party objective, led to a bitter split with Massachusetts senator Ted Kennedy, who fought Carter for the 1980 presidential nomination. Carter did sign legislation to ensure solvency in the Social Security system, but the measure increased both employer and employee contributions, thereby increasing the tax burden on lower- and middle-income Americans.

By contrast, corporations and wealthy individuals gained from new legislation, such as a sharp cut in the capital gains tax. When the Chrysler Corporation approached bankruptcy in 1979, Congress provided $1.5 billion in loan guarantees to bail out the tenth-largest corporation in the country. Congress also acted on Carter's proposals to deregulate airlines in 1978 and the banking, trucking, and railroad industries in 1980. Carter's successor, Ronald Reagan, would move much further, implementing conservatives' attachment to a free market and unfettered private enterprise.

Energy and Environmental Reform

Complicating the government's efforts to deal with stagflation was the nation's enormous consumption of energy and its dependence on foreign nations to fill one-third of its energy demands. Consequently, Carter proposed a comprehensive program to conserve energy, and he elevated its importance by establishing the Department of Energy. Beset with competing demands among energy producers and consumers, Congress picked Carter's program apart. The **National Energy Act of 1978** penalized manufacturers of gas-guzzling automobiles and provided other incentives for conservation and development of alternative fuels, such as wind and solar power, but the act fell far short of a long-term, comprehensive program, and Carter's successor dismantled much of the regulation that did succeed.

In 1979, a new upheaval in the Middle East, the Iranian revolution, created the most severe energy crisis yet. In midsummer, shortages caused 60 percent of gasoline stations to close down; frustrated drivers waited in long lines and paid unprecedentedly high prices for gas. "We are struggling with a profound transition from a time of abundance to a time of growing scarcity in energy," Carter told the nation, asking for additional measures to address the shortages. Congress reduced controls on the oil and gas industry to stimulate American production and imposed a windfall profits tax on producers to redistribute some of the profits they would reap from deregulation.

Congress rejected a key Carter proposal to conserve oil by taxing it at the wellhead and thus ultimately increasing its cost to consumers. European nations were just as dependent on foreign oil as was the United States, but they more successfully controlled consumption. They levied high taxes on gasoline, which impelled people to rely more on public transportation and manufacturers to produce more energy-efficient cars. In the automobile-dependent United States, however, with inadequate public transit, people accustomed to driving long distances, and an aversion to taxes, politicians dismissed that approach. By the end of the century, the United States, with 6 percent of the world's population, would consume more than 25 percent of global oil production (Map 30.1).

One alternative fuel, nuclear energy, aroused opposition from a vigorous environmental movement. Activists warned of radiation leakage, potential accidents, and the hazards of radioactive wastes from nuclear power plants, which provided about 10 percent of the nation's electricity in the 1970s. In 1976, hundreds of members of the Clamshell Alliance went to jail for attempting to block construction of a nuclear power plant in Seabrook, New Hampshire; other groups sprang up across the country to demand an environment safe from nuclear radiation and waste. The perils of nuclear energy claimed international attention in March 1979, when a meltdown of the reactor core was narrowly averted at the **Three Mile Island** nuclear facility near Harrisburg, Pennsylvania. Popular opposition and the great expense of building nuclear power plants stalled further development of the industry. The explosion of a nuclear reactor in Chernobyl, Ukraine, in 1986 further solidified antinuclear concerns as part of the environmental movement.

A disaster at Love Canal in Niagara Falls, New York, advanced other environmental goals by underscoring the human costs of unregulated development. Residents

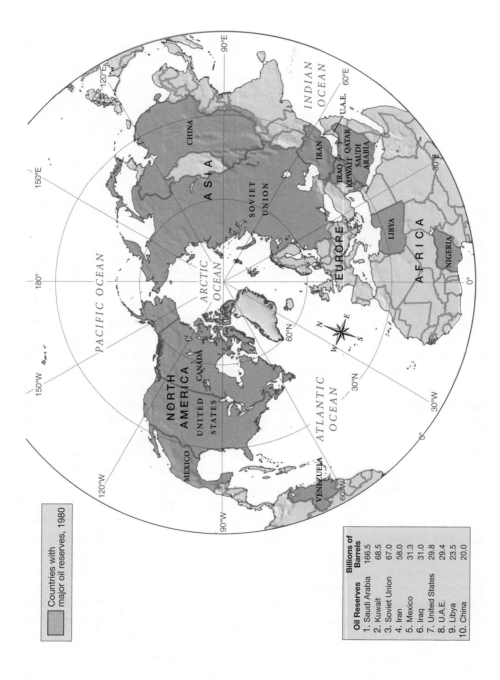

Countries with major oil reserves, 1980

Oil Reserves	Billions of Barrels
1. Saudi Arabia	166.5
2. Kuwait	68.5
3. Soviet Union	67.0
4. Iran	58.0
5. Mexico	31.3
6. Iraq	31.0
7. United States	29.8
8. U.A.E.	29.4
9. Libya	23.5
10. China	20.0

suffering high rates of serious illness discovered that their homes sat amid highly toxic waste products from a nearby chemical company. One resident, Lois Gibbs, who eventually led a national movement against toxic wastes, explained how women were galvanized to become environmentalists: "I never thought of myself as an activist. I was a housewife, a mother, but all of a sudden it was my family, my children, and my neighbors." Finally responding to the residents' claims in 1978, the state of New York agreed to help families relocate, and the Carter administration sponsored legislation in 1980 that created the so-called Superfund, $1.6 billion for cleanup of hazardous wastes left by the chemical industry around the country.

Carter's environmental legislation did not stop there. He signed bills to improve clean air and water programs; to expand the Arctic National Wildlife Refuge (ANWR) preserve in Alaska; and to control strip-mining, which left destructive scars on the land. During the 1979 gasoline crisis, Carter attempted to balance the development of domestic fuel sources with environmental concerns, winning legislation to conserve energy and to provide incentives for the development of solar energy and environmentally friendly alternative fuels.

Promoting Human Rights Abroad

"We're ashamed of what our government is as we deal with other nations around the world," Jimmy Carter charged. Asserting that his predecessors' foreign policy violated the nation's principles of freedom and dignity, he promised to reverse the cynical support of dictators, secret diplomacy, interference in the internal affairs of other countries, and excessive reliance on military solutions.

Human rights formed the cornerstone of his approach. The Carter administration applied economic pressure on governments that denied their citizens basic rights, refusing aid or trading privileges to nations such as Chile and El Salvador, as well as to the white minority governments of Rhodesia and South Africa, which brutally violated the rights of their black majorities. Yet in other instances, Carter sacrificed human rights ideals to strategic and security considerations. He invoked no sanctions against repressive governments in Iran, South Korea, and the Philippines, for example, and he established formal diplomatic relations with the People's Republic of China in 1979, even though its government blatantly withheld democratic rights.

Carter's human rights principles faced another test when a popular movement overthrew an oppressive dictatorship in Nicaragua. U.S. officials were uneasy about the leftist Sandinistas who led the rebellion and had ties to Cuba. Once they

◀ MAP 30.1

Worldwide Oil Reserves, 1980
Data produced by geologists and engineers enable experts to estimate the size of "proved oil reserves," quantities that are recoverable with existing technology and prices. In 1980, the total worldwide reserves were estimated at 645 billion barrels. The recovery of reserves depends on many factors, including the precise location of the oil. Large portions of the U.S. reserves, for example, lie under deep water in the Gulf of Mexico, where it is expensive to drill and where operations can be disrupted by hurricanes. But the U.S. government is much more generous than most nations in allowing oil companies to take oil from public land, imposing relatively low taxes and royalty payments.

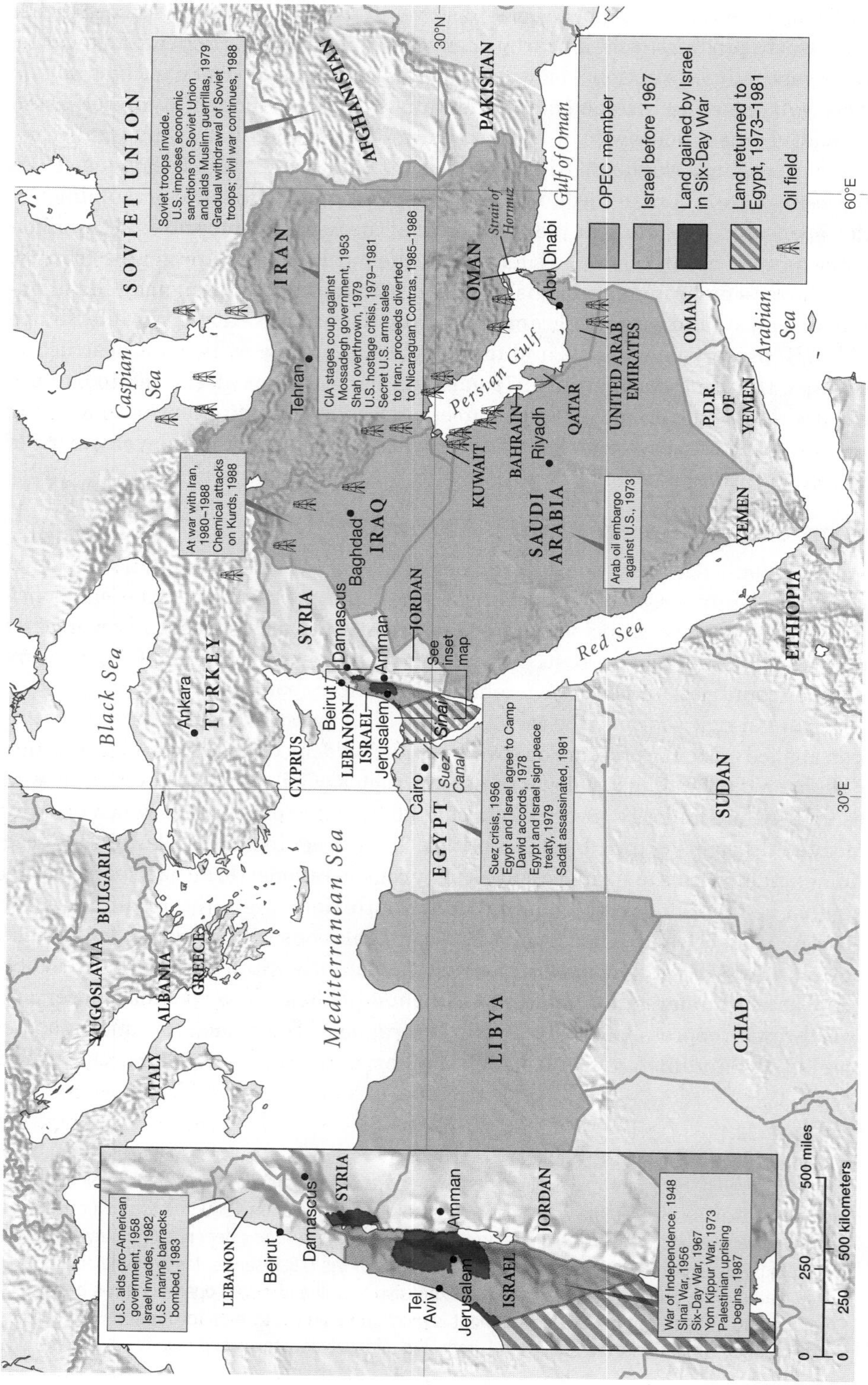
SOVIET UNION
Soviet troops invade.
U.S. imposes economic sanctions on Soviet Union and aids Muslim guerrillas, 1979
Gradual withdrawal of Soviet troops; civil war continues, 1988
AFGHANISTAN
PAKISTAN
IRAN
CIA stages coup against Mossadegh government, 1953
Shah overthrown, 1979
U.S. hostage crisis, 1979–1981
Secret U.S. arms sales to Iran; proceeds diverted to Nicaraguan Contras, 1985–1986
Tehran
Caspian Sea
At war with Iran, 1980–1988
Chemical attacks on Kurds, 1988
IRAQ
Baghdad
KUWAIT
BAHRAIN
QATAR
Riyadh
SAUDI ARABIA
Arab oil embargo against U.S., 1973
UNITED ARAB EMIRATES
Abu Dhabi
OMAN
Strait of Hormuz
Gulf of Oman
Persian Gulf
P.D.R. OF YEMEN
YEMEN
Arabian Sea
OPEC member
Israel before 1967
Land gained by Israel in Six-Day War
Land returned to Egypt, 1973–1981
Oil field
30°N
60°E
30°E
Black Sea
TURKEY
Ankara
SYRIA
Damascus
Amman
JORDAN
See inset map
Beirut
LEBANON
ISRAEL
Jerusalem
Sinai
CYPRUS
Cairo
Suez Canal
EGYPT
Suez crisis, 1956
Egypt and Israel agree to Camp David accords, 1978
Egypt and Israel sign peace treaty, 1979
Sadat assassinated, 1981
Red Sea
ETHIOPIA
SUDAN
CHAD
LIBYA
Mediterranean Sea
BULGARIA
YUGOSLAVIA
ALBANIA
GREECE
ITALY
U.S. aids pro-American government, 1958
Israel invades, 1982
U.S. marine barracks bombed, 1983
LEBANON
Beirut
Damascus
SYRIA
Amman
JORDAN
Tel Aviv
Jerusalem
ISRAEL
War of Independence, 1948
Sinai War, 1956
Six-Day War, 1967
Yom Kippur War, 1973
Palestinian uprising begins, 1987
0 250 500 miles
0 250 500 kilometers

assumed power in 1979, however, Carter recognized the new government and sent economic aid, signaling that the way a government treated its citizens was as important as how anti-Communist and friendly to American interests it was.

Applying moral principles to relations with Panama, Carter sped up negotiations over control of the Panama Canal and in 1977 signed a treaty providing for Panama's takeover of the canal in 2000. Supporters viewed the treaty as recompense for the barefaced use of U.S. power to obtain the canal in 1903. Opponents insisted on retaining the vital waterway. "We bought it, we paid for it, it's ours," claimed Ronald Reagan during the presidential primaries of 1976. It took a massive effort by the administration to get Senate ratification of the **Panama Canal treaty**, which passed by just one vote.

Seeking to promote peace in the Middle East, Carter seized on the courage of Egyptian president Anwar Sadat, the first Arab leader to risk his political career by talking directly with Israeli officials. In 1979, Carter invited Sadat and Israeli prime minister Menachem Begin to the presidential retreat at Camp David, Maryland, where he applied his tenacious diplomacy for thirteen days. These talks led to the **Camp David accords**, whereby Egypt became the first Arab state to recognize Israel, and Israel agreed to gradual withdrawal from the Sinai Peninsula, which it had seized in the 1967 Six-Day War (Map 30.2). Although the issues of Palestinian self-determination in other Israeli-occupied territories (the West Bank and Gaza) and the plight of Palestinian refugees remained unresolved, Carter had nurtured the first meaningful steps toward peace in the Middle East.

The Cold War Intensifies

Consistent with his human rights approach, Carter preferred to pursue national security through nonmilitary means and initially sought accommodation with the nation's Cold War enemies. In June 1979, Carter and Soviet premier Leonid Brezhnev signed a second strategic arms reduction treaty, setting limits on strategic missiles. Earlier that year, Carter had also followed up on another Nixon initiative, formally recognizing the People's Republic of China.

Yet that same year, Carter decided to pursue a military buildup when the Soviet Union invaded neighboring Afghanistan (see Map 30.2). Afghanistan's recently installed Communist government was threatened by Muslim opposition, which even before the invasion had received secret support from the CIA. Announcing that the Soviet action "could pose the greatest threat to peace since the Second World War," Carter imposed economic sanctions on the Soviet Union, barred U.S. participation in the 1980 Summer Olympic Games in Moscow, and obtained legislation requiring all nineteen-year-old men to register for the draft.

◀ **MAP 30.2**
The Middle East, 1948–1989
Determination to preserve access to the rich oil reserves of the Middle East and commitment to the security of Israel were the fundamental — and often conflicting — principles of U.S. foreign policy in that region.

Claiming that Soviet actions jeopardized oil supplies from the Middle East, the president announced the "Carter Doctrine," threatening the use of any means necessary to prevent an outside force from gaining control of the Persian Gulf. His human rights policy fell by the wayside as the United States stepped up aid to the military dictatorship in Afghanistan's neighbor, Pakistan, and the CIA funneled secret aid through Pakistan to the Afghan rebels. Finally, Carter called for hefty increases in defense spending.

Events in Iran also encouraged this hard-line approach. All the U.S. arms and aid had not enabled the shah to crush Iranian dissidents who still resented the CIA's role in the overthrow of the Mossadegh government in 1953 (see chapter 27). Dissidents condemned the shah's savage attempts to silence opposition and detested his adoption of Western culture and values. These grievances erupted into a revolution in 1979 that forced the shah out of Iran and brought to power Shiite Islamic fundamentalists led by Ayatollah Ruholla Khomeini, whom the shah had exiled in 1964.

Carter's decision to allow the shah into the United States for medical treatment enraged Iranians, who believed that the United States would restore the shah to power as it had done in 1953. Anti-American demonstrations escalated in the capital city of Teheran. On November 4, 1979, a crowd broke into the U.S. Embassy and seized sixty-six U.S. diplomats, CIA officers, citizens, and military attachés. Refusing the captors' demands that the shah be returned to Iran for trial, Carter froze Iranian assets in U.S. banks and placed an embargo on Iranian oil. In April 1980, he sent a small military operation into Iran, but the rescue mission failed.

The disastrous rescue attempt and scenes of blindfolded U.S. citizens paraded before TV cameras fed Americans' feelings of impotence, simmering since the defeat in Vietnam. These frustrations in turn increased support for a more militaristic foreign policy. Opposition to Soviet-American détente, combined with the Soviet invasion of Afghanistan, nullified the thaw in superpower relations that had begun in the 1960s. The **Iran hostage crisis** dominated the news during the 1980 presidential campaign and contributed to Carter's defeat. Iran freed the hostages the day he left office, but relations with the United States remained tense.

REVIEW How and where did Carter implement his commitment to human rights, and where and why did human rights give way to other priorities?

▶ Ronald Reagan and the Conservative Ascendancy

The election of Ronald Reagan in 1980 marked the most important turning point in politics since Franklin D. Roosevelt won the presidency in 1932. Eisenhower and Nixon were middle-of-the-road Republicans, but Reagan's victory established conservatism's dominance in the Republican Party. Since the 1930s, the Democrats had defined the major issues. In the 1980s, the Republicans assumed that initiative, while Democrats searched for voter support by moving toward the right. The United States was not alone in this political shift. Conservatives rose to power in Britain with Prime Minister Margaret Thatcher, and they led governments in Germany, Canada, and Sweden, while socialist and social democratic governments elsewhere trimmed their welfare states.

On the domestic front, the Reagan administration embraced the conservative Christian values of the New Right, but it left its most important mark on the economy: victory over inflation, deregulation of industry, enormous tax cuts, and a staggering federal budget deficit. Economic expansion, which took off after 1983, helped the middle class and brought great wealth to some, but the percentage of poor Americans increased, and income inequality grew. Although the Reagan era did not see a policy revolution comparable to that of the New Deal, it dealt a sharp blow to the liberalism that had informed American politics since the 1930s.

Appealing to the New Right and Beyond

Sixty-nine-year-old **Ronald Reagan** was the oldest candidate ever nominated for the presidency. Born in Tampico, Illinois, Reagan attended a small religious college and worked as a sportscaster before becoming a movie actor. He initially shared the politics of his staunchly Democratic father but moved to the right in the 1940s and 1950s and campaigned for Goldwater in 1964.

Reagan's political career took off when he was elected governor of California in 1966. He ran as a conservative, but in office he displayed considerable flexibility, approving a major tax increase, a strong water pollution bill, and a liberal abortion law. Displaying similar agility in the 1980 presidential campaign, he softened earlier attacks on programs such as Social Security and chose the moderate George H. W. Bush as his running mate.

Nonetheless, some Republicans balked at his nomination and at the party platform, which reflected the concerns of the party's right wing. For example, after Phyllis Schlafly persuaded the party to reverse its forty-year support for the Equal Rights Amendment, moderate and liberal Republican women protested outside the convention hall. Some Republicans found a more acceptable presidential candidate in Illinois representative John B. Anderson, who deserted his party to run as an independent.

Reagan's campaign capitalized on the economic recession and the international challenges symbolized by the Americans held hostage in Iran. Repeatedly, Reagan asked voters, "Are you better off now than you were four years ago?" He promised to "take government off the backs of the people" and to restore Americans' morale and other nations' respect. Fifty-one percent of voters responded favorably to Reagan's upbeat message, while Carter won 41 percent, and 7 percent went to Anderson. Republicans won control of the Senate for the first time since the 1950s.

While the economy and the Iran hostage crisis sealed Reagan's victory, he also benefited from the burgeoning grassroots conservative movements. An extraordinarily adept politician, Reagan appealed to a wide spectrum of groups and sentiments: free market advocates, militant anti-Communists, fundamentalist Christians, white southerners, and white working-class Democrats — the so-called Reagan Democrats disenchanted with the Great Society and suffering from the stagflation of the 1970s.

Reagan's support from religious conservatives, predominantly Protestants, constituted a relatively new phenomenon in politics known as the **New Right** or **New Christian Right**. During the 1970s, evangelical and fundamentalist Christianity claimed thousands of new adherents. Evangelical ministers such as Pat Robertson preached to huge television audiences, attacking feminism, abortion, and homosexuality and calling for the restoration of old-fashioned "family values." They wanted prayer back in the schools and sex education out of them. A considerable number of Catholics, such as Phyllis Schlafly, shared the fundamentalists' goal of a return to "Christian values."

Conservatives created political organizations such as the Moral Majority, founded by the Reverend Jerry Falwell in 1979, to fight "left-wing, social welfare bills, . . . pornography, homosexuality, [and] the advocacy of immorality in school textbooks." Dr. James Dobson, a clinical psychologist with a popular Christian talk show, founded the Family Research Council in 1983 to lobby Congress for measures to curb abortion, divorce, homosexuality, and single motherhood. The instruments of more traditional conservatives, who stressed limited government at home and militant anticommunism abroad, likewise flourished. Decades-old institutions like the *National Review* and the American Enterprise Institute were joined by new institutions such as the Heritage Foundation, a think tank that formulated and promoted conservative ideas. The monthly *Phyllis Schlafly Report* merged the sentiments of the old and new right.

Reagan embraced the full spectrum of conservatism, but he actually delivered more to the traditional right. He spoke for the New Right on such issues as abortion and school prayer, but he did not push hard for so-called moral or social policies. Instead, his major achievements fulfilled goals of the older right — strengthening the nation's anti-Communist posture and reducing taxes and government restraints on free enterprise. "In the present crisis," Reagan declared, "government is not the solution to our problem, government is the problem."

Reagan's admirers stretched far beyond conservatives. The extraordinarily popular president was liked even by Americans who opposed his policies and even when he made glaring mistakes. Reagan's optimism, confidence, and easygoing humor formed a large part of his appeal. Ignoring the darker moments of the American past, he presented a version of history that Americans could feel good about. Listeners understood his declaration that it was "morning in America" as a promise that the best was yet to come. Reagan also gained public sympathy after being shot by a would-be assassin in March 1981. Just before surgery to remove the bullet, Reagan joked to physicians, "I hope you're Republicans." His tremendous popularity helped him withstand serious charges of executive branch misconduct in his second term.

Unleashing Free Enterprise

Reagan's first domestic objective was a massive tax cut. Although tax cuts in the face of a large budget deficit contradicted traditional Republican economic doctrine, Reagan relied on a new theory called **supply-side economics**, which held that cutting taxes would actually increase revenue by enabling businesses to expand and encouraging individuals to work harder because they could keep more of their earnings. Business expansion would increase the production of goods and services — the supply — which in turn would boost demand. Reagan promised that the economy would grow so much that the government would recoup the lost taxes, but instead it incurred a galloping deficit.

In the summer of 1981, Congress passed the **Economic Recovery Tax Act**, the largest tax reduction in U.S. history. Rates were cut from 14 percent to 11 percent for the lowest-income individuals and from 70 percent to 50 percent for the wealthiest. The law gave corporations tax breaks and reduced levies on capital gains, gifts, and inheritances. A second measure, the Tax Reform Act of 1986, went even further, lowering the maximum rate on individual income to 28 percent and on business income to 35 percent. Although the 1986 law narrowed loopholes used primarily by the wealthy, affluent Americans saved far more on their tax bills than did average taxpayers, and the distribution of wealth tipped further in favor of the rich. Moreover, the total federal tax burden barely declined, from 19.4 percent of national income in 1981 to 19.3 percent in 1989.

"Hack, chop, crunch!" were *Time* magazine's words for Reagan's efforts to free private enterprise from government restraints. Carter had confined deregulation to particular industries, such as air transportation and banking, while increasing health, safety, and environmental regulations. The Reagan administration, by contrast, pursued across-the-board deregulation. It declined to enforce the Sherman Antitrust Act (see chapter 18), which limited monopolies, against an unprecedented number of business mergers and takeovers. Reagan also loosened regulations protecting employee health and safety, and he weakened labor unions. When members of the Professional Air Traffic Controllers Organization — one of the few unions to support him in 1980 — struck in 1981, Reagan pointed to the illegality of the strike, gave workers two days to go back to work, and then fired thousands who didn't. Although federal workers had struck before without being penalized, Reagan demonstrated decisiveness and toughness, destroying the union and intimidating organized labor.

Ronald Reagan loved the outdoors and his remote ranch in southern California, where altogether he spent nearly one-eighth of his two-term presidency. Yet he blamed environmental laws for the nation's sluggish economic growth and targeted them for deregulation. His first secretary of the interior, James Watt, declared, "We will mine more, drill more, cut more timber," and released federal lands to private exploitation. Meanwhile, the head of the Environmental Protection Agency relaxed enforcement of air and water pollution standards. Of environmentalists, Reagan wisecracked, "I don't think they'll be happy until the White House looks like a bird's nest," but their numbers grew in opposition to his policies. Popular support for environmental protection forced several officials to resign and blocked full realization of Reagan's deregulatory goals.

Deregulation of the banking industry, begun under Carter with bipartisan support, created a crisis in the savings and loan industry. Some of the newly deregulated savings and loan institutions (S&Ls) extended enormous loans to real estate developers and invested in other high-yield but risky ventures. S&L

owners reaped lavish profits, and their depositors enjoyed high interest rates. But when real estate values began to plunge, hundreds of S&Ls went bankrupt. After Congress voted to bail out the S&L industry in 1989, American taxpayers bore the burden of the largest financial scandal in U.S. history, estimated at more than $100 billion.

Deregulation did little to reduce the size of government or the federal deficit. The administration cut funds for food stamps, job training, student aid, and other social welfare programs, and hundreds of thousands of people lost benefits. Yet increases in defense spending far exceeded the budget cuts, and the deficit climbed from $74 billion in 1981 to a high of $220 billion in 1986. Under Reagan, the nation's debt tripled to $2.3 trillion, and interest on the debt consumed one-seventh of all federal expenditures. Despite Reagan's antigovernment rhetoric, the number of federal employees increased from 2.9 million to 3.1 million during his presidency.

It took the severest recession since the 1930s to squeeze inflation out of the U.S. economy. Unemployment approached 11 percent late in 1982, and record numbers of banks and businesses closed. The threat of unemployment further undermined organized labor, forcing unions to make concessions that management insisted were necessary for industry's survival. In 1983, the economy recovered and entered a period of unprecedented growth.

That economic upswing and Reagan's own popularity posed a formidable challenge to the Democrats in the 1984 election. They nominated Carter's vice president, Walter F. Mondale, to head the ticket, but even his precedent-breaking move in choosing a woman as his running mate — New York representative Geraldine A. Ferraro — did not save the Democrats from a humiliating defeat. Reagan charged his opponents with concentrating on America's failures, while he emphasized success and possibility. Democrats, he claimed, "see an America where every day is April 15th [the deadline for income tax returns] . . . we see an America where every day is the Fourth of July."

Voters responded to the president's sunny vision and the economic comeback, giving him a landslide victory with 59 percent of the popular vote and every state but Minnesota. Stung by Republican charges that the Democratic Party was captive to "special interests" such as labor, women, and minorities, some Democratic leaders, including the young Arkansas governor, Bill Clinton, urged the party to shift more toward the right.

Winners and Losers in a Flourishing Economy

After the economy took off in 1983, some Americans won great fortunes. Popular culture celebrated making money and displaying wealth. Books by business wizards topped best seller lists, the press described lavish million-dollar parties, and a new television show, *Lifestyles of the Rich and Famous*, drew large audiences. College students listed making money as their primary ambition.

Participating conspicuously in the new affluence were members of the baby boom generation, known popularly as "yuppies," short for "young urban professionals." These mostly white, well-educated young men and women lived in urban condominiums and consumed lavishly—fancy cars, health clubs, expensive vacations, and electronic gadgets. Though definitely a minority, they established consumption standards that many tried to emulate. And, in fact, millions of Americans enjoyed larger houses that they filled with such new products as VCRs, microwave ovens, and personal computers.

Many of the newly wealthy got rich from moving assets around rather than from producing goods. Notable exceptions included Steven Jobs, who invented the Apple computer in his garage; Bill Gates, who transformed the software industry; and Liz Claiborne, who created a billion-dollar fashion enterprise. But many others made money by manipulating debt and restructuring corporations through mergers and takeovers. "To say these guys are entrepreneurs is like saying Jesse James was an entrepreneur," said Texas businessman Ross Perot, who defined entrepreneurship as making things rather than making money. Most financial wizards operated within the law, but greed sometimes led to criminal convictions.

Older industries faced increasing international pressures. Americans bought more Volkswagens and Hondas and fewer Fords and Chevrolets, as German and Japanese corporations overtook U.S. manufacturing in steel, automobiles, and electronics. International competition forced the collapse of some older companies. Others moved factories and jobs abroad to be closer to foreign markets or to benefit from the low wages in countries such as Mexico and Korea. Service industries expanded and created new jobs at home, but this work paid substantially lower wages than did manufacturing jobs. When David Ramos was laid off in 1982 from his $12.75-an-hour job in a steel plant, his wages fell to $5 an hour as a security guard, forcing his family to rely on food stamps. The number of full-time workers earning wages below the poverty level ($12,195 for a family of four in 1990) rose from 12 percent to 18 percent of all workers in the 1980s.

The weakening of organized labor combined with the decline in manufacturing to erode the position of blue-collar workers. Chicago steelworker Ike Mazo, who contemplated the $6-an-hour jobs available to him, fumed, "It's an attack on the living standards of workers." Increasingly, a second income was needed to stave off economic decline. By 1990, nearly 60 percent of married women with young children worked outside the home. Yet even with two incomes, families struggled. Speaking of her children, Mazo's wife confessed, "I worry about their future every day. Will we be able to put them through college?" The average $10,000 gap between men's and women's annual earnings made things even harder for the nearly 20 percent of families headed by women.

In keeping with conservative philosophy, Reagan adhered to trickle-down economics, insisting that a booming economy would benefit everyone. Average personal income did rise during his tenure, but the trend toward greater economic inequality that had begun in the 1970s intensified in the 1980s, encouraged in part by his tax policies. Between 1979 and 1987, personal income shot up sharply for the wealthiest 20 percent of Americans, while it fell by 9.8 percent for the poorest. During Reagan's presidency, the percentage of Americans living in poverty increased from 11.7 to 13.5, the highest poverty rate in the industrialized world.

Social Security and Medicare helped to stave off destitution among the elderly. Less fortunate were other groups that the economic boom had bypassed: racial minorities, female-headed families, and children. One child in five lived in poverty.

Even as the economy boomed, affluent urbanites walked past men and women sleeping in subway stations and on park benches. Experts debated the number of homeless Americans — estimates ranged from 350,000 upward — but no one doubted that homelessness had increased. Those without shelter included the victims of long-term unemployment, the erosion of welfare benefits, and slum clearance, as well as Vietnam veterans and individuals suffering from mental illness, drug addiction, and alcoholism.

REVIEW   Why did economic inequality increase during the Reagan administration?

▶ Continuing Struggles over Rights

The rise of conservatism put liberal social movements on the defensive, as the Reagan administration moved away from the national commitment to equal opportunity undertaken in the 1960s and the president's federal court appointments reflected that shift. Feminists and minority groups fought to keep protections they had recently won, and they achieved some limited gains. The gay and lesbian rights movement actually grew in numbers, edging attitudes toward greater tolerance and winning important protections in some states and cities.

Battles in the Courts and Congress

Ronald Reagan agreed with conservatives that the nation had moved too far in guaranteeing rights to minority groups. Crying "reverse discrimination," conservatives maintained that affirmative action unfairly hurt whites. Brian Weber, a Kaiser Aluminum production worker, filed a lawsuit when some African Americans with less seniority were admitted to a training program to which he had applied. Ignoring the discrimination that had prevented blacks from accruing seniority, he insisted that he should not "be made to pay for what someone did 150 years ago." Weber and other critics of affirmative action called for "color-blind" policies, ignoring statistics showing that minorities and white women still lagged far behind white men in opportunities and income.

Intense mobilization by civil rights groups, educational leaders, labor, and even corporate America prevented the administration from abandoning affirmative action, and the Supreme Court upheld important antidiscrimination policies, including the one that Weber challenged. Moreover, against Reagan's wishes, Congress voted to extend the Voting Rights Act with veto-proof majorities. The administration did, however, put the brakes on civil rights enforcement by appointing conservatives to the Justice Department, the Civil Rights Commission, and other agencies and by slashing their budgets.

Congress stepped in to defend antidiscrimination programs after the Justice Department persuaded the Supreme Court to severely weaken Title IX of the

Education Amendments Act of 1972, a key law promoting equal opportunity in education. *Grove City v. Bell* (1984) allowed the Justice Department to abandon dozens of civil rights cases against schools and colleges, which in turn galvanized a coalition of civil rights organizations and groups representing women, the aged, and the disabled, along with their allies. In 1988, Congress passed the Civil Rights Restoration Act over Reagan's veto, reversing the administration's victory in *Grove City* and banning government funding of any organization that practiced discrimination on the basis of race, color, national origin, sex, disability, or age.

The *Grove City* decision reflected a rightward movement in the federal judiciary, upon which liberals had counted as a powerful ally. With the opportunity to appoint half of the 761 federal court judges and three new Supreme Court justices, President Reagan encouraged this trend by carefully selecting conservative candidates. He endured only one setback, when in 1987 the Senate denied confirmation of arch-conservative Robert Bork. Thus, Reagan's appointments turned the tide back toward strict construction — the literal interpretation of the Constitution that narrowly adheres to the words of its authors, thereby limiting judicial power to protect individual rights. The full impact of these appointments became clear after Reagan left office, as the Court allowed states to impose restrictions that weakened access to abortion for poor and uneducated women, reduced protections against employment discrimination, and whittled down legal safeguards against the death penalty.

Feminism on the Defensive

A signal achievement of the New Right was taking control of the Republican Party's position on women's rights. For the first time in its history, the Republican Party took an explicitly antifeminist tone, opposing both the **Equal Rights Amendment (ERA)** and a woman's right to abortion, key goals of women's rights activists. When the time limit for ratification of the ERA ran out in 1982, Phyllis Schlafly celebrated victory on the issue that had first galvanized her antifeminist campaign, while amendment supporters looked for the silver lining. Sonia Johnson, who was excommunicated by the Mormon Church for her feminism in 1979, exaggerated only somewhat when she called the ratification struggle "the greatest political training ground for women in the history of the world."

Cast on the defensive, feminists focused more on women's economic and family problems, where they found some common ground with the Reagan administration. The Child Support Enforcement Amendments Act helped single and divorced mothers collect court-ordered child support payments from absent fathers. The Retirement Equity Act of 1984 benefited divorced and older women by strengthening their claims to their husbands' pensions and enabling women to qualify more easily for private retirement pensions.

The Reagan administration had its own concerns about women, specifically about the gender gap in voting — women's tendency to support liberal and Democratic candidates in larger numbers than men did. Reagan eventually appointed three women to cabinet posts and, in 1981, selected the first woman,

The Abortion Debate

After the Supreme Court upheld women's right to abortion in *Roe v. Wade* in 1973, several state legislatures instituted restrictions on that right that fell within the parameters outlined by the Court. In 1989, the Court upheld a Missouri law that prohibited public employees from performing abortions not necessary to save the life of the woman, banned the use of public buildings for providing abortions, and required physicians to perform viability tests on the fetus in pregnancies beyond the twentieth week. Here, activists on both sides of the issue rally before the Supreme Court on the day of its decision. AP Images/Ron Edmonds.

Sandra Day O'Connor, a moderate conservative, for the Supreme Court, despite the Christian Right's objection to her support of abortion. But these actions accompanied a general decline in the number of women and minorities in high-level government positions. And with higher poverty rates than men, women suffered most from Reagan's cuts in social programs.

A powerful antiabortion movement won Supreme Court decisions that placed restrictions on women's ability to obtain abortions, but feminists fought successfully to retain the basic principles of *Roe v. Wade*. Moreover, they won a key decision from the Supreme Court ruling that sexual harassment in the workplace constituted sex discrimination. Feminists also made some gains at the state level in such areas as pay equity, rape, and domestic violence.

The Gay and Lesbian Rights Movement

In contrast to feminism and other social movements, gay and lesbian rights activism grew during the 1980s, galvanized in part by the discovery in 1981 of a devastating disease, **acquired immune deficiency syndrome (AIDS)**. Because initially the disease disproportionately affected male homosexuals in the United States, activists mobilized to promote public funding for AIDS education, prevention, and treatment. Such efforts, along with the death from AIDS of a friend, movie star Rock Hudson, spurred President Reagan during his second term to attack the epidemic, which he had previously refused to address.

The gay and lesbian rights movement helped closeted homosexuals experience the relief of "coming out," and their visibility increased awareness, if not always acceptance, of homosexuality among the larger population. Beginning with the election of Elaine Noble to the Massachusetts legislature in 1974, several openly gay politicians won offices ranging from mayor to member of Congress, and the Democrats began to include gay rights in their party platforms. Activists organized gay rights marches throughout the country, turning out half a million people in New York City in 1987.

Popular attitudes about homosexuality moved toward greater tolerance but remained complex, leading to uneven changes in policies. Dozens of cities banned job discrimination against homosexuals, and beginning with Wisconsin in 1982, eleven states made sexual orientation a protected category under civil rights laws. Local governments and large corporations began to offer health insurance and other benefits to same-sex domestic partners.

Yet a strong countermovement challenged the drive for recognition of gay rights. The Christian Right targeted gays and lesbians as symbols of national immorality and succeeded in overturning some homosexual rights measures, which already lagged far behind antidiscrimination guarantees for minorities and women.

Gay Pride Parades
Since June 1970, when gays and lesbians marched in New York City on the first anniversary of Stonewall (see chapter 28), annual gay pride parades have taken place throughout the United States. According to history professor Robert Dawidoff, the parades are not about "flaunting private things in public," as some people charged, but a way for gay men and lesbians to express "pride . . . in having survived the thousand petty harassments and reminders of a special status we neither seek nor merit." Friends and families of homosexuals participate in the parades, as this sign from a parade in Los Angeles indicates. © Bettmann/Corbis.

Many states removed antisodomy laws from the books, but in 1986 the Supreme Court upheld the constitutionality of such laws. Until the Court reversed that opinion in 2003, more than a dozen states retained statutes that left homosexuals vulnerable to criminal charges for private consensual behavior.

REVIEW What gains and setbacks did minorities, feminists, and gays and lesbians experience during the Reagan years?

▶ Ronald Reagan Confronts an "Evil Empire"

Campaigning for president in the wake of the Soviet invasion of Afghanistan and the Iran hostage crisis, Reagan accused Carter of weakening the military and losing the confidence of the nation's allies and the respect of its enemies. As president, he accelerated Carter's arms buildup and harshly censured the Soviet Union, calling it "an evil empire." Yet despite the new aggressiveness — or, as some argued, because of it — Reagan presided over the most impressive thaw in superpower conflict since the Cold War had begun.

On the periphery of the Cold War, however, Reagan practiced militant anticommunism, assisting antileftist movements in Asia, Africa, and Central America and dispatching troops to the Middle East and the Caribbean. When Congress blocked Reagan's efforts to help overthrow the leftist government in Nicaragua, administration officials resorted to secret and illegal means to achieve their agenda.

Militarization and Interventions Abroad

Reagan expanded the military with new bombers and missiles, an enhanced nuclear force in Europe, a larger navy, and a rapid-deployment force. Despite the growing budget deficit, Congress approved most of these programs, and military expenditures shot up by one-third in the first half of the 1980s. Throughout Reagan's presidency, defense spending averaged $216 billion a year, up from $158 billion in the Carter years and higher even than in the Vietnam era.

Reagan startled many of his own advisers in March 1983 by announcing plans for research on the **Strategic Defense Initiative (SDI)**. Immediately dubbed "Star Wars" by critics who doubted its feasibility, the project would deploy lasers in space to destroy enemy missiles before they could reach their targets. Reagan conceded that SDI could appear to be "an aggressive policy" that would allow the United States to strike first and not fear retaliation. The Soviets reacted angrily because SDI violated the 1972 Antiballistic Missile Treaty and because they would have to make huge investments to develop their own Star Wars technology. Nonetheless, Reagan persisted, and subsequent administrations continued to spend billions on SDI research without producing a working system.

Reagan justified the military buildup and SDI as a means to negotiate with the Soviets from a position of strength, but he provoked an outburst of pleas to halt the arms race. In 1982, a rally demanding a freeze on additional nuclear weapons drew 700,000 people in New York City. That same year the National Conference of Catholic Bishops issued a strong call for nuclear disarmament. Hundreds of thousands demonstrated across Europe, stimulated by fears of new U.S. missiles scheduled for deployment there in 1983.

The U.S. military buildup was impotent before the growing threat of terrorism by nonstate organizations that sought political objectives by attacking civilian populations. Terrorism had a long history throughout the world, but in the 1970s and 1980s Americans saw it escalate in the Middle East, used by Palestinians after the Israeli occupation of the West Bank and by other groups hostile to Western policies. The terrorist organization Hezbollah, composed of Shiite Muslims and backed by Iran and Syria, arose in Lebanon in 1982 after Israeli forces invaded that country to stop the Palestine Liberation Organization from using sanctuaries in Lebanon to launch attacks on Israel.

Reagan's effort to stabilize Lebanon by sending 2,000 Marines to join an international peacekeeping mission failed. In April 1983, a suicide attack on the U.S. Embassy in Beirut killed 63 people, and in October a Hezbollah fighter drove a bomb-filled truck into a U.S. barracks there, killing 241 Marines (see Map 30.2). The attack prompted the withdrawal of U.S. troops, and Lebanon remained in chaos, while incidents of murder, kidnapping, and hijacking by various Middle Eastern extremist groups continued.

Following a Cold War pattern begun under Eisenhower, the Reagan administration sought to contain leftist movements across the globe. In October 1983, 5,000 U.S. troops invaded Grenada, a small island nation in the Caribbean where Marxists had staged a successful coup. In Asia, the United States moved more quietly, aiding the Afghan rebels' war against Afghanistan's Soviet-backed government. In the African nation of Angola, the United States armed rebel forces against the government supported by both the Soviet Union and Cuba. Reagan also sided with the South African government, which was brutally suppressing black protest against apartheid, forcing Congress to override his veto in order to impose economic sanctions against South Africa.

Administration officials were most fearful of left-wing movements in Central America, which Reagan claimed could "destabilize the entire region from the Panama Canal to Mexico." When a leftist uprising occurred in El Salvador in 1981, the United States sent money and military advisers to prop up the authoritarian government even though it had committed murderous human rights violations. In neighboring Nicaragua, the administration secretly aided the Contras (literally, "opposers"), an armed coalition seeking to unseat the left-wing Sandinistas, who had toppled a long-standing dictatorship.

The Iran-Contra Scandal

The Reagan administration's commitment to the Contras highlighted the issue of presidential versus congressional authority in using force abroad. Fearing another Vietnam, many Americans opposed aligning the United States with reactionary forces not supported by the majority of Nicaraguans. Congress repeatedly instructed the president to stop aiding the Contras, but the administration continued to secretly provide them with weapons and training and helped wreck the Nicaraguan economy. With support for his government undermined, Nicaragua's president, Daniel Ortega, agreed to a political settlement, and when he was defeated by a coalition of all the opposition groups, he stepped aside.

Secret aid to the Contras was part of a larger project that came to be known as the **Iran-Contra scandal**. It began in 1985 when officials of the National Security Council and CIA secretly arranged to sell arms to Iran, then in the midst of an eight-year war with neighboring Iraq, even while the United States openly supplied Iraq with funds and weapons. The purpose was to get Iran to pressure Hezbollah to release seven American hostages being held in Lebanon (see Map 30.2). Funds from the arms sales were then channeled through Swiss bank accounts to aid the Nicaraguan Contras. Over the objections of his secretary of state and secretary of defense, Reagan approved the arms sales, but the three subsequently denied knowing that the proceeds were diverted to the Contras.

When news of the affair surfaced in November 1986, the Reagan administration faced serious charges. The president's aides had defied Congress's express ban on military aid for the Contras. Investigations by an independent prosecutor appointed by Reagan led to a trial in which seven individuals pleaded guilty or were convicted of lying to Congress and destroying evidence. One felony conviction was later overturned on a technicality, and President George H. W. Bush pardoned the other six officials in December 1992. The independent prosecutor's final report found no evidence that Reagan had broken the law, but it concluded that he had known about the diversion of funds to the Contras and had "knowingly participated or at least acquiesced" in covering up the scandal — the most serious case of executive branch disregard for the law since Watergate.

A Thaw in Soviet-American Relations

A momentous reduction in Cold War tensions soon overshadowed the Iran-Contra scandal. The new Soviet-American accord depended in part on Reagan's flexibility, his profound desire to end the possibility of nuclear war, and his fortitude in standing up to conservatives and the national security establishment. It also depended on an innovative Soviet head of state who recognized that his country's domestic problems demanded an easing of Cold War antagonism. **Mikhail Gorbachev** assumed power in 1985 determined to revitalize an inefficient Soviet economy incapable of delivering basic consumer goods. As Reagan remarked privately, Gorbachev knew that "his economy is a basket case." Hoping to stimulate production and streamline distribution, Gorbachev introduced some elements of free enterprise and proclaimed a new era of *glasnost* (greater freedom of expression), eventually allowing contested elections and challenges to Communist rule.

Concerns about immense defense budgets moved both Reagan and Gorbachev to the negotiating table. Enormous military expenditures stood between the Soviet premier and his goal of economic revival. With growing popular support for arms reductions, along with a push from his wife, Nancy, Reagan made disarmament a major goal in his last years in office and readily responded when Gorbachev

The Fireside Summit
This photograph captures the warmth that developed between President Ronald Reagan and Soviet leader Mikhail Gorbachev at their first meeting at Geneva in November 1985. Although the meeting did not produce any key agreements, the two men spent much more time in private meetings than had been scheduled. They began to appreciate each other's concerns and to build trust, launching a relationship that would lead to nuclear arms reductions and the end of the Cold War. Ronald Reagan Presidential Library.

took the initiative. A positive personal chemistry developed between them, and they met four times between 1985 and 1988. Although Reagan's insistence on proceeding with SDI nearly killed the talks, by December 1987 the superpowers had completed an **intermediate-range nuclear forces (INF) agreement**. The treaty marked a major turning point in U.S.-Soviet relations. It eliminated all short- and medium-range missiles from Europe and provided for on-site inspection for the first time. This was also the first time that either nation had agreed to eliminate weapons already in place.

In 1988, Gorbachev further reduced tensions by announcing a gradual withdrawal from Afghanistan, which had become the Soviet equivalent of America's Vietnam. In addition, the Soviet Union, the United States, and Cuba agreed on a political settlement of the civil war in the African nation of Angola. In the Middle East, both superpowers supported a cease-fire and peace talks in the eight-year war between Iran and Iraq. Within three years, the Cold War that had defined the world for nearly half a century would be history.

REVIEW How did anticommunism shape Reagan's foreign policy?

► Conclusion: Reversing the Course of Government

"Ours was the first revolution in the history of mankind that truly reversed the course of government," boasted Ronald Reagan in his farewell address in 1989. The word *revolution* exaggerated the change, but his administration did mark the slowdown or reversal of expanding federal budgets for domestic programs and regulations that had taken off in the 1930s. Although he did not deliver on the social or moral issues dear to the heart of the New Right, Reagan represented the "choice not an echo" that Phyllis Schlafly had called for in 1964, as he used his skills as "the Great Communicator" to cultivate antigovernment sentiment and undo the liberal assumptions of the New Deal.

Antigovernment sentiment grew along with the backlash against the reforms of the 1960s and the conduct of the Vietnam War. Watergate and other lawbreaking by Nixon administration officials further disillusioned Americans. Presidents Ford and Carter restored morality to the White House, but neither could solve the gravest economic problems since the Great Depression — slow economic growth, stagflation, and an increasing trade deficit. Even the Democrat Carter gave higher priority to fiscal austerity than to social reform, and he began the government's retreat from regulation of key industries.

A new conservative movement helped Reagan win the presidency and flourished during his administration. Reagan's tax cuts, combined with hefty increases in defense spending, created a federal deficit crisis that justified cuts in social welfare spending, made new federal initiatives unthinkable, and burdened the country for years to come. These policies also contributed to a widening income gap between the rich and poor, weighing heavily especially on minorities, female-headed families, and children. Many Americans continued to support specific federal programs — especially those, such as Social Security and Medicare, that reached beyond the poor — but public sentiment about the government in general had taken a U-turn from the Roosevelt era. Instead of seeing the government as a helpful and problem-solving institution, many believed that not only was it ineffective at solving national problems, but it also often made things worse. As Reagan appointed new justices, the Supreme Court retreated from liberalism, curbing the government's authority to protect individual rights and regulate the economy.

With the economic recovery that set in after 1982 and his optimistic rhetoric, Reagan lifted the confidence of Americans about their nation and its promise — confidence that had eroded with the economic and foreign policy blows of the 1970s. He began his presidency voicing harsh rhetoric against the Soviet Union and intensifying the military buildup begun by Carter; he left office having helped move the two superpowers to the highest level of cooperation since the Cold War began. Although that accord was not welcomed by strong anti-Communist conservatives like Phyllis Schlafly, it signaled developments that would transform American-Soviet relations — and the world — in the next decade.

Reviewing Chapter 30

REVIEW QUESTIONS

1. How did Nixon's policies reflect the increasing influence of conservatives on the Republican Party? (pp. 907–915)

2. How and where did Carter implement his commitment to human rights, and where and why did human rights give way to other priorities? (pp. 915–922)

3. Why did economic inequality increase during the Reagan administration? (pp. 922–928)

4. What gains and setbacks did minorities, feminists, and gays and lesbians experience during the Reagan years? (pp. 928–932)

5. How did anticommunism shape Reagan's foreign policy? (pp. 932–935)

MAKING CONNECTIONS

1. What was Watergate's legacy for American politics in the following decade? In your answer, explain what led to Nixon's resignation. How did Congress try to prevent such abuses of power in the future?

2. Both the Republican and Democratic parties changed significantly in the 1970s and 1980s. Describe these changes, and discuss how they shaped contemporary American politics. In your answer, be sure to cite specific political developments.

3. Recent experiences in Vietnam hung over the foreign policy decisions of Presidents Carter and Reagan. How did each president try to reconcile the lessons of that conflict and the ongoing Cold War? In your answer, be sure to discuss the impact of the Vietnam War on specific policies in the 1970s and 1980s.

4. American regional politics shifted in significant ways during the 1970s and 1980s. Why was grassroots conservatism particularly strong in the Sun Belt? What was its relationship to the civil rights and equal opportunity developments of the 1960s? What was its relationship to economic development?

LINKING TO THE PAST

1. How were the conservatives of the 1980s similar to and different from the conservatives who opposed the New Deal in the 1930s? (See chapter 24.)

2. Presidents Jimmy Carter and Woodrow Wilson both claimed human rights as a central principle of their foreign policy. Which one do you think pursued human rights more consistently? Which one was more successful in spreading human rights? Explain your answers. (See chapter 22.)

TIMELINE 1966–1988

1966 • Republican Ronald Reagan elected governor of California.

1968 • Republican Richard Nixon elected president.

1969 • Warren E. Burger appointed chief justice of U.S. Supreme Court.

1971 • Nixon vetoes comprehensive child care bill.

1972 • Nixon campaign aides arrested at Watergate complex.
• Nixon reelected president.

1974 • Nixon resigns; Gerald Ford becomes president.
• Ford pardons Nixon of any crimes he may have committed while president.

1976 • Democrat Jimmy Carter elected president.

1977 • United States signs Panama Canal treaty.

1978 • *Regents of University of California v. Bakke.*
• Congress deregulates airlines.

1979 • Camp David accords signed.
• Carter establishes formal diplomatic relations with China.

• Soviet Union invades Afghanistan.
• Hostage crisis in Iran begins.
• Moral Majority founded.

1980 • Congress deregulates banking, trucking, and railroad industries.
• Congress passes Superfund legislation.
• Republican Ronald Reagan elected president.

1981 • Researchers discover AIDS virus.
• Economic Recovery Tax Act.

1982 • Large demonstrations against nuclear weapons.

1983 • Terrorist bomb kills 241 U.S. Marines in Beirut, Lebanon.
• Reagan announces plans for Strategic Defense Initiative ("Star Wars").
• Family Research Council founded.
• Reagan reelected president.

1986 • Iran-Contra scandal.

1987 • INF agreement signed.

1988 • Civil Rights Restoration Act.

▶ FOR AN ONLINE BIBLIOGRAPHY, PRACTICE QUIZZES, WEB SITES, IMAGES, AND DOCUMENTS RELATED TO THIS CHAPTER, see the Book Companion Site at **bedfordstmartins.com/roarkvalue**.

▶ FOR DOCUMENTS RELATED TO THIS PERIOD, see Michael Johnson, ed., *Reading the American Past*, Fifth Edition.

31

The Promises and Challenges of Globalization

Since 1989

IN HIS MOSCOW HOTEL ROOM ON APRIL 22, 1988, RONALD REAGAN'S national security adviser, Colin L. Powell, contemplated the plans that Premier Mikhail Gorbachev had just announced, which would dramatically alter the Soviet Union's government and economy. "Lying there in bed," Powell recalled, "I realized that one phase of my life had ended, and another was about to begin. Up until now, as a soldier, my mission had been to confront, contain, and, if necessary, combat communism. Now I had to think about a world without a Cold War." For the next sixteen years, Powell labored to redefine his country's role in a world transformed.

Colin Powell was born in Harlem in 1937 and grew up in the Bronx, the son of Jamaican immigrants. His father headed the shipping department in a garment factory, where his mother worked as a seamstress. After attending public schools, Powell enrolled in City College of New York. There he joined the army's Reserve Officers Training Corps (ROTC) program, the defining experience of his college years. "The discipline, the structure, the camaraderie, the sense of belonging," he said, "were what I craved." When he graduated in 1958, Powell began a lifelong career in military and public service, rising to the highest rank of four-star general. He chose to stay in the army primarily because "I loved what I was doing." But he also recognized that "for a black, no other avenue in American society offered so much opportunity."

Secretary of State Colin Powell
Colin Powell's loyalty and discretion helped him rise through the ranks of the army and serve in four presidential administrations. The U.S. invasion of Iraq in March 2003 ran counter to Powell's commitment to acting through the international community and sacrificing American lives only when a vital interest was at stake and an exit plan had been established. Nonetheless, he stayed in his job until 2005 and defended administration policy. In this photo taken at the White House in February 2003, Powell listens to Secretary of Defense Donald Rumsfeld. National Security Adviser Condoleezza Rice stands behind them. Charles Ommanney/Contact Press Images for *Newsweek*.

Powell's two tours of duty in Vietnam taught him that "you do not squander courage and lives without clear purpose, without the country's backing, and without full commitment." In his subsequent positions as national security adviser to Ronald Reagan, chairman of the Joint Chiefs of Staff in the George H. W. Bush and Bill Clinton administrations, and secretary of state under George W. Bush, Powell endeavored to keep his country out of "halfhearted warfare for half-baked reasons that the American people could not understand or support."

Powell's sense that Gorbachev's reforms would ring down the curtain on the Cold War became a reality more quickly than anyone anticipated. Eastern Europe broke free from Communist control in 1989, and the Soviet Union disintegrated in 1991. Throughout the 1990s, as the lone superpower, the United States deployed both military and diplomatic power during episodes of instability in Latin America, the Middle East, eastern Europe, and Asia, almost always in concert with the major nations of Europe and Asia. In 1991, in its first full-fledged war since Vietnam, the United States led a United Nations–authorized force of twenty-eight nations to repel Iraq's invasion of Kuwait.

During a temporary retirement from public service in the 1990s, Powell remarked that "neither of the two major parties fits me comfortably." Many Americans seemed to agree: They turned Republican George H. W. Bush out of office in 1992 but elected Republican Congresses during Democrat Bill Clinton's administration. When Republican George W. Bush (son of George H. W. Bush) entered the White House in 2001, he faced a nearly evenly divided Congress. Between 1989 and 2000, domestic policies reflected a slight retreat from the conservatism of the Reagan years. The first Bush administration approved tighter environmental protections and new rights for people with disabilities, and President Clinton signed measures strengthening gun control and aiding low-wage earners. But the pendulum swung back to the right in the second Bush presidency.

All three presidents shared a commitment to hastening the globalization processes that were linking nations together in an increasingly connected economy. As capital, products, information, and people crossed national boundaries in greater numbers and at greater speed, a surge of immigration rivaled the stream of a century earlier that had brought Powell's parents to the United States. Powell cheered globalization, predicting that the world would become "defined by trade relations, by the flow of information, capital, technology, and goods, rather than by armies glaring at each other across borders."

He was not so naive as to anticipate a world "without war or conflict," recognizing challenges such as nuclear proliferation, nationalist passions in areas of former Soviet dominance and the Middle East, civil wars in Africa, and Islamic extremism. But he shared other Americans' shock when in September 2001 deadly terrorist attacks in New York City and Washington, D.C., exposed American vulnerability to new and horrifying threats and sent U.S. soldiers into Afghanistan to overthrow the government that harbored the attackers. The administration's response to terrorism overwhelmed Secretary of State Powell's commitments to internationalism, multilateralism, and military restraint. In 2003, George W. Bush began a second war against Iraq, implementing a distinct shift to a foreign policy based on preemptive attacks against presumed threats and going it alone if necessary. The unpopularity of that war and a severe financial crisis helped the Democrats regain power and elect Barack Obama as the first African American president.

▶ Domestic Stalemate and Global Upheaval: The Presidency of George H. W. Bush

Announcing his bid for the presidency in 1988, Vice President **George H. W. Bush** declared, "We don't need radical new directions." Generally satisfied with the agenda set by Ronald Reagan and facing a Democratic-controlled Congress, Bush proposed few domestic initiatives. His dispatch of troops to oust the corrupt dictator of Panama, Manuel Noriega, represented a much longer continuity, following a century of U.S. intervention in Latin America.

Yet as the most dramatic changes since the 1940s swept through the world, Bush confronted situations that did not fit the simpler free world versus communism framework that had guided foreign policy since World War II. Most Americans approved of Bush's handling of two challenges to U.S. foreign policy: the disintegration of the Soviet Union and its hold over Eastern Europe, and Iraq's invasion of neighboring Kuwait. But voters' concern over a sluggish economy limited Bush to one term in the White House.

Gridlock in Government

The son of a wealthy New England senator, George Herbert Walker Bush fought in World War II, earned a Yale degree, and then settled in Texas to make his own way in the oil industry and politics. He served in Congress during the 1960s and headed the CIA during the Nixon and Ford years. When Ronald Reagan achieved a commanding lead in the 1980 presidential primaries, Bush adjusted his more moderate policy positions to fit Reagan's conservative agenda and accepted second place on the Republican ticket. At the end of Reagan's second term, Republicans rewarded him with the presidential nomination.

Several candidates competed for the Democratic nomination in 1988. The Reverend Jesse Jackson — whose Rainbow Coalition campaign centered on the needs of minorities, women, the working class, and the poor — made an impressive bid, winning several primaries and seven million votes. But a more centrist candidate, Massachusetts governor Michael Dukakis, won the nomination. On election day, half the eligible voters stayed home, indicating their disgust with the negative campaigning or their satisfaction with the Republican record on peace and prosperity. Divided government would remain, however, as Bush won 54 percent of the vote but the Democrats gained seats in Congress.

Although President Bush saw himself primarily as guardian and beneficiary of the Reagan legacy, he promised "a kinder, gentler nation" and was more inclined than Reagan to approve government activity in the private sphere. An oil spill from an Exxon tanker that ruined eight hundred miles of Alaska shoreline in 1989 heightened environmental awareness and helped Bush convince Congress to approve the **Clean Air Act of 1990**, the strongest, most comprehensive environmental law in history.

"Let the shameful wall of exclusion finally come tumbling down," proclaimed Bush when he signed another regulatory measure in 1990, the **Americans with**

Disabilities Act. Benefiting some forty million Americans, this measure banned discrimination in employment, transportation, public accommodation, communications, and governmental activities, requiring that private businesses and public facilities be accessible to people with disabilities. Cynthia Jones, publisher of a magazine on disability politics, noticed a breeze stirring over the White House lawn at the signing of the bill. She said, "It was kind of like a new breath of air was sweeping across America. . . . People knew they had rights. That was wonderful."

Yet Bush also needed to satisfy conservatives whose strength in the Republican Party continued to rise. His most famous campaign pledge had been "Read my lips: No new taxes," and he opposed most proposals requiring additional federal funds. Bush vetoed thirty-six bills, including those lifting abortion restrictions, extending unemployment benefits, raising taxes, and mandating family and medical leave for workers. Press reports increasingly used the words *stalemate, gridlock,* and *divided government.*

Continuing a trend begun during the Reagan years, states tried to compensate for this paralysis, becoming more innovative than Washington. States passed bills to block corporate takeovers, establish parental leave policies, improve food labeling, and protect the environment. In the 1980s, a few states began to pass measures guaranteeing gay and lesbian rights. In the 1990s, dozens of cities passed ordinances requiring businesses receiving tax abatements or other city benefits to pay wages well above the federal minimum wage. And in 1999, California passed a gun control bill with much tougher restrictions on assault weapons than reformers had been able to get through Congress.

The huge federal budget deficit inherited from the Reagan administration impelled the president in 1990 to abandon his "no new taxes" pledge, outraging conservatives. The new law, which Bush depended on Democrats to pass, authorized modest tax increases for high-income Americans and higher taxes on gasoline, cigarettes, alcohol, and luxury items. Yet it had little effect on the massive tax reductions of the early 1980s, leaving intact a key element of Reagan's legacy. Neither the new revenues nor controls on spending curbed the deficit, which was boosted by rising costs for Social Security, Medicare, and Medicaid and spending on war and natural disasters.

Bush also continued Reagan's efforts to create a more conservative Supreme Court. His first nominee, federal appeals court judge David Souter, was a moderate. But in 1991, when the only African American on the Court, Justice Thurgood Marshall, retired, Bush set off a national controversy. He nominated Clarence Thomas, a conservative black appeals court judge who had opposed affirmative action as head of the Equal Employment Opportunity Commission (EEOC) under Reagan. Charging that Thomas would not protect minority rights, civil rights groups and other liberal organizations fought the nomination. Then Anita Hill, a black law professor, accused Thomas of sexually harassing her while she was his employee at the EEOC.

Thomas angrily denied the charges, claiming that he was the victim of a "high-tech lynching for uppity blacks." Hill's testimony failed to sway the Senate, which voted narrowly to confirm Thomas. The hearings angered many women,

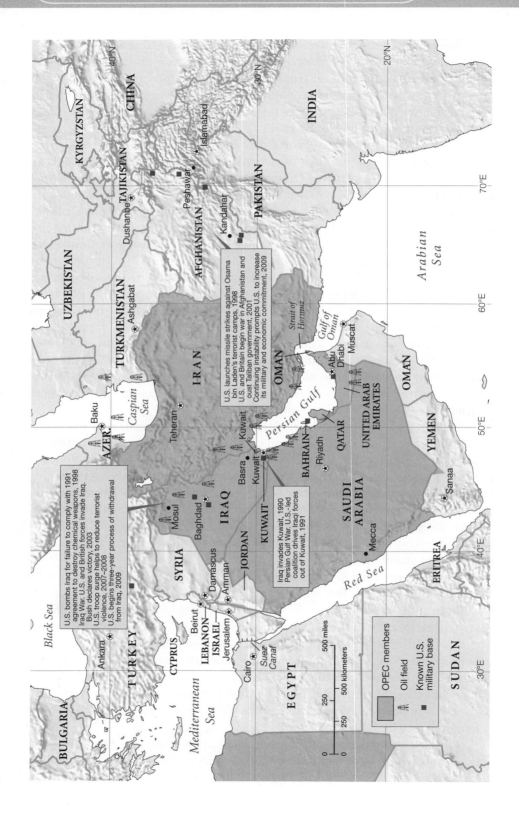

BULGARIA

Black Sea

TURKEY

Ankara ✾

Mediterranean Sea

CYPRUS

LEBANON
Beirut
ISRAEL
Jerusalem

SYRIA
Damascus
Amman

JORDAN

IRAQ
Mosul
Baghdad

Basra
Kuwait
KUWAIT

EGYPT
Cairo ✾

Suez Canal

Red Sea

SAUDI ARABIA

Mecca

Riyadh ✾

BAHRAIN
QATAR

UNITED ARAB EMIRATES
Abu Dhabi
Muscat

OMAN

YEMEN

Sanaa ✾

ERITREA

SUDAN

Gulf of Oman

Strait of Hormuz

Persian Gulf

Arabian Sea

IRAN

Teheran ✾

Caspian Sea

Baku
AZER.

TURKMENISTAN
Ashgabat ✾

UZBEKISTAN

Dushanbe ✾
TAJIKISTAN

KYRGYZSTAN

CHINA

AFGHANISTAN
Kandahar

Peshawar
Islamabad ✾

PAKISTAN

INDIA

U.S. bombs Iraq for failure to comply with 1991 agreement to destroy chemical weapons, 1998
Iraq War. U.S. and British forces invade Iraq, Bush declares victory, 2003
U.S. troop surge helps to reduce terrorist violence, 2007–2008
U.S. begins three-year process of withdrawal from Iraq, 2009

Iraq invades Kuwait, 1990
Persian Gulf War. U.S.-led coalition drives Iraqi forces out of Kuwait, 1991

U.S. launches missile strikes against Osama bin Laden's terrorist camps, 1998
U.S. and Britain begin war in Afghanistan and oust Taliban government, 2001
Continuing instability prompts U.S. to increase its military and economic commitment, 2009

OPEC members

Oil field

Known U.S. military base

0   250   500 miles

0   250   500 kilometers

20°N

30°N

40°N

30°E   40°E   50°E   60°E   70°E

who noted that only two women sat in the Senate and denounced the male senators for failing to take sexual harassment seriously. Feminists complained that men "still don't get it" and redirected their anger to electoral politics, making 1992 a banner year for female candidates. Thomas's confirmation solidified the Supreme Court's shift to the right.

Going to War in Central America and the Persian Gulf

President Bush won greater support for his actions abroad than for his domestic policy, and he twice sent U.S. soldiers into battle. In Central America, the United States had tolerated and, in fact, paid Panamanian dictator Manuel Noriega for helping the Contras in Nicaragua and providing the CIA with information about Communist activities in the region. But in 1989, after Noriega was indicted for drug trafficking by an American grand jury and after his troops killed an American Marine, President Bush ordered 25,000 military personnel into Panama. In **Operation Just Cause**, U.S. forces quickly overcame Noriega's troops, sustaining 23 deaths, while hundreds of Panamanians, including many civilians, died. Chairman of the Joint Chiefs of Staff Colin Powell noted that "our euphoria over our victory in Just Cause was not universal." Both the United Nations and the Organization of American States censured the unilateral action by the United States.

By contrast, Bush's second military engagement rested solidly on international approval. Considering Iran to be America's major enemy in the Middle East, U.S. officials had quietly assisted the Iraqi dictator **Saddam Hussein** in the Iran-Iraq war, which began in 1980 and ended inconclusively in 1988. In August 1990, Hussein sent troops into the small, oil-rich country of Kuwait to the south (Map 31.1), and within days the invasion neared the Saudi Arabian border, threatening the world's largest oil reserves. President Bush quickly ordered a massive mobilization of American forces and assembled an international coalition to stand up to Iraq. He invoked principles of national self-determination and international law, but long-standing interests in Middle Eastern oil also drove the U.S. response. As the largest importer of oil, the United States consumed one-fourth of the world's supply, 20 percent of which came from Iraq and Kuwait.

Reflecting the easing of Cold War tensions, the Soviet Union voted for a UN resolution declaring an embargo on Iraqi oil and authorizing the use of force if

◀ **MAP 31.1**

Events in the Middle East, 1989–2011

During the Persian Gulf War of 1991, Egypt, Syria, and other Middle Eastern nations joined the coalition against Iraq, and the twenty-two-member Arab League supported the war as a means to liberate Kuwait. After September 11, 2001, the Arab League approved of U.S. military operations in Afghanistan because the attacks "were an attack on the common values of the world, not just on the United States." Yet, except for the countries where the United States had military bases — Bahrain, Kuwait, Qatar, and Saudi Arabia — no Arab country supported the American invasion and occupation of Iraq in 2003. Arab hostility toward the United States also reflected the deterioration of Israeli-Palestinian relations after 1999, as Arabs charged that the United States allowed Israel to deny Palestinians land and liberty.

Iraq did not withdraw from Kuwait by January 15, 1991. By then, the United States had deployed more than 400,000 soldiers to Saudi Arabia, joined by 265,000 troops from some two dozen other nations, including several Arab states. "The community of nations has resolutely gathered to condemn and repel lawless aggression," Bush announced. "With few exceptions, the world now stands as one."

With Iraqi forces still in Kuwait, in January 1991 Bush asked Congress to approve war. Considerable sentiment favored waiting to see if the embargo and other means would force Hussein to back down, a position quietly urged within the administration by Colin Powell. Linking the crisis to the failure of U.S. energy conservation, Democratic senator Edward M. Kennedy insisted, "Not a single American life should be sacrificed in a war for the price of oil." Congress debated for three days and then authorized war by a margin of five votes in the Senate and sixty-seven in the House, with most Democrats in opposition. On January 17, 1991, the U.S.-led coalition launched Operation Desert Storm, a forty-day bombing campaign against Iraqi military targets, power plants, oil refineries, and transportation networks. Having severely crippled Iraq by air, the coalition then stormed into Kuwait with massive ground forces, forcing Iraqi troops to withdraw (see Map 31.1).

"By God, we've kicked the Vietnam syndrome once and for all," President Bush exulted on March 1. Most Americans found no moral ambiguity in the **Persian Gulf War** and took pride in the display of military prowess. In contrast to the loss of 58,000 American lives in Vietnam, 270 U.S. service members perished in Desert Storm. The United States stood at the apex of global leadership, steering a coalition in which Arab nations fought beside their former colonial rulers.

Some Americans criticized the Bush administration for ending the war without deposing Hussein. But Bush pointed to the UN mandate that limited the mission to driving Iraqi forces out of Kuwait and to Middle Eastern leaders' concern that an invasion of Iraq would destabilize the region. His secretary of defense, Richard Cheney, doubted that coalition forces could secure a stable government to replace Hussein and considered the price of a long occupation too high. Administration officials counted on economic sanctions and Hussein's pledges not to rearm or develop weapons of mass destruction, secured by a system of UN inspections, to contain the dictator.

Yet Middle Eastern stability remained elusive. Israel, which had endured Iraqi missile attacks, was more secure, but the Israeli-Palestinian conflict remained intractable. Despite military losses, Saddam Hussein remained in power and turned his war machine on Iraqi Kurds and Shiite Muslims whom the United States had encouraged to rebel. Hussein also found ways to conceal arms from UN weapons inspectors before he threw them out in 1998. Finally, the decision to keep U.S. troops based in Saudi Arabia, the holy land of Islam, fueled the hatred and determination of Muslim extremists like Osama bin Laden and served as a recruiting tool.

The Cold War Ends

Soviet support in the Persian Gulf War marked a momentous change in relations between the United States and the Soviet Union. The progressive forces that

Gorbachev had encouraged in the Communist world (see chapter 30) swept through Eastern Europe in 1989, when popular uprisings in Hungary, Poland, East Germany, and elsewhere demanded an end to state repression and inefficient economic bureaucracies. Communist governments toppled like dominoes (Map 31.2), virtually without bloodshed, because Gorbachev refused to prop them up with Soviet armies. East Germany opened its border with West Germany, and in November 1989 ecstatic Germans danced on the Berlin Wall and swung sledge-hammers to demolish that dominant symbol of the Cold War, which had separated East and West since 1961. An amazed East Berliner crossed the line exclaiming, "They just let us go. I can't believe it."

Bush assured Gorbachev that he would not "climb the Berlin Wall and make high-sounding pronouncements," taking care not to weaken the Soviet leader at home. The president persuaded Gorbachev that unification of East and West Germany was inevitable, and it sped to completion in 1990. Soon former iron curtain countries such as Hungary and Poland lined up to join NATO. Although U.S. military forces remained in Europe as part of NATO, Europe no longer depended on the United States for its security. Its economic clout also grew as Western Europe formed a common economic market in 1992. The destiny of Europe, to which the United States and the Soviet Union had held the key for forty-five years, now lay in European hands.

Inspired by the liberation of Eastern Europe, republics within the Soviet Union soon sought their own independence. In December 1991, Boris Yeltsin, president of the Russian Republic, announced that Russia and eleven other republics had formed a new entity, the Commonwealth of Independent States, and other former Soviet states declared their independence. With nothing left to govern, Gorbachev resigned. The Soviet Union had dissolved, and with it the Cold War conflict that had defined U.S. foreign policy for decades.

Colin Powell joked that he was "running out of villains. I'm down to Castro and Kim Il Sung," the North Korean dictator who, along with China's leaders, resisted the liberalizing tides sweeping the world. In 1989, Chinese soldiers killed hundreds of pro-democracy demonstrators in Tiananmen Square in Beijing, and the Communist government arrested some ten thousand reformers. North Korea remained a Communist dictatorship, committed to developing nuclear weapons. "The post–Cold War world is decidedly not post-nuclear," declared one U.S. official. In 1990, the United States and the Soviet Union signed the Strategic Arms Reduction Talks (START) treaty, which cut about 30 percent of each superpower's nuclear arsenal. And in 1996, the UN General Assembly overwhelmingly approved a total nuclear test ban treaty. Yet India and Pakistan, hostile neighbors, refused to sign the treaty, and both exploded atomic devices in 1998, increasing the nuclear risk in South Asia. Moreover, the Republican-controlled Senate defeated U.S. ratification of the test ban treaty in October 1999, halting a decade of progress on nuclear weapons control. The potential for rogue nations and terrorist groups to develop nuclear weapons posed an ongoing threat to international peace and security.

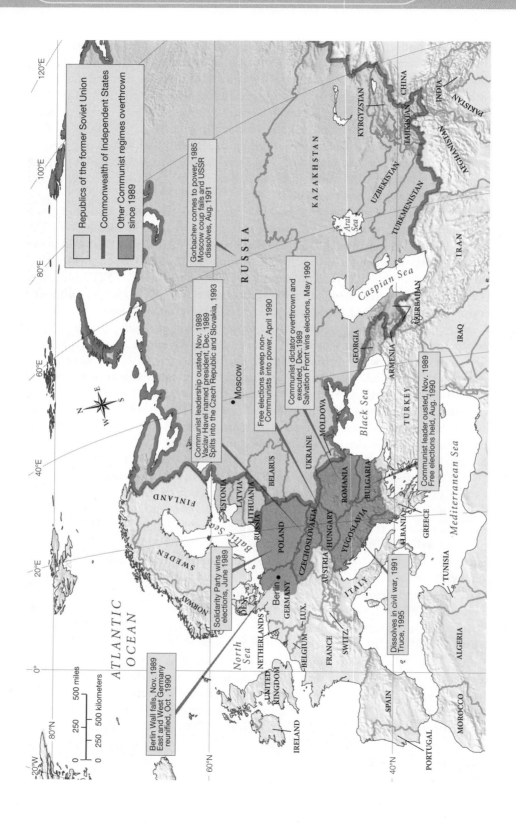

Republics of the former Soviet Union

Commonwealth of Independent States

Other Communist regimes overthrown since 1989

Gorbachev comes to power, 1985
Moscow coup fails and USSR dissolves, Aug. 1991

Communist leadership ousted, Nov. 1989
Vaclav Havel named president, Dec. 1989
Splits into the Czech Republic and Slovakia, 1993

Free elections sweep non-Communists into power, April 1990

Communist dictator overthrown and executed, Dec. 1989
Salvation Front wins elections, May 1990

Communist leader ousted, Nov. 1989
Free elections held, Aug. 1990

Solidarity Party wins elections, June 1989

Dissolves in civil war, 1991
Truce, 1995

Berlin Wall falls, Nov. 1989
East and West Germany reunified, Oct. 1990

Fall of the Berlin Wall
After 1961, the Berlin Wall stood as the prime symbol of the Cold War and the iron grip of communism over Eastern Europe and the Soviet Union. More than four hundred Eastern Europeans were killed trying to flee to the West. After Communist authorities opened the wall on November 9, 1989, permitting free travel between East and West Germany, Berliners from both sides gathered at the wall to celebrate. Eric Bouvet/Gamma Press Images

The 1992 Election

In March 1991, Bush's chances for reelection in 1992 looked golden. The Gulf War victory catapulted his approval rating to 88 percent, causing the most prominent Democrats to opt out of the presidential race. But that did not deter **William Jefferson "Bill" Clinton**, who at age forty-five had served as governor of Arkansas for twelve years. Like Carter in 1976, Clinton and his running mate, Tennessee senator Albert Gore Jr., presented themselves as "New Democrats" and sought to rid the party of its liberal image.

Clinton promised to work for the "forgotten middle class," who "do the work, pay the taxes, raise the kids, and play by the rules." Disavowing the "tax and spend" label that Republicans pinned on his party, he promised a tax cut for the middle class, pledged to reinvigorate government and the economy, and vowed "to put an end to welfare as we know it." Bush was vulnerable to voters' concerns about the ailing economy, as unemployment reached 7 percent, and to the Clinton

◀ **MAP 31.2**
Events in Eastern Europe, 1989–2002
The overthrow of Communist governments throughout Eastern Europe and the splintering of the Soviet Union into more than a dozen separate nations were the most momentous changes in world history since World War II.

campaign's emphasis on bread-and-butter issues. The popularity of a third candidate, self-made Texas billionaire H. Ross Perot, revealed Americans' frustrations with government and the major parties. Railing against the huge federal budget deficit, Perot mobilized a sizable grassroots movement and established the deficit as a key campaign issue.

Fifty-five percent of those eligible voted, just barely reversing the thirty-year decline in voter turnout. Clinton won 43 percent of the popular vote, Bush 38 percent, and Perot 19 percent — the strongest third-party finish in eighty years. By casting nearly two-thirds of their votes against Bush, voters suggested a mandate for change but not the direction that change should take.

> **REVIEW** How did George H. W. Bush respond to threats to U.S. interests as the Cold War came to an end?

▶ The Clinton Administration's Search for the Middle Ground

Bill Clinton's assertion that "the era of big government is over" reflected the Democratic Party's move to the right that had begun with Jimmy Carter in the 1970s. Clinton did not completely abandon liberal principles. He extended benefits for the working poor; delivered incremental reforms to feminists, environmentalists, and other groups; and spoke out in favor of affirmative action and gay rights. Yet his administration attended more to the concerns of middle-class Americans than to the needs of the disadvantaged.

Clinton's eight-year presidency witnessed the longest economic boom in history and ended with a budget surplus. Although various factors generated the prosperity, many Americans identified Clinton with the buoyant economy, elected him to a second term, and continued to support him even when his reckless sexual behavior resulted in impeachment. The Senate failed to convict the president, but the scandal crippled Clinton's leadership in his last years in office.

Clinton's Reforms

Clinton wanted to restore confidence in government as a force for good while not alienating antigovernment voters. The huge budget deficit that he inherited — $4.4 trillion in 1993 — further precluded substantial federal initiatives. Moreover, Perot's challenges denied Clinton a majority of the popular vote in both 1992 and 1996, and the Republicans controlled Congress for all but his first two years in office. Throughout most of his presidency, Clinton was burdened by investigations into past financial activities and private indiscretions. While the president had an extraordinary knack for making voters feel that he liked and understood them, he struggled to translate that appeal into gains for his agenda.

Despite these obstacles, Clinton achieved a number of incremental reforms. He used his executive authority to ease restrictions on abortion and signed several bills that Republicans had previously blocked. In 1993, Congress enacted gun control legislation and the Family and Medical Leave Act, which entitled workers in larger companies to unpaid leave for childbirth, adoption, and family medical emergencies. The Violence against Women Act of 1994 authorized $1.6 billion and new remedies for combating sexual assault and domestic violence. Clinton won stricter air pollution controls and greater protection for national forests and parks. Other liberal measures included a minimum-wage increase, the largest expansion of aid for college students since the GI Bill (see chapter 25), and the creation of AmeriCorps, which enabled students to pay for their education with community service.

Most significantly, Clinton pushed through a substantial increase in the **Earned Income Tax Credit (EITC)** for low-wage earners, a program begun in 1975. The EITC gave tax cuts to people who worked full-time at meager wages or, if they paid no taxes, a subsidy to lift their family income above the poverty line. By 2003, some fifteen million low-income families were benefiting from the EITC, almost half of them minorities. One expert called it "the largest antipoverty program since the Great Society."

Shortly before Clinton took office, the economy had begun to rebound, and the boom that followed helped boost his popularity through the 1990s. Economic expansion, along with spending cuts, tax increases, and declining unemployment, produced a budget surplus in 1998, the first since 1969. Despite a substantial tax cut in 1997 that reduced levies on estates and capital gains and provided tax credits for families with children and for higher education, the surplus grew. The seemingly inexorable growth of government debt had turned around.

Clinton failed, however, to provide universal health insurance and to curb skyrocketing medical costs. Under the direction of First Lady Hillary Rodham Clinton and with very little congressional consultation, the administration proposed a complicated plan that drew criticism from both sides. Liberals wanted a single-payer plan similar to Medicare, while conservatives charged that the proposal would increase taxes and government interference in medical decisions. Congress enacted smaller reforms enabling workers who changed jobs to retain health insurance and underwriting health care for five million uninsured children, but affordable health care for all remained elusive.

Pledging to change the face of government to one that "looked like America," Clinton built on the gradual progress women and minorities had made since the 1960s. For example, African Americans and women had become mayors in major cities from New York to San Francisco. Virginia had elected the first black governor since Reconstruction, and Florida the first Latino. In the executive branch, Clinton appointed the most diverse group of department heads ever assembled, including six women, three African Americans, and two Latinos. Secretary of Commerce Norman Y. Mineta became the first Asian American to hold a cabinet post. Janet Reno became the first female attorney general and Madeleine K. Albright the first female secretary of state. Clinton's judicial appointments had a similar cast, and in 1993 he named the second woman to the Supreme Court, Ruth Bader Ginsburg, whose arguments before she became an appeals court judge had won key women's rights rulings from the Supreme Court.

Accommodating the Right

Although much of Clinton's agenda fell within the liberal tradition, the continuing strength of conservatism and his own determination to move his party to the center led him to make compromises with the right. The 1994 midterm elections swept away the Democratic majorities in Congress. Led by Representative Newt Gingrich of Georgia, Republicans claimed the 1994 election as a mandate for their "contract with America," a conservative platform to end "government that is too big, too intrusive, and too easy with the public's money" and to elect "a Congress that respects the values and shares the faith of the American family." Opposition from Democrats and moderate Republicans blocked passage of most of the contract's pledges, but Gingrich succeeded in moving the debate to the right.

The most extreme antigovernment sentiment developed far from Washington in the form of grassroots armed militias. They celebrated white Christian supremacy and reflected conservatives' hostility to such diverse institutions as taxes and the United Nations. Claiming the need to defend themselves from government tyranny, they stockpiled weapons. The militia movement grew in reaction to the passage of new gun control legislation and after government agents stormed the headquarters of an armed religious cult in Waco, Texas, in April 1993, killing more than 80. On the second anniversary of that event, a bomb leveled a federal building in Oklahoma City, taking 169 lives in the worst terrorist attack in the nation's history up to that point.

Clinton bowed to conservative views on gay and lesbian rights, backing away from a campaign promise to lift the ban on gays in the military. Although many other nations, including France and Israel, welcomed homosexual soldiers, U.S. military leaders and key legislators objected to the proposal, and Clinton reverted to a **"don't ask, don't tell" policy** in 1993. Officials were forbidden to ask military personnel about their sexuality, but soldiers who said they were gay or who engaged in homosexual behavior could be dismissed. Eventually, more than ten thousand homosexuals were discharged, including army Arabic linguist Cathleen Glover, who lamented, "The army preaches integrity, but asks you to lie to everyone around you." In 1996, Clinton signed the Defense of Marriage Act, prohibiting the federal government from recognizing state-licensed marriages between same-sex couples.

Nonetheless, gays and lesbians continued to make strides as attitudes about homosexuality became more tolerant. By 2006, more than half of the country's five hundred largest companies provided health benefits to same-sex domestic partners and included sexual orientation in their nondiscrimination policies. More than twenty-five states banned discrimination in public employment, and many of those laws extended to private employment, housing, and education. By 2010, gay marriage was legal in Massachusetts, Connecticut, Vermont, Iowa, Maine, New Hampshire, and the District of Columbia; moreover, several states recognized civil unions and domestic partnerships, extending to same-sex couples rights available to married couples such matters as inheritance, taxation, and medical decisions.

Clinton's efforts to cast himself as a centrist were apparent in his handling of the New Deal program Aid to Families with Dependent Children (AFDC), which most people called welfare. Public sentiment about poverty had shifted since the 1960s. Instead of blaming poverty on the lack of adequate jobs or other external circumstances, more people blamed the poor themselves and believed that welfare programs trapped the poor in cycles of dependency. Many questioned why they should subsidize poor mothers now that so many women had joined the labor force. Nearly everyone considered work to be better than welfare, but supporters of AFDC doubted that the economy could provide sufficient jobs at decent wages.

After vetoing two welfare reform bills, Clinton forced through a less punitive measure, which he signed as the 1996 election approached. The **Personal Responsibility and Work Opportunity Reconciliation Act** abolished AFDC and with it the nation's fifty-year pledge to provide a minimum level of subsistence for all children. The law provided grants to the states to assist the poor, but it limited welfare payments to two years, regardless of whether the recipient could find a job, and it set a lifetime limit of aid at five years. Reflecting growing controversy over immigration, it also barred legal immigrants from obtaining food stamps and other benefits and allowed states to stop Medicaid for legal immigrants. New York senator Daniel Patrick Moynihan called it "the most brutal act of social policy since Reconstruction."

In its first decade, the law produced neither the horrors predicted by its critics nor the successes promised by its advocates. As intended, it did force single mothers to seek employment, cutting welfare rolls from 12.5 million to 4.5 million between 1996 and 2006. Yet not all former welfare recipients became self-supporting. Forty percent of former welfare mothers were not working regularly after being cut from the rolls, and those who did find jobs earned on average only about $12,000 a year. More than one-third of children living in female-headed families still lived in poverty.

Clinton's signature on the new law denied Republicans a partisan issue in the 1996 presidential campaign. The president ran as a moderate who would save the country from extremist Republicans, while the Republican Party also moved to the center, nominating Kansan Robert Dole, a World War II hero and former Senate majority leader. Clinton won 49 percent of the votes; 41 percent went to Dole and 9 percent to third-party candidate Ross Perot. Although Clinton won reelection with room to spare, voters sent a Republican majority back to Congress.

In 1999, Clinton and Congress bowed to calls from the financial industry for deregulation by repealing key aspects of the Glass-Steagall Act, passed during the New Deal to avoid another Great Depression. This Financial Services Modernization Act ended the separation between banking, securities, and insurance services, allowing financial institutions to engage in all three, practices that leading economists would link to the severe financial meltdown of 2008.

Impeaching the President

Clinton's magnetic and articulate style, his ability to capture the middle ground of the electorate, and the nation's economic resurgence enabled the self-proclaimed "comeback kid" to survive scandals and an impeachment trial in 1999. Early in his presidency, charges related to firings of White House staff, political use of FBI records, and "Whitewater" — the nickname for real estate investments that the Clintons had made in Arkansas — led to an official investigation by an independent prosecutor. The president also faced a sexual harassment lawsuit filed in 1994 by a state employee. A federal court threw out that case in 1998, but another sexual scandal more seriously threatened Clinton's presidency.

In January 1998, Kenneth Starr, independent prosecutor for Whitewater, began to investigate the charge that Clinton had had sexual relations with a twenty-one-year-old White House intern and then lied about it to a federal grand jury. At first, Clinton vehemently denied the charge, but subsequently he bowed to the mounting evidence against him. Starr prepared a case for the House of Representatives, which in December 1998 voted to impeach the president on two counts: perjury and obstruction of justice. Clinton became the second president (after Andrew Johnson, in 1868) to be impeached by the House and tried by the Senate.

The Senate trial took place in early 1999. Most Americans condemned the president's behavior but approved of the job he was doing and opposed his removal from office. Some saw Starr as a fanatic invading individuals' privacy. One man said, "Let him get a divorce from his wife. Don't take him out of office and disrupt the country." Those favoring removal insisted that the president must set a high moral standard for the nation and that lying to a grand jury, even over a private matter, was a serious offense. A number of senators did not believe that Clinton's actions constituted the high crimes and misdemeanors required by the Constitution for conviction. With a two-thirds majority needed for that result, the Senate voted 45 to 55 on the perjury count and 50 to 50 on the obstruction of justice count. A majority, including some Republicans, seemed to agree with a Clinton supporter that the president's behavior, though "indefensible, outrageous, unforgivable, shameless," did not warrant his removal from office.

The investigation that triggered events leading up to impeachment ended in 2000 when the independent prosecutor reported insufficient evidence of illegalities related to the Whitewater land deals. Although more than 60 percent of Americans gave Clinton high marks on his job performance throughout the scandal, it distracted him from domestic and international problems and precluded the possibility of significant policy advances in his last years in office.

The Booming Economy of the 1990s

Clinton's ability to weather the impeachment crisis owed much to the prosperous economy, which in 1991 began its longest period of expansion in U.S. history. During the 1990s, the gross domestic product grew by more than one-third, thirteen million new jobs were created, inflation remained in check, unemployment reached 4 percent — its lowest point in twenty-five years — and the stock market soared.

The president took credit for the thriving economy, and his policies did contribute to the boom. He made deficit reduction a priority, and in exchange the

Federal Reserve Board and bond market traders lowered interest rates, encouraging economic expansion by making money easier to borrow. Businesses also prospered because they had lowered their costs through restructuring and laying off workers. Economic problems in Europe and Asia helped American firms become more competitive in the international market. And the computer revolution and the application of information technology boosted productivity.

People at all income levels benefited from the economic boom, but the gaps between the rich and the poor and between the wealthy and the middle class, which had been growing since the 1970s, endured. This persistence of inequality was linked in part to the growing use of information technology, which increased demand for highly skilled workers, while the movement of manufacturing jobs abroad diminished opportunities and wages for the less skilled. In addition, deregulation and the continuing decline of unions hurt lower-skilled workers, tax cuts had favored the better-off, and the national minimum wage failed to keep up with inflation.

Although more minorities than ever attained middle-class status, in general people of color remained lowest on the economic ladder, reflecting Colin Powell's observation that "race still casts a shadow over our society." For instance, in 1999 the median income for white households surpassed $45,000, but it stood at only $29,423 and $33,676 for African American and Latino households, respectively. In 2000, poverty afflicted about 22 percent of blacks, 21 percent of Latinos, and 10 percent of Asian Americans, in contrast to 7.5 percent of whites.

REVIEW What policies of the Clinton administration moved the Democratic Party to the right?

▶ The United States in a Globalizing World

America's economic success in the 1990s was linked to its dominance in the world economy. From that position, President Clinton tried to shape the tremendous transformations occurring in a process called **globalization** — the growing integration and interdependence of national citizens and economies. Building on the initiatives of Reagan and Bush, Clinton lowered a number of trade barriers, despite stiff opposition from critics who emphasized the economic deprivation and environmental devastation that often resulted. Debates likewise arose over the large numbers of immigrants entering the United States.

Clinton agreed with Bush that the United States must retain its economic and military dominance over all other nations. The president took military action in Somalia, Haiti, the Middle East, and eastern Europe, and he pushed hard to ease the conflict between Israel and the Palestinians. Yet no new global strategy emerged to replace the containment of communism as the decisive factor in the exercise of American power abroad. And safeguarding American interests from terrorist attacks around the world proved much more difficult than combating communism.

Defining America's Place in a New World Order

In 1991, President George H. W. Bush declared a "new world order" emerging from the ashes of the Cold War. As the sole superpower, the United States was determined to let no nation challenge its military superiority or global leadership. Yet policymakers struggled to define guiding principles for deciding when and how to use the nation's military and diplomatic power in a post–Cold War world. Combating Saddam Hussein's naked aggression seemed the obvious course of action in 1991, but dealing with other areas of instability proved more difficult.

Africa, where civil wars and extreme human suffering rarely evoked a strong American response, was a case in point. In 1992, guided largely by humanitarian concern, President Bush had attached U.S. forces to a UN operation in the small northern African country of Somalia, where famine and civil war raged. In 1993, President Clinton allowed that humanitarian mission to turn into "nation building" — an effort to establish a stable government — and eighteen U.S. soldiers were killed. After Americans saw film of Somalis dragging a soldier's corpse through the streets, the outcry at home suggested that most citizens were unwilling to sacrifice lives when no vital interest seemed threatened. Indeed, both the United States and the United Nations stood by in 1994 when more than half a million people were massacred in a brutal civil war in the central African nation of Rwanda.

As always, the United States was more inclined to use force nearer its borders, but in the case of Haiti it gained international support for intervention. In 1994, after a military coup overthrew Jean-Bertrand Aristide, Haiti's democratically elected president, Clinton persuaded the United Nations to impose economic sanctions on Haiti and to authorize military intervention. Hours before U.S. forces were to invade, Haitian military leaders promised to step down. U.S. forces peacefully landed, and Aristide was restored to power. Initially a huge success, U.S. policy continued to be tested as Haiti faced grave economic challenges and political instability.

In eastern Europe, the collapse of communism ignited a severe crisis, triggering U.S.-NATO intervention in Yugoslavia. During the Cold War, the Communist government of Yugoslavia, a federation of six republics, had held ethnic tensions in check, and many Muslims, Croats, and Serbs had grown accustomed to living and working together. After the Communists were swept out in 1989, ruthless leaders exploited ethnic differences to bolster their power, and Yugoslavia splintered into separate states and fell into civil war.

The Serbs' aggression under President Slobodan Milosevic against Bosnian Muslims in particular horrified much of the world, but European and U.S. leaders hesitated to use military force. As reports of rape, torture, and mass killings in Bosnia increased, American leaders worried about the image of the world's strongest nation being unwilling to stop the violence. Finally, in 1995, Clinton ordered U.S. fliers to join NATO forces in intensive bombing of Serbian military concentrations. That effort and successful offensives by the Croatian and Bosnian armies forced Milosevic to the bargaining table. After representatives from Serbia, Croatia, and Bosnia hammered out a peace treaty, Clinton then agreed to send twenty thousand American troops to Bosnia as part of a NATO peacekeeping mission.

In 1998, new fighting broke out in the southern Serbian province of Kosovo, where ethnic Albanians, who constituted 90 percent of the population, demanded independence. The Serbian army brutally retaliated, driving out one-third of Kosovo's 1.8 million Albanian Muslims. In 1999, NATO launched a U.S.-led bombing attack on Serbian military and government targets that, after three months, forced Milosevic to agree to a peace settlement. Serbians voted Milosevic out of office in October 2000, and he died in 2006 while on trial for genocide by a UN war crimes tribunal.

Elsewhere, Clinton remained willing to deploy U.S. power when he could send missiles rather than soldiers, and he was prepared to act without international support or UN sanction. In August 1998, bombs exploded at the U.S. embassies in Kenya and Tanzania, killing 12 Americans and more than 250 Africans. Clinton retaliated with missile attacks on terrorist training camps in Afghanistan and facilities in Sudan controlled by **Osama bin Laden**, a Saudi-born millionaire who financed the Islamic-extremist terrorist network linked to the embassy attacks. Clinton also launched air strikes against Iraq in 1993 when a plot to assassinate former president Bush was uncovered, in 1996 after Saddam Hussein attacked the Kurds in northern Iraq, and repeatedly between 1998 and 2000 after Hussein expelled UN weapons inspectors. Whereas Bush had acted in the Gulf War with the support of an international force that included Arab states, Clinton acted unilaterally and in the face of Arab opposition.

To defuse the Israeli-Palestinian conflict, a major source of Arab hostility toward the West, Clinton used diplomatic rather than military power. In 1993, largely because of the efforts of the Norwegian government, Yasir Arafat, head of the Palestine Liberation Organization (PLO), and Yitzhak Rabin, Israeli prime minister, recognized the existence of each other's states for the first time and agreed to Israeli withdrawal from the Gaza Strip and Jericho, allowing for Palestinian self-government there. In July 1994, Clinton presided over another turning point as Rabin and King Hussein of Jordan signed a declaration of peace. Yet difficult issues remained to be settled: control of Jerusalem; the fate of Palestinian refugees; and the presence of more than 200,000 Israeli settlers in the West Bank, the land seized by Israel in 1967, where 3 million Palestinians were determined to establish their own state. Clinton's last effort to broker negotiations between the PLO and Israel failed in 2000, and continuing violence between Israelis and Palestinians strengthened anti-American sentiment among Arabs, who saw the United States as Israel's ally.

Debates over Globalization

The Clinton administration moved energetically on the economic side to speed up the growth of a "global marketplace." The process of globalization had begun in the fifteenth century, when Europeans began to penetrate other parts of the world. Between the U.S. Civil War and World War I, products, capital, and labor crossed national boundaries in ever-larger numbers. In that era, globalization was based on imperialism; Western nations took direct control of foreign territories, extracted their natural resources, and restricted manufacturing. By contrast, late-twentieth-century globalization advanced among sovereign nations and involved the industrialization of less developed areas, such as Korea and China. Other distinguishing marks of the more recent globalization were its scope and intensity: New communications technologies such as the Internet and cell phones connected nations, corporations, and individuals at much greater speed and much less cost than ever before.

Building on efforts by Presidents Reagan and Bush, Clinton sought to speed up globalization, seeking new measures to ease restrictions on international commerce. In November 1993, he won congressional approval of the **North American Free Trade Agreement (NAFTA)**, which eliminated all tariffs and trade barriers among the United States, Canada, and Mexico. Organized labor and others fearing loss of jobs and industries to Mexico lobbied vigorously against NAFTA, and a majority of Democrats opposed it, but Republican support ensured approval. In 1994, the Senate ratified the General Agreement on Tariffs and Trade, establishing the **World Trade Organization (WTO)** to enforce substantial tariff reductions and elimination of import quotas among some 135 member nations. And in 2005, Clinton's successor, George W. Bush, lowered more trade barriers with the passage of the Central American–Dominican Republic Free Trade Agreement.

The free trade issue was intensely contested. Much of corporate America welcomed the elimination of trade barriers. "Ideally, you'd have every plant you own on a barge," remarked Jack Welch, CEO of General Electric. Critics linked globalization to the loss of manufacturing jobs, the erosion of the social safety net provided for workers since the 1930s, and the growing gap between rich and poor. Demanding "fair trade" rather than simply free trade, critics wanted trade treaties to require decent wage and labor standards. Environmentalists insisted that countries seeking increased commerce with the United States agree to eliminate or reduce pollution and prevent the destruction of endangered species.

Globalization controversies often centered on relationships between the United States, which dominated the world's industrial core, and the developing nations on the periphery, whose cheap labor and lax environmental standards caught the eye of investors. United Students against Sweatshops, for example, attacked the international conglomerate Nike, which paid Chinese workers $1.50 to produce a pair of shoes selling for more than $100 in the United States. Yet leaders of developing nations actively sought foreign investment, insisting that wages deemed pitiful by Americans offered their impoverished people a much better living than they could otherwise obtain. At the same time, developing countries often pointed to American hypocrisy in advocating free trade in industry while heavily subsidizing the U.S. agricultural sector. "When countries like America, Britain and France subsidize their farmers," complained a grower in Uganda, "we get hurt."

Whereas globalization's cheerleaders argued that everyone would benefit in the long run, critics focused on the short-term victims. American businessman

George Soros conceded that international trade and investments generated wealth, "but they cannot take care of other social needs, such as the preservation of peace, alleviation of poverty, protection of the environment, labor conditions, or human rights." The critics enjoyed a few successes. In 2000, President Clinton signed an executive order requiring an environmental impact review before the signing of any trade agreement. Beyond the United States, officials from the World Bank and the International Monetary Fund, along with representatives from wealthy economies, promised in 2000 to provide poor nations more debt relief and a greater voice in decisions about loans and grants. According to World Bank president James D. Wolfensohn, "Our challenge is to make globalization an instrument of opportunity and inclusion — not fear."

The Internationalization of the United States

Globalization was typically associated with the expansion of American enterprise and culture to other countries, yet the United States experienced the dynamic forces of globalization within its own borders. Already in the 1980s, Japanese, European, and Middle Eastern investors had purchased American stocks and bonds, real estate, and corporations such as Firestone and 20th Century Fox. Local communities welcomed foreign capital, and states competed to recruit foreign automobile plants. American non-union workers began to produce Hondas in Marysville, Ohio, and BMWs in Spartanburg, South Carolina. By 2002, the paychecks of nearly four million American workers came from foreign-owned companies.

Globalization was transforming not just the economy but American society as well, as the United States experienced a tremendous surge of immigration, part of a worldwide trend that counted some 214 million immigrants across the globe in 2010. By 2006, the United States' 35.7 million immigrants constituted 12.4 percent of the population. The 20 million who arrived between 1980 and 2005 surpassed the previous peak immigration of the first two decades of the twentieth century and exhibited a striking difference in country of origin. Eighty-five percent of the earlier immigrants had come from Europe; by the 1980s, the vast majority came from Asia and Latin America. Consequently, immigration changed the racial and ethnic composition of the nation. By 2004, Asian Americans numbered 13 million, while 41 million Latinos constituted — at 14 percent — the largest minority group in the nation.

The promise of economic opportunity, as always, lured immigrants to America, and the Immigration and Nationality Act of 1965 enabled them to come. Although the law set an annual limit of 270,000 immigrants, it allowed close relatives of U.S. citizens to enter above the ceiling, thus creating family migration chains. In addition, the Cold War dispersal of U.S. military and other personnel around the world enabled foreigners to learn about the nation and form relationships with citizens. Moreover, during the Cold War, U.S. immigration policy was generous to refugees from communism, welcoming more than 800,000 Cubans after Castro's revolution in 1959 and more than 600,000 Vietnamese, Laotians, and Cambodians after the Vietnam War.

Unlike in the earlier immigration, women comprised more than half of all newcomers to the United States in the 1990s. But it was the racial composition of the new immigration that heightened the century-old wariness of native-born Americans toward newcomers. Pressure for more restrictive policies stemmed from beliefs that immigrants took jobs from the native-born, suppressed wages by accepting low pay, strained the capability of social services, or eroded the dominant culture and language. Americans expressed particular hostility toward immigrants who were in the country illegally — an estimated 12 million in 2008 — even though the economy depended on their cheap labor. The Immigration Reform and Control Act of 1986 did little to stem the tide. It penalized employers who hired undocumented aliens but also granted amnesty to some 2 million illegal immigrants who had been in the country before 1982.

The new immigration was once again making America an international, interracial society. The largest numbers of immigrants flocked to California, New York, Texas, Florida, New Jersey, and Illinois, but new immigrants dispersed throughout the country. Taquerias, sushi bars, and Vietnamese restaurants appeared in southeastern and midwestern towns; cable TV companies

Immigrant Labor

Large commercial farms depended on Latino workers, who constituted more than 45 percent of agricultural labor in 2002. A majority of these workers were citizens, and not all were immigrants, but growers insisted that they could not supply Americans with fresh produce without the labor of immigrants, legal and illegal. The dependence of agriculture and service industries on immigrant labor helped block movements for greater immigration restrictions. The workers here are harvesting strawberries near Carlsbad, California. In 2002, the median weekly pay for migrant farmworkers was $300. Sandy Huffaker/Getty Images.

added Spanish-language stations; and the international sport of soccer soared in popularity. Mixed marriages displayed the growing fusion of cultures, recognized in 2000 on Census Bureau forms, where Americans could check more than one racial category. Only half-joking, the famous golfer Tiger Woods called himself a "Cablinasian" to reflect his mixed heritage of Caucasian, black, American Indian, and Asian.

Like their predecessors, the majority of post-1965 immigrants were unskilled and poor. They took the lowest-paying jobs, constituting, for example, nearly half of all farmworkers and housekeepers and performing other work that employers insisted native-born Americans would not do. Yet a significant number of immigrants were highly skilled workers, sought after by burgeoning high-tech industries. By 2006, nearly one-third of all software developers were foreign-born, as were 28 percent of all physicians.

REVIEW Who criticized free trade agreements and why?

▶ President George W. Bush: Conservatism at Home and Radical Initiatives Abroad

The election of **George W. Bush** in 2000 marked the second time that a son of a former president gained the White House. But the younger Bush pushed an agenda that was closer to Ronald Reagan's than to that of George H. W. Bush. He signed key legislation to improve public school education and to subsidize prescription drugs for elderly citizens. But he also persuaded Congress to pass enormous tax cuts favoring the wealthy, reduced environmental protections, and tipped the balance on the Supreme Court with two conservative appointments. The tax cuts, along with spending on new international and domestic crises, turned the substantial budget surplus that Bush had inherited into the largest deficit in the nation's history, and a financial crisis near the end of his presidency sent the economy into a recession.

As Islamist terrorism replaced communism as the primary threat to U.S. security, the Bush administration launched a war in Afghanistan in 2001 and expanded the federal government's powers to investigate and detain individuals. In distinct contrast to his father's multilateral and cautious approach to foreign policy, George W. Bush adopted a policy of unilateralism and preemption by going to war against Iraq in 2003. He won reelection in 2004, but stability in Iraq and Afghanistan, despite huge costs, remained elusive, and Bush confronted serious foreign and domestic crises in his second term. Democrats capitalized on widespread dissatisfaction with his administration to gain control of Congress in 2006.

The Disputed Election of 2000

Clinton's presidency ended with a flourishing economy, and public opinion polls indicated that a majority of Americans agreed with the Democrats on most issues.

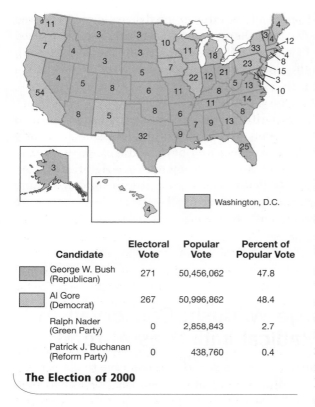

Candidate	Electoral Vote	Popular Vote	Percent of Popular Vote
George W. Bush (Republican)	271	50,456,062	47.8
Al Gore (Democrat)	267	50,996,862	48.4
Ralph Nader (Green Party)	0	2,858,843	2.7
Patrick J. Buchanan (Reform Party)	0	438,760	0.4

The Election of 2000

Yet his vice president, Albert Gore, failed to succeed him in 2000. To many voters, Gore seemed stiff and pompous and too willing to change his positions for political advantage. He was further burdened with the taint of Clinton administration scandals.

George W. Bush won the Republican nomination after a series of richly funded, hard-fought primaries. The oldest son of former president George H. W. Bush, he had earned degrees from Yale and Harvard, worked in the oil industry, and served as governor of Texas since 1994. Inexperienced in national and international affairs, Bush chose for his running mate a seasoned official, Richard B. Cheney, who had served in the Nixon, Ford, and first Bush administrations.

Many observers predicted that the amazingly strong economy would give Gore the edge, and he did surpass Bush by more than half a million votes. Once the polls closed, however, it became clear that Florida's 25 electoral college votes would decide the presidency. Bush's tiny margin in Florida prompted an automatic recount of the votes, which eventually gave him an edge of 537 votes in that state.

Meanwhile, the Democrats asked for hand-counting of Florida ballots in several heavily Democratic counties where machine errors and confusing ballots may have left thousands of Gore votes unrecorded. The Republicans, in turn, went to court to try to stop the hand-counts. The outcome of the 2000 election hung in the balance for weeks as cases went all the way to the Supreme Court. Finally, a bitterly divided Court ruled five to four against further recounts, and Gore conceded the presidency to Bush on December 13, 2000. For the first time since 1888, a president who failed to win the popular vote took office (Map 31.3). Despite the lack of a popular mandate, the Bush administration set out to make dramatic policy changes.

The Domestic Policies of a "Compassionate Conservative"

Bush's appointments, like Clinton's, brought significant diversity to the executive branch. He chose African Americans Colin Powell as secretary of state and

Condoleezza Rice first as national security adviser and subsequently as secretary of state when Powell resigned in January 2005. Five of Bush's top-level appointees were women, including Secretary of Labor Elaine L. Chao, the first Asian American woman to serve in the cabinet.

Bush had promised to govern as a "compassionate conservative." A devout born-again Christian, he immediately established the White House Office of Faith-Based and Community Initiatives to encourage religious groups to participate in government programs aimed at prison inmates, the unemployed, and others. The religious right praised the initiatives, but others charged that they violated the constitutional separation of church and state, and federal courts ruled in several dozen cases that faith ministries were using government funds to indoctrinate the people they served.

Bush's fiscal policies were more compassionate toward the rich than toward average Americans. In 2001, he signed a bill reducing taxes over the next ten years by $1.35 trillion. A 2003 tax law slashed another $320 billion. The laws heavily favored the rich by reducing income taxes, phasing out estate taxes, and cutting tax rates on capital gains and dividends. They also provided benefits for married couples and families with children and offered tax deductions for college expenses.

The administration insisted that the tax cuts would promote economic growth and jolt the economy out of the recession that had begun in 2000. The economy did recover, but opponents stressed inequities in the tax cuts and pointed to a mushrooming federal deficit — the highest in U.S. history — that surpassed $400 billion in 2004, although Republicans had traditionally railed against budget deficits. In 2009, the deficit surpassed $1 trillion as the government struggled to combat a recession. By then, the national debt had risen to $9.6 trillion, making the United States increasingly dependent on China and other foreign investors, who held more than half of the debt.

Bush used regulatory powers that did not require congressional approval to weaken environmental protection as part of his larger goals of reducing government regulation, promoting economic growth, and increasing energy production. The administration opened millions of wilderness acres to mining, oil, and timber industries and relaxed environmental requirements under the Clean Air and Clean Water Acts. To worldwide dismay, the administration withdrew from the **Kyoto Protocol** on global warming, signed in 1997 by 178 nations to reduce greenhouse gas emissions.

While environmentalists pushed for measures to limit American energy consumption, the administration called for more rapid development of energy resources. During his second term, as gasoline prices reached all-time highs in 2005, Bush signed the Energy Policy Act, a compromise bill providing $14 billion in subsidies to producers of oil, coal, nuclear power, and alternative sources of energy. But when gas prices shot up even higher in 2008 and Bush sought to lift restrictions on offshore drilling for oil, Congress blocked the president's efforts, and it continued to thwart his calls to allow drilling for oil in the Arctic National Wildlife Refuge.

Bush had the opportunity to replace two Supreme Court justices, and conservatives hailed his choices. In 2005, John Roberts, who had served in the Reagan and George H. W. Bush administrations, was named chief justice. Bush then replaced the moderate Sandra Day O'Connor with Samuel A. Alito, a staunch conservative who won confirmation by a narrow margin. While the Court stood up to the administration in rulings on the rights of accused terrorists, it tilted right on cases concerning abortion, gun control, sex discrimination in employment, campaign financing, and regulation of business.

In contrast to the partisan conflict over judicial appointments and tax and environmental policy, Bush won bipartisan support for the **No Child Left Behind Act** of 2002, marking the greatest change in federal education policy since the 1960s and substantially extending the role of the federal government in public education. Promising to end, in Bush's words, "the story of children being just shuffled through the system," the law required every school to meet annual testing standards, penalized failing schools, and allowed parents to transfer their children out of such schools. It authorized an increase in federal aid, but not enough for Senator Paul Wellstone of Minnesota, one of the few critics of the measure, who asked, "How can you reach the goal of leaving no child behind on a tin cup budget?" In addition to struggling to finance the new standards, school officials began to criticize the one-size-fits-all approach and pointed to family and community impoverishment as sources of student deficiencies.

The Bush administration's second major effort to co-opt Democratic Party issues constituted what the president hailed as "the greatest advance in health care coverage for America's seniors" since the start of Medicare in 1965. In 2003, Bush signed a bill authorizing prescription drug benefits for the elderly and at the same time expanding the role of private insurers in the Medicare system. Most Democrats opposed the legislation, charging that it left big gaps in coverage, subsidized private insurers with federal funds to compete with Medicare, banned imports of low-priced drugs, and prohibited the government from negotiating with drug companies to reduce prices. Legislators of both parties worried about the cost of the new drug benefit. More than 80 percent of the elderly who signed up for the benefit were at least "somewhat satisfied" with the program, but medical costs overall continued to soar, and the number of uninsured Americans surpassed forty million in 2008.

One domestic undertaking of the Bush administration found little approval anywhere: its handling of **Hurricane Katrina**, which in August 2005 devastated the coasts of Alabama, Louisiana, and Mississippi and ultimately resulted in some fifteen hundred deaths. The catastrophe that ensued when New Orleans's levees broke, flooding 80 percent of the city, shook a deeply rooted assumption held by Americans: that government owed its citizens protection from natural disasters. Federal, state, and local officials failed the citizens of New Orleans in two ways: They had not built the levees to withstand such a deluge, and they failed to rescue citizens when the levees broke and flooded their homes.

New Orleans residents who were too old, too poor, or too sick to flee the flooding spent anguished days waiting on rooftops for help; wading in filthy, toxic water; and enduring the heat, disorder, and lack of basic necessities at the convention center

9/11

The magnitude of the destruction and loss of lives in the 9/11 attacks made Americans feel more vulnerable than they had since the Cold War ended. In the aftermath of the attacks, a surge of patriotism swept the United States, and people around the world streamed to U.S. embassies to express their shock and sympathy. Steve Ludlum/The New York Times/Redux.

and Superdome, where they had been told to go for safety and protection. "How can we save the world if we can't save our own people?" wondered one Louisianan. Thousands of volunteers rushed to help, and millions more opened their pocketbooks to aid the victims. Yet the immense private generosity and the superb response of a few groups, such as the U.S. Coast Guard and the Louisiana Department of Wildlife and Fisheries, could not make up for the feeling that the nation had failed some of its citizens when they needed it most. Since so many of Katrina's hardest-hit victims were poor and black, the disaster also highlighted the severe injustices and deprivations remaining in American society.

The Globalization of Terrorism

The response to Hurricane Katrina contrasted sharply with the Bush administration's decisive reaction to the horror that had unfolded four years earlier on the morning of **September 11, 2001**. In the most deadly attack ever launched on American soil, nineteen terrorists hijacked four planes and flew two of them into the twin towers of New York City's World Trade Center and one into the Pentagon in Washington, D.C.; the fourth crashed in a field in Pennsylvania. The attacks took nearly 2,800 lives, including U.S. citizens and people from ninety countries. The nation, indeed the world, was stunned.

The hijackers belonged to Osama bin Laden's **Al Qaeda** international terrorist network, and some of them had been living in the United States for several years. Organized from bin Laden's sanctuaries in Afghanistan, where the radical Muslim Taliban government had taken control, the attacks reflected Islamic extremists' rage at the spread of Western goods, culture, and values into the Muslim world, as well as their opposition to the 1991 Persian Gulf War against Iraq and the stationing of American troops in Saudi Arabia. Bin Laden sought to rid the Middle East of Western influence and install puritanical Muslim control.

The 9/11 terrorists and others who came after them ranged from poor to middle-class; some lived in Middle Eastern homelands governed by undemocratic and corrupt governments, others in Western cities where they felt alienated and despised. All saw the West, especially the United States, as the evil source of their humiliation and the supporter of Israel's oppression of Palestinian Muslims. In the wake of the September 11 attacks, President Bush's public approval rating skyrocketed as he sought a global alliance against terrorism and won at least verbal support from most governments.

On October 11, the United States and Britain began bombing Afghanistan, and American special forces aided the Northern Alliance, the Taliban government's main opposition. By December, the Taliban government was destroyed, but bin Laden eluded capture, continuing to direct Al Qaeda forces throughout the world, until U.S. special forces killed him in Pakistan in 2011. Afghans elected a new national government, but the Taliban remained strong in large parts of the county, and economic stability and physical security remained out of reach.

At home, the balance between liberty and security tilted. Throughout the country, anti-immigrant sentiment revived, and anyone appearing to be Middle Eastern or practicing Islam was likely to arouse suspicion. Even though President Bush reminded Americans that "the enemy of America is not our many Muslim friends," authorities arrested more than a thousand Arabs and Muslims, and a Justice Department study later reported that many people with no connection to terrorism spent months in jail, denied their rights. "I think America overreacted . . . by singling out Arab-named men like myself," said Shanaz Mohammed, who was jailed for eight months for an immigration violation.

In October 2001, Congress passed the **USA Patriot Act** by huge majorities. The law gave the government new powers to monitor suspected terrorists and their associates, including the ability to access personal information, while allowing more exchange of information between criminal investigators and those investigating foreign threats. It soon provoked calls for revision from both conservatives and liberals. Kathleen MacKenzie, a councilwoman in Ann Arbor, Michigan, explained why the council opposed the Patriot Act: "As concerned as we were about national safety, we felt that giving up [rights] was too high a price to pay." A security official countered, "If you don't violate someone's human rights some of the time, you probably aren't doing your job."

Insisting that presidential powers were virtually limitless in times of national crisis, Bush stretched his authority as commander in chief until he met resistance from the courts and Congress. In 2001, the administration established special military commissions to try prisoners captured in Afghanistan and taken to the U.S. military base at Guantánamo, Cuba. But in 2006, responding to a suit filed by one of the approximately five hundred detainees who had languished there for years, the Supreme Court ruled five to three that Congress had not authorized such tribunals and that they violated international law. That year, congressional leaders became openly critical of the administration for wiretapping phone conversations of U.S. residents without obtaining the warrants required by law.

The government also sought to protect Americans from future terrorist attacks through the greatest reorganization of the executive branch since 1948. In November 2002, Congress authorized the new **Department of Homeland Security**, combining 170,000 federal employees from twenty-two agencies that had responsibilities for various aspects of domestic security. Chief among the department's duties were intelligence analysis; immigration and border security; chemical, biological, and nuclear countermeasures; and emergency preparedness and response.

Unilateralism, Preemption, and the Iraq War

The Bush administration sought collective action against the Taliban, but on most other international issues it adopted a go-it-alone approach. In addition to withdrawing from the Kyoto Protocol on global warming and violating international rules about the treatment of military prisoners, it scrapped the 1972 Antiballistic Missile Treaty in order to develop the space-based Strategic Defense Initiative first proposed by Ronald Reagan. Bush also withdrew the nation from the UN's International Criminal Court, and he rejected an agreement to enforce bans on the development and possession of biological weapons — an agreement signed by all of America's European allies.

Nowhere was the new policy of unilateralism more striking than in a new war against Iraq, a war endorsed by Vice President Dick Cheney and Secretary of Defense Donald H. Rumsfeld, but not by Secretary of State Colin Powell. Addressing West Point graduates in June 2002, President Bush proclaimed a new policy for American security based not on containment but on preemption: "Traditional concepts of deterrence will not work against a terrorist enemy whose avowed tactics are wanton destruction and the targeting of innocents; whose so-called soldiers seek martyrdom in death and whose most potent protection is statelessness." Because nuclear, chemical, and biological weapons enabled "even weak states and small groups [to] attain a catastrophic power to strike great nations," the United States had to "be ready for preemptive action." The president's claim that the United States had the right to start a war was at odds with international law and with many Americans' understanding of their nation's ideals. It distressed most of America's great-power allies.

The Bush administration moved deliberately to apply the doctrine of preemption to Iraq, whose dictator, Saddam Hussein, appeared to be in violation of UN resolutions from the 1991 Gulf War requiring Iraq to destroy and stop further development of nuclear, chemical, and biological weapons. In November 2002, the United States persuaded the UN Security Council to pass a resolution requiring Iraq to disarm or face "serious consequences." When Iraq failed to comply fully with new UN inspections, the Bush administration decided on war. Making claims (subsequently refuted) that Hussein had links to Al Qaeda and harbored terrorists and that Iraq possessed weapons of mass destruction, the president insisted that the threat was immediate and great enough to justify preemptive action. In opposition were the Arab world and most major nations — including France, Germany, China, and Russia — which preferred to give the UN inspectors more time. Nevertheless, the United States and Britain invaded Iraq on March 19, 2003, supported by some thirty nations (see Map 31.1). Coalition forces won an easy and decisive victory, and Bush declared the end of the **Iraq War** on May 1. Saddam Hussein remained at large until December 2003.

Chaos followed the quick victory over Hussein. Damage from U.S. bombing and widespread looting resulting from the failure of U.S. troops to secure order and provide basic necessities left Iraqis wondering how much they had gained. "With Saddam there was tyranny, but at least you had a salary to put food on your family's table," said a young father from Hussein's hometown of Tikrit. A Baghdad hospital worker complained, "They can take our oil, but at least they should let us have electricity and water." Five years after the invasion, Iraqis had less electricity than they had had before the war, and a majority lacked access to clean water. Continuing violence had caused 2 million to flee their country and displaced 1.9 million within Iraq.

The administration had not planned adequately for the occupation and sent far fewer forces to Iraq than it had deployed in 1991 in response to Iraq's invasion of Kuwait. The 140,000 American forces in Iraq came under attack almost daily from remnants of the former Hussein regime, religious extremists, and hundreds of foreign terrorists now entering the chaotic country. Seeking to divide Iraqis and undermine the occupation, terrorists launched deadly assaults on such targets as the UN mission in Baghdad, as well as on major mosques and Iraqi citizens, resulting in the death of tens of thousands.

The war became an issue in the presidential campaign of 2004, which registered the highest voter turnout since 1968. Massachusetts senator John Kerry, the Democratic nominee, criticized Bush's unilateralist foreign policy and the administration's conduct of the war. A slim majority of voters, however, indicated their belief that Bush would better protect American security from terrorist threats than Kerry. The president eked out a 286 to 252 victory in the electoral college, winning 50.7 percent of the popular vote to Kerry's 48.3 percent and carrying Republican majorities into Congress.

In June 2004, the United States transferred sovereignty to an interim Iraqi government, and in January 2005 Iraqis elected a national assembly. The daunting challenge facing the national assembly was to organize a government satisfactory to Iraq's three major groups — Sunnis, Shiites, and Kurds. Violence escalated against government officials, Iraqi civilians, and occupation forces. A nineteen-year-old Iraqi confined to his house by his parents, who feared he could be killed or lured into terrorist activities, said, "If I'm killed, it doesn't even matter because I'm dead right now." By 2006, when U.S. military deaths approached 3,000 and Iraqi civilian casualties reached tens of thousands, public opinion polls in the United States found that a majority of Americans believed that the Iraq War was a mistake.

The president's father, George H. W. Bush, had refused to invade Iraq at the end of the 1991 Gulf War. He explained that Colin Powell, Dick Cheney, and other advisers agreed that "unilaterally exceeding the United Nations' mandate would have destroyed the precedent of international response to aggression that we hoped to establish." The first Bush administration resisted making the nation "an occupying power in a bitterly hostile land," refusing to incur the "incalculable human and political costs" that such an invasion would produce.

By 2006, his son's very different approach was subject to criticism that crossed party lines and included leading military figures. Critics acknowledged that the U.S. military had felled a brutal dictator, but coalition forces were not large enough or adequately prepared for the turmoil that followed the invasion. Nor did they find the weapons of mass destruction or links to Osama bin Laden that administration officials had insisted made the war necessary. Rather, in the chaos induced by the invasion, more than a thousand terrorists entered Iraq — the place, according to one expert, "for fundamentalists to go . . . to stick it to the West."

The war and occupation exacted a steep price not only in dollars but also in American and Iraqi lives, U.S. relations with the other great powers, and the nation's reputation in the world, especially among Arab nations. Revelations of prisoner abuse in the Abu Ghraib prison in Iraq and in the Guantánamo detention camp housing captives from the Afghan war further tarnished the United States' image. Anti-Americanism around the world rose to its highest point in history. The budget deficit swelled, and resources were diverted to Iraq from other national security challenges, including the stabilization of Afghanistan, the elimination of bin Laden and Al Qaeda, and the threats posed by North Korea's and Iran's pursuit of nuclear weapons.

Voters registered their dissatisfaction in 2006, turning control of both houses of Congress over to the Democrats for the first time since 1994. President Bush replaced Secretary of Defense Donald Rumsfeld, and the administration displayed more willingness to work with other nations in dealing with Iraq, Iran, and North Korea. Yet Bush clung to the goal of bringing democracy to the Middle East, even as the situation in Iraq deteriorated. Despite opposition from Democrats in Congress, who wanted a timetable for withdrawal from Iraq, in 2007 the administration began a troop surge that increased U.S. forces there to 160,000. The surge, along with actions by Iraqi leaders, contributed to a significant reduction in terrorist violence, and the administration began planning for the eventual withdrawal of U.S. forces by the end of 2011.

REVIEW Why did the United States invade Iraq in March 2003?

▶ The Obama Presidency: Reform and Backlash

Despite the improving situation in Iraq, President Bush's approval ratings sank below 30 percent, posing severe difficulties for the Republican Party in the 2008 elections. The Republicans nominated John McCain, a Vietnam War hero and longtime senator from Arizona, who chose as his running mate Alaska governor Sarah Palin, the second woman to run for vice president on a major party ticket. Even more historic changes occurred in the Democratic Party when, for the first time, an African American and a woman were the top two contenders. In hard-fought

The Inauguration of Barack Obama
President Barack Obama and his wife, Michelle, walk down Pennsylvania Avenue after his inauguration at the Capitol on January 20, 2009. In his inaugural address, Obama spoke of "this winter of our hardship," referring to economic crisis, wars in Iraq and Afghanistan, and other challenges facing the nation. While the most people ever to attend an inauguration absorbed his sober message, they also radiated feelings of sheer joy and hope. AP Images/Doug Mills/Pool.

battles that continued until the last primaries in June, **Barack Obama** edged out New York senator and former First Lady **Hillary Rodham Clinton**, for the presidential nomination.

Born to a white mother and a Kenyan father and raised in Hawai'i and Indonesia, Obama was the first African American to head the *Harvard Law Review*. He settled in Chicago, served in the Illinois Senate, and won election to the U.S. Senate in 2004. At the age of forty-seven, Obama won the Democratic nomination with a combination of a brilliant campaign strategy based on grass-roots and Internet organizing and the ability to speak to deep-seated longings for a new kind of politics and racial reconciliation. He won 53 percent of the popular vote and defeated McCain 365 to 173 in the electoral college, while Democrats increased their majorities in the House and Senate.

Obama hoped to work across party lines, nodding to both conservatives and liberals when he defined "individual responsibility and mutual responsibility" as "the essence of the American promise." The first African American president pledged to pursue a series of reforms in health care, education, the environment, and immigration policy, but he confronted the worst economic crisis since the 1980s. A recession struck in 2008, fueled by a breakdown in financial institutions that had accumulated trillions of dollars of bad debt, largely from the making of loans for overpriced houses to people who lacked the capacity to repay them. As the recession spread to other parts of the world, home mortgage foreclosures skyrocketed, major companies went bankrupt, and unemployment rose to 9.8 percent in late 2010, the highest rate in more than twenty-five years. The financial crisis was so severe that Congress passed the Bush administration's $700 billion Troubled Assets Relief Program in 2008 to inject credit into the economy and shore up banks and other businesses. Obama followed with the **American Recovery and Reinvestment Act of 2009**, $787 billion worth of spending and tax cuts to stimulate the economy and relieve unemployment. Finally, in an effort to prevent the conditions that triggered the financial crisis, he persuaded Congress to expand governmental regulation with the **Wall Street Reform and Consumer Protection Act** in 2010.

Obama's judicial appointments increased the number of women on the Supreme Court to three and included the first ever Latina justice. The president implemented reforms in education, and he signed laws strengthening women's right to equal pay and protecting credit-card holders. His most substantial domestic achievement was passage of a health care reform bill over unanimous Republican opposition. The **Patient Protection and Affordable Care Act** of 2010 extended health insurance to thirty million Americans. It provided subsidies and compelled larger businesses to offer coverage, imposed new regulations on insurance companies to protect their customers, and contained provisions to limit health care costs. Although liberals failed to get a public option to allow government-managed programs to compete with private insurance plans, the law represented the largest expansion of government since the Great Society. One journalist remarked that its passage made Obama "a figure in history for reasons far beyond the color of his skin."

In foreign affairs, Obama reached out to Muslim nations, recommitted the United States to multilateralism, and worked to contain the proliferation of nuclear weapons. He continued the Bush administration's plan to withdraw from Iraq. When the last combat troops departed in 2010, 50,000 U.S. military personnel remained to train and assist Iraqi security forces while leaders struggled to build a stable government that could win the confidence of the three major factions. On Afghanistan, even though corruption permeated its government and a majority of Americans opposed that war, Obama accepted the advice of military leaders that more troops were needed to contain the Taliban insurgents and secure the government. He dispatched an additional 50,000 military personnel to Afghanistan with the promise that the United States could begin to draw down its commitment in mid-2011.

Voters were much more concerned with domestic issues when they issued a sharp rebuke to Obama in the 2010 midterm elections, turning over the House to the Republicans and cutting into the Democratic majority in the Senate. Nearly 10 percent of American workers were unemployed, the federal deficit that Obama had inherited from the Bush administration soared to $1.4 trillion, and a vocal minority of older and mostly white voters expressed their fury at what they considered an overreaching government by joining grassroots movements that took the name the Tea Party revolt. As one Tea Party supporter put it, "The government is taking over everything — I want my freedom back." The intensely polarized political environment would complicate Obama's efforts to reduce unemployment and cut into the enormous federal debt and would imperil his agenda of reform in environmental and immigration policy.

REVIEW   What obstacles stood in the way of Obama's reform agenda?

▶ Conclusion: Defining the Government's Role at Home and Abroad

More than two hundred years after the birth of the United States, Colin Powell referred to the unfinished nature of the American promise when he declared that the question of America's role in the world "isn't answered yet." In fact, the end of the Cold War, the rise of international terrorism, and the George W. Bush administration's doctrines of preemption and unilateralism sparked new debates over the long-standing question of how the United States should act beyond its borders.

Nor had Americans set to rest questions about the role of government at home. In a population so greatly derived from people fleeing oppressive governments, Americans had debated for more than two centuries what responsibilities the government should shoulder and what was best left to private enterprise, families, churches, and other voluntary institutions. Far more than most industrialized democracies, the United States had relied on private rather than public obligation, individual rather than collective solutions. In the twentieth century, Americans had significantly enlarged the federal government's powers and responsibilities, but the years since the 1960s had seen a decline of trust in government's ability to improve people's lives, even as a poverty rate of 20 percent among children and a growing gap between rich and poor survived the economic boom of the 1990s.

The shifting of control of the government back and forth between Republicans and Democrats from 1989 to 2010 revealed a dynamic debate over government's role in domestic affairs. The protections enacted for people with disabilities during the first Bush administration and Bill Clinton's incremental reforms both built on a deep-rooted tradition that sought to realize the American promise of justice and human well-being. Those who mobilized against the ravages of globalization worked internationally for what populists, progressives, New Deal reformers, and many activists of the 1960s had sought for the domestic population: protection of individual rights, curbs on capitalism, assistance for victims of rapid economic change, and fiscal policies that placed greater responsibility on those best able to pay for the collective good. Even the second Bush administration, which sought to limit government's reach, supported the No Child Left Behind Act and the Medicare prescription drug program, and it departed from traditional conservative policy in the gigantic program to bail out failing businesses when the financial crisis hit the economy in 2008. The bitter controversy surrounding Obama's health care reform replayed America's long-standing debate about the government's appropriate role.

The United States became ever more deeply embedded in the global economy as products, information, and people crossed borders with amazing speed and frequency. Although the end of the Cold War brought about unanticipated cooperation between the United States and its former enemies, globalization also contributed to international instability and the threat of deadly terrorism to a nation unaccustomed to foreign attacks within its own borders. In response to those dangers, the second Bush administration departed from the multilateral approach to foreign policy that had been built up by Republican and Democratic administrations alike since World War II. Toward the end of his second term, however, Bush worked to improve international relationships, and Obama promised a new approach in American relations with the world.

Reviewing Chapter 31

REVIEW QUESTIONS

1. How did George H. W. Bush respond to threats to U.S. interests as the Cold War came to an end? (pp. 942–950)

2. What policies of the Clinton administration moved the Democratic Party to the right? (pp. 950–955)

3. Who criticized free trade agreements and why? (pp. 955–961)

4. Why did the United States invade Iraq in March 2003? (pp. 961–969)

5. What obstacles stood in the way of Obama's reform agenda? (pp. 969–972)

MAKING CONNECTIONS

1. How did George H. W. Bush continue the policies of his predecessor, Ronald Reagan? How did he depart from them?

2. President Bill Clinton called himself a "New Democrat." How did his policies and goals differ from those of Democrats in the past?

3. In the late twentieth century, economic globalization transformed the United States. Explain what globalization is, and describe how it affected the U.S. economy and population in the 1990s.

4. The terrorist attacks of September 11, 2001, were unprecedented. What gave rise to the attacks? How did the nation respond?

LINKING TO THE PAST

1. How did George W. Bush's doctrine of preemption differ from the doctrine of containment? (See chapter 26.)

2. What features did the immigration after 1980 have in common with the immigration between 1880 and 1920? What was different? (See chapter 19.)

TIMELINE 1988–2011

1988 • Republican George H. W. Bush elected president.

1989 • Communism collapses in Eastern Europe.
• United States invades Panama.

1990 • Americans with Disabilities Act.

1991 • Persian Gulf War.

1992 • Democrat William Jefferson "Bill" Clinton elected president.

1993 • Israel and PLO sign peace accords.
• North American Free Trade Agreement (NAFTA).

1994 • United States sends troops to Haiti.
• General Agreement on Tariffs and Trade establishes World Trade Organization (WTO).

1995 • Bombing of federal building in Oklahoma City.
• United States, with NATO, bombs Serbia.

1996 • Personal Responsibility and Work Opportunity Reconciliation Act.
• President Clinton reelected.

1998 • United States bombs terrorist sites in Afghanistan and Sudan.

1998–2000 • United States bombs Iraq

1999 • Senate trial fails to approve impeachment of Clinton.

2000 • Republican George W. Bush elected president.

2001 • September 11. Terrorists attack World Trade Center and Pentagon.
• U.S.-led coalition attacks Afghanistan, driving out Taliban government.
• USA Patriot Act.
• $1.35 trillion tax cut.

2002 • No Child Left Behind Act.
• Department of Homeland Security established.

2003 • United States attacks Iraq.
• Prescription drug coverage added to Medicare.

2004 • George W. Bush reelected president.

2005 • Hurricane Katrina.

2007 • Bush begins troop surge in Iraq.

2008 • Worst financial crisis since the Great Depression.
• Troubled Asset Relief Program.
• Democrat Barack Obama elected president.

2009 • American Recovery and Reinvestment Act.

2010 • Patient Protection and Affordable Care Act.
• Wall Street Reform and Consumer Protection Act.
• United States ends combat operations in Iraq, increases troops in Afghanistan.

2011 • U.S. forces kill Osama bin Laden in Pakistan

▶ **FOR AN ONLINE BIBLIOGRAPHY, PRACTICE QUIZZES, WEB SITES, IMAGES, AND DOCUMENTS RELATED TO THIS CHAPTER,** see the Book Companion Site at **bedfordstmartins.com/roarkvalue**.

▶ **FOR DOCUMENTS RELATED TO THIS PERIOD,** see Michael Johnson, ed., *Reading the American Past*, Fifth Edition.

Appendix

THE DECLARATION OF INDEPENDENCE

In Congress, July 4, 1776,

The Unanimous Declaration of the Thirteen United States of America

When in the course of human events, it becomes necessary for one people to dissolve the political bands which have connected them with another, and to assume, among the powers of the earth, the separate and equal station to which the laws of nature and of nature's God entitle them, a decent respect to the opinions of mankind requires that they should declare the causes which impel them to the separation.

We hold these truths to be self-evident, that all men are created equal; that they are endowed by their Creator with certain unalienable rights; that among these, are life, liberty, and the pursuit of happiness. That, to secure these rights, governments are instituted among men, deriving their just powers from the consent of the governed; that, whenever any form of government becomes destructive of these ends, it is the right of the people to alter or to abolish it, and to institute a new government, laying its foundation on such principles, and organizing its powers in such form, as to them shall seem most likely to effect their safety and happiness. Prudence, indeed, will dictate that governments long established, should not be changed for light and transient causes; and, accordingly, all experience hath shown, that mankind are more disposed to suffer, while evils are sufferable, than to right themselves by abolishing the forms to which they are accustomed. But, when a long train of abuses and usurpations, pursuing invariably the same object, evinces a design to reduce them under absolute despotism, it is their right, it is their duty, to throw off such government and to provide new guards for their future security. Such has been the patient sufferance of these colonies, and such is now the necessity which constrains them to alter their former systems of government. The history of the present King of Great Britain is a history of repeated injuries and usurpations, all having, in direct object, the establishment of an absolute tyranny over these States. To prove this, let facts be submitted to a candid world:

He has refused his assent to laws the most wholesome and necessary for the public good.

He has forbidden his governors to pass laws of immediate and pressing importance, unless suspended in their operation till his assent should be obtained; and, when so suspended, he has utterly neglected to attend to them.

He has refused to pass other laws for the accommodation of large districts of people, unless those people would relinquish the right of representation in the legislature; a right inestimable to them, and formidable to tyrants only.

He has called together legislative bodies at places unusual, uncomfortable, and distant from the depository of their public records, for the sole purpose of fatiguing them into compliance with his measures.

He has dissolved representative houses repeatedly for opposing, with manly firmness, his invasions on the rights of the people.

He has refused, for a long time after such dissolutions, to cause others to be elected; whereby the legislative powers, incapable of annihilation, have returned to the people at large for their exercise; the state remaining in the mean-time exposed to all the danger of invasion from without, and convulsions within.

He has endeavoured to prevent the population of these States; for that purpose, obstructing the laws for naturalization of foreigners, refusing to pass others to encourage their migration hither, and raising the conditions of new appropriations of lands.

He has obstructed the administration of justice, by refusing his assent to laws for establishing judiciary powers.

He has made judges dependent on his will alone, for the tenure of their offices, and the amount and payment of their salaries.

He has erected a multitude of new offices, and sent hither swarms of officers to harass our people, and eat out their substance.

He has kept among us, in times of peace, standing armies, without the consent of our legislature.

He has affected to render the military independent of, and superior to, the civil power.

He has combined, with others, to subject us to a jurisdiction foreign to our Constitution, and unacknowledged by our laws; giving his assent to their acts of pretended legislation:

For quartering large bodies of armed troops among us:

For protecting them by a mock trial, from punishment, for any murders which they should commit on the inhabitants of these States:

For cutting off our trade with all parts of the world:

For imposing taxes on us without our consent:

For depriving us, in many cases, of the benefit of trial by jury:

For transporting us beyond seas to be tried for pretended offences:

For abolishing the free system of English laws in a neighboring province, establishing therein an arbitrary government, and enlarging its boundaries, so as to render it at once an example and fit instrument for introducing the same absolute rule into these colonies:

For taking away our charters, abolishing our most valuable laws, and altering, fundamentally, the powers of our governments:

For suspending our own legislatures, and declaring themselves invested with power to legislate for us in all cases whatsoever.

He has abdicated government here, by declaring us out of his protection, and waging war against us.

He has plundered our seas, ravaged our coasts, burnt our towns, and destroyed the lives of our people.

He is, at this time, transporting large armies of foreign mercenaries to complete the works of death, desolation, and tyranny, already begun, with circumstances of cruelty and perfidy scarcely paralleled in the most barbarous ages, and totally unworthy the head of a civilized nation.

He has constrained our fellow citizens, taken captive on the high seas, to bear arms against their country, to become the executioners of their friends, and brethren, or to fall themselves by their hands.

He has excited domestic insurrections amongst us, and has endeavored to bring on the inhabitants of our frontiers, the merciless Indian savages, whose known rule of warfare is an undistinguished destruction of all ages, sexes, and conditions.

In every stage of these oppressions, we have petitioned for redress; in the most humble terms; our repeated petitions have been answered only by repeated injury. A prince, whose character is thus marked by every act which may define a tyrant, is unfit to be the ruler of a free people.

Nor have we been wanting in attention to our British brethren. We have warned them, from time to time, of attempts made by their legislature to extend an unwarrantable jurisdiction over us. We have reminded them of the circumstances of our emigration and settlement here. We have appealed to their native justice and magnanimity, and we have conjured them, by the ties of our common kindred, to disavow these usurpations, which would inevitably interrupt our connections and correspondence. They, too, have been deaf to the voice of justice and consanguinity. We must, therefore, acquiesce in the necessity which denounces our separation, and hold them as we hold the rest of mankind, enemies in war, in peace, friends.

We, therefore, the representatives of the United States of America, in general Congress assembled, appealing to the Supreme Judge of the world for the rectitude of our intentions, do, in the name, and by authority of the good people of these colonies, solemnly publish and declare, that these united colonies are, and of right ought to be, free and independent states: that they are absolved from all allegiance to the British Crown, and that all political connection between them and the state of Great Britain is, and ought to be, totally dissolved; and that, as free and independent states, they have full power to levy war, conclude peace, contract alliances, establish commerce, and to do all other acts and things which independent states may of right do. And, for the support of this declaration, with a firm reliance on the protection of Divine Providence, we mutually pledge to each other our lives, our fortunes, and our sacred honor.

The foregoing Declaration was, by order of Congress, engrossed, and signed by the following members:

John Hancock

New Hampshire
Josiah Bartlett
William Whipple
Matthew Thornton

Massachusetts Bay
Samuel Adams
John Adams
Robert Treat Paine
Elbridge Gerry

Rhode Island
Stephen Hopkins
William Ellery

Connecticut
Roger Sherman
Samuel
   Huntington
William Williams
Oliver Wolcott

New York
William Floyd
Phillip Livingston
Francis Lewis
Lewis Morris

New Jersey
Richard Stockton
John Witherspoon
Francis Hopkinson
John Hart
Abraham Clark

Pennsylvania
Robert Morris
Benjamin Rush
Benjamin Franklin
John Morton
George Clymer
James Smith
George Taylor
James Wilson
George Ross

Delaware
Caesar Rodney
George Read
Thomas M'Kean

Maryland
Samuel Chase
William Paca
Thomas Stone
Charles Carroll,
   of Carrollton

North Carolina
William Hooper
Joseph Hewes
John Penn

South Carolina
Edward Rutledge
Thomas
   Heyward, Jr.
Thomas Lynch, Jr.
Arthur Middleton

Virginia
George Wythe
Richard Henry Lee
Thomas Jefferson
Benjamin Harrison
Thomas Nelson, Jr.
Francis Lightfoot
   Lee
Carter Braxton

Georgia
Button Gwinnett
Lyman Hall
George Walton

Resolved, That copies of the Declaration be sent to the several assemblies, conventions, and committees, or councils of safety, and to the several commanding officers of the continental troops; that it be proclaimed in each of the United States, at the head of the army.

THE ARTICLES OF CONFEDERATION AND PERPETUAL UNION

Agreed to in Congress, November 15, 1777.
Ratified March 1781.

BETWEEN THE STATES OF NEW HAMPSHIRE, MASSACHUSETTS BAY, RHODE ISLAND AND PROVIDENCE PLANTATIONS, CONNECTICUT, NEW YORK, NEW JERSEY, PENNSYLVANIA, DELAWARE, MARYLAND, VIRGINIA, NORTH CAROLINA, SOUTH CAROLINA, GEORGIA.*

Article 1

The stile of this confederacy shall be "The United States of America."

Article 2

Each State retains its sovereignty, freedom and independence, and every power, jurisdiction, and right, which is not by this confederation expressly delegated to the United States, in Congress assembled.

Article 3

The said states hereby severally enter into a firm league of friendship with each other for their common defence, the security of their liberties and their mutual and general welfare; binding themselves to assist each other against all force offered to, or attacks made upon them, or any of them, on account of religion, sovereignty, trade, or any other pretence whatever.

Article 4

The better to secure and perpetuate mutual friendship and intercourse among the people of the different states in this union, the free inhabitants of each of these states, paupers, vagabonds, and fugitives from justice excepted, shall be entitled to all privileges and immunities of free citizens in the several states; and the people of each State shall have free ingress and regress to and from any other State, and shall enjoy therein all the privileges of trade and commerce, subject to the same duties, impositions, and restrictions, as the inhabitants thereof respectively; provided, that such restrictions shall not extend so far as to prevent the removal of property, imported into any State, to any other State of which the owner is an inhabitant; provided also, that no imposition, duties, or restriction, shall be laid by any State on the property of the United States, or either of them.

If any person guilty of, or charged with treason, felony, or other high misdemeanor in any State, shall flee from justice and be found in any of the United States, he shall, upon demand of the governor or executive power of the State from which he fled, be delivered up and removed to the State having jurisdiction of his offence.

Full faith and credit shall be given in each of these states to the records, acts, and judicial proceedings of the courts and magistrates of every other State.

---

*This copy of the final draft of the Articles of Confederation is taken from the *Journals*, 9:907–925, November 15, 1777.

Article 5

For the more convenient management of the general interests of the United States, delegates shall be annually appointed, in such manner as the legislature of each State shall direct, to meet in Congress, on the 1st Monday in November in every year, with a power reserved to each State to recall its delegates, or any of them, at any time within the year, and to send others in their stead for the remainder of the year.

No State shall be represented in Congress by less than two, nor by more than seven members; and no person shall be capable of being a delegate for more than three years in any term of six years; nor shall any person, being a delegate, be capable of holding any office under the United States, for which he, or any other for his benefit, receives any salary, fees, or emolument of any kind.

Each State shall maintain its own delegates in a meeting of the states, and while they act as members of the committee of the states.

In determining questions in the United States, in Congress assembled, each State shall have one vote.

Freedom of speech and debate in Congress shall not be impeached or questioned in any court or place out of Congress: and the members of Congress shall be protected in their persons from arrests and imprisonments, during the time of their going to and from, and attendance on Congress, except for treason, felony, or breach of the peace.

Article 6

No State, without the consent of the United States, in Congress assembled, shall send any embassy to, or receive any embassy from, or enter into any conference, agreement, alliance, or treaty with any king, prince, or state; nor shall any person, holding any office of profit or trust under the United States, or any of them, accept of any present, emolument, office or title, of any kind whatever, from any king, prince, or foreign state; nor shall the United States, in Congress assembled, or any of them, grant any title of nobility.

No two or more states shall enter into any treaty, confederation, or alliance, whatever, between them, without the consent of the United States, in Congress assembled, specifying accurately the purposes for which the same is to be entered into, and how long it shall continue.

No state shall lay any imposts or duties which may interfere with any stipulations in treaties entered into by the United States, in Congress assembled, with any king, prince, or state, in pursuance of any treaties already proposed by Congress to the courts of France and Spain.

No vessels of war shall be kept up in time of peace by any State, except such number only as shall be deemed necessary by the United States, in Congress assembled, for the defence of such State or its trade; nor shall any body of forces be kept up by any State, in time of peace, except such number only as, in the judgment of the United States, in Congress assembled, shall be deemed requisite to garrison the forts necessary for the defence of such State; but every State shall always keep up a well regulated and disciplined militia, sufficiently armed and accoutred, and shall provide, and constantly have ready for use, in public stores, a due number of field pieces and tents, and a proper quantity of arms, ammunition and camp equipage.

No State shall engage in any war without the consent of the United States, in Congress assembled, unless such State be actually invaded by enemies, or shall have received certain advice of a resolution being formed by some nation of Indians to invade such State, and the danger is so imminent as not to admit of a delay till the United States, in Congress assembled, can be consulted; nor shall any State grant commissions to any ships or vessels of war, nor letters of marque or reprisal, except it be after a declaration of war by the United States, in Congress assembled, and then only against the kingdom or state, and the subjects thereof, against which war has been so declared, and under such regulations as shall be established by the United States, in Congress assembled, unless such State be infested by pirates, in which case vessels of war may be fitted out for that occasion, and kept so long as the danger shall continue, or until the United States, in Congress assembled, shall determine otherwise.

Article 7

When land forces are raised by any State for the common defence, all officers of or under the rank of colonel, shall be appointed by the legislature of each State respectively, by whom such forces shall be raised, or in such manner as such State shall direct; and all vacancies shall be filled up by the State which first made the appointment.

Article 8

All charges of war and all other expences, that shall be incurred for the common defence or general welfare, and allowed by the United States, in Congress assembled, shall be defrayed out of a common treasury, which shall be supplied by the several states, in proportion to the value of all land within each State, granted to or surveyed for any person, as such land and the buildings and improvements thereon shall be estimated according to such mode as the United States, in Congress assembled, shall, from time to time, direct and appoint.

The taxes for paying that proportion shall be laid and levied by the authority and direction of the legislatures of the several states, within the time agreed upon by the United States, in Congress assembled.

Article 9

The United States, in Congress assembled, shall have the sole and exclusive right and power of determining on peace and war, except in the cases mentioned in the 6th article; of sending and receiving ambassadors; entering into treaties and alliances, provided that no treaty of commerce shall be made, whereby the legislative power of the respective states shall be restrained from imposing such imposts and duties on foreigners as their own people are subjected to, or from prohibiting the exportation or importation of any species of goods or commodities whatsoever; of establishing rules for deciding, in all cases, what captures on land or water shall be legal, and in what manner prizes, taken by land or naval forces in the service of the United States, shall be divided or appropriated; of granting letters of marque and reprisal in times of peace; appointing courts for the trial of piracies and felonies committed on the high seas, and establishing courts for receiving and determining, finally, appeals in all cases of captures; provided, that no member of Congress shall be appointed a judge of any of the said courts.

The United States, in Congress assembled, shall also be the last resort on appeal in all disputes and differences now subsisting, or that hereafter may arise between two or more states concerning boundary, jurisdiction or any other cause whatever; which authority shall always be exercised in the manner following: whenever the legislative or executive authority, or lawful agent of any State, in controversy with another, shall present a petition to Congress, stating the matter in question, and praying for a hearing, notice thereof shall be given, by order of Congress, to the legislative or executive authority of the other State in controversy, and a day assigned for the appearance of the parties by their lawful agents, who shall then be directed to appoint, by joint consent, commissioners or judges to constitute a court for hearing and determining the matter in question; but, if they cannot agree, Congress shall name three persons out of each of the United States, and from the list of such persons each party shall alternately strike out one, the petitioners beginning, until the number shall be reduced to thirteen; and from that number not less than seven, nor more than nine names, as Congress shall direct, shall, in the presence of Congress, be drawn out by lot; and the persons whose names shall be so drawn, or any five of them, shall be commissioners or judges to hear and finally determine the controversy, so always as a major part of the judges who shall hear the cause shall agree in the determination; and if either party shall neglect to attend at the day appointed, without shewing reasons which Congress shall judge sufficient, or, being present, shall refuse to strike, the Congress shall proceed to nominate three persons out of each State, and the secretary of Congress shall strike in behalf of such party absent or refusing; and the judgment and sentence of the court to be appointed, in the manner before prescribed, shall be final and conclusive; and if any of the parties shall refuse to submit to the authority of such court, or to appear or defend their claim or cause, the court shall nevertheless proceed to pronounce sentence or judgment, which shall, in like manner, be final and decisive, the judgment or sentence and other proceedings begin, in either case, transmitted to Congress, and lodged among the acts of Congress for the security of the parties concerned: provided, that every commissioner, before he sits in judgment, shall take an oath, to be administered by one of the judges of the supreme or superior court of the State where the cause shall be tried, "well and truly to hear and determine the matter in question, according to the best of his judgment, without favour, affection, or hope of reward:" provided, also, that no State shall be deprived of territory for the benefit of the United States.

All controversies concerning the private right of soil, claimed under different grants of two or more states, whose jurisdictions, as they may respect such lands and the states which passed such grants, are adjusted, the said grants, or either of them, being at the same time claimed to have originated antecedent to such settlement of jurisdiction, shall, on the petition of either party to the Congress of the United States, be finally determined, as near as may be, in the same manner as is before prescribed for deciding disputes respecting territorial jurisdiction between different states.

The United States, in Congress assembled, shall also have the sole and exclusive right and power of regulating the alloy and value of coin struck by their own authority, or by that of the respective states; fixing the standard of weights and measures throughout the United States; regulating the trade and managing all affairs with the Indians not members of any of the states; provided that the legislative right of any State within its own limits be not infringed or violated; establishing and regulating post offices from one State to another throughout all the United States, and exacting such postage on the papers passing through the same as may be requisite to defray the expences of the said office; appointing all officers of the land forces in the service of the United States, excepting regimental officers; appointing all the officers of the naval forces, and commissioning all officers whatever in the service of the United States; making rules for the government and regulation of the said land and naval forces, and directing their operations.

The United States, in Congress assembled, shall have authority to appoint a committee to sit in the recess of Congress, to be denominated "a Committee of the States," and to consist of one delegate from each State, and to appoint such other committees and civil officers as may be necessary for managing the general affairs of the United States, under their direction; to appoint one of their number to preside; provided that no person be allowed to serve in the office of president more than one year in any term of three years; to ascertain the necessary sums of money to be raised for the service of the United States, and to appropriate and apply the same for defraying the public expences; to borrow money or emit bills on the credit of the United States, transmitting, every half year, to the respective states, an account of the sums of money so borrowed or emitted; to build and equip a navy; to agree upon the number of land forces, and to make requisitions from each State for its quota, in proportion to the number of white inhabitants in such State; which requisitions shall be binding; and thereupon, the legislature of each State shall appoint the regimental officers, raise the men, and cloathe, arm, and equip them in a soldier-like manner, at the expence of the United States; and the officers and men so cloathed, armed, and equipped, shall march to the place appointed and within the time agreed on by the United States, in Congress assembled; but if the United States, in Congress assembled, shall, on consideration of circumstances, judge proper that any State should not raise men, or should raise a smaller number than its quota, and that any other State should raise a greater number of men than the quota thereof, such extra number shall be raised, officered, cloathed, armed, and equipped in the same manner as the quota of such State, unless the legislature of such State shall judge that such extra number cannot be safely spared out of the same, in which case they shall raise, officer, cloathe, arm, and equip as many of such extra number as they judge can be safely spared. And the officers and men so cloathed, armed, and equipped, shall march to the place appointed and within the time agreed on by the United States, in Congress assembled.

The United States, in Congress assembled, shall never engage in a war, nor grant letters of marque and reprisal in time of peace, nor enter into any treaties or alliances, nor coin money, nor regulate the value thereof, nor ascertain the sums and expences necessary for the defence and welfare of the United States, or any of them: nor emit bills, nor borrow money on the credit of the United States, nor appropriate money, nor agree upon the number of vessels of war to be built or purchased, or the number of land or sea forces to be raised, nor appoint a commander in chief of the army or navy, unless nine states assent to the same; nor shall a question on any other point, except for adjourning from day to day, be determined, unless by the votes of a majority of the United States, in Congress assembled.

The Congress of the United States shall have power to adjourn to any time within the year, and to any place within the United States, so that no period of adjournment be for a longer duration than the space of six months, and shall publish the journal of their proceedings monthly, except such parts thereof, relating to treaties, alliances or military operations, as, in their judgment, require secrecy; and the yeas and nays of the delegates of each State on any question shall be entered on the journal, when it is desired by any delegate; and the delegates of a State, or any of them, at his, or their request, shall be furnished with a transcript of the said journal, except such parts as are above excepted, to lay before the legislatures of the several states.

Article 10

The committee of the states, or any nine of them, shall be authorized to execute, in the recess of Congress, such of the powers of Congress as the United States, in Congress assembled, by the consent of nine states, shall, from time to time, think expedient to vest them with; provided, that no power be delegated to the said committee, for the exercise of which, by the articles of confederation, the voice of nine states, in the Congress of the United States assembled, is requisite.

Article 11

Canada acceding to this confederation, and joining in the measures of the United States, shall be admitted into and entitled to all the advantages of this union; but no other colony shall be admitted into the same, unless such admission be agreed to by nine states.

Article 12

All bills of credit emitted, monies borrowed and debts contracted by, or under the authority of Congress before the assembling of the United States, in pursuance of the present confederation, shall be deemed and considered as a charge against the United States, for payment and satisfaction whereof the said United States and the public faith are hereby solemnly pledged.

Article 13

Every State shall abide by the determinations of the United States, in Congress assembled, on all questions which, by this confederation, are submitted to them. And the articles of this confederation shall be inviolably observed by every State, and the union shall be perpetual; nor shall any alteration at any time hereafter be made in any of them, unless such alteration be agreed to in a Congress of the United States, and be afterwards confirmed by the legislatures of every State.

These articles shall be proposed to the legislatures of all the United States, to be considered, and if approved of by them, they are advised to authorize their delegates to ratify the same in the Congress of the United States; which being done, the same shall become conclusive.

THE CONSTITUTION OF THE UNITED STATES*

Agreed to by Philadelphia Convention, September 17, 1787.
Implemented March 4, 1789.

Preamble

We the people of the United States, in order to form a more perfect union, establish justice, insure domestic tranquility, provide for the common defense, promote the general welfare, and secure the blessings of liberty to ourselves and our posterity, do ordain and establish this Constitution for the United States of America.

Article I

Section 1 All legislative powers herein granted shall be vested in a Congress of the United States, which shall consist of a Senate and a House of Representatives.

Section 2 The House of Representatives shall be composed of members chosen every second year by the people of the several States, and the electors in each State shall have the qualifications requisite for electors of the most numerous branch of the State Legislature.

No person shall be a Representative who shall not have attained to the age of twenty-five years, and been seven years a citizen of the United States, and who shall not, when elected, be an inhabitant of that State in which he shall be chosen.

---

*Passages no longer in effect are in italic type.

Representatives and direct taxes shall be apportioned among the several States which may be included within this Union, according to their respective numbers, *which shall be determined by adding to the whole number of free persons, including those bound to service for a term of years and excluding Indians not taxed, three-fifths of all other persons.* The actual enumeration shall be made within three years after the first meeting of the Congress of the United States, and within every subsequent term of ten years, in such manner as they shall by law direct. The number of Representatives shall not exceed one for every thirty thousand, but each State shall have at least one Representative; *and until such enumeration shall be made, the State of New Hampshire shall be entitled to choose three, Massachusetts eight, Rhode Island and Providence Plantations one, Connecticut five, New York six, New Jersey four, Pennsylvania eight, Delaware one, Maryland six, Virginia ten, North Carolina five, South Carolina five, and Georgia three.*

When vacancies happen in the representation from any State, the Executive authority thereof shall issue writs of election to fill such vacancies.

The House of Representatives shall choose their Speaker and other officers; and shall have the sole power of impeachment.

Section 3   The Senate of the United States shall be composed of two Senators from each State, *chosen by the legislature thereof,* for six years; and each Senator shall have one vote.

Immediately after they shall be assembled in consequence of the first election, they shall be divided as equally as may be into three classes. The seats of the Senators of the first class shall be vacated at the expiration of the second year, of the second class at the expiration of the fourth year, and of the third class at the expiration of the sixth year, so that one-third may be chosen every second year; *and if vacancies happen by resignation or otherwise, during the recess of the legislature of any State, the Executive thereof may make temporary appointments until the next meeting of the legislature, which shall then fill such vacancies.*

No person shall be a Senator who shall not have attained to the age of thirty years, and been nine years a citizen of the United States, and who shall not, when elected, be an inhabitant of that State for which he shall be chosen.

The Vice-President of the United States shall be President of the Senate, but shall have no vote, unless they be equally divided.

The Senate shall choose their other officers, and also a President *pro tempore,* in the absence of the Vice-President, or when he shall exercise the office of President of the United States.

The Senate shall have the sole power to try all impeachments. When sitting for that purpose, they shall be on oath or affirmation. When the President of the United States is tried, the Chief Justice shall preside: and no person shall be convicted without the concurrence of two-thirds of the members present.

Judgment in cases of impeachment shall not extend further than to removal from the office, and disqualification to hold and enjoy any office of honor, trust or profit under the United States: but the party convicted shall nevertheless be liable and subject to indictment, trial, judgment and punishment, according to law.

Section 4   The times, places and manner of holding elections for Senators and Representatives shall be prescribed in each State by the legislature thereof; but the Congress may at any time by law make or alter such regulations, except as to the places of choosing Senators.

The Congress shall assemble at least once in every year, and such meeting *shall be on the first Monday in December, unless they shall by law appoint a different day.*

Section 5   Each house shall be the judge of the elections, returns and qualifications of its own members, and a majority of each shall constitute a quorum to do business; but a smaller number may adjourn from day to day, and may be authorized to compel the attendance of absent members, in such manner, and under such penalties, as each house may provide.

Each house may determine the rules of its proceedings, punish its members for disorderly behavior, and with the concurrence of two-thirds, expel a member.

Each house shall keep a journal of its proceedings, and from time to time publish the same, excepting such parts as may in their judgment require secrecy; and the yeas and nays of the members of either house on any question shall, at the desire of one-fifth of those present, be entered on the journal.

Neither house, during the session of Congress, shall, without the consent of the other, adjourn for more than three days, nor to any other place than that in which the two houses shall be sitting.

Section 6   The Senators and Representatives shall receive a compensation for their services, to be ascertained by law and paid out of the treasury of the United States. They shall in all cases except treason, felony and breach of the peace, be privileged from arrest during their attendance at the session of their respective houses, and in going to and returning from the same; and for any speech or debate in either house, they shall not be questioned in any other place.

No Senator or Representative shall, during the time for which he was elected, be appointed to any civil office under the authority of the United States, which shall have been created, or the emoluments whereof shall have been increased, during such time; and no person holding any office under the United States shall be a member of either house during his continuance in office.

Section 7   All bills for raising revenue shall originate in the House of Representatives; but the Senate may propose or concur with amendments as on other bills.

Every bill which shall have passed the House of Representatives and the Senate, shall, before it become a law, be presented to the President of the United States; if he approve he shall sign it, but if not he shall return it with objections to that house in which it shall have originated, who shall enter the objections at large on their journal, and proceed to reconsider it. If after such reconsideration two-thirds of that house shall agree to pass the bill, it shall be sent, together with the objections, to the other house, by which it shall likewise be reconsidered, and, if approved by two-thirds of that house, it shall become a law. But in all such cases the votes of both houses shall be determined by yeas and nays, and the names of the persons voting for and against the bill shall be entered on the journal of each house respectively. If any bill shall not be returned by the President within ten days (Sundays excepted) after it shall have been presented to him, the same shall be a law, in like manner as if he had signed it, unless the Congress by their adjournment prevent its return, in which case it shall not be a law.

Every order, resolution, or vote to which the concurrence of the Senate and House of Representatives may be necessary (except on a question of adjournment) shall be presented to the President of the United States; and before the same shall take effect, shall be approved by him, or being disapproved by him, shall be repassed by two-thirds of the Senate and House of Representatives, according to the rules and limitations prescribed in the case of a bill.

Section 8   The Congress shall have power

To lay and collect taxes, duties, imposts, and excises, to pay the debts and provide for the common defense and general welfare of the United States; but all duties, imposts and excises shall be uniform throughout the United States;

To borrow money on the credit of the United States;

To regulate commerce with foreign nations, and among the several States, and with the Indian tribes;

To establish an uniform rule of naturalization, and uniform laws on the subject of bankruptcies throughout the United States;

To coin money, regulate the value thereof, and of foreign coin, and fix the standard of weights and measures;

To provide for the punishment of counterfeiting the securities and current coin of the United States;

To establish post offices and post roads;

To promote the progress of science and useful arts by securing for limited times to authors and inventors the exclusive right to their respective writings and discoveries;

To constitute tribunals inferior to the Supreme Court;

To define and punish piracies and felonies committed on the high seas and offences against the law of nations;

To declare war, grant letters of marque and reprisal, and make rules concerning captures on land and water;

To raise and support armies, but no appropriation of money to that use shall be for a longer term than two years;

To provide and maintain a navy;

To make rules for the government and regulation of the land and naval forces;

To provide for calling forth the militia to execute the laws of the Union, suppress insurrections and repel invasions;

To provide for organizing, arming, and disciplining the militia, and for governing such part of them as may be employed in the service of the United States, reserving to the States respectively the appointment of the officers, and the authority of training the militia according to the discipline prescribed by Congress;

To exercise exclusive legislation in all cases whatsoever, over such district (not exceeding ten miles square) as may, by cession of particular States, and the acceptance of Congress, become the seat of the government of the United States, and to exercise like authority over all places purchased by the consent of the legislature of the State, in which the same shall be, for erection of forts, magazines, arsenals, dock-yards, and other needful buildings;—and

To make all laws which shall be necessary and proper for carrying into execution the foregoing powers, and all other powers vested by this Constitution in the government of the United States, or in any department or officer thereof.

Section 9   *The migration or importation of such persons as any of the States now existing shall think proper to admit shall not be prohibited by the Congress prior to the year one thousand eight hundred and eight; but a tax or duty may be imposed on such importation, not exceeding ten dollars for each person.*

The privilege of the writ of habeas corpus shall not be suspended, unless when in cases of rebellion or invasion the public safety may require it.

No bill of attainder or ex post facto law shall be passed.

No capitation, or other direct, tax shall be laid, unless in proportion to the census or enumeration herein before directed to be taken.

No tax or duty shall be laid on articles exported from any State.

No preference shall be given by any regulation of commerce or revenue to the ports of one State over those of another; nor shall vessels bound to, or from, one State be obliged to enter, clear, or pay duties in another.

No money shall be drawn from the treasury, but in consequence of appropriations made by law; and a regular statement and account of the receipts and expenditures of all public money shall be published from time to time.

No title of nobility shall be granted by the United States: and no person holding any office of profit or trust under them, shall, without the consent of the Congress, accept of any present, emolument, office, or title, of any kind whatever, from any king, prince, or foreign state.

Section 10 No State shall enter into any treaty, alliance, or confederation; grant letters of marque and reprisal; coin money; emit bills of credit; make anything but gold and silver coin a tender in payment of debts; pass any bill of attainder, ex post facto law, or law impairing the obligation of contracts, or grant any title of nobility.

No State shall, without the consent of Congress, lay any imposts or duties on imports or exports, except what may be absolutely necessary for executing its inspection laws: and the net produce of all duties and imposts, laid by any State on imports or exports, shall be for the use of the treasury of the United States; and all such laws shall be subject to the revision and control of the Congress.

No State shall, without the consent of Congress, lay any duty of tonnage, keep troops, or ships of war in time of peace, enter into any agreement or compact with another State, or with a foreign power, or engage in war, unless actually invaded, or in such imminent danger as will not admit of delay.

Article II

Section 1 The executive power shall be vested in a President of the United States of America. He shall hold his office during the term of four years, and, together with the Vice-President, chosen for the same term, be elected as follows:

Each State shall appoint, in such manner as the legislature thereof may direct, a number of electors, equal to the whole number of Senators and Representatives to which the State may be entitled in the Congress; but no Senator or Representative, or person holding an office of trust or profit under the United States, shall be appointed an elector.

The electors shall meet in their respective States, and vote by ballot for two persons, of whom one at least shall not be an inhabitant of the same State with themselves. And they shall make a list of all the persons voted for, and of the number of votes for each; which list they shall sign and certify, and transmit sealed to the seat of government of the United States, directed to the President of the Senate. The President of the Senate shall, in the presence of the Senate and House of Representatives, open all the certificates, and the votes shall then be counted. The person having the greatest number of votes shall be the President, if such number be a majority of the whole number of electors appointed; and if there be more than one who have such majority, and have an equal number of votes, then the House of Representatives shall immediately choose by ballot one of them for President; and if no person have a majority, then from the five highest on the list said house shall in like man-ner choose the President. But in choosing the President the votes shall be taken by States, the representation from each State having one vote; a quorum for this purpose shall consist of a member or members from two-thirds of the States, and a majority of all the States shall be necessary to a choice. In every case, after the choice of the President, the person having the greatest number of votes of the electors shall be the Vice-President. But if there should remain two or more who have equal votes, the Senate shall choose from them by ballot the Vice-President.

The Congress may determine the time of choosing the electors, and the day on which they shall give their votes; which day shall be the same throughout the United States.

No person except a natural-born citizen, *or a citizen of the United States at the time of the adoption of this Constitution*, shall be eligible to the office of President; neither shall any person be eligible to that office who shall not have attained to the age of thirty-five years, and been fourteen years a resident within the United States.

In cases of the removal of the President from office or of his death, resignation, or inability to discharge the powers and duties of the said office, the same shall devolve on the Vice-President, and the Congress may by law provide for the case of removal, death, resignation, or inability, both of the President and Vice-President, declaring what officer shall then act as President, and such officer shall act accordingly, until the disability be removed, or a President shall be elected.

The President shall, at stated times, receive for his services a compensation, which shall neither be increased nor diminished during the period for which he shall have been elected, and he shall not receive within that period any other emolument from the United States, or any of them.

Before he enter on the execution of his office, he shall take the following oath or affirmation:—"I do solemnly swear (or affirm) that I will faithfully execute the office of the President of the United States, and will to the best of my ability preserve, protect and defend the Constitution of the United States."

Section 2   The President shall be commander in chief of the army and navy of the United States, and of the militia of the several States, when called into the actual service of the United States; he may require the opinion, in writing, of the principal officer in each of the executive departments, upon any subject relating to the duties of their respective offices, and he shall have power to grant reprieves and pardons for offenses against the United States, except in cases of impeachment.

He shall have power, by and with the advice and consent of the Senate, to make treaties, provided two-thirds of the Senators present concur; and he shall nominate, and by and with the advice and consent of the Senate, shall appoint ambassadors, other public ministers and consuls, judges of the Supreme Court, and all other officers of the United States, whose appointments are not herein otherwise provided for, and which shall be established by law: but Congress may by law vest the appointment of such inferior officers, as they think proper, in the President alone, in the courts of law, or in the heads of departments.

The President shall have power to fill up all vacancies that may happen during the recess of the Senate, by granting commissions which shall expire at the end of their next session.

Section 3   He shall from time to time give to the Congress information of the state of the Union, and recommend to their consideration such measures as he shall judge necessary and expedient; he may, on extraordinary occasions, convene both houses, or either of them, and in case of disagreement between them, with respect to the time of adjournment, he may adjourn them to such time as he shall think proper; he shall receive ambassadors and other public ministers; he shall take care that the laws be faithfully executed, and shall commission all the officers of the United States.

Section 4   The President, Vice-President and all civil officers of the United States shall be removed from office on impeachment for, and on conviction of, treason, bribery, or other high crimes and misdemeanors.

Article III

Section 1   The judicial power of the United States shall be vested in one Supreme Court, and in such inferior courts as the Congress may from time to time ordain and establish. The judges, both of the Supreme and inferior courts, shall hold their offices during good behavior, and shall, at stated times, receive for their services a compensation which shall not be diminished during their continuance in office.

Section 2   The judicial power shall extend to all cases, in law and equity, arising under this Constitution, the laws of the United States, and treaties made, or which shall be made, under their authority;—to all cases affecting ambassadors, other public ministers and consuls;—to all cases of admiralty and maritime jurisdiction;—to controversies to which the United States shall be a party;—to controversies between two or more States;—*between a State and citizens of another State;*—between citizens of different States;—between citizens of the same State claiming lands under grants of different States, and between a State, or the citizens thereof, and foreign states, citizens or subjects.

In all cases affecting ambassadors, other public ministers and consuls, and those in which a State shall be party, the Supreme Court shall have original jurisdiction. In all the other cases before mentioned, the Supreme Court shall have appellate jurisdiction, both as to law and fact, with such exceptions, and under such regulations, as the Congress shall make.

The trial of all crimes, except in cases of impeachment, shall be by jury; and such trial shall be held in the State where said crimes shall have been committed; but when not committed within any State, the trial shall be at such place or places as the Congress may by Law have directed.

Section 3   Treason against the United States shall consist only in levying war against them, or in adhering to their enemies, giving them aid and comfort. No person shall be convicted of treason unless on the testimony of two witnesses to the same overt act, or on confession in open court.

The Congress shall have power to declare the punishment of treason, but no attainder of treason shall work corruption of blood, or forfeiture except during the life of the person attainted.

Article IV

Section 1   Full faith and credit shall be given in each State to the public acts, records, and judicial proceedings of every other State. And the Congress may by general laws prescribe the manner in which such acts, records, and proceedings shall be proved, and the effect thereof.

Section 2   The citizens of each State shall be entitled to all privileges and immunities of citizens in the several States.

A person charged in any State with treason, felony, or other crime, who shall flee from justice, and be found in another State, shall on demand of the executive authority of the State from which he fled, be delivered up, to be removed to the State having jurisdiction of the crime.

No Person held to service or labor in one State, under the laws thereof, escaping into another, shall, in consequence of any law or regulation therein, be discharged from such service or labor, but shall be delivered up on claim of the party to whom such service or labor may be due.

Section 3   New States may be admitted by the Congress into this Union; but no new State shall be formed or erected within the jurisdiction of any other State; nor any State be formed by the junction of two or more States, or parts of States, without the consent of the legislatures of the States concerned as well as of the Congress.

The Congress shall have power to dispose of and make all needful rules and regulations respecting the territory or other property belonging to the United States; and nothing in this Constitution shall be so construed as to prejudice any claims of the United States, or of any particular State.

Section 4   The United States shall guarantee to every State in this Union a republican form of government, and shall protect each of them against invasion; and on application of the legislature, or of the executive (when the legislature cannot be convened), against domestic violence.

Article V

The Congress, whenever two-thirds of both houses shall deem it necessary, shall propose amendments to this Constitution, or, on the application of the legislatures of two-thirds of the several States, shall call a convention for proposing amendments, which, in either case, shall be valid to all intents and purposes, as part of this Constitution, when ratified by the legislatures of three-fourths of the several States, or by conventions in three-fourths thereof, as the one or the other mode of ratification may be proposed by the Congress; provided *that no amendments which may be made prior to the year one thousand eight hundred and eight shall in any manner affect the first and fourth clauses in the ninth section of the first article*; and that no State, without its consent, shall be deprived of its equal suffrage in the Senate.

Article VI

All debts contracted and engagements entered into, before the adoption of this Constitution, shall be as valid against the United States under this Constitution, as under the Confederation.

This Constitution, and the laws of the United States which shall be made in pursuance thereof; and all treaties made, or which shall be made, under the authority of the United States, shall be the supreme law of the land; and the judges in every State shall be bound thereby, anything in the Constitution or laws of any State to the contrary notwithstanding.

The Senators and Representatives before mentioned, and the members of the several State legislatures, and all executive and judicial officers, both of the United States and of the several States, shall be bound by oath or affirmation to support this Constitution; but no religious test shall ever be required as a qualification to any office or public trust under the United States.

Article VII

The ratification of the conventions of nine States shall be sufficient for the establishment of this Constitution between the States so ratifying the same.

Done in convention by the unanimous consent of the States present, the seventeenth day of September in the year of our Lord one thousand seven hundred and eighty-seven and of the Independence of the United States of America the twelfth. In witness whereof we have hereunto subscribed our names.

George Washington
PRESIDENT AND DEPUTY FROM VIRGINIA

New Hampshire
John Langdon
Nicholas Gilman

Massachusetts
Nathaniel Gorham
Rufus King

Connecticut
William Samuel
    Johnson
Roger Sherman

New York
Alexander
    Hamilton

New Jersey
William Livingston
David Brearley
William Paterson
Jonathan Dayton

Pennsylvania
Benjamin Franklin
Thomas Mifflin
Robert Morris
George Clymer
Thomas
    FitzSimons
Jared Ingersoll
James Wilson
Gouverneur Morris

Delaware
George Read
Gunning Bedford, Jr.
John Dickinson
Richard Bassett
Jacob Broom

Maryland
James McHenry
Daniel of St.
    Thomas Jenifer
Daniel Carroll

Virginia
John Blair
James Madison, Jr.

North Carolina
William Blount
Richard Dobbs
    Spaight
Hugh Williamson

South Carolina
John Rutledge
Charles Cotesworth
    Pinckney
Charles Pinckney
Pierce Butler

Georgia
William Few
Abraham Baldwin

AMENDMENTS TO THE CONSTITUTION

(including the six unratified amendments)

Although the first ten amendments to the Constitution are commonly known as the Bill of Rights, only Amendments 1–8 actually provide guarantees of individual rights. Amendments 9 and 10 deal with the structure of power within the constitutional system. The Bill of Rights was promised to appease Antifederalists who refused to ratify the Constitution without guarantees of individual liberties and limitations to federal power. After studying more than two hundred amendments recommended by the ratifying conventions of the states, Federalist James Madison presented a list of seventeen to Congress, which used Madison's list as the foundation for the twelve amendments that were sent to the states for ratification. Ten of the twelve were adopted in 1791. The first on the list of twelve, known as the Reapportionment Amendment, was never adopted (see page A-19). The second proposed amendment was adopted in 1992 as Amendment 27 (see page A-26).

Amendment I

Congress shall make no law respecting an establishment of religion, or prohibiting the free exercise thereof; or abridging the freedom of speech, or of the press; or the right of the people peaceably to assemble, and to petition the government for a redress of grievances.

Amendment II

A well-regulated militia being necessary to the security of a free State, the right of the people to keep and bear arms shall not be infringed.

Amendment III

No soldier shall, in time of peace, be quartered in any house without the consent of the owner, nor in time of war, but in a manner to be prescribed by law.

Amendment IV

The right of the people to be secure in their persons, houses, papers, and effects, against unreasonable searches and seizures, shall not be violated, and no warrants shall issue but upon probable cause, supported by oath or affirmation, and particularly describing the place to be searched, and the persons or things to be seized.

Amendment V

No person shall be held to answer for a capital, or otherwise infamous crime, unless on a presentment or indictment of a grand jury, except in cases arising in the land or naval forces, or in the militia, when in actual service in time of war or public danger; nor shall any person be subject for the same offence to be twice put in jeopardy of life or limb; nor shall be compelled in any criminal case to be a witness against himself, nor be deprived of life, liberty, or property, without due process of law; nor shall private property be taken for public use without just compensation.

Amendment VI

In all criminal prosecutions, the accused shall enjoy the right to a speedy and public trial, by an impartial jury of the State and district wherein the crime shall have been committed, which district shall have been previously ascertained by law, and to be informed of the nature and cause of the accusation; to be confronted with the witnesses against him; to have compulsory process for obtaining witnesses in his favor, and to have the assistance of counsel for his defence.

Amendment VII

In suits at common law, where the value in controversy shall exceed twenty dollars, the right of trial by jury shall be preserved, and no fact tried by a jury shall be otherwise re-examined in any court of the United States, than according to the rules of the common law.

Amendment VIII

Excessive bail shall not be required, nor excessive fines imposed, nor cruel and unusual punishments inflicted.

Amendment IX

The enumeration in the Constitution, of certain rights, shall not be construed to deny or disparage others retained by the people.

Amendment X

The powers not delegated to the United States by the Constitution, nor prohibited by it to the States, are reserved to the States respectively, or to the people.

Unratified Amendment

Reapportionment Amendment (proposed by Congress September 25, 1789, along with the Bill of Rights)

After the first enumeration required by the first article of the Constitution, there shall be one Representative for every thirty thousand, until the number shall amount to one hundred, after which the proportion shall be so regulated by Congress, that there shall be not less than one hundred Representatives, nor less than one Representative for every forty thousand persons, until the number of Representatives shall amount to two hundred; after which the proportion shall be so regulated by Congress, that there shall not be less than two hundred Representatives, nor more than one Representative for every fifty thousand persons.

Amendment XI

[Adopted 1798]

The judicial power of the United States shall not be construed to extend to any suit in law or equity, commenced or prosecuted against one of the United States by citizens of another State, or by citizens or subjects of any foreign state.

Amendment XII

[Adopted 1804]

The electors shall meet in their respective States, and vote by ballot for President and Vice-President, one of whom, at least, shall not be an inhabitant of the same State with themselves; they shall name in their ballots the person voted for as President, and in distinct ballots the person voted for as Vice-President, and they shall make distinct lists of all persons voted for as President, and of all persons voted for as Vice-President, and of the number of votes for each, which lists they shall sign and certify, and transmit sealed to the seat of government of the United States, directed to the President of the Senate;—the President of the Senate shall, in the presence of the Senate and House of Representatives, open all the certificates and the votes shall then be counted;—the person having the greatest number of votes for President shall be the President, if such number be a majority of the whole number of electors appointed; and if no person have such majority, then from the persons having the highest numbers not exceeding three on the list of those voted for as President, the House of Representatives shall choose immediately, by ballot, the President. But in choosing the President, the votes shall be taken by States, the representation from each State having one vote; a quorum for this purpose shall consist of a member or members from two-thirds of the States, and a majority of all the States shall be necessary to a choice. And if the House of Representatives shall not choose a President whenever the right of choice shall devolve upon them, before *the fourth day of March* next following, then the Vice-President shall act as President, as in the case of the death or other constitutional disability of the President.

The person having the greatest number of votes as Vice-President shall be the Vice-President, if such number be a majority of the whole number of electors appointed; and if no person have a majority, then from the two highest numbers on the list the Senate shall choose the Vice-President; a quorum for the purpose shall consist of two-thirds of the whole number of Senators, and a majority of the whole number shall be necessary to a choice. But no person constitutionally ineligible to the office of President shall be eligible to that of Vice-President of the United States.

Unratified Amendment

Titles of Nobility Amendment (proposed by Congress May 1, 1810)

If any citizen of the United States shall accept, claim, receive or retain any title of nobility or honor or shall, without the consent of Congress, accept and retain any present, pension, office or emolument of any kind whatever, from any emperor, king, prince or foreign power, such person shall cease to be a citizen of the United States, and shall be incapable of holding any office of trust or profit under them or either of them.

The Civil War and Reconstruction Amendments (Thirteenth, Fourteenth, and Fifteenth Amendments)

In the four months between the election of Abraham Lincoln and his inauguration, more than 200 proposed constitutional amendments were presented to Congress as part of a desperate attempt to hold the rapidly dissolving Union together. Most of these were efforts to appease the southern states by protecting the right to own slaves or by disfranchising African Americans through constitutional amendment. None were able to win the votes required from Congress to send them to the states. The relatively innocuous Corwin Amendment seemed to be the only hope for preserving the Union by amending the Constitution.

The northern victors in the Civil War tried to restructure the Constitution just as the war had restructured the nation. Yet they were often divided in their goals. Some wanted to end slavery; others hoped for social and economic equality regardless of race; others hoped that extending the power of the ballot box to former slaves would help create a new political order. The debates over the Thirteenth, Fourteenth, and Fifteenth Amendments were bitter. Few of those who fought for these changes were satisfied with the amendments themselves; fewer still were satisfied with their interpretation. Although the amendments put an end to the legal status of slavery, it took nearly a hundred years after the amendments' passage before most of the descendants of former slaves could begin to experience the economic, social, and political equality the amendments had been intended to provide.

Unratified Amendment

Corwin Amendment (proposed by Congress March 2, 1861)

No amendment shall be made to the Constitution which will authorize or give to Congress the power to abolish or interfere, within any State, with the domestic institutions thereof, including that of persons held to labor or service by the laws of said State.

Amendment XIII

[Adopted 1865]

Section 1   Neither slavery nor involuntary servitude, except as a punishment for crime whereof the party shall have been duly convicted, shall exist within the United States, or any place subject to their jurisdiction.

Section 2   Congress shall have power to enforce this article by appropriate legislation.

Amendment XIV

[Adopted 1868]

Section 1   All persons born or naturalized in the United States, and subject to the jurisdiction thereof, are citizens of the United States and of the State wherein they reside.

No State shall make or enforce any law which shall abridge the privileges or immunities of citizens of the United States; nor shall any State deprive any person of life, liberty, or property, without due process of law; nor deny to any person within its jurisdiction the equal protection of the laws.

Section 2   Representatives shall be appointed among the several States according to their respective numbers, counting the whole number of persons in each State, excluding Indians not taxed. But when the right to vote at any election for the choice of Electors for President and Vice-President of the United States, Representatives in Congress, the executive and judicial officers of a State, or the members of the legislature thereof, is denied to any of the male inhabitants of such State, being twenty-one years of age and citizens of the United States, or in any way abridged, except for participation in rebellion, or other crime, the basis of representation therein shall be reduced in the proportion which the number of such male citizens shall bear to the whole number of male citizens twenty-one years of age in such State.

Section 3   No person shall be a Senator or Representative in Congress, or Elector of President and Vice-President, or hold any office, civil or military, under the United States, or under any State, who, having previously taken an oath, as a member of Congress, or as an officer of the United States, or as a member of any State legislature, or as an executive or judicial officer of any State, to support the Constitution of the United States, shall have engaged in insurrection or rebellion against the same, or given aid or comfort to the enemies thereof. Congress may, by a vote of two-thirds of each house, remove such disability.

Section 4   The validity of the public debt of the United States, authorized by law, including debts incurred for payment of pensions and bounties for services in suppressing insurrection or rebellion, shall not be questioned. But neither the United States nor any State shall assume or pay any debt or obligation incurred in aid of insurrection or rebellion against the United States, or any claim for the loss or emancipation of any slave; but all such debts, obligations, and claims shall be held illegal and void.

Section 5   The Congress shall have power to enforce, by appropriate legislation, the provisions of this article.

Amendment XV
[Adopted 1870]

Section 1   The right of citizens of the United States to vote shall not be denied or abridged by the United States or by any State on account of race, color, or previous condition of servitude.

Section 2   The Congress shall have power to enforce this article by appropriate legislation.

The Progressive Amendments (Sixteenth–Nineteenth Amendments)

No amendments were added to the Constitution between the Civil War and the Progressive Era. America was changing, however, in fundamental ways. The rapid industrialization of the United States after the Civil War led to many social and economic problems. Hundreds of amendments were proposed, but none received enough support in Congress to be sent to the states. Some scholars believe that regional differences and rivalries were so strong during this period that it was almost impossible to gain a consensus on a constitutional amendment. During the Progressive Era, however, the Constitution was amended four times in seven years.

Amendment XVI
[Adopted 1913]

The Congress shall have power to lay and collect taxes on incomes, from whatever source derived, without apportionment among the several States, and without regard to any census or enumeration.

Amendment XVII
[Adopted 1913]

Section 1   The Senate of the United States shall be composed of two Senators from each State, elected by the people thereof, for six years; and each Senator shall have one vote. The electors in each State shall have the qualifications requisite for electors of [voters for] the most numerous branch of the State legislatures.

Section 2   When vacancies happen in the representation of any State in the Senate, the executive authority of such State shall issue writs of election to fill such vacancies: Provided, that the Legislature of any State may empower the executive thereof to make temporary appointments until the people fill the vacancies by election as the Legislature may direct.

Section 3   This amendment shall not be so construed as to affect the election or term of any Senator chosen before it becomes valid as part of the Constitution.

Amendment XVIII
[Adopted 1919; repealed 1933 by Amendment XXI]

Section 1   After one year from the ratification of this article the manufacture, sale, or transportation of intoxicating liquors within, the importation thereof into, or the exportation thereof from the United States and all territory subject to the jurisdiction thereof, for beverage purposes, is hereby prohibited.

Section 2   The Congress and the several States shall have concurrent power to enforce this article by appropriate legislation.

Section 3   This article shall be inoperative unless it shall have been ratified as an amendment to the Constitution by the legislatures of the several States, as provided by the Constitution, within seven years from the date of the submission thereof to the States by the Congress.

Amendment XIX
[Adopted 1920]

Section 1   The right of citizens of the United States to vote shall not be denied or abridged by the United States or by any State on account of sex.

Section 2   Congress shall have the power to enforce this article by appropriate legislation.

Unratified Amendment

Child Labor Amendment (proposed by Congress June 2, 1924)

Section 1   The Congress shall have power to limit, regulate, and prohibit the labor of persons under eighteen years of age.

Section 2   The power of the several States is unimpaired by this article except that the operation of State laws shall be suspended to the extent necessary to give effect to legislation enacted by Congress.

Amendment XX

[Adopted 1933]

Section 1   The terms of the President and Vice-President shall end at noon on the 20th day of January, and the terms of Senators and Representatives at noon on the 3rd day of January, of the years in which such terms would have ended if this article had not been ratified; and the terms of their successors shall then begin.

Section 2   The Congress shall assemble at least once in every year, and such meeting shall begin at noon on the 3rd day of January, unless they shall by law appoint a different day.

Section 3   If, at the time fixed for the beginning of the term of the President, the President-elect shall have died, the Vice-President-elect shall become President. If a President shall not have been chosen before the time fixed for the beginning of his term, or if the President-elect shall have failed to qualify, then the Vice-President-elect shall act as President until a President shall have qualified; and the Congress may by law provide for the case wherein neither a President-elect nor a Vice-President-elect shall have qualified, declaring who shall then act as President, or the manner in which one who is to act shall be selected, and such person shall act accordingly until a President or Vice-President shall have qualified.

Section 4   The Congress may by law provide for the case of the death of any of the persons from whom the House of Representatives may choose a President whenever the right of choice shall have devolved upon them, and for the case of the death of any of the persons from whom the Senate may choose a Vice-President whenever the right of choice shall have devolved upon them.

Section 5   Sections 1 and 2 shall take effect on the 15th day of October following the ratification of this article.

Section 6   This article shall be inoperative unless it shall have been ratified as an amendment to the Constitution by the Legislatures of three-fourths of the several States within seven years from the date of its submission.

Amendment XXI

[Adopted 1933]

Section 1   The eighteenth article of amendment to the Constitution of the United States is hereby repealed.

Section 2   The transportation or importation into any State, Territory, or Possession of the United States for delivery or use therein of intoxicating liquors, in violation of the laws thereof, is hereby prohibited.

Section 3 This article shall be inoperative unless it shall have been ratified as an amendment to the Constitution by conventions in the several States, as provided in the Constitution, within seven years from the date of the submission thereof to the States by the Congress.

Amendment XXII
[Adopted 1951]

Section 1 No person shall be elected to the office of the President more than twice, and no person who has held the office of President, or acted as President, for more than two years of a term to which some other person was elected President shall be elected to the office of President more than once. But this article shall not apply to any person holding the office of President when this Article was proposed by the Congress, and shall not prevent any person who may be holding the office of President, or acting as President, during the term within which this Article becomes operative from holding the office of President or acting as President during the remainder of such term.

Section 2 This article shall be inoperative unless it shall have been ratified as an amendment to the Constitution by the legislatures of three-fourths of the several States within seven years from the date of its submission to the States by the Congress.

Amendment XXIII
[Adopted 1961]

Section 1 The District constituting the seat of Government of the United States shall appoint in such manner as the Congress may direct: A number of electors of President and Vice-President equal to the whole number of Senators and Representatives in Congress to which the District would be entitled if it were a State, but in no event more than the least populous State; they shall be in addition to those appointed by the States, but they shall be considered for the purposes of the election of President and Vice-President, to be electors appointed by a State; and they shall meet in the District and perform such duties as provided by the twelfth article of amendment.

Section 2 The Congress shall have the power to enforce this article by appropriate legislation.

Amendment XXIV
[Adopted 1964]

Section 1 The right of citizens of the United States to vote in any primary or other election for President or Vice-President, for electors for President or Vice-President, or for Senator or Representative in Congress, shall not be denied or abridged by the United States or any State by reason of failure to pay any poll tax or other tax.

Section 2 The Congress shall have the power to enforce this article by appropriate legislation.

Amendment XXV
[Adopted 1967]

Section 1 In case of the removal of the President from office or of his death or resignation, the Vice-President shall become President.

Section 2   Whenever there is a vacancy in the office of the Vice-President, the President shall nominate a Vice-President who shall take office upon confirmation by a majority vote of both Houses of Congress.

Section 3   Whenever the President transmits to the President pro tempore of the Senate and the Speaker of the House of Representatives his written declaration that he is unable to discharge the powers and duties of his office, and until he transmits to them a written declaration to the contrary, such powers and duties shall be discharged by the Vice-President as Acting President.

Section 4   Whenever the Vice-President and a majority of either the principal officers of the executive departments or of such other body as Congress may by law provide, transmit to the President pro tempore of the Senate and the Speaker of the House of Representatives their written declaration that the President is unable to discharge the powers and duties of his office, the Vice-President shall immediately assume the powers and duties of the office as Acting President.

Thereafter, when the President transmits to the President pro tempore of the Senate and the Speaker of the House of Representatives his written declaration that no inability exists, he shall resume the powers and duties of his office unless the Vice-President and a majority of either the principal officers of the executive department[s] or of such other body as Congress may by law provide, transmit within four days to the President pro tempore of the Senate and the Speaker of the House of Representatives their written declaration that the President is unable to discharge the powers and duties of his office. Thereupon Congress shall decide the issue, assembling within forty-eight hours for that purpose if not in session. If the Congress, within twenty-one days after receipt of the latter written declaration, or, if Congress is not in session, within twenty-one days after Congress is required to assemble, determines by two-thirds vote of both Houses that the President is unable to discharge the powers and duties of his office, the Vice-President shall continue to discharge the same as Acting President; otherwise, the President shall resume the powers and duties of his office.

Amendment XXVI

[Adopted 1971]

Section 1   The right of citizens of the United States, who are eighteen years of age or older, to vote shall not be denied or abridged by the United States or by any State on account of age.

Section 2   The Congress shall have power to enforce this article by appropriate legislation.

Unratified Amendment

Equal Rights Amendment (proposed by Congress March 22, 1972; seven-year deadline for ratification extended to June 30, 1982)

Section 1   Equality of rights under the law shall not be denied or abridged by the United States or by any State on account of sex.

Section 2   The Congress shall have the power to enforce, by appropriate legislation, the provisions of this article.

Section 3 This amendment shall take effect two years after the date of ratification.

Unratified Amendment

D.C. Statehood Amendment (proposed by Congress August 22, 1978)

Section 1 For purposes of representation in the Congress, election of the President and Vice-President, and article V of this Constitution, the District constituting the seat of government of the United States shall be treated as though it were a State.

Section 2 The exercise of the rights and powers conferred under this article shall be by the people of the District constituting the seat of government, and as shall be provided by Congress.

Section 3 The twenty-third article of amendment to the Constitution of the United States is hereby repealed.

Section 4 This article shall be inoperative, unless it shall have been ratified as an amendment to the Constitution by the legislatures of three-fourths of the several states within seven years from the date of its submission.

Amendment XXVII

[Adopted 1992]

No law, varying the compensation for the services of the Senators and Representatives, shall take effect, until an election of Representatives shall have intervened.

Glossary of Historical Vocabulary

A NOTE TO STUDENTS: This list of terms is provided to help you with historical and economic vocabulary. Many of these terms refer to broad, enduring concepts that you may encounter not only in further studies of history but also when following current events. The terms appear in bold at their first use in each chapter. For definitions and discussions of words not included here, consult a dictionary and the book's index, which will point you to topics covered at greater length in the book.

affirmative action Policies established in the 1960s and 1970s by governments, businesses, universities, and other institutions to overcome the effects of past discrimination against specific groups such as racial and ethnic minorities and women. Measures to ensure equal opportunity include setting goals for admission, hiring, and promotion; considering minority status when allocating resources; and actively encouraging victims of past discrimination to apply for jobs and other resources.

agribusiness Farming on a large scale, using the production, processing, and distribution methods of modern business. Farming became a big business, not just a way to feed a family and make a living, in the late nineteenth century as farms got larger and more mechanized. In the 1940s and 1950s, specialized commercial farms replaced many family-run operations and grew to an enormous scale.

alliance system The military and diplomatic system formulated in an effort to create a balance of power in pre–World War I Europe. Nations were bound together by rigid and comprehensive treaties that promised mutual aid in the case of attack by specific nations. The system swung into action after the Austrian archduke Franz Ferdinand was assassinated in Sarajevo on June 28, 1914, dragging most of Europe into war.

anarchist A person who rebels against established order and authority. An anarchist is someone who believes that government of any kind is unnecessary and undesirable and should be replaced with voluntary cooperation and free association. Anarchists became increasingly visible in the United States in the late nineteenth and early twentieth centuries. They advocated revolution and grew in numbers through appeals to discontented laborers. Anarchists frequently employed violence in an attempt to achieve their goals. In 1901, anarchist Leon Czolgosz assassinated President William McKinley.

antebellum A term that means "before a war" and commonly refers to the period prior to the Civil War.

antinomian A person who does not obey societal or religious laws. In colonial Massachusetts, Puritan authorities accused Anne Hutchinson of antinomianism because she believed that Christians could achieve salvation by faith alone. They further asserted, incorrectly, that Hutchinson also held the belief that it was not necessary to follow God's laws as set forth in the Bible.

archaeology A social science devoted to learning about people who lived in the past through the study of physical artifacts created by humans. Most but not all archaeological study focuses on the history of people who lived before the use of the written word.

Archaic A term applied to various hunting and gathering cultures that descended from Paleo-Indians. The term also refers to the period of time when these cultures dominated ancient America, roughly from 8000 BP to between 2000 and 1000 BP.

artifacts Material remains studied and used by archaeologists and historians to support their interpretations of human history. Examples of artifacts include bones, pots, baskets, jewelry, furniture, tools, clothing, and buildings.

artisan A term commonly used prior to 1900 to describe a skilled craftsman, such as a cabinetmaker.

Bill of Rights The commonly used term for the first ten amendments to the U.S. Constitution. The Bill of Rights (the last of which was ratified in 1791) guarantees individual liberties and defines limitations to federal power. Many states made the promise of the prompt addition of a bill of rights a precondition for their ratification of the Constitution.

black nationalism A term linked to several African American movements emphasizing racial pride, separation from whites and white institutions, and black autonomy. Black nationalism gained in popularity with the rise of Marcus Garvey and the Universal Negro Improvement Association (1917–1927) and later with the Black Panther Party, Malcolm X, and other participants of the black power movements of the 1960s.

bloody shirt A refrain used by Republicans in the late nineteenth century to remind the voting public that the Democratic Party, dominated by the South, was largely responsible for the Civil War and that the Republican Party had led the victory to preserve the Union. Republicans urged their constituents to "vote the way you shot."

***bracero* program** A policy begun during World War II to help with wartime agriculture in which Mexican laborers (*braceros*) were permitted to enter the United States and work for a limited period of time but not to gain citizenship or permanent residence. The program officially ended in 1964.

brinksmanship A cold war practice of appearing willing and able to resort to nuclear war in order to make an enemy back down. Secretary of State John Foster Dulles was the foremost proponent of this policy.

Calvinism The religious doctrine of which the primary tenet is that salvation is predestined by God. Founded by John Calvin of Geneva during the Protestant Reformation, Calvinism required its adherents to live according to a strict religious and moral code. The Puritans who settled in colonial New England were devout Calvinists. *See also* predestination.

capitalism An economic system in which private individuals and corporations own and operate most means of production. Free-market competition—in which supply and demand is minimally regulated by the state or not regulated at all—determines the prices of goods and services. There are three major aspects of capitalism. First, a capitalist system generally includes many workers who do not own what they produce, but instead perform labor for wages. Second, capitalist societies move beyond local trade to the specialized production of goods for large-scale cash markets. Third, people in a capitalist society internalize a social mentality that emphasizes rationality and the pursuit of profit as the primary goal of economic life. In the United States, most regions made the transition to capitalism by the early nineteenth century. Over the following two hundred years, the United States developed an industrial capitalist system, based on new technologies that allowed for self-sustaining economic growth.

checks and balances A system in which the executive, legislative, and judicial branches of the government curb each other's power. Checks and balances were written into the U.S. Constitution during the Constitutional Convention of 1787.

civil disobedience The public and peaceful violation of certain laws or government orders on the part of individuals or groups who act out of a profound conviction that the law or directive is unjust or immoral and who are prepared to accept the consequences of their actions. Civil disobedience was practiced most famously in U.S. history in the black freedom struggle of the 1960s.

civil service The administrative service of a government. This term often applies to reforms following the passage of the Pendleton Act in 1883, which set qualifications for U.S. government jobs and sought to remove such jobs from political influence. *See also* spoils system.

closed shop An establishment in which every employee is required to join a union in order to obtain a job.

cold war The hostile and tense relationship that existed between the Soviet Union on the one hand and the United States and other Western nations on the other from 1947 to 1989. This war was said to be "cold" because the hostility stopped short of armed (hot) conflict, which was warded off by the strategy of nuclear deterrence. *See also* deterrence.

collective bargaining Negotiation by a group of workers (usually through a union) and their employer concerning rates of pay and working conditions.

collective security An association of independent nations that agree to accept and implement decisions made by the group, including going to war in defense of one or more members. The United States resolutely avoided such alliances until after World War II, when it created the North Atlantic Treaty Organization (NATO) in response to the threat posed by the Soviet Union. *See also* North Atlantic Treaty Organization.

colonization The process by which a country or society gains control over another, primarily through settlement.

Columbian exchange The transatlantic exchange of goods, peoples, and ideas that began when Columbus arrived in the Caribbean in 1492, ending the age-old separation of the hemispheres.

communism (Communist Party) A system of government and political organization, based on Marxist-Leninist ideals, in which a single authoritarian party controls the economy through state ownership of production, as a means toward reaching the final stage of Marxist theory in which the state dissolves and economic goods are distributed evenly for the common good. Communists around the globe encouraged the spread of communism in other nations in hopes of fomenting worldwide revolution. At its peak in the 1930s, the Communist Party of the United States worked closely with labor unions and insisted that only the overthrow of the capitalist system by its workers could save the victims of the Great Depression. After World War II, the Communist power and aspirations of the Soviet Union were held to be a direct threat to American democracy, prompting the cold war. *See also* cold war.

conscription Compulsory military service. Americans were first subject to conscription during the Civil War. The Selective Service Act of 1940 marked the first peacetime use of conscription. *See also* draft.

conservatism A political and moral outlook dating back to Alexander Hamilton's belief in a strong central government resting on a solid banking foundation. Currently associated with the Republican Party, conservatism today places a high premium on military preparedness, free market economics, low taxes, and strong sexual morality.

consumer culture (consumerism) A society that places high value on, and devotes substantial resources to, the purchase and display of material goods. Elements of American consumerism were evident in the nineteenth century but really took hold in the twentieth century with installment buying and advertising in the 1920s and again with the postwar prosperity of the 1950s.

containment The U.S. foreign policy developed after World War II to hold in check the power and influence of the Soviet Union and other groups or nations espousing communism. The strategy was first fully articulated by diplomat George F. Kennan in 1946–1947.

covenant An agreement or pact; in American history, this refers to a religious agreement. The Pilgrims used this term in the Mayflower Compact to refer to the agreement among themselves to establish a law-abiding community in which all members would work together for the common good. Later, New England Puritans used this term to refer to the agreement they made with God and each other to live according to God's will as revealed through Scripture. *See also* Halfway Covenant.

cult of domesticity The nineteenth-century belief that women's place was in the home, where they should create a haven for harried men working in the outside world. This ideal was made possible by the separation of the workplace and the home and was used to sentimentalize the home and women's role in it. *See also* separate spheres.

culture A term used here to connote what is commonly called "way of life." It refers not only to how a group of people supplied themselves with food and shelter but also to their family relationships, social groupings, religious ideas, and other features of their lives.

de-industrialization A long period of decline in the industrial sector. The term often refers specifically to the decline of manufacturing and the growth of the service sector of the economy in post–World War II America. This shift and the loss of manufacturing resulting from it were caused by more efficient and automated production techniques at home, increased competition from foreign-made goods, and the use of cheap labor abroad by U.S. manufacturers.

democracy A system of government in which the people have the power to rule, either directly or indirectly, through their elected representatives. Believing that direct democracy was dangerous, the framers of the Constitution created a government that gave direct voice to the people only in the House of Representatives and that placed a check on that voice in the Senate by offering unlimited six-year terms to senators, elected by the state legislatures to protect them from the whims of democratic majorities. The framers further curbed the perceived dangers of democracy by giving each of the three branches of government (legislative, executive, and judicial) the ability to check the power of the other two. *See also* checks and balances.

détente French for "loosening." The term refers to the easing of tensions between the United States and the Soviet Union during the Nixon administration.

deterrence The linchpin of U.S. military strategy during the cold war. The strategy of deterrence dictated that the United States would maintain a nuclear arsenal so substantial that the Soviet Union would refrain from attacking the United States and its allies out of fear that the United States would retaliate in devastating proportions. The Soviets pursued a similar strategy.

disfranchisement The denial of suffrage to a group or individual through legal or other means. Beginning in 1890, southern progressives preached the disfranchisement of black voters as a "reform" of the electoral system. The most common means of eliminating black voters were poll taxes and literary tests.

domino theory The assumption underlying U.S. foreign policy from the early cold war until the end of the Vietnam War. The theory was that if one country fell to communism, neighboring countries also would fall under Communist control.

doves Peace advocates, particularly during the Vietnam War.

draft (draftee) A system for selecting individuals for compulsory military service. A draftee is an individual selected through this process. *See also* conscription.

emancipation The act of freeing from slavery or bondage. The emancipation of American slaves, a goal shared by slaves and abolitionists alike, occurred with the passage of the Thirteenth Amendment in 1865.

English Reformation *See* Reformation.

Enlightenment An eighteenth-century philosophical movement that emphasized the use of reason to reevaluate previously accepted doctrines and traditions.

evangelicalism The trend in Protestant Christianity stressing salvation through conversion, repentance of sin, adherence to Scripture, and the importance of preaching over ritual. During the Second Great Awakening in the 1830s, evangelicals worshipped at camp meetings and religious revivals led by exuberant preachers. *See also* Second Great Awakening.

fascism An authoritarian system of government characterized by dictatorial rule, disdain for international stability, and a conviction that warfare is the only means by which a nation can attain greatness. Nazi Germany and Mussolini's Italy are the prime examples of fascism.

federal budget deficit The situation resulting when the government spends more money than it takes in.

feminism The belief that men and women have the inherent right to equal social, political, and economic opportunities. The suffrage movement and second-wave feminism of the 1960s and 1970s were the most visible and successful manifestations of feminism, but feminist ideas were expressed in a variety of statements and movements as early as the late eighteenth century and continue to be expressed in the twenty-first.

finance capitalism Refers to investment sponsored by banks and bankers and the profits garnered from the sale of financial assets such as stocks and bonds. The decades at the end of the twentieth century are known as a period of finance capitalism because banks and financiers increasingly took on the role of stabilizing markets and reorganizing industries.

franchise The right to vote. The franchise was gradually widened in the United States to include groups such as women and African Americans, who had no vote when the Constitution was ratified. *See also* suffrage.

free labor Work conducted free from constraint and in accordance with the laborer's personal inclinations and will. Prior to the Civil War, free labor became an ideal championed by Republicans (who were primarily Northerners) to articulate individuals' right to work how and where they wished and to accumulate property in their own name. The ideal of free labor lay at the heart of the North's argument that slavery should not be extended into the western territories.

free silver The late-nineteenth-century call by silver barons and poor American farmers for the widespread coinage of silver and for silver to be used as a base upon which to expand the paper money supply. The coinage of silver created a more inflationary monetary system that benefited debtors. *See also* gold standard.

free soil The idea advanced in the 1840s that Congress should prohibit slavery within the western territories. "Free soil, free speech, free labor, and free men" became the rallying cry of the short-lived Free-Soil Party.

frontier A borderland area. In U.S. history, this refers to the borderland between the areas primarily inhabited by Europeans or their descendants and the areas solely inhabited by Native Americans.

fundamentalism Strict adherence to core, often religious beliefs. The term has varying meanings for different religious groups. Protestant fundamentalists adhere to a literal interpretation of the Bible and thus deny the possibility of evolution. Muslim fundamentalists believe that traditional Islamic law should govern nations and that Western influences should be banned.

gag rule A procedural rule invoked to prohibit discussion or debate on a particular subject in a legislative body. From 1836 to 1844, a series of gag rules prevented the House of Representatives from discussing the large number of antislavery petitions from abolitionist groups that flooded that chamber.

gender gap An electoral phenomenon that became apparent in the 1980s when men and women began to display different preferences in voting. Women tended to favor liberal candidates, and men tended to support conservatives. The key voter groups contributing to the gender gap were single women and women who worked outside the home.

globalization The spread of political, cultural, and economic influences and connections among countries, businesses, and individuals around the world through trade, immigration, communication, and other means. In the late twentieth century, globalization was intensified by new communications technology that connected individuals, corporations, and nations with greater speed at low prices. This led to an increase in political and economic interdependence and mutual influence among nations.

gold standard A monetary system in which any circulating currency was exchangeable for a specific amount of gold. Advocates for the gold standard believed that gold alone should be used for coinage and that the total value of paper banknotes should never exceed the government's supply of gold. The triumph of gold standard supporter William McKinley in the 1896 presidential election was a big victory for supporters of this policy. *See also* free silver.

gospel of wealth The idea that wealth garnered from earthly success should be used for good works. Andrew Carnegie promoted this view in an 1889 essay in which he maintained that the wealthy should serve as stewards and act in the best interests of society as a whole.

government bonds Promissory notes issued by a government in order to borrow money from members of the public. Such bonds are redeemable at a set future date. Bondholders earn interest on their investments.

Great Awakening The widespread movement of religious revitalization in the 1730s and 1740s that emphasized vital religious faith and personal choice. It was characterized by large, open-air meetings at which emotional sermons were given by itinerant preachers.

Great Society President Lyndon Johnson's domestic program, which included civil rights legislation, antipoverty programs, government subsidy of medical care, federal aid to education, consumer protection, and aid to the arts and humanities.

gross domestic product (GDP) A measure of economic production. GDP is the value of all the goods and services produced within a country during a year, regardless of the nationality of the owners of those goods and services.

gross national product (GNP) A measure of economic production. GNP is the value of all the goods and services produced by a country's citizens, regardless of where production takes place.

guerrilla warfare Fighting carried out by an irregular military force usually organized into small, highly mobile groups. Guerrilla combat was common in the Vietnam War and during the American Revolution. Guerrilla warfare is often effective against opponents who have greater material resources.

Halfway Covenant A Puritan compromise that allowed the unconverted children of the "visible saints" to become "halfway" members of the church and to baptize their own children even though they were not full members of the church themselves because they had not experienced full conversion. Massachusetts ministers accepted this compromise in 1662, but the compromise remained controversial throughout the seventeenth century.

hard currency (hard money) Money coined directly from, or backed in full by, precious metals (particularly gold).

hawks Advocates of aggressive military action or all-out war, particularly during the Vietnam War. *See also* War Hawks.

holding company A system of business organization whereby competing companies are combined under one central administration in order to curb competition and ensure profit. Pioneered in the late 1880s by John D. Rockefeller, holding companies, such as Standard Oil, exercised monopoly control even as the government threatened to outlaw trusts as a violation of free trade. *See also* monopoly; trust.

horizontal integration A system in which a single person or corporation creates several subsidiary businesses to sell a product in different markets. John D. Rockefeller pioneered the use of horizontal integration in the 1880s to control the refining process, giving him a virtual monopoly on the oil-refining business. *See also* vertical integration; monopoly.

impeachment The process by which formal charges of wrongdoing are brought against a president, a governor, or a federal judge.

imperialism The system by which great powers gain control of overseas territories. The United States became an imperialist power by gaining control of Puerto Rico, Guam, the Philippines, and Cuba as a result of the Spanish-American War.

indentured servitude A system that committed poor immigrants to four to seven years of labor in exchange for passage to the colonies and food and shelter after they arrived. An indenture is a type of contract.

iron curtain A metaphor coined by Winston Churchill during his commencement address at Westminster College in Fulton, Missouri, in 1946, to refer to the political, ideological, and military barriers that separated Soviet-controlled Eastern Europe from the rest of Europe and the West following World War II.

isolationism A foreign policy perspective characterized by a desire to have the United States withdraw from the conflicts of the world and enjoy the protection of two vast oceans.

Jim Crow The system of racial segregation that developed in the post–Civil War South and extended well into the twentieth century; it replaced slavery as the chief instrument of white supremacy. Jim Crow laws segregated African Americans in public facilities such as trains and streetcars and denied them basic civil rights, including the right to vote. It was also at this time that the doctrine of "separate but equal" became institutionalized.

Keynesian economics A theory developed by economist John Maynard Keynes that guided U.S. economic policy from the New Deal to the 1970s. According to Keynesians, the federal government has a duty to stimulate and manage the economy by spending money on public works projects and by making general tax cuts in order to put more money into the hands of ordinary people, thus creating demand.

laissez-faire The doctrine, based on economic theory, that government should not interfere in business or the economy. Laissez-faire ideas guided American government policy in the late nineteenth century and conservative politics in the twentieth century. Business interests that supported laissez-faire in the late nineteenth century accepted government interference when it took the form of tariffs or subsidies that worked to their benefit. A broader use of the term refers to the simple philosophy of abstaining from interference.

land grant A gift of land from a government, usually intended to encourage settlement or development. The British government issued several land grants to encourage development in the American colonies. In the mid-nineteenth century, the U.S. government issued land grants to encourage railroad development and, through the passage of the Land-Grant College Act (also known as the Morrill Act) in 1862, set aside public land to support universities.

liberalism The political doctrine that government rests on the consent of the governed and is duty-bound to protect the freedom and property of the individual. In the twentieth century, liberalism became associated with the idea that government should regulate the economy and ensure the material well-being and individual rights of all people.

liberty The condition of being free or enjoying freedom from control. This term also refers to the possession of certain social, political, or economic rights, such as the right to own and control property. Eighteenth-century American colonists invoked the principle to argue for strict limitations on government's ability to tax its subjects.

manifest destiny A term coined by journalist John O'Sullivan in 1845 to express the popular nineteenth-century belief that the United States was destined to expand westward to the Pacific Ocean and had an irrefutable right and God-given responsibility to do so. This idea provided an ideological shield for westward expansion and masked the economic and political motivations of many of those who championed it.

McCarthyism The practice of searching out suspected Communists and others outside mainstream American society, discrediting them, and hounding them from government and other employment. The term derives from Senator Joseph McCarthy, who gained notoriety for leading such repressive activities from 1950 to 1954.

mercantilism A set of policies that regulated colonial commerce and manufacturing for the enrichment of the mother country. Mercantilist policies ensured that the American colonies in the mid-seventeenth century produced agricultural goods and raw materials to be shipped to Britain, where they would increase wealth in the mother country through reexportation or manufacture into finished goods that would then be sold to the colonies and elsewhere.

Middle Passage The crossing of the Atlantic (as a slave destined for auction) in the hold of a slave ship in the eighteenth and nineteenth centuries. Conditions were unimaginably bad, and many slaves died during these voyages.

military-industrial complex A term first used by President Dwight D. Eisenhower to refer to the aggregate power and influence of the armed forces in conjunction with the aerospace, munitions, and other industries that produced supplies for the military in the post–World War II era.

miscegenation The sexual mixing of races. In slave states, despite the social stigma and legal restrictions on interracial sex, masters' almost unlimited power over their female slaves meant that liaisons inevitably occurred. Many states maintained laws against miscegenation into the 1950s.

monopoly Exclusive control and domination by a single business entity over an entire industry through ownership, command of supply, or other means. Gilded Age businesses monopolized their industries quite profitably, often organizing holding companies and trusts to do so. *See also* holding company; trust.

Monroe Doctrine President James Monroe's 1823 declaration that the Western Hemisphere was closed to any further colonization or interference by European powers. In exchange, Monroe pledged that the United States would not become involved in European struggles. Although Monroe could not back his policy with action, it was an important formulation of national goals.

nationalism A strong feeling of devotion and loyalty toward one nation over others. Nationalism encourages the promotion of the nation's common culture, language, and customs.

nativism Bias against immigrants and in favor of native-born inhabitants. American nativists especially favor persons who come from white, Anglo-Saxon, Protestant lines over those from other racial, ethnic, and religious heritages. Nativists may include former immigrants who view new immigrants as incapable of assimilation. Many nativists, such as members of the Know-Nothing Party in the nineteenth century and the Ku Klux Klan through the contemporary period, voice anti-immigrant, anti-Catholic, and anti-Semitic sentiments.

Navigation Acts British acts of 1650, 1651, and 1660 that, together with a 1663 law (the Staple Act), set forth three fundamental regulations governing colonial trade. First, all colonial goods imported into England had to be transported on English ships using primarily English crews. Second, specific colonial products could be shipped only to England or to other English colonies. Third, all goods imported into the colonies had to pass through England. The 1660 Navigation Act assessed an explicit import tax of two pence on every pound of colonial tobacco; these tobacco taxes yielded about a quarter of all English customs revenues in the 1660s. The Navigation Acts fueled tension between the colonies and the monarchy in the century leading up to the Revolutionary War (1775–1783).

New Deal The group of social and economic programs that President Franklin Roosevelt developed to provide relief for the needy, speed economic recovery, and reform economic and government institutions. The New Deal was a massive effort to bring the United States out of the Great Depression and ensure its future prosperity.

New Right Politically active religious conservatives who became particularly vocal in the 1980s. The New Right criticized feminism, opposed abortion and homosexuality, and promoted "family values" and military preparedness.

New South A vision of the South, promoted after the Civil War by Henry Grady, editor of the *Atlanta Constitution*, that urged the South to abandon its dependence on agriculture and use its cheap labor and natural resources to compete with northern industry. Many Southerners migrated from farms to cities in the late nineteenth century, and Northerners and foreigners invested a significant amount of capital in railroads, cotton and textiles, mining, lumber, iron, steel, and tobacco in the region.

North Atlantic Treaty Organization (NATO) North Atlantic Treaty Organization (NATO) A post–World War II alliance that joined the United States, Canada, and Western European nations into a military coalition designed to counter the Soviet Union's efforts to expand. Each NATO member pledged to go to war if any member was attacked. Since the end of the cold war, NATO has been expanding to include the formerly Communist countries of Eastern Europe.

nullification The idea that states can disregard federal laws when those laws represent an overstepping of congressional powers. The controversial idea was first proposed by opponents of the Alien and Sedition Acts of 1798 and later by South Carolina politicians in 1828 as a response to the Tariff of Abominations.

oligopoly A competitive system in which several large corporations dominate an industry by dividing the market so each business has a share of it. More prevalent than outright monopolies during the late 1800s, the oligopolies of the Gilded Age successfully muted competition and benefited the corporations that participated in this type of arrangement.

paternalism The idea that slavery was a set of reciprocal obligations between masters and slaves, with slaves providing labor and obedience and masters providing basic care and direction. The concept of paternalism denied that the slave system was brutal and exploitative. Although paternalism did provide some protection against the worst brutality, it did not guarantee decent living conditions, reasonable work, or freedom from physical punishment.

planters Owners of large farms (or, more specifically, plantations) that were worked by twenty or more slaves. By 1860, planters had accrued a great deal of local, statewide, and national political power in the South despite the fact that they represented a minority of the white electorate. Planters' dominance of southern politics demonstrated both the power of tradition and stability among southern voters and the planters' success at convincing white voters that the slave system benefited all whites, even those without slaves.

plutocracy A society ruled by the richest members. The excesses of the Gilded Age and the fact that just 1 percent of the population owned more than half the real and personal property in the country led many to question whether the United States was indeed a plutocracy.

pogrom An organized and often officially encouraged massacre of an ethnic minority; usually used in reference to attacks on Jews.

popular sovereignty The idea that government is subject to the will of the people. Before the Civil War, this was the idea that the residents of a territory should determine, through their legislatures, whether to allow slavery.

Populism A political movement that led to the creation of the People's Party, primarily comprising southern and western farmers who railed against big business and advocated business and economic reforms, including government ownership of the railroads. The movement peaked in the late nineteenth century. The Populist ticket won more than 1 million votes in the presidential election of 1892 and 1.5 million in the congressional elections of 1894. The term *populism* has come to mean any political movement that advocates on behalf of the common person, particularly for government intervention against big business.

predestination The idea that individual salvation or damnation is determined by God at, or just prior to, a person's birth. The concept of predestination invalidated the idea that salvation could be obtained through either faith or good works. *See also* Calvinism.

progressivism (progressive movement) A wide-ranging twentieth-century reform movement that advocated government activism to mitigate the problems created by urban industrialism. Progressivism reached its peak in 1912 with the creation of the Progressive Party, which ran Theodore Roosevelt for president. The term *progressivism* has come to mean any general effort advocating for social welfare programs.

Protestantism A powerful Christian reform movement that began in the sixteenth century with Martin Luther's critiques of the Roman Catholic Church. Over the centuries, Protestantism has taken many different forms, branching into numerous denominations with differing systems of worship.

Protestant Reformation *See* Reformation.

Puritanism The ideas and religious principles held by dissenters from the Church of England, including the belief that the church needed to be purified by eliminating the elements of Catholicism from its practices.

Reformation The reform movement that began in 1517 with Martin Luther's critiques of the Roman Catholic Church, which led to the formation of Protestant Christian groups. The English Reformation began with Henry VIII's break with the Roman Catholic Church, which established the Protestant Church of England. Henry VIII's decision was politically motivated; he had no particular quarrel with Catholic theology and remained an orthodox Catholic in most matters of religious practice.

reform Darwinism A social theory, based on Charles Darwin's theory of evolution, that emphasized activism, arguing that humans could speed up evolution by altering the environment. A challenge to social Darwinism, reform Darwinism condemned laissez-faire and demanded that the government take a more active approach to solving social problems. It became the ideological basis for progressive reform in the late nineteenth and early twentieth centuries. *See also* laissez-faire; social Darwinism.

republicanism The belief that the unworkable model of European-style monarchy should be replaced with a form of government in which supreme power resides in the hands of citizens with the right to vote and is exercised by a representative government answerable to this electorate. In Revolutionary-era America, republicanism became a social philosophy that embodied a sense of community and called individuals to act for the public good.

scientific management A system of organizing work, developed by Frederick Winslow Taylor in the late nineteenth century, to increase efficiency and productivity by breaking tasks into their component parts and training workers to perform specific parts. Labor resisted this effort because it de-skilled workers and led to the speedup of production lines. Taylor's ideas were most popular at the height of the Progressive Era.

Second Great Awakening A popular religious revival that preached that salvation was available to anybody who chose to take it. The revival peaked in the 1830s, and its focus on social perfection inspired many of the reform movements of the Jacksonian era. *See also* evangelicalism.

separate spheres A concept of gender relations that developed in the Jacksonian era and continued well into the twentieth century, holding that women's proper place was in the world of hearth and home (the private sphere) and men's was in the world of commerce and politics (the public sphere). The doctrine of separate spheres eroded slowly over the nineteenth and twentieth centuries as women became more and more involved in public activities. *See also* cult of domesticity.

social Darwinism A social theory, based on Charles Darwin's theory of evolution, that argued that all progress in human society came as the result of competition and natural selection. Gilded Age proponents such as William Graham Sumner and Herbert Spencer claimed that reform was useless because the rich and poor were precisely where nature intended them to be and intervention would retard the progress of humanity. *See also* reform Darwinism.

social gospel movement A religious movement in the late nineteenth and early twentieth centuries founded on the idea that Christians have a responsibility to reform society as well as individuals. Social gospel adherents encouraged people to put Christ's teachings to work in their daily lives by actively promoting social justice.

socialism A governing system in which the state owns and operates the largest and most important parts of the economy.

social purity movement A movement to end prostitution and eradicate venereal disease, often accompanied by the censorship of materials deemed "obscene."

spoils system An arrangement in which party leaders reward party loyalists with government jobs. This slang term for *patronage* comes from the saying "To the victor go the spoils." Widespread government corruption during the Gilded Age spurred reformers to curb the spoils system through the passage of the Pendleton Act in 1883, which created the Civil Service Commission to award government jobs on the basis of merit. *See also* civil service.

state sovereignty A state's autonomy or freedom from external control. The federal system adopted at the Constitutional Convention in 1787 struck a balance between state sovereignty and national control by creating a strong central government while leaving the states intact as political entities. The states remained in possession of many important powers on which the federal government cannot intrude.

states' rights A strict interpretation of the Constitution that holds that federal power over the states is limited and that the states hold ultimate sovereignty. First expressed in 1798 through the passage of the Virginia and Kentucky Resolutions, which were based on the assumption that the states have the right to judge the constitutionality of federal laws, the states' rights philosophy became a cornerstone of the South's resistance to federal control of slavery.

strict constructionism An approach to constitutional law that attempts to adhere to the original intent of the writers of the Constitution. Strict construction often produces Supreme Court decisions that defer to the legislative branch and to the states and restrict the power of the federal government. Opponents of strict construction argue that the Constitution is an organic document that must be interpreted to meet conditions unimagined when it was written.

suffrage The right to vote. The term *suffrage* is most often associated with the efforts of American women to secure voting rights. *See also* franchise.

Sun Belt The southern and southwestern regions of the United States, which grew tremendously in industry, population, and influence after World War II.

supply-side economics An economic theory based on the premise that tax cuts for the wealthy and for corporations encourage investment and production (supply), which in turn stimulate consumption. Embraced by the Reagan administration and other conservative Republicans, this theory reversed Keynesian economic policy, which assumes that the way to stimulate the economy is to create demand through federal spending on public works and general tax cuts that put more money into the hands of ordinary people. *See also* Keynesian economics.

temperance movement The reform movement to end drunkenness by urging people to abstain from the consumption of alcohol. Begun in the 1820s, this movement achieved its greatest political victory with the passage of a constitutional amendment in 1919 that prohibited the manufacture, sale, and transportation of alcohol. That amendment was repealed in 1933.

third world Originally a cold war term linked to decolonization, *third world* was first used in the late 1950s to describe newly independent countries in Africa and Asia that were not aligned with either Communist nations (the second world) or non-Communist nations (the first world). Later, the term was applied to all poor, nonindustrialized countries, in Latin America as well as in Africa and Asia. Many international experts see *third world* as a problematic category when applied to such a large and disparate group of nations, and they criticize the discriminatory hierarchy suggested by the term.

trickle-down economics The theory that financial benefits and incentives given to big businesses in the top tier of the economy will flow down to smaller businesses and individuals and thus benefit the entire nation. President Herbert Hoover unsuccessfully used the trickle-down strategy in his attempt to pull the nation out of the Great Depression, stimulating the economy through government investment in large economic enterprises and public works such as construction of the Hoover Dam. In the late twentieth century, conservatives used this economic theory to justify large tax cuts and other financial benefits for corporations and the wealthy.

Truman Doctrine President Harry S. Truman's assertion that American security depended on stopping any Communist government from taking over any non-Communist government—even nondemocratic and repressive dictatorships—anywhere in the world.

Beginning in 1947 with American aid to help Greece and Turkey stave off Communist pressures, this approach became a cornerstone of American foreign policy during the cold war.

trust A corporate system in which corporations give shares of their stock to trustees, who coordinate the industry to ensure profits to the participating corporations and curb competition. Pioneered by Standard Oil, such business practices were deemed unfair, were moderated by the Sherman Antitrust Act (1890), and were finally abolished by the combined efforts of Presidents Theodore Roosevelt and William Howard Taft and the sponsors of the 1914 Clayton Antitrust Act. The term *trust* is also loosely applied to all large business combinations. *See also* holding company.

vertical integration A system in which a single person or corporation controls all processes of an industry from start to finished product. Andrew Carnegie first used vertical integration in the 1870s, controlling every aspect of steel production from the mining of iron ore to the manufacturing of the final product, thereby maximizing profits by eliminating the use of outside suppliers or services.

virtual representation The notion, propounded by the British Parliament in the eighteenth century, that the House of Commons represented all British subjects—wherever they lived and regardless of whether they had directly voted for their representatives. Prime Minister George Grenville used this idea to argue that the Stamp Act and other parliamentary taxes on British colonists did not constitute taxation without representation. The American colonists rejected this argument, insisting that political representatives derived authority only from explicit citizens' consent (indicated by elections), and that members of a distant government body were incapable of adequately representing their interests.

War Hawks Young Republicans elected to the U.S. Congress in the fall of 1810 who were eager for war with Britain in order to legitimize attacks on Indians, end impressment, and avenge foreign insults. *See also* hawks.

welfare capitalism The idea that a capitalistic, industrial society can operate benevolently to improve the lives of workers. The notion of welfare capitalism became popular in the 1920s as industries extended the benefits of scientific management to improve safety and sanitation in the workplace as well as institute paid vacations and pension plans. *See also* scientific management.

welfare state A nation or state in which the government assumes responsibility for some or all of the individual and social welfare of its citizens. Welfare states commonly provide education, health care, food programs for the poor, unemployment compensation, and other social benefits. The United States dramatically expanded its role as a welfare state with the provisions of the New Deal in the 1930s.

Yankee imperialism A cry raised in Latin American countries against the United States when it intervened militarily in the region without invitation or consent from those countries.

yeoman A farmer who owned a small plot of land that was sufficient to support a family and was tilled by family members and perhaps a few servants.

Index

Abenaki Indians, 17
ABMs. See Antiballistic missiles
Abolition and abolitionism, 324–325, 360–361, 369, 395
    "gag rule" and, 327
    Lincoln and, 441, 442
    in Massachusetts, 216
    violence against, 325
    wartime reconstruction and, 462
    women and, 325–326, 358–359
Abortion and abortion rights, 867, 870, 906, 911
    debate over, 930(i)
Abraham Lincoln Brigade, 754
Abstract expressionism, 832
Abu Ghraib prison abuse, 969
Abundance. See also Consumers; Prosperity; Wealth
    culture of, 827–832
Academies, for women, 286, 289–290, 320
Accommodation
    by Indians, 267–268
    by slaves, 381
    Washington, Booker T., and, 646, 647
Acheson, Dean, 786, 795
Acoma pueblo, 13
    revolt in, 41
Acquired immune deficiency syndrome (AIDS), 931
Action painting, 832
Activism. See also Protest(s); Revolts and rebellions; specific individuals and movements
    civil rights movement and, 832–836, 840–842, 850–858
    feminist, 540–541
    gay and lesbian, 863
    Latino, 859–861
    Native American, 858–860
    of New Left and Counterculture, 861–863
    progressivism and, 619
    women's, 358–360, 540–541, 597–600, 863–868
Act of Supremacy (England, 1534), 84
AD (date notation), 5

ADA. See Americans with Disabilities Act
Adams, Abigail, 176, 178, 179, 187, 215, 271
Adams, Charles Francis, 399, 419–420
Adams, John, 115, 187
    Alien and Sedition Acts and, 262–264
    Boston Massacre and, 160
    on Boston Tea Party, 163
    cabinet of, 260–261
    Declaration of Independence and, 180
    election of 1796 and, 260
    election of 1800 and, 270
    at First Continental Congress, 165
    on French Revolution, 256–257
    Hamilton and, 240
    at Second Continental Congress, 176
    as vice president, 242, 243
    on voting rights, 214, 216
Adams, John Quincy, 269
    cabinet of, 296, 297
    election of 1824 and, 290, 295–296
    election of 1828 and, 310, 311(m)
    Monroe Doctrine and, 294–295
    presidency of, 296–297
Adams, Louisa Catherine, 295
Adams, Samuel, 161
    Articles of Confederation and, 213
    at First Continental Congress, 165
    at Second Continental Congress, 176
    on Shays's Rebellion, 226
    Stamp Act resistance by, 153
    Townshend duties and, 157
Adams-Onís Treaty (1819), 294
Adaptation, Native American, 18
Addams, Jane, 618(i), 638, 648
    Hull House and, 617–619, 620, 621
    woman suffrage and, 623–624
    World War I and, 667
Adding machine, 568
Adena culture, 14
Administrative Reorganization Act (1938), 743
Adventures of Huckleberry Finn, The (Twain), 522
Advertising
    in 1920s, 690
    on television, 829

Advice to American Women (Graves), 319
Advocate of Moral Reform (newspaper), 323
AEF. *See* American Expeditionary Force
Aerospace industry, 816(i), 825
AFDC. *See* Aid to Families with Dependent
    Children
Affirmative action. *See also* African
        Americans; specific groups
    Bakke case and, 911
    critics of, 928
    Johnson, L. B., executive order for (1965),
        855
    Nixon and, 870
    Thomas, Clarence, and, 943
    for women, 855, 864, 870
Affluent society. *See also* Wealth
    Galbraith on, 821
    in 1950s, 827–832
    during Reagan era, 926–927
Afghanistan
    Bush, G. W., and, 961
    Obama and, 972
    Soviets and, 921, 932, 935
    Taliban in, 966
    U.S. aid to rebels in, 933
AFL. *See* American Federation of Labor
Africa. *See also* African Americans; North
        Africa; Slaves and slavery
    Barbary Wars and, 272–273
    expeditions to, 30–31
    foods from, 127
    human emigration from, 5–6
    immigrants from, 112, 122–123
    influence on slaves' Christianity, 381
    Nixon and, 895
    Portugal and, 30–31
    slavery and, 31, 71
African Americans. *See also* Africa; Africans;
        Civil rights; Civil rights movement;
        Free blacks; Freedmen; Race and rac-
        ism; Race riots; Rights; Slaves and
        slavery; Voting and voting rights
    as abolitionists, 360–361
    accommodationism and, 646, 647
    in armed forces, 425–426, 443–444,
        444(i), 795
    black codes and, 466
    in Boston Massacre, 160, 160(i)
    as buffalo soldiers, 506
    Carter appointments of, 915, 916
    Christianity of, 381
    in cities, 561
    civil rights and, 794–795
    civil rights movement and, 832–836
    in Civil War, 449
    college enrollment in 1950s, 827
    Colored Farmers' Alliance and, 589
    in Continental army, 182
    as cowboys, 514
    departure from United States, 218
    discrimination against, 460, 466, 477,
        506, 538, 794
    education for, 645

election of 1960 and, 843
emancipation of, 216, 425, 427, 442–443
in government, 460(i), 475, 855, 951
in Great Depression, 712, 732
in House of Representatives, 460
Jim Crow laws and, 477, 538, 561
labor unions and, 573, 596
lineages of, 126
as loyalists, 202
lynchings of, 538–540, 561, 745
migration by, 699(m), 822
Montgomery bus boycott and,
    834–836
New Deal and, 731(i), 738–739, 745
in New Jersey, 215
as New Negroes, 694–696
in New York City, 694
in 1950s, 811
Obama and, 970–971
People's Party and, 602–603
in political office, 855
in presidential cabinet, 915
as presidential candidate, 911–912
in Progressive Era, 645–647
Red scare of 1950s and, 800
in Republican Party, 473
Revolution and, 197–198
rock and roll and, 831
school integration and, 910
Second Reconstruction and, 850–858
segregation of, 538, 563
sharecropping and, 478–479
as slaveholders, 388
Social Security and, 737
in South, 537
terrorism against, 483–484
as U.N. ambassador, 915
in Vietnam War, 887–888
wealth of, 341
in West, 506
women and, 287, 539, 540, 567, 666, 692
women's movement and, 866
in World War I, 660, 662
in World War II, 761, 767–768
African Methodist Episcopal Church, 464
Africans. *See also* African Americans; Slaves
        and slavery
    as indentured servants, 63
    as slaves, 63, 122
Agawam Indians, 92
Age. *See* Elderly
Agencies of government. *See* Departments of
        government; Government (U.S.);
        specific agencies
Agent Orange, 884, 889, 901
Age of Reason, The (Paine), 179(i)
Aggression. *See* specific conflicts
Agnew, Spiro T., 892, 913
Agrarianism, transformation of, 517
Agribusiness, 515, 517
Agricultural Adjustment Act (AAA)
    first (1933), 727, 730, 731(i)
    second (1938), 744

Agricultural rural domain (global economic region), 556(m), 557
Agriculture. *See also* Crops; Farms and farming; Rural areas; specific crops
    of ancient Americans, 11–12
    commercial, 515, 517
    in Confederacy, 446
    in 1840s and 1850s, 335–336
    for export trade, 245
    in Great Depression, 743–744
    Hispanic workers in, 739
    immigrant labor in, 960
    income (1920–1940), 708(f)
    Jefferson and, 271
    manufacturing and, 249
    markets for, 516
    migrant workers in, 515
    Native American, 18
    in New Deal, 727–728, 730–732, 743–744
    in New England, 94
    settlements, chiefdoms, and, 12–15
    sharecropping system of, 478–479, 515
    Social Security and, 737
    in South, 371–372, 371(m), 537
    technology and, 515, 821–822
    tobacco and, 62
    in Woodland cultures, 11–12
    in World War II, 767
Agriculture Department, creation of, 448
Aguinaldo, Emilio, 613
AIDS. *See* Acquired immune deficiency syndrome
Aid to Families with Dependent Children (AFDC), 846, 952–953
AIM. *See* American Indian Movement
Air-conditioning, 825
Air force
    Allied (World War II), 771
    in England, 757
    German, 757, 771
Airline industry, deregulation of, 916
Airplane, Sun Belt growth and, 823
Air pollution, 870, 951. *See also* Clean Air Act; Environment
    Carter and, 919
    Reagan and, 925
    from steamboats, 304
    from steelworks, 533(i)
Akan culture, 122
Alabama, 292, 368(m), 420, 459, 460. *See also* Birmingham; Montgomery
Alabama (Confederate cruiser), 440
Alamo, Battle of the, 348
Alaska, 350, 480
    humans in, 6
Albanians, ethnic, 957
Albany, New York, in Revolution, 192
Albany Congress, 144–145
Albany Plan of Union, 140, 145
Albright, Madeleine, 951
Albuquerque, 41
Alcatraz, Indian seizure of, 859

Alcohol and alcoholism. *See also* Temperance
    Indians and, 255, 344
    progressivism and, 621
    prohibition and, 691–692
    after World War I, 664–665
Algeciras, Spain, conference in, 635
Algiers, 272
Algonquian Indians, 17, 54, 56, 69, 143(m)
Alien and Sedition Acts (1798), 262–264, 317
Alien Land Law (California, 1913), 645
Aliens. *See* Illegal immigrants
Alito, Samuel A., 964
Allen, Doris, 901
Allende, Salvador, 895
Alliance(s). *See also* specific alliances
    with France, 196, 201, 261
    French-Indian, 142–143
    in peacetime, 789, 790
    in Revolutionary War, 196
    SEATO as, 818
    Washington on, 260
    in World War I, 655–657, 656(m)
    in World War II, 757, 758, 759, 777
Alliance for Progress, 880
Allies, in UN, 772–773
Allies (World War I), 655, 658–659, 662, 663. *See also* World War I; specific countries
    at Paris Peace Conference, 668–673
Allies (World War II), 755. *See also* World War II; specific countries
    after World War II, 782–783
Allotment policy, 498, 499–500, 727
Alphabet, Cherokee, 315
Al Qaeda, 966, 968, 969
Altgeld, John Peter, 596
Amalgamated Association of Iron and Steel Workers, 573, 591–592
Amalgamated Clothing Workers, 736
Amendments. *See also* specific amendments
    to Articles of Confederation, 210, 235
    Bill of Rights as, 243–244
    Tallmadge, 293
America(s). *See also* Central America; Exploration; North America; South America
    Monroe Doctrine and, 295
    naming of, 34
American Bell (telephone company), 530
American Civil Liberties Union (ACLU), 676–677
American Colonization Society, 324, 361
American Communist Party. *See* Communist Party
American Enterprise Institute, 905, 924
American Equal Rights Association, 469
American Expeditionary Force (AEF), 651, 661, 663
American Federation of Labor (AFL), 570, 573, 574, 575, 592, 601, 664, 675. *See also* Labor unions; Strikes
    CIO merger with, 822

American Federation of Labor *(continued)*
  in Great Depression, 711, 736
  women workers and, 621–622, 623
American GI Forum, 796, 796(i), 825, 861
American Historical Association, 489
American Independent Party, 892, 893
American Indian Movement (AIM), 859
American Indians. *See* Native Americans
Americanization
  immigrants and, 561
  of Vietnam War, 886–887, 891
American Liberty League, 730, 737
American Medical Association, 693, 737
American National Exhibition (Moscow, 1959), 810(i)
American Party. *See* Know-Nothing Party
American Philosophical Society, 130
American Psychiatric Association, gays classified by, 863
American Railway Union (ARU), Pullman strike and, 596, 597
American Recovery and Reinvestment Act (2009), 971
American Red Cross, 449
American Revolution. *See* Revolutionary War
American Sugar Refining Company, 547
Americans with Disabilities Act (ADA, 1990), 943
American system, of manufacturing, 337
American System, of Clay, 295
American Telephone and Telegraph (AT&T), 530
American Temperance Society, 322
American Tobacco Company, 537, 628
American Woman Suffrage Association (AWSA), 599
Amherst, Jeffery, 148, 149
Amish, 117
Amoco, 529
Amusement parks, 577
Anaconda Plan, 432
Anarchism, 574
  Sacco and Vanzetti trial and, 700
  unionism and, 593
Anasazi culture, 13
Ancient Americans, 1–22, 2(i). *See also* specific groups
Anderson, "Bloody Bill," 438
Anderson, John B., 923
Anderson, Robert, 428
Andros, Edmund, 104
Angel Island immigration station, 562
Anglican Church. *See* Church of England
Anglo-Americans
  in California gold rush, 356
  in Mexican borderlands, 347
  in Southwest, 507
Angola, 933, 935
  culture of, 122
  slaves from, 63

Animals. *See also* Hunters and hunting; specific animals
  ancient hunting of, 7–8, 9–10
Ann Arbor, Michigan, antidiscrimination ordinance in, 863
Annexation(s)
  of Florida, 336
  Hawai'i and, 606–607
  after Mexican-American War, 336
  of Oregon, 336
  Santo Domingo and, 480
  of Texas, 349
Anschluss, 755, 769
Antebellum era, 367, 456
Anthony, Susan B., 409, 469, 469(i), 540, 599–600
Anthracite coal strike (1902), 628–630
Antiabortion movement, 930
Anti-Americanism
  Iraq War and, 969
  support for Israel and, 896
Antiballistic missiles (ABMs), 895
Antiballistic Missile Treaty (1972), 932, 967
Anticommunism, 905, 906
  Eisenhower and, 803
  Kennedy, John F., and, 876, 882
  Nixon and, 894
  Reagan and, 932
Antietam, Battle of (1862), 435(m), 436–437
Antifederalists, 232–234, 236
  Bill of Rights and, 241–242
Antifeminism, 929
Anti-German sentiment, during World War I, 665, 667
Antigovernment sentiment, 907
Anti-immigrant sentiment, 408, 505
Anti-imperialism, 613
Antilynching legislation, 539
Antilynching movement, 538–540
Anti-Nazi League, 780
Antinomians, 93
Antipoverty programs. *See also* Great Society
  of Clinton, 951
  of Johnson, L. B., 845
  of Kennedy, 844
Antiquities Act (1906), 632
Anti-Saloon League, 621
Anti-Semitism. *See also* Jews and Judaism
  of Hitler, 753
Antislavery movement, 395, 400. *See also* Abolition and abolitionism
  Republican Party and, 408–409
  Whig party and, 399
Antisodomy laws, 932
Antitax movement, 909(i), 910
Antitrust activities
  legislation, 547
  Roosevelt, T., and, 627–628
  Taft and, 637
  of Wilson, 641
Antiwar movement, in Vietnam War, 889–890, 889(i), 892, 897–898

Apache Indians, 17, 18, 350, 501–502
Apollo program, 879
Appalachian Mountains, settlement and, 119
Appeal to the Christian Women of the South, An (Angelina Grimké), 302
Appeal . . . to the Coloured Citizens of the World, An (Walker), 324, 366
Appeal to the Women of the Nominally Free States, An (Angelina Grimké), 302
Appeasement, before World War II, 755, 783–785
Apple computer, 927
Appliances, in 1950s, 827
Appomattox Court House, Virginia, 455
Apprentices, in trades, 321
Apprenticeship, laws in black codes, 466
Arab-Israeli wars
　Six-Day War (1967), 895–896, 917
　Yom Kippur War (1973), 896
Arab world. *See also* Arab-Israeli wars; Iraq War; Middle East; specific locations
　Clinton and, 957
　Eisenhower and, 819
　energy crisis and, 869
　Israel and, 791, 819
　Jews and, 670
　Nixon and, 895
　Obama and, 972
Arafat, Yasir, 957
Aragon, 25–26
Arapaho Indians, 344, 498, 503
Arbella (ship), 87, 89
Arbenz, Jacobo, 818
Arbitration, in strikes, 594, 596
Arbitration treaties, Taft and, 637
Archaeologists, 3
Archaic Indians, 8–12
Architecture, skyscrapers and, 578–579, 578(i)
Arctic National Wildlife Refuge, 919, 963
Argonne Cemetery, 680
Arikara Indians, 500
Aristide, Jean-Bertrand, 956
Aristocracy, in Carolina, 75
Arizona, 7(i), 13, 493
Ark (ship), 67
Arkansas, 277, 368, 418, 429, 462
　school integration in, 833
Arkansas River region, Osage in, 273–274
Armada (Spain), 56
Armed forces. *See* Continental army; Military; specific battles and wars
Armed neutrality policy, 659
Armenian immigrants, 559
Arminianism, 93
Armistice
　in Korean War, 804–805
　World War I and, 663
Arms and armaments. *See* Weapons; specific weapons
Arms limitation treaties, 894–895

Arms race, 816(i). *See also* Disarmament; Nuclear arms race; Nuclear weapons
　Eisenhower and, 816–817, 820–821
　Reagan and, 932–933
Armstrong, Louis, 696
Army Air Corps, in World War II, 749
Army of Northern Virginia, 436
Army of the Potomac, 434, 437, 451
Army of the Republic of Vietnam (ARVN), 818, 875, 883, 888, 891, 896, 897
Arnaz, Desi, 829
Arnold, Benedict, 183, 199–200, 199(i)
"Arsenal of democracy," U.S. as, 762
Art(s). *See also* Literature; Painting; Poets and poetry; specific arts and artists
　Chumash, 11(i)
　Great Depression and, 732
　in Harlem Renaissance, 695–696
　Lost Generation and, 691, 697–698
　National Arts and Humanities Act and, 847
　in 1950s, 831–832
　WPA support for, 734
Arthur, Chester A., 542–543
Article 231 (World War I peace treaty), 670
Articles of Confederation (1781–1789), 208–213. *See also* Constitution (U.S.)
　amendments to, 235
　Article 8 of, 210
　Indians and, 253
　problems of, 218–227
　ratification of, 211, 212(m)
　revising, 227
　war debts and, 210, 218–219, 225
Artifacts, ancient American, 22
Artisans, 565
　slaves as, 379
ARVN. *See* Army of the Republic of Vietnam
Asante culture, 122
Asia. *See also* specific countries and regions
　immigrants from, 507–508, 700
　Japan and, 758–759
　Open Door policy in, 608, 609, 633, 635
　Pacific ports for trade with, 343
　Portugal and, 31
　sailing to, 31–32, 34–35
　Taft and, 637
　trade with, 605, 608
　U.S. role in, 805, 933
　World War I and, 670–671
Asian Americans
　McCarran-Walter Act and, 798
　New Deal and, 739–740
Assassinations
　of Garfield, 543
　of Kennedy, J. F., 841, 844, 884
　of Kennedy, R. F., 892
　of King, Martin Luther, Jr., 855, 858, 892
　of Lincoln, 455–456, 465
　of McKinley, 626
　Reagan shooting and, 924

Assemblies. *See also* Legislatures; specific colonies and states
  colonial, 136, 164, 165
  protests by, 154–155, 157
  in Seven Years' War, 146
  two-chamber, 214
  in Virginia, 60
Assembly lines, 684, 689
Assimilation
  immigrants and, 561
  of Indians, 498, 499–500, 813
Astrolabe, 30
Astronauts, 879
Astronomy, of Anasazi, 13
Aswan Dam, 819
Atahualpa (Incas), 39
Atchison, David Rice, 411–412
Athapascan Indians, 18
Atlanta
  fall of (1864), 452(m), 454
  race riot in, 647
Atlanta Compromise, 646
Atlanta Constitution, 537
Atlantic and Pacific Railroad, 525
Atlantic Charter (1941), 758
Atlantic Ocean region
  Civil War in, 439
  commerce in, 111, 115–116, 129
  European exploration of, 31–36
  slave trade in, 122–125
  trade in, 114(m), 115–116
  in World War II, 760, 764
Atomic bomb. *See also* Nuclear weapons
  Soviet, 788–789
  in World War II, 750–751, 775–776, 776(i)
Attorney general, 242
Attucks, Crispus, 160, 160(i)
Audiotapes, Watergate, 913
Augusta, Georgia, 197
Auschwitz, Poland, concentration camp in, 770
Austin, Stephen F., 347
Australia, 559, 763
Austria, *Anschluss* with Nazi Germany and, 755
Austria-Hungary, World War I and, 656, 656(m), 670
Automobiles and automobile industry, 688–689. *See also* Suburbs
  consumer safety and, 847
  Ford and, 683–685
  foreign-owned companies in, 927
  non-union labor and, 959
  Sun Belt growth and, 823
  UAW strike in (1937), 736
Axis powers, 751, 759, 776. *See also* World War II; specific countries
Ayllón, Lucas Vázquez de, 39
Aztecs. *See* Mexica (people)

B-17 Flying Fortress (bomber), 749, 770–771
B-29 Super Fortress (bomber), 750, 750(i)

Babington School District v. Schemta (1963), 850
Baby boom, 828
Baby boom generation, affluence and, 926–927
Backcountry
  immigrants in, 122
  in Revolutionary War, 200
"Back to Africa" movement, 694
Bacon, Nathaniel, 70
Bacon's Laws (1676), 70
Bacon's Rebellion, 69–71
Baer, George, 629
Baker, Ella, 836, 841(i), 851
Baker, Isaac Wallace, 356(i)
Baker, Newton D., 660–661
Baker v. Carr (1963), 849
Bakke case, 911
Balance of power
  Roosevelt, T., and, 635
  World War I and, 656, 671
Balboa, Vasco Núñez de, 34
Balkan region, 670
Ball, Lucille, 829
"Ballad of Pretty Boy Floyd, The," 711
Ballparks, 577
Baltimore (Lord), 67, 105
Baltimore, Maryland, Democratic convention in, 418
Baltimore and Ohio Railroad, 305, 571
Bambara culture, 122
"Banana republics," 608
Bank(s) and banking, 307. *See also* Bank of the United States; Federal Reserve Board; Panics
  charters for, 318
  during Civil War, 448
  commercial, 247
  deregulation and, 746, 916, 925–926
  finance capitalism and, 532–534
  in Great Depression, 705–706, 707, 723–725
  Hamilton on, 240
  national bank and, 248–249, 317–319
  in South, 373
  Wilson and, 640–641
"Bank holiday" (1933), 723
Banknotes, 307, 318
Bank of England, 249
Bank of the United States
  first, 248–249
  Jackson and, 312
  second, 307, 308, 318
Bank runs. *See also* Panics
  in 1839, 329
Bank runs. *See also* Great Depression
Bankruptcies
  of farmers (1920s), 686
  in S&L industry, 926
Banks, Dennis, 859
Bank War, 317–319
Bannock Shoshoni Indians, 505

Baptist and Commoner (magazine), 702
Baptists, 130, 380, 386, 464
women and, 288
Barbados, 73, 74
Barbary Wars (1801–1805), 272–273
Barbed wire, 514
Barboncito (Navajo leader), 494
Barrios, in California, 507
Barry, Leonora, 573
Barter, among yeomen, 384
Barton, Clara, 449
Baruch, Bernard, 664
Baseball, 577
integration of, 696, 795
move by Brooklyn Dodgers and, 823
Bastogne, in World War II, 771
Bataan Death March, 763
Batista, Fulgencio, 752, 819
Baton Rouge, Louisiana, bus boycott in, 834
Battle of Britain (1940), 757
Battle of the Bulge (1944–1945), 771–772
Battles. *See* specific battles and wars
Bay of Pigs invasion (1961), 879, 882
Bayonet rule, in South, 482, 484
Beals, Melba Patillo, 833
Bear Flag Revolt, 348
Beat generation, 831–832, 862
Beautification, environmental, 847
Beaver furs, 142. *See also* Fur trade
Beecher, Catharine, 289
Beecher, Lyman, 322. *See also* Stowe,
Harriet Beecher
Begin, Menachem, 921
Belgium, German invasion of, 755
Bell, Alexander Graham, 530
Bell, John, 407(m), 418
Belleau Wood, battle at, 663
Bends (medical condition), building of
Brooklyn Bridge and, 553–554
Benét, Stephen Vincent, 417
Bentley, Elizabeth, 798
Benton, Thomas Hart (senator), 343, 409
Beringia (land bridge), 6
Berkeley, California, free speech movement
in, 861–862
Berkeley, William, 68, 69
Berkman, Alexander, 593
Berlin, Germany
Allied occupation of, 788
Red Army capture of, 773
Berlin, Treaty of (1899), 608
Berlin airlift, 788, 788(i)
Berlin crisis (1961), 880
Berlin Wall, 880, 947, 949(i)
Bernard, Francis, 153, 157, 159
Berry, Chuck, 831
Bessemer, Henry, 527
Bethlehem, Pennsylvania, 120(i)
Bethlehem Steel, 534
Bethune, Mary McLeod, 739
Bett, Mum (Elizabeth Freeman), 216
Bevin, Ernest, 787

Bibb, Henry, 360
Bible, King James version of, 85
Bicycle, 587(i)
"Big Bonanza," 505
Big business. *See also* Business; Economy
farming as, 515, 517
in Great Depression, 723
railroads as, 525–527
regulation of, 535, 641
Roosevelt, T., and, 639
Big-city boss. *See* Bosses (political)
Bight of Biafra, 109, 124
Big Knives, Americans as, 267
"Big stick" foreign policy, of Roosevelt,
Theodore, 633–635
Big Three (World War II), 772
"Billion Dollar Congress," 546
Bill of rights
under Articles of Confederation, 214, 216
in state constitutions, 243
Bill of Rights (U.S.), 241, 243–244. *See also*
Amendments; Constitution (U.S.);
specific Amendments
equal protection in, 849
Red scare of 1950s and, 799
Bin Laden, Osama, 946, 957, 966, 969
Biological weapons, Bush, George W., and,
967
Biracialism, in South, 369
Bird reservations, 632
"Birds of passage" (immigrants), 560
Birmingham, Alabama, 537, 852
Birney, James G., 350
Birth control movement, 643–644, 694, 862
Birthrate. *See also* Baby boom
baby boom and, 828
in Great Depression, 710
in 1950s, 827
of slaves, 125
Bison (buffalo)
Archaic Indian hunters of, 7, 9
Plains Indians and, 17, 344, 493
slaughter of, 495
Black Cabinet, of Roosevelt, Franklin D.,
739
Black codes, 466, 467, 468
Black Death, 29
Black Elk (Oglala holy man), 498
Blackfeet Indians, 17
Black Hawk (Sauk and Fox Indians), 315
Black Hawk War (1832), 315, 432
Black Hills, Indians and, 497–498
Black Kettle (Cheyenne leader), 494
Blacklist, in movie industry, 799
Black market, in Revolution, 191
Black Muslims, 857
Black Panther Party for Self-Defense, 858
Black power, 857–858
Blacks. *See* Africa; African Americans;
Africans; Free blacks; Freedmen;
Slaves and slavery
Black Star Line, 694

Black suffrage, 460(i), 462, 470. *See also* African Americans; Voting and voting rights
Black Thursday (October 24, 1929), 705
Black Tuesday (October 29, 1929), 706
Blackwell, Unita, 855
Blaine, James G., 542, 543–544, 544(m), 545, 608
Bleeding Kansas, 411–412
"Bleeding Sumner," 412
Blitzkrieg ("lightning war"), 755, 756(i)
Blockade runners, 425, 439
Blockades
    in Civil War, 432, 439
    in Cuban missile crisis, 881
    in Vietnam War, 898
    in World War I, 657, 659, 669
"Bloody Sunday," in Montgomery, 853
Bloomers, 359(i)
Blue-collar workers, 907, 927
    Great Depression and, 713
Blue Eagle campaign (NRA), 729
Blue Jacket (Shawnee Indians), 253, 255
Boarding schools, for Indians, 499
Board of Indian Commissioners, 499
Board of Trade (Britain), 136
Boeing, 816(i)
Boleyn, Anne, 85
Bolsheviks and Bolshevism. *See also* Communism; Russia; Soviet Union
    Bolshevik Revolution and, 660, 677, 752
    after World War I, 675–676
Bombs and bombings. *See also* Atomic bomb; Nuclear weapons
    of Cambodia, 896–897
    of England, 756–757
    of German targets, 773
    Haymarket, 574–575, 593
    in Iraq War, 967
    of Oklahoma City federal building, 952
    of Vietnam, 884, 885, 886–887, 898, 899
    in World War II, 749–751, 770–771
Bomb shelters, 820
Bonanza farms, 515
Bond, Julian, 913
Bonds, 247–248
    under Articles of Confederation, 210
    to finance Civil War, 433
Bonfield, John ("Blackjack"), 575
Bonus Marchers, in Great Depression, 711–712, 734
Book of Mormon, The, 346
Boom and bust cycles, 308–309, 525–526, 640–641
Boonesborough, Kentucky, 194
Bootblacks, 567, 567(i)
Booth, John Wilkes, 455–456, 465
Borah, William, 672
Border(s). *See also* Boundaries
    with Canada, 221
    Venezuela–British Guiana dispute and, 608
Borderlands

of English colonies, 131–135
    Mexican, 347–348, 349
    Spanish, 72–73
Border states (Civil War), 430, 450
    Emancipation Proclamation and, 442
    freedom for blacks and, 441
    secession and, 429, 429(m)
Boré, Étienne de, 371
Bork, Robert, 929
Borrowing. *See also* Credit
    consumer, 828
Bosch, Juan, 886
Bosnia, 956–957
    peacekeeping in, 957
Bosque Redondo Reservation, 494
Bosses (political), 542, 543, 580–582
Boston, 87, 403, 560. *See also* Massachusetts
    British military occupation of, 141
    police strike in (1919), 675
    resistance in, 153, 157
    school busing in, 910–911
    wealth in, 115
Boston *Courier,* 569
Boston Massacre, 159–161, 160(i)
Boston Port Act (1774), 163
Boston Public Library, 579–580
Boston Tea Party (1773), 162–163
Boudry, Nancy, 378
Boundaries. *See also* Border(s)
    with Canada, 285
    of Connecticut, 211
    with Creek Indians, 252
    of Louisiana Purchase, 294
    Mason-Dixon line as, 366–367, 368
    with Mexico, 351–352
    of Missouri, 293
    of 1763, 149
    of Texas, 400, 401
    of Virginia, 211
Bow, Clara, 696
Bow and arrow, as Native American weapons, 9
Bowdoin, James, 226
Bowie, James, 348
Boxer Protocol (1901), 607
Boxer uprising (China), 607
Boxing, 696–697
Boycotts
    anti-British, 157–159
    colonial, 157, 165
    grape, 861
    against integration, 910
    of Pullman cars, 596
    against segregation, 834–836
    Soviet, of UN Security Council, 801
Boyer, LaNada, 859
Boys. *See also* Men
    in workforce, 567, 567(i)
Bozeman Trail, 497
BP (years before the present, date notation), 5
Bracero program, 825, 826(i)
Braddock, Edward, 146

Bradford, William, 85, 86
Brady, Mathew, 419(i), 455(i)
Branches of government. *See also* specific
    branches
    in Constitution, 230
Brandeis, Louis, 641
Brant, Joseph (Thayendanegea), 188,
    192–193, 194, 203, 221
Bray, Rosemary, 848
Brazil, 34
    slavery in, 369, 371
Bread riots, 446
Breaker boys (child labor), 629(i)
Breckinridge, John C., 407(m), 418, 419
Br'er Rabbit and Br'er Fox stories, 381
Brest-Litovsk, treaty of (1918), 662
Brezhnev, Leonid, 921
Briand, Aristide, 688
Bridges, 528
    Brooklyn, 553–555, 565, 578
Briggs, Laura, 783
Brinksmanship, 817
Britain. *See* England (Britain)
Britain, Battle of, 757. *See also* England
    (Britain)
British Empire. *See also* Colonies and coloniza-
    tion; England (Britain); specific colonies
    colonial politics in, 101–105, 135–136
British Guiana, Venezuela and, 608
British North America. *See also* Colonies
    and colonization; England (Britain);
    Navigation Acts; North America
    expansion of, 111–135
    French, Spanish, and, 131–135, 132(m)
    unifying elements in, 128–136
Brooklyn Bridge, 553–555, 565, 578
Brooklyn Dodgers, move by, 823
Brooks, Gwendolyn, 795
Brooks, Preston, 412
Brotherhood of Sleeping Car Porters, 767–768
Brown, Edmund, 908
Brown, John, 396(i)
    Harpers Ferry raid by, 395–396, 417
    Pottawatomie Creek killings by, 395, 412
Brown, Joseph E., 445
Brown, Oliver, 833
Brown, William Wells, 360
Browne, George ("Brownie"), 651–653,
    652(i), 663
Brown power, 861
Brownsville (Brooklyn, New York), birth con-
    trol clinic in, 643
Brownsville incident (1906), 646
Brown v. Board of Education (1954), 796–
    797, 833, 849
Bruce, Blanche K., 475
Brunauer, Esther, 799
Bryan, William Jennings
    election of 1896 and, 603–605
    election of 1904 and, 630
    election of 1908, 636
    Scopes trial and, 701

as secretary of state, 654
on U.S expansionism, 613
World War I and, 658
Bryce, James, 581
Bubonic plague. *See* Black Death
Buchanan, James, 407(m), 410–411, 415,
    421, 868
Buckley v. Valeo (1976), 914
Bucktails, 310
Budget. *See* Federal budget
Buena Vista, Mexico, battle at, 352, 353
Buffalo. *See* Bison (buffalo)
Buffalo soldiers, 506
Buffalo Telegraph, 544
Bulgaria, 785
Bulge, Battle of the (1944–1945), 771–772
Bull Moose Party. *See* Progressive Party, of
    1912
Bull Run (Manassas)
    first Battle of (1861), 434, 435(m)
    second Battle of (1862), 435(m), 436
"Bully pulpit," Roosevelt, Theodore, on, 626,
    627(i)
Bunche, Ralph J., 795
Bundy, McGeorge, 884
Bunker Hill, Battle of (1775), 177, 181
Bureaucracy, 543. *See also* Departments of
    government; specific departments
    Reagan and, 926
Bureau of Corporations, 628
Bureau of Indian Affairs, 503
    Indian relocation and, 496
Bureau of Refugees, Freedmen, and
    Abandoned Lands. *See* Freedmen's
    Bureau
Burger, Warren E., 911
Burgoyne, John, 177, 185(m), 192, 193
Burial mounds
    Adena, 14
    in Cahokia, 1–3, 2(i)
Burials, by Woodland peoples, 11, 14
Burleson, Albert, 668
Burma, 773
Burnham, Daniel, 582
Burns, Anthony, 403
Burnside, Ambrose, 437
Burr, Aaron, 208(i)
    duel with Hamilton, 271(i)
    election of 1796 and, 260
    election of 1800 and, 270
Bus boycott, in Montgomery, 834–836,
    850
Bush, George H. W., 907, 923
    Central America and, 945–946
    election of 1988 and, 942
    election of 1992 and, 941, 949
    end of Cold War and, 947
    foreign policy of, 942–945, 956
    government under, 942–945
    Iran-Contra scandal pardons by, 934
    Iraq and, 945–946, 969
    Persian Gulf War and, 946

Bush, George W., 941
  cabinet of, 963
  domestic policy of, 962–967
  economy and, 963
  election of 2000 and, 961
  election of 2004 and, 961, 968
  foreign policy and, 961
  presidential powers and, 967
  Supreme Court and, 064
  trade and, 958
Business. *See also* Big business;
    Corporations; Finance capitalism
  campaign contributions and, 543
  foreign markets and, 608, 690
  foreign policy and, 606–607
  in Gilded Age, 523–525, 525–531,
    531–534, 535
  Great Depression and, 723–725
  management changes in, 689
  mechanization in, 568
  monopolies in, 526, 530
  in New Deal, 728–729
  New Deal reforms of, 729–730
  in 1920s, 685, 686
  in 1990s, 955
  private development and, 339
  Reagan administration and, 925–926,
    927
  regulation of trusts and, 529, 627–628
  telephones and, 530
  in World War I, 664
Business organization. *See also* Corporations
  horizontal integration, 529
  vertical integration, 528
Busing, school integration and, 906, 910
Butler, Andrew P., 412
Butler, Benjamin F., 441
Butler, Nicholas Murray, 667
Byington, Margaret, 576, 577
Byles, Mather, 189

Cabinet (presidential). *See* specific presidents
    and posts
Cable cars, 579
Cabot, John, 34, 48
Cabral, Pedro Álvars, 34
Cady, Elizabeth. *See* Stanton, Elizabeth
    Cady
Cahokia, 1–3, 2(i), 14, 15(i), 17
Caissons, 553, 554(i)
Calhoun, John C., 282–283, 326, 397, 400
  election of 1824 and, 295–296
  nullification and, 312, 316–317
  on slavery, 327, 370, 398–399, 414
California, 400, 401. *See also* Los Angeles
  acquisition of, 348, 349, 350
  Asians in, 635, 645
  Bear Flag Revolt in, 348
  Chinese in, 355–356, 356(i), 507–508
  conservatism in, 908
  cultures of, 10
  discrimination in, 855
  gold rush in, 349, 354–357

  gun control in, 943
  higher education in, 826
  manifest destiny and, 493
  Mexican Americans in, 507, 711, 825
  Mexican-American War in, 352
  Mexican migration to, 348
  population growth in, 823
  progressivism in, 626
  Reagan as governor of, 908, 923
  tax revolt in, 909(i), 910
  woman suffrage and, 600
California Indians, 348
California peoples, 10
California Trail, 348
Californios, 349, 356, 507
Calley, William, 898
Calvin, John, and Calvinism, 90
Cambodia, 883, 899
  bombing of, 896–897
  U.S. invasion of (1970), 897
Cambridge (ship), 425
Camden, Battle of (1780), 198(m), 199
Campaigns (military). *See* specific battles
    and wars
Campaigns (political). *See also* Elections
  financing of, 914
Camp David accords, 921
Camp followers, in Revolution, 192
Camp meetings, 386, 386(i)
Canada, 459, 559. *See also* New France;
    specific locations
  African Americans in, 218
  black loyalists in, 202, 217(i)
  border with, 221, 285
  Catholicism in, 163
  England and, 49, 147
  immigrants from, 504
  loyalists in, 189
  Mohawk relocation to, 203
  NAFTA and, 958
  Oregon and, 350
  in Revolutionary War, 183, 184(m), 192
  slave movement to, 169, 403
  War of 1812 and, 269, 283, 285
Canals, 304–305. *See also* Panama Canal
Canal Zone. *See* Panama Canal
Canary Islands, 32
Cane Ridge revival, 321
Cannon, Joseph, 632
Cantigny, battle at, 662
CAP. *See* Community Action Program
Cape of Good Hope, 31
Cape Verde Islands, Portugal and, 31
Capital (financial), of national bank, 249
Capital city. *See also* Washington, D.C.
  under Articles of Confederation, 212–213
  at Potomac site, 248
Capital gains tax, 916
Capitalism
  corporate, 565
  crony, 527
  finance, 532–534
  in Great Depression, 712, 723

panic of 1837 and, 329
welfare, 689
Capitol, British burning of, 285
Capone, Alphonse ("Big Al"), 691–692
Caputo, Philip, 899
Caravel, 31
Caribbean region. *See also* specific locations
exploration of, 36
Haitian Revolution in, 258–259
immigrants from, 859
Roosevelt, T., and, 633
slavery in, 74–77, 251
sugar in, 73–75
Taft and, 637
U.S. involvement in, 480, 608, 878(m), 933
Carleton, Guy, 202
Carlisle Indian School, 499
Carmel, California, mission in, 134(i)
Carmichael, Stokely, 841(i), 857–858
Carnegie, Andrew, 523, 557–559, 568, 570
and gospel of wealth, 535
Homestead strike and, 537, 591–592, 593
Morgan, J. P., and, 533, 534
social Darwinism and, 535
steel industry and, 527–528
Carnegie Endowment for International
Peace, 666–667
Carney, Kate, 377
Carolina(s). *See also* North Carolina; South
Carolina
emancipation in, 218
in 17th century, 74(m)
slavery in, 75
western settlement in, 119
Carpetbaggers, 459, 473–474
Carranza, Venustiano, 654
Cars. *See* Automobiles and automobile
industry
Carson, Rachel, 870
Carter, James Earl, Jr. ("Jimmy"), 906–907,
950
cabinet of, 915
domestic policy of, 915–916
election of 1976 and, 907, 914–915
election of 1980, 916, 922, 923
energy and, 917
environment and, 919
foreign policy of, 921–922
human rights and, 919–921
Iran hostage crisis and, 922
Carter Doctrine, 922
Cartier, Jacques, 48
Casablanca meeting (1943), 765
Cash-and-carry foreign trade policy, 754, 757
Cash crops, 371–372. *See also* specific crops
Cash register, 568
Cass, Lewis, 399, 407(m)
Castile, 25
Castle Garden, 562
Castro, Fidel, 818–819, 879
Bay of Pigs invasion and, 879
CIA illegal activities against, 914
Casualties. *See also* specific wars and battles

Brooklyn Bridge construction and,
553–554
in Iraq War, 969
in Mexican War, 353
in Revolutionary War, 183
Catechism for Colored Persons (Jones), 381
Cathay Company, 49
Catholicism. *See also* Missions and missionaries; Protestant Reformation; Religion(s)
in Canada, 163
in colonies, 130
in England, 104
in Maryland, 67
in New France, 105
in New Mexico and Florida, 72–73
vs. Protestantism, 90, 408
Protestant Reformation and, 47–48
of Smith, Alfred, 702
Catlin, George, 344
Catt, Carrie Chapman, 666
Cattell, James McKeen, 667
Cattle. *See* Ranching
Cattle trails, 512(m)
Cayuga Indians, 17, 188
Cell phones, 958
Censorship, of mail, 643
Census
of 1790, 247(i)
of 1810, 282
racial categories on forms of, 961
Central America. *See also* Latin America;
specific countries and regions
ancient cultures of, 8
U.S. intervention in, 608, 878(m), 933–934
Central American–Dominican Republic Free
Trade Agreement, 958
Central Intelligence Agency (CIA)
Chilean destabilization by, 895
covert operations of, 922
creation of, 789–790
Cuba and, 818–819, 879, 881
Eisenhower and, 810, 816
Guatemala and, 818
illegal activities by, 914
Iran-Contra scandal and, 934
secret operations of, 816–817
spying on peace advocates, 890
Watergate and, 912
Central Pacific Railroad, 507
Central Park (New York City), 579, 580
Century of Dishonor, A (Jackson), 500
Cerro Gordo, Mexico, battle at (1847), 353
Certificates of debt
financing after Revolution, 248
in Revolution, 191
Cession, of Indian land. *See* Land; Native
Americans
Chacoan culture and Chaco Canyon, 13
Chamberlain, Neville, 755
Chamber of Commerce, 729–730, 737
Chambers, Whittaker, 798
Champlain, Lake, 146
Chancellorsville, battle at (1863), 436

Chao, Elaine L., 963
Chaplin, Charlie, 696
Chapultepec, Battle of (1847), 353–354
Charities, in Great Depression, 709
Charles I (England), 67, 85, 86, 94
Charles I (Spain). *See* Charles V (Holy Roman Empire)
Charles II (England), 75, 99, 100, 104
Charles V (Charles I of Spain, Holy Roman Empire), 34, 47–48
Charleston, South Carolina, 75
    Democratic convention in, 418
    Fort Sumter attack in, 428
    in Revolutionary War, 197, 201
Charlestown. *See* Bunker Hill, Battle of
Charles Towne. *See* Charleston
Charter(s)
    bank, 249, 318
    of Bank of the United States, 307, 318
    of Carolina, 75
    of Massachusetts, 86, 91, 104, 220
    of New York, 220
    UN, 772–773
    of Virginia Company, 60
Charter of Privileges (Pennsylvania), 101
Chase, Salmon P., 400, 401, 433, 465, 472
Château-Thierry, battle at, 662
Chattanooga, Battle of (1863), 451, 452(m)
Chavez, Cesar, 860, 860(i)
"Checkers speech" (Nixon), 803
Checks and balances, 230
Chemical weapons, 889
Cheney, Richard B.
    Iraq War and, 967
    Persian Gulf War and, 969
    as vice president, 962
Chernobyl, Ukraine, nuclear reactor explosion at, 917
Cherokee Indians, 133, 437
    constitution of, 315
    during Revolution, 194–195
    Trail of Tears and, 315, 316, 493, 494
Cherokee strip, land rush in, 513
Cherry Valley, 194
Chesapeake (ship), 279–280
Chesapeake region. *See also* Maryland; South; Tobacco and tobacco industry; Virginia
    English colonies in, 53–55, 60–71, 61(m)
    hierarchy in, 67–71
    population in, 122
    religion in, 66–67
    servants in, 65
    slavery in, 71–77, 124, 126
    tobacco society in, 60–71
    trade in, 103
Chesnut, Mary Boykin, 377, 391
Chevron oil company, 529
Cheyenne Indians, 17, 344, 494, 497, 498, 503
Chiang Kai-shek. *See* Jiang Jieshi (Chiang Kai-shek)

Chicago, 528, 555
    African Americans in, 561, 822
    de facto segregation in, 855
    Democratic National Convention in (1968), 892
    Fort Dearborn and, 283
    Great Fire of 1871 in, 578
    Haymarket bombing in, 574–575
    Hull House in, 617–619
    immigrants in, 560
    King, Martin Luther, Jr., in, 858
    skyscrapers in, 578–579, 578(i)
    World's Columbian Exposition in, 489, 582–583
Chicago Bears (football team), 697
Chicago Daily Tribune, 797
Chicago Inter-Ocean, 539
"Chicago school" of architecture, 579
Chicago Tribune, 467
    on Pullman strike, 597
Chicanos, 861
    antiwar protest, 897
    use of term, 860
Chickamauga, Battle of (1863), 451, 452(m)
Chickasaw Indians, 17, 304, 315, 316, 437, 493
Chiefdoms, agricultural, 12–15
Chief Joseph (Nez Percé chief), 501, 501(i)
Chief justice, Jay as, 242–243
Child, Lydia Maria, 358, 410(i)
Childbirth
    by indentured servants, 65
    by pioneer women, 345
Child care, Nixon and, 870, 911
Child labor, 340
    in coal mines, 629(i)
    Keating-Owen Act and, 642
    in late 19th century, 566–567, 567(i)
    in textile mills, 537
Children
    black codes, apprenticeship laws, and, 466
    education for, 476–477
    Farmers' Alliance and, 589
    of freedmen, 477, 478
    in garment industry, 566
    of immigrants, 508, 558(m), 560
    Indian, 494, 498, 499
    in poverty, 928
    slave, 378
    in textile mills, 537
    working class, 566–567, 567(i)
Children's Bureau (Labor Department), 637
Child Support Enforcement Amendments Act, 929
Chile, 294
    Carter and, 919
    CIA and, 895
    immigrants from, 504
China
    Boxer uprising in, 607
    Carter and, 919, 921
    Communists vs. Nationalists in, 790–791

immigrants from, 700
Japan and, 758
Korean War and, 800
missionaries in, 607
Nasser and, 819
Nixon and, 877, 893–894, 894(i)
Open Door policy in, 608, 633, 635
Portugal and, 31
Soviet Union and, 791, 893
Tiananmen Square protests in, 947
World War I and, 670
World War II and, 772, 773
after World War II, 777
Chinese Exclusion Act (1882, 1902), 508,
    561, 562, 645, 678–679
Chinese immigrants, 505
    in California, 355–356, 356(i), 507–508,
        508(i)
    in cities, 561–562
    in mining, 504
    railroads and, 508(i)
    work of, 507
Chino (racial category), 44(i)
Chippewa Indians, 17
    Northwest Territory land ordinances and,
        222
Chisholm, Shirley, 911–912
Chisholm Trail, 514
Chivalry, in South, 376, 377
Chivington, John M., 494
Choctaw Indians, 17, 315, 316, 437, 493
Choice Not an Echo, A (Schlafly), 906
Cholera, 494
"Christian guardianship" (paternalism), 374
Christianity. See also Protestant
        Reformation; specific groups
    African American, 381
    in China, 607
    in colonies, 129–131
    evangelical, 924
    Indians and, 57, 58, 313
    new conservatives and, 907
    in New Spain, 43
    slaves and, 380–381
Chrysler Corporation, bail out of (1976), 916
Chumash Indians, 10, 11(i)
Churches. See also Religion(s); specific
        groups
    black, 464
    Catholic, 72–73
    in government, 90–91
    in Jamestown, 66(i)
    membership in, 828–829
    Puritan, 89–91, 95–96
    women and, 288
Churchill, Winston. See also World War II
    Atlantic Charter and, 758
    at Casablanca, 765
    iron curtain speech of, 785–786
    Nazi Germany and, 756–757
    at Teheran, 771
    at Yalta, 772

Church of England (Anglican), 66–67, 87, 88,
    128, 130
Church of Jesus Christ of Latter-Day Saints.
    See Mormons
Churubusco, Battle of (1847), 353
CIA. See Central Intelligence Agency
Cigarettes, 537. See also Tobacco and tobacco
    industry
Cincinnati, Ohio, 253
CIO. See Congress of Industrial
    Organizations
Circumnavigation of globe, 34
Cisler, Lucinda, 867
Cities and towns. See also Urban areas; spe-
        cific locations
    African Americans in, 388, 561, 677, 678,
        822
    architecture of, 578–579, 578(i)
    Asian immigrants in, 561–562
    automobile and, 688–689
    bosses (political) in, 580–582
    decline of, 823
    electric lights in, 530–531
    in Gilded Age, 553–564, 578–583
    global migration and, 555–557
    growth of, 555–557
    immigrants in, 560
    leisure in, 575, 577
    mass transit in, 563
    mining towns, 505, 506
    movement to, 537
    neighborhoods in, 563
    in New England, 92
    parks in, 579
    population in, 555
    poverty in, 563–564, 580
    progressivism and, 619–621, 621–624,
        625
    public works in, 579–580
    segregation in, 563
    slaves in, 378
    social geography of, 563–564
    in South, 372–373, 475
    urban renewal and, 843–844
Citizens and citizenship
    Alien and Sedition Acts and (1798), 262
    Asians and, 507, 508
    for Californios, 507
    Fourteenth Amendment and, 468
    gender and, 538, 540
    Native Americans and, 500
    Supreme Court and, 413, 481
City upon a hill, Massachusetts Bay colony
        as, 87, 105
Civil Defense Administration, 820
Civil disobedience, 645
Civilian Conservation Corps (CCC), 725–726,
    769
Civil liberties
    in 1920s, 687
    Red scare and, 675–677, 799
    World War I and, 668

Civil rights. *See also* Civil rights movement
  for African Americans, 468, 477, 794–795
  Eisenhower and, 833
  for gays and lesbians, 931
  in Great Depression, 732
  Great Society and, 847
  legislation in 1950s, 834
  for Mexican Americans, 795–796,
    825–826
  Reagan and, 928–929
  Second Reconstruction and, 850–858
  Truman and, 795
Civil Rights Act. *See also* Title VII
  of 1866, 468
  of 1875, 481
  of 1957, 834
  of 1964, 845, 847, 853, 861, 870, 909
  of 1968, 848, 855
Civil Rights Commission, 928
Civil rights movement, 832–836, 840–842,
    850–858. *See also* King, Martin
    Luther, Jr.; specific leaders and events
Civil Rights Restoration Act (1988), 929
Civil service, 480
  as Jackson's "spoils system," 312
Civil Service Commission, 543
Civil service reform, 542, 543
Civil war(s). *See also* Civil War (U.S.,
    1861–1865)
  in China, 791
  in Guatemala, 818
  in Kansas, 412
  in Rwanda, 956
  in Saint Domingue, 258
  in Spain, 754
  Vietnam War as, 876, 885
Civil War (U.S., 1861–1865). *See also*
    Reconstruction
  African Americans in, 425–426, 443–444,
    444(i)
  armed forces in, 433
  battles in (1861–1862), 434–439, 435(m)
  battles in (1863–1865), 450–454, 452(m),
    454–455
  casualties in, 427, 436, 437, 438, 444, 453,
    453(i), 455
  diplomacy in, 431, 439–440
  draft in, 443, 446, 449
  in East, 434–437
  effects of, 456
  emancipation and, 440–443
  events leading to, 395–421
  financing of, 433
  Fort Sumter attack and, 428
  home fronts during, 444–447, 447–450
  Indians in, 437–438, 437(i)
  Lee's surrender and, 455
  mobilization for, 432–433
  navy in, 425, 426, 426(i), 432, 438
  resources of North and South in, 431–432
  secession and, 419–421, 428–429, 429(m)
  slavery and, 427

  strategy in, 431–432
  as total war, 445
  weapons in, 433
  in West, 429–430, 437–438
Civil Works Administration (CWA), 725
Claiborne, Liz, 927
Clamshell Alliance, 917
Clark, George Rogers, 196
Clark, William, 275
Classes. *See also* Hierarchy; specific classes
  conflict in Gilded Age, 546
  Jackson on, 318
  social stratification and, 44(i), 45
  in South, 370
  voting rights and, 216
Classical liberalism, Gilded Age and, 619
Clay, Henry, 282–283, 430
  American System of, 295
  Bank War and, 318
  California compromise of, 400
  "corrupt bargain" and, 296
  election of 1824 and, 295, 296, 310
  election of 1828 and, 310
  election of 1844 and, 349
  Missouri Compromise and, 293
  nullification and, 317
Clay, Henry, Jr., 352
Clayton Antitrust Act (1914), 641
Clean Air Act
  of 1970, 870
  of 1990, 942, 963
Clean Water Act (1972), 870, 963
Clemenceau, Georges, 662, 669
Clemens, Samuel Langhorne. *See* Twain,
    Mark
Clerical jobs, in 1950s, 822
Clermont (steamboat), 304
Cleveland, Grover, 608
  election of 1884 and, 543–544, 544(m)
  election of 1888 and, 545, 546
  election of 1892 and, 545, 546
  election of 1896 and, 603–605
  gold standard and, 549
  Hawai'i and, 606–607
  on immigration restriction, 563
  Pullman strike and, 596–597
  tariff reform and, 546
Cleveland, Ohio, 563
  progressive government in, 625
Climate, in Americas, 6
Clinton, DeWitt, 283
Clinton, Henry, 177, 197, 199
Clinton, Hillary Rodham, 951
  election of 2008 and, 971
Clinton, William Jefferson ("Bill"), 606(i),
    926, 941
  appointments of, 951
  cabinet of, 951
  economy and, 950, 954–955
  election of 1992 and, 949–950
  election of 1996 and, 953
  foreign policy of, 956–957

gays in military and, 952
globalization and, 955–961
impeachment of, 950, 953–954
presidency of, 950–955
Clodfelter, Mike, 887
Closed shops, 687
Clothing. *See also* Cotton and cotton indus-
try; Garment industry; Textiles and
textile industry
of slaves, 375
Clovis culture, 7, 7(i), 8
Clovis point, 7
Coal and coal industry, 337
child labor in, 629(i)
strikes against, 628–630
Coalitions
in New Deal, 718, 719, 720(m), 741,
768–769
in Persian Gulf War, 946
Cobb, Howell, 420
Cobb, Thomas R. R., 370
Cockran, Bourke, 613
Code (military), German, 757
Cody, William F. ("Buffalo Bill"), 490–491,
490(i)
Coeducational colleges, 320
Coerced labor, in New Spain, 43
Coercive (Intolerable) Acts (1774), 163–164,
166
Cohan, George M., 660
Coins. *See* Currency
Cold Harbor, Battle of (1864), 452(m), 453
Cold War, 783–791, 805. *See also* Soviet
Union; Vietnam War
beginning of, 783–786
Carter and, 921–922
Central America and, 878(m)
defense research in, 826
end of, 935, 935(i), 946–948
Gorbachev and, 939, 940
Helsinki Accords and, 895
immigration during, 959
interventions during, 787
Kennedy, John F., and, 877–884
Korean War and, 800–805
Latin America and, 878(m)
opening of, 783–786
racism and, 795
Reagan and, 932, 933, 934–935
Truman and, 780–782
Vietnam War and, 876–877, 890, 901–902
Colfax, Schuyler, 480
Colfax massacre, 484
"Collapse of the Armed Forces, The" (1971
report), 898
Collective bargaining, 664, 797, 822
Collective security
in national security state, 789
after World War I, 671–672
College of William and Mary, 366
Colleges. *See* Universities and colleges; spe-
cific schools

Colleton, John, 75
Collier, John, 740
Colombia, 294
Panama Canal and, 633
Colonialism. *See also* Colonies and colonization
third world and, 556(m), 557
in West, 491–493, 494
Colonies and colonization. *See also* British
North America; France; Native
Americans; New France; New Spain;
Revolutionary War; Spain; specific col-
onies and regions
African Americans and, 324, 361, 441–
442
British military occupation in, 159–161
in Chesapeake region, 53–55, 60–71, 61(m)
Dutch, 98–99
economy of, 112
English, 49, 54–77, 101–105
English and Spanish compared, 77
European, 42(m), 605
intercolonial political action by, 154–155
in late 17th century, 102(m)
middle colonies and, 97–101
Monroe Doctrine and, 294–295
Native Americans and, 133–134
New England and, 83–97, 88(m)
in North (17th century), 81–105
politics in, 101–105, 135–136
population growth in, 111–112
religion in, 129–131
resistance strategies in, 152–154
before Revolution, 175–177
smuggling in, 147
society in, 128–136
southern, 121–128
Spanish, 47–48
trade in, 69, 101–103, 131–135
after World War I, 670
Colorado, 493, 494
voting by women in, 599(i), 600
Color barrier, breaking after World War II, 795
Colored Farmers' Alliance, 589
Colored Orphan Asylum, 449
Columbian exchange, 35–36, 35(i), 46
Columbian Patriot, A (pseud.), 232
Columbia River region, 18, 277
Columbia University
as King's College, 239
protests at, 892
Columbus, Christopher, 25–27, 26(i),
32–34, 498
Comanche Indians, 17, 274, 276(m), 278–279,
344, 350, 495, 496, 500
Comanchería, 496–497
Combine (farm machine), 515
Comintern, 675
Commerce. *See also* Trade
in Atlantic region, 111, 115–116, 129
colonial, 101–103, 129
voting rights and, 291
Commerce and Labor Department, 628

Commercial agriculture, 515, 516, 517
Commercial banking, 247. *See also* Bank(s) and banking
Commercialization, of leisure, 577
Commercial law, 308
Committee for Industrial Organization, 736
Committee of Vigilance, in San Francisco, 355
Committee on Civil Rights (1946). *See* President's Committee on Civil Rights (1946)
Committee on Fair Employment Practices (1941), 768
Committees of correspondence, 161–162, 164, 165, 250
Committees of public safety, 165
Commodity Credit Corporation, 727–728, 744
Commodity loans, 728
Common laborers, 553, 565
Common market, in Western Europe, 947
Common Sense (Paine), 178, 179(i)
Commonwealth, Massachusetts as, 89
Commonwealth of Independent States, 947
Communication(s)
    expansion of, 303
    hot line, 882
    railroads and, 339, 526
    technologies in, 958
    telegraph and, 339, 526
Communism. *See also* Red scare; Russia; Soviet Union
    in Afghanistan, 921
    in Cambodia, 900
    in China, 790–791
    conservatives and, 905, 906, 907
    in Cuba, 879
    Eastern Europe and, 947, 948(m), 956
    in East Germany, 880
    Eisenhower and, 815
    in Great Depression, 712, 740
    Johnson, L. B., and, 884–888
    Kennedy, J. F., and, 877–879
    Laos, 900
    after liberation movements, 790
    national liberation movements and, 880
    New Deal and, 732
    in postwar Eastern Europe, 785
    Red scare and, 675–677
    in Southeast Asia, 817
    in Vietnam, 877, 883(m), 900
Communist bloc, 784(m)
Communist Party. *See also* Communism
    in Great Depression, 712, 713, 732
    in Guatemala, 818
    in Italy, 790
    McCarthyism and, 800
    prosecution of members, 799
Communities
    African American, 506
    utopian, 358
Community Action Program (CAP), 845
Community colleges, 826

Commutation, of military pensions, 220
Commutation certificates, 225
Commuters, 689
Compass, 30
Compensation, to Indians, 814
Competition
    antitrust laws and, 547
    international, 927
    Morgan and, 532–534
    in petroleum industry, 529
    in railroad industry, 526–527
    unfair, 641
Complex marriage (Oneida community), 358
Compromise of 1850, 400–401, 402(m), 403
Compromise of 1877, 485
Comstock, Anthony, 643
Comstock, Henry, 504
Comstock Lode (Nevada), 397, 491, 504–506
Concentration camps
    in Cuba, 609
    in Holocaust, 769–770
Concentration policy, for Indians, 344
Concord, battle at, 166–167, 167(m), 170
Condren, Dan, 794
Conestoga Indians, 148–149
Coney Island, New York, 577
Confederacy, of Tecumseh, 269
Confederate Congress, 445
Confederate States of America (Civil War South)
    "belligerent" status for, 440
    birth of, 420
    bread riots in, 446
    centralization in, 445
    cotton famine and, 432
    diplomacy and, 439–440
    draft in, 445
    emancipation of slaves and, 443
    financing War by, 433
    industry in, 433, 445
    inflation in, 433, 445
    mobilization of, 432–433
    nationalism in, 446
    Native Americans and, 437–438
    resources of, 431–432
    secession and, 420, 430
    slavery in, 446–447
Confederation. *See* Articles of Confederation
Confiscation Act
    of 1861, 441, 463
    of 1862, 442, 463
Conflict. *See also* War(s) and warfare; specific types
    in borderlands, 131–135
    among Native Americans, 19
    in 1920s, 685
Conformity
    in Cold War, 813
    Puritan, 89–90, 91
Congo, slaves from, 124

Congregationalism, 130, 325, 620
Congress (U.S.). *See also* Congressional
    Reconstruction; Continental Congress;
    Elections; House of Representatives;
    Senate
  under Articles of Confederation, 209–213
  "Billion Dollar," 546
  Eighty-ninth, 846
  under Eisenhower, 815
  election of 1876 and, 484–485
  election of 2006 and, 969
  ex-Confederates in, 467
  gag rule in, 327
  in Gilded Age, 521–522, 541
  intelligence agency oversight by, 914
  New Jersey Plan and, 229
  override of presidential vetoes, 471
  Reconstruction and, 461, 462, 470–471,
    475, 481, 482
  slavery and, 400, 401, 413, 441
  Virginia Plan and, 228–229
  women in, 780–782
Congressional Reconstruction, 468–473
Congress of Industrial Organizations (CIO),
    575, 736
  AFL merger with, 822
Congress of Racial Equality (CORE), 768,
    834, 851, 857
Conkling, Roscoe, 542, 543
Connecticut, 94, 135, 136
  gradual emancipation in, 217
  western boundary of, 211
ConocoPhillips, 529
Conquistadors, 39–40, 41
Conscientious objectors, in Vietnam War, 890
Conscription. *See also* Draft (military)
  by Confederacy, 445
Conservation. *See also* Environment
  of energy, 917
  environmentalism and, 869
  New Deal programs and, 725–727
  Roosevelt, T., and, 632–633
  Taft and, 636
Conservatives and conservatism, 905–907.
        See also specific politicians and move-
        ments
  Bush, G. H. W., and, 943
  Bush, G. W., and, 943, 961
  Clinton and, 952
  in education, 909
  Eisenhower and, 812, 822
  grassroots, 908–910, 923–924
  minority rights and, 928–929
  New Deal and, 719, 720, 737, 739,
    741–742, 743, 746
  Nixon and, 907–908, 910–911
  Reagan and, 907, 922–923, 923–926,
    928–929
  religious, 924
  of Supreme Court, 741–742, 911
Consolidation, of business, 523–524, 526,
    531, 535

Constitution. *See also* Constitution (U.S.)
  of Cherokees, 315
  Cuban, 611
  Lecompton, 415
  reconstruction, in South, 466, 470, 475
  state, 208, 213–214, 243
Constitution (U.S.), 227–231, 398. *See also*
    Amendments; Bill of Rights; Supreme
    Court (U.S.); specific Amendments
  Hamilton and, 239
  Jefferson and, 271
  Madison and, 209, 227, 228–229
  ratification of, 231–235
  slavery and, 402
  strict construction of, 911, 929
  Supreme Court on, 272
  three-fifths clause in, 229
Constitutional convention (1787), 227–231
Constitutional Union Party, 418
Consumer culture
  in 1950s, 827–828
  advertising and, 690
  in Gilded Age, 570
  in 1920s, 689–690
  in 1950s, 826
Consumer goods, 877
  in colonies, 129
  in World War II, 767
Consumers
  auto safety and, 847
  economic cycles and, 308
  after World War II, 792
Consumption
  colonial commerce and, 129
  mass production and, 690
  in 1950s, 827–828
  of oil, 917
  underconsumption and, 723
  yuppies and, 927
Containment policy, 782, 786
  Eisenhower and, 810
  Kennan and, 786
  Kennedy and, 877
  Korean War and, 800–802, 804
  Nixon and, 894
  Truman and, 786, 789
  in Vietnam, 817–818
  Vietnam War and, 900
Continental army, 176, 177–178, 181–182.
        See also Revolutionary War
  African Americans in, 182
  Newburgh conspiracy and, 219–220
  northern strategy of, 183–186, 184(m),
    192–193
  southern strategy of, 197–203, 198(m)
  at Valley Forge, 193
  western strategy of, 193–196, 195(m)
Continental Association, 165
Continental Congress, 228(i). *See also* Articles
    of Confederation; Congress (U.S.)
  Articles of Confederation and, 209–210
  First (1774), 165–166

Continental Congress *(continued)*
  Madison in, 208
  in Revolution, 182, 191
  Second (1775), 166, 175–178, 180–181
Continental dollars, 176–177
Continental drift, 5(m)
Contraband of war, runaway slaves as,
  441
Contraception, 694. *See also* Birth Control
  defined, 643
Contract labor
  freedmen and, 463
  Populists and, 591
Contract with America, 952
Contras, in Nicaragua, 933–934
Conventions. *See* Nominating conventions;
  specific political parties
Conversion (religious)
  in Great Awakening, 131, 321–322
  of Native Americans to Christianity, 43,
  72, 313
  to Protestantism, 88
  of slaves, 380
Coode, John, 104
Coolidge, Calvin, 685, 686–687, 705
"Coolie labor," 508
Cooperatives, farmers', 590
Coral Sea, Battle of (1942), 764, 773
Corbin, Hannah, 215
CORE. *See* Congress of Racial Equality
Corinth, Mississippi, in Civil War, 435(m),
  438
Corn (maize), 19, 36
  of Eastern Woodland peoples, 11–12, 17
  in Jamestown, 57, 58–59
  in Southwest, 12–13
Cornplanter (Seneca Indians), 221
Cornstalk (Shawnee Indians), 194
Cornwallis, Charles, 198–199, 200
Coronado, Francisco Vásquez de, 39–40,
  40(i)
Corporate capitalism, 565
Corporations. *See also* Business
  assembly line and management changes
  in, 689
  private, 339
  Rockefeller and, 529
  Supreme Court and, 535
  tax cuts for, 925
"Corrupt bargain" (1824), 296, 310
Corruption
  in city government, 580–581
  in Gilded Age, 541–542
  under Grant, 480, 521
  under Nixon, 912–913
  in Revolutionary War, 191
  in southern Republican governments,
  477
  in territorial government, 509–510
Cortés, Hernán, 26(i), 36–39, 41
Cortés Montezuma, Isabel Tolosa, 41
Costa Rica, 608

Cotton, John, 93
Cotton and cotton industry, 245. *See also*
  Cotton gin; Textiles and textile industry
  in Carolina, 75
  Civil War and, 431, 439–440
  cotton famine in, 432, 440
  panic of 1837 and, 328
  price decline in, 306
  sharecropping and, 479
  slaves and, 368–369, 368(m), 378
  in southern agricultural economy, 371(m),
  372
  in Texas, 515
  westward movement and, 367–369
  yeomen farmers in, 383
Cotton Club, 695(i), 696
Cotton gin, 245, 372
Cotton kingdom, 368–369
Coughlin, Charles, 732, 737
Council of Economic Advisers, 792
Counterculture, 862
Counterinsurgency forces, Kennedy, J.F.,
  and, 881
Country-born (creole) slaves, 124
Coups. *See also* specific countries
  against Diem, 884
  military (Latin America), 886
Court-packing plan, of Roosevelt, F. D.,
  741–742
Courts. *See also* Supreme Court (U.S.);
  specific cases
  church, 67
  in Massachusetts, 164
Courtship, working-class, 577
Covenant, Puritan, 87, 89–90, 92
Covenant Chain, 145
Covenant of grace, 93
Covert operations. *See* Secret operations
Cowboys, 513–514, 610
  industrial, 517
Cowpens, Battle of (1781), 198(m), 200
Cox, Archibald, 913
Cox, James M., 679, 686, 719
Coxey, Jacob S., 600–602
Coxey's army, 600–602, 601(i)
Craft unions, 573
Crashes (financial). *See* Depressions (finan-
  cial); Panics
Crater Lake National Park, 634(m)
Crawford, William H., 295, 296, 297
Crazy Horse (Sioux chief), 497, 498
Credit, 373. *See also* National debt
  Bank War and, 318
  economic panics and, 309
  farmers and, 516, 728
  installment buying and, 690
  restoration under Hamilton, 250
  by United States, 687
Creek Indians, 17, 367, 437
  African Americans and, 218
  removal of, 313, 316, 493
  in Southwest, 251–253

War of 1812 and, 283, 286
  in Yamasee War, 133
Creek War (1813–1814), 283–284, 367
Creoles, slave, 45, 124
Crime and criminals
  during prohibition, 691–692
  Warren Court and, 849–850
Cripple Creek, Colorado, 505
  miners' strike in (1894), 594
Croatia, 956–957
Croatoan, discovery of word, 49
Croats, in former Yugoslavia, 956
Crocker, Charles, 507
Crockett, Davy, 348
Crogman, William, 647
Croly, Jane Cunningham (Jennie June), 540
Cromwell, Oliver, 94
Cronkite, Walter, 889, 891
Crook, George, 497, 502
Crop lien system, 479, 537, 589
Crops, 371. *See also* Agriculture; Farms and
    farming; specific crops
  in Carolina, 75
  cash, in South, 371–372, 371(m)
  in Chesapeake, 66
  of Eastern Woodland peoples, 11–12
  in 1840s and 1850s, 336
  food, 383, 384
  in Jamestown, 58–59
  markets for, 66
  in middle colonies, 120
  prices for, 308
Cross-dressing, by Sampson, Deborah, 174,
    201
"Cross of gold" speech, of Bryan, 603
Crow Dog, Mary, 859
Crow Indians, 17, 500–501
Crusade for Justice (Wells), 539
Cuba. *See also* Cuban missile crisis
  Angola and, 933
  Bay of Pigs invasion in, 879
  British invasion of, 146
  Platt Amendment and, 611–613
  revolution in (1930s), 752
  revolution in (1959), 818–819, 879
  slavery in, 369, 371
  Spain and, 36, 147, 294
  Spanish-American War and, 609–610
  United States and, 405, 611–613, 879
  U.S. naval base in, 613
Cuban missile crisis, 877, 881–882, 882(i)
Cuffe, Paul and **John,** 216
Cullen, Countee, 696
Cult of domesticity, 576, 598
Culture(s). *See also* specific groups
  Adena, 14
  of African immigrants, 122–123, 124
  Anasazi, 13
  of ancient Americas, 1–22
  consumer, 689–690
  counterculture and, 862
  Eastern Woodland, 11–12, 14–15, 17

  of Great Basin, 9–10
  Hohokam, 13
  Mimbres, 13
  Mississippian, 14–15
  Mogollon, 13
  Native American, 12–19, 494, 499, 500
  Pacific Coast, 10
  of plain folk, 385–386
  popular, 696, 901
  shifts in mid-1800s, 319–326
  slave, 126–127, 380–381
  southern, 128, 369, 446
  southwestern, 12–13
Currency, 640. *See also* Money
  banknotes as, 318, 319
  Continental dollars as, 176–177
  national, 448
  Populist reforms and, 591
  in Revolution, 191
Curriculum
  in Indian schools, 499
  in women's schools, 289
Curtis, Benjamin R., 413–414
Cushman, Belle, 570
Custer, George Armstrong, 497–498
"Custer's Last Stand," 490, 498
Customs. *See also* Duties; Taxation
  British collection of, 154
Czechoslovakia, 670
  Nazi invasion of, 755
  Soviets and, 785, 787
Czolgosz, Leon, 626

Da Gama, Vasco, 31
Daguerreotypes. *See* Photography
Dakotas. *See* North Dakota
Dakota Sioux, 496
Dallas, Kennedy, J. F., assassination in, 844
Dalles, The (fishing site), 18
Dams
  in Great Depression, 735(i)
  for irrigation, 632
Dance halls, 577
Darrow, Clarence, 701
Darwin, Charles, 532, 534, 701. *See also*
    Reform Darwinism; Social Darwinism
Daughters of Liberty, 158–159
Davis, Henry Winter, 462
Davis, James J., 565
Davis, Jefferson, 400
  as president of Confederacy, 420, 427–428,
    432, 445, 446
Davis, John W., 687
Davis, Paula Wright, 360
Dawes, Charles, 688
Dawes, Henry, 500
Dawes, William, 166
Dawes Allotment Act (1887), 500, 814
Dawes Plan, 688
Dawidoff, Robert, 931(i)
Day care, Nixon and, 911
D-Day invasion, 771

Deadwood Dick (Nat Love), 514
Dean, John, 913
Dearborn, Fort, 283
Death camps, Nazi, 769–770
Death rate. *See* Mortality rate
Debates
    Lincoln-Douglas, 415–416
    presidential (1960), 843
Debs, Eugene V.
    election of 1912 and, 639, 640(m), 642
    Espionage Act and, 668
    IWW and, 643
    as progressive, 639
    Pullman strike and, 596, 597
    Socialist Party and, 597, 642
Debt. *See also* National debt
    Confederate, 466
    credit and, 309, 318
    farm, 516
    foreign, after Revolution, 225
    of railroads, 532
    after Revolutionary War, 210, 218–219,
        225, 240
    after Seven Years' War, 150
Decatur, Stephen, 273
Decimal system, 297
"Declaration of Dependence, A" (loyalist
    document), 189
Declaration of Independence (1776), 180–
    181, 209
Declaration of rights, at First Continental
    Congress, 165
"Declaration on the Causes and Necessity of
    Taking Up Arms, A" (Jefferson), 176
Declaratory Act (1766), 155
Deep South. *See also* Slaves and slavery;
    South (U.S. region)
    emancipation in, 218
Deere, John, 336
Defender (Chicago newspaper), 561
Defense. *See also* National security
    Eisenhower and, 816
    national security state and, 788–790
Defense industry, African Americans in,
    767–768
Defense of Marriage Act (1996), 952
Defense spending
    Adams, John, and, 261
    Carter and, 921
    Kennedy, John F., and, 879, 880
    Korean War and, 804–805
    NSC 68 and, 805
    Reagan and, 926, 932–933, 934
    in World War II, 766
    after World War II, 789, 794
Deferments, college, in Vietnam War, 887
Deficit
    in federal budget, 932, 943, 954–955
    foreign trade, 914
    Vietnam War and, 900
Deflation, 547
Deforestation, steamboat use and, 304

Deism, in colonies, 130
Delany, Martin R., 360
Delaware, 61(m), 116, 429. *See also* Middle
    colonies
    Articles of Confederation and, 211
    slavery in, 218
Delaware (Lenni Lenape) Indians, 98(i), 100,
    144, 146, 255, 282
    Fort Stanwix Treaty and, 221, 253
    Northwest Territory land ordinances and,
        222
    during Revolution, 188, 195(m)
Delaware River region, 119, 185–186
Demilitarized zone, in Korea, 804
Demobilization, after World War I, 673–674
Democracy
    direct, 213
    vs. republicanism, 230–231
    spread of, 309–312
    after World War I, 673–680
Democratic National Convention
    of 1860, 418
    of 1896, 603
    of 1948, 781(i)
    of 1964, 841(i)
    of 1968, 892, 912
Democratic Party (Democrats), 330, 482. *See
    also* Elections; specific presidents
    during Civil War, 449–450
    emancipation and, 441, 443
    free silver issue and, 549, 603
    in Gilded Age, 536, 541
    Jackson and, 310, 312–319
    Peace Democrats in, 450, 454
    popular sovereignty and, 408
    Populists and, 603–604
    progressives in, 626
    Roosevelt coalition and, 718, 719, 720,
        741, 768–769
    South and, 390, 418, 482–484, 536, 720,
        798, 911
    southern Republican state governments
        and, 475, 477, 482–483
    Vietnam War and, 889
    Watergate break-in and, 912
    white supremacy and, 482–484
    women in, 911–912, 926
    World War I and, 668
Democratic societies, 255
Democratization
    of higher education, 826–827
    of politics, 389–390
    of voting, 389
Demonstration(s). *See* Protest(s); Revolts and
    rebellions; specific demonstrations
Dempsey, Jack, 696–697
Denby, Charles, 607
Denmark, 755
Dennis v. United States (1951), 799
Departments of government, 242. *See also*
    specific departments
Department stores, 570

Deportation
of immigrants, 562
of Mexican Americans, in Great
Depression, 709–710, 709(i)
Depressions (financial). *See also* Great
Depression; Panics; Recessions
in 1870s, 481, 508, 548, 565, 570–571
in 1890s, 491, 565, 582, 594, 600–605,
606, 614
Deregulation
by Carter, 916, 925
by Clinton, 955
financial collapse and, 746
of oil and gas industries, 917
by Reagan, 916, 925–926
Desegregation. *See also* Segregation
of armed forces, 795
Eisenhower and, 833
Nixon and, 910–911
of schools, 833–834, 849, 870
Desertion, in Civil War, 446
De Soto, Hernando, 39, 46(i)
Détente policy, 894–895, 914
Detroit
race riot in (1967), 857
in War of 1812, 283
Detroit, Fort, 148, 194, 195(m)
Developing nations, United States and, 880
Dew, Thomas R., 366, 370, 377
Dewey, George, 610
Dewey, John, 664
Dewey, Thomas E., 797
Dias, Bartolomeu, 31
Díaz, Porfirio, 678
Dickinson, John, 156, 176, 178, 180
Dictators. *See* specific individuals
Diem, Ngo Dinh, 818, 883, 884
Dien Bien Phu, 817
Diet (food). *See also* Food(s)
Columbian exchange and, 36
of slaves, 375
Dinwiddie, Robert, 144
Diphtheria, 494
Diplomacy. *See also* Foreign policy; specific
presidents, treaties, and countries
in Civil War, 431, 439–440
of Clinton, 957
with Cuba, 819
dollar diplomacy, 637
with France, 261
jugular, 898
King Cotton, 431, 439–440
Monroe Doctrine and, 294–295, 608
by Washington, 251, 257
Direct democracy, 213
Direct election of senators, 416, 542, 591, 637
Direct primary, 626
Dirksen, Everett, 845
Disabled people, ADA and, 943
Disarmament
calls for, 933
naval, 688

Reagan, Gorbachev, and, 934–935
Rush-Bagot treaty and (1817), 286
Discovery. *See* Exploration
Discovery (ship), 56
Discrimination. *See also* Civil rights; Civil
rights movement; Integration; Race
and racism; Segregation
affirmative action and, 855
against African Americans, 366, 387,
460(i), 466, 477, 506, 538
against Asians, 356, 507–508, 645
black codes and, 468
gender, 538, 864
homosexuals and, 863, 952
job, 853
legislation against, 847
Mexican Americans and, 507
during Reconstruction, 481
reverse, 928
women and, 566
after World War II, 794
Disease. *See also* Medicine; specific conditions
AIDS, 931
in cities, 563
European in Americas, 35–36, 35(i), 46
Indians and, 46, 344, 348, 494
from mining, 506
in New England, 87–88, 95
slaves and, 124, 372
in Vietnam War veterans, 901
in Virginia, 57
after World War I, 675
Disfranchisement. *See also* Voting and voting
rights
of African Americans, 645
of ex-Confederates, 470, 475
of women, 473
Disqualification Act, 226
Dissent and dissenters, 914. *See also* Civil
rights movement; Protest(s); specific
issues
in 1950s, 830–832
in North (Civil War), 449–450
World War I and, 664, 667, 668, 676
Distribution, transportation and, 305
District of Columbia. *See also* Washington,
D.C.
slavery in, 325
Diversification, economic, 372, 373
Diversity
California gold rush and, 355
in middle colonies, 101, 106
Native American, 18
in South, 367
in West, 506–509
of workforce, 565–566
Division of labor, sexual, 560
Divorce, 287, 376
Dix, Dorothea, 449
Dixiecrats, 797, 911
Dobson, James, 924
Doctors. *See* Medicine

Dole, Robert, 953
Dollar diplomacy (Taft), 637
"Domestic allotment plan" in New Deal, 727
Domesticity
    cult of, 576
    in 1950s, 828
    women and, 320
Domestic partners, 952
Domestic policy. See specific presidents
Domestics (domestic servants), 387. See also
        Servants
    black women as, 567
    women as, 576
Domestic workers, Social Security and, 737
Dominican Republic, 480, 633
    Jewish refugees to, 769
    U.S. intervention in, 637, 654, 884, 886
Dominion of New England, 104
Dominis, Lydia Kamakaeha. See
        Lili'uokalani
Domino theory, 787, 817, 900
Donelson, Fort, capture of (1862), 435(m), 438
Donnelly, Ignatius, 600
"Don't ask, don't tell" policy, 952
Double V campaign, 767–768
"Doughboys," 652
"Doughfaces," northerners as, 405, 410
Douglas, Aaron, 696
Douglas, Helen Gahagan, 780, 781(i), 797
    economy and, 792
    equal pay and, 793
    "Hollywood Ten" and, 799
    Truman Doctrine and, 787
Douglas, Melvyn, 780
Douglas, Stephen A., 334, 407(m), 428
    Compromise of 1850 and, 401
    debates with Lincoln, 415–416
    election of 1860 and, 418–419
    Freeport Doctrine of, 416
    Kansas-Nebraska Act of, 405–406
    on Lecompton constitution, 415
    popular sovereignty and, 408, 411
Douglass, Frederick, 360, 361(i), 396, 400,
        405, 441, 469
    on Civil War, 427, 440
Dove (ship), 67
Doves, in Vietnam War, 891
Downs, Frederick, 875–876, 876(i), 877,
        887, 888, 900, 901, 902
Draft (military)
    Carter and, 921
    in Civil War, 443, 445, 446, 449
    Kennedy, J. F., and, 880
    peacetime, 789
    in Vietnam War, 887, 890
    in World War I, 660, 661, 676
    in World War II, 760–761
Draft card burnings, in Vietnam War, 889
Drake, Edwin, 528
Drake, Francis, 344
Dred Scott decision (1857), 412–414, 415, 416
Drift and Mastery (Lippmann), 624

Drought
    on Great Plains (1880s-1890s), 513
    in Southwest, 13
Drugs (illegal), student protests and, 862
Drugs (legal), 631, 964. See also Prescription
        medication
Du Bois, W. E. B., 539, 646(i), 647, 660, 694
Dueling
    Hamilton-Burr duel and, 271(i)
    among planters, 376
Due process, 468, 535, 849–850
Dukakis, Michael, 942
Duke family, 537
Duke of York. See James II (Duke of York,
        England)
Dulles, John Foster, 815–817, 819
Dunkirk, withdrawal from, 756
Dunmore (Lord), 149, 168
Du Pont, 628
Duquesne, Fort, 144, 146, 148
Dürer, Albrecht, 48
Dust Bowl, in Great Depression, 717
Dutch
    British North America and, 133
    German invasion of Netherlands and,
        755
    in Indonesia, 758
    in New Amsterdam, 61(m)
    in New Netherland, 97–98
Dutch East India Company, 98
Dutch East Indies (Indonesia), 31, 758, 763
Dutch Reformed Church, 99
Duties. See also Tariffs; Taxation; specific acts
    Grenville, 150–152
    Townshend, 156–157
Duty, women's vs. men's, 320
DuVall, Peggy, 887
Dylan, Bob, 862
Dynamic Sociology (Ward), 624

Earned Income Tax Credit (EITC), 951
East (U.S. region)
    Civil War in, 434–437, 451, 452(m)
    immigrants in, 560, 562
East (worldwide), sea route to, 31. See also
        Asia
East Berlin, 788
    Berlin Wall and, 947, 949(i)
Eastern Europe. See also Europe and
        Europeans; specific locations
    communism in, 785
    conditions after communism in, 956
    end of Cold War and, 947, 948(m), 949(i)
    events in (1989-2002), 948(m)
    Soviet Union and, 771, 772, 777, 783, 895
Eastern Hemisphere, competition for trade
        in, 608
Eastern Woodland peoples, 11–12, 14–17
East Germany, 788
    Berlin Wall and, 880, 947, 949(i)
    end of communism in, 947
East India Company, British, 162

East Indies. *See also* Dutch East Indies
    Columbus and, 32, 34
    Portugal and, 31
East River, 553
East St. Louis, Illinois, race riot in, 678
Eaton, William, 273
Ecology, of Great Plains, 495
Economic cycles. *See* Boom and bust cycles
Economic Opportunity Act (1964), 845
Economic Recovery Tax Act (1981), 925
Economics
    laissez-faire and, 535, 600
    supply-side, 924–925
    trickle-down, 706–707, 927–928
Economic sanctions, by Carter, 921
Economy. *See also* Depressions; Exploration;
        Globalization; New Deal; Panics;
        Tariffs; Trade; Wealth
    in 1830s, 318–319, 326, 328–329
    in 1840s and 1850s, 335–339
    in 1929, 704–705
    in 1950s, 821, 827–828
    in 1990s, 954–955
    auto industry and, 688–689
    banking and, 317–319
    banking deregulation and, 746
    boom and bust cycles in, 308–309
    Carter and, 916
    in Civil War, 433, 445, 447–448
    Clinton and, 950
    colonial, 112
    Embargo Act (1807) and, 280
    expansion of, 343
    family, 566–567
    Ford administration and, 914
    global regions of world, 556(m), 557
    before Great Crash, 707
    in Great Depression, 707–710, 722–729
    Great Society and, 848
    Hamilton and, 245–251
    inequality and, 340–341
    interdependence of, 367
    Jackson and, 312
    Japanese, 791
    Kennedy, John F., and, 844
    legal foundation for, 308
    manufacturing and mechanization in, 337
    market revolution and, 303–309
    in New England, 94, 113–116
    Nixon and, 868–869
    Obama and, 971, 972
    plantation, 370–373
    Reagan and, 923, 924–925, 926–928
    recession of 1937–1938 and, 740–741
    in Reconstruction South, 477
    in Revolutionary War, 186, 191
    in South, 477, 536, 537
    in Spain, 48
    stagflation and, 907, 915, 916
    in Sun Belt, 825
    tariffs and, 545–546
    Truman and, 792–794

    in Vietnam War, 877
    in Western Europe, 787
    westward movement and, 339
    women in, 693
    after World War I, 674–675, 687–688
    in World War II, 759–760, 761–762, 777
    after World War II, 783
Edenton, North Carolina, women protesters
        in, 158(i)
Edison, Thomas Alva, 530–531, 531(i)
Education. *See also* Academies; Higher edu-
        cation; School(s)
    for African Americans, 476(i), 645
    Bush, G. W., and, 964
    desegregation of schools and, 833–834,
        849
    in 1830s, 320–321
    equal opportunity in, 929
    for Indians, 499
    Johnson, Lyndon B., and, 846–847
    for Mexican Americans, 796–797
    plain folk and, 385–386
    sex discrimination in, 867
    sex education and, 909
    in South, 373, 385–386, 476–477
    universal, 340
    for women, 286, 288–290, 377
    of youth, 320–321
Education Amendments Act (1972), Title IX
        of, 867, 928–929
Edward VI (England), 84
Edwards, Jay Dearborn, 373(i)
Edwards, Jonathan, 131
EEOC. *See* Equal Employment Opportunity
        Commission
Efficiency, 624, 625, 689
Efik people (Africa), 109
Egypt
    Eisenhower administration and, 819–820
    recognition of Israel by, 921
    Six-Day War and, 895–896
    Suez crisis and, 819–820
    in World War II, 764
    Yom Kippur War and, 896
Eighteenth Amendment, 665, 691, 692
Eighth Amendment, 243
Eight-hour workday, 574, 575, 591, 594, 637,
        642, 664
Eighty-ninth Congress, 846
Einstein, Albert, 789
Eisenhower, Dwight D., 876
    arms race and, 817, 820–821
    civil rights and, 833, 834
    containment policy and, 817–818
    Cuba and, 819
    D-Day invasion and, 771
    election of 1952 and, 802–803, 804(i)
    election of 1956 and, 815
    foreign policy of, 816–817
    Geneva summit (1955) and, 820
    Korean War and, 802–805
    Latin America and, 818–819

Eisenhower, Dwight D. *(continued)*
  Middle East and, 819–820
  North Africa and, 765
  politics of, 811–815
  Soviet Union and, 810–811
  television and, 829
  Vietnam and, 817–818
  women in cabinet of, 812
  on women in military, 789
Eisenhower Doctrine, 820
EITC. *See* Earned Income Tax Credit
El-Alamein, Battle of (1942), 764
Elastic clause, 230
Elderly. *See also* Pensions
  in Great Society, 848
  during Reagan era, 928
  as slaves, 378
"Elect," Puritans as, 90
Elections. *See also* Voting and voting rights
  of 1789, 242
  of 1796, 260–261
  of 1800, 263–264, 269–270
  of 1804, 279
  of 1808, 279, 280
  of 1812, 283
  of 1816, 290
  of 1820, 290
  of 1824, 290, 295–296, 327
  of 1828, 309–311, 311(m), 327
  of 1832, 326, 327
  of 1836, 326–328
  of 1840, 329
  of 1844, 349–350
  of 1848, 399–400, 407(m)
  of 1852, 405, 407, 407(m)
  of 1856, 407, 407(m), 409–411
  of 1860, 407(m), 417–419
  of 1862, 443
  of 1864, 454, 465
  of 1865, 466
  of 1866, 469–470
  of 1868, 459, 473, 479–480
  of 1872, 460, 480
  of 1874, 460, 482
  of 1876, 484–485, 542
  of 1880, 542–543
  of 1884, 543–544, 544(m)
  of 1888, 545, 546
  of 1890, 546
  of 1892, 545, 546, 602–603
  of 1896, 603–605
  of 1900, 627
  of 1904, 630
  of 1908, 635–636
  of 1910, 637
  of 1912, 638–639, 640(m), 642
  of 1914, 641
  of 1916, 641–642, 658
  of 1920, 679–680, 686
  of 1924, 687
  of 1928, 702–703, 719
  of 1932, 720–721, 721(m)
  of 1934, 732
  of 1936, 741
  of 1938, 745
  of 1940, 722, 757
  of 1944, 769
  of 1946, 797
  of 1948, 795, 797
  of 1952, 802–803, 804(i)
  of 1956, 815
  of 1958, 815
  of 1960, 843
  of 1964, 845–846, 885, 905, 908
  of 1968, 868, 891, 892–893, 906, 910
  of 1972, 906, 908, 910, 911–912
  of 1976, 907, 914–915
  of 1980, 907, 916, 922–924
  of 1984, 926
  of 1988, 942
  of 1992, 949–950
  of 1994, 952
  of 1996, 953
  of 2000, 961–962
  of 2004, 961, 968
  of 2006, 969
  of 2008, 536, 970–971, 970(i)
  of 2010, 972
  electoral college and, 291
  money in, 829
  of senators, 416, 542, 591, 637
  in South, 391
  to Virginia House of Burgesses, 68–69
Electoral college, 291
  in election of 2000, 962
Electoral commission, for 1876 election,
    484–485
Electric industry, 531
Electricity
  in cities, 530–531
  hydroelectricity and, 726–727, 726(m)
  in rural areas, 726–727
Electric streetcar, 563
Electronic trolleys, 689
Elementary and Secondary Education Act
    (ESEA, 1965), 846–847
Elevated trains, 528, 579
Eliot, John, 88
Elites. *See also* Classes
  free black, 388
  of Mexica, 21
  planter, 68
  southern, 391
  voting rights and, 292
  women as, 286
Elitism, progressive, 625, 648
Elizabeth I (England), 85
Elkins Act (1903), 628, 630
Ellington, Duke, 695(i), 696
Ellis Island, 562
Ellison William, 388
El Salvador
  Carter and, 919
  uprising in, 933
Emancipation, 464
  colonization in Africa and, 441–442

Congress and, 441, 442
contraband status of slaves and, 440–442
in deep South, 218
gradual, 217
individual, 218
Lincoln and, 425
as military necessity, 443
preliminary proclamation of, 442
after Revolution, 202, 387
whites and, 324
Emancipation Proclamation (1863), 425, 427, 442–443
Embargo
against Japan, 759
by Jefferson, 280
before World War II, 753–754
Embargo Act (1807), 280
Embassies
in Saigon, 899(i)
terrorist attacks on U.S., 933
Emergency Banking Act (1933), 723
Emerging nations, 790
Emerson, Ralph Waldo, 357, 417
Emigrant aid societies, Kansas settlement and, 411
Emigration. *See* Immigrants and immigration; Migration
Eminent domain, 308
Emmons, Glenn, 813
Empires. *See also* specific empires
British, 101–105
Comanchería, 496
in eastern North America, 132(m)
Holy Roman, 47
Mexica, 20–21
Portuguese commercial, 31
of United States, 349, 611–613, 612(m)
Employment. *See also* Unemployment; Women; Workforce
of African Americans, 677–678
fair, 767–768
in Great Depression, 710, 734
in manufacturing, 249
of women, 828
in World War II, 762
after World War II, 794
Employment Act (1946), 792
Empresario, 347
Encomendero, 42–43
Encomienda system, 42–43, 77
Energy. *See also* Steam power; specific types and sources
Carter and, 915, 917, 919
coal and, 337
consumption of, 917
hydroelectric, 726–727, 726(m)
Nixon and, 868–869
nuclear, 813, 917
Energy crisis, 869, 917
Energy Department, 917
Energy Policy Act (2005), 963
England (Britain). *See also* British Empire; Colonies and colonization; Revolution-

ary War; World War I; World War II; specific colonies
African Americans in, 218
Civil War (U.S.) and, 431, 440
colonies of, 53–77
cotton from South and, 372, 440
exploration by, 34, 48–49
France and, 142–144, 146–147
Glorious Revolution in, 104
immigrants from, 112, 117, 504, 559, 700
impressment by, 279–280, 285
loyalists in, 189
Nazi bombings of, 756–757
Oregon Country and, 342, 343–344, 350
Protestantism in, 84–85
Puritan Revolution in, 94
reasons for Revolutionary War loss by, 203–204
in Revolutionary War, 182–186, 192–203
Rush-Bagot treaty with, 286
settlement house movement in, 620
in Seven Years' War, 142–147, 143(m)
Texas and, 349
U.S. support for, 757–758
Venezuelan-British Guiana borders and, 608
Vietnam War and, 900
war materiel purchases by, 757
War of 1812 and, 269, 282–286
women's rights in, 645
in World War I, 657, 659
after World War I, 670
World War II and, 754
English Reformation, 84–85
Enlightenment, 130
Enola Gay (airplane), 750–751, 750(i), 776(i)
Entertainment. *See also* Leisure
in Great Depression, 710–711
in 1920s, 696–697
television in, 829–830
Entrepreneurship, 927
Enumerated goods, 102–103
Environment. *See also* Air pollution
Agent Orange and, 889
ancient humans and, 6, 8, 9–10, 11
beautification of, 847
Bush, G. W., and, 963
Carter and, 919
Clinton and, 951
damage in 1950s and, 823
farming changes in, 120(i)
fires and, 19
Johnson, Lyndon B., and, 847
Love Canal and, 917–919
Native Americans and, 18
Nixon and, 869–870
pollution and, 870
Reagan and, 925
of Sun Belt, 825
Superfund for cleanup of, 919
Three Mile Island and, 917
trade and, 958
white settlement and, 494

Environmental Protection Agency (EPA), 870, 925
Epidemics. *See also* specific diseases
  Plains Indians and, 494
  of smallpox, 494
  of Spanish influenza, 675
Equal Employment Opportunity Commission (EEOC), 861, 870, 943
Equality. *See also* Civil rights movement; Gender and gender issues; Slaves and slavery; specific rights and groups
  in Chesapeake region, 67–71
  gender, 793, 793(i), 864
  Johnson, Lyndon B., on, 855
  racial, 461, 462, 481
  slavery and, 216–218
  in World War II, 766
Equal Pay Act (1963), 864
Equal pay for equal work principle, 622
Equal protection, in Fourteenth Amendment, 849
Equal Rights Amendment (ERA)
  of 1923, 693
  of 1972, 866, 867, 906, 923, 929
Equiano, Olaudah, 123, 123(i), 131
Erie, Lake
  battle in, 283
  in Seven Years' War, 146
Erie Canal, 305
Ervin, Samuel J., 913
Espionage. *See* Spies and spying
Espionage Act (1917), 668
Ethiopia, Italian invasion of, 754
Ethiopian Regiment, 168
Ethnic Albanians, 957
Ethnic groups. *See also* specific groups
  in cities, 563
  in colonies, 137
  in former Yugoslavia, 956
  immigration and, 959
  Mexican migrants and, 679
  politics and, 536
  racism and, 561
  women's movement and, 866
  after World War I, 670
Ethnocentrism, toward Indians, 813
Eugenics, birth control and, 694
Europe and Europeans. *See also* Colonies and colonization; World War I; World War II; specific countries
  Civil War (U.S.) and, 431, 439–440
  division after World War II, 784(m)
  exploration by, 27–41
  financial crisis in (1819), 308
  immigrants from, 559–560
  investments in U.S. by, 959
  Marshall Plan and, 787
  New World and, 22, 47–49
  oil consumption by, 917
  Roosevelt, T., and, 635
  Spain's impact on, 48–49
  tobacco in, 61
  trade routes of, 28(m)

World War I and, 655–659, 670
  after World War I, 671(m)
  World War II and, 764–765, 772(m)
European Recovery Program. *See* Marshall Plan
European Union, Marshall Plan and, 787
Evangelicalism, 319, 321–322, 380. *See also* Revivals and revivalism
  in 1950s, 829
  in 1970s, 924
  Plain folk and, 386, 386(i)
  reform and, 357
Evans, Hiram Wesley, 701
Everett, Sarah, 346
Everett, Wesley, 676
Evers, Medgar, 795, 851–852
Evolution, 534, 701
Exceptionalism, 490, 491
Excise tax, on whiskey, 250–251
Executive. *See also* Presidency; President; specific presidents and departments
  under Articles of Confederation, 210, 213
  New Jersey Plan and, 229
  Virginia Plan and, 229
Executive departments, under Articles of Confederation, 213
Executive Orders
  9066, 760
  9835, 799
  for affirmative action (1965), 855
  desegregating armed services, 795
Executive privilege, Nixon and, 913
Exodusters, 514
Expansion and expansionism. *See also* Imperialism; Monroe Doctrine; Open door policy; Westward movement
  colonial, 111–135
  economic, 343
  by 1860, 354(m)
  as foreign policy, 605
  missionaries and, 607
  politics of, 349
  of railroads, 338, 338(m)
  Spanish-American War and, 610
  trade and, 606–607
  U.S. overseas through 1900, 612(m)
  War of 1812 and, 283
  in West, 253–255, 254(m), 491–493
  westward, 342–348
Expertise, 624, 641
Exploration
  by Columbus, 26–27, 32–34
  Dutch, 98–99
  by England, 34, 48–49
  European, 27–41
  by France, 48
  by Lewis and Clark, 275–277, 276(m)
  by Portugal, 30–31
  space, 877, 879
  Spanish, 32–33, 36–46
Exports
  from Britain, 129
  business and, 606

colonial, 77–78, 103
of cotton, 372, 432
from middle colonies, 120
from New England, 113, 115
from South, 127, 371
External taxes, 153, 156
Extinction, of ancient large mammals, 7–8
ExxonMobil, 529
oil spill and, 942

Factionalism, 477, 541–543
Factions. See Political parties; specific parties
Factories
in Confederacy, 433
slaves in, 378
textile, 565–566
workers and, 305–307
in World War II, 761–762
Fair Deal, 792–800
Fair Labor Standards Act (1938), 745
Fall, Albert, 686
Fallen Timbers, Battle of (1794), 255, 267
Fall line, 61(m)
Falwell, Jerry, 924
Families. See also Kinship
birth control movement and, 643
in Chesapeake region, 65
Civil War and, 427, 430, 447
in 1830s, 319–320
farm, 589
of free blacks, 388
of freedmen, 464, 477–478, 478–479
government and, 952
in Great Depression, 710
in mid-1830s, 319
Native American, 499
in New England, 89
in 1950s, 827
of planters, 374
in Reagan era, 927
separate spheres idea and, 319–320
slave, 380
southern, 385
in working class, 566–567, 576–577
in World War II, 766–767
yeoman, 127, 383–384
Family and Medical Leave Act (1993), 951
Family economy, 566–567
Family law, 179. See also Law(s); Marriage
divorce and, 287
Family Research Council, 924
Family values, 924
Famine, in Ireland, 342
Farewell address
of Eisenhower, 821
of Reagan, 936
of Washington, 260
Farm Credit Act (FCA, 1933), 728
Farmers' Alliance, 589–590
Farms and farming. See also Agriculture;
Bracero program; Rural areas; Shays's
Rebellion; Tenant farmers

in 1840s and 1850s, 335–336
in 1920s, 686
in 1929, 705
in 1950s, 821–822
by ancient peoples, 12–13, 14
in Chesapeake region, 66–67
commercial, 491, 515, 517
cooperatives and, 590
debt of, 516
electrification for, 726–727, 726(m)
environmental changes from, 120(i)
free silver issue and, 547–548
on Great American Desert, 513
in Great Depression, 711, 727–728
immigrants and, 63, 960
income decline and, 588–589
Jefferson and, 271
labor for, 336, 960(i), 961
mechanization in, 336, 448, 515
Mexican workers and, 679, 700, 861
in New England, 113–115
protests by, 588–590
railroads and, 546, 589
sharecropping and, 478–479, 515
in South, 483
tariffs and, 545
tenant, 515
in West, 448, 510–513, 515–517
women and, 448
yeomen and, 382–384
Farm Security Administration (FSA, 1937),
743–744
Fascism, 751, 753. See also Mussolini,
Benito; Nazi Germany
Hitler and, 753
in Spain, 754
Fathers. See Families; Men
Faubus, Orval, 833
FBI. See Federal Bureau of Investigation
Federal budget
Carter and, 916
Clinton and, 951
deficit in, 943, 963
Vietnam War and, 877
Federal Bureau of Investigation (FBI)
illegal activities by, 914
infiltration of peace movement by, 890
King, Martin Luther, Jr., and, 853
Federal Communications Commission, 830
Federal Deposit Insurance Corporation
(FDIC), 723
Federal Election Campaign Act (1974), 914
Federal Emergency Relief Administration
(FERA), 725
Federal government. See Government (U.S.)
Federal Housing Administration, 823
Federalist Papers, The, 234–235, 239
Federalists, 231, 234, 264
collapse of, 290
election of 1796 and, 260–261
election of 1800 and, 270
election of 1816 and, 290
Embargo Act of 1807 and, 280

Federalists *(continued)*
    Hartford Convention and, 285–286
    Republicans (Jeffersonian) and, 259–264,
        297
    War of 1812 and, 269, 283, 285
    XYZ affair and, 261–262
Federal Republic of Germany. *See* West
        Germany
Federal Reserve Act (1913), 640, 641
Federal Reserve Board, 640, 641, 916
Federal slave code, 418
Federal Surplus Commodities Corporation, 744
Federal Trade Commission (FTC), 641, 687
Female academies, 289
Females. *See* Feminism and feminists; Women
Female suffrage. *See* Woman suffrage
Feme covert doctrine, 287, 292, 298
Feminine Mystique, The (Friedan), 828
Feminism and feminists, 906. *See also*
        Women; specific individuals
    countermovement to, 866–868
    Fifteenth Amendment and, 473
    in 1960s and 1970s, 863–868
    radical, 864, 865
    Reagan and, 929–930
    on Thomas, Clarence, appointment, 945
Fences, ranching and, 507, 514
Ferdinand (Spain), 25–26, 26(i), 32, 47
Ferraro, Geraldine A., 926
Ferris, George Washington Gale, Jr., 582
Ferris wheel, 489, 582
Fetterman, William, 497
Field, Stephen J., 535
Fifteenth Amendment, 472–473, 486, 599
"Fifty-four Forty or Fight," 350
Filipinos. *See also* Philippines
    in war against U.S., 613
Fillmore, Millard, 401, 407(m), 409
Films. *See* Movies
Finance capitalism, 532–534
Finances. *See also* Economy; Hamilton,
        Alexander
    under Articles of Confederation, 210, 225
    for Civil War, 433
    of Comstock Lode operations, 504
    credit and, 309
    government spending in 1950s and, 822
    in Great Depression, 723–725
    of presidential campaigns, 914
    Revolution and, 191
    tariffs and, 317
Financial institutions
    Glass-Steagall Act repeals and, 953
    2008 economic collapse and deregulation
        of, 971
Financial Services Modernization Act (1999),
        953
Finney, Charles Grandison, 321–322, 323
Fire, Indian uses of, 19
"Fire-eaters" (radical southerners), 400
Fireside chats, of Roosevelt, Franklin D.,
        724, 724(i)
Firestone, 959

First Amendment, 243, 314
    "Hollywood Ten" and, 799
    school prayer and, 850
First Bank of the United States, 248–249
First Congress, 243
    Hamilton and, 245
First Continental Congress (1774), 165–166
First hundred days. *See* Hundred Days
First Lady. *See* specific individuals
First World War. *See* World War I
Fishing and fishing industry
    Native Americans and, 18, 825
    in New England, 94–95, 115
    in Pacific Northwest, 10
Fitzgerald, Ella, 795
Fitzhugh, George, 370, 376
Five Civilized Tribes, 437, 493
Five-Power Naval Treaty (1922), 688
Flag, burnings in Vietnam War, 889
Flaming Youth, 685, 697
Flappers, 685, 691, 693, 693(i)
Flexible response, 880
Florida, 72–73, 368
    African Americans in, 218
    annexation and, 336
    ceded to United States, 294
    election of 2000 and, 962
    Indians in, 73, 502
    secession of, 420
    Spain and, 39, 40
Floyd, John, 365
Floyd, Kitty, 208(i)
Flying Fortress. *See* B-17 Flying Fortress
Foch, Ferdinand, 662
Folk music, 862
Folsom culture and points, 9
Food(s). *See also* Agriculture; Crops; Diet
        (food); Hunters and hunting; Plants;
        specific crops and foods
    from Africa, 127
    of ancient Americans, 7–8, 9–10, 11–12
    in Columbian exchange, 36
    in Confederacy, 433
    in Jamestown, 57, 58
    New Deal distribution of, 744(i)
    of Pacific Coast cultures, 10
Food Administration, in World War I, 664, 686
Food stamp program, 846, 868, 926, 927
Football, 697
Foote, Henry S., 400
Force Bill (1833), 317
Ford, Gerald, 907, 908, 913–914, 915
Ford, Henry, 683–685, 684(i), 688, 690, 711
Fordney-McCumber tariff (1922), 686
Ford's Theatre, Lincoln at, 455
Foreclosures
    on farms, 589
    in Great Depression, 711
Foreign aid
    to developing nations, 880
    to friendly countries, 789
    Marshall Plan and, 787
    Truman Doctrine and, 787

Foreign debt, after Revolution, 225
Foreigners. *See* Immigrants and immigration
Foreign markets, 690
Foreign policy. *See also* Cold War; Diplomacy;
    specific presidents and policies
  Bush, George H.W., and, 945–947, 956
  Bush, George W., and, 961
  business and, 606–607
  Clinton and, 956–957
  détente policy in, 894–895, 914
  Eisenhower Doctrine and, 820
  Eisenhower's "New Look" in, 816–817
  isolationism and expansionism in, 605
  militarization of, 800
  Monroe and, 290
  Monroe Doctrine and, 294–295, 605,
    607–608, 609
  Nixon and, 868
  Obama and, 972, 973
  Open Door policy and, 608, 609, 633, 635
  racism and, 745, 795, 832–833
  Truman Doctrine and, 786–787
  U.S. as world power and, 607
  Washington Disarmament Conference
    and, 688
  after World War II, 782–791
Forest reserves, 632
  deforestation and, 304
Forrestal, James V., 783–785
Fort(s). *See also* specific forts
  British along frontier, 257
  in Ohio River region, 144, 253, 257
  on Oregon Trail, 344
  presidios as, 134, 135
  in Seven Years' War, 144, 146, 148
Fort Laramie
  Treaty of (1851), 494, 496
  Treaty of (1868), 497, 498
Fort Laramie conference, 344–345, 493–494
Fort Sill reservation, 498, 500, 502
Fort Stanwix. *See* Stanwix, Fort
Fort Stanwix, Treaty of (1784), 221, 253
Fortune, Emanuel, 483
Fort Wayne, Treaty of, 282
Founding fathers, 240. *See also* Constitution
    (U.S.); specific individuals
Four Freedoms, 758
Fourier, Charles, 358
Fourierist phalanxes, 358
Fourteen Points, 668–669, 672
Fourteenth Amendment, 468–469, 481, 486,
    540
  corporations and, 535
  equal rights in, 849
  Mexican American rights and, 826
  ratification by southern states, 469, 470,
    475
  voting rights and, 468–469, 599
"Fraggings," in Vietnam War, 898
Framers. *See* Constitution (U.S.)
France. *See also* French Revolution; New
    France; World War I
  Adams, John, and, 262–263

Civil War (U.S.) and, 431
colonies of, 105
England and, 142–144, 146–147
exploration by, 48
Haiti and, 275
immigrants from, 504
Indochina and, 758, 790, 805
Louisiana Territory and, 274–275
Mexico and, 480
Mississippi River region and, 274
Morocco crisis and, 635
Nazi Germany and, 756
Revolutionary War alliance with, 196,
    201, 203
in Seven Years' War, 142–144, 143(m),
    146–147
Vietnam and, 817
war materiel purchases by, 757
West Indies and, 196, 257
World War I and, 657, 659, 662–663
after World War I, 670, 688
World War II and, 754
XYZ affair and, 261–262
Franchise. *See also* Voting and voting rights
  for free black men, 292
Franco, Francisco, 754
Frank Leslie's Illustrated Weekly, 554(i)
Franklin, Benjamin, 113, 121, 131, 176, 227
  Albany Plan of Union and, 145
  on American soldiers, 147
  Constitution and, 228
  Declaration of Independence and, 180–181
  as deist, 130
  on right to taxation, 151
  slavery and, 118
  on work, 137
Franklin, Deborah, 121
Franklin family, Anne, Josiah, and Abiah
    as, 113
Franz Ferdinand (Archduke, Austria-
    Hungary), 656, 656(m)
Fredericksburg, Battle of (1862), 435(m),
    437
Free blacks, 119. *See also* African Americans
  abolitionism and, 360–361
  laws restricting, 366, 387
  in Pennsylvania, 217
  rights of, 216, 413
  in South, 387–389, 459–460
  in Virginia, 218
Freedmen, 459, 460, 462
  black codes and, 466
  education and, 464, 476, 476(i)
  as Exodusters, 514
  freedom and, 464
  labor code and, 463
  labor of, 463, 477–478
  land for, 463–464, 466, 471, 477, 478
  in Republican Party, 473, 474
  search for families by, 464
  sharecropping by, 478–479
  voting rights for, 471, 473
Freedmen's Bureau, 463–464, 466, 470, 476

Freedmen's Bureau Acts (1865 and 1866), 463, 467–468
Freedom(s)
  in Bill of Rights, 243
  of free blacks, 388–389
  for freedmen, 464
  McCarthyism and, 800
  for slaves, 168, 461
  for women, 867
"Freedom papers," 387
Freedom Rides, 851, 853
"Freedom schools," 861
Free enterprise, Coolidge and, 687
Free labor, 339–342, 474
  immigrants and, 341–342
  vs. slavery, 370, 463
  in West, 398, 415
Free-labor ideal, 340
  economic inequality and, 340–341
  woman's rights and, 360
Freeman, Elizabeth. See Bett, Mum
Freemen
  in colonies, 68–69
  Massachusetts Bay Company stockholders as, 91
Freeport Doctrine, 416
Free silver, 547–549, 591, 603
Free soil doctrine, 398, 400, 441
Free-Soil Party, 399, 405, 406
Free speech, 450
  gag rule and, 327
"Free speech" movement, 861–862
Free states. See also specific states
  Missouri Compromise and, 293, 294(m)
  vs. slave states, 400–401
  Texas, Oregon, and, 350
Free trade, 958
Freewill Baptists, 288
Frémont, Jessie Benton, 409–410, 410(i)
Frémont, John C., 348, 407(m), 409–410, 410(i), 442, 509
French and Indian War. See Seven Years' War
French Revolution (1789), 245, 255–257
  Haitian Revolution and, 258
Freud, Sigmund, 690–691
Frick, Henry Clay, 592, 593
Friedan, Betty, 828, 864, 865(i)
Friends of the Earth, 869
Frobisher, Martin, 49
Front. See also Home front
  in World War I, 662
Frontier
  in Revolutionary War, 201
  in Seven Years' War, 147
  violence along, 133, 148
  westward movement and, 342–343
  women on, 511
Frontier thesis (Turner), 489–490, 491
Frowne, Sadie, 566
FTC. See Federal Trade Commission

Fuels. See also Energy; Gasoline; Oil and oil industry
  alternative, 917
  of homesteaders, 511
Fugitive Slave Act (1850), 403, 404(i), 418
Fugitive slaves, 361, 402–403, 441
  in Civil War, 425–426, 446–447
  in Northwest Territory, 224–225
  resistance by, 382
  underground railroad and, 403
Fulbright, J. William, 889
Fuller, Margaret, 357
Fulton, Robert, 304
Fundamental Constitutions of Carolina, 75
Fundamentalism
  Islamic in Iran, 922
  Protestant, 701–702, 924
  Scopes trial and, 701–702
Fundamental Orders of Connecticut, 94
Fur trade, 94, 105, 119, 133, 142
  Covenant Chain and, 145
  England and, 257

Gabler, Mel and Norma, 909
Gabriel's rebellion (1800), 270
Gadsden, James, 405
Gadsden Purchase (1853), 405
Gage, Thomas, 149, 163, 164, 166, 168, 177
"Gag rule," in Congress, 327
Galbraith, John Kenneth, 821
Galloway, Joseph, at First Continental Congress, 165
Galveston, Texas, 39
Gambian culture, 122
Gambling, Jefferson on, 249
Gandhi, Mohandas (Mahatma)
  Chavez, Cesar, and, 860(i)
  King, Martin Luther, Jr., and, 835(i)
Gangsters, in prohibition, 691–692
García, Héctor Peréz, 796(i)
Garfield, James A., 470, 480, 542–543
Garment industry, 566, 622–623
Garnet, Henry Highland, 360
Garrison, William Lloyd, 324, 366, 400, 485
Garvey, Marcus, 694
Gary, Martin, 483
Gas. See Poison gas
Gasoline. See also Energy; Oil and oil industry
  shortages of, 917
Gaspée (ship), 161
Gates, Bill, 927
Gates, Horatio, 193, 198(m), 199
Gates, John ("Bet a Million"), 514
Gates, Merrill, 499
GATT. See General Agreement on Tariffs and Trade
Gay Liberation Front, 863
Gay pride parades, 931(i)
Gays and lesbians. See also Homosexuals and homosexuality
  Christian Right and, 931

gay rights protests and (1960s), 863
lesbian collectives and, 866
in military, 952
protecting rights of, 943
Reagan administration and, 931
rights movement for, 930–931
rights of, 906, 932
Gaza Strip, 896, 921, 957
Gender and gender issues. *See also* Men;
    Women; specific issues
in Chesapeake colonies, 64
churches and, 288
cult of domesticity and, 576
education and, 287–289, 320–321
lynching of black men and, 539
marriage inequality and, 287
Native Americans and, 313
in 1950s, 828, 830
politics and, 538–540
progressivism and, 644–645
separate spheres idea and, 319–320
voting rights and, 214–215, 244
women in workplace and, 569–570
General Agreement on Tariffs and Trade,
    958
General Assembly (UN), 772, 947
General Court (Massachusetts), 91
General Electric, 531, 705, 958
General Federation of Women's Clubs
    (GFWC), 540
Generall Historie of Virginia (Smith), 53–54
General Managers Association, 596, 597
General Motors (GM), 736
General strike, in Seattle, 675
*General Theory of Employment, Interest, and
    Money, The* (Keynes), 743
"General welfare" clause, 249
Geneva accords (1954), 817
Geneva summit (1955), 820
Genocide, Holocaust as, 769–770
"Gentlemen's Agreement" (1907), 635
Gentry, in South, 127, 128
Geographic regions, global, 556(m), 557
Geographic revolution, 34
George III (England), 150, 156, 180
Revolutionary War and, 178, 182
Georgia
Cherokee removal and, 314(m), 315–316,
    493
Civil War in, 452(m), 454
Creeks in, 251
emancipation in, 218
founding of, 122
population of, 121
power of planters in, 391
Revolutionary War and, 197–199, 198(m)
secession and, 420
Spanish exploration of, 46(i)
German Americans, 341
Pennsylvania Dutch as, 116–117
in Revolutionary War, 192
World War I and, 667

German-language regions, immigrants from,
    112
Germany. *See also* East Germany; Nazi
    Germany; West Germany; World War
    I; World War II
colonies of, 670
immigrants from, 116–117, 121–122, 341,
    504, 559
Morocco crisis and, 635
Protestant Reformation in, 47–48, 84
reparations after World War I, 688
U-boats of, 657–658, 659
unification of, 947
U.S. navy and, 608
Venezuela confrontation and, 633
World War I and, 655–658, 659, 660,
    662–663, 665
after World War I, 669–670, 688
after World War II, 785
zones of occupation in, 785
Geronimo (Apache shaman), 502
Gettysburg, Battle of (1863), 443, 451,
    452(m)
Ghent, Treaty of (1814), 285, 295
Ghettos
Harlem as, 696
uprisings in, 856(m)
urban, 555–557
Ghost Dance, 502–503
Gibbon, John, 497, 498
Gibbs, Lois, 919
GI Bill (1944), 769, 794
Gideon v. Wainwright (1963), 850
GI Forum. *See* American GI Forum
Gift exchange, with Indians, 148
Gilbert, Humphrey, 49
Gilbert Islands, 773
Gilded Age, 521–523
cities in, 553–564, 578–583
classical liberalism and, 619
consolidation in, 523–525, 526, 531
depression of 1890s in, 549, 550
economy during, 523, 545–549
finance capitalism and, 532–534
free silver issue in, 547–549
gender, race, and politics in, 538–540
industry during, 523–531
labor in, 564–570
materialism of, 499, 521
New South during, 536–537
politics in, 523, 526, 536, 545–549
poverty in, 534, 535, 563–564
presidency during, 541, 630
presidential politics in, 541–544
social Darwinism and, 534–535
Supreme Court during, 535
wealthy in, 526, 534, 564
West in, 517–518, 550
women in, 538–540, 540–541
Gilded Age, The (Twain and Warner), 517,
    521–522
Gin, cotton, 245

Gingrich, Newt, 952
Ginsberg, Allen, 831
Ginsburg, Ruth Bader, 951
Girdling, of trees, 62
Girls. *See* Women
Glaciers, 6
Gladden, Washington, 620
Glasnost, 934
Glass-Steagall Banking Act (1933), 953
Glenn, John, 879
Glidden, Joseph F., 514
Global issues. *See also* Economy; Foreign
    policy; Immigrants and immigration;
    Imperialism; Migration; specific pres-
    idents
  economy as, 973
  environment and, 963, 967
  migration and, 555–557
Globalization, 955–961
  debates over, 957–959
  since 1989, 939–941
  Nixon in China and, 894
  of terrorism, 965–967, 965(i)
Global migration, growth of cities and,
    555–557
Global warming, 963, 967
Glorieta Pass, battle at (1862), 438
Glorious Revolution (England), 104
Gods and goddesses. *See* Religion; specific
    deities and peoples
Godspeed (ship), 56
God's Trombones (James Weldon Johnson),
    696
Golan Heights, 896
Gold. *See also* Gold standard
  in California, 349, 354–357
  discoveries of, 497, 504
  exploration and, 30
  Indians and discoveries of, 497
  in Mexico, 37
  from Peru, 39
  U.S. reserves of, 548, 549
Gold, Blackie, 725–726
Gold Coast, slaves from, 124
Goldman, Emma, 676
Goldmark, Josephine, 623
Gold rush (California), 354–357, 397, 504
Gold standard, 548, 549
  election of 1896 and, 603
  vs. free silver, 547
Goldwater, Barry M., 845–846, 885, 905,
    908, 909
Goliad, massacre at (1836), 348
Gompers, Samuel, 570, 573, 574, 575, 622,
    643, 675
Gonzales, Rodolfo ("Corky"), 861
Good neighbor policy, 752–753
Goods and services. *See* Consumer culture;
    specific goods and services
"Goo goos" (good government proponents), 581
Gorbachev, Mikhail, 934–935, 935(i)
  end of Cold War and, 939, 940, 947

Gordon (slave), 375(i)
Gore, Albert, Jr., 949, 962
Gorgas, Josiah, 433
Gospel of wealth, 535, 620
Gould, Jay, 523, 525, 526, 527, 573
Gould, William, 425–426, 427, 443, 456
Gould and Curry mine, 505
Government. *See also* Chiefdoms;
    Government (U.S.); Legislation;
    State(s); specific programs
  Adams, John Quincy, and, 297
  aid to railroads by, 339
  under Articles of Confederation, 209–213
  assistance programs of, 868
  of Carolina, 75
  in Chesapeake region, 68–69
  city, 580–582
  Cold War and, 800
  colonial, 135–136
  of English royal colonies, 104–105, 135
  limited, 140
  of Maryland, 67
  of Massachusetts, 91–92, 140–142
  of Massachusetts Bay, 85–86
  Mayflower Compact and, 85
  Mexica, 21–22
  of military districts in South, 470
  in New Deal, 725
  of New England, 90–91, 104, 113
  in New Netherland, 99
  of Pennsylvania, 100–101
  progressive, 619, 623, 625–626
  Puritan, 91–92
  under Second Continental Congress,
    175–177
  territorial, 509–510
  of Virginia, 60, 68, 69–71
Government (U.S.). *See also* Constitution
    (U.S.); Federal budget; Legislation;
    specific programs
  business control of, 686–687
  Civil War and, 427, 447–448, 456
  departments of, 242
  depression of 1893 and, 600
  deregulation and, 926
  Eisenhower and, 811, 812
  in Great Depression, 709, 711–712
  Revolution and, 203, 241–245
  role in 20th and 21st centuries, 972–973
  Roosevelt, Franklin D., and, 719
  Virginia Plan and, 228–229
Governors
  colonial, 135–136, 140, 156–157, 163
  territorial, 509
Gradual emancipation, 217–218, 225
Gradualism policy, of Washington, Booker T.,
    647
Grady, Henry, 537
Graham, Billy, 829
Grain, from middle colonies, 120
Grand Allies. *See* Allies (World War II)
Grand Canyon National Park, 632, 634(m)

Grand Coulee Dam, 735(i)
Grandees, 70, 73. *See also* Elites
Grandfather clause, black voters and, 645
Grange, 546, 589
Grange, Harold ("Red"), 697
Grant, Ulysses S.
    in Civil War, 438, 450, 451, 453–454, 455
    corruption and, 480, 521, 541
    election of 1868 and, 459, 473, 479–480
    election of 1872 and, 480
    foreign policy of, 480
    peace policy for Indians, 496
    Reconstruction and, 480–481, 482
Grants, federal, 847
Grape boycott, 861
Grapes of Wrath, The (Steinbeck), 731
Grasse (Comte de), 201
Grassroots conservatism, 908–910, 923–924
Grateful Dead, 862
Graves, A. J. (Mrs.), 319
Gray, Thomas R., 366
Great American Desert, farmers in, 513
Great Awakening, 131
    Second, 319, 321–322
Great Basin region, cultures of, 9–10
Great Britain. *See* England (Britain)
Great Compromise, 229
Great Depression (1930s), 641. *See also* New
        Deal; Roosevelt, Franklin Delano
    agriculture in, 727–728
    Asian Americans and, 739–740
    crash of 1929 and, 705–706
    economy during, 706–707, 707–710
    Hispanics in, 739
    industrial recovery in, 728–729
    labor in, 706, 735–737, 745
    lifestyle in, 707–712
    migrant labor during, 717, 731–732
    Native Americans in, 740
    politics in, 732–733
    welfare in, 726, 733–740
    working-class militancy in, 711–712
Great East River Bridge. *See* Brooklyn
        Bridge
Greater East Asia Co-Prosperity Sphere, 758
Great Fire (Chicago, 1871), 578
Great Lakes region, 105, 146
    Indians of, 17, 133, 147–149
    steamboats in, 304
    in World War I, 667–668
Great migration
    of African Americans, 677–678, 678(i)
    of Mexican Americans, 678–679
Great Northern Railroad, 525
Great Plains. *See also* Plains Indians
    bison hunters in, 9
    buffalo on, 495
    dust storms in, 513, 717
    ecology of, 495
    farming in, 510–513
    horses on, 9
    Indians of, 17

Great Railroad Strike (1877), 570–572,
        571(i), 594, 596
Great Salt Lake, 346
Great Sioux Reservation, 498
Great Sioux Uprising (1862), 496
Great Society, 841, 842–843, 845–849
    civil rights legislation and, 847
    Nixon and, 868, 907
    reforms of (1964–1968), 845–849
    Vietnam War and, 885, 900
Great Southwest Strike (1885), 573
"Great War." *See* World War I
Great White Fleet, 635
Greece, 670, 786–787
    immigrants from, 504
Greeley, Horace, 433, 480, 555
Green, William, 711
Greenback Labor Party, 548, 589
Greenbacks (paper money), 448, 547, 548,
        591
Green Berets, 881
Greene, Nathanael, 198(m)
Greenfield Village, 685
Greenhouse gas emissions, 963
Greensboro, North Carolina, sit-in in, 851
Greenville, Treaty of (1795), 255, 256(i), 267
Greenwich Village, 692
Grenada, U.S. invasion of, 933
Grenville, George, 150–152
Grey, Edward, 657
Grimké sisters, 325–326, 327, 330
        Angelina, 302–303, 302(i)
        Sarah, 301–302, 302(i)
Grinnell, Julius S., 575
Griswold, Roger, 263(i)
Gross national product (GNP), in 1950s,
        827–828
Grove City v. Bell (1984), 929
Guadalcanal, Battle of, 773
Guadalupe Hidalgo, Treaty of (1848), 354, 507
Guadeloupe, 146, 147, 150
Guam, 610, 612(m), 613, 763
Guantánamo, Cuba
    detention camp in, 967, 969
    U.S. base at, 613
Guatemala, 608, 818
    revolution in, 752
Guerrilla warfare
    during Civil War, 438
    with Filipino nationalists, 609
    in Kansas, 412
    in Revolutionary War, 197, 200
    in Vietnam, 818, 884, 900–901
Guiteau, Charles, 543
Gulf of Mexico region, 39, 918(m)
Gulf of Tonkin Resolution (1964), 885, 897
Gulf War. *See* Persian Gulf War
Gun(s), manufacture of, 337
Gunboats, in Civil War, 438
Gun control
    in California, 943
    legislation (1993), 951

Gunpowder, Powder Alarm and, 164
Guthrie, Woody, 710–711, 740

Habeas corpus, Lincoln and, 429
Haires, Francis, 64
Haiti, 461
    French loss of, 275
    republic in, 258
    revolution in, 245, 258–259
    UN and, 956
    U.S. intervention in, 654, 955
    U.S. withdrawal from, 752
Hakluyt, Richard, 56
Hale, John P., 407(m)
Half Breeds, 542
Halfway Covenant, 96
Hallidie, Andrew Smith, 579
Hamer, Fannie Lou, 840–842, 847, 851
Hamilton, Alexander, 208, 239–241, 240(i),
    545
    Constitution and, 227, 234
    duel with Burr, 271(i)
    economic policies of, 245–251
    election of 1796 and, 260–261
    election of 1800 and, 270
    Federalist Papers and, 234–235, 239
    national debt and, 240, 245, 247–248
    Report on Manufactures, 249
    Report on Public Credit, 247
    as treasury secretary, 242
Hamilton, Fort, 253
Hammond, James H., 379
Hampton Institute (Indian boarding school),
    499
Hancock, John, 153, 168, 181
Hancock, Winfield Scott, 542–543
Haney-López, Ian, 826
Hanna, Mark, 604, 610, 626, 630
Hanoi. *See* Vietnam; Vietnam War
Harding, Florence, 680
Harding, Warren Gamaliel, 679–680,
    686–687
Hard money, 307
Harlem, 694
    migration to, 678
Harlem Renaissance, 695–696
Harmar, Josiah, 253
Harpers Ferry, Virginia, Brown's raid on
    (1859), 395–396, 417
Harper's Weekly, 483(i), 580
Harrington, Michael, 843
Harris, David Golightly, 478
Harris, Frank, 554
Harrison, Benjamin, 503, 545, 546
Harrison, Carter, 575
Harrison, William Henry, 268, 282, 283,
    328, 329, 349, 545
Harrows, 515
Hartford, 94
Hartford Convention (1814), 285–286
Hartford Seminary, 289
Hawai'i. *See also* Pearl Harbor
    annexation and, 606–607

Hawai'i's Story by Hawai'i's Queen
    (Liliuokalani), 606(i)
Hawks, in Vietnam War, 890–891
Hay, John, 608, 609, 633
Hayden, Casey, 864
Hayes, Rutherford B., 541
    election of 1876 and, 484–485, 542
    Great Railroad Strike and, 572
    presidency of, 542
Haymarket bombing, 574–575, 593
Haymarket martyrs, 575
Haywood, William Dudley ("Big Bill"),
    643
Headright, 62
Head Start, 845, 868
Health, Education, and Welfare, Department
    of, 812
Health and health care. *See also* Disease;
    Medicine; specific conditions
    Bush, George W., and, 964
    Carter and, 916
    Clinton and, 951
    national health insurance and, 964, 971
    Obama and, 971
    public health nursing and, 620
    Truman and, 792
Hearst, William Randolph, 609
Hegemony, of U.S., 608
Helicopters, in Vietnam War, 875
Helms, Jesse, 911
Helsinki accords (1975), 895
Hendrick (Mohawk Indians), 145
Hendricks, Thomas A., 481
Henry IV (Castile), 25, 26
Henry VII (England), 34
Henry VIII (England), 84, 85
Henry, Patrick, 149, 152–153, 161, 227
    as Antifederalist, 234
    at First Continental Congress, 165
Henry the Navigator (Portugal), 30
Henry, Fort, 195(m)
    capture of (1862), 435(m), 438
Henry Street settlement, 620
Hepburn Act (1906), 630–631
Herbicide, Agent Orange as, 884
Heresy, Hutchinson and, 93
Heritage Foundation, 924
Hernandez, Aileen, 866
Hernandez, Pete, 825
Hernandez v. Texas (1954), 825–826
Herndon, William, 414
Hessians, 183, 192. *See also* Mercenaries
Hester Street (New York City), 560, 580
Hezbollah, 920(m), 933, 934
Hidatsa Indians, 494
Hierarchy
    in Chesapeake society, 67–71
    in Quaker society, 100
    social, 303
Higby, Richard, 65
Higher education. *See also* Universities and
    colleges; specific schools
    democratization of, 826–827

GI Bill and, 794
for women, 864
Higher Education Act (1965), 847
"Higher law" doctrine (Seward), 401, 403
High schools, 579. *See also* Education;
    School(s)
Highways. *See* Roads and highways
Hill, Aaron (Mohawk Indians), 221
Hill, Anita, 943–945
Hillman, Sidney, 736
Hillsborough (Lord), 157, 159
Hippies, 862
Hirohito (Japan), 759
Hiroshima, bombing of, 750–751, 775, 776(i)
Hispanics and Hispanic Americans. *See also*
    Latinos; specific groups
    movement to South and West, 699(m)
    New Deal and, 739
    in Southwest, 507
    use of term, 859
Hispaniola
    Haitian Revolution and, 258
    Spain and, 36
Hiss, Alger, 798
"History of the Standard Oil Company"
    (Tarbell), 529–530
Hitler, Adolf, 680, 751. *See also* Nazi
    Germany
    anti-Semitism of, 753
    suicide by, 773
    on United States, 776
Hobby, Oveta Culp, 812
Hoboes, in Great Depression, 712
Ho Chi Minh, 817, 818, 882
Ho Chi Minh City, 899
Ho Chi Minh Trail, 883
Hohokam culture, 13
Holding companies, 529, 547
Holland. *See* Dutch
Hollywood
    and movies in 1920s, 696
    and movies in Great Depression,
    710–711
"Hollywood Ten," 799
Holmes, George F., 404
Holmes, Oliver Wendell (Supreme Court
    Justice), 676
Holocaust, 769–770, 791
Home, as women's sphere, 320
Home front
    in Civil War, 444–447, 447–450
    in Revolutionary War, 186–191
    in World War I, 663
    in World War II, 760, 765–770
Homeland Security, Department of, 967
Homelessness, of children, 567
"Home protection" ballot, woman's suffrage
    and, 598, 599
Home rule, for South, 480, 482
Homespun cloth, 158
Homestead Act (1862), 448, 510
Homesteaders, 510–513
    women as, 511, 511(i)

Homestead steelworks, 533(i)
    strike at, 591–593
Homo erectus, 5
Homo sapiens, 4, 5, 6
Homosexuals and homosexuality. *See also*
    Gays and lesbians
    AIDS and, 931
    attitudes toward, 863, 952
    gay and lesbian organization in 1960s
    and, 863
    loyalty and, 799
    in military, 761, 952
Honduras, 608, 637
Hone, Philip, 328
Honor, in South, 376
Hood, John B., 454
Hooker, Thomas, 93–94
Hoover, Herbert, 685
    crash of 1929 and, 703–704
    election of 1928 and, 702, 703(i)
    election of 1932 and, 720
    as Food Administration head, 664, 704
    Great Depression and, 706–707, 709,
    710
    as Secretary of Commerce, 687, 704
Hoover, J. Edgar, Red scare (1919) and,
    676
Hoovervilles, 710
Hopi Indians, 13
Hopkins, Harry, 722, 725
Horizontal integration, 529
Horse car, 563
Horses, Plains Indians and, 9, 344, 494,
    496
Horseshoe Bend, Battle of (1814), 284
Hostages, in Iran, 922
Hotchkiss rapid-fire guns, 503
"Hot line," U.S.-Soviet, 882
Hourglass, 30
House Judiciary Committee, 913
House of Burgesses, 60, 68, 128
House of Representatives (U.S.), 229, 460.
    See also Congress (U.S.)
    Antifederalists on, 233
    election of 1800 and, 270
    election of 1824 and, 290, 296
    presidential impeachment by, 471, 913
House Un-American Activities Committee
    (HUAC), 782, 799
Housewives. *See* Domesticity
Housing
    in cities, 579
    discrimination in, 855
    Eisenhower and, 812, 823
    of free black elite, 388
    of homesteaders, 510–511
    Johnson, Lyndon B., and, 848
    in New Deal, 744
    in 1950s, 821, 827–828
    on plantations, 374, 478, 478(m)
    for slaves, 127, 375
    slums and, 557
    sod houses, 510–511, 511(i)

Housing (continued)
  tenements as, 563–564
  Truman and, 792
  veterans and, 794
  working class, 576–577, 594–595
Housing Act (1949), 797
Houston, Sam, 348
Howard University, African Americans students at, 862
Howe, Eleanor, 909
Howe, William, 177, 183, 185, 189, 190, 192, 197
Howl (Ginsberg), 831
How the Other Half Lives (Riis), 563–564
HUAC. *See* House Un-American Activities Committee
Huang Zunxian (poet), 562
Hudson, Carrie, 378
Hudson, Henry, 98
Hudson, Rock, 931
Hudson River region, 192
Huerta, Dolores, 860, 860(i)
Huerta, Victoriano, 654
Hughes, Charles Evans, 658, 688, 742
Hughes, Langston, 696
Huguenots, 130
Huitzilopochtli (god), 21
Hull, Charles, 617
Hull, Cordell, 752
Hull House, 617–619, 620, 621
Human rights, Carter and, 919–921, 922
Humans, in ancient Americas, 1–22
Human sacrifice
  by Mexica, 20(i), 21, 37
  Native American, 19
Humphrey, Hubert H., 880, 892–893
Hunchback (ship), 426(i)
Hundred Days (F. D. Roosevelt), 722
  legislation of, 723, 725–729
Hungary, 670
  immigrants from, 504, 559
  in NATO, 947
  revolt in 1956, 817
  Soviets and, 785
Hunkpapa Sioux Indians, 497
Huns, in World War I, 660
Hunter, David, 442
Hunter-gatherers, Archaic, 8–12
Hunters and hunting
  ancient, 4–5, 6
  Native American, 19
  Paleo-Indians and, 7–8
Huron Indians, 148
Hurricane Katrina, 964–965
Hurston, Zora Neale, 696
Husbands. *See also* Men
  rights of, 376
Hussein, Saddam, 945, 956
  Clinton and, 957
  Iraq War and, 967–968
  in Persian Gulf War, 946
Hutchinson, Anne, 92–93

Hutchinson, Thomas, 141(i), 159, 163, 168
  Albany Plan of Union and, 140, 145
  Boston Tea Party and, 161, 162–163
  as loyalist, 140–142, 187
  taxation and, 152, 154
Hydroelectricity, 633, 636
  New Deal programs for, 726–727, 726(m)
Hydrogen bomb, 789

Iberian Peninsula. *See also* Portugal; Spain
  Reconquest and, 30
ICBMs. *See* Intercontinental ballistic missiles
Idaho, voting rights for women in, 599(i), 600
Identity. *See* specific groups
Igbo culture, 122
Illegal immigrants, 826(i). *See also* Undocumented aliens
Illinois, 282, 292, 336
  Indian removal and, 315
  Lincoln in, 334, 334(i)
Illiteracy, 386, 476
Illness. *See* Disease
I Love Lucy (TV program), 829
Immigrants and immigration. *See also* Migration; specific groups
  Addams, Jane, and, 617
  anti-immigrant sentiment and, 408
  Asian, 507–508, 561–562, 645
  to California, 348
  California gold rush and, 355–356
  from Caribbean region, 859
  in cities, 560
  to colonies, 112, 116–117, 135
  Comstock Lode and, 504–505
  as domestic servants, 576
  free labor and, 341–342
  German, 116–117, 121–122
  global migration, urbanization, and, 557–560
  illegal, 826(i)
  impact to 1910, 558(m)
  indenture of, 63–64
  from Ireland, 112, 116, 117
  Jews and, 769
  McCarran-Walter Act and, 798
  in middle colonies, 116–118
  to New England, 89
  to New Netherland, 99
  in 1920s, 699–700
  old and new immigration, 559
  political bosses and, 581
  population growth through, 111–112
  racism and, 560–563
  restrictions on, 508, 561, 562, 563, 635, 645, 700, 959
  Scots-Irish, 112, 116, 117
  as servant labor, 62–64
  South and, 121–122, 373
  in textile industry, 566
  transportation conditions of, 117–118
  by 2006, 959

Immigration and Nationality Act (1965), 847,
    959
Immigration Reform and Control Act (1986),
    960
Impartial Administration of Justice Act
    (1774), 163
Impeachment
    of Clinton, 950, 953–954
    of Johnson, Andrew, 471–472, 954
    of Nixon and, 913
Imperialism
    debate over, 613
    Indians and, 498
    by Japan, 758, 759
    national liberation movements and, 790
    by United States, 480, 609
    in West, 491–493
    "Yankee," 886
Imperial presidency, 912
Imports
    colonial, 115
    under Nixon, 869
Impost (import tax), 219, 225
Impressment, 279–280, 285
    in Confederacy, 445
Inauguration
    of Adams, John, 260
    of Eisenhower, 815
    of Jackson, 311–312
    of Jefferson (1800), 263–264, 271
    of Lincoln, 421, 427, 461–462
    of Obama, 970 (i)
    of Roosevelt, T., 502
    Twentieth Amendment and, 421
Incandescent light bulb, 530
Incan empire, 39
Income. See also Wages
    of African Americans families, 768
    of farm families, 727
    national, 707
    by race, 955
    redistribution of, 849
    stagflation and, 907
Income tax, 535, 637, 640, 925
    Vietnam War and, 890
Incorporation, laws of, 308
Indentured servants, 63–66, 68, 117–118. See
    also Slaves and slavery
    redemptioners as, 117–118
    in South, 122
Independence. See also Revolutionary War;
    specific locations
    for California, 348
    colonial, 178–181
    in Cuba, 609
    for Philippines, 790
    third world movements for, 879
    after World War I, 670
Independence Hall, 228
Independent magazine, 565–566, 568, 572
India
    British withdrawal from, 790

nuclear test ban treaty and, 947
Portugal and, 31
Indian(s). See also Native Americans; specific
    groups
    use of term, 32
Indiana, 282, 292, 336
Indian Claims Commission (1946), 814
Indian country. See also Indian Territory;
    Oklahoma; West
    in Revolutionary War, 193–196, 195(m)
Indian Ocean region, 34
Indian policy. See also Native Americans
    allotment as, 498, 499–500
    assimilation as, 498, 499–500
    in colonies, 140
    concentration policy as, 344
    of Jackson, 313–316
    peace policy as, 496
    removal as, 313–315, 314(m), 493–495
    reservations and, 492(m), 493–495, 496,
        497, 498, 499–500
Indian Relocation Program (1948), 814
Indian Removal Act (1830), 313–314, 314(m)
Indian Reorganization Act (1934), 740
Indian Rights Association, 500
Indian Territory, 314(m), 316, 493, 501(i),
        513. See also Indian country
Indian wars, in West, 491, 493, 496, 497–
        498, 500–503, 506
Indies. See also East Indies; specific locations
    Northwest Passage to, 34
Indigenous people. See Native Americans;
    specific groups
Indigo, 75, 122, 127
Indochina, 758. See also Cambodia; Laos;
    Vietnam
    France and, 790
    U.S. and, 805
Indonesia. See also Dutch East Indies
    Dutch in, 758
Industrial core (global economic region),
        556(m), 557
Industrialism
    rise of, 523
    western commercial farming and, 516–517
Industrialization, Civil War and, 427, 445
Industrial Workers of the World (IWW), 643,
        675, 676
Industry. See also specific industries
    buffalo slaughter and, 495
    in Confederacy, 433, 445
    in Gilded Age, 523–532
    Great Depression and, 728–729
    infant industry, tariffs and, 545
    in 1929, 705
    in North (Civil War), 448–449
    railroads and, 339
    in Reagan era, 927
    in South, 537
    southern plantations and northern, 372
    technology in 1950s and, 822–823
    after World War II, 792

Inequality. *See also* Equality
  economic, 534, 927–928
  social Darwinism and, 534
  wealth and, 705
Infant industries, 545
Inflation. *See also* Economy; Stagflation
  Carter and, 916
  in Civil War, 433, 445
  in 1990s, 953
  Nixon and, 869
  unemployment and, 907
  Vietnam War and, 900
  after World War I, 674
  after World War II, 792
Influenza. *See* Spanish influenza epidemic
Infrastructure, WPA jobs and, 734
Inheritance
  in New England, 113
  by women, 287
In His Steps (Sheldon), 620
Initiative, 625, 626
Injunctions, 641
  in Pullman strike, 597
Inoculation, against smallpox, 177
Installment buying, 690
Instruments (musical), African American, 127
Insurance
  national health, 964, 971
  Social Security and, 737
Integration. *See also* Segregation
  of armed forces, 795
  Eisenhower and, 833, 834
  of interstate transportation, 851
  in Little Rock, 833
  Nixon and, 870
  of public schools, 833–834, 910–911
Intellectual thought. *See also* Art(s);
    Education; Harlem Renaissance;
    Literature; specific works and individ-
    uals
  Enlightenment and, 130
  in Great Depression, 732
  in 1920s, 697–698
  in 1950s, 831–832
  proslavery, 369–370
  transcendentalists and, 357
  utopians and, 358
Intelligence agencies, congressional oversight
    of, 914
Interchangeable parts, 337
Intercontinental ballistic missiles (ICBMs),
    820, 881
Interesting Narrative (Equiano), 123(i)
Interlocking directorates, 641
Intermarriage, 44(i), 45. *See also* Marriage
Intermediate-range nuclear forces (INF)
    agreement, 935
Internal taxes, 153
International Criminal Court (UN), 967
International Ladies' Garment Workers
    Union (ILGWU), 622
International Monetary Fund, 959
Internet, 958

Internment camps, for Japanese Americans,
    760, 761(m)
Interracial marriage, 849, 961
Interstate commerce, steamboats and, 304
Interstate Commerce Act (1887), 547
Interstate Commerce Commission (ICC), 547,
    630–631
Interstate Highway and Defense System Act
    (1956), 812, 813(m). *See also* Roads
    and highways
Intervention and interventionism. *See* spe-
    cific incidents and countries
Intolerable (Coercive) Acts (1774), 163–164
Inventions and inventors. *See also*
    Electricity; specific types
  telegraph and, 526
  telephone and, 530
Investment, finance capitalism and, 532
Investment banks, 723
Iowa, 336
Iran, 933. *See also* Iran hostage crisis
  Bush, G. H. W., and, 945
  Carter and, 917, 919, 922
  CIA and, 819
  Nixon administration and, 895
  nuclear weapons and, 969
  revolution in (1979), 917, 922
  Soviet troops in, 785
Iran-Contra scandal, Reagan and, 933–934
Iran hostage crisis, 922, 923
Iran-Iraq war, 935, 945
Iraq, 670. *See also* Iraq War (2003–2011)
  Bush, George W., and, 967
  occupation of, 968
  Persian Gulf War and, 945–946
Iraq War (2003–2011), 945, 961, 967–969
Ireland. *See also* Scots-Irish
  immigrants from, 112, 116, 117, 341, 342,
    504, 505, 554, 554(i), 560, 561
Irish Americans, 449
Iron and iron industry, 339, 537, 565
Ironclad warships, 439
Iron curtain, 784(m), 785–786, 817. *See also*
    Soviet Union
Iroquoian Indians, 17, 119
Iroquois Confederacy
  at Albany Congress, 145
  Fort Stanwix Treaty and, 220, 221
  in Revolutionary War, 192, 195(m)
Iroquois Indians, fur trade and, 119, 133,
    143(m)
Irreconcilables, in Congress, 672
"Irrepressible conflict" speech (Seward), 418
Irrigation, 12, 346, 632
Isabella (Spain), 25–26, 26(i), 30, 32, 47
Isham, Edward, 384–385
Islam. *See* Muslims
Islamic fundamentalists, in Iran, 922
Island-hopping campaign, 773
Isolationism
  foreign policy and, 605, 757
  in 1930s, 751–752
  World War II in Europe and, 755–757

Israel. *See also* Arab world; Middle East
  Camp David Accords and, 921
  creation of, 791
  Eisenhower and, 819
  Nixon and, 895
  after Persian Gulf War, 946
  Six-Day War and (1967), 895–896, 917
  Suez crisis and, 819–820
  terrorism against, 933
  Truman and, 791
  Yom Kippur War and (1973), 896
Isthmus of Panama. *See* Panama Canal region
Italy. *See also* Mussolini, Benito
  Communist Party in, 790
  Ethiopian invasion by, 754
  immigrants from, 504, 559
  trade and, 28(m)
  in Tripartite Pact, 759
  after World War I, 669, 670
  World War II and, 754, 765
Iwo Jima, Battle of, 774
IWW. *See* Industrial Workers of the World

Jackson, Andrew ("Old Hickory"), 313(i)
  banking, currency, and, 308
  Bank of the United States and, 317–318
  Bank War and, 317–319
  cabinet of, 312
  California and, 348
  Creek War and, 283–284
  election of 1824 and, 296, 298
  election of 1828 and, 310–311, 311(m)
  election of 1832 and, 326
  Florida and, 294
  Indians and, 294, 312, 313–316, 493
  marriage of, 310–311
  nullification and, 316–317
  second American party system and, 309
  spoils system under, 312
  Van Buren and, 312, 326, 327
  in War of 1812, 285
Jackson, Helen Hunt, 500
Jackson, Jesse, 942
Jackson, Rachel, 310–311
Jackson, Thomas J. ("Stonewall"), 436
Jackson State College, Mississippi, killings at, 897
Jamaica, Spain and, 36
James I (England), 55, 60, 85
James II (Duke of York, England), 99, 104
Jamestown, 53–55, 56–57, 59(i), 66(i)
Japan
  atomic bombing of, 750–751
  immigrants from, 504, 508, 562, 700
  investments in U.S. by, 959
  Korea and, 800
  League of Nations and, 752
  Manchuria and, 635
  Pearl Harbor and, 758–759
  "Rape of Nanking" by, 754
  Roosevelt, T., and, 635
  Soviet Union and, 772

  in Tripartite Pact, 759
  Vietnam and, 817
  in World War I, 657
  after World War I, 670–671
  World War II and, 754, 763(i), 773–776
  after World War II, 791
Japanese Americans
  discrimination against, 645, 739–740
  internment of, 760, 761(m)
  McCarran-Walter Act and, 798
  World War II and, 760
Jarvis, Howard, 909(i), 910
Jay, John. *See also* Jay Treaty
  as chief justice, 242–243
  as envoy to England, 257
  Federalist Papers and, 226–227, 234–235
Jay Treaty, 257–258, 261
Jazz, 696
Jazz Age, 685
Jefferson, Fort, 253
Jefferson, Isaac, 379(i)
Jefferson, Mary, 379(i)
Jefferson, Thomas
  Articles of Confederation and, 208
  cabinet of, 272
  Declaration of Independence and, 180, 214
  "Declaration on the Causes and Necessity of Taking Up Arms, A," 176
  election of 1796 and, 260, 261
  election of 1800 and, 263–264, 269–270
  election of 1804 and, 279
  Gaspée and, 161
  Haitian Revolution and, 259
  Hamilton and, 241, 248
  inauguration of (1800), 263–264, 271
  Indians and, 268–269
  intellectual thought and, 130
  Louisiana Purchase and, 274–275
  Missouri Compromise and, 293
  Northwest Territory and, 222, 224, 224(i)
  Osage Indians and, 278
  presidency of, 269–273
  on republican simplicity, 270–271
  Revolution and, 200–201
  as secretary of state, 242
  slavery and, 124–125, 128, 374, 379(i)
  western lands and, 211, 276(m)
  Whiskey Rebellion and, 251
Jeffersonian Republicans. *See* Republicans (Jeffersonian)
Jenney, William Le Baron, 578(i)
Jericho, Israeli withdrawal from, 957
Jersey (British prisoner of war ship), 190
Jerusalem, 957
Jews and Judaism. *See also* Anti-Semitism
  Arabs and, 670
  in Great Depression, 732
  Holocaust and, 769–770
  as immigrants, 559, 560
  Israel and, 791
  in middle colonies, 99
  pogroms against, 560
  Spanish Reconquest and, 26

Jiang Jieshi (Chiang Kai-Shek), 753, 772, 790–791
Jim Crow laws, 477, 538, 561, 645
Job Corps, 845
Job discrimination, 853
Jobs. *See also* Employment; Unemployment
    patronage and, 536
Jobs, Steven, 927
John II (Castile), 25
John Birch Society, 908
Johnson, Andrew
    assumption of presidency, 456, 465
    black codes and, 466, 467
    Fourteenth Amendment and, 469–470
    Freedmen's Bureau bill and, 467–468
    impeachment of, 471–472, 954
    Reconstruction plan of, 465–466
Johnson, Dorothy, 766(i)
Johnson, Hiram, 625, 626, 638, 645, 672
Johnson, James Weldon, 695–696
Johnson, Jane, 379
Johnson, "Lady Bird," 847
Johnson, Lyndon B., 844–845
    assumption of presidency, 844
    civil rights and, 841, 842, 848, 909
    election of 1960 and, 843
    election of 1964 and, 845, 885, 905, 908
    election of 1968 and, 891
    foreign policy of, 884–888
    Great Society and, 841, 842–843, 845–849
    Latin America and, 886
    Mexican Americans and, 861
    Vietnam War and, 848, 876, 884–885, 886, 888, 889, 890, 891
Johnson, Martha, 652, 653
Johnson, Sonia, 929
Johnson, Thomas Loftin (Tom), 625, 626
Johnson, William, 146, 149
Johnson-Reed Act (1924), 700
Johnston, Albert Sidney, 438
Johnston, Joseph, 436
Joint Chiefs of Staff, Powell and, 940
Joint-stock companies, 86
Jones, Charles Colcock, 381
Jones, Cynthia, 943
Jones, Isaac, 151(i)
Jones, William ("Billy"), 568
Joplin, Janis, 862
Jordan
    Eisenhower and, 820
    Rabin and, 957
    Six-Day War and, 895–896
Joseph (Nez Percé chief), 501, 501(i)
Journalism. *See also* Newspapers
    depression of 1890s and, 602
    muckraking in, 631
    photojournalism, 563–564
    yellow, 609
Judaism. *See* Jews and Judaism
Judiciary. *See also* Courts; Supreme Court
    under Articles of Confederation, 210
    Carter and, 916

in Constitution, 230
    rightward movement in, 929
    Virginia Plan and, 229
    Warren Court and, 849–850
Judiciary Act (1789), 272
Jugular diplomacy, 898
Jungle, The (Sinclair), 631
Juries
    discrimination in selection of, 855
    free blacks on, 388
    Mexican Americans excluded from, 825–826
Justice Department, in Reagan era, 928–929

Kaintwakon. *See* Cornplanter
Kaiser. *See* Wilhelm II
Kaiser, The: The Beast of Berlin (musical), 667
Kamikaze pilots, 774
Kansas, 395, 514
    "Bleeding Kansas," 411–412
    Coronado in, 40
    free vs. slave state settlers in, 411–412, 415
Kansas-Nebraska Act (1854), 402, 405–406, 409, 413, 414, 415
Kaskaskia, battle at, 196
Katrina, Hurricane, 964–965
Kearny, Stephen Watts, 352
Kearsarge (ship), 440
Keating-Owen Act (1916), 642
Kelley, Florence, 623
Kellogg, Frank, 688
Kellogg-Briand Pact (1928), 688
Kendall, Mary, 377
Kennan, George F., 786, 789
Kennedy, Edward M. ("Ted"), 847, 916, 946
Kennedy, Jacqueline, 843
Kennedy, John F.
    assassination of, 841, 844, 884
    Bay of Pigs invasion and, 879, 882
    Cuban missile crisis and, 881–882
    economy and, 844
    foreign policy of, 877–884
    New Frontier of, 842
    Soviet Union and, 879–880
    television and, 829
    third world initiatives of, 880–881
    Vietnam War and, 876, 882–883, 884
Kennedy, Joseph P., 725
Kennedy, Robert F., 851, 860(i), 892
Kennesaw Mountain, Battle of (1864), 452(m), 454
Kent State University, Ohio, killings at, 897
Kentucky, 430, 438
    Revolutionary War and, 193
    Unionism in, 429
    Virginia and Kentucky Resolutions and, 262
    western settlement in, 149
Kerouac, Jack, 831–832
Kerry, John, 968
Kettle Hill, 610
Keynes, John Maynard, 709, 743

Keynesian economics, 743
Khmer Rouge (Cambodia), 897
Khomeini, Ayatollah Ruholla, 922
Khrushchev, Nikita
    Cuban missile crisis and, 881–882
    Kennedy, J. F., and, 879–880
    Nixon and, 809–810, 810(i), 820, 823,
        877–879
    nuclear arms race and, 820–821
Kim Il Sung, 800, 947
King, Boston, 202
King, Martin Luther, Jr., 850–853, 915
    assassination of, 855, 858, 892
    in Birmingham, 852
    in Chicago, 858
    March on Washington for Jobs and
        Freedom (1963), 852
    Montgomery bus boycott and, 835–836,
        835(i)
    on Vietnam War, 877, 889
King, Mary, 864
King, Rufus, 290
King Cotton diplomacy, 431, 439–440
King George, Grandy, 109, 111
King James version, of Bible, 85
King Philip (Metacomet, Wampanoag
    Indians), 103–104
King Philip's War (1675–1676), 101, 103–105
Kings Canyon National Park, 634(m)
King's College (Columbia University), 239
Kingsley, Bathsheba, 131
King's Mountain, Battle of (1780), 198(m), 200
King William's War (1689–1697), 105
Kinsey, Alfred, 830
Kinship. *See also* Families
    in West Africa, 126–127
Kiowa Indians, 344, 350, 495, 500
Kissinger, Henry A., 893, 894, 895, 896,
    897, 898
Kitchen debate, 823, 827, 877–879. *See also*
    Nixon, Richard
Klamath Indians, 814
Klan. *See* Ku Klux Klan
Knights of Labor, 562, 570, 572–573, 574,
    575, 587
    WCTU and, 598
Know-Nothing Party, 408, 409, 414
Knox, Henry, 242, 251, 252–253
Korea. *See also* Korean War; North Korea;
    South Korea
    Soviet Union and, 772
Korean War (1950–1953), 795, 800–805,
    801(m)
Korematsu decision, 760
Ku Klux Klan, 459, 474–475, 474(i), 480, 685
    in 1920s, 699, 700–701
Ku Klux Klan Acts (1870 and 1871), 481
Kurds, 946, 968
Kuwait
    Bush, G. H. W., and, 945–946
    Persian Gulf War and, 941
Kyoto Protocol, Bush, George W., and, 963, 967

Labor. *See also* Child labor; Free labor;
        Labor unions; Servants; Slaves and
        slavery; Strikes; Wages; Workforce
    agricultural, 62–64, 336
    black codes and, 466
    changes in, 570
    child, 340
    Chinese, 507–508
    common laborers and, 563, 565
    of freed slaves, 463, 477–479
    in Gilded Age, 564–570
    in Great Depression, 706, 732, 735–737
    immigration and, 557–560, 960–961,
        960(i)
    in later 19th century., 564–570
    for manufacturing, 337
    mechanization and, 559
    Mexican, 678–679
    migrant, 515, 517
    in mining, 504–505
    Native American, 46
    in New Deal, 745
    in New Spain, 43
    in 1950s, 822–823
    non-union, 959
    organization of, 570–575
    pick-and-shovel, 565
    Populists and, 591, 604
    slavery as, 125–127, 378–379
    in South, 537
    Taft-Hartley Act and, 797
    Truman and, 792–793
    WCTU and, 598
    women as, 320, 665
    in World War I, 664
    after World War I, 674–675, 674(i)
    in World War II, 766–767
Labor code, in Reconstruction, 463
Labor Department
    Children's Bureau of, 637
    Nixon and, 871
Labor force. *See* Workforce
Labor unions. *See also* Labor; Strikes; spe-
        cific unions and leaders
    African Americans in, 768
    antitrust laws used against, 547, 628
    during Great Depression, 735–737
    immigrants and, 699–700
    injunctions and, 597, 641
    in mining, 506
    NAFTA and, 958
    in 1920s, 687
    in 1950s, 822
    non-union labor and, 959
    Reagan and, 925, 927
    settlement house movement and, 621
    Supreme Court and, 535
    Taft-Hartley Act and, 797
    WCTU and, 598
    welfare capitalism and, 689
    after World War II, 793
    in World War II, 762

Labor wars, 591–597
Ladies Association (Philadelphia), 187
Lafayette (Marquis de), 218
La Follette, Robert M. ("Fighting Bob"), 625, 626, 638, 664, 687
Laissez-faire
    toward business, 619, 627
    depression of 1890s and, 600
    Great Depression and, 719
    Republican Party and, 704
    social Darwinism and, 535
Lakes. *See* specific lake regions
Lakewood development, in California, 826
Lakota Sioux Indians, 494, 497, 859
Lancaster Turnpike, 245
Land. *See also* Agriculture; Conservation;
        Farms and farming
    annexations to 1860, 336
    under Articles of Confederation, 210, 211
    of Californios, 507
    in Chesapeake region, 66–67
    Dawes Act and, 500
    in 1840s and 1850s, 335–336
    for freedmen, 463–464, 466, 471, 477, 478
    in Great Depression, 711
    Homestead Act and, 448, 510
    Indian, 119, 149, 202–203, 252, 278, 284, 313, 367, 492(m), 493, 497, 498, 500, 814, 859, 871
    Indian cessions in Northwest Territory (1795–1809), 254(m)
    Jackson and, 312
    in middle colonies, 119–120
    Morrill Act and, 448
    New Deal conservation of, 726, 726(m)
    in New England, 92, 104, 112–113
    New York-Massachusetts conflict over, 220–221
    in Ohio River region, 252
    ordinances and Northwest Territory, 222–225
    Osage and, 278
    Quebec and, 163
    return to ex-Confederates, 466
    speculation in, 113, 149, 318, 511–513
    state, 211
    in Texas, 347
    in West, 211, 212(m), 510, 512(m)
Land bridge, between Siberia and Alaska, 6
Land-Grant College Act (Morrill Act, 1863), 448
Land grants
    to railroads, 512(m), 513, 526
    Spanish and Mexican, 507
Landon, Alfred ("Alf"), 741
Land ordinances, Northwest Ordinance (1787), 222–225
Landowners, in Chesapeake, 68
Land rush, in Oklahoma, 513
Lange, Dorothea, 717(i), 718
Language(s). *See also* Writing
    of California peoples, 10
    of Eastern Woodland peoples, 17

L'Anse aux Meadows, Newfoundland, 27
Lansing, Robert, 658, 670
Laos, 883, 899
Laramie, Fort
    Indian conference at, 493–494
    Treaty of (1851), 344, 494, 496
    Treaty of (1868), 497, 498
La Raza Unida, 861
Las Casas, Bartolomé de, 43
Las Manos Negras (the Black Hands), 507
Lassen Volcanic National Park, 634(m)
Latin America. *See also* America(s); Central
        America; South America; specific lead-
        ers and countries
    Alliance for Progress and, 880
    good neighbor policy and, 752–753
    interventions in, 818–819
    Johnson, L. B., and, 886
    Monroe and, 290
    Monroe Doctrine and, 294–295
    Roosevelt Corollary and, 633
    Soviets and, 785
    U.S. involvement in, 608, 878(m)
    Wilson and, 654
Latinos/Latinas. *See also* Hispanics and
        Hispanic Americans; specific groups
    as Carter appointees, 916
    equal rights struggle by, 859–861
    in population, 959
    use of term, 859
Latitude, determining, 30
Law(s). *See also* Legislation; specific laws
    colonial, 136
    commercial, 308
    constitutionality of, 272
    criminal justice system and, 849
    Puritan, 91
    against southern free blacks, 366, 387
    women and, 286, 287
Lawless Decade, 686
Lawrence, Kansas, sack of, 412
Lawson, James, 851
Lazarus, Emma, 562
League of Five Nations, 17
League of Nations, 669, 671–672, 679, 687, 752
League of United Latin-American Citizens
        (LULAC), 796, 825, 860, 861
League of Women Voters, 693
Lebanon
    American hostages in, 920(m), 934
    Hezbollah in, 933
    intervention in (1958), 820
Lecompton constitution (Kansas), 415
Le Dru, Pierre, 268(i)
Lee, Fort, 185
Lee, George Washington Custis, 455(i)
Lee, Richard Henry, 161, 215
Lee, Robert E., 433, 482
    in Civil War, 436, 451, 453, 454, 455, 455(i)
    Harpers Ferry raid and, 396
Leftist movements, Reagan and, 933–934

Left wing (political). *See also* Communism; Socialism and socialists
  in Great Depression, 712, 732
  New Left and, 861
Legal Services program, 868
Legal Tender Act (1862), 448
Legislation. *See also* Law(s); specific laws
  of New Deal's first Hundred Days, 723, 725–729
  to protect working women, 623
  welfare (New Deal), 733–740
Legislatures. *See also* Assemblies; Congress (U.S.); specific legislative bodies
  in Kansas, 412
  in Pennsylvania, 101
  southern, 128, 390
Leisler, Jacob, 104
Leisure. *See also* Entertainment
  of plain folk, 385–386
  of working class, 575, 577
Lemlich, Clara, 622
Lend-Lease Act (1941), 758, 760
Lenni Lenape (Delaware) Indians. *See* Delaware Indians
Leopard (ship), 279–280
Lesbians. *See* Gays and lesbians; Homosexuals and homosexuality
Letters from a Farmer in Pennsylvania (Dickinson), 156, 176
Letters on the Equality of the Sexes (Sarah Grimké), 302
"Levees" (audiences), 242
Levitt, William J., 823
Levittown, 823
Lewelling, Lorenzo, 600
Lewis, John (SNCC), 853
Lewis, John L. (United Mine Workers), 735, 736
Lewis, Meriwether, 272, 275–277, 276(m)
Lewis and Clark expedition, 274, 275–277, 276(m)
Lexington, battle at, 166–167, 167(m)
Leyte Gulf, Battle of, 773–774
Liberal Party, 480
Liberals and liberalism. *See also* Classical liberalism; Progressivism
  Carter and, 915–916
  in 1960s, 842–850
  Reagan era and, 923
Liberation movements, 777
  in Vietnam, 882–883
  after World War II, 790
Liberator (newspaper), 302, 324, 366
Liberia, former slaves in, 324, 361
Liberty(ies). *See also* Civil liberties; Freedom(s); specific rights and liberties
  under Articles of Confederation, 214
  colonial, 155
Liberty Party, 350
Libraries, 527, 579–580
Lien, crop. *See* Crop lien system
Life, liberty, and property, 155
Life magazine, 889

Lifestyle. *See also* Society
  of ancient peoples, 6
  automobile and, 688–689
  of free black elite, 388
  in Great Depression, 707–712
  in middle colonies, 121
  Native American, 18–19
  of planters, 374–377
  of servants, 65
  in South, 127, 128, 385, 738
  in Vietnam War, 888
  wealth and, 926–927
  of working class families, 566–567
  of yeomen, 383–384
Lifestyles of the Rich and Famous (TV program), 926
"Lift Every Voice," 695–696
Light bulb, 530
Lili'uokalani (Hawai'i), 606, 606(i)
Limited government, 140, 549
  Jackson on, 312
Limited test ban treaty (1963), 882
Lin, Maya, 901
Lincoln, Abraham, 333–335, 397, 405, 419(i), 421, 427–428, 438
  assassination of, 455–456, 465
  cabinet of, 432–433
  in Civil War, 428, 429, 432, 434, 439
  election of 1860 and, 407(m), 417–419
  election of 1864 and, 454
  emancipation and, 441–442, 442–443
  first inaugural address (1861), 421, 422, 427
  on free labor, 340, 415
  at Gettysburg, 443, 465
  on Harpers Ferry raid, 396
  leadership by, 432
  Mexican-American War and, 352
  reconstruction plan of, 461–462
  second inaugural address of, 461–462
  slavery and, 414
  Springfield home of, 334(i)
  wealth of, 341
Lincoln, Abraham (grandfather), 119–120
Lincoln, John, 119
Lincoln, Mary Todd, 333, 334–335, 334(i)
Lincoln, Mordecai, 119
Lincoln, Nancy, 334
Lincoln, Thomas, 120, 333, 334
Lincoln-Douglas debates, 415–416
"Lincoln states," 462
Lindbergh, Charles, 697
Lineages, African American, 126
Lippmann, Walter, 624
Lipscomb family, 385
Liquor. *See* Alcohol and alcoholism
Liquor lobby, 621
Lisbon, Portugal, 31
Literacy, 568
  black, 464
  Johnson, L. B., and, 845
  in South, 476–477
  tests of, 472, 563, 645, 847

Literacy (continued)
    for voting, 292, 472, 645
    for women, 320
Literature. See also specific works and authors
    on cowboys, 514
    by ex-slaves, 404–405
    of Farmers' Alliance, 589–590
    in Harlem Renaissance, 695–696
    transcendentalist, 357
    Uncle Tom's Cabin, 402, 403–405
Little Big Horn, Battle of (1876), 490(i),
    497–498
"Little Boy" (bomb), 750–751
Little Crow (Dakota Sioux), 496
Little Rock, Arkansas, school integration in,
    833
"Little Rock Nine," 833
Little Turtle (Miami Indians), 253, 255
Livingston, Robert R., 274
Lloyd, Henry Demarest, 542
Lloyd George, David, 669
Loans. See also Bank(s) and banking;
        Economy
    agricultural, 743
    banking, 307
    commodity, 728
    money supply contraction and, 308
    in World War I, 659
    after World War II, 794
Lobo (racial category), 44(i)
Local government. See also Cities and towns
    loyalty oaths in, 800
    women's rights and, 867–868
Locke, Alain, 695
Locke, John, 75
Locomotives, 338
Lodge, Henry Cabot, 562–563, 672, 687
Lodge, Henry Cabot, Jr., 795
Loggers, 516(i)
Lonely Crowd, The (Riesman), 830
Lone Star Republic, 348, 349
Long, Huey, 733, 737
Longfellow, Henry Wadsworth, 404
"Long Walk" of Navajo, 494
Looms, 306, 306(i), 565
Lord Dunmore's War, 149
Los Alamos, New Mexico, 775
Los Angeles, 897. See also Watts riots
    Mexican American deportation in Great
        Depression, 710
Lost Cause, 482
Lost Generation, 691, 697–698
Louis XIV (France), 669
Louisiana, 274, 462. See also New Orleans
    secession and, 420
    War of 1812 and, 285
Louisiana Purchase, 268–269, 274–275,
    276(m), 294, 336, 405
Louisiana Territory, 273–274, 275, 278, 397
Love, Nat (Deadwood Dick), 514
Love Canal, 917–919
Lovejoy, Elijah, 325
Loving v. Virginia (1967), 849

Lowell, Massachusetts, 305
    mills in, 305, 321
Lowell Offering, 306
Lower house, in states, 214
Lower South, 126, 418, 419, 427. See also
        South
    black population in, 369
    as cotton kingdom, 368–369
    secession and, 420
Loyalists (Spain), 754
Loyalists (U.S.), 140–142, 181, 186, 200
    black, 202, 217(i)
    Indians as, 188
    in Revolutionary War, 187–189
    strength of, 187
    as traitors, 189
Loyalty, in World War I, 664, 667
Loyalty oaths, in state and local govern-
        ments, 800
Loyalty program
    Eisenhower and, 812
    of Truman, 799
Lozen (Apache female warrior), 502
Luftwaffe (Germany), 757, 771
LULAC. See League of United Latin-
        American Citizens
Lumber industry, 537
    loggers in, 516(i)
Lunch counter sit-ins, 851
Lusitania (ship), 658
Luther, Martin, 47
Lutherans, German immigrants as, 117
Lux, Charles, 517
Luxembourg, German invasion of, 755
Lynchings
    of African Americans, 538–540, 561, 745
    of Prager, Robert, 667
    after World War I, 678
Lynd, Robert and Helen, 689
Lynn, Massachusetts, 307
Lyon, Mary, 320
Lyon, Matthew, 263(i)

MacArthur, Douglas, 763, 801, 802
Machine (political), 580
Machinery. See also Factories;
        Industrialization; Mechanization
    industrial, 305
    standardization and, 337
MacKenzie, Kathleen, 966
Mackintosh, Ebenezer, 153
MAD. See Mutually assured destruction
Madison, Dolley, 208(i), 279, 280–281,
    281(i), 285, 286
Madison, James, 207–209, 208(i)
    Articles of Confederation and, 208–209, 213
    Barbary Wars and, 273
    Bill of Rights and, 243
    Constitution and, 209, 227, 234
    election of 1808 and, 279, 280
    election of 1812 and, 283
    Federalist Papers and, 234–235, 236
    Hamilton and, 240–241

national bank and, 249
political power and, 214
as Secretary of State, 272
Virginia Plan and, 228–229
western lands and, 211
Magazines, 692. *See also* specific magazines
Magellan, Ferdinand, 34–35
Mahan, Alfred Thayer, 606, 607
Mail service, 245, 304
birth control information and, 643
by Pony Express, 448, 526
Maine, 293, 294(m), 322
Maine (ship), explosion of, 610
Maine laws, 540
Mainland colonies. *See* British North
America; Colonies and colonization;
specific colonies
Maize (corn). *See* Corn
Malcolm X, 857
Male, use of term in Constitution, 469, 540
Male suffrage, 215–216, 389–390, 475, 647.
See also Voting and voting rights
Malinali (Marina, Mexico), 37
Malls, in 1950s, 823, 826
Mammals, 4–5. *See also* Animals
Mammoths, 4, 7
Management, business, 689
Managers, in workforce, 565, 568, 596
Manassas, Battle of. *See* Bull Run
Manchuria, 635
Soviet Union and, 772
Mandan Indians, 17, 275–277, 494
Mandate system, after World War I, 670
Mandinga culture, 122
Manhate Indians, 98
Manhattan Island, 98, 98(i), 99
Manhattan Project, 775
Manifest destiny, 343, 605
Indian removal and, 493
Pierce and, 405
Polk and, 350
westward movement and, 343
Manila, U.S. navy in, 610, 611(m)
Mansfield, Lord, 110–111
Mansfield, Mike, 885, 889
Manufacturing
American system of, 337
automobile, 688–689
expansion of, 305–307
globalization of, 894, 927
Hamilton and, 249
income (1920–1940), 708(f)
mechanization and, 305
under Nixon, 869
tariffs and, 545
women in, 448
Manumission, of slaves, 218
Mao Zedong, 790–791
Maps, of New World, 34
Marbury v. Madison (1803), 272
March on Washington (1941), 767–768
March on Washington for Jobs and Freedom
(1963), 852

Margin purchases, of stocks, 705
Marina. *See* Malinali (Marina, Mexico)
Marines (U.S.). *See also* Military; specific
battles and wars
in Barbary Wars, 273
in Dominican Republic, 884
Hezbollah terrorism against, 920(m), 933
in Latin America, 637
in Mexico, 654
Market(s). *See also* Stock market; Trade
in China, 894
colonial, 129
expansion of, 606–607
international, 545, 608, 690
tobacco, 66
transportation and, 304
for western agriculture, 516
Market revolution, 302–303, 303–309
Marne River, battle at, 663
Marriage
African American, 287
in Chesapeake, 64
by free blacks, 388
gay, 952
in Great Depression, 710
Indian-English, 57
interracial, 849, 961
in New England, 112–113
in 1950s, 827
in Oneida community, 358
plural (polygamy), 509
Puritan, 91
of slaves, 380
women and, 286, 287, 360, 377, 566, 567,
569–570
women in college and, 827
Married women
rights of, 215, 376, 409
in workforce, 566, 567, 927
Marshall, George C., 787
Marshall, James, 355
Marshall, Thurgood, 796–797, 833, 943
Marshall Islands, 773
Marshall Plan, 787, 880
Martin, Anna, 189
Martin, Joseph W., Jr., 792
Martinique, 146, 147, 150
Mary (textile worker), 565–566
Mary I (England), 84–85
Mary II (England), 104
Maryland, 61(m), 136. *See also* Chesapeake
region; Tobacco and tobacco industry
Articles of Confederation and, 211
Catholicism in, 67, 104
in Civil War, 436
government of, 67, 135
population of, 121
Protestant Association in, 104–105
secession and, 429
slavery in, 218
Unionism in, 429
Masculine power, of planters, 376
Masculinity, in 1950s, 830

Mason, George, 216, 234
Mason-Dixon line, 366–367, 368
Massachusetts. *See also* Boston; New
    England
  abolition in, 216
  charter of, 86, 91, 104
  committee of correspondence in, 161–162
  constitution in, 216
  Fort Stanwix Treaty and, 220–221
  government of, 91–92, 140–142
  King Philip's War and, 103
  Pilgrims in, 85
  protests in, 157
  Shays's Rebellion in, 225–227
  Williams, Roger, in, 81–83
Massachusetts Bay Company, 83, 86–89,
    87(i), 91
Massachusetts Government Act (1774), 163,
    164
Massacres. *See* specific massacres
Massasoit (Wampanoag Indians), 86, 103
Mass communication. *See* Communication(s);
    specific media
Masses. *See* People, the
Massive retaliation policy, 817
Mass media. *See also* specific media
  in 1920s, 692, 697
  women's movement and, 866
Mass production, 689
Mass transit, 563
Matamoros, 351
Materialism, in Gilded Age, 499, 521
Mather, Increase, 91
Mathews, John, 379
Mathews, Mary McNair, 506
Matrilineal descent, Iroquoian, 17
Maximilian (Mexico), 480
May Day rally (Chicago, 1886), 574
Mayflower (ship), 85
Mayflower Compact, 85
Mayors, reform, 581
Maysville Road veto, 312
Mazo, Ike, 927
McCain, John, 970, 971
McCarran-Walter Act (1952), 798
McCarthy, Eugene, 892
McCarthy, Joseph R., and McCarthyism,
    798–800, 812
McClellan, George B., 434–436, 454
McClure's Magazine, 529
McCormick, Cyrus, 336, 448
McCormick, Cyrus, Jr., 574
McCormick reaper works, strike at, 574
McDonough, Clarence, 910
McGillivray, Alexander (Creek Indians),
    251–252
McGovern, George S., 889, 912
McIntosh, Fort, Treaty of (1785), 222
McJunkin, George, 9
McKay, Claude, 696
McKinley, William, 541, 607
  assassination of, 626
  election of 1896 and, 603–605
  Spanish-American War and, 610, 613
McKinley tariff (1890), 546, 606
McNamara, Robert, 884, 891
Measles, 46, 494
Meat Inspection Act (1906), 631
Mechanical reapers, 336, 448, 515
Mechanization
  in business, 568
  in farming, 336, 448, 515
  in garment industry, 566
  labor changes and, 570
  manufacturing and, 337
  in textile industry, 305, 565–566
Media. *See* Mass media; specific media
Medicaid (1965), 847, 867, 868
Medicare (1965), 846(i), 847, 928, 964
Medicine. *See also* Disease; Health and
    health care
  Medicare, Medicaid, and, 847, 849
  polio vaccine and, 812
  regulation of patent, 631
Medicine Lodge Creek, Treaty of (1867),
    495
Mediterranean region
  Barbary Wars in, 272–273
  trade in, 29–30
  in World War II, 764, 765
Mellon, Andrew, 686, 687
Memphis
  in Civil War, 435(m), 438
  King assassination in, 858
  violence against blacks in, 539
Men. *See also* Gender
  on Comstock Lode, 505
  in Great Depression, 710
  as immigrants, 570
  separate spheres for, 538
  in Vietnam War, 887
  voting rights for, 291–292, 538
Mencken, H. L., 701, 702
Mendez v. Westminster (1947), 796–797
Menéndez de Avilés, Pedro, 41
Mennonites, 117
Menominee Indians, 814
Mercantilism, in English colonies, 69
Mercenaries, German, 180, 183, 192, 193
Mercer, Frederick W., 375(i)
Merchants
  in middle colonies, 121
  in New England, 115
  in sharecropping, 479
  in South, 372–373
Meredith, James H., 853
Mergers, 533, 925, 927
  of AFL and CIO, 822
Merrimack (frigate), 435(m), 439
Mesa Verde, Colorado, 13, 634(m)
Mescalero Apache Agency, 499
Mesoamerica, Mexica people in, 19–22,
    20(i)
Mestizos, 44(i), 45

Metacomet (Wampanoag Indians). *See* King Philip
Metals. *See* Gold; Silver
Methodists, 380, 386, 464
Meuse-Argonne offensive, 653, 663
Mexica (people), 19–22, 20(i), 37–39
Mexican Americans
    as agricultural labor, 700, 731
    arrests of, 826(i)
    civil rights for, 795–796
    in Civil War, 438
    as cowboys, 514–515
    in Great Depression, 739
    population growth of, 825
    as scapegoats in Great Depression, 709–710, 709(i)
    in Southwest, 859–860
    women's movement and, 866
    in World War II armed forces, 761
    zoot-suit riots and, 768
Mexican-American War (1846–1848), 349, 350–354, 351(m), 397, 398, 432, 507
    land cessions after, 421
    manifest destiny and, 493
    Treaty of Guadalupe Hidalgo and, 507
Mexican borderlands, 347–348
Mexican cession (1848), 400
    slavery in, 396–397, 398, 407, 421
Mexican immigrants, 504. *See also* Mexican Americans; Migrant laborers
    to Southwest, 700
Mexico. *See also* Mexican-American War
    borderlands of, 347–348, 349
    Gadsden Purchase and, 405
    independence of, 294
    Mexica people of, 19–22, 20(i), 37–38
    NAFTA and, 958
    nationalization of oil in, 752
    revolution in (1911), 637
    silver from, 41
    Southwest and, 347
    Spain and, 36–39
    Texas and, 348, 349
    U.S. intervention in, 480
    Wilson and, 654
    workers from, 731
Mexico City, Cortés in, 38
Meyers, John, 553–554
Miami, Fort, 255
Miami Indians, 253, 255, 282
Michigan, 282, 336
Middle class
    black, 647
    in cities, 563
    during Civil War, 449
    domestics and, 576
    in Gilded Age, 568–570
    Great Railroad Strike and, 572
    by 1960, 827
    Vietnam War and, 887
    wealthy and, 564
    in workforce, 568–569

Middle colonies. *See also* specific locations
    farming in, 119–120
    founding of, 97–101
    immigrants in, 116–118
    population of, 116
    Revolutionary War and, 178
    slaves in, 118–119
Middle East. *See also* Arab world; Israel; specific countries and wars
    1948–1989, 920(m)
    1989–2011, 946(m)
    Bush, George W., and, 967–969
    Carter and, 921, 922
    Clinton and, 955
    Eisenhower and, 819–820
    interventions in, 819–820
    investments in U.S. by, 959
    Iranian revolution in, 917
    Iran-Iraq cease-fire in, 935
    Israel policy and, 791
    Nixon and, 895
    oil in, 917, 918(m), 921
    Persian Gulf War and, 945–946
    terrorism and, 933
"Middle ground," of southern free blacks, 387
Middlemen, in cotton export, 372
Middle Passage, 123–124, 126
    Second, 369
Middletown (1929), 689–690
"Middle way," of Eisenhower, 811–815
Middling class. *See also* Middle class
    German immigrants as, 117
"Midnight judges," 272
Midway Island, Battle of, 764, 773
Midway Plaisance, 489, 582
Midwest, 604. *See also* specific regions
    Indians of, 17
    population of, 336
Migrant laborers, 515, 517, 780, 781, 960(i)
    in Great Depression, 717, 731–732
Migrant Mother (Lange photo), 717(i), 718
Migrants, arrests of, 826(i)
Migration. *See also* Immigrants and immigration; Slave trade; Westward movement; specific groups
    African American, 677–678, 678(i), 699(m), 768, 822
    to Americas, 6
    forced, of slaves, 111
    German, 116–117
    global, 555–560
    of Indians, 814
    Mexican American, 678–679
    Native American, 17
    westward, 342–348
Miles, Dora, 766
Miles, Nelson, 501(i), 502
Militancy. *See also* Protest(s); specific groups
    working-class, 711–712

Military. *See also* Defense; Defense spending; Soldiers; specific battles and wars; specific branches
    African Americans in, 425–426
    attitude toward Native Americans, 494–495
    Boxer uprising and, 607
    British colonial, 159–161
    Carter and, 921
    Clinton and, 955
    desegregation of, 795
    Eisenhower and, 816–817
    in Great Railroad Strike, 572
    Green Berets in, 881
    homosexuals in, 761, 952
    in Iraq War, 969
    Jefferson and, 272
    Kennedy, John F., and, 879, 880
    McCarthy and, 812
    NSC 68 and, 805
    in Pullman strike, 596–597
    Reagan and, 932–933
    in Revolutionary War, 181–182
    segregation of, 660
    third world and U.S., 881
    in Vietnam War, 876, 883, 883(m), 884, 885, 896
    women in, 789
    in World War II, 760–761
Military districts, in South, 470
Military Reconstruction Act (1867), 470–471
Militia. *See also* Military; National Guard
    in Civil War, 428
    in Constitution, 243
    in Great Railroad Strike, 571, 572
    Homestead strike and, 593
    in New England, 164
    in Revolutionary War, 166–167, 176, 181
Militia Act (1862), 443
Militia movement, 952
Miller, Henry, 517
Miller & Lux (agribusiness), 517
Milliken's Bend, Battle of, 444
Mills, textile, 305, 537, 565–566
Milosevic, Slobodan, 956
Mimbres culture, 13
Minavavana (Chippewa, Ojibwa), 147–148
Mines and mining, 337. *See also* Coal and coal industry; Gold rush
    "Big Bonanza" and, 505
    Comstock Lode and, 397, 491, 504–506
    immigrants in, 504–505
    Indians and, 496, 497
    mining towns, 505, 506
    in New South, 537
    safety and, 505–506, 637
    silver and, 43–44, 547, 549
    strikes and, 594
    strip-mining and, 919
    technology for, 505–506
    in West, 504–506, 512(m)
Mineta, Norman Y., 951

Mingo Indians, 144
    Fort Stanwix Treaty and, 221
Miniconjou Sioux Indians, 503
Minimum wage, 664, 687, 745, 812, 951
Minneapolis Lakers, move by, 823
Minnesota, 496
Minorities. *See also* Ethnic groups; specific groups
    Clinton and, 951
    in Eisenhower years, 815
    Great Society and, 847, 848
    Hispanics as, 507
    New Deal and, 738–740
    rights of, 928–929
    Vietnam War and, 900
Minow, Newton, 830
Minuit, Peter, 98
Miranda v. Arizona (1966), 850
Miscegenation, 370, 538
    planters and, 376, 377
Miss America pageant, 864–865
Missiles, 816(i), 820. *See also* Cuban missile crisis; Intercontinental ballistic missiles
    INF agreement and, 935
    SALT and, 895
    SDI and, 932
Missionary societies, women in, 322
Missions and missionaries
    in California, 134(i), 135
    in China, 607
    in Florida, 72–73
    Indians and, 43, 135, 313
    in New Mexico, 72–73
    Spanish, 40(i), 43
Mississippi, 292, 368(m), 450–451, 477
    black disfranchisement in, 645, 840–842
    secession and, 420
    state elections in (1876), 484
Mississippian culture, 14–15, 17
Mississippi Freedom Democratic Party (MFDP), 841(i)
Mississippi Freedom Summer Project (1964), 852–853
Mississippi River region. *See also* Mississippian culture; specific locations
    Civil War in, 435(m), 437, 438
    Louisiana Purchase and, 274–275
    settlement west of, 342–343
    in Seven Years' War, 147
    travel in, 304
Mississippi Valley State College, 842
Missouri, 292–293, 294(m), 390
    Civil War in, 437–438, 442
    slavery in Kansas and, 411
    Unionism in, 429
Missouri Compromise (1820), 269, 292–293, 294(m), 397, 406, 413–414
Mitchell, George (Chippewa Indians), 859
Mixed-race people
    in Haiti, 258
    in New Spain, 44(i), 45

Mobilization
    in Civil War, 431, 432–433
    for Persian Gulf War, 945
    for World War II, 755, 759–762, 777
Model T Ford, 684, 684(i)
"Modern Republicanism" (Eisenhower), 812–813
Mogollon culture, 13
Mohammed, Shanaz, 966
Mohawk Indians, 17, 145, 188, 203
Mohawk Valley region, 192, 193, 194, 195(m)
Molasses Act (1733), 150
Monarchs and monarchies. *See* specific rulers
Mondale, Walter F., 915, 926
Money
    banknotes as, 307
    gold standard and, 547, 548
    paper, 433, 445, 448, 547, 548
    in Revolution, 191
Money supply
    contraction of, 308, 916
    market revolution and, 303
"Money trust" of Morgan, 640
Monitor (ironclad), 435(m), 439
Moniz, Felipa (wife of Columbus), 32
"Monkey trial." *See* Scopes trial
Monks Mound, Cahokia, 1, 2
Monmouth, Battle of, 182
Monongahela, Battle of the, 146
Monopolies, business, 526, 530, 627, 628
Monroe, Elizabeth, 290, 295
Monroe, James, 269, 290–295, 607. *See also* Monroe Doctrine (1823)
    Missouri Compromise and, 293
Monroe Doctrine (1823), 294–295
    foreign policy and, 605, 607–608
    Roosevelt, T., and, 633
    Wilson and, 654
Montana, in World War I, 667
Monterey, California, 135
Monterrey, Mexico, battle at (1846), 352
Montezuma (Mexico), 37–38
Montgomery, Alabama
    bus boycott in, 834–836, 850
    voting rights march to, 852(i), 853
Montgomery, Richard, 183
Montgomery Improvement Association (MIA), 834–835
Monticello, 201, 379(i)
Montreal, 146, 183, 192
Moon landing, 879
Morality
    alcohol ban and, 664–665
    after Civil War, 477
    conservatism and, 909–910
    movie code for, 710
Moral Majority, 924
Moral reform movement, 322–323
Moravians, 117
Morgan, Anne, 622
Morgan, Daniel, 198(m)
Morgan, J. P., and Company, 532, 640

Morgan, J. P., 523, 628, 630
    depression of 1890s and, 549, 550
    finance capitalism and, 532–534
    panic of 1907 and, 631, 640
    U.S. Steel and, 533–534
Morgan, J. P., Jr., 705–706
Morisco, 44(i)
Mormons, 343, 346–347, 509, 929
Mormon War (1857), 347
Morocco, 272, 505, 635
Morrill, Justin, 448
Morrill (Land-Grant College) Act (1863), 448
Morris, Robert, 208, 213, 219, 220
Morristown, New Jersey, Washington in, 186
Morrow, E. Frederick, 834
Morse, Samuel F. B., 339, 526
Mortality rate
    in Chesapeake region, 68
    from European diseases, 46
    in Great Depression, 710
    in Middle Passage, 124
    in New England, 113
    of slave children, 125
    of southern slaves, 125
    in Virginia colony, 60
Morton, Jelly Roll, 696
Mossadegh, Mohammed, 819, 922
Motels, 688
Mothers. *See* Families; Women
Motion picture camera, 530
Moudy, Ross, 505–506
Mound builders, 1–3, 2(i), 14–15
Mount Holyoke Seminary, 320
Movies
    in Great Depression, 710–711
    in 1920s, 696
Moynihan, Daniel Patrick, 953
Ms. magazine, 866
Muckraking, 631
Mugwumps, 542, 543, 544
Muhammad Ali (boxer), 890
Muir, John, 632
Mulattos, 44(i), 377
Muller v. Oregon (1908), 623
Mumford, Lewis, 823
Muncie, Indiana, study of, 689
Munich conference (1938), 755
Municipal housekeeping concept, 624
Munn v. Illinois (1877), 546
Murray, Judith Sargent, 244, 289
Murray, Pauli, 864
Music
    African American, 127, 795
    folk, 862
    hymns, 386
    jazz, 696
    in 1920s, 696
    in 1950s, 831
    in 1960s, 862
    rock and roll, 831, 862
    spirituals, 386
Music halls, 577

Muskogean Indians, 17
Muslims
    in Afghanistan, 921
    encomienda and, 42
    in former Yugoslavia, 956
    as fundamentalists in Iran, 922
    in Iran, 922
    Reconquest and, 26
    terrorist attacks and, 966
Muslim states, on Barbary Coast, 272–273
Mussolini, Benito, 751, 765
Mustangs (airplane), 771
Mutually assured destruction (MAD), 817
Mutual security pact, with Japan, 791
Myer, Dillon S., 814
My Lai massacre, 898, 900

NAACP. *See* National Association for the
    Advancement of Colored People
Nader, Ralph, 847
NAFTA. *See* North American Free Trade
    Agreement
Nagasaki, bombing of, 751, 775
Names, of slaves, 126
Nanjing (Nanking), China, Japanese capture
    of, 754
Napalm, 884
Napoleon I Bonaparte (France), 274
Napoleonic Wars, 245
Narragansett Indians, 103
Narragansett region, 83
*Narrative of the Life of Frederick Douglass,
    as Told by Himself* (Douglass), 405
Narváez, Pánfilo de, 39
NASA. *See* National Aeronautics and Space
    Administration
Nashville, Battle of (1864), 452(m), 454
Nasser, Gamal Abdel, 819
Nast, Thomas, on Tweed ring, 580–581
Natchez Indians, 17
Natchitoches, Louisiana, Comanches in,
    278–279
Natick Indians, 160
National Aeronautics and Space
    Administration (NASA, 1958), 820
National American Woman Suffrage
    Association (NAWSA), 599, 645, 666
National Arts and Humanities Act (1965),
    847
National Association for the Advancement of
    Colored People (NAACP), 539(i), 647,
    694, 768, 794, 795
    Brown v. Board of Education and, 833
National Association of Colored Women
    (NACW), 539(i)
National Association of Manufacturers,
    729–730, 737
National Banking Act (1863), 448
National banking system, 240
National Black Feminist Organization, 866
National Coalition of Labor Union Women, 866
National Conference of Catholic Bishops, 933
National Consumers' League (NCL), 623

National Council of Churches of Christ,
    women in, 866
National Council of Negro Women, 739, 866
National debt, 248. *See also* Debt
    Clinton and, 951
    disappearance of, 318–319
    Hamilton and, 240, 245, 247–248
    Obama and, 971
    Reagan and, 907, 926
National defense, interstate highway system
    and, 812
National Defense Education Act (NDEA, 1958),
    820
National Energy Act (1978), 917
National Era (antislavery journal), 403
National Farmers' Holiday Association
    (1932), 711
National Federation of Republican Women,
    905
National Gay and Lesbian Task Force, 863
National Guard, 880
    in Great Depression strikes, 735
    at Homestead strike, 593
    at Kent State, 897
    in Little Rock, 833
    Selma civil rights marchers and, 853
    Vietnam War and, 887
National health insurance. *See also* Health
    and health care
    Carter and, 916
    Clinton and, 951
    Obama and, 971
    Truman and, 792
National Housing Act
    of 1937, 744
    of 1968, 848–849
Nationalism
    Confederate, 446
    after War of 1812, 286
Nationalist movements, third world, 880
Nationalists, in China, 790–791
Nationalist Spain, 754
Nationalization, in Guatemala, 818
National Labor Relations (Wagner) Act
    (NLRA, 1935), 735–736, 742
National Labor Relations Board (NLRB), 736
National Liberation Front (NLF, Vietnam),
    883, 886, 891–892
National liberation movements, 777, 790
National Miners Union, 712
National Organization for Women (NOW), 864
National parks, 632–633, 634(m)
National Recovery Administration (NRA,
    1933), 728–729, 730
National Republicans, 310
National Review, 924
National Road, 304
National security
    Bush, George W., on, 967
    Carter and, 921–922
    Kennedy, John F., and, 879
    after September 11, 2001, 966
    in World War II, 760

National Security Act (1947), 789
National Security Council (NSC)
  creation of, 789
  Iran-Contra and, 934
  NSC 68 and, 805
National security state, 788–790
National self-determination. *See* Self-
  determination
National Socialist Party, 751. *See also* Nazi
  Germany
National Union for Social Justice (Union
  Party), 733
National Union Party, 469–470
National War Labor Policies Board, 664
National Welfare Rights Organization, 846,
  866
National Woman's Party (NWP), 645, 693
National woman's rights convention, 358–359
National Woman Suffrage Association
  (NWSA), 540, 599
National Women's Political Caucus, 842
National Youth Administration, Division of
  Negro Affairs, 739
Nation of Islam. *See* Black Muslims
Native Americans. *See also* specific groups
    and regions
  ancient, 1–22
  assimilation of, 498, 499
  Bacon's Rebellion and, 69–70
  in Black Hills, 497–498
  buffalo and, 344, 493, 495
  buffalo soldiers and, 506
  in California, 356
  in Carolina, 75
  Christianity and, 57, 58, 88
  citizenship and, 500
  Civil Rights Act of 1964 and, 853
  in Civil War, 437–438, 437(i)
  Columbus and, 32–33
  Comstock Lode discovery and, 505
  concentration policy for, 344
  conversion of, 72, 135
  cultures of, 8, 15–19, 496, 500
  Dawes Act and, 500
  diseases and, 35–36, 35(i), 46, 344, 348, 494
  Dutch and, 98
  encomienda and, 42–43
  English colonial attitudes toward, 87(i)
  English settlements and, 57–60, 78
  environmental damage and, 825
  Europeans and, 22
  in Florida, 73
  Fort Stanwix Treaty and, 220–221, 253
  in 1490s, 15–19, 16(m)
  French alliances with, 142–143
  Ghost Dance of, 502–503
  in Great Depression, 740
  imperialism, colonialism, and, 491–493, 498
  Jackson and, 294, 312
  as labor, 46
  Lewis and Clark expedition and, 275–277
  loss of lands (1850-1890), 492(m)
  mass execution of, 496

  in Mississippi River region, 274
  in New England, 86, 94, 113
  in New France, 105(i)
  Nixon and, 868, 871
  of Northwest, 10, 253–255
  in Northwest Territory, 223–224
  in Ohio River region, 147–149, 194, 221,
    251, 253–255, 254(m)
  of Pacific Coast, 10, 18
  peace policy for, 496
  in Pennsylvania, 100, 119
  as Plains Indians, 17, 277–279, 344
  protests by, 858–859
  removal and, 313–315, 314(m), 367,
    493–495
  reservations for, 493–495, 497, 498,
    499–500
  resistance by, 500–503
  after Revolution, 218
  Revolutionary War and, 188, 192–193,
    202–205
  Sand Creek massacre against, 494–495
  scorched-earth policy against, 104, 496–497
  as servants, 63
  Seven Years' War and, 134, 144–145,
    147–149
  smallpox deaths and, 177
  in Southwest, 251–253
  Spanish and, 39, 46(i)
  Tecumseh and, 267–269, 281–282
  termination and relocation of, 813–814
  tobacco and, 60–61, 62
  trade and, 133, 149
  transcontinental railroad and, 405, 406
  treaties with, 494, 496, 497, 498
  Vietnam War and, 900
  "Walking Purchase" and, 119
  warfare by, 101, 103–105, 491, 493, 496,
    497–498, 500–503
  War of 1812 and, 269, 298
  in West, 492(m), 493–498
  women's movement and, 866
  in World War II armed forces, 761
  Wounded Knee Massacre against, 503
Nativism, 408, 621
NATO. *See* North Atlantic Treaty
  Organization
Natural increase, of population, 111–112,
  121
Naturalization. *See* Citizens and citizenship
Natural resources. *See also* specific resources
  CCC and, 726
  conservation of, 632–633, 726–728,
    726(m)
Natural rights, 180
Nature. *See* Environment
Nauvoo, Illinois, Mormons in, 346
Navajo Indians, 18, 494, 502
Navies. *See also* Navy (U.S.)
  British, 103, 657
Navigation Acts, 129
  of 1650, 69, 102
  of 1651, 69, 102

Navigation Acts *(continued)*
    of 1660, 69, 102
    of 1663, 102
Navigation aids, 30
Navy (U.S.), 528
    African Americans in, 425, 426, 426(i)
    in Civil War, 425, 426(i), 432, 438, 439
    Great White Fleet of, 635
    at Guantánamo, 613
    in Manila, 610, 611(m)
    at Pearl Harbor, 759
    SEALS of, 881
    in Spanish-American War, 610
    Washington Disarmament Conference
        and, 688
    World War I and, 669
    World War II and, 762, 773–774, 774(m)
Nazi Germany. *See also* Germany; Hitler,
        Adolf; World War II
    anti-Semitism in, 753
    Austrian *Anschluss* with, 755
    Holocaust and, 769–770
    Italian occupation by, 765
    in North Africa, 764–765
    rearmament of, 752
    Rhineland and, 754
    Soviet invasion by, 758
    as Third Reich, 755
    in Tripartite Pact, 759
Nazi-Soviet nonaggression treaty (1939), 755
NBC television, 829
Nebraska, as free state, 405–406
"Necessary evil" argument, for slavery, 370
Necessity, Fort, 144
Negro. *See* African Americans
"Negro domination," southern politics and, 475
"Negro first" strategy, 472–473
Neighborhoods, 563
Nelson, Knute, 613
Neolin (Delaware Indians), 148
Netherlands. *See also* Dutch
    German invasion of, 755
Neutrality
    U.S. policy before World War II, 757
    in World War I, 657–658
Neutrality Acts, of 1935–1937, 753–754, 757
Neutrality Proclamation (1793), 257
Nevada, 350, 509
    Comstock Lode in, 397, 491, 504–506
Neville, John, 250
New Amsterdam, 61(m), 88, 98. *See also* New
        York (city)
Newark, race riot in (1967), 857
Newburgh Conspiracy, 219–220, 242
New Christian Right. *See* New Right
New Deal, 718, 720, 721(m), 805. *See also*
        Economy; Fair Deal; Great
        Depression; Roosevelt, Franklin
        Delano
    agriculture in, 727–728
    Asian Americans and, 739–740
    banking and finance reform in, 723–725

challenges to, 729–733
    conservation programs in, 725–727
    conservatism in, 719, 720, 737, 739,
        741–742, 743, 746
    Eisenhower and, 811
    food distribution in, 744(i)
    Hispanics in, 739
    industrial recovery in, 728–729
    labor in, 706, 735–737, 745
    later period in, 740–745
    legislation of first hundred days, 723,
        725–729
    Native Americans in, 740
    objectives of, 722–723
    relief programs in, 725–727
    in rural areas, 730–732
    Social Security and, 737–738
    Truman and, 797
    welfare in, 726, 733–740
    women in, 725–726
    workers and, 738–740
New Deal coalition, 718, 719, 720(m), 741,
        768–769
New England, 83–97, 88(m). *See also* Native
        Americans; specific groups; specific lo-
        cations
    as city upon a hill, 87
    Dominion of, 104
    economy in, 94, 113–116
    farming in, 113–115
    government in, 90–91
    Hartford Convention and (1814), 285–286
    land in, 92, 104
    manufacturing in, 337
    militias in, 164
    population and society in, 95, 112–116
    protests in, 164–165
    Puritanism in, 83–97
    Puritan Revolution (England) and, 94
    Puritans in, 83–97
    religion in, 81–94, 95–97, 130
    in Revolutionary War, 166–167, 167(m),
        177–178, 192
    society in, 89–97
    in War of 1812, 283
    water in, 82(m)
New England Anti-Slavery Society, 324
New England Emigrant Aid
        Company, 411
"New Era," 1920s as, 685–690
Newfoundland, 27, 34, 49
New France, 105. *See also* Canada
    British North America and, 133
    English colonies and, 113
    Indians and, 105(i)
New Freedom, The, (Wilson), 639, 641
New Frontier (Kennedy), 842, 843–844
New Guinea, 773
New Hampshire, taxation in, 225
New immigration, 559
New Jersey, 97, 99–100, 116. *See also* Middle
        colonies

Articles of Confederation and, 211
    gradual emancipation in, 217
    in Revolutionary War, 185–186, 192
    voting rights for women in, 215
New Jersey Plan, 229
New Jerusalem, New York, 288
Newlands Reclamation Act (1902), 632
"New Left," 861, 864
"New Look" (Eisenhower), 816–817
Newly independent nations, U.S. racism and, 795
New Mexico, 72–73, 400, 401
    ancient Americans in, 9
    Anglo-Americans in, 507
    Hispanics in, 507
    manifest destiny and, 493
    Mogollon culture in, 13
    Spanish colony in, 41
    Villa, Pancho, in, 654–655, 655(i)
New Nationalism, The, 639, 641
"New Negro," in 1920s, 685, 691, 694–696
New Negroes (newly-arrived slaves), 124, 126
New Netherland, 97–98
New Orleans
    Battle of (1815), 285
    Civil War in, 435(m), 438
    control of, 274
    cotton trade in, 373(i)
    Hurricane Katrina in, 964–965
    Spanish in, 147
    U.S. purchase of, 274
New (Christian) Right, 924
    gay rights and, 931
    Reagan and, 923
    women's rights and, 929
New South, 461, 536–537, 538
New Spain
    British North America and, 133
    California and, 134–135, 134(i)
    English colonies compared with, 77
    Indian conversions in, 43
    mixed-race people in, 44(i), 45
    in 16th century, 41–45
Newspapers. See also Journalism; specific newspapers
    antislavery, 324, 366
    in elections, 310
    Pullman strike coverage in, 596
Newton, Huey, 858
New World, 22. See also America(s); Colonies and colonization; Exploration; specific countries; specific regions
    in Atlantic region, 31–36
    map of, 34
    16th-century Europe and, 47–49
    Spain in, 42(m)
"New world order," of Bush, G. H. W., 956
New York (city), 528, 553. See also New Amsterdam
    African Americans in, 561
    as arts center, 832

British troops in, 185(i)
    Central Park in, 579, 580
    Harlem in, 694
    immigrants in, 560, 562
    public schools in, 579
    in Revolutionary War, 201
    settlement houses in, 620
    Tammany Hall in, 580–581
    travel times from, 246, 246(m)
    world finance in, 687
New York (colony), 97, 99, 116. See also Middle colonies
    Albany Congress in, 144–145
    assembly suspension in, 156–157
    Leisler in, 104
    in Revolutionary War, 183–185, 192
New York (state)
    canals in, 305
    constitutional ratification and, 234–235
    election of 1828 and, 310
    Fort Stanwix Treaty and, 220–221
    slavery in, 327
    in War of 1812, 285
New York, Treaty of, 252
New York Age, 539
New York Central Railroad, 564
New York City draft riots, 449
New York Female Moral Reform Society, 323
New York Journal, 609
New-York Loyal Gazette, 188(i)
New York Society of Pewterers, 233(i)
New York Stock Exchange, 525–526, 705
New York Suspending Act, 156–157
New York Times, 572, 889
    Pentagon Papers in, 898
New York Tribune, 433, 434, 480
New York World, 564, 609
New Zealand, in World War II, 763
Nez Percé Indians, 501, 501(i)
Nez Percé war (1877), 501
Niagara, Fort, 146, 194, 221
Niagara movement (1905), 647
Nicaragua
    Reagan and, 932, 933–934
    revolution in, 752
    Sandinistas in, 919–921
    Taft and, 637
    U.S. intervention in, 654, 933
Nicholas II (Russia), 660
Nicodemas, Kansas, 506
Niedermeyer, George, 846(i)
Night riders, 483
Nike, overseas production by, 958
Nimitz, Chester W., 763–764
Niña (ship), 32
Nineteenth Amendment, 600, 666, 865(i)
92nd Division, in World War I, 662
Ninth Amendment, 243
Nipmuc Indians, 103
Nixon, E. D., 834
Nixon, Isaac, lynching of, 795
Nixon, Pat, 804(i), 894(i)

Nixon, Richard M., 888, 893
  as anti-Communist, 894
  China and, 877, 893–894, 894(i)
  civil rights and, 842
  conservatism and, 907–908, 910–911
  Douglas, Helen Gahagan, and, 782
  economy and, 868–869
  election of 1950 and, 782
  election of 1952 and, 803, 804(i)
  election of 1960 and, 843
  election of 1968 and, 868, 892–893, 906, 910
  election of 1972 and, 906, 908, 910, 911–912
  environment and, 869–870
  foreign policy of, 868, 893–898
  impeachment of, 913
  Israel and, 896
  Khrushchev and, 809–810, 810(i), 820, 823, 877–879
  liberal reform and, 868–871
  Native Americans and, 868, 871
  pardon of, 914
  resignation of, 913
  social justice under, 870–871
  Soviet Union and, 893, 894
  Supreme Court appointments by, 911
  Vietnam War and, 876, 896–897, 899–900
  Watergate and, 899, 907, 912–913
  welfare state and, 868
  women's rights and, 911
Nobel Peace Prize
  for Bunche, Ralph J., 795
  for King, 835(i)
  for Roosevelt, T., 635
Noble, Elaine, 863, 931
Noble and Holy Order of the Knights of Labor. *See* Knights of Labor
No Child Left Behind (NCLB) Act (2002), 964
Nominating conventions, 326–327
Nonaggression treaty, Nazi-Soviet (1939), 755
Nonconsumption, 157
Nonimportation
  agreements among merchants, 157
  law, of Jefferson, 279–280
Non-Intercourse Act (1809), 282
Nonintervention policy, 752–753
Nonviolent resistance, in civil rights movement, 851, 852
Nonwhites. *See also* specific groups
  immigrant, 508
  Northwest Territory and, 223–224
Noriega, Manuel, 942, 945
"Normalcy," Harding on, 679–680, 686
Normandy, D-Day invasion at, 771–772
Norris, Frank, 626
Norsemen, 27
North (Civil War)
  draft in, 449
  emancipation and, 449
  freedom for slaves and, 441
  government and economy in, 447–448
  inflation in, 433
  Lincoln's leadership of, 432–433
  mobilization of, 433
  politics and dissent in, 449–450
  resources of, 431–432
  revenues in, 433
  women in, 448–449
North (U.S. region)
  African American migration to, 677–678, 678(i)
  African Americans in, 218, 369, 561, 646
  Civil War impact on, 456
  colonies in 17th century, 81–105
  cotton export and, 372
  de facto segregation in, 855
  demographic changes in, 694–695
  free soil support in, 398
  Indian removal and, 314, 315
  investment in southern industry by, 537
  mixed economy of, 372
  Reconstruction and, 475, 480–482
  Revolutionary War in, 183–186, 184(m)
  runaway slaves in, 403
  school integration in, 910–911
  school segregation in, 833–834
  slaves in, 397
  South compared with, 367
  southern Republican Party and, 473–474
North, Frederick (Lord), 161, 166, 197
North Africa, World War II in, 764–765
North America. *See also* America(s); Colonies and colonization; Latin America; South America; specific regions
  ancient peoples of, 1–22, 2(i)
  British, 111–135
  human migration to, 5–6
  Native Americans of, 1–19
  Spanish exploration of, 39–40
  zones of empire in, 132(m)
North American Free Trade Agreement (NAFTA), 958
North Atlantic Treaty Organization (NATO), 782, 784(m), 789
  after Cold War, 947
  interventions by, 956
  military aid to, 789
North Carolina, 122, 390. *See also* Carolina(s)
  English settlement of, 49
  population of, 121
  in Revolutionary War, 194–195, 200
  secession of, 429
North Dakota, 275
Northern Alliance (Afghanistan), 966
Northern Pacific Railroad, 497, 525
Northern Paiute Indians, 505
Northern Securities Company, 628
North Korea, 800–804, 801(m), 947
  nuclear weapons and, 969
Northup, Solomon, 404–405

North Vietnam, 818, 882, 883, 885, 899. *See also* Vietnam; Vietnam War
  army of, 887, 891
  bombing of, 886–887, 898
Northwest (U.S. region)
  expansion in, 253–255, 254(m)
  Indians of, 10, 253–255
Northwestern Farmers' Alliance, 589
Northwest Ordinance (1787), 222–225, 292–293, 397
Northwest Passage, search for, 34, 48, 49
Northwest peoples, 10
Northwest Territory, 224(i), 282
  Indian land cessions in, 253
  land ordinances and, 222–225, 223(m)
  slavery in, 222, 224
Norton, Eleanor Holmes, 841(i)
Norway, 755
Nova Scotia, African American loyalists in, 202, 217(i)
NOW. *See* National Organization for Women
Noyes, John Humphrey, 358
NSC 68, 805. *See also* National Security Council
Nuclear arms race, 881–882. *See also* Arms race; Nuclear weapons
Nuclear disarmament. *See* Disarmament
Nuclear energy
  accidents in, 917–919
  Eisenhower and, 813
Nuclear test ban treaty
  limited (1963), 882
  total, 947
Nuclear weapons. *See also* Atomic bomb; Nuclear arms race
  Bush, George W., and, 969
  after Cold War, 947
  containment of, 877
  Cuban missile crisis and, 881–882
  disarmament and, 935
  Eisenhower and, 810, 820
  hydrogen bomb and, 789
  Kennedy and, 880
  in 1950s, 817
Nueces River, 351
Nullification
  crises, 400
  slavery and, 317
  of tariff of 1828, 312, 316–317
Nursing
  in Civil War, 449
  public health, 620
  in Vietnam War, 887
Nye, Gerald, and Nye Committee, 753

Oakland, California, 507
Oath of allegiance, in Lincoln's Reconstruction plan, 462
Obama, Barack, 970–972
  domestic policy of, 971, 972
  economy and, 971, 972

  election of 2008 and, 970–971, 970(i)
  foreign policy of, 972, 973
Obama, Michelle, 970(i)
Oberlin College, 320
Occupation (military)
  British, of Boston, 159–161
  of Germany, 785
  of Iraq, 968
  of Japan, 791
  of Korea, 800
Occupational Safety and Health Act (OSHA, 1970), 637, 870
Occupations (jobs). *See also* Employment; Work
  women in, 693
O'Connor, Sandra Day, 930, 964
Octopus, The (Norris), 626
O'Dell, Jack, 800
O'Donnell, Hugh, 592, 593
Officeholders
  African Americans as, 460(i), 475, 855, 951
  in antebellum South, 390
  campaign contributions and, 543
  Chicanos as, 861
  ex-Confederate, 462, 467
  gay, 863, 931
  women as, 867, 951
Office of Economic Opportunity (OEO), 849, 868
Oglala Sioux Indians, 497
Ohio, 253
Ohio Company, 144, 149
Ohio gang, of Harding, 686
Ohio River region
  Indians in, 147–149, 194, 221, 251, 253–255, 254(m)
  population of, 282
  Quebec Act and, 163
  in Revolutionary War, 188, 192, 193–196
  Seven Years' War in, 142–147
  travel in, 304
Oil and oil industry. *See also* Energy crisis
  Bush, George W, and, 963
  energy shortage and, 869, 917
  Exxon spill and, 942
  gasoline shortages and, 917
  Iran and, 785, 819, 895
  in Middle East, 917, 921
  Rockefeller in, 528–530
  superpower rivalry and, 790
  in World War II, 765
  worldwide reserves of (1980), 918(m)
Oil embargo (1973), 896
Ojibwa Indians, 146, 147–148
Okies, 717, 731, 732
Okinawa, battle at, 774
Oklahoma. *See also* Indian Territory
  as Indian Territory, 314(m), 316
  land runs in, 513
Oklahoma City, terrorism in, 952
Oklahoma Tenant Farmers' Union, 728
Okra, 127

Old Age Revolving Pension, 733
Older Americans. *See* Elderly
Old immigration, 559
Old North Bridge, Concord, 167
Olesdater, Beret, 511(i)
Oligarchy, in South, 128
Oligopoly
    in mining industry, 505
    in steel industry, 534
Olive Branch Petition, 178
Oliver, Andrew, 153
Olives, in Carolina, 75
Olmsted, Frederick Law, 579, 582
Olney, Richard B., 596–597
Olympic Games, U.S. non-participation in
    1980, 921
Omnibus Bill (1850), 401
Oñate, Juan de, 41, 507
Oneida community, 358
Oneida Indians, 17, 146, 192
"One person, one vote" principle, 849
Onondaga Indians, 17, 188
Ontario, Lake, 146
On the Origin of Species (Darwin), 534
On the Road (Kerouac), 832
"On to Washington" movement, 600
Opechancanough (Algonquian leader), 59, 69
Open Door policy, 608, 609, 633, 635
Open range, 507, 514
Operation Desert Storm, 946
Operation Just Cause, 945
Operation Rolling Thunder, 885, 886, 889
Oppenheimer, J. Robert, 775–776
Ordinances. *See also* Northwest Ordinance
    (1787)
    of 1784, 222
    of 1785, 222, 223(m)
Ordnance Bureau (Confederacy), 433
Oregon, 346, 350, 493
    annexation of, 336
    joint occupation of, 344
    Texas annexation and, 349–350
Oregon Country, 343–346
    British in, 342, 350
Oregon Trail, 344
Organization Man, The (Whyte), 830
Organization of American States (OAS), 886
Organized labor. *See* Labor unions
Organized Trades and Labor Unions, 573
Oriskany, Battle of (1777), 192–193, 194
Orlando, Vittorio, 669
Ortega, Daniel, 934
Osage Indians, 273–274, 276(m), 277–278,
    292
OSHA. *See* Occupational Safety and Health
    Act
O'Sullivan, John L. (editor), 343
O'Sullivan, Mary Kenney, 621
Oswald, Lee Harvey, 844
Other America, The (Harrington), 843
Ottawa Indians, 146, 148, 255
    Northwest Territory land ordinances and,
    222

Ottoman empire, after World War I, 670
Ouachita River, 277
"Outing system," at Carlisle Indian School, 499
Outwork, 565
Overcapitalization, 532
Overlord, second-front operation as, 771
Overseers, 374, 383
"Over There" (song), 660
"Overwork," by slaves, 380
Owens, Florence, and family, in Great
    Depression, 716–718, 717(i), 727, 737

P-51 Mustang (fighter), 771
Pacific Coast cultures, 10, 18
Pacific Northwest Indians, 10
Pacific Ocean region
    Asian immigrants in, 561–562
    Asian trade and, 343
    exploration in, 34–35
    immigrants from, 505
    Lewis and Clark at, 277
    Spain and, 134–135
    U.S. involvement in, 608
    World War II in, 763–764, 773–775, 774(m)
Pacific Railroad Act (1862), 448
Pacific Slope. *See* Pacific Ocean region
Pacifism, of Bryan, 654
Packard, Vance, 830
Pago Pago, Samoa, 608
Pahlavi, Mohammad Reza (Shah of Iran),
    819, 922
Paine, Thomas, 178, 179(i)
Painting. *See also* Art(s); specific artists
    in Harlem Renaissance, 696
    in 1950s, 832
Paiute Indians, 502–503, 505
Pakistan
    nuclear test ban treaty and, 947
    U.S. intervention in, 922
Palatine Germans, in Mohawk Valley region,
    192
Paleo-Indians, 6, 7–8
Palestine and Palestinians. *See also* Middle
    East
    Cold War and, 791
    Israel and, 791, 896, 946
    refugees from, 896, 917, 957
    self-determination and, 917
    terrorism by, 933
    after World War I, 670
Palestine Liberation Organization (PLO),
    933, 957
Palin, Sarah, 970
Palmer, A. Mitchell, 676, 677
Palo Alto, battle at (1846), 352
Palo Duro Canyon, Battle of, 496
Panama
    intervention in, 633
    Noriega and, 942, 945
Panama Canal region, 34, 633, 886
    U.S. control of, 921
Panama Canal treaty, 921
Panama Canal Zone, riots in, 886

Pan-American Exposition, 626
Pangaea, 5
Panics (financial). *See also* Depressions
    (financial)
    of 1819, 303, 308
    of 1837, 303, 326, 328–329, 390
    of 1857, 415
    of 1873, 481, 523, 548, 570
    of 1893, 491, 516, 523, 532, 545, 549,
        594
    of 1907, 631, 640
Pan-Indian confederation, 268
Pan-Indian movement, 814
Pankhurst family (Emmeline, Cristabel,
    and Sylvia), 645
Paper money. *See* Money
Pardons
    for Confederates, 462, 465, 471
    for Nixon, 914
Paris
    peace accords in (1973), 898–899
    peace negotiations in (1968), 891–892
    World War II liberation of, 771
Paris, Treaty of
    of 1763, 146, 147
    of 1783, 202, 203, 253
    of 1898, 613
Paris Peace Conference (1919), 669–672
Parker, Alton B., 630
Parker, Charlie ("Bird"), 795
Parker, Theodore, 401, 403
Parkhurst, Charles H., 620
Parks, Rosa, 834–835
Parliament (England)
    Charles I and, 86
    colonial control by, 153, 156, 163, 170
    virtual representation in, 152, 154–155
Parsons, Albert, 574, 575
Partible inheritance, in New England, 113
Partisanship, 543
    in southern politics, 390
Partition. *See also* Zones of occupation
    of Vietnam, 817–818
Party politics, 260, 264 309–310, 668. *See
    also* Political parties
Patent medicines, regulation of, 631
Paternalism, of planters, 374–375
Patient Protection and Affordable Care Act
    (2010), 971
Patriarchy, 538, 539
Patriot Act (2001). *See* USA Patriot Act
Patriotism
    in Civil War, 449
    in Revolutionary War, 186–187
    September 11, 2001, attacks, and, 965–967,
        965(i)
    by women, 157–159, 187
    in World War I, 663–664, 666–667
Patronage, 536, 541
    Adams, John Quincy, and, 297
    Jackson and, 312
Patrons of Husbandry. *See* Grange
Patton, George, 761, 765

Paul, Alice, 645, 665
Pawnee Indians, 17, 500, 503
Paxton Boys, 148–149
Payne-Aldrich bill, 636, 637
Peace accords, in Vietnam War, 898–899,
    900
Peace Corps, 880
Peace Democrats, 450, 454
Peacekeeping, in Bosnia, 957
Peace movement. *See also* Antiwar movement
    in Vietnam War, 889–890
    World War I and, 667
Peace of Paris (1783), 202, 203, 253
Peale, Charles Willson, 208(i)
Pea Ridge, Battle of (1862), 438
Pearl Harbor, Japanese attack on, 758–759
Pell grants, 868
Pendleton Civil Service Act (1883), 543
Peninsula campaign (1862), 436, 453(i)
Peninsulares, 45
Penn family (Pennsylvania), 100, 119
    William, 97, 99–100
Pennsylvania, 97, 100–101, 116, 528. *See
        also* Middle colonies
    Articles of Confederation and, 211
    Bethlehem, 120(i)
    canals in, 305
    Civil War in, 451, 452(m)
    constitution in, 216
    gradual emancipation in, 217
    Native Americans in, 119
    September 11, 2001, terrorist attack and,
        966
    standard of living in, 121
    statehouse in, 228(i)
    Whiskey Rebellion in, 250
Pennsylvania Dutch, Germans as,
    116–117
Pennsylvania Railroad, 526, 527, 529
Penobscot Indians, 17
Pensions
    old-age, 565
    for Revolutionary War soldiers, 218–219,
        220
    Social Security and, 737
    Townsend on, 733
Pentagon, terrorist attack on, 965–966
Pentagon Papers, 898
People, the
    defined, 214–216
    entertainment for, 696–697
    state constitutions and, 213
    voting and, 291
People of color. *See also* Minorities; specific
        groups
    as immigrants, 559
People's (Populist) Party, 583, 587(i), 588,
        590–591, 598. *See also* Populist move-
        ment
    Debs and, 597
    election of 1892 and, 602–603
    election of 1896 and, 603–605
    subtreasury plan of, 590

People's Republic of China (PRC), 791, 801. *See also* China
People's Republic of North Korea, 800. *See also* North Korea
People's Revolutionary Government (Vietnam), 898
Pepper, Claude, 846(i)
Pequot War, 103
Peralta family, 507
Percy, George, 57
Perfection, 303
    transcendentalists, utopians, and, 357–358
Perkins, Frances, 722
Perot, H. Ross, 927, 950, 953
Perry, Oliver Hazard, 283
Pershing, John J. ("Black Jack")
    in Mexico, 655, 655(i)
    in World War I, 661–662
Persian Gulf region, Carter Doctrine and, 921
Persian Gulf War (1991), 941, 945–946
Personal liberty laws, 403, 418
Personal Responsibility and Work Opportunity Reconciliation Act (1996), 953
Peru, 294
    gold from, 39
    Incan empire in, 39
Petersburg, Virginia, siege of (1864–1865), 452(m), 453–454, 455
Peterson, Esther, 864
Petition
    abolition, 327
    against Indian removal, 315
    for redress of grievances by women, 314–315
    right of, 243
Petrified Forest National Park, 634(m)
Petroleum. *See* Oil and oil industry
Philadelphia, 555, 560, 561
    British occupation in Revolutionary War, 193
    constitutional convention in, 209, 227–231
    First Continental Congress in, 165–166
    Quakers in, 121
    Second Continental Congress in, 175
Philadelphia (ship), 273
Philadelphia Centennial Exposition (1876), 530
Philanthropy, of Carnegie, 527, 528
Philip, King. *See* King Philip
Philip II (Spain), 47–48, 84
Philippines
    Carter and, 919
    independence of, 790
    Japan and, 758, 763
    Magellan and, 34
    Spanish-American War and, 610
    Taft as governor of, 635–636
    U.S. acquisition of, 613, 635
    warfare against U.S., 609, 613
    in World War II, 773–774
Phillips, Wendell, 400, 462, 473
Philosophy, social Darwinism as, 532, 534–535

Phonograph, 530
Photography
    Brady and, 419(i), 455(i)
    daguerreotypes, 379(i)
    by Edwards, Jay Dearborn, 373(i)
    of slave, 375(i)
Photojournalism, 563–564
Phyllis Schlafly Report, The, 906, 906(i), 924
Physicians. *See* Medicine
Pickering, Timothy, 259
Pickett, George E., 451
Piecework, 565, 566, 567, 625
Pierce, Franklin, 405, 407(m)
Pike, Zebulon, 276(m), 277
Pilgrims, 85–86
Pilgrim's Progress, 631
Pill, the. *See* Birth control
Pinchot, Gifford, 632, 633, 636
Pinckney, Charles Cotesworth, 279, 280
Pinckney, Thomas, 260
Pine Ridge Reservation, 497, 503
Pingree, Hazen S., 581
Pinkerton Detective Agency
    Homestead lockout and, 592
    McCormick reaper works strike and, 574
Pinochet, Augusto, 895
Pinta (ship), 32
Pioneers. *See also* Settler(s)
    on trails, 345
Pitt, Fort, 148, 194
Pitt, William, 146, 147, 156
Pittsburgh, 571(i), 572
Pittsburgh Courier, The, 767
Pizarro, Francisco, 39
Plague. *See* Black Death
Plain folk
    politics and, 390–391
    in South, 382–386
Plains Indians, 406, 493–494. *See also* Great Plains; specific groups
    buffalo decimation and, 493, 495
    horse-centered lifestyle of, 496
    westward movement and, 344
Plantation belt, yeomen in, 383
Plantation economy, 370–373
Plantation labor, slavery and, 31
Planters and plantations
    in Carolina, 75
    in Chesapeake region, 68, 71
    after Civil War, 478–479
    during Civil War, 446, 447
    distinguished from farmers, 371
    in 1860 and 1881, 478(m)
    families of, 374
    honor and, 375–376
    housing of, 374, 375
    Johnson, Andrew, and, 465, 466
    labor code and, 463
    paternalism of, 374–375
    power of, 376, 390–391
    slaves and, 371, 376, 377
    southern economy and, 371–373
    sugar and, 71, 73–75

tobacco and, 63–64
westward movement of, 368–369
white women and, 376–377
yeomen and, 383
Plants. *See also* Agriculture; Food(s)
foraging for, 8, 10
Native Americans and, 10, 11
Platt, Thomas C., 627
Platt Amendment (1898), 611–613
Playboy magazine, 830
Plenty Coups (Crow chief), 500–501
Plessy v. Ferguson (1896), 646, 833
PLO. *See* Palestine Liberation
Organization
Plow, steel, 336, 515
Plural marriage (polygamy), 346, 347
Plutocracy, 564
Plymouth settlement, 85–86
Pocahontas, 53, 54(i), 62
Poets and poetry. *See also* specific poets
in Harlem Renaissance, 696
Pogroms, against Jews, 560
Point IV Program (1949), 790
Poison gas, in World War I, 653, 662
Poland
concentration camps in, 770
immigrants from, 504, 559
in NATO, 947
Nazi Germany and, 755, 756(i)
pogroms in, 560
Soviets and, 783, 785
after World War I, 670
after World War II, 783
Polaris nuclear submarines, 820
Police
antiwar protests and, 897
Coxey's army and, 602
at Democratic National Convention
(1968), 892
Haymarket bombing and, 575
Polio
Roosevelt, Franklin, and, 719
vaccine for, 812
Political action committees (PACs), 914
Political campaigns. *See also* Elections
of 1884, 543–544
federal employees and, 543
Political cartoons. *See also* specific subjects
Jackson and, 313(i)
by Nast, 580–581
portrayal of senators in, 542
Political office. *See* Officeholders
Political parties, 264–265, 330. *See also* specific parties
after 1828, 309–310
after 1836, 326, 327–328
factionalism and, 541–543
in Gilded Age, 536
Jackson and, 312
money in elections and, 829
nominating conventions of, 326–327
one-party system and, 290
realignment of, 406–411, 545–549

second American party system and, 309
sectionalism and, 406
Political refugees. *See* Refugees
Politics. *See also* Party politics; Political
parties; specific groups
African Americans in, 855
in colonies, 135–136
communication and, 303
democratization of, 389–390
during depression of 1890s, 600–605
ethnicity and, 536
gender and, 538–540
in Gilded Age, 523, 536
in Great Depression, 732–733
Ku Klux Klan and, 474–475
in North (Civil War), 449–450
polarization of, 259–260
political wives and, 295
presidential, 541–544
reformers and, 618
religion and, 536
sectionalism in, 397, 400–401, 405–406
of slavery, 389–391
tariffs and, 545–546
television and, 829
women and, 244–245, 540–541, 692
Polk, James K., 348, 354
election of 1844 and, 349–350
Mexican-American War and, 349,
350–351
Pollock, Jackson, 832
Poll tax, for voting, 645, 745
Pollution, 870. *See also* Air pollution;
Environment; Water pollution
Polygamy, 346, 347, 509
Ponce de León, Juan, 39
Pontiac (Ottawa Indians), rebellion by,
147–149
Pony Express, 448, 526
Pools (business), 526, 547
Poor people. *See* Poverty
Poor Richard's Almanack (Franklin), 121
Popé (Pueblo Indians), 73
Pope, John, 436
Popular culture. *See also* specific issues
in 1920s, 696
in 1980s, 926
Vietnam War in, 901
Popular Front, in 1930s, 740
Popular sovereignty, 399, 401, 406, 408, 410,
411, 416, 418
Popular vote, in 1828, 309–310, 311. *See also*
Voting and voting rights
Population. *See also* Immigrants and immi-
gration
Black Death and, 29
of British America, 111
of Californios, 507
of Chesapeake region, 61, 70, 74–75
of Chinese immigrants, 508, 561
of cities, 555
during Civil War, 431
in 1800, 247, 247(i)

Population (continued)
  of free blacks in South, 387
  immigrants in, 504–505
  increase from 1950 to 1960, 828
  Latinos in, 959
  Mexican American, 825
  of middle colonies, 116
  of Midwest, 336
  in mining towns, 504–505
  movement from rural areas, 341
  Native American, 15–17, 498
  of New England, 95, 112–113
  of New York City, 694
  in 1790, 247, 247(i), 253
  shift from rural to urban (1920-1930), 699(m)
  slave, 124–125, 368(m), 392, 421
  of southern colonies, 121–122
  in Sun Belt, 824(m)
  taxes on, 272
  of wageworkers, 564–565
  of Western Hemisphere (1490s), 19–20
  of West Indies, 73
Populist movement, 590–591, 601, 614. See also People's (Populist) Party
  Cripple Creek strike and, 594
  in election of 1896, 603–605
  Homestead strike and, 593
Pork barrel programs, 546
Port cities. See also specific locations
  immigrants in, 555, 560
  in Revolutionary War, 183
  in South, 372, 373
Port Hudson, Battle of (1863), 444
Portolá, Gaspar de, 135
Portugal
  Africa and, 30–31
  Brazil and, 34
  exploration by, 29(m), 30–31, 34
  immigrants from, 505
  slavery and, 31, 71
"Positive good" argument, for slavery, 370
Postal service. See Mail service; U.S. Post Office
Post-traumatic stress disorder, in Vietnam War veterans, 901
Potatoes, 36
  famine in Ireland and, 342
Potawatomi Indians, 146, 148, 255, 282
Potsdam, Germany, conference at, 775
Pottawatomie Creek, Brown, John, at, 395, 412
Pottery, in Woodland cultures, 12
Poverty. See also specific programs
  of African Americans, 768
  in cities, 563–564, 580
  Clinton policies and, 953
  in Confederacy, 445–446
  in Eisenhower years, 811, 815
  of free blacks, 387
  in Great Depression, 707–710, 713
  Great Society and, 845–849
  of Indians, 814

Kennedy, John F., and, 843, 844
  in 1950s, 828
  by race, 955
  Reagan and, 927–928, 930
  on reservations, 494, 500
  Roosevelt, Franklin D., and, 720
  rural, 822
  social Darwinism and, 534, 535
  in Vietnam War, 887
  of whites in South, 384–385
  of women, 930
  of working-class families, 566–567
Powder Alarm, 164
Powderly, Terence V., 562, 573, 574, 587
Powell, Colin L., 939–941, 940(i)
  after Cold War, 947
  Iraq War and, 967
  Persian Gulf War and, 946, 969
  on race, 955
  as secretary of state, 962
Power (energy). See Energy; Energy crisis
Power (political)
  executive vs. legislative, 471
  Madison and, 214
  of planters, 390–391
Power loom, 306, 306(i)
Powhatan (Indian leader), 53, 54, 56, 57–58, 78
Prager, Robert, lynching of, 667
Prayer, in public schools, 850
PRC. See People's Republic of China
Preaching. See also Revivals and revivalism
  by women, 288
Predestination, 90
Preemption doctrine, of Bush, G. W., 966–967
Pregnancy, of indentured servants, 65
Prejudice. See Discrimination; specific groups
Presbyterians, 130
  Scots-Irish as, 117
Prescription medication. See also Medicine
  for elderly, 964
Preservationists, 632
Presidency. See also President; specific individuals
  in Constitution, 230
  imperial, 912
  Jackson and, 312
  New Jersey Plan and, 229
  power of, 541, 897
  Republicans in, 720
  Roosevelt, F. D., and, 718, 719
  Roosevelt, T., and, 626, 627, 628, 630, 633, 636
  Wilson and, 639–640
President. See also Elections; Executive; Twelfth Amendment; specific individuals
  use of title, 242
Presidential debates, of 1960, 843
Presidential Reconstruction, 465–468
President's Commission on the Status of Women (PCSW), 864

President's Committee on Civil Rights (1946), 795
Presidios, 134, 135
Presley, Elvis, 831, 831(i)
Preston, John Smith, 420
Preston, Thomas, 159, 163
Prices
    freeze in, 869
    in World War I, 664
    after World War II, 792
Princeton, battle at, 186
Prisoners of war (POWs). *See also* specific wars
    during Revolution, 189–191
Private corporations, 339
Privateers, French, 261
Private property, vs. workers' rights, 593, 597
Private welfare state, 822
Proclamation of 1763, 149
Proclamation of Amnesty and Reconstruction (1863), 462
Production, cotton, 368, 368(m)
Production code, in movies, 710
Productivity
    in steel industry, 528
    Taylor and, 625
Professional Air Traffic Controllers Organization (PATCO), strike by, 925
Professions, women in, 866–867
Profiteers, 271
Progressive Era, 619
    business-government cooperation in, 631–632
    1920s and, 685
    World War I and, 660–661
Progressive Party
    of 1912, 638–639, 640
    of 1924, 687
    of 1948, 797
Progressivism, 587(i), 619, 637, 647–648
    Addams, Jane, and, 617–619
    African Americans and, 645–647
    in city and state government, 625–626
    conservation and, 626
    grassroots, 619–624
    limitations of, 642–647
    racism and, 619, 645–647
    reform Darwinism and, 624
    Roosevelt, T., and, 626–635
    settlement house movement and, 619, 620
    Taft and, 636, 637
    theoretical basis for, 624–625
    urban, 620–621
    Wilson and, 640, 641–642
    woman suffrage and, 644–645
    working class and, 621–624
    World War I and, 653, 660–661, 663, 664–665
Prohibition, 691–692. *See also* Alcohol and alcoholism; Temperance
    nativism and, 621
    after World War I, 665
Prohibition Party, 541, 598

Propaganda
    for national security, 789, 790
    in World War I, 662, 664, 667
Property
    of African Americans, 341
    slaves as, 370
    voting rights and, 214, 216, 244, 291, 475
    of women, 341
Property rights, Supreme Court on, 535
Prophet, Tenskwatawa as, 268
Prophetstown, Indiana, 282
Proposition 13 (California), 909(i)
Proprietary colonies, 75, 97–98, 100–101, 135
Proslavery arguments, 369–370
Prosperity
    in 1920s, 687–688
    in 1960s, 849
    culture of abundance and, 827–832
    in middle colonies, 121
    slavery and, 127–128
    in World War II, 767
Prossor, Thomas, 270
Prostitution, 620–621
    World War I and, 662
Protective legislation, for working women, 623
Protective tariffs, 295, 545–546. *See also* Tariffs
Protest(s). *See also* Civil rights movement; Resistance; Revolts and rebellions
    by African Americans, 832–836
    antiwar, 889–890, 892
    at Chicago Democratic National Convention (1968), 892
    colonial, 161–163
    by farmers, 588–590
    by gays and lesbians, 863
    in Great Depression, 711–712
    by Latinos, 859–861
    by Native Americans, 858–859
    in New England, 164–165
    pro-Vietnam War, 890
    student, 861–862, 890–891
    against Vietnam War, 862, 889–890, 892
Protestant Association (Maryland), 104
Protestantism. *See also* Evangelicalism; Great Awakening; specific groups
    vs. Catholicism, 47, 408
    in Chesapeake region, 66–67
    in colonies, 81–97
    conservatism and, 924
    evangelical, 319, 321–322
    fear of Catholic and Jewish immigrants, 700
    German Americans and, 341
    Native Americans and, 88
Protestant Reformation, 47–48
    in England, 84–85
Psychology, Freud and, 690–691
Pubic domain, land in, 318
Public assistance. *See also* Welfare and welfare system
    federal government and, 737–738

Public credit. *See* Credit
Public debt. *See* Debt; National debt
Public facilities, segregation of, 645
Public financing, for presidential campaigns, 914
Public housing. *See also* Housing
    Eisenhower and, 812
Public land. *See* Land
Public libraries, 527, 579–580
Public Opinion (journal), 562
Public schools, 320. *See also* Education; School(s)
    in cities and towns, 579
    for females, 288–290
    integration of, 910–911
    segregation of Asians in, 635
    in South, 373, 476–477
Public transportation, 303
Public works
    in cities, 579–580
    Coxey on, 600–601
    New Deal programs for, 734
Puddlers, in iron industry, 565
Pueblo Indians, 39–40, 40(i)
Pueblo Revolt, 73
Pueblos, revolt in Acoma and, 13, 18, 41
Puerto Rican people, 859
Puerto Rico, 36, 610, 611, 612(m), 613
Pulitzer, Joseph, 609, 628
Pullman (town), 594–595
Pullman, George M., 594–595, 596, 597
Pullman boycott, 596
Pullman Palace cars, 595(i)
Pullman strike (1894), 594–597
Punishment
    of free blacks, 387
    of indentured servants, 65
    of slaves, 118, 119, 375, 375(i)
Pure Food and Drug Act (1906), 631
Puritan Revolution (England), 67, 94
Puritans and Puritanism, 84
    in Chesapeake region, 67
    colonial, 81–94
    in Massachusetts, 81
    in New England, 81–94
    splintering of, 92–94
Pynchon, William, 92
Pyramids, in Cahokia, 1

Quadrant, 30
Quakers, 96, 99–100, 117
    Grimké sisters and, 301
    in Philadelphia, 121
    wealth of, 121
    women and, 288
Quantrill, William Clarke, 438
Quarantine policy, 754
Quartering Act (1765), 156–157, 163
Quasi-War (1798–1800), 261, 263
Quebec, 146
    in Revolutionary War, 183, 184(m), 192
Quebec Act (1774), 163

Queen Anne's War (1702–1713), 116–117
Quincy, Josiah, Boston Massacre and, 160
Quotas, on immigration, 798, 847

Rabin, Yitzak, 957
Race and racism. *See also* Abolition and abolitionism; African Americans; Civil rights movement; Segregation; specific groups
    against African Americans, 426, 443, 561, 677–678, 832–834
    against Asians, 561–562, 678
    in California mining camps, 356
    in Chesapeake, 76
    civil rights movement and, 832–836
    Cold War and, 795
    in colonies, 119
    conservatism and, 908–909
    foreign policy and, 745, 795, 832–833
    free blacks and, 387
    in Great Depression, 739
    Haitian Revolution and, 258–259
    immigrants and, 559, 560–563, 959, 960
    imperialism and, 613
    against Indians, 814
    of Johnson, Andrew, 465
    left wing fight against, 712
    lynchings and, 538
    Mexicans and, 678–679
    Missouri Compromise and, 293
    mixed races in New Spain, 44(i)
    New Deal and, 745
    politics and, 538–540
    Populists and, 602–603
    Powell, Colin, on, 955
    progressivism and, 619, 645–647
    Reconstruction and, 476
    scientific racism and, 535
    social Darwinism and, 535, 561
    in South, 122, 127–128, 369, 477, 645
    suburban development and, 823
    voting rights and, 215, 244, 645
    women's movement and, 866
    after World War I, 670–671
    in World War II, 761, 768
Race riots
    in Atlanta, 647
    during Reconstruction, 470
    urban (1965-1968), 857
    in Watts (1965), 856(m), 857, 908
    after World War I, 678
    in World War II, 768
Racial segregation. *See* Segregation
Radar, 757, 764
Radical feminism, 864, 865
Radical Reconstruction, 470–471
Radical Republicans, 470–471
Radicals and radicalism. *See also* specific groups
    birth control movement and, 643–644
    black, 857–858
    in Great Depression, 712, 732

Grimké sisters and, 302
IWW and, 643
labor, 574–575
Socialist Party and, 642
student protests and, 862
after World War I, 675–677
Radio, 697
fireside chats on, 724, 724(i)
Radioactive fallout, from nuclear testing,
882
Railroad Administration, 664
Railroads, 305, 337–339, 338(m)
as big business, 525–527
buffalo hunting and, 495
Chinese workers on, 507, 508(i), 561
in Civil War, 433, 448
competition and, 526–527
deregulation of, 916
expansion of, 524(m), 526
farming and, 515, 589
land grants to, 512(m), 513, 526
Morgan and reorganization of, 532–533,
628
ranching and, 515
rate wars and, 628
rebates from, 529, 589, 628, 630
regulation of, 535, 546–547
safety legislation for, 637
in South, 373, 391, 476, 537
steel use by, 527
strikes against, 570–572, 594–597
telegraph communication and, 526
transcontinental, 405, 448, 507, 510, 525,
526
in West, 510, 512(m), 524(m)
workday on, 642
Rainbow Coalition, 942
Raleigh, Walter, 49
Ramos, David, 927
Rancheros, 348
Ranching, 507, 512(m), 513–514, 517
vaqueros in, 514–515
Ranchos, 348, 507
Randolph, A. Philip, 767–768, 852
Randolph, Edmund, 242, 375–376
Rape
lynching and, 539
women's rights and, 865, 868
"Rape of Nanking," 754
Rapier, James T., 459–450, 460(i), 475
Rapier, John, 459
Ratification
of Articles of Confederation, 210, 211
of Bill of Rights, 243
of Constitution, 231–235
of Versailles Treaty, 672–673
Rationing, in World War II, 767
Raza Unida, La. See La Raza Unida
Reading, Pennsylvania, strike in, 571
Readjusters, 538
Reagan, Nancy, 934
Reagan, Ronald, cabinet of, 929

Reagan, Ronald, 923, 935(i)
AIDS epidemic and, 931
assassination attempt on, 924
as California governor, 908, 923
conservatism of, 907, 922, 924, 928,
929
deregulation and, 916, 925–926
election of 1976 and, 914, 922–924
election of 1980 and, 907, 922–924
election of 1984 and, 926
environment and, 925
farewell address of, 936
feminism and, 929
foreign policy of, 932–933, 939
Iran-Contra scandal and, 933–934
judicial appointments by, 929
Lebanon and, 933
minority rights and, 928–929
on Panama Canal, 921
Soviet Union and, 932–933, 934–935
supply-side economics and, 924–925
Supreme Court and, 929–930
trickle-down economics and, 927–928
Reagan Democrats, 924
Reapers, mechanical, 336, 448, 515
Rearmament, of Nazi Germany, 752
Rebates, railroad, 529, 589, 628, 630
Rebellions. See Protest(s); Revolts and
rebellions
Recall
Populists on, 591
progressives and, 625, 626
Recessions. See also Depressions; Economy;
Panics
in 1937–1938, 742–743
in 1957, 815
in 2008–, 971
Recién llegados, los, 679
Reconquest (Spain), 26, 30
Reconstruction, second, 486, 850–858
Reconstruction (1863–1877), 459–486
carpetbaggers and, 459, 473–474
collapse of, 479–485, 542
congressional, 468–473
Johnson impeachment and, 471–472
Ku Klux Klan and, 474–475
labor code and, 463
military rule during, 470, 482
North and, 480–482
politics in, 473–475
presidential, 465–468
Radical, 470–471
Redeemers and, 482
scalawags and, 474
South and, 459–461, 473–479, 482–484,
485(m)
southern Republican Party and, 473–474,
482–484
Supreme Court and, 481
wartime, 461–464
white supremacy and, 482–484
Reconstruction Acts (1867), 471, 472, 475

Reconstruction Amendments. *See* Thirteenth
    Amendment; Fourteenth Amendment;
    Fifteenth Amendment
Reconstruction Finance Corporation (RFC,
    1932), 706, 723
Recovery, in New Deal, 728–729, 742–743, 746
Recreation. *See* Leisure
Red Army (Soviet Union), 755, 771, 773
Red-baiting, 798
Redbook magazine, "flappers" in, 693(i)
Red Cloud (Sioux chief), 497
Redcoats, 183
Red Cross, 665, 707
Redeemers, in South, 482, 484, 486, 537
Redemptioners, 117–118
Red Hawk (Shawnee Indians), 194
Redistricting, voting rights and, 849
Redress of grievances, petition for, 314–315
Red River, 277
Red scare
    in 1950s, 798–800
    after World War I, 675–677
    after World War II, 782, 798
Red Stockings, 577
Referendum, 591, 625, 626
Reform and reform movements. *See also*
        Great Society; specific movements
    in cities, 625, 626
    civil service, 542, 543
    Clinton and, 950–951
    in 1830s, 322–326
    evangelicalism and, 357
    Kennedy, John F., and, 843–844
    monetary, 549
    moral reform movement and, 322–323
    in New Deal, 729–730, 737–738, 743–745
    Nixon and, 868–871
    political, 389–390
    Populist movement, 590–591, 614
    progressive, 619–626, 645
    Roosevelt, T., and, 630–632
    settlement house movement and,
        617–619
    southern Republican governments and,
        475–476
    tariff, 546
    temperance and, 540–541, 621
    Wilson and, 639–641, 641–642
    women and, 358–360, 540–541, 586–588,
        598–599, 617–619, 620, 863–868
    in World War I, 667
Reformation. *See* Protestant Reformation
Reform Darwinism, 624
Refugees
    African Americans, 217(i)
    Haitian, 258
    Indian, 194
    Jewish, 769–770
    Palestinian, 896, 921, 957
    Vietnam War and, 888, 891
*Regents of the University of California v.
    Bakke* (1978), 911
Regions (U.S.). *See* specific regions

Regulation
    of business, 630–631, 631–632
    of colonial trade, 101–103
    in Great Depression, 725
    under Nixon, 868–869
    progressives and government, 623, 625,
        626
    of railroads, 535, 546–547
    of trusts, 547, 628
Reid, Whitelaw, 466
Relief programs. *See also* Welfare and wel-
        fare system
    in New Deal, 725–727, 734, 739, 746
Religion(s). *See also* Churches; Missions and
        missionaries; specific religions
    church attendance and, 130
    colonial, 129–131
    conservatives and, 924
    evangelical, 319, 321–322, 357
    of freedmen, 464
    of Indians, 148, 502–503
    in middle colonies, 99
    in New England, 81–94, 95–97, 130
    in 1950s, 827, 828–829
    of plain folk, 386
    politics and, 536
    school prayer and, 850
    of Scots-Irish immigrants, 117
    of slaves, 380–381
    of Smith, Alfred, 702–703
    social gospel and, 620
    social purity movement and, 620–621
    of Taino people, 32–33
    women and, 286, 288
Religious toleration
    in New York, 99, 106
    in Pennsylvania, 101, 106
Relocation. *See also* Removal policy
    of Indians, 813–814
    of Japanese Americans, 760, 761(m)
Remington, Frederic, 609
Removal policy, for Indians, 313–316,
        314(m), 367, 493–495
Rent controls, after World War II, 792
Reparations, after World War I, 688
Repartimiento, 43, 71
Report on Manufactures (Hamilton), 249
Report on Public Credit (Hamilton), 247
Report on the Causes and Reasons for War,
        283
Representation
    Antifederalists on, 285
    census and, 247(i)
    colonial, 136, 152, 163, 165
    Constitution on, 229
    taxation without, 152, 154, 157, 162, 170
    virtual, 152
Representative government, in New
        Netherland, 99
Republic(s), independence of Soviet, 947
Republicanism, 213–214, 235–236, 241
    democracy and, 213, 230–231
    Paine on, 178

Republican motherhood, 244–245
Republican Party, 330. *See also* Elections; specific presidents
   abortion rights and, 911
   business and, 526
   during Civil War, 447–448, 449–450
   conservatism and, 907, 922–923
   on *Dred Scott* decision, 413, 414
   Eisenhower and, 812–813
   ex-Confederates in Congress and, 467
   factionalism in, 542, 543
   Fifteenth Amendment and, 472
   Fourteenth Amendment and, 469
   during Gilded Age, 526, 536, 541, 542
   Klan and political violence against, 483–484
   Liberal Party and, 480
   in 1950s, 815
   presidential Reconstruction and, 467–468
   progressives in, 626, 638
   Radical Reconstruction and, 470–471
   Roosevelt, T., and, 630, 631
   sectionalism and, 408–409
   Social Security and, 737
   in South, 473–474, 475–477, 481, 482, 483, 911
   tariffs and, 545–546
   tax revolts and, 909(i)
   War of 1812 and, 286
   women and, 409, 929
   World War I and, 668
Republicans (Jeffersonian), 259–264, 269
   election of 1808 and, 279, 280
   election of 1828 and, 310
   Federalists and, 259–264, 297
   philosophy of, 271–272
   XYZ affair and, 261–262
Republicans (Spain), 754
Republican societies, 255
Republic of Texas, 350
Republic Steel, strike at, 736
Requisition, of money by Articles of Confederation, 210
Resaca de la Palma, battle at (1846), 352
Research, in 1950s, 826
Reservations (Indian), 492(m), 493–495, 496, 497, 498, 499–500, 814, 859
Reserve Officers Training Corps (ROTC), 889
Reservoirs, 632
Residential apartments ("French flats"), 579
Residential segregation, 563
Resistance. *See also* Revolts and rebellions
   colonial, 152–154, 170
   by Indians, 491, 493, 496, 497–498, 500–503
   by slaves, 126, 168, 169, 170, 365–366, 381–382
   to Stamp Act, 153–154
Resources. *See also* Natural resources; specific resources
   on Indian lands, 813–814
Reston, James, 844
Retirement Equity Act (1984), 929

Reuther, Walter, 822
Revel, James, 65
Revenue Act (1764, Sugar Act), 150–151
Revenues. *See* Finances
Revere, Paul, 166
Reverse discrimination, 855, 928
Revivals and revivalism, 303
   in Great Awakening, 321–322
   Plain folk and, 131, 386, 386(i)
Revolts and rebellions. *See also* Resistance
   at Acoma pueblo, 41
   Bacon's, 69
   Boxer uprising as, 607
   Gabriel's rebellion, 270
   in Hawai'i, 606(i)
   in Hungary (1956), 817
   by Indians against Spanish, 73
   by Leisler, 104
   by Pontiac, 147–149
   1774-1775, 166–169
   Shays's Rebellion, 225–227
   by slaves, 365–366, 382
   Stono rebellion, 126
   by students, 861–862
   by Turner, Nat, 365–366, 366(i), 382
   urban, 856(m)
   by urban blacks, 855–857
   Whiskey Rebellion and, 245, 250–251
Revolution(s). *See also* Market revolution; Revolutionary War
   Bolshevism and, 660, 677
   in Cuba, 609, 818, 879
   French, 255–257
   in Haiti, 245, 258–259
   in Iran (1979), 919, 922
   in Mexico (1911), 637
   Puritan (England), 67
   in Russia (1917), 660
   in transportation, 304–305
Revolutionary War (1775–1783). *See also* Continental army; specific leaders and battles
   British strategy in, 182–183
   campaigns of 1777–1779 in, 192–196
   finances during, 191
   first year of (1775–1776), 181–186
   French alliance during, 196, 201, 203
   home front in, 186–191
   Indians in, 188, 193–196, 195(m), 202–203
   Lexington, Concord, and, 166–167, 167(m)
   loyalists in, 187–189
   in North, 183–186, 184(m), 192–193
   patriotism in, 186–187
   prisoners of war in, 189–191
   reasons for British loss, 203–204
   in South, 197–203, 198(m)
   treason and guerrilla warfare in, 189, 199–200
   war debts after, 210, 218–219, 225, 240, 257
   in West, 193–196, 195(m)

Revolutionary War (continued)
  women in, 173–175, 181–182
  Yorktown surrender and, 200–202
Rhee, Syngman, 800
Rhineland, Nazis in, 754
Rhode Island, 135, 136
  Articles of Confederation and, 211
  gradual emancipation in, 217
Rhodesia, 919
Rice
  in Carolina, 75
  slavery and, 127, 372
  in South, 122, 371–372
Rice, Condoleezza, 940(i), 962–963
Richmond, Virginia
  Civil War in, 436, 455
  Democratic convention in, 418
Ridgway, Matthew B., 805
Riesman, David, 830
Rifles, 495
Rights. See also Bill of Rights (U.S.); specific
      groups
  declaration of (1774), 165
  national security and, 966
  natural, 180
  private property vs. workers', 593, 597
  Reagan and, 928–929
  state vs. federal, 481
  for women, 286, 287, 326, 357, 358–360
Rights of Man, The (Paine), 179(i)
Right-to-work laws, 797
Right wing (political). See also Conservatives
      and conservatism
  Clinton and, 952
  Reagan and, 923
Riis, Jacob, 563–564, 566, 631
Rio Grande region, border in, 354, 826(i)
Riots. See also Protest(s); Race riots
  antidraft, 449
  for bread, in Confederacy, 446
  against Chinese immigrants, 508
  during Great Railroad Strike, 572
River Rouge factory (Ford), 685, 711
Rivers. See also specific river regions
  navigable, 66
  travel on, 246(m)
Rivington, James, 188(i)
Roads and highways
  auto use and, 688
  interstate system and, 812, 813(m)
  in 1790s, 245–246
  transportation revolution and, 304–305
Roanoke Island, 49
Roaring Twenties, 685, 690–703
Robards, Rachel Donelson. See Jackson,
      Rachel
"Robber barons," 532
Roberts, John, 964
Roberts, Owen, 742
Robertson, Pat, 924
Robin John family, 109–111
Robinson, Jackie, 795, 834
Robinson, Jo Ann, 834, 835–836

Robinson, Solon, 373(i)
Rochambeau (Comte de), 201
Rock and roll music, 831, 862
Rockefeller, "Big Bill," 528
Rockefeller, John D., 523, 528–530, 563,
      568, 606
  criticism of, 620, 627
Rockefeller, John D., Jr., 534
Rockies, 277
Rockingham (Marquess of), 155, 156
Rockne, Knute, 697
Roebling family
  Emily Warren, 555
  John, 553, 583
  Washington, 555, 583
Roe v. Wade (1973), 867, 911, 930, 930(i)
Rolfe, John, 54, 54(i), 62, 63
Rolfe, Thomas, 54, 55
Roman Catholicism. See Catholicism
Romania, 670
Rommel, Erwin, 764, 771
Roosevelt, Eleanor, 719, 722, 725, 739
Roosevelt, Franklin Delano, 718–720. See
      also Great Depression; New Deal
  Atlantic Charter and, 758
  Black Cabinet of, 739
  at Casablanca, 765
  court-packing plan of, 741–742
  death of, 773
  Democratic coalition of, 718, 719, 720(m),
      741, 768–769
  election of 1920 and, 679
  election of 1928 and, 719
  election of 1932 and, 720
  election of 1936 and, 741
  election of 1940 and, 722, 757
  election of 1944 and, 769
  fireside chats of, 724, 724(i)
  isolationism and, 751–752
  Latin America and, 752–753
  minority groups and, 739–740
  as New York governor, 719
  at Teheran, 771
  World War II and, 759–762
  at Yalta, 772
Roosevelt, Theodore, 502, 626–627, 627(i),
      642, 719
  anthracite coal strike and, 629–630
  assumption of presidency, 626
  conservation and, 632–633, 634(m)
  election of 1904 and, 630
  election of 1912 and, 638–639, 640(m)
  foreign policy of, 633–635
  racism and, 646
  as reformer, 630–632
  Spanish-American War and, 610–611
  Square Deal of, 630
  Taft and, 635, 636, 637
  as trustbuster, 628
  Washington, Booker T., and, 646
Roosevelt Corollary, 633, 637
Root-Takahira agreement (1908), 635
Rosebud, Battle of (1876), 497

Rosecrans, William, 451
Rosenberg, Ethel and Julius, 799
"Rosie the Riveter", 766, 766(i)
Ross, John (Cherokee chief), 315–316, 437(i)
ROTC. See Reserve Officers Training Corps
Roughing It (Twain), 517
Rough Riders, 610–611
Rowlandson, Mary, 103–104
Royal Air Force (England), 757
Royal colonies
    British, 104–105, 135
    Virginia as, 60
"Royal fifth," 41
Royal Navy. See Navies, British
Ruby, Jack, 844
Ruhr Valley region, France and, 688
Rum, molasses tax and, 150, 151(i)
Rumsfeld, Donald, 940(i), 967, 969
Runaway slaves. See Fugitive slaves
Rural areas. See also Agriculture; Farms and farming
    electricity and, 726–727
    in Great Depression, 708–709
    New Deal and, 730–732
    population in, 515
    population movement from, 341, 537, 557
    poverty in, 822
    TVA and, 726–727
    vs. urban values, 702
Rural Electrification Administration (REA), 727
Rush, Benjamin, 244
Rush-Bagot disarmament treaty (1817), 286
Rusk, Dean, 883, 884
Russell, Martha, 403
Russia. See also Soviet Union
    Bolshevism in, 675–676
    immigrants from, 504, 559, 700
    Pacific Coast region and, 134–135
    pogroms in, 560
    purchase of Alaska from, 480
    revolution of 1917 in, 660
    World War I and, 660
Russian Republic, 947. See also Russia; Soviet Union
Russo-Japanese War, 635
Rustin, Bayard, 852
Ruth, George Herman ("Babe"), 696
Rwanda, civil war in, 956

Sabbath, Quakers and, 96
Sacajawea (Shoshoni Indians), 277
Sacco, Nicola, 700
"Sack of Lawrence," 412
Sacrifice. See Human sacrifice
Sadat, Anwar, 921
Saddam Hussein. See Hussein, Saddam
Safety legislation. See Occupational Safety and Health Act (OSHA, 1970)
Sager family, 345(i)
Saigon. See Vietnam War

Sailors. See Exploration; Impressment; Navies; Navigation; Ships and shipping
St. Augustine, Florida, 41
St. Clair, Arthur, 253–254
Saint Domingue, 258
St. Lawrence River region, 48, 119
St. Louis, Missouri, 275, 555
St. Louis Exposition (1904), 502
St.-Mihiel, battle at, 652–653
"Saints," Puritan elect as, 90, 95
St. Valentine's Day massacre, 692
Salem, Massachusetts
    Williams, Roger, in, 82
    witch trials in, 96–97
Salesclerks, 570, 623
Saloons, 540
SALT. See Strategic Arms Limitation Talks
Salta abas (mixed race group), 44(i)
Salt Lake City, 347, 509
Salvation
    by faith alone, 47
    Puritans on, 93
Salvation Army, 665
Same-sex couples, rights of, 952
Samoan Islands, 608
Samoset, 86
Sampson, Deborah (Robert Shurtliff), 173–175, 174(i), 201
Samuelson, Robert, 827
San Carlos Borroméo de Carmelo (mission), 135
San Carlos Reservation, 502
Sand Creek massacre (1864), 494–495
San Diego
    in Mexican War, 352
    mission in, 135
San Diego de Alcalá, 135
S&L crisis. See Savings and loan crisis
Sandoz, Jules, 503
San Francisco, 355, 504, 555, 561, 579
Sanger, Margaret, 643–644, 693–694
San Jacinto, battle at, 348
San Juan Hill, Roosevelt, Theodore, at, 611
San Miguel de Gualdape, 39
San Salvador, Columbus in, 32
Santa Anna, Antonio López de, 347, 348, 352–354
Santa Clara County v. Southern Pacific Railroad, 535
Santa Fe, New Mexico, 41, 278, 347
    battle at, 352, 438
Santa Fe Trail, 347
Santa Maria (ship), 32
Santee (Dakota) Indians, 496
Santee Uprising (1862), 496
Santo Domingo, 480
Saratoga, Battle of (1777), 192–193
Satak (Sitting Bear) (Kiowa chief), 495
Satellite countries, Soviet, 785
Saturday Evening Post, 667, 692
Saudi Arabia, 945
    U.S. soldiers in, 946
Sauk and Fox Indians, 315

Savannah, Georgia, 578
    Civil War in, 452(m), 454
    in Revolution, 197, 201
Savings and loan (S&L) crisis, 925–926
"Scabs" (strikebreakers), 572, 574
Scalawags, 474
Scandals. *See* specific scandals
Scandinavia, immigrants from, 504, 559
Scapegoats, in Great Depression, 709–710
Scarlet fever, 494
Schenck, Charles, 676
Schenck v. United States (1919), 676
Schlafly, Fred, 905
Schlafly, Phyllis, 867, 905–906, 906(i), 907,
    908, 923, 924, 929, 936
Schneiderman, Rose, 623
School(s). *See also* Education; Higher educa-
        tion; Public schools; specific locations
    conservatives on curriculum of, 909
    desegregation of, 833–834, 849, 870
    for females, 288–289
    Freedmen's, 476(i)
    Indian, 499
    integration of, 910–911
    prayer in, 850
    segregation in, 739
    for women, 449
Schreiber, Marie, 793
Schurz, Carl, 460, 486, 543
Schuyler, Betsey, 239
Schuylkill Canal, 305
Sciences, exploration and, 30
Scientific management, 619, 624–625
Scientific racism, 535
SCLC. *See* Southern Christian Leadership
        Conference
Scopes, John, 701
Scopes trial, 701–702
Scorched-earth policy
    in Civil War, 454
    against Indians, 104, 496–497
Scotland. *See also* Scots-Irish immigrants
    immigrants from, 112, 116, 117, 504
Scots-Irish immigrants, 112, 117, 121–122, 566
Scott, Dred, 412–413, 413(i)
Scott, Hugh, 913
Scott, Tom, 527
Scott, Winfield, 353, 405, 407(m)
Scottsboro Boys, 712
Scriven, Abream, 380
SDI. *See* Strategic Defense Initiative
SDS. *See* Students for a Democratic Society
Seabrook, New Hampshire, nuclear power
        plant in, 917
Seale, Bobby, 858
SEALs, 881
Seaports. *See* Port cities
Sea routes. *See* Exploration; Trade
Seasonal laborers. *See* Migrant laborers
SEATO. *See* Southeast Asia Treaty
        Organization
Seattle, general strike in (1919), 675

SEC. *See* Securities and Exchange Commission
Secession, 417
    repudiation of, 466
    of South, 419–421, 428–429, 429(m)
Secessionists, 420
"Second American Revolution," Civil War as,
        456
Secondary schools, 579. *See also* Education;
        School(s)
Second Bank of the United States, 307, 308,
        318
Second Continental Congress (1775), 166,
        175–181
    on traitors, 189
Second front, in World War II, 764, 770
Second Great Awakening, 319, 321–322
"Second Middle Passage," 369, 380
Second Reconstruction, 486, 850–858. *See
        also* Reconstruction
Second World War. *See* World War II
Secretarial work, women in, 568–570
Secret ballot, Populists on, 591
Secret operations, of CIA, 789–790, 816–817,
        914
Secret Service, 543
Sectionalism. *See also* Civil War
        (U.S., 1861–1865)
    Dred Scott case and, 412–414
    election of 1860 and, 417–419
    expansion and, 349
    Mexican-American War and, 396
    Missouri Compromise and, 293, 298
    New South and, 536–537
    People's Party and, 600
    in politics, 397, 400–401, 405–406, 406–411
    slavery and, 225, 407(m)
    transcontinental railroad and, 405
    in War of 1812, 283
Securities and Exchange Commission
        (SEC, 1934), 725
Security. *See* Defense; National security;
        National security state
Security Council (UN), 772
    Iraq War (2003–2011) and, 968
    Korean War and, 801
Sedition Act
    of 1798, 262–264
    of 1918, 668
Segregation. *See also* Desegregation
    of armed forces, 443, 660
    in California, 635
    in cities, 561
    Civil Rights Act (1964) and, 853
    de facto in North, 855
    Jim Crow and, 538, 645
    in Levittowns, 823
    in 1950s, 811
    of public transportation, 477
    residential, 563, 823
    of schools, 739
    social, 563
    in South, 477, 481, 538, 645

of southern universities, 794
Supreme Court on, 646
Wilson and, 647
Selective Service Act
of 1917, 660
of 1940, 760–761
Self-determination, 670, 790
Palestinian, 921
Self-fulfillment, in 1960s, 862
Selma, Alabama, voting rights march in, 852(i), 853
Seminaries. *See* Academies
Seminole Indians, 218, 294, 313, 315, 316, 437, 493
Senate (U.S.), 229, 472. *See also* Congress (U.S.)
election to, 416, 542, 591, 637
slavery violence in, 412
Versailles treaty and, 672–673
Seneca Falls, New York, women's rights convention at, 359, 599, 600, 665
Seneca Falls Declaration of Sentiments (1848), 359, 360
Seneca Indians, 17, 188, 221
Senegambia, 124
"Sentiments of an American Woman, The," 187
"Separate but equal" doctrine, 646, 739, 833
Separate spheres idea, 319–320, 410(i), 538
Separation of church and state, school prayer and, 850
Separation of powers, Nixon and, 913
Separatism, southern, 397
Separatists, Pilgrims as, 85, 87
September 11, 2001, attacks, 965–967, 965(i)
Sequoia National Park, 634(m)
Serbs and Serbia
in former Yugoslavia, 956
World War I and, 656
Serra, Junípero, 135
Servants. *See also* Domestics (domestic servants); Indentured servants; Slaves and slavery
in Chesapeake region, 63–67, 71, 76
colonial, 118
as labor, 62–64
slaves as, 378
women as, 65–66
Servicemen's Readjustment Act (1944). *See* GI Bill (1944)
Service occupations, in 1950s, 822
Settlement(s). *See also* Colonies and colonization; Exploration; Land; specific locations
agricultural, 12–15, 66
ancient, 9, 10, 11–12
in New England, 113
in Ohio River region, 253
Spanish North American, 40
Settlement house movement, 617–619, 620, 621

Settler(s). *See also* Homesteaders
on Great Plains, 510–513
recruitment of, 510
"Settlers' wars," 496
Seven Cities of Cíbola, wealth of, 39
Seven Days Battle (1862), 435(m), 436
Seventeenth Amendment, 416, 637
Seven Years' (French and Indian) War (1754–1763), 134, 140, 142–147
costs to Britain, 147
European areas of influence in, 143(m)
Sewall, Arthur M., 603
Seward, William H., 401, 411, 418, 421, 433, 480
"Seward's Ice Box," 480
Sewing machine, 566
Sex and sexuality. *See also* Homosexuals and homosexuality
in 1920s, 690–691, 693
in 1950s, 830
in 1960s, 862
double standard of, 621
Freud and, 690–691
moral reform movement and, 322–323
among servants, 64
slave women and, 376
social purity movement and, 620–621
working class women and, 577
Sex discrimination, 864, 870
in education, 867
Sex education, 909
Sexual Behavior in the Human Female (Kinsey), 830
Sexual Behavior in the Human Male (Kinsey), 830
Sexual division of labor. *See also* Gender and gender issues
female immigrants and, 560
Sexual harassment, in workplace, 943, 945
Sexual revolution (1960s), 862
Seymour, Horatio, 479–480
Seymour, Jane (England), 84
Shadrach (runaway slave), 403
Shafter, William, 611
Shah of Iran. *See* Pahlavi, Mohammad Reza
"Shame of the Cities, The" (Steffens), 581
Shandong (Shan-tung) Province, Boxers in, 607, 670
Shantung Peninsula, as Japanese mandate, 670
Shantytowns, in Great Depression, 713
Sharecroppers and sharecropping, 478–479, 515, 712, 728, 731(i)
"Share Our Wealth" plan (Long), 733
Shawnee Indians, 144, 146, 255
Fort Stanwix Treaty and, 221, 253
during Revolution, 188, 194, 195(m)
Tecumseh and, 267–269, 281–282
Shays, Daniel, 226
Shays's Rebellion (1786–1787), 225–227
Sheldon, Charles M., 620
Shelters, for battered women, 868

Shenandoah River region
    Civil War in, 454
    settlement in, 119
Sheppard-Towner Act (1921), 692
Sheridan, Philip H., 454, 495
Sherman, John, 495
Sherman, William Tecumseh, 451, 454,
    455, 463, 466, 496
Sherman Antitrust Act (1890), 547, 627–628,
    925
Sherman Silver Purchase Act (1890), 548–549
Sherman's March to the Sea, 452(m), 454
Shiite Muslims, 968
    Hezbollah and, 933
    in Iran, 922
    in Iraq, 946
Shiloh, Battle of (1862), 435(m), 438
Shipping Board, 664
Ships and shipping. *See also* Navies; Navy
        (U.S.); Slave trade; Submarines
    Barbary Wars and, 272–273
    British seizure of, 257
    in Civil War, 438, 439
    colonial trade and, 69, 102–103
    costs of, 305
    impressment and, 279–280
    on Mississippi River, 274
    in New England, 115
    Portuguese, 31
    in slave trade, 110, 110(i), 123–124
    steamboat travel and, 304
    transportation improvements and, 304
    in World War I, 658
    in World War II, 764
Shoe industry, 305, 307
Shopping centers, in 1950s, 823, 826
Shoshoni Indians, 277, 344, 500, 501, 503, 505
Shurtliff, Robert. *See* Sampson, Deborah
Siberia, humans in, 6
Sicily, 765
Sierra Club, 632
Sierra Leone, 125(i), 217(i)
    African Americans in, 218
"Significance of the Frontier on American
        History, The" (Turner), 489
Silent Spring (Carson), 870
Silver
    banknotes and, 318
    Comstock Lode and, 504–506
    free silver issue, 547–549, 603
    from New Spain, 43–44
    from Peru, 39
Simpson, Jim ("Dead Shot"), 610
Sin
    moral reform movement and, 323
    in Puritan New England, 96
Sinai Peninsula, 896, 921
Sinatra, Frank, 799
Sinclair, Upton, 631, 732
Sioux Indians, 344, 496, 498, 500, 503
    Black Hills and, 497–498
    Teton Sioux, 17
    Wounded Knee massacre against, 503, 859

Sit-down strike, at GM, 736
Sit-ins
    at Woolworth's, 851
    during World War II, 768
Sitting Bear (Satak, Kiowa chief), 495
Sitting Bull (Sioux leader), 490(i), 495, 497,
    498, 503
Six-Day War (1967), 895–896, 917
Sixteenth Amendment, 637
Skilled workers, 560–561, 565, 568, 573
Skin color, 388, 460(i), 561
Skyscrapers, 528, 578–579, 578(i)
Slade, Mark, 909(i)
Slater, Samuel, 305
Slaughterhouse cases (1873), 481
Slave codes (laws), 369, 418
Slave drivers, 379
Slaveholders, 369, 370–371. *See also*
        Planters and plantations
    black, 388
    in Civil War, 430, 446, 447
    labor code and, 463
    secession and, 420
    in southern legislatures, 390
    westward movement of, 367
Slave patrols, 383
Slave Power, 409, 412, 414
Slaves and slavery. *See also* Abolition and
        abolitionism; African Americans;
        Fugitive slaves; Revolts and rebellions
    African, 109–111, 110(i)
    in Caribbean, 73–77, 251
    in Carolina, 75
    in Chesapeake region, 63, 71–77
    Civil War and, 425–426, 427, 440–443, 445
    colonial, 78, 142
    Constitution and, 229–230, 243
    cotton and, 368–369, 372
    Declaration of Independence and, 180
    defense of, 366, 369–370
    destruction of, 446–447, 456
    in District of Columbia, 325
    emancipation and, 441–443
    equality and, 216–218
    families and, 380
    free labor vs., 463
    geographic expansion of, 368–369
    in Georgia, 122
    gradual emancipation and, 217–218
    Grimké sisters on, 301–302
    Haitian Revolution and, 258–259
    Indians and, 36
    as labor system, 125–127
    liberty and, 155
    Lincoln-Douglas debates on, 416
    Lincoln on, 414
    as loyalists, 202
    manumission and, 218
    marriage and, 380
    in middle colonies, 118–119
    Missouri Compromise and, 293, 397
    movement to Canada and, 169
    mulatto children and, 377

in New England, 116
in Northwest Territory, 222, 224
nullification and, 317
organizing against, 324–326
paternalism and, 374–375
plantations and, 31, 378–382
politics of, 389–391
prohibition in Northwest Territory states, 222
punishment of, 119, 375, 375(i)
rebellions by, 365–366, 382
religion and, 130, 380–381
Republican Party on, 409
resistance and, 126, 168–169, 170, 365–366, 381–382
in Revolutionary War, 197–199, 201
for rice crops, 372
search for families of former, 464
sectionalism and, 407(m)
in South, 121–128, 365–382
sugar and, 372
Tallmadge amendments and, 293
in territories, 397–399, 400–401, 405–406, 411–412, 412–414
tobacco and, 372
Van Buren and, 327
women and, 287, 377, 378
work of, 378–379
Slave states, 398. See also specific states
Texas, Oregon, and, 350
Slave trade, 109–111, 110(i), 122–125, 125(i), 418
close of, 401
Constitution and, 229
domestic, 369
Slums, 557, 849
Smallpox
Indians and, 35, 35(i), 46, 494
in Revolution, 177
Smith, Alfred E. (Al), 702–703, 703(i)
Smith, Bessie, 696
Smith, Gerrit, 361
Smith, John, 53–54, 55, 57, 58
Smith, Joseph, Jr., 346
Smith Act (1940), 799
Smoking. See Tobacco and tobacco industry
Smuggling, colonial, 147, 150, 162
SNCC. See Student Nonviolent Coordinating Committee
Snelling, Fort, mass execution at, 496
Social conservatism, 911
Social Darwinism, 534, 561, 629
depression of 1890s and, 600
racism and, 535, 561
reform Darwinism and, 624
social gospel and, 620
Social Democratic Party. See Socialist Party
Social engineering, 624
Social geography, of cities, 563–564
Social gospel, 620
Socialism and socialists, 574, 642
in Great Depression, 712
after liberation movements, 790

New Deal and, 732
panic of 1837 and, 329
Socialist Labor Party, 642
Socialist Party
Debs and, 597, 642
in Great Depression, 713
in 1912, 639
Social purity movement, 620–621
Social Security, 737–738, 742, 916, 928
Eisenhower and, 812
Medicare, Medicaid, and, 847
Nixon and, 868
Social Security Act (1935), 738
Social segregation, 563
Social welfare. See Welfare and welfare system
Social work, as profession, 620
Society. See also Culture(s); Great Society; Progressivism; Reform and reform movements; specific issues
in British colonies, 111–112, 128, 129–131
in Chesapeake, 60–71, 61(m)
colonial, 41–45, 77–78, 128–136
in Gilded Age, 546
globalization and, 959
hierarchy in, 303
Mexica, 21
in New England, 89–97
Nixon, social justice, and, 870–871
reforms of, 358–361
slave, 365–392
of South, 367
Spanish American, 44–46
in Spanish borderland colonies, 72–73
yeomen, 382–384
Society of Friends. See Quakers
"Sodbusters," 510
Sod houses, 510–511, 511(i)
Software industry, Gates in, 927
Solar energy, 919
Soldiers. See also Armed forces; Military; Veterans; specific battles and wars
black, 506
in Civil War, 453(i), 482
Newburgh Conspiracy and, 219–220
in Revolution, 173–175
in Vietnam War, 875–876, 883(m), 887–888
in World War I, 651–653, 652(i), 661(i)
Solid South, 536, 702–703, 911
Solomon Islands, 773
Somalia, 955, 956
Somoza, Anastasio, 752
Sonoran Desert, 501
Sons of Liberty, 153, 158–159
Boston Tea Party and, 162–163
Soros, George, 959
Sorosis Club, 540
Souls of Black Folk, The (Du Bois), 646(i), 647
Sousa, John Philip, 609
Souter, David, 943

South (U.S. region). *See also* Civil rights movement; Civil War (U.S.); Colonies and colonization; Confederacy (Civil War South); New South; Reconstruction; Slaves and slavery; Sun Belt; specific locations
  African Americans and, 124–125, 218, 369, 537, 645, 677–678, 678(i), 738, 832
  agricultural economy of, 371(m), 537
  black codes in, 466, 467, 468
  black migration from, 561
  Brown's raid and, 417
  cash crops of, 371–372, 371(m)
  cities in, 372–373
  during Civil War, 444–447
  cotton and, 245, 372
  crop lien system in, 589
  defense industry and, 823
  economy in, 477, 536, 537
  Fourteenth Amendment and, 469, 470
  free blacks in, 387–389
  free silver and, 547–548
  grassroots conservatism in, 908–910
  Great Depression in, 720
  Hartford Convention and, 285–286
  home rule for, 480, 482
  honor in, 376
  immigrants in, 373
  impact of Civil War on, 456, 475–476
  Indian removal in, 315
  integration in, 910
  Jim Crow laws in, 477, 538, 561, 645
  Klan in, 474–475, 480
  land sales in, 318
  military rule in, 470–471, 482, 484, 537
  North compared with, 367
  plain folk in, 382–386
  politics of slavery in, 389–391
  Populists in, 602–603, 604
  public education in, 476–477
  racial violence in, 470
  railroads in, 373, 537
  Reconstruction and, 459–461, 473–479, 482–484, 485(m)
  Redeemers in, 482, 484, 486, 537
  Republican governments in, 475–477, 482–483
  Republican Party in, 473–474
  Revolutionary War and, 197–203, 198(m)
  school segregation in, 833
  secession of, 419–421, 428–429, 429(m)
  segregation in, 477, 481, 538
  separatism of, 397
  settlement in, 119
  sharecropping in, 478–479
  slavery in, 121–128, 365–382
  Sun Belt in, 823
  Unionists in, 418, 420, 427, 429–430
  upcountry in, 383–384
  voting in, 128, 389–390, 475, 645

South Africa
  Carter and, 919
  Reagan and, 933
South America. *See also* Latin America; North America; specific countries; specific cultures
  ancient cultures of, 8
  exploration of, 34
  human migration to, 7
  Monroe Doctrine and, 294–295
South Boston High School, 910
South Carolina, 122, 390. *See also* Carolina(s)
  Civil War in, 428, 455
  nullification and, 316–317
  population of, 121
  Revolutionary War in, 197–199, 198(m), 200
  secession and, 420
  slaves in, 122, 124, 126
  Spanish in, 39
Southeast (U.S. region), economy of, 631
Southeast Asia. *See also* specific locations
  communism in, 817
Southeast Asia Treaty Organization (SEATO), 818
Southeast region, Indians of, 17
Southern Arapaho Indians, 495
Southern Christian Leadership Conference (SCLC), 836, 841(i), 851
Southern Democrats, 798
Southern Farmers' Alliance, 589
Southern Farm Tenants Union, 730
Southern Literary Messenger, 403
Southern Pacific Railroad, 525, 626
Southern strategy, of Nixon, 910–911
Southern Unionists, 420. *See also* Unionists, in South
South Korea, 800–804, 801(m)
  Carter and, 919
South Vietnam, 818, 885. *See also* Vietnam War
  army of, 875, 888, 891, 896
  bombing of, 887
  evacuation of, 899, 899(i)
  government of, 884, 888, 896
Southwest (U.S. region)
  Anglo-Americans in, 347
  Civil War in, 438
  cultures of, 12–13
  Hispanics in, 507
  Indians in, 251–253, 494, 501–503
  Mexican Americans in, 797, 859–860
  Mexican control of, 342, 347–348
  Mexican immigrants in, 678–679, 700, 709(i)
  movement to, 811
  native cultures of, 12–13
  Spain and, 41
  Sun Belt and, 823
Sovereignty. *See* Popular sovereignty; State(s); State sovereignty

Soviet Union. *See also* Bolsheviks and
    Bolshevism; Cold War; Russia; Stalin,
    Joseph
    Afghanistan and, 921, 932, 935
    antiballistic missiles and, 932
    arms race with, 933
    atomic bomb of, 788–789
    Berlin and, 787–788
    Bolshevism in, 752
    China and, 791, 893
    in Cold War, 783–786, 946–947
    Cuba and, 819, 879, 881–882
    Czechoslovakia and, 785, 787
    détente with, 894–895
    Eastern Europe and, 771, 772, 777, 783,
      895
    economic sanctions against, 921
    Eisenhower and, 810–811, 815–816
    end of, 940–941
    German nonaggression treaty with, 755
    Gorbachev in, 934–935
    Hungarian revolt and (1956), 817
    hydrogen bomb of, 789
    independence of republics in, 947
    Korean War and, 800, 802
    Lend-Lease for, 758
    Nazi invasion of, 758
    Nazi treaty with, 755
    Nixon and, 893, 894
    Reagan and, 932–933, 934–935
    Red scare and, 798–800
    Roosevelt, F. D., and, 752
    satellite countries of, 785
    third world and, 879
    World War II and, 770
Space exploration
    Soviet orbit of earth and, 879
    Sputnik and, 820
    by United States, 877
Spain. *See also* Colonies and colonization;
    New Spain; Spanish-American War;
    specific locations
    borderland settlements of, 41–45, 72–73
    Columbus and, 26–27, 32–33
    Comanche and, 278
    Creek Indians and, 252
    Cuba and, 294, 609–610
    economy of, 48
    England and, 56
    exploration and conquest by, 36–46
    Florida and, 39, 41
    immigrants from, 504
    Incan empire and, 39
    Mexico and, 36–39
    Mississippi River region and, 274, 275,
      276(m)
    Monroe Doctrine and, 294–295
    Pacific Coast region and, 134–135
    Protestant Reformation and, 47–48
    Reconquest in, 26, 30
    Seven Years' War and, 143(m), 146, 147
    slavery and, 71

Texas and, 294
Treaty of Paris (1898) and, 613
Spanish-American War (1898), 588, 605,
    609–611, 611(m), 614, 635
    treaty ending, 613
Spanish civil war, 754
Spanish influenza epidemic, 675
"Speakeasy," 691
Speaker of the House, 418
Special interests, territorial appointees and,
    509–510
Specie payments, 307, 308
Speculation
    in Great Depression, 723
    Jefferson on, 271
    in land, 113, 149, 222, 318, 511–513
    in mining, 504
    national debt and, 248
    in railroads, 525, 526–527
    in stocks, 525–526, 527, 705
Spencer, Herbert, 534
Spending. *See* Defense spending; Finances
    in Sun Belt, 823
Spheres of influence
    of U.S., 605, 607–608, 633
    Western Hemisphere and, 607–608, 633
Spice trade, 34
Spies, August, 574, 575
Spies and spying
    in Cold War, 788–789, 798–800
    U-2 incident and, 820–821
    in World War II, 760
Spinning, 305
Spirit of St. Louis, The (airplane), 697
Spoils system, 312, 480, 536, 541, 543
Sports, in 1920s, 696–697
Spotsylvania Court House, Battle of (1864),
    452(m), 453
Springfield, Illinois, Lincoln in, 334, 334(i),
    414, 421
Springfield, Massachusetts, 92
    gun factory in, 337
Sputnik, 820
Squanto, 86
Square Deal, 630
Squatters, 507
Stagecoach travel, 246, 304
Stagflation, 869, 907, 917, 924
    Carter and, 915, 916
Stalin, Joseph, 758
    Cold War and, 783–786
    Nazi agreement with, 755
    at Potsdam, 775
    second front and, 764, 770
    at Teheran, 771
    in World War II, 765
    at Yalta, 772
Stalingrad, battle at (1942–1943), 770
Stalwarts, 542, 543
Stamp Act (1765), 141, 151–152
    resistance to, 153–155, 157–158
Stamp Act Congress (1765), 154–155

Standard of living. *See* Consumer entries; Lifestyle; Wealth
Standard Oil Company, 528, 529–530, 534, 547, 606, 627, 628
Standing Bear, Luther, 495
Standing Rock Reservation, 503
Stanton, Edwin M., 471, 472
Stanton, Elizabeth Cady, 289, 358–359, 359(i), 469(i), 540
　on "Negro first" strategy, 472–473
　woman's suffrage movement and, 469, 599–600
Stanwix, Fort
　battle at (1777), 192, 193
　Treaty of (1784), 220–221, 222, 253
Starr, Ellen Gates, 618(i)
Starr, Kenneth, 954
START treaty. *See* Strategic Arms Reduction Talks treaty
Starvation
　during depression of 1893, 600
　on reservations, 494
"Starving time," in Jamestown, 57
"Star Wars," SDI as, 932
State(s). *See also* State sovereignty; specific states
　under Articles of Confederation, 210
　bank charters from, 318
　Bill of Rights (U.S.) and, 243, 849–850
　civil unions and domestic partnerships in, 952
　Cold War and, 800
　constitutions of, 208, 213–214
　Eisenhower and, 813
　election of 1800 and, 270
　financing for, 248
　innovation by, 943
　laws of incorporation in, 308
　in Northwest Territory, 222, 224(i)
　progressive reforms and, 625–626
　public colleges and universities in, 826
　during Reconstruction, 475–477
　restoration to Union, 462, 465–466, 475
　slavery in, 397–398, 421
　taxation by, 225
　voting rights in, 244, 291, 475
　women's rights in, 867–868
State Department, 242
　Jefferson and, 272
Statehood. *See also* specific states
　Missouri Compromise and, 292–293, 292(m)
　for territories, 222–223, 405–406, 415, 509
　for Texas, 350
　voting and, 291–292
State legislatures, 637, 930(i)
State sovereignty, under Articles of Confederation, 213–218
States' rights
　Confederate centralization and, 445
　election of 1824 and, 295
　federal power vs., 316–317

Johnson, Andrew, on, 465, 466
　Wilson and, 638, 639
States' Rights Party. *See* Dixiecrats
Statue of Liberty, 562
Status Seekers, The (Packard), 830
Steam power, 515
　steamboats, 304, 373(i)
　steam engine and, 337
　steamships and global migration, 559
Steel and steel industry
　Bessemer process in, 527
　Carnegie in, 527–528
　in Great Depression, 707
　Morgan, J. P., in, 533–534
　in New South, 537
　strikes against, 591–593, 675, 736–737
　structural steel and, 578
Steele, Walter L., 391
Steeplechase Park, 577
Steffens, Lincoln, 581, 625
Steinbacher, Joseph, 773, 774–775
Steinbeck, John, 731
Steinem, Gloria, 866
Stenographers, 569, 569(i)
Stephens, Alexander, 420, 467
Stephens, Uriah, 572
Stephenson, David, 701
Stern, Edith, 828
Stevens, Thaddeus, 470, 471
Stevenson, Adlai E., 803, 815
Stewart, Maria, 324
Stirrups, Spanish, 72, 72(i)
Stock(s)
　bank, 247, 249
　of railroads, 532–533
　speculation in, 525–526, 705
Stock market
　crash of (1929), 705–706
　regulation of, 725
　in San Francisco, 504
Stone Mountain, Georgia, Klan in, 701
Stonewall riots (1969), 863, 931(i)
Stono rebellion, 126
Stowe, Harriet Beecher, 289, 403
　Uncle Tom's Cabin, 402, 403–405
Strategic Arms Limitation Talks (SALT), 895
Strategic Arms Reduction Talks (START) treaty, 947
Strategic arms reduction treaty (1979), second, 921
Strategic Defense Initiative (SDI, "Star Wars"), 932, 935, 967
Strategic hamlets (Vietnam), 884
Streetcars, 688
Strict construction, 911, 929
Strikebreakers, 572, 574, 593, 596
Strikes. *See also* Labor; Labor unions
　by air traffic controllers, 925
　during Civil War, 449
　by coal miners, 628–630
　by Cripple Creek miners, 594
　by garment workers, 622
　in Great Depression, 712, 735–736

Great Railroad Strike (1877), 570–572,
    571(i), 594, 596
Great Southwest Strike, 573
Homestead, 591–593
Knights of Labor and, 573
at McCormick reaper works, 574
Pullman, 594–597
against railroads, 570–572, 594–597
after World War I, 674(i), 675
in World War II, 762
after World War II, 792–793
Strip-mining, 919
Stuart, Gilbert, 281(i)
Stuart, James E. B. ("Jeb"), 436
Student Nonviolent Coordinating Committee
    (SNCC), 851, 857
Students. *See also* Young people
    protests by, 861–862, 890–891, 892, 897
Students for a Democratic Society (SDS),
    861, 889
Submarines
    in Civil War, 439
    Polaris nuclear submarine, 820
    in World War I, 657–658, 659
    in World War II, 758, 760, 762, 764
Subsidies
    in Great Society, 849
    in New Deal, 730
Subsistence lifestyle. *See* Hunter-gatherers
Substitutes, in Civil War draft, 449
Subtreasury plan, of Populists, 590
Suburbs
    growth of, 811, 812, 823
    racism and, 823
    white flight to, 910–911
Subversives, in Red scare of 1950s, 799
Subway system, 579
Sudetenland, 755
Suez Canal, 764
Suez crisis (1956), 819–820
Suffrage. *See also* Voting and voting rights;
        Woman suffrage
    black, 216, 460(i), 462, 470, 599
    Fourteenth Amendment and, 468–469
    for men, 215–216, 389–390, 475, 647
    in states, 291–292, 475
    World War I and, 665–666
Sugar Act (Revenue Act, 1764), 141, 150–
    151, 151(i), 156
Sugar and sugar industry
    in Hawai'i, 606
    Portuguese plantations and, 31
    slavery and, 73–75, 372
    in South, 371–372
    trade and, 115
    in West Indies, 73–75
Sugar islands. *See* Guadeloupe; Martinique
Sugarman, Tracy, 771
Sullivan, John, 194, 196
Sullivan, Louis, 579
Summit meetings, at Geneva (1955), 820
Sumner, Charles, 399, 412, 469, 470
Sumner, William Graham, 534

Sumter, Fort, attack on, 428
Sun Belt, 811, 821, 823–826, 824(m)
    conservatism in, 908
Sunday closings, of commercial establish-
        ments, 621
Sun Falcon. *See* Ancient Americans
Sunni Muslims, 968
Sunoco, 529
Super Fortress. *See* B-29 Super Fortress
Superfund, 919
Superpowers
    in arms race, 820–821
    after Cold War, 947
    global rivalry of, 790–791
    U.S. as, 776–777, 783
Supply-side economics, 924–925
Supreme Court (U.S.). *See also* specific cases
    on abortion rights, 930, 930(i)
    African American challenges to, 832–834
    Agricultural Adjustment Act and, 730
    antidiscrimination policies and, 928
    on antisodomy laws, 932
    antitrust law and, 547, 627–628
    Burger Court and, 911
    Bush, G. H. W., and, 943
    Bush, G. W., and, 961, 964
    business and, 535
    Californio land claims and, 507
    on campaign spending, 914
    Cherokee removal and, 315
    on Colfax massacre attackers, 484
    conservatism of, 911, 929, 943
    on Constitution, 272
    Coolidge and, 686
    on election of 2000, 962
    Jay as chief justice, 242–243
    on labor unions, 535
    liberalism of, 909
    National Recovery Administration and, 730
    Nixon and, 911
    Obama and, 971
    on *Pentagon Papers,* 898
    on personal liberty laws, 418
    on railroad regulation, 546–547
    Reagan and, 929–930
    reconstruction and, 481–482
    Roosevelt, F. D., and, 741–742
    separate but equal doctrine and, 646
    on slavery in territories, 413–414
    Title IX and, 928–929
    Warren Court and, 911
    Wilson and, 641
    women on, 929–930, 951, 964, 971
    on women's equality, 867
    on workday, 623
Surplus (agricultural), in Great Depression,
    744(i)
Surplus (financial), 546
    under Clinton, 951
"Survival of the fittest," 534
Susan Constant (ship), 56
Sweatshops, 565, 566
Switzerland, immigrants from, 504

Syphilis, 36
Syria, 933
    Six-Day War and, 895–896
    Yom Kippur War and, 896
"Systematized shop management" (Taylor),
        624–625

Taft, Robert A., 803
Taft, William Howard, 626
    dollar diplomacy of, 637
    election of 1908 and, 635–636
    election of 1912 and, 638–639, 640(m)
    tariffs and, 636
Taft-Hartley Act (1947), 797
Taino people, 32–33
Taiwan, Nationalist Chinese on, 791
Takeovers, 925, 927
Taliban (Afghanistan), 966, 972
Tallmadge, James, Jr., 293
Tammany Hall, 580–581, 702
Tanaghrisson (Mingo Indians), 144
Taney, Roger B., 413, 418
Tarbell, Ida M., 529–530
Tariffs. See also specific tariffs
    of Abominations (1828), 312, 316–317
    American System and, 295
    Fordney-McCumber (1922), 686
    McKinley, 546, 606
    on molasses, 150
    NAFTA and, 958
    Payne-Aldrich, 636, 637
    Taft and, 636
    as trade barriers, 958
    Underwood (1913), 640
    Wilson and, 640
Tarleton, Banastre, 199, 200–201
Task system, 126
Taverns, 151(i), 540
Taxation. See also Duties; Income tax; specific
        presidents and acts
    under Articles of Confederation, 210, 219
    Bush, G. H. W., and, 943
    Bush, G. W., and, 963
    capital gains, 916
    Carter and, 916
    census and, 247(i)
    Civil War and, 433, 448
    Clinton and, 951
    in colonies, 69, 140, 150–152, 155, 162
    Constitution on, 229, 230
    Eisenhower and, 813
    external and internal, 153
    income tax and, 637, 640, 925
    Jefferson and, 272
    Johnson, L. B., and, 890
    Kennedy, John F., and, 844
    New Deal reforms in, 738
    Proposition 13 revolt against, 909(i)
    Reagan and, 924–925
    revolts against, 909(i), 910
    right of, 151
    on slaves, 391
    in South, 477, 483

    Stamp Act and, 141, 151–152, 153–155
    by states, 225
    on tea, 161–163
    Townshend duties and, 156–157
    Vietnam War and, 890
    on whiskey, 245, 250–251
    windfall profits, 917
Taxation without representation, 152, 154,
        157, 162, 170
    women's voting rights and, 215
Tax Reform Act (1986), 925
Taylor, Frederick Winslow, 624–625
Taylor, Maxwell, 883
Taylor, Walter H., 455(i)
Taylor, Zachary, 401
    election of 1848 and, 399–400, 407(m)
    free soil and, 400
    in Mexican American War, 351
Tea
    Dutch, 162
    protests against British, 161–163
    tax on, 162
Tea Act (1773), 141, 162
Teachers, women as, 320, 340, 568
Tea Party revolt, 972
Teapot Dome scandal, 686
Technocrats, 624
Technology. See also Automobiles; Weapons;
        specific types
    agriculture, industry, and, 821–823
    communications, 958
    Eisenhower and, 816
    European in New World, 35
    for mining, 505–506
Tecumseh (Shawnee Indians), 267–269,
        268(i), 283
    Tippecanoe and, 281–282
Teenagers. See Young people
Teheran, U.S. hostages in, 922
Teheran conference (1943), 771
Tejanos, 347, 507, 515
Telegraph, 339, 448, 526, 530
Telephone, 530
Television
    culture, politics, and (1950s), 829–830
    presidential debates on, 843
    Vietnam War on, 888
Temperance, 357. See also Alcohol and alco-
        holism; Prohibition
    movement, 322, 540–541
    "pledge," 323(i)
    women and, 540–541, 586, 587, 598–599
Temporary Emergency Relief Administration
        (New York), 720
Tenant farmers
    New Deal and, 728, 731(i), 743
    poor southern whites as, 384
    in Revolutionary War, 187
    in South, 127
    in West, 515
Tenements, 577
    photography of, 563–564
Tennent, William, 131

Tennessee, 429, 462, 469, 493
  Civil War in, 435(m), 438, 451, 452(m)
  Revolutionary War in, 194
Tennessee Coal and Iron Company, 631, 637
Tennessee Valley Authority (TVA), 726–727, 726(m)
Tenochtitlán, 20, 37, 38, 39
Tenskwatawa (Prophet, Shawnee Indians), 267–268, 282
Tenth Amendment, 243
Tenure of Office Act (1867), 471, 472
Termination program, for Indians, 813–814
Term limits, under Articles of Confederation, 210
Territories. See also specific types
  government in, 509–510
  popular sovereignty in, 399
  slavery in, 397–399, 400–401, 405–406, 412–414, 415, 441
  statehood for, 405–406
Terrorism
  by Klan, 474–475, 480, 481
  in Middle East, 957
  by nonstate organizations, 933
  in Oklahoma City, 952
  September 11, 2001, attacks, and, 965–967, 965(i)
  southern Democratic party and, 483–484
Tet Offensive (1968), 891
Teton Sioux Indians, 17
Texas, 368, 368(m)
  Anglo-Americans in, 347–348, 507
  annexation of, 349
  boundary of, 351
  Britain and, 349
  immigrants in, 341
  independence from Mexico, 348
  Lone Star Republic in, 348
  manifest destiny and, 493
  Mexican Americans in, 507, 825
  Mexico and, 349
  New Mexico boundary with, 400, 401
  secession and, 420
  Spain and, 39, 275, 294
  Tejanos in, 347, 507, 515
Texas Rangers, 507
Texcoco, Lake, 20
Textbooks, free labor and, 340
Textiles and textile industry. See also
    Clothing; Cotton and cotton industry
  immigrants in, 566
  mechanization in, 305, 565–566
  in South, 537
Thames, Battle of the (1813), 269, 283
Thatcher, Margaret, 923
Thayendanegea (Joseph Brant). See Brant, Joseph
Their Eyes Were Watching God (Hurston), 696
Thieu, Nguyen Van, 899(i)
Third parties, 330, 536, 893, 950. See also
    specific groups
Third Reich, Nazi Germany as, 755
Third world, 556(m), 557, 879

Kennedy, J.F., and, 880–881
  Vietnam War and, 900
Thirteenth Amendment, 466, 486
Thirty-eighth parallel (Korea), 802, 804
Thomas, Clarence, 943–945
Thomas, Norman, 712
Thoreau, Henry David, 357
Three-fifths clause, 229, 285
Three Mile Island nuclear facility, 917
Threshers, 515
Thurmond, J. Strom, 797, 911
Thygeson, Sylvie, 568, 570
Tiananmen Square demonstrations, Beijing, 947
Tianjin (Tientsin) treaty (1858), 607
Tibbets, Paul, 749–751, 750(i), 760, 770, 775
Ticonderoga, Fort, 146, 192
Tiffany, William, 610
Tilden, Samuel J., 484–485
Till, Emmett, 833
Tillman, Benjamin, 603
Tilyou, George, 577
Time magazine, 925
Tippecanoe
  Battle of (1811), 282
  Tecumseh and, 281–282
Title(s), of President, 242
Title VII, of Civil Rights Act (1964), 853, 861
Title IX, of Education Amendments Act (1972), 867, 870–871, 928–929
Tlaxcala and Tlaxcalan people, 38
Tobacco and tobacco industry
  in Carolina, 75
  in Chesapeake, 60–67
  European consumers of, 36
  slavery and, 63, 127
  in South, 122, 371–372, 537
  taxation on, 69
  trade in, 66
  wrapper for, 76(i)
Tobasco people, 36, 37
Tocqueville, Alexis de, 367
Todd, Albert, 378
Todd, Dolley Payne. See Madison, Dolley
Tojo, Hideki (Japan), 759
Toleration. See Religious toleration
Tools, of ancient Americans, 4, 8–9
Toombs, Robert, 399, 417, 428
Tordesillas, Treaty of (1494), 33, 41, 42(m)
Tories, loyalists as, 187, 189
Toronto (York), in War of 1812, 283
Tosques, Nick, 804
Tourism, in World War I, 662
Toussaint L'Ouverture, 258, 259(i)
Town meetings, in New England, 91–92
Townsend, Francis, 733, 737
Townshend, Charles, 156–157
Townshend duties, 141, 156–157, 161
Townships, in Northwest Territory, 223(m)
Toxic wastes
  Love Canal disaster and, 917–919
  Superfund for cleanup of, 919

Trade. *See also* Commerce; Exploration; Free trade; Market(s); Ships and shipping; Slave trade; Transportation; specific products
agricultural export, 245
under Articles of Confederation, 210
with Asia, 343
in Atlantic region, 30–31, 114(m), 115–116
with China, 608, 633, 635
during Civil War, 440
in Cold War, 790
colonial, 69, 101–103, 131–135, 165
with Comanche, 279
deficits, 914
expansion of, 606–607
Mediterranean, 29–30
Native Americans and, 18, 58, 98, 142–143, 149
neutrality and, 257
in New England, 94, 112
in West Indies, 257
Trade barriers, NAFTA and, 958
Trade routes, European (15th century), 28(m)
Trades (occupations), apprenticeships in, 321
Trade unions, 573, 689. *See also* Labor unions
Trading posts, 148. *See also* Fort(s)
Trading with the Enemy Act (1917), 668
Trail(s). *See also* specific trails
cattle, 512(m)
pioneers on, 345
Trail of Tears, 314, 316
Traitors, in Revolution, 189
Transatlantic region, trade in, 245
Transcendentalism, 357
Transcontinental railroad, 344, 405, 448, 507, 510, 525, 526, 561
Trans-Mississippi West, 274
land rush in, 510
railroad growth in, 524(m)
Transportation. *See also* Railroads; Roads and highways; specific types
in cities, 563, 579
of crops, 66
improvements in, 304–305
integration of, 851
mass transit, 563
in New England, 113
segregation of, 477
Travel
improvements in, 245–246
times from New York City, 246, 246(m)
Treason. *See also* Red scare, in 1950s; Traitors
in Civil War, 450
in Revolutionary War, 182, 199–200, 199(i)
Treasury Department, 242
under Articles of Confederation, 210
Hamilton and, 239
Jefferson and, 272
Treaties. *See also* specific treaties and wars
with France, 263

with Indians, 69, 220–221, 222, 252, 313, 315, 813–814
with Tripoli, 273
Tredegar Iron Works, 445
Trees, agriculture and, 336
Trench warfare, in World War I, 651–652, 662
Triangle Shirtwaist Company
fire at, 621–622
strike at, 621
Tribes. *See* Native Americans; specific groups
Tribute, to Mexica, 21
Trickle-down economics, 706–707, 927–928
Tripartite Pact (1940), 759
Triple Alliance, 655
Triple Entente, 655, 658–659
Tripoli, 272–273
Trolleys, 689
Troubled Assets Relief Program (2008), 971
Troy Female Seminary, New York, 289
Trucking industry, deregulation of, 916
Truman, Harry S., 876, 911
assumption of presidency, 773
atomic bomb and, 750(i), 775
China and, 885
civil rights and, 795
Cold War and, 782, 786–790
containment and, 786
desegregation of armed forces by, 795
economy and, 783, 792–794
election of 1944 and, 769
election of 1948 and, 795, 797
election of 1952 and, 803
Fair Deal and, 792–800
Indian policies and, 814
on Jewish state, 791
Korean War and, 801–802
loyalty oaths and, 799
MacArthur and, 801, 802
national security state and, 788–790
at Potsdam, 776
Soviet Union and, 785, 790–791
Truman Doctrine, 786–788, 800
Trumbull, John, 240(i)
Trumbull, Lyman, 467
Trust(s), 529, 547, 627–628, 637, 638, 641
Truth, Sojourner, 360
Tubman, Harriet, 361, 403
Tunis, 272
Tunney, Gene, 697
Turkey, 881
Greece and, 670
immigrants from, 505, 559
after World War II, 786–787
Turner, Frederick Jackson, 489–490, 491, 517, 518
Turner, Nat, 365–366, 366(i), 382
Turner, West, 379
Turnpikes, 245, 304
Tuskegee Institute, 645
Twain, Mark (Samuel Langhorne Clemens), 521–523, 522(i), 613
on baseball, 577

on Comstock Lode, 504
on Gilded Age, 517, 521–522
Tweed, William Marcy ("Boss"), 580–581
Twelfth Amendment (1804), 270, 296
Twelve Years a Slave (Northup), 404–405
20th Century Fox, 959
Twentieth Amendment, 421
Twenty-first Amendment, 692
"Twenty-Negro law," 446
Twenty-sixth Amendment, 870
Two Moons (Cheyenne chief), 498
Tyler, John, 349
Tyler, William, 68–69
Typewriter (machine), 568
"Typewriters" (secretarial workers), 565, 568, 569

U-boats. *See also* Submarines
    in World War I, 657–658, 659
    in World War II, 758, 760, 762, 764
UFW. *See* United Farm Workers
UN. *See* United Nations
Uncle Tom's Cabin (Stowe), 402, 403–405, 404(i)
Unconscious, Freud on, 690
Underconsumption, Great Depression and, 723, 728
Underground railroad, 361, 403
Underwood tariff (1913), 640
Undocumented aliens, 960. *See also* Illegal immigrants
Unemployment
    Carter and, 916
    in depression of 1870s, 481, 565
    in depression of 1890s, 549, 565, 594, 600–602
    in Great Depression, 706, 707, 710, 743
    indentured servitude and, 63
    inflation and, 907
    Kennedy, John F., and, 844
    New Deal relief for, 734
    in 1920s, 686
    Nixon and, 869
    Obama and, 971
    panic of 1819 and, 308–309
    after World War I, 674
Unemployment insurance, 565, 737
Unification. *See also* Albany Plan of Union
    of Germany, 947
    Hutchinson on colonial, 140
Unilateralism, in foreign policy of Bush, G. W., 961
Union (labor). *See* Labor unions
Union (U.S.). *See also* North (Civil War)
    under Articles of Confederation, 210
    collapse of, 416–421
    Lincoln on, 421, 427
Union blockade. *See* Blockades, in Civil War
Unionists, in South, 418, 420, 427, 429–430, 465
Union Party, 733
Union Signal, 598
United Auto Workers (UAW), 736

United Farm Workers (UFW), 860–861
United Fruit Company, 608, 818
United Mine Workers (UMW), 628–629, 630, 735, 762
United Nations (UN), 772, 777, 915
    Charter of, 773
    Iraq War (2003–2011) and, 968
    Korean War and, 800–805
    Persian Gulf War and, 945–946
    Somalia and, 956
    total nuclear test ban treaty and, 947
United States. *See* Constitution (U.S.);
    Government (U.S.); specific issues
U.S. Communist Party. *See* Communist Party
U.S. Congress. *See* Congress (U.S.)
U.S. Constitution. *See* Constitution (U.S.)
U.S. Government. *See* Government (U.S.)
U.S. Post Office, 245, 304
U.S. Sanitary Commission, 449
U.S. Steel (USX), 533–534, 631, 637, 736
U.S. Supreme Court. *See* Supreme Court (U.S.)
United States v. Cruikshank (1876), 481
United States v. E. C. Knight Company (1895), 547
United Students against Sweatshops, 958
Universal education, 340
Universal male suffrage, 475, 538, 647
Universal Negro Improvement Association (UNIA), 694
Universal woman suffrage act (1870, Utah), 509
Universities and colleges. *See also* Higher education; specific schools
    antiwar protest in, 889
    Bakke case and, 911
    in 1830s, 320
    Morrill Act and, 448
    women in, 864
University of California, 908
    free speech movement at Berkeley, 861–862
University of Chicago, women at, 862
University of Mississippi, African Americans in, 853
Unsafe at Any Speed (Nader), 847
Unskilled workers, 559–560, 643
Unterseebooten. See U-boats
Upcountry, yeomen in, 383–384
Upper house, in states, 214
Upper South, 122. *See also* South
    secession and, 421, 427, 428–429
"Uprising of the twenty thousand" (garment workers' strike), 622
Uprisings. *See* Protest(s); Revolts and rebellions
Upward mobility, poor southern whites and, 385
Urban areas. *See also* Cities and towns; specific locations
    housing in, 744
    vs. rural values, 702
    uprisings in, 855–858, 857(m)

Urban industrialism, 504, 575, 583
    progressivism and, 619, 648
    social problems of, 617
    women activists and, 598
Urbanization. *See also* Cities and towns
    produce markets and, 515
Urban renewal, 843–844, 849
USA Patriot Act (2001), 966
USX. *See* U.S. Steel
Utah, 346–347, 401, 493, 505, 508
    women's voting rights in, 599(i), 600
Utopians, 357, 358
U-2 spy plane incident, 820

Vaccines, polio, 812
Vagrancy, black codes and, 466
Valentino, Rudolph, 696
Vallandigham, Clement, 450
Vallejo, Mariano, 356
Valley Forge, Continental Army at, 193
Van Buren, Martin
    election of 1832 and, 326
    election of 1836 and, 326–328
    election of 1840 and, 329
    election of 1848 and, 399, 407(m)
    Indian removal and, 316
    as secretary of state, 312
    South and, 327
Vandenberg, Arthur, 786
Vanderbilt family
    Alice, 564
    Alva, 564
    Cornelius ("Commodore"), 526, 527, 564,
        568
    William K., 564
Vanzetti, Bartolomeo, 700
Vaqueros, 514–515
Vaux, Calvert, 579
Venezuela, 608, 633
Veracruz
    Marines in, 654
    in Mexican-American War, 353
Verrazano, Giovanni da, 48
Versailles, Paris Peace Conference at, 669
Versailles treaty (1919), 672–673, 754
Vertical integration, 528
Vesey, Denmark, 388
Vespucci, Amerigo, 34
Veterans
    African American, 678, 794–795
    in colleges and universities, 827
    in Great Depression, 711–712, 734
    of Vietnam War, 897–898, 900–901
    after World War I, 673, 674(i)
    after World War II, 794
Veterans Administration (VA), 823, 876(i),
    901
Vetoes
    by Bush, George H. W., 943
    by Cleveland, 563
    by Jackson, 312, 318
    by Johnson, Andrew, 468, 471

    by Nixon, 911
    presidential, 230
    by Reagan, 929
    Virginia Plan and, 229
Vice, urban, 620–621
Vice president. *See* Elections; specific indi-
    viduals
Vichy France, 756
Vicksburg, Mississippi (1863), siege of, 450–
    451, 452(m)
Victoria (England), 490(i)
Victory Gardens, 767
Vienna, Austria, Kennedy-Khrushchev meet-
    ing in, 879–880
Vietcong, 882, 884, 887, 891, 898
Vietminh, 817
Vietnam. *See also* Indochina
    China and, 900
    containment policy toward, 817–818
Vietnamization policy, in Vietnam War, 891,
    896
Vietnam Veterans Memorial (1982), 901
Vietnam War (1964–1975), 875–876, 883(m),
    911. *See also* Vietnam
    African Americans soldiers in, 887–888
    Americanization of, 886–887
    antiwar protests against, 889–891, 889(i)
    atrocities in, 898, 900–901
    bombings in, 884, 885, 886–887, 899
    casualties in, 877, 884, 888, 891, 896
    as civil war, 876, 885, 900–901
    costs and effects of, 901–902
    helicopters in, 875
    Johnson, L. B., and, 848, 876, 884–885,
        886
    Kennedy and, 876, 882–884
    legacy of, 900–901
    morale in, 898
    Nixon and, 876, 896–897, 899–900
    peace accords and, 898–899, 900
    peace negotiations in (1968), 891–892
    pro-war demonstrations, 890
    refugees in, 888, 891, 899, 899(i)
    soldiers in, 875–876, 883(m), 887–888
    student protests against, 862
    Tet Offensive in, 891
    veterans of, 897–898, 900–901
Vigilance committees, runaway slaves and, 403
Vigilantes
    against African Americans, 739, 795
    Paxton Boys as, 148–149
    in World War I, 667
Vikings, 27
Villa, Francisco ("Pancho"), 654–655, 655(i)
Villages. *See also* Settlement(s)
    Indian, 59
    Mogollon, 13
Vincennes, Fort, battle at, 196
Violence. *See also* Race riots; Riots; Strikes;
        specific conflicts
    at female antislavery convention, 325
    Klan and political, 483–484

Violence against Women Act (1994), 951
Virginia, 462. *See also* Chesapeake region;
        House of Burgesses; Jamestown;
        Tobacco and tobacco industry
    Bacon's Rebellion in, 69–71
    bill of rights in, 214, 216
    Civil War in, 434, 435(m), 452(m), 453–454,
        455
    as colony, 60, 61(m), 68–69
    constitutional ratification and, 234, 235
    Jamestown colony in, 53–55
    national capital and, 248
    population of, 121
    Readjusters in, 538
    secession of, 429
    slavery in, 218
    Turner rebellion in, 365–366
    voting rights in, 128
    western lands of, 119, 149, 208, 211
Virginia (ironclad), 435(m), 439
Virginia and Kentucky Resolutions (1798),
        262, 316–317
Virginia City, 504, 505
Virginia Company, 55, 56, 57, 60
Virginia Convention, 207–208
Virginia Plan, 228–229
Virginia Resolves, 152, 154
Virtual representation, 152, 154–155
Virtue
    feminine, in South, 376
    republican motherhood and, 244
    use of term, 245
    women's vs. men's, 320
Visible saints, Puritan, 90
VISTA. *See* Volunteers in Service to America
Vitascope, 531(i)
Volunteers, in Civil War, 449
Volunteers in Service to America (VISTA),
        845
Voter Education Project (1961), 851
Voting and voting rights. *See also* Elections;
        Popular vote; Woman suffrage
    African Americans and, 292, 461, 466,
        471, 472, 599, 645, 795, 832, 840–842,
        852–853, 852(i), 853–854, 854(m),
        856(m)
    Baker v. Carr and, 849
    in colonies, 60, 68–69
    Constitution on, 243–244
    in election of 1824, 296
    in election of 1860, 419
    Fifteenth Amendment and, 472–473
    Fourteenth Amendment and, 468–469
    for free blacks, 292
    for freedmen, 471
    gender gap in, 929
    in Massachusetts, 91–92
    New Deal and, 745
    in 1920s, 692–693
    Nineteenth Amendment and, 600
    property qualifications and, 214, 291
    during Reconstruction, 460, 475

    in South, 128, 389–390, 483(i)
    voter turnout and, 536
    in West, 298, 665, 666(m)
    for women, 179, 215, 292, 461, 469, 598,
        599–600, 623–624, 644–645, 665–666,
        666(m)
    for young people, 870, 887
Voting Rights Act (1965), 847, 853
    extension of, 870, 928
Voyages of exploration. *See also* Exploration
    by Columbus, 26–27, 32–34
    of Magellan, 34–35

Wabash v. Illinois (1886), 547
Waco, Texas, religious cult in, 952
Wade, Benjamin, 462
Wade-Davis bill (1864), 462
Wage labor, 306–307, 514, 515, 559, 564–565,
        570. *See also* Free labor; Labor
    freedmen and, 478
Wages
    in Comstock, 506
    equal pay for equal work, 622, 864
    at Ford, 690
    freeze in, 869
    in Gilded Age, 565
    in Great Depression, 725
    of management, 568
    in manufacturing, 566, 689
    for men vs. women, 927
    in 1929, 705
    in Pullman, 595
    in shoe industry, 307
    for women, 448–449, 566, 767
    in World War I, 664
Wagner, Fort, Battle of (1863), 444
Wagner, Robert, 735, 744
Wagner Act (NLRA, 1935), 735–736, 742
Wagon trains, 344, 345, 345(i)
Waite, Davis H., 594
Wake Island, 763
Wald, Lillian, 620
Waldseemüller, Martin, 34
Walker, David, 324, 366
Walker, Quok, 216
Walking city, 563
"Walking Purchase," 119
Wallace, George C., 892, 893
Wallace, Henry A., 786, 797
Wall Street
    crash of 1929 and, 705
    New Deal and, 723
    Roosevelt, T., and, 628
Wall Street Journal, 889
Wall Street Reform and Consumer Protection
        Act (2010), 971
Wampanoag Indians, 86
    King Philip's War and, 103
War(s) and warfare. *See* Guerrilla war;
        specific battles, wars, and leaders
War crimes. *See also* Milosevic, Slobodan
    in Vietnam War, 898

Ward, Lester Frank, 624
War debts. *See also* Debt
    after Revolution, 210, 218–219, 225, 240,
      257
War Department, 242
War Hawks, War of 1812 and, 282–283, 286
War Industries Board (WIB), 664
Warm Springs, Georgia, 719
Warner, Charles Dudley, 521, 526–527
War of 1812, 269, 279, 282–286, 284(m)
    Native Americans and, 298
    Washington City in, 285
War of attrition
    Grant and, 438, 451
    Westmoreland and, 887
War on Poverty, 845, 846, 849
War Powers Act (1973), 900
War Production Board, 762
Warren, Earl, 833, 844, 849–850, 911
Warren, Mercy Otis, 232–233
Warriors, Mexica, 21
Wars of liberation, Khrushchev and, 879
Wartime Reconstruction (Civil War), 461–
    464
Washington (state), 516(i)
Washington, Booker T., 476(i), 645–646, 647
Washington, D.C., 578. *See also* Capital city;
    March on Washington entries;
    Washington City
    abolition of slavery in, 401, 441
    antiwar protests in, 889
    Bonus Marchers in, 711–712
    Coxey's army in, 601–602
    integration of public facilities in, 834
    race riot in (1968), 857
    terrorist attack on Pentagon in, 965–966
    woman suffrage march in, 644, 644(i)
Washington, Fort, 185, 253
Washington, George
    cabinet of, 242–243
    Constitution and, 228, 234
    Continental army and, 176
    diplomacy by, 251
    at First Continental Congress, 165
    Indians and, 194, 252–253
    Newburgh Conspiracy and, 220
    as president, 242
    on prisoners of war, 190
    in Revolutionary War, 177–178, 183,
      185–186, 192–194, 201
    in Seven Years' War, 144, 145
    slaves of, 218
    Whiskey Rebellion and, 250–251
Washington, Lawrence and **Augustine,**
    142–144
Washington, Martha, 271
    slaves freed by, 218
Washington City, 271. *See also* Washington,
    D.C.
    burning of (1814), 285–286
Washington Disarmament Conference, 688
Washington Monument, 528
Washington Post, on U.S. empire, 613

Water
    in New England, 82(m)
    travel by, 304
Watergate scandal, 899, 907, 908, 912–913,
    914
Water pollution, 870, 919, 925. *See also*
    Environment
Water power, 633
Watson, Tom, 589, 600, 604
Watt, James, 925
Watts riots (1965), 856(m), 857, 908
"Waving the bloody shirt," 480, 484, 536
Wayne, Anthony ("Mad Anthony"), 255
WCTU. *See* Woman's Christian Temperance
    Union
We (Lindbergh), 697
Wealth
    of adult white men, 341
    distribution of, 564, 925
    exploration and, 36
    in Gilded Age, 526, 534, 564, 619
    in gold rush, 356–357
    in Mexica society, 21, 37–38
    in middle colonies, 121
    in New England, 115–116
    in 1920s, 686
    in 1929, 705
    under Reagan, 925, 926–927
    social Darwinism on, 534, 535
    in South, 127–128, 476
    Spanish colonial, 47–48, 49
    tax cuts and, 925
    of women, 341
Wealth gap, 564, 619
    in 1979-1987, 927–928
    in 1990s, 955
Weapons. *See also* Nuclear weapons; specific
    types
    ancient, 4, 7, 7(i), 9
    biological, 967
    in Civil War, 433
    Eisenhower and, 818
    Hotchkiss rapid-fire guns, 503
    Native American, 18
    poison gas in World War I as, 653, 662
    in Vietnam War, 884
    in World War II, 757
Weapons of mass destruction, Iraq War
    (2003–2011) and, 968
Webb, Sheyann, 850
Weber, Brian, 928
Webster, Daniel, 328, 400–401
Wehrmacht (German army), 755, 758, 770
Weights and measures, decimal system of,
    297
Welch, Jack, 958
Weld, Ezra Greenleaf, 361(i)
Welfare and welfare system
    AFDC and, 952–953
    Clinton and, 952–953
    in Confederacy, 446
    Eisenhower and, 812
    in New Deal, 726, 733–740, 746

Nixon and, 868–869
Reagan and, 926
women's movement and, 866
Welfare capitalism, 689
Welfare state
in New Deal, 733–740
private, 822
Wells, Ida B., antilynching campaign of, 538–540, 539(i), 550
Wellstone, Paul, 964
Welsh immigrants, 504
Werowance (subordinate chief), 54
Wesley, John and **Charles,** 111
West (U.S. region). *See also* Pacific Ocean region; Sun Belt; Westward movement
Articles of Confederation and, 210, 211
Civil War in, 429–430, 435(m), 437–438, 450–451, 452(m)
cowboys in, 513–514
diversity in, 506–509
economy in, 516
farming in, 448, 510–513, 515–517, 589
free labor in, 398
free silver and, 547–548, 549, 603
in Gilded Age, 517–518
grassroots conservatism in, 908
Homestead Act and, 448
homesteaders in, 510–513
Indians and, 491, 492(m), 493–498
Indian war in Revolution and (1777–1782), 195(m)
irrigation in, 632
land in, 149, 212(m), 493, 510, 512(m), 513
manifest destiny and, 493
mining in, 504–506, 512(m)
movement to, 811
railroads in, 513, 524(m)
ranching in, 507, 513–514
Revolutionary War in, 193–196, 195(m)
and settlement after Revolution, 218
southern and northern views of, 397
Sun Belt and, 823
territorial annexations and, 336
territorial government in, 509–510
Turner on, 489–490, 491
voting in, 298
woman suffrage in, 509, 599(i), 600, 644–645, 665
West Africa
kinship in, 126–127
slaves from, 109
West Bank, 896, 921, 933, 957
West Berlin, 788
Soviets and, 880
West Coast. *See* Pacific Ocean region
Western Electric, 530
Western Europe. *See also* Europe and Europeans; specific locations
common economic market in, 947
after World War II, 786–787
Western Federation of Miners (WFM), 594, 643

Western Hemisphere. *See also* America(s); Exploration; Latin America; specific locations
European exploration and, 35
human habitation of, 5–6
Monroe Doctrine and, 294–295, 607–608, 654
Western Union, 526
Western world, U.S. dominance in, 777
West Florida, Spain and, 275
West Germany, 785, 788
Berlin Wall and, 880, 947, 949(i)
West India Company (Dutch), 98, 99
West Indies
Carolina and, 75
English, 196
France and, 196, 257
in 17th century, 74(m)
slaves and, 71, 73–75, 118, 124
sugar in, 71, 73–75
Westinghouse, George W., 530
Westmoreland, William, 887
West Point, 199–200
West Virginia, 430, 571
Westward movement, 342–348. *See also* West (U.S. region)
cotton kingdom and, 367–369
economy and, 339
Indians and, 251–253
Jefferson and, 273–279
Louisiana Purchase and, 274–275
manufacturing and, 337
in Ohio Valley, 144
into Oregon Country, 343–346
by pioneers, 345, 345(i)
"Wetbacks," use of term, 826(i)
Weyler, Valeriano ("Butcher"), 609
What Social Classes Owe to Each Other (Sumner), 534
Wheat, 120, 515
Wheatley, Phillis, 168, 169(i)
Whig Party (Whigs), 310
Bank War and, 317–318
collapse of, 407–408
election of 1828 and, 311
election of 1836 and, 328
election of 1840 and, 329
election of 1848 and, 399–400
Lincoln in, 414
Mexican-American War and, 352
sectionalism in, 407
in South, 390
Whippings, of blacks, 375, 375(i), 463
Whiskey, taxation of, 245, 250–251, 272
Whiskey Rebellion (1794), 245, 250–251
White, Hugh Lawson, 328
White, John, 49
White, William Allen, 610
White City (World's Columbian Exposition), 489, 582
White-collar workers, 565, 568–570
Great Depression and, 713
White Eyes (Delaware Indians), 194

Whitefield, George, 131
White House
    British burning of, 285
    naming of, 281
White Lion (ship), 63
"White list" of NCL, 623
White male suffrage, 389–390
Whites
    abolitionism and, 360
    in Chesapeake, 76–77, 122
    emancipation and, 324, 464
    as immigrants, 559
    in Indian lands, 313
    in Mexican War, 352
    movement to South and West by, 699(m)
    in 1950s, 826
    opportunities for, 339–340
    patriotism of women in Revolutionary
        War and, 186
    progressivism for male, 644–647
    vs. slaves as servants, 125
    social Darwinism and, 535, 561
    in South, 127, 459, 538
    in southern Democratic Party, 482–483,
        536
    as southern poor, 384–385
    in southern Republican Party, 474, 482
    voting qualifications for, 214–215
    in World War I, 662
White supremacy
    African Americans in North and, 361
    Ku Klux Klan and, 475
    Reconstruction and, 482–484
    in South, 369, 538, 645, 720
    support for, 646
"White terror," 474–475
Whitewater scandal, 954
Whitman, Marcus and Narcissa, 345(i)
Whitman, Walt, 427
Whitney, Eli, 245, 372
Whyte, William H., Jr., 830
Wichita Indians, 344
Wigglesworth, Michael, 95
Wilderness, preservation of, 632
Wilderness, Battle of the (1864), 452(m), 453
Wilhelm II (Germany), 655, 657, 663
Wilkinson, Eliza, 187
Wilkinson, Jemima, 288
Willard, Emma Hart, 289, 289(i)
Willard, Frances, 586–588, 587(i), 614
    Woman's Christian Temperance Union
        and, 541, 597, 598–599
William III (of Orange, English king), 104
William and Mary, College of, 366
Williams, Roger, 81–83, 92
Williamsburg, Virginia, battle at, 200
Willkie, Wendell, 757
Wilmot, David, 396, 398, 421
Wilmot Proviso (1846), 396, 397–399, 401,
    410
Wilson, Charles, 818
Wilson, Edith, 666

Wilson, Woodrow, 637, 638
    election of 1912 and, 639, 640(m)
    election of 1916 and, 641–642, 658
    election of 1920 and, 679
    foreign policy of, 653–657
    Fourteen Points of, 668–669
    League of Nations and, 669, 671–672
    progressivism and, 640, 641–642
    reforms and, 639–641, 641–642
    segregation and, 647
    on women's rights, 644, 666
    World War I and, 653, 657, 658, 664
Wind Cave National Park, 634(m)
Windfall profits tax, 917
Winnemucca, Sarah, 494
Winthrop, John (father), 81, 82, 86–87, 89,
    92, 105
Winthrop, John (son), 87
Wiretapping, 967
Wisconsin, 336, 412, 625
Witches and witchcraft, 96–97, 97(i)
Wives. *See* Married women; Women
Wobblies. *See* Industrial Workers of the World
Wolfensohn, James D., 959
Woman Rebel (newspaper), 643
Woman's Christian Temperance Union
    (WCTU), 541, 597–598, 621
Woman's Crusade, 540–541
Woman's rights. *See also* Feminism; Women
    conventions, 359–360
    movement, 358–360, 598
    organization for, 540
    Reagan administration and, 929–930
Woman suffrage, 409, 598
    14th Amendment and, 469, 540
    15th Amendment and, 472–473
    19th Amendment and, 600
    march for, 644, 644(i)
    movement for, 599–600, 599(i)
    progressivism and, 623–624
    in West, 509, 599(i), 600, 644–645, 665
    Willard and, 586, 587, 598
    Wilson and, 644
    World War I and, 665, 680
Women. *See also* Feminism; Gender and gen-
        der issues; Slaves and slavery; Voting
        and voting rights; specific individuals
    abolitionist movement and, 324, 325–326,
        361(i)
    abortion rights for, 867
    academies for, 286, 289–290, 320
    activism of, 540–541, 597–600
    affirmative action for, 855, 864, 870
    ancient, 6
    antiwar protests by, 889(i)
    birth control movement and, 643–644
    in cabinet, 929, 963
    Carter appointments of, 915, 916
    in Chesapeake region, 64
    in Civil War, 427, 446, 448–449
    Clinton appointments of, 951
    college enrollment in 1950s, 827

colonial, 91–92
on Comstock, 505
in Congress, 780–782
conservatism and, 905–906, 907
cult of domesticity and, 576
as Daughters of Liberty, 156, 158–159
as domestic servants, 576
in early republic, 286–290
economic roles in 1920s, 693
as Edenton tea ladies, 158(i)
education for, 286, 288–290
equality and, 923
Equal Rights Amendment (1972) and, 867
ex-slave, 477–478
Farmers' Alliance and, 589
feme covert doctrine and, 287, 292, 298
feminist movement in 1960s and 1970s,
    863–868
First Lady and, 280–281
Fourteenth Amendment and, 469
French Revolution and, 256
in garment industry, 566
GI Bill and, 794
in government, 812, 951
in Great Depression, 710
Grimké sisters and, 301–302, 302(i)
as homesteaders, 511, 511(i)
as immigrants, 570, 960
Indian, 17
inheritance by, 287
Irish American, 342
labor unions and, 573, 621–622, 623
law and, 286, 287
literacy of, 320
marriage and, 215, 286, 287, 376, 409,
    566, 567, 927
minimum-wage law for, 687
in mining towns, 505, 506
in missionary societies, 322
in moral reform movement, 323
Native American, 502
in New Deal, 725–726
in New England, 112
new woman and, 685, 691, 692–694
in 1950s, 828
Nixon and, 911
occupations for, 693, 822–823
patriotism of, 187
petition for redress of grievances by,
    314–315
on plantations, 376–377
in political office, 867
as political wives, 295
politics and, 241, 244–245, 538–541
property and, 930
in Quaker society, 100
religion and, 286, 288
as republican mothers, 244–245
in Republican Party, 409
in revolutionary period, 173–175, 192
rights for, 286, 287, 326, 357, 358–360,
    929

separate spheres doctrine and, 319–320,
    538
as servants, 65
in settlement house movement, 617–619,
    620
shelters for, 868
slave, 287, 376, 377, 378
Social Security and, 737
southern, 538
student protests and, 862
on Supreme Court, 929–930, 951, 964,
    971
as teachers, 320
in temperance movement, 540–541, 586,
    587, 598–599
in textile industry, 305, 537, 565–566
as vice presidential candidate, 926
in Vietnam War, 887
voting rights for, 179, 215, 292, 461, 469,
    472–473, 508, 540, 598, 599–600,
    623–624, 644–645
wealth of, 341
as wives of loyalists, 189
of Woodland cultures, 11–12
workday for, 623
in workforce, 321, 448–449, 565, 567,
    568–570, 620–623, 687, 793, 793(i),
    927
working class, 566–567, 577
World War I and, 663, 665–666
in World War II, 761, 766–767
yeomen, 383–384
Women's clubs, 540
Women's International League for Peace and
    Freedom, 667
Women's liberation movement, 864–866
Women's movement. *See also* Feminism and
    feminists; Women
    race, ethnicity, and, 866
Women's Peace Party, 667
Women's Political Council (WPC), 834
Women's Strike for Equality, 865(i)
Women's Trade Union League (WTUL),
    621–622, 623
Women Strike for Peace (WSP), 889(i)
Wood, Leonard, 502
Woodhenges, 14–15
Woodland peoples, 14–17, 494. *See also*
    Eastern Woodland peoples
Woodley, Arthur E., Jr., 888
Woods, Tiger, 961
Woodside, John A., 291(i)
Woodstock Music Festival, 862
Woolworth's, lunch counter sit-in at, 851
Worcester v. Georgia (1832), 315–316
Work. *See* Labor; Workers; Workplace
Workday
    eight-hour, 574, 575, 591, 637, 642
    in mining industry, 594, 628
    of slaves, 375
    in steel industry, 528
    ten-hours, for women, 623

Workday *(continued)*
 in textile mills, 566
 twelve- vs. eight-hour, 574
Workers. *See also* Factories; Labor; Labor
  unions; Strikes; Women; Workforce;
  Working class
 African American, 677–678, 678(i), 739
 assembly lines and, 689
 blue-collar, 713, 907, 927
 on Brooklyn Bridge, 553–555
 in caissons, 553, 554(i)
 Carnegie and, 528, 591
 in Civil War, 448–449
 as common laborers, 553, 565
 factories and, 305–307
 in Gilded Age, 546, 564–570
 in Great Depression, 706, 707, 711–712
 Hispanic, 739
 industrial, 822
 Irish immigrants as, 342
 for manufacturing, 337
 Mexican, 825
 migrant, 515, 517
 in mills, 305–306, 306(i)
 New Deal and, 738–740
 in 1920s, 687
 in 1929, 705
 organization of, 570–575
 OSHA and, 870
 population of, 564
 private property vs. rights of, 593, 597
 in Pullman, 594–595
 in Reagan era, 925, 927
 scientific management and, 624–625
 skilled, 560–561, 565, 568, 573
 Social Security and, 737
 in Sun Belt, 825
 in textile mills, 305–306
 unskilled, 559, 560–561, 643
 wages of, 534
 wealth gap and, 925
 white-collar, 565, 568–570, 713
 women as, 565, 568–570, 598, 687, 793,
  793(i)
 after World War I, 674–675, 674(i)
 in World War II, 766–767
 after World War II, 792–793
Workers' compensation, 565, 642
Workforce
 of Carnegie, 559
 in Great Depression, 707
 immigrants in, 559
 in mining, 506
 in 1950s, 821–823
 unionization of, 736
 women in, 321, 565, 567, 568–570, 710,
  822–823, 927
Working class. *See also* Workers
 in cities, 563
 families in, 566–567, 576–577
 leisure of, 577
 militancy of, 711–712

 progressives and, 621–624
 prohibition movement and, 621
 school busing and, 910
 in Vietnam War, 887, 890
Workingmen's Party, 508
Workplace
 as men's sphere, 320
 scientific management in, 625
 sexual harassment in, 943
 women in, 693
Works Progress Administration (WPA), 734,
  769
World Bank, 959
World Boxing Association, 890
World Jewish Congress, 770
World's Columbian Exposition (Chicago,
  1893), 489, 582–583
World Trade Center, September 11, 2001,
  destruction of, 965–966, 965(i)
World Trade Organization (WTO), 958
World War I (1914–1918). *See also* Allies
  (World War I); specific countries
 AEF in, 651, 661, 663
 African Americans and, 660, 662, 677–
  678
 alliances in, 655–657, 656(m)
 armed forces in, 651–653
 armistice in, 663
 Asia and, 651–653, 670–671
 casualties in, 657, 662, 663, 680
 democracy after, 673–680
 democracy during, 663–668
 Europe after, 670, 671(m)
 events leading to, 655–657
 France and, 659, 662–663
 Germany and, 662–663
 home front in, 663–668
 legacy of, 751
 Ottoman empire after, 670
 patriotism during, 663–664, 666–667
 peace treaty after, 670–672
 Red scare after, 675–677
 Russian withdrawal from, 660
 soldiers in, 651–653, 652(i), 661(i)
 submarine warfare in, 657–658
 trench warfare in, 651–652
 United States and, 658–663
 woman suffrage and, 665–666
 women and, 664–665
World War II (1939–1945). *See also* Allies
  (World War II); Nazi Germany; specific countries
 African American veterans after, 794
 atomic bomb and, 750–751, 775–776,
  776(i)
 bombing campaigns during, 770–771
 casualties in, 773, 777
 economy and, 759–760, 761–762, 777
 in Europe, 764–765, 772(m)
 home front in, 760, 765–770
 military in, 760–761
 mobilization for, 759–762

navy in, 762
opening of, 755
in Pacific Ocean region, 763–764, 773–775, 774(m)
Pearl Harbor attack in, 758–759
Red Scare after, 782
second front in, 764, 770
U.S. entry into, 759
women in, 761, 766–767
Wounded Knee, South Dakota
AIM takeover of, 859
massacre at (1890), 503
Wovoka (Paiute shaman), 502–503
WPA. *See* Works Progress Administration
Wright, Frank Lloyd, 823
Writing
Native Americans and, 18
origins of, 4
WTO. *See* World Trade Organization
Wyandot Indians, Northwest Territory land ordinances and, 222
Wyoming, voting by women in, 509, 598, 599(i)

Ximenes, Vicente T., 861

Yalta Conference, 772
Yamamoto, Isoroku (Japan), 763, 764
Yamasee Indians, 133
Yamasee War (1715), 133
Yams, 127
Yellow journalism, 609
Yellowstone National Park, 634(m)
Yellow Wolf (Nez Percé), 501
Yeltsin, Boris, 947
Yeomen, 68, 382–383
during Civil War, 446

lifestyle of, 127
plantation belt, 383
in southern Republican Party, 483
upcountry, 383–384
Yippies. *See* Youth International Party
YMCA, 665
Yom Kippur War (1973), 869, 896
York (slave), 277
York, Canada. *See* Toronto
York, Duke of. *See* James II (Duke of York, England)
Yorktown, Battle of (1781), 198(m), 200–201
Yosemite National Park, 632, 634(m)
Young, Andrew, 915
Young, Brigham, 346, 347, 509
Young, Lewis, 379
Young Americans for Freedom (YAF), 908
Young Men's Christian Association. *See* YMCA
Young people. *See also* Students
education and training of, 320–321
in Vietnam War, 887
working class, 577
Youth International Party (Yippies), 892
Youth movement, voting and, 870
Yucatán peninsula, Cortés in, 36–37
Yugoslavia, 670
breakup of, 956
Yuppies, 927–928
Zacatecas, Mexico, silver from, 41
Zimmermann, Arthur, and Zimmermann telegram, 659
Zion National Park, 634(m)
Zones of occupation, in postwar Germany, 785
"Zoot suit riots," 768
Zuñi Indians, 13, 39–40, 40(i)

About the authors

JAMES L. ROARK (Ph.D., Stanford University) is Samuel Candler Dobbs Professor of American History at Emory University. In 1993, he received the Emory Williams Distinguished Teaching Award, and in 2001–2002 he was Pitt Professor of American Institutions at Cambridge University. He has written *Masters without Slaves: Southern Planters in the Civil War and Reconstruction* and coauthored *Black Masters: A Free Family of Color in the Old South* with Michael P. Johnson.

MICHAEL P. JOHNSON (Ph.D., Stanford University) is professor of history at Johns Hopkins University. His publications include *Toward a Patriarchal Republic: The Secession of Georgia*; *Abraham Lincoln, Slavery, and the Civil War: Selected Speeches and Writings*; and *Reading the American Past: Selected Historical Documents*, the documents reader for *The American Promise*. He has also coedited *No Chariot Let Down: Charleston's Free People of Color on the Eve of the Civil War* with James L. Roark.

PATRICIA CLINE COHEN (Ph.D., University of California, Berkeley) is professor of history at the University of California, Santa Barbara, where she received the Distinguished Teaching Award in 2005–2006. She has written *A Calculating People: The Spread of Numeracy in Early America* and *The Murder of Helen Jewett: The Life and Death of a Prostitute in Nineteenth-Century New York*, and she has coauthored *The Flash Press: Sporting Male Weeklies in 1840s New York*.

SARAH STAGE (Ph.D., Yale University) has taught U.S. history at Williams College and the University of California, Riverside, and she was visiting professor at Beijing University and Szechuan University. Currently she is professor of women's studies at Arizona State University. Her books include *Female Complaints: Lydia Pinkham and the Business of Women's Medicine* and *Rethinking Home Economics: Women and the History of a Profession*.

SUSAN M. HARTMANN (Ph.D., University of Missouri) is Arts and Humanities Distinguished Professor of History at Ohio State University. In 1995 she won the university's Exemplary Faculty Award in the College of Humanities. Her publications include *Truman and the 80th Congress*; *The Home Front and Beyond: American Women in the 1940s*; *From Margin to Mainstream: American Women and Politics since 1960*; and *The Other Feminists: Activists in the Liberal Establishment*.

About the cover image

Jeannette Rankin with American Flag, 1918

Congresswoman Jeannette Rankin (1880–1973) is shown receiving the flag that flew over the Capitol when the House of Representatives passed the Nineteenth Amendment, which, when it was ratified in 1920, gave women the right to vote. Rankin, who held office from 1917 to 1919 and from 1941 to 1943, was the first woman elected to Congress and an ardent supporter of woman suffrage. Her election solidified the necessity of a female voice in government and ushered in a new era in women's struggle for equality.